PROFESSIONAL

ASP.NET 4.5 in C# and VB

Jason N. Gaylord
Christian Wenz
Pranav Rastogi
Todd Miranda
Scott Hanselman

wrox™

A Wiley Brand

Professional ASP.NET 4.5 in C# and VB

Published by
John Wiley & Sons, Inc.
10475 Crosspoint Boulevard
Indianapolis, IN 46256
www.wiley.com

Copyright © 2013 by John Wiley & Sons, Inc., Indianapolis, Indiana

Published simultaneously in Canada

ISBN: 978-1-118-31182-0
ISBN: 978-1-118-42438-4 (ebk)
ISBN: 978-1-118-33205-4 (ebk)
ISBN: 978-1-118-33534-5 (ebk)

Manufactured in the United States of America

10 9 8 7 6 5 4 3 2 1

For general information on our other products and services please contact our Customer Care Department within the United States at (877) 762-2974, outside the United States at (317) 572-3993 or fax (317) 572-4002.

Wiley publishes in a variety of print and electronic formats and by print-on-demand. Some material included with standard print versions of this book may not be included in e-books or in print-on-demand. If this book refers to media such as a CD or DVD that is not included in the version you purchased, you may download this material at http://book support.wiley.com. For more information about Wiley products, visit www.wiley.com.

Library of Congress Control Number: 2013933610

To my loving wife, Lisa, and our four awesome children.

—Jason N. Gaylord

I would like to dedicate this book with the following quote, to my mother who has been instrumental in my upbringing and is an integral part of my life. Abraham Lincoln said, "All that I am, or hope to be, I owe to my angel mother."

—Pranav Rastogi

To Kelly, Amber, and Sydney

—Todd Miranda

To my wife and the two little boys I work for.

—Scott Hanselman

ABOUT THE AUTHORS

JASON N. GAYLORD is an application developer and Director of Technology at United One Resources in Wilkes-Barre, Pennsylvania. His programming career started with a simple GOTO statement and continued over 15 years of developing Windows and web applications. During this time, Jason has had the opportunity to plan, build, test, and deploy several enterprise applications including integrations with accounting and operating systems and B2B web applications used by some of the top banks in the United States.

Outside of the normal day to day activities, Jason blogs, speaks, and organizes technology events including TECHbash and NEPA GiveCamp. He's the group leader for the .NET Valley technology user group. Recently, Jason was recognized as a Microsoft MVP for 10 consecutive years. He remains a member of the ASPInsiders, a group that provides product feedback directly to the ASP.NET team. You can find out more about Jason by visiting his website at jasongaylord.com. You can follow him on Twitter at @jgaylord.

CHRISTIAN WENZ started working almost exclusively with web technologies in 1993 and has not looked back since. As a developer and project manager he has been responsible for websites from medium–sized companies up to large, international enterprises. As an author, he has written or co-written over 100 books that have been translated into 10 languages. As a consultant, he helped companies and teams of developers to make their applications more reliable, better performing, and more secure. Christian frequently writes for various IT magazines, is a sought-after speaker at developer conferences around the world, and is always keen on sharing technologies he is excited about with others. He contributes to various open source projects, is a Microsoft ASP.NET MVP and an ASPInsider, and co-author of several developer certifications. You can follow him on Twitter at @chwenz.

PRANAV RASTOGI is a member of the Microsoft ASP.NET product team and is based in Seattle. Over the past years, Pranav has worked on a variety of areas such as ASP.NET Web Forms, Dynamic Data, and more recently ASP.NET SignalR. He is passionate about understanding web developer woes with the Microsoft stack and helps champion tools, packages, or libraries that will enhance the web development experience on the Microsoft stack. Pranav is also a regular speaker on a variety of ASP.NET related topics at various worldwide conferences. He blogs about his experiences at http://blogs.msdn.com/b/pranav_rastogi/. Before joining Microsoft, Pranav graduated from the University Of Florida with a masters in Computer Science.

Pranav is also a food junkie who sometimes works as a Chef de Cuisine at home. He is an adventure seeker and can be often found backpacking in the wilderness. In this spare time Pranav regularly practices his bartending skills on his friends. If you know anyone who is looking to throw a party and needs a bartender, then get in touch with him. You can follow Pranav on Twitter at @rustd.

TODD MIRANDA is an active proponent of .NET technologies and software craftsmanship as a whole. He has been developing on various platforms for over 20 years and has been involved with .NET since it was previewed in 2000. He has worked with many of the .NET platforms but focuses primarily on ASP.NET. He is the owner of NxtDimension Solutions and provides consulting and training on the Microsoft stack. As a Microsoft MVP, Todd works closely with Microsoft. He is the co-founder of the Birmingham .NET User Group and remains active in the development community. He has recorded hundreds of online training videos on Microsoft development topics including security, JavaScript, Silverlight, WPF, Expression, and ASP.NET. He is an INETA speaker and regularly presents at user groups, community events, and technical conferences. You can follow Todd on Twitter @tmiranda.

SCOTT HANSELMAN is a web developer who has been blogging at http://hanselman .com for over a decade. He works on Azure and ASP.NET for Microsoft out of his home office in Portland, Oregon. Scott has three podcasts, http://hanselminutes.com for tech talk, http://thisdeveloperslife.com on developers' lives and loves, and http:// ratchetandthegeek.com for pop culture and tech media. He's written a number of books and spoken in person to almost a half million developers worldwide. You can follow Scott on Twitter at @shanselman.

ABOUT THE TECHNICAL EDITORS

KEN COX has been creating web applications with Microsoft technologies since the earliest betas of ASP Classic in the mid-1990s. He has worked on dozens of ASP.NET sites, large and small, and is the author of *ASP.NET 3.5 For Dummies* published by John Wiley & Sons. Ken was honored as a Microsoft Most Valuable Professional (MVP) for ASP.NET for 15 consecutive years prior to his retirement and remains an ASPInsider. Ken does consulting work from his home in Nipissing Township, Ontario, Canada.

BIPIN JOSHI is an independent blogger and author who writes about apparently unrelated topics—yoga and technology. A former software consultant and trainer by profession, Bipin has been programming since 1995 and has worked with the .NET Framework since its inception. He is a published author and has authored or co-authored more than a half dozen books and numerous articles on .NET technologies. Bipin was a Microsoft Most Valuable Professional (MVP) and a Microsoft Certified Trainer (MCT) during his tenure as a software consultant and trainer. He has also penned a few books on yoga. Having embraced the yoga way of life, he enjoys the intoxicating presence of God and writes about yoga, life, and technology. He can be reached at www.bipinjoshi.com.

JOHN PETERSEN, an early adopter of the Microsoft .NET Platform, has over 20 years of experience architecting and developing software. Currently, John is a practice director in the Technology Platform Group at Neudesic, LLC, a Microsoft National Systems Integrator and Gold ISV Partner and is a 10-time recipient of Microsoft's Most Valuable Professional Award. John is a current ASP.NET/IIS MVP. John has spoken at numerous industry events, including VSLive and DevConnections, as well as at many regional events and Code Camps. John is also a regular contributor to *CODE Magazine*.

JEFFERY TAY has been developing and designing .NET solutions since 2002, specializing in solutions for the education and medical sectors. He was awarded Microsoft Most Valuable Professional for the last 3 years. He has experience in Java and most Microsoft technologies such as Silverlight, SQL Server, and Windows Server. He is an associate director at the National University of Singapore where he leads a team that manages the university's Learning Management System and comes up with new solutions where the use of IT can enhance teaching. You can reach Jeffery at taykwama@hotmail.com.

DEEPAK VERMA has been developing and designing web solutions for the last 10 years. During these years, Deepak has been involved in technologies such as Flash Scripting, Flex, ColdFusion, Silverlight, Java, and PHP and now is mostly working on Microsoft stack. He is currently working as a Software Development Engineer in Test for Microsoft. At Microsoft he has contributed to Visual Studio Dynamic data tooling, multi-targeting, Razor editor and tooling, Azure SDK for Java, PHP & .NET, Visual Studio HTML and CSS editors, Azure Mobile Services, and NuGet. He lives in Redmond, Washington, with his wife, Madhu, and children, Adya and Kian. You can reach him at deepu_verma@yahoo.com.

CREDITS

ACKNOWLEDGMENTS

I'D LIKE TO THANK the time and dedication of the team at Wrox Press and John Wiley & Sons. Without their support, this book would not be possible. Thanks to Scott Hunter, Scott Hanselman, Damian Edwards, and the rest of the ASP.NET team for their current leadership to bring ASP.NET 4.5 to market. Thanks to Scott Guthrie, Steve Smith, and Rob Howard for allowing me to join the ASPInsiders program and helping me get my content off the ground. Thanks to all of the ASPInsiders and Microsoft MVPs for their support over the years. Thanks to Frank Sorokach in allowing me to spend the time necessary to get my development career off the ground. Thanks to Louis Cesare and Sean Higgins for supporting my community initiatives and giving me time when I've needed to provide feedback to the ASP.NET team. Thanks to Luzerne County Community College and Penn State University for allowing our user group to prosper in Northeastern Pennsylvania. Finally, thanks to my family, specifically my parents, Deb and Tom Gaylord; my grandparents; my aunts and uncles; my wife, Lisa; and my children for their support. It's not easy writing a book and they've certainly understood the time and dedication needed to get this book to ship.

—JASON N. GAYLORD

EVERY BOOK IS A TEAM EFFORT with all the editors (acquisition, development, technical, etc.) involved, but with this title, the authors are quite a large team, too! So thank you to Jason, Pranav, Scott, and Todd, it has been an honor working with you. Also we are indebted to the authors of the previous editions, to everyone involved at Wiley, and to our tech editors.

About 7 years ago, I was working on another book for the Wrox imprint of Wiley, and promised Yvonne that I would invite her to a really sumptuous dinner at one of Europe's top restaurants after it has been published. Things did not turn out as planned, including co-authors dropping out, so the book (and the dinner) never materialized. So let's try again—would June 13 work?

—CHRISTIAN WENZ

I WOULD LIKE TO THANK all the coffee shops owners in Seattle. The relaxing environment and a good coffee was my inspiration in writing the book.

—PRANAV RASTOGI

THANKS to Kelly for putting up with more late nights than normal and to my two princesses, Amber and Sydney, for putting up with less time and attention! I love you all. Thanks to Kevin, Mary, and the rest of the team at Wiley for their help and support on this book project. Also a big thank you to my co-authors. It has been great working with you on this book.

—TODD MIRANDA

BIG THANKS to Pranav Rastogi, Scott Hunter, Damian Edwards, Eilon Lipton, and the whole ASP.NET team that does the real work.

—SCOTT HANSELMAN

CONTENTS

PART VII: CLIENT-SIDE DEVELOPMENT

FOREWORD

ASP.NET has continued to evolve over the years as the web has changed. When it was first released, Web Forms was a revolutionary model for bringing object-oriented programming to the web by using rich controls to encapsulate web behavior. Next when Ajax was starting to be a common term, ASP.NET evolved to contain a rich Ajax Library and an UpdatePanel control that simplified Ajax programming. Then as the Model-View-Controller pattern started becoming popular, we shipped ASP.NET MVC which provided a framework for building ASP.NET applications using the MVC pattern. And then ASP.NET went back to its original roots with ASP.NET Web Pages, which provided a simple PHP style of programming to help people learn to program for the web. As connected devices such as smartphones and tablets started appearing, programmers needed a way to build APIs that can be called from devices, and ASP.NET Web API was born. The latest addition is ASP.NET SignalR, which provides a programming model for applications that need to have real time events showing live updates of data, such as stock quotes.

Each time the web has changed, ASP.NET has changed with it, and we will continue to keep each ASP.NET framework in sync with the latest developments in the future. With ASP.NET 4.5, one of our goals was to make sure that Web Forms remained up to date with the advancements in the other frameworks listed above. Features like Model Binding, Unobtrusive JavaScript, and NuGet Libraries were added to Web Forms so Web Forms developers had access to the new features that were created in the newer frameworks. Tooling was added so ASP.NET Web APIs can be added to any ASP.NET project. You are witnessing the evolution of One ASP.NET which will enable all of our frameworks and features to work together.

Enjoy the beginning of One ASP.NET and ASP.NET.NET 4.5 with *Professional ASP.NET 4.5 in C# and VB*!

—Scott Hunter

Principal Program Manager, Web Platform Team, Microsoft

INTRODUCTION

SIMPLY PUT, ASP.NET 4.5 is an amazing technology to use to build your web applications! Since the inception of ASP.NET, numerous technologies have been introduced that make it one of the most ambitious web frameworks available today. ASP.NET 4.5 continues to build on the foundation laid by the previous releases of ASP.NET by focusing on the area of developer productivity.

This book covers nearly all of what ASP.NET has to offer. It not only introduces new topics, but it also shows you examples of these new technologies in action. So sit back, pull up that keyboard, and enjoy!

THE PAST, PRESENT, AND FUTURE OF ASP.NET

ASP.NET 4.5 is another major release of the product and builds on the previous releases with additional capabilities. This release continues on a path to make ASP.NET developers the most productive developers in the web space. With each release of ASP.NET, the Microsoft team has focused its goals on developer productivity, administration, and management, as well as performance and scalability. This book focuses on the new additions to ASP.NET and the .NET Framework.

ASP.NET has been around for over 10 years. When it was first released, the focus was to convert the existing web programming model of using VBScript or Jscript to build Active Server Pages to an object-oriented model. To assist in the transition, several server controls were included to encapsulate common functionality.

As time passed, developers began to require more control over the rendered markup. As a result, ASP.NET changed. Newer web paradigms emerged, and technologies, such as ASP.NET MVC, were born. On the other hand, ASP.NET Web Forms continued to control the majority of the development. Thus, the past few releases of ASP.NET placed an emphasis on proper markup rendering with server controls.

However, as the Visual Studio team, like most Microsoft teams, was on a 2- to 3-year release cycle, the ASP.NET team could not keep up with the changes in web technologies. Chapter 1 of this book provides a more comprehensive explanation as to how the ASP.NET team is handling this dilemma by providing more frequent out-of-band (OOB) releases of their products. This chapter also discusses the open source initiatives that the ASP.NET team has. In fact, many of the ASP.NET technologies have been already released as true open source.

It's a really exciting time for web development on ASP.NET.

WHAT YOU NEED FOR ASP.NET 4.5

You will most likely find that installing Visual Studio 2012 is best to work through the examples in this book. However, you can use Microsoft's Notepad or WebMatrix and the command-line compilers that come with the .NET Framework 4.5. To work through *every* example in this book, you need the following:

- ➤ Windows 8, Windows 7, Windows Vista, Windows Server 2012, or Windows Server 2008
- ➤ Visual Studio 2012 (this installs the .NET Framework 4.5)
- ➤ SQL Server 2012, 2008, 2005, or SQL Server Express Edition

The nice thing is that you are not required to have Microsoft Internet Information Services (IIS) to work with ASP.NET 4.5, because Visual Studio 2012 includes a built-in version of the web server called IIS Express. Moreover, if you do not have a full-blown version of SQL Server, don't be alarmed. Many examples that use this database can be altered to work with Microsoft's SQL Server Express Edition, which you can find free on the Internet.

WHO THIS BOOK IS FOR

This book was written to introduce you to the features and capabilities that ASP.NET 4.5 offers, as well as to give you an explanation of the foundation that ASP.NET provides. We assume you have a general understanding of web technologies, such as previous versions of ASP.NET or other web technologies such as PHP. If you understand the basics of web programming, you should not have much trouble following along with this book's content.

If you are brand new to ASP.NET, be sure to check out Wrox's *Beginning ASP.NET 4.5: In C# and VB* by Imar Spaanjaars (John Wiley & Sons, 2012) to help you understand the basics.

In addition to working with web technologies, we also assume that you understand basic programming constructs, such as variables, For Each loops, and object-oriented programming.

You may also be wondering whether this book is for the Visual Basic developer or the C# developer. We are happy to say that it is for both! When the code differs substantially, this book provides examples in both VB and C#. In these cases, any HTML markup is omitted from the C# example for brevity.

WHAT THIS BOOK COVERS

This book explores the 4.5 release of ASP.NET. It covers each major new feature included in ASP.NET 4.5 in detail. The following list tells you something about the content of each chapter.

➤ **Chapter 1, "One ASP.NET" — Extending a Healthy Web Ecosystem:** The first chapter may just be one of the most interesting chapters in the book. After 10 years of existence, ASP.NET is one of the most prolific web development technologies. In this chapter, the future plans for ASP.NET are detailed, including a new vision: to have one ASP.NET.

➤ **Chapter 2, "HTML5 and CSS3 Design with ASP.NET":** Visual Studio 2012 places an emphasis on building web applications using HTML5 and CSS3. This chapter takes a close look at how you can effectively work with HTML and CSS to design your ASP.NET applications.

➤ **Chapter 3, "ASP.NET Web Forms Structure":** The third chapter covers the frameworks of ASP.NET applications as well as the structure and frameworks provided for single ASP.NET pages. This chapter shows you how to build ASP.NET applications with Visual Studio 2012. It also shows you the folders and files that are part of ASP.NET. It discusses ways to compile code and shows you how to perform cross-page posting. The chapter ends by showing you easy ways to deal with your classes from within Visual Studio 2012.

➤ **Chapters 4 through 7, "Controls":** These four chapters are grouped together because they all deal with server or user controls. This batch of chapters starts by examining the idea of the server control and its pivotal role in ASP.NET development. In addition to looking at the server control framework, these chapters delve into the plethora of server controls that are at your disposal for ASP.NET development projects. Chapter 4, "ASP.NET Server Controls and Client-Side Scripts," looks at the basics of working with server controls. Chapter 5, "ASP.NET Web Server Controls," covers the controls that are part of the latest ASP.NET release. Chapter 6, "Validation Server Controls," describes a special group of server controls: those for validation. You can use these controls to create beginning-to-advanced form validations. Chapter 7, "User and Server Controls," describes building your own server controls and using them within your applications.

➤ **Chapters 8 through 13, "Data Access":** This part of the book discusses data access. Nearly all web applications that exist today interact with at least one type of data source. From relational data to JSON, these chapters cover it all. Chapter 8, "Data Binding," looks at the underlying capabilities that enable you to work with the data programmatically before issuing the data to a control. Chapter 9, "Model Binding," covers the basics of binding and applying model binding to Web Forms. Chapter 10, "Querying with LINQ," introduces you to LINQ and how to effectively use this feature in your web applications today. Chapter 11, "Entity Framework," discusses mapping objects from the database to the objects within your code. Using Visual Studio 2012, you are able to visually design your entity data models. Chapter 12, "ASP.NET Dynamic Data," describes how dynamic data enables you to quickly and easily put together a reporting and data entry application from your database. Chapter 13, "Working with Services," outlines the differences between traditional ASMX Web Services, WCF, and the new WebAPI.

➤ **Chapter 14, "Introduction to the Provider Model":** A number of systems are built into ASP.NET that make the lives of developers so much easier and more productive than ever before. These systems are built on an architecture called a provider model, which is rather extensible. This chapter gives an overview of this provider model and how it is used throughout ASP.NET 4.5.

➤ **Chapter 15, "Extending the Provider Model":** After an introduction of the provider model, this chapter looks at some of the ways to extend the provider model found in ASP.NET 4.5. This chapter also reviews a couple of sample extensions to the provider model.

➤ **Chapter 16, "Working with Master Pages":** Master pages are a great capability of ASP.NET. They provide a means of creating templated pages that enable you to work with the entire application, as opposed to single pages. This chapter examines the creation of these templates and how to apply them to your content pages throughout an ASP.NET application.

➤ **Chapter 17, "Site Navigation":** It is quite apparent that many developers do not simply develop single pages — they build applications. Therefore, they need mechanics that deal with functionality throughout the entire application, not just the pages. One of the application capabilities provided by ASP.NET 4.5 is the site navigation system covered in this chapter. The underlying navigation system enables you to define your application's navigation structure through an XML file, and it introduces a whole series of navigation server controls that work with the data from these XML files.

➤ **Chapter 18, "Personalization":** Developers are always looking for ways to store information pertinent to the end user. After it is stored, this personalization data has to be persisted for future visits or for grabbing other pages within the same application. The ASP.NET team developed a way to store this information — the ASP.NET personalization system. The great thing about this system is that you configure the entire behavior of the system from the web.config file.

➤ **Chapter 19, "Membership and Role Management":** This chapter covers the membership and role management system developed to simplify adding authentication and authorization to your ASP.NET applications. These two systems are extensive; they make some of the more complicated authentication and authorization implementations of the past a distant memory. This chapter focuses on using the web.config file for controlling how these systems are applied, as well as on the server controls that work with the underlying systems.

➤ **Chapter 20, "Security":** This chapter discusses security beyond the membership and role management features provided by ASP.NET 4.5. This chapter provides an in-depth look at the authentication and authorization mechanics inherent in the ASP.NET technology, as well as HTTP access types and impersonations.

➤ **Chapter 21, "State Management":** Because ASP.NET is a request-response–based technology, state management and the performance of requests and responses take on significant importance. This chapter introduces these two separate but important areas of ASP.NET development.

➤ **Chapter 22, "Caching":** Because of the request-response nature of ASP.NET, caching (storing previously generated results, images, and pages) on the server becomes important to the performance of your ASP.NET applications. This chapter looks at some of the advanced caching capabilities provided by ASP.NET, including the SQL cache invalidation feature that is part of ASP.NET 4.5. This chapter also takes a look at object caching and object caching extensibility.

➤ **Chapters 23 through 27, "Client-Side Development":** These five chapters touch upon one of the hottest areas of technology: mobile technologies. The day has come where consumers and businesses have the expectation of having real-time data delivery and applications with fluent designs that work from a cell phone, to a tablet, to a full-blown PC. Chapter 23, "ASP.NET AJAX," takes a look at building your applications using AJAX. Chapter 24, "Ajax Control Toolkit," reviews a series of controls available to make use of the AJAX technology. Chapter 25, "jQuery," provides an overview of the jQuery JavaScript library. Chapter 26, "Real-Time Communication," compares the methods for providing real-time communication traditionally with more modern methods such as using HTML5 Web Sockets or SignalR, which contains a hybrid solution. Chapter 27, "Developing Websites with Mobile in Mind," specifically discusses methods for updating the client side to provide better mobile client support.

➤ **Chapters 28 through 33, "Application Configuration and Deployment":** By this point, you should have a solid understanding of building an ASP.NET application. These six chapters focus on configuring and optimizing your application, and, finally, deploying the application. Chapter 28, "Configuration," teaches you to modify the capabilities and behaviors of ASP.NET using the various configuration files at your disposal. Chapter 29, "Debugging and Error Handling," tells you how to properly structure error handling within your applications and shows you how to use various debugging techniques to find errors that your applications might contain. Chapter 30, "Modules and Handlers," looks at two methods of manipulating the way ASP.NET processes HTTP requests: `HttpModule` and `HttpHandler`. Each method provides a unique level of access to the underlying processing of ASP.NET. Chapter 31, "Asynchronous Communication," discusses methods for performing one-way communication from the client to a method on the server or to a hosted service. Chapter 32, "Building Global Applications," looks at some of the important items to consider when building your web applications for the world. Chapter 33, "Packaging and Deploying ASP.NET Applications," takes the building process one step further and shows you how to package your ASP.NET applications for easy deployment.

➤ **Chapter 34, "ASP.NET MVC":** ASP.NET MVC has generated a lot of excitement from the development community. ASP.NET MVC supplies you with the means to create ASP.NET applications using the Model-View-Controller models that many developers expect. ASP.NET MVC provides developers with the testability, flexibility, and maintainability in the applications they build. It is important to remember that ASP.NET MVC is not meant to be a replacement for the ASP.NET everyone knows and loves, but instead is simply a different way to construct your applications.

➤ **Chapter 35, "ASP.NET Web Pages and Razor":** ASP.NET Web Pages is a newer technology that enables developers to use Razor syntax to build an interactive web application. This chapter provides an overview of building a Web Pages application using Microsoft WebMatrix. It also provides a listing of some of the more popular helpers that use the Razor syntax to render valid HTML and CSS.

➤ **Appendix A, "Migrating Older ASP.NET Projects":** In some cases, you build your ASP.NET 4.5 applications from scratch, starting everything new. In many instances, however, this is not an option. You need to take an existing ASP.NET application that was built on a previous version of the .NET Framework and migrate the application so that it can run on the .NET Framework 4.5.

➤ **Appendix B, "COM Integration":** Invariably, you will have components created with previous technologies that you do not want to rebuild, but that you do want to integrate into new ASP.NET applications. If this is the case, the .NET Framework makes incorporating your previous COM components into your applications fairly simple and straightforward. This appendix also shows you how to build .NET components instead of turning to the previous COM component architecture.

➤ **Appendix C, "ASP.NET Ultimate Tools":** This appendix takes a look at the tools available to you as an ASP.NET developer. Many of the tools here will help you to expedite your development process and, in many cases, make you a better developer.

➤ **Appendix D, "Administration and Management":** Besides making it easier for the developer to be more productive in building ASP.NET applications, the ASP.NET team also put considerable effort into making the managing of applications easier. In the past, using ASP.NET 1.0/1.1, you managed ASP.NET applications by changing values in an XML configuration file. This appendix provides an overview of the GUI tools that come with ASP.NET today that enable you to manage your web applications easily and effectively.

➤ **Appendix E, "Dynamic Types and Languages":** As of the release of ASP.NET 4.5, you can now build your web applications using IronRuby and IronPython. This appendix takes a quick look at using dynamic languages in building your web applications.

➤ **Appendix F, "ASP.NET Online Resources":** This small appendix points you to some of the more valuable online resources for enhancing your understanding of ASP.NET.

➤ **Appendix G, "Visual Studio Extensibility with NuGet":** Visual Studio 2012 provides an extensibility model by using Microsoft's version of NuGet called Package Manager. NuGet enables developers to share files, folders, and binaries by creating a distributable package. The packages can be made available on the public feed or within a private feed.

CONVENTIONS

This book uses a number of different styles of text and layout to help differentiate among various types of information. Here are examples of the styles used and an explanation of what they mean:

➤ New words being defined are shown in *italics*.

➤ Keys that you press on the keyboard, such as Ctrl and Enter, are shown in initial caps and spelled as they appear on the keyboard.

➤ File extensions, URLs, and code that appears in regular paragraph text are shown in a monospaced typeface.

A block of code that you can type as a program and run is shown on separate lines, like this:

```
public static void Main()
{
    AFunc(1,2,"abc");
}
```

or like this:

```
public static void Main()    {        AFunc(1,2,"abc");    }
```

Sometimes you see code in a mixture of styles, like this:

```
    // If we haven't reached the end, return true, otherwise
    // set the position to invalid, and return false.
    pos++;
    if (pos < 4)
        return true;
    else {
        pos = -1;
        return false;
    }
```

When mixed code is shown like this, the bold code is what you should focus on in the current example.

We demonstrate the syntactical usage of methods, properties, and so on using the following format:

```
SqlDependency="database:table"
```

Here, the italicized parts indicate *placeholder text*: object references, variables, or parameter values that you need to insert.

Most of the code examples throughout the book are presented as numbered listings that have descriptive titles, like this:

LISTING I-3: Targeting mobile devices in your ASP.NET pages

Each listing is numbered (for example, Listing 1-3) where the first number represents the chapter number and the number following the hyphen represents a sequential number that indicates where that listing falls within the chapter. Downloadable code from the Wrox website (www.wrox.com) also uses this numbering system (in many cases) so that you can easily locate the examples you are looking for. "In other cases where listing numbers are not used, the authors have included filenames in the chapter that point you to where the code is in the download."

All code is shown in both VB and C#, when warranted. The exception is for code in which the only difference is, for example, the value given to the Language attribute in the Page directive. In such situations, we don't repeat the code for the C# version; the code is shown only once, as in the following example:

```
<%@ Page Language="VB"%>

<html xmlns="http://www.w3.org/1999/xhtml">
<head runat="server">
    <title>DataSetDataSource</title>
</head>
<body>
    <form id="form1" runat="server">
        <asp:DropDownList ID="Dropdownlist1" Runat="server" DataTextField="name"
         DataSourceID="XmlDataSource1">
        </asp:DropDownList>

        <asp:XmlDataSource ID="XmlDataSource1" Runat="server"
         DataFile="◁/Painters.xml">
        </asp:DataSetDataSource>
    </form>
</body>
</html>
```

> **NOTE** *Throughout the book, we may reference the default folder for the .NET Framework at* C:\WINDOWS\Microsoft.NET\Framework\v4.0.xxxxx\. *However, if you are using a 64-bit version of Windows and have the x64 version of the .NET Framework installed, you can find the 64-bit version of the framework at* C:\WINDOWS\Microsoft .NET\Framework64\v4.0.xxxxx\.

SOURCE CODE

As you work through the examples in this book, you may choose either to type all the code manually or to use the source code files that accompany the book. As previously indicated, all the source code used in this book is available for download at www.wrox.com. When you get to the site, simply locate the book's title (either by using the Search box or one of the topic lists) and click the Download Code link. You can then choose to download all the code from the book in one large Zip file or download just the code you need for a particular chapter.

> **NOTE** *Because many books have similar titles, you may find it easiest to search by ISBN; this book's ISBN is 978-1-118-31182-0.*

After you download the code, just decompress it with your favorite compression tool. Alternatively, you can go to the main Wrox code download page at `www.wrox.com/dynamic/books/download.aspx` to see the code available for this book and all other Wrox books. Remember that you can easily find the code you are looking for by referencing the listing number of the code example from the book, such as "Listing 1-2." We used these listing numbers when naming most of the downloadable code files. Those listings that are not named by their listing number are accompanied by the filename so you can easily find them in the downloadable code files. Also, you can download the versions of the AdventureWorks and Northwind databases we used for this book from `www.wrox.com/go/SQLServer2012DataSets`.

ERRATA

We make every effort to ensure that there are no errors in the text or in the code. However, no one is perfect, and mistakes do occur. If you find an error in one of our books, such as a spelling mistake or faulty piece of code, we would be very grateful if you would tell us about it. By sending in errata, you may spare another reader hours of frustration; at the same time, you are helping us provide even higher-quality information.

To find the errata page for this book, go to `www.wrox.com` and locate the title using the Search box or one of the title lists. Then, on the book details page, click the Book Errata link. On this page, you can view all errata that have been submitted for this book and posted by Wrox editors. A complete book list including links to each book's errata is also available at `www.wrox.com/misc-pages/booklist.shtml`.

If you do not spot "your" error already on the Book Errata page, go to `www.wrox.com/contact/techsupport.shtml` and complete the form there to send us the error you have found. We will check the information and, if appropriate, post a message to the book's errata page and fix the problem in subsequent editions of the book.

P2P.WROX.COM

For author and peer discussion, join the P2P forums at `p2p.wrox.com`. The forums are a web-based system for you to post messages relating to Wrox books and technologies and to interact with other readers and technology users. The forums offer a subscription feature that enables you to receive e-mail on topics of interest when new posts are made to the forums. Wrox authors, editors, other industry experts, and your fellow readers are represented in these forums.

At `http://p2p.wrox.com` you will find a number of different forums that will help you not only as you read this book, but also as you develop your own applications. To join the forums, just follow these steps:

1. Go to `p2p.wrox.com` and click the Register link.
2. Read the terms of use and click Agree.
3. Supply the information required to join, as well as any optional information you want to provide, and click Submit.

You will receive an e-mail with information describing how to verify your account and complete the joining process.

> **NOTE** *You can read messages in the forums without joining P2P, but you must join in order to post messages.*

After you join, you can post new messages and respond to other users' posts. You can read messages at any time on the web. If you want to have new messages from a particular forum e-mailed to you, click the Subscribe to this Forum icon by the forum name in the forum listing.

For more information about how the forum software works, as well as answers to many common questions specific to P2P and Wrox books, be sure to read the P2P FAQs. Simply click the FAQ link on any P2P page.

PART I
ASP.NET Fundamentals

One ASP.NET

➤ Introducing One ASP.NET

➤ Exploring and simplifying the complex web ecosystem

➤ Benefiting from One ASP.NET

ASP.NET has been a prominent web development framework that has supported .NET developers in building web applications for years. As the Internet has matured and progressed, so have the ASP.NET framework and the ecosystem around it. Thousands of products, services, and open source projects call ASP.NET home.

The Internet has advanced much faster than ASP.NET. The advancements in HTML, CSS, and JavaScript have led to richer experiences for users, which put pressure on ASP.NET to support these emerging technologies. The ASP.NET framework has had to support the growing needs of web developers. Although all this has led to the development of a healthy ecosystem where web developers from all over have come together to make it better, it's also caused core pieces of ASP.NET to show its age.

This chapter looks at how ASP.NET as a framework has matured, and proposes some ways to fix the problems with the ecosystem. How can ASP.NET be a trusted and reliable framework that the enterprise developer can count on, while still meeting the needs of the advanced web developer who demands the latest standards? The goal of the chapter is to give you an idea of some of the changes that have happened in ASP.NET and where the framework is headed.

INTRODUCING ONE ASP.NET

A few years back when ASP.NET MVC was just coming out, a number of people told me they were being discouraged from making "hybrid" applications. They wanted ASP.NET apps with services components, MVC areas, and Web Forms pieces. Some Microsoft employees made them feel that this was an unsupported thing. "Why would you want to do that? That's not a good idea."

But it is. ASP.NET MVC is ASP.NET. Web Forms is ASP.NET. The pipeline set in place more than 10 years ago is with us today, offering many extensibility points that have been exploited not only by ASP.NET but also by alternative frameworks like NancyFx and ServiceStack.

Why make developers choose from a half dozen different flavors when it's all the same underlying menu? ASP.NET offers core services that you need regardless of your application architecture. Key management, session management, caching, HTTP, authorization, and authentication are all universal web development truths. How you choose to render your angle brackets or curly braces is your preference, but you should feel comfortable using whatever ASP.NET framework or frameworks help you solve your business problem. You should be able to do this not only without guilt, but also in a totally supported and encouraged way. Figure 1-1 shows a breakdown of the different frameworks in ASP.NET and how they all use a common underlying ASP.NET core.

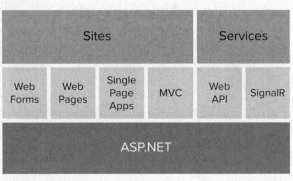

FIGURE 1-1

One ASP.NET is all about making it easier for developers to build applications using ASP.NET and Visual Studio. One ASP.NET is a general term and can mean a lot of things. Let's break it down.

In today's world, you have a lot of choices and options when you think about building web applications. Each one has its own merits and drawbacks. When you set out to build applications, how do you know which framework to choose?

If you choose one and then realize it was not a good choice, how easily can you come back and go another route? Was your framework modular enough for you to swap out the offending piece, or did you have to rewrite everything? Are you able to share code between subsystems?

How often should your framework update itself? The Internet moves far faster than most any framework can handle. How can ASP.NET serve two masters? You want HTML5 and CSS3 now, but you can't break an app your business relies on.

One ASP.NET should give developers the confidence that, no matter what they choose, they are still developing on a trusted underlying framework—ASP.NET. To help you understand One ASP.NET, the following section explores how we got here.

Evolution of ASP.NET

Web development for Microsoft started with Classic ASP (Active Server Pages) in the late 90s. A developer was able to write dynamic pages based on the VB scripting language.

ASP.NET 1.0 was introduced in 2002 and was built on top of the .NET Framework. ASP.NET Web Forms simplified developers' transition from Windows application development to web development by enabling them to build pages composed of controls, similar to a Windows user interface. It was unlike anything we'd ever seen! Visual Basic developers who were used to dragging data grids onto Windows Forms could drag data grids onto Web Forms! It was magic.

It was magic because it layered state on top of stateless HTTP. It allowed developers to react to business-level events like `Button.Click` rather than low-level events like HTTP POST, enabling a whole new generation of developers to create great web applications.

ASP.NET 2.0 was released in 2005 along with Visual Studio 2005. This release took the controls metaphor even further with data-focused enhancements like the SqlDataSource and ObjectDataSource. ASP.NET 3.5 followed in 2008 and brought with it DynamicData, which enables you to rapidly generate data-driven applications in minutes.

Shortly thereafter, ASP.NET MVC was released and introduced the popular Model-View-Controller pattern to ASP.NET web development for the first time. Still based on ASP.NET, ASP.NET MVC provided a level of testability and composition as yet unseen on the .NET platform. ASP.NET MVC was developed to meet the growing needs of a developer community that wanted to easily unit-test their applications and have more granular control over how HTML markup was generated. ASP.NET MVC represented a level of absolute control and power that brought a new kind of developer to the .NET Framework, and perhaps also allowed some older, disenfranchised developers to stay on ASP.NET.

A few things were interesting about MVC. ASP.NET MVC was one of the first releases for the ASP.NET framework where a part of the framework was released by itself "out of band" (OOB). It meant that ASP.NET MVC was released as a standalone installer that developers could optionally download and add onto their existing Visual Studio installation. This was a huge step toward making it possible for developers to get new products quickly rather than waiting for 2 to 3 years. The ASP.NET team didn't realize it was happening, but ASP.NET MVC as an out-of-band release arguably marked the beginning of the ASP.NET team's break from the Visual Studio "ship train."

Over the next 2 years, two more versions of ASP.MVC were released. More significantly, ASP.NET MVC was released under the Microsoft Public License (MS-PL), which allows developers to see the source of their favorite framework. Whispers began that perhaps ASP.NET MVC might be released as proper open source, but Microsoft would never do that, right?

ASP.NET 4 was released along with VS2010. At the same time ASP.NET MVC 4 was released, ASP.NET Web Pages was introduced with a fantastic new syntax for dynamic page creation called Razor. ASP.NET Web Pages and the new Razor syntax provide a fast, approachable, and lightweight way to combine server code with HTML to create dynamic web content. Razor became the new view engine behind ASP.NET MVC. ASP.NET Web Pages brought Razor to a simple new programming model suitable for smaller sites or folks just getting started.

ASP.NET 4.5 was released along with VS2012 in 2012. This release included ASP.NET MVC 4.5 and a new member into the ASP.NET family called ASP.NET Web API, which made it easier to write REST-based web services.

Shortly thereafter, Microsoft released the majority of its Web Stack (including ASP.NET MVC, Razor, and ASP.NET Web API) under an open source license (Apache License 2.0). But it also announced it would be taking contributions from the community—real open source on a strategically important and flagship web framework. The big ship was starting to turn.

This was the beginning of "development in the open." An interested community member can actually read the code checkins while the developers are working inside Microsoft. Even better, contributors can fix bugs, add features, and submit pull requests knowing their code could be used by millions of developers.

Open development was initially scary, but doing so enabled a more open development model where everyone is engaged and can provide feedback on code checkins, bug-fixes, new feature development, and build and test the products on a daily basis using the most up-to-date versions of the source code and tests. This was a gigantic step in getting the ASP.NET ecosystem to come together in a way that developers could work together toward building a better framework.

At this point in the story, we have a large part of ASP.NET and its runtime components shipping out of band as open source. Many features are optional, or easily added on, like Web Optimization, Universal Membership Providers, and test harnesses. How can the tooling be opened up to support a simultaneously more uniform but modular ASP.NET?

The Web Evolves and We Evolve with It

HTML5 isn't done, and unless this chapter is published in 2017, it still won't be done at the time of this writing. However, HTML5, along with its siblings CSS3 and JavaScript, have won the Internet. Now that a reliable and complete version of JavaScript is available on every modern browser, combined with a cohesive document object model (DOM), applications have changed their architecture dramatically.

JavaScript has moved beyond simple `alert()` statements and input type validation and graduated to being a near-complete virtual machine in the browser. HTML5 is very simple as a spec, and CSS3 makes it shine. Take all these ingredients and combine them with a pocket super computer, and you've got a mobile web revolution.

Today, customers are using different form factors, ranging from smartphones to tablets to personal computers. This means that they can access a web application using a phone or tablet, or using a mobile browser, or using the traditional desktop browser. The web is going more social as well. Users are interacting with each other through social means such as Twitter, Facebook, and so on, and they want to carry their social identities in all web applications with which they interact. This means that they want to log in using their social credentials, so that when they log in to the application they can interact with their friends as well. It's a world of connected devices and services for the web developer.

As the web becomes more ubiquitous and web standards continue to evolve, it is crucial that the ASP.NET framework rev at a frequency that matches the advancements in web development.

SIMPLIFYING A COMPLEX ECOSYSTEM

File ⇨ New Project is too scary. It forces an artificial choice and makes developers feel that they've proceeded down a fork in the road that may not be reversible. Perhaps, rather than a fork in the road forcing an unnatural choice, we instead consider a unified face to ASP.NET with some choice to select possible subsystems, libraries, or alternative application frameworks.

So you make your choice. How do you now discover and integrate libraries to easily write services in your application? What if you take the safe choice and choose Empty Web Application? Does that make it easier to add services? If you choose ASP.NET Web Application, how do you add DynamicData functionality to this application?

What about social? You can bring in a social support library, but can you easily integrate it into both MVC and Web Forms? From a developer's perspective, this is a fairly complicated story that leaves you hanging, trying to figure out not just the best way to get started, but also how to extend your application. Figure 1-2 shows the choices you have when creating a new project.

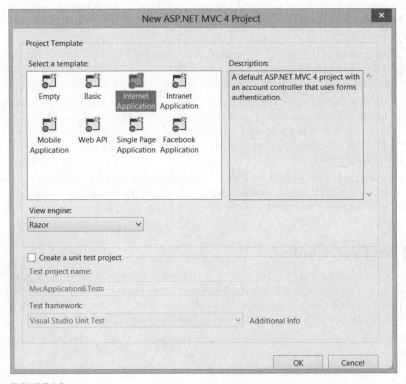

FIGURE 1-2

Web Ecosystem

Web development is an exciting and complicated space to be in. A lot of variables impact the productivity of a web developer. As a web developer, you have to constantly be versed in the latest and greatest in terms of web standards, and once you know what the latest standards are, you then have to worry whether the framework and tools you are using support those standards. Once you know that, how easy is it for you to get the FX, tools, and libraries that you want to use in your application?

A big part of this developer experience is the growing ecosystem. As the web expands and grows, you can find an explosion of libraries that help you develop your applications. These libraries can become popular and widely accepted by the developer community based on the problems they solve. For example, more general libraries such as jQuery are widely popular, and jQuery is the library of choice for many developers who use JavaScript. In addition, lots of specialized libraries are solving unique problems that might not apply to the majority of developers.

We are at a point where lots of such libraries are available, such as Entity Framework, JSON.NET, ELMAH, and so on that are open sourced and can be used in your applications. A big part of your application now comprises a mixture of these open sourced libraries and the ones that come from Microsoft. So the question is that in this growing ecosystem, how easy is it to find such libraries and easily bring them into your applications? Also, once you have these libraries, how do you ensure that they are always updated to the latest versions? Figure 1-3 shows the NuGet gallery with the most popular packages. These packages have been downloaded more than a million times each, and at the time of writing there have been total of 50 million downloads of packages from the NuGet gallery.

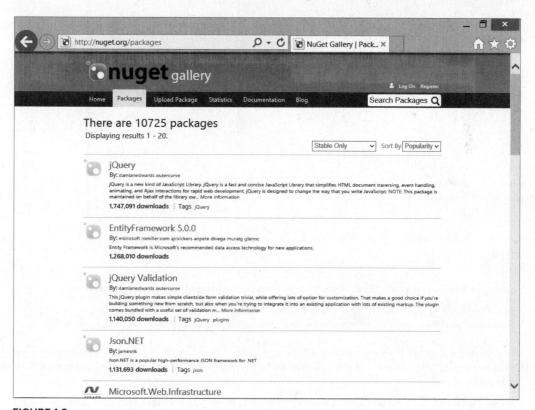

FIGURE 1-3

Web development has definitely evolved over the years, and it is an exciting time to be a web developer. Web developers no longer have to spend time adding basic building blocks to their applications. Features such as logging are so common that developers can reuse a plethora of logging libraries in their applications. How easy is it for you to start with something really small and add these so-called Lego pieces to your application to get the job done more quickly? And how can you now focus on writing code that is central to your applications and bring in these different building blocks as and when required?

The next few sections look at how ASP.NET framework and Visual Studio tooling can help you solve these problems and improve your productivity.

Getting Started Is Easy

In Visual Studio 2012 when you choose File ⇨ New Project, you get lots of choices on what type of project you want to create. You can choose from creating a Single Page Application (SPA) or have an application that uses Social Login, or have an application that uses Windows Authentication. This becomes a problem when you want to create an application where you want to mix these scenarios. There is no easy way to get started built into Visual Studio. The templates represent a static list of options, but things would be simpler with a single One ASP.NET template, as shown in Figure 1-4.

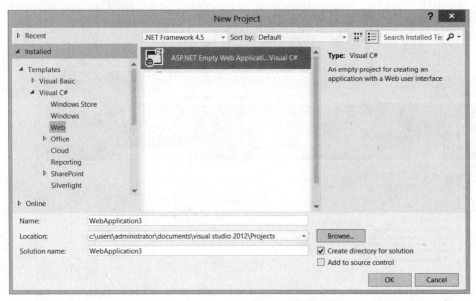

FIGURE 1-4

> **NOTE** *This is just a conceptual idea at the time of writing this book.*

Once you create an ASP.NET project, Visual Studio can guide you through a series of steps that help you get started with an SPA framework of your choice, and then enable you to choose how you want users to log in to your application.

The next section looks at how you can get more Lego pieces, or update the ones you have, once you start with such an application.

Integrating the Ecosystem Is Easy

In the previous section you looked at how easy it would be to create an SPA application with all the required libraries, such as Knockout, jQuery, ASP.NET Web API, and so on. In Visual Studio 2012, all the libraries are installed as NuGet packages. You can see what libraries are installed in your project by right-clicking the project and clicking Manage NuGet Packages. Figure 1-5 shows this option.

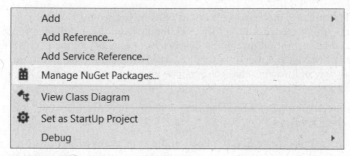

FIGURE 1-5

This launches the Manage NuGet Packages window, where you can choose the Installed packages tab and see all the packages that are installed in your project. Figure 1-6 shows all the packages installed in a project.

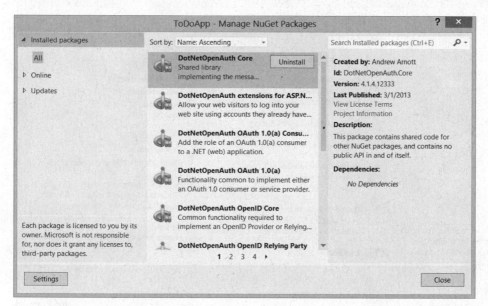

FIGURE 1-6

This window shows you the list of packages that were installed when you created the application. This application has packages that are a mix of Microsoft owned and open sourced libraries as well. This section discusses how NuGet helps you to integrate the ecosystem easily into your project.

NuGet is a Visual Studio extension that makes it easy to add, remove, and update libraries and tools in Visual Studio projects. NuGet works on both Visual Studio 2010 and Visual Studio 2012, and you can download it from the Visual Studio Extension Gallery. If you develop a library that you want to share with other developers, you can create a NuGet package and upload the package to the NuGet gallery. If you want to use a library or tool that someone else has developed, you can download the package from the gallery and install it in your Visual Studio project. Simply put, NuGet is changing the .NET developer ecosystem by making it easy to redistribute and install packages into a project.

Imagine that you had to install ELMAH into your application. Without NuGet, you would have to download an installer and then manually add references to the ELMAH library from the install location. Beyond this, you would have to read the documentation on the ELMAH website to make all the necessary changes to the `web.config` to configure ELMAH. If a new version of ELMAH came out during the course of your development, you would have no way of knowing that the version you have in your project is outdated and that you need to download a new version.

NuGet makes this entire process of finding, installing, configuring, and updating libraries very easy. It is a one-stop solution that can solve all of these problems.

Figure 1-6 showed the packages that were installed in an SPA application. Imagine that you were working on this project for a while and wanted to check for updates to any of the libraries that you were using. To do this, you would simply launch the Manage NuGet Packages window and click the Updates tab. Figure 1-7 shows the updates available for the packages.

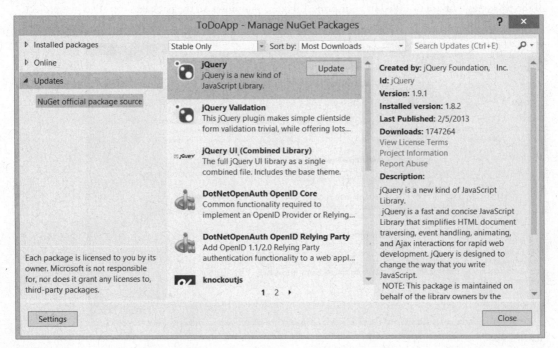

FIGURE 1-7

You click Update on the package that you want to update, and NuGet downloads a new version of that package and updates the references as well. You can easily update any of the packages quickly.

> **NOTE** *When you create any new project in Visual Studio 2012, the project already has NuGet packages installed so you can get these benefits easily.*

Real-World Example

This section shows how you can apply One ASP.NET in a practical real-world application. The following approach by no means represents any best practice, but it is meant to demonstrate how One ASP.NET and the web ecosystem can come together to help you build an ASP.NET application. Assume that you wanted to create a simple single page to-do list web application with the following requirements:

➤ A user should be able to log in using Facebook, Twitter, or register as an account on the website.

➤ A user should be able to create to dos and mark items when done.

➤ An administrator should be able to manage user accounts via an administrative section.

You can get started by choosing the ASP.NET SPA template and configuring the template to use Facebook, Twitter, and Local login. Once you have this template ready, you can start building your application.

First, implement an ASP.NET Web API so you can have a REST-based service to manage to-do items. You can add a Web API by right-clicking your project and adding a new item template—ASP.NET Web API Controller Class (see Figure 1-8).

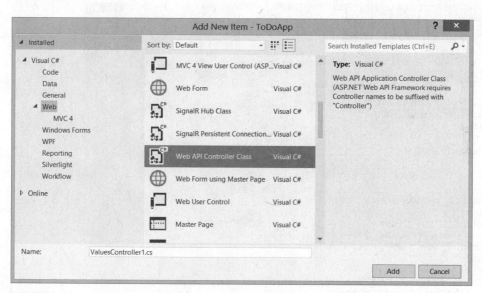

FIGURE 1-8

When you install this item template, it installs all the NuGet packages needed for running a Web API in ASP.NET.

Write some code to implement to-do functionality of your application that includes features such as adding, deleting, modifying, and getting all to dos. Figure 1-9 shows a snippet of code for retrieving a list of to-do items.

```
// GET api/TodoList
public IEnumerable<TodoListDto> GetTodoLists()
{
    return db.TodoLists.Include("Todos")
        .Where(u => u.UserId == User.Identity.Name)
        .OrderByDescending(u => u.TodoListId)
        .AsEnumerable()
        .Select(todoList => new TodoListDto(todoList));
}
```

FIGURE 1-9

While writing this To do Web API, you will want to test out the functionality without running your entire application, because it can become quite cumbersome. You can use NuGet to search for some test clients for testing your To do Web API. A quick search might return a list of packages from which you can choose one based on its rating. For example, you could download the WebApiTestClient NuGet package, which was popular at the time of writing this chapter. Figure 1-10 shows the result when you use this test client to test your Web API.

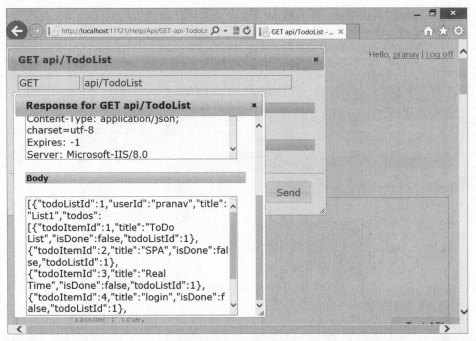

FIGURE 1-10

Now that you have the Web API working, you can start adding SPA libraries so that you can write the front end of the application. Again, you can search on NuGet for an SPA library of your choice. For this example, choose Knockout. Once you install the NuGet package, it brings in all the required libraries for using Knockout.

After you install Knockout, you can create web pages where you can call your To do Web API and bind the results in Knockout views. The Visual Studio editor provides rich support for Knockout syntax highlighting and IntelliSense, which makes it easier to use Knockout. Figure 1-11 shows the syntax highlighting support for Knockout in Visual Studio.

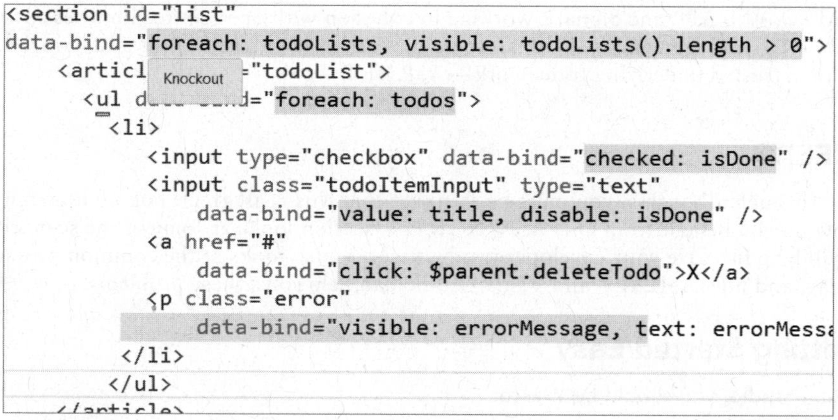

```html
<section id="list"
data-bind="foreach: todoLists, visible: todoLists().length > 0">
    <articl  Knockout  ="todoList">
     <ul d    ="foreach: todos">
       <li>
          <input type="checkbox" data-bind="checked: isDone" />
          <input class="todoItemInput" type="text"
             data-bind="value: title, disable: isDone" />
          <a href="#"
             data-bind="click: $parent.deleteTodo">X</a>
          <p class="error"
             data-bind="visible: errorMessage, text: errorMessa
       </li>
     </ul>
   </article>
```

FIGURE 1-11

Once you have the client-side data binding working with Knockout, you will have a fully functional SPA application. If you want to receive updates about your to-do items, you can get real-time update functionality by installing ASP.NET SignalR. You can do this by downloading the Microsoft.AspNet.SignalR NuGet package. Once you install this package, you can modify your application code to add real-time functionality. Figure 1-12 shows the to-do application that you just developed.

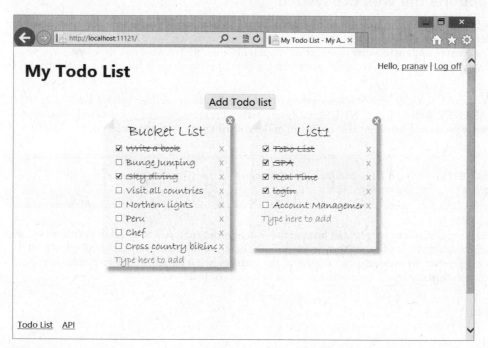

FIGURE 1-12

The final part in creating your application is to build some user account management for administrators. You can quickly build this part using ASP.NET Web Forms and Dynamic Data, which is a good framework for rapidly building data-driven applications. You can also secure this section with ASP.NET authorization using roles so that only administrators can access this section of the website.

Finally, if you look at this application, it is a mixture of ASP.NET frameworks and technologies such as ASP.NET Web Forms, MVC, Web API, and SignalR working in cohesion with open source libraries such as Knockout, jQuery, JSON.NET, and many more. With all these different sets of frameworks and libraries, you are still developing on a trusted underlying framework—ASP.NET.

HOW DO YOU BENEFIT?

Now that you have read through all of this, you must be thinking that this is all great, but what is in it for you as a developer? How do you benefit from One ASP.NET? This section looks at some of the scenarios where One ASP.NET will help increase your developer productivity. It also looks at the common problems faced by developers today, and how ASP.NET and Visual Studio can help solve these problems.

ASP.NET Makes Getting Started Easy

With ASP.NET and Visual Studio, you should be able to:

> ➤ Start with nothing (an empty project) and add the required pieces of the framework and libraries needed to build your application.

> ➤ Choose the set of frameworks and libraries you need to build your application.

One ASP.NET will make the ASP.NET framework more modular so you can get started with an application and be able to easily add the required set of pieces needed to build your application.

ASP.NET Supports the Web Ecosystem

We all know by now that future web applications will be much richer in terms of the user experience that they will offer. Also, with the growth of the .NET developer community, there has been an explosion of libraries being created and distributed amongst developers. In the .NET ecosystem, developers are now relying more and more on open sourced libraries and are contributing to these libraries to make them even better.

The majority of the Microsoft Web Stack is now open sourced. Products such as ASP.NET MVC, ASP.NET Web Pages, ASP.NET Web API, ASP.NET SignalR, and Entity Framework are open sourced. This means that developers who do not work for Microsoft can make contributions to these projects.

> **NOTE** *Even though these products are open sourced, they continue to be fully supported and staffed by Microsoft.*

Apart from making contributions, you can browse the source code, subscribe to checkin notifications, and browse through the active list of issues that developers on these products are working on. By doing all of this, you, as a developer, have more direct impact to the features being designed and developed in these products, which eventually results in a better product being developed.

ASP.NET Makes Finding, Adding, and Updating Lego Blocks to Your Site Easy

Although the growing ecosystem is a great sign for the web developer community, today there is a problem of discovering and installing all these great libraries in this ecosystem. The installation experience for such libraries has centered around downloading an installer and running through the installation steps. This makes the process of adding, configuring, and updating libraries in the project very hard. In contrast, NuGet is a giant step forward in this space. Libraries/frameworks can be redistributed as NuGet packages, which can be easily installed into your project through Visual Studio.

ASP.NET Helps You Apply Concepts from One Framework to Another

The ASP.NET umbrella has lots of different features that were developed in one framework, such as ASP.NET MVC, and have now made their way into other frameworks, such as ASP.NET Web Forms, and vice versa. For example:

➤ There was a feature called Data Annotation Attributes that was introduced in ASP.NET Dynamic Data and later introduced in ASP.NET MVC.

➤ Routing and model binding were some of the highlights of ASP.NET MVC that eventually made their way into ASP.NET Web Forms.

➤ ASP.NET Web Pages had a simple routing model called Smarty Routes that let you generate cleaner looking URLs without any configuration. This feature made its way into ASP.NET Web Forms and is now called ASP.NET FriendlyURLs.

This means that if you are an ASP.NET developer, you can use these well-known concepts or features and apply them to any framework of your choice. If you like model binding and are a Web Forms developer, now you can continue building Web Forms applications while using new and well-known features such as model binding. You do not have to switch to another framework such as ASP.NET MVC, just for the simple reason that ASP.NET MVC supports model binding.

ASP.NET Moves as Fast as the Web

The web is evolving at a crazy pace. This is caused by many factors. The proliferation of devices and services has caused new kinds of applications to emerge that need to be more closely interconnected. The web is going more social, where users want to collaborate with each other in real time. To support all these changes, the Web Standards Consortium is pushed to make sure the specifications of HTML, JavaScript, and CSS are updated quickly to support these demands. Given all these changes, developers are pushed as well to stay abreast of all of them and demand that the frameworks and tools they use are updated to these latest standards as well.

ASP.NET and Visual Studio have been responding to these changes as well. When ASP.NET 2.0 was released, it was released with VS2005, which was released 3 years after ASP.NET 1.0. This meant that developers had to wait for 3 years to get the latest framework that supported the latest web standards. We are moving to a new world now where parts of ASP.NET can be released more frequently and updated easily without waiting for the next release of Visual Studio.

ASP.NET MVC, Web Pages, Web API, and SignalR are released as NuGet packages on the NuGet gallery so you can update these frameworks by updating the NuGet packages installed in your project. Microsoft ASP.NET and Web Frameworks 2012.2 and Microsoft Web Developer Tools 2012.2 add support for a number of improvements to make it easy to write web applications in VS and publish them to Azure. Visual Studio 2012 shipped with 1.0 version of Microsoft Web Developer Tools, but by the time this book is published this would be 1.2. This means in a matter of a few months as a developer you were able to get the latest tools to increase your productivity while building web applications. The ASP.NET team is moving toward a more frequent release schedule to be able to deliver updated tools and libraries to make web development more relevant for the emerging standards and libraries.

SUMMARY

ASP.NET should be a reliable, fun, modular, powerful, and scalable platform for building web applications. Whether you're using a reporting control in Web Forms from a third-party control builder, or writing your own custom HTML Helper, ASP.NET can be a platform you should feel confident to have underlying your work.

Perhaps your solution is developed using TDD and Agile with SpecFlow and targeting ASP.NET MVC, or perhaps you prefer Ember.js and ASP.NET Web API. Likely you'll mix and match, and as well you should. ASP.NET is certainly becoming a web framework with choices.

Don't be afraid to try new things, swap out components, or explore new open source libraries. ASP.NET and the team will try to solve the big, hard problems of scale, security, and performance. How you architect your application is a personal choice, and you should have no concerns about ASP.NET's ability to rise to the occasion and support your architecture.

With the release of ASP.NET and Web Tools 2012.2, ASP.NET is about halfway to the dream of One ASP.NET. Someday soon perhaps Microsoft project templates will live side by side with community templates, and project templates will be easily shared and distributed as NuGet packages. The most recent version of ASP.NET doesn't make it too hard to imagine that future.

HTML5 and CSS3 Design with ASP.NET

➤ Understanding the basics of HTML5
➤ Understanding the basics of CSS3
➤ Using HTML5 and CSS3 in ASP.NET applications

WROX.COM CODE DOWNLOADS FOR THIS CHAPTER

Please note that all the code examples in this chapter are available as a part of this chapter's code download on the book's website at www.wrox.com on the Download Code tab.

When HTML was first introduced by Tim Berners-Lee, it was intended to be a simple way for researchers using the Internet to format and cross-link their research documents. At the time, the web was still primarily text-based; therefore, the formatting requirements for these documents were fairly basic. HTML needed only a small handful of basic layout concepts, such as a page title, section headers, paragraphs, and lists. As the web was opened up to the general public, graphical browsers were introduced, and as requirements for formatting web pages continued to expand, newer versions of HTML were introduced. These newer versions expanded the original capabilities of HTML to accommodate the new, rich graphical browser environment, allowing table layouts, richer font styling, images, and frames. In 1997, HTML was standardized to HTML4.

Although all of these improvements to HTML were helpful, HTML still proved to be inadequate for allowing developers to create complex, highly stylized web pages. In 1994, a new technology called Cascading Style Sheets (CSS) was introduced. CSS served as a complementary technology to HTML, giving developers of web pages the power they needed to control the style of their web pages.

As the web has matured, CSS has gained popularity as developers realized that it has significant advantages over standard HTML styling capabilities. Unlike HTML, which was originally conceived as primarily a layout mechanism, CSS was conceived from the beginning to provide rich styling capabilities to web pages. The cascading nature of CSS makes it easy to apply styles with a broad stroke to an entire application and overrides those styles only where necessary. CSS allows externally defining website style information easy, allowing for a clear separation of web page style and structure. CSS also allows developers to greatly reduce the file size of a web page, which translates into faster page load times and reduced bandwidth consumption.

Since the turn of the century, mobile devices and multimedia streaming have gained in popularity. As Web 2.0 applications continue to evolve, so has HTML and CSS. Over the past couple of years, HTML5 and CSS3 have become more prevalent. The chapter starts with a brief overview of HTML5 and CSS3, and finishes with creating websites in Visual Studio using HTML and CSS. It's a good idea to review these technologies because the project templates found in Visual Studio 2012 have been reworked using HTML5 and CSS3.

CAVEATS

Although this chapter includes a lot of great information about HTML and CSS, and how you can use them in conjunction with ASP.NET and Visual Studio, you should be aware of several caveats.

First, because there is no way that a single chapter can begin to cover the entire breadth of HTML and CSS, if you are looking for an in-depth discussion of these topics, you can check out the Wrox title *HTML5 24-Hour Trainer,* by Joseph W. Lowery and Mark Fletcher (Wiley, 2011).

Second, because CSS is simply a recommended specification, the interpretation and implementation of that specification is up to each browser vendor. As is so often the case in web development, each browser has its own quirks in how it implements (or sometimes does not implement) different CSS features. Even though the samples in this chapter were tested on Internet Explorer 10, be sure to thoroughly test your websites in multiple browsers on multiple platforms to ensure that your CSS is rendering appropriately in each browser you are targeting.

Finally, both HTML5 and CSS3 are works in progress. CSS3 is unlike previous versions in that it's made up of multiple modules. As of this book's publication date, four modules have been published as formal recommendations. Although the CSS3 recommendation has not been finalized, the first official draft of CSS4 has been published in September, 2011 by the World Wide Web Consortium (W3C). HTML5 is still in its draft phase. In July 2012, the HTML5 specification editor Ian Hickson, announced that the W3C plans to take a snapshot of the HTML5 specification in 2014. This snapshot will be known as HTML5. The Web Hypertext Application Technology Working Group (WHATWG) will continue to maintain the specification beyond that period.

HTML5 OVERVIEW

From the beginning of the web, continuing to today, HTML serves as the primary mechanism for defining the content blocks of your web page, and is the easiest way to define the layout of your page. HTML includes a variety of layout tags you can use, including table, list, and grouping elements. You can combine these elements to create highly complex layouts in your page. Figure 2-1 illustrates a single web page that defines a basic layout using a variety of HTML elements.

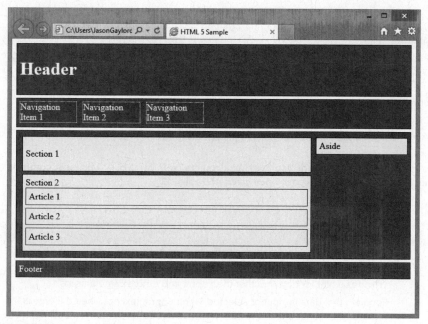

FIGURE 2-1

Looking at this figure, you may quickly notice that the web page contains a page title, a few headings, a list, and a few paragraphs. However, unlike typical HTML4, this page is using a few new semantic elements as part of HTML5. We'll take a look at the source of this page and explain the new elements in greater detail next.

> **NOTE** *If you want to learn more about the differences between the HTML4 and HTML5 specification beyond what is mentioned within this chapter, be sure to visit the W3C website at* www.w3.org *and search for HTML5.*

New Elements, Attributes, and Values in HTML5

The official HTML5 specification that has been documented by the W3C includes several new semantic elements. These elements include, but are not limited to, the ones shown in Table 2-1.

TABLE 2-1

ELEMENT	DESCRIPTION
section	A web page as a whole or a portion of that web page such as featured content
article	A piece of information on a web page such as a news posting, blog post, or status message
header	The top portion of a web page that can contain logos or other page headings
nav	A specific section that is designated for navigation elements such as a menu or breadcrumbs
aside	A portion of a web page that provides content that partially relates to the overall content such as a side bar or advertisements

continues

TABLE 2-1 *(continued)*

ELEMENT	DESCRIPTION
figure	An area designated to represent a piece of content that displays information related to the web page such as a chart or video
footer	The bottom portion of a web page that can contain copyright information, privacy notices, or other information about an author
video	Displays a multimedia video
audio	Plays audio sounds and is the replacement for bgsound

There have been quite a few new attributes added to existing elements from HTML4. The most common attributes added include, but are not limited to, the ones listed in Table 2-2.

TABLE 2-2

ATTRIBUTE	DESCRIPTION
autofocus	Allows an input (except when the type is hidden), select, textarea, and button element to gain focus when a page is loaded.
placeholder	Provides a hint for data input for the input and textarea elements.
required	Requires that data is input or selected for an input (except when the type is hidden, image, or one of the button types), select, or textarea element.
min, max, step, multiple, pattern	Specifies constraints for input elements.
async	Loads script elements asynchronously.
seemless	Provides a borderless frame for an iframe element. When a link is clicked within an iframe with the seemless attribute, the content is loaded in the parent frame unless the _blank value is used with the target attribute.
reversed	Reverses the order of an ol element's list items.

In addition to the semantic elements and new attributes introduced in HTML5, several new values have been added to the input element's type attribute. At the time of publication, the following values are included:

➤ tel: A string value that doesn't force the user to enter a valid telephone number, as the possible values change based on location. However, the input validation can be made by applying the pattern attribute and setting a value to that attribute.

➤ search: A string value that is very similar to the text type, but allows certain browsers or applications to identify it differently.

➤ url: A string value that conforms to a single, absolute URL.

➤ email: A string value that conforms to a valid e-mail address. When specifying the multiple attribute, the e-mail addresses are split by using a comma.

➤ datetime: A string value that conforms to a valid global date and time value. A valid global date and time value consists of a Gregorian date and a time. The Gregorian date consists of a year, a month, and a day. The time consists of an hour, a minute, a second, and a fraction of a second, expressed with a time-zone offset.

➤ date: A string value that conforms to a valid date value. A valid date value consists of a year, a month, and a day separated by hyphens. A valid date does not include a time-zone offset.

➤ month: A string value that conforms to a valid month value that is represented by a four-digit year, a hyphen, followed by a two-digit month.

➤ week: A string value that conforms to a valid week value that is represented by a four-digit year, a hyphen, followed by a two-digit week number. The maximum value for a week number can be 53 if a particular year has 53 weeks. Otherwise, the maximum week number is 52. A week is counted if it starts on a Monday.

➤ `time`: A string value that conforms to a valid time that consists of an hour, a minute, and a second. Optionally, a fraction of a second up to three digits can be included. A valid time does not include a time-zone offset.

➤ `datetime-local`: A string value that conforms to a valid local date and time value. Much like a `datetime` value, a valid local date and time value consists of a Gregorian date and a time. However, this value does not include a time-zone offset.

➤ `number`: A string value that consists of a positive or negative floating point number. As of the date of publication, the bounds of this value are between 2^{1024} and -2^{1024}.

➤ `range`: A string value that consists of a positive or negative floating point number, as defined previously. However, this value can be further restricted when using the `min`, `max`, and `step` attributes. If no `min`, `max`, or `step` attributes are provided, the minimum value defaults to 0 and the maximum value defaults to 100.

➤ `color`: A string value that consist of a simple color value. A simple color value is defined as a valid sRGB value represented by the number sign (#) followed by the lowercase hexadecimal value of the sRGB color. For example, white would be represented as #ffffff. The value must be exactly seven characters in length.

As an example, Listing 2-1 shows the HTML source produced by the web page that was rendered in Figure 2-1. The style elements were removed for better clarity.

LISTING 2-1: The web page source output for Figure 2-1

```
<!DOCTYPE html>
<html>
<head>
    <title>HTML 5 Sample</title>
</head>
<body>
    <header>
        <h1>Header</h1>
    </header>
    <nav>
        <ul>
            <li>Navigation Item 1</li>
            <li>Navigation Item 2</li>
            <li>Navigation Item 3</li>
        </ul>
    </nav>
    <div id="mainContent">
        <aside>
            Aside
        </aside>
        <section>
            <p>
                Section 1
            </p>
        </section>
        <section>
            Section 2
            <article>
                Article 1
            </article>
            <article>
                Article 2
```

continues

LISTING 2-1 *(continued)*

```
                </article>
                <article>
                    Article 3
                </article>
            </section>
        </div>
        <footer>
            Footer
        </footer>
    </body>
</html>
```

When inspecting the source, one of the first changes you'll notice in HTML5 is the shortened DOCTYPE name. The reasoning behind the shortened DOCTYPE is that modern browsers will load the document and switch to the appropriate DOCTYPE based on the content loaded.

The next set of changes you'll notice are the semantic elements that are used. You've already read about the purpose of these elements. However, when you look at the HTML source, it's easier to read. Another developer with limited experience with your website will be able to understand the content layout and the separation between the header, section, article, aside, and footer.

Using the New HTML5 Markup

At this point, you've learned about most of the markup changes within HTML5. To gain a better understanding of how to use the new elements, attributes, and values, you'll now step through two example projects.

Scenario 1: Implementing a Top Ten Countdown

Let's assume that for your first task, you've been asked to provide markup for a sports article. The article will contain a list of the top ten high school baseball teams in your area. However, instead of listing the teams as one through ten, you're tasked with listing them in countdown order. If you were using HTML4, you can accomplish this task by breaking the HTML 4.01 specification. In this case, you would produce HTML similar to what is shown in Listing 2-2 (abbreviated sample for demonstrative purposes).

LISTING 2-2: Creating a reversed order list in HTML4

```
<h1>Top Three Teams</h1>
<ol>
    <li value="3">Third Place</li>
    <li value="2">Runner Up</li>
    <li value="1">Top Team</li>
</ol>
```

Now that you are using HTML5, you can use the article element and the reversed attribute of an ordered list, as shown in Listing 2-3.

LISTING 2-3: Using the article element and reversed attribute

```
<article>
    <h1>Top Ten Baseball Teams</h1>
    <ol reversed="reversed">
        <li>Coughlin</li>
        <li>Hazleton Area</li>
        <li>Pittston Area</li>
        <li>Nanticoke Area</li>
        <li>Hanover Area</li>
```

```
            <li>Lake Lehman</li>
            <li>Crestwood</li>
            <li>Wyoming Valley West</li>
            <li>Dallas</li>
            <li>Wyoming Area</li>
        </ol>
    </article>
```

When viewing this in Internet Explorer, you will continue to see the teams listed one through ten. As mentioned earlier, the HTML5 specification has not been finalized. In this case, not all browsers support the reversed Boolean value. However, in Google Chrome, for instance, you will see the correct rendering, as shown in Figure 2-2. Later in this chapter, you'll learn how you can force compatibility in most browsers.

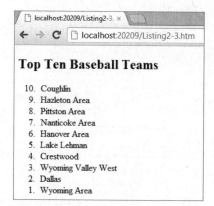

FIGURE 2-2

Scenario 2: Capturing a Valid Dollar Amount

You are building an e-commerce application. One of your user stories can be summed up to allow a product entry clerk to enter a valid price for a product. A valid price has the following requirements:

➤ The lowest price for a product can be $1.00.
➤ The highest price for a product can be $99.95.
➤ Product prices must be in increments of a nickel ($0.05).
➤ A product price is required.

If you were using pure HTML4, you could not accomplish this task. The best you would be able to do is create a drop-down with list items ranging from 1.00 to 99.95. Furthermore, if you were to use client-side code only, JavaScript would be required to force a value to be entered into the field.

Much like the first scenario, this is a piece of cake when using HTML5. In fact, most modern browsers, including Internet Explorer, provide a user-friendly validation message without needing to add custom JavaScript. As shown here by adding a simple input element, you can meet all of the requirements:

```
<input name="price" type="number" min="1" max="99.95" step="0.05" required />
```

As you can see, the input element has the type attribute set to number. Remember that the number type allows a positive or negative floating number. Next, you've added new attributes to the input element. To meet the requirements, you've set the min attribute value to 1 and the max attribute value to 99.95. This ensures that the data entry clerk can only enter a value between and including the min and max values. You've also added a value of 0.05 for the step attribute. With this attribute value, you're allowing prices to increment only five cents at a time. Finally, you've added the required attribute to force a value for this input element. When entering an incorrect value, such as 1.01, users will receive the validation message as shown in Figure 2-3.

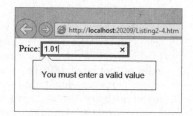

FIGURE 2-3

New APIs in HTML5

In addition to the markup language changes already mentioned, the HTML5 specification includes many new APIs to access using JavaScript. The new APIs that are currently in the HTML5 specification include, but are not limited to, the following:

➤ Media
➤ Offline web application support
➤ Drag and drop

➤ Session browser history

➤ Printing

➤ Base64 conversion

➤ Search providers

There are other APIs that are not officially part of the HTML5 specification. These include, but are not limited to, the following:

➤ Microdata

➤ Canvas and SVG

➤ Background scripts

➤ Client-side data storage

➤ WebSocket (bidirectional client-server communication)

➤ EventSource (server-to-client communication)

➤ Geolocation

> **NOTE** *If you want to learn more about these APIs, be sure to visit the WHATWG website at* www.whatwg.org *or search online for HTML5 API.*

CSS3 OVERVIEW

Earlier, in Listing 2-1, you reviewed HTML markup with semantic elements. Although the organization of this web page is interesting, it lacks all but the most basic styling. To solve this problem, many developers would be tempted to add HTML-based formatting tags. For example, if I wanted to change the font and color of the text in the first paragraph, I might change its HTML to something like this:

```
<font face="Arial" color="blue">
```

In fact, in the early days of web design tools, this code was generated when users added styling to their web pages, and for a while, using `<font>` tags seemed like a great solution to the problem of styling your web pages.

Web developers and designers quickly learned, however, that using the `<font>` tag quickly lead to a mess of spaghetti HTML, with `<font>` tags being splattered throughout the HTML. Imagine that if, in Listing 2-1, you not only wanted to set the color, but some of the text also needed to be bold, a different color or font face, a different font size, underlined, and displayed as superscript. Imagine how many `<font>` tags you would need then, and how it would increase the weight of the web page and decrease its maintainability. Using `<font>` tags (and other style-related tags) meant that a clear and clean separation no longer existed between the structure and content of the web page. Instead, both were mashed together into a single complex document.

The introduction of cascading style sheets (CSS) to the web development and design world brought back a clean and elegant solution for styling web pages. CSS meant a style could be defined in a single location for the entire website, and simply referenced on the elements requiring the style. Using CSS brings back the logical separation between web page content and the styles used to display it.

> **NOTE** *Since CSS has become so popular with web development, the HTML5 specification has deprecated certain HTML elements that have represented style in the past, such as the* font, center, *and* strike *elements.*

Creating Style Sheets

Like HTML, CSS is an interpreted language. When a web page request is processed by a web server, the server's response can include style sheets, which are simply collections of cascading style instructions. The style sheets can be included in the server's response in three ways: through external style sheet files, through internal style sheets embedded directly in the web page, or through inline style sheets.

External Sheets

External style sheets are collections of CSS styles stored outside of the web pages that will use them—generally files using the .css extension. Visual Studio makes adding external style sheet files to your application simple by including a Style Sheet file template in the Add New Item dialog box, as shown in Figure 2-4.

> **NOTE** *You can access the Add New Item dialog box by right-clicking on your project and choosing Add ⇨ Add New Item, going to File ⇨ New ⇨ File, or by pressing Ctrl+N.*

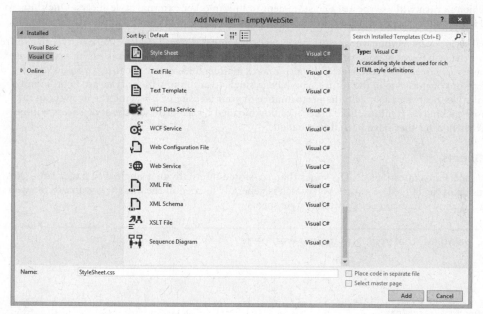

FIGURE 2-4

After Visual Studio creates the style sheet, inserting new styles is easy. Visual Studio even provides CSS IntelliSense when working with styles in the document, as shown in Figure 2-5.

You link external style sheets into web pages by using the HTML `<link>` tag. A single web page can contain multiple style sheet references, as shown in Listing 2-4.

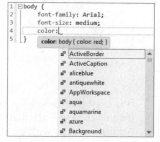

FIGURE 2-5

LISTING 2-4: Adding multiple style sheet references

```
<!DOCTYPE html>
<html>
<head>
    <title>HTML 5 Sample</title>
    <link href="primary.css" type="text/css" rel="stylesheet" />
    <link href="secondary.css" type="text/css" rel="stylesheet" />
</head>
<body>
    <div>Lorem Ipsum</div>
</body>
</html>
```

You can also use the CSS import statement directly in your style sheet to actually link multiple style sheets together:

```
@import url("secondary.css");
```

Using the import statement has the advantage that you can alter the style sheets linked together without having to modify every web page in your site. Instead, you can simply link each page to a master external style sheet, which in turn will use the import statement to link in other external style sheets. One thing to keep in mind is that older browsers may not understand this syntax and will simply ignore the command.

Using external style sheets in your website offers several advantages. First, because external style sheets are kept outside of the web pages in your site, adding a link tag to all of your web pages is easier than trying to manage the styles directly in each page. This also makes maintenance easier because if you decide to update the style of your website in the future, you have a single location in which styles are kept. Finally, using external style sheets can also help the performance of your website by allowing the browser to take advantage of its caching capabilities. Like other files downloaded by the browser, the style sheets will be cached on the client after they have been downloaded.

Internal Style Sheets

Internal style sheets are collections of CSS styles that are stored internally in a single web page. The styles are located inside of the HTML <style> tag, which is generally located in the <head> section of the web page. Listing 2-5 shows an example of internal style sheets.

LISTING 2-5: Using internal style sheets in a web page

```
<!DOCTYPE html>
<html>
<head>
    <title>HTML 5 Sample</title>
    <style type="text/css">
        body {
            font-family: Arial;
            font-size: medium;
        }
    </style>
</head>
<body>
    <div>Lorem Ipsum</div>
</body>
</html>
```

It is important when you create internal style sheets that when you create style blocks, you make sure to include the type attribute with the style tag so the browser knows how to properly interpret the block. Additionally, as with external style sheets, Visual Studio gives you IntelliSense support to make adding properties easy for you.

Inline Styles

Inline styles are CSS styles that are applied directly to an individual HTML element using the element's `style` attribute, which is available on most HTML elements. Listing 2-6 shows an example of inline styles.

LISTING 2-6: Using inline styles in a web page

```
<!DOCTYPE html>
<html>
<head>
    <title>Inline CSS Sample</title>
</head>
<body>
    <div style="font-family: Arial;">Lorum Ipsum</div>
</body>
</html>
```

CSS Rules

Regardless of how they are stored, after CSS styles are sent from the server to the client, the browser is responsible for parsing the styles and applying them to the appropriate HTML elements in the web page. If a style is stored in either an external or internal style sheet, the styles will be defined as a CSS rule. Rules are what the browser uses to determine what styling to apply to which HTML elements.

> **NOTE** *Inline styles do not need to be defined as a rule because they are automatically applied to the element they are included with. Therefore, the browser does not need to select the elements to apply it to.*

A rule is made up of two parts: the selector and its properties. Figure 2-6 shows an example of a CSS rule.

Selectors

The *selector* is the portion of the rule that dictates exactly how the web browser should select the elements to apply the style to. CSS includes a variety of types of selectors, each of which defines a different element selection technique.

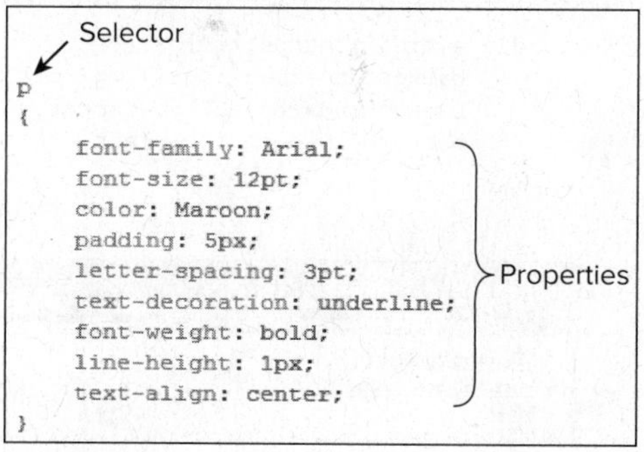

Universal Selectors

The Universal selector indicates that the style should apply to any element in the web page. The sample that follows shows a Universal selector, which would change the font of any element that supports the `font-family` property to Arial.

FIGURE 2-6

```
*
{
    font-family: Arial;
}
```

Type Selectors

The Type selector allows you to create a style that applies to a specific type of HTML element. The style will then be applied to all elements of that type in the web page. The following sample shows a Type selector configured for the HTML paragraph tag, which will change the font family of all <p> tags in the web page to Arial:

```
p
{
    font-family: Arial;
}
```

Descendant Selectors

Descendant selectors allow you to create styles that target HTML elements that are descendants of a specific type of element. The following sample demonstrates a style that will be applied to any `<span>` tag that is a descendant of a `<div>`:

```
div span
{
    font-family: Arial;
}
```

Child Selectors

The Child selector is similar to the Descendant selector except unlike the Descendant selector, which searches the entire descendant hierarchy of an element, the Child selector restricts its element search to only those elements that are direct children of the parent element. The following code shows a modification of the Descendant selector, making it a Child selector:

```
div > span
{
    font-family:Arial;
}
```

Attribute Selectors

Attribute selectors enable you to define a style that is applied to elements based on the existence of element attributes rather than the actual element name. For example, the following sample creates a style that is applied to any element in the web page that has the `href` attribute set:

```
*[href]
{
    font-family:Arial;
}
```

CSS3 adds some additional behavior to attribute selectors. Beginning with CSS3, you can now specify not only attributes, but attribute values. For example, let's say you want to display a list of web links as shown in Figure 2-7. For each link that begins with `https://`, you want to place a lock icon to the left of the link:

```
div a[href^="https://"] {
    background-image: url(img/lock-icon.png);
    background-repeat: no-repeat;
    background-position: left;
}
```

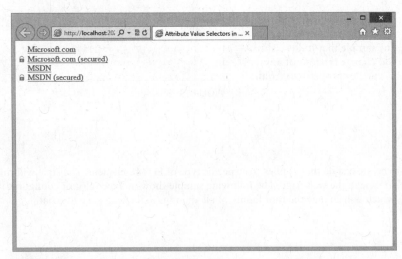

FIGURE 2-7

> **NOTE** *Attribute selectors are not supported by older browsers such as Internet Explorer 6, but as a web developer, you can decide whether you're willing to support older browsers. You can find the current percentage of PCs with Internet Explorer 6 installed by visiting* www.ie6countdown.com.

Adjacent Selectors

Adjacent selectors enable you to select HTML elements that are immediately adjacent to another element type. For example, in an unordered list, you might want to highlight the first list item and then have all the following items use a different style. You can use an Adjacent selector to do this, as shown in the following sample:

```
li
{
    color: maroon;
}
li+li
{
    color: silver;
}
```

In this sample, a default Type selector has been created for the list item element (`<li>`), which will change the color of the text in the element to maroon. However, a second Adjacent selector has been created, which will override the Type selector for all list items after the first, changing the color to silver.

Class Selectors

A Class selector is a special type of CSS selector that allows you to apply a style to any element with a specific class name. The class name is defined in HTML using the `class` attribute, which is present on almost every element. Class selectors are distinguished from other selector types by prefixing them with a single period (.):

```
.title
{
    font-size: larger;
    font-weight: bold;
}
```

This CSS rule would then be applied to any element whose class attribute value matched the rule name, an example of which is shown here:

```
<div class="title">Lorum Ipsum</div>
```

When creating Class selectors, note that the class name may not begin with a numeric character. Also, CSS class names can contain alphanumeric characters. Hyphens and underscores are also allowed. However, spaces and symbols are not allowed anywhere in the class name. Class names also cannot start with two hyphens or an underscore. Finally, make sure that you match the casing of your class name when using it in the HTML. Although CSS itself is not case sensitive, some HTML DocTypes dictate that the `class` and `id` attributes be treated as case sensitive.

ID Selectors

An ID selector is another special type of CSS selector that allows you to create styles that target elements with specific ID values. ID selectors are distinguished from other selector types by prefixing them with a hash mark (#):

```
#title
{
    font-size: larger;
    font-weight: bold;
}
```

This CSS rule would be applied to any element whose id attribute value matched the rule name, an example of which is shown here:

```
<div id="title">Lorum Ipsum</div>
```

Pseudo-Classes

CSS also includes a series of pseudo-class selectors that give you additional options in creating style rules. You can add pseudo-classes to other selectors to allow you to create more complex rules.

First-Child Pseudo-Class

The first-child pseudo-class allows you to indicate that the rule should select the first child element *M* of an element *N*. The following is an example of using the first-child pseudo-class:

```
#title p:first-child
{
    font-size: xx-small;
}
```

The previously defined rule states that the style should be applied to the first paragraph tag found within any element with an id attribute value of title. In the following HTML, that means that the text First Child would have the style applied to it:

```
<div id="title">
    Lorum
    <p>First Child</p>
    <p>Second Child</p>
    Ipsum
</div>
```

CSS includes a number of pseudo-classes specifically related to anchor tags. These special pseudo-classes allow you to define styles for the different states of an anchor tag:

```
a:link
{
    color: maroon;
}
a:visited
{
    color: silver;
}
```

In this sample, two rules have been created, the first of which applies a style to the unvisited links in a page, whereas the second applies a different style to the visited links.

Dynamic Pseudo-Classes

The dynamic pseudo-classes are special CSS classes that are applied by the browser based on actions performed by the end user, such as hovering over an element, activating an element, or giving an element focus.

```
a:hover
{
    color: maroon;
}
a:active
{
    color: silver;
}
a:focus
{
    color: olive;
}
```

Although the sample demonstrates the use of the dynamic pseudo-classes with the anchor tag, you can use them with any HTML element. Note, however, that support for the dynamic pseudo-classes in different browsers varies.

Language Pseudo-Class

The language pseudo-class allows you to define specific rules based on the end user's language settings.

```
:lang(de)
{
    quotes: '<<' '>>' '\2039' '\203A'
}
```

In this sample, the `lang` pseudo-class is used to set the quotes for a web page that is German.

> **NOTE** *IE 7 does not support the* `lang` *pseudo-class.*

Pseudo-Elements

CSS also includes several pseudo-elements that allow you to make selections of items in the web page that are not true elements.

The pseudo-elements available are `first-line`, `first-letter`, `before`, and `after`. The following samples demonstrate the use of these elements:

```
p:first-line
{
    font-style: italic;
}
p:first-letter
{
    font-size: xx-large;
}
```

The pseudo-`first-line` and `first-letter` elements allow you to apply special styling to the first line and first letter of a content block.

```
p:before
{
    content: url(images/quote.gif);
}
p:after
{
    content: '<<end>>';
}
```

The pseudo-`before` and `after` elements allow you to insert content before or after the targeted element, in this case a paragraph element. The content you insert can be a URL, string, quote character, counter, or the value of an attribute of the element.

Selector Grouping

When creating CSS rules, CSS allows you to group several selectors together into a single rule. The following sample demonstrates a single rule that combines three Type selectors:

```
h1, h2, h3
{
    color: maroon;
}
```

This rule then results in the forecolor of the text content of any h1, h2, or h3 tag being maroon.

Selector Combinations

CSS also allows you to combine multiple selector types (see Listing 2-7). For example, you can create Class selectors that target specific HTML elements in addition to matching the `class` attribute value.

LISTING 2-7: Combining multiple selector types in a single CSS rule

```
<!DOCTYPE html>
<html>
<head>
    <title>Combining Selector Types</title>
    <style type="text/css">
        .title
        {
            font-family:'Courier New';
        }

        div.title
        {
            font-family:Arial;
        }
    </style>
</head>
<body>
    <article>
        <p class="title">Lorum Ipsum</p>
        <div class="title">Lorum Ipsum</div>
    </article>
</body>
</html>
```

Merged Styles

CSS also merges styles when several style rules are defined that apply to a given HTML element. For example, in the sample code shown in Listing 2-8, a Class and Type selector are defined. Both of these selectors apply to the paragraph element in the HTML. When the browser interprets the styles, it merges both onto the element.

LISTING 2-8: Merging styles from multiple rules onto a single element

```
<!DOCTYPE html>
<html>
<head>
    <title>Merging Styles</title>
    <style type="text/css">
        .title
        {
            text-decoration:underline;
        }

        p
        {
            font-family:'Courier New';
        }
    </style>
</head>
<body>
    <article>
        <p class="title">Lorum Ipsum</p>
    </article>
</body>
</html>
```

As you can see in Figure 2-8, both the font and the text decoration of the single paragraph element have been styled, even though two separate style rules defined the style.

FIGURE 2-8

You can also merge multiple styles by defining multiple rules using different selector types. If a single HTML element matches all the rules, the styles from each rule will be merged. Listing 2-9 shows an example where a single element matches multiple rules.

LISTING 2-9: Multiple selector matches on a single element

```
<!DOCTYPE html>
<html>
<head>
    <title>Multiple Selector matches</title>
    <style type="text/css">
        p
        {
            font-family: Arial;
            color: blue;
        }

        p#book
        {
            font-size: xx-large;
        }

        p.title
        {
            font-family: 'Courier New';
        }
    </style>
</head>
<body>
    <article>
        <p id="book" class="title" style="letter-spacing:5pt;">Lorum Ipsum</p>
    </article>
</body>
</html>
```

In this case, because the paragraph tag defines the `id`, `class`, and `style` attributes, each of the Style rules match; therefore, each of their styles are merged onto the element.

Finally, you can use the `class` attribute to merge multiple styles onto the same element, as shown in Listing 2-10. The `class` attribute allows you to specify multiple class names in a space-delimited string.

LISTING 2-10: Assigning multiple class selectors to a single element

```html
<!DOCTYPE html>
<html>
<head>
    <title>Multiple Class Selectors</title>
    <style type="text/css">
        p.title
        {
            font-family: 'Courier New';
            letter-spacing: 5pt;
        }

        p.summer
        {
            color: Blue;
        }

        p.newproduct
        {
            font-weight: bold;
            color: red;
        }
    </style>
</head>
<body>
    <article>
        <p class="title newproduct summer">Lorum Ipsum</p>
    </article>
</body>
</html>
```

In this case, the three classes—`title`, `summer`, and `newproduct`—have all been defined in the `class` attribute. This means that these three styles will be merged onto the paragraph element.

Note that, in this case, the order in which the CSS classes are defined in the internal style sheet also influences how the styles are merged onto the paragraph tag. Even though the `summer` class is last in the list of classes defined in the `class` attribute, the `newproduct` rule overrides the summer rule's `color` property because the `newproduct` rule is defined after the `summer` rule in the internal style sheet.

CSS Inheritance

CSS includes the concept of style inheritance, and it works because the browser views the different locations that a style can be defined in (external, internal, or inline) as a hierarchical structure. Figure 2-9 shows this inheritance by demonstrating how the `font-family` property of a paragraph Type selector rule, defined in three different locations, can be overridden by other style rules.

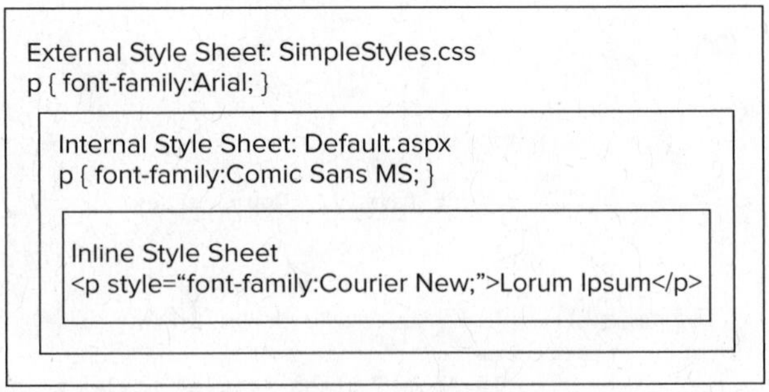

As you can see in Figure 2-9, the general rule is that the closer the style definition is to the

```
External Style Sheet: SimpleStyles.css
p { font-family:Arial; }

    Internal Style Sheet: Default.aspx
    p { font-family:Comic Sans MS; }

        Inline Style Sheet
        <p style="font-family:Courier New;">Lorum Ipsum</p>
```

FIGURE 2-9

element it applies to, the more precedence it will take. In this case, the paragraph text would ultimately be displayed using the Courier New font family because that is defined in the inline style.

Inheritance not only applies to styles kept in separate file locations, but also to styles within the same location, which means that sometimes you also must think about the order in which you define your styles. For example, Listing 2-11 shows a style sheet that contains two Type selectors, both targeting the paragraph element, both setting the `font-family` style property. Obviously, both of these cannot be applied to the same element, so CSS simply chooses the selector that is closest to the paragraph tags.

LISTING 2-11: Using style overriding within the same internal style sheet

```
<!DOCTYPE html>
<html>
<head>
    <title>Styling Overriding</title>
    <style type="text/css">
        p
        {
            font-family: Arial;
        }
        p
        {
            font-family: 'Courier New';
        }
    </style>
</head>
<body>
    <article>
        <p>Lorum Ipsum</p>
    </article>
</body>
</html>
```

Running this sample, you will see that the Courier New font is applied.

Note that you should be careful when combining styles from external style sheets and internal style sheets. Remember that the browser will ultimately choose the style that is defined closest to the specific elements. This means that as the browser begins to parse the web page, internal styles defined before external styles are considered farther away from the HTML elements. Thus, the browser will use the styles located in the external style sheet. If you plan on storing style rules in both internal and external style sheets, remember to include the external style sheets `<link>` tags before the internal style sheets `<style>` block in your web page.

Element Layout and Positioning

CSS is useful not only for styling elements in a page, but also for positioning elements. CSS actually gives you a much more flexible system for positioning elements than HTML itself. CSS bases the positioning of elements in a web page on the *box model*. After an element's box behavior has been determined, you can position it using several techniques.

The CSS Box Model

A core element of positioning in CSS is the box model. The box model defines how every element in HTML is treated by the browser as a rectangular box. The box is comprised of different parts, including margins, padding, borders, and content. Figure 2-10 shows how all of these elements are combined to form the box.

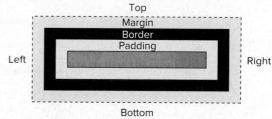

FIGURE 2-10

All the separate elements that make up the box can influence its position within the web page, and unless otherwise specified, each is given a default value of zero. The height and width of the element is equal to the height and width of the outer edge of the margin, which, as you can see in the previous image, is not necessarily the height and width of the content.

HTML provides you with two types of boxes: the block box and the inline box. Block boxes are typically represented by tags such as `<p>`, `<div>`, or `<table>`, as well as any of the new HTML5 semantic elements such as `<article>`, `<section>`, `<header>`, `<aside>`, `<nav>`, or `<footer>`. For block boxes, the containing block is used to determine the position of its child blocks. Additionally, block boxes can contain only inline or block boxes, but not both.

Listing 2-12 shows an example of a page containing a single parent block and two child block elements.

LISTING 2-12: Creating block box elements

```
<div>
    Lorem ipsum dolor sit amet, consectetuer adipiscing elit.
    <div>
        Donec et velit a risus convallis porttitor.
        Vestibulum nisi metus, imperdiet sed, mollis
        condimentum, nonummy eu, magna.
    </div>
    <div>
        Duis lobortis felis in est. Nulla eu velit ut nisi
        consequat vulputate.
    </div>
    Vestibulum vel metus. Integer ut quam. Ut dignissim, sapien
    sit amet malesuada aliquam, quam quam vulputate nibh, ut
    pulvinar velit lorem at eros. Sed semper lacinia diam. In
    faucibus nonummy arcu. Duis venenatis interdum quam. Aliquam
    ut dolor id leo scelerisque convallis. Suspendisse non velit.
    Quisque nec metus. Lorum ipsum dolor sit amet, consectetuer
    adipiscing elit. Praesent pellentesque interdum magna.
</div>
```

The second box type is the inline box. Inline boxes are typically represented by tags such as `strong`, `i`, and `span` as well as actual text and content. Listing 2-13 shows how you can modify the previous listing to include inline boxes.

LISTING 2-13: Creating inline box elements

```
<div>
    Lorem <strong>ipsum</strong> dolor sit amet, consectetuer adipiscing elit.
    <div>
        Donec et velit a risus <strong>convallis</strong> porttitor.
        Vestibulum nisi mets, imperdiet sed, mollis
        condimentum, nonummy eu, magna.
    </div>
    <div>Duis lobortis felis in est.
        <span>Nulla eu velit ut nisi consequat vulputate.</span>
    </div>
    <i>Vestibulum vel metus.</i> Integer ut quam. Ut dignissim, sapien
    sit amet malesuada aliquam, quam quam vulputate nibh, ut
    pulvinar velit lorem at eros. Sed semper lacinia diam. In
    faucibus nonummy arcu. Duis venenatis interdum quam. Aliquam
    ut dolor id leo scelerisque convallis. Suspendisse non velit.
    Quisque nec metus. Lorem ipsum dolor sit amet, consectetuer
    adipiscing elit. Praesent pellentesque interdum magna
</div>
```

Rendering this page results in each block beginning a new line. Figure 2-11 shows the markup rendered in the browser.

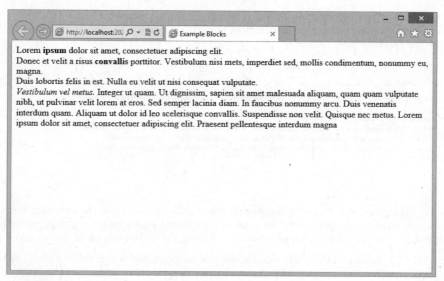

FIGURE 2-11

The Visual Studio design surface can help you get a clear picture of the layout of a div as well. When you select an individual div element, the design surface highlights the selected element, as shown in Figure 2-12.

```
div em ipsum dolor sit amet, consectetuer adipiscing elit.
Donec et velit a risus convallis porttitor. Vestibulum nisi mets, imperdiet sed, mollis condimentum, nonummy eu, magna.
Duis lobortis felis in est. Nulla eu velit ut nisi consequat vulputate.
Vestibulum vel metus. Integer ut quam. Ut dignissim, sapien sit amet malesuada aliquam, quam quam vulputate nibh, ut pulvinar velit lorem at
eros. Sed semper lacinia diam. In faucibus nonummy arcu. Duis venenatis interdum quam. Aliquam ut dolor id leo scelerisque convallis.
Suspendisse non velit. Quisque nec metus. Lorem ipsum dolor sit amet, consectetuer adipiscing elit. Praesent pellentesque interdum magna
```

FIGURE 2-12

At the beginning of this section, I stated that a block will always contain either inline or block boxes, but it's interesting to note that in this case, because the first line of text contains an inline box, and the next contains a block box, it looks like the parent div is violating that rule. However, what is actually happening is that the browser is automatically adding an anonymous block box around the first line of text when the page is rendered. Figure 2-13 highlights the block boxes as the browser sees them.

You can explicitly set which box behavior an element will exhibit by using the position attribute. For example, setting the position property on the second div, as shown here, results in the layout of the content changing.

```html
<div>
    Lorem <strong>ipsum</strong> dolor sit amet, consectetuer adipiscing elit.
    <div>
        Donec et velit a risus <strong>convallis</strong> porttitor.
        Vestibulum nisi mets, imperdiet sed, mollis
        condimentum, nonummy eu, magna.
    </div>
    <div>Duis lobortis felis in est.
        <span>Nulla eu velit ut nisi consequat vulputate.</span>
    </div>
    <i>Vestibulum vel metus.</i> Integer ut quam. Ut dignissim, sapien
    sit amet malesuada aliquam, quam quam vulputate nibh, ut
    pulvinar velit lorem at eros. Sed semper lacinia diam. In
    faucibus nonummy arcu. Duis venenatis interdum quam. Aliquam
    ut dolor id leo scelerisque convallis. Suspendisse non velit.
    Quisque nec metus. Lorem ipsum dolor sit amet, consectetuer
    adipiscing elit. Praesent pellentesque interdum magna
</div>
```

FIGURE 2-13

```
<div style="display: inline;">
    Donec et velit a risus <strong>convallis</strong> porttitor.
    Vestibulum nisi metus, imperdiet sed, mollis condimentum.
</div>
```

Figure 2-14 shows how adding this property changes the rendering of the markup on the Visual Studio design surface. You can see that now, rather than the element being displayed on a new line, its content is simply continued from the previous block.

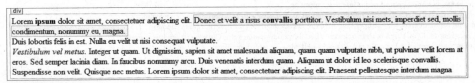

FIGURE 2-14

You can also set the display property to none to completely remove the element from the web page layout. If you have elements whose display property is set to none, or an element whose visibility property is set to hidden, Visual Studio gives you the option of showing or hiding these elements on its design surface.

As shown in Figure 2-15, two options on the View menu allow you to toggle the design surface visibility of elements with these properties set.

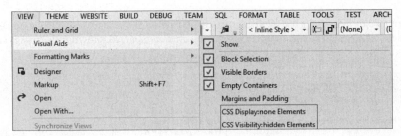

FIGURE 2-15

Positioning CSS Elements

CSS provides you with three primary positioning mechanisms: normal, absolute, and relative. Each type offers a different behavior you can use to lay out the elements in your page. To specify the type of layout behavior you want an element to use, you can set the CSS position property. Each element can have its own position property set, allowing you to use multiple positioning schemes within the same web page.

Normal Positioning

Using normal positioning, block items flow vertically, and inline items flow horizontally, left to right. This behavior is the default, and is used when no other value is provided for the position property. Figure 2-16 demonstrates the layout of four separate blocks using normal positioning.

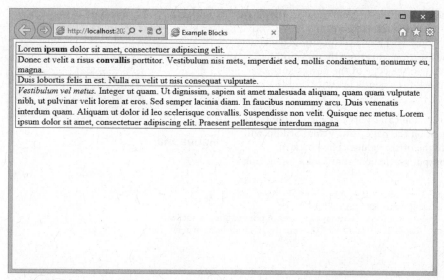

FIGURE 2-16

As you can see, each block item flows vertically as expected.

Relative Positioning

Using relative positioning, elements are initially positioned using normal layout. The surrounding boxes are positioned, and then the box is moved based on its offset properties: `top`, `bottom`, `left`, and `right`. Figure 2-17 shows the same content as in the prior section, but now the third block box has been styled

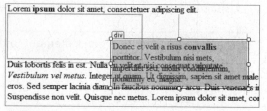

FIGURE 2-17

to use relative positioning. Visual Studio is helping you out by providing positioning lines for the block, showing you that its top offset is being calculated based on the normal top position of the block, and the left offset from the normal left position. Visual Studio even lets you visually position the block by grabbing the element's tag label and dragging it over the design surface.

As you position the element on the design surface, the element's top and left values are being updated. You will end up with an element looking something like this:

```
<div style="position: relative;top: 214px;left: 62px;
        width: 239px;height: 81px">
    Donec et velit a risus <strong>convallis</strong> porttitor. Vestibulum
    nisi metus, imperdiet sed, mollis condimentum, nonummy eu, magna.
</div>
```

If you are using relative positioning and have both left and right offsets defined, the right will generally be ignored.

Absolute Positioning

Absolute positioning works much like relative positioning, except instead of an element calculating its offset position based on its position in the normal positioning scheme, the offsets are calculated based on the position of its closest absolutely positioned ancestor. If no element exists, then the ancestor is the browser window itself.

Figure 2-18 shows how blocks using absolute positioning are displayed on the Visual Studio design surface. As you can see, unlike the display of the relative positioned element shown in the previous section, this time the positioning lines extend all the way to the edge of the design surface. This is because the block is using the browser window to calculate its offset.

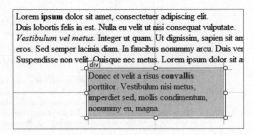

FIGURE 2-18

As with relative blocks, you can use the element's tag label to position the element on the page, and Visual Studio will automatically update the offset values. The block in Figure 2-18 would output an element that looks something like this:

```
<div style="position: absolute; top: 180px; left:94px;
        width: 239px; height: 81px;">
    Donec et velit a risus <b>convallis</b> porttitor. Vestibulum
    nisi metus, imperdiet sed, mollis condimentum, nonummy eu, magna.
</div>
```

Floating Elements

Another option for controlling the position of elements using CSS is the `float` property. The `float` property allows you to float an element to the left or right side of a block. The floating block is positioned vertically as it would normally be in normal position, but horizontally shifted as far left or right as possible. Listing 2-14 demonstrates floating the same block used in previous samples in this section.

LISTING 2-14: Floating a block element to the right

```
<!DOCTYPE html>
<html>
<head>
    <title>Box Elements</title>
</head>
<body>
    <div id="asdas" class="werwer">
        Lorem ipsum dolor sit amet, consectetuer adipiscing elit.
    </div>
    <div style="float: right; width: 236px;">
        Donec et velit a risus <strong>convallis</strong> porttitor.
        Vestibulum nisi metus, imperdiet sed, mollis
        condimentum, nonummy eu, magna.
    </div>
    <div>
        Duis lobortis felis in est. Nulla eu velit ut nisi consequat.
    </div>
    <div>
        Sit amet malesuada aliquam, quam quam vulputate nibh, ut
        pulvinar velit lorem at eros. Sed semper lacinia diam. In
        faucibus nonummy arcu. Duis venenatis interdum quam. Aliquam
        ut dolor id leo scelerisque convallis. Suspendisse non velit.
        Quisque nec metus. Lorem ipsum dolor sit amet, consectetuer
        adipiscing elit. Praesent pellentesque interdum magna.
    </div>
</body>
</html>
```

The block has been modified to include the `float` property in its style. When this is done, Visual Studio correctly positions the element to the far right side of the page, as shown in Figure 2-19.

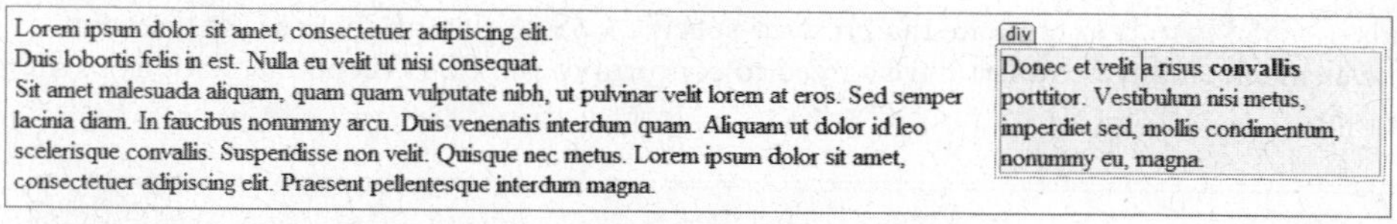

Lorem ipsum dolor sit amet, consectetuer adipiscing elit.
Duis lobortis felis in est. Nulla eu velit ut nisi consequat.
Sit amet malesuada aliquam, quam quam vulputate nibh, ut pulvinar velit lorem at eros. Sed semper
lacinia diam. In faucibus nonummy arcu. Duis venenatis interdum quam. Aliquam ut dolor id leo
scelerisque convallis. Suspendisse non velit. Quisque nec metus. Lorem ipsum dolor sit amet,
consectetuer adipiscing elit. Praesent pellentesque interdum magna.

div
Donec et velit a risus **convallis**
porttitor. Vestibulum nisi metus,
imperdiet sed, mollis condimentum,
nonummy eu, magna.

FIGURE 2-19

The !important Attribute

As you saw earlier in this chapter, the browser will apply the closest style to the element, which can mean that properties of other applied styles might be overridden. As with many other rules in CSS this, too, is not absolute. CSS provides a mechanism to circumvent this rule called the `!important` attribute. Properties that have this attribute applied can prevent other CSS rules from overriding its value. Listing 2-11 showed how the `font-family` property can be overridden. You can see how the `!important` attribute works by modifying this sample to use the attribute. This is shown in Listing 2-15.

LISTING 2-15: Using the !important attribute to control style overriding

```
<!DOCTYPE html>
<html>
<head>
    <title>Box Elements</title>
    <style type="text/css">
        p {
            font-family: Arial !important;
        }
        p {
            font-family: 'Courier New';
        }
    </style>
</head>
<body>
    <p>
        Lorem ipsum dolor sit amet, consectetuer adipiscing elit.
    </p>
</body>
</html>
```

In this case, rather than the paragraph being shown in Courier New, it will use the Arial font because it has been marked with the `!important` attribute.

New Features in CSS3

As mentioned earlier, the CSS3 recommendation has several modules that have been proposed. Many of these proposed modules have already been implemented in most modern browsers. In combination with HTML5, CSS3 allows web developers to implement more advanced designs without the need of ActiveX plug-ins or JavaScript libraries.

For many years, developers had to add browser-specific CSS to accomplish specific tasks. For instance, to add opacity to elements in most browsers, you could use CSS similar to:

```
opacity:.8;
```

However, Internet Explorer did not render the element with the desired opacity. Instead, to accomplish the same result for Internet Explorer users, developers used:

```
-ms-filter:"progid:DXImageTransform.Microsoft.Alpha(opacity=80)";
    filter:alpha(opacity=80);
```

One of the goals of CSS3 is to help mitigate the browser-specific CSS. Although there are still several browser-specific elements, many browsers have agreed to conform to the CSS3 recommendations as they become formalized.

> **NOTE** *There are many features and style rules with CSS3. Although I touch upon some of the new features and rules, it is recommended that you search for CSS3 on the Internet for additional features and rules.*

Using the New Border Features

One of the most common features of CSS3 is the implementation of the borders module. In the past, developers needed to use multiple `div` elements or images with rounded corners to accomplish rounded corners. In CSS3, this can be accomplished simply by adding a few style rules:

```
div {
    border-radius: 15px;
    box-shadow: 5px 5px rgba(0,0,0,0.2);
}
```

Besides adding a rounded border of 15 pixels, there is also a 5px shadow around the `div` element. Listing 2-16 enhances this further by defining a `border-radius` on only the lower-right corner and placing an inset shadow at the bottom. This produces the rendering you see in Figure 2-20.

LISTING 2-16: Using enhanced rules with CSS3 borders

```
<!DOCTYPE html>
<html>
<head>
    <title>CSS3 Borders</title>
    <style type="text/css">
        .pageFeel {
            padding: 5px;
            height: 240px;
            border: 1px solid #cccccc;
            background-color: #eeeeee;
            width: 240px;
            -moz-border-radius-bottomright: 50px 25px;
            border-bottom-right-radius: 50px 25px;
            -moz-box-shadow: inset -5px -5px 5px #aaa;
            -webkit-box-shadow: inset -5px -5px 5px #aaa;
            box-shadow: inset -3px -3px 20px #aaa;
        }
    </style>
</head>
<body>
    <div class="pageFeel">
        Lorem ipsum dolor sit amet, consectetuer adipiscing elit.
    </div>
</body>
</html>
```

You'll notice that for the `border-radius` rule, there is a special rule designated with the `-moz-` prefix. This allows for Mozilla Firefox 3.5 support. For the `box-shadow` rule, you'll notice that in addition to the rule with the `-moz-` prefix, there is another rule with the `-webkit-` prefix. This rule allows for Safari and Google Chrome support.

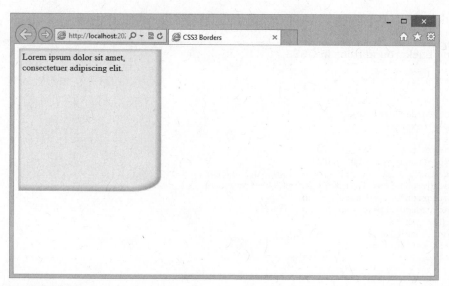

FIGURE 2-20

Enhancing Backgrounds

Another style issue that developers have faced in the past is the ability to have multiple backgrounds or layer backgrounds. This was commonly resolved by having multiple div elements with various z-index values. In CSS3, multiple backgrounds can be applied in the same style rule.

Another common issue that developers had was creating a background image for their site that would tile or scale appropriately based on the variety of screen sizes. Many times, a separate CSS file had to be used to capture the screen resolution. If not, you would have to design an image that would tile without the user noticing the edges of the images. An example of this is shown in Figure 2-21.

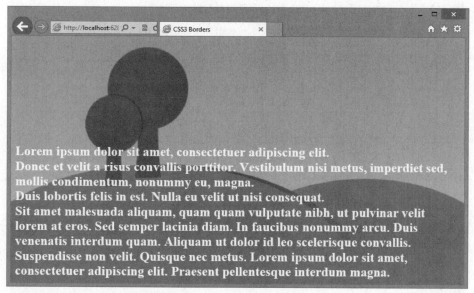

FIGURE 2-21

To resolve both of these issues, you can use the new features of CSS3, as shown in Listing 2-17.

LISTING 2-17: Using background rules in CSS3

```
<!DOCTYPE html>
<html>
<head>
    <title>CSS3 Borders</title>
    <style type="text/css">
        body {
            margin-top: 200px;
            background-color: #33BEF2;
            background-image: url(clouds.png), url(background.png);
            background-position: top center, bottom center;
            background-size: auto, cover;
            background-repeat: no-repeat, repeat-y;
            color: white;
            font-size: 18pt;
            font-weight: bold;
        }
    </style>
</head>
<body>
    <div>
        Lorem ipsum dolor sit amet, consectetuer adipiscing elit.
    </div>
    <div>
        Donec et velit a risus <strong>convallis</strong> porttitor.
        Vestibulum nisi metus, imperdiet sed, mollis
        condimentum, nonummy eu, magna.
    </div>
    <div>
        Duis lobortis felis in est. Nulla eu velit ut nisi consequat.
    </div>
    <div>
        Sit amet malesuada aliquam, quam quam vulputate nibh, ut
        pulvinar velit lorem at eros. Sed semper lacinia diam. In
        faucibus nonummy arcu. Duis venenatis interdum quam. Aliquam
        ut dolor id leo scelerisque convallis. Suspendisse non velit.
        Quisque nec metus. Lorem ipsum dolor sit amet, consectetuer
        adipiscing elit. Praesent pellentesque interdum magna.
    </div>
</body>
</html>
```

As you can see, the background-image rule has two images specified. Each will be rendered separately. The background.png file will be rendered to the back of the page. The clouds.png will be placed on top of that background. The background-size rule has two values as well. The first value for the background-size applies to the first background-image, whereas the second value applies to the second background-image. This is shown in Figure 2-22.

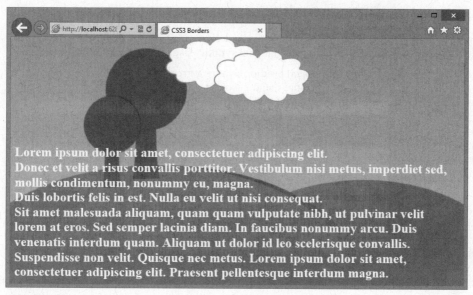

FIGURE 2-22

Adding a Drop Shadow to Text

Before CSS2, the best way to add a shadow to some text was to generate an image representing the desired output. CSS2 introduced a new rule that can be specified on text called `text-shadow`. Although this rule was introduced with CSS2, it hadn't been widely adopted until more modern browsers. This rule accepts four values as shown here:

```
text-shadow: 5px 5px 2px #000000;
```

The first value is the number of pixels to offset to the right. The second value is the number of pixels to offset to the left. The third value is to set the number of pixels to blur. The last value is to set the color of the drop shadow.

HTML and CSS Compatibility

Much of what has been discussed thus far will not work in older browsers such as Internet Explorer 8, which is the web browser installed on most machines running Windows 7. To assist developers with compatibility, the ASP.NET team has included the Modernizr.js JavaScript library in all of the new ASP.NET project templates. Although this JavaScript library doesn't add HTML5 elements that aren't supported on older browsers, it does help to ease the compatibility issues between older browsers and more current ones.

Developers should use the HTML5Shiv.js file, which is not part of the Modernizr library, if they want to add more HTML5 support to their page renderings in older Internet Explorer browsers. This file is also known as the HTML5 *shim* file.

> **NOTE** *For more information about the Modernizr library, be sure to visit* `http://modernizr.com/`. *If you have an existing website or web application, you can update your application to include Modernizr by installing it using NuGet. You can find out more about NuGet in Appendix G. For more information about the HTML5Shiv file, be sure to search online for HTML5Shiv or HTML5Shim.*

WORKING WITH HTML AND CSS IN VISUAL STUDIO

Working with HTML and CSS to create compelling website designs can be quite daunting. Thankfully, Visual Studio provides you with a variety of tools that help simplify page layout and CSS management.

As you are probably already familiar with, Visual Studio includes a great WYSIWYG design surface for editing HTML. When editing HTML, the Format menu becomes available. When the Design view has focus, the Format and Table menus both become available as shown in Figure 2-23.

FIGURE 2-23

The Table menu, as you might guess, includes a set of tools that allow you to insert, delete, select, and modify the HTML tables in your web page. Selecting the Insert Table option from the Table menu opens the Insert Table dialog box shown in Figure 2-24, which allows you to easily specify properties of your table. You can define the number of table rows and columns, the cell padding and spacing, and the border attributes. When you click OK, Visual Studio automatically generates the appropriate table HTML in your web page.

When you select an existing table in your web page, the Table menu lets you insert and delete table rows, columns, and cells. The Modify menu option also allows you to split an existing cell into two separate cells, merge two cells into a single cell, and configure row and column sizing.

The Format menu includes basic element formatting options such as accessing the elements CSS class; setting fore- and background colors, font, and position; and converting content to different types of lists.

Working with CSS in Visual Studio

Visual Studio offers a variety of tools specifically designed to make working with CSS a great experience. To create a new style for your web page, simply select the New Style option from the Format menu. The New Style dialog box opens, as shown in Figure 2-25.

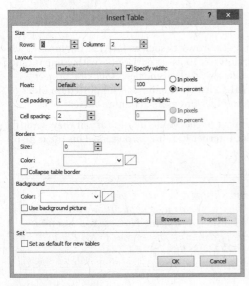

FIGURE 2-24

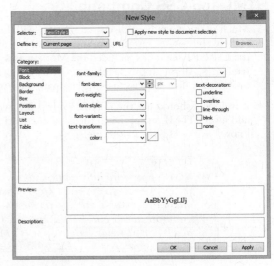

FIGURE 2-25

This dialog box makes creating a new style a snap. To start, select the type of selector you want to create from the Selector drop-down list, which includes all the available element types. If you want to create a Class or ID selector, simply type the Style name into the Selector combo box.

Next, you select where you want to create the style from the Define In combo box. You can select Current Page to create an internal style sheet, New Style Sheet to create a new external style sheet file, or Existing Style Sheet to insert the style into an existing style sheet file. If you select either New Style Sheet or Existing Style Sheet, you must provide a value for the URL combo box.

Finally, to have this style apply to the element (or elements) currently selected in the design surface, select the Apply New Style to Document check box.

After you have entered the selector you want to use and chosen a location to define the style, you can set the style's properties. Simply select the property category from the Category list box and set the property values. The Preview area gives you a real-time preview of your new style. Additionally, the Description area shows you the actual property syntax created by Visual Studio. Click OK to close the dialog box.

After you begin to create styles for your application, you need to be able to manage and apply those styles to elements in your application. Visual Studio includes three tool windows you can use to manage style sheets, apply styles to elements, and easily inspect the style properties applied to an element.

Manage Styles Tool Window

The first tool to explore is the Manage Styles tool window, which you can open by selecting Manage Styles from the CSS Styles submenu of the View menu. This tool window, shown in Figure 2-26, gives you the bird's-eye view of all the styles available to the current web page open in Visual Studio.

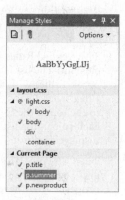

If you examine the contents of this tool, you see that the very top portion includes two important links: New Style, which opens the New Style dialog box and allows you to create new CSS styles as described earlier in this section; and the Attach Style Sheet link, which allows you to import new style sheets into a web page. Using this option to attach style sheets to the web page causes Visual Studio to insert `<link>` tags into your web page for you.

Remember that you must be careful about the order of your link tags and style blocks to make sure that your styles are applied correctly.

FIGURE 2-26

The next portion of the tool includes a preview area allowing you to see a real-time preview of each style.

Finally, the bottom portion of the tool window displays all the styles available to the page. Styles are color coded according to their selector type using colored bullets: blue for Type selectors, green for Class selectors, and red for ID selectors. Styles used within the page are shown with a gray circle surrounding the colored bullet. Should your web page contain multiple linked style sheets, or inline style sheets, these styles would be grouped together, making it easy to determine where a style is defined.

Also, as you can see in Figure 2-26, the tool window lets you view style sheets attached to the web page via the CSS Imports statement. By expanding the `light.css` node shown in the figure, you can see a listing of all the styles included in that style sheet.

Apply Styles Tool Window

The second tool to help you use CSS in Visual Studio is the Apply Styles tool window. As with the Manage Styles tool window, the Apply Styles tool window gives you an easy way to view the CSS Styles available in your application and apply them to elements in a web page. From the tool window, you can attach CSS files to the web page, making external CSS Styles available; select page styles to apply or remove from an element; and modify styles. As with the other CSS tool windows, the Apply Styles tool window displays the available styles based on the CSS inheritance order, with external styles being shown first, then the page styles section, and finally the inline styles shown last. The Apply Styles window also is contextually sensitive to the currently selected element and will show only those styles in your application that can be applied to the element type. Styles are also grouped according to the CSS selector style, with a different visual indicator for each selector type.

The tool window shown in Figure 2-27 shows the styles available for an anchor tag `<a>`. The tool first shows all styles in the attached `layout.css` file, then the styles in the current page, and finally, if applied, the element's inline styles. You can click on styles in any of these sections to apply them to the element.

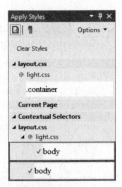

FIGURE 2-27

The Apply Styles tool also includes the intelligence to properly apply multiple Class selectors (hold down the Ctrl key while you click Class selectors in the list), but prevent you from selecting multiple ID selectors because that would result in invalid CSS. The tool will also not let you deselect Type selectors or inline styles.

CSS Properties Tool Window

The final tool is the CSS Properties tool window shown in Figure 2-28. This handy tool window shows you all the CSS properties that have been applied to the currently selected element. The tool window is composed of two separate parts: the Applied Rules list and the CSS properties grid.

The Applied Rules list shows all the CSS rules that are applied to the selected element. The list is automatically sorted to show you the inheritance chain of the applied rules with the outermost rules at the top, moving down to the innermost rules. That means that rules contained in external CSS files are automatically sorted to the top of the list, and inline styles are sorted to the bottom. You can click on each rule in the list and alter the properties that are shown in the CSS Properties grid displayed below.

FIGURE 2-28

The CSS Properties grid works in a similar fashion to the standard .NET properties grid, showing you all the CSS properties available for the element and showing properties that have values set in bold. Additionally, you can set property values for a CSS rule directly from the CSS property grid. Also in the CSS Properties tool window is a Summary button that allows you to change the display of the CSS Properties grid to show only properties that have values set. This feature can be very useful because HTML elements can have a large number of CSS properties.

Because CSS also includes the concept of property inheritance, which is generally not available in a standard .NET object, the CSS Rules list and CSS Properties grid have been designed to help you fully understand where a specific property value applied to an element is being defined. As you click on each rule in the CSS Rules list, the CSS Properties grid updates to reflect that rule's properties. What you will notice, however, is that certain properties have a strikethrough. (See Figure 2-29.)

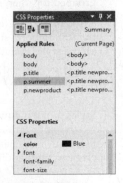

FIGURE 2-29

The strikethrough of a property indicates that the value of that property is being overridden by a rule closer to the element.

Styling ASP.NET Controls

Because ASP.NET controls simply render HTML markup, using CSS to style them is fairly easy. In fact, by default, the controls actually already use inline CSS styles. You can see this in action by looking at the standard ASP.NET Button control. The standard method for styling ASP.NET controls like the Button is to provide values for the style-related properties exposed by the control, which is shown here:

```
<asp:Button ID="Button1" runat="server" BackColor="#3333FF"
    BorderColor="Silver" BorderStyle="Double" BorderWidth="3px"
    Font-Bold="True" Font-Size="Large" ForeColor="White"
    Text="Button" />
```

When ASP.NET processes the web page containing this control, it converts a button into a standard HTML Input tag, and it also converts the style properties you have set into CSS styles and applies them to the `input` tag. The HTML and CSS rendered by the button is shown here:

```
<input type="submit" name="Button1" value="Button" id="Button1"
    style="color:White;background-color:#3333FF;border-color:Silver;
border-width:3px;
        border-style:Double;font-size:Large;font-weight:bold;" />
```

Setting style properties directly on the ASP.NET controls is a fast and simple way to style the ASP.NET controls in your application. Additionally, because these are standard properties on the controls, you can also set them at run time using code.

```
protected void Page_Load(object sender, EventArgs e)
{
    this.Button1.BackColor =
        System.Drawing.ColorTranslator.FromHtml("#3333FF");
    this.Button1.BorderColor = System.Drawing.Color.Silver;
    this.Button1.BorderStyle= BorderStyle.Double;
    this.Button1.BorderWidth = Unit.Pixel(3);
    this.Button1.Font.Bold=true;
    this.Button1.Font.Size=FontUnit.Large;
    this.Button1.ForeColor=System.Drawing.Color.White;
}
```

Although using properties to set style info is easy and convenient, it does have some drawbacks, especially when you use the same technique with larger repeating controls. One drawback is that using inline styles makes controlling the styling of your website at a higher, more abstract level difficult. If you want every button in your website to have a specific style, generally you would have to manually set that style on every Button control in your entire site. Themes can help solve this problem but are not always useful, especially when you are mixing ASP.NET controls with standard HTML controls.

Another drawback is that for controls that generate a large amount of repetitive HTML, such as the GridView, having inline styles on every element of each iteration of HTML adds a lot of extra markup to your web page.

Thankfully, every ASP.NET server control exposes a `CssClass` property. This property allows you to provide one or more Class selector rules to the control. Although this technique is helpful, and usually better than letting the control render inline styles, it still requires you to be familiar with the HTML that the control will render at run time. Listing 2-18 shows how you can use the `CssClass` attribute to style the ASP.NET Button control.

LISTING 2-18: Styling a standard ASP.NET Button control using CSS

```
<%@ Page Language="C#" %>

<!DOCTYPE html>

<html xmlns="http://www.w3.org/1999/xhtml">
<head runat="server">
    <link href="SpringStyles.css" rel="stylesheet" type="text/css" />
    <style>
        .search
        {
            color:White;
            font-weight:bolder;
            background-color:Green;
        }
```

continues

LISTING 2-18 *(continued)*

```
        </style>
    </head>
    <body>
        <form id="form1" runat="server">
            <asp:Button ID="Button1"
                CssClass="search" runat="server" Text="Button" />
        </form>
    </body>
</html>
```

In this case, the button will have the search class applied to it.

HTML and CSS Improvements in Visual Studio 2012

In each version of Visual Studio, Microsoft improves the HTML development capabilities in the software. Visual Studio 2012 is no different. There have been several improvements added for HTML in Visual Studio 2012 including, but not limited to:

➤ WAI-ARIA support, which allows elements to include the role attribute and other attributes that begin with aria.

➤ Matching HTML and ASP.NET server control tags are renamed when the other tag is renamed.

➤ HTML5 elements are now available as snippets within Visual Studio.

➤ The `TextBox` ASP.NET server control was updated to support the new HTML5 input types such as `email` and `datetime`.

➤ The `FileUpload` ASP.NET server control supports multiple file uploads in modern browsers.

There are also several improvements with CSS in Visual Studio 2012 including, but not limited to:

➤ Improved IntelliSense showing only the items that are available as well as new CSS3 rules such as browser-specific rules starting with `-moz` and `-webkit`.

➤ Hierarchical indentation to show logical separation of your CSS rules (as shown in Figure 2-30).

➤ Commenting (using shortcut keys), regions, and code snippets are available for CSS just as they have been for source code.

➤ A new color palette helps you choose the colors you're looking for (as shown in Figure 2-31).

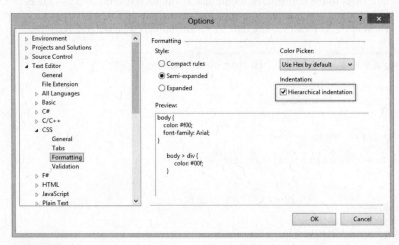

FIGURE 2-30

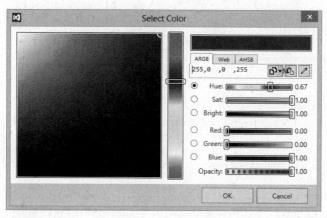

FIGURE 2-31

Page Inspector

Page Inspector is a new tool that comes with Visual Studio 2012. This tool allows developers to see the rendered markup for the related server-side code. In other words, when choosing controls from your Web Forms or MVC pages, you will see the corresponding markup highlighted in the preview window (as shown in Figure 2-32). Currently, Page Inspector uses Internet Explorer 9 or later to render the markup.

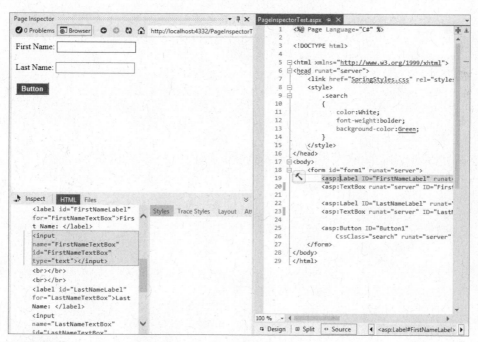

FIGURE 2-32

> **NOTE** *Chapter 28 covers how to optimize CSS even more by walking through a new feature in ASP.NET 4.5 called Bundling and Minification.*

SUMMARY

CSS is a great way to add style to your website. It's a powerful and convenient mechanism that allows you to create complex styles and layouts for your website, especially when paired with HTML5. A full discussion of CSS would require much more time and space than available here, so this chapter focused on showing you some of the basic concepts of HTML and CSS, as well as the new features in Visual Studio 2012 and ASP .NET 4.5.

This chapter provided an overview of HTML5 by introducing you to new elements, attributes, attribute values, and APIs. You learned about using the new HTML5 elements and attributes in real-world situations.

Next you were provided an overview of CSS3, introducing you to external, internal, and inline style sheets. You learned about the various selector types that CSS offers and about basic layout and positioning of CSS elements, including how the box model works to influence element positions in your web page. You also learned about backward compatibility of HTML5 and CSS3.

Finally, you reviewed the tools available in Visual Studio, including the Style Manager and CSS Properties tool windows that make working with CSS easy. You looked at how to use CSS with the ASP.NET server controls. You also learned about several new features of HTML and CSS in Visual Studio 2012 and Page Inspector.

ASP.NET Web Forms Structure

WHAT'S IN THIS CHAPTER?

➤ Choosing application location and page structure options

➤ Working with page directives, page events, and application folders

➤ Choosing compilation options

WROX.COM CODE DOWNLOADS FOR THIS CHAPTER

Please note that all the code examples in this chapter are available as a part of this chapter's code download on the book's website at www.wrox.com on the Download Code tab.

The progression from Active Server Pages 3.0 to ASP.NET 1.0 was revolutionary, to say the least. And now the revolution continues with the latest release of ASP.NET—version 4.5. The original introduction of ASP.NET 1.0 fundamentally changed the way websites and applications were developed. ASP.NET 4.5 is just as revolutionary in the way it will increase your productivity. As of late, the primary goal of ASP.NET is to enable you to build powerful, secure, dynamic applications using the least possible amount of code. Although this book covers the new features provided by ASP.NET 4.5, it also covers all the offerings of ASP.NET technology.

If you are new to ASP.NET and building your first set of applications in ASP.NET 4.5, you may be amazed by the vast amount of server controls it provides. You may marvel at how it enables you to work with data more effectively using a series of data providers. You may be impressed at how easily you can build in security and personalization.

The outstanding capabilities of ASP.NET 4.5 do not end there, however. This chapter looks at many options that facilitate working with ASP.NET web pages and applications. One of the first steps you, the developer, should take when starting a project is to become familiar with the foundation you are building on and the options available for customizing that foundation.

APPLICATION LOCATION OPTIONS

With ASP.NET 4.5, you have the option—using Visual Studio 2012—to create an application with a virtual directory mapped to IIS or a standalone application outside the confines of IIS. Whereas the early Visual Studio .NET 2002/2003 IDEs forced developers to use IIS for all web applications, Visual Studio 2008/2010 (and Visual Web Developer 2008/2010 Express Edition, for that matter) included a built-in web server, known as Cassini, that you used for development, much like the one used in the past with the ASP.NET WebMatrix. In Visual Studio 2012, the built-in web server is IIS Express.

> **NOTE** *IIS Express is a light-weight, self-contained version of IIS optimized for developers and Visual Studio. Additional information about it can be found at* www.iis.net. *IIS Express is also installed if you download WebMatrix as discussed later in Chapter 35.*

The following section shows you how to use IIS Express, which comes with Visual Studio 2012.

Using File System (IIS Express)

By default, Visual Studio 2012 builds applications by using IIS Express. You can see this when you select File ⇨ New ⇨ Web Site in the IDE. By default, the location provided for your application is in C:\Users\ JasonGaylord\Documents\Visual Studio 2012\WebSites if you are using Windows 8 (shown in Figure 3-1). It is not C:\Inetpub\wwwroot\ as it would have been in Visual Studio .NET 2002/2003. By default, any site that you build and host inside C:\Users\JasonGaylord\Documents\ Visual Studio 2012\WebSites (or any other folder you create) uses IIS Express, which is built into Visual Studio 2012. If you use the built-in web server from Visual Studio 2012, you are not locked into the WebSites folder. Rather, you can create and use any folder you like.

To change from this default, you have a handful of options. Click the Browse button in the New Web Site dialog box. The Choose Location dialog box opens, shown in Figure 3-2.

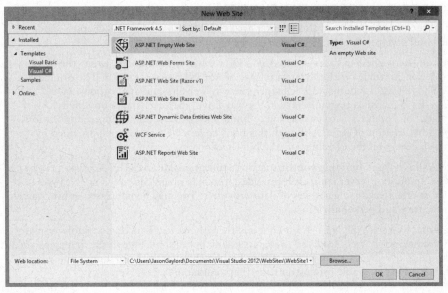

FIGURE 3-1

If you continue to use the built-in IIS Express that Visual Studio 2012 provides, you can choose a new location for your website from this dialog box. To choose a new location, select a new folder and save your .aspx pages and any other associated files to this directory. When using Visual Studio 2012, you can run your application completely from this location. This way of working with the ASP.NET pages you create is ideal if you do not have access to a web server because it enables you to build applications that do not reside on a machine with the full version of IIS.

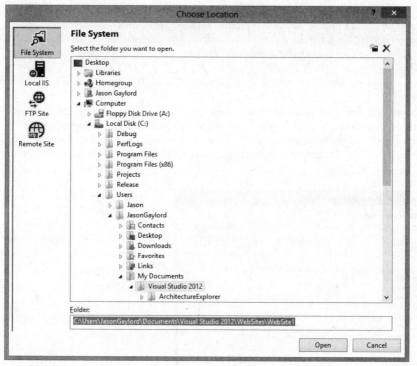

FIGURE 3-2

After you create the new website, you have access to modify the IIS Express settings right in the Visual Studio properties pane. An example of this is shown in Figure 3-3.

Using IIS

From the Choose Location dialog box (as shown in Figure 3-4), you can also change where your application is saved and which type of web server your application employs. To use IIS, select the Local IIS button in the dialog box. This changes the results in the text area to show you a list of all the virtual application roots on your machine.

FIGURE 3-3

> **NOTE** *You are required to run Visual Studio as an administrator user if you want to see your local IIS instance.*

To create a new virtual root for your application, highlight Default Web Site. Two accessible buttons appear at the top of the dialog box (see Figure 3-4). When you look from left to right, the first button in the upper-right corner of the dialog box is for creating a new site. This is used for adding new sites to IIS Express. The second button is for creating a new web application—or a virtual root. The third button enables you to create virtual directories for any of the virtual roots you created. The last button is a Delete button, which allows you to delete any selected sites, virtual directories, or virtual roots.

> **NOTE** *Notice from the IIS option, shown in Figure 3-4, that you can see all the sites that have been set up for IIS Express. From this window, you can also delete sites that are no longer valid. You can also create a new site, web application, or virtual directory under each site.*

After you have created the virtual directory you want, click the Open button. Visual Studio 2012 then goes through the standard process to create your application. Now, however, instead of depending on IIS Express, your application will use the full version of IIS. When you invoke your application, the URL consists of something like `http://localhost/MyWeb/Default.aspx`, which means it is using IIS.

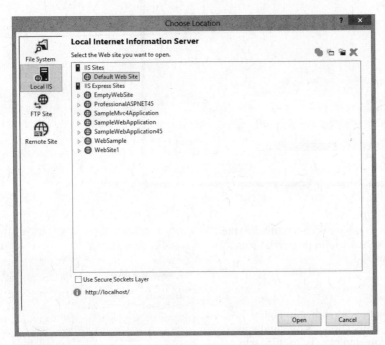

FIGURE 3-4

Using FTP

Not only can you decide on the type of web server for your web application when you create it using the Choose Location dialog box, but you can also decide where your application is going to be located. With the previous options, you built applications that resided on your local server. The FTP option enables you to actually store and even code your applications while they reside on a server somewhere else in your enterprise—or on the other side of the planet. You can also use the FTP capabilities to work on different locations within the same server. Using this capability provides a wide range of possible options. You can see this in Figure 3-5.

To create your application on a remote server using FTP, simply provide the server name, the port to use, and the directory—as well as any required credentials. If the correct information is provided, Visual Studio 2012 reaches out to the remote server and creates the appropriate files for the start of your application, just as if it were doing the job locally. From this point on, you can open your project and connect to the remote server using FTP.

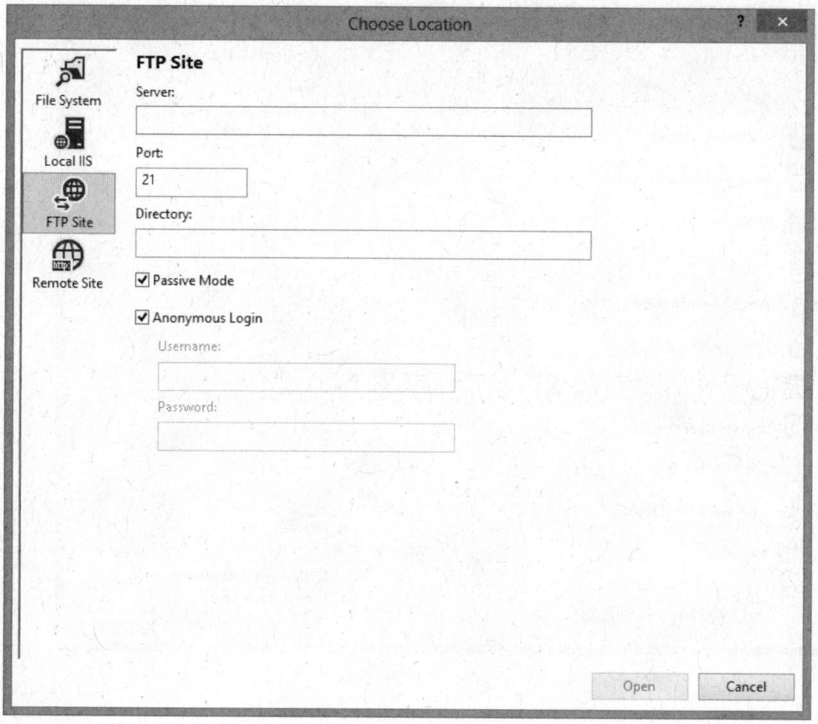

FIGURE 3-5

THE ASP.NET PAGE STRUCTURE OPTIONS

ASP.NET provides two paths for structuring the code of your ASP.NET pages. The first path utilizes the code-inline model. This model should be familiar to classic ASP developers because all the code is contained within a single `.aspx` page. The second path uses ASP.NET's code-behind model, which allows for code separation of the page's business logic from its presentation logic. In this model, the presentation logic for the page is stored in an `.aspx` page, whereas the logic piece is stored in a separate class file: `.aspx.vb` or `.aspx.cs`. Using the code-behind model is considered the best practice because it provides a clean model in separation of pure UI elements from code that manipulates these elements. It is also seen as a better means in maintaining code.

Inline Coding

With the .NET Framework 1.0/1.1, developers went out of their way (and outside Visual Studio .NET) to build their ASP.NET pages inline and avoid the code-behind model that was so heavily promoted by Microsoft and others. Visual Studio 2012 (as well as Visual Studio Express 2012 for Web) allows you to build your pages easily using this coding style. To build an ASP.NET page inline instead of using the code-behind model, you simply select the page type from the Add New Item dialog box and make sure that the Place Code in Separate File check box is not selected. You can get at this dialog box (see Figure 3-6) by right-clicking the project or the solution in the Solution Explorer and selecting Add New Item.

From here, you can see the check box you need to unselect if you want to build your ASP.NET pages inline. In fact, many page types have options for both inline and code-behind styles. Table 3-1 shows your inline options when selecting files from this dialog box.

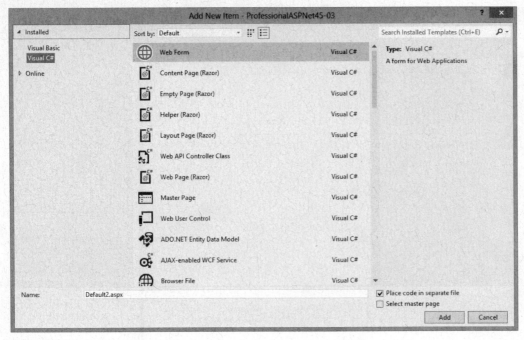

FIGURE 3-6

TABLE 3-1

OPTION	FILE CREATED
Web Form	.aspx file
Master Page	.master file
Web User Control	.ascx file
Web Service	.asmx file

> **NOTE** *In addition to the file types that are listed in Table 3-1, the file types designated with (Razor) after the name also allow inline code options. These files are covered in Chapter 35.*

By using the Web Form option with a few controls, you get a page that encapsulates not only the presentation logic, but the business logic as well. This is illustrated in Listing 3-1 (Listing03-01.aspx in this chapter's code download).

LISTING 3-1: A simple page that uses the inline coding model

VB

```vb
<%@ Page Language="vb" %>
<script runat="server">
    Protected Sub Button1_Click(sender As Object, e As EventArgs)
```

```
            Literal1.Text = "Hello " & TextBox1.Text
        End Sub
</script>
<!DOCTYPE html>

<html xmlns="http://www.w3.org/1999/xhtml">
<head runat="server">
    <title>Simple Page</title>
</head>
<body>
    <form id="form1" runat="server">
        <div>
            What is your name?<br />
            <asp:TextBox ID="TextBox1" runat="server"></asp:TextBox>
            <asp:Button ID="Button1" runat="server" Text="Submit"
                OnClick="Button1_Click" />
        </div>
        <div>
            <asp:Literal ID="Literal1" runat="server" />
        </div>
    </form>
</body>
</html>
```

C#

```
<%@ Page Language="C#" %>
<script runat="server">
    protected void Button1_Click1(object sender, EventArgs e)
    {
        Literal1.Text = "Hello " + TextBox1.Text;
    }
</script>
```

From this example, you can see that all the business logic is encapsulated in between `<script>` tags. The nice feature of the inline model is that the business logic and the presentation logic are contained within the same file. Some developers find that having everything in a single viewable instance makes working with the ASP.NET page easier. Another great thing is that Visual Studio 2012 provides IntelliSense when working with the inline coding model and ASP.NET 4.5. Before Visual Studio 2005, this capability did not exist.

Code-Behind Model

The other option for constructing your ASP.NET 4.5 pages is to build your files using the code-behind model. The idea of using the code-behind model is to separate the business logic and presentation logic into separate files. Doing this makes working with your pages easier, especially if you are working in a team environment where visual designers work on the UI of the page and coders work on the business logic that sits behind the presentation pieces.

> **NOTE** *It is important to note that the code-behind model is preferred over the inline model. You will find that many of the examples in this book use an inline coding model simply because it's easier to show an example in one listing. Even though the example is using an inline coding style, it is recommended that you move the code to the code-behind model.*

To create a new page in your ASP.NET solution that uses the code-behind model, select the page type you want from the New File dialog box. To build a page that uses the code-behind model, you first select the page in the Add New Item dialog box and make sure the Place Code in Separate File check box is selected. Table 3-2 shows you the options for pages that use the code-behind model.

TABLE 3-2

FILE OPTION	FILE CREATED
Web Form	`.aspx` file; `.aspx.vb` or `.aspx.cs` file
Master Page	`.master` file; `.master.vb` or `.master.cs` file
Web User Control	`.ascx` file; `.ascx.vb` or `.ascx.cs` file
Web Service	`.asmx` file; `.vb` or `.cs` file

In Listing 3-1, you saw how to create a page using the inline coding style. In Listings 3-2 and 3-3, you see how to convert the inline model to the code-behind model. You can find the code for Listing 3-2 as Listing03-02.aspx in this chapter's download. You can find the code for Listing 3-3 in this chapter's download as Listing03-02.aspx.vb and Listing03-02.aspx.cs.

LISTING 3-2: An .aspx page that uses the ASP.NET 4.5 code-behind model

VB

```
<%@ Page Language="vb" AutoEventWireup="false" CodeBehind="Listing03-02.aspx.vb"
    Inherits="ProfessionalASPNet45_03VB.Listing03_02" %>
<!DOCTYPE html>

<html xmlns="http://www.w3.org/1999/xhtml">
<head id="Head1" runat="server">
    <title>Simple Page</title>
</head>
<body>
    <form id="form1" runat="server">
        <div>
            What is your name?<br />
            <asp:TextBox ID="TextBox1" runat="server"></asp:TextBox>
            <asp:Button ID="Button1" runat="server" Text="Submit"
                OnClick="Button1_Click" />
        </div>
        <div>
            <asp:Literal ID="Literal1" runat="server" />
        </div>
    </form>
</body>
</html>
```

C#

```
<%@ Page Language="C#" AutoEventWireup="true" CodeBehind="Listing03-02.aspx.cs"
    Inherits="ProfessionalASPNet45_03CS.Listing03_02" %>
```

LISTING 3-3: A code-behind page

VB

```
Partial Public Class Listing03_02
```

```
    Inherits System.Web.UI.Page

    Protected Sub Button1_Click(sender As Object, e As EventArgs)
        Literal1.Text = "Hello " & TextBox1.Text
    End Sub

End Class
```

C#

```
public partial class Listing03_02 : System.Web.UI.Page
{
    protected void Button1_Click1(object sender, EventArgs e)
    {
        Literal1.Text = "Hello " + TextBox1.Text;
    }
}
```

The `.aspx` page using this ASP.NET code-behind model has some attributes in the `Page` directive that you should pay attention to when working in this mode. The first attribute needed for the code-behind model to work is the `CodeBehind` attribute. This attribute in the `Page` directive is meant to point to the code-behind page that is used with this presentation page. In this case, the value assigned is `Listing03-02.aspx.vb` or `Listing03-02.aspx.cs`. The second attribute needed is the `Inherits` attribute. This attribute was available in previous versions of ASP.NET, but was little used before ASP.NET 2.0. This attribute specifies the name of the class that is bound to the page when the page is compiled. The directives are simple enough in ASP.NET 4.5. Look at the code-behind page from Listing 3-3.

The code-behind page is rather simple in appearance because of the partial class capabilities that .NET 4.5 provides. You can see that the class created in the code-behind file uses partial classes, employing the `Partial` keyword in Visual Basic 2012 and the `partial` keyword from C# 2012. This enables you to simply place the methods that you need in your page class. In this case, you have a button-click event and nothing else.

Later in this chapter, you look at the compilation process for both of these models.

ASP.NET 4.5 PAGE DIRECTIVES

ASP.NET directives are part of every ASP.NET page. You can control the behavior of your ASP.NET pages by using these directives. Here is an example of the `Page` directive:

```
<%@ Page Language="vb" AutoEventWireup="false" CodeBehind="Listing03-02.aspx.vb"
    Inherits="ProfessionalASPNet45_03VB.Listing03_02" %>
```

Twelve directives, shown in Table 3-3, are at your disposal in your ASP.NET pages or user controls. You use these directives in your applications whether the page uses the code-behind model or the inline coding model.

Basically, these directives are commands that the compiler uses when the page is compiled. Directives are simple to incorporate into your pages. A directive is written in the following format:

```
<%@ [Directive] [Attribute=Value] %>
```

From this, you can see that a directive is opened with a `<%@` and closed with a `%>`. Putting these directives at the top of your pages or controls is best because this is traditionally where developers expect to see them (although the page still compiles if the directives are located at a different place). Of course, you can also add more than a single attribute to your directive statements, as shown in the following:

```
<%@ [Directive] [Attribute=Value] [Attribute=Value] %>
```

TABLE 3-3

DIRECTIVE	DESCRIPTION
@Assembly	Links an assembly to the page or user control for which it is associated.
@Control	Page directive meant for use with user controls (.ascx).
@Implements	Implements a specified .NET Framework interface.
@Import	Imports specified namespaces into the page or user control.
@Master	Enables you to specify master page–specific attributes and values to use when the page parses or compiles. This directive can be used only with master pages (.master).
@MasterType	Associates a class name to a page to get at strongly typed references or members contained within the specified master page.
@OutputCache	Controls the output caching policies of a page or user control.
@Page	Enables you to specify page–specific attributes and values to use when the page parses or compiles. This directive can be used only with ASP.NET pages (.aspx).
@PreviousPageType	Enables an ASP.NET page to work with a postback from another page in the application.
@Reference	Links a page or user control to the current page or user control.
@Register	Associates aliases with namespaces and class names for notation in the custom server control syntax.
@WebHandler	Enables a page to be used as an HttpHandler. This will be covered more in Chapter 30.

The following sections provide a quick review of each of these directives. Some of these directives are valid only within specific page types.

@Page

The @Page directive enables you to specify attributes and values for an ASP.NET page (.aspx) to be used when the page is parsed or compiled. This is the most frequently used directive from Table 3-3. Because the ASP.NET page is such an important part of ASP.NET, there are quite a few attributes for the directive. Table 3-4 summarizes the attributes available through the @Page directive.

TABLE 3-4

ATTRIBUTE	DESCRIPTION
AspCompat	Permits the page to be executed on a single-threaded apartment thread when given a value of True. The default setting for this attribute is False.
Async	Specifies whether the ASP.NET page is processed synchronously or asynchronously.
AsyncTimeout	Specifies the amount of time in seconds to wait for the asynchronous task to complete. The default setting is 45 seconds.
AutoEventWireup	Specifies whether the page events are autowired when set to True. The default setting for this attribute is True.
Buffer	Enables HTTP response buffering when set to True. The default setting for this attribute is True.
ClassName	Specifies the name of the class that is bound to the page when the page is compiled.
ClientIDMode	Specifies the algorithm that the page should use when generating ClientID values for server controls that are on the page. The default value is AutoID (the mode that was used for ASP.NET pages prior to ASP.NET 4).

`ClientTarget`	Specifies the target user agent a control should render content for. This attribute needs to be tied to an alias defined in the `<clientTarget>` section of the `web.config` file.
`CodeBehind`	References the compiled code-behind file with which the page is associated. This attribute is used for web application projects.
`CodeFile`	References the code-behind file with which the page is associated. This attribute is used for website projects.
`CodeFileBaseClass`	Specifies the type name of the base class to use with the code-behind class, which is used by the `CodeFile` attribute.
`CodePage`	Indicates the code page value for the response.
`CompilationMode`	Specifies whether ASP.NET should compile the page or not. The available options include `Always` (the default), `Auto`, or `Never`. A setting of `Auto` means that if possible, ASP.NET will not compile the page.
`CompilerOptions`	Compiler string that indicates compilation options for the page.
`ContentType`	Defines the HTTP content type of the response as a standard MIME type.
`Culture`	Specifies the culture setting of the page. ASP.NET 3.5 and later include the capability to give the `Culture` attribute a value of `Auto` to enable automatic detection of the culture required.
`Debug`	Compiles the page with debug symbols in place when set to `True`.
`Description`	Provides a text description of the page. The ASP.NET parser ignores this attribute and its assigned value.
`EnableEventValidation`	Specifies whether to enable validation of events in postback and callback scenarios. The default setting of `True` means that events will be validated.
`EnableSessionState`	Session state for the page is enabled when set to `True`. The default setting is `True`.
`EnableTheming`	Page is enabled to use theming when set to `True`. The default setting for this attribute is `True`.
`EnableViewState`	ViewState is maintained across the page when set to `True`. The default value is `True`.
`EnableViewStateMac`	Page runs a machine-authentication check on the page's ViewState when the page is posted back from the user when set to `True`. The default value is `False`.
`ErrorPage`	Specifies a URL to post to for all unhandled page exceptions.
`Explicit`	Visual Basic `Explicit` option is enabled when set to `True`. The default setting is `False`.
`Language`	Defines the language being used for any inline rendering and script blocks.
`LCID`	Defines the locale identifier for the web form's page.
`LinePragmas`	`Boolean` value that specifies whether line pragmas are used with the resulting assembly.
`MasterPageFile`	Takes a `String` value that points to the location of the master page used with the page. This attribute is used with content pages.
`MaintainScrollPosition OnPostback`	Takes a `Boolean` value, which indicates whether the page should be positioned exactly in the same scroll position or whether the page should be regenerated in the uppermost position for when the page is posted back to itself.
`MetaDescription`	Allows you to specify a page's description in a Meta tag for SEO purposes.
`MetaKeywords`	Allows you to specify a page's keywords in a Meta tag for SEO purposes.

continues

TABLE 3-4 *(continued)*

ATTRIBUTE	DESCRIPTION
ResponseEncoding	Specifies the response encoding of the page content.
SmartNavigation	Specifies whether to activate the ASP.NET Smart Navigation feature for richer browsers. This returns the postback to the current position on the page. The default value is `False`. Since ASP.NET 2.0, `SmartNavigation` has been deprecated. Use the `SetFocus()` method and the `MaintainScrollPositionOnPostback` property instead.
Src	Points to the source file of the class used for the code-behind of the page being rendered.
Strict	Compiles the page using the Visual Basic `Strict` mode when set to `True`. The default setting is `False`.
StylesheetTheme	Applies the specified theme to the page using the ASP.NET themes feature. The difference between the `StylesheetTheme` and `Theme` attributes is that `StylesheetTheme` will not override preexisting style settings in the controls, whereas `Theme` will remove these settings.
Theme	Applies the specified theme to the page using the ASP.NET themes feature.
Title	Applies a page's title. This is an attribute mainly meant for content pages that must apply a page title other than what is specified in the master page.
Trace	Page tracing is enabled when set to `True`. The default setting is `False`.
TraceMode	Specifies how the trace messages are displayed when tracing is enabled. The settings for this attribute include `SortByTime` or `SortByCategory`. The default setting is `SortByTime`.
Transaction	Specifies whether transactions are supported on the page. The settings for this attribute are `Disabled`, `NotSupported`, `Supported`, `Required`, and `RequiresNew`. The default setting is `Disabled`.
UICulture	The value of the `UICulture` attribute specifies what UI Culture to use for the ASP.NET page. ASP.NET 3.5 and later include the capability to give the `UICulture` attribute a value of `Auto` to enable automatic detection of the `UICulture`.
ValidateRequest	When this attribute is set to `True`, the form input values are checked against a list of potentially dangerous values. This helps protect your web application from harmful attacks such as JavaScript attacks. The default value is `True`.
ViewStateEncryptionMode	Specifies how the ViewState is encrypted on the page. The options include `Auto`, `Always`, and `Never`. The default is `Auto`.
ViewStateMode	Determines whether the ViewState is maintained for controls on a page.
WarningLevel	Specifies the compiler warning level at which to stop compilation of the page. Possible values are 0 through 4.

Here is an example of how to use the `@Page` directive:

```
<%@ Page Language="C#" AutoEventWireup="true" CodeBehind="Listing03-02.aspx.cs"
    Inherits="ProfessionalASPNet45_03CS.Listing03_02" %>
```

@Master

The `@Master` directive is quite similar to the `@Page` directive except that the `@Master` directive is meant for master pages (`.master`). In using the `@Master` directive, you specify properties of the templated page that you will be using in conjunction with any number of content pages on your site. Any content pages (built using the @Page directive) can then inherit from the master page all the master content (defined in the master page using the @Master directive). Although they are similar, the @Master directive has fewer attributes available to it than does the @Page directive. The available attributes for the @Master directive are shown in Table 3-5.

TABLE 3-5

ATTRIBUTE	DESCRIPTION
AutoEventWireup	Specifies whether the master page's events are autowired when set to True. The default setting is True.
ClassName	Specifies the name of the class that is bound to the master page when compiled.
CodeBehind	References the compiled code-behind file with which the master page is associated.
CodeFile	References the code-behind file with which the master page is associated.
CompilationMode	Specifies whether ASP.NET should compile the page. The available options include Always (the default), Auto, or Never. A setting of Auto means that if possible, ASP .NET will not compile the page.
CompilerOptions	Compiler string that indicates compilation options for the master page.
Debug	Compiles the master page with debug symbols in place when set to True.
Description	Provides a text description of the master page. The ASP.NET parser ignores this attribute and its assigned value.
EnableTheming	Indicates the master page is enabled to use theming when set to True. The default setting for this attribute is True.
EnableViewState	Maintains the ViewState for the master page when set to True. The default value is True.
Explicit	Indicates that the Visual Basic Explicit option is enabled when set to True. The default setting is False.
Inherits	Specifies the CodeBehind class for the master page to inherit.
Language	Defines the language that is being used for any inline rendering and script blocks.
LinePragmas	Boolean value that specifies whether line pragmas are used with the resulting assembly.
MasterPageFile	Takes a String value that points to the location of the master page used with the master page. It is possible to have a master page use another master page, which creates a nested master page.
Src	Points to the source file of the class used for the code-behind of the master page being rendered.
Strict	Compiles the master page using the Visual Basic Strict mode when set to True. The default setting is False.
WarningLevel	Specifies the compiler warning level at which you want to abort compilation of the page. Possible values are from 0 to 4.

Here is an example of how to use the @Master directive:

```
<%@ Master Language="C#" AutoEventWireup="true"
    CodeBehind="ProfessionalASPNet45-Layout.master.cs"
    Inherits="ProfessionalASPNet45_03CS.ProfessionalASPNet45_Layout" %>
```

@Control

The @Control directive is similar to the @Page directive except that you use it when you build an ASP.NET user control. The @Control directive allows you to define the properties to be inherited by the user control. These values are assigned to the user control as the page is parsed and compiled. The available attributes are fewer than those of the @Page directive, but they allow for the modifications you need when building user controls. Table 3-6 details the available attributes.

TABLE 3-6

ATTRIBUTE	DESCRIPTION
AutoEventWireup	Specifies whether the user control's events are autowired when set to True. The default setting is True.
ClassName	Specifies the name of the class that is bound to the user control when the page is compiled.
ClientIDMode	Specifies the algorithm that the page should use when generating ClientID values for server controls that are on the page. The default value is AutoID (the mode that was used for ASP.NET pages prior to ASP.NET 4).
CodeBehind	References the compiled code-behind file with which the master page is associated. In ASP.NET 2.0 or earlier, CodeFile should be used along with Inherits.
CodeFile	References the code-behind file with which the user control is associated.
CodeFileBaseClass	Specifies the type name of the base class to use with the code-behind class, which is used by the CodeFile attribute.
CompilationMode	Specifies whether the control should be compiled.
CompilerOptions	Compiler string that indicates compilation options for the user control.
Debug	Compiles the user control with debug symbols in place when set to True.
Description	Provides a text description of the user control. The ASP.NET parser ignores this attribute and its assigned value.
EnableTheming	User control is enabled to use theming when set to True. The default setting for this attribute is True.
EnableViewState	ViewState is maintained for the user control when set to True. The default value is True.
Explicit	Visual Basic Explicit option is enabled when set to True. The default setting is False.
Inherits	Specifies the CodeBehind class for the user control to inherit.
Language	Defines the language used for any inline rendering and script blocks.
LinePragmas	Boolean value that specifies whether line pragmas are used with the resulting assembly.
Src	Points to the source file of the class used for the code-behind of the user control being rendered.
Strict	Compiles the user control using the Visual Basic Strict mode when set to True. The default setting is False.
WarningLevel	Specifies the compiler warning level at which to stop compilation of the user control. Possible values are 0 through 4.

The @Control directive is meant to be used with an ASP.NET user control. The following is an example of how to use the directive:

```
<%@ Control Language="C#" AutoEventWireup="true"
   CodeBehind="RegistrationUserControl.ascx.cs"
   Inherits="ProfessionalASPNet45_03CS.RegistrationUserControl" %
```

@Import

The @Import directive allows you to specify a namespace to be imported into the ASP.NET page or user control. By importing, all the classes and interfaces of the namespace are made available to the page or user control. This directive supports only a single attribute: Namespace.

The Namespace attribute takes a String value that specifies the namespace to be imported. The @Import directive cannot contain more than one attribute/value pair. Because of this, you must place multiple namespace imports in multiple lines as shown in the following example:

```
<%@ Import Namespace="System.Data" %>
<%@ Import Namespace="System.Data.SqlClient" %>
```

Several assemblies are already being referenced by your application. You can find a list of these imported namespaces by looking in the root web.config file found at C:\Windows\Microsoft.NET\Framework\ v4.0.xxxxx\Config. You can find this list of assemblies being referenced from the <assemblies> child element of the <compilation> element. The settings in the root web.config file are as follows:

```
<assemblies>
    <add assembly="Microsoft.VisualStudio.Web.PageInspector.Loader,
      Version=1.0.0.0, Culture=neutral, PublicKeyToken=b03f5f7f11d50a3a" />
    <add assembly="mscorlib" />
    <add assembly="Microsoft.CSharp, Version=4.0.0.0, Culture=neutral,
      PublicKeyToken=b03f5f7f11d50a3a" />
    <add assembly="System, Version=4.0.0.0, Culture=neutral,
      PublicKeyToken=b77a5c561934e089" />
    <add assembly="System.Configuration, Version=4.0.0.0, Culture=neutral,
      PublicKeyToken=b03f5f7f11d50a3a" />
    <add assembly="System.Web, Version=4.0.0.0, Culture=neutral,
      PublicKeyToken=b03f5f7f11d50a3a" />
    <add assembly="System.Data, Version=4.0.0.0, Culture=neutral,
      PublicKeyToken=b77a5c561934e089" />
    <add assembly="System.Web.Services, Version=4.0.0.0, Culture=neutral,
      PublicKeyToken=b03f5f7f11d50a3a" />
    <add assembly="System.Xml, Version=4.0.0.0, Culture=neutral,
      PublicKeyToken=b77a5c561934e089" />
    <add assembly="System.Drawing, Version=4.0.0.0, Culture=neutral,
      PublicKeyToken=b03f5f7f11d50a3a" />
    <add assembly="System.EnterpriseServices, Version=4.0.0.0, Culture=neutral,
      PublicKeyToken=b03f5f7f11d50a3a" />
    <add assembly="System.IdentityModel, Version=4.0.0.0, Culture=neutral,
      PublicKeyToken=b77a5c561934e089" />
    <add assembly="System.Runtime.Serialization, Version=4.0.0.0, Culture=neutral,
      PublicKeyToken=b77a5c561934e089" />
    <add assembly="System.ServiceModel, Version=4.0.0.0, Culture=neutral,
      PublicKeyToken=b77a5c561934e089" />
    <add assembly="System.ServiceModel.Activation, Version=4.0.0.0,
      Culture=neutral, PublicKeyToken=31bf3856ad364e35" />
    <add assembly="System.ServiceModel.Web, Version=4.0.0.0, Culture=neutral,
      PublicKeyToken=31bf3856ad364e35" />
    <add assembly="System.Activities, Version=4.0.0.0, Culture=neutral,
      PublicKeyToken=31bf3856ad364e35" />
    <add assembly="System.ServiceModel.Activities, Version=4.0.0.0,
      Culture=neutral, PublicKeyToken=31bf3856ad364e35" />
    <add assembly="System.WorkflowServices, Version=4.0.0.0, Culture=neutral,
      PublicKeyToken=31bf3856ad364e35" />
    <add assembly="System.Core, Version=4.0.0.0, Culture=neutral,
      PublicKeyToken=b77a5c561934e089" />
```

```
      <add assembly="System.Web.Extensions, Version=4.0.0.0, Culture=neutral,
        PublicKeyToken=31bf3856ad364e35" />
      <add assembly="System.Data.DataSetExtensions, Version=4.0.0.0,
        Culture=neutral, PublicKeyToken=b77a5c561934e089" />
      <add assembly="System.Xml.Linq, Version=4.0.0.0, Culture=neutral,
        PublicKeyToken=b77a5c561934e089" />
      <add assembly="System.ComponentModel.DataAnnotations, Version=4.0.0.0,
        Culture=neutral, PublicKeyToken=31bf3856ad364e35" />
      <add assembly="System.Web.DynamicData, Version=4.0.0.0, Culture=neutral,
        PublicKeyToken=31bf3856ad364e35" />
      <add assembly="System.Web.ApplicationServices, Version=4.0.0.0,
        Culture=neutral, PublicKeyToken=31bf3856ad364e35" />
      <add assembly="*" />
      <add assembly="System.Web.WebPages.Deployment, Version=1.0.0.0,
        Culture=neutral, PublicKeyToken=31bf3856ad364e35" />
      <add assembly="System.Web.WebPages.Deployment, Version=2.0.0.0,
        Culture=neutral, PublicKeyToken=31bf3856ad364e35" />
</assemblies>
```

Because of this reference in the root `web.config` file, these assemblies do not need to be referenced in the References folder, as you would have done in ASP.NET 1.0/1.1. You can actually add or delete assemblies that are referenced from this list. For example, if you have a custom assembly referenced continuously by every application on the server, you can simply add a similar reference to your custom assembly next to these others. You can perform this same task through the application-specific `web.config` file of your application as well.

> **NOTE** *Although you can edit the* `.config` *files located in the* `C:\Windows\Microsoft`
> `.NET\Framework\vX.X.XXXX\config` *folders, it's highly recommended that these files
> remain untouched as future updates may remove customizations. Also, if you are
> deploying your application(s) to a web farm, any machine-specific changes must be
> made on each server.*

Even though assemblies might be referenced, you must still import the namespaces of these assemblies into your pages. The same root `web.config` file contains a list of namespaces automatically imported into every page of your application. This is specified through the `<namespaces>` child element of the `<pages>` element.

```
<namespaces>
    <add namespace="System" />
    <add namespace="System.Collections" />
    <add namespace="System.Collections.Generic" />
    <add namespace="System.Collections.Specialized" />
    <add namespace="System.ComponentModel.DataAnnotations" />
    <add namespace="System.Configuration" />
    <add namespace="System.Linq" />
    <add namespace="System.Text" />
    <add namespace="System.Text.RegularExpressions" />
    <add namespace="System.Web" />
    <add namespace="System.Web.Caching" />
    <add namespace="System.Web.DynamicData" />
    <add namespace="System.Web.SessionState" />
    <add namespace="System.Web.Security" />
    <add namespace="System.Web.Profile" />
    <add namespace="System.Web.UI" />
    <add namespace="System.Web.UI.WebControls" />
    <add namespace="System.Web.UI.WebControls.WebParts" />
    <add namespace="System.Web.UI.HtmlControls" />
    <add namespace="System.Xml.Linq" />
</namespaces>
```

From this XML list, you can see that quite a few namespaces are imported into every one of your ASP.NET pages. Again, you can feel free to modify this selection in the root `web.config` file or even make a similar selection of namespaces from within your application's `web.config` file.

For instance, you can import your own namespace in the `web.config` file of your application to make the namespace available on every page where it is utilized.

```xml
<?xml version="1.0"?>
<configuration>
    <system.web>
        <compilation debug="true" targetFramework="4.5" />
        <httpRuntime targetFramework="4.5" />
        <pages>
            <namespaces>
                <add namespace="Widgets" />
            </namespaces>
        </pages>
    </system.web>
</configuration>
```

Remember that importing a namespace into your ASP.NET page or user control gives you the opportunity to use the classes without fully identifying the class name. For example, by importing the namespace `System.IO` into the ASP.NET page, you can refer to classes within this namespace by using the singular class name (`Directory` instead of `System.IO.Directory`).

@Implements

The `@Implements` directive gets the ASP.NET page to implement a specified .NET Framework interface. This directive supports only a single attribute: `Interface`.

The `Interface` attribute directly specifies the .NET Framework interface. When the ASP.NET page or user control implements an interface, it has direct access to all its events, methods, and properties.

Here is an example of the `@Implements` directive:

```
<%@ Implements Interface="System.Web.UI.IValidator" %>
```

@Register

The `@Register` directive associates aliases with namespaces and class names for notation in custom server control syntax. You can see the use of the `@Register` directive when you drag and drop a user control onto any of your `.aspx` pages. Dragging a user control onto the `.aspx` page causes Visual Studio 2012 to create a `@Register` directive at the top of the page. This registers your user control on the page so that the control can then be accessed on the `.aspx` page by a specific name.

The `@Register` directive supports five attributes, as described in Table 3-7.

TABLE 3-7

ATTRIBUTE	DESCRIPTION
Assembly	The assembly you are associating with the TagPrefix
Namespace	The namespace to relate with the TagPrefix
Src	The location of the user control
TagName	The alias to relate to the class name
TagPrefix	The alias to relate to the namespace

Here is an example of how to use the `@Register` directive to import a user control to an ASP.NET page:

```
<%@ Register TagPrefix="MyTag" Namespace="MyNamespace"
  Assembly="MyAssembly" %>
```

@Assembly

The `@Assembly` directive attaches assemblies, the building blocks of .NET applications, to an ASP.NET page or user control as it compiles, thereby making all the assembly's classes and interfaces available to the page. This directive supports two attributes, as shown in Table 3-8.

TABLE 3-8

ATTRIBUTE	DESCRIPTION
Name	Enables you to specify the name of an assembly used to attach to the page files. The name of the assembly should include the filename only, not the file's extension. For instance, if the file is `MyAssembly.vb`, the value of the name attribute should be `MyAssembly`.
Src	Enables you to specify the source of the assembly file to use in compilation.

The following provides some examples of how to use the `@Assembly` directive:

```
<%@ Assembly Name="MyAssembly" %>
<%@ Assembly Src="MyAssembly.vb" %>
```

@PreviousPageType

This directive is used to specify the page from which any cross-page postings originate. Cross-page posting between ASP.NET pages is explained later in the section "Cross-Page Posting."

The `@PreviousPageType` works with the cross-page posting capability that ASP.NET 4.5 provides. This directive contains two attributes as shown in Table 3-9.

TABLE 3-9

ATTRIBUTE	DESCRIPTION
TypeName	Sets the name of the derived class from which the postback will occur
VirtualPath	Sets the location of the posting page from which the postback will occur

@MasterType

The `@MasterType` directive associates a class name to an ASP.NET page to get at strongly typed references or members contained within the specified master page. This directive supports two attributes, as shown in Table 3-10.

TABLE 3-10

ATTRIBUTE	DESCRIPTION
TypeName	Sets the name of the derived class from which to get strongly typed references or members
VirtualPath	Sets the location of the page from which these strongly typed references and members will be retrieved

Details of how to use the @MasterType directive are shown in Chapter 16. Here is an example of its use:

```
<%@ MasterType VirtualPath="~/Wrox.master" %>
```

@OutputCache

The @OutputCache directive controls the output caching policies of an ASP.NET page or user control. This directive supports the attributes described in Table 3-11.

TABLE 3-11

ATTRIBUTE	DESCRIPTION
CacheProfile	Allows for a central way to manage an application's cache profile. Use the CacheProfile attribute to specify the name of the cache profile detailed in the web.config file.
Duration	The duration of time in seconds that the ASP.NET page or user control is cached.
Location	Location enumeration value. The default is Any. This is valid for .aspx pages only and does not work with user controls (.ascx). Other possible values include Client, Downstream, None, Server, and ServerAndClient.
NoStore	Specifies whether to send a no-store header with the page.
Shared	Specifies whether a user control's output can be shared across multiple pages. This attribute takes a Boolean value and the default setting is False.
SqlDependency	Enables a particular page to use SQL Server cache invalidation.
VaryByContentEncodings	Semicolon-separated list of strings used to vary the output cache based on content encodings.
VaryByControl	Semicolon-separated list of strings used to vary the output cache of a user control.
VaryByCustom	String specifying the custom output caching requirements.
VaryByHeader	Semicolon-separated list of HTTP headers used to vary the output cache.
VaryByParam	Semicolon-separated list of strings used to vary the output cache.

Here is an example of how to use the @OutputCache directive:

```
<%@ OutputCache Duration="180" VaryByParam="None" %>
```

Remember that the Duration attribute specifies the amount of time in *seconds* during which this page is to be stored in the system cache.

@Reference

The @Reference directive declares that another ASP.NET page or user control should be compiled along with the active page or control. This directive contains a single attribute, the VirtualPath attribute. VirtualPath contains a location of the page or user control from which the active page will be referenced.

Here is an example of how to use the @Reference directive:

```
<%@ Reference VirtualPath="~/MyControl.ascx" %>
```

ASP.NET PAGE EVENTS

ASP.NET developers consistently work with various events in their server-side code. Many of the events that they work with pertain to specific server controls. For instance, if you want to initiate some action when the end user clicks a button on your web page, you create a button-click event in your server-side code, as shown in Listing 3-4 (Listing03-04.aspx.cs in the code download for this chapter).

LISTING 3-4: A sample button-click event shown in C#

```csharp
protected void VerifyDataButton_Click(object sender, EventArgs e)
{
    // Verify Data
}
```

In addition to the server controls, developers also want to initiate actions at specific moments when the ASP.NET page is being either created or destroyed. The ASP.NET page itself has always had a number of events for these instances. Since the inception of ASP.NET, the following page events are available:

➤ AbortTransaction

➤ CommitTransaction

➤ DataBinding

➤ Disposed

➤ Error

➤ Init

➤ Load

➤ PreRender

➤ Unload

One of the more popular page events from this list is the Load event, which is used in C# as shown in Listing 3-5 (Listing03-05.aspx.cs in the code download for this chapter).

LISTING 3-5: Using the Page_Load event

```csharp
protected void Page_Load(object sender, EventArgs e)
{
    Response.Write("This is the Page_Load event");
}
```

Besides the page events just shown, ASP.NET 4.5 has the following events:

➤ InitComplete: Indicates the initialization of the page is completed

➤ LoadComplete: Indicates the page has been completely loaded into memory

➤ PreInit: Indicates the moment immediately before a page is initialized

➤ PreLoad: Indicates the moment before a page has been loaded into memory

➤ PreRenderComplete: Indicates the moment directly before a page has been rendered in the browser

An example of using any of these events, such as the PreInit event, is shown in Listing 3-6 (Listing03-06.aspx.vb and Listing03-06.aspx.cs in the code download for this chapter).

LISTING 3-6: Using page events

VB

```vb
Private Sub Page_PreInit(sender As Object, e As EventArgs) Handles Me.PreInit
    Page.Theme = Request.QueryString("ThemeChange")
End Sub
```

C#

```csharp
protected void Page_PreInit(object sender, EventArgs e)
{
    Page.Theme = Request.QueryString["ThemeChange"];
}
```

If you create an ASP.NET 4.5 page and turn on tracing, you can see the order in which the main page events are initiated. They are fired in the order shown in Figure 3-7.

With the addition of these choices, you can now work with the page and the controls on the page at many points in the page-compilation process. You see these useful page events in code examples throughout the book.

DEALING WITH POSTBACKS

When you are working with ASP.NET pages, be sure you understand the page events just listed. They are important because you place a lot of your page behavior inside these events at specific points in a page lifecycle.

In Active Server Pages 3.0, developers had their pages post to other pages within the application. ASP.NET pages typically post back to themselves to process events (such as a button-click event).

For this reason, you must differentiate between posts for the first time a page is loaded by the end user and *postbacks*. A postback is just that—a posting back to the same page. The postback contains all the form information collected on the initial page for processing if required.

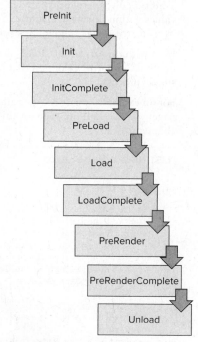

FIGURE 3-7

> **NOTE** *Postbacks use an HTTP POST action instead of an HTTP GET. An HTTP POST sends form data in the message body of an HTTP Request. A HTTP GET sends form data in the URL of an HTTP Request.*

Because of all the postbacks that can occur with an ASP.NET page, you want to know whether a request is the first instance for a particular page or is a postback from the same page. You can make this check by using the `IsPostBack` property of the `Page` class, as shown in the following example:

VB

```vb
If Not Page.IsPostBack Then
    ' Do processing
End If
```

C#

```csharp
if (!Page.IsPostBack) {
    // Do processing
}
```

CROSS-PAGE POSTING

One common feature in ASP 3.0 that was difficult to achieve in early versions of ASP.NET is the capability to do cross-page posting. Cross-page posting enables you to submit a form (say, `Page1.aspx`) and have this form and all the control values post themselves to another page (`Page2.aspx`).

Traditionally, any page created in ASP.NET 1.0/1.1 simply posted to itself, and you handled the control values within this page instance. You could differentiate between the page's first request and any postbacks by using the `Page.IsPostBack` property, as shown earlier in this chapter.

Even with this capability, many developers still wanted to be able to post to another page and deal with the first page's control values on that page. This is something that is possible in ASP.NET 4.5, and it is quite a simple process.

For an example, create a page called `Page1.aspx` that contains a simple form. Listing 3-7 shows this page; you can find the code for this listing in Listing03-07 (Page 1).aspx in the code download for the chapter.

LISTING 3-7: Page1.aspx

VB

```vb
<%@ Page Language="vb" %>
<!DOCTYPE html>
<script runat="server">
    Protected Sub Button1_Click(sender As Object,
        e As System.EventArgs)
        Label1.Text = "Hello " & TextBox1.Text & "<br />" &
            "Date Selected: " & Calendar1.SelectedDate.ToShortDateString()
    End Sub
</script>
<html xmlns="http://www.w3.org/1999/xhtml">
<head runat="server">
    <title>First Page</title>
</head>
<body>
    <form id="form1" runat="server">
        Enter your name:<br />
        <asp:Textbox ID="TextBox1" Runat="server"></asp:Textbox>
        <p>
            When do you want to fly?<br />
            <asp:Calendar ID="Calendar1" Runat="server"></asp:Calendar>
        </p>
        <br />
        <asp:Button ID="Button1" Runat="server" Text="Submit page to itself"
            OnClick="Button1_Click" />
        <asp:Button ID="Button2" Runat="server" Text="Submit page to Page2.aspx"
            PostBackUrl="Page2.aspx" />
        <p>
            <asp:Label ID="Label1" Runat="server"></asp:Label>
        </p>
    </form>
</body>
</html>
```

C#

```csharp
<%@ Page Language="C#" %>
<!DOCTYPE html>
<script runat="server">
    protected void Button1_Click(Object sender, EventArgs e)
    {
        Label1.Text = "Hello " + TextBox1.Text + "<br />" +
            "Date Selected: " + Calendar1.SelectedDate.ToShortDateString();
    }
</script>
```

The code from `Page1.aspx`, as shown in Listing 3-7, is quite interesting. Two buttons are shown on the page. Both buttons submit the form, but each submits the form to a different location. The first button submits the form to itself. This is the behavior that has been the default for ASP.NET 1.0/1.1. In fact, nothing is different about `Button1`. It submits to `Page1.aspx` as a postback because of the use of the `OnClick` property in the button control. A `Button1_Click` method on `Page1.aspx` handles the values that are contained within the server controls on the page.

The second button, `Button2`, works quite differently. This button does not contain an `OnClick` method as the first button did. Instead, it uses the `PostBackUrl` property. This property takes a string value that points to the location of the file to which this page should post. In this case, it is `Page2.aspx`. This means that `Page2.aspx` now receives the postback and all the values contained in the `Page1.aspx` controls. Look at the code for `Page2.aspx`, shown in Listing 3-8 (Listing03-08 (Page 2).aspx in the code download for this chapter).

LISTING 3-8: Page2.aspx

VB

```
<%@ Page Language="vb" %>
<script runat="server">
    Protected Sub Page_Load(ByVal sender As Object, ByVal e As System.EventArgs)
        Dim pp_Textbox1 As TextBox
        Dim pp_Calendar1 As Calendar
        pp_Textbox1 = CType(PreviousPage.FindControl("Textbox1"), TextBox)
        pp_Calendar1 = CType(PreviousPage.FindControl("Calendar1"), Calendar)
        Label1.Text = "Hello " & pp_Textbox1.Text & "<br />" & _
            "Date Selected: " & pp_Calendar1.SelectedDate.ToShortDateString()
    End Sub
</script>
<!DOCTYPE html>

<html xmlns="http://www.w3.org/1999/xhtml">
<head runat="server">
    <title>Second Page</title>
</head>
<body>
    <form id="form1" runat="server">
        <asp:Label ID="Label1" Runat="server"></asp:Label>
    </form>
</body>
</html>
```

C#

```
<%@ Page Language="C#" %>
<script runat="server">
    protected void Page_Load(Object sender, EventArgs e)
    {
        TextBox pp_TextBox1;
        Calendar pp_Calendar1;
        pp_TextBox1 = (TextBox)PreviousPage.FindControl("TextBox1");
        pp_Calendar1 = (Calendar)PreviousPage.FindControl("Calendar1");
        Label1.Text = "Hello " + pp_TextBox1.Text + "<br />" +
            "Date Selected: " + pp_Calendar1.SelectedDate.ToShortDateString();
    }
</script>
```

You have a couple of ways of getting at the values of the controls that are exposed from `Page1.aspx` from the second page. The first option is displayed in Listing 3-8. To get at a particular control's value that is carried over from the previous page, you simply create an instance of that control type and populate this instance using the `FindControl()` method from the `PreviousPage` property. The `String` value assigned to the `FindControl()` method is the `Id` value, which is used for the server control from the previous page. After this is assigned, you can work with the server control and its carried-over values just as if it had originally resided on the current page. You can see from the example that you can extract the `Text` and `SelectedDate` properties from the controls without any problem.

Another way of exposing the control values from the first page (`Page1.aspx`) is to create a `Property` for the control, as shown in Listing 3-9 (code file Listing03-09 (Page 1).aspx in the code download for this chapter).

LISTING 3-9: Exposing the values of the control from a property

VB

```
<%@ Page Language="vb" %>
<script runat="server">
    Public ReadOnly Property pp_TextBox1() As TextBox
        Get
            Return TextBox1
        End Get
    End Property
    Public ReadOnly Property pp_Calendar1() As Calendar
        Get
            Return Calendar1
        End Get
    End Property
</script>
```

C#

```
<%@ Page Language="C#" %>
<!DOCTYPE html>
<script runat="server">
    public TextBox pp_TextBox1 { get { return TextBox1; } }
    public Calendar pp_Calendar1 { get { return Calendar1; } }
</script>
```

Now that these properties are exposed on the posting page, the second page (`Page2.aspx`) can more easily work with the server control properties that are exposed from the first page. Listing 3-10 shows you how `Page2.aspx` works with these exposed properties (Listing03-10 (Page 2).aspx in the code download for this chapter).

LISTING 3-10: Consuming the exposed properties from the first page

VB

```
<%@ Page Language="vb" %>
<%@ PreviousPageType VirtualPath="Page1.aspx" %>
<script runat="server">
    Protected Sub Page_Load(ByVal sender As Object, ByVal e As System.EventArgs)
        Label1.Text = "Hello " & PreviousPage.pp_Textbox1.Text & "<br />" & _
            "Date Selected: " & _
                PreviousPage.pp_Calendar1.SelectedDate.ToShortDateString()
    End Sub
</script>
```

C#

```
<%@ Page Language="C#" %>
<%@ PreviousPageType VirtualPath="Page1.aspx" %>
<script runat="server">
    protected void Page_Load(Object sender, EventArgs e)
    {
        Label1.Text = "Hello " + PreviousPage.pp_TextBox1.Text + "<br />" +
            "Date Selected: " +
                PreviousPage.pp_Calendar1.SelectedDate.ToShortDateString();
    }
</script>
```

To be able to work with the properties that `Page1.aspx` exposes, you have to strongly type the `PreviousPage` property to `Page1.aspx`. To do this, you use the `PreviousPageType` directive. This directive allows you to specifically point to `Page1.aspx` with the use of the `VirtualPath` attribute.

Notice that when you are cross posting from one page to another, you are not restricted to working only with the postback on the second page. In fact, you can still create methods on `Page1.aspx` that work with the postback before moving onto `Page2.aspx`. To do this, you simply add an `OnClick` event for the button in `Page1.aspx` and a method. You also assign a value for the `PostBackUrl` property. You can then work with the postback on `Page1.aspx` and then again on `Page2.aspx`.

What happens if users request `Page2.aspx` before they work their way through `Page1.aspx`? Determining whether the request is coming from `Page1.aspx` or whether someone just hit `Page2.aspx` directly is actually quite easy. You can work with the request through the use of the `IsCrossPagePostBack` property that is quite similar to the `IsPostBack` property. The `IsCrossPagePostBack` property enables you to check whether the request is from `Page1.aspx`. Listing 3-11 (Listing03-11.aspx in the code download for this chapter) shows an example of this.

LISTING 3-11: Using the IsCrossPagePostBack property

VB

```
<%@ Page Language="vb" %>
<%@ PreviousPageType VirtualPath="Page1.aspx" %>
<script runat="server">
    Protected Sub Page_Load(ByVal sender As Object, ByVal e As System.EventArgs)
        If PreviousPage IsNot Nothing AndAlso PreviousPage.IsCrossPagePostBack Then
            Label1.Text = "Hello " & PreviousPage.pp_Textbox1.Text & "<br />" &
                "Date Selected: " &
                    PreviousPage.pp_Calendar1.SelectedDate.ToShortDateString()
        Else
            Response.Redirect("Page1.aspx")
        End If
    End Sub
</script>
```

C#

```
<%@ Page Language="C#" %>
<%@ PreviousPageType VirtualPath="Page1.aspx" %>
<script runat="server">
    protected void Page_Load(Object sender, EventArgs e)
    {
        if (PreviousPage != null && PreviousPage.IsCrossPagePostBack)
```

continues

LISTING 3-11 *(continued)*

```
        {
            Label1.Text = "Hello " + PreviousPage.pp_TextBox1.Text + "<br />" +
                "Date Selected: " +
                    PreviousPage.pp_Calendar1.SelectedDate.ToShortDateString();
        }
        else
        {
            Response.Redirect("Page1.aspx");
        }
    }
</script>
```

ASP.NET APPLICATION FOLDERS

When you create ASP.NET applications, notice that ASP.NET 4.5 uses a file-based approach. When working with ASP.NET, you can add as many files and folders as you want within your application without recompiling every time a new file is added to the overall solution. ASP.NET 4.5 includes the capability to automatically precompile your ASP.NET applications dynamically.

ASP.NET 1.0/1.1 compiled everything in your solution into a DLL. This is no longer necessary because ASP.NET applications now have a defined folder structure. By using the ASP.NET-defined folders, you can have your code automatically compiled for you, your application themes accessible throughout your application, and your globalization resources available whenever you need them. To gain a better understanding, let's review each of the defined folders to see how they work. The first folder reviewed is the App_Code folder.

App_Code Folder

The App_Code folder is meant to store your classes, .wsdl files, and typed data sets. Any of these items stored in this folder are then automatically available to all the pages within your solution. The nice thing about the App_Code folder is that when you place something inside it, Visual Studio 2012 automatically detects this and compiles it if it is a class (.vb or .cs), automatically creates your XML web service proxy class (from the .wsdl file), or automatically creates a typed data set for you from your .xsd files. After the files are automatically compiled, these items are then instantaneously available to any of your ASP.NET pages that are in the same solution. Look at how to employ a simple class in your solution using the App_Code folder.

The first step is to create an App_Code folder. To do this, simply right-click the solution and choose Add ⇨ Add ASP.NET Folder ⇨ App_Code. After the App_Code folder is in place, right-click the folder and select Add New Item. The Add New Item dialog box (as shown in Figure 3-8) that appears gives you a few options for the types of files that you can place within this folder. The available options include an Ajax-enabled WCF Service, a Class file, a LINQ to SQL Class, an ADO.NET Entity Data Model, an ADO .NET EntityObject Generator, a Sequence Diagram, a Text Template, a Text file, a DataSet, a Report, and a Class Diagram if you are using Visual Studio 2012. Visual Studio 2012 Express for Web offers only a subset of these files. For the first example, select the file of type Class and name the class **Calculator .vb** or **Calculator.cs**. Listing 3-12 shows this class, and it can be found in this chapter's code download as Calculator.vb and Calculator.cs.

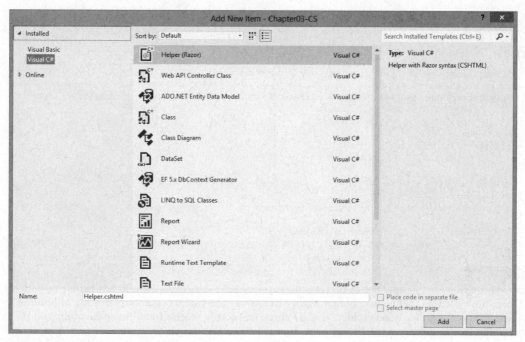

FIGURE 3-8

LISTING 3-12: The Calculator class

VB

```
Public Class Calculator
    Public Function Add(a As Integer, b As Integer) As Integer
        Return (a + b)
    End Function
End Class
```

C#

```
public class Calculator
{
    public int Add(int a, int b)
    {
        return (a + b);
    }
}
```

What's next? Just save this file, and it is now available to use in any pages that are in your solution. To see this in action, create a simple .aspx page that has just a single Label server control. Listing 3-13 (Calculator .aspx in the code download) shows you the code to place within the Page_Load event to make this new class available to the page.

LISTING 3-13: An .aspx page that uses the Calculator class

VB

```vb
<%@ Page Language="vb" %>
<script runat="server">
    Protected Sub Page_Load(ByVal sender As Object, ByVal e As System.EventArgs)
        Dim myCalc As New Calculator
        Label1.Text = myCalc.Add(12, 12)
    End Sub
</script>
```

C#

```csharp
<%@ Page Language="C#" %>
<script runat="server">
    protected void Page_Load(Object s, EventArgs e)
    {
        Calculator myCalc = new Calculator();
        Label1.Text = myCalc.Add(12, 12).ToString();
    }
</script>
```

When you run this .aspx page, notice that it utilizes the Calculator class without any problem, with no need to compile the class before use. In fact, right after saving the Calculator class in your solution or moving the class to the App_Code folder, you also instantaneously receive IntelliSense capability on the methods that the class exposes (as illustrated in Figure 3-9).

FIGURE 3-9

To see how Visual Studio 2012 works with the App_Code folder, open the Calculator class again in the IDE and add a Subtract method. Your class should now appear as shown in Listing 3-14, which can be found in this chapter's code download as Calculator.vb and Calculator.cs.

LISTING 3-14: Adding a Subtract method to the Calculator class

VB

```vb
Public Class Calculator
    Public Function Add(a As Integer, b As Integer) As Integer
        Return (a + b)
    End Function
    Public Function Subtract(a As Integer, b As Integer) As Integer
        Return (a - b)
    End Function
End Class
```

C#

```csharp
public class Calculator
{
    public int Add(int a, int b)
    {
        return (a + b);
    }

    public int Subtract(int a, int b)
    {
        return (a - b);
    }
}
```

After you have added the `Subtract` method to the `Calculator` class, save the file and go back to your `.aspx` page. Notice that the class has been recompiled by the IDE, and the new method is now available to your page. You see this directly in IntelliSense. Figure 3-10 shows this in action.

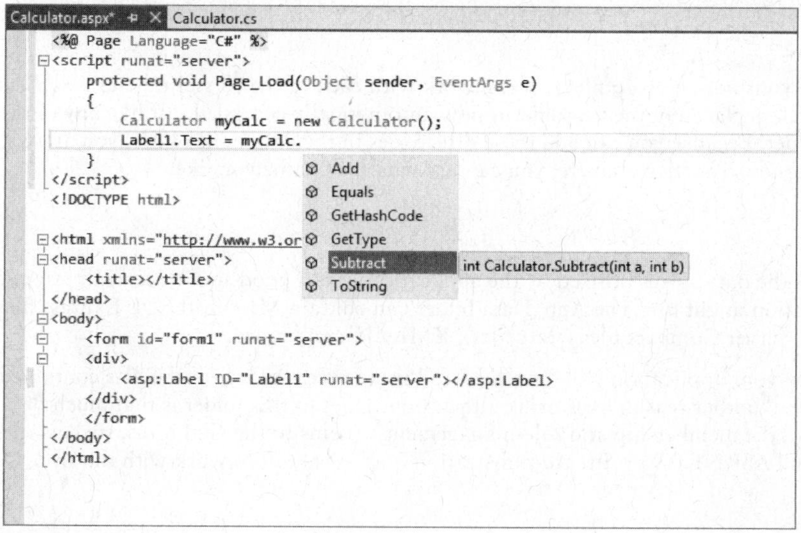

FIGURE 3-10

Everything placed in the App_Code folder is compiled into a single assembly. The class files placed within the App_Code folder are not required to use a specific language. This means that even if all the pages of the solution are written in Visual Basic, the `Calculator` class in the App_Code folder of the solution can be built in C# (`Calculator.cs`).

Because all the classes contained in this folder are built into a single assembly, you *cannot* have classes of different languages sitting in the root App_Code folder, as in the following example:

```
\App_Code
    Calculator.cs
    AdvancedMath.vb
```

Having two classes made up of different languages in the App_Code folder (as shown here) causes an error to be thrown. It is impossible for the assigned compiler to work with two different languages. Therefore, to be able to work with multiple languages in your App_Code folder, you must make some changes to the folder structure and to the web.config file.

The first step is to add two new subfolders to the App_Code folder—a VB folder and a CS folder. This gives you the following folder structure:

```
\App_Code
  \VB
    Add.vb
  \CS
    Subtract.cs
```

This still will not correctly compile these class files into separate assemblies, at least not until you make some additions to the web.config file. Most likely, you do not have a web.config file in your solution at this moment, so add one through the Solution Explorer. After it is added, change the <compilation> node so that it is structured as shown in Listing 3-15 (web.config in the code download for this chapter).

LISTING 3-15: Structuring the web.config file so that classes in the App_Code folder can use different languages

```
<compilation debug="false" targetFramework="4.5">
    <codeSubDirectories>
        <add directoryName="VB"></add>
        <add directoryName="CS"></add>
    </codeSubDirectories>
</compilation>
```

Now that this is in place in your web.config file, you can work with each of the classes in your ASP.NET pages. In addition, any C# class placed in the CS folder is now automatically compiled just like any of the classes placed in the VB folder. Because you can add these directories in the web.config file, you are not required to name them VB and CS as they are here; you can use whatever name you like.

App_Data Folder

The App_Data folder holds the data stores utilized by the application. It is a good spot to centrally store all the data stores your application might use. The App_Data folder can contain Microsoft SQL Express files (.mdf files), Microsoft SQL Server Compact files (.sdf files), XML files, and more.

The user account utilized by your application will have read and write access to any of the files contained within the App_Data folder. Another reason for storing all your data files in this folder is that much of the ASP.NET system—from the membership and role-management systems to the GUI tools, such as the ASP.NET MMC snap-in and ASP.NET Web Site Administration Tool—is built to work with the App_Data folder.

App_GlobalResources Folder

Resource files are string tables that can serve as data dictionaries for your applications when these applications require changes to content based on things such as changes in culture. You can add Assembly Resource Files (.resx) to the App_GlobalResources folder, and they are dynamically compiled and made part of the solution for use by all your .aspx pages in the application. When using ASP.NET 1.0/1.1, you had to use the `resgen.exe` tool and had to compile your resource files to a `.dll` or `.exe` for use within your solution. Dealing with resource files in ASP.NET 4.5 is considerably easier. Simply placing your application-wide resources in this folder makes them instantly accessible. Localization is covered in detail in Chapter 32.

App_LocalResources Folder

Even if you are not interested in constructing application-wide resources using the App_GlobalResources folder, you may want resources that can be used for a single `.aspx` page. You can do this very simply by using the App_LocalResources folder.

You can add resource files that are page-specific to the App_LocalResources folder by constructing the name of the `.resx` file in the following manner:

➤ `Default.aspx.resx`
➤ `Default.aspx.fi.resx`
➤ `Default.aspx.ja.resx`
➤ `Default.aspx.en-gb.resx`

Now, the resource declarations used on the `Default.aspx` page are retrieved from the appropriate file in the App_LocalResources folder. By default, the `Default.aspx.resx` resource file is used if another match is not found. If the client is using a culture specification of `fi-FI` (Finnish), however, the `Default.aspx.fi.resx` file is used instead. Localization of local resources is covered in detail in Chapter 32.

App_WebReferences Folder

The App_WebReferences folder is a new name for the previous Web References folder that was used in versions of ASP.NET prior to ASP.NET 3.5. Now you can use the App_WebReferences folder and have automatic access to the remote web services referenced from your application. Chapter 13 covers web services in ASP.NET.

App_Browsers Folder

The App_Browsers folder holds `.browser` files, which are XML files used to identity the browsers making requests to the application and understanding the capabilities these browsers have. You can find a list of globally accessible `.browser` files at `C:\Windows\Microsoft.NET\Framework\v4.0.xxxxx\Config\Browsers`. In addition, if you want to change any part of these default browser definition files, just copy the appropriate `.browser` file from the Browsers folder to your application's App_Browsers folder and change the definition.

COMPILATION

You already saw how Visual Studio 2012 compiles pieces of your application as you work with them (for instance, by placing a class in the App_Code folder). The other parts of the application, such as the `.aspx` pages, can be compiled just as they were in earlier versions of ASP.NET by referencing the pages in the browser.

When an ASP.NET page is referenced in the browser for the first time, the request is passed to the ASP.NET parser that creates the class file in the language of the page. It is passed to the ASP.NET parser based on the file's extension (`.aspx`) because ASP.NET realizes that this file extension type is meant for its handling and processing. After the class file has been created, the class file is compiled into a DLL and then written to the disk of the web server. At this point, the DLL is instantiated and processed, and an output is generated for the initial requester of the ASP.NET page. This is detailed in Figure 3-11.

On the next request, great things happen. Instead of going through the entire process again for the second and respective requests, the request simply causes an instantiation of the already-created DLL, which sends out a response to the requester. This is illustrated in Figure 3-12.

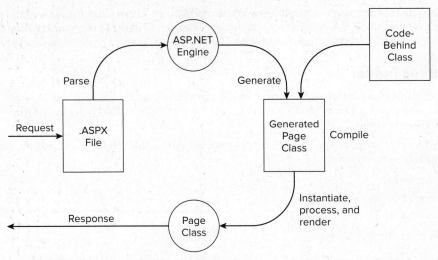

FIGURE 3-11

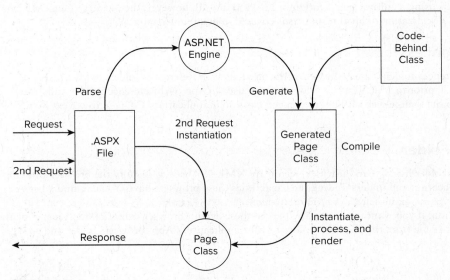

FIGURE 3-12

Because of the mechanics of this process, if you made changes to your .aspx code-behind pages, you found it necessary to recompile your application. This was quite a pain if you had a larger site and did not want your end users to experience the extreme lag that occurs when an .aspx page is referenced for the first time after compilation. Many developers, consequently, began to develop their own tools that automatically go out and hit every single page within their application to remove this first-time lag hit from the end user's browsing experience.

ASP.NET provides a few ways to precompile your entire application with a single command that you can issue through a command line. One type of compilation is referred to as *in-place precompilation*. To precompile your entire ASP.NET application, you must use the aspnet_compiler.exe tool that comes with ASP.NET. You navigate to the tool using the Command window. Open the Command window and navigate to C:\Windows\Microsoft.NET\Framework\v4.0.*xxxxx*\. When you are there, you can work with the `aspnet_compiler` tool. You can also get to this tool directly from the Developer Command Prompt for VS2012. In Windows 8, choose the Search charm and enter Developer Command Prompt. Choose the appropriate application from the search results.

After you get the command prompt, you use the `aspnet_compiler.exe` tool to perform an in-place precompilation using the following command:

```
aspnet_compiler -p "C:\Inetpub\wwwroot\WROX" -v none
```

> **NOTE** *IIS 8 on Windows 8 and Windows Server 2012 includes a feature for Application Initialization, which is very similar to precompiling your application using the* `aspnet_compiler.exe` *utility. For more information, search online for IIS8 Application Initialization.*

You then get a message stating that the precompilation is successful. The other great thing about this precompilation capability is that you can also use it to find errors on any of the ASP.NET pages in your application. Because it hits every page, if one of the pages contains an error that won't be triggered until run time, you get notification of the error immediately as you employ this precompilation method.

The next precompilation option is commonly referred to as *precompilation for deployment.* This outstanding capability of ASP.NET enables you to compile your application down to some DLLs, which can then be deployed to customers, partners, or elsewhere for your own use. Not only are minimal steps required to do this, but also after your application is compiled, you simply have to move around the DLL and some placeholder files for the site to work. This means that your website code is completely removed and placed in the DLL when deployed.

However, before you take these precompilation steps, create a folder in your root drive called, for example, Wrox. This folder is the one to which you will direct the compiler output. When it is in place, you can return to the compiler tool and give the following command:

```
aspnet_compiler -v [Application Name] -p [Physical Location] [Target]
```

Therefore, if you have an application called `ThomsonReuters` located at `C:\Websites\ThomsonReuters`, you use the following commands:

```
aspnet_compiler -v /ThomsonReuters -p C:\Websites\ThomsonReuters C:\Wrox
```

Press the Enter key, and the compiler either tells you that it has a problem with one of the command parameters or that it was successful (shown in Figure 3-13). If it was successful, you can see the output placed in the target directory.

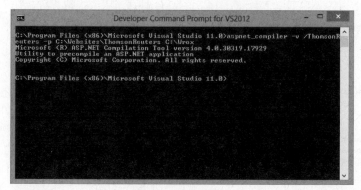

FIGURE 3-13

In Figure 3-13, `-v` is a command for the virtual path of the application, which is provided by using `/ThomsonReuters`. The next command is `-p`, which is pointing to the physical path of the application. In this case, it is `C:\Websites\ThomsonReuters`. Finally, the last bit, `C:\Wrox`, is the location of the compiler output. Table 3-12 describes some of the possible commands for the `aspnet_compiler.exe` tool.

TABLE 3-12

COMMAND	DESCRIPTION
`-m`	Specifies the full IIS metabase path of the application. If you use the `-m` command, you cannot use the `-v` or `-p` command.
`-v`	Specifies the virtual path of the application to be compiled. If you also use the `-p` command, the physical path is used to find the location of the application.
`-p`	Specifies the physical path of the application to be compiled. If this is not specified, the IIS metabase is used to find the application.
`-u`	If this command is utilized, it specifies that the application is updatable.
`-f`	Specifies to overwrite the target directory if it already exists.
`-d`	Specifies that the debug information should be excluded from the compilation process.
`-c`	Specifies that the application to be compiled should be completely rebuilt.
`[targetDir]`	Specifies the target directory where the compiled files should be placed. If this is not specified, the output files are placed in the application directory.

After compiling the application, you can go to `C:\Wrox` to see the output. Here you see all the files and the file structures that were in the original application. However, if you look at the content of one of the files, notice that the file is simply a placeholder. In the actual file, you find the following comment:

```
This is a marker file generated by the precompilation tool
and should not be deleted!
```

In fact, you find one or more `App_Web_XXXXXXXX.dll` files in the bin folder where all the page code is located. Because it is in a DLL file, it provides great code obfuscation as well. From here on, all you do is move these files to another server using FTP or Windows Explorer, and you can run the entire web application from these files. When you have an update to the application, you simply provide a new set of compiled files. Figure 3-14 shows a sample output.

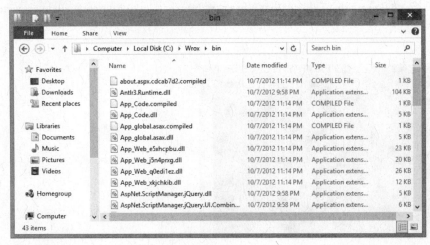

FIGURE 3-14

Note that this compilation process does not compile *every* type of web file. In fact, it compiles only the ASP.NET-specific file types and leaves out of the compilation process the following types of files:

➤ HTML files

➤ XML files

➤ XSD files

➤ web.config files

➤ Text files

You cannot do much to get around this, except in the case of the HTML files and the text files. For these file types, just change the file extensions of these file types to .aspx; they are then compiled into the *App_Web_XXXXXXXX*.dll like all the other ASP.NET files.

BUILD PROVIDERS

As you review the various ASP.NET folders, note that one of the more interesting folders is the App_Code folder. You can simply drop code files, XSD files, and even WSDL files directly into the folder for automatic compilation. When you drop a class file into the App_Code folder, the class can automatically be utilized by a running application. In the early days of ASP.NET, if you wanted to deploy a custom component, you had to precompile the component before being able to utilize it within your application. Now ASP.NET simply takes care of all the work that you once had to do. You do not need to perform any compilation routine.

Which file types are compiled in the App_Code folder? As with most things in ASP.NET, this is determined through settings applied in a configuration file. Listing 3-16 shows a snippet of configuration code taken from the master web.config file found in ASP.NET 4.5. Please note that this listing is not included in the source code available for download because the web.config listed here is installed with the .NET 4.5 Framework.

LISTING 3-16: Reviewing the list of build providers

```
<buildProviders>
    <add extension=".aspx" type="System.Web.Compilation.PageBuildProvider" />
    <add extension=".ascx"
      type="System.Web.Compilation.UserControlBuildProvider" />
    <add extension=".master"
      type="System.Web.Compilation.MasterPageBuildProvider" />
    <add extension=".asmx" type="System.Web.Compilation.WebServiceBuildProvider" />
    <add extension=".ashx" type="System.Web.Compilation.WebHandlerBuildProvider" />
    <add extension=".soap" type="System.Web.Compilation.WebServiceBuildProvider" />
    <add extension=".resx" type="System.Web.Compilation.ResXBuildProvider" />
    <add extension=".resources"
      type="System.Web.Compilation.ResourcesBuildProvider" />
    <add extension=".wsdl" type="System.Web.Compilation.WsdlBuildProvider" />
    <add extension=".xsd" type="System.Web.Compilation.XsdBuildProvider" />
    <add extension=".js" type="System.Web.Compilation.ForceCopyBuildProvider" />
    <add extension=".lic" type="System.Web.Compilation.IgnoreFileBuildProvider" />
    <add extension=".licx" type="System.Web.Compilation.IgnoreFileBuildProvider" />
    <add extension=".exclude"
      type="System.Web.Compilation.IgnoreFileBuildProvider" />
    <add extension=".refresh"
      type="System.Web.Compilation.IgnoreFileBuildProvider" />
    <add extension=".edmx"
      type="System.Data.Entity.Design.AspNet.EntityDesignerBuildProvider" />
    <add extension=".xoml"
      type="System.ServiceModel.Activation.WorkflowServiceBuildProvider,
      System.WorkflowServices, Version=4.0.0.0, Culture=neutral,
```

continues

LISTING 3-16 *(continued)*

```
            PublicKeyToken=31bf3856ad364e35" />
        <add extension=".svc"
            type="System.ServiceModel.Activation.ServiceBuildProvider,
            System.ServiceModel.Activation, Version=4.0.0.0, Culture=neutral,
            PublicKeyToken=31bf3856ad364e35" />
        <add extension=".xamlx" type="System.Xaml.Hosting.XamlBuildProvider,
            System.Xaml.Hosting, Version=4.0.0.0, Culture=neutral,
            PublicKeyToken=31bf3856ad364e35" />
    </buildProviders>
```

This section contains a list of build providers that can be used by two entities in your development cycle. The build provider is first used during development when you are building your solution in Visual Studio 2012. For instance, placing a `.wsdl` file in the App_Code folder during development in Visual Studio causes the IDE to give you automatic access to the dynamically compiled proxy class that comes from this `.wsdl` file. The other entity that uses the build providers is ASP.NET itself. As stated, simply dragging and dropping a `.wsdl` file in the App_Code folder of a deployed application automatically gives the ASP.NET application access to the created proxy class.

A build provider is simply a class that inherits from `System.Web.Compilation.BuildProvider`. The `<buildProviders>` section in the `web.config` file allows you to list the build provider classes that will be utilized. The capability to dynamically compile any WSDL file is defined by the following line in the configuration file:

```
<add extension=".wsdl" type="System.Web.Compilation.WsdlBuildProvider" />
```

This means that any file utilizing the `.wsdl` file extension is compiled using the `WsdlBuildProvider`, a class that inherits from `BuildProvider`. Microsoft provides a set number of build providers out-of-the-box for you to use. As you can see from the set in Listing 3-16, a number of providers are available in addition to the `WsdlBuildProvider`, including providers such as the `XsdBuildProvider`, `PageBuildProvider`, `UserControlBuildProvider`, `MasterPageBuildProvider`, and more. Just by looking at the names of some of these providers you can pretty much understand what they are about. The next section, however, reviews some other providers whose names might not ring a bell right away.

Using the Built-In Build Providers

Two providers that this section covers are `ForceCopyBuildProvider` and `IgnoreFileBuildProvider`, both of which are included in the default list of providers.

The `ForceCopyBuildProvider` copies only those files for deployment that use the defined extension. (These files are not included in the compilation process.) An extension that utilizes the `ForceCopyBuildProvider` is shown in the predefined list in Listing 3-16. This is the `.js` file type (a JavaScript file extension). Any `.js` files are simply copied and not included in the compilation process (which makes sense for JavaScript files). You can add other file types that you want to be a part of this copy process with the command shown here:

```
<add extension=".chm" type="System.Web.Compilation.ForceCopyBuildProvider" />
```

In addition to the `ForceCopyBuildProvider`, you should also be aware of the `IgnoreFileBuildProvider` class. This provider causes the defined file type to be ignored in the deployment or compilation process. This means that any file type defined with `IgnoreFileBuildProvider` is simply ignored. Visual Studio will not copy, compile, or deploy any file of that type. So, if you are including Visio diagrams in your project, you can simply add the following `<add>` element to the `web.config` file to have this file type ignored. An example is presented here:

```
<add extension=".vsd" type="System.Web.Compilation.IgnoreFileBuildProvider" />
```

With this in place, all `.vsd` files are ignored.

Using Your Own Build Providers

In addition to using the predefined build providers out-of-the-box, you can also take this build provider stuff one step further and construct your own custom build providers to use within your applications.

For example, suppose you wanted to construct a Car class dynamically based upon settings applied in a custom .car file that you have defined. You might do this because you are using this .car definition file in multiple projects or many times within the same project. Using a build provider makes defining these multiple instances of the Car class simpler.

Listing 3-17, found in Listing03-17.car in the code download, presents an example of the .car file type.

LISTING 3-17: An example of a .car file

```xml
<?xml version="1.0" encoding="utf-8" ?>
<car name="AspNetCar">
    <color>White</color>
    <door>4</door>
    <seats>8</seats>
</car>
```

In the end, this XML declaration specifies the name of the class to compile as well as some values for various properties and a method. These elements make up the class. Now that you understand the structure of the .car file type, the next step is to construct the build provider. To accomplish this task, create a new Class Library project in the language of your choice within Visual Studio. Name the project **CarBuildProvider**. The CarBuildProvider contains a single class—Car.vb or Car.cs. This class inherits from the base class BuildProvider and overrides the GenerateCode() method of the BuildProvider class. Listing 3-18 (Listing03-18.vb and Listing03-18.cs in the code download for this chapter) presents this class.

LISTING 3-18: The CarBuildProvider

VB

```vb
Imports System.IO
Imports System.Web.Compilation
Imports System.Xml
Imports System.CodeDom
Public Class Car
    Inherits BuildProvider
    Public Overrides Sub GenerateCode(ByVal myAb As AssemblyBuilder)
        Dim carXmlDoc As XmlDocument = New XmlDocument()
        Using passedFile As Stream = Me.OpenStream()
            carXmlDoc.Load(passedFile)
        End Using
        Dim mainNode As XmlNode = carXmlDoc.SelectSingleNode("/car")
        Dim selectionMainNode As String = mainNode.Attributes("name").Value
        Dim colorNode As XmlNode = carXmlDoc.SelectSingleNode("/car/color")
        Dim selectionColorNode As String = colorNode.InnerText
        Dim doorNode As XmlNode = carXmlDoc.SelectSingleNode("/car/door")
        Dim selectionDoorNode As String = doorNode.InnerText
        Dim seatsNode As XmlNode = carXmlDoc.SelectSingleNode("/car/seats")
        Dim selectionseatsNode As String = seatsNode.InnerText
        Dim ccu As CodeCompileUnit = New CodeCompileUnit()
        Dim cn As CodeNamespace = New CodeNamespace()
        Dim cmp1 As CodeMemberProperty = New CodeMemberProperty()
        Dim cmp2 As CodeMemberProperty = New CodeMemberProperty()
        Dim cmm1 As CodeMemberMethod = New CodeMemberMethod()
        cn.Imports.Add(New CodeNamespaceImport("System"))
```

continues

LISTING 3-18 *(continued)*

```
        cmp1.Name = "Color"
        cmp1.Type = New CodeTypeReference(GetType(System.String))
        cmp1.Attributes = MemberAttributes.Public
        cmp1.GetStatements.Add(New CodeSnippetExpression("return """ &
            selectionColorNode & """"))
        cmp2.Name = "Doors"
        cmp2.Type = New CodeTypeReference(GetType(System.Int32))
        cmp2.Attributes = MemberAttributes.Public
        cmp2.GetStatements.Add(New CodeSnippetExpression("return " &
            selectionDoorNode))
        cmm1.Name = "Go"
        cmm1.ReturnType = New CodeTypeReference(GetType(System.Int32))
        cmm1.Attributes = MemberAttributes.Public
        cmm1.Statements.Add(New CodeSnippetExpression("return " &
            selectionseatsNode))
        Dim ctd As CodeTypeDeclaration = New CodeTypeDeclaration(selectionMainNode)
        ctd.Members.Add(cmp1)
        ctd.Members.Add(cmp2)
        ctd.Members.Add(cmm1)
        cn.Types.Add(ctd)
        ccu.Namespaces.Add(cn)
        myAb.AddCodeCompileUnit(Me, ccu)
    End Sub
End Class
```

C#

```
using System.IO;
using System.Web.Compilation;
using System.Xml;
using System.CodeDom;
namespace CarBuildProvider
{
    class Car : BuildProvider
    {
        public override void GenerateCode(AssemblyBuilder myAb)
        {
            XmlDocument carXmlDoc = new XmlDocument();
            using (Stream passedFile = OpenStream())
            {
                carXmlDoc.Load(passedFile);
            }
            XmlNode mainNode = carXmlDoc.SelectSingleNode("/car");
            string selectionMainNode = mainNode.Attributes["name"].Value;
            XmlNode colorNode = carXmlDoc.SelectSingleNode("/car/color");
            string selectionColorNode = colorNode.InnerText;
            XmlNode doorNode = carXmlDoc.SelectSingleNode("/car/door");
            string selectionDoorNode = doorNode.InnerText;
            XmlNode seatsNode = carXmlDoc.SelectSingleNode("/car/seats");
            string selectionseatsNode = seatsNode.InnerText;
            CodeCompileUnit ccu = new CodeCompileUnit();
            CodeNamespace cn = new CodeNamespace();
            CodeMemberProperty cmp1 = new CodeMemberProperty();
            CodeMemberProperty cmp2 = new CodeMemberProperty();
            CodeMemberMethod cmm1 = new CodeMemberMethod();
            cn.Imports.Add(new CodeNamespaceImport("System"));
            cmp1.Name = "Color";
            cmp1.Type = new CodeTypeReference(typeof(string));
            cmp1.Attributes = MemberAttributes.Public;
            cmp1.GetStatements.Add(new CodeSnippetExpression("return \"" +
```

```
                    selectionColorNode + "\""));
          cmp2.Name = "Doors";
          cmp2.Type = new CodeTypeReference(typeof(int));
          cmp2.Attributes = MemberAttributes.Public;
          cmp2.GetStatements.Add(new CodeSnippetExpression("return " +
             selectionDoorNode));
          cmm1.Name = "Go";
          cmm1.ReturnType = new CodeTypeReference(typeof(int));
          cmm1.Attributes = MemberAttributes.Public;
          cmm1.Statements.Add(new CodeSnippetExpression("return " +
             selectionseatsNode));
          CodeTypeDeclaration ctd = new CodeTypeDeclaration(selectionMainNode);
          ctd.Members.Add(cmp1);
          ctd.Members.Add(cmp2);
          ctd.Members.Add(cmm1);
          cn.Types.Add(ctd);
          ccu.Namespaces.Add(cn);
          myAb.AddCodeCompileUnit(this, ccu);
      }
   }
}
```

As you look over the GenerateCode() method, you can see that it takes an instance of AssemblyBuilder. This AssemblyBuilder object is from the System.Web.Compilation namespace and, because of this, your Class Library project must have a reference to the System.Web assembly. With all the various objects used in this Car class, you also have to import in the following namespaces:

```
using System.IO;
using System.Web.Compilation;
using System.Xml;
using System.CodeDom;
```

When you have done this, one of the tasks remaining in the GenerateCode() method is loading the .car file. Because the .car file is using XML for its form, you are able to load the document easily using the XmlDocument object. From there, by using the CodeDom, you can create a class that contains two properties and a single method dynamically. The class that is generated is an abstract representation of what is defined in the provided .car file. On top of that, the name of the class is also dynamically driven from the value provided via the name attribute used in the main <Car> node of the .car file.

The AssemblyBuilder instance that is used as the input object then compiles the generated code along with everything else into an assembly.

What does it mean that your ASP.NET project has a reference to the CarBuildProvider assembly in its project? It means that you can create a .car file of your own definition and drop this file into the App_Code folder. The second you drop the file into the App_Code folder, you have instant programmatic access to the definition specified in the file.

To see this in action, you need a reference to the build provider in either the server's machine.config or your application's web.config file. A reference is shown in Listing 3-19 (web.config in the code download for this chapter).

LISTING 3-19: Making a reference to the build provider in the web.config file

```xml
<?xml version="1.0"?>
<configuration>
    <system.web>
        <compilation debug="true" targetFramework="4.5">
            <buildProviders>
                <add extension=".car" type="CarBuildProvider.Car" />
            </buildProviders>
```

continues

LISTING 3-19 *(continued)*

```
            </compilation>
            <httpRuntime targetFramework="4.5" />
        </system.web>
    </configuration>
```

`<buildProviders>` is a child element of the `<compilation>` element. The `<buildProviders>` element takes a couple of child elements to add or remove providers. In this case, because you want to add a reference to the custom `CarBuildProvider` object, you use the `<add>` element. The `<add>` element can take two attributes—`extension` and `type`. You must use both of these attributes. In the `extension` attribute, you define the file extension that this build provider will be associated with. In this case, you use the `.car` file extension. This means that any file using this file extension is associated with the class defined in the `type` attribute. The `type` attribute then takes a reference to the `CarBuildProvider` class that you built—`CarBuildProvider.Car`.

With this reference in place, you can create the `.car` file that was shown earlier in Listing 3-17. Place the created `.car` file in the App_Code folder. You instantly have access to a dynamically generated class that comes from the definition provided via the file. For example, because I used `AspNetCar` as the value of the name attribute in the `<Car>` element, this will be the name of the class generated, and I will find this exact name in IntelliSense as I type in Visual Studio.

If you create an instance of the `AspNetCar` class, you also find that you have access to the properties and the method that this class exposes. This is shown in Figure 3-15.

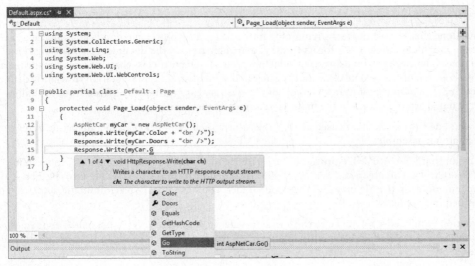

FIGURE 3-15

In addition to getting access to the properties and methods of the class, you also gain access to the values that are defined in the `.car` file. This is shown in Figure 3-16. The simple code example shown in Figure 3-15 is used for this browser output.

Although a `Car` class is not the most useful thing in the
world, this example shows you how to take the build
provider mechanics into your own hands to extend
your application's capabilities.

GLOBAL.ASAX

If you add a new item to your ASP.NET application, you
get the Add New Item dialog box. From here, you can
see that you can add a Global Application Class to your
applications. This adds a `Global.asax` file. This file is
used by the application to hold application-level events,
objects, and variables—all of which are accessible
application-wide. Active Server Pages developers had
something similar with the `Global.asa` file.

FIGURE 3-16

Your ASP.NET applications can have only a single `Global.asax` file. This file supports a number of items.
When it is created, you are given the following template:

```
public class Global : System.Web.HttpApplication
{
    protected void Application_Start(object sender, EventArgs e) { }
    protected void Session_Start(object sender, EventArgs e) { }
    protected void Application_BeginRequest(object sender, EventArgs e) { }
    protected void Application_AuthenticateRequest(object sender, EventArgs e) { }
    protected void Application_Error(object sender, EventArgs e) { }
    protected void Session_End(object sender, EventArgs e) { }
    protected void Application_End(object sender, EventArgs e) { }
}
```

Just as you can work with page-level events in your `.aspx` pages, you can work with overall application
events from the `Global.asax` file. In addition to the events listed in this code example, the following list
details some of the events you can structure inside this file:

➤ `Application_Start`: Called when the application receives its very first request. It is an ideal spot
   in your application to assign any application-level variables or state that must be maintained
   across all users.

➤ `Session_Start`: Similar to the `Application_Start` event except that this event is fired when an
   individual user accesses the application for the first time. For instance, the `Application_Start` event
   fires once when the first request comes in, which gets the application going, but the `Session_Start` is
   invoked for each user who requests something from the application for the first time.

➤ `Application_BeginRequest`: Although it is not listed in the preceding template provided by Visual
   Studio 2012, the `Application_BeginRequest` event is triggered before each request that comes
   its way. This means that when a request comes into the server, before this request is processed, the
   `Application_BeginRequest` is triggered and dealt with before any processing of the request occurs.

➤ `Application_AuthenticateRequest`: Triggered for each request and enables you to set up custom
   authentications for a request.

➤ `Application_Error`: Triggered when an error is thrown anywhere in the application by any user of
   the application. This is an ideal spot to provide application-wide error handling or an event recording
   the errors to the server's event logs.

➤ `Session_End`: When running in `InProc` mode, this event is triggered when a user leaves the application.

➤ `Application_End`: Triggered when the application comes to an end. This is an event that most
   ASP.NET developers won't use that often because ASP.NET does such a good job of closing and
   cleaning up any objects that are left around.

In addition to the global application events that the `Global.asax` file provides access to, you can also use directives in this file as you can with other ASP.NET pages. The `Global.asax` file allows for the following directives:

➤   `@Application`

➤   `@Assembly`

➤   `@Import`

These directives perform in the same way when they are used with other ASP.NET page types.

An example of using the `Global.asax` file is shown in Listing 3-20 (Global.asax in the code download). It demonstrates how to log when the ASP.NET application domain shuts down. When the ASP.NET application domain shuts down, the ASP.NET application abruptly comes to an end. Therefore, you should place any logging code in the `Application_End` method of the `Global.asax` file.

LISTING 3-20: Using the Application_End event in the Global.asax file

VB

```vb
<%@ Application Language="vb" %>
<%@ Import Namespace="System.Reflection" %>
<%@ Import Namespace="System.Diagnostics" %>
<script runat="server">
    Sub Application_End(ByVal sender As Object, ByVal e As EventArgs)
        Dim MyRuntime As HttpRuntime =
            GetType(System.Web.HttpRuntime).InvokeMember("_theRuntime", _
            BindingFlags.NonPublic Or BindingFlags.Static Or _
            BindingFlags.GetField, _
            Nothing, Nothing, Nothing)
        If (MyRuntime Is Nothing) Then
            Return
        End If
        Dim shutDownMessage As String =
            CType(MyRuntime.GetType().InvokeMember("_shutDownMessage", _
            BindingFlags.NonPublic Or BindingFlags.Instance Or _
            BindingFlags.GetField,
            Nothing, MyRuntime, Nothing), System.String)
        Dim shutDownStack As String =
            CType(MyRuntime.GetType().InvokeMember("_shutDownStack", _
            BindingFlags.NonPublic Or BindingFlags.Instance Or _
            BindingFlags.GetField, _
            Nothing, MyRuntime, Nothing), System.String)
        If (Not EventLog.SourceExists(".NET Runtime")) Then
            EventLog.CreateEventSource(".NET Runtime", "Application")
        End If
        Dim logEntry As EventLog = New EventLog()
        logEntry.Source = ".NET Runtime"
        logEntry.WriteEntry(String.Format( _
            "shutDownMessage={0}\r\n\r\n_shutDownStack={1}", _
            shutDownMessage, shutDownStack), EventLogEntryType.Error)
    End Sub
</script>
```

C#

```csharp
<%@ Application Language="C#" %>
<%@ Import Namespace="System.Reflection" %>
<%@ Import Namespace="System.Diagnostics" %>
<script runat="server">
    void Application_End(object sender, EventArgs e)
```

```
    {
        HttpRuntime runtime =
            (HttpRuntime)typeof(System.Web.HttpRuntime)
            .InvokeMember("_theRuntime", BindingFlags.NonPublic |
            BindingFlags.Static | BindingFlags.GetField,
            null, null, null);
        if (runtime == null)
        {
            return;
        }
        string shutDownMessage =
            (string)runtime.GetType().InvokeMember("_shutDownMessage",
            BindingFlags.NonPublic | BindingFlags.Instance |
            BindingFlags.GetField, null, runtime, null);
        string shutDownStack =
            (string)runtime.GetType().InvokeMember("_shutDownStack",
            BindingFlags.NonPublic | BindingFlags.Instance |
            BindingFlags.GetField, null, runtime, null);
        if (!EventLog.SourceExists(".NET Runtime"))
        {
            EventLog.CreateEventSource(".NET Runtime", "Application");
        }
        EventLog logEntry = new EventLog();
        logEntry.Source = ".NET Runtime";
        logEntry.WriteEntry(String.Format("\r\n\r\n_" +
            "shutDownMessage={0}\r\n\r\n_shutDownStack={1}",
            shutDownMessage, shutDownStack), EventLogEntryType.Error);
    }
</script>
```

With this code in place in your `Global.asax` file, start your ASP.NET application. Next, do something to cause the application to restart. You could, for example, make a change to the `web.config` file while the application is running. This triggers the `Application_End` event, and you see the following addition (shown in Figure 3-17) to the event log.

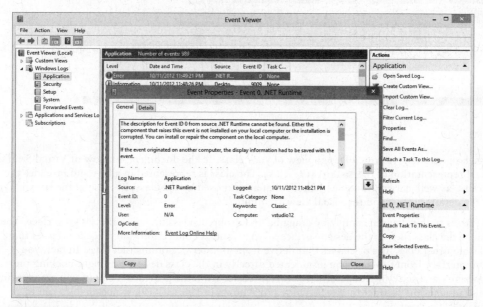

FIGURE 3-17

WORKING WITH CLASSES THROUGH VISUAL STUDIO 2012

So far, this chapter has shown you how to work with classes within your ASP.NET projects. In constructing and working with classes, you will find that Visual Studio 2012 is quite helpful. One particularly useful item is the class designer file. The class designer file has an extension of .cd and gives you a visual way to view your class, as well as all the available methods, properties, and other class items it contains.

To see this designer in action, create a new Class Library project in the language of your choice. This project has a single class file, Class1.vb or .cs. Delete this file and create a new class file called **Calculator.vb** or **.cs**, depending on the language you are using. From here, complete the class by creating a simple Add() and Subtract() method. Each of these methods takes in two parameters (of type Integer) and returns a single Integer with the appropriate calculation performed.

After you have the Calculator class in place, the easiest way to create your class designer file for this particular class is to right-click the Calculator.vb file directly in the Solution Explorer and select View Class Diagram from the menu. This creates a ClassDiagram1.cd file in your solution.

Figure 3-18 presents the visual file, ClassDiagram1.cd.

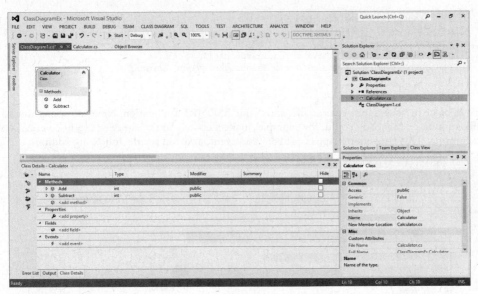

FIGURE 3-18

The new class designer file gives you a Design view of your class. In the document window of Visual Studio, you see a visual representation of the Calculator class. The class is represented in a box and provides the name of the class, as well as two available methods that are exposed by the class. Because of the simplicity of this class, the details provided in the visual view are limited.

You can add classes to this diagram simply by dragging and dropping class files onto the design surface. You can then arrange the class files on the design surface as you want. A connection is in place for classes that are inherited from other class files or classes that derive from an interface or abstract class. In fact, you can extract an interface from the class you just created directly in the class designer by right-clicking the Calculator class box and selecting Refactor ⇨ Extract Interface from the provided menu (if you are working with C#). This launches the Extract Interface dialog box (shown in Figure 3-19), which enables you to customize the interface creation.

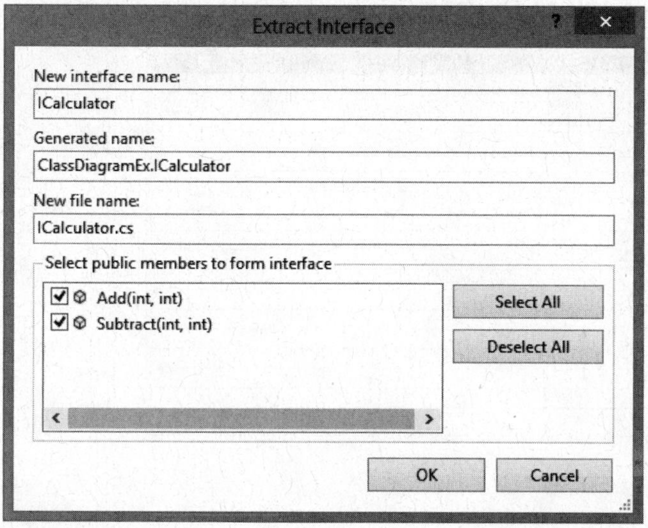

Extract Interface

New interface name:

ICalculator

Generated name:

ClassDiagramEx.ICalculator

New file name:

ICalculator.cs

Select public members to form interface

☑ ⚙ Add(int, int)
☑ ⚙ Subtract(int, int)

Select All

Deselect All

OK   Cancel

FIGURE 3-19

After you click OK, the `ICalculator` interface is created and is then visually represented in the class diagram file, as illustrated in Figure 3-20.

In addition to creating items such as interfaces on-the-fly, you can also modify your `Calculator` class by adding additional methods, properties, events, and more through the Class Details pane found in Visual Studio (see Figure 3-21).

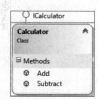

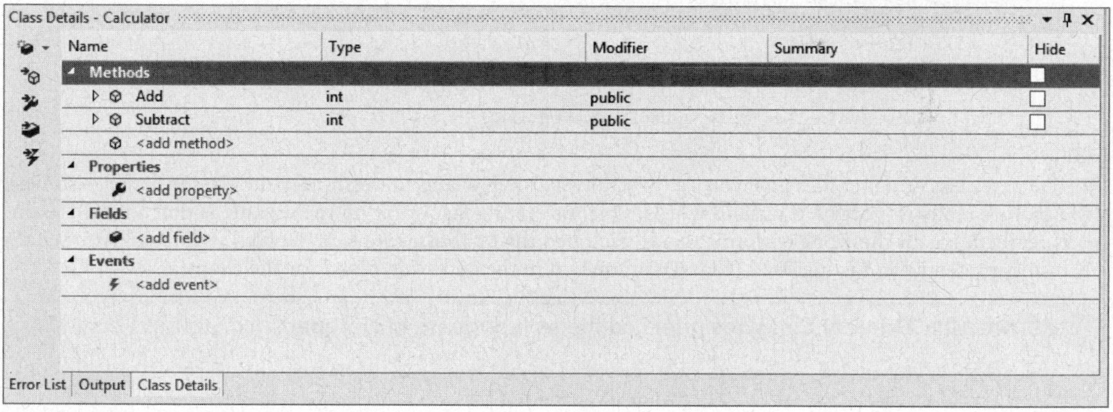

FIGURE 3-20

Class Details - Calculator   ▼ ╤ ✕

	Name	Type	Modifier	Summary	Hide
	◢ **Methods**				☐
	▷ ⚙ Add	int	public		☐
	▷ ⚙ Subtract	int	public		☐
	⚙ <add method>				
	◢ **Properties**				
	🔧 <add property>				
	◢ **Fields**				
	🔩 <add field>				
	◢ **Events**				
	⚡ <add event>				

Error List | Output | Class Details

FIGURE 3-21

From this view of the class, you can directly add other methods, properties, fields, or events without directly typing code in your class file. When you enter these items in the Class Details view, Visual Studio generates the code for you on your behalf. For an example of this, add the additional `Multiply()` and `Divide()` methods that the `Calculator` class needs. Expanding the plus sign next to these methods shows the parameters needed in the signature. This is where you add the required a and b parameters. When you have finished, your Class Details screen should appear as shown in Figure 3-22.

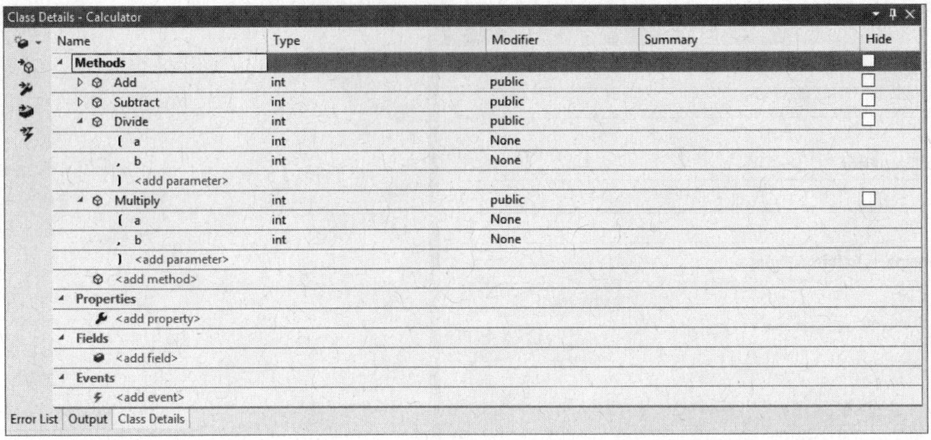

FIGURE 3-22

After you have added new `Multiply()` and `Divide()` methods and the required parameters, you see that the code in the `Calculator` class has changed to indicate these new methods are present. When the framework of the method is in place, you also see that the class has not been implemented in any fashion. The C# version of the `Multiply()` and `Divide()` methods created by Visual Studio is presented in Listing 3-21 (Calculator.cs in the code download for the chapter).

LISTING 3-21: The framework provided by Visual Studio's class designer

```
public int Divide(int a, int b)
{
    throw new System.NotImplementedException();
}


public int Multiply(int a, int b)
{
    throw new System.NotImplementedException();
}
```

The new class designer files give you a powerful way to view and understand your classes better—sometimes a picture really is worth a thousand words. One interesting last point on the `.cd` file is that Visual Studio is really doing all the work with this file. If you open the `ClassDesigner1.cd` file in Notepad, you see the results presented in Listing 3-22 (ClassDiagram1.cd in the code download for the chapter).

LISTING 3-22: The real ClassDesigner1.cd file as it appears in Notepad

```xml
<?xml version="1.0" encoding="utf-8"?>
<ClassDiagram MajorVersion="1" MinorVersion="1">
  <Class Name="ClassDiagramEx.Calculator">
    <Position X="0.5" Y="0.5" Width="1.5" />
    <TypeIdentifier>
      <HashCode>AAIAAAAAQAAAAAAAADAAAAAAAAAAAAAAAAAAAAA=</HashCode>
      <FileName>Calculator.cs</FileName>
    </TypeIdentifier>
    <Lollipop Position="0.2" />
  </Class>
  <Font Name="Segoe UI" Size="9" />
</ClassDiagram>
```

As you can see, it is a rather simple XML file that defines the locations of the class and the items connected to the class.

SUMMARY

This chapter covered a lot of ground. It discussed some of the issues concerning ASP.NET applications as a whole and the choices you have when building and deploying these new applications. With the help of Visual Studio 2012, you have options about which web server to use when building your application and whether to work locally or remotely through the built-in FTP capabilities.

ASP.NET 4.5 and Visual Studio 2012 make it easy to build your pages using an inline coding model or to select a code-behind model that is simpler to use and easier to deploy than in the past. You also learned about the cross-posting capabilities and the fixed folders that ASP.NET 4.5 has incorporated to make your life easier. These folders make their resources available dynamically with no work on your part. You saw some of the outstanding compilation options that are at your disposal. Finally, you looked at ways in which Visual Studio 2012 makes it easy to work with the classes of your project.

PART II
Controls

ASP.NET Server Controls and Client-Side Scripts

WHAT'S IN THIS CHAPTER?

➤ Building ASP.NET pages with server controls

➤ Working with HTML server controls

➤ Identifying server controls

➤ Modifying server controls with JavaScript

WROX.COM CODE DOWNLOADS FOR THIS CHAPTER

Please note that all the code examples in this chapter are available as a part of this chapter's code download on the book's website at www.wrox.com on the Download Code tab.

As discussed in the previous chapter, ASP.NET evolved from Microsoft's earlier web technology called Active Server Pages (referred to as ASP then and classic ASP today). This model was completely different from today's ASP.NET. Classic ASP used interpreted languages to accomplish the construction of the final HTML document before it was sent to the browser. ASP.NET, on the other hand, uses true compiled languages to accomplish the same task. The idea of building web pages based on objects in a compiled environment is one of the main focuses of this chapter.

This chapter looks at how to use a particular type of object in ASP.NET pages called a *server control* and how you can profit from using this control. This chapter introduces a particular type of server control—the HTML server control. Then it demonstrates how you can use JavaScript in ASP.NET pages to modify the behavior of server controls.

The rest of this chapter shows you how to use and manipulate server controls, both visually and programmatically, to help with the creation of your ASP.NET pages.

ASP.NET SERVER CONTROLS

In the past, one of the difficulties of working with classic ASP was that you were in charge of the entire HTML output from the browser by virtue of the server-side code you wrote. Although this might seem ideal, it created a problem because each browser interpreted the HTML given to it in a slightly different manner.

The two main browsers at the time were Microsoft's Internet Explorer and Netscape Navigator. This meant that not only did developers have to be cognizant of the browser type to which they were outputting HTML, but they also had to take into account which versions of those particular browsers might be making a request to their application. Some developers resolved the issue by creating two separate applications. When an end user made an initial request to the application, the code made a browser check to see what browser type was making the request. Then, the ASP page would redirect the request down one path for an IE user or down another path for a Netscape user.

Because requests came from so many versions of the same browser, the developer often designed for the lowest possible version that might be used to visit the site. Essentially, everyone lost out by using the lowest common denominator as the target. This technique ensured that the page was rendered properly in most browsers making a request, but it also forced the developer to dumb-down the application. If applications were always built for the lowest common denominator, the developer could never take advantage of some of the more advanced features offered by newer browser versions.

ASP.NET server controls overcome these obstacles. When using the server controls provided by ASP.NET, you are not specifying the HTML to be output from your server-side code. Rather, you are specifying the functionality you want to see in the browser and letting ASP.NET decide on the output to be sent to the browser.

When a request comes in, ASP.NET examines the request to see which browser type is making the request, as well as the version of the browser, and then it produces HTML output specific to that browser. This process is accomplished by processing a User Agent header retrieved from the HTTP request to sniff the browser. This means that you can now build for the best browsers without worrying about whether features will work in the browsers making requests to your applications. Because of the previously described capabilities, you will often hear these controls referred to as *smart controls*.

Types of Server Controls

ASP.NET provides two distinct types of server controls—HTML server controls and web server controls. Each type of control is quite different and, as you work with ASP.NET, you will see that much of the focus is on the web server controls. This does not mean that HTML server controls have no value. They do provide you with many capabilities—some that web server controls do not give you.

You might be asking yourself which is the better control type to use. The answer is that it really depends on what you are trying to achieve. HTML server controls map to specific HTML elements. You can place an `HtmlTable` server control on your ASP.NET page that works dynamically with a `<table>` element. On the other hand, web server controls map to specific functionality that you want on your ASP.NET pages. This means an `<asp:Panel>` control might use a `<table>` or another element altogether—it really depends on the capability of the browser making the request.

Table 4-1 provides a summary of information on when to use HTML server controls and when to use web server controls.

TABLE 4-1

CONTROL TYPE	WHEN TO USE THIS CONTROL TYPE
HTML Server	When converting traditional ASP 3.0 web pages to ASP.NET web pages and speed of completion is a concern. It is a lot easier to change your HTML elements to HTML server controls than it is to change them to web server controls. When you prefer a more HTML-type programming model. When you want to explicitly control the code that is generated for the browser. Using ASP.NET MVC for this (covered in Chapter 34) might be a better answer.
Web Server	When you require a richer set of functionality to perform complicated page requirements. When you are developing web pages that will be viewed by a multitude of browser types and that require different code based upon these types. When you prefer a more Visual Basic–type programming model that is based on the use of controls and control properties.

Of course, some developers like to separate certain controls from the rest and place them in their own categories. For instance, you may see references to the following types of controls:

➤ **List controls:** These control types allow data to be bound to them for display purposes of some kind.

➤ **Rich controls:** Controls, such as the Calendar control, that display richer content and capabilities than other controls.

➤ **Validation controls:** Controls that interact with other form controls to validate the data that they contain.

➤ **User controls:** These are not really controls, but page templates that you can work with as you would a server control on your ASP.NET page.

➤ **Custom controls:** Controls that you build yourself and use in the same manner as the supplied ASP .NET server controls that come with the default install of ASP.NET 4.5.

When you are deciding between HTML server controls and web server controls, remember that no hard and fast rules exist about which type to use. You might find yourself working with one control type more than another, but certain features are available in one control type that might not be available in the other. If you are trying to accomplish a specific task and you do not see a solution with the control type you are using, look at the other control type because it may very well hold the answer. Also, realize that you can mix and match these control types. There are no barriers to using both HTML server controls and web server controls on the same page or within the same application.

Building with Server Controls

You have a couple of ways to use server controls to construct your ASP.NET pages. You can actually use tools that are specifically designed to work with ASP.NET 4.5 that enable you to visually drag and drop controls onto a design surface and manipulate the behavior of the control. You can also work with server controls directly through code input.

Working with Server Controls on a Design Surface

Visual Studio 2012 enables you to visually create an ASP.NET page by dragging and dropping visual controls onto a design surface. You can get to this visual design option by clicking the Design tab at the bottom of the IDE when viewing your ASP.NET page. You can also show the Design view and the Source Code view in the same document window. This feature was introduced in Visual Studio 2008. When the

Design view is present, you can place the cursor on the page in the location where you want the control to appear and then double-click the control you want in the Toolbox window of Visual Studio.

In the Design view of your page, you can highlight a control and the properties for the control appear in the Properties window. For example, Figure 4-1 shows a Button control selected in the Design panel and its properties are displayed in the Properties window on the lower right.

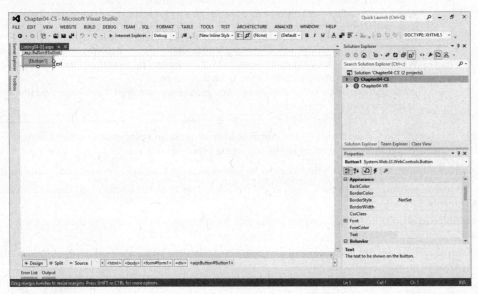

FIGURE 4-1

Changing the properties in the window changes the appearance or behavior of the highlighted control. Because all controls inherit from a specific base class (`WebControl`), you can also highlight multiple controls at the same time and change the base properties of all the controls at once. You do this by holding down the Ctrl key as you make your control selections.

Coding Server Controls

You also can work from the code page directly. Because many developers prefer this, it is the default when you first create your ASP.NET page. Hand-coding your own ASP.NET pages may seem to be a slower approach than dragging and dropping controls onto a design surface, but it isn't as slow as you might think. You get plenty of assistance in coding your applications from Visual Studio 2012. As you start typing in Visual Studio, the IntelliSense features kick in and help you with code auto-completion. Figure 4-2, for example, shows an IntelliSense drop-down list of possible code completion statements that appeared as the code was typed.

The IntelliSense focus is on the most commonly used attribute or statement for the control or piece of code that you are working with. Using IntelliSense effectively as you work is a great way to code with great speed.

FIGURE 4-2

As with Design view, the Source view of your page lets you drag and drop controls from the Toolbox onto the code page itself. For example, dragging and dropping a TextBox control onto the code page produces the same results as dropping it on the design page:

```
<asp:TextBox ID="TextBox1" runat="server"></asp:TextBox>
```

You can also highlight a control in Source view or place your cursor in the code statement of the control, and the Properties window displays the properties of the control. Now, you can apply properties directly in the Properties window of Visual Studio, and these properties are dynamically added to the code of your control.

Working with Server Control Events

ASP.NET uses an event-driven model. Items or coding tasks are initiated only when a particular event occurs. A common event in the ASP.NET programming model is `Page_Load`, which is illustrated in Listing 4-1.

LISTING 4-1: Working with specific page events

VB

```
Protected Sub Page_Load(sender As Object, e As EventArgs)
    'Insert code here
End Sub
```

C#

```
protected void Page_Load(Object sender, EventArgs e)
{
    // Insert code here
}
```

Not only can you work with the overall page—as well as its properties and methods at particular moments in time through page events—but you can also work with the server controls contained on the page through particular control events. For example, one common event for a button on a form is `Button_Click`, which is illustrated in Listing 4-2.

LISTING 4-2: Working with a Button Click event

VB

```
Protected Sub Button1_Click(sender As Object, e As EventArgs)
    'Insert code here
End Sub
```

C#

```
protected void Button1_Click(object sender, EventArgs e)
{
    // Insert code here
}
```

The event shown in Listing 4-2 is fired only when the end user actually clicks the button on the form that has an `OnClick` attribute value of `Button1_Click`. Therefore, not only does the event handler exist in the server-side code of the ASP.NET page, but that handler is also hooked up using the `OnClick` property of the server control in the associated ASP.NET page markup, as illustrated in the following code:

```
<asp:Button ID="Button1" runat="server" Text="Button" OnClick="Button1_Click" />
```

How do you handle these events for server controls? You have a couple of ways to go about it. The first way is to pull up your ASP.NET page in the Design view and double-click the control for which you want to create a server-side event. For instance, double-clicking a Button server control in Design view creates the structure of the `Button1_Click` event within your server-side code, whether the code is in a code-behind file or inline. This creates a stub handler for that server control's most popular event.

With that said, be aware that a considerable number of additional events are available to the Button control that you cannot get at by double-clicking the control. To access them, from any of the views within the IDE, choose the control from the Properties dialog box. Then you find a lightning bolt icon that provides you with a list of all the control's events. From here, you can double-click the event you are interested in, and Visual Studio creates the stub of the function you need. Figure 4-3 shows the event list. You might, for example, want to work with the Button control's `PreRender` event rather than its `Click` event. The handler for the event you choose is placed in your server-side code.

After you have an event structure in place, you can program specific actions that you want to occur when the event is fired.

Applying Styles to Server Controls

FIGURE 4-3

More often than not, you want to change the default style (which is basically no style) to the server controls you implement in your applications. You most likely want to build your web applications so that they reflect your own look-and-feel. One way to customize the appearance of the controls in your pages is to change the controls' properties.

As stated earlier in this chapter, to get at the properties of a particular control you highlight the control in the Design view of the page from Visual Studio. If you are working from the Source view, place the cursor in the code of the control. The properties presented in the Properties window allow you to control the appearance and behavior of the selected control.

> **NOTE** *Most websites and applications today use CSS instead of inline styles. For more information about CSS, please refer to Chapter 2.*

Examining the Controls' Common Properties

Many of the default server controls that come with ASP.NET 4.5 are derived from the WebControl class and share similar properties that enable you to alter their appearance and behavior. Not all the derived controls use all the available properties (although many are implemented). Another important point is that not all server controls are implemented from the WebControl class. For instance, the Literal, PlaceHolder, Repeater, and XML server controls do not derive from the WebControl base class, but instead from the Control class.

HTML server controls also do not derive from the WebControl base class because they are more focused on the set attributes of particular HTML elements. Table 4-2 lists the common properties the server controls share.

TABLE 4-2

PROPERTY	DESCRIPTION
AccessKey	Enables you to assign a character to be associated with the Alt key so that the end user can activate the control using quick-keys on the keyboard. For instance, you can assign a Button control an AccessKey property value of K. Now, instead of clicking the button on the ASP.NET page (using a pointer controlled by the mouse), the end user can press Alt+K.
Attributes	Enables you to define additional attributes for a web server control that are not defined by a public property.
BackColor	Controls the color shown behind the control's layout on the ASP.NET page.
BorderColor	Assigns a color that is shown around the physical edge of the server control.
BorderWidth	Assigns a value to the width of the line that makes up the border of the control. Placing a number as the value assigns the number as a pixel-width of the border. The default border color is black if the BorderColor property is not used in conjunction with the BorderWidth property setting.
BorderStyle	Enables you to assign the design of the border that is placed around the server control. By default, the border is created as a straight line, but a number of different styles can be used for your borders. Other possible values for the BorderStyle property include Dotted, Dashed, Solid, Double, Groove, Ridge, Inset, None, NotSet, and Outset.
ClientIDMode	Allows you to get or set the algorithm that is used to create the value of the ClientID property.
CssClass	Assigns a custom CSS (Cascading Style Sheet) class to the control.
Enabled	Enables you to turn off the functionality of the control by setting the value of this property to False. By default, the Enabled property is set to True.
EnableTheming	Enables you to turn on theming capabilities for the selected server control. The default value is True.
EnableViewState	Enables you to specify whether view state should be persisted for this control.

continues

TABLE 4-2 *(continued)*

PROPERTY	DESCRIPTION
Font	Sets the font for all the text that appears anywhere in the control.
ForeColor	Sets the color of all the text that appears anywhere in the control.
Height	Sets the height of the control.
SkinID	Sets the skin to use when theming the control.
Style	Enables you to apply CSS styles to the control.
TabIndex	Sets the control's tab position in the ASP.NET page. This property works in conjunction with other controls on the page.
ToolTip	Assigns text that appears in a yellow box in the browser when a mouse pointer is held over the control for a short length of time. This can be used to add more instructions for the end user.
Width	Sets the width of the control.

You can see these common properties in many of the server controls you work with. Some of the properties of the WebControl class presented here work directly with the theming system built into ASP.NET such as the EnableTheming and SkinID properties. You also see additional properties that are specific to the control you are viewing. Learning about the properties from the preceding table enables you to quickly work with web server controls and to modify them to your needs.

CSS Rendering in ASP.NET 4.5

In ASP.NET 3.5 and earlier, the rendered HTML from the ASP.NET server controls that you used weren't always compliant with the latest HTML standards. As an example, in ASP.NET 3.5, you could set the Enabled property of the server control to False. This would render the control on the page but with a disabled attribute as illustrated here:

```
<span id="Label1" disabled="disabled">Hello there!</span>
```

This is not valid HTML as the span element does not have a disabled attribute.

In ASP.NET 4 and ASP.NET 4.5, the <pages> element within the web.config file instructs ASP.NET what version style to use when rendering controls. The default value is 4.0 as shown in the following code:

```
<pages controlRenderingCompatibilityVersion="4.0" />
```

If this value is set to 4.0, ASP.NET will disable the control using CSS correctly as shown here:

```
<span id="Label1" class="aspNetDisabled">Hello there!</span>
```

> **NOTE** *The value of the* controlRenderingCompatibilityVersion *attribute can be any value formatted with a single digit and a single decimal value. Any value less than* 4.0 *renders the disabled attribute. A value of* 4.0 *or greater renders the class attribute.*

As you can see, ASP.NET sets the class attribute rather than the disabled attribute. To revert to the old way of control rendering, you can set the controlRenderingCompatibilityVersion value to 3.5.

HTML SERVER CONTROLS

ASP.NET enables you to take HTML elements and, with relatively little work on your part, turn them into server-side controls. Afterward, you can use them to control the behavior and actions of elements implemented in your ASP.NET pages.

Of course, you can place any HTML you want in your pages and you have the option of using the HTML as a server-side control. You can also find a list of HTML elements contained in the Toolbox of Visual Studio (shown in Figure 4-4).

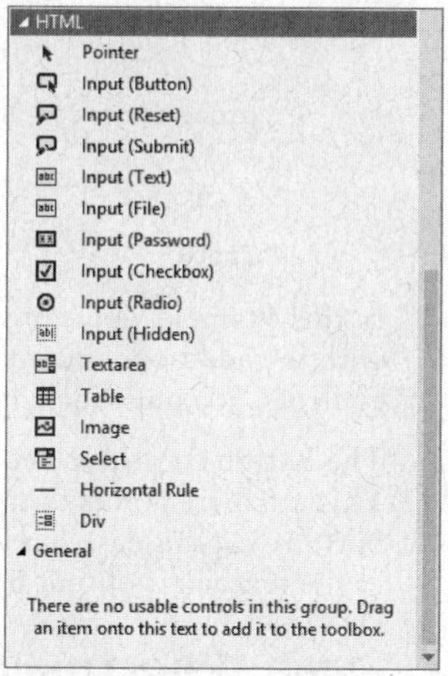

Dragging and dropping any of these HTML elements from the Toolbox to the Design or Source view of your ASP.NET page in the Document window simply produces the appropriate HTML element. For instance, placing an HTML Button control on your page produces the following results in your code:

```
<input id="Button1" type="button" value="button" />
```

In this state, the Button control is not a server-side control. It is simply an HTML element and nothing more. You can turn this into an HTML server control very easily. In Source view, you change the HTML element by adding a `runat="server"` to the control:

```
<input id="Button1" type="button" value="button" runat="server" />
```

After the element is converted to a server control (through the addition of the `runat="server"` attribute and value), you can work with the selected element on the server side as you would work with any of the web server controls. Listing 4-3 shows an example of some HTML server controls.

FIGURE 4-4

LISTING 4-3: Working with HTML server controls

VB

```vb
<%@ Page Language="VB" %>
<!DOCTYPE html>
<script runat="server">
    Protected Sub Button1_ServerClick(sender As Object, e As EventArgs)
        Response.Write(«Hello « & Text1.Value)
    End Sub
</script>
<html xmlns="http://www.w3.org/1999/xhtml">
<head runat="server">
    <title>Using HTML Server Controls</title>
</head>
<body>
    <form id="form1" runat="server">
    <div>
        What is your name?<br />
        <input id="Text1" type="text" runat="server" />
        <input id="Button1" type="button" value="Submit" runat="server"
            onserverclick="Button1_ServerClick" />
    </div>
    </form>
</body>
</html>
```

C#

```csharp
<%@ Page Language="C#" %>
<!DOCTYPE html>
<script runat="server">
```

continues

LISTING 4-3 *(continued)*

```
    protected void Button1_ServerClick(object sender, EventArgs e)
    {
        Response.Write("Hello " + Text1.Value);
    }
</script>
```

In this example, you can see two HTML server controls on the page. Both are typical HTML elements with the additional `runat="server"` attribute added. If you are working with HTML elements as server controls, you must include an `id` attribute so that the server control can be identified in the server-side code.

The Button control includes a reference to a server-side event using the `OnServerClick` attribute. This attribute points to the server-side event handler code that is executed when an end user clicks the button—in this case, `Button1_ServerClick`. Within the `Button1_ServerClick` method, the value placed in the textbox is output by using the `Value` property.

Looking at the HtmlControl Base Class

All the HTML server controls use a class that is derived from the `HtmlControl` base class (fully qualified as `System.Web.UI.HtmlControls.HtmlControl`). These classes expose many properties from the control's derived class. Table 4-3 details some of the properties available from this base class. Some of these items are themselves derived from the base `Control` class.

TABLE 4-3

METHOD OR PROPERTY	DESCRIPTION
Attributes	Provides a collection of name/value pairs of all the available attributes specified in the control, including custom attributes.
Disabled	Allows you to get or set whether the control is disabled using a Boolean value.
EnableTheming	Enables you, using a Boolean value, to get or set whether the control takes part in the page-theming capabilities.
EnableViewState	Allows you to get or set a Boolean value that indicates whether the control participates in the page's view state capabilities.
ID	Allows you to get or set the unique identifier for the control.
Page	Allows you to get a reference to the `Page` object that contains the specified server control.
Parent	Gets a reference to the parent control in the page control hierarchy.
Site	Provides information about the container in which the server control belongs.
SkinID	When the `EnableTheming` property is set to `True`, the `SkinID` property specifies the named skin that should be used in setting a theme.
Style	Makes references to the CSS style collection that applies to the specified control.
TagName	Provides the name of the element that is generated from the specified control.
Visible	Specifies whether the control is visible (rendered) on the generated page.

> **NOTE** *There are many more attributes than those listed. You can find a more comprehensive list in the MSDN documentation.*

Looking at the HtmlContainerControl Class

The `HtmlControl` base class is used for those HTML classes that are focused on HTML elements that can be contained within a single node. For instance, the `<img>`, `<input>`, and `<link>` elements work from classes derived from the `HtmlControl` class.

Other HTML elements, such as `<a>`, `<form>`, and `<select>`, require an opening and closing set of tags. These elements use classes that are derived from the `HtmlContainerControl` class, a class specifically designed to work with HTML elements that require a closing tag.

Because the `HtmlContainerControl` class is derived from the `HtmlControl` class, you have all the `HtmlControl` class's properties and methods available to you as well as some new items that have been declared in the `HtmlContainerControl` class itself. The most important of these are the `InnerText` and `InnerHtml` properties:

➤ `InnerHtml` — Enables you to specify content that can include HTML elements to be placed between the opening and closing tags of the specified control

➤ `InnerText` — Enables you to specify raw text to be placed between the opening and closing tags of the specified control

Looking at All of the HTML Classes

It is quite possible to work with every HTML element because a corresponding class is available for each one of them. Table 4-4 contains a partial list of the server control classes that render HTML.

TABLE 4-4

CLASS	HTML ELEMENT RENDERED
HtmlAnchor	`<a>`
HtmlArea	`<area>`
HtmlAudio	`<audio>`
HtmlButton	`<button>`
HtmlForm	`<form>`
HtmlHead	`<head>`
HtmlIframe	`<iframe>`
HtmlImage	`<img>`
HtmlInputButton	`<input type="button">`
HtmlInputCheckBox	`<input type="checkbox">`
HtmlInputFile	`<input type="file">`
HtmlInputHidden	`<input type="hidden">`
HtmlInputImage	`<input type="image">`
HtmlInputPassword	`<input type="password">`
HtmlInputRadioButton	`<input type="radio">`
HtmlInputReset	`<input type="reset">`
HtmlInputSubmit	`<input type="submit">`
HtmlInputText	`<input type="text">`
HtmlLink	`<link>`
HtmlMeta	`<meta>`
HtmlSelect	`<select>`

continues

TABLE 4-4 *(continued)*

CLASS	HTML ELEMENT RENDERED
HtmlSource	<source>
HtmlTable	<table>
HtmlTableCell	<td>
HtmlTableRow	<tr>
HtmlTextArea	<textarea>
HtmlTitle	<title>
HtmlTrack	<track>
HtmlVideo	<video>

You gain access to one of these classes when you convert an HTML element to an HTML server control. For example, convert the `<title>` element to a server control this way:

```
<title id="Title1" runat="Server"/>
```

This gives you access to the `HtmlTitle` class for this particular HTML element. Using this class instance, you can perform a number of tasks including providing a text value for the page title dynamically:

VB

```
Title1.Text = DateTime.Now.ToString()
```

C#

```
Title1.Text = DateTime.Now.ToString();
```

You can get most of the HTML elements you need by using these classes, but a considerable number of other HTML elements are at your disposal that are not explicitly covered by one of these HTML classes. For example, the `HtmlGenericControl` class provides server-side access to any HTML element you want.

Using the HtmlGenericControl Class

You should be aware of the importance of the `HtmlGenericControl` class; it gives you some capabilities that you do not get from any other server control offered by ASP.NET. For instance, using the `HtmlGenericControl` class, you can get server-side access to the `<p>`, `<span>`, or other elements that would otherwise be unreachable.

Listing 4-4 shows you how to change the new, HTML5 `<progress>` element in your page using the `HtmlGenericControl` class.

LISTING 4-4: Changing the <progress> element using the HtmlGenericControl class

VB

```
<%@ Page Language="VB" %>
<!DOCTYPE html>
<script runat="server">
    Protected Sub Page_Load(sender As Object, e As EventArgs)
        Progress1.Attributes("max") = 100
        Progress1.Attributes("value") = 25
    End Sub
</script>
<html xmlns="http://www.w3.org/1999/xhtml">
<head runat="server">
    <title>Using the HtmlGenericControl class</title>
</head>
```

```
<body>
    <form id="form1" runat="server">
        <progress id="Progress1" runat="server"></progress>
    </form>
</body>
</html>
```

C#

```
<%@ Page Language="C#" %>
<!DOCTYPE html>
<script runat="server">
    protected void Page_Load(object sender, EventArgs e)
    {
        Progress1.Attributes["max"] = "100";
        Progress1.Attributes["value"] = "25";
    }
</script>
```

In this example, the page's `<meta>` element is turned into an HTML server control with the addition of the `id` and `runat` attributes. Because the `HtmlGenericControl` class (which inherits from `HtmlControl`) can work with a wide range of HTML elements, you cannot assign values to HTML attributes in the same manner as you do when working with the other HTML classes, such as `HtmlInputButton`. You assign values to the attributes of an HTML element using the `HtmlGenericControl` class's `Attributes` property, specifying the attribute you are working with as a string value.

The following is a partial result of running the example page:

```
<html xmlns="http://www.w3.org/1999/xhtml">
<head>
  <meta id="Meta1" Name="description"
  CONTENT="Generated on: 12/25/2012 2:42:52 AM"></meta>
  <title>Using the HtmlGenericControl class</title>
</head>
```

By using the `HtmlGenericControl` class, along with the other HTML classes, you can manipulate every element of your ASP.NET pages from your server-side code.

IDENTIFYING ASP.NET SERVER CONTROLS

When you create your ASP.NET pages with a series of controls, many of the controls are nested and many are even dynamically laid out by ASP.NET itself. For instance, when you are working with user controls, the GridView, ListView, Repeater, and more, ASP.NET is constructing a complicated control tree that is rendered to the page.

When this occurs, ASP.NET provides these dynamic controls with IDs. When it does, IDs such as `GridView1$ctl02$ctl00` are generated. As with the controls, the IDs are dynamic. Because these IDs are unpredictable, the ID generation makes it difficult to work with the control from client-side code.

To help with this situation, ASP.NET 4.5 includes the ability to control the IDs that are used for your controls. To demonstrate the issue, Listing 4-5 shows some code that results in some unpredictable client IDs for the controls. To start, first create a user control.

LISTING 4-5: A user control with some simple controls

```
<%@ Control Language="C#" ClassName="Listing04_05" %>
<asp:TextBox ID="TextBox1" runat="server" />
<br />
<asp:Button ID="Button1" runat="server" Text="Button" />
```

Then the next step is to use this user control within one of your ASP.NET pages. This is illustrated in Listing 4-6.

LISTING 4-6: Making use of the user control within a simple ASP.NET page

```
<%@ Page Language="C#" Trace="true" %>
<%@ Register src="Listing04-05.ascx" tagname="MyUserControl" tagprefix="muc" %>
<!DOCTYPE html>
<html xmlns="http://www.w3.org/1999/xhtml">
<head runat="server">
    <title>Working with Control IDs</title>
</head>
<body>
    <form id="form1" runat="server">
    <div>
        <muc:MyUserControl ID="MyUserControl1" runat="server" />
    </div>
    </form>
</body>
</html>
```

So this user control contains only two simple server controls that are then rendered onto the page. If you look back at Listing 4-5, you can see that they have pretty simple control IDs assigned to them. There is a TextBox server control with the ID value of TextBox1 and a Button server control with the ID value of Button1.

Looking at the page code from Listing 4-6, you can see in the @Page directive that the Trace attribute is set to True. This enables you to see the UniqueID that is produced in the control tree of the page. Running this page, you see the results in the page, as shown in Figure 4-5.

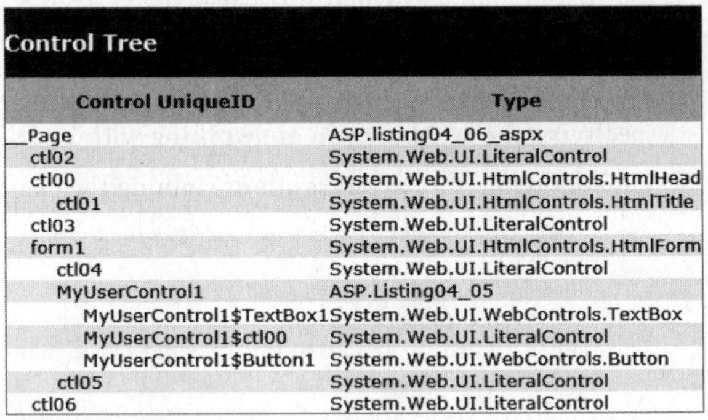

Control Tree

Control UniqueID	Type
Page	ASP.listing04_06_aspx
ctl02	System.Web.UI.LiteralControl
ctl00	System.Web.UI.HtmlControls.HtmlHead
ctl01	System.Web.UI.HtmlControls.HtmlTitle
ctl03	System.Web.UI.LiteralControl
form1	System.Web.UI.HtmlControls.HtmlForm
ctl04	System.Web.UI.LiteralControl
MyUserControl1	ASP.Listing04_05
MyUserControl1$TextBox1	System.Web.UI.WebControls.TextBox
MyUserControl1$ctl00	System.Web.UI.LiteralControl
MyUserControl1$Button1	System.Web.UI.WebControls.Button
ctl05	System.Web.UI.LiteralControl
ctl06	System.Web.UI.LiteralControl

FIGURE 4-5

> **NOTE** *Chapter 7 covers user controls in more detail. Chapter 29 covers tracing within ASP.NET in more detail.*

If you look at the source code for the page, you see the following snippet of code:

```
<div>
<input name="MyUserControl1$TextBox1" type="text" id="MyUserControl1_TextBox1" />
<br />
<input type="submit" name="MyUserControl1$Button1" value="Button"
  id="MyUserControl1_Button1" />
</div>
```

From this, you can see that the ASP.NET assigned control IDs are lengthy and something you probably wouldn't choose yourself. The TextBox server control was output with a name value of MyUserControl1$TextBox1 and an id value of MyUserControl1_TextBox1. A lot of this is done to make sure that the controls end up with a unique ID.

ASP.NET 4.5 includes the ability to control these assignments through the use of the ClientIDMode attribute. The possible values of this attribute include AutoID, Inherit, Predictable, and Static. An example of setting this value is provided here:

```
<muc:MyUserControl ID="MyUserControl1" runat="server" ClientIDMode="AutoID" />
```

This example uses `AutoID`, which forces the naming style to match the rules set in the .NET Framework 3.5 and earlier. Using this gives you the following results:

➤ **name:** `MyUserControl1$TextBox1 MyUserControl1$Button1`

➤ **id:** `MyUserControl1_TextBox1 MyUserControl1_Button1`

If you use `Inherit`, the same values would be populated as if you used `AutoID`. The reason is that it uses the containing control, the page, or the application in building the control. Therefore, for this example, you would end up with the same values as if you used `AutoID`. The `Inherit` value is the default value for all controls.

`Predictable` is generally used for data-bound controls that have a nesting of other controls (for example, the Repeater control). When used with a `ClientIDRowSuffix` property value, it appends this value rather than increments with a number (for example, `ctrl1`, `ctrl2`).

A value of `Static` gives you the name of the control you have assigned. It is up to you to ensure the uniqueness of the identifiers. Setting the `ClientIDMode` to `Static` for the user control in our example gives you the following values:

➤ **name:** `MyUserControl1$TextBox1 MyUserControl1$Button1`

➤ **id:** `TextBox1 Button1`

You can set the `ClientID` property at the control, container control, user control, page, or even application level via the `<pages>` element in the `machine.config` or `Web.config` file.

Now with this capability, you will find that working with your server controls using technologies like JavaScript on the client is far easier than before. The next section takes a look at using JavaScript within your ASP.NET pages.

MANIPULATING PAGES AND SERVER CONTROLS WITH JAVASCRIPT

Developers generally like to include some of their own custom JavaScript functions in their ASP.NET pages. You have a couple of ways to do this. The first is to apply JavaScript directly to the controls on your ASP .NET pages. For example, look at a simple TextBox server control, shown in Listing 4-7, which displays the current date and time.

LISTING 4-7: Showing the current date and time

VB

```
Protected Sub Page_Load(ByVal sender As Object, ByVal e As System.EventArgs)
    TextBox1.Text = DateTime.Now.ToString()
End Sub
```

C#

```
protected void Page_Load(object sender, EventArgs e)
{
    TextBox1.Text = DateTime.Now.ToString();
}
```

> **NOTE** *Although this chapter does cover a bit about JavaScript, chapters in Part VII of this book explain much more about JavaScript in ASP.NET.*

This little bit of code displays the current date and time on the page of the end user. The problem is that the date and time displayed are correct for the web server that generated the page. If someone sits in the Pacific time zone (PST) and the web server is in the Eastern time zone (EST), the page won't be correct for that viewer. If you want the time to be correct for anyone visiting the site, regardless of where they reside in the world, you can employ JavaScript to work with the TextBox control, as illustrated in Listing 4-8.

LISTING 4-8: Using JavaScript to show the current time for the end user

```
<%@ Page Language="C#" %>
<!DOCTYPE html>
<html xmlns="http://www.w3.org/1999/xhtml">
<head runat="server">
    <title>Using JavaScript</title>
</head>
<body onload="javascript:document.forms[0]['TextBox1'].value=Date();">
    <form id="form1" runat="server">
    <div>
        <asp:TextBox ID="TextBox1" Runat="server" Width="300"></asp:TextBox>
    </div>
    </form>
</body>
</html>
```

In this example, even though you are using a standard TextBox server control from the web server control family, you can get at this control using JavaScript that is planted in the onload attribute of the <body> element. The value of the onload attribute actually points to the specific server control via an anonymous function by using the value of the ID attribute from the server control: TextBox1. You can get at other server controls on your page by employing the same methods. This bit of code produces the result illustrated in Figure 4-6.

ASP.NET uses the Page.ClientScript property to register and place JavaScript functions on your ASP .NET pages. Three of these methods are reviewed here. More methods and properties than just these three are available through the ClientScript object (which references an instance of System.Web .UI.ClientScriptManager), but these are the more useful ones. You can find the rest by searching the documentation online.

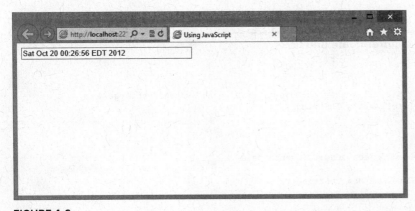

FIGURE 4-6

> **NOTE** *The* `Page.RegisterStartupScript` *and the* `Page`
> `.RegisterClientScriptBlock` *methods from the .NET Framework 1.0/1.1 are now
> considered obsolete. Both of these possibilities for registering scripts required a key/script
> set of parameters. Because two separate methods were involved, there was a possibility that
> some key-name collisions would occur. The* `Page.ClientScript` *property is meant to
> bring all the script registrations under one umbrella, making your code less error–prone.*

Using Page.ClientScript.RegisterClientScriptBlock

The `RegisterClientScriptBlock` method allows you to place a JavaScript function at the top of the page. This means that the script is in place for the startup of the page in the browser. Its use is illustrated in Listing 4-9.

LISTING 4-9: Using the RegisterClientScriptBlock method

VB

```vb
<%@ Page Language="VB" %>
<!DOCTYPE html>
<script runat="server">
    Protected Sub Page_Load(ByVal sender As Object, ByVal e As System.EventArgs)
        Dim myScript As String = "function AlertHello() {alert('Hello ASP.NET');}"
        Page.ClientScript.RegisterClientScriptBlock(Me.GetType(), "MyScript",
            myScript, True)
    End Sub
</script>
<html xmlns="http://www.w3.org/1999/xhtml">
<head runat="server">
    <title>Adding JavaScript</title>
</head>
<body>
    <form id="form1" runat="server">
    <div>
        <asp:Button ID="Button1" Runat="server" Text="Button"
            OnClientClick="AlertHello()" />
    </div>
    </form>
</body>
</html>
```

C#

```csharp
<%@ Page Language="C#" %>
<!DOCTYPE html>
<script runat="server">
    protected void Page_Load(object sender, EventArgs e)
    {
        string myScript = @"function AlertHello() { alert('Hello ASP.NET'); }";
        Page.ClientScript.RegisterClientScriptBlock(this.GetType(),
            "MyScript", myScript, true);
    }
</script>
```

From this example, you can see that you create the JavaScript function `AlertHello()` as a string called `myScript`. Then using the `Page.ClientScript.RegisterClientScriptBlock` method, you program the script to be placed on the page. The two possible constructions of the `RegisterClientScriptBlock` method are the following:

➤   `RegisterClientScriptBlock` (*type, key, script*)

➤   `RegisterClientScriptBlock` (*type, key, script, script tag specification*)

In the example from Listing 4-9, you are specifying the type as `Me.GetType()`, the key, the script to include, and then a Boolean value setting of `True` so that .NET places the script on the ASP.NET page with `<script>` tags automatically. When running the page, you can view the source code for the page to see the results:

```
<!DOCTYPE html
<html xmlns="http://www.w3.org/1999/xhtml">
<head><title>
    Adding JavaScript
</title></head>
<body>
    <form method="post" action="Listing04-09.aspx" id="form1">
<div class="aspNetHidden">
<input type="hidden" name="__VIEWSTATE" id="__VIEWSTATE" value="hbVKLJCpbcKtClOpVO6
+dE5HkSYJIxqrLCZF0BMbiZhhPdOepUjRfUukoZ7ZEg0BGQiZYBg8umPQQs/DvUX21ZQbhL3D4wLmJRxiVN
pCkLY=" />
</div>
<script type="text/javascript">
//<![CDATA[
function AlertHello() { alert('Hello ASP.NET'); }//]]>
</script>
<div class="aspNetHidden">
    <input type="hidden" name="__EVENTVALIDATION" id="__EVENTVALIDATION" value="Sbe6uw
GDqPTxBfbGDMs1s8mWmBtO+sJwDh9YY6hS0PUZGqpOraDf1Mdrhkd3MgX5444UcMM5yv+j6yZi+XNuseFXe
9L9qv+17YKNOLDHUJHJaibcCyLDb3qp0dOPcJkv" />
</div>
    <div>
     <input type="submit" name="Button1" value="Button" onclick="AlertHello();"
        id="Button1" />
    </div>
    </form>
</body>
</html>
```

Button →

From this, you can see that the script specified was indeed included on the ASP.NET page before the relevant page code. Not only were the `<script>` tags included, but the proper comment tags were added around the script (so older browsers will not break).

Using Page.ClientScript.RegisterStartupScript

The `RegisterStartupScript` method is not that different from the `RegisterClientScriptBlock` method. The big difference is that the `RegisterStartupScript` places the script at the bottom of the ASP.NET page instead of at the top. In fact, the `RegisterStartupScript` method even takes the same constructors as the `RegisterClientScriptBlock` method:

➤ `RegisterStartupScript` (*type*, *key*, *script*)

➤ `RegisterStartupScript` (*type*, *key*, *script*, *script tag specification*)

So what difference does it make where the script is registered on the page? A lot, actually!

If you have a bit of JavaScript that is working with one of the controls on your page, in most cases you want to use the `RegisterStartupScript` method instead of `RegisterClientScriptBlock`. For example, you use the following code to create a page that includes a simple `<asp:TextBox>` control that contains a default value of `Hello ASP.NET`:

```
<asp:TextBox ID="TextBox1" Runat="server">Hello ASP.NET</asp:TextBox>
```

Then use the `RegisterClientScriptBlock` method to place a script on the page that utilizes the value in the `TextBox1` control, as illustrated in Listing 4-10.

LISTING 4-10: Improperly using the RegisterClientScriptBlock method

VB

```
Protected Sub Page_Load(ByVal sender As Object, ByVal e As System.EventArgs)
    Dim myScript As String = "alert(document.getElementById('TextBox1').value);"
    Page.ClientScript.RegisterClientScriptBlock(Me.GetType(), "myKey", myScript,
        True)
End Sub
```

C#

```
protected void Page_Load(object sender, EventArgs e)
{
    string myScript = @"alert(document.getElementById('TextBox1').value);";
    Page.ClientScript.RegisterClientScriptBlock(this.GetType(),
        "MyScript", myScript, true);
}
```

Running this page (depending on the version of IE you are using) gives you a JavaScript error, as shown in Figure 4-7.

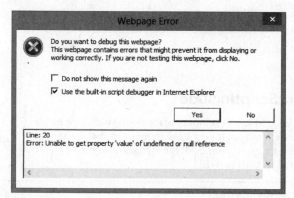

FIGURE 4-7

The reason for the error is that the JavaScript function fired before the textbox was placed on the screen. Therefore, the JavaScript function did not find TextBox1, and that caused an error to be thrown by the page. Now try the RegisterStartupScript method shown in Listing 4-11.

LISTING 4-11: Using the RegisterStartupScript method

VB

```
Protected Sub Page_Load(ByVal sender As Object, ByVal e As System.EventArgs)
    Dim myScript As String = "alert(document.forms[0]['TextBox1'].value);"
    Page.ClientScript.RegisterStartupScript(Me.GetType(), "myKey", myScript,
        True)
End Sub
```

C#

```
protected void Page_Load(object sender, EventArgs e)
{
    string myScript = @"alert(document.forms[0]['TextBox1'].value);";
    Page.ClientScript.RegisterStartupScript(this.GetType(),
        "MyScript", myScript, true);
}
```

This approach puts the JavaScript function at the bottom of the ASP.NET page, so when the JavaScript starts, it finds the TextBox1 element and works as planned. The result is shown in Figure 4-8.

FIGURE 4-8

Using Page.ClientScript.RegisterClientScriptInclude

The final method is RegisterClientScriptInclude. Many developers place their JavaScript inside a .js file, which is considered a best practice because it makes it very easy to make global JavaScript changes to the application. You can register the script files on your ASP.NET pages using the RegisterClientScriptInclude method illustrated in Listing 4-12.

LISTING 4-12: Using the RegisterClientScriptInclude method

VB

```
Dim myScript As String = "myJavaScriptCode.js"
Page.ClientScript.RegisterClientScriptInclude("myKey", myScript)
```

C#

```
string myScript = "myJavaScriptCode.js";
Page.ClientScript.RegisterClientScriptInclude("myKey", myScript);
```

This creates the following construction on the ASP.NET page:

```
<script src="myJavaScriptCode.js" type="text/javascript"></script>
```

SUMMARY

This chapter gave you one of the core building blocks of an ASP.NET page—the server control. The server control is an object-oriented approach to page development that encapsulates page elements into modifiable and expandable components. The chapter also looked at using HTML server controls and adding JavaScript to your pages to modify the behaviors of your controls.

ASP.NET Web Server Controls

WHAT'S IN THIS CHAPTER?

➤ Reviewing key web server controls

➤ Differentiating between web server control features

➤ Removing items from a collection

WROX.COM CODE DOWNLOADS FOR THIS CHAPTER

Please note that all the code examples in this chapter are available as a part of this chapter's code download on the book's website at www.wrox.com on the Download Code tab.

Of the two types of server controls—HTML server controls and web server controls—the latter is considered the more powerful and flexible. The previous chapter looked at how to use HTML server controls in applications. HTML server controls enable you to manipulate HTML elements from your server-side code. On the other hand, web server controls are powerful because they are not explicitly tied to specific HTML elements; rather, they are more closely aligned to the specific functionality that you want to generate. As you will see throughout this chapter, web server controls can be very simple or rather complex depending on the control you are working with.

The purpose of the large collection of controls is to make you more productive. These controls give you advanced functionality that, in the past, you would have had to laboriously program or simply omit. In the classic ASP days, for example, few calendars were used on Internet websites. With the introduction of the Calendar server control in ASP.NET 1.0, calendar creation on a site became a trivial task. Building an image map on top of an image was another task that was difficult to achieve in ASP.NET 1.x, but this capability was introduced as a new server control in ASP.NET 2.0. As ASP .NET evolves through the releases, new controls and functionality are constantly added that help to make you a more productive web developer.

This chapter introduces some of the available web server controls. The first part of the chapter focuses on the web server controls that were around since the early days of ASP.NET. Then the chapter explores the server controls that were introduced after the initial release of ASP.NET. This chapter does not discuss every possible control because some server controls are introduced and covered in other chapters throughout the book.

AN OVERVIEW OF WEB SERVER CONTROLS

The web server control is ASP.NET's most-used component. Although you may have seen a lot of potential uses of the HTML server controls shown in the previous chapter, web server controls are definitely a notch higher in capability. They allow for a higher level of functionality that becomes more apparent as you work with them.

The HTML server controls provided by ASP.NET are translated to specific HTML elements. You control the output by working with the HTML attributes that the HTML element provides. The attributes can be changed dynamically on the server side before they are finally output to the client. There is a lot of power in this, and you have some HTML server control capabilities that you simply do not have when you work with web server controls.

Web server controls work differently. They do not map to specific HTML elements, but instead enable you to define functionality, capability, and appearance without the attributes that are available to you through a collection of HTML elements. When constructing a web page that is made up of web server controls, you are describing the functionality, the look-and-feel, and the behavior of your page elements. You then let ASP.NET decide how to output this construction. The output, of course, is based on the capabilities of the container that is making the request. This means that each requestor might see a different HTML output because each is requesting the same page with a different browser type or version. ASP.NET takes care of all the browser detection and the work associated with it on your behalf.

Unlike HTML server controls, web server controls are not only available for working with common web page form elements (such as textboxes and buttons), but they can also bring some advanced capabilities and functionality to your web pages. For instance, one common feature of many web applications is a calendar. No HTML form element places a calendar on your Web Forms, but a web server control from ASP.NET can provide your application with a full-fledged calendar, including some advanced capabilities. In the past, adding calendars to your web pages was not a small programming task. Today, adding calendars with ASP .NET is rather simple and is achieved with a single line of code!

Remember that when you are constructing your web server controls, you are actually constructing a control—*a set of instructions*—that is meant for the server (not the client). By default, all web server controls provided by ASP.NET use an `asp` prefix at the beginning of the control declaration. The following is a typical web server control:

```
<asp:Label ID="Label1" runat="server" Text="Hello World"></asp:Label>
```

Like HTML server controls, web server controls require an `ID` attribute to reference the control in the server-side code, as well as a `runat="server"` attribute declaration. As you do for other XML-based elements, you need to properly open and close web server controls using XML syntax rules. In the preceding example, you can see that the `<asp:Label>` control has a closing `</asp:Label>` element associated with it. You could have also closed this element using the following syntax:

```
<asp:Label ID="Label1" runat="server" Text="Hello World" />
```

The rest of this chapter examines some of the web server controls available to you in ASP.NET.

THE LABEL SERVER CONTROL

The Label server control is used to display text in the browser. Because this is a server control, you can dynamically alter the text from your server-side code. As you saw from the preceding examples of using the `<asp:Label>` control, the control uses the `Text` attribute to assign the content of the control as shown here:

```
<asp:Label ID="Label1" runat="server" Text="Hello World" />
```

Instead of using the `Text` attribute, however, you can place the content to be displayed between the `<asp:Label>` elements like this:

```
<asp:Label ID="Label1" runat="server">Hello World</asp:Label>
```

You can also provide content for the control through programmatic means, as illustrated in Listing 5-1.

LISTING 5-1: Programmatically providing text to the Label control

VB

```
Label1.Text = "Hello ASP.NET!"
```

C#

```
Label1.Text = "Hello ASP.NET!";
```

The Label server control has always been a control that simply showed text. Ever since ASP.NET 2.0, it has a little bit of extra functionality. The big change since this release of the framework is that you can give items in your form hot-key functionality (also known as *accelerator* keys). This causes the page to focus on a particular server control that you declaratively assign to a specific hot-key press (for example, using Alt+N to focus on the first textbox on the form).

> **NOTE** *Note that the accelerator keys may not work in all browsers and browser versions.*

A hot key is a quick way for the end user to initiate an action on the page. For instance, if you use Microsoft Internet Explorer, you can press Ctrl+N to open a new instance of IE. Hot keys have always been quite common in thick-client applications (Windows Forms), and now you can use them in ASP.NET. Listing 5-2 shows an example of how to give hot-key functionality to two textboxes on a form.

LISTING 5-2: Using the Label server control to provide hot-key functionality

```
<%@ Page Language="C#" %>
<!DOCTYPE html>
<html xmlns="http://www.w3.org/1999/xhtml">
<head runat="server">
    <title>Label Server Control</title>
</head>
<body>
    <form id="form1" runat="server">
        <p>
            <asp:Label ID="Label1" runat="server" AccessKey="N"
                AssociatedControlID="Textbox1">User<u>n</u>ame</asp:Label>
            <asp:TextBox ID="TextBox1" runat="server"></asp:TextBox>
        </p>
        <p>
            <asp:Label ID="Label2" runat="server" AccessKey="P"
                AssociatedControlID="Textbox2"><u>P</u>assword</asp:Label>
            <asp:TextBox ID="TextBox2" runat="server"></asp:TextBox>
        </p>
        <p>
            <asp:Button ID="Button1" runat="server" Text="Submit" />
        </p>
    </form>
</body>
</html>
```

Hot keys are assigned with the `AccessKey` attribute. In this case, `Label1` uses `N`, and `Label2` uses `P`. The second attribute for the Label control is the `AssociatedControlID` attribute. The `string` value placed here associates the Label control with another server control on the form. The value must be one of the other server controls on the form. If not, the page gives you an error when invoked.

With these two controls in place, when the page is called in the browser, you can press Alt+N or Alt+P to automatically focus on a particular textbox in the form. In Figure 5-1, HTML-declared underlines indicate the letters to be pressed along with the Alt key to create focus on the control adjoining the text. This is not required, but it's highly recommended because the end user expects this functionality when working with hot keys. In this example, the letter n in Username and the letter P in Password are underlined.

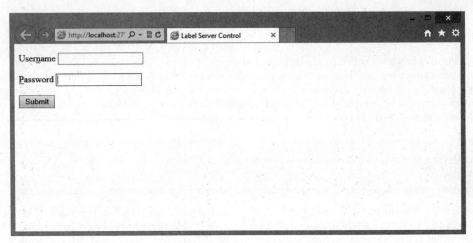

FIGURE 5-1

When working with hot keys, be aware that not all letters are available to use with the Alt key. Microsoft Internet Explorer already uses Alt+A, E, H, I, O, T, V, and W. If you use any of these letters, IE actions supersede any actions you place on the page.

THE LITERAL SERVER CONTROL

The Literal server control works very much like the Label server control does. This control was always used in the past for text that you wanted to push out to the browser but keep unchanged in the process (a literal state). A Label control alters the output by placing `<span>` elements around the text as shown:

```
<span id="Label1">Here is some text</span>
```

The Literal control just outputs the text without the `<span>` elements. One feature found in this server control is the attribute `Mode`. This attribute enables you to dictate how the text assigned to the control is interpreted by the ASP.NET engine.

If you place some HTML code in the string that is output (for instance, `<strong>Here is some text</strong>`), the Literal control outputs just that, and the consuming browser shows the text as bold:

Here is some text

Try using the `Mode` attribute as illustrated here:

```
<asp:Literal ID="Literal1" runat="server" Mode="Encode"
 Text="<strong>Here is some text</strong>"></asp:Literal>
```

Adding `Mode="Encode"` encodes the output before it is received by the consuming application:

```
&lt;b&gt;Label&lt;/b&gt;
```

Now, instead of the text being converted to a bold font, the `<strong>` elements are displayed:

```
<strong>Here is some text</strong>
```

This is ideal if you want to display code in your application. Other values for the Mode attribute include Transform and PassThrough. Transform looks at the consumer and includes or removes elements as needed. For instance, not all devices accept HTML elements, so, if the value of the Mode attribute is set to Transform, these elements are removed from the string before it is sent to the consuming application. A value of PassThrough for the Mode property means that the text is sent to the consuming application without any changes being made to the string.

THE TEXTBOX SERVER CONTROL

One of the main features of web pages is to offer forms that end users can use to submit their information for collection. The TextBox server control is one of the most used controls in this space. As its name suggests, the control provides a textbox on the form that enables the end user to input text. You can map the TextBox control to three different HTML elements used in your forms.

First, the TextBox control can be used as a standard HTML textbox, as shown in the following code snippet:

```
<asp:TextBox ID="TextBox1" runat="server"></asp:TextBox>
```

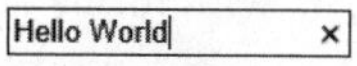

FIGURE 5-2

This code creates a textbox on the form that looks like the one shown in Figure 5-2.

Second, the TextBox control can allow end users to input their passwords into a form. This is done by changing the TextMode attribute of the TextBox control to Password, as illustrated here:

```
<asp:TextBox ID="TextBox1" runat="server" TextMode="Password"></asp:TextBox>
```

When asking end users for their passwords through the browser, it is best practice to provide a textbox that encodes the content placed in this form element. Using an attribute and value of TextMode="Password" ensures that the text is encoded with a star (*) or a dot, as shown in Figure 5-3.

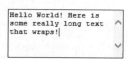

FIGURE 5-3

Third, the TextBox server control can be used as a multiline textbox. The code for accomplishing this task is as follows:

```
<asp:TextBox ID="TextBox1" runat="server" TextMode="MultiLine" Width="300px"
   Height="150px"></asp:TextBox>
```

Giving the TextMode attribute a value of MultiLine creates a multilined textbox in which the end user can enter a larger amount of text in the form. The Width and Height attributes set the size of the text area, but these are optional attributes—without them, the text area is produced in its smallest size. Figure 5-4 shows the use of the preceding code after adding some text.

Hello World! Here is
some really long text
that wraps!

FIGURE 5-4

When working with a multilined textbox, be aware of the Wrap attribute. When set to True (which is the default), the text entered into the text area wraps to the next line if needed. When set to False, the end user can type continuously in a single line until she presses the Enter key, which brings the cursor down to the next line.

Using the Focus() Method

Because the TextBox server control is derived from the base class of WebControl, one of the methods available to it is Focus(). The Focus() method enables you to dynamically place the end user's cursor in an appointed form element (not just the TextBox control, but in any of the server controls derived from the WebControl class). With that said, it is probably most often used with the TextBox control, as illustrated in Listing 5-3.

LISTING 5-3: Using the Focus() method with the TextBox control

VB

```
Protected Sub Page_Load(sender As Object, e As EventArgs)
    FirstNameTextBox.Focus()
End Sub
```

C#

```
protected void Page_Load(Object sender, EventArgs e)
{
    FirstNameTextBox.Focus();
}
```

When the page using this method is loaded in the browser, the cursor is already placed inside of the textbox, ready for you to start typing. There is no need to move your mouse to get the cursor in place so you can start entering information in the form. This is ideal for those folks who take a keyboard approach to working with forms.

Using AutoPostBack

ASP.NET pages work in an event-driven way. When an action on a web page triggers an event, server-side code is initiated. One of the more common events is an end user clicking a button on the form. If you double-click the button in Design view of Visual Studio 2012, you can see the code page with the structure of the `Button1_Click` event already in place. This is because `OnClick` is the most common event of the Button control. Double-clicking the TextBox control constructs an `OnTextChanged` event. This event is triggered when the end user moves the cursor focus outside the textbox, either by clicking another element on the page after entering something into a textbox, or by simply tabbing out of the textbox. The use of this event is shown in Listing 5-4.

LISTING 5-4: Triggering an event when a TextBox change occurs

VB

```
<%@ Page Language="VB" %>
<!DOCTYPE html>
<script runat="server">
    Protected Sub TextBox1_TextChanged(sender As Object, e As EventArgs)
        Response.Write("OnTextChanged event triggered")
    End Sub
    Protected Sub Button1_Click(sender As Object, e As EventArgs)
        Response.Write("OnClick event triggered")
    End Sub
</script>
<html xmlns="http://www.w3.org/1999/xhtml">
<head runat="server">
    <title>Triggering an event when a TextBox</title>
</head>
<body>
    <form id="form1" runat="server">
        <div>
            <asp:TextBox ID="TextBox1" runat="server" AutoPostBack="True"
                OnTextChanged="TextBox1_TextChanged"></asp:TextBox>
            <asp:Button ID="Button1" runat="server" Text="Button"
                OnClick="Button1_Click" />
        </div>
    </form>
</body>
</html>
```

C#

```
<%@ Page Language="C#" %>
<!DOCTYPE html>
<script runat="server">
    protected void TextBox1_TextChanged(object sender, EventArgs e)
    {
        Response.Write("OnTextChanged event triggered");
    }
    protected void Button1_Click(object sender, EventArgs e)
    {
        Response.Write("OnClick event triggered");
    }
</script>
```

As you build and run this page, notice that you can type something in the textbox, but once you tab out of it, the `OnTextChanged` event is triggered and the code contained in the `TextBox1_TextChanged` event runs. To make this work, you must add the `AutoPostBack` attribute to the TextBox control and set it to `True`. This causes the web page to look for any text changes prior to an actual page postback. For the `AutoPostBack` feature to work, the browser viewing the page must support ECMAScript.

Using AutoCompleteType

You want the forms you build for your web applications to be as simple to use as possible. You want to make them easy and quick for the end user to fill out the information and proceed. If you make a form too onerous, the people who come to your site may leave without completing it.

One of the great capabilities for any Web Form is smart auto-completion. You may have seen this yourself when you visited a site for the first time. As you start to fill out information in a form, a drop-down list appears below the textbox as you type, showing you a value that you have typed in a previous form. The plain textbox you were working with has become a smart textbox. Figure 5-5 shows an example of this feature.

FIGURE 5-5

A great aspect of the TextBox control is the `AutoCompleteType` attribute, which enables you to apply the auto-completion feature to your own forms. You have to help the textboxes on your form to recognize the type of information that they should be looking for. What does that mean? To answer this, first look at the possible values of the `AutoCompleteType` attribute:

Disabled	Company	HomeFax
BusinessCity	DisplayName	Homepage
BusinessCountryRegion	HomeState	HomePhone
BusinessFax	HomeStreetAddress	JobTitle
BusinessPhone	HomeZipCode	LastName
BusinessState	Email	MiddleName
BusinessStreetAddress	Enabled	Notes
BusinessUrl	FirstName	Office
BusinessZipCode	Gender	Pager
Cellular	HomeCity	Search
Department	HomeCountryRegion	

From this list, you can see that if your textbox is asking for the end user's home street address, you want to use the following in your TextBox control:

```
<asp:TextBox ID="TextBox1" runat="server"
    AutoCompleteType="HomeStreetAddress"></asp:TextBox>
```

As you view the source of the textbox you created, you can see that the following construction has occurred:

```
<input name="TextBox1" type="text" vcard_name="vCard.Home.StreetAddress"
    id="TextBox1" />
```

This feature makes your forms easier to work with. Yes, it is a simple thing but sometimes the little things keep visitors coming back again and again to your website.

THE BUTTON SERVER CONTROL

Another common control for your Web Forms is a button that can be constructed using the Button server control. Buttons are the usual element used to submit forms. Most of the time you are simply dealing with items contained in your forms through the Button control's OnClick event, as illustrated in Listing 5-5.

LISTING 5-5: The Button control's OnClick event

VB

```
Protected Sub Button1_Click(sender As Object, e As EventArgs)
    'Code here
End Sub
```

C#

```
protected void Button1_Click(object sender, EventArgs e)
{
    // Code here
}
```

The Button control is one of the easier controls to use, but there are a couple of properties of which you must be aware: CausesValidation and CommandName. They are discussed in the following sections.

The CausesValidation Property

If you have more than one button on your web page and you are working with the validation server controls, you may not want to fire the validation for each button on the form. Setting the CausesValidation property to False is a way to use a button that will not fire the validation process. This is explained in more detail in Chapter 6.

The CommandName Property

You can have multiple buttons on your form all working from a single event. The nice thing is that you can also tag the buttons so that the code can make logical decisions based on which button on the form was clicked. You must construct your Button controls in the manner illustrated in Listing 5-6 to take advantage of this behavior.

LISTING 5-6: Constructing multiple button controls to work from a single function

```
<asp:Button ID="Button1" runat="server" OnCommand="Button_Command"
    CommandName="DoSomething1" Text="Button 1" />
<asp:Button ID="Button2" runat="server" OnCommand="Button_Command"
    CommandName="DoSomething2" Text="Button 2" />
```

Looking at these two instances of the Button control, you should pay attention to several things. The first thing to notice is what is not present—any attribute mention of an `OnClick` event. Instead, you use the `OnCommand` event, which points to an event called `Button_Command`. You can see that both Button controls are working from the same event. How does the event differentiate between the two buttons being clicked? Through the value placed in the `CommandName` property. In this case, they are indeed separate values—`DoSomething1` and `DoSomething2`.

The next step is to create the `Button_Command` event to deal with both these buttons by simply typing one out or by selecting the `Command` event from the drop-down list of available events for the Button control from the Code view of Visual Studio. In either case, you should end up with an event like the one shown in Listing 5-7.

LISTING 5-7: The Button_Command event

VB

```
Protected Sub Button_Command(ByVal sender As Object,
    ByVal e As System.Web.UI.WebControls.CommandEventArgs)
    Select Case e.CommandName
        Case "DoSomething1"
            Response.Write("Button 1 was selected")
        Case "DoSomething2"
            Response.Write("Button 2 was selected")
    End Select
End Sub
```

C#

```
protected void Button_Command(object sender,
    System.Web.UI.WebControls.CommandEventArgs e)
{
    switch (e.CommandName)
    {
        case ("DoSomething1"):
            Response.Write("Button 1 was selected");
            break;
        case ("DoSomething2"):
            Response.Write("Button 2 was selected");
            break;
    }
}
```

Notice that this method uses `System.Web.UI.WebControls.CommandEventArgs` instead of the typical `System.EventArgs`. This gives you access to the member `CommandName` used in the `Select Case` (switch) statement as `e.CommandName`. With this object, you can check for the value of the `CommandName` property used by the button that was clicked on the form and take a specific action based upon the value passed.

You can add some parameters to be passed in to the `Command` event beyond what is defined in the `CommandName` property. You do this by using the Button control's `CommandArgument` property. Adding values to the property enables you to define items a bit more granularly if you want. You can get at this value via server-side code using `e.CommandArgument` from the `CommandEventArgs` object.

Buttons That Work with Client-Side JavaScript

Buttons are frequently used for submitting information and causing actions to occur on a web page. Before ASP.NET 1.0/1.1, people intermingled quite a bit of JavaScript in their pages to fire JavaScript events when a button was clicked. The process became more cumbersome in ASP.NET 1.0/1.1, but ever since ASP.NET 2.0, it has been much easier.

You can create a page that has a JavaScript event, as well as a server-side event, triggered when the button is clicked, as illustrated in Listing 5-8.

LISTING 5-8: Two types of events for the button

VB

```vb
<%@ Page Language="VB" %>
<!DOCTYPE html>
<script runat="server">
    Protected Sub Button1_Click(ByVal sender As Object, _
       ByVal e As System.EventArgs)
        Response.Write("Postback!")
    End Sub
</script>
<html xmlns="http://www.w3.org/1999/xhtml">
<head runat="server">
    <title>Button Server Control</title>
</head>
<body>
    <form id="form1" runat="server">
        <asp:Button ID="Button1" runat="server" Text="Button"
            OnClientClick="AlertHello()" OnClick="Button1_Click" />
    </form>
    <script type="text/javascript">
        function AlertHello() {
            alert('Hello ASP.NET');
        }
    </script>
</body>
</html>
```

C#

```csharp
<%@ Page Language="C#" %>
<!DOCTYPE html>
<script runat="server">
    protected void Button1_Click(Object sender, EventArgs e)
    {
        Response.Write("Postback!");
    }
</script>
```

The first thing to notice is the attribute for the Button server control: `OnClientClick`. It points to the client-side function, unlike the `OnClick` attribute that points to the server-side event. This example uses a JavaScript function called `AlertHello()`.

One cool thing about Visual Studio 2012 is that it can work with server-side script tags that are right alongside client-side script tags. It all works together seamlessly. In the example, after the JavaScript alert dialog box is issued (see Figure 5-6) and the end user clicks OK, the page posts back as the server-side event is triggered.

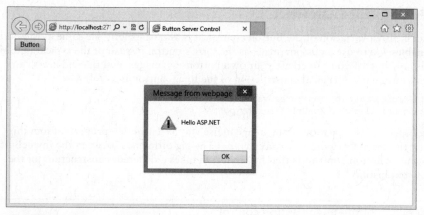

FIGURE 5-6

Another interesting attribute for the Button server controls is `PostBackUrl`. It enables you to perform cross-page posting, instead of simply posting your ASP.NET pages back to the same page, as shown in the following example:

```
<asp:Button ID="Button1" runat="server" Text="Submit to Another Page"
    PostBackUrl="Page2.aspx" />
```

Cross-page posting is covered in greater detail in Chapter 3.

THE LINKBUTTON SERVER CONTROL

The LinkButton server control is a variation of the Button control. It is the same except that the LinkButton control takes the form of a hyperlink. Nevertheless, it is not a typical hyperlink. When the end user clicks the link, it behaves like a button.

A LinkButton server control is constructed as follows:

```
<asp:LinkButton ID="LinkButton1" Runat="server" OnClick="LinkButton1_Click">
    Submit your name to our database
</asp:LinkButton>
```

Using the LinkButton control gives you the results shown in Figure 5-7.

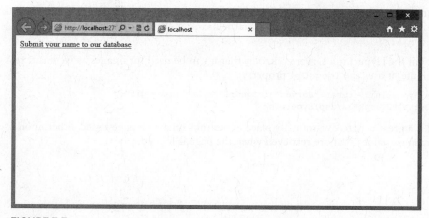

FIGURE 5-7

THE IMAGEBUTTON SERVER CONTROL

The ImageButton control is also a variation of the Button control. It is almost exactly the same as the Button control, except that it enables you to use a custom image as the form's button instead of the typical buttons used on most forms. This means that you can create your own buttons as images, and the end users can click the images to submit form data. A typical construction of the ImageButton is as follows:

```
<asp:ImageButton ID="ImageButton1" runat="server"
    OnClick="ImageButton1_Click" ImageUrl="search.jpg" />
```

The ImageButton control specifies the location of the image in use via the `ImageUrl` property. From this example, you can see that the `ImageUrl` points to `search.jpg`. The big difference between the ImageButton control and the LinkButton or Button controls is that ImageButton takes a different construction for the `OnClick` event. It is shown in Listing 5-9.

LISTING 5-9: The Click event for the ImageButton control

VB

```
Protected Sub ImageButton1_Click(sender As Object, e As ImageClickEventArgs)
    'Code here
End Sub
```

C#

```
protected void ImageButton1_Click(object sender, ImageClickEventArgs e)
{
    // Code here
}
```

The construction uses the `ImageClickEventArgs` object instead of the `System.EventArgs` object usually used with the LinkButton and Button controls. You can use this object to determine where in the image the end user clicked by using both `e.X` and `e.Y` coordinates.

THE HYPERLINK SERVER CONTROL

The HyperLink server control enables you to programmatically work with any hyperlinks on your web pages. Hyperlinks are links that allow end users to transfer from one page to another. You can set the text of a hyperlink using the control's `Text` attribute:

```
<asp:HyperLink ID="HyperLink1" runat="server" Text="Go to this page here"
    NavigateUrl="Default2.aspx"></asp:HyperLink>
```

This server control creates a hyperlink on your page with the text `Go to this page here`. When the link is clicked, the user is redirected to the value that is placed in the `NavigateUrl` property (in this case, the `Default2.aspx` page).

The interesting thing about the HyperLink server control is that it can be used for images as well as text. Instead of the `Text` attribute, it uses the `ImageUrl` property:

```
<asp:HyperLink ID="HyperLink2" runat="server" ImageUrl="MyLinkImage.gif"
    NavigateUrl="Default2.aspx"></asp:HyperLink>
```

The HyperLink control is a great way to dynamically place hyperlinks on a web page based either upon user input in a form or on database values that are retrieved when the page is loaded.

THE DROPDOWNLIST SERVER CONTROL

The DropDownList server control enables you to place an HTML select box on your web page and program against it. It is ideal when you have a large collection of items from which you want the end user to select a single item. It is usually used for a medium- to large-sized collection. If the collection size is relatively small, consider using the RadioButtonList server control (described later in this chapter).

The select box generated by the DropDownList control displays a single item and allows the end user to make a selection from a larger list of items. Depending on the number of choices available in the select box, the end user may have to scroll through a list of items. Note that the appearance of the scroll bar in the drop-down list is automatically created by the browser depending on the browser version and the number of items contained in the list.

Here is the code for a DropDownList control:

```
<asp:DropDownList ID="DropDownList1" runat="server">
    <asp:ListItem>Select an Item</asp:ListItem>
    <asp:ListItem>Car</asp:ListItem>
    <asp:ListItem>Airplane</asp:ListItem>
    <asp:ListItem>Train</asp:ListItem>
</asp:DropDownList>
```

FIGURE 5-8

This code generates a drop-down list in the browser, as shown in Figure 5-8.

The DropDownList control comes in handy when you start binding it to various data stores. The data stores can be arrays, database values, XML file values, or values found elsewhere. For an example of binding the DropDownList control, this next example looks at dynamically generating a DropDownList control from one of three available arrays, as shown in Listing 5-10.

LISTING 5-10: Dynamically generating a DropDownList control from an array

VB

```
<%@ Page Language="VB" %>
<!DOCTYPE html>
<script runat="server">
    Protected Sub DropDownList1_SelectedIndexChanged(ByVal sender As Object,
      ByVal e As System.EventArgs)
        Dim CarArray() As String = {"Ford", "Honda", "BMW", "Dodge"}
        Dim AirplaneArray() As String = {"Boeing 777", "Boeing 747", "Boeing 737"}
        Dim TrainArray() As String = {"Bullet Train", "Amtrack", "Tram"}
        If DropDownList1.SelectedValue = "Car" Then
            DropDownList2.DataSource = CarArray
        ElseIf DropDownList1.SelectedValue = "Airplane" Then
            DropDownList2.DataSource = AirplaneArray
        ElseIf DropDownList1.SelectedValue = "Train" Then
            DropDownList2.DataSource = TrainArray
        End If
        DropDownList2.DataBind()
        DropDownList2.Visible = (DropDownList1.SelectedValue <> _
            "Select an Item")
    End Sub
    Protected Sub Button1_Click(ByVal sender As Object,
        ByVal e As System.EventArgs)
        Response.Write("You selected <b>" & _
        DropDownList1.SelectedValue.ToString() & ": " &
        DropDownList2.SelectedValue.ToString() & "</b>")
    End Sub
</script>
<html xmlns="http://www.w3.org/1999/xhtml">
```

continues

LISTING 5-10 *(continued)*

```
<head runat="server">
    <title>DropDownList Page</title>
</head>
<body>
    <form id="form1" runat="server">
        <div>
            Select transportation type:<br />
            <asp:DropDownList ID="DropDownList1" runat="server"
                OnSelectedIndexChanged="DropDownList1_SelectedIndexChanged"
                AutoPostBack="true">
                <asp:ListItem>Select an Item</asp:ListItem>
                <asp:ListItem>Car</asp:ListItem>
                <asp:ListItem>Airplane</asp:ListItem>
                <asp:ListItem>Train</asp:ListItem>
            </asp:DropDownList> 
            <asp:DropDownList ID="DropDownList2" runat="server" Visible="false">
            </asp:DropDownList>
            <asp:Button ID="Button1" runat="server" Text="Select Options"
                OnClick="Button1_Click" />
        </div>
    </form>
</body>
</html>
```

C#

```
<%@ Page Language="C#" %>
<!DOCTYPE html>
<script runat="server">
    protected void DropDownList1_SelectedIndexChanged(object sender, EventArgs e)
    {
        string[] carArray = new[] { "Ford", "Honda", "BMW", "Dodge" };
        string[] airplaneArray = new[] {"Boeing 777", "Boeing 747",
            "Boeing 737"};
        string[] trainArray = new[] { "Bullet Train", "Amtrack", "Tram" };
        if (DropDownList1.SelectedValue == "Car")
        {
            DropDownList2.DataSource = carArray;
        }
        else if (DropDownList1.SelectedValue == "Airplane")
        {
            DropDownList2.DataSource = airplaneArray;
        }
        else if (DropDownList1.SelectedValue == "Train")
        {
            DropDownList2.DataSource = trainArray;
        }
        DropDownList2.DataBind();
        DropDownList2.Visible = DropDownList1.SelectedValue != "Select an Item";
    }
    protected void Button1_Click(object sender, EventArgs e)
    {
        Response.Write("You selected <b>" +
        DropDownList1.SelectedValue.ToString() + ": " +
        DropDownList2.SelectedValue.ToString() + "</b>");
    }
</script>
```

In this example, the second drop-down list is dynamically generated based upon the value selected from the first drop-down list. For instance, selecting Car from the first drop-down list dynamically creates a second drop-down list on the form that includes a list of available car selections.

This is possible because of the use of the `AutoPostBack` feature of the `DropDownList` control. When the `AutoPostBack` property is set to `True`, the method provided through the `OnSelectedIndexChanged` event is fired when a selection is made. In the example, the `DropDownList1_SelectedIndexChanged` event is fired, dynamically creating the second drop-down list.

In this method, the content of the second drop-down list is created in a string array and then bound to the second DropDownList control through the use of the `DataSource` property and the `DataBind()` method.

When built and run, this page looks like the one shown in Figure 5-9.

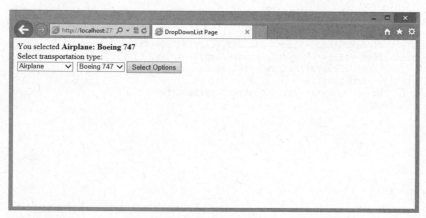

FIGURE 5-9

VISUALLY REMOVING ITEMS FROM A COLLECTION

The DropDownList, ListBox, CheckBoxList, and RadioButtonList server controls give you the capability to visually remove items from the collection displayed in the control, although you can still work with the items that are not displayed in your server-side code.

> **NOTE** *The ListBox, CheckBoxList, and RadioButtonList controls are discussed shortly in this chapter.*

For a quick example of removing items, create a drop-down list with three items, including one that you will not display. On the postback, however, you can still work with the ListItem's `Value` or `Text` property, as illustrated in Listing 5-11.

LISTING 5-11: Disabling certain ListItems from a collection

VB

```vb
<%@ Page Language="VB" %>
<!DOCTYPE html>
<script runat="server">
    Protected Sub DropDownList1_SelectedIndexChanged(ByVal sender As Object,
        ByVal e As System.EventArgs)
        Response.Write("You selected item number " &
            DropDownList1.SelectedValue & "<br>")
        Response.Write("You didn't select item number " &
            DropDownList1.Items(1).Value)
    End Sub
```
```
    End Sub
```

continues

LISTING 5-11 *(continued)*

```
    </script>
    <html xmlns="http://www.w3.org/1999/xhtml">
    <head runat="server">
        <title>DropDownList Server Control</title>
    </head>
    <body>
        <form id="form1" runat="server">
            <div>
                <asp:DropDownList ID="DropDownList1" runat="server"
                    AutoPostBack="True"
                    OnSelectedIndexChanged="DropDownList1_SelectedIndexChanged">
                    <asp:ListItem Value="1">First Choice</asp:ListItem>
                    <asp:ListItem Value="2" Enabled="False">Second
                        Choice</asp:ListItem>
                    <asp:ListItem Value="3">Third Choice</asp:ListItem>
                </asp:DropDownList>
            </div>
        </form>
    </body>
    </html>
```

C#

```
<%@ Page Language="C#" %>
<!DOCTYPE html>
<script runat="server">
    protected void DropDownList1_SelectedIndexChanged(object sender, EventArgs e)
    {
        Response.Write("You selected item number " +
            DropDownList1.SelectedValue + "<br>");
        Response.Write("You didn't select item number " +
            DropDownList1.Items[1].Value);
    }
</script>
```

From the code, you can see that the ListItem server control element has an attribute: `Enabled`. The `boolean` value given to this element dictates whether an item in the collection is displayed. If you use `Enabled="False"`, the item is not displayed, but you still have the capability to work with the item in the server-side code displayed in the `DropDownList1_SelectedIndexChanged` event. The result of the output from these `Response.Write` statements is shown in Figure 5-10.

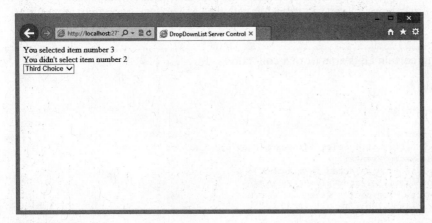

FIGURE 5-10

THE LISTBOX SERVER CONTROL

The ListBox server control has a function similar to the DropDownList control. It displays a collection of items. The ListBox control behaves differently from the DropDownList control in that it displays more of the collection to the end user, and it enables the end user to make multiple selections from the collection—something that is not possible with the DropDownList control.

A typical ListBox control appears in code as follows:

```
<asp:ListBox ID="ListBox1" runat="server">
    <asp:ListItem>ASP.NET 4.5</asp:ListItem>
    <asp:ListItem>ASP.NET MVC 4</asp:ListItem>
    <asp:ListItem>jQuery 1.8.x</asp:ListItem>
    <asp:ListItem>Visual Studio 2012</asp:ListItem>
</asp:ListBox>
```

This generates the browser display illustrated in Figure 5-11.

```
ASP.NET 4.5
ASP.NET MVC 4
jQuery 1.8.x
Visual Studio 2012
```

FIGURE 5-11

Allowing Users to Select Multiple Items

You can use the `SelectionMode` attribute to let your end users make multiple selections from what is displayed by the ListBox control. Here's an example:

```
<asp:ListBox ID="ListBox1" runat="server" SelectionMode="Multiple">
    <asp:ListItem>ASP.NET 4.5</asp:ListItem>
    <asp:ListItem>ASP.NET MVC 4</asp:ListItem>
    <asp:ListItem>jQuery 1.8.x</asp:ListItem>
    <asp:ListItem>Visual Studio 2012</asp:ListItem>
</asp:ListBox>
```

The possible values of the `SelectionMode` property include `Single` and `Multiple`. Setting the value to `Multiple` allows the end user to make multiple selections in the list box. The user must hold down either the Ctrl or Shift keys while making selections. Holding down the Ctrl key enables the user to make a single selection from the list while maintaining previous selections. Holding down the Shift key enables a range of multiple selections.

An Example of Using the ListBox Control

The ListBox control shown in Listing 5-12 allows multiple selections to be displayed in the browser when a user clicks the Submit button. The form should also have an additional textbox and button at the top that enables the end user to add additional items to the ListBox.

LISTING 5-12: Using the ListBox control

VB

```
<%@ Page Language="VB" %>
<!DOCTYPE html>
<script runat="server">
    Protected Sub Button1_Click(ByVal sender As Object,
        ByVal e As System.EventArgs)
        ListBox1.Items.Add(TextBox1.Text.ToString())
    End Sub
    Protected Sub Button2_Click(ByVal sender As Object,
    ByVal e As System.EventArgs)
        Label1.Text = "You selected from the ListBox:<br>"
        For Each li As ListItem In ListBox1.Items
            If li.Selected = True Then
                Label1.Text += li.Text & "<br>"
```

continues

LISTING 5-12 *(continued)*

```
                End If
            Next
        End Sub
    </script>
    <html xmlns="http://www.w3.org/1999/xhtml">
    <head runat="server">
        <title>Using the ListBox</title>
    </head>
    <body>
        <form id="form1" runat="server">
            <div>
                <asp:TextBox ID="TextBox1" runat="server"></asp:TextBox>
                <asp:Button ID="Button1" runat="server" Text="Add an additional item"
                    OnClick="Button1_Click" /><br />
                <asp:ListBox ID="ListBox1" runat="server" SelectionMode="Multiple">
                    <asp:ListItem>ASP.NET 4.5</asp:ListItem>
                    <asp:ListItem>ASP.NET MVC 4</asp:ListItem>
                    <asp:ListItem>jQuery 1.8.x</asp:ListItem>
                    <asp:ListItem>Visual Studio 2012</asp:ListItem>
                </asp:ListBox><br />
                <br />
                <asp:Button ID="Button2" runat="server" Text="Submit"
                    OnClick="Button2_Click" /><br />
                <br />
                <asp:Label ID="Label1" runat="server"></asp:Label>
            </div>
        </form>
    </body>
    </html>
```

C#

```
<%@ Page Language="C#" %>
<!DOCTYPE html>
<script runat="server">
    protected void Button1_Click(object sender, EventArgs e)
    {
        ListBox1.Items.Add(TextBox1.Text.ToString());
    }
    protected void Button2_Click(object sender, EventArgs e)
    {
        Label1.Text = "You selected from the ListBox:<br>";
        foreach (ListItem li in ListBox1.Items)
        {
            if (li.Selected)
            {
                Label1.Text += li.Text + "<br>";
            }
        }
    }
</script>
```

This is an interesting example. First, some default items (four commonly used products in ASP.NET web development) are already placed inside the ListBox control. However, the textbox and button at the top of the form allow the end user to add products to the list. Users can then make one or more selections from the ListBox, including selections from the items that they dynamically added to the collection. After a user makes his or her selection and clicks the button, the Button2_Click event iterates through the ListItem instances in the collection and displays only the items that have been selected.

This control works by creating an instance of a `ListItem` object and using its `Selected` property to see if a particular item in the collection has been selected. The use of the `ListItem` object is not limited to the ListBox control (although that is what is used here). You can dynamically add or remove items from a collection and get at items and their values using the `ListItem` object in the DropDownList, CheckBoxList, and RadioButtonList controls as well. It is a list-control feature. When this page is built and run, you get the results presented in Figure 5-12.

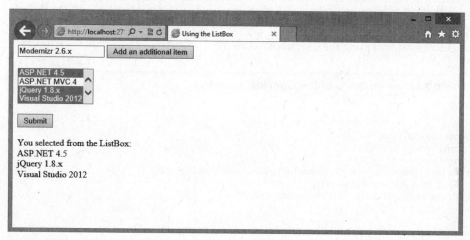

FIGURE 5-12

Adding Items to a Collection

To add items to the collection, you can use the following short syntax:

```
ListBox1.Items.Add(TextBox1.Text)
```

Look at the source code created in the browser, and you should see something similar to the following generated dynamically:

```
<select size="4" name="ListBox1" multiple="multiple" id="ListBox1">
    <option value="ASP.NET 4.5">ASP.NET 4.5</option>
    <option value="ASP.NET MVC 4">ASP.NET MVC 4</option>
    <option value="jQuery 1.8.x">jQuery 1.8.x</option>
    <option value="Visual Studio 2012">Visual Studio 2012</option>
    <option value="Modernizr 2.6.x">Modernizr 2.6.x</option>
</select>
```

You can see that the dynamically added value is a text item, and you can see its value. You can also add instances of the `ListItem` object to get different values for the item name and value:

VB

```
ListBox1.Items.Add(New ListItem("Modernizr 2.6.x", "Modernizr"))
```

C#

```
ListBox1.Items.Add(new ListItem("Modernizr 2.6.x", "Modernizr"));
```

This example adds a new instance of the `ListItem` object—adding not only the textual name and version of the item, but also the value of the item (its name only). It produces the following results in the browser:

```
<option value="Modernizr">Modernizr 2.6.x</option>
```

THE CHECKBOX SERVER CONTROL

Check boxes on a web form enable your users to make selections from a collection of items or to specify a value of an item to be yes/no, on/off, or true/false. Use either the CheckBox control or the CheckBoxList control to include check boxes in your Web Forms.

The CheckBox control allows you to place single check boxes on a form; the CheckBoxList control allows you to place collections of check boxes on the form. You can use multiple CheckBox controls on your ASP .NET pages, but each check box is treated as its own element with its own associated events. On the other hand, the CheckBoxList control allows multiple check boxes and specific events for the entire group.

Listing 5-13 shows an example of using the CheckBox control.

LISTING 5-13: Using a single instance of the CheckBox control

VB

```
<%@ Page Language="VB" %>
<!DOCTYPE html>
<script runat="server">
    Protected Sub CheckBox1_CheckedChanged(ByVal sender As Object,
        ByVal e As System.EventArgs)
        Response.Write("Thanks for your donation!")
    End Sub
</script>
<html xmlns="http://www.w3.org/1999/xhtml">
<head runat="server">
    <title>CheckBox control</title>
</head>
<body>
    <form id="form1" runat="server">
    <div>
    <asp:CheckBox ID="CheckBox1" runat="server" Text="Donate $10 to my cause!"
        OnCheckedChanged="CheckBox1_CheckedChanged" AutoPostBack="true" />
    </div>
    </form>
</body>
</html>
```

C#

```
<%@ Page Language="C#" %>
<!DOCTYPE html>
<script runat="server">
    protected void CheckBox1_CheckedChanged(object sender, EventArgs e)
    {
        Response.Write("Thanks for your donation!");
    }
</script>
```

This produces a page that contains a single check box asking for a monetary donation. Using the CheckedChanged event, OnCheckedChanged is used within the CheckBox control. The attribute's value points to the CheckBox1_CheckedChanged event, which fires when the user checks the check box. It occurs only if the AutoPostBack property is set to True (this property is set to False by default). Running this page produces the results shown in Figure 5-13.

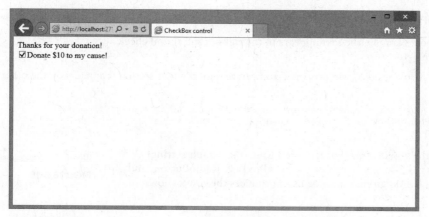

FIGURE 5-13

How to Determine Whether Check Boxes Are Checked

You might not want to use the `AutoPostBack` feature of the check box, but instead want to determine if the check box is checked after the form is posted back to the server. You can make this check through an `If Then` statement, as illustrated in the following example:

VB

```
If (CheckBox1.Checked = True) Then
    Response.Write("Thanks for your donation!")
End If
```

C#

```
if (CheckBox1.Checked == true)
{
    Response.Write("Thanks for your donation!");
}
```

This check is done on the CheckBox value using the control's `Checked` property. The property's value is a `boolean` value, so it is either `True` (checked) or `False` (not checked).

> **NOTE** *In both Visual Basic and C#, you can eliminate the check for a true value and simply call the following (shown in C# here):* `if (CheckBox1.Checked) {. . .}`.

Assigning a Value to a Check Box

You can also use the `Checked` property to make sure a check box is checked based on other dynamic values:

VB

```
If (Member = True) Then
    CheckBox1.Checked = True
End If
```

C#

```
if (Member == true)
{
    CheckBox1.Checked = true;
}
```

Aligning Text around the Check Box

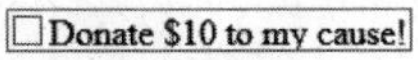

FIGURE 5-14

In the previous check box example, the text appears to the right of the actual check box, as shown in Figure 5-14.

Using the CheckBox control's `TextAlign` property, you can realign the text so that it appears on the other side of the check box:

```
<asp:CheckBox ID="CheckBox1" runat="server" Text="Donate $10 to my cause!"
    OnCheckedChanged="CheckBox1_CheckedChanged" AutoPostBack="true"
    TextAlign="Left" />
```

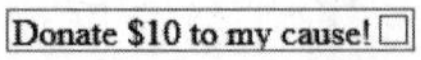

The possible values of the `TextAlign` property are `Right` (the default setting) and `Left`. This property is also available to the CheckBoxList, RadioButton, and RadioButtonList controls. Assigning the value `Left` produces the result shown in Figure 5-15.

FIGURE 5-15

THE CHECKBOXLIST SERVER CONTROL

The CheckBoxList server control is quite similar to the CheckBox control, except that the former enables you to work with a collection of items rather than a single item. The idea is that a CheckBoxList server control instance is a collection of related items, each being a check box unto itself.

To see the CheckBoxList control in action, you can build an example that uses Microsoft's SQL Server to pull information from the Customer table of the AdventureWorks sample database. An example is presented in Listing 5-14.

> **NOTE** *You can download the version of the AdventureWorks database we used for this book from* `www.wrox.com/go/SQLServer2012DataSets`.

LISTING 5-14: Dynamically populating a CheckBoxList

VB

```
<%@ Page Language="VB" %>
<!DOCTYPE html>
<script runat="server">
    Protected Sub Button1_Click(ByVal sender As Object,
      ByVal e As System.EventArgs)
        Label1.Text = "You selected:<br>"
        For Each li As ListItem In CheckBoxList1.Items
            If li.Selected = True Then
                Label1.Text += li.Text & "<br>"
            End If
        Next
    End Sub
</script>
<html xmlns="http://www.w3.org/1999/xhtml">
<head id="Head1" runat="server">
    <title>CheckBoxList control</title>
</head>
<body>
    <form id="form1" runat="server">
        <div>
            <asp:Button ID="Button1" runat="server" Text="Submit Choices"
```

```
                                 OnClick="Button1_Click" /><br />
                    <br />
                    <asp:Label ID="Label1" runat="server"></asp:Label>
                    <br />
                    <asp:CheckBoxList ID="CheckBoxList1" runat="server"
                        DataSourceID="SqlDataSource1" DataTextField="CompanyName"
                        RepeatColumns="3" BorderColor="Black"
                        BorderStyle="Solid" BorderWidth="1px">
                    </asp:CheckBoxList>
                    <asp:SqlDataSource ID="SqlDataSource1" runat="server"
                        SelectCommand="SELECT DISTINCT TOP 12 [CompanyName]
                        FROM [SalesLT].[Customer] ORDER BY [CompanyName]"
                        ConnectionString="
                           <%$ ConnectionStrings:AdventureWorksConnectionString %>">
                    </asp:SqlDataSource>
                </div>
            </form>
    </body>
    </html>
```

C#

```
<%@ Page Language="C#" %>
<!DOCTYPE html>
<script runat="server">
    protected void Button1_Click(object sender, EventArgs e)
    {
        Label1.Text = "You selected:<br>";
        foreach (ListItem li in CheckBoxList1.Items)
        {
            if (li.Selected == true)
            {
                Label1.Text += li.Text + "<br>";
            }
        }
    }
</script>
```

This ASP.NET page has a SqlDataSource control on the page that pulls the information you need from the Adventure Works database. From the SELECT statement used in this control, you can see that you are retrieving the CompanyName field from the top 10 unique listings in the Customer table.

The CheckBoxList control binds itself to the SqlDataSource control using a few properties:

```
<asp:CheckBoxList ID="CheckBoxList1" runat="server"
    DataSourceID="SqlDataSource1" DataTextField="CompanyName"
    RepeatColumns="3" BorderColor="Black"
    BorderStyle="Solid" BorderWidth="1px">
</asp:CheckBoxList>
```

The DataSourceID property is used to associate the CheckBoxList control with the results that come back from the SqlDataSource control. Then the DataTextField property is used to retrieve the name of the field you want to work with from the results. In this example, there is only one that is available: the CompanyName. That's it! CheckBoxList generates the results you want.

The remaining code consists of styling properties, which are pretty interesting. The BorderColor, BorderStyle, and BorderWidth properties enable you to put a border around the entire check box list. The most interesting property is the RepeatColumns property, which specifies how many columns (three in this example) can be used to display the results.

When you run the page, you get the results shown in Figure 5-16.

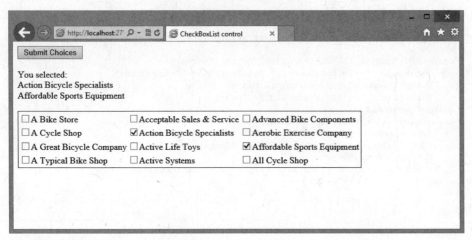

FIGURE 5-16

The RepeatDirection property instructs the CheckBoxList control about how to lay out the items bound to the control on the web page. Possible values include Vertical and Horizontal. The default value is Vertical. Setting it to Vertical with a RepeatColumn setting of 3 gives the following results:

CheckBox1	CheckBox4	CheckBox7
CheckBox2	CheckBox5	CheckBox8
CheckBox3	CheckBox6	CheckBox9

When the RepeatDirection property is set to Horizontal, you get the check box items laid out in a horizontal fashion:

CheckBox1	CheckBox2	CheckBox3
CheckBox4	CheckBox5	CheckBox6
CheckBox7	CheckBox8	CheckBox9

THE RADIOBUTTON SERVER CONTROL

The RadioButton server control is quite similar to the CheckBox server control. It places a radio button on your web page. Unlike a check box, however, a single radio button on a form does not make much sense. Radio buttons are generally form elements that require at least two options. A typical set of RadioButton controls on a page takes the following construction:

```
<asp:RadioButton ID="RadioButton1" runat="server" Text="Yes" GroupName="Set1" />
<asp:RadioButton ID="RadioButton2" runat="server" Text="No" GroupName="Set1"/>
```

Figure 5-17 shows the result.

Yes No

FIGURE 5-17

When you look at the code for the RadioButton control, note the standard Text property that places the text next to the radio button on the web form. The more important property here is GroupName, which can be set in one of the RadioButton controls to match what it is set to in the other. This enables the radio buttons on the web form to work together for the end user. How do they work together? Well, when one of the radio buttons on the form is checked, the circle associated with the item selected appears filled in. Any other filled-in circle from the same group in the collection is removed, ensuring that only one of the radio buttons in the collection is selected.

Listing 5-15 shows an example of using the RadioButton control.

LISTING 5-15: Using the RadioButton server control

VB

```
<%@ Page Language="VB" %>
<!DOCTYPE html>
<script runat="server">
    Protected Sub RadioButton_CheckedChanged(ByVal sender As Object,
        ByVal e As System.EventArgs)
        If RadioButton1.Checked = True Then
            Response.Write("You selected Visual Basic")
        Else
            Response.Write("You selected C#")
        End If
    End Sub
</script>
<html xmlns="http://www.w3.org/1999/xhtml">
<head id="Head1" runat="server">
    <title>RadioButton control</title>
</head>
<body>
    <form id="form1" runat="server">
        <div>
            <asp:RadioButton ID="RadioButton1" runat="server" Text="Visual Basic"
                GroupName="LanguageChoice"
                OnCheckedChanged="RadioButton_CheckedChanged"
                AutoPostBack="True" />
            <asp:RadioButton ID="RadioButton2" runat="server" Text="C#"
                GroupName="LanguageChoice"
                OnCheckedChanged="RadioButton_CheckedChanged"
                AutoPostBack="True" />
        </div>
    </form>
</body>
</html>
```

C#

```
<%@ Page Language="C#" %>
<!DOCTYPE html>
<script runat="server">
    protected void RadioButton_CheckedChanged(object sender, EventArgs e)
    {
        if (RadioButton1.Checked == true)
        {
            Response.Write("You selected Visual Basic");
        }
        else
        {
            Response.Write("You selected C#");
        }
    }
</script>
```

Like the CheckBox, the RadioButton control has a CheckedChanged event that puts an OnCheckedChanged attribute in the control. The attribute's value points to the server-side event that is fired when a selection is made using one of the two radio buttons on the form. Remember that the AutoPostBack property needs to be set to True for this to work correctly.

Figure 5-18 shows the results.

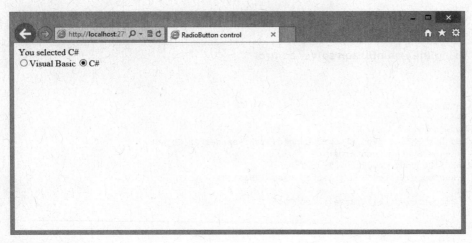

FIGURE 5-18

One advantage that the RadioButton control has over a RadioButtonList control (which is discussed next) is that it enables you to place other items (text, controls, or images) between the RadioButton controls themselves. RadioButtonList, however, is always a straight list of radio buttons on your web page.

THE RADIOBUTTONLIST SERVER CONTROL

The RadioButtonList server control lets you display a collection of radio buttons on a web page. The RadioButtonList control is quite similar to the CheckBoxList and other list controls in that it allows you to iterate through to see what the user selected, to make counts, or to perform other actions.

A typical RadioButtonList control is written to the page in the following manner:

```
<asp:RadioButtonList ID="RadioButtonList1" runat="server">
    <asp:ListItem Selected="True">English</asp:ListItem>
    <asp:ListItem>Russian</asp:ListItem>
    <asp:ListItem>Finnish</asp:ListItem>
    <asp:ListItem>Swedish</asp:ListItem>
</asp:RadioButtonList>
```

Like the other list controls, this one uses instances of the `ListItem` object for each of the items contained in the collection. From the example, you can see that if the `Selected` property is set to `True`, one of the `ListItem` objects is selected by default when the page is generated for the first time. This produces the results shown in Figure 5-19.

FIGURE 5-19

The `Selected` property is not required, but it is a good idea if you want the end user to make some sort of selection from this collection. Using it makes it impossible to leave the collection blank.

You can use the RadioButtonList control to check for the value selected by the end user in any of your page methods. Listing 5-16 shows a `Button1_Click` event that pushes out the value selected in the RadioButtonList collection.

LISTING 5-16: Checking the value of the item selected from a RadioButtonList control

VB

```
<%@ Page Language="VB" %>
<!DOCTYPE html>
<script runat="server">
    Protected Sub Button1_Click(ByVal sender As Object,
        ByVal e As System.EventArgs)
        Label1.Text = "You selected: " &
        RadioButtonList1.SelectedItem.ToString()
    End Sub
</script>
<html xmlns="http://www.w3.org/1999/xhtml">
<head id="Head1" runat="server">
    <title>RadioButtonList Control</title>
</head>
<body>
    <form id="form1" runat="server">
        <div>
            <asp:Label ID="Label1" runat="server" />
            <asp:RadioButtonList ID="RadioButtonList1" runat="server">
                <asp:ListItem Selected="True">English</asp:ListItem>
                <asp:ListItem>Russian</asp:ListItem>
                <asp:ListItem>Finnish</asp:ListItem>
                <asp:ListItem>Swedish</asp:ListItem>
            </asp:RadioButtonList>
            <asp:Button ID="Button1" runat="server" Text="Submit"
                OnClick="Button1_Click" />
        </div>
    </form>
</body>
</html>
```

C#

```
<%@ Page Language="C#" %>
<!DOCTYPE html>
<script runat="server">
    protected void Button1_Click(object sender, EventArgs e)
    {
        Label1.Text = "You selected: " + RadioButtonList1.SelectedItem.ToString();
    }
</script>
```

This bit of code gets at the item selected from the RadioButtonList collection of `ListItem` objects. It is how you work with other list controls that are provided in ASP.NET. The RadioButtonList also affords you access to the `RepeatColumns` and `RepeatDirection` properties (these were explained in the CheckBoxList section). You can bind this control to items that come from any of the data source controls so that you can dynamically create radio button lists on your web pages.

IMAGE SERVER CONTROL

The Image server control enables you to work with the images that appear on your web page from the server-side code. It is a simple server control, but it can give you the power to determine how your images are displayed on the browser screen. A typical Image control is constructed in the following manner:

```
<asp:Image ID="Image1" runat="server" ImageUrl="~/Images/Windows.jpg" />
```

The important property here is `ImageUrl`. It points to the file location of the image. In this case, the location is specified as the `Windows.jpg` file.

Listing 5-17 shows an example of how to change the `ImageUrl` property dynamically.

VB

```vb
<%@ Page Language="VB" %>
<!DOCTYPE html>
<script runat="server">
    Protected Sub Button1_Click(ByVal sender As Object,
      ByVal e As System.EventArgs)
        Image1.ImageUrl = "~/Images/Windows8.jpg"
    End Sub
</script>
<html xmlns="http://www.w3.org/1999/xhtml">
<head id="Head1" runat="server">
    <title>Image Control</title>
</head>
<body>
    <form id="form1" runat="server">
        <div>
            <asp:Image ID="Image1" runat="server"
              ImageUrl="~/Images/Windows.jpg" /><br />
            <br />
            <asp:Button ID="Button1" runat="server" Text="Change Image"
                OnClick="Button1_Click" />
        </div>
    </form>
</body>
</html>
```

C#

```csharp
<%@ Page Language="C#" %>
<!DOCTYPE html>
<script runat="server">
    protected void Button1_Click(object sender, EventArgs e)
    {
        Image1.ImageUrl = "~/Images/Windows8.jpg";
    }
</script>
```

In this example, an image (`Windows.jpg`) is shown in the browser when the page is loaded for the first time. When the end user clicks the button on the page, a new image (`Windows8.jpg`) is loaded in the postback process.

Special circumstances can prevent end users from viewing an image that is part of your web page. They might be physically unable to see the image, or they might be using a text-only browser. In these cases, their browsers look for the `<img>` element's `longdesc` attribute that points to a file containing a long description of the image that is displayed.

For these cases, the Image server control includes a `DescriptionUrl` attribute. The value assigned to it is a text file that contains a thorough description of the image with which it is associated. Here is how to use it:

```
<asp:Image ID="Image1" runat="server" ImageUrl="~/Images/Windows.jpg"
    DescriptionUrl="~/WindowsImage.txt" />
```

This code produces the following results in the browser:

```
<img id="Image1" src="Images/Windows.jpg" longdesc="WindowsImage.txt" />
```

Remember that the image does not support the user clicking the image. If you want to program events based on button clicks, use the ImageButton server control discussed earlier in this chapter.

TABLE SERVER CONTROL

Tables are one of the web page's more common elements because the HTML `<table>` element is one of the most common formats utilized for displaying numerous records of information. The typical construction of the Table server control is as follows:

```
<asp:Table ID="Table1" runat="server">
    <asp:TableRow ID="TableRow1" runat="server" Font-Bold="True"
        ForeColor="White" BackColor="DarkGray">
        <asp:TableHeaderCell>First Name</asp:TableHeaderCell>
        <asp:TableHeaderCell>Last Name</asp:TableHeaderCell>
    </asp:TableRow>
    <asp:TableRow>
        <asp:TableCell>Jason</asp:TableCell>
        <asp:TableCell>Gaylord</asp:TableCell>
    </asp:TableRow>
    <asp:TableRow>
        <asp:TableCell>Scott</asp:TableCell>
        <asp:TableCell>Hanselman</asp:TableCell>
    </asp:TableRow>
    <asp:TableRow>
        <asp:TableCell>Todd</asp:TableCell>
        <asp:TableCell>Miranda</asp:TableCell>
    </asp:TableRow>
    <asp:TableRow>
        <asp:TableCell>Pranav</asp:TableCell>
        <asp:TableCell>Rastogi</asp:TableCell>
    </asp:TableRow>
</asp:Table>
```

First Name	Last Name
Jason	Gaylord
Scott	Hanselman
Todd	Miranda
Pranav	Rastogi
Christian	Wenz

FIGURE 5-20

This produces the simple two-rowed table shown in Figure 5-20.

You can do a lot with the Table server control. For example, you can dynamically add rows to the table, as illustrated in Listing 5-18.

LISTING 5-18: Dynamically adding rows to the table

VB

```
<%@ Page Language="VB" %>
<!DOCTYPE html>
<script runat="server">
    Protected Sub Page_Load(ByVal sender As Object, ByVal e As System.EventArgs)
        Dim tr As New TableRow()
        Dim fname As New TableCell()
        fname.Text = "Christian"
        tr.Cells.Add(fname)
        Dim lname As New TableCell()
        lname.Text = "Wenz"
        tr.Cells.Add(lname)
        Table1.Rows.Add(tr)
    End Sub
</script>
```

C#

```
<%@ Page Language="C#" %>
<!DOCTYPE html>
<script runat="server">
    protected void Page_Load(object sender, EventArgs e)
    {
        TableRow tr = new TableRow();
        TableCell fname = new TableCell();
```

continues

LISTING 5-18 *(continued)*

```
                fname.Text = "Christian";
                tr.Cells.Add(fname);
                TableCell lname = new TableCell();
                lname.Text = "Wenz";
                tr.Cells.Add(lname);
                Table1.Rows.Add(tr);
        }
    </script>
```

To add a single row to a Table control, you have to create new instances of the `TableRow` and `TableCell` objects. You create the `TableCell` objects first and then place them within a `TableRow` object that is added to a `Table` object.

The Table server control obviously contains some extra features beyond what has been presented. One of the simpler features is the capability to add captions to the tables on web pages. Figure 5-21 shows a table with a caption.

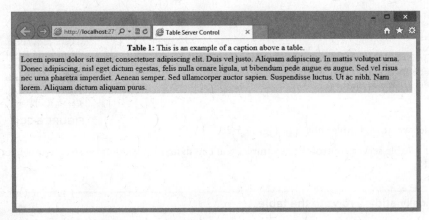

FIGURE 5-21

To give your table a caption, simply use the `Caption` attribute in the Table control, as illustrated in Listing 5-19.

LISTING 5-19: Using the Caption attribute

```
<%@ Page Language="C#" %>
<html xmlns="http://www.w3.org/1999/xhtml">
<head runat="server">
    <title>Table Server Control</title>
</head>
<body>
    <form id="form1" runat="server">
        <asp:Table ID="Table1" runat="server"
            Caption="<b>Table 1:</b> This is an example of a caption above a
                table."
            BackColor="Gainsboro">
            <asp:TableRow ID="Tablerow1" runat="server">
                <asp:TableCell ID="Tablecell1" runat="server">
                    Lorem ipsum dolor sit
                    amet, consectetuer adipiscing elit. Duis vel justo. Aliquam
                    adipiscing. In mattis volutpat urna. Donec adipiscing, nisl ege
                    dictum egestas, felis nulla ornare ligula, ut bibendum pede aug
                    eu augue. Sed vel risus nec urna pharetra imperdiet. Aenean
```

```
                    semper. Sed ullamcorper auctor sapien. Suspendisse luctus. Ut a
                    nibh. Nam lorem. Aliquam dictum aliquam purus.
                </asp:TableCell>
            </asp:TableRow>
        </asp:Table>
    </form>
</body>
</html>
```

By default, the caption is placed at the top center of the table, but you can control where it is placed by using another attribute—`CaptionAlign`. Its settings include `Bottom`, `Left`, `NotSet`, `Right`, and `Top`.

In the early days of ASP.NET, an `<asp:Table>` element contained any number of `<asp:TableRow>` elements. In ASP.NET 4.5, you can nest some additional elements within the `<asp:Table>` element. These elements include `<asp:TableHeaderRow>` and `<asp:TableFooterRow>`. They add either a header or footer to your table, enabling you to use the Table server control to page through lots of data but still retain some text in place to indicate the type of data being handled. This is quite a powerful feature when you work with mobile applications that dictate that sometimes end users can move through only a few records at a time.

THE CALENDAR SERVER CONTROL

The Calendar server control is a rich control that enables you to place a full-featured calendar directly on your web pages. It allows for a high degree of customization to ensure that it looks and behaves in a unique manner. The Calendar control, in its simplest form, is coded in the following manner:

```
<asp:Calendar ID="Calendar1" runat="server"></asp:Calendar>
```

This code produces a calendar on your web page without any styles added, as shown in Figure 5-22.

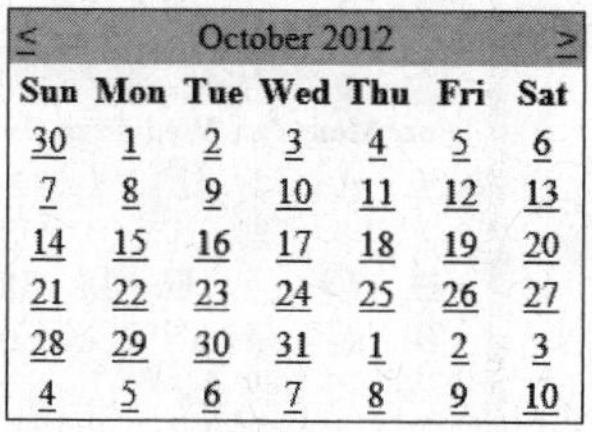

Making a Date Selection from the Calendar Control

The calendar allows you to navigate through the months of the year and to select specific days in the exposed month. A simple application that enables the user to select a day of the month is shown in Listing 5-20.

FIGURE 5-22

LISTING 5-20: Selecting a single day in the Calendar control

VB

```vb
<%@ Page Language="VB" %>
<!DOCTYPE html>
<script runat="server">
    Protected Sub Calendar1_SelectionChanged(ByVal sender As Object,
        ByVal e As System.EventArgs)
        Response.Write("You selected: " &
            Calendar1.SelectedDate.ToShortDateString())
    End Sub
</script>
<html xmlns="http://www.w3.org/1999/xhtml">
<head id="Head1" runat="server">
    <title>Using the Calendar Control</title>
</head>
<body>
    <form id="form1" runat="server">
        <div>
            <asp:Calendar ID="Calendar1" runat="server"
                OnSelectionChanged="Calendar1_SelectionChanged"></asp:Calendar>
        </div>
```

continues

LISTING 5-20 *(continued)*

```
            </form>
        </body>
        </html>
```

C#

```
<%@ Page Language="C#" %>
<!DOCTYPE html>
<script runat="server">
    protected void Calendar1_SelectionChanged(object sender, EventArgs e)
    {
        Response.Write("You selected: " +
            Calendar1.SelectedDate.ToShortDateString());
    }
</script>
```

Running this application pulls up the calendar in the browser. The end user can then select a single date in it. After a date is selected, the `Calendar1_SelectionChanged` event is triggered and makes use of the `OnSelectionChange` attribute. This event writes the value of the selected date to the screen. The result is shown in Figure 5-23.

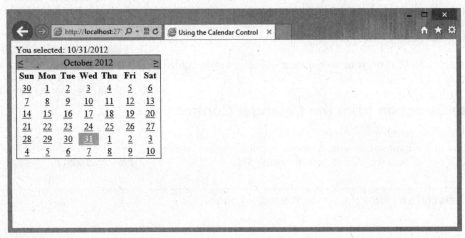

FIGURE 5-23

Choosing a Date Format to Output from the Calendar

When you use the `Calendar1_SelectionChanged` event, the selected date is written out using the `ToShortDateString()` method. The Calendar control also allows you to write out the date in a number of other formats, as detailed in the following list:

➤ `ToFileTime`: Converts the selection to the local operating system file time: `129961296000000000`.

➤ `ToFileTimeUtc`: Converts the selection to the operating system file time, but instead of using the local time zone, the UTC time is used: `129961152000000000`.

➤ `ToLocalTime`: Converts the current coordinated universal time (UTC) to local time: `10/30/2012 8:00:00 PM`.

➤ `ToLongDateString`: Converts the selection to a human-readable string in a long format: `Wednesday, October 31, 2012`.

➤ `ToLongTimeString`: Converts the selection to a time value (no date is included) of a long format: `12:00:00 AM`.

➤ ToOADate: Converts the selection to an OLE Automation date equivalent: 41213.

➤ ToShortDateString: Converts the selection to a human-readable string in a short format: 10/31/2012.

➤ ToShortTimeString: Converts the selection to a time value (no date is included) in a short format: 12:00 AM.

➤ ToString: Converts the selection to the following: 10/31/2012 12:00:00 AM.

➤ ToUniversalTime: Converts the selection to universal time (UTC): 10/31/2012 4:00:00 AM.

Making Day, Week, or Month Selections

By default, the Calendar control enables you to make single day selections. You can use the SelectionMode property to change this behavior to allow your users to make week or month selections from the calendar instead. The possible values of this property include Day, DayWeek, DayWeekMonth, and None.

The Day setting enables you to click a specific day in the calendar to highlight it (this is the default). When you use the setting of DayWeek, you can still make individual day selections, but you can also click the arrow next to the week (see Figure 5-24) to make selections that consist of an entire week. Using the setting of DayWeekMonth lets users make individual day selections or week selections. A new arrow appears in the upper-left corner of the calendar that enables users to select an entire month (also shown in Figure 5-24). A setting of None means that it is impossible for the end user to make any selections, which is useful for calendars on your site that are informational only.

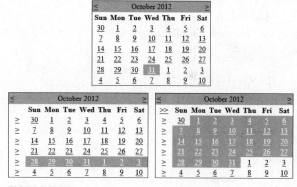

FIGURE 5-24

Working with Date Ranges

Even if an end user makes a selection that encompasses an entire week or an entire month, you get back from the selection only the first date of this range. If, for example, you allow users to select an entire month and one selects October 2012, what you get back (using ToShortDateString()) is 10/1/2012 — the first date in the date range of the selection. That might work for you, but if you require all the dates in the selected range, Listing 5-21 shows you how to get them.

LISTING 5-21: Retrieving a range of dates from a selection

VB

```
<%@ Page Language="VB" %>
<!DOCTYPE html>
<script runat="server">
    Protected Sub Calendar1_SelectionChanged(ByVal sender As Object,
        ByVal e As System.EventArgs)
        Label1.Text = "<b><u>You selected the following date/dates:</u></b><br>"
        For i As Integer = 0 To (Calendar1.SelectedDates.Count - 1)
            Label1.Text += Calendar1.SelectedDates.Item(i).ToShortDateString() &
                "<br>"
        Next
    End Sub
</script>
<html xmlns="http://www.w3.org/1999/xhtml">
<head id="Head1" runat="server">
```

continues

LISTING 5-21 *(continued)*

```
        <title>Using the Calendar Control</title>
    </head>
    <body>
        <form id="form1" runat="server">
            <div>
                <asp:Calendar ID="Calendar1" runat="server"
                    OnSelectionChanged="Calendar1_SelectionChanged"
                    SelectionMode="DayWeekMonth"></asp:Calendar>
                <p>
                    <asp:Label ID="Label1" runat="server"></asp:Label>
                </p>
            </div>
        </form>
    </body>
</html>
```

C#

```
<%@ Page Language="C#" %>
<!DOCTYPE html>
<script runat="server">
    protected void Calendar1_SelectionChanged(object sender, EventArgs e)
    {
        Label1.Text = "<b><u>You selected the following date/dates:</u></b><br>";
        for (int i = 0; i < Calendar1.SelectedDates.Count; i++)
        {
            Label1.Text += Calendar1.SelectedDates[i].ToShortDateString() +
            "<br>";
        }
    }
</script>
```

In this example, the Calendar control lets users make selections that can be an individual day, a week, or even a month. Using a `For Next` loop, you iterate through a selection by using the `SelectedDates.Count` property. The code produces the results shown in Figure 5-25.

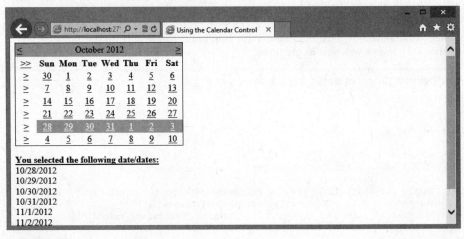

FIGURE 5-25

You can get just the first day of the selection by using the following:

VB

```
Calendar1.SelectedDates.Item(0).ToShortDateString()
```

C#

```
Calendar1.SelectedDates[0].ToShortDateString();
```

And you can get the last date in the selected range by using:

VB

```
Calendar1.SelectedDates.Item(Calendar1.SelectedDates.Count-1).ToShortDateString()
```

C#

```
Calendar1.SelectedDates[Calendar1.SelectedDates.Count-1].ToShortDateString();
```

As you can see, this is possible using the `Count` property of the `SelectedDates` object.

Modifying the Style and Behavior of Your Calendar

There is a lot to the Calendar control—definitely more than can be covered in this chapter. One nice thing about the Calendar control is the ease of extensibility that it offers. Begin exploring new ways to customize this control further by looking at one of the easiest ways to change it—applying a style to the control.

Using Visual Studio, you can give the controls a new look-and-feel from the Design view of the page you are working with. Highlight the Calendar control and open the control's smart tag to see the Auto Format link. That gives you a list of available styles that can be applied to your Calendar control.

> **NOTE** *The Calendar control is not alone in this capability. Many other rich controls offer a list of styles. You can always find this capability in the control's smart tag.*

Some of the styles are shown in Figure 5-26.

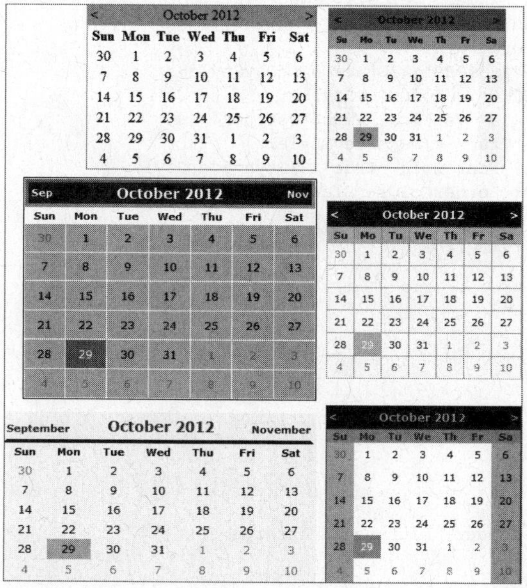

FIGURE 5-26

In addition to changing the style of the Calendar control, you can work with the control during its rendering process. The Calendar control includes an event called `DayRender` that allows you to control how a single date or all the dates in the calendar are rendered. Listing 5-22 shows an example of how to change one of the dates being rendered in the calendar.

LISTING 5-22: Controlling how a day is rendered in the calendar

VB

```vb
<%@ Page Language="VB" %>
<!DOCTYPE html>
<script runat="server">
    Protected Sub Calendar1_DayRender(ByVal sender As Object,
        ByVal e As System.Web.UI.WebControls.DayRenderEventArgs)
        e.Cell.VerticalAlign = VerticalAlign.Top
        If (e.Day.DayNumberText = "25") Then
            e.Cell.Controls.Add(New LiteralControl("<p>User Group Meeting!</p>"))
            e.Cell.BorderColor = Drawing.Color.Black
            e.Cell.BorderWidth = 1
            e.Cell.BorderStyle = BorderStyle.Solid
            e.Cell.BackColor = Drawing.Color.LightGray
        End If
    End Sub
</script>
<html xmlns="http://www.w3.org/1999/xhtml">
<head id="Head1" runat="server">
    <title>Using the Calendar Control</title>
</head>
<body>
    <form id="form1" runat="server">
        <div>
            <asp:Calendar ID="Calendar1" runat="server"
                OnDayRender="Calendar1_DayRender" Height="190px"
                BorderColor="White"
                Width="350px" ForeColor="Black" BackColor="White" BorderWidth="1px"
                NextPrevFormat="FullMonth" Font-Names="Verdana" Font-Size="9pt">
                <SelectedDayStyle ForeColor="White"
                    BackColor="#333399"></SelectedDayStyle>
                <OtherMonthDayStyle ForeColor="#999999"></OtherMonthDayStyle>
                <TodayDayStyle BackColor="#CCCCCC"></TodayDayStyle>
                <NextPrevStyle ForeColor="#333333" VerticalAlign="Bottom"
                    Font-Size="8pt" Font-Bold="True"></NextPrevStyle>
                <DayHeaderStyle Font-Size="8pt" Font-Bold="True"></DayHeaderStyle>
                <TitleStyle ForeColor="#333399" BorderColor="Black"
                    Font-Size="12pt" Font-Bold="True"
                    BackColor="White" BorderWidth="4px">
                </TitleStyle>
            </asp:Calendar>
        </div>
    </form>
</body>
</html>
```

C#

```csharp
<%@ Page Language="C#" %>
<!DOCTYPE html>
<script runat="server">
    protected void Calendar1_DayRender(object sender, DayRenderEventArgs e)
    {
        e.Cell.VerticalAlign = VerticalAlign.Top;
        if (e.Day.DayNumberText == "18")
        {
```

```
                e.Cell.Controls.Add(new LiteralControl("<p>User Group Meeting!</p>"));
                e.Cell.BorderColor = System.Drawing.Color.Black;
                e.Cell.BorderWidth = 1;
                e.Cell.BorderStyle = BorderStyle.Solid;
                e.Cell.BackColor = System.Drawing.Color.LightGray;
            }
        }
    </script>
```

In this example, you use a Calendar control with a little style to it. When the page is built and run in the browser, you can see that the 18th of every month in the calendar has been changed by the code in the `Calendar1_DayRender` event. The calendar is shown in Figure 5-27.

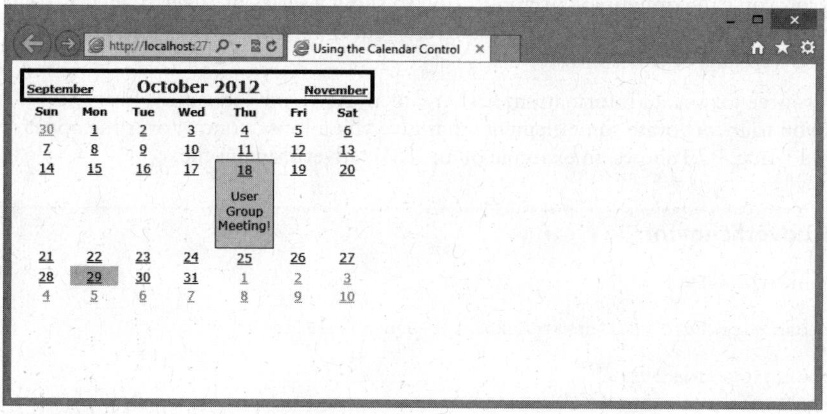

FIGURE 5-27

The Calendar control in this example adds an `OnDayRender` attribute that points to the `Calendar1_DayRender` event. The method is run for each of the days rendered in the calendar. The class constructor shows that you are not working with the typical `System.EventArgs` class, but instead with the `DayRenderEventArgs` class. It gives you access to each of the days rendered in the calendar.

The two main properties from the `DayRenderEventArgs` class are `Cell` and `Day`. The `Cell` property gives you access to the space in which the day is being rendered, and the `Day` property gives you access to the specific date being rendered in the cell.

From the actions being taken in the `Calendar1_DayRender` event, you can see that both properties are used. First, the `Cell` property sets the vertical alignment of the cell to `Top`. If it didn't, the table might look a little strange when one of the cells has content. Next, a check is made to determine if the day being rendered (checked with the `Day` property) is the 25th of the month. If it is, the `If Then` statement runs using the `Cell` property to change the styling of just that cell. The styling change adds a control, as well as makes changes to the border and color of the cell.

As you can see, working with individual dates in the calendar is fairly straightforward. You can easily give them the content and appearance you want.

A nice feature of the `Day` property is that you can turn off the option to select a particular date or range of dates by setting the `Day` property's `IsSelectable` property to `False`:

VB

```
Public Sub Calendar1_DayRender(sender As Object, e As DayRenderEventArgs)
    If (e.Day.Date < DateTime.Now) Then
        e.Day.IsSelectable = False
    End If
End Sub
```

C#

```
public void Calendar1_DayRender(Object sender, DayRenderEventArgs e)
{
    if (e.Day.Date < DateTime.Now)
    {
        e.Day.IsSelectable = false;
    }
}
```

ADROTATOR SERVER CONTROL

Although web users find ads rather annoying, advertising continues to be prevalent everywhere on the web. With the AdRotator control, you can configure your application to show a series of advertisements to the end users. With this control, you can use advertisement data from sources other than the standard XML file that was used with the early versions of this control.

If you are using an XML source for the ad information, first create an XML advertisement file. The advertisement file allows you to incorporate some elements that give you a lot of control over the appearance and behavior of your ads. Listing 5-23 shows an example of an XML advertisement file.

LISTING 5-23: The XML advertisement file

```
<?xml version="1.0" encoding="utf-8" ?>
<Advertisements
  xmlns="http://schemas.microsoft.com/AspNet/AdRotator-Schedule-File">
    <Ad>
        <ImageUrl>book1.jpg</ImageUrl>
        <NavigateUrl>http://www.wrox.com</NavigateUrl>
        <AlternateText>Beginning ASP.NET</AlternateText>
        <Impressions>50</Impressions>
        <Keyword>ASP.NET</Keyword>
    </Ad>
    <Ad>
        <ImageUrl>book2.jpg</ImageUrl>
        <NavigateUrl>http://www.wrox.com</NavigateUrl>
        <AlternateText>Beginning Visual C#</AlternateText>
        <Impressions>50</Impressions>
        <Keyword>C#</Keyword>
    </Ad>
</Advertisements>
```

This XML file, used for storing information about the advertisements that appear in your application, has just a few elements detailed in Table 5-1. Remember that all elements are optional.

TABLE 5-1

ELEMENT	DESCRIPTION
ImageUrl	Takes a string value that indicates the location of the image to use.
NavigateUrl	Takes a string value that indicates the URL to post to when the image is clicked.
AlternateText	Takes a string value that is used for display if images are turned off in the client's browser or if the image is not found.
Impressions	Takes a numerical value that indicates the likelihood of the image being selected for display.
Keyword	Takes a string value that sets the category of the image in order to allow for the filtering of ads.

Now that the XML advertisement file is in place, you can simply use the AdRotator control to read from this file. Listing 5-24 shows an example of this in action.

LISTING 5-24: Using the AdRotator control as a banner ad

```
<%@ Page Language="C#" %>

<!DOCTYPE html>
<html xmlns="http://www.w3.org/1999/xhtml">
<head runat="server">
    <title>AdRotator Page</title>
</head>
<body>
    <form id="form1" runat="server">
        <div>
            <asp:AdRotator ID="AdRotator1" runat="server"
                AdvertisementFile="Listing05-23.xml" />
            <p>
                Lorem ipsum dolor sit
amet, consectetuer adipiscing elit. Duis vel justo. Aliquam
adipiscing. In mattis volutpat urna. Donec adipiscing, nisl eget
dictum egestas, felis nulla ornare ligula, ut bibendum pede augue
eu augue. Sed vel risus nec urna pharetra imperdiet. Aenean
semper. Sed ullamcorper auctor sapien. Suspendisse luctus. Ut ac
nibh. Nam lorem. Aliquam dictum aliquam purus.
            </p>
        </div>
    </form>
</body>
</html>
```

The example shows the ad specified in the XML advertisement file as a banner ad at the top of the page.

You are not required to place all your ad information in the XML advertisement file. Instead, you can use another data source to which you bind the AdRotator. For instance, you bind the AdRotator to a `SqlDataSource` object that is retrieving the ad information from SQL Server in the following fashion:

```
<asp:AdRotator ID="AdRotator1" runat="server"
    DataSourceId="SqlDataSource1" AlternateTextField="AlternateTF"
    ImageUrlField="Image" NavigateUrlField="NavigateUrl" />
```

The `AlternateTextField`, `ImageUrlField`, and `NavigateUrlField` properties point to the column names that are used in SQL Server for those items.

THE XML SERVER CONTROL

The Xml server control provides a means of getting XML and transforming it using an XSL style sheet. The Xml control can work with your XML in a couple of ways. The simplest method is by using the construction shown in Listing 5-25.

LISTING 5-25: Displaying an XML document

```
<asp:Xml ID="Xml1" runat="server" DocumentSource="Food.xml"
    TransformSource="FoodTemplate.xslt"></asp:Xml>
```

This method takes only a couple of attributes to make it work: `DocumentSource`, which points to the path of the XML file, and `TransformSource`, which provides the XSLT file to use in transforming the XML document.

The other way to use the Xml server control is to load the XML into an object and then pass the object to the Xml control, as illustrated in Listing 5-26.

LISTING 5-26: Loading the XML file to an object before providing it to the Xml control

VB

```
<%@ Page Language="VB" %>
<%@ Import Namespace="System.Xml.Xsl" %>
<%@ Import Namespace="System.Xml.XPath" %>
<!DOCTYPE html>
<script runat="server">
    Protected Sub Page_Load(sender As Object, e As EventArgs)
        Dim MyXmlDoc = New XPathDocument(Server.MapPath("Food.xml"))
        Dim MyXsltDoc = New XslTransform()
        MyXsltDoc.Load(Server.MapPath("FoodTemplate.xslt"))
        Xml1.XPathNavigator = MyXmlDoc.CreateNavigator()
        Xml1.Transform = MyXsltDoc
    End Sub
</script>
```

C#

```
<%@ Page Language="C#" %>
<%@ Import Namespace="System.Xml.Xsl" %>
<%@ Import Namespace="System.Xml.XPath" %>
<!DOCTYPE html>
<script runat="server">
    protected void Page_Load(Object sender, EventArgs e)
    {
        XPathDocument MyXmlDoc = new XPathDocument(Server.MapPath("Food.xml"));
        XslTransform MyXsltDoc = new XslTransform();
        MyXsltDoc.Load(Server.MapPath("FoodTemplate.xslt"));
        Xml1.XPathNavigator = MyXmlDoc.CreateNavigator();
        Xml1.Transform = MyXsltDoc;
    }
</script>
```

> **NOTE** XslTransform *has been deprecated to* XslCompiledTransform. *The XML web control has not been updated to accommodate* XslCompiledTransform. *You can continue to use* XslTransform. *However, you will receive a warning when you compile.*

To make this work, you have to ensure that the System.Xml and System.Xml.Xsl namespaces are imported into your page. The example loads both the XML and XSL files and then assigns these files as the values of the Document and Transform properties.

PANEL SERVER CONTROL

The Panel server control encapsulates a set of controls you can use to manipulate or lay out your ASP.NET pages. It is basically a wrapper for other controls, enabling you to take a group of server controls along with other elements (such as HTML and images) and turn them into a single unit.

The advantage of using the Panel control to encapsulate a set of other elements is that you can manipulate these elements as a single unit using one attribute set in the Panel control itself. For example, setting the Font-Bold attribute to True causes each item within the Panel control to adopt this attribute.

The Panel control also has the capability to scroll with scrollbars that appear automatically depending on the amount of information that Panel control holds. You can even specify how the scrollbars should appear.

For an example of using scrollbars, look at a long version of the Lorem Ipsum text (found at `www.lipsum.com`) and place that text within the Panel control, as shown in Listing 5-27.

LISTING 5-27: Using the Scrollbar feature with the Panel server control

```
<%@ Page Language="C#" %>
<!DOCTYPE html>
<html xmlns="http://www.w3.org/1999/xhtml">
<head runat="server">
    <title>Panel Server Control Page</title>
</head>
<body>
    <form id="form1" runat="server">
        <asp:Panel ID="Panel1" runat="server" Height="300" Width="300"
            ScrollBars="auto">
            <p>Lorem ipsum dolor sit amet . . . </p>
        </asp:Panel>
    </form>
</body>
</html>
```

By assigning values to the `Height` and `Width` attributes of the Panel server control and using the `ScrollBars` attribute (in this case, set to `Auto`), you can display the information it contains within the defined area using scrollbars (see Figure 5-28).

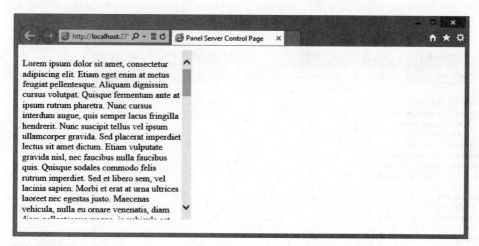

FIGURE 5-28

As you can see, a single vertical scrollbar has been added to the set area of 300 × 300 pixels. The Panel control wraps the text by default as required. To change this behavior, use the `Wrap` attribute, which takes a boolean value:

```
<asp:Panel ID="Panel1" runat="server" Height="300" Width="300"
    ScrollBars="auto" Wrap="False" />
```

Turning off wrapping may cause the horizontal scrollbar to turn on (depending on what is contained in the panel section).

If you do not want to let the ASP.NET engine choose which scrollbars to activate, you can actually make that decision by using the `ScrollBars` attribute. In addition to `Auto`, its values include `None`, `Horizontal`, `Vertical`, and `Both`.

Another interesting attribute that enables you to change the behavior of the Panel control is `HorizontalAlign`. It enables you to set how the content in the Panel control is horizontally aligned. The possible values of this attribute include `NotSet`, `Center`, `Justify`, `Left`, and `Right`. Figure 5-29 shows a collection of Panel controls with different horizontal alignments.

    Center-aligned   Justified   Left-aligned   Right-aligned

FIGURE 5-29

It is also possible to move the vertical scrollbar to the left side of the Panel control by using the `Direction` attribute. `Direction` can be set to `NotSet`, `LeftToRight`, and `RightToLeft`. A setting of `RightToLeft` is ideal when you are dealing with languages that are written from right to left (some Asian languages, for example). However, that setting also moves the scrollbar to the left side of the Panel control. If the scrollbar is moved to the left side and the `HorizontalAlign` attribute is set to `Left`, your content resembles Figure 5-30.

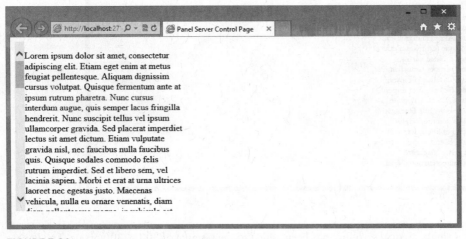

FIGURE 5-30

THE PLACEHOLDER SERVER CONTROL

The PlaceHolder server control works just as its name implies—it is a placeholder for you to interject objects dynamically into your page. Think of it as a marker with which you can add other controls. The capability to add controls to a page at a specific point also works with the Panel control.

To see how it works, insert a PlaceHolder control into your page and then add controls to it from your server-side code in the manner shown in Listing 5-28.

LISTING 5-28: Using the PlaceHolder server control to add controls to a page dynamically

VB

```
<%@ Page Language="VB" %>
<!DOCTYPE html>
<script runat="server">
    Protected Sub Page_Load(sender As Object, e As EventArgs)
        Dim MyNameLabel As New Label()
        MyNameLabel.Text = "Welcome, Jason!"
        PlaceHolder1.Controls.Add(MyNameLabel)
    End Sub
</script>
<html xmlns="http://www.w3.org/1999/xhtml">
<head runat="server">
    <title>PlaceHolder Control</title>
</head>
<body>
    <form id="form1" runat="server">
    <div>
        <asp:PlaceHolder ID="PlaceHolder1" runat="server" />
    </div>
    </form>
</body>
</html>
```

C#

```
<%@ Page Language="C#" %>
<!DOCTYPE html>
<script runat="server">
    protected void Page_Load(Object sender, EventArgs e)
    {
        Label MyNameLabel = new Label();
        MyNameLabel.Text = "Welcome, Jason!";
        PlaceHolder1.Controls.Add(MyNameLabel);
    }
</script>
```

This example creates a new instance of a Label control and populates it with a value before it is added to the PlaceHolder control. You can add more than one control to a single instance of a PlaceHolder control.

BULLETEDLIST SERVER CONTROL

One common HTML web page element is a collection of items in a bulleted list. The BulletedList server control is meant to display a bulleted list of items easily in an ordered (using the HTML `<ol>` element) or unordered (using the HTML `<ul>` element) fashion. In addition, the control can determine the style used for displaying the list.

The BulletedList control can be constructed of any number of `<asp:ListItem>` controls or can be data-bound to a data source of some kind and populated based upon the contents retrieved. Listing 5-29 shows a bulleted list in its simplest form.

LISTING 5-29: A simple BulletedList control

```
<%@ Page Language="C#" %>
<!DOCTYPE html>
<html xmlns="http://www.w3.org/1999/xhtml">
<head runat="server">
    <title>BulletedList Server Control</title>
</head>
<body>
    <form id="form1" runat="server">
        <asp:BulletedList ID="Bulletedlist1" runat="server">
            <asp:ListItem>United States</asp:ListItem>
            <asp:ListItem>United Kingdom</asp:ListItem>
            <asp:ListItem>Finland</asp:ListItem>
            <asp:ListItem>Russia</asp:ListItem>
            <asp:ListItem>Sweden</asp:ListItem>
            <asp:ListItem>Estonia</asp:ListItem>
        </asp:BulletedList>
    </form>
</body>
</html>
```

The use of the `<asp:BulletedList>` element, along with `<asp:ListItem>` elements, produces a simple bulleted list output like the one shown in Figure 5-31.

FIGURE 5-31

The BulletedList control also enables you to easily change the style of the list with just one or two attributes. The `BulletStyle` attribute changes the style of the bullet that precedes each line of the list. It has possible values of `Numbered`, `LowerAlpha`, `UpperAlpha`, `LowerRoman`, `UpperRoman`, `Disc`, `Circle`, `Square`, `NotSet`, and `CustomImage`. Figure 5-32 shows examples of these styles (minus the `CustomImage` setting that enables you to use any image of your choice).

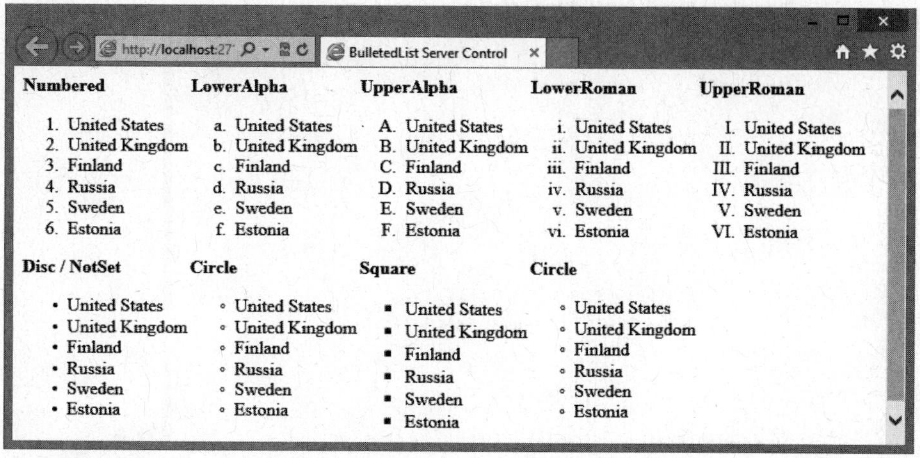

FIGURE 5-32

You can change the starting value of the first item in any of the numbered styles (Numbered, LowerAlpha, UpperAlpha, LowerRoman, UpperRoman) by using the FirstBulletNumber attribute. If you set the attribute's value to 5 when you use the UpperRoman setting, for example, you get the format illustrated in Figure 5-33.

FIGURE 5-33

To employ images as bullets, use the CustomImage setting in the BulletedList control. You must also use the BulletImageUrl attribute in the following manner:

```
<asp:BulletedList ID="Bulletedlist1" BulletStyle="CustomImage"
    BulletImageUrl="~/search.jpg" runat="server">
```

Figure 5-34 shows an example of image bullets.

FIGURE 5-34

The BulletedList control has an attribute called `DisplayMode`, which has three possible values: `Text`, `HyperLink`, and `LinkButton`. `Text` is the default and has been used so far in the examples. Using `Text` means that the items in the bulleted list are laid out only as text. `HyperLink` means that each of the items is turned into a hyperlink—any user clicking the link is redirected to another page, which is specified by the `<asp:ListItem>` control's `Value` attribute. A value of `LinkButton` turns each bulleted list item into a hyperlink that posts back to the same page. It enables you to retrieve the selection that the end user makes, as illustrated in Listing 5-30.

LISTING 5-30: Using the LinkButton value for the DisplayMode attribute

VB

```
<%@ Page Language="VB" %>
<!DOCTYPE html>
<script runat="server">
    Protected Sub BulletedList1_Click(sender As Object, e As BulletedListEventArgs)
        Label1.Text = "The index of item you selected: " & e.Index & _
            "<br>The value of the item selected: " & _
            BulletedList1.Items(e.Index).Text
    End Sub
</script>
<html xmlns="http://www.w3.org/1999/xhtml">
<head runat="server">
    <title>BulletedList Server Control</title>
</head>
<body>
    <form id="form1" runat="server">
        <asp:BulletedList ID="BulletedList1" runat="server"
            OnClick="BulletedList1_Click" DisplayMode="LinkButton">
            <asp:ListItem>United States</asp:ListItem>
            <asp:ListItem>United Kingdom</asp:ListItem>
            <asp:ListItem>Finland</asp:ListItem>
            <asp:ListItem>Russia</asp:ListItem>
            <asp:ListItem>Sweden</asp:ListItem>
            <asp:ListItem>Estonia</asp:ListItem>
        </asp:BulletedList>
        <asp:Label ID="Label1" runat="server">
```

```
        </asp:Label>
    </form>
</body>
</html>
```

C#

```
<%@ Page Language="C#" %>
<!DOCTYPE html>
<script runat="server">
    protected void BulletedList1_Click(object sender, BulletedListEventArgs e)
    {
        Label1.Text = "The index of item you selected: " + e.Index +
            "<br>The value of the item selected: " +
            BulletedList1.Items[e.Index].Text;
    }
</script>
```

In this example, the `DisplayMode` attribute is set to `LinkButton`, and the `OnClick` attribute is used to point to the `BulletedList1_Click` event. `BulletedList1_Click` uses the `BulletedListEventArgs` object, which only exposes the `Index` property. Using that, you can determine the index number of the item selected.

You can directly access the `Text` value of a selected item by using the `Items` property, or you can use the same property to populate an instance of the `ListItem` object, as shown here:

VB

```
Dim blSelectedValue As ListItem = BulletedList1.Items(e.Index)
```

C#

```
ListItem blSelectedValue = BulletedList1.Items[e.Index];
```

Now that you have seen how to create bulleted lists with items that you declaratively place in the code, look at how to create dynamic bulleted lists from items that are stored in a data store. The following example shows how to use the BulletedList control to data-bind to results coming from a data store; in it, all information is retrieved from an XML file.

The first step is to create the XML in Listing 5-31.

LISTING 5-31: An XML listing of books

```
<?xml version="1.0" encoding="utf-8" ?>
<Books>
    <Book
     Title="Professional ASP.NET 4.5"
     Year="2013"
     Price="$59.99" />
    <Book
     Title="Beginning ASP.NET 4.5"
     Year="2012"
     Price="$59.99" />
    <Book
     Title="Beginning Visual C#"
     Year="2012"
     Director="$59.99" />
</Books>
```

To populate the BulletedList server control with the `Title` attribute from the `Listing05-31.xml` file, use an XmlDataSource control to access the file, as illustrated in Listing 5-32.

LISTING 5-32: Dynamically populating a BulletedList server control

```
<%@ Page Language="C#" %>
<!DOCTYPE html>
<html xmlns="http://www.w3.org/1999/xhtml">
<head runat="server">
    <title>BulletedList Server Control</title>
</head>
<body>
    <form id="form1" runat="server">
        <asp:BulletedList ID="BulletedList1" runat="server"
            DataSourceID="XmlDataSource1" DataTextField="Title">
        </asp:BulletedList>
        <asp:XmlDataSource ID="XmlDataSource1" runat="server"
            DataFile="~/Listing05-31.xml" XPath="Books/Book"></asp:XmlDataSource>
    </form>
</body>
</html>
```

In this example, you use the `DataSourceID` attribute to point to the XmlDataSource control (as you would with any control that can be bound to one of the data source controls). After you are connected to the data source control, you specifically point to the `Title` attribute using the `DataTextField` attribute. After the two server controls are connected and the page is run, you get a bulleted list that is completely generated from the contents of the XML file. Figure 5-35 shows the result.

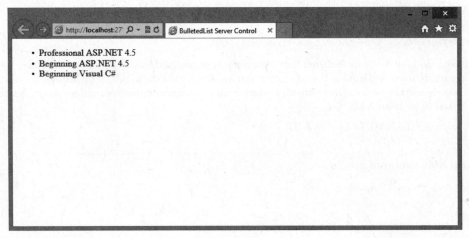

FIGURE 5-35

> **NOTE** *The XmlDataSource server control has some limitations in that the binding to the BulletedList server control worked in the previous example only because the* `Title` *value was an XML attribute and not a subelement. The XmlDataSource control exposes XML attributes as properties only when data binding. If you want to work with subelements, you must perform an XSLT transform using the XmlDataSource control's* `TransformFile` *attribute to turn elements into attributes.*

HIDDENFIELD SERVER CONTROL

For many years now, developers have been using hidden fields in their web pages to work with state management. The `<input type="hidden">` element is ideal for storing items that have no security context to them. These items are simply placeholders for data points that you want to store in the page itself instead of using the `Session` object or intermingling the data with the view state of the page. ViewState (discussed in more detail in Chapter 7) is another great way to store information in a page, but many developers turn off this feature to avoid corruption of the ViewState or possible degradation of page performance.

Any time a hidden field is placed within a web page, it is not interpreted in the browser in any fashion, although it is completely viewable by end users if they look at the source of the HTML page.

Listing 5-33 is an example of using the HiddenField server control to hold a GUID that can be used from page to page simply by carrying over its value as the end user navigates through your application.

LISTING 5-33: Working with the HiddenField server control

VB

```
<%@ Page Language="VB" %>
<!DOCTYPE html>
<script runat="server">
    Protected Sub Page_Load(sender As Object, e As EventArgs)
        HiddenField1.Value = Guid.NewGuid().ToString()
    End Sub
</script>
<html xmlns="http://www.w3.org/1999/xhtml">
<head id="Head1" runat="server">
    <title>HiddenField Server Control</title>
</head>
<body>
    <form id="form1" runat="server">
        <asp:HiddenField ID="HiddenField1" runat="Server" />
    </form>
</body>
</html>
```

C#

```
<%@ Page Language="C#" %>
<!DOCTYPE html>
<script runat="server">
    protected void Page_Load(Object sender, EventArgs e)
    {
        HiddenField1.Value = Guid.NewGuid().ToString();
    }
</script>
```

In this example, the `Page_Load` event populates the `HiddenField1` control with a GUID. You can see the hidden field and its value by looking at the source of the blank HTML page that is created. You should see a result similar to the following (the GUID will have a different value, of course):

```
<input type="hidden" name="HiddenField1" id="HiddenField1"
    value="d447f6b9-bfbe-4eaa-859a-fb4136e95cd2" />
```

On the page postback, ASP.NET can detect whether the HiddenField server control has changed its value since the last post. This enables you to change the HiddenField value with client-side script and then work with the changes in a page event.

The HiddenField server control has an event called `ValueChanged` that you can use when the value is changed:

VB

```
Protected Sub HiddenField1_ValueChanged(ByVal sender As Object,
   ByVal e As System.EventArgs)
   ' Handle event here
End Sub
```

C#

```
protected void HiddenField1_ValueChanged(object sender, EventArgs e)
{
   // Handle event here
}
```

The `ValueChanged` event is triggered when the ASP.NET page is posted back to the server if the value of the HiddenField server control has changed since the last time the page was drawn. If the value has not changed, the method is never triggered. Therefore, the method is useful to act upon any changes to the HiddenField control—such as recording a value to the database or changing a value in the user's profile.

FILEUPLOAD SERVER CONTROL

In the very early days of ASP.NET, you could upload files using the HTML FileUpload server control. This control put an `<input type="file">` element on your web page to enable the end user to upload files to the server. To use the file, however, you had to make a couple of modifications to the page. For example, you were required to add `enctype="multipart/form-data"` to the page's `<form>` element.

Ever since ASP.NET 2.0, you have been able to use the FileUpload server control that makes the process of uploading files to a server even simpler. When giving a page the capability to upload files, you simply include the `<asp:FileUpload>` control, and ASP.NET takes care of the rest, including adding the `enctype` attribute to the page's `<form>` element.

Uploading Files Using the FileUpload Control

After the file is uploaded to the server, you can also take hold of the uploaded file's properties and either display them to the end user or use these values yourself in your page's code-behind. Listing 5-34 shows an example of using the FileUpload control. The page contains a single FileUpload control, plus a Button and a Label control.

LISTING 5-34: Uploading files using the FileUpload control

VB

```
<%@ Page Language="VB" %>
<!DOCTYPE html>
<script runat="server">
    Protected Sub Button1_Click(ByVal sender As Object,
       ByVal e As System.EventArgs)
        If FileUpload1.HasFile Then
            Try
                FileUpload1.SaveAs("C:\Uploads\" &
                    FileUpload1.FileName)
                Label1.Text = "File name: " &
                    FileUpload1.PostedFile.FileName & "<br>" &
                    "File Size: " & _
                    FileUpload1.PostedFile.ContentLength & " kb<br>" &
```

```
                            "Content type: " &
                        FileUpload1.PostedFile.ContentType
                Catch ex As Exception
                    Label1.Text = "ERROR: " & ex.Message.ToString()
                End Try
            Else
                Label1.Text = "You have not specified a file."
            End If
        End Sub
    </script>
    <html xmlns="http://www.w3.org/1999/xhtml">
    <head runat="server">
        <title>FileUpload Server Control</title>
    </head>
    <body>
        <form id="form1" runat="server">
            <asp:FileUpload ID="FileUpload1" runat="server" />
            <p>
                <asp:Button ID="Button1" runat="server" Text="Upload"
                    OnClick="Button1_Click" />
            </p>
            <p>
                <asp:Label ID="Label1" runat="server"></asp:Label>
            </p>
        </form>
    </body>
    </html>
```

C#

```
<%@ Page Language="C#" %>
<!DOCTYPE html>
<script runat="server">
    protected void Button1_Click(object sender, EventArgs e)
    {
        if (FileUpload1.HasFile)
            try
            {
                FileUpload1.SaveAs("C:\\Uploads\\" + FileUpload1.FileName);
                Label1.Text = "File name: " +
                    FileUpload1.PostedFile.FileName + "<br>" +
                    FileUpload1.PostedFile.ContentLength + " kb<br>" +
                    "Content type: " +
                    FileUpload1.PostedFile.ContentType;
            }
            catch (Exception ex)
            {
                Label1.Text = "ERROR: " + ex.Message.ToString();
            }
        else
        {
            Label1.Text = "You have not specified a file.";
        }
    }
</script>
```

From this example, you can see that the entire process is rather simple. The single button on the page initiates the upload process. The FileUpload control itself does not initiate the uploading process. You must initiate it through another event such as Button_Click.

When compiling and running this page, you may notice a few things in the generated source code of the page. An example of the generated source code is presented here:

```
<!DOCTYPE html>
<html xmlns="http://www.w3.org/1999/xhtml">
<head><title>
    FileUpload Server Control
</title></head>
<body>
    <form method="post" action="Listing05-34.aspx" id="form1"
      enctype="multipart/form-data">
<div class="aspNetHidden">
<input type="hidden" name="__VIEWSTATE" id="__VIEWSTATE" value="YkgBQVHMwxdJnFcwbHY
G5i9hOlxcWnVeP+bjjdfpcRzkW30vLjxP75xY0wPaGlfa6YBcCAKm7gdi/7tonGDExufgpgIGwHE4yb0t6
jWepmD1DxH9i0/G69Pmr76WXQjPZcoaO7Uxyh9sbhqER1zcqg==" />
</div>
<div class="aspNetHidden">
        <input type="hidden" name="__EVENTVALIDATION" id="__EVENTVALIDATION"
          value="gNlwD1eVXBy2QmFixsfWZQGK7o0wSftXvY9Ff6ULdXYbqETya2cdZ5Ta2AmMcsvGIR
          BNBJ3tCi8FgYsxjwfTlGGECrta3LiwFjipySbNhzhtwnY8sGfd9ygP96s9/aSE" />
</div>
        <input type="file" name="FileUpload1" id="FileUpload1" />
        <p>
            <input type="submit" name="Button1" value="Upload" id="Button1" />
        </p>
        <p>
            <span id="Label1"></span>
        </p>
    </form>
</body>
</html>
```

The first thing to notice is that because the FileUpload control is on the page, ASP.NET 4.5 modified the page's `<form>` element on your behalf by adding the appropriate `enctype` attribute. Also notice that the FileUpload control was converted to an HTML `<input type="file">` element.

After the file is uploaded, the first check (done in the file's `Button1_Click` event handler) examines whether a file reference was actually placed within the `<input type="file">` element. If a file was specified, an attempt is made to upload the referenced file to the server using the `SaveAs()` method of the FileUpload control. That method takes a single `String` parameter, which should include the location where you want to save the file. In the `String` parameter used in Listing 5-34, you can see that the file is being saved to a folder called Uploads, which is located in the `C:\` drive.

The `PostedFile.FileName` attribute is used to give the saved file the same name as the file it was copied from. If you want to name the file something else, simply use the `SaveAs()` method in the following manner:

```
FileUpload1.SaveAs("C:\Uploads\UploadedFile.txt")
```

You could also give the file a name that specifies the time it was uploaded:

```
FileUpload1.SaveAs("C:\Uploads\" & System.DateTime.Now.ToFileTimeUtc() & ".txt")
```

After the upload is successfully completed, the Label control on the page is populated with metadata of the uploaded file. In the example, the file's name, size, and content type are retrieved and displayed on the page for the end user. When the file is uploaded to the server, the page generated is similar to that shown in Figure 5-36.

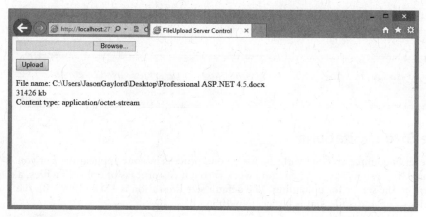

FIGURE 5-36

Uploading files to another server can be an error-prone affair. It is vital to upload files in your code using proper exception handling. That is why the file in the example is uploaded using a `Try Catch` statement.

Giving ASP.NET Proper Permissions to Upload Files

You might receive errors when your end users upload files to your web server through the FileUpload control in your application. Errors may occur because the destination folder on the server is not writable for the account used by ASP.NET. If ASP.NET is not enabled to write to the folder you want, you can enable it using the folder's properties.

First, right-click on the folder where the ASP.NET files should be uploaded and select Properties from the provided menu. The Properties dialog box for the selected folder opens. Click the Security tab to make sure the IIS_IUSRS account is included in the list and has the proper permissions to write to disk. If it is enabled, you see something similar to what is presented in Figure 5-37.

If you do not see the IIS_IUSRS account in the list of users allowed to access the folder, add it by clicking the Add button and entering IIS_IUSRS in the text area provided (see Figure 5-38).

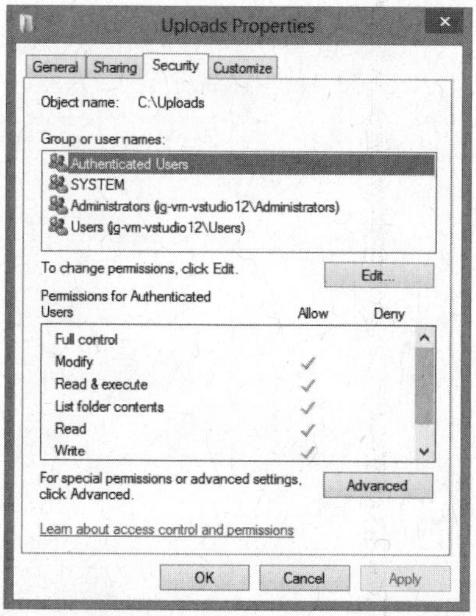

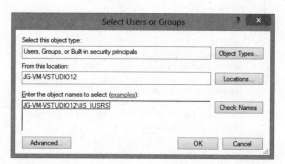

FIGURE 5-37

FIGURE 5-38

Click OK, and you can then click the appropriate check boxes to provide the permissions needed for your application.

> **NOTE** *Prior to IIS 7.0, the ASP.NET user account (aspnet_user) was used to control permissions.*

Understanding File Size Limitations

Your end users might never encounter an issue with the file upload process in your application, but you should be aware that some limitations exist. When users work through the process of uploading files, a size restriction is actually sent to the server for uploading. The default size limitation is 4MB (4096KB); the transfer fails if a user tries to upload a file that is larger than 4096KB.

A size restriction protects your application. You want to prevent malicious users from uploading numerous large files to your web server in an attempt to tie up all the available processes on the server. Such an occurrence is called a *denial of service attack*. It ties up the web server's resources so that legitimate users are denied responses from the server.

One of the great things about .NET, however, is that it usually provides a way around limitations. You can usually change the default settings that are in place. To change the limit on the allowable upload file size, you make some changes to either the root web.config file (found in the ASP.NET 4.5 configuration folder at C:\WINDOWS\Microsoft.NET\Framework\v4.0.*xxxxx*\CONFIG) or to your application's web.config file.

In the web.config file, you can create a node called <httpRuntime>. In this file, you apply the settings so that the default allowable file size is dictated by the actual request size permitted to the web server (4096KB). The <httpRuntime> section of the web.config.comments file is shown in Listing 5-35.

LISTING 5-35: Changing the file size limitation setting in the web.config file

```
<httpRuntime
    asyncPreloadMode="None"
    executionTimeout="110"
    maxRequestLength="4096"
    requestLengthDiskThreshold="80"
    useFullyQualifiedRedirectUrl="false"
    minFreeThreads="8"
    minLocalRequestFreeThreads="4"
    appRequestQueueLimit="5000"
    enableKernelOutputCache="true"
    enableVersionHeader="true"
    requireRootedSaveAsPath="true"
    enable="true"
    defaultRegexMatchTimeout="00:00:00"
    shutdownTimeout="90"
    delayNotificationTimeout="0"
    waitChangeNotification="0"
    maxWaitChangeNotification="0"
    enableHeaderChecking="true"
    sendCacheControlHeader="true"
    apartmentThreading="false"
    encoderType="System.Web.Util.HttpEncoder"
    requestValidationMode="4.0"
```

```
requestValidationType="System.Web.Util.RequestValidator"
requestPathInvalidCharacters="&lt;,&gt;,*,%,&amp;,:,\,?"
maxUrlLength="260"
maxQueryStringLength="2048"
relaxedUrlToFileSystemMapping="false"
allowDynamicModuleRegistration="true"
fcnMode="NotSet" />
```

You can do a lot with the <httpRuntime> section of the web.config file, but two properties—maxRequestLength and executionTimeout—are especially interesting.

The maxRequestLength property dictates the size of the request made to the web server. When you upload files, the file is included in the request; you alter the size allowed to be uploaded by changing the value of this property. The value presented is in kilobytes. To allow files larger than the default of 4MB, change the maxRequestLength property as follows:

```
maxRequestLength="10240"
```

This example changes the maxRequestLength property's value to 10,240KB (10MB). With this setting in place, your end users can upload 10MB files to the server. When changing the maxRequestLength property, be aware of the setting provided for the executionTimeout property. This property sets the time (in seconds) for a request to attempt to execute to the server before ASP.NET shuts down the request (whether or not it is finished). The default setting is 90 seconds. The end user receives a timeout error notification in the browser if the time limit is exceeded. If you are going to permit larger requests, remember that they take longer to execute than smaller ones. If you increase the size of the maxRequestLength property, you should examine whether to increase the executionTimeout property as well.

> **NOTE** *If you are working with smaller files, it is advisable to reduce the size allotted for the request to the web server by decreasing the value of the* maxRequestLength *property. This helps safeguard your application from a denial of service attack.*

Making these changes in the web.config file applies this setting to all the applications that are on the server. If you want to apply this only to the application you are working with, apply the <httpRuntime> node to the web.config file of your application, overriding any setting that is in the root web.config file. Make sure this node resides between the <system.web> nodes in the configuration file.

Uploading Multiple Files from the Same Page

So far, you have seen some good examples of how to upload a file to the server without much hassle. Now, let's look at how to upload multiple files to the server from a single page.

No built-in capabilities in the Microsoft .NET Framework enable you to upload multiple files from a single ASP.NET page. With a little work, however, you can easily accomplish this task just as you would have in the past using .NET 1.x.

The trick is to import the System.IO class into your ASP.NET page and then to use the HttpFileCollection class to capture all the files that are sent in with the Request object. This approach enables you to upload as many files as you want from a single page.

If you wanted to, you could simply handle each FileUpload control on the page individually, as shown in Listing 5-36.

LISTING 5-36: Handling each FileUpload control individually

VB

```vb
If FileUpload1.HasFile Then
    ' Handle this upload
End If
If FileUpload2.HasFile Then
    ' Handle this upload
End If
```

C#

```csharp
if (FileUpload1.HasFile) {
    /// Handle this upload
}
if (FileUpload2.HasFile) {
    /// Handle this upload
}
```

If you are working with a limited number of file upload boxes, this approach works; but at the same time you may, in certain cases, want to handle the files using the `HttpFileCollection` class. This is especially true if you are working with a dynamically generated list of server controls on your ASP.NET page.

For an example of this, you can build an ASP.NET page that has three FileUpload controls and one Submit button (using the Button control). After the user clicks the Submit button and the files are posted to the server, the code-behind takes the files and saves them to a specific location on the server. After the files are saved, the file information that was posted is displayed in the ASP.NET page (see Listing 5-37).

LISTING 5-37: Uploading multiple files to the server

VB

```vb
<%@ Page Language="VB" %>
<%@ Import Namespace="System.IO" %>
<!DOCTYPE html>
<script runat="server">
    Protected Sub Button1_Click(ByVal sender As Object,
        ByVal e As System.EventArgs)
        Dim filepath As String = "C:\Uploads"
        Dim uploadedFiles As HttpFileCollection = Request.Files
        Dim i As Integer = 0
        Do Until i = uploadedFiles.Count
            Dim userPostedFile As HttpPostedFile = uploadedFiles(i)
            Try
                If (userPostedFile.ContentLength > 0) Then
                    Label1.Text += "<u>File #" & (i + 1) & "</u><br>"
                    Label1.Text += "File Content Type: " &
                        userPostedFile.ContentType & "<br>"
                    Label1.Text += "File Size: " &
                        userPostedFile.ContentLength & "kb<br>"
                    Label1.Text += "File Name: " &
                        userPostedFile.FileName & "<br>"
                    userPostedFile.SaveAs(filepath & "\" &
                    Path.GetFileName(userPostedFile.FileName))
                    Label1.Text += "Location where saved: " &
                        filepath & "\" &
                        Path.GetFileName(userPostedFile.FileName) &
                        "<p>"
                End If
```

```
                        Catch ex As Exception
                            Label1.Text += "Error:<br>" & ex.Message
                        End Try
                        i += 1
                Loop
        End Sub
    </script>
    <html xmlns="http://www.w3.org/1999/xhtml">
    <head runat="server">
        <title>FileUpload Server Control</title>
    </head>
    <body>
        <form id="form1" runat="server">
            <p>
                <asp:FileUpload ID="FileUpload1" runat="server" />
            </p>
            <p>
                <asp:FileUpload ID="FileUpload2" runat="server" />
            </p>
            <p>
                <asp:FileUpload ID="FileUpload3" runat="server" />
            </p>
            <p>
                <asp:Button ID="Button1" runat="server" Text="Upload"
                    OnClick="Button1_Click" />
            </p>
            <p>
                <asp:Label ID="Label1" runat="server"></asp:Label>
            </p>
        </form>
    </body>
    </html>
```

C#

```
<%@ Page Language="C#" %>
<%@ Import Namespace="System.IO" %>
<!DOCTYPE html>
<script runat="server">
    protected void Button1_Click(object sender, EventArgs e)
    {
        string filepath = "C:\\Uploads";
        HttpFileCollection uploadedFiles = Request.Files;
        for (int i = 0; i < uploadedFiles.Count; i++)
        {
            HttpPostedFile userPostedFile = uploadedFiles[i];
            try
            {
                if (userPostedFile.ContentLength > 0)
                {
                    Label1.Text += "<u>File #" + (i + 1) +
                      "</u><br>";
                    Label1.Text += "File Content Type: " +
                      userPostedFile.ContentType + "<br>";
                    Label1.Text += "File Size: " +
                      userPostedFile.ContentLength + "kb<br>";
                    Label1.Text += "File Name: " +
                      userPostedFile.FileName + "<br>";
                    userPostedFile.SaveAs(filepath + "\\" +
                  Path.GetFileName(userPostedFile.FileName));
                    Label1.Text += "Location where saved: " +
                  filepath + "\\" +
                  Path.GetFileName(userPostedFile.FileName) +
```

continues

LISTING 5-37 *(continued)*

```
                    "<p>";
                }
            }
            catch (Exception Ex)
            {
                Label1.Text += "Error: <br>" + Ex.Message;
            }
        }
    }
</script>
```

This ASP.NET page enables the end user to select up to three files and click the Upload Files button, which initializes the `Button1_Click` event. Using the `HttpFileCollection` class with the `Request.Files` property lets you gain control over all the files that are uploaded from the page. When the files are in this state, you can do whatever you want with them. In this case, the files' properties are examined and written to the screen. In the end, the files are saved to the Uploads folder in the root directory of the server. The result of this action is illustrated in Figure 5-39.

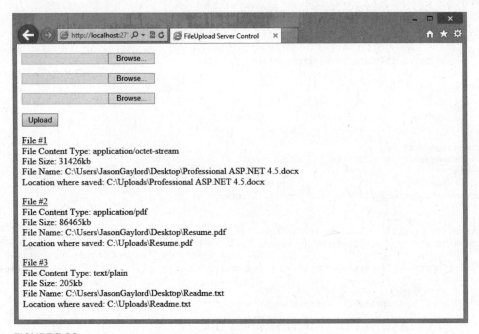

FIGURE 5-39

Placing the Uploaded File into a Stream Object

One nice feature of the FileUpload control is that it not only gives you the capability to save the file to disk, but it also lets you place the contents of the file into a `Stream` object. You do this by using the `FileContent` property, as demonstrated in Listing 5-38.

LISTING 5-38: Uploading the file contents into a Stream object

VB

```
Dim myStream As Stream
myStream = FileUpload1.FileContent
```

C#

```
Stream myStream;
myStream = FileUpload1.FileContent;
```

In this short example, an instance of the `Stream` object is created. Then, using the FileUpload control's `FileContent` property, the content of the uploaded file is placed into the object. This is possible because the `FileContent` property returns a `Stream` object.

Moving File Contents from a Stream Object to a Byte Array

Because you have the capability to move the file contents to a `Stream` object of some kind, it is also fairly simple to move the contents of the file to a `Byte` array (useful for such operations as placing files in a database of some kind). To do so, first move the file contents to a `MemoryStream` object and then convert the object to the necessary `Byte` array object. Listing 5-39 shows the process.

LISTING 5-39: Uploading the file contents into a Byte array

VB

```
Dim myByteArray() As Byte
Dim myStream As MemoryStream
myStream = FileUpload1.FileContent
myByteArray = myStream.ToArray()
```

C#

```
MemoryStream myStream;
myStream = (MemoryStream)FileUpload1.FileContent;
Byte[] myByteArray = new Byte[FileUpload1.PostedFile.ContentLength];
myByteArray = myStream.ToArray();
```

In this example, instances of a `Byte` array and a `MemoryStream` object are created. First, the `MemoryStream` object is created using the FileUpload control's `FileContent` property as you did previously. Then it's fairly simple to use the `MemoryStream` object's `ToArray()` method to populate the `myByteArray()` instance. After the file is placed into a `Byte` array, you can work with the file contents as necessary. This is a common method to save files as an `Image` format for Microsoft SQL Server.

MULTIVIEW AND VIEW SERVER CONTROLS

The MultiView and View server controls work together to give you the capability to turn on/off sections of an ASP.NET page. Turning sections on and off, which means activating or deactivating a series of View controls within a MultiView control, is similar to changing the visibility of Panel controls. For certain operations, however, you may find that the MultiView control is easier to manage and work with.

The sections, or views, do not change on the client-side; rather, they change with a postback to the server. You can put any number of elements and controls in each view, and the end user can work through the views based upon the sequence numbers that you assign to the views.

You can build these controls (like all server controls) from the Source view or Design view. If working with Visual Studio 2012, you can drag and drop a MultiView control onto the design surface and then drag and drop any number of View controls inside the MultiView control. Place the elements you want within the View controls. When you are finished, you have something like the view shown in Figure 5-40.

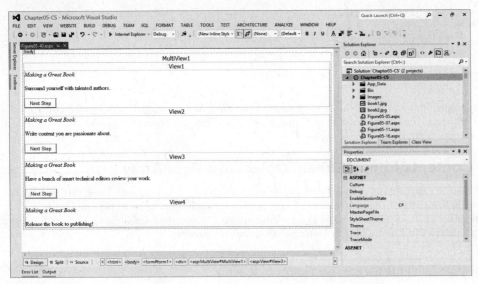

FIGURE 5-40

You also can create your controls directly in the code, as shown in Listing 5-40.

LISTING 5-40: Using the MultiView and View server controls

VB

```
<%@ Page Language="VB" %>
<script runat="server">
    Protected Sub Page_Load(ByVal sender As Object, ByVal e As System.EventArgs)
        If Not Page.IsPostBack Then
            MultiView1.ActiveViewIndex = 0
        End If
    End Sub
    Sub NextView(ByVal sender As Object, ByVal e As System.EventArgs)
        MultiView1.ActiveViewIndex += 1
    End Sub
</script>
<html xmlns="http://www.w3.org/1999/xhtml">
<head id="Head1" runat="server">
    <title>MultiView Server Control</title>
</head>
<body>
    <form id="form2" runat="server">
        <asp:MultiView ID="MultiView1" runat="server">
            <asp:View ID="View1" runat="server">
                <em>Making a Great Book</em><br />
                <br />
                Surround yourself with talented authors.<br />
                <br />
                <asp:Button ID="Button1" runat="server" Text="Next Step"
                  OnClick="NextView" />
            </asp:View>
```

```
            <asp:View ID="View2" runat="server">
                <em>Making a Great Book</em><br />
                <br />
                Write content you are passionate about.<br />
                <br />
                <asp:Button ID="Button2" runat="server" Text="Next Step"
                  OnClick="NextView" />
            </asp:View>
            <asp:View ID="View3" runat="server">
                <em>Making a Great Book</em><br />
                <br />
                Have a bunch of smart technical editors review your work.<br />
                <br />
                <asp:Button ID="Button3" runat="server" Text="Next Step"
                  OnClick="NextView" />
            </asp:View>
            <asp:View ID="View4" runat="server">
                <em>Making a Great Book</em><br />
                <br />
                Release the book to publishing!
            </asp:View>
        </asp:MultiView>
    </form>
</body>
</html>
```

C#

```
<%@ Page Language="C#" %>
<!DOCTYPE html>
<script runat="server">
    protected void Page_Load(object sender, EventArgs e)
    {
        if (!Page.IsPostBack)
        {
            MultiView1.ActiveViewIndex = 0;
        }
    }
    void NextView(object sender, EventArgs e)
    {
        MultiView1.ActiveViewIndex += 1;
    }
</script>
```

This example shows four views expressed in the MultiView control. Each view is constructed with an `<asp:View>` server control that also needs `ID` and `Runat` attributes. A button is added to each of the first three views (`View1`, `View2`, and `View3`) of the MultiView control. The buttons point to a server-side event that triggers the MultiView control to progress onto the next view within the series of views.

Before either of the buttons can be clicked, the MultiView control's `ActiveViewIndex` attribute is assigned a value. By default, the `ActiveViewIndex`, which describes the view that should be showing, is set to `-1`. This means that no view shows when the page is generated. To start on the first view when the page is drawn, set the `ActiveViewIndex` property to `0`, which is the first view because this is a zero-based index. Therefore, the code from Listing 5-40 first checks to see if the page is in a postback situation, and if not, the `ActiveViewIndex` is assigned to the first View control.

Each of the buttons in the MultiView control triggers the `NextView` method. `NextView` simply adds one to the `ActiveViewIndex` value, thereby showing the next view in the series until the last view is shown. The view series is illustrated in Figure 5-41.

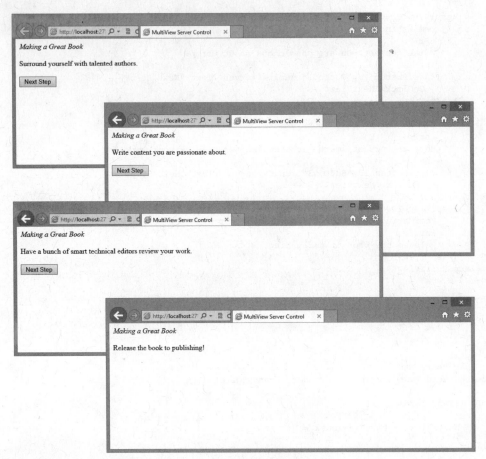

FIGURE 5-41

In addition to the Next Step button on the first, second, and third views, you could place a button in the second, third, and fourth views to enable the user to navigate backward through the views. To do this, create three buttons titled Previous Step in the last three views and point them to the following method in their OnClick events:

VB

```
Sub PreviousView(ByVal sender As Object, ByVal e As System.EventArgs)
    MultiView1.ActiveViewIndex -= 1
End Sub
```

C#

```
void PreviousView(object sender, EventArgs e)
{
    MultiView1.ActiveViewIndex -= 1;
}
```

Here, the PreviousView method subtracts one from the ActiveViewIndex value, thereby showing the previous view in the view series.

Another option is to spice up the MultiView control by adding a step counter that displays (to a Label control) which step in the series the end user is currently performing. In the Page_PreRender event, you add the following line:

VB

```
Label1.Text = "Step " & (MultiView1.ActiveViewIndex + 1).ToString() &
    " of " & MultiView1.Views.Count.ToString()
```

C#

```
Label1.Text = "Step " + (MultiView1.ActiveViewIndex + 1).ToString() +
    " of " + MultiView1.Views.Count.ToString();
```

Now when working through the MultiView control, the end user sees `Step 1 of 3` on the first view, which changes to `Step 2 of 3` on the next view, and so on.

WIZARD SERVER CONTROL

Much like the MultiView control, the Wizard server control enables you to build a sequence of steps that is displayed to the end user. Web pages are all about either displaying or gathering information and, in many cases, you don't want to display all the information at once—nor do you always want to gather everything from the end user at once.

When you are constructing a step-by-step process that includes logic on the steps taken, use the Wizard control to manage the entire process. The first time you use the Wizard control, notice that it allows for a far greater degree of customization than does the MultiView control.

In its simplest form, the Wizard control can be just an `<asp:Wizard>` element with any number of `<asp:WizardStep>` elements. Listing 5-41 creates a Wizard control that works through three steps.

LISTING 5-41: A simple Wizard control

```
<%@ Page Language="C#" %>
<!DOCTYPE html>
<html xmlns="http://www.w3.org/1999/xhtml">
<head runat="server">
    <title>Wizard server control</title>
</head>
<body>
    <form id="form1" runat="server">
        <asp:Wizard ID="Wizard1" runat="server" DisplaySideBar="True"
            ActiveStepIndex="0">
            <WizardSteps>
                <asp:WizardStep ID="WizardStep1" runat="server" Title="Step 1">
                    This is the first step.
                </asp:WizardStep>
                <asp:WizardStep ID="WizardStep2" runat="server" Title="Step 2">
                    This is the second step.
                </asp:WizardStep>
                <asp:WizardStep ID="WizardStep3" runat="server" Title="Step 3">
                    This is the third and final step.
                </asp:WizardStep>
            </WizardSteps>
        </asp:Wizard>
    </form>
</body>
</html>
```

In this example, three steps are defined with the `<asp:WizardSteps>` control. Each step contains content—simply text in this case, although you can put in anything you want, such as other web server controls or even user controls. The order in which the `WizardSteps` are defined is based completely on the order in which they appear within the `<WizardSteps>` element.

The `<asp:Wizard>` element contains a couple of important attributes. The first is `DisplaySideBar`. In this example, it is set to `True` by default—meaning that a side navigation system in the displayed control enables the end user to quickly navigate to other steps in the process. The `ActiveStepIndex` attribute of the Wizard control defines the first wizard step. In this case, it is the first step—`0`.

The three steps of the example Wizard control are shown in Figure 5-42.

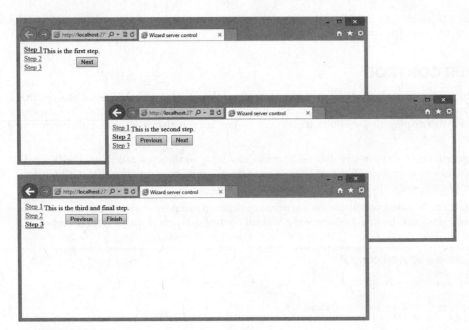

FIGURE 5-42

The side navigation allows for easy access to the defined steps. The Wizard control adds appropriate buttons to the steps in the process. The first step has simply a Next button, the middle step has Previous and Next buttons, and the final step has Previous and Finish buttons. The user can navigate through the steps using either the side navigation or the buttons on each of the steps. You can customize the Wizard control in so many ways that it's reminiscent of the other rich web server controls from ASP.NET, such as the Calendar control. Because so much is possible, only a few of the basics are covered—the ones you are most likely to employ in some of the Wizard controls you build.

Customizing the Side Navigation

The steps in the Figure 5-42 example are defined as Step 1, Step 2, and Step 3. The links are created based on the `Title` property's value that you give to each of the `<asp:WizardStep>` elements in the Wizard control:

```
<asp:WizardStep ID="WizardStep1" runat="server" Title="Step 1">
    This is the first step.
</asp:WizardStep>
```

By default, each wizard step created in Design view is titled `Step X` (with `X` being the number in the sequence). You can easily change the value of the `Title` attributes of each of the wizard steps to define the steps as you see fit. Figure 5-43 shows the side navigation of the Wizard control with renamed titles.

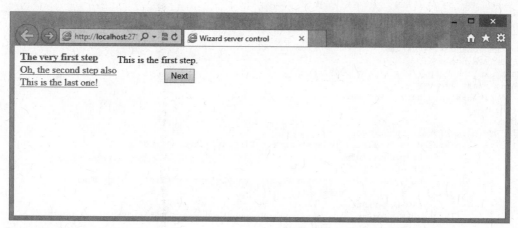

FIGURE 5-43

Examining the AllowReturn Attribute

Another interesting point of customization for the side navigation piece of the Wizard control is the `AllowReturn` attribute. By setting this attribute on one of the wizard steps to `False`, you can remove the capability for end users to go back to this step after they have viewed it. The end user cannot navigate backward to any viewed steps that contain the attribute, but he would be able to return to any steps that do not contain the attribute or that have it set to `True`:

```
<asp:WizardStep ID="WizardStep1" runat="server" AlowReturn="False"
    Title="The very first step">This is the first step.</asp:WizardStep>
```

Working with the StepType Attribute

Another interesting attribute in the `<asp:WizardStep>` element is `StepType`. The `StepType` attribute defines the structure of the buttons used on the steps. By default, the Wizard control places only a Next button on the first step. It understands that you do not need the Previous button there. It also knows to use a Next and Previous button on the middle step, and it uses Previous and Finish buttons on the last step. It draws the buttons in this fashion because, by default, the `StepType` attribute is set to `Auto`, meaning that the Wizard control determines the placement of buttons. You can, however, take control of the `StepType` attribute in the `<asp:WizardStep>` element to make your own determination about which buttons are used for which steps.

In addition to `Auto`, `StepType` value options include `Start`, `Step`, `Finish`, and `Complete`. `Start` means that the step defined has only a Next button. It simply allows the user to proceed to the next step in the series. A value of `Step` means that the wizard step has Next and Previous buttons. A value of `Finish` means that the step includes a Previous and a Finish button. `Complete` enables you to give some final message to the end user who is working through the steps of your Wizard control. In the Wizard control shown in Listing 5-42, for example, when the end user gets to the last step and clicks the Finish button, nothing happens and the user just stays on the last page. You can add a final step to give an ending message, as shown in Listing 5-42.

LISTING 5-42: Having a complete step in the Wizard step collection

```
<%@ Page Language="C#" %>
<!DOCTYPE html>
<html xmlns="http://www.w3.org/1999/xhtml">
<head runat="server">
    <title>Wizard server control</title>
</head>
<body>
    <form id="form1" runat="server">
        <asp:Wizard ID="Wizard1" runat="server" DisplaySideBar="True"
            ActiveStepIndex="0">
            <WizardSteps>
                <asp:WizardStep ID="WizardStep1" runat="server" Title="Step 1">
                    This is the first step.
                </asp:WizardStep>
                <asp:WizardStep ID="WizardStep2" runat="server" Title="Step 2">
                    This is the second step.
                </asp:WizardStep>
                <asp:WizardStep ID="WizardStep3" runat="server" Title="Step 3">
                    This is the third and final step.
                </asp:WizardStep>
                <asp:WizardStep ID="WizardStep4" runat="server" Title="Final Step"
                    StepType="Complete">
                    Thanks for working through the steps.
                </asp:WizardStep>
            </WizardSteps>
        </asp:Wizard>
    </form>
</body>
</html>
```

When the end user clicks the Finish button in Step 3, the last step—Final Step—is shown and no buttons appear with it.

Adding a Header to the Wizard Control

The Wizard control enables you to place a header at the top of the control by means of the HeaderText attribute in the main <asp:Wizard> element. Listing 5-43 provides an example.

LISTING 5-43: Working with the HeaderText attribute

```
<asp:Wizard ID="Wizard1" runat="server" DisplaySideBar="True"
    ActiveStepIndex="0" HeaderText="Step by Step with the Wizard Control"
    HeaderStyle-BackColor="DarkGray" HeaderStyle-Font-Bold="true"
    HeaderStyle-Font-Size="20">
    . . .
</asp:Wizard>
```

This code creates a header that appears on each of the steps in the wizard. The result of this snippet is shown in Figure 5-44.

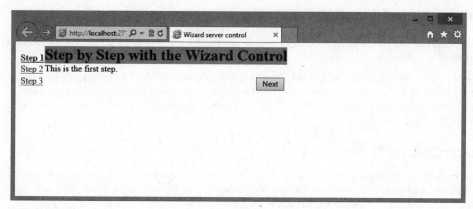

FIGURE 5-44

Working with the Wizard's Navigation System

As stated earlier, the Wizard control allows for a very high degree of customization—especially in the area of style. You can customize every aspect of the process, as well as how every element appears to the end user.

Pay particular attention to the options that are available for customization of the navigation buttons. By default, the wizard steps use Next, Previous, and Finish buttons throughout the entire series of steps. From the main `<asp:Wizard>` element, you can change everything about these buttons and how they work.

First, if you look through the long list of attributes available for this element, notice that one available button is not shown by default: the Cancel button. Set the value of the `DisplayCancelButton` attribute to `True`, and a Cancel button appears within the navigation created for each step, including the final step in the series. Figure 5-45 shows a Cancel button in a step.

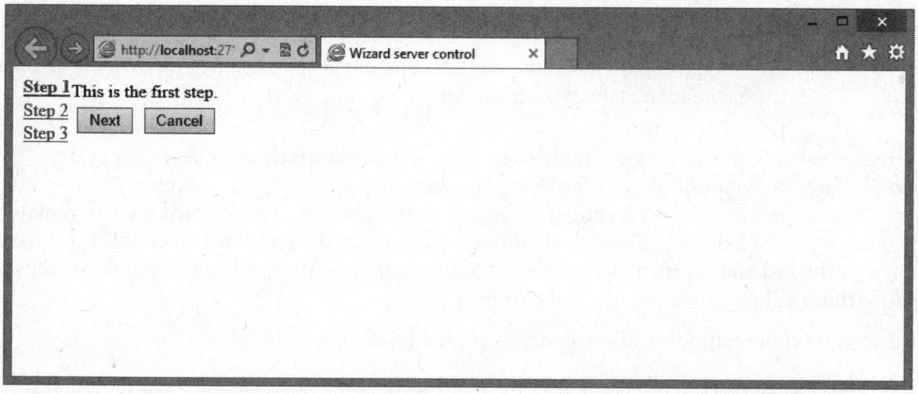

FIGURE 5-45

After you decide which buttons to use within the Wizard navigation, you can choose their style. By default, regular buttons appear; you can change the button style with the `CancelButtonType`, `FinishStepButtonType`, `FinishStepPreviousButtonType`, `NextStepButtonType`, `PreviousStepButtonType`, and `StartStepNextButtonType` attributes. If you use any of these button types and want all the buttons consistently styled, you must change each attribute to the same value. The possible values of these button-specific elements include `Button`, `Image`, and `Link`. `Button` is the default and means that the navigation system uses buttons. A value of `Image` enables you to use image buttons, and `Link` turns a selected item in the navigation system into a hyperlink.

In addition to these button-specific attributes of the `<asp:Wizard>` element, you can also specify a URL to which the user is directed when the user clicks the Cancel or Finish buttons. To redirect the user with one of these buttons, you use the `CancelDestinationPageUrl` or the `FinishDestinationPageUrl` attributes and set the appropriate URL as the destination.

Finally, you are not required to use the default text included with the buttons in the navigation system. You can change the text of each of the buttons using the `CancelButtonText`, `FinishStepButtonText`, `FinishStepPreviousButtonText`, `NextStepButtonText`, `PreviousStepButtonText`, and `StartStepNextButtonText` attributes.

Utilizing Wizard Control Events

One of the most convenient capabilities of the Wizard control is that it enables you to divide large forms into logical pieces. The end user can then work systematically through each section of the form. The developer, dealing with the inputted values of the form, has a few options because of the various events that are available in the Wizard control.

The Wizard control exposes events for each of the possible steps that an end user might take when working with the control. Table 5-2 describes each of the available events.

TABLE 5-2

EVENT	DESCRIPTION
`ActiveStepChanged`	Triggers when the end user moves from one step to the next. It does not matter if the step is the middle or final step in the series. This event simply covers each step change generically.
`CancelButtonClick`	Triggers when the end user clicks the Cancel button in the navigation system.
`FinishButtonClick`	Triggers when the end user clicks the Finish button in the navigation system.
`NextButtonClick`	Triggers when the end user clicks the Next button in the navigation system.
`PreviousButtonClick`	Triggers when the end user clicks the Previous button in the navigation system.
`SideBarButtonClick`	Triggers when the end user clicks one of the links contained within the sidebar navigation of the Wizard control.

By working with these events, you can create a multi-step form that saves all the end user's input information when he changes from one step to the next. You can also use the `FinishButtonClick` event to save everything that was stored in each of the steps at the end of the process. The Wizard control remembers all the end user's input in each of the steps by means of the view state in the page, which enables you to work with all these values in the last step. It also gives the end user the capability to go back to previous steps and change values before those values are saved to a data store.

The event appears in your code-behind or inline code, as shown in Listing 5-44.

LISTING 5-44: The FinishButtonClick event

VB

```
<%@ Page Language="VB" %>
<!DOCTYPE html>
<script runat="server">
    Protected Sub Wizard1_FinishButtonClick(sender As Object,
      e As WizardNavigationEventArgs)
      . . . .
```

```
        End Sub
</script>
<html xmlns="http://www.w3.org/1999/xhtml">
<head runat="server">
    <title>Wizard server control</title>
</head>
<body>
    <form id="form1" runat="server">
        <asp:Wizard ID="Wizard1" runat="server" DisplaySideBar="True"
            ActiveStepIndex="0" OnFinishButtonClick="Wizard1_FinishButtonClick">
            <WizardSteps>
                <asp:WizardStep ID="WizardStep1" runat="server" Title="Step 1">
                    This is the first step.
                </asp:WizardStep>
                <asp:WizardStep ID="WizardStep2" runat="server" Title="Step 2">
                    This is the second step.
                </asp:WizardStep>
                <asp:WizardStep ID="WizardStep3" runat="server" Title="Step 3">
                    This is the third and final step.
                </asp:WizardStep>
            </WizardSteps>
        </asp:Wizard>
    </form>
</body>
</html>
```

C#

```
<%@ Page Language="C#" %>
<!DOCTYPE html>
<script runat="server">
    protected void Wizard1_FinishButtonClick(object sender,
      WizardNavigationEventArgs e)
    {
        . . .
    }
</script>
```

The `OnFinishButtonClick` attribute should be added to the main `<asp:Wizard>` element to point at the `Wizard1_FinishButtonClick` event. Listing 5-45 shows how to do this.

LISTING 5-45: The `<asp:Wizard>` element changes

```
<asp:Wizard ID="Wizard1" runat="server" DisplaySideBar="True"
    ActiveStepIndex="0" OnFinishButtonClick="Wizard1_FinishButtonClick">
```

The Wizard control is one of the great controls that enable you to break up longer workflows into more manageable pieces for your end users. By separating longer Web Forms into various wizard steps, you can effectively make your forms easy to understand and less daunting to the end user.

Using the Wizard Control to Show Form Elements

So far, you have learned how to work with each of the Wizard control steps, including how to add steps to the process and how to work with the styling of the control. Now look at how you put form elements into the Wizard control to collect information from the end user in a stepped process. This is just as simple as the first examples of the Wizard control that used only text in each of the steps.

One nice thing about putting form elements in the Wizard step process is that the Wizard control remembers each input into the form elements from step to step, enabling you to save the results of the entire form at the last step. It also means that when the end user presses the Previous button, the data that is entered into the form previously is still there and can be changed.

Listing 5-46 shows the first part of a process that steps through entering form information by building a registration process. The last step of the process saves the results to a database of your choice, although in this example, you just push the results to a Label control on the page.

LISTING 5-46: Building the form in the Wizard control

```
<asp:Wizard ID="Wizard1" runat="Server">
    <WizardSteps>
        <asp:WizardStep ID="WizardStep1" runat="server"
            Title="Provide Personal Info">
            First name:<br />
            <asp:TextBox ID="fnameTextBox" runat="server"></asp:TextBox><br />
            Last name:<br />
            <asp:TextBox ID="lnameTextBox" runat="server"></asp:TextBox><br />
            Email:<br />
            <asp:TextBox ID="emailTextBox" runat="server"></asp:TextBox><br />
        </asp:WizardStep>
        <asp:WizardStep ID="WizardStep2" runat="server"
            Title="Membership Information">
            Are you already a member of our group?<br />
            <asp:RadioButton ID="RadioButton1" runat="server" Text="Yes"
                GroupName="Member" />
            <asp:RadioButton ID="RadioButton2" runat="server" Text="No"
                GroupName="Member" />
        </asp:WizardStep>
        <asp:WizardStep ID="WizardStep3" runat="server"
            Title="Provided Information"
            StepType="Complete" OnActivate="WizardStep3_Activate">
            <asp:Label ID="Label1" runat="server" />
        </asp:WizardStep>
    </WizardSteps>
</asp:Wizard>
```

This Wizard control has three steps. The first step asks for the user's personal information, and the second asks for the user's membership information. The third step contains a Label control that pushes out all the information that was input. This is done through the Activate event that is specific for the WizardStep object on the third WizardStep control. The code for the WizardStep3_Activate event is shown in Listing 5-47.

LISTING 5-47: Adding an Activate event to a WizardStep object

VB

```
<%@ Page Language="VB" %>
<!DOCTYPE html>
<script runat="server">
    Protected Sub WizardStep3_Activate(ByVal sender As Object,
        ByVal e As System.EventArgs)
        ' You could save the inputted data to the database here instead
        Label1.Text = "First name: " & fnameTextBox.Text.ToString() & "<br>" & _
            "Last name: " & lnameTextBox.Text.ToString() & "<br>" &
            "Email: " & emailTextBox.Text.ToString()
    End Sub
</script>
```

C#

```
<%@ Page Language="C#" %>
<!DOCTYPE html>
<script runat="server">
    protected void WizardStep3_Activate(object sender, EventArgs e)
    {
        Label1.Text = "First name: " + fnameTextBox.Text.ToString() + "<br>" +
            "Last name: " + lnameTextBox.Text.ToString() + "<br>" +
            "Email: " + emailTextBox.Text.ToString();
    }
</script>
```

When the end user comes to the third step in the display, the `WizardStep3_Activate` method from Listing 5-47 is invoked. Using the `OnActivate` attribute in the third WizardStep control, the content provided by the end user in earlier steps is used to populate a Label control. The three steps are shown in Figure 5-46.

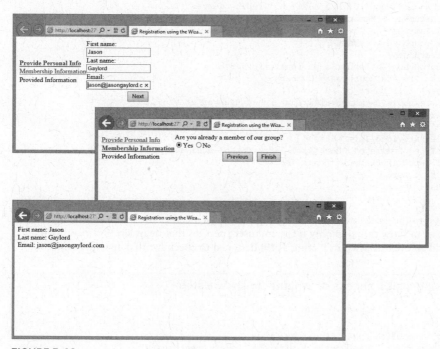

FIGURE 5-46

This example is simple and straightforward, but you can increase the complexity a little bit. Imagine you want to add another WizardStep control to the process, and you want to display it only if a user specifies that he is a member in `WizardStep2`. If he answers from the radio button selection that he is not a member, you have him skip the new step and go straight to the final step where the results are displayed in the Label control. First, add a `WizardStep` to the Wizard control, as shown in Listing 5-48.

LISTING 5-48: Adding a WizardStep

```
<asp:Wizard ID="Wizard1" runat="Server">
    <WizardSteps>
        <asp:WizardStep ID="WizardStep1" runat="server"
            Title="Provide Personal Info">
            First name:<br />
            <asp:TextBox ID="fnameTextBox" runat="server"></asp:TextBox><br />
            Last name:<br />
            <asp:TextBox ID="lnameTextBox" runat="server"></asp:TextBox><br />
            Email:<br />
            <asp:TextBox ID="emailTextBox" runat="server"></asp:TextBox><br />
        </asp:WizardStep>
        <asp:WizardStep ID="WizardStep2" runat="server"
            Title="Membership Information">
            Are you already a member of our group?<br />
            <asp:RadioButton ID="RadioButton1" runat="server" Text="Yes"
                GroupName="Member" />
            <asp:RadioButton ID="RadioButton2" runat="server" Text="No"
                GroupName="Member" />
        </asp:WizardStep>
        <asp:WizardStep ID="MemberStep" runat="server"
            Title="Provide Membership Number">
            Membership Number:<br />
            <asp:TextBox ID="mNumberTextBox" runat="server"></asp:TextBox>
        </asp:WizardStep>
        <asp:WizardStep ID="WizardStep3" runat="server"
            Title="Provided Information"
            StepType="Complete" OnActivate="WizardStep3_Activate">
            <asp:Label ID="Label1" runat="server" />
        </asp:WizardStep>
    </WizardSteps>
</asp:Wizard>
```

A single step was added to the workflow—one that simply asks the member for his or her membership number. Since you want to show this step only if the end user specifies that he or she is a member in WizardStep2, you add an event (shown in Listing 5-49) designed to check for that specification.

LISTING 5-49: Applying logical checks on whether to show a step

VB

```
Sub Wizard1_NextButtonClick(ByVal sender As Object,
    ByVal e As System.Web.UI.WebControls.WizardNavigationEventArgs)
    If e.NextStepIndex = 2 Then
        If RadioButton1.Checked = True Then
            Wizard1.ActiveStepIndex = 2
        Else
            Wizard1.ActiveStepIndex = 3
        End If
    End If
End Sub
```

C#

```
void Wizard1_NextButtonClick(object sender, WizardNavigationEventArgs e)
{
    if (e.NextStepIndex == 2)
    {
        if (RadioButton1.Checked == true)
        {
```

```
            Wizard1.ActiveStepIndex = 2;
        }
        else
        {
            Wizard1.ActiveStepIndex = 3;
        }
    }
}
```

To check whether you should show a specific step in the process, use the NextButtonClick event from the Wizard control. The event uses the WizardNavigationEventArgs class instead of the typical EventArgs class that gives you access to the NextStepIndex number, as well as to the CurrentStepIndex number.

In the example from Listing 5-49, you check whether the next step to be presented in the process is 2. Remember that this is index 2 from a zero-based index (0, 1, 2, and so on). If it is Step 2 in the index, you check which radio button is selected from the previous WizardStep. If the RadioButton1 control is checked (meaning that the user is a member), the next step in the process is assigned as index 2. If the RadioButton2 control is selected, the user is not a member, and the index is then assigned as 3 (the final step), thereby bypassing the membership step in the process.

You could also take this example and alter it a bit so that you show a WizardStep only if the user is contained within a specific role (such as an Admin role).

> **NOTE** *Role management is covered in Chapter 19.*

Showing only a WizardStep when the user is contained within a certain role is demonstrated in Listing 5-50.

LISTING 5-50: Applying logical checks on whether to show a step based upon roles

VB
```
Sub Wizard1_NextButtonClick(ByVal sender As Object,
    ByVal e As System.Web.UI.WebControls.WizardNavigationEventArgs)
    If e.NextStepIndex = 2 Then
        If (Roles.IsUserInRole("ManagerAccess")) Then
            Wizard1.ActiveStepIndex = 2
        Else
            Wizard1.ActiveStepIndex = 3
        End If
    End If
End Sub
```

C#
```
void Wizard1_NextButtonClick(object sender, WizardNavigationEventArgs e)
{
    if (e.NextStepIndex == 2)
    {
        if (Roles.IsUserInRole("ManagerAccess"))
        {
            Wizard1.ActiveStepIndex = 2;
        }
        else
        {
            Wizard1.ActiveStepIndex = 3;
        }
    }
}
```

IMAGEMAP SERVER CONTROL

The ImageMap server control enables you to turn an image into a navigation menu. In the past, many developers would break an image into multiple pieces and put it together again in a table, reassembling the pieces into one image. When the end user clicked a particular piece of the overall image, the application picked out which piece of the image was chosen and based actions upon that particular selection.

With the ImageMap control, you can take a single image and specify particular hotspots on the image using coordinates. An example is shown in Listing 5-51.

LISTING 5-51: Specifying sections of an image that are clickable

VB

```
<%@ Page Language="VB" %>
<!DOCTYPE html>
<script runat="server">
    Protected Sub ImageMap1_Click(sender As Object, e As ImageMapEventArgs)
        Response.Write("You selected: " & e.PostBackValue)
    End Sub
</script>
<html xmlns="http://www.w3.org/1999/xhtml">
<head runat="server">
    <title>ImageMap Control</title>
</head>
<body>
    <form id="form1" runat="server">
        <asp:ImageMap ID="ImageMap1" runat="server" HotSpotMode="PostBack"
          ImageUrl="~/Images/kids.jpg" OnClick="ImageMap1_Click">
            <asp:CircleHotSpot PostBackValue="Addison" Radius="26" X="145"
              Y="372" />
            <asp:CircleHotSpot PostBackValue="Brayden" Radius="20" X="181"
              Y="314" />
            <asp:CircleHotSpot PostBackValue="Arianna" Radius="28" X="245"
              Y="344" />
        </asp:ImageMap>
    </form>
</body>
</html>
```

C#

```
<%@ Page Language="C#" %>
<!DOCTYPE html>
<script runat="server">
    protected void ImageMap1_Click(object sender, ImageMapEventArgs e)
    {
        Response.Write("You selected: " + e.PostBackValue);
    }
</script>
```

This page brings up an image of me and my children at an aquarium. If you click one of the children's faces, the child's name will be written to the Response stream, as shown in Figure 5-47.

FIGURE 5-47

The ImageMap control enables you to specify hotspots in a couple of different ways. From the example in Listing 5-51, you can see that hotspots are placed in a circular fashion using the `<asp:CircleHotSpot>` element. Besides the `<asp:CircleHotSpot>` control, you can also use the `<asp:RectangleHotSpot>` and the `<asp:PolygonHotSpot>` controls. Each control takes coordinates appropriate to its shape.

After you define the hotspots on the image, you can respond to the end user click of the hotspot in several ways. You first specify how to deal with the hotspot clicks in the root `<asp:ImageMap>` element with the use of the `HotSpotMode` attribute.

The `HotSpotMode` attribute can take the values `PostBack`, `Navigate`, or `InActive`. In the previous example, the `HotSpotMode` value is set to `PostBack`—meaning that after the end user clicks the hotspot, you want to postback to the server and deal with the click at that point.

Because the `HotSpotMode` is set to `PostBack` and you have created several hotspots, you must determine which hotspot is selected. You make this determination by giving each hotspot (`<asp:CircleHotSpot>`) a postback value with the `PostBackValue` attribute. The example uses `Arianna`, `Addison`, and `Brayden` as the values of the three hotspots.

The `PostBackValue` attribute is also the helper text that appears in the browser (in the yellow box) directly below the mouse cursor when the end user hovers the mouse over the hotspot.

After the user clicks one of the hotspots, the event procedure displays the value that was selected in a `Response.Write` statement.

Instead of posting back to the server, you can also navigate to an entirely different URL when a particular hotspot is selected. To accomplish this, change the `HotSpotMode` attribute in the main `<asp:ImageMap>` element to the value `Navigate`. Then, within the `<asp:CircleHotSpot>` elements, simply use the

`NavigateUrl` attribute and assign the location to which the end user should be directed if that particular hotspot is clicked:

```
<asp:ImageMap ID="ImageMap1" runat="server" ImageUrl="~/Images/kids.jpg"
    HotSpotMode="Navigate">
    <asp:CircleHotSpot AlternateText="Addison" NavigateUrl="Addison.aspx"
        Radius="26" X="145" Y="372" />
    <asp:CircleHotSpot AlternateText="Brayden" NavigateUrl="Brayden.aspx"
        Radius="20" X="181" Y="314" />
    <asp:CircleHotSpot AlternateText="Arianna" NavigateUrl="Arianna.aspx"
        Radius="28" X="245" Y="344" />
</asp:ImageMap>
```

SUMMARY

This chapter explored numerous server controls, their capabilities, and the features they provide. With ASP .NET 4.5, you have more than 50 server controls at your disposal.

Because you have so many server controls at your disposal when you are creating your ASP.NET applications, you have to think carefully about which is the best control for the task. Many controls seem similar, but they offer different features. These controls guarantee that you can build the best possible applications for all browsers.

Server controls are some of the most useful tools you will find in your ASP.NET arsenal. They are quite useful and can save you a lot of time. This chapter introduced you to some of these controls and to the different ways you might incorporate them into your next projects. All these controls are wonderful options to use on any of your ASP.NET pages and make it much easier to develop the functionality that your pages require.

Validation Server Controls

➤ Understanding the provided validation server controls

➤ Working with both client- and server-side validations

➤ Enabling unobtrusive validation

WROX.COM CODE DOWNLOADS FOR THIS CHAPTER

Please note that all the code examples in this chapter are available as a part of this chapter's code download on the book's website at www.wrox.com.

When you look at the Toolbox window in Visual Studio 2012—especially if you've read Chapters 4 and 5, which cover the various server controls at your disposal—you may be struck by the number of server controls that come with ASP.NET 4.5. This chapter takes a look at a specific type of server control you find in the Toolbox window: the *validation server control*.

Validation server controls are a series of controls that enable you to work with the information your end users input into the form elements of the applications you build. These controls work to ensure the validity of the data being placed in the form.

Before you learn how to use these controls, however, this chapter first takes a look at the process of validation.

UNDERSTANDING VALIDATION

Developers have been constructing web applications for a number of years. Usually the motivation is to provide or gather information. In this chapter, you focus on the information-gathering and validation aspects of web applications. If you collect data with your applications, collecting *valid* data should be important to you. If the information isn't valid, there really isn't much point in collecting it.

Validation is a set of rules that you apply to the data you collect. These rules can be many or few and enforced either strictly or in a lax manner: It really depends on your business rules and requirements. No perfect validation process exists because some users may find a way to cheat to some degree, no matter what rules you establish. The trick is to find the right balance of the fewest rules and the proper strictness, without compromising the usability of the application.

The data you collect for validation comes from the Web Forms you provide in your applications. Web Forms are made up of different types of HTML elements that are constructed using raw HTML form elements, ASP.NET HTML server controls, or ASP.NET Web Form server controls. In the end, your forms are made up of many different types of HTML elements, such as textboxes, radio buttons, check boxes, drop-down lists, and more.

As you work through this chapter, you see the different types of validation rules that you can apply to your form elements. Remember that you have no way to validate the *truthfulness* of the information you collect; instead, you apply rules that respond to such questions as:

➤ Is something entered in the textbox?

➤ Is the data entered in the textbox in the form of an e-mail address?

Notice from these questions that you can apply more than a single validation rule to an HTML form element (examples of this appear later in this chapter). In fact, you can apply as many rules to a single element as you want. Applying more rules to elements increases the strictness of the validation applied to the data.

CLIENT-SIDE VERSUS SERVER-SIDE VALIDATION

If you are new to web application development, you might not be aware of the difference between client-side and server-side validation. Suppose that the end user clicks the Submit button on a form after filling out some information. What happens in ASP.NET is that this form is packaged in a *request* and sent to the server where the application resides. At this point in the request/response cycle, you can run validation checks on the information submitted. Doing this is called *server-side validation* because it occurs on the server.

On the other hand, it's also possible to supply a client-side script (usually in the form of JavaScript) in the page that is posted to the end user's browser to perform validations on the data entered in the form *before* the form is posted back to the originating server. In this case, *client-side validation* has occurred.

Client-side validation is quick and responsive for the end user. It is something end users expect of the forms that they work with. If something is wrong with the form, using client-side validation ensures that the end user knows about it as soon as possible. The reason for this is that the client-side validation, if called properly, executes before the form is posted back to the server. Client-side validation also pushes the processing power required of validation to the client, meaning that you don't need to spin CPU cycles on the server to process the same information because the client can do the work for you.

With this said, client-side validation is the more insecure form of validation. When a page is generated in an end user's browser, this end user can look at the code of the page quite easily (simply by right-clicking his mouse in the browser and selecting View Code). When he or she does so, in addition to seeing the HTML code for the page, all of the JavaScript that is associated with the page can be viewed. If you are validating your form client-side, it doesn't take much for the crafty hacker to repost a form (containing the values he wants in it) to your server as valid. Cases also exist in which clients have simply disabled the client-scripting capabilities in their browsers—thereby making your validations useless. Therefore, client-side validation should be considered a convenience and a courtesy to the end user and never a security mechanism. However, even with the risks, client-side validation is quite popular as it does provide a better user experience.

The more secure form of validation is server-side validation. Server-side validation means that the validation checks are performed on the server instead of on the client. It is more secure because these checks cannot be easily bypassed. Instead, the form data values are checked using server code (C# or VB) on the server. If the form data isn't valid, the page that is sent back to the client as invalid. Although it is more secure, server-side validation can be slow. It is sluggish simply because the page has to be posted to a remote location and checked. Your end user might not be the happiest surfer in the world if, after waiting 20 seconds for a form to post, he is told his e-mail address isn't in the correct format.

So what is the correct path? Well, actually, both! The best approach is always to perform client-side validation first and then, after the form passes and is posted to the server, to perform the validation checks again using server-side validation. This approach provides the best of both worlds. It is secure because hackers can't simply bypass the validation. They may bypass the client-side validation, but they quickly find that their form data is checked once again on the server after it is posted. This validation technique is also highly effective—giving you both the quickness and snappiness of client-side validation.

ASP.NET VALIDATION SERVER CONTROLS

Getting the forms that are present on your web pages to deal with validation is a common task in web development. For this reason, with the initial release of ASP.NET, the ASP.NET team introduced a series of validation server controls meant to make implementing sound validation for forms a snap.

ASP.NET not only introduces form validations as server controls, but it also makes these controls rather smart. When developing using some other web technologies, developers have to determine where to perform form validation—either on the client or on the server. The ASP.NET validation server controls eliminate this dilemma because ASP.NET performs browser detection when generating the ASP.NET page and makes decisions based on the information it gleans.

This means that if the browser can support the JavaScript that ASP.NET can send its way, the validation occurs on the client-side. If the client cannot support the JavaScript meant for client-side validation, this JavaScript is omitted and the validation occurs on the server.

The best part about this scenario is that even if client-side validation is initiated on a page, ASP.NET still performs the server-side validation when it receives the submitted page, thereby ensuring that security won't be compromised. This decisive nature of the validation server controls means that you can build your ASP.NET web pages to be the best they can possibly be—rather than dumbing-down your web applications for the lowest common denominator.

> **NOTE** *As mentioned earlier, server-side validation can be slower than client-side validation. However, since the server-side validation is only happening when the page is submitted and control postback can be disabled, the performance impact is not as severe.*

Presently, seven validation controls are available to you in ASP.NET 4.5. No new validation server controls have been added to ASP.NET since the initial release of the technology. However, ASP.NET 4.5 did introduce a new validation technique by using unobtrusive JavaScript capabilities, and this is discussed later in this chapter.

The available validation server controls include:

- ➤ `RequiredFieldValidator`
- ➤ `CompareValidator`
- ➤ `RangeValidator`
- ➤ `RegularExpressionValidator`
- ➤ `CustomValidator`
- ➤ `DynamicValidator`
- ➤ `ValidationSummary`

> **NOTE** *All of the validation server controls can be found in the Validation toolbox with the exception of the* `DynamicValidator`. *This can be found in the Dynamic Data toolbox.*

Working with ASP.NET validation server controls is no different from working with any other ASP.NET server control. Each of these controls allows you to drag and drop it onto a design surface or to work with it directly from the code of your ASP.NET page. You can also configure these controls so that they appear exactly as you want—ensuring the visual uniqueness that your applications might require. You see some aspects of both of these items throughout this chapter.

> **NOTE** *If the ASP.NET Validation controls don't meet your needs, you can certainly write your own custom validation controls. However, third-party controls are available, such as Peter Blum's Validation and More (VAM) from* www.peterblum.com/DES, *which includes more than 50 ASP.NET validation controls.*

Table 6-1 describes the functionality of each of the available validation server controls.

TABLE 6-1

VALIDATION SERVER CONTROL	DESCRIPTION
RequiredFieldValidator	Ensures that the user does not skip a form entry field.
CompareValidator	Allows for comparisons between the user's input and another item using a comparison operator (equals, greater than, less than, and so on).
RangeValidator	Checks the user's input based upon a lower- and upper-level range of numbers or characters.
RegularExpressionValidator	Checks that the user's entry matches a pattern defined by a regular expression. This control is good to use to check e-mail addresses and phone numbers.
CustomValidator	Checks the user's entry using custom-coded validation logic.
DynamicValidator	Works with exceptions that are thrown from entity data models and extension methods. This control is part of the ASP.NET Dynamic Data Framework. For more information about this control, be sure to search the Internet for DynamicValidator.
ValidationSummary	Displays all the error messages from the validators in one specific spot on the page.

Validation Causes

Validation doesn't just happen; it occurs in response to an event. In most cases, it is a button click event. The Button, LinkButton, and ImageButton server controls all have the capability to cause a page's form validation to initiate. This is the default behavior. Dragging and dropping a Button server control onto your form gives you the following initial result:

```
<asp:Button ID="Button1" runat="server" Text="Button" />
```

If you look through the properties of the Button control, you can see that the CausesValidation property is set to True. As stated, this behavior is the default—all buttons on the page, no matter how many there are, cause the form validation to fire.

If you have multiple buttons on an ASP.NET page, and you don't want every button to initiate the form validation, you can set the CausesValidation property to False for all the buttons you want to ignore in the validation process (for example, a form's Cancel button or pressing enter in another form element such as a search box):

```
<asp:Button ID="Button1" runat="server" Text="Cancel" CausesValidation="false" />
```

Unobtrusive Validation in ASP.NET 4.5

Traditionally, validation is handled on the server-side by using a built-in control or writing a method to check the values on the form. On the client-side, JavaScript would be omitted to the browser. In this scenario, the end user may be overwhelmed with validation messages. In addition, if the JavaScript itself contains errors, the page may not load properly. To circumvent this, the jQuery validation plugin was updated to support *unobtrusive validation.*

Unobtrusive validation helps to reduce the invasion on the user's interaction with the web application. Instead of rendering JavaScript inline, HTML5 data-* attributes are added to the appropriate form elements. In ASP.NET 4.5, the jQuery validation plugin is used and the unobtrusive validation functionality is enabled by default.

Unlike previous versions of Visual Studio, Visual Studio 2012 contains an empty project template that is truly empty. This means that a project is added to a solution with only a `web.config` file. If you choose to create a new website, the `web.config` file contains only the following:

```
<?xml version="1.0"?>
<configuration>
    <system.web>
        <compilation debug="true" targetFramework="4.5"/>
        <httpRuntime targetFramework="4.5"/>
    </system.web>
</configuration>
```

One of the validation controls available to you in ASP.NET is the RequiredFieldValidator. Listing 6-1 shows a simple use of the RequiredFieldValidator control.

LISTING 6-1: A simple use of the RequiredFieldValidator server control

VB

```
<%@ Page Language="VB" %>
<!DOCTYPE html>
<script runat="server">
    Protected Sub Button1_Click(ByVal sender As Object, ByVal e As System.EventArgs)
        If Page.IsValid Then
            Label1.Text = "Page is valid!"
        End If
    End Sub
</script>
<html xmlns="http://www.w3.org/1999/xhtml">
<head runat="server">
    <title></title>
</head>
<body>
    <form id="form1" runat="server">
        <div>
            <asp:TextBox ID="TextBox1" runat="server"></asp:TextBox>
            <asp:RequiredFieldValidator ID="RequiredFieldValidator1"
                runat="server" Text="Required!" ControlToValidate="TextBox1"
                EnableClientScript="true">
            </asp:RequiredFieldValidator>
            <br />
            <asp:Button ID="Button1" runat="server" Text="Submit"
                OnClick="Button1_Click" />
            <br />
            <br />
            <asp:Label ID="Label1" runat="server"></asp:Label>
        </div>
    </form>
```

continues

LISTING 6-1 *(continued)*

```
    </body>
    </html>
```

C#

```
<%@ Page Language="C#" %>
<!DOCTYPE html>
<script runat="server">
    protected void Button1_Click(Object sender, EventArgs e)
    {
        if (Page.IsValid)
        {
            Label1.Text = "Page is valid!";
        }
    }
</script>
```

If you run this page as is, leaving the textbox blank and submitting the form, you'll receive an exception, as shown in Figure 6-1.

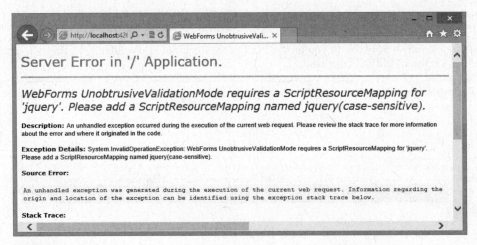

FIGURE 6-1

This exception occurs because ASP.NET is expecting you to define how validation should be rendered. You can enable unobtrusive validation by adding the following to the web.config file:

```
<appSettings>
    <add key="ValidationSettings:UnobtrusiveValidationMode" value="WebForms" />
</appSettings>
```

The value of `ValidationSettings:UnobtrusiveValidationMode` can be `None` or `WebForms`.

➤   `WebForms` means that you would like to use the Web Forms unobtrusive validation mode.

➤   `None` means that you do not want to use unobtrusive validation.

Instead of setting this value in the web.config file, you can also set this value in the global.asax file's Application_Start method, as shown here:

VB

```
ValidationSettings.UnobtrusiveValidationMode = UnobtrusiveValidationMode.WebForms
```

C#

```
ValidationSettings.UnobtrusiveValidationMode = UnobtrusiveValidationMode.WebForms;
```

If you want to set this value on a page-by-page basis, you can. In the `Page_Load` event, add the following:

VB

```
Page.UnobtrusiveValidationMode = UnobtrusiveValidationMode.WebForms
```

C#

```
Page.UnobtrusiveValidationMode = UnobtrusiveValidationMode.WebForms;
```

If you set the `UnobtrusiveValidationMode` to use `WebForms`, you're not done yet. You still have to register the jQuery JavaScript library with the ASP.NET Ajax ScriptManager (see sidebar).

> **NOTE** *jQuery is discussed further in Chapter 25.*

INSTALLING NUGET PACKAGES TO ENABLE UNOBTRUSIVE VALIDATION

If you don't already have jQuery installed in Visual Studio, here's how you do it. Using the Package Manager in Visual Studio 2012, you'll install two different packages. To access Package Manager, go to View ➪ Other Windows ➪ Package Manager Console.

1. The first package we need to install is jQuery. This allows ASP.NET to use the jQuery JavaScript framework. When the package is installed, the scripts are placed in a scripts folder. To install jQuery using the Package Manager, enter `install-package jQuery`. When executing this, the latest version of jQuery is installed.

2. The second package we need to install will add jQuery to the ScriptManager object in the `PreApplicationStartupMethod`. To install this package using the Package Manager, enter `install-package AspNet.ScriptManager.jQuery`.

The RequiredFieldValidator Server Control

The RequiredFieldValidator control simply checks to see whether any characters were entered into the HTML form element. It is a simple validation control, but it is one of the most frequently used. You must have a RequiredFieldValidator control for each form element on which you want to enforce a value-required rule.

> **NOTE** *All validator server controls, except for the validation summary control, which does not perform validation, can only validate one input control at a time. Therefore, if you would like every input control within your form to be required, each input control would need to have a separate RequiredFieldValidator control.*

In the previous section on unobtrusive validation when you tried to use the RequiredFieldValidator control, an exception was thrown. However, since then, you have added jQuery and told ASP.NET to register the scripts with the ScriptManager to resolve this exception. A simple textbox and button appear on the page. Don't enter any value inside the textbox, but click the Submit button. Figure 6-2 shows the result.

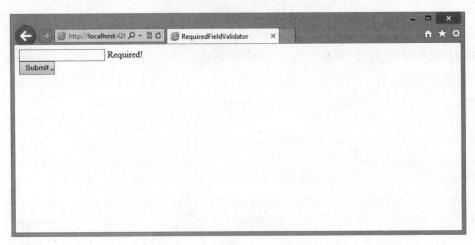

FIGURE 6-2

Now look at the code from this example back in Listing 6-1. First, nothing is different about the TextBox, Button, or Label controls. They are constructed just as they would be if you were not using any type of form validation. This page does contain a simple RequiredFieldValidator control, however. Several properties of this control are especially notable because you will use them in most of the validation server controls you create.

The first property to look at is the Text property. This property is the value that is shown to the end user via the web page if the validation fails. In this case, it is a simple `Required!` string. The second property to look at is the `ControlToValidate` property. This property is used to make an association between this validation server control and the ASP.NET form element that requires the validation. In this case, the value specifies the only element in the form — the textbox.

> **NOTE** *The WebControls that can be validated by using the* ControlToValidate *property are:*
>
> ➤ *DropDownList*
> ➤ *FileUpload*
> ➤ *ListBox*
> ➤ *RadioButtonList*
> ➤ *TextBox*
>
> *The HtmlControls that can be validated by using the* ControlToValidate *property are:*
>
> ➤ *HtmlInputFile*
> ➤ *HtmlInputPassword*
> ➤ *HtmlInputText*
> ➤ *HtmlSelect*
> ➤ *HtmlTextArea*

As you can see from this example, the error message is constructed from an attribute within the `<asp:RequiredFieldValidator>` control.

You can also express this error message between the `<asp:RequiredFieldValidator>` opening and closing nodes, as shown in Listing 6-2.

LISTING 6-2: Placing values between nodes

```
<asp:RequiredFieldValidator ID="RequiredFieldValidator1"
    runat="server" ControlToValidate="TextBox1"
    EnableClientScript="true">
    Required!
</asp:RequiredFieldValidator>
```

> **NOTE** *The RequiredFieldValidator is the only validation control that verifies that a value is submitted. The other validation controls do not require a value to be submitted.*

Looking at the Results Generated

The RequiredFieldValidator control uses client-side validation if the browser allows it. You can see how the client-side validation works by right-clicking on the page and selecting View Source from the menu. In the page code, you'll see the markup shown in Listing 6-3.

LISTING 6-3: Partially generated markup

```
<!-- Abbreviated for clarity -->
<input name="TextBox1" type="text" id="TextBox1" />
<span data-val-controltovalidate="TextBox1" id="RequiredFieldValidator1" data-val="true"
  data-val-evaluationfunction="RequiredFieldValidatorEvaluateIsValid"
  data-val-initialvalue="" style="visibility:hidden;">
    Required!
</span>
<br />
<input type="submit" name="Button1" value="Submit" onclick="javascript:WebForm_
DoPostBackWithOptions(new WebForm_PostBackOptions(&quot;Button1&quot;, &quot;&quot;, true,
&quot;&quot;, &quot;&quot;, false, false))" id="Button1" />
```

The `WebForm_DoPostBackWithOptions` JavaScript function initiates the client-side validation. Notice that the span element includes four attributes that begin with `data-val`. These attributes help the JavaScript functions determine which elements should be used for validation and how the validation should be handled.

> **NOTE** *The data-* attributes are only rendered when unobtrusive validation is turned on. When unobtrusive validation is not turned on, JavaScript will be emitted to the browser to handle the validation such as:*
>
> ```
> <script type="text/javascript">
> //<![CDATA[
> var RequiredFieldValidator1 = document.all ? document.all
>   ["RequiredFieldValidator1"] : document.getElementById("RequiredFieldVal
> idator1");
> RequiredFieldValidator1.controltovalidate = "TextBox1";
> RequiredFieldValidator1.evaluationfunction =
>   "RequiredFieldValidatorEvaluateIsValid";
> RequiredFieldValidator1.initialvalue = "";
> //]]>
> </script>
> ```

Using the InitialValue Property

One important property of the RequiredFieldValidator control is the `InitialValue` property. In Listing 6-3, you can see that the initial value is rendered as an attribute named `data-val-initialvalue` on the span element. Sometimes you have form elements that are populated with some default properties (for example, from a datastore), and these form elements might present the end user with values that require changes before the form can be submitted to the server.

When using the `InitialValue` property, you specify to the RequiredFieldValidator control the initial text of the element. The end user is then required to change that text value before he or she can submit the form. Listing 6-4 shows an example of using this property.

LISTING 6-4: Working with the InitialValue property

```
<asp:TextBox ID="TextBox1" runat="server" Text="Wrox"></asp:TextBox>
<asp:RequiredFieldValidator ID="RequiredFieldValidator1"
  runat="server" ControlToValidate="TextBox1" InitialValue="Wrox"
  EnableClientScript="true" Text="Please change the value of the textbox!" />
```

In this case, you can see that the `InitialValue` property contains a value of `Wrox`. When the page is built and run, the textbox contains this value as well. The RequiredFieldValidator control requires a change in this value for the page to be considered valid.

Disallowing Blank Entries and Requiring Changes at the Same Time

In the preceding example of the use of the `InitialValue` property, an interesting problem arises. If you run the associated example, one thing the end user can do to get past the form validation is to submit the page with no value entered in this particular textbox. A blank textbox does not fire a validation error because the RequiredFieldValidator control is now reconstructed to force the end user only to *change* the default value of the textbox (which he did when he removed the old value). When you reconstruct the RequiredFieldValidator control in this manner, nothing in the validation rule requires that *something* be entered in the textbox—just that the initial value be changed. The possibility exists for the user to completely bypass the form validation process by just removing anything entered in this textbox.

A way around this problem exists, however, and it goes back to the earlier discussion about how a form is made up of multiple validation rules—some of which are assigned to the same form element. To both require a change to the initial value of the textbox and disallow a blank entry (thereby making the element a required element), you must put an additional RequiredFieldValidator control on the page. This second RequiredFieldValidator control is associated with the same textbox as the first RequiredFieldValidator control. This method is illustrated in the example shown in Listing 6-5.

LISTING 6-5: Using two RequiredFieldValidator controls for one form element

```
<asp:TextBox ID="TextBox1" runat="server" Text="Wrox"></asp:TextBox>
<asp:RequiredFieldValidator ID="RequiredFieldValidator1"
    runat="server" ControlToValidate="TextBox1" InitialValue="Wrox"
    EnableClientScript="true" Text="Please change the value of the textbox!" />
<asp:RequiredFieldValidator ID="RequiredFieldValidator2"
    runat="server" ControlToValidate="TextBox1"
    EnableClientScript="true" Text="Please do not leave this field blank!" />
```

In this example, you can see that the textbox does indeed have two RequiredFieldValidator controls associated with it. The first, `RequiredFieldValidator1`, requires a change to the default value of the textbox through the use of the `InitialValue` property. The second RequiredFieldValidator control, `RequiredFieldValidator2`, simply makes the `TextBox1` control a form element that requires a value. You get the behavior you want by applying two validation rules to a single form element.

Validating Drop-Down Lists with the RequiredFieldValidator Control

So far, you have seen several examples of using the RequiredFieldValidator control with the TextBox control, but you can just as easily use this validation control with other form elements as well.

For example, you can use the RequiredFieldValidator control with an `<asp:DropDownList>` server control. Suppose that you have a drop-down list that requires the end user to select her profession from a list of items. The first line of the drop-down list includes instructions to the end user about what to select, and you want to make this line a required form element as well. Listing 6-6 shows the code to do so.

LISTING 6-6: Drop-down list validations

```
<asp:DropDownList ID="DropDownList1" runat="server">
    <asp:ListItem Selected="True">Select a profession</asp:ListItem>
    <asp:ListItem>Programmer</asp:ListItem>
    <asp:ListItem>Lawyer</asp:ListItem>
    <asp:ListItem>Doctor</asp:ListItem>
    <asp:ListItem>Artist</asp:ListItem>
</asp:DropDownList>
 
<asp:RequiredFieldValidator ID="RequiredFieldValidator1"
    runat="server" Text="Please make a selection"
    ControlToValidate="DropDownList1"
    InitialValue="Select a profession">
</asp:RequiredFieldValidator>
```

Just as when you work with the textbox, the RequiredFieldValidator control in this example associates itself with the DropDownList control using the `ControlToValidate` property. The drop-down list to which the validation control is bound has an initial value—`Select a profession`. You obviously don't want your end user to retain that value when she posts the form back to the server. So again, you use the `InitialValue` property of the RequiredFieldValidator control. The value of this property is assigned to the initial selected value of the drop-down list. This value forces the end user to select one of the provided professions in the drop-down list before she can post the form.

The CompareValidator Server Control

The CompareValidator control enables you to compare two form elements as well as to compare values contained within form elements to a constant value that you specify. For example, you can specify that a form element's value must be an integer and greater than a specified number. You can also state that values must be strings, dates, or other data types that are at your disposal for comparison purposes.

Validating against Other Controls

One of the more common ways of using the CompareValidator control is to make a comparison between two form elements. For example, suppose that you have an application that requires users to have passwords in order to access the site. You create one textbox asking for the user's password and a second textbox that asks the user to confirm the password. Because the textbox is in password mode, the end user cannot see what she is typing—just the number of characters that she has typed. To reduce the chances of the end user mistyping her password and inputting this incorrect password into the system, you ask her to confirm the password. After the form is input into the system, you simply have to make a comparison between the two textboxes to see whether they match. If they match, it is likely that the end user typed the password correctly, and you can input the password choice into the system. If the two textboxes do not match, you want the form to be invalid. Listing 6-7 demonstrates this situation.

LISTING 6-7: Using the CompareValidator to test values against other control values

VB

```
<%@ Page Language="VB" %>
<!DOCTYPE html>
<script runat="server">
    Protected Sub Button1_Click(sender As Object, e As EventArgs)
        If Page.IsValid Then
            Label1.Text = "Passwords match"
        End If
    End Sub
</script>
<html xmlns="http://www.w3.org/1999/xhtml">
<head id="Head1" runat="server">
    <title>CompareFieldValidator</title>
</head>
<body>
    <form id="form1" runat="server">
        <p>
            Password<br />
            <asp:TextBox ID="TextBox1" runat="server"
                TextMode="Password"></asp:TextBox>
             
            <asp:CompareValidator ID="CompareValidator1"
                runat="server" Text="Passwords do not match!"
                ControlToValidate="TextBox2"
                ControlToCompare="TextBox1"></asp:CompareValidator>
        </p>
        <p>
            Confirm Password<br />
            <asp:TextBox ID="TextBox2" runat="server"
                TextMode="Password"></asp:TextBox>
        </p>
        <p>
            <asp:Button ID="Button1" OnClick="Button1_Click"
                runat="server" Text="Login"></asp:Button>
        </p>
        <p>
            <asp:Label ID="Label1" runat="server"></asp:Label>
        </p>
    </form>
</body>
</html>
```

C#

```
<%@ Page Language="C#" %>
<!DOCTYPE html>
<script runat="server">
    protected void Button1_Click(Object sender, EventArgs e) {
        if (Page.IsValid)
            Label1.Text = "Passwords match";
    }
</script>
```

Looking at the CompareValidator control on the form, you can see that it is similar to the RequiredFieldValidator control. The CompareValidator control has a property called `ControlToValidate` that associates itself with one of the form elements on the page. In this case, you need only a single CompareValidator control on the page because a single comparison is made. In this example, you are making a comparison between the value of `TextBox2` and that of `TextBox1`. Therefore, you use the `ControlToCompare` property. This specifies what value is compared to `TextBox2`. In this case, the value is `TextBox1`.

> **NOTE** *A common mistake developers make with the CompareValidator control is to switch the values of the* ControlToValidate *and* ControlToCompare *properties. Be sure to double-check these values.*

It's as simple as that. If the two textboxes do not match after the end user posts the page, the value of the Text property from the CompareValidator control appears in the browser. Figure 6-3 shows an example of this situation.

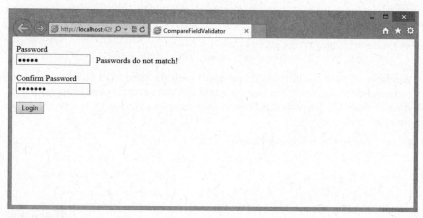

FIGURE 6-3

Validating against Constants

Besides being able to validate values against values in other controls, you can also use the CompareValidator control to make comparisons against constants of specific data types. For example, suppose you have a textbox on your registration form that asks for the age of the user. In most cases, you want to get back an actual number and not something such as aa or bb as a value. Listing 6-8 shows you how to ensure that you get back an actual number.

LISTING 6-8: Using the CompareValidator to validate against constants

```
Age:
<asp:TextBox ID="TextBox1" runat="server" MaxLength="3">
</asp:TextBox>
 
<asp:CompareValidator ID="CompareValidator1" runat="server"
    Text="You must enter a number"
    ControlToValidate="TextBox1" Type="Integer"
    Operator="DataTypeCheck"></asp:CompareValidator>
```

In this example, the end user is required to type a number into the textbox. If he attempts to bypass the validation by entering a fake value that contains anything other than a number, the page is identified as invalid, and the CompareValidator control displays the value of the Text property.

To specify the data types that you want to use in these comparisons, you simply use the Type property. The Type property can take the following values:

➤ Currency

➤ Date

➤ Double

➤ Integer

➤ String

Not only can you make sure that what is entered is of a specific data type, but you can also make sure that what is entered is valid when compared to specific constants. For example, you can make sure what is entered in a form element is greater than, less than, equal to, greater than or equal to, or less than or equal to a specified value. Listing 6-9 shows an example of this situation.

LISTING 6-9: Making comparisons with the CompareValidator control

```
Age:
<asp:TextBox ID="TextBox1" runat="server" MaxLength="3">
</asp:TextBox>
 
<asp:CompareValidator ID="CompareValidator1" runat="server"
    Text="You must be at least 18 to join"
    ControlToValidate="TextBox1" Type="Integer"
    Operator="GreaterThanEqual" ValueToCompare="18"></asp:CompareValidator>
```

In this case, the CompareValidator control not only associates itself with the TextBox1 control and requires that the value must be an integer, but it also uses the Operator and the ValueToCompare properties to ensure that the number is greater than 18. Therefore, if the end user enters a value of 18 or less, the validation fails, and the page is considered invalid.

The Operator property can take one of the following values:

➤ Equal

➤ NotEqual

➤ GreaterThan

➤ GreaterThanEqual

➤ LessThan

➤ LessThanEqual

➤ DataTypeCheck

The ValueToCompare property is where you place the constant value used in the comparison. In the preceding example, it is the number 18.

The RangeValidator Server Control

The RangeValidator control is quite similar to that of the CompareValidator control, but it makes sure that the end-user value or selection provided is within a specified range as opposed to being just greater than or less than a specified constant. For an example of this control, think back to the textbox element that asks for the age of the end user and performs a validation on the value provided. Listing 6-10 demonstrates this validation.

LISTING 6-10: Using the RangeValidator control to test an integer value

```
Age:
<asp:TextBox ID="TextBox1" runat="server" MaxLength="3">
</asp:TextBox>
 
<asp:RangeValidator ID="RangeValidator1" runat="server"
    ControlToValidate="TextBox1" Type="Integer"
    Text="You must be between 30 and 40"
    MaximumValue="40" MinimumValue="30"></asp:RangeValidator>
```

In this example, this page consists of a textbox asking for the age of the end user. The RangeValidator control makes an analysis of the value provided and makes sure the value is somewhere in the range, including the minimum and maximum values, of 30 to 40. You set the range using the MaximumValue and

`MinimumValue` properties. The RangeValidator control also makes sure that what is entered is an integer data type. It uses the `Type` property, which is set to `Integer`. The other possible data types for the RangeValidator control include the same values used, and as mentioned earlier, for the CompareValidator control. The collection of screenshots in Figure 6-4 shows this example in action.

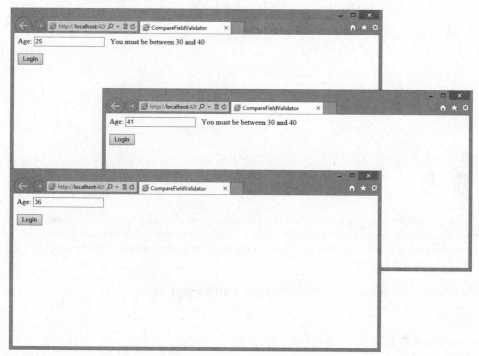

FIGURE 6-4

As you can see from the screenshots in Figure 6-4, a value of less than 30 causes the RangeValidator control to fire, as does a number greater than 40. A value that is somewhere between 30 and 40 (in this case 36) conforms to the validation rule of the control.

The RangeValidator control is not only about validating numbers (although it is most often used in this fashion). It can also be about validating a range of string characters as well as other items, including calendar dates. By default, the `Type` property of any of the validation controls is set to `String`, which allows you to ensure that the string's ASCII value submitted is within a particular range. You can use the RangeValidator control to make sure that what is entered in another server control (such as a Calendar control) is within a certain range of dates.

For example, suppose that you are building a Web Form that asks for a customer's arrival date, and the arrival date needs to be within two weeks of the current date. You can use the RangeValidator control to test for these scenarios quite easily.

Because the date range that you want to check is dynamically generated, you assign the `MaximumValue` and `MinimumValue` properties programmatically in the `Page_Load` event. In the Designer, your sample page for this example should look like Figure 6-5.

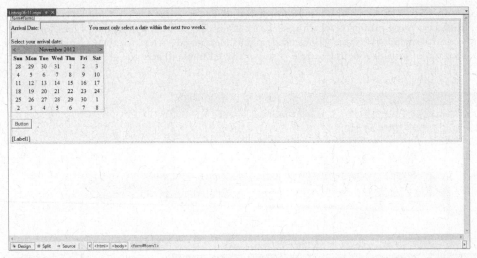

FIGURE 6-5

The idea is that the end user will select a date from the Calendar control, which will then populate the TextBox control. Then, when the end user clicks the form's button, he is notified if the date selected is invalid. If the date selected is valid, that date is presented through the Label control on the page. Listing 6-11 presents the code for this example.

LISTING 6-11: Using the RangeValidator control to test a string date value

VB

```
<%@ Page Language="VB" %>
<!DOCTYPE html>
<script runat="server">
    Protected Sub Page_Load(ByVal sender As Object, ByVal e As System.EventArgs)
        RangeValidator1.MinimumValue = DateTime.Now.ToShortDateString()
        RangeValidator1.MaximumValue = DateTime.Now.AddDays(14).ToShortDateString()
    End Sub
    Protected Sub Calendar1_SelectionChanged(ByVal sender As Object, _
        ByVal e As System.EventArgs)
        TextBox1.Text = Calendar1.SelectedDate.ToShortDateString()
    End Sub
    Protected Sub Button1_Click(ByVal sender As Object, _
        ByVal e As System.EventArgs)
        If Page.IsValid Then
            Label1.Text = "You are set to arrive on: " & TextBox1.Text
        End If
    End Sub
</script>
<html xmlns="http://www.w3.org/1999/xhtml">
<head runat="server">
    <title>Date Validation Check</title>
</head>
<body>
    <form id="form1" runat="server">
        Arrival Date:
```

```
            <asp:TextBox ID="TextBox1" runat="server"></asp:TextBox> 
            <asp:RangeValidator ID="RangeValidator1" runat="server"
                Text="You must only select a date within the next two weeks."
                ControlToValidate="TextBox1" Type="Date"></asp:RangeValidator>
            <br />
            <br />
            Select your arrival date:<br />
            <asp:Calendar ID="Calendar1" runat="server"
                OnSelectionChanged="Calendar1_SelectionChanged"></asp:Calendar>
             
            <br />
            <asp:Button ID="Button1" runat="server" Text="Button"
                OnClick="Button1_Click" />
            <br />
            <br />
            <asp:Label ID="Label1" runat="server"></asp:Label>
        </form>
    </body>
</html>
```

C#

```
<%@ Page Language="C#" %>
<!DOCTYPE html>
<script runat="server">
    protected void Page_Load(object sender, EventArgs e)
    {
        RangeValidator1.MinimumValue = DateTime.Now.ToShortDateString();
        RangeValidator1.MaximumValue =
            DateTime.Now.AddDays(14).ToShortDateString();
    }
    protected void Calendar1_SelectionChanged(object sender, EventArgs e)
    {
        TextBox1.Text = Calendar1.SelectedDate.ToShortDateString();
    }
    protected void Button1_Click(object sender, EventArgs e)
    {
        if (Page.IsValid)
        {
            Label1.Text = "You are set to arrive on: " + TextBox1.Text.ToString();
        }
    }
</script>
```

From this code, you can see that when the page is loaded, the `MinimumValue` and `MaximumValue` attributes are assigned a dynamic value. In this case, the `MinimumValue` gets the `DateTime.Now` `.ToShortDateString()` value, whereas the `MaximumValue` gets a date of 14 days later.

After the end user selects a date, the selected date is populated in the `TextBox1` control using the `Calendar1_SelectionChanged` event. After the user selects a date and clicks the button on the page, the `Button1_Click` event is fired and the page is checked for form validity using the `Page.IsValid` property. By using the `Page.IsValid` property, each of the validation controls are checked to ensure that validation passes. If it does, the value returned is true. Otherwise, a false value is returned. An invalid page gives you the result shown in Figure 6-6.

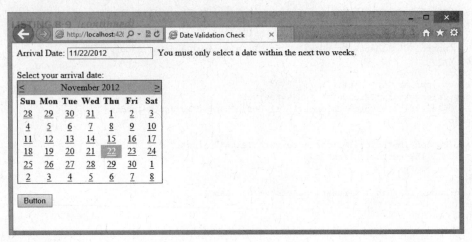

FIGURE 6-6

The RegularExpressionValidator Server Control

One exciting control that developers like to use is the RegularExpressionValidator control. This control offers a lot of flexibility when you apply validation rules to your Web Forms. Using the RegularExpressionValidator control, you can check a user's input based on a pattern that you define using a regular expression.

This means that you can define a structure that a user's input will be applied against to see whether its structure matches the one that you define. For example, you can define that the structure of the user input must be in the form of an e-mail address or an Internet URL; if it doesn't match this definition, the page is considered invalid. Listing 6-12 shows you how to validate what is typed into a textbox by making sure it is in the form of an e-mail address.

LISTING 6-12: Making sure the textbox value is an e-mail address

```
<asp:TextBox ID="TextBox1" runat="server"></asp:TextBox>
<asp:RegularExpressionValidator ID="RegularExpressionValidator1" runat="server"
    Text="You must enter an email address"
    ValidationExpression="\w+([-+.']\w+)*@\w+([-.]\w+)*\.\w+([-.]\w+)*"
    ControlToValidate="TextBox1"></asp:RegularExpressionValidator>
```

Just like the other validation server controls, the RegularExpressionValidator control uses the `ControlToValidate` property to bind itself to the TextBox control, and it includes a `Text` property to push out the error message to the screen if the validation test fails. The unique property of this validation control is the `ValidationExpression` property. This property takes a string value, which is the regular expression you are going to apply to the input value.

Visual Studio makes using regular expressions a little easier through the use of the Regular Expression Editor. This editor provides a few commonly used regular expressions that you might want to apply to your RegularExpressionValidator. To get at this editor, you work with your page from the Design view. Be sure to highlight the RegularExpressionValidator1 server control in this Design view to see the control's properties. In the Property window of Visual Studio, click the button found next to the `ValidationExpression` property to launch the Regular Expression Editor. Figure 6-7 shows this editor.

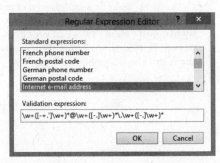

FIGURE 6-7

Using this editor, you can find regular expressions for things like e-mail addresses, Internet URLs, ZIP codes, phone numbers, and social security numbers.

> **NOTE** *In addition to working with the Regular Expression Editor to help you with these sometimes-complicated regular expression strings, you can also find a good-sized collection of them at an Internet site called RegExLib found at* www.regexlib.com.

The CustomValidator Server Control

So far, you have seen a wide variety of validation controls that are at your disposal. In many cases, these validation controls address many of the validation rules that you want to apply to your Web Forms. Sometimes, however, none of these controls works for you, and you have to go beyond what they offer. This is where the CustomValidator control comes into play.

The CustomValidator control enables you to build your own client-side or server-side validations that you can then easily apply to your Web Forms. Doing so enables you to make validation checks against values or calculations performed in the data tier (for example, in a database), or to make sure that the user's input validates against some arithmetic validation (for example, determining whether a number is even or odd). You can do quite a bit with the CustomValidator control.

Using Client-Side Validation

One of the worthwhile functions of the CustomValidator control is its capability to easily provide custom client-side validations. Many developers have their own collections of JavaScript functions that they employ in their applications, and using the CustomValidator control is one easy way of getting these functions implemented with minimal changes to the functions. As an example, in most cases, the JavaScript function signature must be updated to adhere to a specific signature.

For example, look at a simple form that asks for a number from the end user. This form uses the CustomValidator control to perform a custom client-side validation on the user input to make sure that the number provided is divisible by 5. Listing 6-13 shows the code for this validation.

LISTING 6-13: Using the CustomValidator control to perform client-side validations

VB

```
<%@ Page Language="VB" %>
<!DOCTYPE html>
<script runat="server">
    Protected Sub Button1_Click(ByVal sender As Object, ByVal e As System.EventArgs)
        Label1.Text = "VALID NUMBER!"
    End Sub
</script>
<html xmlns="http://www.w3.org/1999/xhtml">
<head id="Head1" runat="server">
    <title>CustomValidator</title>
    <script type="text/javascript">
        function validateNumber(oSrc, args) {
            args.IsValid = (args.Value % 5 == 0);
        }
    </script>
</head>
<body>
    <form id="form1" runat="server">
        <p>
            Number:
```

continues

LISTING 6-13 *(continued)*

```
            <asp:TextBox ID="TextBox1"
                runat="server"></asp:TextBox>
             
            <asp:CustomValidator ID="CustomValidator1"
                runat="server" ControlToValidate="TextBox1"
                Text="Number must be divisible by 5"
                ClientValidationFunction="validateNumber">
            </asp:CustomValidator>
        </p>
        <p>
            <asp:Button ID="Button1" OnClick="Button1_Click"
                runat="server" Text="Button"></asp:Button>
        </p>
        <p>
            <asp:Label ID="Label1" runat="server"></asp:Label>
        </p>
    </form>
</body>
</html>
```

C#

```
<%@ Page Language="C#" %>
<!DOCTYPE html>
<script runat="server">
    protected void Button1_Click(Object sender, EventArgs e)
    {
        Label1.Text = "VALID NUMBER!";
    }
</script>
```

Looking over this Web Form, you can see a couple of things happening. It is a simple form with only a single textbox requiring user input. The user clicks the button that triggers the `Button1_Click` event, which in turn populates the `Label1` control on the page. It carries out this simple operation only if all the validation checks are performed and the user input passes these tests.

One item that is different about this page is the inclusion of the second `<script>` block found within the `<head>` section. This is the custom JavaScript. Note that Visual Studio 2012 is very friendly toward these kinds of constructions, even when you are switching between the Design and Code views of the page—something Visual Studio editions prior to 2008 were rather poor at dealing with. This JavaScript function—`validateNumber`—is shown here:

```
<script type="text/javascript">
    function validateNumber(oSrc, args) {
        args.IsValid = (args.Value % 5 == 0);
    }
</script>
```

This second `<script>` section is the client-side JavaScript that you want the CustomValidator control to use when making its validation checks on the information entered into the textbox. Similarly to the server-side validation methods, the client-side validation method will require two parameters: the source parameter and the arguments parameter. The source parameter is a reference to the validation control itself. The arguments parameter is an object containing two properties, `args.IsValid` and `args.Value`. The JavaScript functions you employ are going to use the `args.IsValid` property and set this property to `True` or `False`, depending on the outcome of the validation check. In this case, the user input (`args.Value`) is checked to see whether it is divisible by 5. The Boolean value returned is then assigned to the `args.IsValid` property, which is then used by the CustomValidator control.

The CustomValidator control, like the other controls before it, uses the `ControlToValidate` property to associate itself with a particular element on the page. The property that you are interested in here is the `ClientValidationFunction` property. The string value provided to this property is the name of the client-side function that you want this validation check to employ when the CustomValidator control is triggered. In this case, it is `validateNumber`:

```
ClientValidationFunction="validateNumber"
```

> **NOTE** *The ClientValidationFunction can be set from code or by using the property window.*

If you run this page and make an invalid entry, you produce the result shown in Figure 6-8.

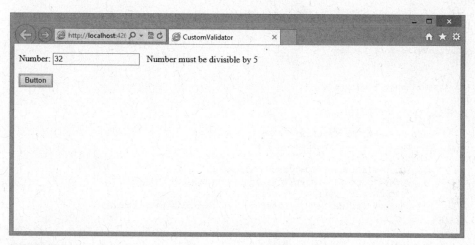

FIGURE 6-8

Using Server-Side Validation

Now let's move this same validation check from the client to the server. The CustomValidator control enables you to make custom server-side validations a reality as well. You will find that creating your server-side validations is just as easy as creating client-side validations.

If you create your own server-side validations, you can make them as complex as your applications require. For example, using the CustomValidator for server-side validations is something you do if you want to check the user's input against dynamic values coming from XML files, databases, or elsewhere.

For an example of using the CustomValidator control for some custom server-side validation, you can work with the same example as you did when creating the client-side validation. Now, create a server-side check that makes sure a user input number is divisible by 5, as shown in Listing 6-14.

LISTING 6-14: Using the CustomValidator control to perform server-side validations

VB

```vb
<%@ Page Language="VB" %>
<!DOCTYPE html>
<script runat="server">
    Protected Sub Button1_Click(ByVal sender As Object, ByVal e As System.EventArgs)
        If Page.IsValid Then
            Label1.Text = "VALID ENTRY!"
        End If
    End Sub
    Sub ValidateNumber(sender As Object, args As ServerValidateEventArgs)
        Try
            Dim num As Integer = Integer.Parse(args.Value)
            args.IsValid = ((num Mod 5) = 0)
        Catch ex As Exception
            args.IsValid = False
        End Try
    End Sub
</script>
<html xmlns="http://www.w3.org/1999/xhtml">
<head runat="server">
    <title>CustomValidator</title>
</head>
<body>
    <form id="form1" runat="server">
        <div>
            <p>
                Number:
                <asp:TextBox ID="TextBox1"
                    runat="server"></asp:TextBox>
                 
                <asp:CustomValidator ID="CustomValidator1"
                    runat="server" ControlToValidate="TextBox1"
                    Text="Number must be divisible by 5"
                    OnServerValidate="ValidateNumber"></asp:CustomValidator>
            </p>
            <p>
                <asp:Button ID="Button1" OnClick="Button1_Click"
                    runat="server" Text="Button"></asp:Button>
            </p>
            <p>
                <asp:Label ID="Label1" runat="server"></asp:Label>
            </p>
        </div>
    </form>
</body>
</html>
```

C#

```csharp
<%@ Page Language="C#" %>
<!DOCTYPE html>
<script runat="server">
    protected void Button1_Click(Object sender, EventArgs e)
    {
        if (Page.IsValid)
        {
            Label1.Text = "VALID ENTRY!";
        }
    }
```

```
void ValidateNumber(object source, ServerValidateEventArgs args)
{
    try
    {
        int num = int.Parse(args.Value);
        args.IsValid = ((num % 5) == 0);
    }
    catch (Exception ex)
    {
        args.IsValid = false;
    }
}
</script>
```

Instead of a client-side JavaScript function in the code, this example includes a server-side function—ValidateNumber. The server-side function accepts the same two parameters that the client-side function uses. The ValidateNumber function, as well as all functions that are being constructed to work with the CustomValidator control, must use the ServerValidateEventArgs object as one of the parameters in order to get the data passed to the function for the validation check. The ValidateNumber function itself is nothing fancy. It simply checks to see whether the provided number is divisible by 5.

From within your custom function, which is designed to work with the CustomValidator control, you actually get at the value coming from the form element through the args.Value object. Then you set the args.IsValid property to True or False, depending on your validation checks. From the preceding example, you can see that the args.IsValid is set to False if the number is not divisible by 5 and also that an exception is thrown (which would occur if a string value were input into the form element). After the custom function is established, the next step is to apply it to the CustomValidator control, as shown in the following example:

```
<asp:CustomValidator ID="CustomValidator1"
    runat="server" ControlToValidate="TextBox1"
    Text="Number must be divisible by 5"
    OnServerValidate="ValidateNumber"></asp:CustomValidator>
```

To make the association between a CustomValidator control and a function that you have in your server-side code, you simply use the OnServerValidate server-side event. The value assigned to this property is the name of the function—in this case, ValidateNumber.

Running this example causes the postback to come back to the server and the validation check (based on the ValidateNumber function) to be performed. From here, the page reloads and the Page_Load event is called. In the example from Listing 6-14, you can see that a check is done to determine whether the page is valid. This check uses the Page.IsValid property:

```
if (Page.IsValid)
{
    Label1.Text = "VALID ENTRY!";
}
```

Using Client-Side and Server-Side Validation Together

As stated earlier in this chapter, you have to think about the security of your forms and to ensure that the data you are collecting from the forms is valid. For this reason, when you decide to employ client-side validations (as you did in Listing 6-13), you should take steps to also reconstruct the client-side function as a server-side function. When you have done this task, you should associate the CustomValidator control to both the client-side and server-side functions. In the case of the number check validation from Listings 6-13 and 6-14, you can use both validation functions in your page and then change the CustomValidator control to point to both of these functions, as shown in Listing 6-15.

LISTING 6-15: The CustomValidator control with client- and server-side validations

```
<asp:CustomValidator ID="CustomValidator1"
    runat="server" ControlToValidate="TextBox1"
    Text="Number must be divisible by 5"
    OnServerValidate="ValidateNumber"
    ClientValidationFunction="validateNumber"></asp:CustomValidator>
```

From this example, you can see it is simply a matter of using the `ClientValidationFunction` and `OnServerValidate` attributes at the same time.

The ValidationSummary Server Control

The ValidationSummary control does not perform validations on the content input into your Web Forms. Instead, it's a reporting control that the other validation controls on a page use. You can use this validation control to consolidate error reporting for all the validation errors that occur on a page instead of leaving it up to each individual validation control.

You might want this capability for larger forms, which have a comprehensive form-validation process. In this case, you may find having all the possible validation errors reported to the end user in a single and easily identifiable manner to be rather user-friendly. You can display these error messages in a list, bulleted list, or paragraph.

By default, the ValidationSummary control shows the list of validation errors as a bulleted list, as shown in Listing 6-16.

LISTING 6-16: A partial page example of the ValidationSummary control

```
<p>
    First name
    <asp:TextBox ID="TextBox1" runat="server"></asp:TextBox>
     
    <asp:RequiredFieldValidator ID="RequiredFieldValidator1"
        runat="server" ErrorMessage="You must enter your first name"
        ControlToValidate="TextBox1"></asp:RequiredFieldValidator>
</p>
<p>
    Last name
    <asp:TextBox ID="TextBox2" runat="server"></asp:TextBox>
     
    <asp:RequiredFieldValidator ID="RequiredFieldValidator2"
        runat="server" ErrorMessage="You must enter your last name"
        ControlToValidate="TextBox2"></asp:RequiredFieldValidator>
</p>
<p>
    <asp:Button ID="Button1" OnClick="Button1_Click" runat="server"
        Text="Submit"></asp:Button>
</p>
<p>
    <asp:ValidationSummary ID="ValidationSummary1" runat="server"
        HeaderText="You received the following errors:"></asp:ValidationSummary>
</p>
<p>
    <asp:Label ID="Label1" runat="server"></asp:Label>
</p>
```

This example asks the end user for her first and last name. Each textbox in the form has an associated RequiredFieldValidator control assigned to it. When the page is built and run, the user's clicking the Submit button with no values placed in either of the textboxes causes both validation errors to fire. Figure 6-9 shows this result.

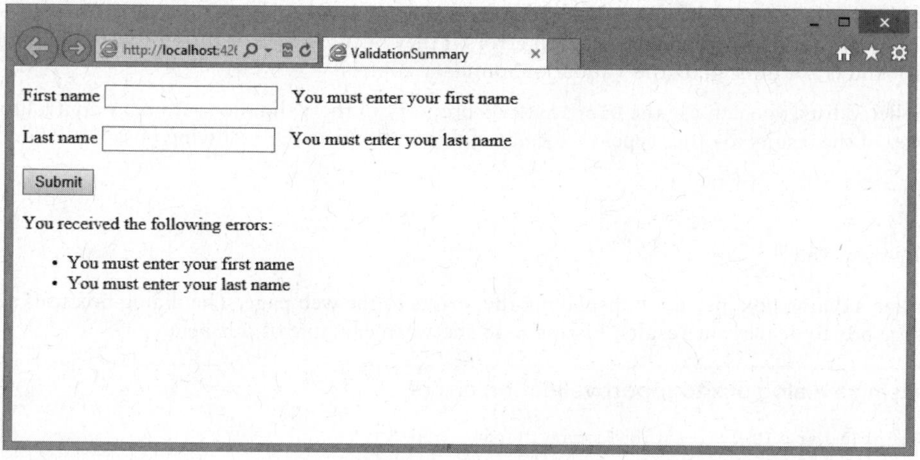

FIGURE 6-9

As in earlier examples of validation controls on the form, these validation errors appear next to each of the textboxes. You can see, however, that the ValidationSummary control also displays the validation errors as a bulleted list at the location of the control on the Web Form. In most cases, you do not want these errors to appear twice on a page for the end user. You can change this behavior by using the `Text` property of the validation controls, in addition to the `ErrorMessage` property, as you have typically done throughout this chapter. The `Text` property is the value of the text displayed within the validation control. The `ErrorMessage` property is the value of the text displayed within the validation summary (if added to the page). Listing 6-17 shows this approach.

LISTING 6-17: Using the Text property of a validation control

```
<asp:RequiredFieldValidator ID="RequiredFieldValidator1"
    runat="server" ErrorMessage="You must enter your first name"
    Text="*" ControlToValidate="TextBox1"></asp:RequiredFieldValidator>
```

Making this type of change to the validation controls produces the results shown in Figure 6-10.

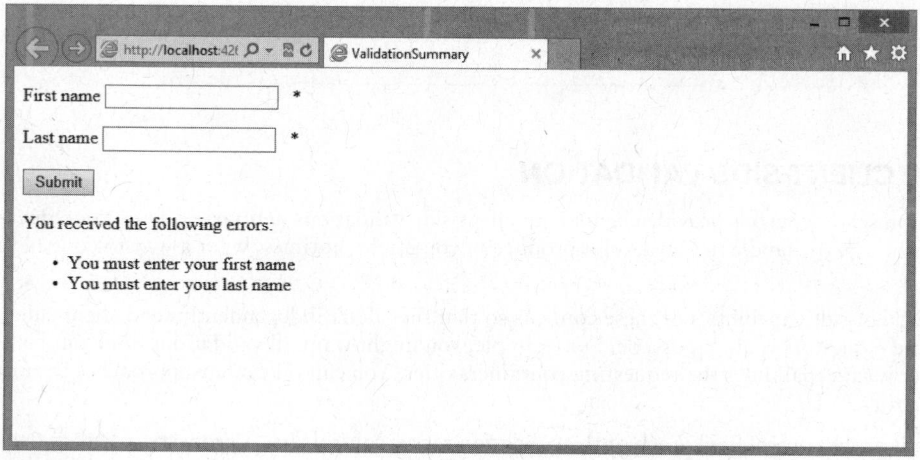

FIGURE 6-10

To get this result, just remember that the ValidationSummary control uses the validation control's `ErrorMessage` property for displaying the validation errors if they occur. The `Text` property is used by the validation control and is not utilized by the ValidationSummary control.

In addition to bulleted lists, you can use the `DisplayMode` property of the ValidationSummary control to change the display of the results to other types of formats. This control has the following possible values:

- `BulletList`
- `List`
- `SingleParagraph`

You can also utilize a dialog box instead of displaying the results to the web page. The dialog box uses a JavaScript message box to display the results. Listing 6-18 shows an example of this behavior.

LISTING 6-18: Using a dialog box to report validation errors

```
<asp:ValidationSummary ID="ValidationSummary1" runat="server"
    ShowMessageBox="true" ShowSummary="false"></asp:ValidationSummary>
```

From this code example, you can see that the `ShowSummary` property is set to `false`—meaning that the bulleted list of validation errors are not shown on the actual web page. However, because the `ShowMessageBox` property is set to `true`, you now get these errors reported in a message box, as shown in Figure 6-11.

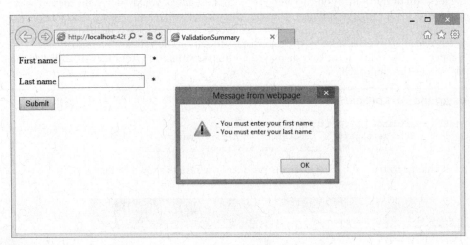

FIGURE 6-11

TURNING OFF CLIENT-SIDE VALIDATION

Because validation server controls provide clients with client-side validations automatically (if the requesting container can properly handle the JavaScript produced), you might, at times, want a way to control this behavior.

Turning off the client-side capabilities of these controls so that they don't independently send client-side capabilities to the requestors is quite possible. For example, you might want all validations done on the server, no matter what capabilities the requesting containers offer. You can take a few approaches to turning off this functionality.

The first option is at the control level. Each of the validation server controls has a property called `EnableClientScript`. This property is set to `True` by default, but setting it to `False` prevents the control from sending out a JavaScript function for validation on the client. Instead, the validation check is done on the server. Listing 6-19 shows the use of this property.

LISTING 6-19: Disabling client-side validations in a validation control

```
<asp:RequiredFieldValidator ID="RequiredFieldValidator1"
    runat="server" ErrorMessage="You must enter your first name"
    Text="*" ControlToValidate="TextBox1" EnableClientScript="false">
</asp:RequiredFieldValidator>
```

You can also remove a validation control's client-side capability programmatically (shown in Listing 6-20).

LISTING 6-20: Removing the client-side capabilities programmatically

VB
```
Protected Sub Page_Load(ByVal sender As Object, ByVal e As System.EventArgs)
    RequiredFieldValidator1.EnableClientScript = False
    RequiredFieldValidator2.EnableClientScript = False
End Sub
```

C#
```
protected void Page_Load(Object sender, EventArgs e)
{
    RequiredFieldValidator1.EnableClientScript = false;
    RequiredFieldValidator2.EnableClientScript = false;
}
```

Another option is to turn off the client-side script capabilities for all the validation controls on a page from within the `Page_Load` event. This method can be rather helpful if you want to dynamically decide not to allow client-side validation. Listing 6-21 shows this option.

LISTING 6-21: Disabling all client-side validations from the Page_Load event

VB
```
Protected Sub Page_Load(ByVal sender As Object, ByVal e As System.EventArgs)
    For Each bv As BaseValidator In Page.Validators
        bv.EnableClientScript = False
    Next
End Sub
```

C#
```
protected void Page_Load(Object sender, EventArgs e)
{
    foreach (BaseValidator bv in Page.Validators)
    {
        bv.EnableClientScript = false;
    }
}
```

By looking for each instance of a `BaseValidator` object in the validators contained on an ASP.NET page, this `For Each` loop turns off client-side validation capabilities for each validation control the page contains.

USING IMAGES AND SOUNDS FOR ERROR NOTIFICATIONS

So far, you have been displaying simple textual messages for the error notifications that come from the validation server controls. In most instances, you are going to do just that—display some simple textual messages to inform end users that they typed something into the form that doesn't pass your validation rules.

An interesting tip regarding the validation controls is that you are not limited to just text—you can also use images and sounds for error notifications.

To use an image for the error, you use the `Text` property of any of the validation controls. You simply place some appropriate HTML as the value of this property, as shown in Listing 6-22.

LISTING 6-22: Using images for error notifications

```
<asp:RequiredFieldValidator ID="RequiredFieldValidator1"
    runat="server" Text="<img src='error.jpg' alt='Error!' />"
    ControlToValidate="TextBox1" EnableClientScript="true">
</asp:RequiredFieldValidator>
```

As you can see from this example, instead of some text being output to the web page, the value of the `Text` property is an HTML string. This bit of HTML is used to display an image. Be sure to notice the use of the single and double quotation marks so you won't get any errors when the browser generates the page. This example produces something similar to Figure 6-12.

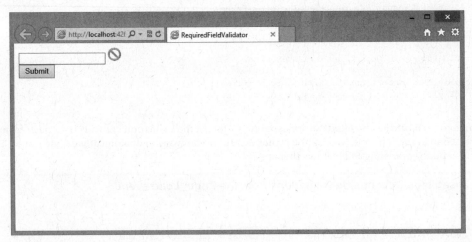

FIGURE 6-12

The other interesting twist you can create is to add a sound notification when an error occurs. You can do so the same way you display an image for error notifications. Listing 6-23 shows an example of this.

LISTING 6-23: Using sound for error notifications

```
<asp:RequiredFieldValidator ID="RequiredFieldValidator1"
    runat="server" ControlToValidate="TextBox1" EnableClientScript="false"
    Text="<audio controls='' src='C:\Windows\Media\tada.wav' autoplay='autoplay'></audio>">
</asp:RequiredFieldValidator>
```

You can find a lot of the Windows system sounds in the `C:\Windows\Media` directory. In this example, the `Text` uses the `<audio>` element to place a sound on the Web Form (works only with HTML5-compliant browsers). The sound plays only when the end user triggers the validation control.

> **NOTE** *When referencing a sound file (such as this one), you must be sure that the web application has proper permissions to listen to the sound. It is recommended that the sounds be hosted within the application or on a content delivery network (CDN). Also note that the audio element does not support .wav files in Internet Explorer. However, several other browsers do support .wav files. Search the Internet for "HTML5 audio supported types" to determine which formats your browsers support.*

When working with sounds for error notifications, you have to disable the client-side script capability for that particular control because if you do not, the sound plays when the page loads in the browser, whether or not a validation error has been triggered.

WORKING WITH VALIDATION GROUPS

In many instances, developers want to place more than one form on a single page. Different validation controls are often assigned to two distinct forms on the page. However, in this example, unexpected behavior may occur. For instance, when the end user submits one form, the validation controls in the other form may be fired even though the user is not working with that form. This will cause the first form from being submitted. In other scenarios, developers may want to simply break up a form and validate controls differently.

Figure 6-13, for example, shows a basic page for the .NET Valley User Group that includes two forms.

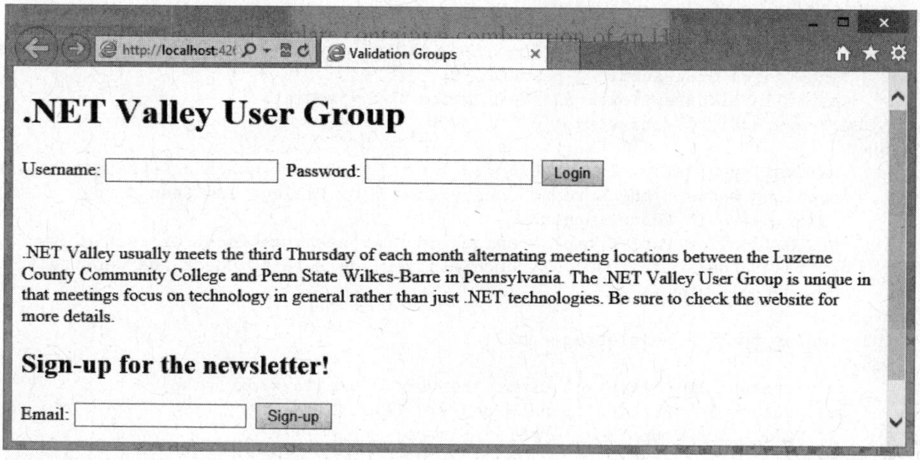

FIGURE 6-13

One of the forms is for members of the site to supply their usernames and passwords to log into the Members Only section of the site. The second form on the page is for anyone who wants to sign up for the user group's newsletter. Each form has its own button and some validation controls associated with it. The problem arises when someone submits information for one of the forms. For example, if you are a member of the group, you supply your username and password, and click the Login button. The validation controls for the newsletter form would fire because no e-mail address was placed in that particular form. If someone interested in getting the newsletter places an e-mail address in the last textbox and clicks the Sign-up button, the validation controls in the first form fire because no username and password were input in that form.

ASP.NET Web Controls contains a `ValidationGroup` property that enables you to separate the validation controls into separate groups. It enables you to activate only the required validation controls when an end user clicks a button on the page. Listing 6-24 shows an example of separating the validation controls on a user group page into different buckets.

LISTING 6-24: Using the ValidationGroup property

```
<%@ Page Language="C#" %>
<!DOCTYPE html>
<html xmlns="http://www.w3.org/1999/xhtml">
<head runat="server">
    <title>Validation Groups</title>
</head>
<body>
```

continues

LISTING 6-24 *(continued)*

```
<form id="form1" runat="server">
    <div>
        <h1>.NET Valley User Group</h1>
        Username:
            <asp:TextBox ID="TextBox1" runat="server"></asp:TextBox>  Password:
            <asp:TextBox ID="TextBox2" runat="server"
                TextMode="Password"></asp:TextBox> 
            <asp:Button ID="Button1" runat="server" Text="Login"
                ValidationGroup="Login" />
        <br />
        <asp:RequiredFieldValidator ID="RequiredFieldValidator1" runat="server"
            Text="* You must submit a username!"
            ControlToValidate="TextBox1" ValidationGroup="Login">
        </asp:RequiredFieldValidator>
        <br />
        <asp:RequiredFieldValidator ID="RequiredFieldValidator2" runat="server"
            Text="* You must submit a password!"
            ControlToValidate="TextBox2" ValidationGroup="Login">
        </asp:RequiredFieldValidator>
        <p>
            .NET Valley usually meets the third Thursday of each month alternating meeting
            locations between the Luzerne County Community College and Penn State
            Wilkes-Barre in Pennsylvania.
            The .NET Valley User Group is unique in that meetings focus on technology in
            general rather than just .NET technologies. Be sure to check the website for
            more details.<br />
        </p>
        <h2>Sign-up for the newsletter!</h2>
        Email:
            <asp:TextBox ID="TextBox3" runat="server"></asp:TextBox> 
            <asp:Button ID="Button2" runat="server" Text="Sign-up"
                ValidationGroup="Newsletter" /> 
            <br />
        <asp:RegularExpressionValidator ID="RegularExpressionValidator1"
            runat="server"
            Text="* You must submit a correctly formatted email address!"
            ControlToValidate="TextBox3" ValidationGroup="Newsletter"
            ValidationExpression="\w+([-+.]\w+)*@\w+([-.]\w+)*\.\w+([-.]\w+)*">
        </asp:RegularExpressionValidator>
        <br />
        <asp:RequiredFieldValidator ID="RequiredFieldValidator3" runat="server"
            Text="* You forgot your email address!"
            ControlToValidate="TextBox3" ValidationGroup="Newsletter">
        </asp:RequiredFieldValidator>
    </div>
</form>
</body>
</html>
```

You can see that the `ValidationGroup` property takes a `String` value. The core server controls also have the `ValidationGroup` property because things like button clicks must be associated with specific validation groups.

In this example, each of the buttons has a distinct validation group assignment. The first button on the form uses `Login` as a value, and the second button on the form uses `Newsletter` as a value. Then each of the validation controls is associated with one of these validation groups. Because of these associations, when the end user clicks the Login button on the page, ASP.NET recognizes that it should work only with the validation server controls that have the same validation group name. ASP.NET ignores the validation controls assigned to other validation groups.

Using this enhancement, you can now have multiple sets of validation rules that fire only when you want them to fire (see Figure 6-14).

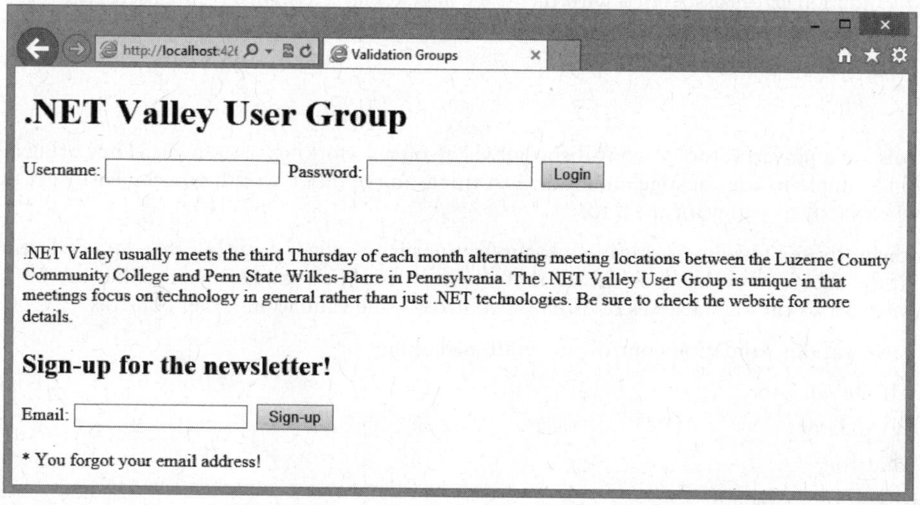

FIGURE 6-14

Another great feature with the validation controls is a property called `SetFocusOnError`. This property takes a Boolean value and, if a validation error is thrown when the form is submitted, the property places the page focus on the form element that receives the error. The `SetFocusOnError` property is used in the following example:

```
<asp:RequiredFieldValidator ID="RequiredFieldValidator1" runat="server"
    Text="* You must submit a username!" SetFocusOnError="true"
    ControlToValidate="TextBox1" ValidationGroup="Login">
</asp:RequiredFieldValidator>
```

If `RequiredFieldValidator1` throws an error because the end user didn't place a value in `TextBox1`, the page is redrawn with the focus on `TextBox1`, as shown in Figure 6-15.

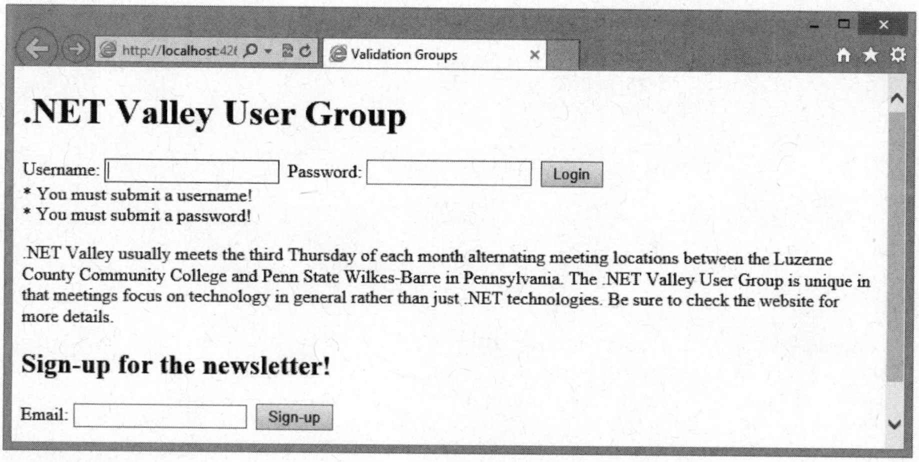

FIGURE 6-15

Note that if you have multiple validation controls on your page with the `SetFocusOnError` property set to `True`, and more than one validation error occurs, the uppermost form element that has a validation error gets the focus. In the previous example, if both the username textbox (`TextBox1`) and the password textbox (`TextBox2`) have validation errors associated with them, the page focus is assigned to the username textbox because it is the first control on the form with an error.

SUMMARY

Validation controls are a powerful tool at your disposal when you are working with forms. They bring a lot of functionality in a simple-to-use package and, like most things in the .NET world, you can easily get them to look and behave exactly as you want them to.

Remember that the purpose of having forms in your applications is to collect data, but this data collection has no meaning if the data is not valid. This means that you must establish validation rules that can be implemented in your forms through a series of different controls—the validation server controls.

This chapter covered various validation controls in detail, including:

- ➤ RequiredFieldValidator
- ➤ CompareValidator
- ➤ RangeValidator
- ➤ RegularExpressionValidator
- ➤ CustomValidator
- ➤ ValidationSummary

In addition to looking at the basic validation controls, this chapter also discussed how to apply client-side and server-side validations. You also had a chance to see how ASP.NET 4.5 introduced unobtrusive validation and the impact that has with your client-side validation.

User and Server Controls

WHAT'S IN THIS CHAPTER?

➤ Creating, interacting with, and loading user controls

➤ Working with server controls

➤ Optimizing your server controls for developers

WROX.COM CODE DOWNLOADS FOR THIS CHAPTER

Please note that all the code examples in this chapter are available as a part of this chapter's code download on the book's website at www.wrox.com on the Download Code tab.

In an object-oriented environment like .NET, the encapsulation of code into small, single-purpose, reusable objects is one of the keys to developing a robust system. For example, if your application deals with customers, you might consider creating a Customer object to represent a single instance of a Customer. This object encapsulates all the properties and behaviors a Customer can perform in the system. The advantage of creating this object is that you create a single point with which other objects can interact, and a single point of code to create, debug, deploy, and maintain. Objects like a Customer object are typically known as business objects because they encapsulate all of the business logic needed for a specific entity in the system.

.NET, being an object-oriented framework, includes many other types of reusable objects. The focus of this chapter is to discuss and demonstrate how you can use the .NET Framework to create two different types of reusable visual components for an ASP.NET application — user controls and server controls:

➤ A *user control* encapsulates existing ASP.NET controls into a single container control, which you can then easily reuse throughout your web project.

➤ A *server control* encapsulates the raw HTML and client and server logic into a single object. You can program against the server control, and its contents are ultimately rendered to the client to allow the user to interact with on the web page.

Because the topics of user controls and server controls are so large, and because discussing the intricacies of each could easily fill an entire book by itself, this chapter can't possibly investigate every option available to you. Instead, it attempts to give you a brief overview of building and using user controls and server controls and demonstrates some common scenarios for each type of control. By the end of this chapter, you should have learned enough to start building basic controls of each type and be able to continue to learn on your own.

USER CONTROLS

User controls represent the most basic form of ASP.NET visual encapsulation. Because they are the most basic, they are also the easiest to create and use. Essentially, a user control is used to group existing server controls into a single-container control. This enables you to create powerful objects that you can use easily throughout an entire web project.

Creating User Controls

Creating user controls is very simple in Visual Studio 2012. To create a new user control, you first add a new User Control file to your website. From the Website menu, select the Add New Item option. After the Add New File dialog box appears, select the Web User Control File template from the list and click Add. Notice that after the file is added to the project, the file has an .ascx extension. This extension signals to ASP.NET that this file is a user control. If you attempt to load the user control directly into your browser, ASP.NET returns an error telling you that this type of file cannot be served to the client.

If you look at the HTML source shown in Listing 7-1, you see several interesting differences from a standard ASP.NET web page.

LISTING 7-1: A web user control file template

```
<%@ Control Language="C#" ClassName="Listing07_01" %>

<script runat="server">

</script>
```

Notice that the source uses the @Control directive rather than the @Page directive that a standard web page would use. Also notice that unlike a standard ASP.NET web page, no other HTML tags besides the <script> tags exist in the control. The web page containing the user control provides the basic HTML, such as the <body> and <form> tags. In fact, if you try to add a server-side form tag to the user control, ASP.NET returns an error when the page is served to the client. The error message tells you that only one server-side form tag is allowed in your web page.

To add controls to the form, simply drag them from the Toolbox onto your user control. Listing 7-2 shows the user control after a label and a button have been added.

LISTING 7-2: Adding controls to the web user control

```
<%@ Control Language="C#" ClassName="Listing07_02" %>

<script runat="server">

</script>
<asp:Label ID="Label1" runat="server" Text="Label"></asp:Label>
<asp:Button ID="Button1" runat="server" Text="Button" />
```

After you add the controls to the user control, you put the user control onto a standard ASP.NET web page. To do this, drag the file from the Solution Explorer onto your web page.

Figure 7-1 shows the user control after it has been dropped onto a host web page.

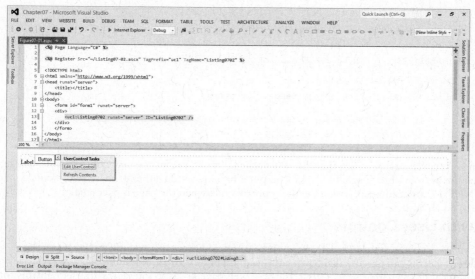

FIGURE 7-1

After you have placed the user control onto a web page, open the page in a browser to see the fully rendered web page.

User controls participate fully in the page-rendering life cycle, and controls contained within a user control behave just as they would if placed onto a standard ASP.NET web page. This means that the user control has its own page events (such as `Init`, `Load`, and `Prerender`) that execute as the page is processed, and that controls within the user control will also fire events as they normally would. Listing 7-3 shows how to use the user control's `Page_Load` event to populate the label and to handle a button's `Click` event.

LISTING 7-3: Creating control events in a user control

VB

```vb
<%@ Control Language="VB" ClassName="Listing07_03" %>
<script runat="server">
    Protected Sub Page_Load(ByVal sender As Object,
                            ByVal e As System.EventArgs)
        Me.Label1.Text = "The quick brown fox jumped over the lazy dog"
    End Sub

    Protected Sub Button1_Click(ByVal sender As Object,
                                ByVal e As System.EventArgs)
        Me.Label1.Text =
                "The quick brown fox clicked the button on the page"
    End Sub
</script>
<asp:Label ID="Label1" runat="server" Text="Label"></asp:Label>
<asp:Button ID="Button1" runat="server" Text="Button" />
```

C#

```csharp
<%@ Control Language="C#" ClassName="Listing07_03" %>
<script runat="server">
    protected void Page_Load(object sender, EventArgs e)
```

continues

LISTING 7-3 *(continued)*

```
    {
        this.Label1.Text = "The quick brown fox jumped over the lazy dog";
    }

    protected void Button1_Click(object sender, EventArgs e)
    {
        this.Label1.Text = "The quick brown fox clicked the button on the page";
    }
</script>
```

When you render the web page, you see that the text of the label changes as the user control loads, and again when you click the bottom of the page. In fact, if you put a breakpoint on either of these two events, you can see that ASP.NET does indeed break inside the user control code when the page is executed.

Interacting with User Controls

So far, you have learned how you can create user controls and add them to a web page. You have also learned how user controls can execute their own code and fire events. Most user controls, however, are not isolated islands within their parent page. Often, the host web page needs to interact with user controls that have been placed on it. For instance, you may decide that the text you want to load in the label must be given to the user control by the host page. To do this, you simply add a public property to the user control, and then assign text using the property. Listing 7-4 shows the modified user control.

LISTING 7-4: Exposing user control properties

VB

```
<%@ Control Language="VB" ClassName="Listing07_04" %>
<script runat="server">
    Public Property Text() As String
    Protected Sub Page_Load(ByVal sender As Object, ByVal e As System.EventArgs)
        Me.Label1.Text = Me.Text
    End Sub
</script>
<asp:Label ID="Label1" runat="server" Text="Label"></asp:Label>
```

C#

```
<%@ Control Language="C#" ClassName="Listing07_04" %>
<script runat="server">
    public string Text { get; set; }
    protected void Page_Load(object sender, EventArgs e)
    {
        this.Label1.Text = this.Text;
    }
</script>
<asp:Label ID="Label1" runat="server" Text="Label"></asp:Label>
```

After you modify the user control, you simply populate the property from the host web page. Listing 7-5 shows how to set the Text property in code.

LISTING 7-5: Populating user control properties from the host web page

VB

```
Protected Sub Page_Load(sender As Object, e As EventArgs)
    Listing0704.Text = "The quick brown fox jumped over the lazy dog"
End Sub
```

C#

```
protected void Page_Load(Object sender, EventArgs e)
{
    Listing0704.Text = "The quick brown fox jumped over the lazy dog";
}
```

Note that public properties exposed by user controls are also exposed by the Property Browser, so you can set a user control's properties using it as well.

User controls are simple ways of creating powerful, reusable components in ASP.NET. They are easy to create using the built-in templates. Because they participate fully in the page life cycle, you can create controls that can interact with their host page and even other controls on the host page.

Loading User Controls Dynamically

You can also create and add user controls to the Web Form dynamically at run time. The ASP.NET `Page` object includes the `LoadControl` method, which enables you to load user controls at run time by providing the method with a virtual path to the user control you want to load. The method returns a generic `Control` object that you can then add to the page's `Controls` collection. Listing 7-6 demonstrates how you can use the `LoadControl` method to dynamically add a user control to a web page.

LISTING 7-6: Dynamically adding a user control

VB

```
<%@ Page Language="VB" %>
<!DOCTYPE html>
<script runat="server">
    Protected Sub Page_Load(ByVal sender As Object, ByVal e As System.EventArgs)
        Dim myForm As Control = Page.FindControl("Form1")
        Dim c1 As Control = LoadControl("Listing07-04.ascx")
        myForm.Controls.Add(c1)
    End Sub
</script>
<html xmlns="http://www.w3.org/1999/xhtml">
<head runat="server">
    <title>Dynamically adding a user control</title>
</head>
<body>
    <form id="form1" runat="server">
    </form>
</body>
</html>
```

C#

```
<%@ Page Language="C#" %>
<!DOCTYPE html>
<script runat="server">
```

continues

LISTING 7-6 *(continued)*

```
    protected void Page_Load(object sender, EventArgs e)
    {
        Control myForm = Page.FindControl("Form1");
        Control c1 = LoadControl("Listing07-04.ascx");
        myForm.Controls.Add(c1);
    }
</script>
```

The first step in adding a user control to the page is to locate the page's Form control using the `FindControl` method. Should the user control contain ASP.NET controls that render form elements such as a button or textbox, you must add the user control to the form element's `Controls` collection.

> **NOTE** *Adding user controls that contain certain ASP.NET elements such as a Label, HyperLink, or Image directly to the* `Page` *object's* `Controls` *collection is possible; however, it is generally safer to be consistent and add them to the Form. Adding a control that must be contained within the Form, such as a Button control, to the* `Page` *object's* `Controls` *collection results in a runtime parser error.*

After the form has been found, the sample uses the page's `LoadControl()` method to load an instance of the user control. The method accepts a virtual path to the user control you want to load and returns the loaded user control as a generic `Control` object.

Finally, you add the control to the `Form` object's `Controls` collection. You can also add the user control to other container controls that may be present on the web page, such as a Panel or Placeholder control.

> **NOTE** *Remember that you need to re-add your control to the ASP.NET page each time the page performs a postback.*

After you have the user control loaded, you can also work with its object model, just as you can with any other control. To access properties and methods that the user control exposes, you need to cast the control from the generic control type to its actual type. To do that, you also need to add the `@Reference` directive to the page. This tells ASP.NET to compile the user control and link it to the ASP.NET page so that the page knows where to find the user control type. Listing 7-7 demonstrates how you can access a custom property of your user control by casting the control after loading it. The sample loads a modified user control that hosts an ASP.NET TextBox control and exposes a public property that enables you to access the TextBox control's `Text` property.

LISTING 7-7: Casting a user control to its native type

VB

```
<%@ Page Language="VB" %>
<!DOCTYPE html>
<script runat="server">
    Protected Sub Page_Load(ByVal sender As Object, ByVal e As System.EventArgs)
        Dim myForm As Control = Page.FindControl("Form1")
        Dim c1 As Listing07_04 = CType(LoadControl("Listing07-04.ascx"), Listing07_04)
        myForm.Controls.Add(c1)
        c1.ID = "Listing07_04"
        c1.Text = "Text about our custom user control."
```

```
        End Sub
    </script>
```

C#

```
<%@ Page Language="C#" %>
<!DOCTYPE html>
<script runat="server">
    protected void Page_Load(object sender, EventArgs e)
    {
        Control myForm = Page.FindControl("Form1");
        Listing07_04 c1 = (Listing07_04)LoadControl("Listing07-04.ascx");
        myForm.Controls.Add(c1);
        c1.ID = "Listing07_04";
        c1.Text = "Text about our custom user control.";
    }
</script>
```

Notice that the sample adds the control to the Form's `Controls` collection and then sets the `Text` property. The ordering of this is important because after a page postback occurs the control's ViewState is not calculated until the control is added to the `Controls` collection. Therefore, if you set the `Text` value (or any other property of the user control) before the control's ViewState is calculated, the value is not persisted in the ViewState.

One additional twist to adding user controls dynamically occurs when you are using output caching to cache the user controls. In this case, after the control has been cached, the `LoadControl` method does not return a new instance of the control. Instead, it returns the cached copy of the control. This presents problems when you try to cast the control to its native type because, after the control is cached, the `LoadControl` method returns it as a `PartialCachingControl` object rather than as its native type. Therefore, the cast in the previous sample results in an exception being thrown.

To solve this problem, you simply test the object type before attempting the cast. This is shown in Listing 7-8.

LISTING 7-8: Detecting cached user controls

VB

```
<%@ Page Language="VB" %>
<!DOCTYPE html>
<script runat="server">
    Protected Sub Page_Load(ByVal sender As Object, ByVal e As System.EventArgs)
        Dim myForm As Control = Page.FindControl("Form1")
        Dim c1 As Control = LoadControl("Listing07-04.ascx")
        myForm.Controls.Add(c1)

        If c1.GetType() Is GetType(Listing07_04) Then
            CType(c1, Listing07_04).ID = "Listing07_04"
            CType(c1, Listing07_04).Text = "Text about our custom user control (not cached)"
        ElseIf c1.GetType() Is GetType(PartialCachingControl) _
            And Not (IsNothing(CType(c1, PartialCachingControl).CachedControl)) Then
            Dim listingControl As Listing07_04 = _
                CType(CType(c1, PartialCachingControl).CachedControl, Listing07_04)
            listingControl.ID = "Listing07_04"
            listingControl.Text = "Text about our custom user control (partially cached)"
        End If
    End Sub
</script>
```

continues

LISTING 7-8 *(continued)*

C#

```csharp
<%@ Page Language="C#" %>
<!DOCTYPE html>
<script runat="server">
    protected void Page_Load(object sender, EventArgs e)
    {
        Control myForm = Page.FindControl("Form1");
        Control c1 = LoadControl("Listing07-04.ascx");
        myForm.Controls.Add(c1);

        if (c1 is Listing07_04)
        {
            ((Listing07_04)c1).ID = "Listing07_04";
            ((Listing07_04)c1).Text = "Text about our custom user control (not cached)";
        }
        else if ((c1 is PartialCachingControl) &&
            ((PartialCachingControl)c1).CachedControl != null)
        {
            Listing07_04 listingControl =
                ((Listing07_04)((PartialCachingControl)c1).CachedControl);
            listingControl.ID = "Listing07_04";
            listingControl.Text = "Text about our custom user control (partially cached)";
        }
    }
</script>
```

The sample demonstrates how you can test to see what type the `LoadControl` returns and set properties based on the type. For more information on caching, check out Chapter 22.

Finally, in the previous samples user controls have been added dynamically during the `Page_Load` event. But there may be times when you want to add the control in a different event, such as a Button's `Click` event or the `SelectedIndexChanged` event of a DropDownList control. Using these events to add user controls dynamically presents new challenges. Because these events may not be raised each time a page postback occurs, you need to create a way to track when a user control has been added so that it can be re-added to the web page as additional postbacks occur.

A simple way to do this is to use the ASP.NET session to track when the user control is added to the web page. Listing 7-9 demonstrates this.

LISTING 7-9: Tracking added user controls across postbacks

VB

```vb
<%@ Page Language="VB" %>
<!DOCTYPE html>
<script runat="server">
    Protected Sub Page_Load(ByVal sender As Object, ByVal e As System.EventArgs)
        If IsNothing(Session("Listing07-04")) Or
            Not (CBool(Session("Listing07-04"))) Then

            Dim myForm As Control = Page.FindControl("Form1")
            Dim c1 As Control = LoadControl("Listing07-04.ascx")
            CType(c1, Listing07_04).Text = "Loaded after first page load"
            myForm.Controls.Add(c1)

            Session("Listing07-04") = True
        End If
```

```
        End Sub

        Protected Sub Button1_Click(ByVal sender As Object, ByVal e As System.EventArgs)
            If Not IsNothing(Session("Listing07-04")) And
                (CBool(Session("Listing07-04"))) Then

                Dim myForm As Control = Page.FindControl("Form1")
                Dim c1 As Control = LoadControl("Listing07-04.ascx")
                CType(c1, Listing07_04).Text = "Loaded after a postback"
                myForm.Controls.Add(c1)
            End If
        End Sub
    </script>
    <html xmlns="http://www.w3.org/1999/xhtml">
    <head runat="server">
        <title>Untitled Page</title>
    </head>
    <body>
        <form id="form1" runat="server">
        <div>
            <asp:Button ID="Button1" runat="server" Text="Load Control"
                OnClick="Button1_Click" />
        </div>
        </form>
    </body>
    </html>
```

C#

```
<%@ Page Language="C#" %>
<!DOCTYPE html>
<script runat="server">
    protected void Page_Load(object sender, EventArgs e)
    {
        if ((Session["Listing07-04"] == null) ||
            (!(bool)Session["Listing07-04"]))
        {
            Control myForm = Page.FindControl("Form1");
            Control c1 = LoadControl("Listing07-04.ascx");
            ((Listing07_04)c1).Text = "Loaded after first page load";
            myForm.Controls.Add(c1);

            Session["Listing07-04"] = true;
        }
    }

    protected void Button1_Click(object sender, EventArgs e)
    {
        if ((Session["Listing07-04"] != null) &&
            ((bool)Session["Listing07-04"]))
        {
            Control myForm = Page.FindControl("Form1");
            Control c1 = LoadControl("Listing07-04.ascx");
            ((Listing07_04)c1).Text = "Loaded after a postback";
            myForm.Controls.Add(c1);
        }
    }
</script>
```

This sample uses a simple Session variable to track whether the user control has been added to the page. When the Button1 Click event fires, the session variable is set to True, indicating that the user control has been added. Then, each time the page performs a postback, the Page_Load event checks to see whether the session variable is set to True, and if so, it re-adds the control to the page.

SERVER CONTROLS

The power to create server controls in ASP.NET is one of the greatest tools you can have as an ASP.NET developer. Creating your own custom server controls and extending existing controls are actually both quite easy. In ASP.NET, all controls are derived from two basic classes: `System.Web.UI.WebControls.WebControl` or `System.Web.UI.ScriptControl`. Classes derived from the `WebControl` class have the basic functionality required to participate in the Page framework. These classes include most of the common functionality needed to create controls that render a visual HTML representation and provide support for many of the basic styling elements such as Font, Height, and Width. Because the `WebControl` class derives from the `Control` class, the controls derived from it have the basic functionality to be designable controls, meaning you can add them to the Visual Studio Toolbox, drag them onto the page designer, and display their properties and events in the Property Browser.

Controls derived from the `ScriptControl` class build on the functionality that the `WebControl` class provides by including additional features designed to make working with client-side script libraries easier. The class tests to ensure that a ScriptManager control is present in the hosting page during the control's PreRender stage, and also ensures that derived controls call the proper ScriptManager methods during the Render event.

Server Control Projects

To make creating a custom server control easy, Visual Studio provides two different project templates that set up a basic project structure including the files you need to create a server control. Figure 7-2 shows the ASP.NET Server Control and ASP.NET AJAX Server Control projects in Visual Studio's New Project dialog box.

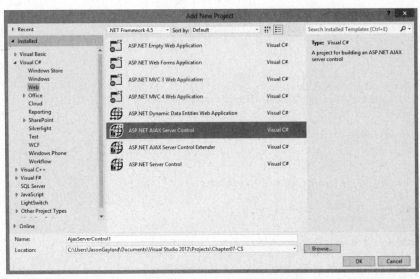

FIGURE 7-2

The ASP.NET Server Control project creates a basic class library project with a single server control class included by default that derives from `WebControl`. The ASP.NET AJAX Server Control project also creates a basic class library project, but includes a single server control class derived from `ScriptControl` and a Resource file and a JavaScript file. Creating either of these project types results in a runnable, though essentially functionless, server control.

You can add additional server control classes to the project by selecting the ASP.NET Server Control file template from the Add New Item dialog box. Note that this template differs slightly from the default template included in the server control projects. It uses a different filename scheme and includes slightly different code in the default control template.

After you've created a new project, you can test the control by adding a new Web Project to the existing solution, rebuilding the entire solution, and opening the default web page. Visual Studio automatically adds the server control to the Toolbox as shown in Figure 7-3.

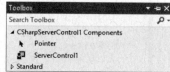

Visual Studio does this for any controls contained in projects in the currently open solution.

Now simply drag the control onto the Web Form. Visual Studio adds a reference to the control to the project, and the control is added to the web page. Listing 7-10 shows you what the web page source code looks like after you have added the control.

FIGURE 7-3

LISTING 7-10: Adding a web control library to a web page

```
<%@ Page Language="C#" %>
<%@ Register Assembly="CSharpServerControl1" Namespace="CSharpServerControl1"
  TagPrefix="cc1" %>
<!DOCTYPE html>
<html xmlns="http://www.w3.org/1999/xhtml">
<head runat="server">
    <title>Adding a Custom Web Control</title>
</head>
<body>
    <form id="form1" runat="server">
    <div>
        <cc1:ServerControl1 ID="ServerControl1" runat="server" />
    </div>
    </form>
</body>
</html>
```

After you drag the control onto the Web Form, take a look at its properties in the Properties window. Figure 7-4 shows the properties of your custom control.

Notice that the control has all the basic properties of a visual control, including various styling and behavior properties. The properties are exposed because the control was derived from the `WebControl` class. The control also inherits the base events exposed by `WebControl`.

Make sure the control is working by entering a value for the `Text` property and viewing the page in a browser. Figure 7-5 shows what the page looks like if you set the `Text` property to `"Hello World!"`.

As expected, the control has rendered the value of the `Text` property to the web page.

Now that you have a basic server control project up and running, you can go back and take a look at the template class created for you by the ASP.NET Server Control project. The default template is shown in Listing 7-11 (ServerControl1.vb and ServerControl1.cs in the code download for this chapter).

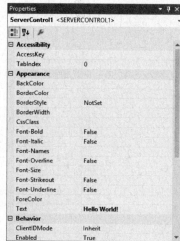

FIGURE 7-4

FIGURE 7-5

LISTING 7-11: The Visual Studio ASP.NET Server Control class template

VB

```vb
Imports System
Imports System.Collections.Generic
Imports System.ComponentModel
Imports System.Text
Imports System.Web
Imports System.Web.UI
Imports System.Web.UI.WebControls


<DefaultProperty("Text"), ToolboxData("<{0}:ServerControl1 runat=server>
  </{0}:ServerControl1>")>
Public Class ServerControl1
    Inherits WebControl

    <Bindable(True), Category("Appearance"), DefaultValue(""), Localizable(True)>
    Property Text() As String
        Get
            Dim s As String = CStr(ViewState("Text"))
            If s Is Nothing Then
                Return "[" & Me.ID & "]"
            Else
                Return s
            End If
        End Get

        Set(ByVal Value As String)
            ViewState("Text") = Value
        End Set
    End Property

    Protected Overrides Sub RenderContents(ByVal output As HtmlTextWriter)
        output.Write(Text)
    End Sub
End Class
```

C#

```csharp
using System;
using System.Collections.Generic;
using System.ComponentModel;
using System.Linq;
using System.Text;
using System.Threading.Tasks;
using System.Web;
using System.Web.UI;
using System.Web.UI.WebControls;

namespace CSharpServerControl1
{
    [DefaultProperty("Text")]
    [ToolboxData("<{0}:ServerControl1 runat=server></{0}:ServerControl1>")]
    public class ServerControl1 : WebControl
    {
        [Bindable(true)]
        [Category("Appearance")]
        [DefaultValue("")]
        [Localizable(true)]
        public string Text
        {
            get
            {
                String s = (String)ViewState["Text"];
                return ((s == null)? "[" + this.ID + "]" : s);
            }

            set
            {
                ViewState["Text"] = value;
            }
        }

        protected override void RenderContents(HtmlTextWriter output)
        {
            output.Write(Text);
        }
    }
}
```

You can see a number of interesting things about the default server control template generated by the project. First, notice that both the class declaration and the Text property are decorated by attributes. ASP.NET server controls make heavy use of attributes to indicate different types of runtime and design-time behaviors. You learn more about the attributes you can apply to server control classes and properties later in this chapter.

Second, by default the template includes a single property called Text and a simple overridden method called RenderContents that renders the value of that property to the screen. The RenderContents method of the control is the primary method used to output content from the server control.

If you view the HTML source of the previous sample, you will see that not only has ASP.NET added the value of the Text property to the HTML markup, but it has surrounded the text with a <SPAN> block. If you look at the code for the WebControl class's render method, you can see that, in addition to calling the RenderContents method, it also includes calls to render a begin and end tag by inserting the Span tag around the control's content.

```csharp
protected internal override void Render(HtmlTextWriter writer)
{
    this.RenderBeginTag(writer);
    this.RenderContents(writer);
    this.RenderEndTag(writer);
}
```

If you have provided an ID value for your control, the Span tag also, by default, renders an ID attribute. Having the Span tags can sometimes be problematic, so if you want to prevent ASP.NET from automatically adding the Span tags you can override the Render method in your control and call the RenderContents method directly:

VB

```
Protected Overrides Sub Render(ByVal writer As System.Web.UI.HtmlTextWriter)
    Me.RenderContents(writer)
End Sub
```

C#

```
protected override void Render(HtmlTextWriter writer)
{
    this.RenderContents(writer);
}
```

The default server control template does a good job of demonstrating how easy it is to create a simple server control, but of course, this control does not have much functionality and lacks many of the features you might find in a typical server control. The rest of this chapter focuses on how you can use different features of the .NET Framework to add additional runtime and design-time features to a server control.

Control Attributes

Much of the design-time experience a server control offers developers is configured by adding attributes to the server control class and properties. For example, when you look at the default control template from the previous section (Listing 7-11), notice that attributes have been applied to both the class and to the Text property. This section describes the attributes that you can apply to server controls and how they affect the behavior of the control.

Class Attributes

Class attributes for server controls can be divided into three general categories: global control runtime behaviors, how the control looks in the Visual Studio Toolbox, and how it behaves when placed on the design surface. Table 7-1 describes some of these attributes.

TABLE 7-1

ATTRIBUTE	DESCRIPTION
Designer	Indicates the designer class this control should use to render a design-time view of the control on the Visual Studio design surface
TypeConverter	Specifies what type to use as a converter for the object
DefaultEvent	Indicates the default event created when the user double-clicks the control on the Visual Studio design surface
DefaultProperty	Indicates the default property for the control
ControlBuilder	Specifies a ControlBuilder class for building a custom control in the ASP.NET control parser
ParseChildren	Indicates whether XML elements nested within the server control's tags are treated as properties or as child controls
TagPrefix	Indicates the text that prefixes the control in the web page HTML

Property/Event Attributes

You use property attributes to control a number of different aspects of server controls, including how your properties and events behave in the Visual Studio Property Browser and how properties and events are serialized at design time. Table 7-2 describes some of the property and event attributes you can use.

TABLE 7-2

ATTRIBUTE	DESCRIPTION
Bindable	Indicates that the property can be bound to a data source
Browsable	Indicates whether the property should be displayed at design time in the Property Browser
Category	Indicates the category this property should be displayed under in the Property Browser
Description	Displays a text string at the bottom of the Property Browser that describes the purpose of the property
EditorBrowsable	Indicates whether the property should be editable when shown in the Property Browser
DefaultValue	Indicates the default value of the property shown in the Property Browser
DesignerSerializationVisibility	Specifies the visibility a property has to the design-time serializer
NotifyParentProperty	Indicates that the parent property is notified when the value of the property is modified
PersistChildren	Indicates whether, at design time, the child controls of a server control should be persisted as nested inner controls
PersistanceMode	Specifies how a property or an event is persisted to the ASP.NET page
TemplateContainer	Specifies the type of INamingContainer that will contain the template after it is created
Editor	Indicates the UI Type Editor class this control should use to edit its value
Localizable	Indicates that the property contains text that can be localized
Themable	Indicates whether this property can have a theme applied to it

Obviously, the class and property/event attribute tables present a lot of information up front. You already saw a demonstration of some of these attributes in Listing 7-11; as you go through the rest of this chapter, the samples leverage other attributes listed in the tables.

Control Rendering

So far in this chapter you have seen how easy it is to develop a very basic server control using the Visual Studio project templates and how you can apply attributes in the server control to influence some basic control behaviors. The rest of the chapter focuses on how you can use features of ASP.NET to add more advanced control capabilities to your server controls.

The Page Event Life Cycle

Before digging deeper into server controls, spending a moment to look at the general ASP.NET page life cycle that server controls operate within is helpful. As the control developer, you are responsible for overriding methods that execute during the life cycle and implementing your own custom rendering logic.

Remember that when a web browser makes a request to the server, it is using HTTP, a stateless protocol. ASP.NET provides a page-execution framework that helps create the illusion of state in a web application. This framework is basically a series of methods and events that execute every time an ASP.NET page is processed. Figure 7-6 shows the events and methods called during the control's life cycle.

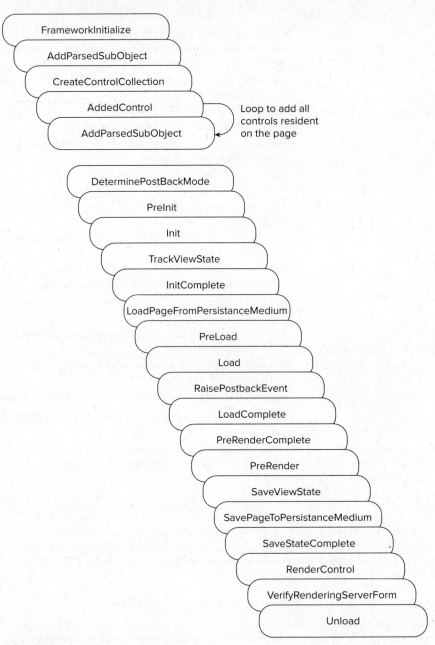

FIGURE 7-6

As you read through the rest of this chapter, you will see that a server control uses many of these events and methods. Understanding them and the order in which they execute is helpful so that as you are adding features to your server control, you can structure your logic to follow the page life cycle.

Rendering HTML Tags

The main job of a server control is to render some type of markup language to the HTTP output stream, which is returned to and displayed by the client. If your client is a standard browser, the control should emit HTML; if the client is something like a mobile device, the control may need to emit a different type of markup. As stated earlier, your responsibility as the control developer is to tell the server control what markup to render. The overridden RenderContents method, called during the control's life cycle, is the primary location where you tell the control what you want to emit to the client. In Listing 7-12, notice that the RenderContents method is used to tell the control to print the value of the Text property (see ServerControl1.vb and ServerControl1.cs in the code download for this chapter).

LISTING 7-12: Overriding the Render method

VB

```
Protected Overrides Sub RenderContents(ByVal output As HtmlTextWriter)
    output.Write(Text)
End Sub
```

C#

```
protected override void RenderContents(HtmlTextWriter output)
{
    output.Write(Text);
}
```

Also notice that the RenderContents method has one method parameter called output. This parameter is an HtmlTextWriter class, which is what the control uses to render HTML to the client. This special writer class is specifically designed to emit HTML 4.0–compliant HTML to the browser.

> **NOTE** *Even though the* HtmlTextWriter *class emits HTML 4.0–compliant HTML, you have complete control over the elements and attributes being written. Therefore, the* HtmlTextWriter *class can also emit valid HTML5.*

The HtmlTextwriter class has a number of methods you can use to emit your HTML, including RenderBeginTag and WriteBeginTag. Listing 7-13 shows how you can modify the control's Render method to emit an HTML <input> tag.

LISTING 7-13: Using the HtmlTextWriter to render an HTML tag

VB

```
Protected Overrides Sub RenderContents(ByVal output As HtmlTextWriter)
    output.RenderBeginTag(HtmlTextWriterTag.Input)
    output.RenderEndTag()
End Sub
```

C#

```
protected override void RenderContents(HtmlTextWriter output)
{
    output.RenderBeginTag(HtmlTextWriterTag.Input);
    output.RenderEndTag();
}
```

First, notice that the `RenderBeginTag` method is used to emit the HTML. The advantage of using this method to emit HTML is that it requires you to select a tag from the `HtmlTextWriterTag` enumeration. Using the `RenderBeginTag` method and the `HtmlTextWriterTag` enumeration enables you to have your control automatically support down-level browsers that cannot understand HTML 4.0 or later syntax.

Second, notice that the `RenderEndTag` method is also used. As the name suggests, this method renders the closing tag. Notice, however, that you do not have to specify in this method which tag you want to close. `RenderEndTag` automatically closes the last begin tag rendered by the `RenderBeginTag` method, which in this case is the `<input>` tag. If you want to emit multiple HTML tags, make sure you order your `Begin` and `End` render methods properly. Listing 7-14, for example, adds a `<div>` tag to the control. The `<div>` tag surrounds the `<input>` tag when rendered to the page.

LISTING 7-14: Using the HtmlTextWriter to render multiple HTML tags

VB

```
Protected Overrides Sub RenderContents(ByVal output As HtmlTextWriter)
    output.RenderBeginTag(HtmlTextWriterTag.Div)
    output.RenderBeginTag(HtmlTextWriterTag.Input)
    output.RenderEndTag()
    output.RenderEndTag()
End Sub
```

C#

```
protected override void RenderContents(HtmlTextWriter output)
{
    output.RenderBeginTag(HtmlTextWriterTag.Div);
    output.RenderBeginTag(HtmlTextWriterTag.Input);
    output.RenderEndTag();
    output.RenderEndTag();
}
```

Now that you have a basic understanding of how to emit simple HTML, look at the output of your control. Figure 7-7 shows the source for the page.

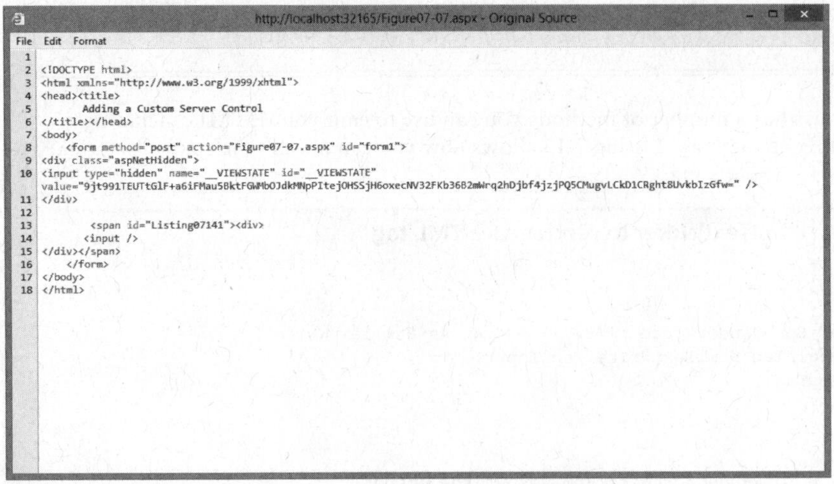


```

<!DOCTYPE html>
<html xmlns="http://www.w3.org/1999/xhtml">
<head><title>
      Adding a Custom Server Control
</title></head>
<body>
    <form method="post" action="Figure07-07.aspx" id="form1">
<div class="aspNetHidden">
<input type="hidden" name="__VIEWSTATE" id="__VIEWSTATE"
value="9jt991TEUTtGlF+a6iFMau5BktFGWMbOJdkMNpPItejOHSSjH6oxecNV32FKb3682mWrq2hDjbf4jzjPQ5CMugvLCkD1CRght8UvkbIzGfw=" />
</div>

        <span id="Listing07141"><div>
        <input />
</div></span>
    </form>
</body>
</html>
```

FIGURE 7-7

You can see that the control emitted some simple HTML markup. Also notice that the control was smart enough to realize that the input control did not contain any child controls and, therefore, the control did not need to render a full closing tag. Instead, it automatically rendered the shorthand />, rather than </input>.

Adding Tag Attributes

Emitting HTML tags is a good start to building the control, but perhaps this is a bit simplistic. Normally, when rendering HTML you would emit some tag attributes (such as ID or Name) to the client in addition to the tag. Listing 7-15 shows how you can easily add tag attributes.

LISTING 7-15: Rendering HTML tag attributes

VB

```
Protected Overrides Sub RenderContents(ByVal output As HtmlTextWriter)
    output.RenderBeginTag(HtmlTextWriterTag.Div)
    output.AddAttribute(HtmlTextWriterAttribute.Type, "text")
    output.AddAttribute(HtmlTextWriterAttribute.Id, Me.ClientID & "_i")
    output.AddAttribute(HtmlTextWriterAttribute.Name,
                        Me.ClientID & "_i")
    output.AddAttribute(HtmlTextWriterAttribute.Value, Me.Text)
    output.RenderBeginTag(HtmlTextWriterTag.Input)
    output.RenderEndTag()
    output.RenderEndTag()
End Sub
```

C#

```
protected override void RenderContents(HtmlTextWriter output)
{
    output.RenderBeginTag(HtmlTextWriterTag.Div);
    output.AddAttribute(HtmlTextWriterAttribute.Type, "text");
    output.AddAttribute(HtmlTextWriterAttribute.Id,
                        this.ClientID + "_i");
    output.AddAttribute(HtmlTextWriterAttribute.Name,
                        this.ClientID + "_i");
    output.AddAttribute(HtmlTextWriterAttribute.Value, this.Text);
    output.RenderBeginTag(HtmlTextWriterTag.Input);
    output.RenderEndTag();
    output.RenderEndTag();
}
```

You can see that by using the AddAttribute method, you have added three attributes to the <input> tag. Also notice that, once again, you are using an enumeration, HtmlTextWriterAttribute, to select the attribute you want to add to the tag. This serves the same purpose as using the HtmlTextWriterTag enumeration, allowing the control to degrade its output to down-level browsers.

As with the Render methods, the order in which you place the AddAttributes methods is important. You place the AddAttributes methods directly before the RenderBeginTag method in the code. The AddAttributes method associates the attributes with the next HTML tag that is rendered by the RenderBeginTag method — in this case, the <input> tag.

Now browse to the test page and check out the HTML source with the added tag attributes. Figure 7-8 shows the HTML source rendered by the control.

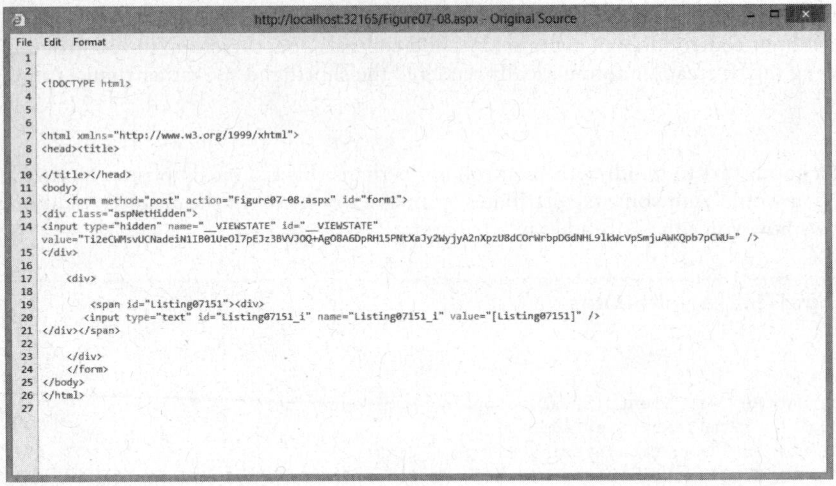

FIGURE 7-8

You can see that the tag attributes you added in the server control are now included as part of the HTML tag rendered by the control.

A Word about Control IDs

Notice that in Listing 7-15, using the control's `ClientID` property as the value of both the `Id` and `Name` attributes is important. Controls that derive from the `WebControl` class automatically expose three different types of ID properties: `ID`, `UniqueID`, and `ClientID`. Each of these properties exposes a slightly altered version of the control's `ID` for use in a specific scenario.

The `ID` property is the most obvious. Developers use it to get and set the control's `ID`. It must be unique to the page at design time.

The `UniqueID` property is a read-only property generated at run time that returns an `ID` that has been prepended with the containing control's `ID`. This is essential so that ASP.NET can uniquely identify each control in the page's control tree, even if the control is used multiple times by a container control such as a Repeater or GridView. For example, if you add this custom control to a Repeater, the `UniqueID` for each custom control rendered by the Repeater is modified to include the Repeater's `ID` when the page is executed:

```
MyRepeater:Ctrl0:MyCustomControl
```

Beginning with ASP.NET 4.0, the `ClientID` property can be generated differently depending on the value of the `ClientIDMode` property. The `ClientIDMode` property enables you to select one of four mechanisms that ASP.NET uses to generate the `ClientID`:

➤ **AutoID:** Equivalent to the behavior used in earlier versions of ASP.NET.

➤ **Static:** Specifies that the `ClientID` value will be the same as the `ID`, without concatenating the IDs of parent containers.

➤ **Predictable:** Primarily for use in data controls, it concatenates the IDs of a control's naming containers, but generated client ID values do not contain strings like `ctlxxx`. Instead, you can set the `ClientIDRowSuffix` property to provide a unique value for each control generated. This is the default value for `ClientIDMode`.

➤ **Inherit:** Specifies that the control's ID generation is the same as its parent.

Additionally, to ensure that controls can generate a unique ID, they should implement the INamingContainer interface. This is a marker interface only, meaning that it does not require any additional methods to be implemented; it does, however, ensure that the ASP.NET run time guarantees that the control always has a unique name within the page's tree hierarchy, regardless of its container.

Styling HTML

So far, you have seen how easy it is to build a simple server control and emit the proper HTML, including attributes. However, modern web development techniques generally restrict the use of HTML to a basic content description mechanism, relying instead on CSS for the positioning and styling of HTML elements in a web page. In this section, you learn how you can have your control render style information.

As mentioned at the very beginning of this section, you are creating controls that inherit from the WebControl class. Because of this, these controls already have the basic infrastructure for emitting most of the standard CSS-style attributes. In the Property Browser for this control, you should see a number of style properties already listed, such as background color, border width, and font. You can also launch the style builder to create complex CSS styles. These basic properties are provided by the WebControl class, but it is up to you to tell your control to render the values set at design time. To do this, you simply execute the AddAttributesToRender method. Listing 7-16 shows you how to do this.

LISTING 7-16: Rendering style properties

VB

```vb
Protected Overrides Sub RenderContents(ByVal output As HtmlTextWriter)
    output.RenderBeginTag(HtmlTextWriterTag.Div)
    output.AddAttribute(HtmlTextWriterAttribute.Type, "text")
    output.AddAttribute(HtmlTextWriterAttribute.Id, Me.ClientID & "_i")
    output.AddAttribute(HtmlTextWriterAttribute.Name,
                        Me.ClientID & "_i")
    output.AddAttribute(HtmlTextWriterAttribute.Value, Me.Text)
    Me.AddAttributesToRender(output)
    output.RenderBeginTag(HtmlTextWriterTag.Input)
    output.RenderEndTag()
    output.RenderEndTag()
End Sub
```

C#

```csharp
protected override void RenderContents(HtmlTextWriter output)
{
    output.RenderBeginTag(HtmlTextWriterTag.Div);
    output.AddAttribute(HtmlTextWriterAttribute.Type, "text");
    output.AddAttribute(HtmlTextWriterAttribute.Id,
                        this.ClientID + "_i");
    output.AddAttribute(HtmlTextWriterAttribute.Name,
                        this.ClientID + "_i");
    output.AddAttribute(HtmlTextWriterAttribute.Value, this.Text);
    this.AddAttributesToRender(output);
    output.RenderBeginTag(HtmlTextWriterTag.Input);
    output.RenderEndTag();
    output.RenderEndTag();
}
```

Executing this method tells the control to render any style information that has been set. It not only causes the style-related properties to be rendered, but also several other attributes, including ID, tabindex, and tooltip. If you are manually rendering these attributes earlier in your control, you may end up with duplicate attributes being rendered.

Additionally, being careful about where you execute the `AddAttributesToRender` method is important. In Listing 7-16, it is executed immediately before the `Input` tag is rendered, which means that the attributes are rendered both on the `Input` element and on the `Span` element surrounding the `Input` element. Placing the method call before the beginning `Div` tag is rendered ensures that the attributes are now applied to the `Div` and its surrounding span. Placing the method call after the end `Div` means the attribute is applied only to the span.

Using the Property Browser, you can set the background color of the control to `Silver` and the font to `Bold`. When you set these properties, they are automatically added to the control tag in the ASP.NET page. After you have added the styles, the control tag looks like this:

```
<cc1:Listing0716 ID="Listing07161" runat="server" BackColor="Silver"
    Font-Bold="True" Text="Hello World!" />
```

The style changes have been persisted to the control as attributes. When you execute this page in the browser, the style information should be rendered to the HTML, making the background of the textbox silver and its font bold. Figure 7-9 shows the page in the browser.

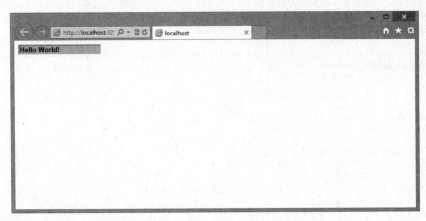

FIGURE 7-9

Once again, look at the source for this page. The style information has been rendered to the HTML as a style tag. Figure 7-10 shows the HTML emitted by the control.

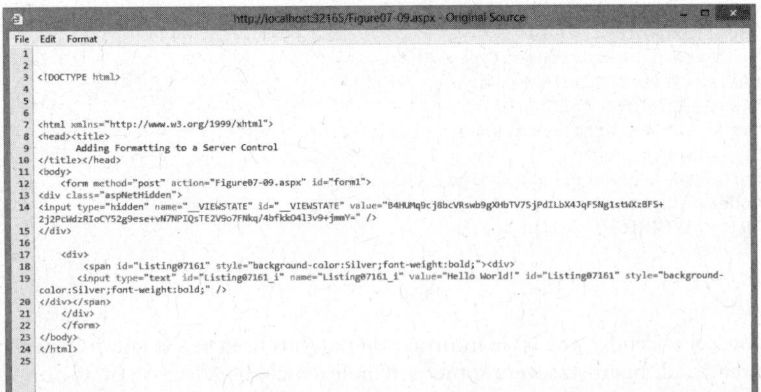

FIGURE 7-10

If you want more control over the rendering of styles in your control you can use the `HtmlTextWriter`'s `AddStyleAttribute` method. Similar to the `AddAttribute` method, the `AddStyleAttribute` method enables you to specify CSS attributes to add to a control using the `HtmlTextWriterStyle` enumeration. However, unlike the `AddAttribute` method, attributes you add using `AddStyleAttribute` are defined inside of a style attribute on the control. Listing 7-17 demonstrates the use of the `AddStyleAttribute` method.

LISTING 7-17: Adding control styles using AddStyleAttribute

VB

```
Protected Overrides Sub RenderContents(ByVal output As HtmlTextWriter)
    output.RenderBeginTag(HtmlTextWriterTag.Div)
    output.AddAttribute(HtmlTextWriterAttribute.Type, "text")
    output.AddAttribute(HtmlTextWriterAttribute.Id, Me.ClientID & "_i")
    output.AddAttribute(HtmlTextWriterAttribute.Name,
                    Me.ClientID & "_i")
    output.AddAttribute(HtmlTextWriterAttribute.Value, Me.Text)
    output.AddStyleAttribute(HtmlTextWriterStyle.BackgroundColor, "Silver")
    output.RenderBeginTag(HtmlTextWriterTag.Input)
    output.RenderEndTag()
    output.RenderEndTag()
End Sub
```

C#

```
protected override void RenderContents(HtmlTextWriter output)
{
    output.RenderBeginTag(HtmlTextWriterTag.Div);
    output.AddAttribute(HtmlTextWriterAttribute.Type, "text");
    output.AddAttribute(HtmlTextWriterAttribute.Id,
                    this.ClientID + "_i");
    output.AddAttribute(HtmlTextWriterAttribute.Name,
                    this.ClientID + "_i");
    output.AddAttribute(HtmlTextWriterAttribute.Value, this.Text);
    output.AddStyleAttribute(HtmlTextWriterStyle.BackgroundColor, "Silver");
    output.RenderBeginTag(HtmlTextWriterTag.Input);
    output.RenderEndTag();
    output.RenderEndTag();
}
```

Running this sample results in a silver background color being applied to the control.

Adding Client-Side Features

Although the capability to render and style HTML is quite powerful by itself, you can send other resources to the client, such as client-side scripts, images, and resource strings. ASP.NET provides you with some powerful tools for using client-side scripts in your server controls and exposing other resources to the client along with the HTML your control emits. Additionally, ASP.NET includes an entire model that enables you to make asynchronous callbacks from your web page to the server.

Emitting Client-Side Script

Having your control emit client-side script like JavaScript enables you to add powerful client-side functionality to your control. Client-side scripting languages take advantage of the client's browser to create more flexible and easy-to-use controls. ASP.NET provides a wide variety of methods for emitting client-side script that you can use to control where and how your script is rendered.

Most of the properties and methods needed to render client script are available from the `ClientScriptManager` class, which you can access using `Page.ClientScript`. Listing 7-18 demonstrates how you can use the `RegisterStartupScript` method to render JavaScript to the client. This listing adds the code into the `OnPreRender` method, rather than into the `Render` method used in previous samples. This method allows every control to inform the page about the client-side script it needs to render. After the `Render` method is called, the page is able to render all the client-side script it collected during the `OnPreRender` method. If you call the client-side script registration methods in the `Render` method, the page has already completed a portion of its rendering before your client-side script can render itself.

LISTING 7-18: Rendering a client-side script to the browser

VB

```vb
Protected Overrides Sub OnPreRender(ByVal e As System.EventArgs)
    Page.ClientScript.RegisterStartupScript(GetType(Page),
        "ControlFocus", "document.getElementById('" &
        Me.ClientID & "_i" & "').focus();", True)
End Sub
```

C#

```csharp
protected override void OnPreRender(EventArgs e)
{
    Page.ClientScript.RegisterStartupScript(typeof(Page),
        "ControlFocus", "document.getElementById('" +
        this.ClientID + "_i" + "').focus();", true);
}
```

In this listing, the code emits client-side script to automatically move the control focus to the TextBox control when the web page loads. When you use the `RegisterStartupScript` method, notice that it now includes an overload that lets you specify whether the method should render surrounding script tags. This can be handy if you are rendering more than one script to the page.

Also notice that the method requires a key parameter. This parameter is used to uniquely identify the script block; if you are registering more than one script block in the web page, make sure that each block is supplied a unique key. You can use the `IsStartupScriptRegistered` method and the key to determine whether a particular script block has been previously registered on the client using the `RegisterStartupScript` method.

When you execute the page in the browser, notice that the focus is automatically placed into a textbox. If you look at the source code for the web page, you should see that the JavaScript was written to the bottom of the page, as shown in Figure 7-11.

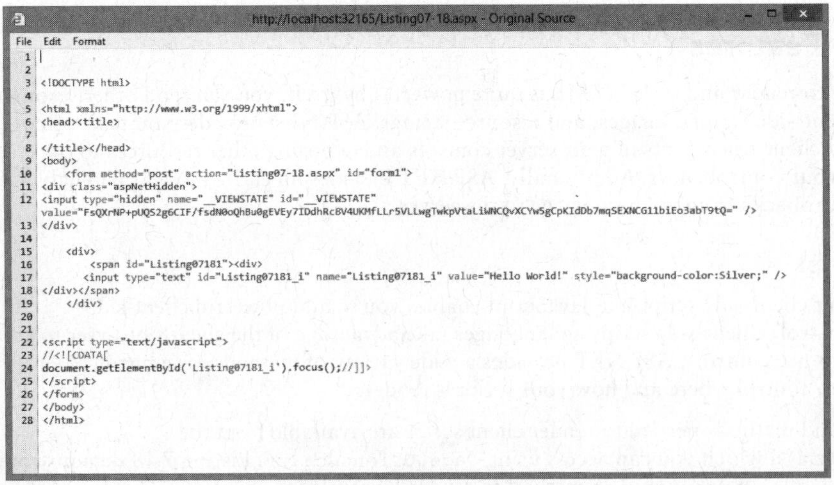

FIGURE 7-11

If you want the script to be rendered to the top of the page, you use the `RegisterClientScriptBlock` method that emits the script block immediately after the opening `<form>` element.

Keep in mind that the browser parses the web page from top to bottom, so if you emit client-side script at the top of the page that is not contained in a function, any references in that code to HTML elements further down the page will fail. The browser has not parsed that portion of the page yet.

Being able to render script that executes automatically when the page loads is nice, but it is more likely that you will want the code to execute based on an event fired from an HTML element on your page, such as the `Click`, `Focus`, or `Blur` events. To do this, you add an attribute to the HTML element you want the event to fire from. Listing 7-19 shows how you can modify your control's `Render` and `PreRender` methods to add this attribute.

LISTING 7-19: Using client-side script and event attributes to validate data

VB

```vb
Protected Overrides Sub RenderContents(ByVal output As HtmlTextWriter)
    output.RenderBeginTag(HtmlTextWriterTag.Div)
    output.AddAttribute(HtmlTextWriterAttribute.Type, "text")
    output.AddAttribute(HtmlTextWriterAttribute.Id, Me.ClientID & "_i")
    output.AddAttribute(HtmlTextWriterAttribute.Name,
                    Me.ClientID & "_i")
    output.AddAttribute(HtmlTextWriterAttribute.Value, Me.Text)
    output.AddAttribute("OnBlur", "ValidateText(this)")
    output.RenderBeginTag(HtmlTextWriterTag.Input)
    output.RenderEndTag()
    output.RenderEndTag()
End Sub

Protected Overrides Sub OnPreRender(ByVal e As System.EventArgs)
    Page.ClientScript.RegisterStartupScript(GetType(Page),
        "ControlFocus", "document.getElementById('" & Me.ClientID &
            "_i" & "').focus();", True)
    Page.ClientScript.RegisterClientScriptBlock(
        GetType(Page),
        "ValidateControl",
        "function ValidateText() {" &
            "if (ctl.value=='') {" &
                "alert('Please enter a value.');ctl.focus(); }" &
        "}", True)
End Sub
```

C#

```csharp
protected override void RenderContents(HtmlTextWriter output)
{
    output.RenderBeginTag(HtmlTextWriterTag.Div);
    output.AddAttribute(HtmlTextWriterAttribute.Type, "text");
    output.AddAttribute(HtmlTextWriterAttribute.Id,
                    this.ClientID + "_i");
    output.AddAttribute(HtmlTextWriterAttribute.Name,
                    this.ClientID + "_i");
    output.AddAttribute(HtmlTextWriterAttribute.Value, this.Text);
    output.AddAttribute("OnBlur", "ValidateText(this)");
    output.RenderBeginTag(HtmlTextWriterTag.Input);
    output.RenderEndTag();
    output.RenderEndTag();
```

continues

LISTING 7-19 *(continued)*

```
    }

    protected override void OnPreRender(EventArgs e)
    {
        Page.ClientScript.RegisterStartupScript(
            typeof(Page),
            "ControlFocus", "document.getElementById('" +
            this.ClientID + "_i" + "').focus();", true);

        Page.ClientScript.RegisterClientScriptBlock(
            typeof(Page),
            "ValidateControl",
            "function ValidateText(ctl) {" +
                "if (ctl.value=='') {" +
                    "alert('Please enter a value.'); ctl.focus(); }" +
            "}", true);
    }
```

As you can see, the TextBox control is modified to check for an empty string. An attribute that adds the JavaScript `OnBlur` event to the textbox is also included. The `OnBlur` event fires when the control loses focus. When this happens, the client-side `ValidateText` method is executed, which is rendered to the client using `RegisterClientScriptBlock`.

The rendered HTML is shown in Figure 7-12.

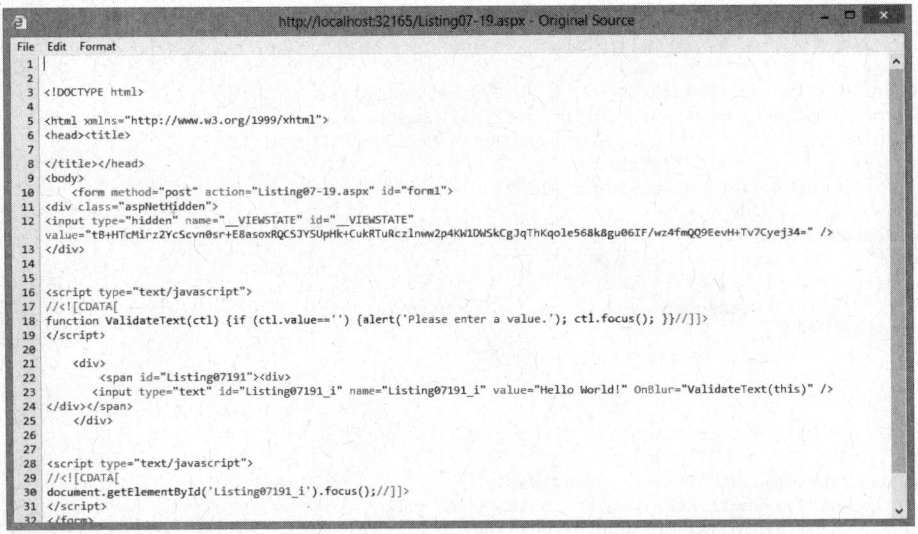

FIGURE 7-12

Embedding JavaScript in the page is powerful, but if you are writing large amounts of client-side code, you might want to consider storing the JavaScript in an external file. You can include this file in your HTML by using the `RegisterClientScriptInclude` method. This method renders a script tag using the URL you provide to it as the value of its `src` element:

```
<script src="[url]" type="text/javascript"></script>
```

Listing 7-20 shows how you can modify the validation added to the input element in Listing 7-18 to store the JavaScript validation function in an external file.

LISTING 7-20: Adding client-side script include files to a web page

VB

```
Protected Overrides Sub OnPreRender(ByVal e As System.EventArgs)
    Page.ClientScript.RegisterClientScriptInclude(
        "UtilityFunctions", "Listing07-21.js")
    Page.ClientScript.RegisterStartupScript(GetType(Page),
        "ControlFocus", "document.getElementById('" &
        Me.ClientID & "_i" & "').focus();",
        True)
End Sub
```

C#

```
protected override void OnPreRender(EventArgs e)
{
    Page.ClientScript.RegisterClientScriptInclude(
        "UtilityFunctions", "Listing07-21.js");
    Page.ClientScript.RegisterStartupScript(
        typeof(Page),
        "ControlFocus", "document.getElementById('" +
        this.ClientID + "_i" + "').focus();",
        true);
}
```

You have modified the `OnPreRender` event to register a client-side script file include, which contains the `ValidateText` function. You need to add a JavaScript file to the project and create the `ValidateText` function, as shown in Listing 7-21.

LISTING 7-21: The validation JavaScript

```
function ValidateText(ctl)
{
    if (ctl.value=='') {
        alert('Please enter a value.');
        ctl.focus();
    }
}
```

The `ClientScriptManager` also provides methods for registering hidden HTML fields and adding script functions to the `OnSubmit` event.

Accessing Embedded Resources

A great way to distribute application resources like JavaScript files, images, or resource files is to embed them directly into the compiled assembly. ASP.NET makes this easy by using the `RegisterClientScriptResource` method, which is part of the `ClientScriptManager`.

This method makes it possible for your web pages to retrieve stored resources — like JavaScript files — from the compiled assembly at run time. It works by using an `HttpHandler` to retrieve the requested resource from the assembly and return it to the client. The `RegisterClientScriptResource` method emits a `<script>` block whose `src` value points to this `HttpHandler` (Note that in the code download MiscEmbeddedScript.cs, AssemblyInfo.cs, and MiscEmbeddedScript.aspx are used to generate this):

```
<script
src="/WebResource.axd?d=ktqObNC8c8uwwm_pAVTdak1ofzyXH33vOZkC2Pqa7gWUvT7XCNmAeT5Jig-
FTrYk2SaMtNk3sR42AEFFZgrf7vQ_knZp3JtuIRq9xHCIDZBhHD0zyFRsRo-3AU0VeOyQ0rJ15SnnA-9ScC-
bwU0-PQ2&amp;t=634880142370628393" type="text/javascript"></script>
```

As you can see, the `WebResource.axd` handler is used to return the resource — in this case, the JavaScript file. You can use this method to retrieve any resource stored in the assembly, such as images or localized content strings from resource files.

Asynchronous Callbacks

Finally, ASP.NET also includes a convenient mechanism for enabling basic Ajax behavior, or client-side callbacks, in a server control. Client-side callbacks enable you to take advantage of the XmlHttp components found in most modern browsers to communicate with the server without actually performing a complete postback. Figure 7-13 shows how client-side callbacks work in the ASP.NET Framework.

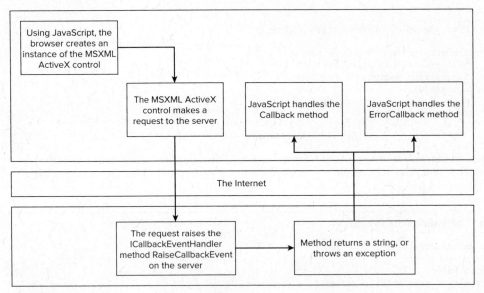

FIGURE 7-13

To enable callbacks in your server control, you implement the `System.Web.UI.ICallBackEventHander` interface. This interface requires you to implement two methods: the `RaiseCallbackEvent` method and the `GetCallbackResult` method. These server-side events fire when the client executes the callback. After you implement the interface, you want to tie your client-side events back to the server. You do this by using the `Page.ClientScript.GetCallbackEventReference` method. This method enables you to specify the two client-side functions: one to serve as the callback handler and one to serve as an error handler. Listing 7-22 demonstrates how you can modify the TextBox control's `Render` methods and add the `RaiseCallbackEvent` method to use callbacks to perform validation.

LISTING 7-22: Adding an asynchronous callback to validate data

VB

```
Protected Overrides Sub OnPreRender(ByVal e As System.EventArgs)
    Page.ClientScript.RegisterClientScriptInclude(
        "UtilityFunctions", "Listing07-23.js")

    Page.ClientScript.RegisterStartupScript(GetType(Page),
        "ControlFocus", "document.getElementById('" &
```

```
            Me.ClientID & "_i" & "').focus();",
            True)

        Page.ClientScript.RegisterStartupScript(
            GetType(Page), "ClientCallback",
            "function ClientCallback() {" &
                "args=document.getElementById('" &
                Me.ClientID & "_i" & "').value;" &
                Page.ClientScript.GetCallbackEventReference(Me, "args",
                    "CallbackHandler", Nothing, "ErrorHandler", True) &
            "}",
            True)
    End Sub

    Public Sub RaiseCallbackEvent(ByVal eventArgument As String) _
        Implements System.Web.UI.ICallbackEventHandler.RaiseCallbackEvent

        Dim result As Int32
        If (Not Int32.TryParse(eventArgument, result)) Then
            Throw New Exception("The method or operation is not implemented.")
        End If
    End Sub

    Public Function GetCallbackResult() As String _
        Implements System.Web.UI.ICallbackEventHandler.GetCallbackResult

        Return "Valid Data"
    End Function
```

C#

```
    protected override void RenderContents(HtmlTextWriter output)
    {
        output.RenderBeginTag(HtmlTextWriterTag.Div);
        output.AddAttribute(HtmlTextWriterAttribute.Type, "text");
        output.AddAttribute(HtmlTextWriterAttribute.Id, this.ClientID + "_i");
        output.AddAttribute(HtmlTextWriterAttribute.Name, this.ClientID + "_i");
        output.AddAttribute(HtmlTextWriterAttribute.Value, this.Text);
        output.AddAttribute("OnBlur", "ClientCallback();");
        output.RenderBeginTag(HtmlTextWriterTag.Input);
        output.RenderEndTag();
        output.RenderEndTag();
    }
    protected override void OnPreRender(EventArgs e)
    {
        Page.ClientScript.RegisterClientScriptInclude(
            "UtilityFunctions", "Listing07-23.js");

        Page.ClientScript.RegisterStartupScript(
            typeof(Page),
            "ControlFocus", "document.getElementById('" + this.ClientID + "_i" + "').focus();",
            true);

        Page.ClientScript.RegisterStartupScript(
            typeof(Page), "ClientCallback",
            "function ClientCallback() {" +
                "args=document.getElementById('" + this.ClientID + "_i" + "').value;" +
                Page.ClientScript.GetCallbackEventReference(this, "args",
                    "CallbackHandler", null, "ErrorHandler", true) + "}",
            true);
```

continues

LISTING 7-22 *(continued)*

```
    }

    public void RaiseCallbackEvent(string eventArgument)
    {
        int result;
        if (!Int32.TryParse(eventArgument, out result))
            throw new Exception("The method or operation is not implemented.");
    }

    public string GetCallbackResult()
    {
        return "Valid Data";
    }
```

As you can see, the `OnBlur` attribute has again been modified, this time by simply calling the `ClientCallback` method. This method is created and rendered during the `PreRender` event. The main purpose of this event is to populate the client-side `args` variable and call the client-side callback method.

The `GetCallbackEventReference` method is used to generate the client-side script that actually initiates the callback. The parameters passed to the method indicate which control is initiating the callback, the names of the client-side callback method, and the names of the callback method parameters. Table 7-3 provides more details on the `GetCallbackEventReference` arguments.

TABLE 7-3

PARAMETER	DESCRIPTION
`Control`	Server control that initiates the callback.
`Argument`	Client-side variable used to pass arguments to the server-side event handler.
`ClientCallback`	Client-side function serving as the `Callback` method. This method fires when the server-side processing has completed successfully.
`Context`	Client-side variable that gets passed directly to the receiving client-side function. The context does not get passed to the server.
`ClientErrorCallback`	Client-side function serving as the `Callback` error-handler method. This method fires when the server-side processing encounters an error.

In the code, you call two client-side methods: `CallbackHandler` and `ErrorHandler`, respectively. The two method parameters are `args` and `ctx`.

In addition to the server control code changes, you add the two client-side callback methods to the JavaScript file. Listing 7-23 shows these new functions.

LISTING 7-23: The client-side callback JavaScript functions

```
var args;
var ctx;

function ValidateText(ctl)
{
    if (ctl.value='') {
        alert('Please enter a value.');
        ctl.focus();
```

```
    }
}

function CallbackHandler(args,ctx)
{
    alert("The data is valid");
}

function ErrorHandler(args,ctx)
{
    alert("Please enter a number");
}
```

Now, when you view your web page in the browser, as soon as the textbox loses focus, you perform a client-side callback to validate the data. The callback raises the `RaiseCallbackEvent` method on the server, which validates the value of the textbox that was passed to it in the `eventArguments`. If the value is valid, you return a string and the client-side `CallbackHandler` function fires. If the value is invalid, you throw an exception, which causes the client-side `ErrorHandler` function to execute.

Browser Capabilities

So far this chapter has described many powerful features, such as styling and emitting client-side scripts that you can utilize when writing your own custom control. But if you are taking advantage of these features, you must also consider how you can handle certain browsers, often called down-level browsers, which might not understand these advanced features or might not have them enabled. Being able to detect and react to down-level browsers is an important consideration when creating your control. ASP.NET includes some powerful tools you can use to detect the type and version of the browser making the page request, as well as what capabilities the browser supports.

.browser Files

ASP.NET uses a highly flexible method for configuring, storing, and discovering browser capabilities. All browser identification and capability information is stored in `.browser` files. ASP.NET stores these files in the `C:\Windows\Microsoft.NET\Framework\v4.0.xxxxx\CONFIG\Browsers` directory. If you open this folder, you see that ASP.NET provides you with a variety of `.browser` files that describe the capabilities of most of today's common desktop browsers, as well as information on browsers in devices such as PDAs and cellular phones. Open one of the browser files, and you see that the file contains all the identification and capability information for the browser. Listing 7-24 shows the contents of the iPhone capabilities file, which can usually be found on your machine at `C:\Windows\Microsoft.NET\Framework\v4.0.30319\Config\Browsers\iphone.browser`.

> **NOTE** *As a reminder, if you are using the x64 version of the .NET Framework, you can also browse to* `C:\Windows\Microsoft.NET\Framework64\v4.0.xxxxx\CONFIG\Browsers`*.*

LISTING 7-24: A sample browser capabilities file

```
<browsers>
    <!-- Mozilla/5.0 (iPhone; U; CPU like Mac OS X; en) AppleWebKit/420+ (KHTML, like Gecko)
        Version/3.0 Mobile/1A543a Safari/419.3   -->
    <gateway id="IPhone" parentID="Safari">
        <identification>
            <userAgent match="iPhone" />
```

continues

LISTING 7-24 *(continued)*

```
        </identification>

        <capabilities>
          <capability name="isMobileDevice"               value="true" />
          <capability name="mobileDeviceManufacturer" value="Apple" />
          <capability name="mobileDeviceModel"          value="IPhone" />
          <capability name="canInitiateVoiceCall"       value="true" />
        </capabilities>
      </gateway>

      <!-- Mozilla/5.0 (iPod; U; CPU like Mac OS X; en) AppleWebKit/420.1 (KHTML, like Gecko)
        Version/3.0 Mobile/4A93 Safari/419.3  -->
      <gateway id="IPod" parentID="Safari">
          <identification>
            <userAgent match="iPod" />
          </identification>

          <capabilities>
            <capability name="isMobileDevice"               value="true" />
            <capability name="mobileDeviceManufacturer" value="Apple" />
            <capability name="mobileDeviceModel"          value="IPod" />
          </capabilities>
      </gateway>

    <!-- Mozilla/5.0 (iPad; U; CPU OS 4_3 like Mac OS X; en-us) AppleWebKit/533.17.9
      (KHTML, like Gecko) Version/5.0.2 Mobile/8F191 Safari/6533.18.5  -->
    <gateway id="IPad" parentID="Safari">
      <identification>
        <userAgent match="iPad" />
      </identification>

      <capabilities>
        <capability name="isMobileDevice"               value="true" />
        <capability name="mobileDeviceManufacturer" value="Apple" />
        <capability name="mobileDeviceModel"          value="IPad" />
      </capabilities>
    </gateway>
  </browsers>
```

The advantage of this method for storing browser capability information is that as new browsers are created or new versions are released, developers simply create or update a `.browser` file to describe the capabilities of that browser.

Accessing Browser Capability Information

Now that you have seen how ASP.NET stores browser capability information, you need to know how you can access this information at run time and program your control to change what it renders based on the browser. To access capability information about the requesting browser, you can use the `Page.Request .Browser` property. This property gives you access to the `System.Web.HttpBrowserCapabilities` class, which provides information about the capabilities of the browser making the current request. The class provides you with a myriad of attributes and properties that describe what the browser can support and render and what it requires. Lists use this information to add capabilities to the TextBox control. Listing 7-25 shows how you can detect browser capabilities to make sure a browser supports JavaScript.

LISTING 7-25: Detecting browser capabilities in server-side code

VB

```vb
Protected Overrides Sub OnPreRender(ByVal e As System.EventArgs)
    If (Page.Request.Browser.EcmaScriptVersion.Major > 0) Then

        Page.ClientScript.RegisterClientScriptInclude(
            "UtilityFunctions", "Listing07-23.js")

        Page.ClientScript.RegisterStartupScript(
            GetType(Page), "ClientCallback",
            "function ClientCallback() {" &
                "args=document.getElementById('" &
                    Me.ClientID & "_i" & "').value;" &
                Page.ClientScript.GetCallbackEventReference(Me, "args",
                    "CallbackHandler", Nothing, "ErrorHandler", True) +
                    "}",
            True)

        Page.ClientScript.RegisterStartupScript(GetType(Page),
            "ControlFocus", "document.getElementById('" &
            Me.ClientID & "_i" & "').focus();",
            True)
    End If
End Sub
```

C#

```csharp
protected override void OnPreRender(EventArgs e)
{
    if (Page.Request.Browser.EcmaScriptVersion.Major > 0)
    {
        Page.ClientScript.RegisterClientScriptInclude(
            "UtilityFunctions", "Listing07-23.js");

        Page.ClientScript.RegisterStartupScript(
            typeof(Page), "ControlFocus", "document.getElementById('" +
                this.ClientID + "_i" + "').focus();",
            true);

        Page.ClientScript.RegisterStartupScript(
            typeof(Page), "ClientCallback",
            "function ClientCallback() {" +
                "args=document.getElementById('" + this.ClientID + "_i" +
                "').value;" +
                Page.ClientScript.GetCallbackEventReference(this, "args",
                    "CallbackHandler", null, "ErrorHandler", true) + "}",
            true);
    }
}
```

This is a very simple sample, but it gives you an idea of what is possible using the `HttpBrowserCapabilities` class.

Using ViewState

When you are developing web applications, remember that they are built on the stateless HTTP protocol. ASP.NET gives you a number of ways to give users the illusion that they are using a stateful application, but perhaps the most ubiquitous is called ViewState. ViewState enables you to maintain the state of the objects and controls that are part of the web page through the page's life cycle by storing the state of the controls in a hidden form field that is rendered as part of the HTML. The state contained in the form field can then be used by the application to reconstitute the page's state when a postback occurs. Figure 7-14 shows how ASP.NET stores ViewState information in a hidden form field.

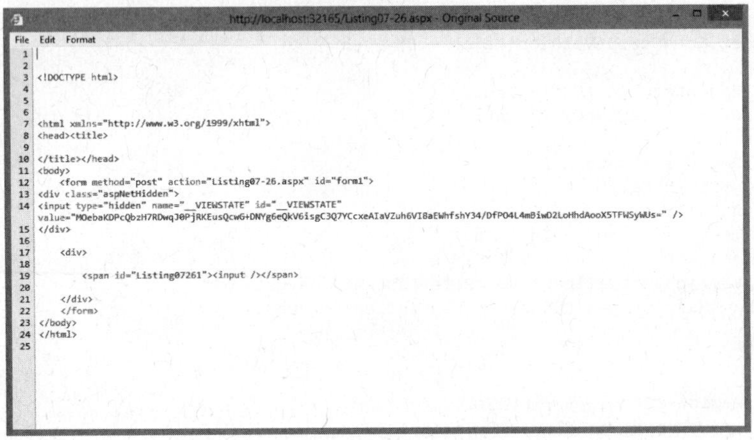

```
                    http://localhost:32165/Listing07-26.aspx - Original Source        _  □  ×
File  Edit  Format
 1 |
 2
 3 <!DOCTYPE html>
 4
 5
 6
 7 <html xmlns="http://www.w3.org/1999/xhtml">
 8 <head><title>
 9
10 </title></head>
11 <body>
12     <form method="post" action="Listing07-26.aspx" id="form1">
13 <div class="aspNetHidden">
14 <input type="hidden" name="__VIEWSTATE" id="__VIEWSTATE"
   value="MOebaKDPcQbzH7RDwqJ0PjRKEusQcwG+DNYg6eQkV6isgC3Q7YCcxeAIaVZuh6VI8aEWhfshY34/DfPO4L4mBiwD2LoHhdAooX5TFWSyWUs=" />
15 </div>
16
17     <div>
18
19         <span id="Listing07261"><input /></span>
20
21     </div>
22     </form>
23 </body>
24 </html>
25
```

FIGURE 7-14

Notice that the page contains a hidden form field named _ViewState. The value of this form field is the ViewState for your web page. By default, ViewState is enabled in all in-box server controls shipped with ASP.NET. If you write customer server controls, however, you are responsible for ensuring that a control is participating in the use of ViewState by the page.

The ASP.NET ViewState is basically a storage format that enables you to save and retrieve objects as key/value pairs. As you see in Figure 7-14, these objects are then serialized by ASP.NET and persisted as an encrypted string, which is pushed to the client as a hidden HTML form field. When the page posts back to the server, ASP.NET can use this hidden form field to reconstitute the StateBag, which you can then access as the page is processed on the server.

> **NOTE** *Because the ViewState can sometimes grow to be very large and can therefore affect the overall page size, you might consider an alternate method of storing the ViewState information. You can create your own persistence mechanism by deriving a class from the* System.Web.UI.PageStatePersister *class and overriding the class's* Load *and* Save *methods.*

As shown in Listing 7-26, by default, the Text property included with the ASP.NET Server Control template is set up to store its value in ViewState.

LISTING 7-26: The Text property's use of ViewState

VB

```
Property Text() As String
    Get
        Dim s As String = CStr(ViewState("Text"))
        If s Is Nothing Then
            Return "[" & Me.ID & "]"
        Else
            Return s
        End If
```

```
        End Get

      Set(ByVal Value As String)
         ViewState("Text") = Value
      End Set
   End Property
```

C#

```
public string Text
{
    get
    {
        String s = (String)ViewState["Text"];
        return ((s == null)? "[" + this.ID + "]" : s);
    }

    set
    {
        ViewState["Text"] = value;
    }
}
```

When you are creating new properties in an ASP.NET server control, you should remember to use this same technique to ensure that the values set by the end user in your control will be persisted across page postbacks.

> **NOTE** *Note that the loading of ViewState happens after the* OnInit *event has been raised by the page. If your control makes changes to itself or another server control before the event has been raised, the changes are not saved to the ViewState.*

Types and ViewState

As mentioned in the preceding section, the ViewState is basically a generic collection of objects, but not all objects can be added to the ViewState. Only types that can be safely persisted can be used in the ViewState, so objects such as database connections or file handles should not be added to the ViewState.

Additionally, certain data types are optimized for use in the ViewState. When adding data to the ViewState, try to package the data into these types:

➤   Primitive Types (`Int32`, Boolean, and so on).

➤   Arrays of Primitive Types.

➤   `ArrayList`, `HashTable`.

➤   `Pair`, `Triplet`.

➤   `Color`, `DataTime`.

➤   `String`, `IndexedString`.

➤   `HybridDictionary` of these types.

➤   Objects that have a `TypeConverter` available. Be aware, however, that there is a reduction in performance if you use these types.

➤   Objects that are serializable (marked with the `Serializable` attribute).

Control State

At times, your control must store small amounts of critical, usually private, information across postbacks. To allow for the storage of this type of information, even if a developer disables ViewState, ASP.NET includes a separate type of ViewState called ControlState. ControlState is essentially a private ViewState for your control only.

> **NOTE** *To ensure that your data is available across postbacks, use ControlState as opposed to ViewState for storing the information. ViewState can be disabled within a web application or site, which can cause the control to fail if it's reliant on ViewState.*

Two methods, `SaveViewState` and `LoadViewState`, provide access to ControlState; however, the implementation of these methods is left up to you. Listing 7-27 shows how you can use the `LoadControlState` and `SaveViewState` methods.

LISTING 7-27: Using ControlState in a server control

VB

```vb
<DefaultProperty("Text")>
<ToolboxData("<{0}:Listing0727 runat=server></{0}:Listing0727>")>
Public Class Listing0727
    Inherits WebControl

    Dim state As String
    Protected Overrides Sub OnInit(ByVal e As System.EventArgs)
        Page.RegisterRequiresControlState(Me)
        MyBase.OnInit(e)
    End Sub

    Protected Overrides Sub LoadControlState(ByVal savedState As Object)
        state = CStr(savedState)
    End Sub

    Protected Overrides Function SaveControlState() As Object
        Return CType("ControlSpecificData", Object)
    End Function

    Protected Overrides Sub Render(ByVal output As System.Web.UI.HtmlTextWriter)
        output.Write("Control State: " & state)
    End Sub

End Class
```

C#

```csharp
[DefaultProperty("Text")]
[ToolboxData("<{0}:Listing0727 runat=server></{0}:Listing0727>")]
public class Listing0727 : WebControl
{
    string state;
    protected override void OnInit(EventArgs e)
    {
        Page.RegisterRequiresControlState(this);

        base.OnInit(e);
    }

    protected override void LoadControlState(object savedState)
    {
        state = (string)savedState;
    }

    protected override object SaveControlState()
    {
        return (object)"ControlSpecificData";
```

```
        }

        protected override void RenderContents(HtmlTextWriter output)
        {
            output.Write("Control State: " + state);
        }
    }
```

Controls intending to use ControlState must call the `Page.RegisterRequiresControlState` method before attempting to save control state data. Additionally, the `RegisterRequiresControlState` method must be called for each page load because the value is not retained through page postbacks.

Raising Postback Events

As you have seen in this chapter, ASP.NET provides a very powerful set of tools you can use to develop server controls and emit them to a client browser. But this is still one-way communication because the server only pushes data to the client. It would be useful if the server control could send data back to the server. The process of sending data back to the server is generally known as a *page postback*. You experience a page postback any time you click a form button or link that causes the page to make a new request to the web server.

ASP.NET provides a rich framework for handling postbacks from ASP.NET web pages. A development model that mimics the standard Windows Forms event model is provided that enables you to use controls that, even though they are rendered in the client browser, can raise events in server-side code. It also provides an easy mechanism for plugging a server control into that framework, enabling you to create controls that can initiate a page postback. Figure 7-15 shows the ASP.NET postback framework.

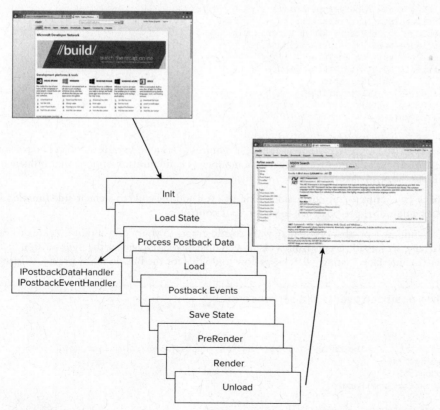

FIGURE 7-15

To initiate a page postback, by default ASP.NET uses client-side scripting. If you want your control to be able to initiate a postback, you must attach the postback initiation script to an HTML element event using the `GetPostBackEventReference` method during the control's render method. Listing 7-28 shows how you can attach the postback client script to the `onClick` event of a standard HTML Button element.

LISTING 7-28: Adding postback capabilities to a server control

VB

```vb
Protected Overrides Sub RenderContents(ByVal output As HtmlTextWriter)
    Dim p As New PostBackOptions(Me)
    output.AddAttribute(HtmlTextWriterAttribute.Onclick,
        Page.ClientScript.GetPostBackEventReference(p))
    output.AddAttribute(HtmlTextWriterAttribute.Value, "My Button")
    output.AddAttribute(HtmlTextWriterAttribute.Id,
                    Me.ClientID & "_i")
    output.AddAttribute(HtmlTextWriterAttribute.Name,
                    Me.ClientID & "_i")
    output.RenderBeginTag(HtmlTextWriterTag.Button)
    output.Write("My Button")
    output.RenderEndTag()
End Sub
```

C#

```csharp
protected override void RenderContents(HtmlTextWriter output)
{
    PostBackOptions p = new PostBackOptions(this);
    output.AddAttribute(HtmlTextWriterAttribute.Onclick,
        Page.ClientScript.GetPostBackEventReference(p));
    output.AddAttribute(HtmlTextWriterAttribute.Id,
                    this.ClientID + "_i");
    output.AddAttribute(HtmlTextWriterAttribute.Name,
                    this.ClientID + "_i");
    output.RenderBeginTag(HtmlTextWriterTag.Button);
    output.Write("My Button");
    output.RenderEndTag();
}
```

When the `GetPostBackEventReference` method is called, it requires a `PostBackOptions` object be passed to it. The `PostBackOptions` object enables you to specify a number of configuration options that influence how ASP.NET will initiate the postback.

You can add the postback JavaScript to any client-side event, or even add the code to a client-side function if you want to include some additional pre-postback logic for your control.

Now that the control can initiate a postback, you may want to add events to your control that execute during the page's postback. To raise server-side events from a client-side object, you implement the `System.Web .IPostBackEventHandler` interface. Listing 7-29 shows how to do this for the Button in the previous listing.

LISTING 7-29: Handling postback events in a server control

VB

```vb
<DefaultProperty("Text"), ToolboxData("<{0}:Listing0729 runat=server></{0}:Listing0729>")>
Public Class Listing0729
    Inherits WebControl
    Implements IPostBackEventHandler

    <Bindable(True), Category("Appearance"), DefaultValue(""), Localizable(True)>
```

```vbnet
    Property Text() As String
        Get
            Dim s As String = CStr(ViewState("Text"))
            If s Is Nothing Then
                Return "[" & Me.ID & "]"
            Else
                Return s
            End If
        End Get

        Set(ByVal Value As String)
            ViewState("Text") = Value
        End Set
    End Property

    Public Event Click()
    Public Sub OnClick(ByVal args As EventArgs)
        RaiseEvent Click()
    End Sub

    Public Sub RaisePostBackEvent(ByVal eventArgument As String) _
      Implements System.Web.UI.IPostBackEventHandler.RaisePostBackEvent
        OnClick(EventArgs.Empty)
    End Sub

    Protected Overrides Sub RenderContents(ByVal output As HtmlTextWriter)
        Dim p As New PostBackOptions(Me)
        output.AddAttribute(HtmlTextWriterAttribute.Onclick,
            Page.ClientScript.GetPostBackEventReference(p))
        output.AddAttribute(HtmlTextWriterAttribute.Value, "My Button")
        output.AddAttribute(HtmlTextWriterAttribute.Id,
                        Me.ClientID & "_i")
        output.AddAttribute(HtmlTextWriterAttribute.Name,
                        Me.ClientID & "_i")
        output.RenderBeginTag(HtmlTextWriterTag.Button)
        output.Write("My Button")
        output.RenderEndTag()
    End Sub
End Class
```

C#

```csharp
[DefaultProperty("Text")]
[ToolboxData("<{0}:Listing0729 runat=server></{0}:Listing0729>")]
public class Listing0729 : WebControl, IPostBackEventHandler
{
    public event EventHandler Click;

    public virtual void OnClick(EventArgs e)
    {
        if (Click != null)
        {
            Click(this, e);
        }
    }

    public void RaisePostBackEvent(string eventArgument)
    {
        OnClick(EventArgs.Empty);
    }

    protected override void RenderContents(HtmlTextWriter output)
```

continues

LISTING 7-29 *(continued)*

```
    {
        PostBackOptions p = new PostBackOptions(this);
        output.AddAttribute(HtmlTextWriterAttribute.Onclick,
            Page.ClientScript.GetPostBackEventReference(p));
        output.AddAttribute(HtmlTextWriterAttribute.Id,
                         this.ClientID + "_i");
        output.AddAttribute(HtmlTextWriterAttribute.Name,
                         this.ClientID + "_i");
        output.RenderBeginTag(HtmlTextWriterTag.Button);
        output.Write("My Button");
        output.RenderEndTag();
    }
}
```

When the user clicks the Button, a page postback occurs, and ASP.NET calls the `RaisePostBackEvent` method in the control, which lets you raise a server-side event. If several different client events in your control can initiate a postback, you can change the behavior of your control by using the `RaisePostBackEvent` method's `eventArgument` parameter to determine which element caused the postback. You set the `eventArgument` parameter using the `PostBackOptions` object mentioned previously.

Handling Postback Data

Now that you have learned how to store control data in ViewState and add postback capabilities to a control, you can enable the control to handle data a user has entered into form fields on the page. When an ASP.NET control initiates a postback, all the form data from the page is posted to the server. A server control can access and interact with that data, storing the information in ViewState and completing the illusion of a stateful application.

To access postback data, your control must implement the `System.Web.IPostBackDataHandler` interface. This interface allows ASP.NET to hand to your control the form data that is passed back to the server during the postback.

The `IPostBackDataHandler` interface requires you to implement two methods: the `LoadPostData` and `RaisePostBackDataChangedEvent` methods. Listing 7-30 shows how you implement the `IPostBackDataHandler` interface method in a simple text input control.

LISTING 7-30: Accessing postback data in a server control

VB

```
<DefaultProperty("Text"),
ToolboxData("<{0}:Listing0730 runat=server></{0}:Listing0730>")>
Public Class Listing0730
    Inherits WebControl
    Implements IPostBackEventHandler, IPostBackDataHandler

    <Bindable(True), Category("Appearance"),
    DefaultValue(""), Localizable(True)>
    Property Text() As String
        Get
            Dim s As String = CStr(ViewState("Text"))
            If s Is Nothing Then
                Return String.Empty
            Else
                Return s
```

```
                    End If
            End Get

        Set(ByVal Value As String)
            ViewState("Text") = Value
        End Set
    End Property

    Protected Overrides Sub RenderContents( _
                        ByVal output As HtmlTextWriter)
        Dim p As New PostBackOptions(Me)
        output.AddAttribute(HtmlTextWriterAttribute.Id, Me.ClientID)
        output.AddAttribute(HtmlTextWriterAttribute.Name, Me.ClientID)
        output.AddAttribute(HtmlTextWriterAttribute.Value, Me.Text)
        output.RenderBeginTag(HtmlTextWriterTag.Input)
        output.RenderEndTag()
    End Sub

    Public Function LoadPostData(ByVal postDataKey As String, _
        ByVal postCollection As  _
            System.Collections.Specialized.NameValueCollection) _
        As Boolean Implements _
            System.Web.UI.IPostBackDataHandler.LoadPostData
        Me.Text = postCollection(postDataKey)
        Return False
    End Function

    Public Sub RaisePostDataChangedEvent() _
        Implements _
            System.Web.UI.IPostBackDataHandler.RaisePostDataChangedEvent
    End Sub

    Public Event Click()
    Public Sub OnClick(ByVal args As EventArgs)
        RaiseEvent Click()
    End Sub

    Public Sub RaisePostBackEvent(ByVal eventArgument As String) _
      Implements System.Web.UI.IPostBackEventHandler.RaisePostBackEvent
        OnClick(EventArgs.Empty)
    End Sub
End Class
```

C#

```csharp
[DefaultProperty("Text")]
[ToolboxData("<{0}:Listing0730 runat=server></{0}:Listing0730>")]
public class Listing0730 : WebControl, IPostBackEventHandler, IPostBackDataHandler
{
    [Bindable(true)]
    [Category("Appearance")]
    [DefaultValue("")]
    [Localizable(true)]
    public string Text
    {
        get
        {
            String s = (String)ViewState["Text"];
            return ((s == null) ? "[" + this.ID + "]" : s);
        }
        set
```

continues

LISTING 7-30 *(continued)*

```
        {
            ViewState["Text"] = value;
        }
    }

    protected override void RenderContents(HtmlTextWriter output)
    {
        PostBackOptions p = new PostBackOptions(this);
        output.AddAttribute(HtmlTextWriterAttribute.Id, this.ClientID);
        output.AddAttribute(HtmlTextWriterAttribute.Name,
                            this.ClientID);
        output.AddAttribute(HtmlTextWriterAttribute.Value, this.Text);
        output.RenderBeginTag(HtmlTextWriterTag.Input);
        output.RenderEndTag();
    }

    public bool LoadPostData(string postDataKey,
    System.Collections.Specialized.NameValueCollection postCollection)
    {
        this.Text = postCollection[postDataKey];
        return false;
    }

    public void RaisePostDataChangedEvent()
    {
    }

    public event EventHandler Click;

    public virtual void OnClick(EventArgs e)
    {
        if (Click != null)
        {
            Click(this, e);
        }
    }

    public void RaisePostBackEvent(string eventArgument)
    {
        OnClick(EventArgs.Empty);
    }
}
```

During a postback, ASP.NET calls the LoadPostData method for this control, passing to it as a NameValueCollection any data submitted with the form. The postDataKey method parameter allows the control to access the postback data specific to it from the NameValueCollection.

Using the method parameters you can save the input element's text to the server control's Text property. If you remember the earlier ViewState example, the Text property saves the value to ViewState, allowing the control to automatically repopulate the input element's value when another page postback occurs.

The LoadPostData method requires you to return a boolean value from the method. This value indicates whether ASP.NET should call the RaisePostBackDataChangedEvent method after the LoadPostData method returns. For example, if you created a TextChanged event in the control to notify you that the control's text has changed, you would want to return True from this method so that you could subsequently raise that event in the RaisePostDataChangedEvent method.

Composite Controls

So far, in looking at server controls, you have concentrated on emitting a single HTML element; but this can be fairly limiting. Creating extremely powerful controls often requires that you combine several HTML elements together. Although you can always use the RenderContents method to emit multiple HTML elements, ASP.NET also enables you to emit existing ASP.NET controls from within a custom server control. These types of controls are called *composite controls*.

To demonstrate how easy creating a composite control can be, try changing the control shown in Listing 7-30 into a composite control. Listing 7-31 shows how you can do this.

LISTING 7-31: Creating a composite control

VB

```vb
<DefaultProperty("Text"),
 ToolboxData("<{0}:Listing0731 runat=server></{0}:Listing0731>")>
Public Class Listing0731
    Inherits System.Web.UI.WebControls.CompositeControl

    Protected textbox As TextBox = New TextBox()

    Protected Overrides Sub CreateChildControls()
        Me.Controls.Add(textbox)
    End Sub
End Class
```

C#

```csharp
[DefaultProperty("Text")]
[ToolboxData("<{0}:Listing0731 runat=server></{0}:Listing0731>")]
public class Listing0731 : CompositeControl
{
    protected TextBox textbox = new TextBox();

    protected override void CreateChildControls()
    {
        this.Controls.Add(textbox);
    }
}
```

A number of things in this listing are important. First, notice that the control class is now inheriting from CompositeControl, rather than WebControl. Deriving from CompositeControl gives you a few extra features specific to this type of control.

Second, notice that no Render method appears in this code. Instead, you simply create an instance of another type of server control and add that to the Controls collection in the CreateChildControls method. When you run this sample, you see that it renders a textbox just like the previous control did. In fact, the HTML that it renders is almost identical.

When you drop a composite control (such as the control from the previous sample) onto the design surface, notice that even though you are leveraging a powerful ASP.NET TextBox control within the control, none of that control's properties are exposed to you in the Properties Explorer. To expose child control properties through the parent container, you must create corresponding properties in the parent control. For example, if you want to expose the ASP.NET textbox Text property through the parent control, you create a Text property. Listing 7-32 shows how to do this.

LISTING 7-32: Exposing control properties in a composite control

VB

```vb
<DefaultProperty("Text"),
ToolboxData("<{0}:Listing0732 runat=server></{0}:Listing0732>")>
Public Class Listing0732
    Inherits System.Web.UI.WebControls.CompositeControl

    Protected textbox As TextBox = New TextBox()

    Public Property Text() As String
        Get
            EnsureChildControls()
            Return textbox.Text
        End Get
        Set(ByVal value As String)
            EnsureChildControls()
            textbox.Text = value
        End Set
    End Property

    Protected Overrides Sub CreateChildControls()
        Me.Controls.Add(textbox)
        Me.ChildControlsCreated = True
    End Sub
End Class
```

C#

```csharp
[DefaultProperty("Text")]
[ToolboxData("<{0}:Listing0732 runat=server></{0}:Listing0732>")]
public class Listing0732 : CompositeControl
{
    protected TextBox textbox = new TextBox();

    public string Text
    {
        get
        {
            EnsureChildControls();
            return textbox.Text;
        }
        set
        {
            EnsureChildControls();
            textbox.Text = value;
        }
    }

    protected override void CreateChildControls()
    {
        this.Controls.Add(textbox);
        this.ChildControlsCreated = true;
    }
}
```

Notice that you use this property simply to populate the underlying control's properties. Also notice that before you access the underlying control's properties, you always call the `EnsureChildControls` method. This method ensures that children of the container control have actually been initialized before you attempt to access them.

Templated Controls

In addition to composite controls, you can also create templated controls. *Templated controls* enable the developer to specify a portion of the HTML that is used to render a container control with nested controls. You might be familiar with the Repeater or DataList control. These are both templated controls that let you specify how you would like data to be bound and displayed when the page renders.

To demonstrate a templated control, the following code listings give you a basic example of displaying a simple text message on a web page. Because the control is a templated control, the developer has complete control over how the message is displayed.

To get started, create the Message server control that will be used as the template inside of a container control. Listing 7-33 shows the class that simply extends the existing Panel control by adding two additional properties, `Name` and `Text`, and a new constructor.

LISTING 7-33: Creating the templated control's inner control class

VB

```vb
Public Class Message
    Inherits System.Web.UI.WebControls.Panel
    Implements System.Web.UI.INamingContainer

    Public Property Name() As String
    Public Property Text() As String
End Class
```

C#

```csharp
public class Message : Panel, INamingContainer
{
    public string Name { get; internal set; }
    public string Text { get; internal set; }
}
```

As you see in a moment, you can access the public properties exposed by the `Message` class to insert dynamic content into the template. You also see how you can display the values of the `Name` and `Text` properties as part of the rendered template control.

Next, as shown in Listing 7-34, create a new server control that will be the container for the Message control. This server control is responsible for rendering any template controls nested in it.

LISTING 7-34: Creating the template control container class

VB

```vb
<DefaultProperty("Text")>
<ToolboxData("<{0}:Listing0734 runat=server></{0}:Listing0734>")>
Public Class Listing0734
    Inherits System.Web.UI.WebControls.WebControl

    <Browsable(False)> Public Property TemplateMessage() As Message

    <PersistenceMode(PersistenceMode.InnerProperty),
        TemplateContainer(GetType(Message))>
    Public Property MessageTemplate() As ITemplate

    <Bindable(True), DefaultValue("")>
    Public Property Name() As String

    <Bindable(True), DefaultValue("")>
```

continues

LISTING 7-34 *(continued)*

```
        Public Property Text() As String

        Public Overrides Sub DataBind()
            EnsureChildControls()
            ChildControlsCreated = True

            MyBase.DataBind()
        End Sub

        Protected Overrides Sub CreateChildControls()
            Me.Controls.Clear()
            Me.TemplateMessage = New Message() With {.Name = Name, .Text = Text}

            If Me.MessageTemplate Is Nothing Then
                Me.MessageTemplate = New DefaultMessageTemplate()
            End If

            Me.MessageTemplate.InstantiateIn(Me.TemplateMessage)
            Controls.Add(Me.TemplateMessage)
        End Sub

        Protected Overrides Sub RenderContents(
            ByVal writer As System.Web.UI.HtmlTextWriter)

            EnsureChildControls()
            ChildControlsCreated = True

            MyBase.RenderContents(writer)
        End Sub
    End Class
```

C#

```
[DefaultProperty("Text")]
[ToolboxData("<{0}:Listing0734 runat=server></{0}:Listing0734>")]
public class Listing0734 : WebControl
{
    [Browsable(false)]
    public Message TemplateMessage { get; internal set; }

    [PersistenceMode(PersistenceMode.InnerProperty)]
    [TemplateContainer(typeof(Message))]
    public virtual ITemplate MessageTemplate { get; set; }

    [Bindable(true)]
    [DefaultValue("")]
    public string Name { get; set; }

    [Bindable(true)]
    [DefaultValue("")]
    public string Text { get; set; }

    public override void DataBind()
    {
        EnsureChildControls();
        ChildControlsCreated = true;

        base.DataBind();
    }

    protected override void CreateChildControls()
```

```
    {
        this.Controls.Clear();
        this.TemplateMessage = new Message() { Name = Name, Text = Text };

        if (this.MessageTemplate == null)
        {
            this.MessageTemplate = new DefaultMessageTemplate();
        }

        this.MessageTemplate.InstantiateIn(this.TemplateMessage);
        Controls.Add(this.TemplateMessage);
    }

    protected override void RenderContents(HtmlTextWriter writer)
    {
        EnsureChildControls();
        ChildControlsCreated = true;

        base.RenderContents(writer);
    }
}
```

To start to dissect this sample, first notice the `MessageTemplate` property. This property allows Visual Studio to understand that the control will contain a template and allows it to display the IntelliSense for that template. The property has been marked with the `PersistanceMode` attribute, indicating that the template control should be persisted as an inner property within the control's tag in the ASPX page. Additionally, the property is marked with the `TemplateContainer` attribute, which helps ASP.NET figure out what type of template control this property represents. In this case, it's the Message template control you created earlier.

The container control exposes two public properties: `Name` and `Text`. These properties are used to populate the `Name` and `Text` properties of the Message control because that class does not allow developers to set the properties directly.

Finally, the `CreateChildControls` method, called by the `DataBind` method, does most of the heavy lifting in this control. It creates a new `Message` object, passing the values of `Name` and `Text` as constructor values. After the `CreateChildControls` method completes, the base `DataBind` operation continues to execute. This is important because that is where the evaluation of the `Name` and `Text` properties occurs, which enables you to insert these properties' values into the template control.

One additional thing to consider when creating templated controls is what should happen if you do not specify a template for the control. In the previous code listing, if you removed the `MessageTemplate` from the `TemplateContainer`, a `NullReferenceException` would occur when you tried to run your web page because the container control's `MessageTemplate` property would return a null value. To prevent this, you can include a default template class as part of the container control. An example of a default template is shown in Listing 7-35.

LISTING 7-35: Creating the templated control's default template class

VB

```
Friend Class DefaultMessageTemplate
    Implements ITemplate

    Public Sub InstantiateIn(ByVal container As System.Web.UI.Control) _
        Implements System.Web.UI.ITemplate.InstantiateIn

        Dim l As New Literal()
```

continues

LISTING 7-35 *(continued)*

```
                l.Text = "No MessageTemplate was included."
                container.Controls.Add(l)
        End Sub
End Class
```

C#

```csharp
internal sealed class DefaultMessageTemplate : ITemplate
{
    public void InstantiateIn(Control container)
    {
        Literal l = new Literal();
        l.Text = "No MessageTemplate was included.";
        container.Controls.Add(l);
    }
}
```

Notice that the `DefaultMessageTemplate` implements the `ITemplate` interface. This interface requires that the `InstantiateIn` method be implemented, which you use to provide the default template content.

To include the default template, simply add the class to the `TemplatedControl` class. You also need to modify the `CreateChildControls` method to detect the null `MessageTemplate` and instead create an instance of and use the default template:

VB

```vb
If Me.MessageTemplate Is Nothing Then
    Me.MessageTemplate = New DefaultMessageTemplate()
End If
```

C#

```csharp
if (this.MessageTemplate == null)
{
    this.MessageTemplate = new DefaultMessageTemplate();
}
```

After the control and default template are created, you can drop them onto a test web page. Listing 7-36 shows how you can use the control to customize the display of the data.

LISTING 7-36: Adding a templated control to a web page

VB

```vb
<%@ Page Language="VB" %>
<%@ Register assembly="VbServerControl1" namespace="VbServerControl1" tagprefix="cc1" %>
<!DOCTYPE html>
<script runat="server">
    Protected Sub Page_Load(ByVal sender As Object, ByVal e As System.EventArgs)
        Me.Listing07341.DataBind()
    End Sub
</script>
<html xmlns="http://www.w3.org/1999/xhtml">
<head id="Head1" runat="server">
    <title>Templated Web Controls</title>
</head>
<body>
    <form id="form1" runat="server">
    <div>
        <cc1:Listing0734 ID="Listing07341" runat="server" Name="John Doe"
```

```
                    Text="Hello World!">
                    <MessageTemplate>The user '<%# Container.Name %>' has a
                        message for you: <br />"<%# Container.Text %>"
                    </MessageTemplate>
                </cc1:Listing0734>
            </div>
        </form>
    </body>
    </html>
```

C#

```
<script runat="server">
    protected void Page_Load(object sender, EventArgs e)
    {
        this.Listing07341.DataBind();
    }
</script>
```

As you can see in the listing, the `<cc1:TemplatedControl>` control contains a `MessageTemplate` within it, which has been customized to display the `Name` and `Text` values. Figure 7-16 shows this page after it has been rendered in the browser.

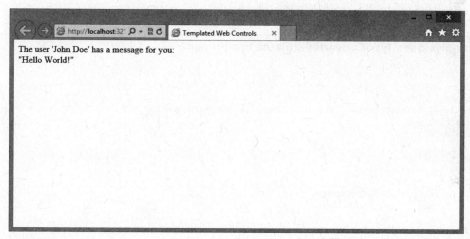

FIGURE 7-16

Design-Time Experiences

So far in this chapter, you concentrated primarily on what gets rendered to the client's browser, but the browser is not the only consumer of server controls. Visual Studio and the developer using a server control are also consumers, and you need to consider their experiences when using your control.

ASP.NET offers numerous ways to give developers using your control a great design-time experience. Some of these require no additional coding, such as the WYSIWYG rendering of user controls and basic server controls. For more complex scenarios, ASP.NET includes a variety of options that enable you to give the developer an outstanding design-time experience when using your control.

When you write server controls, a priority should be to give the developer a design-time experience that closely replicates the runtime experience. This means altering the appearance of the control on the design surface in response to changes in control properties and the introduction of other server controls onto the design surface. Three main components are involved in creating the design-time behaviors of a server control:

➤   Type converters

➤   Designers

➤   UI type editors

Because a chapter can be written for each one of these topics, this section gives you just an overview of each, how they tie into a control's design-time behavior, and some simple examples of their use.

Type Converters

`TypeConverter` is a class that enables you to perform conversions between one type and another. Visual Studio uses type converters at design time to convert object property values to String types so that they can be displayed on the Property Browser, and it returns them to their original types when the developer changes the property.

ASP.NET includes a wide variety of type converters you can use when creating your control's design-time behavior. These range from converters that enable you to convert most numeric types, to converters that let you convert `Fonts`, `Colors`, `DataTimes`, and `Guids`. The easiest way to see what type converters are available to you in the .NET Framework is to search for types in the framework that derive from the `TypeConverter` class using the MSDN Library help.

After you have found a type converter that you want to use on a control property, mark the property with a `TypeConverter` attribute, as shown in Listing 7-37.

LISTING 7-37: Applying the TypeConverter attribute to a property

VB

```
<DefaultProperty("Text"),
ToolboxData("<{0}:ServerControl39 runat=server></{0}:ServerControl39>")>
Public Class Listing0737
    Inherits WebControl

    <Bindable(True)>
    <Category("Appearance")>
    <DefaultValue("")>
    <TypeConverter(GetType(GuidConverter))>
    Property BookId() As System.Guid

    Protected Overrides Sub RenderContents(ByVal output As HtmlTextWriter)
        output.Write(BookId.ToString())
    End Sub
End Class
```

C#

```
[DefaultProperty("Text")]
[ToolboxData("<{0}:Listing0737 runat=server></{0}:Listing0737>")]
public class Listing0737 : WebControl
{
    [Bindable(true)]
    [Category("Appearance")]
    [DefaultValue("")]
    [TypeConverter(typeof(GuidConverter))]
    public Guid BookId { get; set; }

    protected override void RenderContents(HtmlTextWriter output)
    {
        output.Write(BookId.ToString());
    }
}
```

In this example, a property is exposed that accepts and returns an object of type `Guid`. The Property Browser cannot natively display a `Guid` object, so you convert the value to a string so that it can be displayed properly in the Property Browser. Marking the property with the `TypeConverter` attribute and, in this case, specifying the `GuidConverter` as the type converter you want to use, allows complex objects like a `Guid` to display properly in the Property Browser.

Custom Type Converters

Creating your own custom type converters if none of the in-box converters fit into your scenario is also possible. Type converters derive from the `System.ComponentModel.TypeConverter` class. Listing 7-38 shows a custom type converter that converts a custom object called `Name` to and from a string.

LISTING 7-38: Creating a custom type converter

VB

```vb
Imports System
Imports System.ComponentModel
Imports System.Globalization

Public Class Name

    Private _first As String
    Private _last As String

    Public Sub New(ByVal first As String, ByVal last As String)
        _first = first
        _last = last
    End Sub

    Public Property First() As String
        Get
            Return _first
        End Get
        Set(ByVal value As String)
            _first = value
        End Set
    End Property

    Public Property Last() As String
        Get
            Return _last
        End Get
        Set(ByVal value As String)
            _last = value
        End Set
    End Property
End Class

Public Class NameConverter
    Inherits TypeConverter

    Public Overrides Function CanConvertFrom(ByVal context As _
        ITypeDescriptorContext, ByVal sourceType As Type) As Boolean

        If (sourceType Is GetType(String)) Then
            Return True
```

continues

LISTING 7-38 *(continued)*

```vb
        End If

        Return MyBase.CanConvertFrom(context, sourceType)
    End Function

    Public Overrides Function ConvertFrom( _
            ByVal context As ITypeDescriptorContext, _
            ByVal culture As CultureInfo, ByVal value As Object) As Object
        If (value Is GetType(String)) Then
            Dim v As String() = (CStr(value).Split(New [Char]() {" "c}))
            Return New Name(v(0), v(1))
        End If
        Return MyBase.ConvertFrom(context, culture, value)
    End Function

    Public Overrides Function ConvertTo( _
            ByVal context As ITypeDescriptorContext, _
            ByVal culture As CultureInfo, ByVal value As Object, _
            ByVal destinationType As Type) As Object
        If (destinationType Is GetType(String)) Then
            Return (CType(value, Name).First + " " + (CType(value, Name).Last))
        End If
        Return MyBase.ConvertTo(context, culture, value, destinationType)
    End Function
End Class
```

C#

```csharp
using System;
using System.ComponentModel;
using System.Globalization;

public class Name
{
    public Name(string first, string last)
    {
        First = first;
        Last = last;
    }

    public string First { get; set; }
    public string Last { get; set; }
}

public class NameConverter : TypeConverter
{

    public override bool CanConvertFrom(ITypeDescriptorContext context,
        Type sourceType) {

        if (sourceType == typeof(string)) {
            return true;
        }
        return base.CanConvertFrom(context, sourceType);
    }

    public override object ConvertFrom(ITypeDescriptorContext context,
        CultureInfo culture, object value) {
        if (value is string) {
```

```
            string[] v = ((string)value).Split(new char[] {' '});
            return new Name(v[0],v[1]);
        }
        return base.ConvertFrom(context, culture, value);
    }

    public override object ConvertTo(ITypeDescriptorContext context,
        CultureInfo culture, object value, Type destinationType) {

        if (destinationType == typeof(string)) {
            return ((Name)value).First + " " + ((Name)value).Last;
        }
        return base.ConvertTo(context, culture, value, destinationType);
    }
}
```

The `NameConverter` class overrides three methods: `CanConvertFrom`, `ConvertFrom`, and `ConvertTo`. The `CanConvertFrom` method enables you to control what types the converter can convert from. The `ConvertFrom` method converts the string representation back into a `Name` object, and `ConvertTo` converts the `Name` object into a string representation.

After you have built your type converter, you can use it to mark properties in your control with the `TypeConverter` attribute, as you saw in Listing 7-37.

Control Designers

Controls that live on the Visual Studio design surface depend on *control designers* to create the design-time experience for the end user. Control designers, for both WinForms and ASP.NET, are classes that derive from the `System.ComponentModel.Design.ComponentDesigner` class. .NET provides an abstracted base class specifically for creating ASP.NET control designers called the `System.Web.UI.Design .ControlDesigner`. To access these classes you need to add a reference to the `System.Design.dll` assembly to your project.

.NET includes a number of in-box control designer classes that you can use when creating a custom control; but as you develop server controls, you see that .NET automatically applies a default designer. The designer it applies is based on the type of control you are creating. For instance, when you created your first TextBox control, Visual Studio used the `ControlDesigner` class to achieve the WYSIWYG design-time rendering of the textbox. If you develop a server control derived from the `ControlContainer` class, .NET automatically uses the `ControlContainerDesigner` class as the designer.

You can also explicitly specify the designer you want to use to render your control at design time using the `Designer` attribute on your control's class, as shown in Listing 7-39.

LISTING 7-39: Adding a Designer attribute to a control class

VB

```
<DefaultProperty("Text"),
 ToolboxData("<{0}:Listing0739 runat=server></{0}:Listing0739>"),
 Designer(GetType(System.Web.UI.Design.ControlDesigner))>
Public Class Listing0739
    Inherits System.Web.UI.WebControls.WebControl
```

C#

```
[DefaultProperty("Text")]
[ToolboxData("<{0}:Listing0739 runat=server></{0}:Listing0739>")]
[Designer(typeof(System.Web.UI.Design.ControlDesigner))]
public class Listing0739 : WebControl
```

> **NOTE** *In code Listing 7-39, you'll notice that I'm using a control called* `Listing0739`.
> *I've changed the name of this control during the creation of the control. If you leave the*
> *default name, you will most likely end up with a class name of* `WebCustomControl1`.

Notice that you added the `Designer` attribute to the `Listing0739` class. You have specified that the control should use the `ControlDesigner` class (found in the `System.Design` assembly) as its designer. Other in-box designers you could have specified are:

➤ `CompositeControlDesigner`

➤ `TemplatedControlDesigner`

➤ `DataSourceDesigner`

Each designer provides a specific design-time behavior for the control, and you can select one that is appropriate for the type of control you are creating.

Design-Time Regions

As you saw earlier, ASP.NET enables you to create server controls that consist of other server controls and text. ASP.NET enables you to create server controls that have design-time editable portions using a technique called *designer regions*. Designer regions enable you to create multiple, independent regions defined within a single control and respond to events raised by a design region. This might be the designer drawing a control on the design surface or the user clicking an area of the control or entering or exiting a template edit mode.

To show how you can use designer regions, create a container control to which you can apply a custom control designer, as shown in Listing 7-40.

LISTING 7-40: Creating a composite control with designer regions

VB

```vb
Imports System.ComponentModel
Imports System.Web.UI
Imports System.Web.UI.WebControls

<Designer(GetType(MultiRegionControlDesigner))> _
<ToolboxData("<{0}:Listing0740 runat=server width=100%></{0}:Listing0740>")> _
Public Class Listing0740
    Inherits CompositeControl

    ' Define the templates that represent 2 views on the control
    Private _view1 As ITemplate
    Private _view2 As ITemplate

    ' These properties are inner properties
    <PersistenceMode(PersistenceMode.InnerProperty), DefaultValue("")> _
    Public Overridable Property View1() As ITemplate
        Get
            Return _view1
        End Get
        Set(ByVal value As ITemplate)
            _view1 = value
        End Set
    End Property

    <PersistenceMode(PersistenceMode.InnerProperty), DefaultValue("")> _
```

```vb
      Public Overridable Property View2() As ITemplate
          Get
              Return _view2
          End Get
          Set(ByVal value As ITemplate)
              _view2 = value
          End Set
      End Property

      ' The current view on the control; 0= view1, 1=view2, 2=all views
      Private _currentView As Int32 = 0
      Public Property CurrentView() As Int32
          Get
              Return _currentView
          End Get
          Set(ByVal value As Int32)
              _currentView = value
          End Set
      End Property

      Protected Overrides Sub CreateChildControls()
          MyBase.CreateChildControls()

          Controls.Clear()

          Dim template As ITemplate = View1
          If (_currentView = 1) Then
              template = View2
          End If

          Dim p As New Panel()
          Controls.Add(p)

          If (Not template Is Nothing) Then
              template.InstantiateIn(p)
          End If
      End Sub

  End Class
```

C#

```csharp
  [Designer(typeof(MultiRegionControlDesigner))]
  [ToolboxData("<{0}:Listing0740 runat=\"server\" width=\"100%\">" +
      "</{0}:Listing0740>")]
  public class Listing0740 : CompositeControl
  {

      // Define the templates that represent 2 views on the control
      private ITemplate _view1;
      private ITemplate _view2;

      // These properties are inner properties
      [PersistenceMode(PersistenceMode.InnerProperty), DefaultValue(null)]
      public virtual ITemplate View1
      {
          get { return _view1; }
          set { _view1 = value; }
      }

      [PersistenceMode(PersistenceMode.InnerProperty), DefaultValue(null)]
```

continues

LISTING 7-40 *(continued)*

```
        public virtual ITemplate View2
        {
            get { return _view2; }
            set { _view2 = value; }
        }

        // The current view on the control; 0= view1, 1=view2, 2=all views
        private int _currentView = 0;
        public int CurrentView
        {
            get { return _currentView; }
            set { _currentView = value; }
        }

        protected override void CreateChildControls()
        {
            Controls.Clear();

            ITemplate template = View1;
            if (_currentView == 1)
                template = View2;

            Panel p = new Panel();
            Controls.Add(p);

            if (template != null)
                template.InstantiateIn(p);
        }
    }
```

The container control creates two ITemplate objects, which serve as the controls to display. The ITemplate objects are the control containers for this server control, enabling you to drop other server controls or text into this control. The control also uses the Designer attribute to indicate to Visual Studio that it should use the MultiRegionControlDesigner class when displaying this control on the designer surface.

Now you create the control designer that defines the regions for the control. Listing 7-41 shows the designer class.

LISTING 7-41: A custom designer class used to define designer regions

VB

```
    Public Class MultiRegionControlDesigner
        Inherits System.Web.UI.Design.WebControls.CompositeControlDesigner

        Protected _currentView As Int32 = 0
        Private myControl As Listing0740

        Public Overrides Sub Initialize(ByVal component As IComponent)
            MyBase.Initialize(component)
            myControl = CType(component, Listing0740)
        End Sub

        Public Overrides ReadOnly Property AllowResize() As Boolean
            Get
                Return True
            End Get
```

```vb
    End Property

    Protected Overrides Sub OnClick(ByVal e As DesignerRegionMouseEventArgs)

        If (e.Region Is Nothing) Then
            Return
        End If

        If ((e.Region.Name = "Header0") And (Not _currentView = 0)) Then
            _currentView = 0
            UpdateDesignTimeHtml()
        End If

        If ((e.Region.Name = "Header1") And (Not _currentView = 1)) Then

            _currentView = 1
            UpdateDesignTimeHtml()
        End If
    End Sub

    Public Overrides Function GetDesignTimeHtml( _
            ByVal regions As DesignerRegionCollection) As String
        BuildRegions(regions)
        Return BuildDesignTimeHtml()
    End Function

    Protected Overridable Sub BuildRegions( _
            ByVal regions As DesignerRegionCollection)

        regions.Add(New DesignerRegion(Me, "Header0"))
        regions.Add(New DesignerRegion(Me, "Header1"))

        ' If the current view is for all, we need another editable region
        Dim edr0 As New EditableDesignerRegion(Me, "Content" & _currentView, False)
        edr0.Description = "Add stuff in here if you dare:"
        regions.Add(edr0)

        ' Set the highlight, depending upon the selected region
        If ((_currentView = 0) Or (_currentView = 1)) Then
            regions(_currentView).Highlight = True
        End If
    End Sub

    Protected Overridable Function BuildDesignTimeHtml() As String

        Dim sb As New StringBuilder()
        sb.Append(BuildBeginDesignTimeHtml())
        sb.Append(BuildContentDesignTimeHtml())
        sb.Append(BuildEndDesignTimeHtml())

        Return sb.ToString()
    End Function

    Protected Overridable Function BuildBeginDesignTimeHtml() As String
        ' Create the table layout
        Dim sb As New StringBuilder()
        sb.Append("<table ")

        ' Styles that we'll use to render for the design-surface
        sb.Append("height='" & myControl.Height.ToString() & "' width='" & _
            myControl.Width.ToString() & "'>")

        ' Generate the title or caption bar
```

continues

LISTING 7-41 *(continued)*

```vbnet
        sb.Append("<tr height='25px' align='center' " & _
            "style='font-family:tahoma;font-size:10pt;font-weight:bold;'>" & _
            "<td style='width:50%' " & _
            DesignerRegion.DesignerRegionAttributeName & "='0'>")
        sb.Append("Page-View 1</td>")
        sb.Append("<td style='width:50%' " & _
            DesignerRegion.DesignerRegionAttributeName & "='1'>")
        sb.Append("Page-View 2</td></tr>")

        Return sb.ToString()
    End Function

    Protected Overridable Function BuildEndDesignTimeHtml() As String
        Return ("</table>")
    End Function

    Protected Overridable Function BuildContentDesignTimeHtml() As String

        Dim sb As New StringBuilder()
        sb.Append("<td colspan='2' style='")
        sb.Append("background-color:" & _
            myControl.BackColor.Name.ToString() & ";' ")

        sb.Append(DesignerRegion.DesignerRegionAttributeName & "='2'>")

        Return sb.ToString()
    End Function

    Public Overrides Function GetEditableDesignerRegionContent( _
            ByVal region As EditableDesignerRegion) As String

        Dim host As IDesignerHost = _
            CType(Component.Site.GetService(GetType(IDesignerHost)), IDesignerHost)

        If (Not host Is Nothing) Then
            Dim template As ITemplate = myControl.View1

            If (region.Name = "Content1") Then
                template = myControl.View2
            End If

            If (Not template Is Nothing) Then
                Return ControlPersister.PersistTemplate(template, host)
            End If

        End If

        Return String.Empty
    End Function

    Public Overrides Sub SetEditableDesignerRegionContent( _
            ByVal region As EditableDesignerRegion, ByVal content As String)

        Dim regionIndex As Int32 = Int32.Parse(region.Name.Substring(7))

        If (content Is Nothing) Then

            If (regionIndex = 0) Then
```

```
                    myControl.View1 = Nothing
            ElseIf (regionIndex = 1) Then
                    myControl.View2 = Nothing
                    Return
            End If

            Dim host As IDesignerHost = _
                CType(Component.Site.GetService(GetType(IDesignerHost)),
                    IDesignerHost)

            If (Not host Is Nothing) Then
                    Dim template = ControlParser.ParseTemplate(host, content)

                    If (Not template Is Nothing) Then
                        If (regionIndex = 0) Then
                            myControl.View1 = template
                        ElseIf (regionIndex = 1) Then
                            myControl.View2 = template
                        End If
                    End If
            End If
        End If
    End Sub
End Class
```

C#

```csharp
public class MultiRegionControlDesigner :
    System.Web.UI.Design.WebControls.CompositeControlDesigner {

    protected int _currentView = 0;

    private Listing0740 myControl;
    public override void Initialize(IComponent component)
    {
        base.Initialize(component);
        myControl = (Listing0740)component;
    }

    public override bool AllowResize { get { return true;}}

    protected override void OnClick(DesignerRegionMouseEventArgs e)
    {
        if (e.Region == null)
            return;

        if (e.Region.Name == "Header0" && _currentView != 0) {
            _currentView = 0;
            UpdateDesignTimeHtml();
        }

        if (e.Region.Name == "Header1" && _currentView != 1) {
            _currentView = 1;
            UpdateDesignTimeHtml();
        }
    }

    public override String GetDesignTimeHtml(DesignerRegionCollection regions)
    {
        BuildRegions(regions);
        return BuildDesignTimeHtml();
```

continues

LISTING 7-41 *(continued)*

```
    }

    protected virtual void BuildRegions(DesignerRegionCollection regions)
    {
        regions.Add(new DesignerRegion(this, "Header0"));
        regions.Add(new DesignerRegion(this, "Header1"));

        // If the current view is for all, we need another editable region
        EditableDesignerRegion edr0 = new
            EditableDesignerRegion(this, "Content" + _currentView, false);
        edr0.Description = "Add stuff in here if you dare:";
        regions.Add(edr0);

        // Set the highlight, depending upon the selected region
        if (_currentView ==0 || _currentView==1)
            regions[_currentView].Highlight = true;
    }

    protected virtual string BuildDesignTimeHtml()
    {
        StringBuilder sb = new StringBuilder();
        sb.Append(BuildBeginDesignTimeHtml());
        sb.Append(BuildContentDesignTimeHtml());
        sb.Append(BuildEndDesignTimeHtml());

        return sb.ToString();
    }

    protected virtual String BuildBeginDesignTimeHtml()
    {
        // Create the table layout
        StringBuilder sb = new StringBuilder();
        sb.Append("<table ");

        // Styles that we'll use to render for the design-surface
        sb.Append("height='" + myControl.Height.ToString() + "' width='" +
            myControl.Width.ToString() +  "'>");

        // Generate the title or caption bar
        sb.Append("<tr height='25px' align='center' " +
            "style='font-family:tahoma;font-size:10pt;font-weight:bold;'>" +
            "<td style='width:50%' " + DesignerRegion.DesignerRegionAttributeName +
            "='0'>");
        sb.Append("Page-View 1</td>");
        sb.Append("<td style='width:50%' " +
            DesignerRegion.DesignerRegionAttributeName + "='1'>");
        sb.Append("Page-View 2</td></tr>");

        return sb.ToString();
    }

    protected virtual String BuildEndDesignTimeHtml()
    {
        return ("</table>");
    }

    protected virtual String BuildContentDesignTimeHtml()
    {
```

```
            StringBuilder sb = new StringBuilder();
            sb.Append("<td colspan='2' style='");
            sb.Append("background-color:" + myControl.BackColor.Name.ToString() +
                ";' ");

            sb.Append(DesignerRegion.DesignerRegionAttributeName + "='2'>");

            return sb.ToString();
        }

        public override string GetEditableDesignerRegionContent
            (EditableDesignerRegion region)
        {
            IDesignerHost host =
                (IDesignerHost)Component.Site.GetService(typeof(IDesignerHost));

            if (host != null) {
                ITemplate template = myControl.View1;

                if (region.Name == "Content1")
                    template = myControl.View2;

                if (template != null)
                    return ControlPersister.PersistTemplate(template, host);
            }

            return String.Empty;
        }

        public override void SetEditableDesignerRegionContent
            (EditableDesignerRegion region, string content)
        {
            int regionIndex = Int32.Parse(region.Name.Substring(7));

            if (content == null)
            {
                if (regionIndex == 0)
                    myControl.View1 = null;
                else if (regionIndex == 1)
                    myControl.View2 = null;
                return;
            }

            IDesignerHost host =
                (IDesignerHost)Component.Site.GetService(typeof(IDesignerHost));

            if (host != null)
            {
                ITemplate template = ControlParser.ParseTemplate(host, content);

                if (template != null)
                {
                    if (regionIndex == 0)
                        myControl.View1 = template;
                    else if (regionIndex == 1)
                        myControl.View2 = template;
                }
            }
        }
    }
}
```

The designer overrides the `GetDesignTimeHtml` method, calling the `BuildRegions` and `BuildDesignTimeHtml` methods to alter the HTML that the control renders to the Visual Studio design surface.

The `BuildRegions` method creates three design regions in the control: two header regions and an editable content region. The regions are added to the `DesignerRegionCollection`. The `BuildDesignTimeHtml` method calls three methods to generate the actual HTML that is generated by the control at design time.

The designer class also contains two overridden methods for getting and setting the editable designer region content: `GetEditableDesignerRegionContent` and `SetEditableDesignerRegionContent`. These methods get or set the appropriate content HTML, based on the designer region template that is currently active.

Finally, the class contains an `OnClick` method that it uses to respond to click events fired by the control at design time. This control uses the `OnClick` event to switch the current region being displayed by the control at design time.

When you add the control to a Web Form, you see that you can toggle between the two editable regions, and each region maintains its own content. Figure 7-17 shows what the control looks like on the Visual Studio design surface.

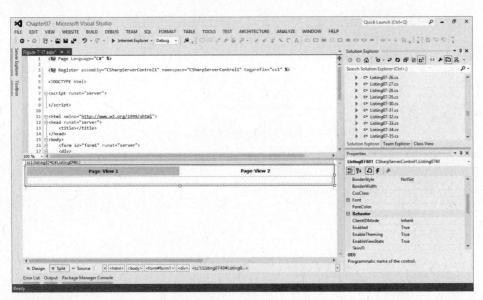

FIGURE 7-17

As you can see in Figure 7-17, the control contains three separate design regions. When you click design regions 1 or 2, the `OnClick` method in the designer fires and redraws the control on the design surface, changing the template area located in design region 3.

Designer Actions

Another great feature of ASP.NET design-time support is control smart tags. Smart tags give developers using a control quick access to common control properties. To add menu items to a server control's smart tag, you create a new class that inherits from the `DesignerActionList` class. The `DesignerActionList` class contains the list of designer action items that are displayed by a server control. Classes that derive from the `DesignerActionList` class can override the `GetSortedActionItems` method, creating their own `DesignerActionItemsCollection` object to which you can add designer action items.

You can add several different types of `DesignerActionItems` to the collection:

- ➤ `DesignerActionTextItem`
- ➤ `DesignerActionHeaderItem`
- ➤ `DesignerActionMethodItem`
- ➤ `DesignerActionPropertyItem`

Listing 7-42 shows a control designer class that contains a private class deriving from `DesignerActionList`.

LISTING 7-42: Adding designer actions to a control designer

VB

```vb
Public Class Listing0742Designer
    Inherits ControlDesigner

    Private _actionLists As DesignerActionListCollection

    Public Overrides ReadOnly Property ActionLists() _
            As DesignerActionListCollection
        Get
            If IsNothing(_actionLists) Then
                _actionLists = New DesignerActionListCollection()
                _actionLists.AddRange(MyBase.ActionLists)
                _actionLists.Add(New ServerControl44ControlList(Me))
            End If
            Return _actionLists
        End Get
    End Property

    Private NotInheritable Class ServerControl44ControlList
        Inherits DesignerActionList

        Public Sub New(ByVal c As Listing0742Designer)
            MyBase.New(c.Component)
        End Sub

        Public Overrides Function GetSortedActionItems() _
                As DesignerActionItemCollection

            Dim c As New DesignerActionItemCollection()
            c.Add(New DesignerActionTextItem("Text Action Item",
                                             "Custom Category"))
            Return c
        End Function
    End Class
End Class
```

C#

```csharp
public class Listing0742Designer : ControlDesigner
{
    private DesignerActionListCollection _actionLists = null;

    public override DesignerActionListCollection ActionLists
    {
        get
        {
            if (_actionLists == null)
```

continues

LISTING 7-42 *(continued)*

```
            {
                _actionLists = new DesignerActionListCollection();
                _actionLists.AddRange(base.ActionLists);
                _actionLists.Add(new ServerControl44ControlList(this));
            }
            return _actionLists;
        }
    }

    private sealed class ServerControl44ControlList :
                         DesignerActionList
    {
        public ServerControl44ControlList(ControlDesigner c)
            : base(c.Component)
        {
        }

        public override DesignerActionItemCollection
            GetSortedActionItems()
        {
            DesignerActionItemCollection c =
                new DesignerActionItemCollection();
            c.Add(new DesignerActionTextItem("Text Action Item",
                                             "Custom Category"));
            return c;
        }
    }
}
```

The control designer class overrides the `ActionsLists` property. The property creates an instance of the `TextControlList` class, which derives from `DesignerActionList` and overrides the `GetSortedActionItems` method. The method creates a new `DesignerActionListCollection`, and a `DesignerActionTextItem` is added to the collection (see Figure 7-18). The `DesignerActionTextItem` class enables you to add text menu items to the smart tag.

FIGURE 7-18

As shown in Figure 7-18, when you add the control to a web page, the control now has a smart tag with the `DesignerActionTextItem` class as content.

UI Type Editors

A UI type editor is a way to provide users of your controls with a custom interface for editing properties directly from the Property Browser. One type of UI type editor you might already be familiar with is the Color Picker you see when you want to change the `ForeColor` attribute that exists on most ASP.NET controls. ASP.NET provides a wide variety of in-box UI type editors that make editing more complex property types easy. The easiest way to find what UI type editors are available in the .NET Framework is to search for types derived from the `UITypeEditor` class in the MSDN Library help or searching the Internet.

After you find the type editor you want to use on your control property, you simply apply the UI type editor to the property using the `Editor` attribute. Listing 7-43 shows how to do this.

LISTING 7-43: Adding a UI type editor to a control property

VB

```vb
<ToolboxData("<{0}:Listing0743 runat=server></{0}:Listing0743>")>
Public Class Listing0743
    Inherits System.Web.UI.WebControls.WebControl

    <Bindable(True), Category("Appearance"), DefaultValue(""),
    Editor(
            GetType(System.Web.UI.Design.UrlEditor),
            GetType(System.Drawing.Design.UITypeEditor))>
    Public Property Url() As String

    Protected Overrides Sub RenderContents(ByVal output As HtmlTextWriter)
        output.Write(Url.ToString())
    End Sub
End Class
```

C#

```csharp
[ToolboxData("<{0}:Listing0743 runat=server></{0}:Listing0743>")]
public class Listing0743 : WebControl
{
    [Bindable(true)]
    [Category("Appearance")]
    [DefaultValue("")]
    [Editor(typeof(System.Web.UI.Design.UrlEditor),
        typeof(System.Drawing.Design.UITypeEditor))]
    public string Url { get; set; }

    protected override void RenderContents(HtmlTextWriter output)
    {
        output.Write(this.Url);
    }
}
```

In this sample, you have created a `Url` property for a control. Because you know this property will be a URL, you want to give the control user a positive design-time experience. You can use the `UrlEditor` type editor to make it easier for users to select a URL. Figure 7-19 shows the URL Editor that appears when the user edits the control property.

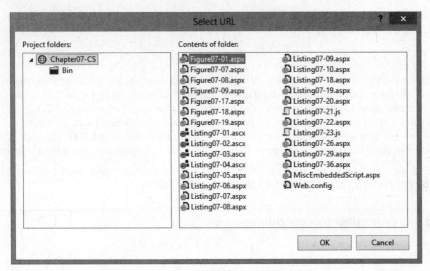

FIGURE 7-19

SUMMARY

In this chapter, you learned a number of ways you can create reusable, encapsulated chunks of code. You first looked at user controls, the simplest form of control creation. You learned how to create user controls and how you can make them interact with their host web pages. Creating user controls is quite easy, but they lack the portability of other control-creation options.

Then, you saw how you can create your own custom server controls. You looked at many of the tools you can create by writing custom server controls, emitting HTML, and creating CSS styles. The chapter also discussed the type of server controls you can create, ranging from server controls that simply inherit from the `WebControl` class to templated controls that give users of the control the power to define the display of the server control.

Finally, you looked at ways you can give the users of your server control a great design-time experience by providing them with type convertors, design surface interactions, and custom property editors in your server control.

PART III
Data Access

Data Binding

WHAT'S IN THIS CHAPTER?

➤ Working with data source controls

➤ Using inline data-binding syntax

➤ Using data-binding expressions

WROX.COM CODE DOWNLOADS FOR THIS CHAPTER

Please note that all the code examples in this chapter are available as a part of this chapter's code download on the book's website at www.wrox.com on the Download Code tab.

When it was originally released, one of the most exciting features of ASP.NET was its ability to bind entire collections of data to controls at run time without requiring you to write large amounts of code. The controls understood they were data-bound and would render the appropriate HTML for each item in the data collection. Additionally, you could bind the controls to any type of data sources, from simple arrays to complex Oracle database query results. This was a huge step forward from classic ASP, in which each developer was responsible for writing all the data access code, looping through a recordset, and manually rendering the appropriate HTML code for each record of data.

This chapter explores the server-side data controls. It shows how you can use the data source controls to easily and quickly bind data to data-bound controls. It also focuses on the power of the data-bound list controls included in ASP.NET. Finally, you take a look at changes in the inline data-binding syntax and inline XML data binding.

DATA SOURCE CONTROLS

In ASP.NET 1.0/1.1, you typically performed a data-binding operation by writing some data access code to retrieve a `DataReader` or a `DataSet` object; then you bound that data object to a server control such as a `DataGrid`, `DropDownList`, or `ListBox`. If you wanted to update or delete the bound data, you were then responsible for writing the data access code to do that. Listing 8-1 shows a typical example of a data-binding operation in ASP.NET 1.0/1.1.

LISTING 8-1: Typical data-binding operation in ASP.NET 1.0/1.1

VB

```
Dim conn As New SqlConnection()
Dim cmd As New SqlCommand("SELECT * FROM Customers", conn)
    Dim da As New SqlDataAdapter(cmd)
    Dim ds As New DataSet()
da.Fill(ds)
    DataGrid1.DataSource = ds
DataGrid1.DataBind()
```

C#

```
SqlConnection conn = new SqlConnection();
SqlCommand cmd = new SqlCommand("SELECT * FROM Customers", conn);
    SqlDataAdapter da = new SqlDataAdapter(cmd);
    DataSet ds = new DataSet();
da.Fill(ds);
    DataGrid1.DataSource = ds;
DataGrid1.DataBind();
```

Since ASP.NET 1.0/1.1, ASP.NET has introduced an additional layer of abstraction through the use of data source controls. As shown in Figure 8-1, these controls abstract the use of an underlying data provider, such as the SQL Data Provider or the OLE DB Data Provider. This means you no longer need to concern yourself with the hows and whys of using the data providers, instead letting the data source controls do the heavy lifting for you. You need to know only where your data is and, if necessary, how to construct a query for performing CRUD (Create, Retrieve, Update, and Delete) operations.

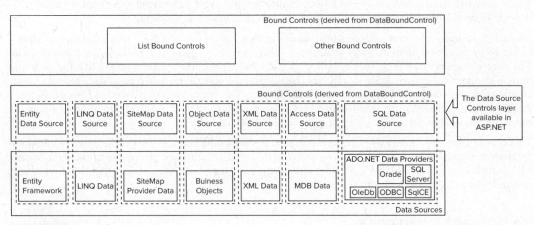

FIGURE 8-1

Additionally, because the data source controls all derive from the `Control` class, you can use them much as you would any other web server control. For instance, you can define and control the behavior of the data source control either declaratively in declarative markup or programmatically. In fact, although you certainly can control the data source controls from code, most of the examples in this chapter show you how to perform powerful database queries using nothing more than the Visual Studio 2012 wizards and declarative syntax.

ASP.NET has seven built-in data source controls, each used for a specific type of data access. Table 8-1 lists and describes each data source control.

TABLE 8-1

CONTROL NAME	DESCRIPTION
SqlDataSource	Provides access to any data source that has an ADO.NET Data Provider available; by default, the control has access to the ODBC, OLE DB, SQL Server, Oracle, and SQL Server Compact providers.
LinqDataSource	Provides access to different types of LinqToSql objects using LINQ queries.
ObjectDataSource	Provides specialized data access to business objects or other classes that return data.
XmlDataSource	Provides specialized data access to XML documents, either physically on disk or in memory.
SiteMapDataSource	Provides specialized access to sitemap data for a website that is stored by the sitemap provider.
AccessDataSource	Provides specialized access to Access databases.
EntityDataSource	Provides specialized access to Entity Framework models.

All the data source controls are derived from either the `DataSourceControl` class or the `HierarchicalDataSourceControl` class, both of which are derived from `Control` and implement the `IDataSource` and `IListSource` interfaces. This means that although each control is designed for use with a specific source of data, they all share a basic set of core functionality. It also means that should you need to, you can easily create your own custom data source controls based on the structure of your specific data sources.

SqlDataSource Control

The SqlDataSource control is the data source control to use if your data is stored in SQL Server, SQL Server Express, SQL Server LocalDb, SQL Server Compact, or Oracle. The control provides an easy-to-use wizard that walks you through the configuration process, or you can modify the control manually by changing the control attributes directly in Source view. In this section you will see how you can create and configure a SqlDataSource control, as well as how you can filter the results. In later sections of this book, you see how in conjunction with other data controls like `GridView`, you can allow users to update and delete data through the SqlDataSource control.

Begin using the control by opening an ASP.NET WebForm page and dragging the SqlDataSource control from the toolbox onto the form. You find all the data-related controls located under the Data section in the Visual Studio toolbox.

Configuring a Data Connection

After the control has been dropped onto the web page, you need to tell it what database connection it should use. The easiest way to do this is by using the Configure Data Source wizard, shown in Figure 8-2. Launch this wizard by selecting the Configure Data Source option from the data source control's smart tag menu.

After the wizard opens, you can select an existing database connection from the drop-down list or create a new connection. Most of the examples shown in this chapter use the Northwind database as their data source, so if it does not already exist, you can create a new connection to the Northwind database.

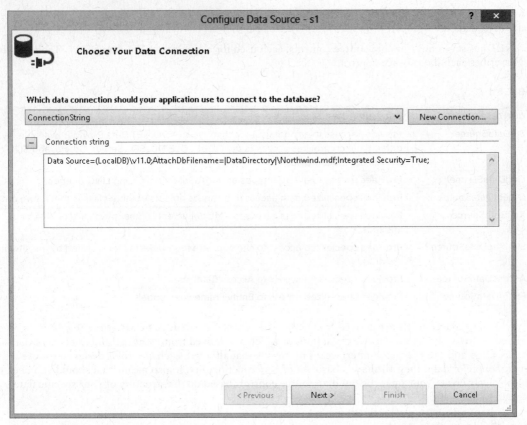

FIGURE 8-2

> **NOTE** *The Northwind database is included as part of the download of the code for this chapter as well.*

To create a new connection, click the New Connection button to open the Choose Data Source dialog box. This dialog box allows you to select the specific data source for this connection and the data provider to use for the data source.

> **NOTE** *The list of providers is generated from the data contained in the* DbProviderFactory *node of the* machine.config *file. If you have additional providers to display in the wizard you can modify your* machine.config *file to include specific providers' information.*

After you've selected the source and provider, click the Continue button to open the Add Connection dialog box. This dialog box allows you to set all the properties of the new database connection. Figure 8-3 shows the window for configuring a SQL Server database connection.

Simply fill in the appropriate information for your database connection, click the Test Connection button to verify that your connection information is correct, and then click OK to return to the Configure Data Source wizard.

Click the Next button to continue to the wizard's next step, which allows you to save your database connection information to your `web.config` file. Storing the connection here can make maintenance and deployment of your application easier. This screen allows you to specify the key under which the connection information should be stored in the configuration file. Should you choose not to store your connection information in the `web.config` file, it is stored in the actual `.aspx` page as a property of the SqlDataSource control named `ConnectionString`. If the provider chosen was not the SQL Data Provider, a property named `ProviderName` will be used to store that setting.

The next step in the wizard allows you to select the data to retrieve from the database. As you can see in Figure 8-4, a drop-down list of all the tables and views available in the database is shown. You can select a table or view, and the specific columns you want to include in the query. Select all columns available using an asterisk (*), or choose specific columns by selecting the check box located next to each column name.

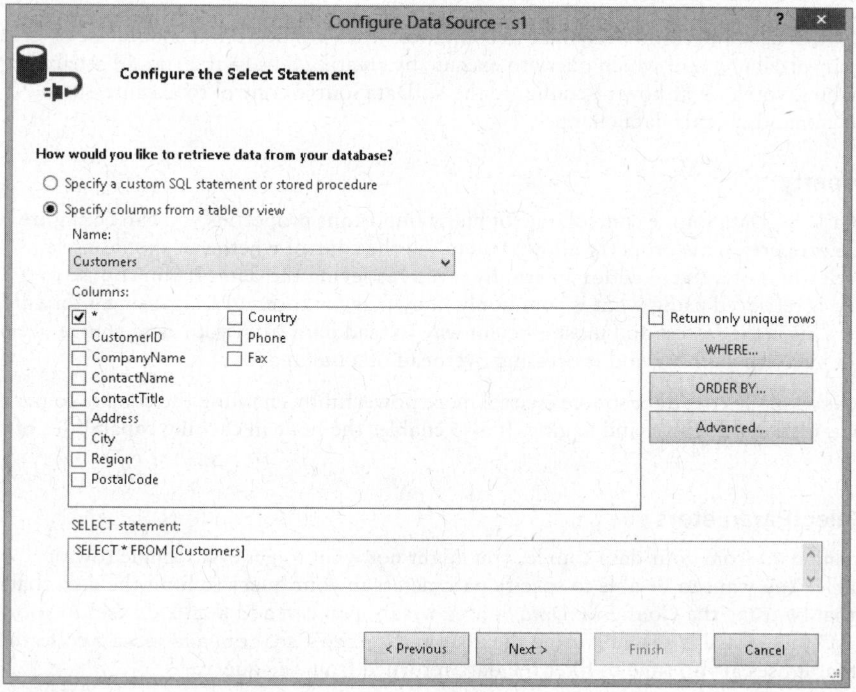

FIGURE 8-3

FIGURE 8-4

The WHERE and ORDER BY buttons allow you to specify WHERE and ORDER BY clauses for filtering and sorting the results of the query. For now, do not enter any additional WHERE or ORDER BY settings.

The Advanced button contains two advanced options. You can have the wizard generate INSERT, UPDATE, and DELETE statements for your data, based on the SELECT statement you created. You can also configure the data source control to use Optimistic Concurrency.

> **NOTE** Optimistic Concurrency *is a database technique that can help you prevent the accidental overwriting of data. When Optimistic Concurrency is enabled, the* UPDATE *and* DELETE *SQL statements used by the SqlDataSource control are modified so that they include both the original and updated values. When the queries are executed, the data in the targeted record is compared to the SqlDataSource controls' original values and if a difference is found, which indicates that the data has changed since it was originally retrieved by the SqlDataSource control, the update or delete will not occur.*

The final screen of the wizard allows you to preview the data selected by your data source control to verify that the query is working as you expect it to. Simply click the Finish button to complete the wizard.

When you are done configuring your data connection, change to Source view in Visual Studio to see how the wizard has generated the appropriate attributes for your control. It should look something like the code in Listing 8-2.

LISTING 8-2: Typical SqlDataSource control generated by Visual Studio

```
<asp:SqlDataSource ID="SqlDataSource1" Runat="server"
  SelectCommand="SELECT * FROM [Customers]"
  ConnectionString="<%$ ConnectionStrings:ConnectionString %>" />
```

You can see that the control uses a declarative syntax to configure which connection it should use by creating a ConnectionString attribute, and which query to execute by creating a SelectCommand attribute. A little later in this chapter, you look at how to configure the SqlDataSource control to execute INSERT, UPDATE, and DELETE commands as this data changes.

Data Source Mode Property

After you've set up a basic SqlDataSource control, one of many important properties you can configure is the DataSourceMode property. This property allows you to tell the control whether it should use a DataSet (the default selection) or a DataReader internally when retrieving the data. If you choose to use a DataReader, data is retrieved using what is commonly known as *firehose mode*, or using a forward-only, read-only cursor. This is the fastest and most efficient way to read data from your data source because a DataReader does not have the memory and processing overhead of a DataSet.

Choosing to use a DataSet makes the data source control more powerful by enabling the control to perform other operations such as filtering, sorting, and paging. It also enables the built-in caching capabilities of the control.

Filtering Data Using SelectParameters

Of course, when selecting data from your data source, you might not want to get every single row of data from a view or table. You want to be able to specify parameters in your query to limit the data that is returned. You saw that by using the Configure Data Source wizard you can add WHERE clauses to your query. "Under the hood" the wizard is actually using the SqlDataSource's SelectParameters collection to create parameters that it uses at run time to filter the data returned from the query.

The SelectParameters collection consists of types that derive from the Parameters class. You can combine any number of parameters in the collection. The data source control then uses these to create a dynamic SQL query. Table 8-2 lists and describes the available parameter types.

TABLE 8-2

PARAMETER	DESCRIPTION
ControlParameter	Uses the value of a property of the specified control
CookieParameter	Uses the key value of a cookie
FormParameter	Uses the key value from the Forms collection
QueryStringParameter	Uses a key value from the QueryString collection
ProfileParameter	Uses a key value from the user's profile
RouteParameter	Uses a key value from the route segment of the requested URL
SessionParameter	Uses a key value from the current user's session

Because all the parameter controls derive from the Parameter class, they all contain several useful common properties. Some of these properties are shown in Table 8-3.

TABLE 8-3

PROPERTY	DESCRIPTION
Type	Allows you to strongly type the value of the parameter
ConvertEmptyStringToNull	Indicates the control should convert the value assigned to it to Null if it is equal to System.String.Empty
DefaultValue	Allows you to specify a default value for the parameter if it is evaluated as Null

The code in Listing 8-3 shows an example of adding a QueryStringParameter to the SelectParameters collection of the SqlDataSource control. As you can see, the SelectCommand query has been modified to include a WHERE clause. When you run this code, the value of the query string field ID is bound to the @CustomerID placeholder in your SelectCommand, allowing you to select only those customers whose CustomerID field matches the value of the query string field.

LISTING 8-3: Filtering select data using SelectParameter controls

```
<asp:SqlDataSource ID="SqlDataSource1" Runat="server"
  SelectCommand="SELECT * FROM [Customers]
        WHERE ([CustomerID] = @CustomerID)"
  ConnectionString="<%$ ConnectionStrings:ConnectionString %>"
  DataSourceMode="DataSet">
  <SelectParameters>
    <asp:QueryStringParameter Name="CustomerID"
      QueryStringField="ID" Type="String">
    </asp:QueryStringParameter>
  </SelectParameters>
</asp:SqlDataSource>
```

In addition to using the Configure Data Source wizard to create the SelectParameters collection, you can manually define them in markup, or create parameters using the Command and Parameter Editor dialog box, which you access by modifying the SelectQuery property of the SqlDataSource control while you are viewing the web page in design mode.

The SqlDataSource control includes an additional way to filter results called the FilterParameters. FilterParameters provide the same basic filtering capabilities as SelectParameters, but use a different technique. The specific differences between SelectParameters and FilterParameters are discussed later in this chapter.

Conflict Detection

The Conflict Detection property allows you to tell the control whether there is a conflict between the value that you are updating and the one in the database. It allows you to prevent users from accidently overriding each other's updates. When this property is set to OverwriteChanges, the user who updated the value last wins.

If the value is set to CompareAllValues, the control compares the original values in the database to the ones received from the user. If the control detects that there is a conflict, it does not update the database; otherwise, it updates the database.

One way to determine whether your update has encountered a concurrency error is by testing the AffectedRows property in the SqlDataSource's Updated event. Listing 8-4 shows one way to do this.

LISTING 8-4: Detecting concurrency errors after updating data

VB

```
Protected Sub SqlDataSource1_Updated(ByVal sender as Object,
  ByVal e As System.Web.UI.WebControls.SqlDataSourceStatusEventArgs)
  If (e.AffectedRows > 0) Then
      Me.lblMessage.Text = "The record has been updated"
  Else
      Me.lblMessage.Text = "Possible concurrency violation"
  End If
End Sub
```

C#

```
protected void SqlDataSource1_Updated(object sender,
  SqlDataSourceStatusEventArgs e)
{
  if (e.AffectedRows > 0)
    this.lblMessage.Text = "The record has been updated";
  else
    this.lblMessage.Text = "Possible concurrency violation";
}
```

Handling Database Errors

The data source control's events are very useful for trapping and handling errors that occur while you are attempting to execute a SQL command against the database. For instance, Listing 8-5 demonstrates how you can use the SqlDataSource control's Updated event to handle a database error that has bubbled back to the application as an exception.

LISTING 8-5: Using the SqlDataSource control's Updated event to handle database errors

VB

```
Protected Sub SqlDataSource1_Updated(ByVal sender As Object,
  ByVal e As System.Web.UI.WebControls.SqlDataSourceStatusEventArgs)
     If (e.Exception IsNot Nothing) Then
    Me.lblMessage.Text = e.Exception.Message
    e.ExceptionHandled = True
  End If
End Sub
```

C#

```
protected void SqlDataSource1_Updated(object sender,
  System.Web.UI.WebControls.SqlDataSourceStatusEventArgs e)
{
  if (e.Exception != null)
  {
    this.lblMessage.Text = e.Exception.Message;
    e.ExceptionHandled = true;
  }
}
```

An extremely important part of this example is the code that sets the `ExceptionHandled` property. By default, this property returns `False`. Therefore, even if you detect that the `Exception` property is not null, and you attempt to handle the error, the exception still bubbles out of the application. Setting the `ExceptionHandled` property to `True` tells .NET that you have successfully handled the exception and that it is safe to continue executing.

AccessDataSource Control

This control gives you specialized access to Access databases using the Jet Data provider, but it still uses SQL commands to perform data retrieval because it is derived from the SqlDataSource.

LinqDataSource Control

Much like the SqlDataSource control, which generates queries for SQL databases by converting its property settings into SQL queries, the LinqDataSource generates Linq queries for LinqToSql data objects in your application.

EntityDataSource Control

The EntityDataSource is a specialized data source control designed for applications that make use of the ADO.NET Entity Framework.

> **NOTE** *For an in-depth discussion of the Entity Framework, see Chapter 11.*

The EntityDataSource control handles selecting, updating, inserting, and deleting data for data controls on a web page as well as automatically enabling sorting and paging of data, allowing you to easily bind to and navigate data from an Entity Framework model. Like all other data source controls, you get started using the EntityDataSource control by dragging it from the Visual Studio toolbox onto the design surface and then selecting the Configure option from the control's smart tag to load the control's Configuration wizard. After the wizard opens, select or supply a connection string for the control, then select the Default Container Name and click Next. An example of selecting a connection to a data model of the Northwind database is shown in Figure 8-5.

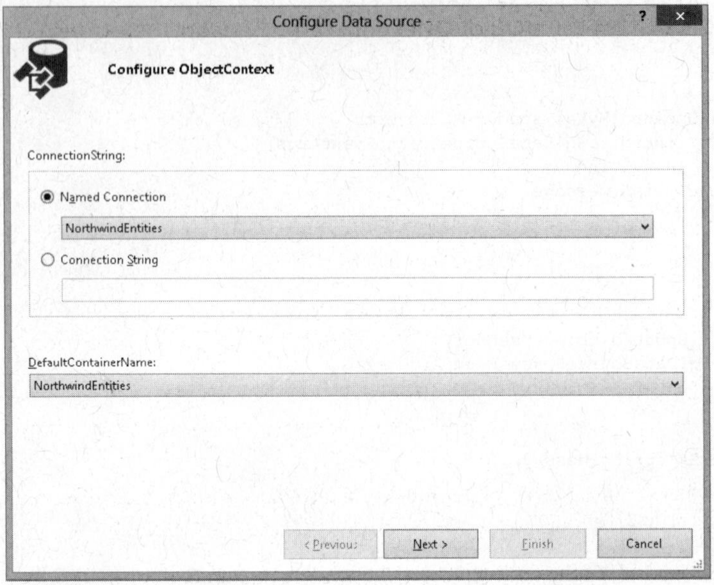

FIGURE 8-5

The next screen allows you to select the specific EntitySetName you want to expose through the data source control. If you want to ensure that only a specific type is returned from the query, you can also specify an EntityTypeFilter. After an EntitySetName is selected, you can create custom projections of properties by selecting them from the list. Figure 8-6 demonstrates selecting the Customers EntitySetName from the Northwind data model.

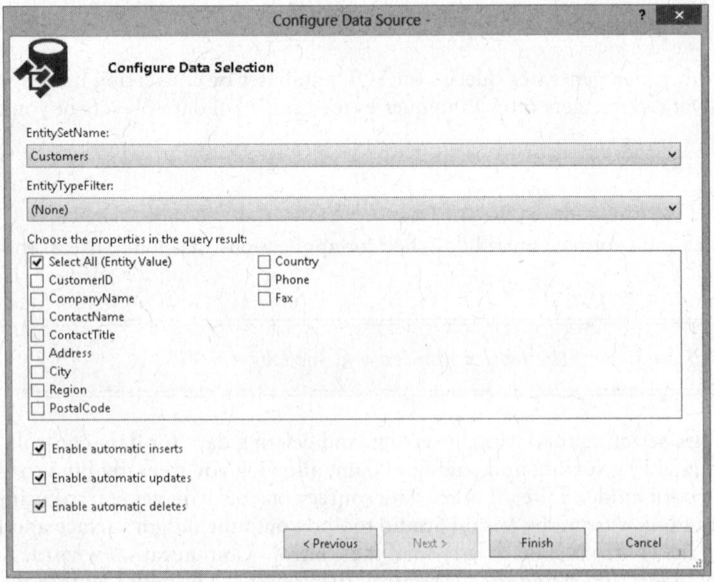

FIGURE 8-6

Finally on this screen you can configure the control to allow automatic inserts, updates, and deletes of data. Note that if you have created a custom projection by selecting specific columns, these options will be disabled.

After you've completed the configuration of the data source control you can now bind any data-bound control to it as normal. Listing 8-6 shows an example of the markup generated by the configuration wizard.

LISTING 8-6: Markup generated by the EntityDataSource Configuration Wizard

```
<asp:EntityDataSource ID="EntityDataSource1" runat="server"
    ConnectionString="name=NorthwindEntities"
    DefaultContainerName="NorthwindEntities" EnableDelete="True"
    EnableFlattening="False" EnableInsert="True" EnableUpdate="True"
    EntitySetName="Customers" EntityTypeFilter="Customer">
</asp:EntityDataSource>
```

The EntityDataSource control includes a variety of other properties and events that you can use to customize even further the behavior of the control.

➤ The query used by the control to select data can be completely customized using the `CommandText` property. This property accepts an Entity SQL command as input. If both `CommandText` and `EntitySetName` are set, the control throws an `InvalidOperationException`.

➤ The control also allows data to be grouped and filtered using the `GroupBy` and `Where` properties. Both properties accept Entity SQL expressions that specify a grouping operation or filtering operation, respectively.

➤ Using the `CommandText` or `GroupBy` properties results in the data source control generating a custom projection, which as discussed earlier means that inserts, updates, and deletes are ignored, even if explicitly enabled.

You can specify parameters that can be used in any of the control's queries as you can in any data source control.

Using the QueryExtender for Complex Filters

Although the EntityDataSource and LinqDataSource controls include built-in capabilities for filtering data, these capabilities do not expose the full power that LINQ provides to create queries that include filters. This is where the QueryExtender comes into play, by allowing you to define complex searches, data range filters, complex multicolumn `OrderBy` clauses, and even completely custom expressions. Table 8-4 shows the available filter expression types.

TABLE 8-4

EXPRESSION TYPE	DESCRIPTION
SearchExpression	Searches a field or fields for string values and compares them to a specified string. The expression can perform "StartsWith," "EndsWith," or "Contains" searches.
RangeExpression	Like the SearchExpression, but uses a pair of values to define a minimum and maximum range.
PropertyExpression	Compares a property value of a column to a specified value.
OrderByExpression	Enables you to sort data by a specified column and sort direction.
CustomExpression	Enables you to provide a custom LINQ expression.
MethodExpression	Enables you to invoke a method containing a custom LINQ query.
OfTypeExpression	Enables you to filter elements in the data source by type.

The QueryExtender works with any data source control that implements the `IQueryableDataSource` interface. By default this includes the LinqDataSource and EntityDataSource controls.

To see how you can use the QueryExtender, start by dragging a QueryExtender control onto the design surface from the toolbox. In the page markup, connect the QueryExtender to the EntityDataSource by specifying the ID of the EntityDataSource control as the QueryExtender's `TargetControlID` property value. Now all you have to do is define the filter expressions you want to use within the QueryExtender. Listing 8-7 demonstrates using a SearchExpression.

LISTING 8-7: Using the QueryExtender control to filter query results

```
<asp:EntityDataSource ID="EntityDataSource1" runat="server"
  ConnectionString="name=NorthwindEntities"
  DefaultContainerName="NorthwindEntities" EnableDelete="True"
  EnableFlattening="False" EnableInsert="True" EnableUpdate="True"
  EntitySetName="Customers" EntityTypeFilter="Customer">
</asp:EntityDataSource>
<asp:QueryExtender ID="QueryExtender2"
  runat="server" TargetControlID=" EntityDataSource1">
  <asp:SearchExpression SearchType="StartsWith"
    DataFields="CustomerID">
    <asp:QueryStringParameter DefaultValue="A"
      QueryStringField="search" />
  </asp:SearchExpression>
</asp:QueryExtender>
```

As you can see, using a `QueryStringParameter`, the expression filters the query results to only `CustomerID`s that start with the value specified by the query string field `"search"`.

XmlDataSource Control

The XmlDataSource control provides you with a simple way of binding XML documents, either in-memory or located on a physical drive. The control provides you with a number of properties that make specifying an XML file containing data and an XSLT transform file for converting the source XML into a more suitable format easy. You can also provide an XPath query to select only a certain subset of data.

Listing 8-8 shows how you might consume an RSS feed from the MSDN website, selecting all the item nodes within it for binding to a bound list control such as the GridView.

LISTING 8-8: Using the XmlDataSource control to consume an RSS feed

```
<asp:XmlDataSource ID="XmlDataSource1" Runat="server"
  DataFile="http://msdn.microsoft.com/rss.xml"
  XPath="rss/channel/item" />
```

In addition to the declarative attributes you can use with the XmlDataSource, a number of other helpful properties and events are available.

Many times your XML is not stored in a physical file, but rather is simply a string stored in your application memory or possibly in a database. The control provides the `Data` property, which accepts a simple string of XML to which the control can bind. Note that if both the `Data` and `DataFile` properties are set, the `DataFile` property takes precedence over the `Data` property.

Additionally, in certain scenarios, you may want to export the bound XML out of the XmlDataSource control to other objects or even save any changes that have been made to the underlying XML if it has been bound to a control such as a GridView. The XmlDataSource control provides two methods to accommodate this. One method is `GetXmlDocument`, which allows you to export the XML by returning a basic `System.Xml.XmlDocument` object that contains the XML loaded in the data source control.

The other way is by using the control's Save method to persist changes made to the XmlDataSource control's loaded XML back to disk. Executing this method assumes you have provided a file path in the DataFile property.

The XmlDataSource control also provides you with a number of specialized events. The Transforming event that is raised before the XSLT transform specified in the Transform or TransformFile properties is applied and allows you to supply custom arguments to the transform.

ObjectDataSource Control

The ObjectDataSource control gives you the power to bind data controls directly to middle-layer business objects that can be hard-coded or automatically generated from programs such as Object Relational (O/R) mappers.

To demonstrate how to use the ObjectDataSource control, create a class in the project that represents a customer and a class that contains methods that allow you to select, insert, update, and delete customers from a collection. Listing 8-9 shows a class that you can use for this demonstration.

LISTING 8-9: A Customer class and CustomerRepository class

VB

```vb
Public Class Customer
  Public Property CustomerID() As String
  Public Property CompanyName() As String
  Public Property ContactName() As String
  Public Property ContactTitle() As String
End Class
    Public Class CustomerRepository
      Public Function [Select](
    ByVal customerID As String) As List(Of Customer)
    ' Implement logic here to retrieve the Customer
    ' data based on the methods customerID parameter
    Dim _customers As New List(Of Customer)
    _customers.Add(New Customer() With {
          .CompanyName = "Acme", .ContactName = "Wiley Cyote",
          .ContactTitle = "President", .CustomerID = "ACMEC"})
      Return _customers
    End Function
      Public Sub Insert(ByVal c As Customer)
    ' Implement Insert logic
    End Sub
      Public Sub Update(ByVal c As Customer)
    ' Implement Update logic
    End Sub
      Public Sub Delete(ByVal c As Customer)
    ' Implement Delete logic
    End Sub
    End Class
```

C#

```csharp
public class Customer
{
  public string CustomerID { get; set; }
  public string CompanyName { get; set; }
  public string ContactName { get; set; }
  public string ContactTitle { get; set; }
}
    public class CustomerRepository
```

continues

LISTING 8-9 *(continued)*

```
{
  public CustomerRepository()
  {
  }
    public List<Customer> Select(string customerId)
  {
    // Implement logic here to retrieve the Customer
    // data based on the methods customerId parameter
    List<Customer> _customers = new List<Customer>();
    _customers.Add(new Customer() {
      CompanyName = "Acme", ContactName = "Wiley Cyote",
      ContactTitle = "President", CustomerID = "ACMEC" });
    return _customers;
  }
    public void Insert(Customer c)
  {
    // Implement Insert logic
  }
    public void Update(Customer c)
  {
    // Implement Update logic
  }
    public void Delete(Customer c)
  {
    // Implement Delete logic
  }
    }
```

To start using the ObjectDataSource, drag the control onto the design surface and open the Configuration wizard from the control's smart tag. When the wizard opens, select the business object you want to use as your data source from the drop-down list. The list shows all the classes located in the App_Code folder of your website that can be successfully compiled. In this case, you want to use the CustomerRepository class shown in Listing 8-9.

The methods that the ObjectDataSource uses to perform CRUD operations must follow certain rules in order for the control to understand. For example, the control's SELECT method must return a DataSet, DataReader, or a strongly typed collection. Each of the control's operation tabs explains what the control expects of the method you specify for it to use. Additionally, if a method does not conform to the rules that specific operation expects, it is not listed in the drop-down list on that tab.

Finally, if your SELECT method contains parameters, the wizard lets you create SelectParameters you can use to provide the method parameter data.

When you have completed configuring the ObjectDataSource, you should have code in your page source like that shown in Listing 8-10.

LISTING 8-10: The ObjectDataSource code generated by the Configuration Wizard

```
<asp:ObjectDataSource ID="ObjectDataSource1" runat="server"
  DeleteMethod="Delete" InsertMethod="Insert"
  SelectMethod="Select" TypeName="CustomerRepository"
  UpdateMethod="Update" DataObjectTypeName="Customer">
  <SelectParameters>
    <asp:QueryStringParameter Name="customerId"
      QueryStringField="ID" Type="string" />
  </SelectParameters>
</asp:ObjectDataSource>
```

As you can see, the wizard has generated the attributes for the `SELECT`, `UPDATE`, `INSERT`, and `DELETE` methods you specified in the wizard. Also notice that it has added the `Select` parameter. Depending on your application, you could change this to any of the `Parameter` objects discussed earlier, such as a `ControlParameter` or `QueryStringParameter` object.

SiteMapDataSource Control

The SiteMapDataSource enables you to work with data stored in your website's SiteMap configuration file if you have one. This can be useful if you are changing your sitemap data at run time, perhaps based on user rights or status.

Note two items regarding the SiteMapDataSource control.

➤ One is that it does not support any of the data caching options that exist in the other data source controls provided (covered in the next section), so you cannot automatically cache your sitemap data.

➤ Another is that the SiteMapDataSource control does not have any configuration wizards like the other data source controls. This is because the SiteMap control can be bound only to the SiteMap configuration data file of your website, so no other configuration is possible.

> **NOTE** *The SiteMapDataSource control has a property called* `SiteMapProvider`, *which allows you to specify which sitemap provider to use. As a rule, it will use the default sitemap provider, but you are free to specify others. See* http://msdn.microsoft .com/en-us/library/system.web.ui.webcontrols.sitemapdatasource. sitemapprovider *for more information.*

DATA SOURCE CONTROL CACHING

ASP.NET includes a great caching infrastructure that allows you to cache on the server arbitrary objects for set periods of time. You can learn more about ASP.NET caching in Chapter 22.

The data source controls leverage this built-in caching infrastructure to allow you to easily cache their query results. Each control uses the same basic syntax for configuring caching, allowing you to create simple caching policies including a cache direction, expiration policies, and key dependencies.

> **NOTE** *The SqlDataSource control's caching features are available only if you have set the* `DataSourceMode` *property to* `DataSet`. *If it is set to* `DataReader`, *the control will throw a* `NotSupportedException`.

The cache duration can be set to a specific number of seconds, or you can set it to `Infinite` to force the cached data to never expire. Listing 8-11 shows how you can easily add caching features to a data source control.

LISTING 8-11: Enabling caching on a SqlDataSource control

```
<asp:SqlDataSource ID="SqlDataSource1" Runat="server"
    SelectCommand="SELECT * FROM [Customers]"
    ConnectionString="<%$ ConnectionStrings:ConnectionString %>"
    DataSourceMode="DataSet" ConflictDetection="CompareAllValues"
    EnableCaching="True" CacheKeyDependency="SomeKey"
    CacheDuration="Infinite" />
```

Some controls also extend the core set of caching features with additional caching functionality specific to their data sources. For example, if you are using the SqlDataSource control you can use that control's `SqlCacheDependency` property to create SQL dependencies.

DATA-BOUND CONTROLS

This section looks at some data-bound controls that can be bound to data source controls and can be used to display, create, edit, and delete data.

GridView

The GridView control is a powerful data grid control that allows you to display an entire collection of data, add sorting and paging, and perform inline editing.

Start using the GridView by dragging the control onto the design surface of an ASP.NET web page. When you do this, you will be prompted to select a data source control to bind to the grid. You can use the SqlDataSource control created earlier in the chapter.

Listing 8-12 shows a simple use of the GridView with a SqlDataSource control. In this example the explicit field definitions have been removed to allow the control to automatically generate columns based on the structure of the data source.

LISTING 8-12: Using the GridView control in an ASP.NET web page

```
<html>
<head runat="server">
  <title>Using the GridView Control</title>
</head>
<body>
  <form id="form1" runat="server">
  <div>
    <asp:GridView ID="GridView1" runat="server"
      DataSourceID="SqlDataSource1">
    </asp:GridView>
        <asp:SqlDataSource ID="SqlDataSource1" Runat="server"
        SelectCommand="SELECT * FROM [Customers]"
        ConnectionString=
          "<%$ ConnectionStrings:ConnectionString %>"
        DataSourceMode="DataSet"
        ConflictDetection="CompareAllValues" EnableCaching="True"
        CacheKeyDependency="MyKey" CacheDuration="Infinite">
      </asp:SqlDataSource>
  </div>
  </form>
</body>
</html>
```

When you run the page, ASP.NET executes the database query using the SqlDataSource control and then binds the results to the GridView control. The GridView control generates a table layout containing all the data returned from the query.

After you assign the GridView a data source, normally the grid updates itself to match the data source schema, setting its `AutoGenerateFields` property to `False` and generating a field in the GridView's Columns collection for each public property or database table column exposed by the data source. Listing 8-13 shows the collection of explicit column definitions.

LISTING 8-13: Explicitly defined GridView columns

```
<asp:GridView ID="GridView1" runat="server" DataSourceID="SqlDataSource1"
  AutoGenerateColumns="False" DataKeyNames="CustomerID">
  <Columns>
    <asp:BoundField DataField="CustomerID"
      HeaderText="CustomerID" ReadOnly="True"
      SortExpression="CustomerID" />
    <asp:BoundField DataField="CompanyName"
      HeaderText="CompanyName" SortExpression="CompanyName" />
    <asp:BoundField DataField="ContactName"
      HeaderText="ContactName" SortExpression="ContactName" />
    <asp:BoundField DataField="ContactTitle"
      HeaderText="ContactTitle" SortExpression="ContactTitle" />
    <asp:BoundField DataField="Address" HeaderText="Address"
      SortExpression="Address" />
    <asp:BoundField DataField="City" HeaderText="City"
      SortExpression="City" />
    <asp:BoundField DataField="Region" HeaderText="Region"
      SortExpression="Region" />
    <asp:BoundField DataField="PostalCode" HeaderText="PostalCode"
      SortExpression="PostalCode" />
    <asp:BoundField DataField="Country" HeaderText="Country"
      SortExpression="Country" />
    <asp:BoundField DataField="Phone" HeaderText="Phone"
      SortExpression="Phone" />
    <asp:BoundField DataField="Fax" HeaderText="Fax"
      SortExpression="Fax" />
  </Columns>
</asp:GridView>
```

Notice that when creating the column definitions, the control by default uses the `BoundField` type for each column. Each `BoundField` has the `DataField` property, which connects the field to a property of the data source, and the `SortExpression` defined. The control also detects read-only properties in the data source and sets the field's `ReadOnly` property.

When the GridView is rendering, it raises a number of events that you can use to alter the control's output or add custom logic to your application. These are described in Table 8-5.

TABLE 8-5

EVENT NAME	DESCRIPTION
DataBinding	Raised as the GridView's data-binding expressions are about to be evaluated.
RowCreated	Raised each time a new row is created in the grid. Before the grid can be rendered, a GridViewRow object must be created for each row in the control. The RowCreated event allows you to insert custom content into the row as it is being created.
RowDataBound	Raised as each GridViewRow is bound to the corresponding data in the data source. This event allows you to evaluate the data being bound to the current row and to affect the output if you need to.
DataBound	Raised after the binding is completed and the GridView is ready to be rendered.

The `RowDataBound` event is especially useful, enabling you to inject logic into the binding process for each data source item being bound to the GridView. Listing 8-14 shows how you can use this event to examine the data being bound to the current grid row and to insert special logic, in this example checking to see whether the item's Region value is `Null`. If a null value is found, logic changes the `ForeColor` and `BackColor` properties of the GridView's row.

LISTING 8-14: Using the RowDataBound to insert custom rendering logic

VB

```
<script runat="server">
  Protected Sub GridView1_RowDataBound(ByVal sender As Object,
    ByVal e As System.Web.UI.WebControls.GridViewRowEventArgs)
        If (e.Row.DataItem IsNot Nothing) Then
      Dim drv As System.Data.DataRowView =
        CType(e.Row.DataItem, System.Data.DataRowView)
          If (drv("Region") Is System.DBNull.Value) Then
          e.Row.BackColor = System.Drawing.Color.Red
          e.Row.ForeColor = System.Drawing.Color.White
      End If
    End If
  End Sub
</script>
```

C#

```
<script runat="server">
  protected void GridView1_RowDataBound(object sender,
                    GridViewRowEventArgs e)
  {
    if (e.Row.DataItem != null)
    {
      System.Data.DataRowView drv =
        (System.Data.DataRowView)e.Row.DataItem;
          if (drv["Region"] == System.DBNull.Value)
      {
        e.Row.BackColor = System.Drawing.Color.Red;
        e.Row.ForeColor = System.Drawing.Color.White;
      }
    }
  }
</script>
```

The GridView also includes events that correspond to selecting, inserting, updating, and deleting data. You will learn more about these events later in the chapter.

Handling Null and Empty Data Conditions

In some cases, the data source bound to the GridView may not contain any data for the control to bind to. In these cases you may want to provide the end users with some feedback informing them of this situation. The GridView includes two mechanisms to do this.

One option is to use the `EmptyDataText` property. This property allows you to specify a string of text that is displayed to the user when no data is present for the GridView to bind to. When the ASP.NET page loads and the GridView determines that no data is available in its bound data source, it creates a special DataRow containing the `EmptyDataText` value and displays that to the users. Listing 8-15 shows how you can add this property to the GridView.

LISTING 8-15: Adding EmptyDataText to the GridView

```
<asp:GridView ID="GridView1" Runat="server"
  DataSourceID="SqlDataSource1" DataKeyNames="CustomerID"
  AutoGenerateColumns="True"
  EmptyDataText="No data was found using your query"></asp:GridView>
```

The other option is to use the EmptyDataTemplate control template to completely customize the special row the user sees when no data exists for the control to bind to.

> **NOTE** *A control template is simply a container that gives you the capability to add other content such as text, HTML controls, or even ASP.NET controls. The GridView control provides you with a variety of templates for various situations, including the EmptyDataTemplate template. This chapter examines these templates throughout the rest of this section.*

You can access the template from the Visual Studio design surface in two ways. One option is to right-click the GridView control, expand the Edit Template option in the context menu, and select the EmptyDataTemplate item from the menu. The other option is to select the Edit Templates option from the GridView's smart tag. Selecting this option puts the GridView into template editing mode and presents you with a dialog box from which you can choose the specific template you want to edit. Simply select EmptyDataTemplate from the drop-down list, as shown in Figure 8-7.

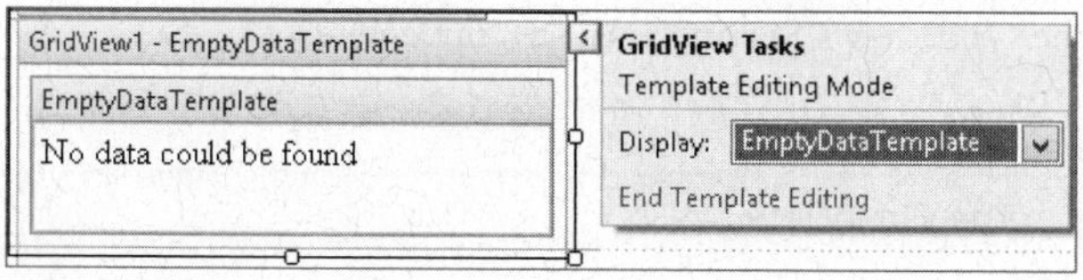

FIGURE 8-7

After you have entered template editing mode, you can add custom text and/or controls to the template editor on the design surface. When you have finished editing the template, right-click, or open the GridView's smart tag and select the End Template Editing option.

Switching to Source view, you see that an `<EmptyDataTemplate>` element has been added to the GridView control. The element contains all the content you added while editing the template. Listing 8-16 shows an example of an `EmptyDataTemplate`.

LISTING 8-16: Using EmptyDataTemplate

```
<EmptyDataTemplate>
        No data could be found based on your query parameters.
        Please enter a new query.
</EmptyDataTemplate>
```

You could, of course, have also added the template and its contents while in Source view.

The GridView also allows you to configure a value to display if the GridView encounters a `Null` value when binding to a data source. For an example of this, add a column using a `<asp:BoundField>` control, as shown in Listing 8-17.

LISTING 8-17: Using the Null value

```
<asp:BoundField DataField="Region" HeaderText="Region"
    NullDisplayText="N/A" SortExpression="Region" />
```

The `<asp:BoundField>` is configured to display the Region column from the `Customers` table. As you look through the data in the Region column, notice that not every row has a value in it. If you don't want to display just a blank cell, you can use the `NullDisplayText` property to configure the GridView to display text in place of the empty items in the column.

Column Sorting

The capability to sort data is one of the most basic tools users have to navigate through data. To enable sorting in the GridView control just set the `AllowSorting` attribute to `True`. The control takes care of all the sorting logic for you internally. Listing 8-18 shows how to add this attribute to your grid.

LISTING 8-18: Adding sorting to the GridView Control

```
<asp:GridView ID="GridView1" Runat="server"
   DataSourceID="SqlDataSource1" DataKeyNames="CustomerID"
   AutoGenerateColumns="True" AllowSorting="True"></asp:GridView>
```

After enabling sorting, you will see that all the grid's column headers have now become hyperlinks.

The GridView sorting can handle both ascending and descending sorting. Repeatedly click on a column header to cause the sort order to switch back and forth between ascending and descending. The GridView also includes a `Sort` method that can accept multiple `SortExpressions` to enable multicolumn sorting. Listing 8-19 shows how you can use the GridView's Sorting event to implement multicolumn sorting.

LISTING 8-19: Adding multicolumn sorting to the GridView

VB

```
<script runat="server">
  Protected Sub GridView1_Sorting(ByVal sender As Object,
                   ByVal e As GridViewSortEventArgs)
       Dim oldExpression As String = GridView1.SortExpression
    Dim newExpression As String = e.SortExpression
         If (oldExpression.IndexOf(newExpression) < 0) Then
    If (oldExpression.Length > 0) Then
        e.SortExpression = newExpression & "," & oldExpression
    Else
        e.SortExpression = newExpression
    End If
    Else
        e.SortExpression = oldExpression
    End If
  End Sub
</script>
```

C#

```
<script runat="server">
  protected void GridView1_Sorting(object sender,
                   GridViewSortEventArgs e)
  {
    string oldExpression = GridView1.SortExpression;
    string newExpression = e.SortExpression;
    if (oldExpression.IndexOf(newExpression) < 0)
    {
      if (oldExpression.Length > 0)
        e.SortExpression = newExpression + "," + oldExpression;
      else
        e.SortExpression = newExpression;
    }
    else
    {
```

```
            e.SortExpression = oldExpression;
        }
    }
</script>
```

The listing uses the `Sorting` event to manipulate the value of the control's `SortExpression` property. The event's parameters enable you to examine the current sort expression, direction of the sort, or even cancel the sort action altogether. The GridView also offers a `Sorted` event, which is raised after the sort has completed.

Paging GridView Data

The GridView also allows you to easily add another common feature — *paging*. To enable paging, set the `AllowPaging` property to `True` or select the Enable Paging check box in the GridView's smart tag. The control defaults to a page size of 10 records and adds the pager to the bottom of the grid. Listing 8-20 shows an example of modifying your grid to enable sorting and paging.

LISTING 8-20: Enabling sorting and paging on the GridView Control

```
<asp:GridView ID="GridView1" Runat="server"
    DataSourceID="SqlDataSource1" DataKeyNames="CustomerID"
    AutoGenerateColumns="True" AllowSorting="True"
    AllowPaging="True"></asp:GridView>
```

The GridView includes a variety of properties that allow you to customize paging. For instance, you can control the number of records displayed on the page using the GridView's `PageSize` attribute. The `PagerSettings` Mode attribute allows you to dictate how the grid's pager is displayed using the various pager modes including `NextPrevious`, `NextPreviousFirstLast`, `Numeric` (the default value), or `NumericFirstLast`. Additionally, specifying the `PagerStyle` element in the GridView, you can customize how the grid displays the pager text, including font color, size, and type, as well as text alignment and a variety of other style options. Listing 8-21 shows how you can customize your GridView control to use the `NextPrevious` mode and style the pager text using the `PagerStyle` element.

LISTING 8-21: Using the PagerStyle and PagerSettings properties in the GridView control

```
<asp:GridView ID="GridView1" Runat="server" DataSourceID="SqlDataSource1"
    DataKeyNames="CustomerID" AutoGenerateColumns="True"
    AllowSorting="True" AllowPaging="True" PageSize="10">
    <PagerStyle HorizontalAlign="Center" />
    <PagerSettings Position=»TopAndBottom»
      FirstPageText=»Go to the first page»
      LastPageText=»Go to the last page»
      Mode=»NextPreviousFirstLast»>
    </PagerSettings>
</asp:GridView>
```

Because the list of `PagerSettings` and `PagerStyle` properties is so long, all the options are not listed here, but you can find a full list of the options in the Visual Studio Help documents.

The GridView control also offers two events you can use to customize the standard paging behavior of the grid. The `PageIndexChanging` and `PageIndexChanged` events are raised before and after the GridView's current page index changes. The page index changes when the user clicks the pager links in the grid. The `PageIndexChanging` event parameters allow you to examine the value of the new page index before it changes or even cancels the paging event altogether.

The GridView also includes the `EnableSortingAndPagingCallbacks` property that allows you to indicate whether the control should use client callbacks to perform sorting and paging. Enabling this property changes the GridView's paging and sorting behaviors to use client-side AJAX callbacks to retrieve data, rather than a full-page postback.

> **NOTE** *If you are interested in learning more about other ways you can integrate AJAX into your ASP.NET applications, Chapter 23 introduces you to the ASP.NET AJAX Framework and explains how you can leverage its capabilities in your applications.*

Customizing Columns in the GridView

Frequently the data you need to display in your grid is not simply text data, but data that you want to display using other types of controls or perhaps don't want to display at all.

If you have your grid configured to automatically generate columns based on the bound data source, the grid creates fields for each public property exposed by the data source. Additionally for all of these properties, except those that return a `Boolean` type, the grid defaults to using its standard `BoundField` type, which treats all types as strings. For `Boolean` types the grid will use the CheckBoxField by default.

These default behaviors might not be optimal in your application. For example you are storing the website address for all of your customers and want the CustomerName column to be displayed as a hyperlink, allowing your users to link directly to a customer's website. The GridView includes a number of specialized Field types that make displaying things like hyperlinks, check boxes, or buttons in grid columns easy.

You have two ways to configure columns in the GridView — through options in the GridView's smart tag or by editing the column markup directly in Source view.

Clicking the Edit Columns link in the GridView's smart tag opens the Fields window, shown in Figure 8-8. From here you can change any existing column's visibility, header text, the usual style options, and many other properties of the column.

Selecting the Add New Column link from the GridView control's smart tag displays the Add Field dialog box, shown in Figure 8-9. This dialog box includes options that allow you to add new columns to your grid. Depending on which column field type you select from the drop-down list, the dialog box presents you with the appropriate options for that column type.

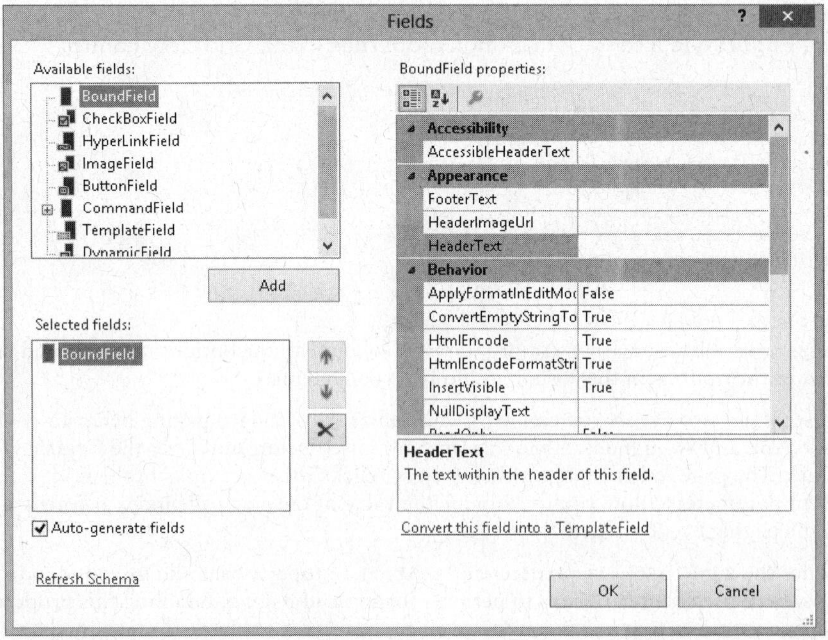

FIGURE 8-8

FIGURE 8-9

The Add Field dialog box lets you select one of the field types described in Table 8-6.

TABLE 8-6

FIELD CONTROL	DESCRIPTION
BoundField	Displays the value of a field in a data source. This is the default column type of the GridView control.
CheckBoxField	Displays a check box for each item in the GridView control. This column field type is commonly used to display fields with a `Boolean` value.
HyperLinkField	Displays the value of a field in a data source as a hyperlink URL. This column field type allows you to bind a second field to the hyperlink's text.
ButtonField	Displays a command button or command link for each item in the GridView control. This allows you to create a column of custom button or link controls, such as an Add or Remove button.
CommandField	Represents a field that displays command buttons or links to perform select, edit, insert, or delete operations in a data-bound control.
ImageField	Automatically displays an image when the data in the field represents an image or displays an image from the URL provided.
TemplateField	Displays user-defined content for each item in the GridView control according to a specified template. This column field type allows you to create a customized column field.

In the example described earlier where you want to allow end users to link to a customer's website, you want to select the HyperLinkField from the drop-down list. The Add Field dialog box changes and lets you enter in the hyperlink information, including the URL, the data field, and a format string for the column.

You can also modify the grid's columns in the Source view, manually adding or editing any of the field types listed in the previous table. Listing 8-22 shows how you can add the appropriate markup in Source view to create a HyperLinkField.

LISTING 8-22: Adding a HyperLinkField control to the GridView

```
<asp:HyperLinkField DataTextField="CompanyName"
  HeaderText="CompanyName" DataNavigateUrlFields="CustomerID,Country"
  SortExpression="CompanyName"
  DataNavigateUrlFormatString=
    http://www.example.com/Customer.aspx?id={0}&country={1} />
```

When you add a field in Source view you need to make sure you specify a property name from your data source on the field. Each field type exposes a different property (or set of properties) that allows you to define this connection between the field and data source. In the previous example you can see that the `HyperLinkField`'s `DataNavigateUrlFields` property allows you to provide a comma-delimited list of data source property names. This allows you to specify multiple data source values to bind to this column. You can then use these fields in your format string to pass two querystring parameters.

Using the TemplateField Column

A key column type available in the GridView control is the `TemplateField` column. This column type allows you to completely customize the contents of column cells by defining templates.

The `TemplateField` provides you with six templates that enable you to customize different areas or states of the column, such as the edit state. Table 8-7 describes the available templates.

TABLE 8-7

TEMPLATE NAME	DESCRIPTION
ItemTemplate	Template used for displaying a TemplateField cell in the data-bound control
AlternatingItemTemplate	Template used for displaying an alternate TemplateField cell
EditItemTemplate	Template used for displaying a TemplateField cell in edit state
InsertItemTemplate	Template used for displaying a TemplateField cell in insert state
HeaderTemplate	Template used for displaying the header section of the TemplateField
FooterTemplate	Template used for displaying the footer section of the TemplateField

To use the `TemplateField` in a GridView, add the column type to a grid using the Add Field dialog box as described in the previous section. The `<asp:TemplateField>` tag serves as a container for the various templates the column can contain. To add content to the templates you can use the template editing features of the Visual Studio 2012 design surface or manually add content directly to the `TemplateField` element in Source view.

The ItemTemplate controls the default contents of each cell of the column. Listing 8-23 demonstrates how you can use the ItemTemplate to customize the contents of the column.

LISTING 8-23: Using ItemTemplate

```
<asp:TemplateField HeaderText="CurrentStatus">
  <ItemTemplate>
    <table>
      <tr>
        <td >
          <asp:Button ID="Button2"
              runat="server" Text="Enable" /></td>
        <td >
          <asp:Button ID="Button3"
              runat="server" Text="Disable" /></td>
      </tr>
    </table>
  </ItemTemplate>
</asp:TemplateField>
```

In the example the ItemTemplate contains a combination of an HTML table and ASP.NET Button controls.

Because the GridView control is data-bound, you can also access the data being bound to the control using data-binding expressions such as the Eval, XPath, or Bind expressions. Listing 8-24 shows how you can add a data-binding expression using the Eval method to set the text field of the Button control. More details about data-binding expressions can be found later in this chapter.

LISTING 8-24: Adding a data-binding expression

```
<asp:TemplateField HeaderText="CurrentStatus">
  <ItemTemplate>
    <table>
      <tr>
        <td>
          <asp:Button ID="Button2" runat="server"
            Text='<%# "Enable " + Eval("CustomerID") %>' />
        </td>
        <td>
          <asp:Button ID="Button3" runat="server"
            Text='<%# "Disable " + Eval("CustomerID") %>' />
        </td>
      </tr>
    </table>
  </ItemTemplate>
</asp:TemplateField>
```

Other common templates available in the TemplateField are InsertTemplate and EditTemplate. These templates are used by the grid when a row enters insert or edit mode. Inserting and editing data in the GridView control, including using the InsertItemTemplate and EditItemTemplate, are reviewed in the next section.

Editing GridView Row Data

Users not only want to view the data in their browsers, but they also want to be able to edit the data and save changes back to the data source. When combined with data source controls, the GridView control makes editing data bound to the grid easy. To demonstrate just how easy enabling editing is, you can modify the SqlDataSource and GridView controls used in the previous examples to allow users to edit the customer's data.

Note that although in this chapter you focus on updating data in a GridView bound to a SqlDataSource control, you can also update data when connecting the GridView to other data source controls. The configuration needed to enable end users to place grid rows into edit mode and insert or delete data via the GridView is identical regardless of the bound data source control. The configuration needed to enable the data source control to persist these changes to the underlying data store is specific to each data source control. If you are using a data source control other than the SqlDataSource, you can refer to the section in this chapter that discusses the details of persisting inserts, updates, and deletes of data for that control.

Configuring the SqlDataSource for Updates

To get started, first modify the SqlDataSource control by adding an UpdateCommand either by using the Configure Data Source wizard or by manually adding the markup in Source view. This property tells the data source control which SQL command it should execute when an update needs to be performed. Listing 8-25 shows the markup needed to add the UpdateCommand property.

LISTING 8-25: Adding an UpdateCommand to a SqlDataSource control

```
<asp:SqlDataSource ID="SqlDataSource1" Runat="server"
  SelectCommand="SELECT * FROM [Customers]"
  ConnectionString="<%$ ConnectionStrings:ConnectionString %>"
  DataSourceMode="DataSet"
  UpdateCommand="UPDATE [Customers] SET [CompanyName] = @CompanyName,
    [ContactName] = @ContactName, [ContactTitle] = @ContactTitle,
    [Address] = @Address, [City] = @City, [Region] = @Region,
    [PostalCode] = @PostalCode, [Country] = @Country,
    [Phone] = @Phone,[Fax] = @Fax
    WHERE [CustomerID] = @ CustomerID">
</asp:SqlDataSource>
```

Notice that the UpdateCommand includes a number of placeholders such as @CompanyName, @Country, @Region, and @CustomerID. These placeholders represent the information that will come from the GridView when a row is updated. Each placeholder corresponds to a Parameter element defined in the SqlDataSource control's UpdateParameters collection. The UpdateParameters collection, shown in Listing 8-26, works much like the SelectParameters element discussed earlier in the chapter.

LISTING 8-26: Adding UpdateParameters to the SqlDataSource Control

```
<UpdateParameters>
  <asp:Parameter Type="String" Name="CompanyName"></asp:Parameter>
  <asp:Parameter Type="String" Name="ContactName"></asp:Parameter>
  <asp:Parameter Type="String" Name="ContactTitle"></asp:Parameter>
  <asp:Parameter Type="String" Name="Address"></asp:Parameter>
  <asp:Parameter Type="String" Name="City"></asp:Parameter>
  <asp:Parameter Type="String" Name="Region"></asp:Parameter>
  <asp:Parameter Type="String" Name="PostalCode"></asp:Parameter>
  <asp:Parameter Type="String" Name="Country"></asp:Parameter>
  <asp:Parameter Type="String" Name="Phone"></asp:Parameter>
  <asp:Parameter Type="String" Name="Fax"></asp:Parameter>
  <asp:Parameter Type="String" Name="CustomerID"></asp:Parameter>
</UpdateParameters>
```

Each Parameter uses two properties to create a connection to the underlying data source, Name, which is the database column name, and Type, which is the database column's data type. In this case, all the parameters are of type String.

Remember that you can also use any of the parameter types mentioned earlier in the chapter, such as the ControlParameter or QueryStringParameter in the UpdateParameters element.

Configuring GridView for Updates

Now that you have configured the SqlDataSource for updates, you need to create a way to place a row in the GridView into edit mode and a way to tell the GridView what the database table's primary key is.

The GridView includes two built-in ways to place a row into edit mode—the `AutoGenerateEditButton` property and the `CommandField`.

When the `AutoGenerateEditButton` property is set to `True`, this tells the grid to add a `ButtonField` column with an edit button for each row. Clicking one of the buttons places the associated row into edit mode. Listing 8-27 shows how to add the `AutoGenerateEditButton` attribute to the GridView control.

LISTING 8-27: Adding the AutoGenerateEditButton property to a GridView

```
<asp:GridView ID="GridView1" Runat="server"
  DataSourceID="SqlDataSource1" DataKeyNames="CustomerID"
  AutoGenerateColumns="True" AllowSorting="True" AllowPaging="True"
  AutoGenerateEditButton="true" />
```

The GridView control also includes `AutoGenerateSelectButton` and `AutoGenerateDeleteButton` properties, which allow you to easily add row selection and row deletion capabilities to the grid.

The `CommandField` column is a special field type that allows you to enable end users to execute different commands on rows in the GridView. Listing 8-28 shows how to configure the `CommandField` to allow the end users to place a row into edit mode.

LISTING 8-28: Adding edit functionality using a CommandField

```
<asp:CommandField ShowHeader="True" HeaderText="Command"
  ShowEditButton="True" />
```

This allows you to display the command as a link, a button, or even an image.

Now if you browse to your web page, you see that a new edit column has been added. Clicking the Edit link allows the user to edit the contents of that particular data row.

The `CommandField` element also has attributes that allow you to control exactly what is shown in the column. You can dictate whether the column displays commands such as Cancel, Delete, Edit, Insert, or Select.

To complete configuring the grid to allow editing, you need to ensure the grid knows which database table columns are configured as its primary key. You can specify this using the GridView's `DataKeyNames` property, which is shown in Listing 8-29.

LISTING 8-29: Adding the DataKeyNames to the GridView control

```
<asp:GridView ID="GridView1" Runat="server"
  DataSourceID="SqlDataSource1" DataKeyNames="CustomerID"
  AutoGenerateColumns="False" AllowSorting="True" AllowPaging="True">
```

If the primary key of the table is more than one column, you can specify more than one column name setting using a comma-delimited list.

You can control which columns the grid allows to be edited by adding the `ReadOnly` property to the columns that you do not want users to edit. Listing 8-30 shows how you can add the `ReadOnly` property to the `ID` column.

LISTING 8-30: Adding the ReadOnly property to a BoundField

```
<asp:BoundField DataField="CustomerID" HeaderText="CustomerID"
  SortExpression="CustomerID" ReadOnly="True" />
```

Now if you browse to the web page again and click the Edit button, you should see that the `ID` column is not editable.

Handling Errors When Updating Data

You can check for errors when updating data through the GridView, using the RowUpdated event. Listing 8-31 shows how to check for errors after an attempt to update data.

LISTING 8-31: Checking for Update errors using the RowUpdated event

VB

```
<script runat="server">
  Protected Sub GridView1_RowUpdated(ByVal sender As Object,
    ByVal e As System.Web.UI.WebControls.GridViewUpdatedEventArgs)
        If e.Exception IsNot Nothing Then
        Me.lblErrorMessage.Text = e.Exception.Message
    End If
  End Sub
</script>
```

C#

```
<script runat="server">
  protected void GridView1_RowUpdated(object sender,
                    GridViewUpdatedEventArgs e)
  {
    if (e.Exception != null)
    {
        this.lblErrorMessage.Text = e.Exception.Message;
    }
  }
</script>
```

The RowUpdated event arguments include an Exception property. The listing checks to see whether this property is null. If not, that indicates an error has occurred, and a message is shown to the end user.

Using the TemplateField's EditItemTemplate

Earlier in the chapter, you were introduced to TemplateField and some of the templates it includes. One of those templates is EditItemTemplate, which the grid uses when a TemplateField column for a row enters edit mode. Using EditItemTemplate allows you to completely customize the data editing experience of the user. For instance, a better editing experience for the Region column would be to present the possible values as a drop-down list rather than as a simple textbox, which is the default editing experience for the BoundField.

To do this, you simply change the Region column from a BoundField to a TemplateField and add ItemTemplate and EditItemTemplate. In EditItemTemplate, you can add a DropDownList control and provide the proper data-binding information so that the control is bound to a unique list of Regions. Listing 8-32 shows how you can add ItemTemplate and EditItemTemplate to the GridView.

LISTING 8-32: Adding ItemTemplate and EditItemTemplate to the GridView

```
<asp:TemplateField HeaderText="Country">
  <ItemTemplate><%# Eval("Country") %></ItemTemplate>
  <EditItemTemplate>
    <asp:DropDownList ID="DropDownList1" runat="server"
      DataSourceID="SqlDataSource2"
      DataTextField="Country" DataValueField="Country">
    </asp:DropDownList>
    <asp:SqlDataSource ID="SqlDataSource2" runat="server"
```

```
            ConnectionString=
              "<%$ ConnectionStrings:ConnectionString %>"
            SelectCommand="SELECT DISTINCT [Country] FROM [Customers]">
          </asp:SqlDataSource>
      </EditItemTemplate>
  </asp:TemplateField>
```

A simple Eval data-binding expression is used in the ItemTemplate to display the value of the column in the row's default display mode. In EditItemTemplate, a DropDownList control bound to a SqlDataSource control is included.

To show the currently selected country in the DropDownList control, you use the RowDataBound event. Listing 8-33 shows how this is done.

LISTING 8-33: Using the RowDataBound event to select a DropDownList item

VB

```vb
<script runat="server">
  Protected Sub GridView1_RowDataBound(ByVal sender As Object,
    ByVal e As System.Web.UI.WebControls.GridViewRowEventArgs)
        'Check for a row in edit mode.
    If ((e.Row.RowState = DataControlRowState.Edit) Or
      (e.Row.RowState = (DataControlRowState.Alternate Or
      DataControlRowState.Edit))) Then
          Dim drv As System.Data.DataRowView =
        CType(e.Row.DataItem, System.Data.DataRowView)
          Dim ddl As DropDownList =
        CType(e.Row.Cells(8).
          FindControl("DropDownList1"), DropDownList)
      Dim li As ListItem = ddl.Items.
        FindByValue(drv("Country").ToString())
      li.Selected = True
    End If
  End Sub
</script>
```

C#

```csharp
<script runat="server">
  protected void GridView1_RowDataBound(object sender,
                    GridViewRowEventArgs e)
  {
    // Check for a row in edit mode.
    if ( (e.Row.RowState == DataControlRowState.Edit) ||
      (e.Row.RowState == (DataControlRowState.Alternate |
            DataControlRowState.Edit)) )
    {
      System.Data.DataRowView drv =
        (System.Data.DataRowView)e.Row.DataItem;
          DropDownList ddl =
        (DropDownList)e.Row.Cells[8].
          FindControl("DropDownList1");
      ListItem li =
          ddl.Items.FindByValue(drv["Country"].ToString());
      li.Selected = true;
    }
  }
</script>
```

To set the DropDownList value, first check that the currently bound GridViewRow is in edit mode by using the RowState property. The RowState property is a bitwise combination of DataControlRowState values. Table 8-8 shows you the possible states for a GridViewRow.

TABLE 8-8

ROWSTATE	DESCRIPTION
Alternate	Indicates that this row is an alternate row
Edit	Indicates the row is currently in edit mode
Insert	Indicates the row is a new row, and is currently in insert mode
Normal	Indicates the row is currently in a normal state
Selected	Indicates the row is currently the selected row in the GridView

To determine the current RowState correctly, you may need to make multiple comparisons against the RowState property. The RowState can be in multiple states at once—for example, alternate and edit—therefore, you need to use a bitwise comparison to properly determine whether the GridViewRow is in an edit state.

After the row is determined to be in an edit state, locate the DropDownList control in the proper cell by using the FindControl method. This method allows you to locate a server control by name. After you find the DropDownList control, locate the appropriate DropDownList ListItem and set its Selected property to True.

You also need to use a GridView event to add the value of the DropDownList control back into the GridView after the user updates the row. For this, you can use the RowUpdating event as shown in Listing 8-34.

LISTING 8-34: Using the RowUpdating event

VB

```
<script runat="server">
  Protected Sub GridView1_RowUpdating(ByVal sender As Object,
    ByVal e As System.Web.UI.WebControls.GridViewUpdateEventArgs)
       Dim gvr As GridViewRow =
      Me.GridView1.Rows(Me.GridView1.EditIndex)
    Dim ddl As DropDownList =
      CType(gvr.Cells(8).
        FindControl("DropDownList1"), DropDownList)
    e.NewValues("Country") = ddl.SelectedValue
  End Sub
</script>
```

C#

```
<script runat="server">
  protected void GridView1_RowUpdating(object sender,
                   GridViewUpdateEventArgs e)
  {
    GridViewRow gvr =
      this.GridView1.Rows[this.GridView1.EditIndex];
    DropDownList ddl =
      (DropDownList)gvr.Cells[8].FindControl("DropDownList1");
    e.NewValues["Country"] = ddl.SelectedValue;
  }
</script>
```

In this event, you determine the GridViewRow that is currently being edited using the `EditIndex`. This property contains the index of the GridViewRow that is currently in an edit state. After you find the row, locate the DropDownList control in the proper row cell using the `FindControl` method, as in the previous listing. After you find the DropDownList control, simply add the `SelectedValue` of that control to the GridView control's `NewValues` collection.

Deleting GridView Data

Deleting data from the table produced by the GridView is even easier than editing data. Just a few additions to the SqlDataSource and GridView enable you to delete an entire row of data from the table.

Like the Edit buttons, you can add a Delete button to the grid by setting the `AutoGenerateDeleteButton` property to `True` or by using the `CommandField`. Using the `AutoGenerateDeleteButton` property is shown in Listing 8-35.

LISTING 8-35: Adding a delete link to the GridView

```
<asp:GridView ID="GridView2" Runat="server"
    DataSourceID="SqlDataSource1" DataKeyNames="CustomerID"
    AutoGenerateColumns="True" AllowSorting="True" AllowPaging="True"
    AutoGenerateEditButton="true" AutoGenerateDeleteButton="true"/>
```

The SqlDataSource control changes are also trivial and can be made using the Configure Data Source wizard or manually in markup. Listing 8-36 shows how you can add the `DeleteCommand` to the control.

LISTING 8-36: Adding delete functionality to the SqlDataSource control

```
<asp:SqlDataSource ID="SqlDataSource1" Runat="server"
    SelectCommand="SELECT * FROM [Customers]"
    ConnectionString="<%$ ConnectionStrings:ConnectionString %>"
    DataSourceMode="DataSet"
    DeleteCommand="DELETE From Customers
            WHERE (CustomerID = @CustomerID)"
    UpdateCommand="UPDATE [Customers]
      SET [CompanyName] = @CompanyName,
      [ContactName] = @ContactName, [ContactTitle] = @ContactTitle,
      [Address] = @Address, [City] = @City, [Region] = @Region,
      [PostalCode] = @PostalCode, [Country] = @Country,
      [Phone] = @Phone, [Fax] = @Fax
      WHERE [CustomerID] = @original_CustomerID">
  <%-- Update parameters removed for clarity --%>
</asp:SqlDataSource>
```

Just like the `UpdateCommand` property, the `DeleteCommand` property makes use of named parameters to determine which row should be deleted. Because of this, you define this parameter from within the SqlDataSource control. To do this, add a `<DeleteParameters>` section to the SqlDataSource control. This is shown in Listing 8-37.

LISTING 8-37: Adding a <DeleteParameters> section to the SqlDataSource control

```
<DeleteParameters>
  <asp:Parameter Name="CustomerID" Type="String">
  </asp:Parameter>
</DeleteParameters>
```

This is the only parameter needed for the `<DeleteParameters>` collection because the SQL command for this deletion requires only the CustomerID from the row to delete the entire row. Running the example displays a Delete link in the grid, which when clicked deletes the selected row.

Remember that just like when you update data, checking for database errors when you delete data is a good idea. Listing 8-38 shows how you can use the GridView's `RowDeleted` event and the SqlDataSource's `Deleted` event to check for errors that might have occurred during the deletion.

LISTING 8-38: Using the RowDeleted event to catch SQL errors

VB

```
<script runat="server">
  Protected Sub GridView1_RowDeleted(ByVal sender As Object,
    ByVal e As GridViewDeletedEventArgs)
        If (Not IsDBNull (e.Exception)) Then
      Me.lblErrorMessage.Text = e.Exception.Message
      e.ExceptionHandled = True
    End If
  End Sub
      Protected Sub SqlDataSource1_Deleted(ByVal sender As Object,
  ByVal e As System.Web.UI.WebControls.SqlDataSourceStatusEventArgs)
        If (e.Exception IsNot Nothing) Then
      Me.lblErrorMessage.Text = e.Exception.Message
      e.ExceptionHandled = True
    End If
  End Sub
</script>
```

C#

```
<script runat="server">
  protected void GridView1_RowDeleted(object sender,
                  GridViewDeletedEventArgs e)
  {
    if (e.Exception != null)
    {
      this.lblErrorMessage.Text = e.Exception.Message;
      e.ExceptionHandled = true;
    }
  }

    protected void SqlDataSource1_Deleted(object sender,
                  SqlDataSourceStatusEventArgs e)
  {
    if (e.Exception != null)
    {
      this.lblErrorMessage.Text = e.Exception.Message;
      e.ExceptionHandled = true;
    }
  }
}
</script>
```

Notice that both events provide `Exception` properties as part of their event arguments. If these properties are not empty, an exception has occurred that you can handle. If you do choose to handle the exception, you should set the `ExceptionHandled` property to `True`; otherwise, the exception will continue to bubble up to the end user.

DetailsView

The DetailsView control is a data-bound control that enables you to work with a single data record at a time. Although the GridView control is excellent for viewing a collection of data, there are many scenarios where you want to show a single record rather than an entire collection. The DetailsView control allows you to do this and provides many of the same data-manipulation and display capabilities as the GridView, including features such as paging, updating, inserting, and deleting data.

To start using the DetailsView, drag the control onto the design surface. Like the GridView, you can use the DetailsView's smart tag to create and set the data source for the control. The examples in this section use the same SqlDataSource control that was used for the GridView examples in the previous section. Set the SqlDataSource as the DetailsView's data source and run the page. Listing 8-39 shows the markup for a DetailsView control bound to a SqlDataSource control.

LISTING 8-39: A DetailsView control bound to a SqlDataSource

```
<asp:DetailsView ID="DetailsView1" Runat="server"
  DataSourceID="SqlDataSource1" DataKeyNames="CustomerID"
  AutoGenerateRows="True"></asp:DetailsView>
    <asp:SqlDataSource ID="SqlDataSource1" Runat="server"
  SelectCommand="SELECT * FROM [Customers]"
  ConnectionString=
    "<%$ ConnectionStrings:ConnectionString %>"
  DataSourceMode="DataSet">
</asp:SqlDataSource>
```

If you simply want to display a single record, you would probably want to change the SqlDataSource control's `SelectCommand` so that it returns only one customer, rather than returning all customers as the query does. However, if you are returning more than a single object from the database, you can allow your end users to page through the data by setting the DetailsView's `AllowPaging` property to `True`, as shown in Listing 8-40.

LISTING 8-40: Enabling paging on the DetailsView control

```
<asp:DetailsView ID="DetailsView1" Runat="server"
  DataSourceID="SqlDataSource1" DataKeyNames="CustomerID"
  AutoGenerateRows="True" AllowPaging="true"></asp:DetailsView>
```

You can select the Enable Paging check box in the DetailsView smart tag or add the property to the control in Source view. Also, like the GridView, the DetailsView control enables you to customize the control's pager using the `PagerSettings-Mode`, as well as the `Pager` style.

Customizing the DetailsView Display

You can customize the appearance of the DetailsView control by choosing which fields the control displays. By default, the control displays each public property from its bound data source. However, using the same basic syntax used for the GridView control, you can specify that only certain properties be displayed. This is illustrated in Listing 8-41.

LISTING 8-41: Customizing the display of the DetailsView control

```
<asp:DetailsView ID="DetailsView1" Runat="server"
  DataSourceID="SqlDataSource1" DataKeyNames="CustomerID"
  AutoGenerateRows="False">
  <Fields>
    <asp:BoundField ReadOnly="True" HeaderText="CustomerID"
      DataField="CustomerID" SortExpression="CustomerID"
      Visible="False" />
    <asp:BoundField ReadOnly="True" HeaderText="CompanyName"
      DataField="CompanyName" SortExpression="CompanyName" />
    <asp:BoundField HeaderText="ContactName"
      DataField="ContactName" SortExpression="ContactName" />
```

continues

LISTING 8-41 *(continued)*

```
        <asp:BoundField HeaderText="ContactTitle"
            DataField="ContactTitle"
            SortExpression="ContactTitle" />
      </Fields>
   </asp:DetailsView>
```

In this example, only four fields from the Customers table are defined using BoundField objects in the DetailsView's Fields collection.

Using the DetailsView and GridView Together

Next, this section looks at a common master/detail display scenario, which uses both the GridView and the DetailsView. In this example, you use the GridView to display a master view of the data and the DetailsView to show the details of the selected GridView row. The Customers table is the data source. Listing 8-42 shows the code needed for this.

LISTING 8-42: Using the GridView and DetailsView together

```
<html>
<head id="Head1" runat="server">
  <title>GridView & DetailsView Controls</title>
</head>
<body>
  <form id="form1" runat="server">
    <p>
      <asp:GridView ID="GridView1" runat="server"
          DataSourceId="SqlDataSource1"
          DataKeyNames="CustomerID"
          AutoGenerateSelectButton="True" AllowPaging="True"
          AutoGenerateColumns="True" PageSize="5">
        <SelectedRowStyle ForeColor="White" BackColor="#738A9C"
            Font-Bold="True" />
      </asp:GridView>
    </p>
    <p><b>Customer Details:</b></p>
    <asp:DetailsView ID="DetailsView1" runat="server"
        DataSourceId="SqlDataSource2"
        AutoGenerateRows="True" DataKeyNames="CustomerID">
    </asp:DetailsView>
      <asp:SqlDataSource ID="SqlDataSource1" runat="server"
      SelectCommand="SELECT * FROM [Customers]"
      ConnectionString=
        "<%$ ConnectionStrings:ConnectionString %>" />
      <asp:SqlDataSource ID="SqlDataSource2" runat="server"
      SelectCommand="SELECT * FROM [Customers]"
      FilterExpression="CustomerID='{0}'"
      ConnectionString=
        "<%$ ConnectionStrings:ConnectionString %>">
      <FilterParameters>
        <asp:ControlParameter Name="CustomerID"
            ControlId="GridView1"
            PropertyName="SelectedValue" />
      </FilterParameters>
    </asp:SqlDataSource>
  </form>
</body>
</html>
```

To see how this works, look at the changes that were made to the second SqlDataSource control, named `SqlDataSource2`. A `FilterExpression` used to filter the data retrieved by the `SelectCommand` has been added. In this case, the value of the `FilterExpression` is set to `CustomerID='{0}'` indicating that the control should filter the data it returns by the `CustomerID` value given to it.

The parameter specified in the `FilterExpression`, `CustomerID`, is defined in the SqlDataSource control's `<FilterParameters>` collection. The example uses an `<asp:ControlParameter>` to specify the GridView control's `SelectedValue` property to populate the parameter's value.

SelectParameters versus FilterParameters

You might have noticed in the previous example that the `FilterParameters` seem to provide the same functionality as the `SelectParameters`, which were discussed in the "SqlDataSource Control" section of this chapter. Although both produce essentially the same result, they use very different methods. As you saw in the previous section, using the `SelectParameters` allows the developer to inject values into a `WHERE` clause specified in the `SelectCommand`. This limits the rows that are returned from the SQL Server and held in memory by the data source control. The advantage is that by limiting the amount of data returned from SQL, you can make your application faster and reduce the amount of memory it consumes. The disadvantage is that you are confined to working with the limited subset of data returned by the SQL query.

`FilterParameters`, on the other hand, do not use a `WHERE`, instead requiring all the data to be returned from the server and then applying a filter to the data source control's in-memory data. The disadvantage of the filter method is that more data has to be returned from the data store. However, in some cases such as when you are performing many filters of one large chunk of data (for instance, to enable paging in DetailsView) this is an advantage as you do not have to call out to your data store each time you need the next record. All the data is stored in cache memory by the data source control.

Inserting, Updating, and Deleting Data Using DetailsView

Inserting data using the DetailsView is similar to inserting data using the GridView control. To insert data using the DetailsView, simply add the `AutoGenerateInsertButton` property to the DetailsView control as shown in Listing 8-43.

LISTING 8-43: Adding an AutoGenerateInsertButton property to the DetailsView

```
<asp:DetailsView ID="DetailsView1" runat="server"
    DataSourceId="SqlDataSource1" DataKeyNames="CustomerID"
    AutoGenerateRows="True" AutoGenerateInsertButton="True" />
```

Then add the `InsertCommand` and corresponding `InsertParameters` elements to the SqlDataSource control, as shown in Listing 8-44.

LISTING 8-44: Adding an InsertCommand to the SqlDataSource control

```
<asp:SqlDataSource ID="SqlDataSource1" runat="server"
  SelectCommand="SELECT * FROM [Customers]"
  InsertCommand="INSERT INTO [Customers] ([CustomerID],
    [CompanyName], [ContactName], [ContactTitle], [Address],
    [City], [Region], [PostalCode], [Country], [Phone], [Fax])
  VALUES (@CustomerID, @CompanyName, @ContactName, @ContactTitle,
  @Address, @City, @Region, @PostalCode,@Country, @Phone, @Fax)"
  DeleteCommand="DELETE FROM [Customers]
        WHERE [CustomerID] = @original_CustomerID"
  ConnectionString="<%$ ConnectionStrings:ConnectionString %>">
```

continues

LISTING 8-44 *(continued)*

```
      <InsertParameters>
        <asp:Parameter Type="String" Name="CustomerID"></asp:Parameter>
        <asp:Parameter Type="String"
              Name="CompanyName"></asp:Parameter>
        <asp:Parameter Type="String"
              Name="ContactName"></asp:Parameter>
        <asp:Parameter Type="String"
              Name="ContactTitle"></asp:Parameter>
        <asp:Parameter Type="String" Name="Address"></asp:Parameter>
        <asp:Parameter Type="String" Name="City"></asp:Parameter>
        <asp:Parameter Type="String" Name="Region"></asp:Parameter>
        <asp:Parameter Type="String" Name="PostalCode"></asp:Parameter>
        <asp:Parameter Type="String" Name="Country"></asp:Parameter>
        <asp:Parameter Type="String" Name="Phone"></asp:Parameter>
        <asp:Parameter Type="String" Name="Fax"></asp:Parameter>
      </InsertParameters>
    </asp:SqlDataSource>
```

Updating and deleting data using the DetailsView control are similar to updating and deleting data using the GridView. Simply specify the `UpdateCommand` or `DeleteCommand` attributes in the DetailsView control; then provide the proper `UpdateParameters` and `DeleteParameters` elements.

ListView

ASP.NET includes another list-style control that bridges the gap between the highly structured GridView control, and the anything goes, unstructured controls like DataList and Repeater.

In the past, many developers who wanted a grid-style data control chose the GridView because it was easy to use and offered powerful features such as data editing, paging, and sorting. Unfortunately, the more developers dug into the control, the more they found that controlling the way it rendered its HTML output was exceedingly difficult. This was problematic if you wanted to lighten the amount of markup generated by the control, or use CSS exclusively to control the control's layout and style.

On the other side of the coin, many developers were drawn to DataList or Repeater because of the enhanced control they achieved over rendering. These controls contained little to no notion of layout and allowed developers total freedom in laying out their data. Unfortunately, these controls lacked some of the basic features of the GridView, such as paging and sorting, or in the case of the Repeater, any notion of data editing.

This is where the ListView can be useful. The control itself emits no runtime generated HTML markup; instead it relies on a series of 11 control templates that represent the different areas of the control and the possible states of those areas. Within these templates you can place markup autogenerated by the control at design time, or markup created by the developer, but in either case the developer retains complete control over not only the markup for individual data items in the control, but also of the markup for the layout of the entire control. Additionally, because the control readily understands and handles data editing and paging, you can let the control do much of the data-management work, allowing you to focus primarily on data display.

Getting Started with the ListView

To get started using the ListView, simply drop the control on the design surface and assign a data source to it just as you would any other data-bound list control. After you assign the data source, however, you will see that no design-time layout preview is available as you might expect. This is because, by default, the ListView has no layout defined and it is completely up to you to define the control's layout. In fact, the design-time rendering of the control even tells you that you need to define at least an ItemTemplate and LayoutTemplate to use the control. The LayoutTemplate serves as the root template for the control, and the ItemTemplate serves as the template for each data item in the control.

You have two options for defining the templates needed by the ListView. You can either edit the templates directly by changing the Current View option in the ListView smart tag, or you can select a predefined layout from the control's smart tag. Changing Current View allows you to see a runtime view of each of the available templates, and edit the contents of those templates directly just as you normally edit any other control template. Figure 8-10 shows the Current View drop-down in the ListView's smart tag.

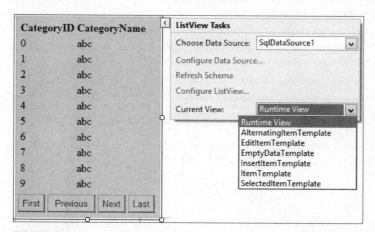

FIGURE 8-10

The second option, and probably the easier to start with, is to choose a predefined layout template from the Configure ListView dialog box. To open this dialog box, simply click the ConfigureListView option from the smart tag. You are presented with a dialog box that lets you select between several predefined layouts, select different style options, and even configure basic behavior options such as editing and paging.

The control includes five layout types—Grid, Tiled, Bulleted List, Flow, and Single Row—and four different style options. A preview of each type is presented in the dialog box, and as you change the currently selected layout and style, the preview is updated.

ListView Templates

After you have applied a layout template to the ListView, if you look at the Source window in Visual Studio, you can see that to provide the layout the control generated a significant chunk of markup. This markup is generated based on the layout that you chose in the Configure ListView dialog box.

If you closely examine the markup that has been generated for the Grid layout used in the previous section, you will see that, by default, the control creates markup for seven control templates: the ItemTemplate, AlternatingItemTemplate, SelectedItemTemplate, InsertItemTemplate, EditItemTemplate, EmptyDataTemplate, and LayoutTemplate. These are just some of the 11 templates that the control exposes, and that you can use to provide markup for the different states of the control. Choosing a different predefined layout option results in the control generating a different collection of templates. Of course, you can also always manually add or remove any of the templates yourself. All 11 templates are listed in Table 8-9.

TABLE 8-9

TEMPLATE NAME	DESCRIPTION
ItemTemplate	Provides a user interface (UI) for each data item in the control
AlternatingItemTemplate	Provides a unique UI for alternating data items in the control
SelectedItemTemplate	Provides a unique UI for the currently selected data item
InsertItemTemplate	Provides a UI for inserting a new data item into the control
EditItemTemplate	Provides a UI for editing an existing data item in the control
EmptyItemTemplate	Provides a unique UI for rows created when there is no more data to display in the last group of the current page
EmptyDataTemplate	The template shown when the bound data object contains no data items
LayoutTemplate	The template that serves as the root container for the ListView control and is used to control the overall layout of the data items
GroupSeparatorTemplate	Provides a separator UI between groups
GroupTemplate	Provides a unique UI for grouped content
ItemSeparatorTemplate	Provides a separator UI between each data item

The use of templates allows the ListView control to retain a very basic level of information about the markup sections and states which can comprise the ListView, while still being able to give you almost total control over the UI of the ListView.

ListView Data Item Rendering

Although the ListView is generally very flexible, allowing you almost complete control over the way it displays its bound data, it does have some basic structure that defines how the templates described in the previous section are related. As described previously, at a minimum, the control requires you to define two templates, the LayoutTemplate and ItemTemplate. The LayoutTemplate is the root control template and therefore is where you should define the overall layout for the collection of data items in the ListView.

For example, if you examine the template markup generated by the Grid layout, you can see the LayoutTemplate includes a `<table>` element definition, a single table row (`<tr>`) definition, and a `<td>` element defined for each column header.

The ItemTemplate, on the other hand, is where you define the layout for an individual data item. If you again look at the markup generated for the Grid layout, its ItemTemplate is a single table row (`<tr>`) element followed by a series of table cell (`<td>`) elements that contain the actual data.

When the ListView renders itself, it knows that the ItemTemplate should be rendered within the Layout Template, but what is needed is a mechanism to tell the control exactly where within the LayoutTemplate to place the ItemTemplate. The ListView control does this by looking within the LayoutTemplate for an item container. The item container is an HTML container element with the `runat = "server"` attribute set and an `id` attribute whose value is `itemContainer`. The element can be any valid HTML container element, although if you examine the default Grid LayoutTemplate you will see that it uses the `<tbody>` element.

```
<tbody id="itemContainer">
</tbody>
```

Adding to the overall flexibility of the control, even the specific `itemContainer` element `id` that ListView looks for can be configured. Although by default the control will attempt to locate an element whose `id` attribute is set to `itemContainer`, you can change the `id` value the control will look for by changing the control's `ItemContainerID` property.

If the control fails to locate an appropriate HTML element designated as the item container, it will throw an exception.

The ListView uses the element identified as the `itemContainer` to position not only the ItemTemplate, but also any item-level template, such as the AlternativeItemTemplate, EditItemTemplate, EmptyItemTemplate, InsertItemTemplate, ItemSeparatorTemplate, and SelectedItemTemplate. During rendering, it simply places the appropriate item template into the item container, depending on the state of the data item (selected, editing, or alternate) for each data item it is bound to.

ListView Group Rendering

In addition to the item container, the ListView also supports another container type, the group container. The *group container* works in conjunction with the GroupTemplate to allow you to divide a large group of data items into smaller sets. The number of items in each group is set by the control's `GroupItemCount` property. This is useful when you want to output some additional HTML after some number of item templates has been rendered. When using GroupTemplate, the same problem exists as was discussed in the prior section. In this case, however, rather than having two templates to relate, introducing the GroupTemplate means you have three templates to relate: the ItemTemplate to the GroupTemplate, and the GroupTemplate to the LayoutTemplate.

When the ListView renders itself, it looks to see whether a GroupTemplate has been defined. If the control finds a GroupTemplate, it checks to see whether a group container is provided in the LayoutTemplate. If you have defined the GroupTemplate, the control requires that you define a group container; otherwise it throws an exception. The group container works the same way as the item container described in the previous section, except that the container element's `id` value should be `groupContainer`, rather than `itemContainer`. As with an item container, the specific `id` value that the control looks for can be changed by altering the `GroupContainerID` property of the control.

You can see an example of the group container being used by looking at the markup generated by the ListView's Tiled layout. The LayoutTemplate of this layout shows a table serving as the group container, shown here:

```
<table id="groupContainer" runat="server" border="0" style="">
</table>
```

After a `groupContainer` is defined, you need to define an item container, but rather than doing this in the LayoutTemplate, you need to do it in the GroupTemplate. Again, looking at the Tiled layout, you can see that within its GroupTemplate, it defined a table row that serves as the item container.

```
<tr id="itemContainer" runat="server">
</tr>
```

Item count has been reached, so the ListView outputs the GroupTemplate, and then the ItemTemplate again, repeating this process for each data item it is bound to.

Using the EmptyItemTemplate

When using the GroupTemplate, it is also important to keep in mind that the number of data items bound to the ListView control may not be perfectly divisible by the `GroupItemCount` value. This is especially important to keep in mind if you have created a ListView layout that is dependent on HTML tables for its data item arrangement because there is a chance that the last row may end up defining fewer table cells than previous table rows, making the HTML output by the control invalid, and possibly causing rendering problems. To solve this, the ListView control includes the EmptyItemTemplate. This template is rendered if you are using the GroupTemplate and there are not enough data items remaining to reach the `GroupItemCount` value.

For example, if the data source bound to the ListView control contains four data items, but the `GroupItemCount` for the control is set to 3, there will be three ItemTemplates rendered in each group. This means for the second group rendered, there will only be a single data item remaining to render; therefore, the control will use the EmptyItemTemplate, if defined, to fill the remaining items.

ListView Data Binding and Commands

Because the ListView does not generate any layout markup at run time and does not include any of the auto field generation logic as you may be used to in the GridView, each template uses the standard ASP.NET inline data-binding syntax to position the values of each data item in the defined layout. The inline data-binding syntax is covered in detail later in this chapter.

You can see an example of inline binding by examining the ItemTemplate of the default Grid layout created by the control. In this template, each column of the bound data source is displayed using an ASP.NET label whose text property is set to a data-binding evaluation expression:

```
<asp:Label ID="ProductNameLabel" runat="server"
  Text='<%# Eval("ProductName") %>' />
```

Because the control uses this flexible model to display the bound data, you can leverage it to place the data wherever you want within the template, and even use the features of ASP.NET data binding to manipulate the bound data before it is displayed.

Every ListView template that displays bound data uses the same ASP.NET binding syntax, and simply provides a different template around it. For example, if you enable editing in the Grid layout you will see that the EditItemTemplate simply replaces the ASP.NET label used by the ItemTemplate with a textbox or check box, depending on the underlying data type.

```
<asp:TextBox ID="ProductNameTextBox" runat="server"
  Text='<%# Bind("ProductName") %>' />
```

Again, this flexibility allows you to choose exactly how you want to allow your end user to edit the data (if you want it to be editable). Instead of a standard ASP.NET textbox, you could easily replace this with a drop-down list, or even a third-party editing control.

To get the ListView to show the EditItemTemplate for a data item, the control uses the same commands concept found in the GridView control. The ItemTemplate provides three commands (see Table 8-10) you can use to change the state of a data item.

TABLE 8-10

COMMAND NAME	DESCRIPTION
Edit	Places the specific data item into edit mode and shows the EditTemplate for the data item
Delete	Deletes the specific data item from the underlying data source
Select	Sets the ListView control's selected index to the index of the specific data item

These commands are used in conjunction with the ASP.NET Button control's CommandName property. You can see these commands used in the ItemTemplate of the ListView's default Grid layout by enabling editing and deleting using the ListView configuration dialog box. Doing this generates a new column with an Edit and Delete button, each of which specified the CommandName property set to Edit and Delete, respectively.

```
<asp:Button ID="DeleteButton" runat="server"
  CommandName="Delete" Text="Delete" />
<asp:Button ID="EditButton" runat="server"
  CommandName="Edit" Text="Edit" />
```

Other templates in the ListView offer other commands, as shown in Table 8-11.

TABLE 8-11

TEMPLATE	COMMAND NAME	DESCRIPTION
EditItemTemplate	Update	Updates the data in the ListView's data source and returns the data item to the ItemTemplate display
EditItemTemplate	Cancel	Cancels the edit and returns the data item to the ItemTemplate
InsertItemTemplate	Insert	Inserts the data into the ListView's data source
InsertItemTemplate	Cancel	Cancels the insert and resets the InsertTemplate controls binding values

ListView Paging and the Pager Control

ASP.NET includes another control called DataPager that the ListView uses to provide paging capabilities. The DataPager control is designed to display the navigation for paging to the end user and to coordinate data paging with any data-bound control that implements the IPagableItemContainer interface, which in ASP.NET is the ListView control. In fact, you will notice that if you enable paging on the ListView control by checking the Paging check box in the ListView configuration dialog box, the control simply inserts a new DataPager control into its LayoutTemplate. The default paging markup generated by the ListView for the Grid layout is shown here:

```
<asp:datapager ID="DataPager1" runat="server">
  <Fields>
    <asp:nextpreviouspagerfield ButtonType="Button" FirstPageText="First"
      LastPageText="Last" NextPageText="Next" PreviousPageText="Previous"
      ShowFirstPageButton="True" ShowLastPageButton="True" />
  </Fields>
</asp:datapager>
```

The markup for the control shows that within the DataPager, a `Fields` collection has been created, which contains a `NextPreviousPagerField` object. As its name implies, using the `NextPreviousPager` object results in the DataPager rendering Next and Previous buttons as its user interface. The DataPager control includes three types of `Field` objects: the `NextPreviousPagerField`; the `NumericPagerField` object, which generates a simple numeric page list; and the `TemplatePagerField`, which allows you to specify your own custom paging user interface. Each of these `Field` types includes a variety of properties that you can use to control exactly how the DataPager displays the user interface. Additionally, because the DataPager exposes a `Fields` collection rather than a simple `Field` property, you can display several `Field` objects within a single DataPager control.

The `TemplatePagerField` is a unique type of `Field` object that contains no user interface itself, but simply exposes a template that you can use to completely customize the pager's user interface. Listing 8-45 demonstrates the use of the `TemplatePagerField`.

LISTING 8-45: Creating a custom DataPager user interface

```
<asp:DataPager ID="DataPager1" runat="server">
  <Fields>
    <asp:TemplatePagerField>
      <PagerTemplate>
        Page
        <asp:Label ID="Label1" runat="server"
          Text=
          "<%# (Container.StartRowIndex/Container.PageSize)+1%>" />
        of
        <asp:Label ID="Label2" runat="server"
```

continues

LISTING 8-45 *(continued)*

```
            Text=
            "<%# Container.TotalRowCount/Container.PageSize%>" />
        </PagerTemplate>
      </asp:TemplatePagerField>
    </Fields>
</asp:DataPager>
```

Notice that the example uses ASP.NET data binding to provide the total page count, page size, and the row that the page should start on; these are values exposed by the DataPager control.

If you want to use custom navigation controls in the PagerTemplate, such as a Button control to change the currently displayed page, you would create a standard Click event handler for the button. Within that event handler, you can access the DataPager's `StartRowIndex`, `TotalRowCount`, and `PageSize` properties to calculate the new `StartRowIndex` the ListView should use when it renders.

Unlike the paging provided by the GridView, DataPager, because it is a separate control, gives you total freedom over where to place it on your web page. The examples you have seen so far have all looked at the DataPager control when it is placed directly in a ListView, but the control can be placed anywhere on the web form. In Listing 8-46, the only significant change you should notice is the use of the `PagedControlID` property.

LISTING 8-46: Placing the DataPager control outside of the ListView

```
<asp:DataPager ID="DataPager1" runat="server"
    PagedControlID="ListView1">
  <Fields>
    <asp:NumericPagerField />
  </Fields>
</asp:DataPager>
```

The `PageControlID` property allows you to specify explicitly which control this pager should work with.

FormView

The FormView control functions like the DetailsView control in that it displays a single data item from a bound data source control and allows adding, editing, and deleting data. What makes it unique is that it displays the data in custom templates, which gives you much greater control over how the data is displayed and edited. The FormView control also contains an EditItemTemplate and InsertItemTemplate that allows you to determine how the control displays when entering edit or insert mode.Listing 8-47 shows the code that Visual Studio generates when designing the FormView control's customized ItemTemplate.

LISTING 8-47: Using a FormView control to display and edit data

```
<html xmlns="http://www.w3.org/1999/xhtml" >
<head runat="server">
  <title>Using the FormView control</title>
</head>
<body>
  <form id="form1" runat="server">
  <div>
    <asp:FormView ID="FormView1" Runat="server"
        DataSourceID="SqlDataSource1"
        DataKeyNames="CustomerID" AllowPaging="True">
      <EditItemTemplate>
```

```
  CustomerID:
  <asp:Label Text='<%# Eval("CustomerID") %>'
     Runat="server" ID="CustomerIDLabel1">
  </asp:Label><br />
  CompanyName:
  <asp:TextBox Text='<%# Bind("CompanyName") %>'
     Runat="server"
     ID="CompanyNameTextBox"></asp:TextBox><br />
  ContactName:
  <asp:TextBox Text='<%# Bind("ContactName") %>'
     Runat="server"
     ID="ContactNameTextBox"></asp:TextBox><br />
  ContactTitle:
  <asp:TextBox Text='<%# Bind("ContactTitle") %>'
    Runat="server"
    ID="ContactTitleTextBox"></asp:TextBox><br />
  Address:
  <asp:TextBox Text='<%# Bind("Address") %>'
     Runat="server"
     ID="AddressTextBox"></asp:TextBox><br />
  City:
  <asp:TextBox Text='<%# Bind("City") %>' Runat="server"
     ID="CityTextBox"></asp:TextBox><br />
  Region:
  <asp:TextBox Text='<%# Bind("Region") %>'
     Runat="server"
     ID="RegionTextBox"></asp:TextBox><br />
  PostalCode:
  <asp:TextBox Text='<%# Bind("PostalCode") %>'
     Runat="server"
     ID="PostalCodeTextBox"></asp:TextBox><br />
  Country:
  <asp:TextBox Text='<%# Bind("Country") %>'
     Runat="server"
     ID="CountryTextBox"></asp:TextBox><br />
  Phone:
  <asp:TextBox Text='<%# Bind("Phone") %>' Runat="server"
     ID="PhoneTextBox"></asp:TextBox><br />
  Fax:
  <asp:TextBox Text='<%# Bind("Fax") %>' Runat="server"
     ID="FaxTextBox"></asp:TextBox><br />
  <br />
  <asp:Button ID="Button2" Runat="server" Text="Button"
     CommandName="update" />
  <asp:Button ID="Button3" Runat="server" Text="Button"
     CommandName="cancel" />
</EditItemTemplate>
<ItemTemplate>
  <table width="100%">
    <tr>
      <td style="width: 439px">
      <b>
      <span style="font-size: 14pt">
        Customer Information</span>
      </b>
      </td>
      <td style="width: 439px" align="right">
        CustomerID:
        <asp:Label ID="CustomerIDLabel"
          Runat="server"
```

continues

LISTING 8-47 *(continued)*

```
                    Text='<%# Bind("CustomerID") %>'>
                  </asp:Label></td>
  </tr>
  <tr>
    <td colspan="2">
      CompanyName:
      <asp:Label ID="CompanyNameLabel"
        Runat="server"
        Text='<%# Bind("CompanyName") %>'>
        </asp:Label><br />
      ContactName:
      <asp:Label ID="ContactNameLabel"
        Runat="server"
        Text='<%# Bind("ContactName") %>'>
        </asp:Label><br />
      ContactTitle:
      <asp:Label ID="ContactTitleLabel"
        Runat="server"
        Text='<%# Bind("ContactTitle") %>'>
        </asp:Label><br />
      <br />
      <table width="100%"><tr>
        <td colspan="3">
          <asp:Label ID="AddressLabel"
            Runat="server"
            Text='<%# Bind("Address") %>'>
              </asp:Label></td>
      </tr>
        <tr>
        <td style="width: 100px">
          <asp:Label ID="CityLabel"
            Runat="server"
            Text='<%# Bind("City") %>'>
              </asp:Label></td>
        <td style="width: 100px">
          <asp:Label ID="RegionLabel"
            Runat="server"
            Text='<%# Bind("Region") %>'>
              </asp:Label></td>
        <td style="width: 100px">
          <asp:Label ID="PostalCodeLabel"
            Runat="server"
           Text='<%# Bind("PostalCode") %>'>
              </asp:Label>
          </td>
        </tr>
        <tr>
        <td style="width: 100px" valign="top">
          <asp:Label ID="CountryLabel"
            Runat="server"
            Text='<%# Bind("Country") %>'>
              </asp:Label></td>
        <td style="width: 100px"></td>
        <td style="width: 100px">Phone:
          <asp:Label ID="PhoneLabel"
            Runat="server"
            Text='<%# Bind("Phone") %>'>
              </asp:Label><br />
          Fax:
```

```
                        <asp:Label ID="FaxLabel"
                            Runat="server"
                            Text='<%# Bind("Fax") %>'>
                            </asp:Label><br />
                    </td>
                </tr></table>
                <asp:Button ID="Button1" Runat="server"
                    Text="Button" CommandName="edit" />
            </td>
        </tr></table>
    </ItemTemplate>
    </asp:FormView>
    <asp:SqlDataSource ID="SqlDataSource1" Runat="server"
        SelectCommand="SELECT * FROM [Customers]"
        ConnectionString=
            "<%$ ConnectionStrings:ConnectionString %>">
        </asp:SqlDataSource>
    </div>
    </form>
</body>
</html>
```

OTHER DATA-BOUND CONTROLS

ASP.NET contains a variety of other simple controls that can be bound to data sources. This section looks at three of the most popular and useful of these other controls and how you can connect them to data in your web application.

TreeView

The TreeView displays hierarchically structured data. Because of this, it can be data-bound only to the XmlDataSource and the SiteMapDataSource controls that are designed to bind to hierarchically structured data sources like a SiteMap file. Listing 8-48 shows an example SiteMap file you can use for your SiteMapDataSource control.

LISTING 8-48: A SiteMap file for your samples

```
<siteMap>
  <siteMapNode url="page3.aspx" title="Home" description="" roles="">
    <siteMapNode url="page2.aspx"
        title="Content" description="" roles="" />
    <siteMapNode url="page4.aspx"
        title="Links" description="" roles="" />
    <siteMapNode url="page1.aspx"
        title="Comments" description="" roles="" />
  </siteMapNode>
</siteMap>
```

Listing 8-49 shows how you can bind a TreeView control to a SiteMapDataSource control to generate navigation for your website.

LISTING 8-49: Using the TreeView with a SiteMapDataSource control

```
<html xmlns="http://www.w3.org/1999/xhtml" >
<head runat="server">
  <title>Using the TreeView control</title>
```

continues

LISTING 8-49 *(continued)*

```
    </head>
    <body>
      <form id="form1" runat="server">
      <div>
        <asp:TreeView ID="TreeView1" Runat="server"
          DataSourceID="SiteMapDataSource1" />
        <asp:SiteMapDataSource ID="SiteMapDataSource1"
          Runat="server" />
      </div>
      </form>
    </body>
    </html>
```

Menu

Like the TreeView control, the Menu control is capable of displaying hierarchical data in a vertical *pop-out style* menu. Also like the TreeView control, it can be data-bound only to the XmlDataSource and the SiteMapDataSource controls. Listing 8-50 shows how you can use the same SiteMap data used earlier in the TreeView control example, and modify it to display using the Menu control.

LISTING 8-50: Using the Menu control with a SiteMapDataSource control

```
    <html xmlns="http://www.w3.org/1999/xhtml" >
    <head runat="server">
      <title>Using the Menu control</title>
    </head>
    <body>
      <form id="form1" runat="server">
      <div>
        <asp:Menu ID="Menu1" Runat="server"
          DataSourceID="SiteMapDataSource1" />
        <asp:SiteMapDataSource ID="SiteMapDataSource1"
          Runat="server" />
      </div>
      </form>
    </body>
    </html>
```

Chart

This is a great control for getting you up and running with some good-looking charts. The Chart server control supports many chart types including:

➤ Point
➤ FastPoint
➤ Bubble
➤ Line
➤ Spline
➤ StepLine
➤ FastLine
➤ Bar

➤ StackedBar
➤ StackedBar100
➤ Column
➤ StackedColumn
➤ StackedColumn100
➤ Area
➤ SplineArea
➤ StackedArea

➤ StackedArea100
➤ Pie
➤ Doughnut
➤ Stock
➤ CandleStick
➤ Range
➤ SplineRange
➤ RangeBar
➤ RangeColumn
➤ Radar

➤ Polar
➤ ErrorBar
➤ BoxPlot
➤ Renko
➤ ThreeLineBreak
➤ Kagi
➤ PointAndFigure
➤ Funnel
➤ Pyramid

Those are a lot of different chart styles! You can find the Chart server control in the toolbox of Visual Studio 2012 underneath the Data tab. It is part of the `System.Web.DataVisualization` namespace.

When you drag it from the toolbox and place it on the design surface of your page, you are presented with a visual representation of the chart type that are you going to use. See Figure 8-11 for an example.

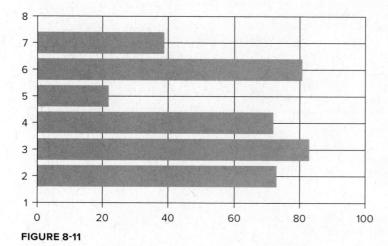

FIGURE 8-11

Open up the smart tag for the control, and you find that you can assign a data provider for the chart as well as select the chart type you are interested in using. Changing the chart type gives you a sample of what that chart looks like (even if you are not yet working with any underlying data) in the Design view of the IDE. There is a lot to this control, probably more than all the others, and this single control could almost warrant a book on its own. To get you up and running with this chart server control, follow this simple example.

Create a new web application and add the Northwind database to your App_Data folder within the application. After that is accomplished, drag and drop the Chart server control onto the design surface of your page. From the smart tag of the control, select <New Data Source> from the drop-down menu when choosing your data source. Work your way through this wizard making sure that you are choosing a SQL data source as your option. As you work through the wizard, you are going to want to choose the option that allows you to choose a custom SQL statement and use the following SQL for this operation:

```
SELECT TOP(5) [ProductName], [UnitsInStock] FROM [Products]
ORDER BY ProductName DESC
```

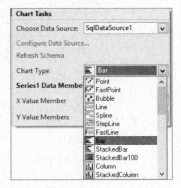

With that in place and the chart server control bound to this data source control, you now find that you have more options in the smart tag of the chart server control. This is presented in Figure 8-12.

Now you can select the series data members and choose what is on the x-axis and what is on the y-axis. I have assigned the Name of the product to be on the x-axis and the quantity ordered to be on the y-axis. After widening the chart's width a bit, you end up with code similar to the following as illustrated here in Listing 8-51.

FIGURE 8-12

LISTING 8-51: Charting with the new Chart server control

```
<%@ Register Assembly="System.Web.DataVisualization, Version=4.0.0.0,
    Culture=neutral, PublicKeyToken=31bf3856ad364e35"
    Namespace="System.Web.UI.DataVisualization.Charting" TagPrefix="asp" %>
<html xmlns="http://www.w3.org/1999/xhtml">
<head id="Head1" runat="server">
    <title>MultiView Server Control</title>
</head>
<body>
    <form id="form1" runat="server">
        <div>
            <asp:Chart ID="Chart1" runat="server"
                DataSourceID="SqlDataSource1"
                Width="500px">
                <Series>
                    <asp:Series ChartType="Bar" Name="Series1"
                        XValueMember="ProductName"
                        YValueMembers="UnitsInStock" YValuesPerPoint="2">
                    </asp:Series>
                </Series>
                <ChartAreas>
                    <asp:ChartArea Name="ChartArea1">
                    </asp:ChartArea>
                </ChartAreas>
            </asp:Chart>
            <asp:SqlDataSource ID="SqlDataSource1" runat="server"
                ConnectionString="<%$ ConnectionStrings:ConnectionString %>"
                SelectCommand="SELECT TOP(5) [ProductName], [UnitsInStock] FROM [Products]
                ORDER BY ProductName DESC"></asp:SqlDataSource>
        </div>
    </form>
</body>
</html>
```

From this, you can see that there isn't much code needed to wire everything up. Most notably, you can see that putting this Chart server control on your page actually added a @Register directive to the top of the page. This is unlike most of the ASP.NET server controls.

Within the <Series> element of this control, you can have as many series as you want, and this is something that is quite common when charting multiple items side by side (such as a time series of prices for two or more stocks).

Running this code, you get results similar to what is presented here in Figure 8-13.

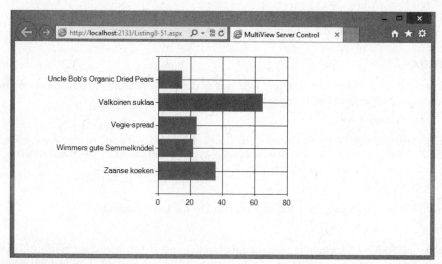

FIGURE 8-13

INLINE DATA-BINDING SYNTAX

Another feature of data binding in ASP.NET is inline data-binding syntax. Inline syntax in ASP.NET 1.0/1.1 was primarily relegated to templated controls such as the DataList or the Repeater controls, and even then it was sometimes difficult and confusing to make it work as you wanted it to. In ASP.NET 1.0/1.1, if you needed to use inline data binding, you might have created something like the procedure shown in Listing 8-52.

LISTING 8-52: USING DATABINDERS IN ASP.NET 1.0

```
<asp:Repeater ID="Repeater1" runat="server"
  DataSourceID="SqlDataSource1">
<HeaderTemplate>
  <table>
</HeaderTemplate>
<ItemTemplate>
  <tr>
   <td>
     <%# Container.DataItem("ProductID")%><BR/>
     <%# Container.DataItem("ProductName")%><BR/>
     <%# DataBinder.Eval(
         Container.DataItem, "UnitPrice", "{0:c}")%><br/>
   </td>
  </tr>
</ItemTemplate>
<FooterTemplate>
  </table>
</FooterTemplate>
</asp:Repeater>
```

As you can see in this example, you are using a Repeater control to display a series of employees. Because the Repeater control is a templated control, you use data binding to output the employee-specific data in the proper location of the template. Using the Eval method also allows you to provide formatting information such as Date or Currency formatting at render time.

In later versions of ASP.NET, the concept of inline data binding remains basically the same, but you are given a simpler syntax and several powerful binding tools to use.

Data-Binding Syntax

ASP.NET contains three ways to perform data binding. One way is that you can continue to use the existing method of binding, using the `Container.DataItem` syntax:

```
<%# Container.DataItem("Name") %>
```

This is good because it means you don't have to change your existing web pages if you are migrating from prior versions of ASP.NET. But if you are creating new web pages, you should probably use the simplest form of binding, which is to use the `Eval` method directly:

```
<%# Eval("Name") %>
```

You can also continue to format data using the formatter overload of the `Eval` method:

```
<%# Eval("HireDate", "{0:mm dd yyyy}" ) %>
```

In addition to these changes, ASP.NET includes a form of data binding called *two-way data binding*. Two-way data binding allows you to support both read and write operations for bound data. This is done using the `Bind` method, which, other than using a different method name, works just like the `Eval` method:

```
<%# Bind("Name") %>
```

The `Bind` method should be used in controls such as the GridView, DetailsView, or FormView, where autoupdates to the data source are implemented.

When working with the data-binding statements, remember that anything between the `<%# %>` delimiters is treated as an expression. This is important because it gives you additional functionality when data binding. For example, you could append additional data:

```
<%# "Foo " + Eval("Name") %>
```

Or you can even pass the evaluated value to a method:

```
<%# DoSomeProcess( Eval("Name") )%>
```

XML Data Binding

Because XML is so prevalent in applications, ASP.NET also includes several ways to bind specifically to XML data sources. These data-binding expressions give you powerful ways of working with the hierarchical format of XML. Additionally, except for the different method names, these binding methods work exactly the same as the `Eval` and `Bind` methods discussed earlier. These binders should be used when you are using the XmlDataSource control. The first binding format that uses the `XPathBinder` class is shown in the following code:

```
<% XPathBinder.Eval(Container.DataItem, "employees/employee/Name") %>
```

Notice that rather than specifying a column name as in the `Eval` method, the `XPathBinder` binds the result of an XPath query. Like the standard `Eval` expression, the XPath data-binding expression also has a shorthand format:

```
<% XPath("employees/employee/Name") %>
```

Also, like the `Eval` method, the XPath data-binding expression supports applying formatting to the data:

```
<% XPath("employees/employee/HireDate", "{0:mm dd yyyy}") %>
```

The `XPathBinder` returns a single node using the XPath query provided. Should you want to return multiple nodes from the XmlDataSource control, you can use the class's `Select` method. This method returns a list of nodes that match the supplied XPath query:

```
<% XPathBinder.Select(Container.DataItem,"employees/employee") %>
```

Or use the shorthand syntax:

```
<% XpathSelect("employees/employee") %>
```

USING EXPRESSIONS AND EXPRESSION BUILDERS

Expressions are statements that are parsed by ASP.NET at run time to return a data value. ASP.NET automatically uses expressions to do things like retrieve the database connection string when it parses the SqlDataSource control, so you may have already seen these statements in your pages. An example of the ConnectionString expression is shown in Listing 8-53.

LISTING 8-53: A CONNECTIONSTRING EXPRESSION

```
<asp:SqlDataSource ID="SqlDataSource1" Runat="server"
  SelectCommand="SELECT * FROM [Customers]"
  ConnectionString="<%$ ConnectionStrings:ConnectionString %>" />
```

When ASP.NET is attempting to parse an ASP.NET web page, it looks for expressions contained in the <%$ %> delimiters. This indicates to ASP.NET that this is an expression to be parsed. As shown in the previous listing, it attempts to locate the NorthwindConnectionString value from the web.config file. ASP.NET knows to do this because of the ConnectionStrings expression prefix, which tells ASP.NET to use the ConnectionStringsExpressionBuilder class to parse the expression.

ASP.NET includes several expression builders, including one for retrieving values from the AppSettings section of the web.config file, one for retrieving ConnectionStrings as shown in Listing 8-53, and one for retrieving localized resource file values. Listings 8-54 and 8-55 demonstrate using the AppSettingsExpressionBuilder and the ResourceExpressionBuilder.

LISTING 8-54: Using AppSettingsExpressionBuilder

```
<asp:Label runat="server" ID="Label1"
  Text="<%$ AppSettings: LabelText %>" />
```

LISTING 8-55: Using ResourceExpressionBuilder

```
<asp:Label runat="server" ID="Label1"
  Text="<%$ Resources: MyAppResources,Label1Text %>" />
```

In addition to using the expression builder classes, you can also create your own expressions by deriving a class from the System.Web.Compilation.ExpressionBuilder base class. This base class provides you with several methods you must override if you want ASP.NET to parse your expression properly. Listing 8-56 shows a simple custom expression builder.

LISTING 8-56: Using a simple custom expression builder

VB

```
<ExpressionPrefix("MyCustomExpression")>
<ExpressionEditor("MyCustomExpressionEditor")>
Public Class MyFirstCustomExpression
  Inherits ExpressionBuilder
    Public Overrides Function GetCodeExpression(
  ByVal entry As BoundPropertyEntry,
```

continues

LISTING 8-56 *(continued)*

```
      ByVal parsedData As Object,
      ByVal context As ExpressionBuilderContext) _
    As System.CodeDom.CodeExpression
        Return New CodeCastExpression("Int64",
      New CodePrimitiveExpression(1000))
  End Function
End Class
```

C#

```
[ExpressionPrefix("MyFirstCustomExpression")]
[ExpressionEditor("MyFirstCustomExpressionEditor")]
public class MyFirstCustomExpression : ExpressionBuilder
{
  public override System.CodeDom.CodeExpression
    GetCodeExpression(BoundPropertyEntry entry, object parsedData,
      ExpressionBuilderContext context)
  {
    return new CodeCastExpression("Int64",
      new CodePrimitiveExpression(1000));
  }
}
```

In examining this listing, notice several items. First, you have derived the `MyCustomExpression` class from `ExpressionBuilder` as discussed earlier. Second, you have overridden the `GetCodeExpression` method. This method supplies you with several parameters that can be helpful in executing this method, and it returns a `CodeExpression` object to ASP.NET that it can execute at run time to retrieve the data value.

> **NOTE** *The* `CodeExpression` *class is a base class in .NET's CodeDom infrastructure. Classes that are derived from the* `CodeExpression` *class provide abstracted ways of generating .NET code, whether VB or C#. This CodeDom infrastructure helps you create and run code dynamically at run time.*

The `BoundPropertyEntry` parameter entry tells you exactly which property the expression is bound to. For example, in Listings 8-54 and 8-55, the Label's `Text` property is bound to the `AppSettings` and `Resources` expressions. The object parameter `parsedData` contains any data that was parsed and returned by the `ParseExpression` method, which you see later on in the chapter. Finally, the `ExpressionBuilderContext` parameter context allows you to reference the virtual path or templated control associated with the expression.

In the body of the `GetCodeExpression` method, you are creating a new `CodeCastExpression` object, which is a class derived from the `CodeExpression` base class. The `CodeCastExpression` tells .NET to generate the appropriate code to execute a cast from one data type to another. In this case, you are casting the value `1000` to an `Int64` data type. When .NET executes the `CodeCastExpression`, it is (in a sense) writing the C# code `((long)(1000))` or (if your application was written in VB) `CType(1000,Long)`. Note that a wide variety of classes derive from the `CodeExpression` class that you can use to generate your final code expression.

The final lines to note are the two attributes that have been added to the class. The `ExpressionPrefix` and `ExpressionEditor` attributes help .NET determine that this class should be used as an expression, and they also help .NET locate the proper expression builder class when it comes time to parse the expression.

After you have created your expression builder class, you let .NET know about it. You do this by adding an `ExpressionBuilders` node to the compilation node in your `web.config` file. Notice that the value of the

`ExpressionPrefix` is added to the `ExpressionBuilder` to help ASP.NET locate the appropriate expression builder class at run time.

```
<compilation debug="true" strict="false" explicit="true">
  <expressionBuilders>
    <add expressionPrefix="MyCustomExpression" type="MyCustomExpression"/>
  </expressionBuilders>
</compilation>
```

The `GetCodeExpression` method is not the only member available for overriding in the `ExpressionBuilder` class. Several other useful members include the `ParseExpression`, `SupportsEvaluate`, and `EvaluateExpression` methods.

The `ParseExpression` method lets you pass parsed expression data into the `GetCodeExpression` method. For example, in Listing 8-56, the `CodeCastExpression` value `1000` was hard-coded. If, however, you want to allow a developer to pass that value in as part of the expression, you simply use the `ParseExpression` method as shown in Listing 8-57.

LISTING 8-57: Using ParseExpression

VB

```vb
<ExpressionPrefix("MyCustomExpression")>
<ExpressionEditor("MyCustomExpressionEditor")>
Public Class MySecondCustomExpression
  Inherits ExpressionBuilder
      Public Overrides Function GetCodeExpression(
    ByVal entry As BoundPropertyEntry,
    ByVal parsedData As Object,
    ByVal context As ExpressionBuilderContext) _
    As System.CodeDom.CodeExpression
        Return New CodeCastExpression("Int64",
      New CodePrimitiveExpression(parsedData))
  End Function
      Public Overrides Function ParseExpression(
    ByVal expression As String,
    ByVal propertyType As Type,
    ByVal context As ExpressionBuilderContext) As Object
        Return expression
  End Function
End Class
```

C#

```csharp
[ExpressionPrefix("MySecondCustomExpression")]
[ExpressionEditor("MySecondCustomExpressionEditor")]
public class MySecondCustomExpression : ExpressionBuilder
{
  public override System.CodeDom.CodeExpression
    GetCodeExpression(BoundPropertyEntry entry, object parsedData,
      ExpressionBuilderContext context)
  {
    return new CodeCastExpression("Int64",
      new CodePrimitiveExpression(parsedData));
  }
  public override object ParseExpression
    (string expression, Type propertyType,
     ExpressionBuilderContext context)
  {
    return expression;
  }
}
```

The last two `ExpressionBuilder` overrides to examine are the `SupportsEvaluate` and `EvaluateExpression` members. You need to override these methods if you are running your website in a no-compile scenario (you have specified `compilationMode = "never"` in your @Page directive). The `SupportEvaluate` property returns a `Boolean` indicating to ASP.NET whether this expression can be evaluated while a page is executing in no-compile mode. If `True` is returned and the page is executing in no-compile mode, the `EvaluateExpression` method is used to return the data value rather than the `GetCodeExpression` method. The `EvaluateExpression` returns an object representing the data value. See Listing 8-58.

LISTING 8-58: Overriding SupportsEvaluate and EvaluateExpression

VB

```vb
<ExpressionPrefix("MyCustomExpression")>
<ExpressionEditor("MyCustomExpressionEditor")>
Public Class MyThirdCustomExpression
  Inherits ExpressionBuilder
    Public Overrides Function GetCodeExpression(
    ByVal entry As BoundPropertyEntry,
    ByVal parsedData As Object,
    ByVal context As ExpressionBuilderContext) _
    As System.CodeDom.CodeExpression
       Return New CodeCastExpression("Int64",
    New CodePrimitiveExpression(parsedData))
  End Function
    Public Overrides Function ParseExpression(
    ByVal expression As String,
    ByVal propertyType As Type,
    ByVal context As ExpressionBuilderContext) As Object
       Return expression
  End Function
  Public Overrides ReadOnly Property SupportsEvaluate As Boolean
    Get
       Return True
    End Get
  End Property
    Public Overrides Function EvaluateExpression(
    ByVal target As Object,
    ByVal Entry As BoundPropertyEntry,
    ByVal parsedData As Object,
    ByVal context As ExpressionBuilderContext) As Object
       Return parsedData
  End Function
  End Class
```

C#

```csharp
[ExpressionPrefix("MyThirdCustomExpression")]
[ExpressionEditor("MyThirdCustomExpressionEditor")]
public class MyThirdCustomExpression : ExpressionBuilder
{
  public override System.CodeDom.CodeExpression
    GetCodeExpression(BoundPropertyEntry entry, object parsedData,
      ExpressionBuilderContext context)
  {
    return new CodeCastExpression("Int64",
      new CodePrimitiveExpression(parsedData));
  }

    public override object ParseExpression
    (string expression, Type propertyType,
     ExpressionBuilderContext context)
  {
```

```
        return expression;
    }

        public override bool SupportsEvaluate
    {
    get
    {
      return true;
    }
    }

        public override object EvaluateExpression(object target,
    BoundPropertyEntry entry, object parsedData,
    ExpressionBuilderContext context)
    {
      return parsedData;
    }
    }
}
```

As shown in Listing 8-58, you can simply return True from the SupportsEvaluate property if you want to override the EvaluateExpression method. Then all you do is return an object from the EvaluateExpression method.

SUMMARY

In this chapter, you examined data binding in ASP.NET. Data source controls such as LinqDataSource, SqlDataSource, and XmlDataSource make querying and displaying data from any number of data sources an almost trivial task. Using the data source controls' own wizards, you learned how easy it is to generate powerful data access functionality with almost no code.

You examined how even a beginning developer can easily combine the data source controls with the GridView, ListView, and DetailsView controls to create powerful data-manipulation applications with a minimal amount of coding.

You saw how ASP.NET includes a multitude of controls that can be data-bound, examining the features of the controls that are included in the ASP.NET toolbox, such as the GridView, TreeView, ListView, FormView, and Menu controls.

Finally, you looked at how the inline data-binding syntax has been improved and strengthened with the addition of the XML-specific data-binding expressions.

Model Binding

WROX.COM CODE DOWNLOADS FOR THIS CHAPTER

Please note that all the code examples in this chapter are available as a part of this chapter's code download on the book's website at www.wrox.com on the Download Code tab.

Model binding was introduced in ASP.NET MVC. Model binding made it easier to bring the data submitted by the client into a format that's suitable for use and validation on the server. Model binding was baked into the ASP.NET MVC 1.0 framework. When ASP.NET MVC 2.0 was released, a new system called "extensible model binding" was introduced. This gave developers more power and flexibility over how the client data is data-bound on the server.

Prior to ASP.NET 4.5 this system was available only in ASP.NET MVC. However, in ASP.NET 4.5 model binding can also be used for building ASP.NET Web Forms applications. The model binding system in ASP.NET4.5 Web Forms is based on the "extensible model binding" system.

In the last chapter you learned how data binding happens with data controls. In this chapter, you look at how you can do data binding with model binding and discover the benefits of using model binding.

MODEL BINDING

Model binding serves two purposes. It provides a way to fetch values from the client and bind them to a model. It also provides a validation mechanism whereby, once the model is bound, you can run validation rules to determine if the model is valid before saving the model. Model binding in ASP.NET Web Forms brings the power of model binding architecture to the controls and provides a system that allows developers to easily integrate patterns, such as PRG (Post-Redirect-Get), Repository, and so on, more easily. It also makes the application code cleaner and makes the application more unit-testable.

Model binding hooks into the existing data-bound controls. You can use model binding to extract the values from the control so that the client values can be used for inspection at the server, and the controls can bind to the values returned from the model binding system. Model binding works with existing data-bound controls so you can use the concepts you learned from the last chapter.

For example, imagine that you have a web page where a user can enter a person's detail using a DetailsView control. When a user enters the details and submits the form to the server, the model binding system extracts the values from the DetailsView control so you can perform some validation operations on the server. If the validation is successful, then you can save the person's detail in the database. In this case, the person is the model that the model binding system interacts with. A model can be either an ADO.NET Entity Framework model or an Entity Framework Code First model.

> **NOTE** *You can learn more about these models in Chapter 11.*

Let's look at some of the common data operations using model binding.

Selecting Data

Begin by creating a new Web Forms page and use a GridView control to select and filter customer data. Listing 9-1 shows how you can configure the GridView control to retrieve data using model binding. The control uses two new properties—ItemType and SelectMethod.

➤ ItemType tells the model binding system which type of model the control should bind to. The ItemType property is optional, but when you include it you get strongly typed IntelliSense for your data-binding expressions. You will look at these strongly typed controls in more detail later in this chapter.

➤ The SelectMethod property determines which method to call on the page to get the records. Listing 9-2 shows how a Select method looks.

LISTING 9-1: GridView using model binding

```
<asp:GridView ID="GridView1" runat="server" ItemType="Customer" AllowPaging="true"
AllowSorting="true" PageSize="2" SelectMethod="SelectCustomers"></asp:GridView>
```

LISTING 9-2: Example of the model binding Select method

VB

```
Dim _context As New CustomerContext()
    Public Function SelectCustomers() As IEnumerable(Of Customer)
        Return _context.Customer.AsEnumerable()
End Function
```

C#

```
CustomerContext _context = new CustomerContext();
    public IEnumerable<Customer> SelectCustomers()
    {
        return _context.Customer.AsEnumerable();
    }
```

In Listing 9-2, the Select method is returning a list of Customers. As shown in this listing we first instantiate CustomerContext, which is used when you are using Entity Framework Code First. When you instantiate a CustomerContext, you can access all the Customers and can perform any LINQ queries to filter the result as shown later in this section.

Paging

The GridView control has built-in paging and sorting features. Using model binding, you can take advantage of these features by returning an `IQueryable<T>` from the model binding `Select` method. Listing 9-3 shows you how to enable paging and sorting. To get paging and sorting, you need to enable paging and sorting on the GridView control as shown in Listing 9-1.

LISTING 9-3: Paging and sorting using model binding

VB

```vb
Private _context As New VB.CustomerContext()
    Public Function SelectCustomers() As IQueryable(Of VB.Customer)
        Return _context.Customer.AsQueryable()
End Function
```

C#

```csharp
CustomerContext _context = new CustomerContext();
    public IQueryable<Customer> SelectCustomers()
    {
        return _context.Customer.AsQueryable();
    }
```

In this listing you will notice that the `Select` method is returning an `IQueryable` instead of `IEnumerable`. GridView can automatically wire up sorting and paging functionality when `IQueryable<T>` is returned from the model binding `Select` method and sorting/paging is enabled on the GridView control.

Filtering

Often, you'll need to filter the results that you want to show the users. You don't want to return all the records of the table. In the last chapter, you learned how to filter data using the `Select` parameters in the SqlDataSource control. Filtering can be achieved in model binding by using `ValueProviders` and `ValueProvider` attributes. Listing 9-4 shows how you can filter data using values from `QueryString`. In this example, adding a query string such as `?ID=5` returns only records where the ID is 5.

LISTING 9-4: Filtering using QueryString

VB

```vb
Public Function SelectCustomers(<System.Web.ModelBinding.QueryString> id As
    System.Nullable(Of Integer)) As IEnumerable(Of VB.Customer)
        If id.HasValue Then
            Return _context.Customer.Where(Function(c) c.ID = id).AsEnumerable()
        Else
            Return _context.Customer.AsEnumerable()
        End If
End Function
```

C#

```csharp
public IEnumerable<Customer> SelectCustomers([System.Web.ModelBinding.QueryString] int? id)
    {
        if(id.HasValue)
            return _context.Customer.Where(c => c.ID == id).AsEnumerable();
        else
            return _context.Customer.AsEnumerable();
    }
```

When you pass in `ID=5` in the `QueryString`, the model binding system takes this value and provides it as a parameter to the `Select` method. Since we are using Entity Framework Code First, we can write a LINQ query to filter the list of customers whose ID is 5 and return the result to the GridView control.

Using Value Providers

Listing 9-4 shows how to use the `QueryString` value provider attribute to filter the results. This attribute tells the model binding system to bind a value from the query string to the `id` parameter at run time. The model binding system performs any type conversion as needed.

The value provider attributes eventually get the value from `ValueProviders` and tell the model binding system which `ValueProvider` to use. Table 9-1 shows the value provider attributes that you can use from the framework.

TABLE 9-1

VALUE PROVIDER ATTRIBUTES	DESCRIPTION
Form	The value is retrieved from the `Form` collection.
Control	The value is retrieved from the specified control.
QueryString	The value is retrieved from the `QueryString` collection.
Cookie	The value is retrieved from the `Cookie` collection.
Profile	The value is retrieved from the `Profile` collection.
RouteData	The value is retrieved from the `RouteData` collection.
Session	The value is retrieved from the `Session` collection.

Filtering Using Control

This section looks at an advanced example where you want to filter a result based on a value coming from another server control. You might often find the need to filter values based on a drop-down list, for example. Listing 9-5 shows how you can use the `Control` value provider attribute to retrieve the value from the drop-down list control. It then uses that value to filter the results and display them in a GridView control.

LISTING 9-5: Filtering using Control

```
<asp:DropDownList ID="DropDown1" runat="server" ItemType="Customer"
            SelectMethod="SelectCustomersForDropDownList" AppendDataBoundItems="true"
            AutoPostBack="true"
            DataTextField="ID" DataValueField="ID">
</asp:DropDownList>
<asp:GridView ID="GridView1" runat="server" ItemType="Customer"
            SelectMethod="SelectCustomers">
</asp:GridView>
```

VB

```
Public Function SelectCustomersForDropDownList() As IEnumerable(Of VB.Customer)
        Return _context.Customer.AsEnumerable()
    End Function
    Public Function SelectCustomers(<System.Web.ModelBinding.Control> DropDown1 As
        System.Nullable(Of Integer)) As IEnumerable(Of VB.Customer)
        If DropDown1.HasValue Then
            Return _context.Customer.Where(Function(c) c.ID = DropDown1).AsEnumerable()
        Else
```

```
              Return _context.Customer.AsEnumerable()
          End If
    End Function
```

C#

```csharp
public IEnumerable<Customer> SelectCustomers([System.Web.ModelBinding.Control] int? DropDown1)
    {
        if (DropDown1.HasValue)
            return _context.Customer.Where(c => c.ID == DropDown1).AsEnumerable();
        else
            return _context.Customer.AsEnumerable();
    }
public IEnumerable<Customer> SelectCustomersForDropDownList()
    {
        return _context.Customer.AsEnumerable();
    }
```

In this listing, when you select a value from the DropDownList control, the GridView gets bounded to the selected value of the DropDownList control. The model binding system takes in the selected value (ID in this case) of the DropDownList control and passes it as an argument to the SelectCustomers method using the Control value provider.

Inserting Data

Recall that, in ASP.NET 4.5, data-bound controls were updated to work with model binding. Now you will take a look at how you can use model binding to insert a record. You can use the DetailsView control to insert a record. On the control, you have to set a new property called InsertMethod, which can be called on the page. Listing 9-6 shows the insert method.

LISTING 9-6: Using the insert method with model binding

```
<asp:DetailsView runat="server" ItemType="Customer" SelectMethod="SelectCustomers"
     InsertMethod="InsertCustomer" AutoGenerateInsertButton="true" AllowPaging="true">
</asp:DetailsView>
```

VB

```vb
Public Sub InsertCustomer(customer As VB.Customer)
    _context = New VB.CustomerContext()
    If ModelState.IsValid Then
        _context.Customer.Add(customer)
    End If
End Sub
```

C#

```csharp
public void InsertCustomer(Customer customer)
    {
        _context = new CustomerContext()
        if(ModelState.IsValid)
        {
            _context.Customer.Add(customer);
        }
    }
```

If you take a closer look at InsertMethod, you will notice that the input to this method is a type called Customer. This is the type of the model that the DetailsView control was bound to. (This was specified via the ItemType property of the control.)

When you insert a value, the model binding system takes the values from the DetailsView control and populates the customer type model so the customer model can be used at the server for any kind of validation. Once the `InsertMethod` is called, you can perform a check to see if there were any validation errors in the model binding system. If everything was successful, then you can add this new `Customer` to the `Customer` collection and save it to the database.

Updating Data

The binding approach that we saw while inserting a record works with simple cases. However, the data control will often not be able to provide values for each member of the model, either because those members are relationship objects or they are not rendered in the control. In these cases, it's best to take in the primary key, load the model from the data storage, and tell the model binding system to bind the values from the data control to the model. Listing 9-7 shows how the update method would work for updating a record.

LISTING 9-7: Model binding update with PrimaryKey as the parameter

```
<asp:DetailsView runat="server" ItemType="Customer" SelectMethod="SelectCustomers"
        UpdateMethod="UpdateCustomer" AutoGenerateEditButton="true" DataKeyNames="ID"
        AllowPaging="true">
</asp:DetailsView>
```

VB

```vb
    Private _context As New VB.CustomerContext()

    Public Function SelectCustomers() As VB.Customer
        Return _context.Customer.First()
    End Function

Public Sub UpdateCustomer(id As Integer)
        _context = New VB.CustomerContext()
        Dim customer = _context.Customer.Where(Function(c) c.ID = id).First()
        TryUpdateModel(customer)
        If ModelState.IsValid Then

        End If
End Sub
```

C#

```csharp
CustomerContext _context = new CustomerContext();

    public Customer SelectCustomers()
    {
        return _context.Customer.First();
    }

    public void UpdateCustomer(int id)
    {
        _context = new CustomerContext();
        var customer = _context.Customer.Where(c => c.ID == id).First();
        TryUpdateModel(customer);
        if(ModelState.IsValid)
        {

        }
    }
```

Listing 9-7 showed how you can update a record. All data-bound controls have a property called `DataKeyNames` that uniquely identifies a record. This property has the names of the primary key fields. When the DetailsView control does an insert operation, the model binding system populates the parameter in the update method with the value of the `DataKeyNames` property. This parameter (id), which now holds the value of the primary key (ID), can be used to retrieve the particular record which was being updated by the user. When you call `TryUpdateModel`, the model binding system updates the values of the customer model with the ones specified by the user when he/she updated the record.

> **NOTE** *Just as you perform an update operation by setting the* `UpdateMethod` *property on the control, you can set the* `DeleteMethod` *to perform a delete operation, on the record.*

Validating Records in a Model Binding System

In the majority of cases, you would want to validate a record for some custom business logic before saving the record in the database. Model binding makes this scenario very easy to implement and results in a much cleaner implementation. If you are using business validation rules with `ObjectDataSource`, there is no easy way to propagate exceptions from the business layer back to the page. You end up throwing an exception in the business layer, which you catch in the control, and then you display a custom error message. This makes the code really messy.

The benefit of the model binding system is that it cleanly separates binding from validation. This means you can use custom validation very easily. The validation errors thrown from the model binding system are displayed through a validation summary, so this makes it easy to customize the UI and helps maintain clean code.

One benefit of enabling model binding in ASP.NET Web Forms is that you can plug in different validation mechanisms. For example, you can use data annotation attributes, which enable you to add attributes to signify some metadata about your model. The model binding system can use that metadata during validation. Listing 9-8 shows you how to tell the model binding system that the `FirstName` field is required.

LISTING 9-8: Adding data annotations

VB

```vb
<Required> _
       Public Property FirstName() As String
           Get
               Return m_FirstName
           End Get
           Set(value As String)
               m_FirstName = value
           End Set
   End Property
```

C#

```csharp
[Required()]
public string FirstName { get; set; }
```

In this case, if you do not enter a value for the `FirstName` field, the call to `TryUpdateModel()` will return `false`. If you have a ValidationSummary control on the page, then you will get the error message displayed in the validation summary. Listing 9-9 shows how you can configure the ValidationSummary control to show errors from the model binding system. The other way to check for any validation errors is to check the `ModelState` property of the page. This property is populated by the model binding system in case any errors happened during model binding.

LISTING 9-9: Configuring the ValidationSummary control to show errors
from the model binding system

```
<asp:ValidationSummary runat="server" ShowModelStateErrors="true" />
```

Separating Business Logic from the page

So far you have been calling the model binding methods on the page. Although this is the more common way to do it, it does result in a lot of code in the page code-behind. The page has to deal with UI logic and business logic. In the last chapter with `ObjectDataSource`, the business logic was in a separate class and the page code dealt only with the UI. Listing 9-10 shows how you can do this in model binding. You have to tell the model binding system where to load the model binding methods. This is done by overriding the `OnCallingDataMethods` method of the data-bound control. The model binding system will then instantiate the `repository` class and will look for the methods in the class. This approach leads to a much cleaner application logic that's more easily testable.

LISTING 9-10: Separating business logic from the page

VB

```vb
Protected Sub GridView1_CallingDataMethods(sender As Object, e As CallingDataMethodsEventArgs)
        e.DataMethodsObject = New VB.CustomerRepository()
End Sub
```

C#

```csharp
protected void GridView1_CallingDataMethods(object sender, CallingDataMethodsEventArgs e)
{
        e.DataMethodsObject = new CustomerRepository();
}
```

USING STRONGLY TYPED CONTROLS

ASP.NET 2.0 Web Forms introduced the concept of templated controls. Templates allow you to customize the markup emitted from server controls and are typically used with data-binding expressions. This section looks at the improvements that have happened in ASP.NET 4.5 to make data binding and HTML encoding easier.

In ASP.NET 2.0 one-way data binding was accomplished with the `Eval()` and `Bind()` helpers. These helpers do a late binding to the data. Listing 9-11 shows how the `Eval()` helper is used.

LISTING 9-11: Data-binding helpers

```
<asp:FormView ID="editCustomer" runat="server">
    <ItemTemplate>
        <div>
            First Name:<%# Eval("FirstName") %>
        </div>
    </ItemTemplate>
</asp:FormView>
```

One drawback of this approach is that since these expressions are late bound, you have to pass in a string to represent the property name. This means you do not get IntelliSense for member names, support for code navigation (like Go To Definition), or compile-time checking support.

When a control is strongly typed, it means that you can declare which type of data the control is going to be bound to, by way of a new property called `ItemType`. When you set this property, the control will have two new properties for the bind expressions—`Item` and `BindItem`.

Item is equivalent to `Eval()`, whereas `BindItem` is equivalent to `Bind()`. Listing 9-12 shows an example of strongly typed controls.

```
<asp:FormView ID="editCustomer" runat="server" ItemType="Customer"
  SelectMethod="SelectCustomer" >
    <ItemTemplate>
        <div>
            First Name:<%# Item.FirstName %>
        </div>
    </ItemTemplate>
</asp:FormView>
```

If you are in Visual Studio and you type `BindItem`, as shown in Listing 9-12, you will get IntelliSense for all the properties in the model `Customer`, as shown in Figure 9-1. If you make a mistake while typing, you will get an error in Visual Studio.

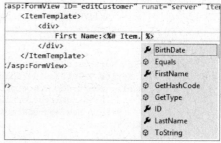

EXTENDING MODEL BINDING

While ASP.NET Web Forms has always been a great web development framework, it has been a bit painful to customize and extend the framework. However, the Model Binding

FIGURE 9-1

system is built in such a way that you can easily customize and extend the model binding system to match your development scenarios. In this section you will learn about customizing value providers and model binders. In the end you will look at extending the `ModelDataSource` to control the workings of the model binding system.

Custom Value Providers

So far you have looked at the `ValueProviders` and `ValueProvider` attributes. These provide basic support for specifying where the model binding system should fetch the value from. However, there are cases when you really don't know where the value might come from, or you want to write your application so you have a fallback mechanism—you want to allow the value to come from `Form collection` or `QueryString collection`. In this case, you can write your own value provider attribute and value provider to take care of this scenario. Listing 9-13 shows what such a custom value provider and value provider attribute would look like.

VB

```
Public Class AggregateValueProvider
        Implements IValueProvider
        Implements IUnvalidatedValueProvider
        Private ReadOnly _valueProviders As New List(Of IUnvalidatedValueProvider)()

        Public Sub New(modelBindingExecutionContext As ModelBindingExecutionContext)
            _valueProviders.Add(New FormValueProvider(modelBindingExecutionContext))
            _valueProviders.Add(New QueryStringValueProvider(modelBindingExecutionContext))
        End Sub

        Public Function ContainsPrefix(prefix As String) As Boolean Implements
          IValueProvider.ContainsPrefix
            Return _valueProviders.Any(Function(vp) vp.ContainsPrefix(prefix))
```

continues

LISTING 9-13 *(continued)*

```vb
        End Function

        Public Function GetValue(key As String) As ValueProviderResult Implements
          IValueProvider.GetValue
            Return GetValue(key, False)
        End Function

        Public Function GetValue(key As String, skipValidation As Boolean) As
          ValueProviderResult Implements IUnvalidatedValueProvider.GetValue
            Return _valueProviders.[Select](Function(vp) vp.GetValue(key,
              skipValidation)).LastOrDefault()
        End Function
    End Class

    Public Class AggregateValueAttribute
        Inherits ValueProviderSourceAttribute
        Public Overrides Function GetValueProvider(modelBindingExecutionContext As
          ModelBindingExecutionContext) As IValueProvider
            Return New AggregateValueProvider(modelBindingExecutionContext)
        End Function
    End Class
```

C#

```csharp
public class AggregateValueProvider : IValueProvider, IUnvalidatedValueProvider
{
    private readonly List<IUnvalidatedValueProvider> _valueProviders = new
      List<IUnvalidatedValueProvider>();

    public AggregateValueProvider(ModelBindingExecutionContext modelBindingExecutionContext)
    {
        _valueProviders.Add(new FormValueProvider(modelBindingExecutionContext))
        _valueProviders.Add(new QueryStringValueProvider(modelBindingExecutionContext));
    }

    public bool ContainsPrefix(string prefix)
    {
        return _valueProviders.Any(vp => vp.ContainsPrefix(prefix));
    }

    public ValueProviderResult GetValue(string key)
    {
        return GetValue(key, false);
    }

    public ValueProviderResult GetValue(string key, bool skipValidation)
    {
        return _valueProviders.Select(vp => vp.GetValue(key, skipValidation))
            .LastOrDefault();
    }
}

public class AggregateValueAttribute : ValueProviderSourceAttribute
{
    public override IValueProvider GetValueProvider(ModelBindingExecutionContext
      modelBindingExecutionContext)
    {
        return new AggregateValueProvider(modelBindingExecutionContext);
    }
}
```

This listing shows a value provider and a value provider attribute that will use this provider. The value provider adds a `Form` and `QueryString` value provider as its sources. This means that when the model binding system calls into this custom value provider, the custom value provider will first check the `Form` collection to retrieve the value, and if there is no value found, then the `QueryString` collection will be checked. Listing 9-14 shows how you can use this custom value provider in your application.

LISTING 9-14: Using a custom value provider

VB

```vb
Private _context As New VB.CustomerContext()
    Public Function SelectCustomers(<VB.AggregateValue> id As System.Nullable(Of Integer))
      As IEnumerable(Of VB.Customer)
        If id.HasValue Then
            Return _context.Customer.Where(Function(c) c.ID = id).AsEnumerable()
        Else
            Return _context.Customer.AsEnumerable()
        End If
    End Function
```

C#

```csharp
CustomerContext _context = new CustomerContext();
    public IEnumerable<Customer> SelectCustomers([AggregateValue] int? id)
    {
        if(id.HasValue)
        return _context.Customer.Where(c => c.ID == id).AsEnumerable();
        else
            return _context.Customer.AsEnumerable();
    }
```

As shown in this listing, you can use your custom value provider by specifying a custom value provider attribute that you defined for your own value provider. The `AggregateValue` attribute works the same way as other value provider attributes such as `QueryString`. The model binding system calls into the `AggregateValue` attribute to bind the value of the parameter `id`. The `AggregateValue` attribute calls into `AggregateValueProvider` to get the value of the parameter `id`.

Custom Model Binders

The implementation of model binding in ASP.NET 4.5 provides support for different kinds of data types. Although the basic implementation takes care of binding to the commonly used data types, there are cases when the model binding system cannot bind to a specific data type. In this case you can write your own model binder and plug it into the model binding system. Whenever the model binding tries to bind a model of this type, your custom model binder will then be called to fetch and save the values and populate the model.

Consider, for example, if you needed to change the behavior of how the out-of-the-box model binders bind the data to a model (such as for `DateTime` types). You want to store the date and time separately or in a different locale format. You can achieve this by implementing your own custom model binder. Because the implementation of the Web Forms model binding system is based on extensible model binding, making this change is really easy. Listing 9-15 shows a custom implementation of a model binder.

To implement a custom model binder, you have to implement a *provider* and a *binder*.

> A **provider** is called by the model binding system to check if the provider can handle a particular type. In the examples in Listings 9-15 and 9-16, you can see the `DateTime` type is being handled. When the provider is called and if the provider can handle the `DateTime` type, the provider calls the binder.

> The **binder** is responsible for parsing the value from the model binding system and populating the model.

LISTING 9-15: Implementing a custom model binder

VB

```vb
Public Class MyDateTimeBinder
        Implements IModelBinder
        Public Function BindModel(modelBindingExecutionContext As ModelBindingExecutionContext,
          bindingContext As ModelBindingContext) As Boolean Implements IModelBinder.BindModel
            Dim valueProviderResult = bindingContext.ValueProvider.GetValue
              (bindingContext.ModelName)
            Dim inputdate = If(valueProviderResult IsNot Nothing,
              valueProviderResult.AttemptedValue, Nothing)
            Dim newDate As New DateTime()
            Dim success As Boolean = DateTime.TryParse(inputdate, CultureInfo.GetCultureInfo
              ("en-GB"), DateTimeStyles.None, newDate)
            bindingContext.Model = newDate
            Return bindingContext.Model IsNot Nothing
        End Function
End Class

Public Class MyDateTimeProvider
        Inherits System.Web.ModelBinding.ModelBinderProvider
        Public Overrides Function GetBinder(modelBindingExecutionContext As
          ModelBindingExecutionContext, bindingContext As ModelBindingContext) As IModelBinder
            If bindingContext.ModelType = GetType(DateTime) Then
                Return New MyDateTimeBinder()
            End If
            Return Nothing
        End Function
End Class
```

C#

```csharp
public class MyDateTimeBinder : IModelBinder
{
    public bool BindModel(ModelBindingExecutionContext modelBindingExecutionContext,
      ModelBindingContext bindingContext)
    {
        var valueProviderResult = bindingContext.ValueProvider.GetValue
          (bindingContext.ModelName);
        var inputdate = valueProviderResult != null ? valueProviderResult.AttemptedValue
          : null;
        DateTime dt = new DateTime();
        bool success = DateTime.TryParse(inputdate, CultureInfo.GetCultureInfo("en-GB"),
          DateTimeStyles.None, out dt);
        bindingContext.Model = dt;
        return bindingContext.Model != null;
    }
}
public class MyDateTimeProvider : System.Web.ModelBinding.ModelBinderProvider
{
    public override IModelBinder GetBinder(ModelBindingExecutionContext
      modelBindingExecutionContext, ModelBindingContext bindingContext)
    {
        if (bindingContext.ModelType == typeof(DateTime))
            return new MyDateTimeBinder();
        return null;
    }
}
```

When the model binding system tries to bind data to a model, it looks through a list of registered providers to see which provider can find a binder to bind a value for a specific type. The registered providers are called in order. You can register your provider as the first one if you are not implementing a generic solution and are not concerned about the fallback behavior in case it can't find a binder for a particular type. Listing 9-16 shows how you can register the model binder with the application.

LISTING 9-16: Registering a custom model binder provider

VB

```
System.Web.ModelBinding.ModelBinderProviders.Providers.Insert(0, NEW MyDateTimeProvider())
```

C#

```
System.Web.ModelBinding.ModelBinderProviders.Providers.Insert(0, new MyDateTimeProvider());
```

Custom ModelDataSource

At the heart of the implementation, the model binding system in Web Forms is based on data controls. The implementation uses the extensible model binding and the controls architecture. Model binding is implemented as a data source called `ModelDataSource`, which implements `IDataSource`. This is the same pattern followed by other `ObjectDataSource` objects. For example, there is also a `ModelDataSourceView` object, which has the logic of executing select, insert, update, and delete calls from the data controls.

This means that this implementation is fully extensible. If you want to override the behavior of how the select calls happen, then you can write your own `ModelDataSource` and `ModelDataSourceView` objects and plug them into the model binding system. This is useful if you want to extend the model binding system to make scenarios such as master-detail binding easier to implement.

Listing 9-17 shows how you can implement custom `ModelDataSource` and `ModelDataSourceView` objects. This custom implementation returns only the first three rows in the table, but it can be easily expanded for more complex scenarios.

LISTING 9-17: Implementing custom ModelDataSouce

VB

```
Public Class MyModelView
        Inherits ModelDataSourceView
        Private ReadOnly _owner As MyModelDataSource

        Public Sub New(owner As MyModelDataSource)
            MyBase.New(owner)
            _owner = owner
        End Sub
        Protected Overrides Function ExecuteSelect(arguments As DataSourceSelectArguments)
          As IEnumerable
            Dim _context As New CustomerContext()
            Return _context.Customer.Take(3).AsEnumerable()
        End Function
End Class

Public Class MyModelDataSource
        Inherits ModelDataSource
        Private _view As MyModelView

        Public Sub New(dataControl As Control)

            MyBase.New(dataControl)
```

continues

LISTING 9-17 *(continued)*

```
            End Sub
        Public Overrides ReadOnly Property View() As ModelDataSourceView
            Get
                If _view Is Nothing Then
                    _view = New MyModelView(Me)
                End If
                Return _view
            End Get
        End Property
    End Class
```

C#

```csharp
public class MyModelView : ModelDataSourceView
{
        private readonly MyModelDataSource _owner;

        public MyModelView(MyModelDataSource owner)
            : base(owner)
        {
            _owner = owner;
        }
        protected override IEnumerable ExecuteSelect(DataSourceSelectArguments arguments)
        {
            CustomerContext _context = new CustomerContext();
            return _context.Customer.Take(3).AsEnumerable();
            //return _context.Customer.Distinct<Customer>().AsEnumerable();
        }
}

public class MyModelDataSource : ModelDataSource
{
        private MyModelView _view;

        public MyModelDataSource(Control dataControl)
            : base(dataControl)
        {

        }
        public override ModelDataSourceView View
        {
            get
            {
                if (_view == null)
                {
                    _view = new MyModelView(this);
                }
                return _view;
            }
        }
}
```

Listing 9-18 shows how you can use this custom ModelDataSource in your application. On the data control, you can override the ModelDataSource that the control should use by overriding an event called OnCreatingModelDataSource.

LISTING 9-18: Calling the custom ModelDataSource

VB

```
Protected Sub GridView1_CreatingModelDataSource(sender As Object, e As
  CreatingModelDataSourceEventArgs)
      e.ModelDataSource = New VB.MyModelDataSource(DirectCast(sender, GridView))
    End Sub
```

C#

```
protected void GridView1_CreatingModelDataSource(object sender,
  CreatingModelDataSourceEventArgs e)
    {
        e.ModelDataSource = new CS.MyModelDataSource((GridView)sender);
    }
```

SUMMARY

The model binding system is the next step in the data-binding story for Web Forms. It uses the power and flexibility of the extensible model binding system and combines it with the power of data controls, which makes application development easy. This also leads to a cleaner implementation, which supports paradigms such as unit testing and IOC containers.

Model binding makes data access more code focused and allows you to reuse the data annotation attributes across ASP.NET. You can use value providers to ease filtering scenarios. Lastly, you saw how you can customize and extend the model binding system for custom binding and selection, which makes this framework very easy to adapt.

10

Querying with LINQ

WHAT'S IN THIS CHAPTER?

➤ Exploring the different types of LINQ queries
➤ Understanding the limitations of traditional query methods
➤ Simplifying query operations with LINQ

WROX.COM CODE DOWNLOADS FOR THIS CHAPTER

Please note that all the code examples in this chapter are available as a part of this chapter's code download on the book's website at www.wrox.com on the Download Code tab.

.NET 3.5 introduced a new technology called Language Integrated Query, or LINQ (pronounced "link"). Since that time LINQ has continued to become an integral technology in .NET development. In both .NET 4.0 and .NET 4.5, Microsoft has continued to provide updates to LINQ to enhance its performance. LINQ is designed to fill the gap that exists between traditional .NET languages, which offer strong typing and object-oriented development, and query languages such as SQL, with syntax specifically designed for query operations. With the introduction of LINQ into the .NET Framework, the query becomes a first-class concept in .NET, whether you are talking about object, XML, or database queries.

Although it is extensible and can be extended to other sources of data, LINQ includes three basic types of queries: LINQ to Objects; LINQ to XML; and LINQ used in the context of databases, like LINQ to SQL or LINQ to Entities. Each type of query offers specific capabilities and is designed to query a specific source of data.

This chapter offers a look at all of the above types of LINQ queries including both LINQ to SQL and LINQ to Entities , and how each enables you to simplify query operations. It also covers some language features of the .NET CLR that you use to create LINQ queries, as well as the tooling support in Visual Studio to support using LINQ.

> **NOTE** *While this chapter focuses primarily on the LINQ capabilities included in the .NET Framework, LINQ is highly extensible and can be used to create query frameworks over just about any data source. How to implement your own LINQ provider is beyond the scope of this chapter. There are many custom implementations of LINQ used to query a wide variety of data stores such as LDAP, SharePoint, and even Amazon.com. Roger Jennings from Oakleaf Systems maintains a list of third-party LINQ providers on his blog at* `http://oakleafblog.blogspot.com/2007/03/third-party-linq-providers.html`*.*

LINQ TO OBJECTS

The first and most basic flavor of LINQ is LINQ to Objects. LINQ to Objects enables you to perform complex query operations against any enumerable object (any object that implements the `IEnumerable` interface). Although the notion of creating enumerable objects that can be queried or sorted is not new to .NET, doing this in versions prior to version 3.5 usually required a significant amount of code. Often that code would end up being so complex that it would be hard for other developers to read and understand, making it difficult to maintain.

Understanding Traditional Query Methods

In order to understand how LINQ improves your ability to query collections, you need to understand how querying is done without it. To do this, take a look at how you might create a simple query that includes a group and sort without using LINQ. Listing 10-1 shows a simple `Movie` class you can use as the basis of these examples.

LISTING 10-1: A Basic Movie class

VB

```vb
Imports Microsoft.VisualBasic

    Public Class Movie
        Public Property Title() As String
        Public Property Director() As String
        Public Property Genre() As Integer
        Public Property Runtime() As Integer
        Public Property ReleaseDate() As DateTime
    End Class
```

C#

```csharp
using System;

public class Movie
{
    public string Title { get; set; }
    public string Director { get; set; }
    public int Genre { get; set; }
    public int RunTime { get; set; }
    public DateTime ReleaseDate { get; set; }
}
```

This basic class is used throughout this section and the following LINQ to Object section.

Now that you have a basic class to work with, it's time to look at how you would normally use the class. Listing 10-2 demonstrates how to create a simple generic list of the Movie objects in an ASP.NET page and then bind that list to a GridView control. The code sample provided for this chapter includes more Movie entries than is shown in Listing 10-2. The GridView displays the values of all public properties exposed by the Movie class. (Note that you need to change the formatting of the dates to what works with the locale of your development machine for this example to work.)

LISTING 10-2: Generating a list of Movie objects and binding to a GridView

VB

```vb
<%@ Page Language="VB" %>
<%@ Import Namespace="System.Collections.Generic" %>

<script runat="server">
  Protected Sub Page_Load(ByVal sender As Object, ByVal e As System.EventArgs)
    Dim movies = GetMovies()

    Me.GridView1.DataSource = movies
    Me.GridView1.DataBind()
  End Sub

  Public Function GetMovies() As List(Of Movie)
   Dim movies As New List(Of Movie) From { _
     New Movie With {.Title = "Shrek", .Director = "Andrew Adamson", _
        .Genre = 0, .ReleaseDate = DateTime.Parse("5/16/2001"), _
        .Runtime = 89}, _
     New Movie With {.Title = "Fletch", .Director = "Michael Ritchie", _
        .Genre = 0, .ReleaseDate = DateTime.Parse("5/31/1985"), _
        .Runtime = 96}, _
     New Movie With {.Title = "Casablanca", .Director = "Michael Curtiz", _
        .Genre = 1, .ReleaseDate = DateTime.Parse("1/1/1942"), _
        .Runtime = 102}, _
     New Movie With {.Title = "Batman", .Director = "Tim Burton", _
        .Genre = 1, .ReleaseDate = DateTime.Parse("6/23/1989"), _
        .Runtime = 126} _
      }

    Return movies

  End Function
</script>

<html>
<head runat="server">
  <title>My Favorite Movies</title>
</head>
<body>
  <form id="form1" runat="server">
  <div>
    <asp:GridView ID="GridView1" runat="server">
    </asp:GridView>
  </div>
  </form>
</body>

</html>
```

continues

LISTING 10-2 *(continued)*

C#

```csharp
<script runat="server">

  protected void Page_Load(object sender, EventArgs e)
  {
    var movies = GetMovies();

    this.GridView1.DataSource = movies;
    this.GridView1.DataBind();
  }

  public List<Movie> GetMovies()
  {
    return new List<Movie> {
      new Movie { Title="Shrek", Director="Andrew Adamson", Genre=0,
        ReleaseDate=DateTime.Parse("5/16/2001"), RunTime=89 },
      new Movie { Title="Fletch", Director="Michael Ritchie", Genre=0,
        ReleaseDate=DateTime.Parse("5/31/1985"), RunTime=96 },
      new Movie { Title="Casablanca", Director="Michael Curtiz", Genre=1,
        ReleaseDate=DateTime.Parse("1/1/1942"), RunTime=102 },
      new Movie { Title="Batman", Director="Tim Burton", Genre=1,
        ReleaseDate=DateTime.Parse("6/23/1989"), RunTime=126 }
    };
  }
</script>
```

Running the sample generates a typical ASP.NET web page that includes a simple grid showing all the `Movie` data on it.

Now, what happens when you want to start performing queries on the list of movies? For example, you might want to filter this data to show only a specific genre of movie. Listing 10-3 shows a typical way you might perform this filtering.

LISTING 10-3: Filtering the list of Movie objects

VB

```vb
Protected Sub Page_Load(ByVal sender As Object, ByVal e As System.EventArgs)
  Dim movies = GetMovies()

  Dim query As New List(Of Movie)()
  For Each m In movies
    If (m.Genre = 0) Then
      query.Add(m)
    End If
  Next

  Me.GridView1.DataSource = query
  Me.GridView1.DataBind()
End Sub
```

C#

```csharp
protected void Page_Load(object sender, EventArgs e)
{
  var movies = GetMovies();

  var query = new List<Movie>();
  foreach (var m in movies)
  {
```

```
        if (m.Genre == 0) query.Add(m);
    }

    this.GridView1.DataSource = query;
    this.GridView1.DataBind();
}
```

As this sample shows, to filter the data so that the page displays movies in a specific genre only requires the creation of a new temporary collection and the use of a `foreach` loop to iterate through the data.

Although this technique seems easy enough, it still requires that you define what you want done (find all movies in the genre) and also that you explicitly define how it should be done (use a temporary collection and a `foreach` loop). Additionally, what happens when you need to perform more complex queries, involving grouping or sorting? Now the complexity of the code dramatically increases, as shown in Listing 10-4.

LISTING 10-4: Grouping and sorting the list of Movie objects

VB

```
Public Class Grouping
  Public Property Genre() As Integer
  Public Property MovieCount() As Integer
End Class

Protected Sub Page_Load(ByVal sender As Object, ByVal e As System.EventArgs)
  Dim movies = GetMovies()

  Dim groups As New Dictionary(Of String, Grouping)

  For Each m In movies

    If (Not groups.ContainsKey(m.Genre)) Then
      groups(m.Genre) = _
        New Grouping With {.Genre = m.Genre, .MovieCount = 0}
    End If

    groups(m.Genre).MovieCount = groups(m.Genre).MovieCount + 1
  Next

  Dim results As New List(Of Grouping)(groups.Values)
  results.Sort(AddressOf MovieSort)

  Me.GridView1.DataSource = results
  Me.GridView1.DataBind()
End Sub

Private Function MovieSort(ByVal x As Grouping, ByVal y As Grouping) As Integer
  Return IIf(x.MovieCount > y.MovieCount, -1, _
    IIf(x.MovieCount < y.MovieCount, 1, 0))
End Function
```

C#

```
public class Grouping
{
  public int Genre { get; set; }
  public int MovieCount { get; set; }
}

protected void Page_Load(object sender, EventArgs e)
{
```

continues

LISTING 10-4 *(continued)*

```
var movies = GetMovies();

Dictionary<int, Grouping> groups = new Dictionary<int, Grouping>();
foreach (Movie m in movies)
{
  if (!groups.ContainsKey(m.Genre))
  {
    groups[m.Genre] = new Grouping { Genre = m.Genre, MovieCount = 0 };
  }
  groups[m.Genre].MovieCount++;
}

List<Grouping> results = new List<Grouping>(groups.Values);
results.Sort(delegate(Grouping x, Grouping y)
{
  return
    x.MovieCount > y.MovieCount ? -1 :
    x.MovieCount < y.MovieCount ? 1 :
    0;
});
this.GridView1.DataSource = results;
this.GridView1.DataBind();
}
```

To group the movie data into genres and count how many movies are in each genre requires the addition of a new class, the creation of a `Dictionary`, and the implementation of a delegate—all fairly complex requirements for such a seemingly simple task. And again, not only do you have to define very specifically what you want done, but also very explicitly how it should be done.

Additionally, because the complexity of the code increases so much, actually determining what this code is doing becomes quite difficult. Consider this: What if you were asked to modify this code in an existing application that you were unfamiliar with? How long would it take you to figure out what it was doing?

Replacing Traditional Queries with LINQ

LINQ was created to address many of the shortcomings of querying collections of objects that were discussed in the previous section. Rather than requiring you to very specifically define exactly how you want a query to execute, LINQ gives you the power to stay at a more abstract level. By defining what you want the query to return, you leave it up to .NET and its compilers to determine the specifics of exactly how the query will run.

In the preceding section, you looked at how you would query collections of objects without the aid of LINQ. In this section, you take a look at LINQ and see how using it can greatly simplify these queries, as well as other types of queries. The samples in this section start out by modifying the samples from the previous section to show you how easy LINQ makes the same tasks.

Before you get started, understand that LINQ is an extension to the core .NET Framework and, therefore, is isolated in its own set of assemblies. The base LINQ functionality is located in the `System.Core.dll` assembly. This assembly does not replace any existing .NET Framework functionality, but augments it. Additionally, by default, projects in Visual Studio include a reference to this assembly so when starting a new ASP.NET web project, LINQ should be readily available to you.

Basic LINQ Queries and Projections

If you remember, the basic sample in Listing 10-2 generates a generic list of movies and binds the list to a GridView control. Listing 10-5 shows how the code can be modified to use LINQ to query the movies list and bind the resulting set of data to the GridView.

LISTING 10-5: Creating a query with LINQ

VB

```
Protected Sub Page_Load(ByVal sender As Object, ByVal e As System.EventArgs)
  Dim movies = GetMovies()

  Dim query = From m In movies _
        Select m

  Me.GridView1.DataSource = query
  Me.GridView1.DataBind()
End Sub
```

C#

```
protected void Page_Load(object sender, EventArgs e)
{
  var movies = GetMovies();

  var query = from m in movies
        select m;

  this.GridView1.DataSource = query;
  this.GridView1.DataBind();
}
```

If you deconstruct the code sample, you can see three basic actions happening. First, the code uses the `GetMovies()` method to obtain the generic `List<Movie>` collection.

Next, the code uses a very simple LINQ query to select all the `Movie` objects from the generic `movies` collection. Notice that this specific LINQ query utilizes language keywords like `from` and `select` in the query statement. These syntax additions are first-class members of the .NET languages; therefore, Visual Studio can offer you development assistance, such as strong type checking and IntelliSense, which makes finding and fixing problems in your code easier.

The query also defines a new variable `m`. This variable is used in two ways in the query. First, by defining it in the `from` statement, `from m`, you are instructing LINQ to use the variable `m` to represent the individual collection item, which in this case is a `Movie` object. Telling LINQ this enables it to understand the structure of the objects you are querying and, as you will see later, also gives you IntelliSense to help create the query.

The second use of `m` in the query is in the `select` statement. Using `m` in the `select` statement tells LINQ to output a projection that matches the structure of `m`. *Projection* refers to the operation of transforming an object into a new form that often consists only of those properties that you need for your particular purposes. In this case, that means LINQ creates a projection that matches the `Movie` object structure.

You could have just as easily created your own custom projection by explicitly defining the fields you wanted returned from the query using the new keyword along with the `select` operator, as shown in Listing 10-6.

LISTING 10-6: Creating a custom projection with LINQ

VB

```
Protected Sub Page_Load(ByVal sender As Object, ByVal e As System.EventArgs)
  Dim movies = GetMovies()

  Dim query = From m In movies _
        Select New With {m.Title, m.Genre}
```

continues

LISTING 10-6 *(continued)*

```
    Me.GridView1.DataSource = query
    Me.GridView1.DataBind()
End Sub
```

C#

```
protected void Page_Load(object sender, EventArgs e)
{
  var movies = GetMovies();

  var query = from m in movies
        select new { m.Title, m.Genre };

  this.GridView1.DataSource = query;
  this.GridView1.DataBind();
}
```

Notice that rather than selecting m, you have defined a new projection containing only the `Title` and `Genre` values.

You can even go so far as to explicitly define the field names that the objects in the resulting set of data will expose. For example, you may want to more explicitly name the `Title` and `Genre` fields to more fully describe their contents. Using LINQ, this naming task is easy, as shown in Listing 10-7.

LISTING 10-7: Creating custom projection field names

VB

```
Protected Sub Page_Load(ByVal sender As Object, ByVal e As System.EventArgs)
  Dim movies = GetMovies()

  Dim query = From m In movies _
        Select New With {.MovieTitle = m.Title, .MovieGenre = m.Genre}

  Me.GridView1.DataSource = query
  Me.GridView1.DataBind()
End Sub
```

C#

```
protected void Page_Load(object sender, EventArgs e)
{
  var movies = GetMovies();

  var query = from m in movies
        select new { MovieTitle = m.Title, MovieGenre = m. Genre };

  this.GridView1.DataSource = query;
  this.GridView1.DataBind();
}
```

This sample explicitly defined the fields that will be exposed by the resultset as `MovieTitle` and `MovieGenre`. You can see in Figure 10-1 that because of this change, the column headers in the GridView have changed to match.

MovieTitle	MovieGenre
Shrek	0
Fletch	0
Casablanca	1
Batman	1
Dances with Wolves	1
Dirty Dancing	1
The Parent Trap	0
Ransom	1
Ocean's Eleven	1
Steel Magnolias	1
Mystic Pizza	1
Pretty Woman	1
Interview with the Vampire	1
Top Gun	2
Mission Impossible	2
The Godfather	1
Carlito's Way	1

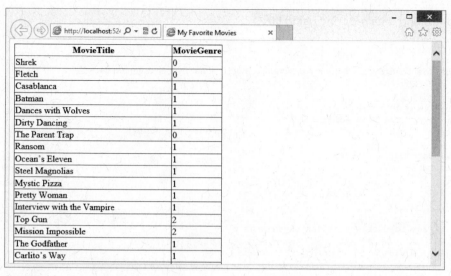

FIGURE 10-1

Finally, the code binds the GridView control to the enumerable list of `Movie` objects returned by the LINQ query.

As shown in Figure 10-2, running the code from Listing 10-5 results in the same vanilla web page as the one generated by Listing 10-2 earlier in the chapter.

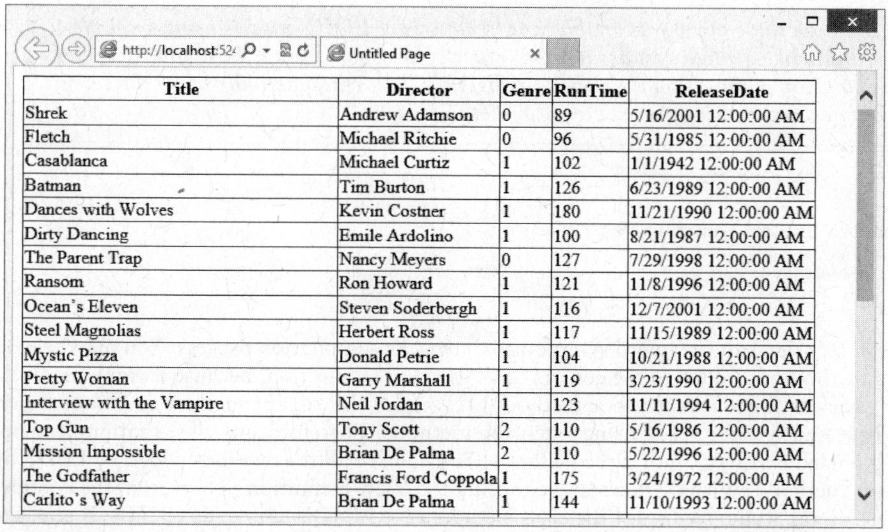

Title	Director	Genre	RunTime	ReleaseDate
Shrek	Andrew Adamson	0	89	5/16/2001 12:00:00 AM
Fletch	Michael Ritchie	0	96	5/31/1985 12:00:00 AM
Casablanca	Michael Curtiz	1	102	1/1/1942 12:00:00 AM
Batman	Tim Burton	1	126	6/23/1989 12:00:00 AM
Dances with Wolves	Kevin Costner	1	180	11/21/1990 12:00:00 AM
Dirty Dancing	Emile Ardolino	1	100	8/21/1987 12:00:00 AM
The Parent Trap	Nancy Meyers	0	127	7/29/1998 12:00:00 AM
Ransom	Ron Howard	1	121	11/8/1996 12:00:00 AM
Ocean's Eleven	Steven Soderbergh	1	116	12/7/2001 12:00:00 AM
Steel Magnolias	Herbert Ross	1	117	11/15/1989 12:00:00 AM
Mystic Pizza	Donald Petrie	1	104	10/21/1988 12:00:00 AM
Pretty Woman	Garry Marshall	1	119	3/23/1990 12:00:00 AM
Interview with the Vampire	Neil Jordan	1	123	11/11/1994 12:00:00 AM
Top Gun	Tony Scott	2	110	5/16/1986 12:00:00 AM
Mission Impossible	Brian De Palma	2	110	5/22/1996 12:00:00 AM
The Godfather	Francis Ford Coppola	1	175	3/24/1972 12:00:00 AM
Carlito's Way	Brian De Palma	1	144	11/10/1993 12:00:00 AM

FIGURE 10-2

LINQ also enables you to order the results using the `order by` statement. As with SQL, you can choose to order the results in ascending or descending order, as shown in Listing 10-8.

LISTING 10-8: Controlling data ordering using LINQ

VB

```vb
Protected Sub Page_Load(ByVal sender As Object, ByVal e As System.EventArgs)
  Dim movies = GetMovies()

  Dim query = From m In movies _
        Order By m.Title Descending _
        Select New With {.MovieTitle = m.Title, .MovieGenre = m.Genre}

  Me.GridView1.DataSource = query
  Me.GridView1.DataBind()
End Sub
```

C#

```csharp
protected void Page_Load(object sender, EventArgs e)
{
  var movies = GetMovies();

  var query = from m in movies
        orderby m.Title descending
        select new { MovieTitle = m.Title, MovieGenre = m. Genre };

  this.GridView1.DataSource = query;
  this.GridView1.DataBind();}
```

Another great feature of the LINQ syntax is the dramatic improvement in readability and understandability that it makes in your code. LINQ enables you to express the intention of your query, indicating to the compiler what you want your code to do, but leaving it up to the compiler to best determine how it should be done.

> **NOTE** *Although these keywords enable you to construct LINQ queries using a simple and clear SQL-like syntax, rest assured no magic is occurring. These keywords actually map to extension methods on the* movies *collection. You could actually write the same LINQ query directly using these extension methods, as follows:*

VB

```vb
Dim query = movies.Select( Function(m as Movie) m )
```

C#

```csharp
var query = movies.Select(m => m);
```

This is what the compiler translates the keyword syntax into during its compilation process. You may be wondering how the Select method was added to the generic List<Movies> collection, because if you look at the object structure of List<T>, there is no Select method. LINQ adds the Select method and many other methods it uses to the base Enumerable class, using extension methods. Therefore, any class that implements IEnumerable will be extended by LINQ with these methods. You can see all the methods added by LINQ by right-clicking the Select method in Visual Studio and choosing the View Definition option from the context menu. Doing this causes Visual Studio to display the class metadata for LINQ's Enumerable class. If you scroll through this class, you will see not only Select, but also other methods such as Where, Count, Min, Max, and many other methods that LINQ automatically adds to any object that implements the IEnumerable interface.

Ordering Results Using a Custom Comparer

When you use either the order by statement or the OrderBy and OrderByDescending extension methods, the default comparer for the type being ordered performs comparisons between values. Sometimes you need more control over the order of the results than the default comparer provides. In these situations, you can create a custom comparer and pass it to the order by operation using an overload of the `OrderBy` or `OrderByDescending` extension methods. In order to create a custom comparer, you create a class that inherits from `IComparer<>`. Given the movie data in Listing 10-2, if you ordered by the director, the result would be ordered by the director's first name because the string contains the first name followed by the last name. If you want the results sorted by last name, you need to create a custom comparer as shown in Listing 10-9.

LISTING 10-9: Custom comparer to sort by director last name

VB

```vb
Imports Microsoft.VisualBasic

Public Class LastNameComparer
    Implements IComparer(Of String)

    Function Compare(x As String, y As String) As Integer _
        Implements IComparer(Of String).Compare

        Dim director1LastName As String
        Dim director2LastName As String
        director1LastName = x.Substring(x.LastIndexOf(" "))
        director2LastName = y.Substring(y.LastIndexOf(" "))
        Return director1LastName.CompareTo(director2LastName)
    End Function

End Class
```

C#

```csharp
using System.Collections.Generic;

public class LastNameComparer : IComparer<string>
{
    public int Compare(string x, string y)
    {
        var director1LastName = x.Substring(x.LastIndexOf(' '));
        var director2LastName = y.Substring(y.LastIndexOf(' '));
        return director1LastName.CompareTo(director2LastName);
    }
}
```

To use this new comparer in the `OrderBy` or `OrderByDescending` extension methods, Listing 10-8 can be rewritten as shown in Listing 10-10.

LISTING 10-10: Using a custom comparer for ordering

VB

```vb
Protected Sub Page_Load(ByVal sender As Object, ByVal e As System.EventArgs)
    Dim movies = GetMovies()

    Dim query = movies.OrderByDescending(Function(m) m.Director, _
        New LastNameComparer()) _
        .Select(Function(m) New With {
            .MovieDirector = m.Director, .MovieTitle = m.Title,
            .MovieGenre = m.Genre })

    Me.GridView1.DataSource = query
```

continues

LISTING 10-10 *(continued)*

```
    Me.GridView1.DataBind()
End Sub
```

C#

```
protected void Page_Load(object sender, EventArgs e)
{
  var movies = GetMovies();

  var query = movies.OrderByDescending(m => m.Director, new LastNameComparer())
    .Select(m => new {MovieDirector = m.Director, MovieTitle = m.Title,
      MovieGenre = m.Genre });

  this.GridView1.DataSource = query;
  this.GridView1.DataBind();}
```

Figure 10-3 shows the result of running the code in Listing 10-10. The director has been added to the results, which are now sorted by the director's last name in descending order.

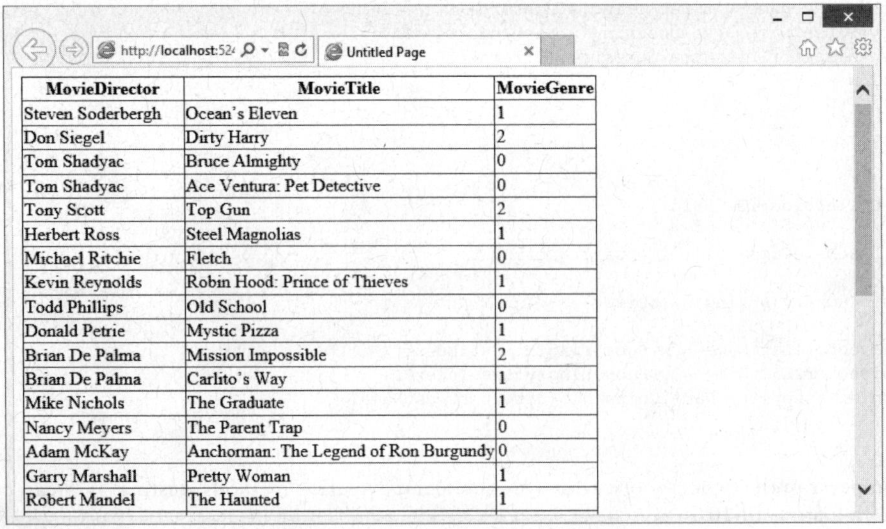

MovieDirector	MovieTitle	MovieGenre
Steven Soderbergh	Ocean's Eleven	1
Don Siegel	Dirty Harry	2
Tom Shadyac	Bruce Almighty	0
Tom Shadyac	Ace Ventura: Pet Detective	0
Tony Scott	Top Gun	2
Herbert Ross	Steel Magnolias	1
Michael Ritchie	Fletch	0
Kevin Reynolds	Robin Hood: Prince of Thieves	1
Todd Phillips	Old School	0
Donald Petrie	Mystic Pizza	1
Brian De Palma	Mission Impossible	2
Brian De Palma	Carlito's Way	1
Mike Nichols	The Graduate	1
Nancy Meyers	The Parent Trap	0
Adam McKay	Anchorman: The Legend of Ron Burgundy	0
Garry Marshall	Pretty Woman	1
Robert Mandel	The Haunted	1

FIGURE 10-3

Deferred Execution

An interesting feature of LINQ is its deferred execution behavior. This means that even though you may execute the query statements at a specific point in your code, LINQ is smart enough to delay the actual execution of the query until it is accessed. For example, in the previous samples, although the LINQ query was written before the binding of the GridView controls, LINQ will not execute the query you have defined until the GridView control begins to enumerate through the query results.

One of the biggest benefits of deferred execution is the ability to modify a LINQ query before it is executed. While a LINQ query returns an `IQueryable`, which inherits from `IEnumerable`, the data is not available until you actual iterate over it. Trying to iterate over the results will cause LINQ to execute the query. There are also methods that cause a LINQ query to be executed immediately, such as methods that start with "To" like `ToList()` and methods that return a single result like `Count()`.

Because the actual execution of the query doesn't happen until you iterate over the results, you can add additional filters to the query before it is executed. Filtering data is discussed in the next section.

Filtering Data Using LINQ

LINQ also supports adding query filters using a familiar SQL-like where syntax. You can modify the LINQ query from Listing 10-3 to add filtering capabilities by adding a where clause to the query, as shown in Listing 10-11.

LISTING 10-11: Adding a filter to a LINQ query

VB

```
Protected Sub Page_Load(ByVal sender As Object, ByVal e As System.EventArgs)
  Dim movies = GetMovies()

  Dim query = From m In movies _
        Where m.Genre = 0 _
        Select m

  Me.GridView1.DataSource = query
  Me.GridView1.DataBind()
End Sub
```

C#

```
protected void Page_Load(object sender, EventArgs e)
{
  var movies = GetMovies();

  var query = from m in movies
        where m.Genre==0
        select m;

  this.GridView1.DataSource = query;
  this.GridView1.DataBind();
}
```

By adding this simple where clause to the LINQ query, the results returned by the query are filtered to show movies from the 0 genre only, as shown in Figure 10-4.

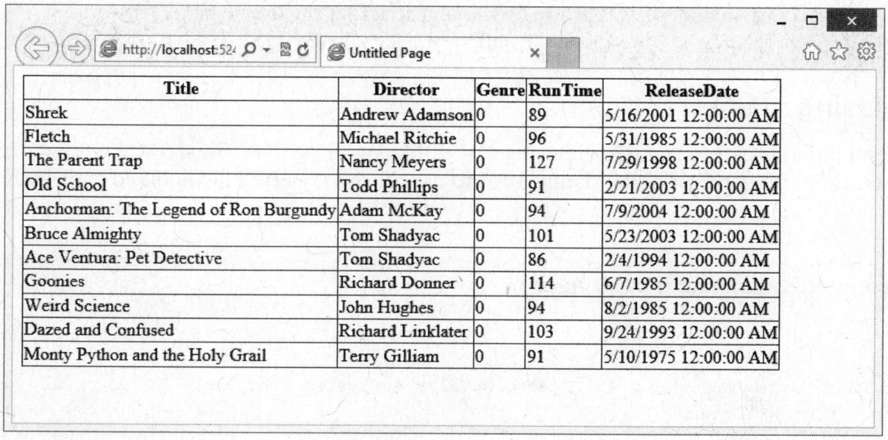

Title	Director	Genre	RunTime	ReleaseDate
Shrek	Andrew Adamson	0	89	5/16/2001 12:00:00 AM
Fletch	Michael Ritchie	0	96	5/31/1985 12:00:00 AM
The Parent Trap	Nancy Meyers	0	127	7/29/1998 12:00:00 AM
Old School	Todd Phillips	0	91	2/21/2003 12:00:00 AM
Anchorman: The Legend of Ron Burgundy	Adam McKay	0	94	7/9/2004 12:00:00 AM
Bruce Almighty	Tom Shadyac	0	101	5/23/2003 12:00:00 AM
Ace Ventura: Pet Detective	Tom Shadyac	0	86	2/4/1994 12:00:00 AM
Goonies	Richard Donner	0	114	6/7/1985 12:00:00 AM
Weird Science	John Hughes	0	94	8/2/1985 12:00:00 AM
Dazed and Confused	Richard Linklater	0	103	9/24/1993 12:00:00 AM
Monty Python and the Holy Grail	Terry Gilliam	0	91	5/10/1975 12:00:00 AM

FIGURE 10-4

Also, notice that, because LINQ is a first-class member of .NET, Visual Studio is able to provide an excellent coding experience as you are constructing your LINQ queries. In this sample, as you enter the where clause, Visual Studio gives you IntelliSense for the possible parameters of m (the Movie object), as shown in Figure 10-5.

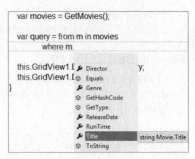

FIGURE 10-5

The where clause in LINQ behaves similarly to the SQL where clause, enabling you to include sub-queries and multiple where clauses, as shown in Listing 10-12.

LISTING 10-12: Adding a where clause to a LINQ query

VB

```
Protected Sub Page_Load(ByVal sender As Object, ByVal e As System.EventArgs)
  Dim movies = GetMovies()

  Dim query = From m In movies _
       Where m.Genre = 0 And m.Runtime > 92 _
       Select m

  Me.GridView1.DataSource = query
  Me.GridView1.DataBind()
 End Sub
```

C#

```
protected void Page_Load(object sender, EventArgs e)
{
  var movies = GetMovies();

  var query = from m in movies
       where m.Genre == 0 && m.RunTime > 92
       select m;

  this.GridView1.DataSource = query;
  this.GridView1.DataBind();
}
```

In this sample, the where clause includes two parameters, one restricting the movie genre, the other restricting the movie's run time.

Grouping Data Using LINQ

LINQ also greatly simplifies grouping data, again using a SQL-like group syntax. To show how easy LINQ makes grouping, you can modify the original Listing 10-4 to use a LINQ query. The modified code is shown in Listing 10-13.

LISTING 10-13: Grouping data using a LINQ query

VB

```
Protected Sub Page_Load(ByVal sender As Object, ByVal e As System.EventArgs)
  Dim movies = GetMovies()

  Dim query = From m In movies _
```

```
        Group By m.Genre Into g = Group, Count()

    Me.GridView1.DataSource = query
    Me.GridView1.DataBind()
End Sub
```

C#

```csharp
protected void Page_Load(object sender, EventArgs e)
{
    var movies = GetMovies();

    var query = from m in movies
            group m by m.Genre into g
            select new { Genre = g.Key, Count = g.Count() };

    this.GridView1.DataSource = query;
    this.GridView1.DataBind();
}
```

This LINQ query uses the `group` keyword, or `Group By` in VB.NET, to group the movie data by genre. Additionally, because a group action does not naturally result in any output, the query creates a custom query projection using the techniques discussed earlier. Figure 10-6 shows the results of this query.

Using LINQ to do this grouping enables you to significantly reduce the lines of code required. If you compare the amount of code required to perform the grouping action in Listing 10-4 with that in the previous listing using LINQ, you can see that the number of lines of code has dropped from 18 to 3, and the readability and clarity of the code has improved.

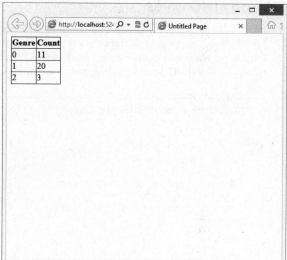

FIGURE 10-6

Using Other LINQ Operators

Besides basic selection, filtering, and grouping, LINQ also includes many operators you can execute on collections. Most of these operators are available for you to use on any collection and are similar to operators you find in SQL, such as `Count`, `Min`, `Max`, `Average`, and `Sum`, as shown in Listing 10-14.

LISTING 10-14: Using LINQ query operators

VB

```vb
Protected Sub Page_Load(ByVal sender As Object, ByVal e As System.EventArgs)
    Dim movies = GetMovies()

    Me.TotalMovies.Text = movies.Count.ToString()
    Me.LongestRuntime.Text = movies.Max(Function(m) m.Runtime).ToString()
    Me.ShortestRuntime.Text = movies.Min(Function(m) m.Runtime).ToString()
    Me.AverageRuntime.Text = movies.Average(Function(m) m.Runtime).ToString()

End Sub
```

continues

LISTING 10-14 *(continued)*

C#

```csharp
protected void Page_Load(object sender, EventArgs e)
{
  var movies = GetMovies();

  this.TotalMovies.Text = movies.Count.ToString();
  this.LongestRuntime.Text = movies.Max(m => m.RunTime).ToString();
  this.ShortestRuntime.Text = movies.Min(m => m.RunTime).ToString();
  this.AverageRuntime.Text = movies.Average(m => m.RunTime).ToString();}
```

This listing demonstrates the use of the Count, Max, Min, and Average operators with the movies collection. Notice that for all but the Count operator, you must provide the method with the specific field you want to execute the operation on. You do this using a Lambda expression.

Making LINQ Joins

LINQ also supports the union of data from different collections using a familiar SQL-like join syntax. For example, in the sample data thus far, you have been able to display the genre only as a numeric ID. Displaying the name of each genre instead would actually be preferable. To do this, you create a Genre class, which defines the properties of the genre, as shown in Listing 10-15.

LISTING 10-15: A simple Genre class

VB

```vb
Public Class Genre

  Public Property ID() As Integer

  Public Property Name() As String
End Class
```

C#

```csharp
public class Genre
{
  public int ID { get; set; }
  public string Name { get; set; }
}
```

Next you can add a GetGenres method to your web page that returns a list of Genre objects, as shown in Listing 10-16.

LISTING 10-16: Populating a collection of genres

VB

```vb
Public Function GetGenres() As List(Of Genre)
  Dim genres As Genre() = { _
    New Genre With {.ID = 0, .Name = "Comedy"}, _
    New Genre With {.ID = 1, .Name = "Drama"}, _
    New Genre With {.ID = 2, .Name = "Action"} _
  }

  Return New List(Of Genre)(genres)
End Function
```

C#

```csharp
public List<Genre> GetGenres()
{
    return new List<Genre> {
        new Genre { ID=0, Name="Comedy" } ,
        new Genre { ID=1, Name="Drama" } ,
        new Genre { ID=2, Name="Action" }
    };
}
```

Finally, you can modify the Page Load event, including the LINQ query, to retrieve the genres list and, using LINQ, join that to the movies list, as shown in Listing 10-17.

LISTING 10-17: Joining genre data with movie data using a LINQ query

VB

```vb
Protected Sub Page_Load(ByVal sender As Object, ByVal e As System.EventArgs)
    Dim movies = GetMovies()
    Dim genres = GetGenres()

    Dim query = From m In movies Join g In genres _
        On m.Genre Equals g.ID _
        Select New With {.Title = m.Title, .Genre = g.Name}

    GridView1.DataSource = query
    GridView1.DataBind()
End Sub
```

C#

```csharp
protected void Page_Load(object sender, EventArgs e)
{
    var movies = GetMovies();
    var genres = GetGenres();

    var query = from m in movies
        join g in genres on m.Genre equals g.ID
        select new { m.Title, Genre = g.Name } ;

    this.GridView1.DataSource = query;
    this.GridView1.DataBind();
}
```

As you can see in this sample, the join syntax is relatively simple. You tell LINQ to include the genres object and then tell LINQ which fields it should associate.

Paging Using LINQ

LINQ also makes including paging logic in your web application much easier by exposing the Skip and Take methods. The Skip method enables you to skip a defined number of records in the resultset. The Take method enables you to specify the number of records to return from the resultset. By calling Skip and then Take, you can return a specific number of records from a specific location of the resultset, as shown in Listing 10-18.

LISTING 10-18: Simple paging using LINQ methods

VB

```vb
Protected Sub Page_Load(ByVal sender As Object, ByVal e As System.EventArgs)
  Dim movies = GetMovies()
  Dim genres = GetGenres()

  Dim query = (From m In movies _
        Join g In genres On m.Genre Equals g.ID _
        Select New With {m.Title, .Genre = g.Name}).Skip(10).Take(10)

  Me.GridView1.DataSource = query
  Me.GridView1.DataBind()
  End Sub
```

C#

```csharp
protected void Page_Load(object sender, EventArgs e)
{
  var movies = GetMovies();
  var genres = GetGenres();

  var query = (from m in movies
        join g in genres on m.Genre equals g.ID
        select new { m.Title, g.Name }).Skip(10).Take(10);

  this.GridView1.DataSource = query;
  this.GridView1.DataBind();
}
```

When running this code, you will see that the results start with the tenth record in the list, and only ten records are displayed.

LINQ TO XML

The second flavor of LINQ is called LINQ to XML. As the name implies, LINQ to XML enables you to use the same basic LINQ syntax to query XML documents. As with the basic LINQ features, the LINQ to XML features of .NET are included as an extension to the basic .NET Framework and do not change existing functionality. Also, as with the core LINQ features, the LINQ to XML features are contained in their own separate assembly, the `System.Xml.Linq` assembly.

This section shows how you can use LINQ to query XML, using the same basic movie data as in the previous section, but converted to XML. Listing 10-19 shows a portion of the movie data converted to a simple XML document. You can find the XML file containing the complete set of converted data in the downloadable code for this chapter.

LISTING 10-19: Sample movies XML data file

```xml
<?xml version="1.0" encoding="utf-8" ?>
<Movies>
 <Movie>
  <Title>Shrek</Title>
  <Director>Andrew Adamson</Director>
  <Genre>0</Genre>
  <ReleaseDate>5/16/2001</ReleaseDate>
  <RunTime>89</RunTime>
 </Movie>
 <Movie>
```

```
    <Title>Fletch</Title>
    <Director>Michael Ritchie</Director>
    <Genre>0</Genre>
    <ReleaseDate>5/31/1985</ReleaseDate>
    <RunTime>96</RunTime>
  </Movie>
  <Movie>
    <Title>Casablanca</Title>
    <Director>Michael Curtiz</Director>
    <Genre>1</Genre>
    <ReleaseDate>1/1/1942</ReleaseDate>
    <RunTime>102</RunTime>
  </Movie>
</Movies>
```

So you can see how to use LINQ to XML to query XML documents, this section walks you through some of the same basic queries you started with in the previous section.

A Simple LINQ to XML Example

Listing 10-20 demonstrates a simple selection query using LINQ to XML.

LISTING 10-20: Querying the XML data file using LINQ

VB

```
<%@ Page Language="VB" %>

<script runat="server">
  Protected Sub Page_Load(ByVal sender As Object, ByVal e As System.EventArgs)
    Dim query = From m In _
          XElement.Load(MapPath("Movies.xml")).Elements("Movie") _
          Select m

    Me.GridView1.DataSource = query
    Me.GridView1.DataBind()
  End Sub
</script>

<html xmlns="http://www.w3.org/1999/xhtml">
<head runat="server">
  <title>My Favorite Movies</title>
</head>
<body>
  <form id="form1" runat="server">
  <div>
    <asp:GridView ID="GridView1" runat="server">
    </asp:GridView>
  </div>
  </form>
</body>
</html>
```

C#

```
<%@ Page Language="C#" %>
<%@ Import Namespace="System.Linq" %>
<%@ Import Namespace="System.Xml.Linq" %>
<script runat="server">
  protected void Page_Load(object sender, EventArgs e)
  {
```

continues

LISTING 10-20 *(continued)*

```
    var query = from m in
            XElement.Load(MapPath("Movies.xml")).Elements("Movie")
        select m;

    this.GridView1.DataSource = query;
    this.GridView1.DataBind();
    }
</script>
```

Notice that in this query, you tell LINQ where to load the XML data from, and from which elements in that document it should retrieve the data, which in this case are all the `Movie` elements. Other than that minor change, the LINQ query is identical to queries you have seen previously.

When you execute this code, you get a page that looks like Figure 10-7.

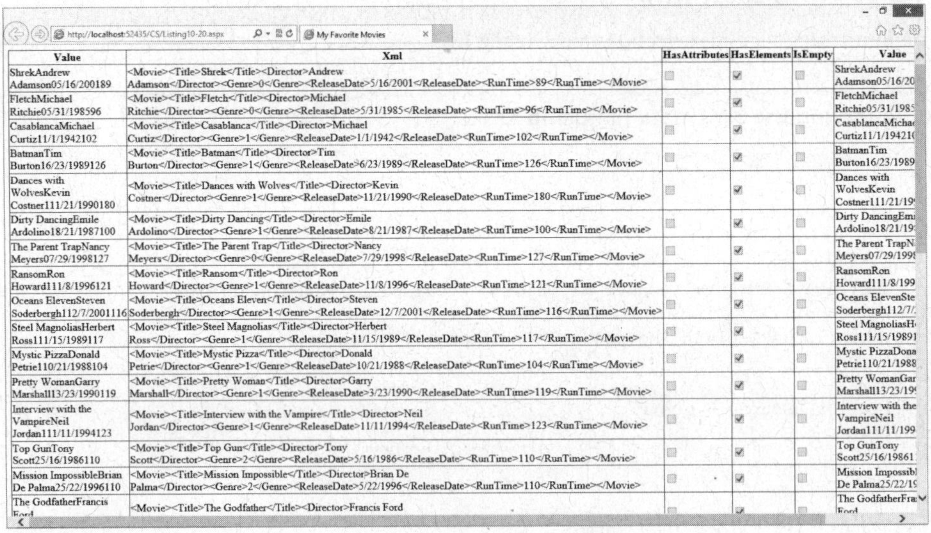

FIGURE 10-7

Notice that the fields included in the resultset of the query don't really show the node data as you might have expected, with each child node as a separate field in the GridView. This is because the query used in the listing returns a collection of generic `XElement` objects, not `Movie` objects as you might have expected. This is because by itself LINQ has no way of identifying what object type each node should be mapped to. Thankfully, you can add a bit of mapping logic to the query to tell it to map each node to a `Movie` object and how the nodes' sub-elements should map to the properties of the `Movie` object, as shown in Listing 10-21.

LISTING 10-21: Mapping XML elements using LINQ

VB

```
Protected Sub Page_Load(ByVal sender As Object, ByVal e As System.EventArgs)
    Dim query = From m In XElement.Load(MapPath("Movies.xml")).Elements("Movie") _
        Select New Movie With { _
                .Title = CStr(m.Element("Title")), _
                .Director = CStr(m.Element("Director")), _
```

```
                    .Genre = CInt(m.Element("Genre")), _
                    .ReleaseDate = CDate(m.Element("ReleaseDate")), _
                    .Runtime = CInt(m.Element("Runtime")) _
                }

    Me.GridView1.DataSource = query
    Me.GridView1.DataBind()
End Sub
```

C#

```
protected void Page_Load(object sender, EventArgs e)
{
    var query = from m in XElement.Load(MapPath("Movies.xml")).Elements("Movie")
        select new Movie {
                Title = (string)m.Element("Title"),
                Director = (string)m.Element("Director"),
                Genre = (int)m.Element("Genre"),
                ReleaseDate = (DateTime)m.Element("ReleaseDate"),
                RunTime = (int)m.Element("RunTime")
            };

    this.GridView1.DataSource = query;
    this.GridView1.DataBind();
}
```

As you can see, the query now includes mapping logic so that LINQ knows what your actual intentions are—to create a resultset that contains the values of the Movie elements' inner nodes. Running this code now results in a GridView that contains what you want, as shown in Figure 10-8.

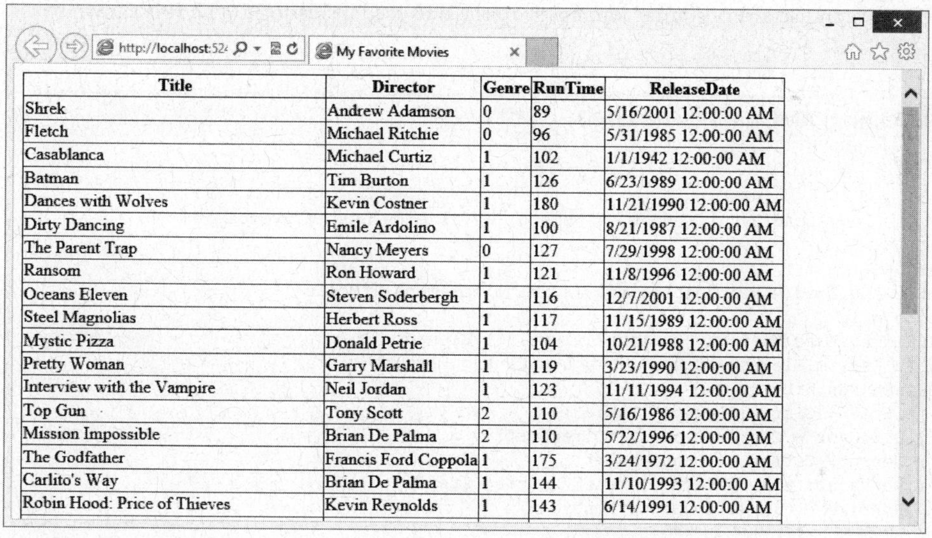

Title	Director	Genre	RunTime	ReleaseDate
Shrek	Andrew Adamson	0	89	5/16/2001 12:00:00 AM
Fletch	Michael Ritchie	0	96	5/31/1985 12:00:00 AM
Casablanca	Michael Curtiz	1	102	1/1/1942 12:00:00 AM
Batman	Tim Burton	1	126	6/23/1989 12:00:00 AM
Dances with Wolves	Kevin Costner	1	180	11/21/1990 12:00:00 AM
Dirty Dancing	Emile Ardolino	1	100	8/21/1987 12:00:00 AM
The Parent Trap	Nancy Meyers	0	127	7/29/1998 12:00:00 AM
Ransom	Ron Howard	1	121	11/8/1996 12:00:00 AM
Oceans Eleven	Steven Soderbergh	1	116	12/7/2001 12:00:00 AM
Steel Magnolias	Herbert Ross	1	117	11/15/1989 12:00:00 AM
Mystic Pizza	Donald Petrie	1	104	10/21/1988 12:00:00 AM
Pretty Woman	Garry Marshall	1	119	3/23/1990 12:00:00 AM
Interview with the Vampire	Neil Jordan	1	123	11/11/1994 12:00:00 AM
Top Gun	Tony Scott	2	110	5/16/1986 12:00:00 AM
Mission Impossible	Brian De Palma	2	110	5/22/1996 12:00:00 AM
The Godfather	Francis Ford Coppola	1	175	3/24/1972 12:00:00 AM
Carlito's Way	Brian De Palma	1	144	11/10/1993 12:00:00 AM
Robin Hood: Price of Thieves	Kevin Reynolds	1	143	6/14/1991 12:00:00 AM

FIGURE 10-8

> **WARNING** Note that the XElement's Load method attempts to load the entire XML document; therefore, trying to load very large XML files using this method is not a good idea.

Joining XML Data

LINQ to XML supports all the same query filtering and grouping operations as LINQ to Objects. It also supports joining data and can actually join data from two different XML documents—a task that previously was quite difficult. Take a look at the same basic join scenario as was presented in the "LINQ to Objects" section. Again, the basic XML data includes only an ID value for the Genre. Showing the actual Genre name with the resultset would, however, be better.

In the case of the XML data, rather than being kept in a separate list, the Genre data is actually stored in a completely separate XML file, shown in Listing 10-22.

LISTING 10-22: Genres XML data

```xml
<?xml version="1.0" encoding="utf-8" ?>
<Genres>
  <Genre>
    <ID>0</ID>
    <Name>Comedy</Name>
  </Genre>
  <Genre>
    <ID>1</ID>
    <Name>Drama</Name>
  </Genre>
  <Genre>
    <ID>2</ID>
    <Name>Action</Name>
  </Genre>
</Genres>
```

To join the data, you can use a very similar join query to the one used in Listing 10-17. It is shown in Listing 10-23.

LISTING 10-23: Joining XML data using LINQ

VB

```vb
Protected Sub Page_Load(ByVal sender As Object, ByVal e As System.EventArgs)

    Dim query = From m In _
        XElement.Load(MapPath("Listing9-18.xml")).Elements("Movie") _
        Join g In _
        XElement.Load(MapPath("Listing9-21.xml")).Elements("Genre") _
          On CInt(m.Element("Genre")) Equals CInt(g.Element("ID")) _
        Select New With { _
          .Title = CStr(m.Element("Title")), _
          .Director = CStr(m.Element("Director")), _
          .Genre = CStr(g.Element("Name")), _
          .ReleaseDate = CDate(m.Element("ReleaseDate")), _
          .Runtime = CInt(m.Element("RunTime")) _
        }

    Me.GridView1.DataSource = query
    Me.GridView1.DataBind()
End Sub
```

C#

```csharp
protected void Page_Load(object sender, EventArgs e)
{
    var query = from m in XElement.Load(MapPath("Movies.xml")).Elements("Movie")
```

```
        join g in XElement.Load(MapPath("Genres.xml")).Elements("Genre")
          on (int)m.Element("Genre") equals (int)g.Element("ID")
        select new {
              Title = (string)m.Element("Title"),
              Director = (string)m.Element("Director"),
              Genre = (string)g.Element("Name"),
              ReleaseDate = (DateTime)m.Element("ReleaseDate"),
              RunTime = (int)m.Element("RunTime")
          };

      this.GridView1.DataSource = query;
      this.GridView1.DataBind();
    }
```

In this sample, you can see that using the `XElement.Load` method as part of the LINQ join statement tells LINQ where to load the `Genre` data from. After the data is joined, you can access the elements of the `Genre` data as you can the elements of the `Movie` data.

LINQ TO SQL

LINQ to SQL, as the name implies, enables you to quickly and easily query SQL-based data sources, such as SQL Server 2005 and above. As with the prior flavors of LINQ, LINQ to SQL is an extension of the core .NET Framework. Its features are located in the `System.Data.Linq` assembly.

Using the O/R Mapper

In addition to the normal IntelliSense and strong type checking that every flavor of LINQ gives you, LINQ to SQL also includes a basic Object/Relation (O/R) mapper directly in Visual Studio. The O/R mapper enables you to quickly map SQL-based data sources to CLR objects that you can then use LINQ to query.

You use the O/R mapper by adding the new LINQ to SQL Classes file to your website project. The LINQ to SQL File document type allows you to easily and visually create data contexts that you can then access and query with LINQ queries. Figure 10-9 shows the LINQ to SQL Classes file type in the Add New Item dialog box.

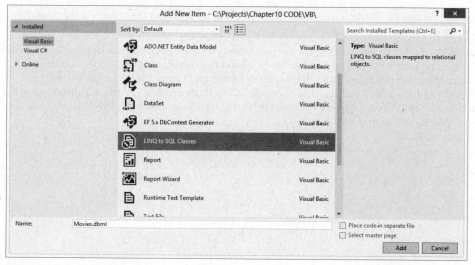

FIGURE 10-9

After you click the Add New Items dialog box's OK button to add the file to your project, Visual Studio notifies you that it wants to add the LINQ to SQL File to your website's App_Code directory. Because the file is located there, the data context created by the LINQ to SQL Classes file will be accessible from anywhere in your website.

After the file has been added, Visual Studio automatically opens it in the LINQ to SQL designer. This simple Object/Relation mapper design tool enables you to add, create, remove, and relate data objects. As you modify objects to the designer, LINQ to SQL generates object classes that mirror the structure of each of those objects. Later, when you are ready to begin writing LINQ queries against the data objects, these classes allow Visual Studio to provide you with design-time IntelliSense support, strong typing, and compile-time type checking. Because the O/R mapper is primarily designed to be used with LINQ to SQL, creating CLR object representations of SQL objects, such as tables, views, and stored procedures, is easy.

The demonstration for LINQ to SQL uses the same sample movie data found in previous sections of this chapter. For this section, the data is stored in a SQL Express LocalDB database.

> **NOTE** *A copy of this database named Movies.mdf is included in the downloadable code from the Wrox website (*www.wrox.com*).*

After the design surface is open and ready, open the Visual Studio Server Explorer tool, locate the Movies database, and expand the database's Tables folder. Drag the Movies table from the Server Explorer onto the design surface. Notice that as soon as you drop the database table onto the design surface, it is automatically interrogated to identify its structure. A corresponding entity class is created by the designer and shown on the design surface.

When you drop table objects onto the LINQ to SQL design surface, Visual Studio examines the table names and will, if necessary, attempt to automatically "singularize" the class names it generates. It does this in order to help you more closely follow the .NET Framework class naming standards. For example, if you drop a table called Products from a database onto the design surface, it would automatically choose the singular name Product as the name of the generated class.

Unfortunately, although the designer generally does a good job at figuring out the correct singular version for the class names, it's not 100 percent accurate. Case in point—look at how it incorrectly singularizes the Movies table to Movy when you drop it onto the design surface. Thankfully, the designer also allows you to change the name of entities on the design surface. You can do so by selecting the entity on the design surface and clicking the entity's name in the designer.

After you have added the Movie entity, drag the Genres table onto the design surface. Again, Visual Studio creates a class representation of this table (and notice it gives it the singular name Genre). Additionally, it detects an existing foreign key relationship between the Movie and Genre. Because it detects this relationship, a dashed line is added between the two tables. The line's arrow indicates the direction of the foreign key relationship that exists between the two tables. Figure 10-10 shows the LINQ to SQL design surface with the Movies and Genres tables added.

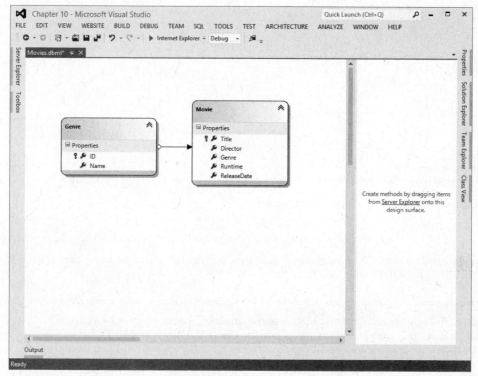

FIGURE 10-10

Accessing and Querying Data

Now that you have set up your LINQ to SQL file, accessing its data context and querying its data is simple.

Accessing Data

To start, you create an instance of the data context in the web form where you will be accessing the data, as shown in Listing 10-24.

LISTING 10-24: Creating a new data context

VB

```vb
<%@ Page Language="VB" %>

<script runat="server">
  Protected Sub Page_Load(ByVal sender As Object, ByVal e As System.EventArgs)
    Dim dc As New MoviesDataContext()
  End Sub
</script>

<html xmlns="http://www.w3.org/1999/xhtml">
<head runat="server">
  <title> My Favorite Movies </title>
</head>
<body>
  <form id="form1" runat="server">
```

continues

LISTING 10-24 *(continued)*

```
  <div>
    <asp:GridView ID="GridView1" runat="server">
    </asp:GridView>

  </div>
  </form>
</body>
</html>
```

C#

```
<script runat="server">
  protected void Page_Load(object sender, EventArgs e)
  {
    .MoviesDataContext dc = new MoviesDataContext();

  }
</script>
```

In this case, you created an instance of the `MoviesDataContext`, which is the name of the data context class generated by the LINQ to SQL file you added earlier.

> **NOTE** *Because the data context class is automatically generated by the LINQ to SQL file, its name will change each time you create a new LINQ to SQL file. The name of this class is determined by appending the name of your LINQ to SQL Class file with the* `DataContext` *suffix, so if you named your LINQ to SQL file* `AdventureWorks` `.dbml`, *the data context class would be* `AdventureWorksDataContext`.

Writing LINQ Queries

After you have added the data context to your page, you can begin writing LINQ queries against it. As mentioned earlier, because LINQ to SQL–generated object classes mirror the structure of the database tables, you get IntelliSense support as you write your LINQ queries. Listing 10-25 shows the same basic movie listing query that has been shown in prior sections.

LISTING 10-25: Querying movie data from LINQ to SQL

VB

```
Protected Sub Page_Load(ByVal sender As Object, ByVal e As System.EventArgs)
  Dim dc As New MoviesDataContext()

  Dim query = From m In dc.Movies _
        Select m

  Me.GridView1.DataSource = query
  Me.GridView1.DataBind()
End Sub
```

C#

```
protected void Page_Load(object sender, EventArgs e)
{
  MoviesDataContext dc = new MoviesDataContext();

  var query = from m in dc.Movies
```

```
                select m;

        this.GridView1.DataSource = query;
        this.GridView1.DataBind();
    }
```

As is shown in Figure 10-11, running the code generates a raw list of the movies in the database.

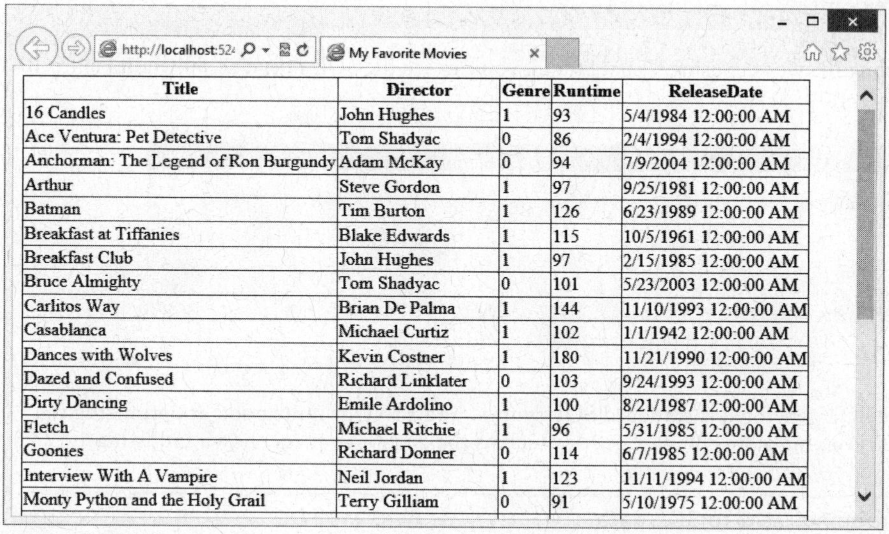

Title	Director	Genre	Runtime	ReleaseDate
16 Candles	John Hughes	1	93	5/4/1984 12:00:00 AM
Ace Ventura: Pet Detective	Tom Shadyac	0	86	2/4/1994 12:00:00 AM
Anchorman: The Legend of Ron Burgundy	Adam McKay	0	94	7/9/2004 12:00:00 AM
Arthur	Steve Gordon	1	97	9/25/1981 12:00:00 AM
Batman	Tim Burton	1	126	6/23/1989 12:00:00 AM
Breakfast at Tiffanies	Blake Edwards	1	115	10/5/1961 12:00:00 AM
Breakfast Club	John Hughes	1	97	2/15/1985 12:00:00 AM
Bruce Almighty	Tom Shadyac	0	101	5/23/2003 12:00:00 AM
Carlitos Way	Brian De Palma	1	144	11/10/1993 12:00:00 AM
Casablanca	Michael Curtiz	1	102	1/1/1942 12:00:00 AM
Dances with Wolves	Kevin Costner	1	180	11/21/1990 12:00:00 AM
Dazed and Confused	Richard Linklater	0	103	9/24/1993 12:00:00 AM
Dirty Dancing	Emile Ardolino	1	100	8/21/1987 12:00:00 AM
Fletch	Michael Ritchie	1	96	5/31/1985 12:00:00 AM
Goonies	Richard Donner	0	114	6/7/1985 12:00:00 AM
Interview With A Vampire	Neil Jordan	1	123	11/11/1994 12:00:00 AM
Monty Python and the Holy Grail	Terry Gilliam	0	91	5/10/1975 12:00:00 AM

FIGURE 10-11

Note that you did not have to write any of the database access code that would typically have been required to create this page. LINQ has taken care of that for you, even generating the SQL query based on the LINQ syntax. You can view the SQL that LINQ generated for the query by writing the query to the Visual Studio output window, as shown in Listing 10-26.

LISTING 10-26: Writing the LINQ to SQL query to the output window

VB

```
Protected Sub Page_Load(ByVal sender As Object, ByVal e As System.EventArgs)
    Dim dc As New MoviesDataContext()

    Dim query = From m In dc.Movies _
        Select m

    System.Diagnostics.Debug.WriteLine(query)

    Me.GridView1.DataSource = query
    Me.GridView1.DataBind()
End Sub
```

C#

```
protected void Page_Load(object sender, EventArgs e)
{
    MoviesDataContext dc = new MoviesDataContext();

    var query = from m in dc.Movies
```

continues

LISTING 10-26 *(continued)*

```
        select m;

    System.Diagnostics.Debug.WriteLine(query);

    this.GridView1.DataSource = query;
    this.GridView1.DataBind();
}
```

Now, when you debug the website using Visual Studio, you can see the SQL query, as shown in Figure 10-12.

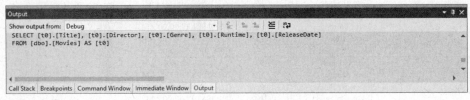

FIGURE 10-12

As you can see, the SQL generated is standard SQL syntax, and LINQ is quite good at optimizing the queries it generates, even for more complex queries such as the grouping query shown in Listing 10-27.

LISTING 10-27: Grouping LINQ to SQL data

VB

```
Protected Sub Page_Load(ByVal sender As Object, ByVal e As System.EventArgs)
    Dim dc As New MoviesDataContext()

    Dim query = From m In dc.Movies _
        Group By m.Genre Into g = Group, Count()

    System.Diagnostics.Debug.WriteLine(query)

    Me.GridView1.DataSource = query
    Me.GridView1.DataBind()

End Sub
```

C#

```
protected void Page_Load(object sender, EventArgs e)
{
    MoviesDataContext dc = new MoviesDataContext();

    var query = from m in dc.Movies
        group m by m.Genre into g
        select new { Genre = g.Key, Count = g.Count() };

    System.Diagnostics.Debug.WriteLine(query);

    this.GridView1.DataSource = query;
    this.GridView1.DataBind();
}
```

Figure 10-13 shows the generated SQL for this query.

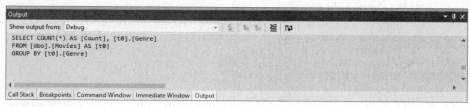

FIGURE 10-13

Note that SQL to LINQ generates SQL that is optimized for the version of SQL Server you're using.

LINQ also includes a logging option you can enable by setting the Log property of the data context.

Using Other SQL Query Methods

Although LINQ to SQL does an excellent job generating the SQL query syntax, there may be times when it's better to use other SQL query methods, such as stored procedures or views.

Using a SQL View

To use a SQL view with LINQ to SQL, you drag the view onto the LINQ to SQL design surface, just as you would a standard SQL table. Views appear on the design surface, just as the tables you added earlier did. After the view is on the design surface, you can execute queries against it, just as you did the SQL tables, as shown in Listing 10-28.

LISTING 10-28: Querying LINQ to SQL data using a view

VB

```
Protected Sub Page_Load(ByVal sender As Object, ByVal e As System.EventArgs)
    Dim dc As New MoviesDataContext()

    Dim query = From m In dc.AllMovies _
        Select m

    System.Diagnostics.Debug.WriteLine(query)

    Me.GridView1.DataSource = query
    Me.GridView1.DataBind()
End Sub
```

C#

```
protected void Page_Load(object sender, EventArgs e)
{
    MoviesDataContext dc = new MoviesDataContext();

    var query = from m in dc.AllMovies
        select m;

    System.Diagnostics.Debug.WriteLine(query);

    this.GridView1.DataSource = query;
    this.GridView1.DataBind();
}
```

Using Stored Procedures

Unlike tables or views, which LINQ to SQL exposes as properties, stored procedures can require parameters. Therefore, LINQ to SQL exposes them from the data context object as method calls, allowing you to provide method parameter values, which are translated by LINQ into stored procedure parameters. Listing 10-29 shows a simple stored procedure you can use to retrieve a specific genre from the database.

LISTING 10-29: Simple SQL stored procedure

```
CREATE PROCEDURE dbo.GetGenre
  (
  @id int
  )

AS
    SELECT * FROM Genre WHERE ID = @id
```

You can add a stored procedure to your LINQ to SQL designer just as you did the tables and views, by dragging them from the Server Explorer onto the LINQ to SQL Classes design surface. If you expect your stored procedure to return a collection of data from a table in your database, you should drop the stored procedure onto the LINQ class that represents the types returned by the query. The stored procedure shown in Listing 10-27 will return all the Genre records that match the provided ID. Therefore, you should drop the GetGenres stored procedure onto the Genres table in the Visual Studio designer. This tells the designer to generate a method that returns a generic collection of Genre objects. When you drop the stored procedure onto the design surface, unlike the tables and views, the stored procedure appears in a list on the right side of the design surface. Figure 10-14 shows the GetGenre stored procedure after it has been added.

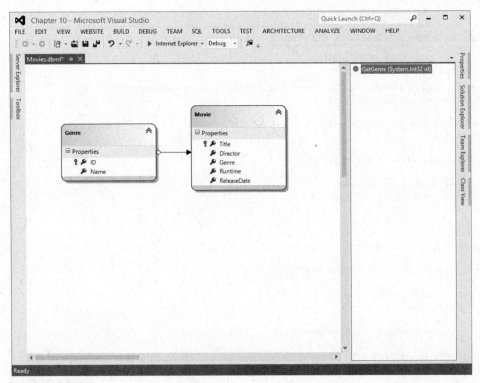

FIGURE 10-14

After you have added the stored procedures, you can access them through the data context, just as you did the table and views you accessed. As stated earlier, however, LINQ to SQL exposes them as method calls. Therefore, they may require you to provide method parameters, as shown in Listing 10-30.

LISTING 10-30: Selecting data from a stored procedure

VB

```vb
Protected Sub Page_Load(ByVal sender As Object, ByVal e As System.EventArgs)
  Dim dc As New MoviesDataContext()

  Me.GridView1.DataSource = dc.GetGenre(1)
  Me.GridView1.DataBind()
End Sub
```

C#

```csharp
protected void Page_Load(object sender, EventArgs e)
{
  MoviesDataContext dc = new MoviesDataContext();

  this.GridView1.DataSource = dc.GetGenre(1);
  this.GridView1.DataBind();
}
```

Making Insert, Update, and Delete Queries through LINQ

Not only can you use LINQ to SQL to create powerful queries that select data from a data source, but you can also use it to manage insert, update, and delete operations. By default, LINQ to SQL does these operations in much the same manner as when selecting data. LINQ to SQL uses the object class representations of the SQL structures and dynamically generates SQL INSERT, UPDATE, and DELETE commands. As with selection, you can also use stored procedures to perform the insert, update, or delete.

Inserting Data Using LINQ

Inserting data using LINQ to SQL is as easy as creating a new instance of the object you want to insert, and adding that to the object collection. The LINQ classes provide two methods—InsertOnSubmit and InsertAllOnSubmit—which make creating and adding any object to a LINQ collection simple. The InsertOnSubmit method accepts a single entity as its method parameter, allowing you to insert a single entity, whereas the InsertAllOnSubmit method accepts a collection as its method parameter, allowing you to insert an entire collection of data in a single method call.

After you have added your objects, LINQ to SQL does require the extra step of calling the Data Context object's SubmitChanges method. Calling this method tells LINQ to initiate the Insert action. Listing 10-31 shows an example of creating a new Movies object, and then adding it to the movies collection and calling SubmitChanges to persist the change back to the SQL database.

LISTING 10-31: Inserting data using LINQ to SQL

VB

```vb
Protected Sub Page_Load(ByVal sender As Object, ByVal e As System.EventArgs)
  Dim dc As New MoviesDataContext()

  Dim m As New Movie With {.Title = "The Princess Bride", _
    .Director = "Rob Reiner", .Genre = 0, _
    .ReleaseDate = DateTime.Parse("9/25/1987"), .Runtime = 98}

  dc.Movies.InsertOnSubmit(m)
```

continues

LISTING 10-31 *(continued)*

```
    dc.SubmitChanges()

End Sub
```

C#

```
protected void Page_Load(object sender, EventArgs e)
{
  MoviesDataContext dc = new MoviesDataContext();

  Movie m = new Movie { Title="The Princess Bride",
    Director="Rob Reiner", Genre=0,
    ReleaseDate=DateTime.Parse("9/25/1987"), Runtime=98 };

  dc.Movies.InsertOnSubmit(m);
  dc.SubmitChanges();
}
```

Using Stored Procedures to Insert Data

Of course, you might already have a complex stored procedure written to handle the insertion of data into your database table. LINQ makes it simple to use an existing stored procedure to insert data into a table. To do this, on the LINQ to SQL design surface, select the entity you want to insert data into, which in this case is the Movies entity. After selecting the entity, open its properties window and locate the Default Methods section, as shown in Figure 10-15.

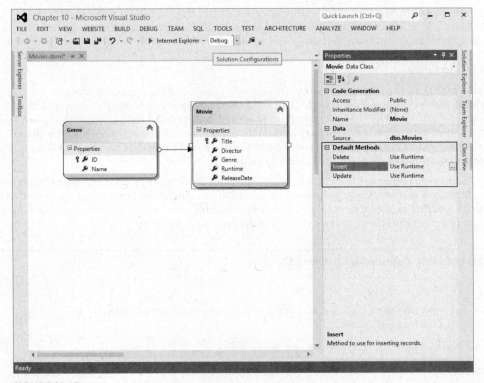

FIGURE 10-15

The Default Methods section contains three properties—`Delete`, `Insert`, and `Update`—which define the behavior LINQ should use when executing these actions on the Movies table. By default, each property is set to the value `UseRuntime`, which tells LINQ to dynamically generate SQL statements at run time. Because you want to insert data into the table using a stored procedure, open the `Insert` property's Configure Behavior dialog box.

In the dialog box, change the Behavior radio button selection from Use Runtime to Customize. Next, select the appropriate stored procedure from the drop-down list below the radio buttons. When you select the stored procedure, LINQ automatically tries to match the table columns to the stored procedure input parameters. However, you can change these manually, if needed.

The final Configure Behavior dialog box is shown in Figure 10-16.

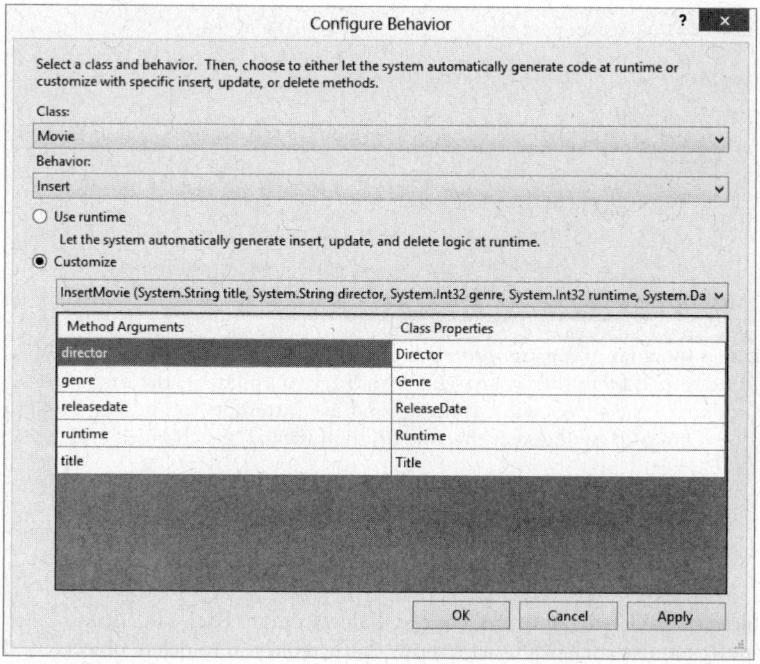

FIGURE 10-16

Now, when you run the code from Listing 10-31, LINQ will use the stored procedure you configured instead of dynamically generating a SQL `INSERT` statement.

Updating Data Using LINQ

Updating data with LINQ is very similar to inserting data. The first step is to get the specific object you want to update. You can do this by using the `Single` method of the collection you want to change. The scalar `Single` method returns a single object from the collection based on its input parameter. If more than one record matches the parameters, the `Single` method returns the first match.

After you have the record you want to update, you change the object's property values and then call the data context's `SubmitChanges` method. Listing 10-32 shows the code required to update a specific movie.

LISTING 10-32: Updating data using LINQ to SQL

VB

```
Protected Sub Page_Load(ByVal sender As Object, ByVal e As System.EventArgs)
  Dim dc As New MoviesDataContext()

  Dim movie = dc.Movies.Single(Function(m) m.Title = "Fletch")
  movie.Genre = 1

  dc.SubmitChanges()
End Sub
```

C#

```
protected void Page_Load(object sender, EventArgs e)
{
  MoviesDataContext dc = new MoviesDataContext();

  var movie = dc.Movies.Single(m => m.Title == "Fletch");
  movie.Genre = 1;

  dc.SubmitChanges();
}
```

HANDLING DATA CONCURRENCY

By default, LINQ to SQL also includes and uses *optimistic concurrency*. That means that if two users retrieve the same record from the database and both try to update it, the first user to submit his or her update to the server wins. If the second user attempts to update the record after the first, LINQ to SQL will detect that the original record has changed and will raise a `ChangeConflictException`.

Deleting Data Using LINQ

Finally, LINQ to SQL also enables you to delete data from your SQL data source. Each data class object generated by the LINQ to SQL designer also includes two methods that enable you to delete objects from the collection, the `DeleteOnSubmit` and `DeleteAllOnSubmit` methods. As their names imply, the `DeleteOnSubmit` method removes a single object from the collection and the `DeleteAllOnSubmit` method removes all records from the collection.

Listing 10-33 shows how you can use LINQ and the `DeleteOnSubmit` and `DeleteAllOnSubmit` methods to delete data from your data source.

LISTING 10-33: Deleting data using LINQ to SQL

VB

```
Protected Sub Page_Load(ByVal sender As Object, ByVal e As System.EventArgs)
  Dim dc As New MoviesDataContext()

  'Select and remove all Action movies
  Dim query = From m In dc.Movies _
       Where (m.Genre = 2) _
```

```
        Select m

    dc.Movies.DeleteAllOnSubmit(query)

    'Select a single movie and remove it
    Dim movie = dc.Movies.Single(Function(m) m.Title = "Fletch")
    dc.Movies.DeleteOnSubmit(movie)

    dc.SubmitChanges()
End Sub
```

C#

```
protected void Page_Load(object sender, EventArgs e)
{
    MoviesDataContext dc = new MoviesDataContext();

    //Select and remove all Action movies
    var query = from m in dc.Movies
            where m.Genre == 2
            select m;

    dc.Movies.DeleteAllOnSubmit(query);

    //Select a single movie and remove it
    var movie = dc.Movies.Single(m => m.Title == "Fletch");
    dc.Movies.DeleteOnSubmit(movie);

    dc.SubmitChanges();
}
```

As with the other SQL commands, you must remember to call the data context's SubmitChanges method in order to commit the changes back to the SQL data source.

LINQ TO ENTITIES

LINQ to SQL is a great tool to use when you need quick construction of your data access code. It also works very well when you have a relatively well-designed database. However, LINQ to SQL supports only one-to-one mapping between entity classes and database tables.

Entity Framework (EF) is an object-relational mapper that enables .NET developers to work with relational data using domain-specific objects, which makes up what is called the conceptual model. EF also allows connections to many different data providers. As such, you can mix and match a number of different database vendors, application servers, or protocols to design an aggregated mash-up of objects that are constructed from a variety of tables, sources, services, etc.

LINQ to Entities enables developers to write queries against the Entity Framework conceptual model using Visual Basic or Visual C#. While LINQ to SQL queries eventually create SQL that is executed against the backing database, LINQ to Entities converts LINQ queries to command tree queries which are understood by the Entity Framework, executes the queries against the Entity Framework, and returns objects that can be used by both the Entity Framework and LINQ. Although the code that is executed behind the scenes when you run a LINQ to Entities query is very different than that of a LINQ to SQL query, the LINQ syntax looks the same.

> **NOTE** *Entity Framework is covered in more detail in Chapter 11.*

Creating an Entity Framework Data Model

In order to work with LINQ to Entities you need to create an EF Data Model. If you have been following along with the chapter, you already have a project with an `App_Code` folder. Right-click on your `App_Code` folder within the Solution Explorer from Visual Studio and select Add ➪ New Item. The Add New Item dialog appears. From this dialog, select the particular language you are working with (found in the left pane of the dialog). The available items you can add include an ADO.NET Entity Data Model item. Select this item and name it `MoviesDM.edmx`. Choose the `Generate from database` option in the Entity Data Model Wizard. Use the existing `MoviesConnectionString` and leave the connection settings name as the default `MovieEntities`. This will be the name of the EF data context you will use later. Choose the `Movies` table in the list of database objects and leave all other settings as the default. Click `Finish` to create the data model. After the entity data model designer opens, you may get a security warning asking whether you want to run a text template. The O/R designer uses T4 templates to automatically generate the DbContext file and files for each of the entities you selected to be generated from the database. This is covered in more detail in Chapter 11. Check the option to not show the message again and click OK.

If you build the solution now, you will get errors indicating that the properties of the `Movie` object already exist in another object. This is because LINQ to SQL also generated an object called `Movie` with all the same properties. In order to prevent these conflicts, you should change the name of the entity classes that are generated by the LINQ to Entities data model designer. Right-click on the `Movie` object in the data model designer and choose Properties. Change the Entity Set Name to **EFMovies** and the Name to **EFMovie**. Figure 10-17 shows the properties pane with the changes made.

After making the changes, save the `MovieDM.edmx` file. Right-click on the `MovieDM.edmx` file and select Run Custom Tool to regenerate the entity classes with the changes you made to the properties.

Accessing Data

FIGURE 10-17

Create a new web form to display the data using the entity data model. In order to start using the entity data model, create an instance of the EF data context in the web form where you will be accessing the data, as shown in Listing 10-34.

LISTING 10-34: Creating a new EF data context

VB

```
<%@ Page Language="VB" %>

<!DOCTYPE html>

<script runat="server">
    Protected Sub Page_Load(ByVal sender As Object, ByVal e As System.EventArgs)
        Dim dc As New MoviesEntities()
    End Sub
</script>

<html xmlns="http://www.w3.org/1999/xhtml">
<head>
    <title> My Favorite Movies </title>
</head>
<body>
    <form id="form1" runat="server">
        <div>
```

```
            <asp:GridView ID="GridView1" runat="server">
            </asp:GridView>
        </div>
        </form>
    </body>
    </html>
```

[C#]

```
    <script runat="server">
        protected void Page_Load(object sender, EventArgs e)
        {
            MoviesEntities dc = new MoviesEntities();
        }
    </script>
```

In this case, you created an instance of the `MoviesEntities`, which is the name of the data context class generated by LINQ to Entities based on the connection settings name specified in the Entity Data Model Wizard.

Writing LINQ Queries

Now that you have an instance of the EF data context, you can begin writing LINQ queries against it. You will notice that writing LINQ queries against an EF data model looks the same as writing the same queries using LINQ to SQL. Just as with other LINQ queries, LINQ to Entities provides IntelliSense support as you write your LINQ queries. Listing 10-35 shows the same basic movie listing query that has been shown in the prior sections using other flavors of LINQ.

LISTING 10-35: Querying movie data using LINQ to Entities

VB

```
    Protected Sub Page_Load(ByVal sender As Object, ByVal e As System.EventArgs)
        Dim dc As New MoviesEntities()

        Dim query = From m In dc.EFMovies Select m

        Me.GridView1.DataSource = query.ToList()
        Me.GridView1.DataBind()
    End Sub
```

C#

```
    protected void Page_Load(object sender, EventArgs e)
    {
        MoviesEntities dc = new MoviesEntities();

        var query = from m in dc.EFMovies select m;

        GridView1.DataSource = query.ToList();
        GridView1.DataBind();
    }
```

Figure 10-18 shows the results of running the code. You can see that, like the prior examples, running the code generates a raw list of the movies in the database.

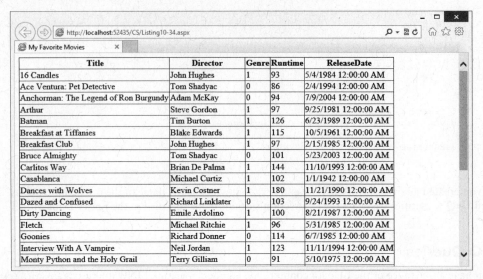

FIGURE 10-18

The similarity in LINQ syntax goes beyond simple queries. You can add filters and other query operations. For example, Listing 10-36 shows the same query modified to include a filter and an ordering operation.

LISTING 10-36: Adding filtering and ordering to LINQ to Entities queries

VB

```
Protected Sub Page_Load(ByVal sender As Object, ByVal e As System.EventArgs)
    Dim dc As New MoviesEntities()

    Dim query = From m In dc.EFMovies
        Where m.Genre = 0
        Order By m.Director
        Select m

    Me.GridView1.DataSource = query.ToList()
    Me.GridView1.DataBind()
End Sub
```

C#

```
protected void Page_Load(object sender, EventArgs e)
{
    MoviesEntities dc = new MoviesEntities();

    var query = from m in dc.EFMovies
        where m.Genre == 0
        orderby m.Director
        select m;

    GridView1.DataSource = query.ToList();
    GridView1.DataBind();
}
```

While the code in Listing 10-36 is using LINQ to Entities, the LINQ syntax is the same as when querying other flavors of LINQ. Figure 10-19 shows the results of running the code in Listing 10-36.

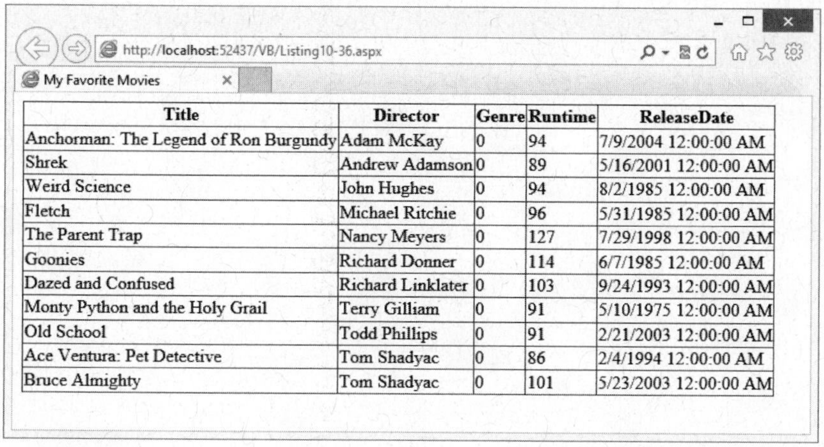

Title	Director	Genre	Runtime	ReleaseDate
Anchorman: The Legend of Ron Burgundy	Adam McKay	0	94	7/9/2004 12:00:00 AM
Shrek	Andrew Adamson	0	89	5/16/2001 12:00:00 AM
Weird Science	John Hughes	0	94	8/2/1985 12:00:00 AM
Fletch	Michael Ritchie	0	96	5/31/1985 12:00:00 AM
The Parent Trap	Nancy Meyers	0	127	7/29/1998 12:00:00 AM
Goonies	Richard Donner	0	114	6/7/1985 12:00:00 AM
Dazed and Confused	Richard Linklater	0	103	9/24/1993 12:00:00 AM
Monty Python and the Holy Grail	Terry Gilliam	0	91	5/10/1975 12:00:00 AM
Old School	Todd Phillips	0	91	2/21/2003 12:00:00 AM
Ace Ventura: Pet Detective	Tom Shadyac	0	86	2/4/1994 12:00:00 AM
Bruce Almighty	Tom Shadyac	0	101	5/23/2003 12:00:00 AM

FIGURE 10-19

SUMMARY

This chapter introduced you to the Language Integrated Query, or LINQ, features of .NET 4.5, which greatly simplify the querying of data in .NET. LINQ makes the query a first-class concept, embedded directly in the .NET Framework.

This review of LINQ presented the current methods for performing object queries, including basic data filtering, grouping, and sorting. You discovered the shortcomings of traditional object query techniques, including the requirement for developers to define not only what the query should do, but also exactly how it should do it. Additionally, you saw how even simple operations can result in highly complex code that can be difficult to read and maintain.

LINQ has three basic types: LINQ to Objects, LINQ to XML, and LINQ to SQL. Each flavor of LINQ uses the same basic query syntax to dramatically simplify the querying of objects, XML, or SQL databases. You can use the basic SQL-like query syntax for selection, filtering, and grouping. This query syntax is clean and easily readable, and also includes many of the same operators as SQL.

The basic O/R mapper that is included with LINQ to SQL makes creating CLR objects that represent SQL structures, such as tables, views, and stored procedures, easy. After the CLR objects are created, you can use LINQ to query the objects.

Using LINQ to SQL, you can easily change the data in your database, using generated SQL statements or using custom stored procedures. With LINQ to Entities you can incorporate the more preferred database access technology, Entity Framework, but use the same LINQ syntax you have become familiar with.

11

Entity Framework

WHAT'S IN THIS CHAPTER?

➤ Understanding mapping and relationships

➤ Creating an Entity Data Model (EDM) using Database First

➤ Using the EntityDataSource control in an EDM

➤ Creating an Entity Data Model using Code First

WROX.COM CODE DOWNLOADS FOR THIS CHAPTER

Please note that all the code examples in this chapter are available as a part of this chapter's code download on the book's website at www.wrox.com on the Download Code tab.

Accessing data is one of the main things almost every application must do. Nearly all applications deal with data in some manner, whether that data comes from memory (in-memory data), databases, XML files, text files, or something else. Many developers find it very difficult to move from the strongly typed object-oriented world of C# or Visual Basic to the data tier where objects are second-class citizens. Before the Entity Framework, the transition from writing code using strongly typed objects to the more loosely typed collections of data returned from a data store was difficult, and often error-prone. Data access can complicate your application development for a number of reasons, not the least of which is the fact that code written to interact with a database and code written to handle application logic are very different from both a design and an implementation perspective.

Microsoft continuously attempts to simplify tasks that are common and laborious for programmers. This is typically done by abstracting the difficulties of these tasks through a combination of new interfaces and IDE assistance. With the latest release of the Entity Framework, you will find that navigating the world between the database and your application is easier than ever. In fact, by using Entity Framework Code First (discussed in this chapter), you now have more options for crossing the chasm between your code and the data in the database.

One of the benefits of working with any one of the available .NET programming languages is that the objects in your code are strongly typed. As a programmer, you can navigate very easily through namespaces, work with a debugger in the Visual Studio IDE, and more. However, when it comes to accessing data, things are dramatically different. You end up in a world that is not strongly typed, where debugging is painful or even non-existent, and you spend most of the time sending strings to the database as queries. As a developer, you must be aware of the underlying data and how it is structured. You must also understand how all the data points relate to one another.

The Entity Framework is a set of ADO.NET technologies that eliminates many of the difficulties mentioned above. Using the Entity Framework (along with LINQ), you now have a lightweight façade that provides a strongly typed interface to the underlying data stores that you are working with. Using these technologies, you can stay within the coding environment you are used to, and you have the ability to access the underlying data as objects that work with the IDE, IntelliSense, and even debugging. You no longer have to worry about the issues developers faced in the past with loosely typed lists of data. Entity Framework allows you to work with data using the same strongly typed objects that you are already comfortable with.

Not only do you have the capability to access and work with data using a more familiar paradigm, but you can do this with data from multiple data stores. The ADO.NET Data Provider model provides a common managed interface in the .NET Framework for connecting to and interacting with a data store. Entity Framework builds on top of the ADO.NET Data Provider model to allow for the use of Entity Framework with any data source for which a supported provider is available. The .NET Framework includes ADO.NET providers for direct access to Microsoft SQL Server and for indirect access to other databases with ODBC and OLE DB drivers. But third-party providers are available to provide direct access to other popular data stores as well, such as Oracle, MySQL, DB2, and many others.

This chapter provides an overview of the latest version of the Entity Framework and how you can use this framework within your ASP.NET applications. The latest version of the Entity Framework is now available as the EntityFramework NuGet package. The NuGet Package Manager is already installed in Visual Studio 2012.

CAN WE SPEAK THE SAME LANGUAGE?

As discussed earlier, building applications that communicate with databases should be an easier task than it is. The difficulty is that objects in code and objects in the database are inherently different beasts. Communicating objects from the database tier to other tiers of your application stack is the primary reason for the added complexity.

The Entity Framework provides the capability to map your application objects to your relational database schemas. For example, when you have an `Orders` table that is full of references to `Customer` objects and `StoreItem` objects, and you are working with a relational database schema, these entities are created using `JOIN` statements between various tables. However, if you are working with this construction from your C# or VB code, then you are creating an `Order` object that includes a property reference to a `Customer` object and a `StoreItem` object. Mapping these disparate representations together has usually been the job of developers.

In the past, an effort was made to address this issue of mapping with the introduction of the `DataSet` object. This object was an in-memory table representation that included with it multiple tables, with the table joins and constraints in place. However, with the pure object-oriented code that people really wanted to develop, the `DataSet` approach was often not recommended.

When you represent your data within the database, you are representing it as a *logical model* through the database's relational schema. However, coding your application is accomplished using a *conceptual model*. Having both logical and conceptual layers forced the creation of a mapping layer. The mapping layer allows you to transfer objects from the .NET classes that you are working with in your code to the relational database schemas that you are working with within the database, as represented in Figure 11-1.

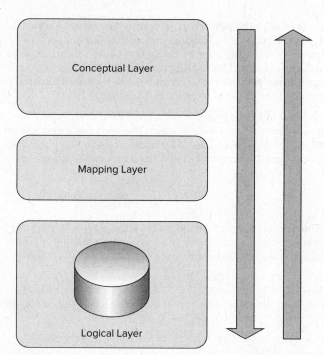

FIGURE 11-1

This mapping layer is sometimes thought of as a data access layer. Microsoft has provided a number of data access technologies over the past few years, and many third-party companies have formed around the concept of making this mapping as simple as possible. Some of the third parties even came on board to provide mapping or data access transformation to specialized databases.

Microsoft has moved forward to make the mapping of objects from the application code to the database schemas as simple as possible. The Entity Framework is in place so that you can write less code to get your applications out the door.

Note that you are going to need both the objects in your application code and the entities that you build within the relational schema of the database for some time to come.

So in the end, the Entity Framework consists of the following:

➤ A model of your database that is represented in the code of your application

➤ A definition of the datastore that you are working with (for example, your data representation within a SQL Server database)

➤ A mapping between the two elements

Development Workflow Options

Developers like options. You have three options for working with data in the Entity Framework:

➤ Database First

➤ Model First

➤ Code First

When you already have a database, you can use the Entity Framework to generate a data model for you. Database First and Model First development workflows utilize the rich designer and tooling support available in Visual Studio 2012. Using Database First, you build your model layer on a design surface from an existing database. Using Model First, you define your model layer using the designer and then use that to generate your database schema. The database schema is then used to create a new database. The designer does this by generating data definition language (DDL) statements to create the database.

The other workflow option was originally introduced in Entity Framework 4. It is called Code First development. Code First development is a more code-centric approach in which you don't use a designer. In Code First development, you define your model using "plain old classes." Database creation and persistence is enabled through the use of a convention over configuration approach, so no explicit configuration is necessary.

The Entity Data Model

The Entity Data Model (EDM) is an abstract conceptual model of data as you want to represent it in your code. It is usually construed as .NET classes that you can manipulate as you would any other object within your code. This first conceptual layer is created using the Conceptual Schema Definition Language (CSDL), which is an XML definition of your objects.

The logical layer is defined using the Store Schema Definition Language (SSDL). The logical layer details the relational schema that you are storing within your database. This includes a definition of the tables, their relations, and their constraints.

The last piece of the Entity Data Model is the mapping layer. This layer maps the CSDL and the SSDL instances using the Mapping Specification Language (MSL).

It is possible for the combination of these three layers to work together for a few reasons. One is that there is a common type system within the Entity Data Model that all three layers can share. This system enables you to specify types that the code of your application will understand and then these same types will be understood by the database that you are working with. The EDM also provides the ability to work with the concept of inheritance as well as complex objects and to make the appropriate mappings between the layers.

The three layers — the conceptual model, the logical model, and the mapping between them — are stored in XML in an `.edmx` file What's nice about Visual Studio 2012 is that you have a graphical designer to create these layers and the corresponding `.edmx` file on your behalf and under your direction. The graphical designer is then used to display and edit the `.edmx` file graphically so you don't have to edit the XML directly.

When using Code First development, you directly define your conceptual model by writing C# or VB classes. You can then use this model to generate a database schema.

CREATING YOUR FIRST ENTITY DATA MODEL

For an example of working with the Entity Framework, the first task is to work through all the steps that are required to read some data from a database and present it in your ASP.NET application using a designer workflow.

For this example, you must have Visual Studio 2010 or Visual Studio 2012. From this IDE, create a new empty ASP.NET web application called `AspnetEntityFx`, a standard ASP.NET application.

> **NOTE** *Next, you must get a database in place to work with. You can download the version of the AdventureWorks database we used for this book from* www.wrox.com/go/SQLSever2012DataSets.
>
> *To create the* App_Data *folder where you will add the database file, right-click on the project and select Add ⇨ Add ASP.NET Folder ⇨ App_Data. To add this database, right-click on the* App_Data *folder from the Solution Explorer and select the option to add an existing item.*

After you have added the database file to your project, you will need to upgrade the database to a SQL Express LocalDB database. Open the Server Explorer by selecting the View from the Visual Studio menu, then selecting Server Explorer. Expand the Data Connections to see the database file you just added. Right-click on the AdventureWorks2012_Data.mdf data connection and select Modify Connection. Click the Advanced button to display the Advanced Properties dialog box. Verify that the Data Source property is set to (LocalDB)\v11.0 and the User Instance property is set to False. Figure 11-2 shows the Advanced Properties dialog box with the correct settings for Data Source and User Instance.

Click OK to dismiss the Advanced Properties dialog box and OK to dismiss the Modify Connection dialog box. You will be presented with a message indicating that the database you are connecting to is not compatible with the current instance of SQL Server. Figure 11-3 shows this window. Click Yes to upgrade the database.

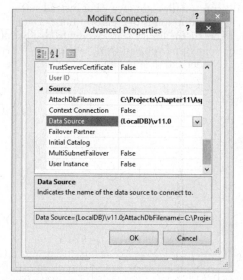

FIGURE 11-2   **FIGURE 11-3**

Once you have upgraded the database, you are ready to create your Entity Data Model. Right-click on your project within the Solution Explorer from Visual Studio and select Add ⇨ New Item. The Add New Item dialog box appears. From this dialog box, select the Data option for the language you are working with (found in the left pane of the dialog box). The available items you can add from the Data option include an ADO.NET Entity Data Model item, as shown in Figure 11-4.

For this example, name your Entity Data Model **EmployeeDM.edmx** (refer to Figure 11-4).

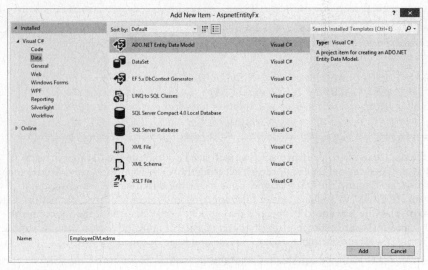

FIGURE 11-4

Working through the EDM Wizard

Adding this file when clicking the Add button does not actually insert a file right away, but instead starts a wizard. You can create an Entity Data Model in two ways. The first option is to create an Entity Data Model based on a preexisting database. The second option is to create the Entity Data Model from a blank slate. The .NET Framework 4.5 really makes the second option something you can work with easily. When you choose this second option, you can create your Entity Data Model and then use a wizard to create the database representation of that model.

The first screen in the wizard presents these options, as Figure 11-5 illustrates.

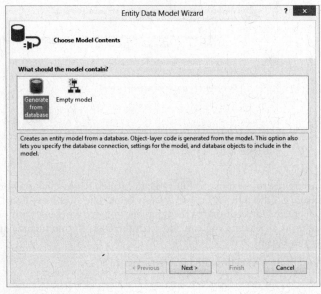

FIGURE 11-5

For this example, select the Generate from Database option. After you click Next in the wizard, the next step is to establish an entity connection string to the database, as shown in Figure 11-6.

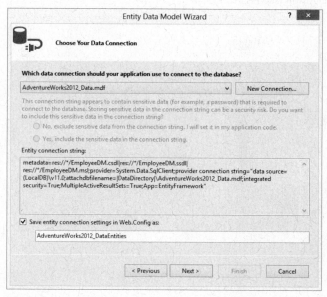

FIGURE 11-6

This wizard enables you to select the database that you want to work with from the first drop-down. The `AdventureWorks2012_Data.mdf` file appears as an option in this drop-down if you have added it to the project as previously instructed.

When selecting this database option in the drop-down, you will be presented with the entity connection string. It is much like a normal connection string:

```
metadata=res://*/EmployeeDM.csdl|res://*/EmployeeDM.ssdl|res://*/EmployeeDM.msl;
provider=System.Data.SqlClient;
provider connection string="Data Source=(LocalDB)\v11.0;
attachdbfilename=|DataDirectory|\AdventureWorks2012_Data.mdf;
integrated security=True; MultipleActiveResultSets=True; App=EntityFramework "
```

Notice that in addition to the normal connection string information that you might have, such as properties for the provider and the provider connection string, you also have the entity definition for what to use for the logical model and the conceptual model, as well as the mapping. The `EmployeeDM.csdl` file is for the conceptual model, `EmployeeDM.ssdl` is for the logical model, and `EmployeeDM.msl` is for the mapping required.

The final option in this dialog box is like most providers' configurations that you have worked with in the past with ASP.NET; it allows you to save the connection string in the `web.config` file of your project.

When you are done with this page of the wizard, click Next to choose the tables, views, and stored procedures that you are going to require for your Entity Data Model.

For this example, expand the Tables option in the tree view and select the Employee (Human Resources) table by selecting the check box next to the option (see Figure 11-7).

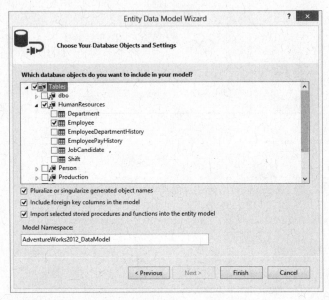

FIGURE 11-7

Notice that this part of the wizard enables you to define the namespace that you would use in accessing it from code. This example uses the default option of `AdventureWorks2012_DataModel`. This step is the last part of the wizard. Click the Finish button and a designer surface for your Entity Data Model then appears. After the designer surface opens, you may get a security warning asking whether you want to run a text template. The designer uses T4 templates to automatically generate a DbContext file and files for each of the entities you selected to be generated from the database. Check the option to not show the message again and click OK.

Using the Entity Framework Designer

The designer built into Visual Studio for working with the Entity Framework is powerful because it allows you to visually configure your conceptual layer and control how it maps to the logical layer.

If you worked through the wizard as defined earlier, then you will have a single `Employee` object represented on the design surface, as demonstrated in Figure 11-8.

When you highlight the `Employee` object in the designer, some basic properties will appear in the Properties pane within Visual Studio, as illustrated in Figure 11-9.

Here you can change the access modifier of the object and provide some basic documentation for the object. Visual Studio also provides you with some views to work with the Entity Framework. After you have created your `.edmx` file, a view is opened on your behalf—the Model Browser.

FIGURE 11-8

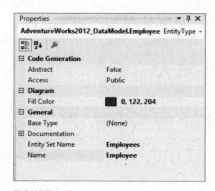

FIGURE 11-9

Another important view is the Entity Data Model Mapping Details window. You can get to this view in a couple of ways. You can select View ⇨ Other Windows ⇨ Entity Data Model Mapping Details from the Visual Studio menu, or you can right-click on the `Employee` object in the designer and select Table Mapping from the provided menu. Figure 11-10 presents both the Entity Data Model Browser and the Entity Data Model Mapping Details windows.

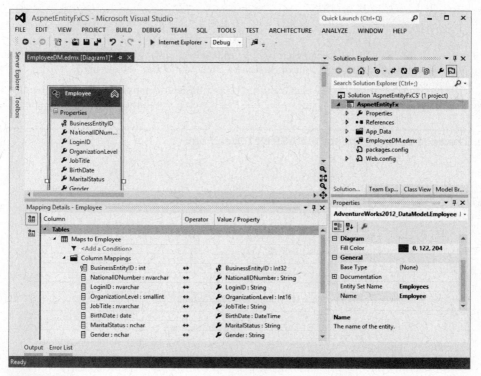

FIGURE 11-10

Now that this simple object is in place and your `.edmx` file is ready to go, the next step is to build a small ASP.NET Web Form that will use this construct.

Building an ASP.NET Web Form Using Your EDM

Now that you have your Entity Data Model in place, this section shows you how to build a simple Web Form that uses this model. The first step is to add a new Web Form to your project called `BasicGrid.aspx`. Add a GridView control on the page. In the end, the code of your ASP.NET Web Form will look like the code presented in Listing 11-1 (BasicGrid.aspx in the code download for this chapter).

LISTING 11-1: A basic ASP.NET Web Form that uses your EDM

```
<%@ Page Language="C#" AutoEventWireup="true"
    CodeBehind="BasicGrid.aspx.cs" Inherits="AspnetEntityFx.BasicGrid" %>

<!DOCTYPE html>

<html xmlns="http://www.w3.org/1999/xhtml" >
<head runat="server">
    <title>My EDM</title>
</head>
<body>
    <form id="form1" runat="server">
    <div>
        <asp:GridView ID="GridView1" runat="server">
        </asp:GridView>
    </div>
    </form>
</body>
</html>
```

This is the C# version of the Web Form. Notice that only a GridView control is on the page. You will use this control to populate the results that come out of the Entity Data Model that you created.

To use the Entity Data Model, Listing 11-2 (BasicGrid.aspx.vb and BasicGrid.aspx.cs in the code download for this chapter) shows you the code-behind page of the ASP.NET Web Form that is presented in Listing 11-1.

LISTING 11-2: The code-behind page for the ASP.NET Web Form

VB

```
Partial Public Class BasicGrid
    Inherits System.Web.UI.Page
    Protected Sub Page_Load(ByVal sender As Object,
      ByVal e As System.EventArgs) Handles Me.Load

        Dim adventureWorks2012_DataEntities As New
            AdventureWorks2012_DataEntities()

        Dim query =
         From emp In adventureWorks2012_DataEntities.Employees
         Select emp

        GridView1.DataSource = query.ToList()
        GridView1.DataBind()
    End Sub

End Class
```

C#

```
using System;
using System.Linq;

namespace AspnetEntityFx
{
    public partial class BasicGrid : System.Web.UI.Page
    {
        protected void Page_Load(object sender, EventArgs e)
        {
            AdventureWorks2012_DataEntities adventureWorks2012_DataEntities =
               new AdventureWorks2012_DataEntities();

            var query = from emp in
                            adventureWorks2012_DataEntities.Employees
                            select emp;
            GridView1.DataSource = query.ToList();
            GridView1.DataBind();
        }
    }
}
```

As you can see, there isn't much code to this page. Running the Web Form produces the results shown in Figure 11-11.

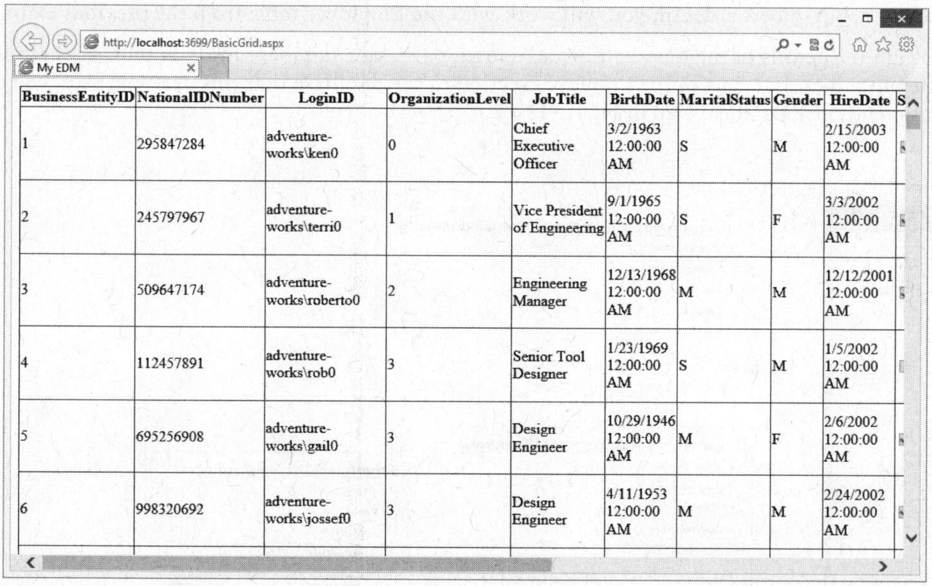

BusinessEntityID	NationalIDNumber	LoginID	OrganizationLevel	JobTitle	BirthDate	MaritalStatus	Gender	HireDate	S
1	295847284	adventure-works\ken0	0	Chief Executive Officer	3/2/1963 12:00:00 AM	S	M	2/15/2003 12:00:00 AM	
2	245797967	adventure-works\terri0	1	Vice President of Engineering	9/1/1965 12:00:00 AM	S	F	3/3/2002 12:00:00 AM	
3	509647174	adventure-works\roberto0	2	Engineering Manager	12/13/1968 12:00:00 AM	M	M	12/12/2001 12:00:00 AM	
4	112457891	adventure-works\rob0	3	Senior Tool Designer	1/23/1969 12:00:00 AM	S	M	1/5/2002 12:00:00 AM	
5	695256908	adventure-works\gail0	3	Design Engineer	10/29/1946 12:00:00 AM	M	F	2/6/2002 12:00:00 AM	
6	998320692	adventure-works\jossef0	3	Design Engineer	4/11/1953 12:00:00 AM	M	M	2/24/2002 12:00:00 AM	

FIGURE 11-11

To work with your new Entity Data Model, an instance of the model is created:

```
Dim adventureWorks2012_DataEntities As New AdventureWorks2012_DataEntities()
```

This instance manages your connection to the database and takes care of feeding in the queries that you might perform over the datastore. The next line is a LINQ statement:

```
Dim query = _
   From emp In adventureWorks2012_DataEntities.Employees _
   Select emp
```

Here you are using an implicitly typed variable, query. The value assigned to the query object is the value of the Employees property, which is of type IQueryable<Employee>. This LINQ query simply pulls the entire contents from the Employee table and places the result in the query object for use within your code.

After the LINQ operation is complete, a list created from the query object is assigned and bound as a source to the GridView1 control.

```
GridView1.DataSource = query.ToList()
GridView1.DataBind()
```

This simple example was of a one-to-one mapping. The next example looks at how to work with a many-to-many relationship.

UNDERSTANDING RELATIONSHIPS

The previous example was a good showing of a one-to-one mapping—an Employee object that mapped to the Employee table. In this section you take look at one-to-one and one-to-many relationships and many-to-one and many-to-many relationships.

One-to-One and One-to-Many Relationships

A one-to-one relationship is a construct in which one table maps to one type within your Entity Data Model. This is also called a Table per Type model (TPT).

To show this relationship in better detail, you will work with the Employee table from the previous example.

If you look through the details of the AdventureWorld2012_Data.mdf database file, you will see that there are a lot of different tables. In terms of the Employee section of the database that this example uses, you can find the database relationships illustrated in Figure 11-12.

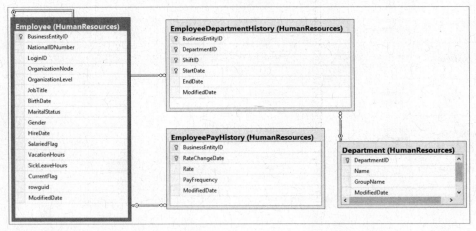

FIGURE 11-12

As you can see, in addition to the Employee table that you worked with earlier, you will find other tables such as the EmployeeDepartmentHistory, Department, and EmployeePayHistory tables with a specific mapping.

You can see from the figure that many of these tables are related through the BusinessEntityID foreign key.

In contrast to this mapping, you can pull up the `EmployeeDM.edmx` file that you created earlier in this chapter. From the design surface of this file, right-click and select Update Model from Database from the provided menu.

An Update Wizard appears, as shown in Figure 11-13.

Expand the Tables node and add references to the missing tables—EmployeeDepartmentHistory, Department, and EmployeePayHistory by selecting the check boxes next to each of them. From this figure, you can see that a one-to-many relationship exists with the other types of employee data.

With this construction in place, you will also find through IntelliSense that now one type (or object) maps to each of the specified tables, as illustrated in Figure 11-14.

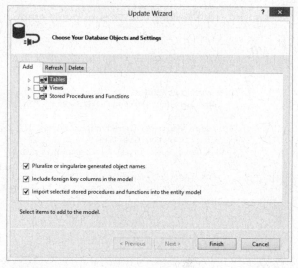

FIGURE 11-13

```csharp
using System;
using System.Linq;

namespace AspnetEntityFx
{
    public partial class BasicGrid : System.Web.UI.Page
    {
        protected void Page_Load(object sender, EventArgs e)
        {
            AdventureWorks2012_DataEntities adventureWorks2012_DataEntities =
                new AdventureWorks2012_DataEntities();

            var query = from emp
                        in adventureWorks2012_DataEntities.e
                        select emp;

            GridView1.DataSource = query.ToList();
            GridView1.DataBind();
        }
    }
}
```

FIGURE 11-14

With these tables in place, you can work with all the objects as demonstrated here. For this example, create a simple ASP.NET Web Form that includes only a single BulletedList control. Then from the code-behind of the Web Form, use the code from Listing 11-3 (OneToMany.aspx.vb and OneToMany.aspx.cs in the code download for this chapter).

LISTING 11-3: Working with one-to-many mappings

VB

```vb
Protected Sub Page_Load(ByVal sender As Object, ByVal e As EventArgs)

    Dim adventureWorks2012_DataEntities As
        New AdventureWorks2012_DataEntities()

    For Each employee In adventureWorks2012_DataEntities.Employees
        Dim li As New ListItem()
        li.Text = employee.BusinessEntityID & " "

        For Each pay In employee.EmployeePayHistories
            li.Text &= "Pay Rate: " & pay.Rate & " "
        Next pay

        BulletedList1.Items.Add(li)
    Next employee
End Sub
```

C#

```csharp
using System;
using System.Web.UI.WebControls;

namespace AspnetEntityFx
{
    public partial class _Default : System.Web.UI.Page
    {
        protected void Page_Load(object sender, EventArgs e)
        {
            AdventureWorks2012_DataEntities adventureWorks2012_DataEntities =
                new AdventureWorks2012_DataEntities();

            foreach (var employee in
                adventureWorks2012_DataEntities.Employees)
            {
                ListItem li = new ListItem();

                li.Text = employee.BusinessEntityID + " ";

                foreach (var pay in employee.EmployeePayHistories)
                {
                    li.Text += "Pay Rate: " + pay.Rate + " ";
                }

                BulletedList1.Items.Add(li);
            }
        }
    }
}
```

At first, the Employees objects are accessed and none of the other objects are actually loaded. The first time the EmployeePayHistory object is accessed, it will be automatically loaded if it has not already been. You no longer have to explicitly load related objects as you did in previous versions of the framework.

If you run this bit of code, you get the results shown in Figure 11-15.

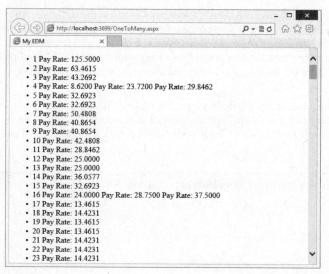

FIGURE 11-15

Many-to-One and Many-to-Many Relationships

In addition to the one-to-one and the one-to-many relationships, the Entity Framework supports many-to-one and many-to-many relationships. In these relationships, the Entity Framework will perform the appropriate table joins for you when you query the database.

Create a new Entity Data Model (Sales.edmx file) that includes the Customer, SalesTerritory, SalesOrderHeader, and the SalesOrderDetail tables.

You end up with a model that looks like Figure 11-16.

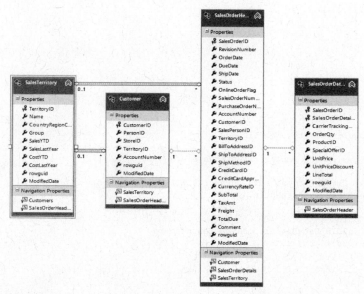

FIGURE 11-16

You can see the relationships by looking at the line that connects the visual objects on the designer. An asterisk on one end of the line indicates *many*. The number 1 appearing on the other side of the connection, as the line that is between the `SalesOrderHeader` and the `Customer` objects, indicates a many-to-one relationship. You can also view details about the relationship in the Properties window of Visual Studio upon highlighting the relationship line itself in the designer, as presented through the two `End` property values in the view.

Now look at a page that will perform some joins on your behalf across the tables. This operation is illustrated in Listing 11-4 (ManyToMany.aspx.vb and ManyToMany.aspx.cs in the code download for this chapter). For this example, just keep the simple Web Form that contains only a GridView control and use the code-behind that is presented here.

LISTING 11-4: Having the Entity Framework perform joins between tables

VB

```vb
Partial Public Class ManyToMany
    Inherits System.Web.UI.Page

Protected Sub Page_Load(ByVal sender As Object,
    ByVal e As EventArgs)

        Dim adventureWorks2012_DataEntities As
            New AdventureWorks2012_DataEntities1()

        Dim query = _
            From o In adventureWorks2012_DataEntities.SalesOrderHeaders
            Where o.SalesOrderDetails.Any(Function(Quantity)
                Quantity.OrderQty > 5)
            Select New With {Key o.PurchaseOrderNumber,
                    Key o.Customer.CustomerID,
                    Key o.SalesPersonID}

        GridView1.DataSource = query.ToList()
        GridView1.DataBind()

    End Sub
End Class
```

C#

```csharp
using System;
using System.Linq;

namespace AspnetEntityFx
{
    public partial class _Default : System.Web.UI.Page
    {
        protected void Page_Load(object sender, EventArgs e)
        {
            AdventureWorks2012_DataEntities1 adventureWorks2012_DataEntities =
                new AdventureWorks2012_DataEntities1();

            var query = from o in
                adventureWorks2012_DataEntities.SalesOrderHeaders
                where o.SalesOrderDetails.Any(Quantity =>
                    Quantity.OrderQty > 5)
```

```
            select new {o.PurchaseOrderNumber,
                o.Customer.CustomerID, o.SalesPersonID};

          GridView1.DataSource = query.ToList();
          GridView1.DataBind();
        }
      }
    }
```

This query pulls content and works from three different tables, and the Entity Framework does all the work of making the appropriate joins for you against the tables.

In this case, you are working with all the items in the SalesOrderHeader table where the quantity of the order is more than five. From the items selected, the fields are pulled for the dynamic object from across a couple of tables. Finally, the result is again bound to a GridView control. Figure 11-17 presents the final result.

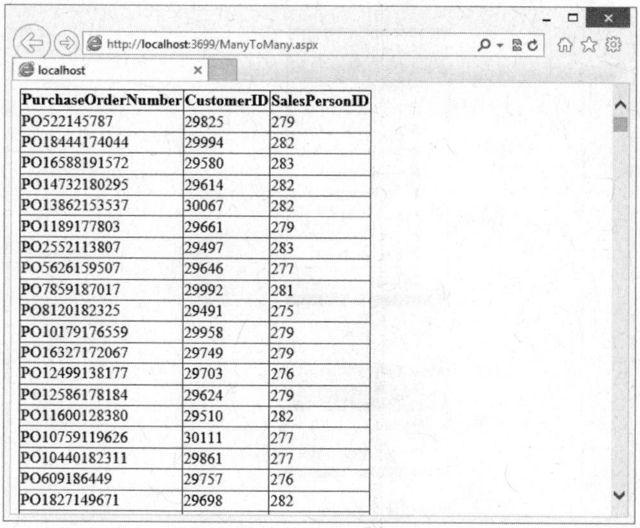

PurchaseOrderNumber	CustomerID	SalesPersonID
PO522145787	29825	279
PO18444174044	29994	282
PO16588191572	29580	283
PO14732180295	29614	282
PO13862153537	30067	282
PO1189177803	29661	279
PO2552113807	29497	283
PO5626159507	29646	277
PO7859187017	29992	281
PO8120182325	29491	275
PO10179176559	29958	279
PO16327172067	29749	279
PO12499138177	29703	276
PO12586178184	29624	279
PO11600128380	29510	282
PO10759119626	30111	277
PO10440182311	29861	277
PO609186449	29757	276
PO1827149671	29698	282

FIGURE 11-17

PERFORMING INHERITANCE WITHIN THE EDM

You can perform inheritance when constructing your Entity Data Model just as easily as you can when dealing with your objects within the CLR.

Inheritance gives you the capability to work with and look for specialized objects that you determine. For an example of this feature, in this section you modify the Vendor object so that you can build a query that will look for inactive vendors by object reference rather than through value interpretation.

Create a new Entity Data Model (Vendor .edmx file) that contains only the Vendor table (Purchasing section). When you open the table definition of the Vendor table within Visual Studio, you will see something like Figure 11-18.

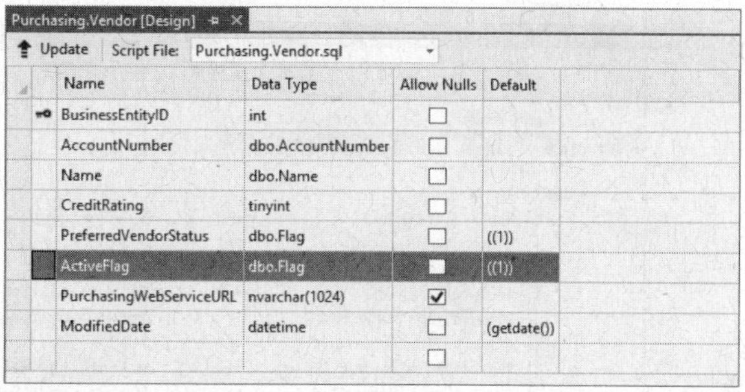

Name	Data Type	Allow Nulls	Default
BusinessEntityID	int	☐	
AccountNumber	dbo.AccountNumber	☐	
Name	dbo.Name	☐	
CreditRating	tinyint	☐	
PreferredVendorStatus	dbo.Flag	☐	((1))
ActiveFlag	dbo.Flag	☐	((1))
PurchasingWebServiceURL	nvarchar(1024)	☑	
ModifiedDate	datetime	☐	(getdate())
		☐	

FIGURE 11-18

As you can see from this figure, the `ActiveFlag` property is of type `bit`, which means it is either a zero or a one representing a False or True, respectively. For this example, you will build a specialized type that is a reference to an inactive vendor so that you can differentiate between active and inactive.

When your Vendor table is in place, right-click on the designer surface and choose Add ⇨ Entity from the provided menu. The Add Entity window then appears.

From this window, provide an entity name of `InactiveVendor` and have it inherit from a base type of `Vendor`. In the end, your Add Entity dialog box should appear as shown in Figure 11-19.

This step will add a visual representation to the mapping, as illustrated in Figure 11-20.

FIGURE 11-19

FIGURE 11-20

The next step is to further tie the two objects together and to provide some logic to their relationship. To accomplish this task you first delete the `ActiveFlag` scalar property from the `Vendor` entity object, because you will not need it in the example.

You then highlight the `Vendor` object within the designer and view the details of the mapping of this object within the Mapping Details view within Visual Studio. From this view, add a condition of `ActiveFlag` being equal to `1`, as demonstrated in Figure 11-21.

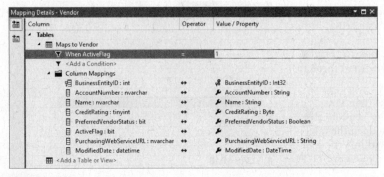

FIGURE 11-21

This setting really means that if the `ActiveFlag` has a value of 1, then the object will be of type `Vendor`. Now you set up the `InactiveVendor` object. Looking at this object within the Mapping Detail view, you first must add the Vendor table in the Mapping Details view. From there, create a condition where the `ActiveFlag` is equal to the value 0, as illustrated in Figure 11-22.

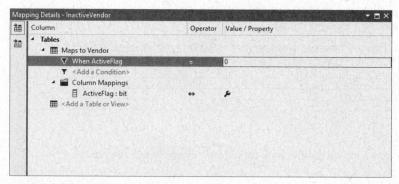

FIGURE 11-22

Now with these conditions all in place, you are really saying that if the `ActiveFlag` value has a value of 1, then it is of type `Vendor` in your Entity Data Model. However, if the `ActiveFlag` has a value of 0, then the object type is of `InactiveVendor`. You can work with this in your code, as illustrated in Listing 11-5 (Inheritance.aspx.vb and Inheritance.aspx.cs in the code download for this chapter).

LISTING 11-5: Using inheritance with your Entity Data Model

VB

```
Partial Public Class Inheritance
    Inherits System.Web.UI.Page

    Protected Sub Page_Load(ByVal sender As Object,
      ByVal e As EventArgs)

        Dim adventureWorks2012_DataEntities As New
            AdventureWorks2012_DataEntities2()

        Dim query =
            From v In adventureWorks2012_DataEntities.Vendors
                .OfType(Of InactiveVendor)()
            Select v

        GridView1.DataSource = query.ToList()
        GridView1.DataBind()
    End Sub

End Class
```

C#

```
using System;
using System.Linq;

namespace AspnetEntityFx
{
```

continues

LISTING 11-5 *(continued)*

```
public partial class Inheritance : System.Web.UI.Page
{
    protected void Page_Load(object sender, EventArgs e)
    {
        AdventureWorks2012_DataEntities3 adventureWorks2012_DataEntities =
            new AdventureWorks2012_DataEntities3();

        var query = from v in adventureWorks2012_DataEntities.Vendors
                        .OfType<InactiveVendor>()
                    select v;
        GridView1.DataSource = query.ToList();
        GridView1.DataBind();
    }
}
```

You can now use the `OfType` extension method to look for objects of type `InactiveVendor`.

USING STORED PROCEDURES

If you have been working with data access prior to using EF or any other ORM technology, you might have had a heavy reliance on stored procedures. Is this technology asking you to abandon the scores of stored procedures that you have built and have ready to use for your applications? Well, the answer is no, because you are able to work with stored procedures just as easily as everything that has been previously shown in this chapter. Many developers building new applications are moving away from the heavy use of stored procedures that was often seen in the past in favor of commands automatically generated by EF. The use of stored procedures is not covered in this chapter, but it is important to note that EF does support their use. If you have a legacy application or are restricted to using stored procedures due to standards or compliance, EF is still a valid option for your data access.

USING THE ENTITYDATASOURCE CONTROL

The EntityDataSource control makes working with your Entity Data Model from your ASP.NET applications easy. The control will handle the LINQ work necessary to bind to any of your controls.

Creating the Base Page

For an example of using the EntityDataSource control, you will go back to the `Sales.edmx` file and work with the `Customer` object within that model.

First, you need to create an ASP.NET Web Form to work with this model. To do so, create the Web Form in your ASP.NET web application project and use the code presented in Listing 11-6 (EntityDataSource.aspx in the code download for the chapter).

LISTING 11-6: Using the EntityDataSource server control

```
<%@ Page Language="C#" AutoEventWireup="true"
    CodeBehind="EntityDataSource.aspx.cs" Inherits="AspnetEntityFx. EntityDataSource" %>

<!DOCTYPE html>

<html xmlns="http://www.w3.org/1999/xhtml" >
```

```
<head runat="server">
    <title> </title>
</head>
<body>
    <form id="form1" runat="server">
    <asp:GridView ID="GridView1" runat="server">
    </asp:GridView>
    <br />
    <asp:EntityDataSource ID="EntityDataSource1" runat="server">
    </asp:EntityDataSource>
    </form>
</body>
</html>
```

With this page in place you can configure the EntityDataSource control on the page to work with the Entity Data Model that you created. Then you can bind the GridView control to this data source control.

Configuring the Data Source Control

Now you configure the data source control on your page so that it will work from your Entity Data Model that you created earlier. To do this, you can either code the EntityDataSource control directly in the code of your ASP.NET Web Form or work through the data source configuration wizard. For this example, you will work through the wizard.

Highlight the data source control in your page, and you will find the Configure Data Source link from the available options. Click the link. The first screen (see Figure 11-23) appears, asking you to configure the ObjectContext.

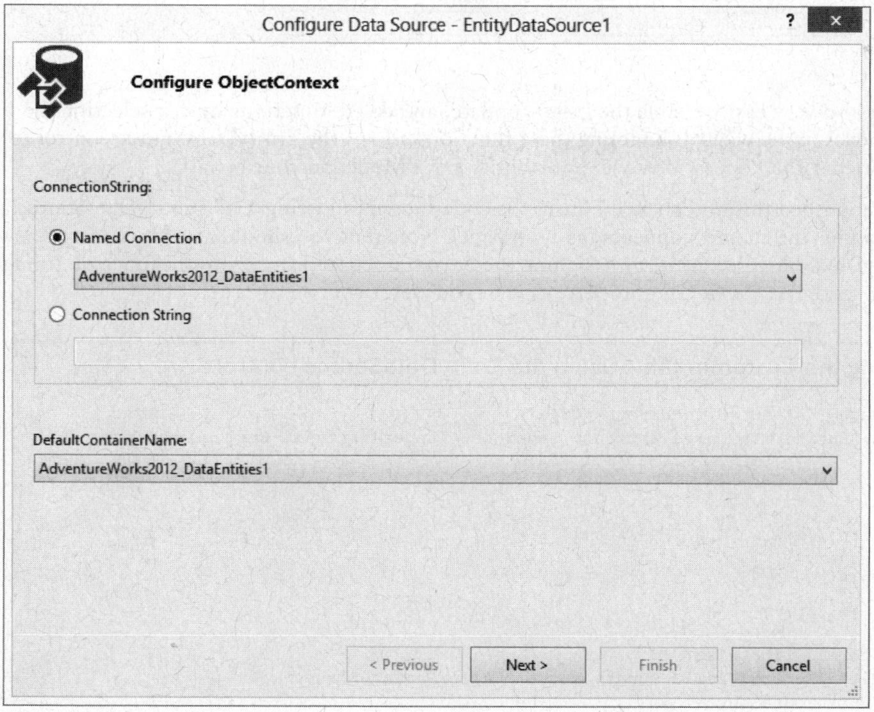

FIGURE 11-23

For this example, you work with the `AdventureWorks2012_DataEntities1` object that you created earlier. Click the Next button to configure your data selection process. In this case, as presented in Figure 11-24, you can select the Customers table.

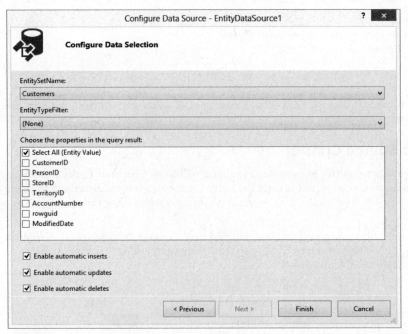

FIGURE 11-24

Notice that you can also very easily enable the insert, update, and delete functions by just selecting the appropriate check boxes in the wizard. Enabling these functions allows the EntityDataSource control to perform the appropriate LINQ operations over your Entity Data Model on your behalf.

After you have accomplished this and clicked Finish, the code shown in Listing 11-7 (EntityDataSource.aspx in the code download for the chapter) appears (as a C# page). Note that you should also tie the GridView1 control to the EntityDataSource1 control by assigning the `DataSourceID` property to this control. It might also be beneficial to set the `AllowPaging` property of the GridView1 control to True.

LISTING 11-7: Pulling the Customer table using the EntityDataSource control

```
<%@ Page Language="C#" AutoEventWireup="true"
    CodeBehind="EntityDataSource.aspx.cs" Inherits="AspnetEntityFx. EntityDataSource" %>

<!DOCTYPE html>

<html xmlns="http://www.w3.org/1999/xhtml" >
<head runat="server">
    <title> </title>
</head>
<body>
    <form id="form1" runat="server">
    <asp:GridView ID="GridView1" runat="server" AllowPaging="True"
DataSourceID="EntityDataSource1">
    </asp:GridView>
```

```
        <asp:EntityDataSource ID="EntityDataSource1" runat="server"
            ConnectionString="name=AdventureWorks2012_DataEntities1NorthwindEntities"
            DefaultContainerName="AdventureWorks2012_DataEntities1NorthwindEntities"
            EnableDelete="True" EnableFlattening="False"
            EnableInsert="True"
            EnableUpdate="True" EntitySetName="Customers">
        </asp:EntityDataSource>
        </form>
    </body>
    </html>
```

Running this Web Form produces the results shown in Figure 11-25 for viewing the items from your Entity Data Model.

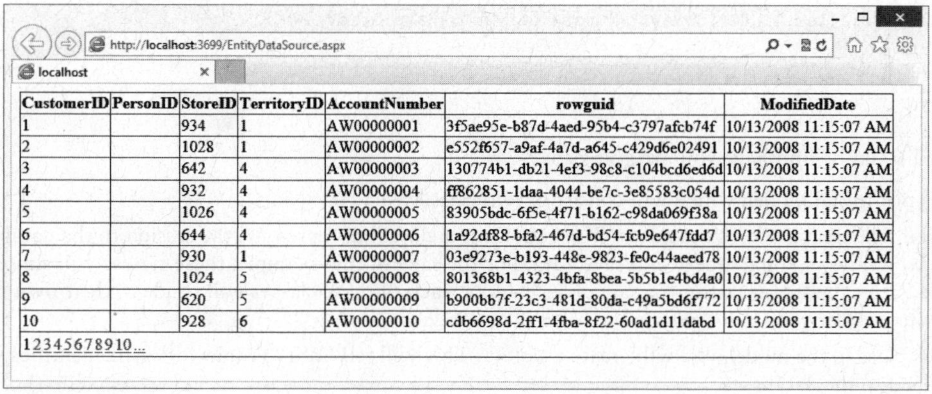

CustomerID	PersonID	StoreID	TerritoryID	AccountNumber	rowguid	ModifiedDate
1		934	1	AW00000001	3f5ae95e-b87d-4aed-95b4-c3797afcb74f	10/13/2008 11:15:07 AM
2		1028	1	AW00000002	e552f657-a9af-4a7d-a645-c429d6e02491	10/13/2008 11:15:07 AM
3		642	4	AW00000003	130774b1-db21-4ef3-98c8-c104bcd6ed6d	10/13/2008 11:15:07 AM
4		932	4	AW00000004	ff862851-1daa-4044-be7c-3e85583c054d	10/13/2008 11:15:07 AM
5		1026	4	AW00000005	83905bdc-6f5e-4f71-b162-c98da069f38a	10/13/2008 11:15:07 AM
6		644	4	AW00000006	1a92df88-bfa2-467d-bd54-fcb9e647fdd7	10/13/2008 11:15:07 AM
7		930	1	AW00000007	03e9273e-b193-448e-9823-fe0c44aeed78	10/13/2008 11:15:07 AM
8		1024	5	AW00000008	801368b1-4323-4bfa-8bea-5b5b1e4bd4a0	10/13/2008 11:15:07 AM
9		620	5	AW00000009	b900bb7f-23c3-481d-80da-c49a5bd6f772	10/13/2008 11:15:07 AM
10		928	6	AW00000010	cdb6698d-2ff1-4fba-8f22-60ad1d11dabd	10/13/2008 11:15:07 AM
12345678910...						

FIGURE 11-25

ENTITY FRAMEWORK CODE FIRST

Code First was introduced in version 4.1 of the Entity Framework. The Code First workflow is a code-centric approach to working with your data and models. It provides an alternative to the Database First and Model First development workflows using the designer interface. Code First uses a convention-over-configuration approach, allowing you to focus on defining your models using C# or VB classes. These classes can then be mapped to an existing database or be used to generate a schema that can be used to generate a new database. If any additional configuration is needed, such as more advanced mapping, you can use data annotations or a fluent API to provide the additional details.

Code First Migrations were introduced in version 4.3.1 of the Entity Framework. Until Migrations were introduced, making changes to your Code First model meant dropping and re-creating your database. This might be acceptable during development of your application. But once you release your application into production, dropping and re-creating it every time there was a change in the model was just not acceptable. Much like Code First allows you to represent your model in code, Code First Migrations allow you to express a database schema migration in code. Each time a change is made to your model that you wish to publish to your database, you create a migration. Each migration is a class representing the changes made to the model since the last migration. As a result, you are able to maintain a history of database changes directly in your project.

Creating a Code First Model

Add a new Web Form to your project called `CodeFirst.aspx`. Add a GridView control on the page. Your ASP.NET page will now look like the code (shown for C#) in Listing 11-8 (CodeFirst.aspx in the code download for this chapter).

LISTING 11-8: The basic page that will use your Code First model

```
<%@ Page Language="C#" AutoEventWireup="true" CodeBehind="CodeFirst.aspx.cs"
Inherits="AspnetEntityFX.CodeFirst" %>

<!DOCTYPE html>

<html xmlns="http://www.w3.org/1999/xhtml">
<head runat="server">
    <title>Code First Model</title>
</head>
<body>
    <form id="form1" runat="server">
    <div>
        <asp:GridView ID="GridView1" runat="server"></asp:GridView>
    </div>
    </form>
</body>
</html>
```

In the ASP.NET code-behind page you are going to:

1. Create your initial model, which will consist of two classes.

2. Then you will create a derived context. The context is a class that represents the session to the database. This is what allows you to query and save data. For the sake of this example, these classes will simply be added after the Page class in the same file. Usually, each of these classes will reside in their own file. The context is derived from System.Data.Entity.DbContext.

3. For each class in the model, you will create a DbSet. This will tell Entity Framework which entities will be mapped to the database.

4. Next, you will add some code to the Page_Load method to add some data to the database and display that data.

Listing 11-9 (CodeFirst.aspx.vb and CodeFirst.aspx.cs in the code download for this chapter) shows the code-behind page after adding the model classes, the context, and the code that uses them.

LISTING 11-9: Code-behind page for the CodeFirst ASP.NET page

VB

```
Imports System.Data.Entity

Public Class CodeFirst
    Inherits System.Web.UI.Page

    Protected Sub Page_Load(ByVal sender As Object, ByVal e As System.EventArgs)
        Handles Me.Load
        Using context As New TeamContextVB()
            Dim team As New Team() With {.TeamName = "Team 1"}
            context.Teams.Add(team)
            team = New Team() With {.TeamName = "Team 2"}
            context.Teams.Add(team)
            team = New Team() With {.TeamName = "Team 3"}
            context.Teams.Add(team)
            context.SaveChanges()

            Dim query = From t In context.Teams Select t

            GridView1.DataSource = query.ToList()
            GridView1.DataBind()
```

```vb
            End Using
        End Sub

End Class

Public Class Team
    Public Property TeamId() As Integer
    Public Property TeamName() As String
End Class

Public Class Player
    Public Property PlayerId() As Integer
    Public Property FirstName() As String
    Public Property LastName() As String
End Class

Public Class TeamContextVB
    Inherits DbContext

    Public Property Teams() As DbSet(Of Team)
    Public Property Players() As DbSet(Of Player)
End Class
```

C#

```csharp
using System;
using System.Collections.Generic;
using System.Data.Entity;
using System.Linq;

namespace AspnetEntityFX
{
    public partial class CodeFirst : System.Web.UI.Page
    {
        protected void Page_Load(object sender, EventArgs e)
        {
            using (var context = new TeamContext())
            {
                var team = new Team { TeamName = "Team 1" };
                context.Teams.Add(team);
                team = new Team { TeamName = "Team 2" };
                context.Teams.Add(team);
                team = new Team { TeamName = "Team 3" };
                context.Teams.Add(team);
                context.SaveChanges();

                var query = from t in context.Teams
                            select t;

                GridView1.DataSource = query.ToList();
                GridView1.DataBind();
            }

        }
    }

    public class Team
    {
        public int TeamId { get; set; }
        public string TeamName { get; set; }
    }

    public class Player
```

continues

LISTING 11-9 *(continued)*

```
    {
        public int PlayerId { get; set; }
        public string FirstName { get; set; }
        public string LastName { get; set; }
    }

    public class TeamContext : DbContext
    {
        public DbSet<Team> Teams { get; set; }
        public DbSet<Player> Players { get; set; }
    }
}
```

That is all the code that is necessary to have Entity Framework create a database based on your model. Notice that you don't have to create a connection to a database or even reference a connection string. That is due to the convention-over-configuration approach of Code First. Executing the page produces the results shown in Figure 11-26.

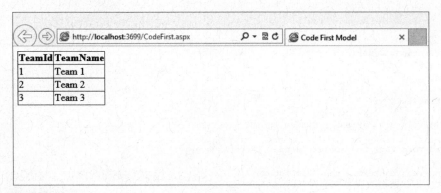

FIGURE 11-26

In order to tell Entity Framework to map your model classes to the database, you create a `DbSet<EntityType>` for each model class.

```
public DbSet<Team> Teams { get; set; };
public DbSet<Player> Players { get; set; };
```

In order to use your new model, you will add some data to the database that will be created for you. You simply need to create a new instance of your class, add it to the `Teams DbSet`, and tell the database context to persist the changes to the database.

```
var team = new Team { TeamName = "Test 3" };
context.Teams.Add(team);
context.SaveChanges();
```

Now you can query the data using the database context just as you did with the Entity Data Model you created using the Database First designer workflow.

```
var query = from t in context.Teams select t
```

Once you have the `IQueryable` returned from the LINQ query, you bind the data to the GridView control.

```
GridView1.DataSource = query.ToList();
GridView1.DataBind();
```

Convention over Configuration

In the previous example, a database was created for you by `DbContext` based on a default convention. The database is created the first time you do anything that causes a connection to the database to be established.

Determining where the database was created depends on what version or versions of SQL Express are installed on your machine. If you have a local SQL Express instance running on your machine, Code First installs your database there. By default, SQL Express was installed with Visual Studio 2010. By default, Visual Studio 2012 installs a new version of SQL Express, called SQL Express LocalDB. If Code First cannot find an instance of SQL Express, the database will be installed using LocalDB.

Regardless of the database used, the database is named using the fully qualified name of the derived context. In this example, the database name is `AspnetEntityFX.TeamContext`.

You can view the database that was created using the Server Explorer in Visual Studio. Add a new data connection. For the server name, specify either (LocalDB)\v11.0 if your database was created using LocalDB or .\SQLExpress if your database was created using SQL Express. Specify the database name as the fully qualified name of the derived context. Figure 11-27 shows the completed Add Connection information.

FIGURE 11-27

After adding the data connection to the database, expand the database tables to view the schema that was created by Code First. Figure 11-28 shows the database schema created for you by Code First.

The `DbContext` determined what classes needed to be included in the model based on the `DbSet` properties you defined. Code First then used a set of default conventions to determine table names, column names, primary keys, data types, and other parts of the database schema. Note that these default conventions can be modified using configuration entries.

Relationships in Code First

Just as you did using the designer, relationships can be created between entities in a Code First model. To demonstrate this, you'll create a one-to-many relationship between the `Team` and the `Player` entities.

The Entity Framework uses navigation properties to represent a relationship between two entity types. Navigation properties can manage relationships in both directions. If the relationship is one-to-one, a property is created referencing the related type. If the relationship is one-to-many or many-to-one, the property is a

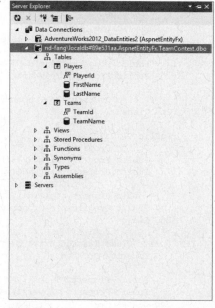

FIGURE 11-28

collection of the type involved in the relationship. Properties can also be used to represent foreign keys on a dependent object using the default Code First conventions. Listing 11-10 (CodeFirst.aspx.vb and CodeFirst .aspx.cs in the code download for the chapter) shows the modified code file after making changes to the classes to create a relationship between the `Team` and `Player` classes.

LISTING 11-10: Code showing a one-to-many Code First relationship

VB

```vb
Imports System.Data.Entity

Public Class CodeFirst
    Inherits System.Web.UI.Page

    Protected Sub Page_Load(ByVal sender As Object, ByVal e As System.EventArgs)
        Handles Me.Load
        Using context As New TeamContextVB()
            Dim team As New Team() With {.TeamName = "Team 1"}
            context.Teams.Add(team)
            team = New Team() With {.TeamName = "Team 2"}
            context.Teams.Add(team)
            team = New Team() With {.TeamName = "Team 3"}
            context.Teams.Add(team)
            context.SaveChanges()

            Dim query = From t In context.Teams Select t

            GridView1.DataSource = query.ToList()
            GridView1.DataBind()
        End Using
    End Sub

End Class

Public Class Team
    Public Sub New()
        Me.Players = New List(Of Player)()
    End Sub
    Public Property TeamId() As Integer
    Public Property TeamName() As String

    Public Overridable Property Players() As ICollection(Of Player)
End Class

Public Class Player
    Public Property PlayerId() As Integer
    Public Property FirstName() As String
    Public Property LastName() As String

    Public Property TeamId() As Integer
    Public Overridable Property Team() As Team
End Class

Public Class TeamContextVB
    Inherits DbContext

    Public Property Teams() As DbSet(Of Team)
    Public Property Players() As DbSet(Of Player)
End Class
```

C#

```csharp
using System;
using System.Collections.Generic;
using System.Data.Entity;
using System.Linq;

namespace AspnetEntityFX
{
    public partial class CodeFirst : System.Web.UI.Page
    {
        protected void Page_Load(object sender, EventArgs e)
        {
            using (var context = new TeamContext())
            {
                var team = new Team { TeamName = "Team 1" };
                context.Teams.Add(team);
                team = new Team { TeamName = "Team 2" };
                context.Teams.Add(team);
                team = new Team { TeamName = "Team 3" };
                context.Teams.Add(team);
                context.SaveChanges();

                var query = from t in context.Teams
                            select t;

                GridView1.DataSource = query.ToList();
                GridView1.DataBind();
            }

        }
    }

    public class Team
    {
        public int TeamId { get; set; }
        public string TeamName { get; set; }

        public virtual List<Player> Players { get; set; }
    }

    public class Player
    {
        public int PlayerId { get; set; }
        public string FirstName { get; set; }
        public string LastName { get; set; }

        public int TeamId { get; set; }
        public virtual Team Team { get; set; }
    }

    public class TeamContext : DbContext
    {
        public DbSet<Team> Teams { get; set; }
        public DbSet<Player> Players { get; set; }
    }
}
```

A relationship was created from a `Team` to a collection of related `Player` entities.

```csharp
public virtual List<Player> Players { get; set; }
```

Note that when you query the database for a particular `Team`, you may not need the collection of `Player` objects to be populated. By making the `Players` property virtual, you are instructing the `DbContext` to lazy load the `Players` collection. Lazy loading means that the collection will automatically be populated from the database when you try to access it.

A relationship was also created from a player back to a team. A navigation property was added to form the relationship to the `Team` object. It is also a virtual property in order to use lazy loading. Another property was added to instruct Code First to create a foreign key to the `Team` database table when the database schema is generated.

```
public int TeamId { get; set; }
public virtual Team Team { get; set; }
```

If you try to execute the new code now, you will get an exception because the database schema no longer matches the model. Before the new code can be executed, the database must be updated. The next section demonstrates how to use Code First Migrations to update the database schema with the changes you have made to the model.

Code First Migrations

Code First Migrations were introduced in Entity Framework 4.3.1. Prior to that, modifying your Code First model meant the database would be dropped and re-created. Obviously that is not a good option for an application in production. Migrations are the answer to pushing model changes to your database. Like Code First models, migrations are also built using code. However, you can use a few Package Manager Console commands to build the migrations for you.

The first step to using Code First Migrations is to enable it.

1. Open the Package Manager Console by clicking on Tools ➪ Library Package Manager ➪ Package Manager Console from the Visual Studio menu.

2. At the console prompt, run the command `Enable-Migrations`.

3. If you have been following along with the other examples in this chapter, you will have multiple derived contexts in the project. Therefore, the `Enable-Migrations` command responds with a message that it cannot determine which context you would like to enable migrations for. You must tell the command which context you want to enable migrations for. In order to do this, run the command `Enable-Migrations -ContextTypeName AspnetEntityFX.TeamContext`.

After the command completes, a new `Migrations` folder is added to your project and two new files have been placed in the folder.

➤ The first file, `Configuration.cs`, contains the configuration settings Migrations will use for the derived context.

➤ The second file is the initial migration file. It contains the changes that have already been applied to the database. The migration filename includes a timestamp used for ordering the migrations.

Now you need to create a new migration that includes the changes you made to the model in the previous section. In order to add a new migration, you will run the add migration command passing in a name for the migration. In the Package Manager Console, run the command `Add-Migration TeamPlayerRelationship`.

When the command runs, it creates a new migration file in the `Migrations` folder. Listing 11-11 (X_TeamPlayerRelationship.cs and X_TeamPlayerRelationship.vb [where X is the timestamp]) shows the contents of the new migration file.

LISTING 11-11: The contents of the new migration file

VB

```vb
Imports System
Imports System.Data.Entity.Migrations

Namespace Migrations
    Public Partial Class TeamPlayerRelationship
        Inherits DbMigration

        Public Overrides Sub Up()
            AddColumn("dbo.Players", "TeamId", Function(c) c.Int(nullable :=
                False))
            AddForeignKey("dbo.Players", "TeamId", "dbo.Teams", "TeamId",
                cascadeDelete := True)
            CreateIndex("dbo.Players", "TeamId")
        End Sub

        Public Overrides Sub Down()
            DropIndex("dbo.Players", New String() { "TeamId" })
            DropForeignKey("dbo.Players", "TeamId", "dbo.Teams")
            DropColumn("dbo.Players", "TeamId")
        End Sub
    End Class
End Namespace
```

C#

```csharp
namespace AspnetEntityFX.Migrations
{
    using System;
    using System.Data.Entity.Migrations;

    public partial class TeamPlayerRelationship : DbMigration
    {
        public override void Up()
        {
            AddColumn("dbo.Players", "TeamId", c => c.Int(nullable: false));
            AddForeignKey("dbo.Players", "TeamId", "dbo.Teams", "TeamId",
                cascadeDelete: true);
            CreateIndex("dbo.Players", "TeamId");
        }

        public override void Down()
        {
            DropIndex("dbo.Players", new[] { "TeamId" });
            DropForeignKey("dbo.Players", "TeamId", "dbo.Teams");
            DropColumn("dbo.Players", "TeamId");
        }
    }
}
```

The add migration command only creates a migration file containing the updates to the database schema. It does not apply those updates automatically. In order to execute the schema changes against the database, you need to run the update database command. Run the `Update-Database` command in the Package Manager Console. After the command completes, you can view the changes to the database in the Server Explorer. Figure 11-29 shows the database schema after the migration has been executed.

You can then continue the process of making updates to the model, creating a new migration, and updating the database.

SUMMARY

This chapter reviewed some of the core principles of the Entity Framework. You as the developer can choose how to work with EF. The EF designer allows you to work with a more graphical interface. You can choose to build your model and generate your database or generate your model from an existing database. Enhanced features have been added and continue to be added to make working with data easier. Features like Code First and Migrations give you options when working with your data to use a code-based workflow in addition to the designer-based workflow.

ASP.NET also includes a control that works with the Entity Framework: the EntityDataSource control.

The Entity Framework provides the ability to work with a multitude of different data sources. It also allows you to explicitly build a mapping layer between your object-oriented business logic layer and the schema-driven database layer or to use a convention-over-configuration approach to mapping your classes to the database layer.

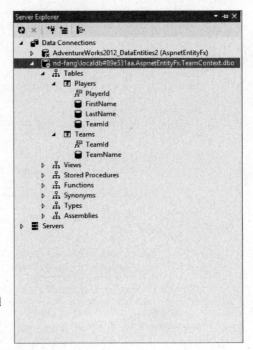

FIGURE 11-29

12

ASP.NET Dynamic Data

WHAT'S IN THIS CHAPTER?

➤ Understanding Dynamic Data features

➤ Understanding model binding

WROX.COM CODE DOWNLOADS FOR THIS CHAPTER

Please note that all the code examples in this chapter are available as a part of this chapter's code download on the book's website at www.wrox.com on the Download Code tab.

ASP.NET offers a feature that enables you to dynamically create data-driven web applications. ASP .NET Dynamic Data is more than purely a code generator, and although it can provide a base application, it is completely modifiable by you. This feature allows you to quickly and easily create data entry or applications that allow your end users to work with and view the backend database.

You can also easily integrate Dynamic Data into your applications and build a rich UI layer that's driven by model binding and data annotation attributes.

This chapter illustrates how to build an ASP.NET Dynamic Data application and use the Dynamic Data features with model binding.

DYNAMIC DATA FEATURES

ASP.NET Dynamic Data's capabilities were introduced with the .NET Framework 3.5 SP1. They have since been enhanced to work with Entity Framework in .NET Framework 4.5. To get started you can create a new Dynamic Data Entities Web Site project.

Visual Studio 2012 will create a base application that is not connected to any database or object model from the start. It's your job to make these connections. Before doing this, however, take a look at what Visual Studio has created for you.

Looking at the Core Files Created in the Default Application

Before you even assign the pre-generated Dynamic Data application to a database, much of the core application is created for you through the Visual Studio process just mentioned.

The items that are generated for you and what is presented here in the Visual Studio Solution Explorer are generally referred to as *scaffolding*. Even though a lot of code seems to be generated for you, rest assured you are not locked into a specific data-driven application. What is generated is termed "scaffolding" because it is a framework that can be taken holistically or modified and extended for any purpose. This framework is the presentation and database layer support that you will need for the autogeneration of your application. You are in no way locked into a specific set of models, looks-and-feels, or even an approach that you are unable to modify to suit your specific needs.

Even though you will find a lot of pre-generated code in your Solution Explorer, you are not even required to use this code to work with ASP.NET Dynamic Data. In fact, you can even add ASP.NET Dynamic Data to preexisting applications and you don't have to start from the ASP.NET Dynamic Data project template.

Next, this chapter looks at the pre-generated application that enables you to work with your backend database.

Application Features

One of the biggest additions to this application operation that is dramatically different from the standard ASP.NET application is a folder called DynamicData. This folder contains the pre-generated ASP.NET application that enables you to work with your database through a browser.

The goal of this application is to enable you to work with your database through the entire CRUD process (Create, Read, Update, and Delete). Again, you can limit the amount of interactivity you provide from your application.

To view how this application works against a database, you must dig further into the controls and pages that make up the application. Expanding the DynamicData folder, you find the following folders:

- ➤ Content
- ➤ CustomPages
- ➤ EntityTemplates
- ➤ FieldTemplates
- ➤ Filters
- ➤ PageTemplates

In addition to these folders, you will find a `web.config` file that is specific to this application.

The Content folder in this part of the application includes a user control that is used in the Page Templates, as well as the underlying images that are used by the style sheet of the application.

The CustomPages folder is a separate folder that allows you to put any custom pages that you might include in the data-driven web application. When you create an application from scratch, you will not find any file in this folder. It is intentionally blank.

The EntityTemplates folder makes getting the layout you want quite easy, thereby not requiring you to build a custom page. Initially, there is a `Default.ascx` (user control), and the edit and insert versions of this control are found in the folder.

The FieldTemplates folder is interesting because it has some of the more granular aspects of the application. The entire application is designed to work off a database, but it really does not have any idea what type of database it is going to be working from. The FieldTemplates folder is a way that the application can present any of the underlying data types that are coming from the database.

The Filters folder is used to create drop-down menus for `Booleans` (`true`/`false` values), foreign keys, and enumerations. These menus enable the end user to filter tables based upon keys within the database.

The PageTemplates folder contains the core pages that you use to bring the application together. Notice that pages exist for many of the core constructs that you will use in representing your tables in the application. The PageTemplates folder includes the following pages:

- ➤ `Details.aspx`
- ➤ `Edit.aspx`
- ➤ `Insert.aspx`
- ➤ `List.aspx`
- ➤ `ListDetails.aspx`

You use the `List.aspx` page for the tables in your connected database. You use the `Details.aspx` pages when you are examining a single row from the table, and you use the `ListDetails.aspx` page for examining master details views of the table and row relationships. You use the `Edit.aspx` and `Insert.aspx` pages, in turn, for the types of operations that they describe.

The `Global.asax` file has the definition of all the routes used by the Dynamic Data application. This means that you can change the URLs without changing the page contents. Since the routes are generic, they work for all the tables in the application.

You can use Data Annotations to customize the column names that will be displayed on the UI and also use them to add validation to the column names being inputted by the users. You'll learn about this in more detail when you read about model binding later in this chapter.

Running the Application

Once the `DynamicDataWebSite` is created, you need to incorporate a database that you are able to work with. For this example, you need to include the Northwind database. After the database is in place, the next step is to establish a defined entity data model layer that will work with the underlying database.

You can register the `NorthwindEntities` object in the overall solution. `NorthwindEntities` is the data model that was built using the LINQ to Entities. You register this `NorthwindEntities` context in the `Global.asax` file, which was created with the project. Listing 12-1 shows how to register the context in `Global.asax`.

LISTING 12-1: Registering the context in Global.asax

VB
```
DefaultModel.RegisterContext(GetType(NORTHWNDModel.NORTHWNDEntities),
    New ContextConfiguration() With {.ScaffoldAllTables = true})
```

C#
```
DefaultModel.RegisterContext(typeof(NORTHWNDModel.NORTHWNDEntities),
    new ContextConfiguration() { ScaffoldAllTables = true });
```

The model is registered as a `DataContext` object of type `NorthwindEntities`, and the `ScaffoldAllTables` property is set to `True` (the default is set to `False`), signifying that you want all the table representations in the model to be included in the generated application.

Results of the Application

As you run the application, notice that the first page allows you to see all the tables that you made a part of your data model, as illustrated in Figure 12-1.

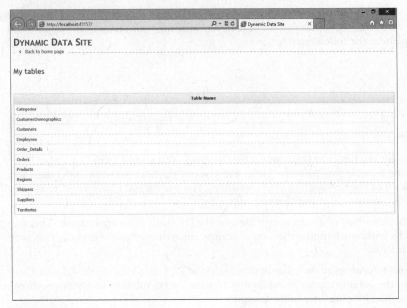

FIGURE 12-1

As an application that reads the contents of your database, it works quite simply. Clicking a table name (which is a hyperlink in the application) provides the contents of the table. Figure 12-2 shows this view.

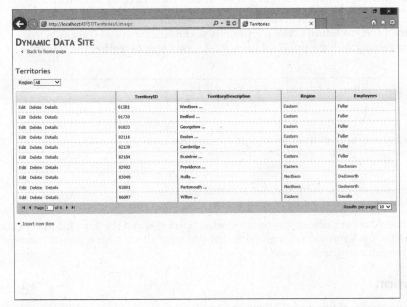

FIGURE 12-2

The table view is nicely styled and includes the ability to edit, delete, or view the details of each row in the database. In cases where a one-to-many relationship exists, you can drill down deeper into it. Another interesting part of the page is the navigation through the table. Pagination appears through the table, as shown at the bottom of the table in Figure 12-2.

In addition to using the edit, delete, or detail view of the row of information in the table, you can insert new rows into the database by clicking the Insert New Item link below the table. A view similar to that shown in Figure 12-3 appears.

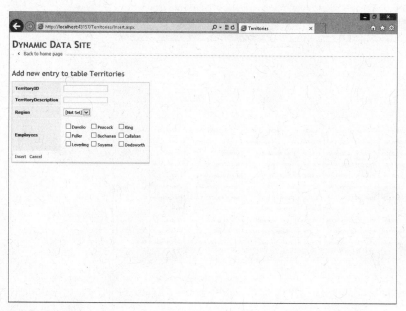

FIGURE 12-3

Editing a row makes the same type of page appear, as shown in Figure 12-4. This page resulted from clicking the Edit link next to one of the rows in the Territories table.

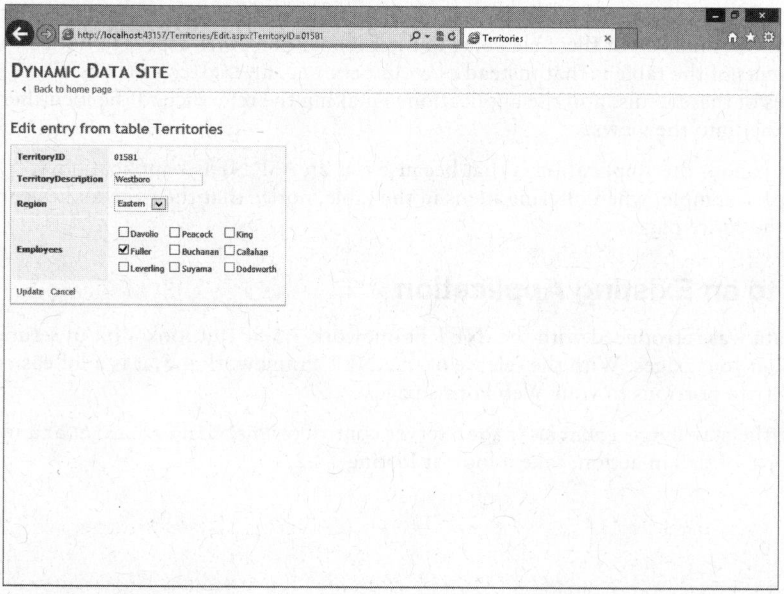

FIGURE 12-4

Another interesting aspect of this application is how it works with the one-to-many relationships of the elements in the data model. For example, clicking the Orders table link produces the view shown in Figure 12-5.

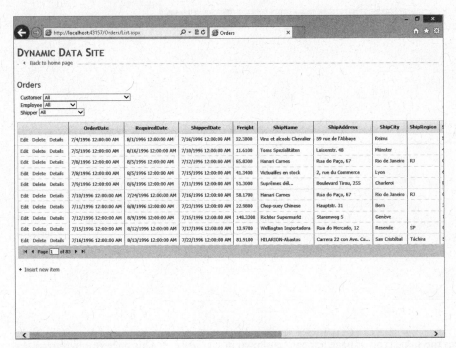

FIGURE 12-5

Here, in addition to the table and its contents, you are presented with a filtering capability via the various drop-down menus at the top of the page. In this case, you can filter the orders by customer, employee, or shipper. You can even use a combination of these elements to filter items. The other aspect to notice in Figure 12-5 about the contents of the table is that instead of a CustomerID, an EmployeeID, or a ShipperID, you see the names of these items, and the application is making the reference to the identifier for these items when drilling further into the views.

The final aspect to understand about this application is that because it is an ASP.NET 4 application, it makes proper use of AJAX. For example, when filtering items in the table, notice that the page makes partial refreshes without refreshing the entire page.

Adding Dynamic Data to an Existing Application

When ASP.NET Dynamic Data was introduced with the .NET Framework 3.5 SP1, it took a bit of setup in order to get dynamic aspects on your pages. With the release of the .NET Framework 4.5, it is a lot easier to add dynamic data functionality to portions to your Web Forms pages.

This is now possible by using the new DynamicDataManager server control or EnablingDynamicData in the Page_Init call. For an example of this in action, take a look at Listing 12-2.

LISTING 12-2: Adding DynamicData to an existing GridView control

```
<%@ Page Language="C#" %>

<script runat="server">
    protected void Page_Init()
    {
        GridView1.EnableDynamicData(typeof(Customer));
    }
</script>
<html xmlns="http://www.w3.org/1999/xhtml">
<head id="Head1" runat="server">
    <title>DynamicDataManager Example</title>
</head>
<body>
    <form id="form1" runat="server">
    <div>
        <asp:GridView ID="GridView1" runat="server" AllowPaging="True"
            DataSourceID="EntityDataSource1"
            AutoGenerateColumns="False" DataKeyNames="RegionID">
            <Columns>
                <asp:BoundField DataField="RegionID" HeaderText="RegionID" ReadOnly="True"
  SortExpression="RegionID"></asp:BoundField>
                <asp:BoundField DataField="RegionDescription"
HeaderText="RegionDescription"
SortExpression="RegionDescription">
</asp:BoundField>

            </Columns>
        </asp:GridView>
        <asp:EntityDataSource ID="EntityDataSource1" runat="server"
            EntitySetName="Regions"
            ConnectionString="name=NORTHWNDEntities"
            DefaultContainerName="NORTHWNDEntities"
            EnableDelete="True" EnableFlattening="False" EnableInsert="True"
            EnableUpdate="True">
        </asp:EntityDataSource>


    </div>
    </form>
</body>
</html>
```

Using the same Northwind object context from the previous examples, you will find that a basic
`EntityDataSource` control has been added to the page to work with the `GridView1` server control.
The `EntityDataSource` has also been assigned to work off the Regions table in this example. What you
want is a grid that shows a list of the customers.

UNDERSTANDING MODEL BINDING

In .NET Framework 4.0, you could finally add Dynamic Data functionality to an existing website, but it
was still hard to take full advantage of the rich support in Dynamic Data. With the introduction of model
binding in .NET Framework 4.5, it is really easy to integrate these features into your application. This
integration provides a developer experience that's similar to ASP.NET MVC in terms of model binding.
This section looks at some of the ways you can integrate Dynamic Data with model binding. All this is also
possible without starting from a Dynamic Data Web Application project template as well. To use model
binding with Dynamic Data, you just have to use model binding with the data-bound controls. If you
want to customize the look-and-feel of the columns and tables, you need to have the FieldTemplates and
EntityTemplates folders in your application.

> **NOTE** *Chapter 9 discusses model binding in detail.*

Attribute Driven UI

This section explains how you can leverage the Field and Entity Templates along with Data Annotation attributes to customize the look of a particular column or table. Table 12-1 lists some of the common attributes that you can use to customize the UI. You can find all these attributes in `System.ComponentModel.DataAnnotations.dll`.

TABLE 12-1

ATTRIBUTE NAME	DESCRIPTION
DataType	Specifies the type that should be associated with this column
Display	Specifies how the columns are displayed by Dynamic Data, such as the name of the column
DisplayFormat	Specifies how data fields are formatted by ASP.NET Dynamic Data
Enum	Enables a .NET Framework enumeration to be mapped to a data column
ScaffoldColumn	Specifies whether the column should be scaffolded by the system
UIHint	Specifies the field template that Dynamic Data uses to display a data field

Field Templates

As you learned earlier, the Field Templates folder contains user controls that map to a particular type of column. For example, `DateTime.ascx` is used by the Dynamic Data system to display a column of type `DateTime`. These user controls are reusable. This means if there are two tables that have the `DateTime` column, you can use the same user control for both tables.

Listing 12-3 shows how you can change the column name that will display the `LastName` column using the `Display` attribute. When you run the page, you will see "Last Part of Name."

LISTING 12-3: Using the Display attribute to change the UI of a column

VB

```
Protected Sub SqlDataSource1_Updated(ByVal sender As Object,
  ByVal e As Systelm.Web.UI.WebControls.SqlDataSourceStatusEventArgs)
      If (e.Exception IsNot Nothing) Then
    Me.lblMessage.Text = e.Exception.Message
    e.ExceptionHandled = True
  End If
End Sub
```

C#

```
[Display(Name="Last Part of Name")]
public string LastName { get; set; }
```

Now assume that you want to change the look-and-feel of the edit/insert view of the `LastName` column. You can do this by creating a new Dynamic Data Field Template user control and using it to change the UI. Listing 12-4 shows how to use the custom field template called `LastName`. The `LastName` user control has to exist in the Field Templates folder.

To add a new field template, right-click the website and choose the Dynamic Data field item template. Figure 12-6 shows how this template looks.

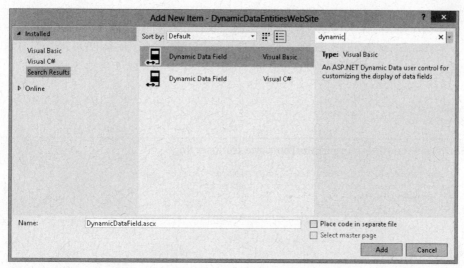

FIGURE 12-6

LISTING 12-4: Using the UIHint attribute to change the FieldTemplate being used

VB

```
Protected Sub SqlDataSource1_Updated(ByVal sender As Object,
    ByVal e As System.Web.UI.WebControls.SqlDataSourceStatusEventArgs)
        If (e.Exception IsNot Nothing) Then
        Me.lblMessage.Text = e.Exception.Message
        e.ExceptionHandled = True
    End If
End Sub
```

C#

```
[UIHint("LastName")]
public string LastName { get; set; }
```

Entity Templates

So far, you have learned how to customize the columns in a table. Say you now want to customize the look-and-feel of the entire table while using the autogeneration of columns with Dynamic Data. Entity templates can be used to achieve this. *Entity templates* are user controls that Dynamic Data uses to show all the columns in a table.

Listing 12-5 shows the markup of an entity template for an insert scenario. This is used by the `FormView` control, as shown in Listing 12-6.

LISTING 12-5: Typical EntityTemplate for inserting a table

```
<asp:EntityTemplate runat="server" ID="EntityTemplate1">
    <ItemTemplate>
        <tr class="td">
            <td class="DDLightHeader">
<asp:Label runat="server" OnInit="Label_Init" OnPreRender=
"Label_PreRender" />
            </td>
            <td>
```

continues

LISTING 12-5 *(continued)*

```
                    <asp:DynamicControl runat="server" ID="DynamicControl" Mode="Insert"
OnInit=
"DynamicControl_Init" />
                </td>
            </tr>
        </ItemTemplate>
</asp:EntityTemplate>
```

LISTING 12-6: FormView control using EntityTemplate for inserting

```
<asp:FormView runat="server" ID="FormView1" DefaultMode="Insert"
        ItemType="Customer" InsertMethod="InsertCustomer">
            <InsertItemTemplate>
                <table>
                    <asp:DynamicEntity ID="DynamicEntity1" runat="server" Mode=
"Insert" />

                    <tr>
                        <td>
                            <asp:LinkButton ID="Insert" runat="server"
                                CommandName="Insert" Text="Insert" />
                            <asp:LinkButton ID="Cancel" runat="server"
                                CommandName="Cancel" Text="Cancel"
                                CausesValidation="false" />
                        </td>
                    </tr>
                </table>
            </InsertItemTemplate>
        </asp:FormView>
```

You can share the entity templates to create a common look-and-feel for all the tables in the database. If you want to customize the view for a particular table, you can create a custom entity template for that particular table. You can do this by creating a subfolder under `DynamicData\EntityTemplates`. The subfolder should be named after the name of the table, `Customer` in this case.

Attribute Driven Validation

Attribute driven validation is a way to add some validation logic to your application by using Data Annotations. You saw some of the attributes that can be used for UI customization, and Table 12-2 shows some of the validation attributes.

TABLE 12-2

ATTRIBUTE NAME	DESCRIPTION
Key	Denotes one or more properties that uniquely identify an entity
Range	Specifies the numeric range constraints for the value of a data field
RegularExpression	Specifies that a data field value in ASP.NET Dynamic Data must match the specified regular expression
Required	Specifies that a data field value is required
StringLength	Specifies the minimum and maximum length of characters that are allowed in a data field

Basic Validation

One of the behaviors that you get out of the box, when you start using data-bound controls with model binding, is validation. When model binding binds the data, the model binding system uses Dynamic Data to handle validation for the columns in the table. This means that the application gets client-side as well as server-side validation for the columns and any validation errors can be viewed in the `ValidationSummary` control.

Data Annotations

You can also customize the type of validation that happens on columns. Listing 12-7 shows how you can add some regular expression validation rules to the column `LastName`. If you then enter a last name that does not start with *a*, you will get the following validation error in the validation summary:

```
The field LastName must match the regular expression 'a*'
```

Note that because you also set the `DisplayName` attribute to change the name of the column, you get the new `DisplayName` in the error message as follows:

```
The field Last Part of Name must match the regular expression 'a*'
```

This is a very compelling use of Dynamic Data, because it customizes your application UI without changing your model.

LISTING 12-7: Using RegularExpression validation

VB

```
Protected Sub SqlDataSource1_Updated(ByVal sender As Object,
  ByVal e As System.Web.UI.WebControls.SqlDataSourceStatusEventArgs)
    If (e.Exception IsNot Nothing) Then
    Me.lblMessage.Text = e.Exception.Message
    e.ExceptionHandled = True
  End If
End Sub
```

C#

```
[Display(Name = "Last Part of Name")]
[RegularExpression("a*")]
public string LastName { get; set; }
```

SUMMARY

This chapter explored the capabilities in ASP.NET for building Dynamic Data-driven applications quickly and easily. These capabilities, in conjunction with Visual Studio, enable you to build a reporting application that provides full CRUD capabilities in less than five minutes.

At the same time, you can use all of these features with model binding and provide a rich consistent experience for your application.

13

Working with Services

WHAT'S IN THIS CHAPTER?

➤ Building and consuming web services

➤ Understanding the Windows Communication Foundation

➤ Working with WebAPI

WROX.COM CODE DOWNLOADS FOR THIS CHAPTER

Please note that all the code examples in this chapter are available as a part of this chapter's code download on the book's website at www.wrox.com on the Download Code tab.

This chapter looks at building XML Web Services and how you can consume XML web service interfaces and integrate them into your ASP.NET applications. It begins with the foundations of XML Web Services in the .NET world by examining some of the underlying technologies such as SOAP, WSDL, and more. The middle part of this chapter focuses on Windows Communication Foundation, also known as WCF. Finally, the last part of this chapter focuses on the latest communication framework, WebAPI. This relatively new framework is something that you can use to quickly and easily expose core functionality through an API.

COMMUNICATION BETWEEN DISPARATE SYSTEMS

It is a diverse world. In a major enterprise, very rarely do you find that the entire organization and its data repositories reside on a single vendor's platform. In most instances, organizations are made up of a patchwork of systems—some based on UNIX, some on Microsoft, and some on other systems. It's unlikely that there will be a day when everything resides on a single platform where all the data moves seamlessly from one server to another in every organization. For that reason, these various systems must be able to talk to one another. If disparate systems can communicate easily, moving unique data sets around the enterprise becomes a simple process—alleviating the need for replication systems and data stores.

When XML (eXtensible Markup Language) was introduced, it became clear that the markup language would be the structure to bring the necessary integration into the enterprise. XML's power comes from the fact that it can be used regardless of the platform, language, or data store of the system using it to expose DataSets.

XML has its roots in the Standard Generalized Markup Language (SGML), which was created in 1986. Because SGML was so complex, something a bit simpler was needed—thus, the birth of XML.

XML is considered ideal for data representation purposes because it enables developers to structure XML documents as they see fit. For this reason, it is also a bit chaotic. Sending self-structured XML documents between dissimilar systems does not make a lot of sense—you would have to custom build the exposure and consumption models for each communication pair.

Vendors and the industry as a whole soon realized that XML needed a specific structure that put some rules in place to clarify communication. The rules defining XML structure make the communication between the disparate systems just that much easier. Tool vendors can now automate the communication process, as well as provide for the automation of the possible creation of all the components of applications using the communication protocol.

The industry settled on using Simple Object Access Protocol (SOAP) to make the standard XML structure work. Previous attempts to solve the communication problem that arose included component technologies such as Distributed Component Object Model (DCOM), Remote Method Invocation (RMI), Common Object Request Broker Architecture (CORBA), and Internet Inter-ORB Protocol (IIOP). These first efforts failed because each of these technologies was either driven by a single vendor or (worse yet) very vendor-specific. Implementing them across the entire industry was, therefore, impossible.

SOAP enables you to expose and consume complex data structures, which can include items such as DataSets, or just tables of data that have all their relations in place. SOAP is relatively simple and easy to understand. Like ASP.NET, XML Web Services are also primarily engineered to work over HTTP. The DataSets you send or consume can flow over the same Internet wires (HTTP), thereby bypassing many firewalls (as they move through port 80).

So what is actually going across the wire? ASP.NET Web Services generally use SOAP over HTTP using the HTTP Post protocol. An example SOAP 1.2 request (from the client to the web service residing on a web server) takes the structure shown in Listing 13-1.

LISTING 13-1: A SOAP request

```
POST /WebService.asmx HTTP/1.1
Host: localhost
Content-Type: application/soap+xml; charset=utf-8
Content-Length: 19
<?xml version="1.0" encoding="utf-8"?>
<soap12:Envelope xmlns:xsi="http://www.w3.org/2001/XMLSchema-instance"
  xmlns:xsd="http://www.w3.org/2001/XMLSchema"
  xmlns:soap12="http://www.w3.org/2003/05/soap-envelope">
    <soap12:Body>
        <HelloWorld xmlns="http://tempuri.org/" />
    </soap12:Body>
</soap12:Envelope>
```

The request is sent to the web service to invoke the `HelloWorld` WebMethod (WebMethods are discussed later in this chapter). Listing 13-2 shows the SOAP response from the web service.

LISTING 13-2: A SOAP response

```
HTTP/1.1 200 OK
Content-Type: application/soap+xml; charset=utf-8
Content-Length: 14
<?xml version="1.0" encoding="utf-8"?>
<soap12:Envelope xmlns:xsi="http://www.w3.org/2001/XMLSchema-instance"
  xmlns:xsd="http://www.w3.org/2001/XMLSchema"
  xmlns:soap12="http://www.w3.org/2003/05/soap-envelope">
    <soap12:Body>
```

```
    <HelloWorldResponse xmlns="http://tempuri.org/">
        <HelloWorldResult>Hello World </HelloWorldResult>
    </HelloWorldResponse>
    </soap12:Body>
</soap12:Envelope>
```

In the examples from Listings 13-1 and 13-2, you can see that what is contained in this message is an XML file. In addition to the normal XML declaration of the `<xml>` node, you see a structure of XML that is the SOAP message. A SOAP message uses a root node of `<soap:Envelope>` that contains the `<soap:Body>` or the body of the SOAP message. Other elements that can be contained in the SOAP message include a SOAP header, `<soap:Header>`, and a SOAP fault, `<soap:Fault>`.

> **NOTE** *For more information about the structure of a SOAP message, be sure to check out the SOAP specifications. You can find them at the W3C website,* `www.w3.org/tr/soap`.

BUILDING A SIMPLE XML WEB SERVICE

Building an XML web service means that you are interested in exposing some information or logic to another entity either within your organization, to a partner, or to your customers. In a more granular sense, building a web service means that you, as a developer, simply make one or more methods from a class you create that is enabled for SOAP communication.

You can use Visual Studio 2012 to build an XML web service. The first step is to actually create a new website by selecting File ⇨ New ⇨ Web Site from the IDE menu. The New Web Site dialog box opens. Select ASP.NET Empty Web Site, as shown in Figure 13-1.

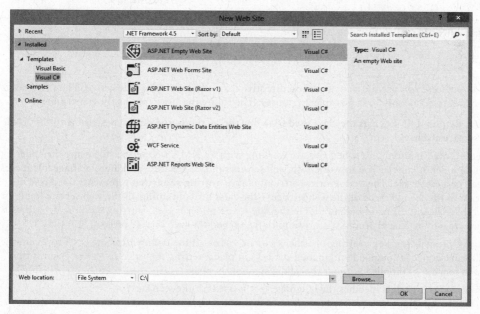

FIGURE 13-1

Once the project is created, right-click to add a new file to the project. Select Web Service (`WebService .asmx`) from the list of options. This creates a single XML web service named `WebService.asmx`. You can find its code-behind file, `WebService.vb` or `WebService.cs`, in the `App_Code` folder (see Figure 13-2).

> **WARNING** *The next few pages of this chapter focus on ASMX Web Services. In 2009, ASMX Web Services were marked as legacy. Therefore, the code found within will not be updated with future ASP.NET releases (the exception would be a security update). However, the information has been included to help with the support of existing ASMX Web Services.*

Check out the `WebService.asmx` file. ASP.NET web service files use the `.asmx` file extension instead of the `.aspx` extension used by typical ASP.NET pages.

> **NOTE** *ASP.NET Web Services are the original method of creating web services using ASP.NET. These are commonly called "ASMX services" in the community as opposed to two other methods, WCF and WebAPI, which are discussed later in this chapter.*

The WebService Page Directive

Open the `WebService.asmx` file in Visual Studio, and you see that the file contains only the `WebService` page directive, as illustrated in Listing 13-3 (WebService.asmx in the code download for this chapter).

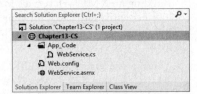

FIGURE 13-2

LISTING 13-3: Contents of the Service.asmx file

```
<%@ WebService Language="C#" CodeBehind="~/App_Code/WebService.cs"
    Class="WebService" %>
```

For `.asmx` web services, you use the `@WebService` directive instead of the `@Page` directive. The simple `@WebService` directive has only four possible attributes. The following list explains these attributes:

➤   `Class`: Required. It specifies the class used to define the methods and data types visible to the XML web service clients.

➤   `CodeBehind`: Required only when you are working with an XML web service file using the code-behind model. It enables you to work with web services in two separate and more manageable pieces instead of a single file. The `CodeBehind` attribute takes a string value that represents the physical location of the second piece of the web service—the class file containing all the web service logic. In ASP.NET, placing the code-behind files in the `App_Code` folder is best, starting with the default web service created by Visual Studio when you initially opened the web service project.

➤   `Debug`: Optional. It takes a setting of either `True` or `False`. If the `Debug` attribute is set to `True`, the XML web service is compiled with debug symbols in place; setting the value to `False` ensures that the web service is compiled without the debug symbols in place.

➤   `Language`: Required. It specifies the language that is used for the web service.

Looking at the Base Web Service Class File

Now look at the `WebService.vb` or `WebService.cs` file—the code-behind file for the XML web service. By default, a structure of code is already in place in the `WebService.vb` or `WebService.cs` file, as shown in Listing 13-4 (/App_Code/WebService.vb and /App_Code/WebService.cs in the code download for the chapter).

LISTING 13-4: Default code structure provided by Visual Studio for your web service

VB

```vb
Imports System.Web
Imports System.Web.Services
Imports System.Web.Services.Protocols

<WebService(Namespace:="http://tempuri.org/")> _
<WebServiceBinding(ConformsTo:=WsiProfiles.BasicProfile1_1)> _
<Global.Microsoft.VisualBasic.CompilerServices.DesignerGenerated()> _
Public Class WebService
    Inherits System.Web.Services.WebService

    <WebMethod()> _
    Public Function HelloWorld() As String
        Return "Hello World"
    End Function
End Class
```

C#

```csharp
using System;
using System.Collections.Generic;
using System.Linq;
using System.Web;
using System.Web.Services;

[WebService(Namespace = "http://tempuri.org/")]
[WebServiceBinding(ConformsTo = WsiProfiles.BasicProfile1_1)]
public class WebService : System.Web.Services.WebService {
    [WebMethod]
    public string HelloWorld() {
        return "Hello World";
    }
}
```

You should take note of a few things here. First, notice that the `System.Linq` namespace is included in the C# solution. Also notice the inclusion of the commented `System.Web.Script.Services.ScriptService` object (removed from Listing 13-3 for brevity) to work with ASP.NET AJAX scripts. To make use of this attribute, you simply uncomment the item.

Also, you can see that the `System.Web.Services.Protocols` namespace is included by default in the VB version. Therefore, in working with SOAP headers and other capabilities provided via this namespace, you do not need to worry about including it.

Finally, you can see the `<WebServiceBinding>` attribute, which builds the XML web service responses that conform to the WS-I Basic Profile 1.0 release (found at `www.ws-i.org/Profiles/BasicProfile-1.0.html`).

Exposing Custom DataSets as SOAP

To build your own web service example, delete the `WebService.asmx` file and create a new file called **Customers.asmx**. This web service will expose the `Customers` table from SQL Server. Then jump into the code shown in Listing 13-5 (/App_Code/Customers.vb and /App_Code/Customers.cs in the code download for the chapter).

> **NOTE** *You can download the version of the AdventureWorks database we used for this book from* www.wrox.com/go/SQLSever2012DataSets.

LISTING 13-5: An XML web service that exposes the Customers table from AdventureWorks

VB

```vb
Imports System.Web
Imports System.Web.Services
Imports System.Web.Services.Protocols
Imports System.Data.SqlClient
Imports System.Data

<WebService(Namespace:="http://adventureworks/customers")> _
<WebServiceBinding(ConformsTo:=WsiProfiles.BasicProfile1_1)> _
<Global.Microsoft.VisualBasic.CompilerServices.DesignerGenerated()> _
Public Class Customers
    Inherits System.Web.Services.WebService

    <WebMethod()> _
    Public Function GetCustomers() As DataSet
        Dim conn As SqlConnection
        Dim myDataAdapter As SqlDataAdapter
        Dim myDataSet As DataSet
        Dim cmdString As String = "Select * From SalesLT.Customer"

        conn = New SqlConnection("Server=(LocalDB)\v11.0;integrated security=True;
          attachdbfilename=|DataDirectory|\AdventureWorksLT2012_Data.mdf;")
        myDataAdapter = New SqlDataAdapter(cmdString, conn)

        myDataSet = New DataSet()
        myDataAdapter.Fill(myDataSet, "Customers")

        Return myDataSet
    End Function
End Class
```

C#

```csharp
using System;
using System.Collections.Generic;
using System.Data;
using System.Data.SqlClient;
using System.Linq;
using System.Web;
using System.Web.Services;

[WebService(Namespace = "http://adventureworks/customers")]
[WebServiceBinding(ConformsTo = WsiProfiles.BasicProfile1_1)]
public class Customers : System.Web.Services.WebService {
    [WebMethod]
    public DataSet GetCustomers() {
        SqlConnection conn;
        SqlDataAdapter myDataAdapter;
        DataSet myDataSet;
        string cmdString = "Select * From SalesLT.Customer";

        conn = new SqlConnection("Server=(LocalDB)\\v11.0;integrated security=True;
          attachdbfilename=|DataDirectory|\\AdventureWorksLT2012_Data.mdf;");
```

```
            myDataAdapter = new SqlDataAdapter(cmdString, conn);

            myDataSet = new DataSet();
            myDataAdapter.Fill(myDataSet, "Customers");

            return myDataSet;
        }
    }
```

The WebService Attribute

All web services are encapsulated within a class. The class is defined as a web service by the `WebService` attribute placed before the class declaration. Here is an example:

```
[WebService(Namespace = "http://adventureworks/customers")]
```

The `WebService` attribute can take a few properties. By default, the `WebService` attribute is used in your web service along with the `Namespace` property, which has an initial value of `http://tempuri.org/`. This is meant to be a temporary namespace, and you should replace it with a more meaningful and original name, such as the URL where you are hosting the XML web service. In the example, the `Namespace` value was changed to `http://adventureworks/customers`. Remember that the value does not have to be an actual URL; it can be any string value you want. The idea is that it should be unique.

Notice that the two languages define their properties within the `WebService` attribute differently. Visual Basic 2012 uses a colon and an equal sign to set the property:

```
Namespace:="http://adventureworks/customers"
```

C# uses just an equal sign to assign the properties within the `WebService` attribute values:

```
Namespace = "http://adventureworks/customers"
```

Other possible `WebService` properties include `Name` and `Description`. `Name` enables you to change how the name of the web service is presented to the developer via the ASP.NET test page (the test page is discussed a little later in the chapter). `Description` enables you to provide a textual description of the web service. The description is also presented on the ASP.NET web service test page. If your `WebService` attribute contains more than a single property, separate the properties using a comma. Here's an example:

```
<WebService(Namespace:="http://adventureworks/customers", Name:="GetCustomers")>
```

The WebMethod Attribute

In Listing 13-5, the class called `Customers` has only a single `WebMethod`. A `WebService` class can contain any number of `WebMethods`, or a mixture of standard methods along with methods that are enabled to be `WebMethods` via the use of the attribute preceding the method declaration. The only methods that are accessible across the HTTP wire are the ones to which you have applied the `WebMethod` attribute.

As with the `WebService` attribute, `WebMethod` can also contain some properties, which are described in the following list:

➤ `BufferResponse`: When `BufferResponse` is set to `True`, the response from the XML web service is held in memory and sent as a complete package. If it is set to `False`, the default setting, the response is sent to the client as it is constructed on the server.

➤ `CacheDuration`: Specifies the number of seconds that the response should be held in the system's cache. The default setting is `0`, which means that caching is disabled. Putting an XML web service's response in the cache increases the web service's performance.

➤ `Description`: Applies a text description to the `WebMethod` that appears on the `.aspx` test page of the XML web service.

➤ `EnableSession`: Setting `EnableSession` to `True` enables session state for a particular `WebMethod`. The default setting is `False`.

➤ MessageName: Applies a unique name to the WebMethod. This step is required if you are working with overloaded WebMethods (discussed later in the chapter).

➤ TransactionOption: Specifies the transactional support for the WebMethod. The default setting is Disabled. If the WebMethod is the root object that initiated the transaction, the web service can participate in a transaction with another WebMethod that requires a transaction. Other possible values include NotSupported, Supported, Required, and RequiresNew.

The XML Web Service Interface

The Customers web service from Listing 13-5 has only a single WebMethod that returns a DataSet containing the complete Customers table from the SQL Server AdventureWorks database.

Running Customers.asmx in the browser pulls up the ASP.NET web service test page. This visual interface to your web service is really meant either for testing purposes or as a reference page for developers interested in consuming the web services you expose. Figure 13-3 shows the page generated for the Customers.asmx web service's GetCustomers WebMethod.

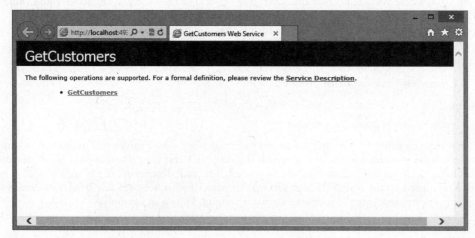

FIGURE 13-3

The interface shows the name of the web service in the blue bar (the dark bar in this black-and-white image) at the top of the page. By default, the name of the class is used unless you changed the value through the Description property of the WebService attribute, as defined earlier. A bulleted list of links to the entire web service's WebMethods is displayed. This example has only one WebMethod: GetCustomers.

A link to the web service's Web Services Description Language (WSDL) document is also available (the link is titled "Service Description" in the figure). The WSDL file is the actual interface with the Customers web service. The XML document (shown in Figure 13-4) is not really meant for human consumption; it is designed to work with tools such as Visual Studio, informing the tool what the web service requires to be consumed. Each web service requires a request that must have parameters of a specific type. When the request is made, the web service response comes back with a specific set of data defined using specific data types. Everything you need for the request and a listing of exactly what you are getting back in a response (if you are the consumer) is described in the WSDL document.

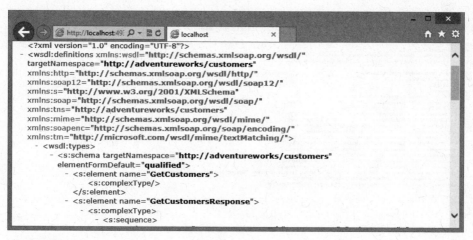

FIGURE 13-4

Clicking the GetCustomers link gives you a new page, shown in Figure 13-5, that not only describes the WebMethod in more detail, but also enables you to test the WebMethod directly in the browser.

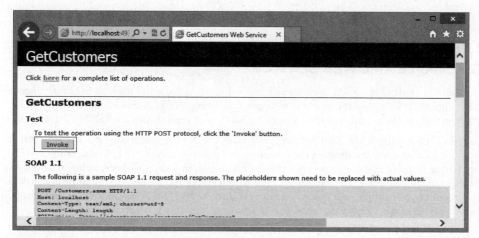

FIGURE 13-5

At the top of the page is the name of the XML web service (Customers); below that is the name of this particular WebMethod (GetCustomers). The page shows you the structure of the SOAP messages that are required to consume the WebMethod, as well as the structure the SOAP message takes for the response. Below the SOAP examples is an example of consuming the XML web service using HTTP Post (with name/value pairs). Using this method of consumption instead of using SOAP is possible.

You can test the WebMethod directly from the page. In the Test section, you find a form. If the WebMethod you are calling requires an input of some parameters to get a response, you see some textboxes included so you can provide the parameters before clicking the Invoke button. If the WebMethod you are calling does not require any parameters, you see only the Invoke button and nothing more.

Clicking Invoke actually sends a SOAP request to the web service, causing a new browser instance with the result to appear, as illustrated in Figure 13-6.

FIGURE 13-6

Now that everything is in place to expose the XML web service, you can consume it in an ASP.NET application.

CONSUMING A SIMPLE XML WEB SERVICE

So far, you have seen only half of the XML web service story. Exposing data and logic as SOAP to disparate systems across the enterprise or across the world is a simple task using .NET, and particularly ASP.NET. The other half of the story is the actual consumption of an XML web service into an ASP.NET application.

You are not limited to consuming XML Web Services only into ASP.NET applications; but because this is an ASP.NET book, it focuses on that aspect of the consumption process in ASP.NET. Consuming XML Web Services into other types of applications is not that difficult and, in fact, is rather similar to how you would consume them using ASP.NET. Remember that the web services you come across can be consumed in Windows Forms, mobile applications, and more. You can even consume XML Web Services with other web services, so you can have a single web service made up of an aggregate of other web services.

Adding a Web Reference

To consume the Customers web service that you created earlier in this chapter, create a new ASP.NET website called **CustomerConsumer**. The first step in consuming an XML web service in an ASP.NET application is to make a reference to the remote object—the web service. You do so by right-clicking the root node of your project from within the Visual Studio Solution Explorer and selecting Add Service Reference. From the Service Reference dialog box, you can enter the URL of your service. However, to get the traditional web service reference dialog box, choose the Advanced button. Then, at the bottom of the Advanced settings page, choose Add Web Reference under the Compatibility section. The Add Web Reference dialog box appears, shown in Figure 13-7.

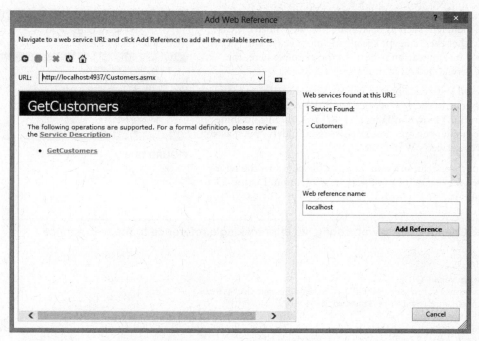

FIGURE 13-7

> **NOTE** *In Visual Studio 2010 and earlier, the Add Web Reference dialog box had its own menu option called Add Web Reference. However, with the emergence of WCF and WebAPI, this menu option has been removed.*

The Add Web Reference dialog box enables you to point to a particular .asmx file to make a reference to it. Understand that the Add Web Reference dialog box is really looking for WSDL files. Microsoft's XML Web Services automatically generate WSDL files based on the .asmx files themselves. To pull up the WSDL file in the browser, simply type in the URL of your web service's .asmx file and add a ?WSDL at the end of the string. For example, you might have the following construction (this is not an actual web service, but simply an example):

```
http://www.contoso.com/WebServices/Customers.asmx?WSDL
```

Because the Add Web Reference dialog box automatically finds where the WSDL file is for any Microsoft-based XML web service, you should simply type in the URL of the actual WSDL file for any non–Microsoft-based XML web service.

> **NOTE** *If you are using Microsoft's Visual Studio and its built-in web server instead of IIS, you will be required to also interject the port number the web server is using into the URL. In this case, your URL would be structured similar to* `http://localhost:4937/Customers.asmx?WSDL.`

In the Add Web Reference dialog box, change the reference from the default name to something a little more meaningful. If you are working on a single machine, the web reference might have the name of `localhost`;

if you are actually working with a remote web service, the name is the inverse of the URL, such as `com.contoso.www`. In either case, renaming it so that the name makes a little more sense and is easy to use within your application is best. In the example here, the web reference is renamed `AdventureWorksCustomers`.

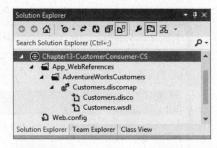

Clicking the Add Reference button causes Visual Studio to make an actual reference to the web service from the `web.config` file of your application (shown in Figure 13-8). You might find some additional files under the `App_WebReferences` folder—such as a copy of the web service's WSDL file.

FIGURE 13-8

Your consuming application's `web.config` file contains the reference to the web service in its `<appSettings>` section. Listing 13-6 shows the addition.

LISTING 13-6: Changes to the web.config file after making a reference to the web service

```xml
<?xml version="1.0"?>
<configuration>
    <system.web>
        <compilation debug="false" targetFramework="4.5"/>
        <httpRuntime targetFramework="4.5"/>
    </system.web>
    <appSettings>
        <add key="AdventureWorksCustomers.Customers"
            value="http://localhost:4473/Customers.asmx"/>
    </appSettings>
</configuration>
```

You can see that the `AdventureWorksCustomers` reference has been made along with the name of the web service, providing a key value of `AdventureWorksCustomers.Customers`. The `value` attribute takes a value of the location of the Customers web service, which is found within the `Customers.asmx` page.

Invoking the Web Service from the Client Application

Now that a reference has been made to the XML web service, you can use it in your ASP.NET application. Create a new Web Form in your project. With this page, you can consume the `Customers` table from the remote AdventureWorks database directly into your application. The data is placed in a GridView control.

On the design part of the page, place a Button and a GridView control so that your page looks something like the one shown in Figure 13-9.

FIGURE 13-9

The idea is that, when the end user clicks the button contained on the form, the application sends a SOAP request to the Customers web service and gets back a SOAP response containing the Customers table, which is then bound to the GridView control on the page. Listing 13-7 shows the code for this simple application.

LISTING 13-7: Consuming the Customers web service in an ASP.NET page

VB

```
<%@ Page Language="VB" %>
<!DOCTYPE html>
<script runat="server">
    Protected Sub Button1_Click(ByVal sender As Object, ByVal e As System.EventArgs)
        Dim ws As New AdventureWorksCustomers.Customers()
        GridView1.DataSource = ws.GetCustomers()
        GridView1.DataBind()
    End Sub
</script>
<html xmlns="http://www.w3.org/1999/xhtml">
<head runat="server">
    <title>Web Service Consumer Example</title>
</head>
<body>
    <form id="form1" runat="server">
        <div>
            <asp:Button ID="Button1" runat="server" Text="Get Customers"
                OnClick="Button1_Click" />
            <br />
            <br />
            <asp:GridView ID="GridView1" runat="server" BorderWidth="1px"
                BackColor="#DEBA84" CellPadding="3" CellSpacing="2" BorderStyle="None"
                BorderColor="#DEBA84">
                <FooterStyle ForeColor="#8C4510" BackColor="#F7DFB5"></FooterStyle>
                <PagerStyle ForeColor="#8C4510" HorizontalAlign="Center"></PagerStyle>
                <HeaderStyle ForeColor="White" Font-Bold="True"
                    BackColor="#A55129"></HeaderStyle>
                <SelectedRowStyle ForeColor="White" Font-Bold="True"
                    BackColor="#738A9C"></SelectedRowStyle>
                <RowStyle ForeColor="#8C4510" BackColor="#FFF7E7"></RowStyle>
            </asp:GridView>
        </div>
    </form>
</body>
</html>
```

C#

```
<%@ Page Language="C#" %>
<!DOCTYPE html>
<script runat="server">
    protected void Button1_Click(Object sender, EventArgs e)
    {
        AdventureWorksCustomers.Customers ws = new AdventureWorksCustomers.Customers();
        GridView1.DataSource = ws.GetCustomers();
        GridView1.DataBind();
    }
</script>
```

The end user is presented with a simple button. Clicking it causes the ASP.NET application to send a SOAP request to the remote XML web service. The returned DataSet is bound to the GridView control, and the page is redrawn, as shown in Figure 13-10.

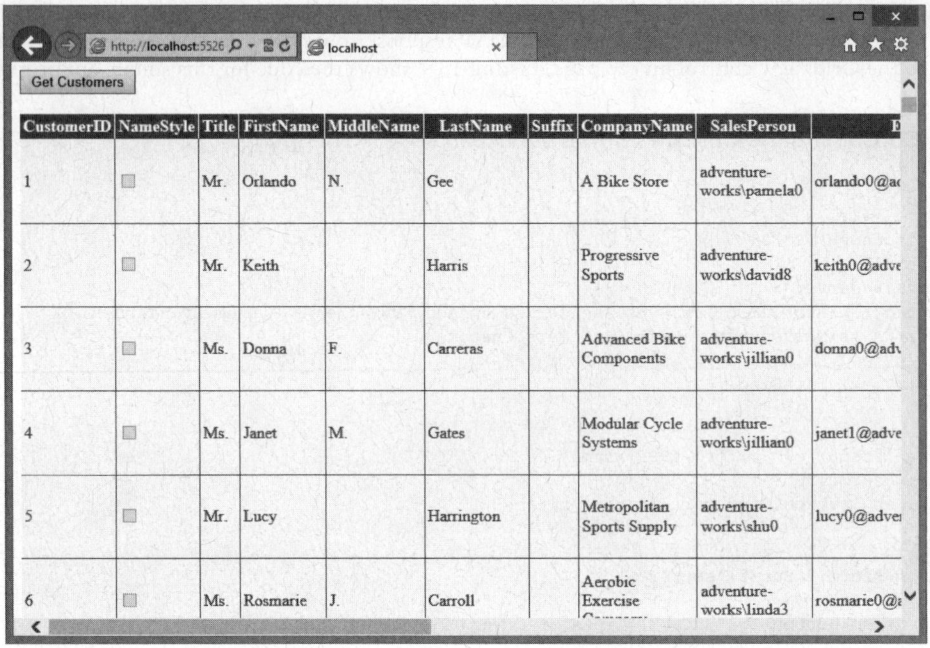

FIGURE 13-10

The Customers web service is invoked by the instantiation of the `AdventureWorksCustomers.Customers` proxy object:

```
AdventureWorksCustomers.Customers ws = new AdventureWorksCustomers.Customers();
```

Then, you can use the `ws` object like any other object within your project. In the code example from Listing 13-7, the result of the `ws.GetCustomers()` method call is assigned to the `DataSource` property of the GridView control:

```
GridView1.DataSource = ws.GetCustomers();
```

As you develop or consume more web services within your applications, you will see more of their power and utility.

OVERLOADING WEBMETHODS

In the object-oriented world of .NET, using method overloading in the code you develop is quite possible. A true object-oriented language has support for *polymorphism*, of which method overloading is a part. Method overloading enables you to have multiple methods that use the same name but have different signatures. With method overloading, one method can be called, but the call is routed to the appropriate method based on the full signature of the request. Listing 13-8 shows an example of standard method overloading.

LISTING 13-8: Method overloading in .NET

VB

```
Public Function HelloWorld() As String
    Return "Hello"
End Function
Public Function HelloWorld(ByVal FirstName As String) As String
```

```
        Return "Hello " & FirstName
    End Function
```

C#

```csharp
public string HelloWorld()
{
    return "Hello";
}
public string HelloWorld(string FirstName)
{
    return "Hello " + FirstName;
}
```

In this example, both methods have the same name, `HelloWorld`. So, which one is called when you invoke `HelloWorld`? Well, it depends on the signature you pass to the method. For example, you might provide the following:

```
Label1.Text = HelloWorld();
```

This yields a result of just `Hello`. However, you might invoke the `HelloWorld()` method using the following signature:

```
Label1.Text = HelloWorld("Jason Gaylord");
```

Then you get back a result of `Hello Jason Gaylord`. As you can see, method overloading is a great feature that your ASP.NET applications can effectively utilize — but how do you go about overloading `WebMethods`?

If you have already tried to overload any of your `WebMethods`, you probably got the following error when you pulled up the web service in the browser:

```
Both System.String HelloWorld(System.String) and System.String HelloWorld() use the message
name 'HelloWorld'.  Use the MessageName property of the WebMethod custom attribute to
specify unique message names for the methods.
```

As this error states, the extra step you have to take to overload `WebMethods` is to use the `MessageName` property. Listing 13-9 shows how (this listing updates the WebService.vb and WebService.cs files from the code download for this chapter, respectively).

LISTING 13-9: WebMethod overloading in .NET

VB

```vb
<WebMethod(MessageName:="HelloWorld")> _
Public Function HelloWorld() As String
    Return "Hello World"
End Function
<WebMethod(MessageName:="HelloWorldWithFirstName")> _
Public Function HelloWorld(ByVal FirstName As String) As String
    Return "Hello " & FirstName
End Function
```

C#

```csharp
[WebMethod(MessageName = "HelloWorld")]
public string HelloWorld() {
    return "Hello World";
}
[WebMethod(MessageName = "HelloWorldWithFirstName")]
public string HelloWorld(string FirstName)
{
    return "Hello " + FirstName;
}
```

In addition to adding the `MessageName` property of the `WebMethod` attribute, you must disable your web service's adherence to the WS-I Basic Profile specification—which it wouldn't be doing if you performed `WebMethod` overloading with your web services. You can disable the conformance to the WS-I Basic Profile specification in a couple of ways. One way is to add the `<WebServiceBinding>` attribute to your code, as illustrated in Listing 13-10.

LISTING 13-10: Changing your web service so it does not conform to the WS-I Basic Profile spec

VB

```
<WebService(Namespace:="http://tempuri.org/")> _
<WebServiceBinding(ConformsTo:=WsiProfiles.None)> _
<Global.Microsoft.VisualBasic.CompilerServices.DesignerGenerated()> _
Public Class WebService
    Inherits System.Web.Services.WebService
    ' Code here...
End Class
```

C#

```
[WebService(Namespace = "http://tempuri.org/")]
[WebServiceBinding(ConformsTo = WsiProfiles.None)]
public class WebService : System.Web.Services.WebService
{
    // Code here...
}
```

The other option is to turn off the WS-I Basic Profile capability in the `web.config` file, as shown in Listing 13-11.

LISTING 13-11: Turning off conformance using the web.config file

```
<configuration>
    <system.web>
        <webServices>
            <conformanceWarnings>
                <remove name="BasicProfile1_1" />
            </conformanceWarnings>
        </webServices>
    </system.web>
</configuration>
```

After you have enabled your web service to overload `WebMethods`, you can see both `WebMethods` defined by their `MessageName` value properties when you pull up the web service's interface test page in the browser (see Figure 13-11).

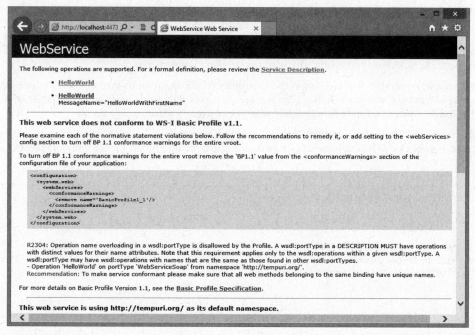

FIGURE 13-11

Although you can see that the names of the `WebMethods` are the same, the `MessageName` property shows that they are distinct methods. When developers consuming the web service make a web reference to your web service, they will see only a single method name available (in this example, `HelloWorld`). It is shown via the Visual Studio 2012 IntelliSense in the application consuming these methods (see Figure 13-12).

```
Figure13-12.aspx*
 1    <%@ Page Language="C#" %>
 2
 3    <!DOCTYPE html>
 4
 5  □<script runat="server">
 6        protected void Page_Load(Object sender, EventArgs e)
 7        {
 8            SampleOverloadService.WebService ws = new SampleOverloadService.WebService();
 9            ws.HelloWorld(
10        }                   ▲ 1 of 2 ▼  string WebService.HelloWorld()
11    </script
12
13  □<html xmlns="http://www.w3.org/1999/xhtml">
14  □<head runat="server">
15        <title></title>
16    </head>
17  □<body>
18  □    <form id="form1" runat="server">
19  □    <div>
20
21        </div>
22        </form>
23    </body>
24    </html>
25
```

FIGURE 13-12

In the box that pops up to guide developers on the signature structure, you can see two options available—one is an empty signature, and the other requires a single string.

CACHING WEB SERVICE RESPONSES

Caching is an important feature in almost every application that you build with .NET. Chapter 22 covers most of the caching capabilities available to you in ASP.NET, but a certain feature of web services in .NET enables you to cache the SOAP response sent to any of the service's consumers.

First, by way of review, remember that caching is the capability to maintain an in-memory store where data, objects, and various items are stored for reuse. This feature increases the responsiveness of the applications you build and manage. Sometimes, returning cached results can greatly affect performance.

XML Web Services use an attribute to control caching of SOAP responses—the `CacheDuration` property. Listing 13-12 (the TimeService.vb and TimeService.cs files in the code download for the chapter) shows its use.

LISTING 13-12: Utilizing the CacheDuration property

VB

```
<WebMethod(CacheDuration:=60)> _
Public Function GetServerTime() As String
    Return DateTime.Now.ToLongTimeString()
End Function
```

C#

```
[WebMethod(CacheDuration = 60)]
public string GetServerTime()
{
    return DateTime.Now.ToLongTimeString();
}
```

As you can see, `CacheDuration` is used within the `WebMethod` attribute much like the `Description` and `Name` properties. `CacheDuration` takes an `Integer` value that is equal to the number of seconds during which the SOAP response is cached.

When the first request comes in, the SOAP response is cached by the server, and the consumer gets the same timestamp in the SOAP response for the next minute. After that minute is up, the stored cache is discarded, and a new response is generated and stored in the cache again for servicing all other requests for the next minute.

Among the many benefits of caching your SOAP responses, you will find that the performance of your application is greatly improved when you have a response that is basically re-created again and again without any change.

USING SOAP HEADERS

One of the more common forms of extending the capabilities of SOAP messages is to add metadata of the request to the SOAP message itself. The metadata is usually added to a section of the SOAP envelope called the *SOAP header*. Figure 13-13 shows the structure of a SOAP message.

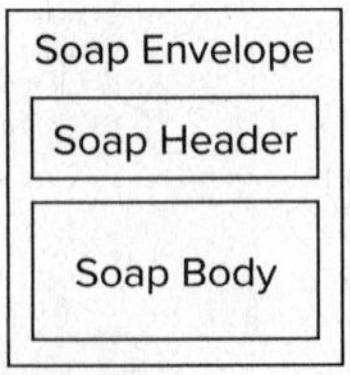

The entire SOAP message is referred to as a *SOAP envelope*. Contained within the SOAP message is the *SOAP body*—a piece of the SOAP message that you have been working with in every example thus far. It is a required element of the SOAP message.

FIGURE 13-13

The one optional component of the SOAP message is the SOAP header. It is the part of the SOAP message in which you can place any metadata about the overall SOAP request instead of incorporating it in the signature of any of your `WebMethods`. Keeping metadata separate from the actual request is important.

What kind of information should you include in a header? It could include many things. One of the more common items placed in the SOAP header is any authentication/authorization functionality required to consume your web service or to get at specific pieces of logic or data. Placing usernames and passwords inside the SOAP headers of your messages is a good example of what you might include.

Building a Web Service with SOAP Headers

You can build upon the sample `HelloWorld` web service that is presented in the default `.asmx` page when it is first pulled up in Visual Studio (from Listing 13-4). Name the new `.asmx` file `HelloSoapHeader.asmx`. The initial step is to add a class that is an object representing what is to be placed in the SOAP header by the client, as shown in Listing 13-13.

LISTING 13-13: A class representing the SOAP header

VB

```
Public Class HelloHeader
    Inherits System.Web.Services.Protocols.SoapHeader
    Public Username As String
    Public Password As String
End Class
```

C#

```
public class HelloHeader : System.Web.Services.Protocols.SoapHeader
{
    public string Username;
    public string Password;
}
```

The class, representing a SOAP header object, has to inherit from the `SoapHeader` class from `System.Web` `.Services.Protocols.SoapHeader`. The `SoapHeader` class serializes the payload of the `<soap:header>` element into XML for you. In the example in Listing 13-13, you can see that this SOAP header requires two elements: simply a username and a password, both of type `String`. The names you create in this class are those used for the sub-elements of the SOAP header construction, so naming them descriptively is important.

Listing 13-14 shows the web service class that creates an instance of the `HelloHeader` class.

LISTING 13-14: A web service class that utilizes a SOAP header

VB

```
<WebService(Namespace:="http://tempuri.org/")> _
<WebServiceBinding(ConformsTo:=WsiProfiles.BasicProfile1_1 ,
    EmitConformanceClaims:=True)> _
<Global.Microsoft.VisualBasic.CompilerServices.DesignerGenerated()> _
Public Class HelloSoapHeader
    Inherits System.Web.Services.WebService

    Public myHeader As HelloHeader

    <WebMethod(), SoapHeader("myHeader")> _
    Public Function HelloWorld() As String
        If (myHeader Is Nothing) Then
            Return "Hello World"
        Else
            Return "Hello " & myHeader.Username & ". " & _
```

continues

LISTING 13-14 *(continued)*

```
                    "<br>Your password is: " & myHeader.Password
            End If
        End Function
    End Class
```

C#

```
[WebService(Namespace = "http://tempuri.org/")]
[WebServiceBinding(ConformsTo = WsiProfiles.BasicProfile1_1, EmitConformanceClaims = true)]
public class HelloSoapHeader : System.Web.Services.WebService {

    public HelloHeader myHeader;

    [WebMethod]
    [SoapHeader("myHeader")]
    public string HelloWorld()
    {
        if (myHeader == null)
        {
            return "Hello World";
        }
        else
        {
            return "Hello " + myHeader.Username + ". " +
                "<br>Your password is: " + myHeader.Password;
        }
    }
}
```

The web service, `HelloSoapHeader`, has a single `WebMethod`—`HelloWorld`. Within the web service class, but outside of the `WebMethod` itself, you create an instance of the `SoapHeader` class. You can do so with the following line of code:

```
Public myHeader As HelloHeader
```

Now that you have an instance of the `HelloHeader` class that you created earlier called `myHeader`, you can use that instantiation in your `WebMethod`. Because web services can contain any number of `WebMethods`, it is not a requirement that all `WebMethods` use an instantiated SOAP header. You specify whether a `WebMethod` will use a particular instantiation of a SOAP header class by placing the `SoapHeader` attribute before the `WebMethod` declaration.

```
[WebMethod]
[SoapHeader("myHeader")]
public string HelloWorld()
{
    // Code here...
}
```

In this example, the `SoapHeader` attribute takes a `string` value of the name of the instantiated `SoapHeader` class—in this case, `myHeader`.

From here, the `WebMethod` actually makes use of the `myHeader` object. If the `myHeader` object is not found (meaning that the client did not send in a SOAP header with his constructed SOAP message), a simple "Hello World" is returned. However, if values are provided in the SOAP header of the SOAP request, those values are used within the returned `string` value.

Consuming a Web Service Using SOAP Headers

Building an ASP.NET application that makes a SOAP request to a web service using SOAP headers is not really difficult. Just as with the web services that do not include SOAP headers, you make a web reference to the remote web service directly in Visual Studio.

For the ASP.NET page, create a simple page with a single Label control. The output of the web service is placed in the Label control. Listing 13-15 shows the code for the ASP.NET page.

LISTING 13-15: An ASP.NET page working with an XML web service using SOAP headers

VB

```
<%@ Page Language="VB" %>
<!DOCTYPE html>
<script runat="server">
    Protected Sub Page_Load(ByVal sender As Object, ByVal e As System.EventArgs)
        Dim ws As New HelloSoap.HelloSoapHeader()
        Dim wsHeader As New HelloSoap.HelloHeader()
        wsHeader.Username = "Jason Gaylord"
        wsHeader.Password = "Lights"
        ws.HelloHeaderValue = wsHeader
        Label1.Text = ws.HelloWorld()
    End Sub
</script>
<html xmlns="http://www.w3.org/1999/xhtml">
<head id="Head1" runat="server">
    <title>Working with SOAP headers</title>
</head>
<body>
    <form id="form1" runat="server">
    <div>
        <asp:Label ID="Label1" Runat="server"></asp:Label>
    </div>
    </form>
</body>
</html>
```

C#

```
<%@ Page Language="C#" %>
<!DOCTYPE html>
<script runat="server">
    protected void Page_Load(object sender, System.EventArgs e)
    {
        helloSoapHeader.HelloSoapHeader ws = new helloSoapHeader.HelloSoapHeader();
        helloSoapHeader.HelloHeader wsHeader = new helloSoapHeader.HelloHeader();
        wsHeader.Username = "Jason Gaylord ";
        wsHeader.Password = "Lights";
        ws.HelloHeaderValue = wsHeader;
        Label1.Text = ws.HelloWorld();
    }
</script>
```

Two objects are instantiated. The first is the actual web service, `HelloSoapHeader`. The second, which is instantiated as `wsHeader`, is the `SoapHeader` object. After both of these objects are instantiated and before making the SOAP request in the application, you construct the SOAP header. This is as easy as assigning values to the `Username` and `Password` properties of the `wsHeader` object. After these properties are assigned, you associate the `wsHeader` object to the `ws` object through the use of the `HelloHeaderValue` property. After you have made the association between the constructed SOAP header object and the actual `WebMethod` object (`ws`), you can make a SOAP request just as you would normally do:

```
Label1.Text = ws.HelloWorld()
```

Running the page produces the result in the browser shown in Figure 13-14.

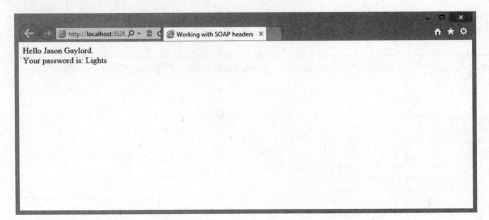

FIGURE 13-14

What is more interesting, however, is that the SOAP request reveals that the SOAP header was indeed constructed into the overall SOAP message, as shown in Listing 13-16.

LISTING 13-16: The SOAP request

```
<?xml version="1.0" encoding="utf-8" ?>
<soap:Envelope xmlns:soap="http://schemas.xmlsoap.org/soap/envelope/"
 xmlns:xsi="http://www.w3.org/2001/XMLSchema-instance"
 xmlns:xsd="http://www.w3.org/2001/XMLSchema">
    <soap:Header>
        <HelloHeader xmlns="http://tempuri.org/">
            <Username>Jason Gaylord</Username>
            <Password>Lights</Password>
        </HelloHeader>
    </soap:Header>
    <soap:Body>
        <HelloWorld xmlns="http://tempuri.org/" />
    </soap:Body>
</soap:Envelope>
```

This code returns the SOAP response shown in Listing 13-17.

LISTING 13-17: The SOAP response

```
<?xml version="1.0" encoding="utf-8" ?>
<soap:Envelope xmlns:soap="http://schemas.xmlsoap.org/soap/envelope/"
 xmlns:xsi="http://www.w3.org/2001/XMLSchema-instance"
 xmlns:xsd="http://www.w3.org/2001/XMLSchema">
    <soap:Body>
        <HelloWorldResponse xmlns="http://tempuri.org/">
            <HelloWorldResult>Hello Jason Gaylord. Your password is:
            Lights</HelloWorldResult>
        </HelloWorldResponse>
    </soap:Body>
</soap:Envelope>
```

Requesting Web Services Using SOAP 1.2

In an ASP.NET application that is consuming a web service, you can control whether the SOAP request is constructed as a SOAP 1.1 message or a 1.2 message. Listing 13-18 changes the previous example so that the request uses SOAP 1.2 instead of the default setting of SOAP 1.1.

LISTING 13-18: An ASP.NET application making a SOAP request using SOAP 1.2

VB

```
<%@ Page Language="VB" %>
<!DOCTYPE html>
<script runat="server">
    Protected Sub Page_Load(ByVal sender As Object, ByVal e As System.EventArgs)
        Dim ws As New HelloSoap.HelloSoapHeader()
        Dim wsHeader As New HelloSoap.HelloHeader()
        wsHeader.Username = "Jason Gaylord"
        wsHeader.Password = "Lights"
        ws.HelloHeaderValue = wsHeader
        ws.SoapVersion = Services.Protocols.SoapProtocolVersion.Soap12
        Label1.Text = ws.HelloWorld()
    End Sub
</script>
```

C#

```
<%@ Page Language="C#" %>
<!DOCTYPE html>
<script runat="server">
    protected void Page_Load(object sender, System.EventArgs e)
    {
        helloSoapHeader.HelloSoapHeader ws = new helloSoapHeader.HelloSoapHeader();
        helloSoapHeader.HelloHeader wsHeader = new helloSoapHeader.HelloHeader();
        wsHeader.Username = "Jason Gaylord";
        wsHeader.Password = "Lights";
        ws.HelloHeaderValue = wsHeader;
        ws.SoapVersion = System.Web.Services.Protocols.SoapProtocolVersion.Soap12;
        Label1.Text = ws.HelloWorld();
    }
</script>
```

In this example, you first provide an instantiation of the web service object and use the `SoapVersion` property. The property takes a value of `System.Web.Services.Protocols.SoapProtocolVersion.Soap12` to work with SOAP 1.2 specifically.

With this bit of code in place, the SOAP request takes the structure shown in Listing 13-19.

LISTING 13-19: The SOAP request using SOAP 1.2

```xml
<?xml version="1.0" encoding="utf-8"?>
<soap:Envelope xmlns:soap="http://www.w3.org/2003/05/soap-envelope"
 xmlns:xsi="http://www.w3.org/2001/XMLSchema-instance"
 xmlns:xsd="http://www.w3.org/2001/XMLSchema">
    <soap:Header>
        <HelloHeader xmlns="http://tempuri.org/">
            <Username>Jason Gaylord</Username>
            <Password>Lights</Password>
        </HelloHeader>
    </soap:Header>
    <soap:Body>
        <HelloWorld xmlns="http://tempuri.org/" />
    </soap:Body>
</soap:Envelope>
```

One difference between the two examples is the `xmlns:soap` namespace that is used. The difference actually resides in the HTTP header. When you compare the SOAP 1.1 and 1.2 messages, you see a difference in the `Content-Type` attribute. In addition, the SOAP 1.2 HTTP header does not use the `soapaction` attribute because this is now combined with the `Content-Type` attribute.

You can turn off either SOAP 1.1 or 1.2 capabilities with the web services that you build by making the proper settings in the `web.config` file, as shown in Listing 13-20.

LISTING 13-20: Turning off SOAP 1.1 or 1.2 capabilities

```xml
<?xml version="1.0"?>
<configuration>
    <system.web>
        <webServices>
            <protocols>
                <remove name="HttpSoap"/>    <!-- Removes SOAP 1.1 abilities -->
                <remove name="HttpSoap1.2"/> <!-- Removes SOAP 1.2 abilities -->
            </protocols>
        </webServices>
    </system.web>
</configuration>
```

CONSUMING WEB SERVICES ASYNCHRONOUSLY

All the web services that you have been working with in this chapter have been done *synchronously*. This means that after a request is sent from the code of an ASP.NET application, the application comes to a complete standstill until a SOAP response is received.

The process of invoking a `WebMethod` and getting back a result can take some time for certain requests. At times, you are not in control of the web service from which you are requesting data and, therefore, you are not in control of the performance or response times of these services. For these reasons, you should consider consuming web services *asynchronously*.

An ASP.NET application that makes an asynchronous request can work on other programming tasks while the initial SOAP request is awaiting a response. When the ASP.NET application is done working on the additional items, it can return to get the result from the web service.

The great news is that to build an XML web service that allows asynchronous communication, you don't have to perform any additional actions. All `.asmx` web services have the built-in capability for asynchronous communication with consumers. The web service in Listing 13-21 is an example. (This listing contains the HelloWorldAsyncService.vb and HelloWorldAsyncService.cs files in their respective projects in the code download for this chapter.)

LISTING 13-21: A slow web service

VB

```vb
Imports System.Web
Imports System.Web.Services
Imports System.Web.Services.Protocols

<WebService(Namespace:="http://tempuri.org/")> _
<WebServiceBinding(ConformsTo:=WsiProfiles.BasicProfile1_1, _
  EmitConformanceClaims:=True)> _
Public Class HelloWorldAsyncService
    Inherits System.Web.Services.WebService

    <WebMethod()> _
    Public Function HelloWorld() As String
        System.Threading.Thread.Sleep(1000)
        Return "Hello World"
    End Function
```

```
End Class
```

C#

```csharp
using System;
using System.Web;
using System.Web.Services;
using System.Web.Services.Protocols;

[WebService(Namespace = "http://tempuri.org/")]
[WebServiceBinding(ConformsTo = WsiProfiles.BasicProfile1_1)]
public class HelloWorldAsyncService : System.Web.Services.WebService {
    [WebMethod]
    public string HelloWorld() {
        System.Threading.Thread.Sleep(1000);
        return "Hello World";
    }
}
```

This web service returns a simple Hello World as a string, but before it does, the web service makes a 1000-millisecond pause. You do this by putting the web service thread to sleep using the Sleep method.

Next, take a look at how an ASP.NET application can consume this slow web service asynchronously, as shown in Listing 13-22.

LISTING 13-22: An ASP.NET application consuming a web service asynchronously

VB

```vb
<%@ Page Language="VB" %>
<!DOCTYPE html>
<script runat="server">
    Protected Sub Page_Load(ByVal sender As Object, ByVal e As System.EventArgs)
        Dim ws As New HelloWorldAsync.HelloWorldAsyncService()
        Dim myIar As IAsyncResult
        myIar = ws.BeginHelloWorld(Nothing, Nothing)
        Dim x As Integer = 0

        Do Until myIar.IsCompleted = True
            x += 1
        Loop

        Label1.Text = "Result from Web service: " & ws.EndHelloWorld(myIar) & _
            "<br>Local count while waiting: " & x.ToString()
    End Sub
</script>
<html xmlns="http://www.w3.org/1999/xhtml">
<head id="Head1" runat="server">
    <title>Async consumption</title>
</head>
<body>
    <form id="form1" runat="server">
    <div>
        <asp:Label ID="Label1" Runat="server"></asp:Label>
    </div>
    </form>
</body>
</html>
```

C#

```csharp
<%@ Page Language="C#" %>
<!DOCTYPE html>
```

continues

LISTING 13-22 *(continued)*

```
<script runat="server">
    protected void Page_Load(object sender, System.EventArgs e)
    {
        helloWorldAsync.HelloWorldAsyncService ws =
          new helloWorldAsync.HelloWorldAsyncService();
        IAsyncResult myIar;
        myIar = ws.BeginHelloWorld(null, null);
        int x = 0;

        while (myIar.IsCompleted == false)
        {
            x += 1;
        }

        Label1.Text = "Result from Web service: " + ws.EndHelloWorld(myIar) +
            "<br>Local count while waiting: " + x.ToString();
    }
</script>
```

When you make the web reference to the remote web service in the consuming ASP.NET application, you not only see the `HelloWorld WebMethod` available to you in IntelliSense, but you also see a `BeginHelloWorld()` and an `EndHelloWorld()`. To work with the web service asynchronously, you must utilize the `BeginHelloWorld()` and `EndHelloWorld()` methods.

Use the `BeginHelloWorld()` method to send a SOAP request to the web service, but instead of the ASP.NET application waiting idly for a response, it moves on to accomplish other tasks. In this case, it is not doing anything that important—just counting the amount of time it is taking in a loop.

After the SOAP request is sent from the ASP.NET application, you can use the `IAsyncResult` object to check whether a SOAP response is waiting. You do this by using `myIar.IsCompleted`. If the asynchronous invocation is not complete, the ASP.NET application increases the value of x by one before making the same check again. The ASP.NET application continues to do this until the XML web service is ready to return a response. The response is retrieved using the `EndHelloWorld()` method call.

The results of running this application are similar to what is shown in Figure 13-15.

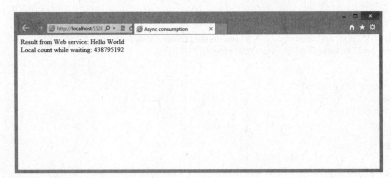

FIGURE 13-15

WINDOWS COMMUNICATION FOUNDATION

In the past, building components that were required to communicate a message from one point to another was not a simple task because Microsoft offered more than one technology that you could use for such an action. Out of this confusion, Microsoft created the Windows Communication Foundation (WCF) to help you decide what path to take with the applications you are trying to build.

WCF is a framework for building *service-oriented architecture* (SOA). Microsoft wanted to provide its developers with a framework to get a proper service-oriented architecture up and running quickly. Using the WCF, you can take advantage of all the items that make distribution technologies powerful. WCF offered an answer and successor to all the other message distribution technologies that came before it.

WCF Overview

As stated, the Windows Communication Foundation is a means to build distributed applications in a Microsoft environment. Although the distributed application is built upon that environment, this does not mean that consumers are required to be Microsoft clients or to take any Microsoft component or technology to accomplish the task of consumption. On the other hand, building WCF services means you are also building services that abide by the core principles of SOA and that these services are vendor-agnostic—thus, they can be consumed by almost anyone.

> **NOTE** *You can build WCF services using Visual Studio 2012. Because this is a .NET Framework 3.0 or greater component, you are actually limited to the operating systems in which you can run a WCF service. An application built with WCF can run only on Windows XP SP2 or later.*

If you are already familiar with WCF, it is interesting to note that some improvements have been made to WCF 4.5. A lot of focus was put on increasing the productivity of developers and providing quick options for common tasks, such as creating asynchronous web services, simplifying the WCF configuration, and enabling HTML5 WebSocket support. Other new features include multiple authentication methods for a single endpoint, improved performance for file streaming, and configuration validation.

Building a WCF Service

Building a WCF service is not hard to accomplish. The assumption here is that you have installed the .NET Framework 4.5 for the purpose of these examples. If you are using Visual Studio 2012, the view of the project from the New Web Site dialog box is as shown in Figure 13-16.

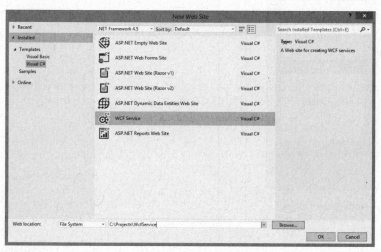

FIGURE 13-16

When you build a WCF project in this manner, the idea is that you build a traditional class library that is compiled down to a DLL that can then be added to another project. The separation of code and project is a powerful division on larger projects. That said, you can, however, just as easily build a WCF service directly in your .NET project, whether that is a console application or a Windows Forms application. The approach taken for the examples in this chapter shows you how to build a WCF service that is hosted in a console application. Keep in mind that for the services you actually build and deploy, building them directly as a WCF Service Library project and using the created DLL in your projects or in IIS itself is usually better.

Before you jump into building a WCF service, first consider what makes up a service built upon the WCF framework.

What Makes a WCF Service

When looking at a WCF service, you should understand that it is made up of three parts: the service, one or more endpoints, and an environment in which to host the service.

A service is a class that is written in one of the .NET-compliant languages. The class can contain one or more methods that are exposed through the WCF service. A service can have one or more endpoints. An endpoint is used to communicate through the service to the client.

Endpoints themselves are also made up of three parts. These parts are usually defined by Microsoft as the ABC of WCF. Each letter of WCF means something in particular in the WCF model, including the following:

➤   "A" is for address.
➤   "B" is for binding.
➤   "C" is for contract.

Basically, you can think of this as follows: "A" is the where, "B" is the how, and "C" is the what. Finally, a hosting environment is where the service is contained. This constitutes an application domain and process. All three of these elements (the service, the endpoints, and the hosting environment) are put together to create a WCF service offering, as depicted in Figure 13-17.

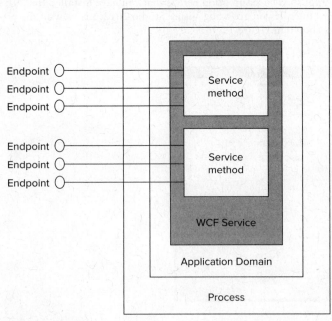

FIGURE 13-17

The next step is to create a basic service using the WCF framework.

Creating Your First WCF Service

To build your service, prior to hosting it, you must perform two main steps. First, you must create a service contract. Second, you must create a data contract. The service contract is really a class with the methods that you want to expose from the WCF service. The data contract is a class that specifies the structure you want to expose from the interface.

After you have a service class in place, you can host it almost anywhere. When running this service from Visual Studio 2012, you will be able to use the same built-in hosting mechanisms that are used by any standard ASP.NET application. To build your first WCF application, choose File ⇨ New ⇨ Web Site from the Visual Studio 2012 menu and leave the default project name of WCFService1.

> **NOTE** *To maintain consistency within this chapter, I'm calling these projects Chapter13-WCFService-CS and Chapter13-WCFService-VB for C# and VB respectively.*

The example this chapter runs through here demonstrates how to build the WCF service by building the interface, followed by the service itself.

Creating the Service Framework

The first step is to create the service framework in the project. To do this, right-click the project and select Add New Item from the provided menu. From the Add New Item dialog box, select WCF Service, and name the service **Calculator.svc**, as illustrated in Figure 13-18.

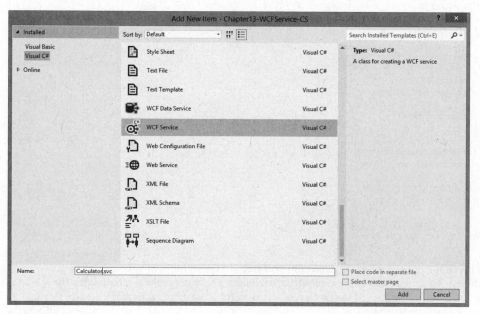

FIGURE 13-18

This step creates a `Calculator.svc` file, a `Calculator.cs` file, and an `ICalculator.cs` file. The `Calculator.svc` file is a simple file that includes only the page directive, whereas the `Calculator.cs` does all the heavy lifting. The `Calculator.cs` file is an implementation of the `ICalculator.cs` interface.

Working with the Interface

To create your service, you need a service contract. The service contract is the interface of the service. This consists of all the methods exposed, as well as the input and output parameters that are required to invoke the methods. To accomplish this task, turn to the `ICalculator.vb` or `ICalculator.cs` file (depending on the language you are using). Listing 13-23 presents the interface you need to create (ICalculator.vb and ICalculator.cs in the Chapter13-WCFService-VB and Chapter13-WCFService-CS folders, respectively, in the code download for this chapter).

LISTING 13-23: Creating the interface

VB

```vb
Imports System.ServiceModel

<ServiceContract()>
Public Interface ICalculator
    <OperationContract()> _
    Function Add(ByVal a As Integer, ByVal b As Integer) As Integer

    <OperationContract()> _
    Function Subtract(ByVal a As Integer, ByVal b As Integer) As Integer

    <OperationContract()> _
    Function Multiply(ByVal a As Integer, ByVal b As Integer) As Integer

    <OperationContract()> _
    Function Divide(ByVal a As Integer, ByVal b As Integer) As Integer
End Interface
```

C#

```csharp
using System.ServiceModel;

[ServiceContract]
public interface ICalculator
{
    [OperationContract]
    int Add(int a, int b);

    [OperationContract]
    int Subtract(int a, int b);

    [OperationContract]
    int Multiply(int a, int b);

    [OperationContract]
    int Divide(int a, int b);
}
```

This is pretty much the normal interface definition you would expect, but with a couple of new attributes included. To gain access to these required attributes, you must make a reference to the `System.ServiceModel` namespace. This gives you access to the `<ServiceContract()>` and `<OperationContract()>` attributes.

You use the <ServiceContract()> attribute to define the class or interface as the service class, and it needs to precede the opening declaration of the class or interface. In this case, the example in the preceding code is based upon an interface:

```
[ServiceContract]
public interface ICalculator
{
    // Code removed for clarity
}
```

Within the interface, four methods are defined. Each method is going to be exposed through the WCF service as part of the service contract. For this reason, each method is required to have the <OperationContract()> attribute applied:

```
[OperationContract]
int Add(int a, int b);
```

Utilizing the Interface

The next step is to create a class that implements the interface. Not only is the new class implementing the defined interface, but it is also implementing the service contract. For this example, add this class to the same Calculator.vb or .cs file. The following code, illustrated in Listing 13-24, shows the implementation of this interface.

LISTING 13-24: Implementing the interface

VB

```
Public Class Calculator
    Implements ICalculator

    Public Function Add(a As Integer, b As Integer) As Integer Implements ICalculator.Add
        Return (a + b)
    End Function

    Public Function Divide(a As Integer, b As Integer) As Integer Implements ICalculator.Divide
        Return (a / b)
    End Function

    Public Function Multiply(a As Integer, b As Integer) As Integer
      Implements ICalculator.Multiply
        Return (a * b)
    End Function

    Public Function Subtract(a As Integer, b As Integer) As Integer
      Implements ICalculator.Subtract
        Return (a - b)
    End Function
End Class
```

C#

```
public class Calculator : ICalculator
{
    public int Add(int a, int b)
    {
        return (a + b);
```

continues

LISTING 13-24 *(continued)*

```
    }

    public int Subtract(int a, int b)
    {
        return (a - b);
    }

    public int Multiply(int a, int b)
    {
        return (a * b);
    }

    public int Divide(int a, int b)
    {
        return (a / b);
    }
}
```

From these new additions, you can see that you don't have to do anything different to the Calculator class. It is a simple class that implements the ICalculator interface and provides implementations of the Add(), Subtract(), Multiply(), and Divide() methods.

With the interface and the class available, you now have your WCF service built and ready to go. The next step is to get the service hosted. Note that this is a simple service—it exposes only simple types, rather than a complex type. This enables you to build only a service contract and not have to deal with the construction of a data contract. You learn about the construction of data contracts later in this chapter.

Hosting the WCF Service in a Console Application

The next step is to take the service just developed and host it in some type of application process. Many hosting options are available, including the following:

- ➤ Console applications
- ➤ Windows Forms applications
- ➤ Windows Presentation Foundation (WPF) applications
- ➤ Managed Windows Services
- ➤ Internet Information Services (IIS) 5.1 and later
- ➤ IIS Express

As stated earlier, this example hosts the service in IIS Express provided by Visual Studio 2012. You can activate hosting a couple of ways—either through the direct coding of the hosting behaviors or through declarative programming (usually done via the configuration file).

Compiling and running this application produces the results illustrated in Figure 13-19.

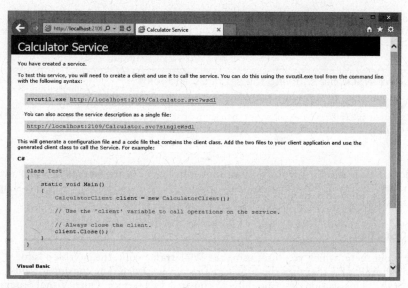

FIGURE 13-19

You will notice that the resulting page is quite similar to how it appears when you build an ASP.NET web service.

Reviewing the WSDL Document

The page presented in Figure 13-19 is the information page about the service. In the image, notice the link to the WSDL file of the service. As with ASP.NET Web Services, a WCF service can also autogenerate the WSDL file. One of the features in WCF 4.5 is an option for a single WSDL file. Clicking the single WSDL link shows the WSDL in the browser, as illustrated in Figure 13-20.

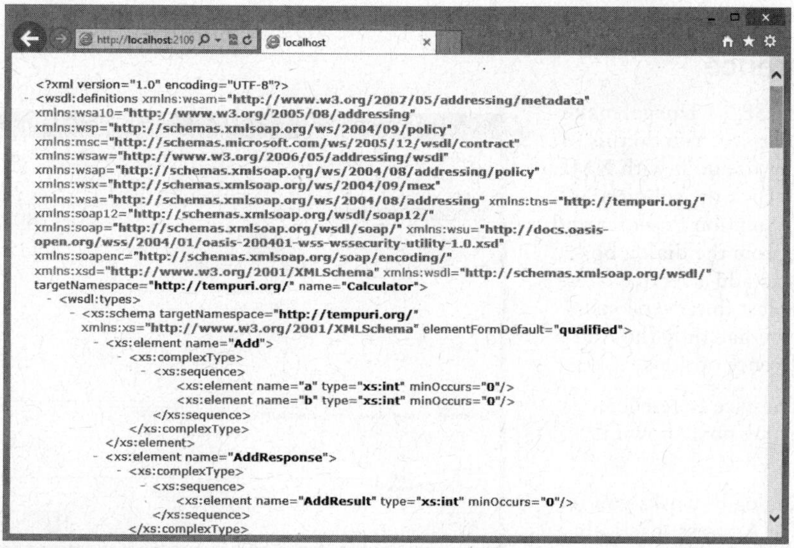

FIGURE 13-20

With this WSDL file, you can consume the service it defines through an HTTP binding. Note the following element at the bottom of the document, as shown in Listing 13-25. (This code listing is taken from the WSDL file when it's generated in the browser.)

LISTING 13-25: The part of the WSDL file showing the service's endpoint

```
<wsdl:service name="Calculator">
    <wsdl:port name="BasicHttpBinding_ICalculator" binding="tns:BasicHttpBinding_ICalculator">
        <soap:address location="http://localhost:2109/Calculator.svc"/>
    </wsdl:port>
</wsdl:service>
```

This element in the XML document indicates that to consume the service, the end user must use SOAP over HTTP. This is indicated through the use of the `<soap:address>` element in the document. Using this simple WSDL document, you can now build a consumer that makes use of this interface.

Building the WCF Consumer

Now that an HTTP service is out there, which you built using the WCF framework, the next step is to build a consumer application in ASP.NET that uses the simple `Calculator` service. The consumer sends its request via HTTP using SOAP. This section describes how to consume this service. Open Visual Studio 2012 and create a new ASP.NET application. Although this example uses an ASP.NET application, you can make this consumer call through any other application type within .NET as well.

Call the new ASP.NET application `WCFConsumer`. This application consumes the `Calculator` service, so it should be laid out with two textboxes and a button to initiate the service call. For this example, you will only use the `Add()` method of the service.

> **NOTE** *To maintain consistency within this chapter, I'm calling these projects Chapter13-CustomerConsumer-CS and Chapter13-CustomerConsumer-VB for C# and VB, respectively.*

Adding a Service Reference

After you have laid out your ASP.NET page, make a reference to the new WCF service. You do this in a manner quite similar to how you do it with XML web service references. Right-click the solution name from the Visual Studio Solution Explorer and select Add Service Reference from the dialog box that appears. This capability to add a service reference has been included in the last three versions of Visual Studio—previously, you had only the Add Reference and Add Web Reference options.

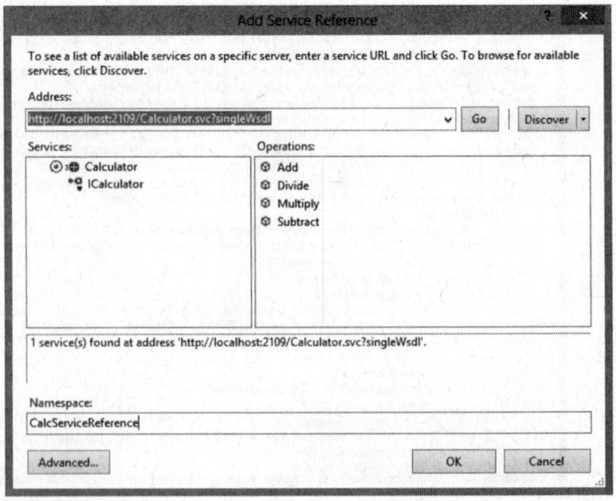

After you have selected Add Service Reference, the Add Service Reference dialog box, shown in Figure 13-21, appears.

The Add Service Reference dialog box asks you for two things: the Service URI or Address (basically a pointer to the WSDL file) and the name you want to give to the reference. The name you provide the

FIGURE 13-21

reference is the name that will be used for the instantiated object that enables you to interact with the service.

Referring to Figure 13-21, you can see that the name provided to the Service Address setting is what is used for the running service from earlier in this chapter. Click OK in the Add Service Reference dialog box. This adds to your project a Service Reference folder containing some proxy files, as shown in Figure 13-22.

Indeed, the Service Reference folder is added and a series of files are contained within this folder. The other important addition to note is the `System.ServiceModel` reference, made for you in the References folder. This reference was not there before you made reference to the service through the Add Service Reference dialog box.

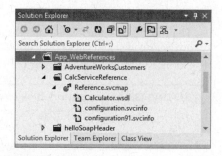

FIGURE 13-22

Configuration File Changes

Looking at the `web.config` file, you can see that Visual Studio has placed information about the service inside the document, as illustrated in Listing 13-26.

LISTING 13-26: Additions made to the web.config file by Visual Studio

```
<system.serviceModel>
    <bindings>
        <basicHttpBinding>
            <binding name="BasicHttpBinding_ICalculator" />
        </basicHttpBinding>
    </bindings>
    <client>
        <endpoint address="http://localhost:2109/Calculator.svc"
            binding="basicHttpBinding"
            bindingConfiguration="BasicHttpBinding_ICalculator"
            contract="CalcServiceReference.ICalculator"
            name="BasicHttpBinding_ICalculator" />
    </client>
</system.serviceModel>
```

The important part of this configuration document is the `<client>` element. This element contains a child element called `<endpoint>` that defines the where and how of the service consumption process.

The `<endpoint>` element provides the address of the service—`http://localhost:2109/Calculator .svc`—and it specifies which binding of the available WCF bindings should be used. In this case, the `basicHttpBinding` is the binding used. Even though you are using an established binding from the WCF framework, from the client side, you can customize how this binding behaves. The settings that define the behavior of the binding are specified using the `bindingConfiguration` attribute of the `<endpoint>` element. In this case, the value provided to the `bindingConfiguration` attribute is `BasicHttpBinding_ ICalculator`, which is a reference to the `<binding>` element contained within the `<basicHttpBinding>` element.

As demonstrated, Visual Studio 2012 makes the consumption of these services fairly trivial. In fact, if you've ever worked with WCF before, you'll notice that the configuration is much more simplistic than previous versions.

The next step is to code the consumption of the service interface into the GUI that you created as one of the first steps earlier in this chapter.

Writing the Consumption Code

The code to consume the interface is quite minimal. The end user places a number in each of the two text-boxes provided and clicks the button to call the service to perform the designated operation on the provided numbers. Listing 13-27 is the code from the button click event.

LISTING 13-27: The button click event to call the service

VB

```
Protected Sub Button1_Click(ByVal sender As Object, ByVal e As System.EventArgs)
    Handles Button1.Click
    Dim ws As New CalcServiceReference.CalculatorClient()
    Dim result As Integer = ws.Add(TextBox1.Text, TextBox2.Text)
    Label1.Text = result.ToString()
    ws.Close()
End Sub
```

C#

```
protected void Button1_Click(object sender, EventArgs e)
{
    CalcServiceReference.CalculatorClient ws = new
        CalcServiceReference.CalculatorClient();
    int result = ws.Add(int.Parse(TextBox1.Text), int.Parse(TextBox2.Text));
    Label1.Text = result.ToString();
    ws.Close();
}
```

This code is quite similar to what is done when working with web references from the XML Web Services world. First is an instantiation of the proxy class, as shown with the creation of the svc object:

```
CalcServiceReference.CalculatorClient ws = new
    CalcServiceReference.CalculatorClient();
```

Working with the ws object now, the IntelliSense options provide you with the appropriate Add(), Subtract(), Multiply(), and Divide() methods. As before, the requests and responses are sent over HTTP as SOAP.

Working with Data Contracts

Thus far, when building the WCF services, the defined data contract has relied upon simple types or primitive data types. In the case of the earlier WCF service, a .NET type of Integer was exposed, which in turn was mapped to an XML schema (XS) type of int. Although you may not be able to see the input and output types defined in the WSDL document provided via the WCF-generated one, they are there. When using a single WSDL file, the types are exposed from within the single WSDL document.

If you are not using a single WSDL file, the XML schema types are defined through an imported .xsd document (Calculator.xsd and Calculator1.xsd). Listing 13-28 presents this bit of the WSDL document.

LISTING 13-28: Imported types in the WSDL document

```
<wsdl:types>
    <xsd:schema targetNamespace="http://tempuri.org/Imports">
        <xsd:import namespace="http://tempuri.org/"
            schemaLocation="http://localhost:2110/Calculator.svc?xsd=xsd0"/>
        <xsd:import
            namespace="http://schemas.microsoft.com/2003/10/Serialization/"
```

```
              schemaLocation="http://localhost:2110/Calculator.svc?xsd=xsd1"/>
    </xsd:schema>
  </wsdl:types>
```

Typing in the XSD location of `http://localhost:2110/Calculator.svc?xsd=xsd0` gives you the input and output parameters of the service. For instance, looking at the definition of the `Add()` method, you will see the following bit of code, as shown in Listing 13-29.

LISTING 13-29: Defining the required types in the XSD

```xml
<xs:element name="Add">
    <xs:complexType>
        <xs:sequence>
            <xs:element minOccurs="0" name="a" type="xs:int" />
            <xs:element minOccurs="0" name="b" type="xs:int" />
        </xs:sequence>
    </xs:complexType>
</xs:element>
<xs:element name="AddResponse">
    <xs:complexType>
        <xs:sequence>
            <xs:element minOccurs="0" name="AddResult" type="xs:int" />
        </xs:sequence>
    </xs:complexType>
</xs:element>
```

This bit of XML code indicates that two required input parameters (a and b) are of type `int`; in return, the consumer gets an element called `<AddResult>`, which contains a value of type `int`.

As a builder of this WCF service, you did not have to build the data contract because this service used simple types. When using complex types, you have to create a data contract in addition to your service contract.

Building a Service with a Data Contract

For an example of working with data contracts, create a new WCF service called `MyCustomDataContractService`. In this case, you still need an interface that defines your service contract, and then another class that implements that interface. In addition to these items, you also need another class that defines the data contract.

As with the service contract, which makes use of the `[ServiceContract]` and the `[OperationContract]` attributes, the data contract uses the `[DataContract]` and `[DataMember]` attributes. To gain access to these attributes, you must make a reference to the `System.Runtime.Serialization` namespace in your project and import this namespace into the file.

The custom type in this case is a `Customer` type, as presented in Listing 13-30 (IMyCustomDataContractService.vb and IMyCustomDataContractService.cs, respectively, in the WCF projects in the code download for this chapter).

LISTING 13-30: Building the Customer type

VB

```vb
Imports System.ServiceModel
Imports System.Runtime.Serialization

<DataContract()>
Public Class Customer
    <DataMember()>
```

continues

LISTING 13-30 *(continued)*

```
    Public FirstName As String

    <DataMember()>
    Public LastName As String
End Class

<ServiceContract()>
Public Interface IMyCustomDataContractService
    <OperationContract()>
    Function HelloFirstName(ByVal cust As Customer) As String

    <OperationContract()>
    Function HelloFullName(ByVal cust As Customer) As String
End Interface
```

C#

```
using System.Runtime.Serialization;
using System.ServiceModel;

[DataContract]
public class Customer
{
    [DataMember]
    public string Firstname;

    [DataMember]
    public string Lastname;
}

[ServiceContract]
public interface IMyCustomDataContractService
{
    [OperationContract]
    string HelloFirstName(Customer cust);

    [OperationContract]
    string HelloFullName(Customer cust);
}
```

Here, you can see that the System.Runtime.Serialization namespace is also imported, and the first class in the file is the data contract of the service. This class, the Customer class, has two members: FirstName and LastName. Both of these properties are of type String. You specify a class as a data contract through the use of the [DataContract] attribute:

```
[DataContract]
public class Customer
{
    // Code removed for clarity
}
```

Now, any of the properties contained in the class are also part of the data contract through the use of the [DataMember] attribute:

```
[DataContract]
public class Customer
{
    [DataMember]
    public string Firstname;

    [DataMember]
    public string Lastname;
}
```

Finally, the `Customer` object is used in the interface, as well as the class that implements the `IMyCustomDataContractService` interface, as shown in Listing 13-31.

LISTING 13-31: Implementing the interface

VB

```vb
Public Class MyCustomDataContractService
    Implements IMyCustomDataContractService

    Public Function HelloFirstName(cust As Customer) As String _
        Implements IMyCustomDataContractService.HelloFirstName
        Return "Hello " & cust.FirstName
    End Function

    Public Function HelloFullName(cust As Customer) As String _
        Implements IMyCustomDataContractService.HelloFullName
        Return "Hello " & cust.FirstName & " " & cust.LastName
    End Function
End Class
```

C#

```csharp
public class MyCustomDataContractService : IMyCustomDataContractService
{
    public string HelloFirstName(Customer cust)
    {
        return "Hello " + cust.Firstname;
    }

    public string HelloFullName(Customer cust)
    {
        return "Hello " + cust.Firstname + " " + cust.Lastname;
    }
}
```

Building the Consumer

Now that the service is running and in place, the next step is to build the consumer. To begin, you're going to update the same web application that you have been using to consume web services. Again, right-click the solution and select Add Service Reference from the options provided in the menu.

From the Add Service Reference dialog box, add the location of the WSDL file for the service and click OK. This adds the changes to the references and the `web.config` file just as before, enabling you to consume the service. The code presented in Listing 13-32 shows what is required to consume the service if you are using a Button control to initiate the call.

LISTING 13-32: Consuming a custom type through a WCF service

VB

```vb
Protected Sub Button1_Click(ByVal sender As Object, ByVal e As System.EventArgs) _
    Handles Button1.Click

    Dim ws As New _
        MyCustomDataContractServiceReference.MyCustomDataContractServiceClient()
    Dim myCustomer As New MyCustomDataContractServiceReference.Customer()

    myCustomer.FirstName = "Jason"
    myCustomer.LastName = "Gaylord"
    Response.Write(ws.HelloFullName(myCustomer))
```

continues

LISTING 13-32 *(continued)*

```vb
        ws.Close()
    End Sub
```

C#

```csharp
    protected void Button1_Click(object sender, EventArgs e)
    {
        MyCustomDataContractServiceReference.MyCustomDataContractServiceClient ws = new
            MyCustomDataContractServiceReference.MyCustomDataContractServiceClient();
        MyCustomDataContractServiceReference.Customer myCustomer = new
            MyCustomDataContractServiceReference.Customer();

        myCustomer.Firstname = "Jason";
        myCustomer.Lastname = "Gaylord";
        Label1.Text = ws.HelloFullName(myCustomer);
        ws.Close();
    }
```

As a consumer, after you make the reference, you will notice that the service reference provides both a `MyCustomDataContractServiceClient` object and the `Customer` object, which was defined through the service's data contract.

Therefore, the preceding code block just instantiates both of these objects and builds the `Customer` object before it is passed into the `HelloFullName()` method provided by the service.

Looking at WSDL and the Schema for MyCustomDataContractService

When you make a reference to the `MyCustomDataContract` service, you will find the following XSD imports in the WSDL:

```xml
<wsdl:types>
    <xsd:schema targetNamespace="http://tempuri.org/Imports">
        <xsd:import namespace="http://tempuri.org/"
          schemaLocation="http://localhost:2109/MyCustomDataContractService.svc?xsd=xsd0"/>
        <xsd:import namespace="http://schemas.microsoft.com/2003/10/Serialization/"
          schemaLocation="http://localhost:2109/MyCustomDataContractService.svc?xsd=xsd1"/>
        <xsd:import namespace="http://schemas.datacontract.org/2004/07/"
          schemaLocation="http://localhost:2109/MyCustomDataContractService.svc?xsd=xsd2"/>
    </xsd:schema>
</wsdl:types>
```

`http://localhost:2109/MyCustomDataContractService.svc?xsd=xsd2` provides the details on your `Customer` object. Here is the code from this file:

```xml
<?xml version="1.0" encoding="UTF-8"?>
<xs:schema xmlns:tns="http://schemas.datacontract.org/2004/07/"
    xmlns:xs="http://www.w3.org/2001/XMLSchema"
    targetNamespace="http://schemas.datacontract.org/2004/07/"
    elementFormDefault="qualified">
    <xs:complexType name="Customer">
        <xs:sequence>
            <xs:element name="Firstname" type="xs:string" nillable="true"
                minOccurs="0"/>
            <xs:element name="Lastname" type="xs:string" nillable="true"
                minOccurs="0"/>
        </xs:sequence>
    </xs:complexType>
    <xs:element name="Customer" type="tns:Customer" nillable="true"/>
</xs:schema>
```

This code is an XSD description of the `Customer` object. Making a reference to the WSDL includes the XSD description of the `Customer` object and enables you to create local instances of this object.

Using this model, you can easily build your services with your own defined types.

Defining Namespaces

Note that the services built in the chapter have no defined namespaces. If you looked at the WSDL files that were produced, you would see that the namespace provided is `http://tempuri.org`. Obviously, you do not want to go live with this default namespace. Instead, you must define your own namespace.

To accomplish this task, the interface's `[ServiceContract]` attribute enables you to set the namespace, as shown here:

```
[ServiceContract(Namespace="http://jasongaylord.com/ns/")]
public interface IMyCustomDataContractService
{
    [OperationContract]
    string HelloFirstName(Customer cust);

    [OperationContract]
    string HelloFullName(Customer cust);
}
```

Here, the `[ServiceContract]` attribute uses the `Namespace` property to provide a namespace.

Using WCF Data Services

An *Entity Data Model (EDM)* is an abstract conceptual model of data as you want to represent it in your code. In recent years, EDMs and their benefits, such as application reusability, have been emphasized.

> **NOTE** *Chapter 11 provides more information on EDMs and how to work with them within Entity Framework.*

Another model that is available is the WCF Data Services framework. This feature enables you to easily create an interface to your client applications that provides everything from simple read capabilities to a full CRUD model (create, read, update, and delete functions). This feature was previously referred to as ADO.NET Data Services.

> **NOTE** *WCF Data Services is commonly known as exposing data using OData and WCF. Although it is not the only way to expose data, it is certainly the easiest. You see later in this chapter how to use this syntax in the URL to construct filters.*

WCF Data Services work to create a services layer to your backend data source. Doing so yourself, especially if you are working with a full CRUD model, means a lot of work. WCF Data Services enables you to get a service layer that is URI-driven. Figure 13-23 shows the general architecture when you're working with WCF Data Services.

As you can see from this figure, the WCF Data Services layer is not the layer that interacts with the database. Instead, you are working with an EDM layer that is the mapping layer between the data store and the cloud-based interface. When working with your EDM, you are able to use LINQ.

WCF Data Services allow you to quickly expose interactions with the application's underlying data source as RESTful-based services. The current version of WCF Data Services enables you to work with the data stores using JSON or Atom-based XML.

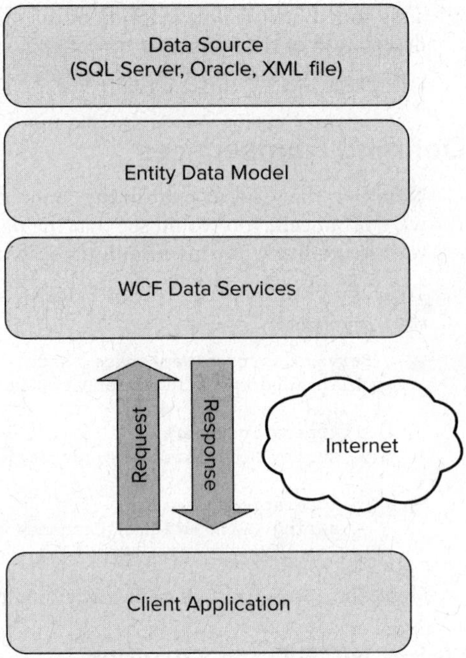

Creating Your First Service

In the past, figuring out how to build a complete services layer to interact with your database for all create, read, update, and delete (CRUD) operations would take some serious time and thought. However, WCF Data Services makes this task much more feasible, as you will see as you work through this first example.

To build a services layer, first create a standard ASP.NET Web Application in either Visual Basic or C#. This, of course, creates a standard web application. Because WCF Data Services works from an underlying database, you will need to add one. For this example, add the AdventureWorks database as you previously used. Place this database within the App_Data folder of your project.

Adding Your Entity Data Model

After you have the database in place, you next create an Entity Data Model that WCF Data Services will work with. To do this, right-click your project and select Add ⇨ New Item from the list of options in the provided menu.

The Add New Item dialog box appears. As illustrated in Figure 13-24, add an ADO.NET Entity Data Model to your project.

FIGURE 13-23

FIGURE 13-24

As shown in the figure, name your ADO.NET Entity Data Model file **AdventureWorks.edmx**. When you create the `AdventureWorks.edmx` file by clicking Add, the Entity Data Model Wizard appears, offering you the option of creating an empty EDM or creating one from a preexisting database. For this example, choose the option to create one from the preexisting (AdventureWorks) database. Then click Next in the wizard.

The next screen of the wizard will find your AdventureWorks database and predefine the connection settings and how they will be stored within your application. Figure 13-25 presents this second screen of the wizard.

In the screenshot in Figure 13-25, notice that the connection string and the locations of the mapping details are going to be stored within the `web.config` file. You can also see on this screen that you are naming the instance of the model **AdventureWorksEntities** in the textbox at the bottom of the wizard. This name is important to note because you will use it later in this example.

The next screen enables you to select the tables, views, or stored procedures that will be part of the model. For this example, select the check box next to the Table item in the tree view to select all the tables in the database, as shown in Figure 13-26.

After selecting the Table check box, click the Finish button to have Visual Studio create the EDM for you. You will notice that Visual Studio creates a visual representation of the model for you in the O/R Designer.

If you look at the `AdventureWorks.designer.vb` or the `AdventureWorks.designer.cs` file in your solution, you will see all the generated code for your EDM in place. This class file is named `AdventureWorksEntities`.

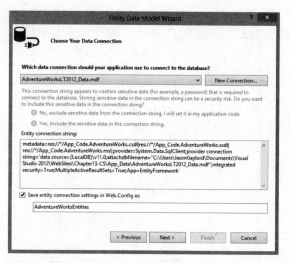

FIGURE 13-25

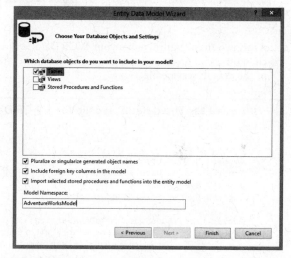

FIGURE 13-26

Creating the Service

Now that the EDM is in place along with the database, the next step is to add your WCF Data Service. To accomplish this, right-click your project within the Visual Studio Solution Explorer and select Add ⇨ New Item from the provided menu. The Add New Item dialog box appears again; select WCF Data Service from the middle section of the provided dialog box (see Figure 13-27).

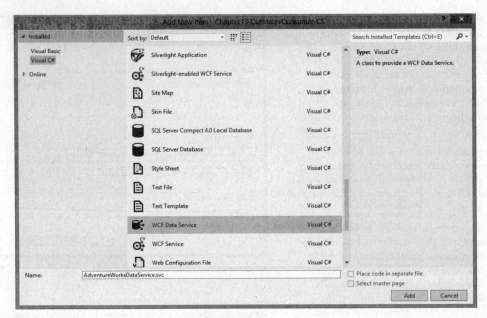

FIGURE 13-27

As shown in the figure, name your WCF Data Service **AdventureWorksDataService.svc**. When you are done, click the Add button and Visual Studio then generates a WCF service for you. Listing 13-33 shows the code of the default service file.

LISTING 13-33: The default .svc file for a WCF Data Service

VB

```vb
Imports System.Data.Services
Imports System.Data.Services.Common
Imports System.Linq
Imports System.ServiceModel.Web

Public Class AdventureWorksDataService
    ' TODO: replace [[class name]] with your data class name
    Inherits DataService(Of [[class name]])

    ' This method is called only once to initialize service-wide
    '       policies.
    Public Shared Sub InitializeService(ByVal config As _
                                    DataServiceConfiguration)
        ' TODO: set rules to indicate which entity sets and service
        '       operations are visible, updatable, etc.
        ' Examples:
        ' config.SetEntitySetAccessRule("MyEntityset",
        '       EntitySetRights.AllRead)
        ' config.SetServiceOperationAccessRule("MyServiceOperation",
        '       ServiceOperationRights.All)
        config.DataServiceBehavior.MaxProtocolVersion = _
            DataServiceProtocolVersion.V3
    End Sub
End Class
```

C#

```csharp
using System;
using System.Data.Services;
using System.Data.Services.Common;
using System.Collections.Generic;
using System.Linq;
using System.ServiceModel.Web;

public class AdventureWorksDataService :
    DataService< /* TODO: put your data source class name here */ >
{
    // This method is called only once to initialize
    //     service-wide policies.
    public static void
        InitializeService(DataServiceConfiguration config)
    {
        // TODO: set rules to indicate which entity sets and
        //     service operations are visible, updatable, etc.
        // Examples:
        // config.SetEntitySetAccessRule("MyEntityset",
        //     EntitySetRights.AllRead);
        // config.SetServiceOperationAccessRule
        //     ("MyServiceOperation", ServiceOperationRights.All);
        config.DataServiceBehavior.MaxProtocolVersion =
            DataServiceProtocolVersion.V3;
    }
}
```

The code generated here is the base framework for what you are going to expose through WCF Data Services. It will not work, however, until you accomplish the big TODO that the code specifies. The first step is to put in the name of the EDM instance using the code presented in Listing 13-34.

LISTING 13-34: Changing the WCF Data Service to work with your EDM

VB

```vb
Public Class AdventureWorksDataService
    Inherits DataService(Of AdventureWorksEntities)

    ' Code removed for clarity
End Class
```

C#

```csharp
public class AdventureWorksDataService :
    DataService<AdventureWorksEntities>
{
    // Code removed for clarity
}
```

Now your application is at a state in which the database, the EDM, and the service to work with the EDM are in place. Upon compiling and pulling up the AdventureWorksDataService.svc file in the browser, you are presented with the following bit of XML:

```xml
<?xml version="1.0" encoding="UTF-8"?>
<service xmlns:atom="http://www.w3.org/2005/Atom"
    xmlns="http://www.w3.org/2007/app"
    xml:base="http://localhost:5526/AdventureWorksDataService.svc/">
    <workspace>
        <atom:title>Default</atom:title>
    </workspace>
</service>
```

> **NOTE** *If you don't see this XML, you need to turn off the feed reading capabilities of your Internet Explorer browser by selecting Tools ⇨ Internet Options. From the provided dialog box, select the Content tab and, within the Feeds section, click the Select button. From there, you will be able to uncheck the "Turn on feed reading" check box.*

The result of the earlier XML is supposed to be a list of all the available sets that are present in the model, but by default, WCF Data Services locks everything down. To unlock these sets from the model, go back to the `InitializeService()` function and add the following bolded code, as illustrated in Listing 13-35.

LISTING 13-35: Opening up the service for reading from the available tables

VB

```
Imports System.Data.Services
Imports System.Data.Services.Common
Imports System.Linq
Imports System.ServiceModel.Web

Public Class AdventureWorksDataService
    Inherits DataService(Of AdventureWorksEntities)

    Public Shared Sub InitializeService(ByVal config As _
                                        DataServiceConfiguration)
        config.SetEntitySetAccessRule("*",
            EntitySetRights.AllRead)
    End Sub
End Class
```

C#

```
using System;
using System.Data.Services;
using System.Data.Services.Common;
using System.Collections.Generic;
using System.Linq;
using System.ServiceModel.Web;

public class AdventureWorksDataService :
    DataService<AdventureWorksEntities>
{
    public static void
        InitializeService(DataServiceConfiguration config)
    {
        config.SetEntitySetAccessRule("*",
            EntitySetRights.AllRead);
    }
}
```

In this case, every table is opened up to access. Everyone who accesses the tables has the ability to read from them, but no writing or deleting abilities. All tables are specified through the use of the asterisk (*), and the right to the underlying data is set to read-only through the `EntitySetRights` enum being set to `AllRead`.

Now, when you compile and run this service in the browser, you see the following bit of XML:

```
<?xml version="1.0" encoding="UTF-8"?>
<service xmlns:atom="http://www.w3.org/2005/Atom"
    xmlns="http://www.w3.org/2007/app"
    xml:base="http://localhost:5526/AdventureWorksDataService.svc/">
```

```
        <workspace>
            <atom:title>Default</atom:title>
            <collection href="BuildVersions">
                <atom:title>BuildVersions</atom:title>
            </collection>
            <collection href="ErrorLogs">
                <atom:title>ErrorLogs</atom:title>
            </collection>
            <collection href="Addresses">
                <atom:title>Addresses</atom:title>
            </collection>
            <collection href="Customers">
                <atom:title>Customers</atom:title>
            </collection>
            <collection href="CustomerAddresses">
                <atom:title>CustomerAddresses</atom:title>
            </collection>
            <collection href="Products">
                <atom:title>Products</atom:title>
            </collection>
            <collection href="ProductCategories">
                <atom:title>ProductCategories</atom:title>
            </collection>
            <collection href="ProductDescriptions">
                <atom:title>ProductDescriptions</atom:title>
            </collection>
            <collection href="ProductModels">
                <atom:title>ProductModels</atom:title>
            </collection>
            <collection href="ProductModelProductDescriptions">
                <atom:title>ProductModelProductDescriptions</atom:title>
            </collection>
            <collection href="SalesOrderDetails">
                <atom:title>SalesOrderDetails</atom:title>
            </collection>
            <collection href="SalesOrderHeaders">
                <atom:title>SalesOrderHeaders</atom:title>
            </collection>
        </workspace>
    </service>
```

The output of this XML is in the AtomPub format, one of the two formats that are made available from WCF Data Services. The other format is JSON, which is used most commonly with JavaScript. The AtomPub example was retrieved due to the following header being in place:

```
GET http://localhost:5526/AdventureWorksDataService.svc/ HTTP/1.1
Accept: text/html, application/xhtml+xml, */*
Accept-Language: en-US
User-Agent: Mozilla/5.0 (compatible; MSIE 10.0; Windows NT 6.2; WOW64; Trident/6.0)
Accept-Encoding: gzip, deflate
Host: localhost:5526
DNT: 1
Connection: Keep-Alive
Pragma: no-cache
```

Changing the Accept header to read `application/json`, such as using jQuery to call the service, will instead give you the following response:

```
{ "d" : {
"EntitySets": [
"BuildVersions", "ErrorLogs", "Addresses", "Customers",
"CustomerAddresses", "Products", "ProductCategories",
"ProductDescriptions", "ProductModels",
```

```
"ProductModelProductDescriptions", "SalesOrderDetails",
"SalesOrderHeaders"
]
} }
```

Querying the Interface

You query the interface using three components: the URI, the action of the HTTP header, and the HTTP verb that you are using in the query. One of the more common ways to query the interface is to perform a read operation against the data store.

Looking back on an example header from earlier in this chapter, you can see something like the code shown in Listing 13-36.

LISTING 13-36: An example request HTTP header

```
GET http://localhost:5526/AdventureWorksDataService.svc/Customers HTTP/1.1
Accept: text/html, application/xhtml+xml, */*
Accept-Language: en-US
User-Agent: Mozilla/5.0 (compatible; MSIE 10.0; Windows NT 6.2; WOW64; Trident/6.0)
Accept-Encoding: gzip, deflate
Host: localhost:5526
DNT: 1
Connection: Keep-Alive
Pragma: no-cache
```

The result that is returned in this case is based on what is returned within the Accept HTTP header. The method that you are calling is determined by the URI used. In the example in Listing 13-36, the URI is `/AdventureWorksDataService.svc/Customers`, meaning that the Customers set from the EDM is called and the results of the Products table from the AdventureWorks database will be returned.

Listing 13-36 is also a read statement because the HTTP verb that is used is a GET statement. Table 13-1 details the list of HTTP verbs and how they map to the data access type.

TABLE 13-1

HTTP VERB	DATA ACCESS TYPE
POST	Create
GET	Read
PUT	Update
DELETE	Delete

The next section looks at different ways to query the underlying interface provided by WCF Data Services for reading content out of the database.

Reading a Table of Data

Reading an entire table of contents is based on the URI that is passed in. You read the contents by specifying the particular entity set that you are interested in. For example, type the following query into the browser's address bar:

```
http://localhost:5526/AdventureWorksDataService.svc/Customers
```

In this case, you are requesting the entire contents of the Customers table by providing only the entity set Customers in the URI. Figure 13-28 shows the result of this request.

FIGURE 13-28

The following syntax is another example of this type of request:

```
http://localhost: 5526/AdventureWorksDataService.svc/Products
```

In this case, you will receive a complete list of products from the Products table in the database. If you look at the table-level information that is available from the URI call, you will find the following (as an example):

```
<id>http://localhost:4113/AdventureWorksDataService.svc/Products</id>
<title type="text">Products</title>
<updated>2012-11-28T04:43:40Z</updated>
<link rel="self" title="Products" href="Products" />
```

Here, you see that you receive a title (the entity name), as well as the full URI as the `<id>` element. You also get the timestamp of when the query was run in the `<updated>` element. Finally, you get a link referencing the item itself (other links also exist to the entity's relationships beyond this one) if you are going to construct URIs programmatically.

Reading a Specific Item from the Table

The previous example showed you how to pull an entire collection from the table or entity set using a URI such as:

```
http://localhost: 5526/AdventureWorksDataService.svc/Products
```

If you look at one of the product items contained within the result collection, you will see something like what's illustrated in Listing 13-37.

LISTING 13-37: Reviewing one of the items from the Products query

```
<entry xml:base="http://localhost:5526/AdventureWorksDataService.svc/"
    xmlns="http://www.w3.org/2005/Atom"
    xmlns:d="http://schemas.microsoft.com/ado/2007/08/dataservices"
    xmlns:m="http://schemas.microsoft.com/ado/2007/08/dataservices/metadata">
    <id>http://localhost:5526/AdventureWorksDataService.svc/Products(710)</id>
```

continues

LISTING 13-37 *(continued)*

```xml
<category  term="AdventureWorksModel.Product"
    scheme="http://schemas.microsoft.com/ado/2007/08/dataservices/scheme" />
<link  rel="edit" title="Product" href="Products(710)" />
<link
    rel="http://schemas.microsoft.com/ado/2007/08/dataservices/
    related/ProductCategory" type="application/atom+xml;type=entry"
    title="ProductCategory" href="Products(710)/ProductCategory" />
<link
    rel="http://schemas.microsoft.com/ado/2007/08/dataservices/
    related/ProductModel" type="application/atom+xml;type=entry"
    title="ProductModel" href="Products(710)/ProductModel" />
<link
    rel="http://schemas.microsoft.com/ado/2007/08/dataservices/
    related/SalesOrderDetails" type="application/atom+xml;type=feed"
    title="SalesOrderDetails" href="Products(710)/SalesOrderDetails" />
<title />
<updated>2012-11-28T04:49:26Z</updated>
<author>
    <name />
</author>
<content type="application/xml">
    <m:properties>
        <d:ProductID m:type="Edm.Int32">710</d:ProductID>
        <d:Name>Mountain Bike Socks, L</d:Name>
        <d:ProductNumber>SO-B909-L</d:ProductNumber>
        <d:Color>White</d:Color>
        <d:StandardCost m:type="Edm.Decimal">3.3963</d:StandardCost>
        <d:ListPrice m:type="Edm.Decimal">9.5000</d:ListPrice>
        <d:Size>L</d:Size>
        <d:Weight  m:type="Edm.Decimal" m:null="true" />
        <d:ProductCategoryID m:type="Edm.Int32">27</d:ProductCategoryID>
        <d:ProductModelID m:type="Edm.Int32">18</d:ProductModelID>
        <d:SellStartDate m:type="Edm.DateTime">
            2001-07-01T00:00:00
        </d:SellStartDate>
        <d:SellEndDate m:type="Edm.DateTime">
            2002-06-30T00:00:00
        </d:SellEndDate>
        <d:DiscontinuedDate  m:type="Edm.DateTime" m:null="true" />
        <d:ThumbNailPhoto m:type="Edm.Binary">
```

```
R0lGODlhUAAxAPcAAAAAAIAAAACAAICAAAAAgIAAgACAgICAgMDAwP8AAAD/AP//AAAA//8A/wD//////wAAAAAA
AAAAAAAAAAAAAAAAAAAAAAAAAAAAAAAAAAAAAAAAAAAAAAAAAAAAAAAAAAAAAAAAAAAAAAAAAAAAAAAAAAAA AAAAAA
AAAAAMwAAZgAAmQAAzAAA/ wAzAAAzMwAAZgAzgAzmQAzzAAz/wBmAABmWBmZgBmmQBmzABm/wCZAACZMwCZZgCZmQCZzACZ/
wDMAADMMwDMZgDMmQDMzADM/wD/AAD/MwD/ZgD/mQD/zAD//zMAADMAMzMAZjMAmTMAzMA/zMzADMzMzMzZjMzmTMzzDMz/
zNmADNmMzNmZjNmmTNmzDNm/zOZADOZMzOZZjOZmTOZzDOZ/zPMADPMMzPMZjPMmTPMzDPM/zP/ADP/MzP/ZjP/mTP/zDP//
2YAAGYAM2YAZmYAmWYAzGYA/2YzAGYzM2YzZmYzmWYzzGYz/2ZmAGZmM2ZmZmZmmWZmzGZm/2aZAGaZM2aZZmaZmWa ZzGa
Z/2bMAGbMM2bMZmbMmWbMzGbM/2b/AGb/M2b/Zmb/mWb/zGb//5kAAJkAM5kAZpkAmZkAzJkA/5kzAJkzM5kzZpkzmZkzzJ
kz/5lmAJlmM5lmZ plmmZlmzJlm/5mZAJmzM5mZZpmZmZmZzJmZ/5nMAJnMM5nMZpnMmZnMzJnM/5n/AJn/M5n/Zpn/mZn/
zJn//8wAAMwAM8wAZswAmcwAzMwA/ 8wzAMwzM8wzZswzmcwzzMwz/8xmAMxmM8xmZsxmmcxmzMxm/8yZAMyZM8yZZsyZmcy
ZzMyZ/8zMAMzMM8zMZszMmczMzMzM/8z/AMz/M8z/Zsz/mcz/zMz///8AAP8AM8AM/8AZsf8Amf8AzP8A//8zAP8zM8zZv8zmf
8zzP8z//9mAP9mM9mZv9mmf9mzP9m//+ZAP+ZM+ZZv+Zmf+ZzP+Z///MAP/MM/MZv/Mmf/MzP/M////AP//M///Zv//
mf//zP///yH5BAEAABAALAAAAABQADEAAAj/AP8JHEiwoMGDCBMqXMiwocOHECNKnEixosWLGDNq3Mixo8ePIEOKHEmypM
mTKFOqXJkRBYqBLhfGZPnQ5ct/MxPmpMnQpsCZNm/CfBnTZ86gQ3HeRMoRadGlQpUqJfoUZ9KnVH9G99KuVhUKtC oVaWKnZrV
K9SmVMPuVHvWrFisPjsPjd+LbuW7tmvb8t6nJ uXIFutfbH2lSt07ta/eeOy3clTYuGtjSjS8yjUy5suXLmDHHdRjWIGPGIjdDBA
3YL2SQVY+mvQsQsVL16yqLOqfuyWtlHZbTv+nYY17G67H38DTs068rGs koMSN+62+fKQqrW2Xe6aem7CSaf6fq7ceevTmcOL
Eh9Pvrz58+jTq1/Pvr379+8DAgA7
```

```
        </d:ThumbNailPhoto>
        <d:ThumbnailPhotoFileName>
            no_image_available_small.gif
        </d:ThumbnailPhotoFileName>
        <d:rowguid m:type="Edm.Guid">
            161c035e-21b3-4e14-8e44-af508f35d80a
        </d:rowguid>
        <d:ModifiedDate m:type="Edm.DateTime">
            2004-03-11T10:01:36.827
        </d:ModifiedDate>
    </m:properties>
  </content>
</entry>
```

If you look at the `<id>` value of this product, you will find the following:

```
http://localhost:5526/AdventureWorksDataService.svc/Products(710)
```

You can see that the reference to this particular product is `Products(710)`, which means that you are interested in the item in the Product collection with a `ProductID` of 710. Typing that URI into the browser's address bar will give you only that particular product.

If you review the XML, you will find that the `<content>` element contains all the data from the specific product that you are looking at. This is constructed as a properties collection.

Although you see a list of properties for this customer, you are also able to get at individual properties themselves through URI declarations such as:

```
http://localhost:5526/AdventureWorksDataService.svc/Products(710)/Name
```

Using a construct like the preceding returns only the `Name` property of this product. Here is the result:

```
<?xml version="1.0" encoding="UTF-8"?>
<d:Name
    xmlns:m="http://schemas.microsoft.com/ado/2007/08/dataservices/metadata"
    xmlns:d="http://schemas.microsoft.com/ado/2007/08/dataservices">
    Mountain Bike Socks, L
</d:Name>
```

It is important to realize that this number reference from `Products(710)` is not an index reference but the ID reference.

Working with Relationships

Working with WCF Data Services obviously makes getting at your database and working with it through a RESTful interface easy. One great advantage to working with the ADO.NET Entity Framework and WCF Data Services is that these items make working with object relationships just as easy.

Going back to the Entity Data Model that was designed earlier in this chapter, you will notice that the objects have a built-in relationship that is visually shown in the O/R Designer. Figure 13-29 presents this view.

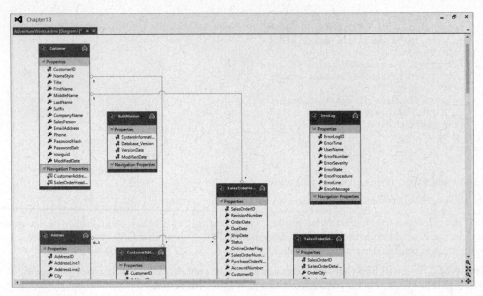

FIGURE 13-29

From this figure, you can see that the `Customers` object has a relationship with the `SalesOrderObjects` object (among others). You can also work down this object chain using WCF Data Services because it is represented in your EDM.

To understand how these relationships are represented, navigate to:

```
http://localhost:5526/AdventureWorksDataService.svc/Customers(1)
```

You will notice the relationships are shown in Listing 13-38.

LISTING 13-38: Reviewing the customer relationships

```
<link
    rel="http://schemas.microsoft.com/ado/2007/08/dataservices/
    related/CustomerAddresses" type="application/atom+xml;type=feed"
    title="CustomerAddresses" href="Customers(1)/CustomerAddresses" />
<link
    rel="http://schemas.microsoft.com/ado/2007/08/dataservices/
    related/SalesOrderHeaders" type="application/atom+xml;type=feed"
    title="SalesOrderHeaders" href="Customers(1)/SalesOrderHeaders" />
```

This snippet shows the two relationships that are in place for this customer. The second is a reference to the `SalesOrderHeaders` relationship. You can see this statement through the `rel` attribute as well as the `title` attribute that is in place within this particular `<link>` element. In addition to just a statement that there is this relationship in place, you will find a link to the relationship itself through the `href` attribute of the `<link>` element. The stated reference is `Customers(1)/SalesOrderHeaders`. This means that you can now type the following URI in the browser:

```
http://localhost:5526/AdventureWorksDataService.svc/Customers(1)/SalesOrderHeaders
```

Typing this URI means that you are interested in drilling down to the customer with the ID of `1` and that customer's sales orders in the system. In response, you get what is presented in Figure 13-30.

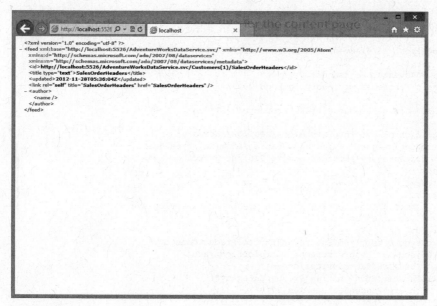

FIGURE 13-30

Expanding on Associations

So far, you have seen the entity associations mentioned through these `<link>` elements and the ability to re-query with a new URI to dig into these associated details. You are also able to pull these associations out in the same query if you want.

Getting these associations is possible through the use of the some query string parameters that have been made available through WCF Data Services. For example, suppose you are making the following query:

```
http://localhost:5526/AdventureWorksDataService.svc/Products(710)
```

This query gives you the output presented earlier in Listing 13-37. You'll notice that one of the links shown is to the ProductCategory entity set. In this mode, if you want the category of this product, you must make an additional call to get this item using `http://localhost:5526/Adventure WorksDataService.svc/ Products(710)/ProductCategory`. Using this gives you a completely separate result.

However, if you want to get this related set of data points for the product in a single call, you can use the expand keyword in your URI query:

```
http://localhost:5526/AdventureWorksDataService.svc/Products(710)
    ?$expand=ProductCategory
```

For this query to work, you can use one of the available keywords in your query string, in this case expand. You simply use a familiar format of `?$expand=` followed by the name of the associated entity sets. This query gives a resultset similar to what is presented in Listing 13-39.

LISTING 13-39: Adding additional entity sets

```xml
<?xml version="1.0" encoding="utf-8" ?>
<entry xml:base="http://localhost:5526/AdventureWorksDataService.svc/"
    xmlns="http://www.w3.org/2005/Atom"
    xmlns:d="http://schemas.microsoft.com/ado/2007/08/dataservices"
    xmlns:m="http://schemas.microsoft.com/ado/2007/08/dataservices/metadata">
    <id>
```

continues

LISTING 13-39 *(continued)*

```
            http://localhost:5526/AdventureWorksDataService.svc/Products(710)
</id>
<category term="AdventureWorksModel.Product"
    scheme="http://schemas.microsoft.com/ado/2007/08/dataservices/scheme"
    />
<link rel="edit" title="Product" href="Products(710)" />
<link
    rel="http://schemas.microsoft.com/ado/2007/08/dataservices/
    related/ProductCategory" type="application/atom+xml;type=entry"
    title="ProductCategory" href="Products(710)/ProductCategory">
    <m:inline>
        <entry>
            <id>
                http://localhost:5526/AdventureWorksDataService.svc/
                ProductCategories(27)
            </id>
            <category term="AdventureWorksModel.ProductCategory"
                scheme="http://schemas.microsoft.com/ado/
                2007/08/dataservices/scheme" />
            <link rel="edit" title="ProductCategory"
                href="ProductCategories(27)" />
            <link rel="http://schemas.microsoft.com/ado/
                2007/08/dataservices/related/Products"
                type="application/atom+xml;type=feed"
                title="Products" href="ProductCategories(27)/Products" />
            <link rel="http://schemas.microsoft.com/ado/
                2007/08/dataservices/related/ProductCategory1"
                type="application/atom+xml;type=feed"
                title="ProductCategory1"
                href="ProductCategories(27)/ProductCategory1" />
            <link rel="http://schemas.microsoft.com/ado/
                2007/08/dataservices/related/ProductCategory2"
                type="application/atom+xml;type=entry"
                title="ProductCategory2"
                href="ProductCategories(27)/ProductCategory2" />
            <title />
            <updated>2012-11-28T05:47:51Z</updated>
            <author>
                <name />
            </author>
            <content type="application/xml">
                <m:properties>
                    <d:ProductCategoryID m:type="Edm.Int32">
                        27
                    </d:ProductCategoryID>
                    <d:ParentProductCategoryID m:type="Edm.Int32">
                        3
                    </d:ParentProductCategoryID>
                    <d:Name>Socks</d:Name>
                    <d:rowguid m:type="Edm.Guid">
                        701019c3-09fe-4949-8386-c6ce686474e5
                    </d:rowguid>
                    <d:ModifiedDate m:type="Edm.DateTime">
                        1998-06-01T00:00:00
                    </d:ModifiedDate>
                </m:properties>
            </content>
        </entry>
    </m:inline>
```

```
            </link>
            <link rel="http://schemas.microsoft.com/ado/
                2007/08/dataservices/related/ProductModel"
                type="application/atom+xml;type=entry" title="ProductModel"
                href="Products(710)/ProductModel" />
            <link rel="http://schemas.microsoft.com/ado/
                2007/08/dataservices/related/SalesOrderDetails"
                type="application/atom+xml;type=feed" title="SalesOrderDetails"
                href="Products(710)/SalesOrderDetails" />
            <title />
            <updated>2012-11-28T05:47:51Z</updated>
            <author>
                <name />
            </author>
            <content type="application/xml">
                <m:properties>
                    <d:ProductID m:type="Edm.Int32">710</d:ProductID>
                    <d:Name>Mountain Bike Socks, L</d:Name>
                    <d:ProductNumber>SO-B909-L</d:ProductNumber>
                    <d:Color>White</d:Color>
                    <d:StandardCost m:type="Edm.Decimal">3.3963</d:StandardCost>
                    <d:ListPrice m:type="Edm.Decimal">9.5000</d:ListPrice>
                    <d:Size>L</d:Size>
                    <d:Weight m:type="Edm.Decimal" m:null="true" />
                    <d:ProductCategoryID m:type="Edm.Int32">
                        27
                    </d:ProductCategoryID>
                    <d:ProductModelID m:type="Edm.Int32">18</d:ProductModelID>
                    <d:SellStartDate m:type="Edm.DateTime">
                        2001-07-01T00:00:00
                    </d:SellStartDate>
                    <d:SellEndDate m:type="Edm.DateTime">
                        2002-06-30T00:00:00
                    </d:SellEndDate>
                    <d:DiscontinuedDate m:type="Edm.DateTime" m:null="true" />
                    <d:ThumbNailPhoto m:type="Edm.Binary">
```
```
R0lGODlhUAAxAPcAAAAAAIAAAACAAICAAAAAgIAAgACAgICAgMDAwP8AAAD/AP//AAAA//8A/wD//////
wAAAAAAAAAAAAAAAAAAAAAAAAAAAAAAAAAAAAAAAAAAAAAAAAAAAAAAAAAAAAAAAAAAAAAAAAAAAAAAAA
AAAAAAAAAAAAAAAAAAAAAAAAMwAAZgAAmQAAzAAA/wAzAAAzMwAzZgAzmQAzzAAz/wBmAABmMwBmZgBmmQBmzABm/
wCZAACZMwCZZgCZmQCZzACZ/wDMAADMMwDMZgDMmQDMzADM/wD/AAD/MwD/ZgD/mQD/zAD//zMAADMAMzMAMZjMAmTMAmDMA/
zMzADMzMzMzMzjMzmTMzzDMz/zNmADNmMzNmZjNmmTNmzDNm/zOZADOZMzOZZjOZmTOZzDOZ/zPMADPMMzPMZjPMmTPMzDPM/
zP/ADP/MzP/ZjP/mTP/zDP//2YAAGYAM2YAZmYAmWYAzGYA/2YzAGYzM2YzZmYzmWYzzGYz/2ZmAGZmM2ZmZmZmmWZ
mzGZm/2aZAGaZM2aZZmaZmWaZzGaZ/2bMAGbMM2bMZmbMmWbMzGbM/2b//GGb/M2b/Zmb/mWb/zGb//5kAAJkAM5kAZ
pkAmZkAzJkA/5kzAJkzM5kzZpkzmZkzzJkz/5lmAJlmM5lmZplmmZlmzJlm/5mZAJmZM5mZZpmZmZmZzJmZ/5nMAJ
nMM5nMZpnMmZnMzJnM/5n//Apn/M5n/Zpn/mZn/zJn//8wAAMwAM8wAZswAmcwAzMwA/8wzAMwzM8wzZswzmcwzzMw
z/8xmAMxmM8xmZsxmmcxmzMxm/8yZAMyZM8yZZsyZmcyZzMyZ/8zMAMzMM8zMZszMmczMzMzM/8z//AMz/M8z/Zsz/
mcz/zMz///8AAP8AM/8AZv8Amf8AzP8A//8zAP8zM/8zZv8zmf8zzP8z//9mAP9mM/9mZv9mmf9mzP9m//+ZAP+ZM/
+ZZv+Zmf+ZzP+Z//+MAP/MM//MZv/Mmf/MzP/M////AP//M///Zv//mf//zP///yH5BAEAABAALAAAAABQADEAAAj/
AP8JHEiwoMGDCBMqXMiwocOHECNKnEixosWLGDNm3Mixo8ePIEOKHEmypMmTKFOqXJkRBYqBLhfGZPnQ5ct/
MxPmpMnQpsCZNm/CfBnTZ86gQ3HeRMoRadGlQpUqfIoFoZ9Gx2GxVhUKtCoVaWKn ZrVK9SmVMPuVHvWWrFisPjd+Lb
uW7tmvb8t6nJuXIIFFutfbH2lSt07ta/ta/eeOy3cl3YuGtjS8n1/8xLmXLLmHHHdRjHrj//////////////////////
LOqfuyWtlHZbTv+nY1 76G67H38DTs068GrSkoMSN+62+fKQqrW2Xe6aem7CSaf6fq7ceevTmcOLEh9Pvrz58+jTq1/
Pvr379+8DAgA7
```
```
                    </d:ThumbNailPhoto>
                    <d:ThumbnailPhotoFileName>
                        no_image_available_small.gif
                    </d:ThumbnailPhotoFileName>
                    <d:rowguid m:type="Edm.Guid">
                        161c035e-21b3-4e14-8e44-af508f35d80a
                    </d:rowguid>
                    <d:ModifiedDate m:type="Edm.DateTime">
                        2004-03-11T10:01:36.827
```

continues

LISTING 13-39 *(continued)*

```
            </d:ModifiedDate>
         </m:properties>
      </content>
   </entry>
```

From this code, you can see that the `<link>` element that was specific for the category is now expanded to include what was once a separate call inline. In addition to expanding a single associated entity set, you can expand multiple items:

```
http://localhost:5526/AdventureWorksDataService.svc/Products(710)
   ?$expand=ProductCategory,ProductModel
```

In this case, both the ProductCategory and the ProductModel sections are expanded within the Product entity set call.

You can also keep digging into the nested associated entity sets. For example, if the ProductCategory entity had a relationship with another entity called SimilarCategories, you would be able to structure your URI as such:

```
http://localhost:5526/AdventureWorksDataService.svc/Products(710)
   ?$expand=ProductCategory/SimilarCategories
```

Using this construct, you are looking at the product with an ID of 710 from the product list and expanding the section for the category of this product. Then, within the category, the similar categories that are related to this category are also included in the resultset. As you can see, there is a lot of power in the ease with which you can drill down into nested relationships.

Ordering in Resultsets

Another way to manipulate the resultset that comes from the URI query is to get the results of the collection placed in a specific order as you define it. You can do so using the `orderby` keyword as a query string command:

```
http://localhost:5526/AdventureWorksDataService.svc/Products
   ?$orderby=Name
```

In this case, you get back a complete list of products that are in alphabetical order according to the entity's Name field value. You are also able to assign an ascending or descending value to the order provided. By default, an ascending order is assigned. This means that the preceding query is the same as the following:

```
http://localhost:5526/AdventureWorksDataService.svc/Products
   ?$orderby=Name asc
```

Notice that there is an actual space between the Name and asc items in the URI. If you want these in the reverse order, or descending order, use the following construct:

```
http://localhost:5526/AdventureWorksDataService.svc/Products
   ?$orderby=Name desc
```

You can also perform nested sorting using WCF Data Services:

```
http://localhost:5526/AdventureWorksDataService.svc/Products
   ?$orderby=Color asc, Name asc
```

Moving around Resultsets

As an end user of this interface, you can probably see that you might be working with fairly large resultsets, depending on what is in the database. If you need only a portion of the database table and you are requesting all of your customers (which might be 100,000 or more), what then?

In this case, WCF Data Services provides the capability to grab just smaller subsets of the content as pages and to navigate through the page that you need. You do this through the combination of two query string commands: `top` and `skip`.

They are also quite powerful in their own right. For instance, with the `top` command, you are able to pull the top *n*-number of items based on the sort that is being used. For example, consider this command:

```
http://localhost:5526/AdventureWorksDataService.svc/Products?$top=5
```

Here, the top five entities, in this case based on the `ID` value, are pulled from the database and returned. If you want the top entities based on a different value, you can use something like the following:

```
http://localhost:5526/AdventureWorksDataService.svc/Products
    ?$orderby=Name desc&$top=5
```

Using this example, the top five products, ordered by the product name, are returned in the resultset.

You are able to use the `skip` command to basically skip the first set of defined items. For instance, you can do something similar to the following:

```
http://localhost:5526/AdventureWorksDataService.svc/Products?$skip=5
```

In this case, the products are returned minus the first five that would normally be returned. There is some question as to the value of this command, but its power is evident when used in combination with the `top` keyword.

```
http://localhost:5526/AdventureWorksDataService.svc/Products?$skip=10&$top=10
```

In this case, you are skipping the first ten entities and then grabbing the following ten entities from that point onward. This means that you are really grabbing page two of sets that consist of ten items each. This would make performing a type of database-pagination process quite easy by using this process to use URI commands to get at the page of data you require.

Filtering Content

The final command is one of the more powerful commands at your disposal. It is a type of screening that enables you to filter the content that you are truly interested in receiving from the database. This is all done through the use of the `filter` command:

```
http://localhost:5526/AdventureWorksDataService.svc/Products
    ?$filter=Color eq 'Red'
```

Using the filter command preceded by a dollar sign ($), the value of this command is `Color eq 'Red'`. With this filtering command, you are requesting a list of products that have a color of `Red`. The database property in this case is `Color`, and within the URI it is important that you are specifying this property in its proper case. This means that if you used `color` instead of `Color`, you would not get any items in the resultset.

The `Red` value is put in single quotes and the operator is specified as a set of characters, rather than a true equals sign (=). When using the `filter` command, you specify the equal operator with the `eq` string. Table 13-2 lists the logical operators that you are able to use.

TABLE 13-2

OPERATOR	DESCRIPTION	EXAMPLE
Eq	Equal	Color eq 'Red'
Ne	Not equal	Color ne 'Red'
Gt	Greater than	$filter = ListPrice gt 20
Ge	Greater than or equal	$filter = ListPrice ge 20
Lt	Less than	$filter = ListPrice lt 20

continues

TABLE 13-2 *(continued)*

OPERATOR	DESCRIPTION	EXAMPLE
Le	Less than or equal	`$filter = ListPrice le 20`
And	Logical and	`$filter = ListPrice gt 0 and StandardCost gt 0`
Or	Logical or	`$filter = ListPrice gt 0 or StandardCost lt 100`
Not	Logical not	`$filter = ListPrice gt 0 not ProductName eq 'Red'`

In addition to logical operators, you can use a number of arithmetic operators, as shown in Table 13-3.

TABLE 13-3

OPERATOR	DESCRIPTION	EXAMPLE
Add	Add	`$filter = ListPrice add 5 gt 20`
Sub	Subtract	`$filter = ListPrice sub 5 gt 20`
Mul	Multiply	`$filter = ListPrice mul 5 gt 20`
Div	Divide	`$filter = ListPrice div 5 gt 20`
Mod	Modulo	`$filter = ListPrice mod 100 gt 20`

A long list of string, date, and math functions is also available:

➤ substringof
➤ startswith
➤ indexof
➤ remove
➤ substring
➤ toupper
➤ concat
➤ hour
➤ month
➤ year
➤ floor
➤ endswith
➤ length
➤ insert
➤ replace
➤ tolower
➤ trim
➤ day
➤ minute
➤ second
➤ round
➤ ceiling

Consuming WCF Data Services in ASP.NET

Now that you understand how to build a WCF Data Service, the next step is to consume this service in an ASP.NET application. Keep in mind that consuming a WCF Data Service in all types of .NET applications is obviously possible, but this chapter focuses on using this technology within ASP.NET itself.

For an example of consuming a data service, create a standard ASP.NET Web Form within your project. On this page, create a simple page that contains only a styled GridView server control. Listing 13-40 presents an example of this page.

LISTING 13-40: A standard ASP.NET page with a GridView control

```
<%@ Page Language="C#" %>
<!DOCTYPE html>
<html xmlns="http://www.w3.org/1999/xhtml">
<head runat="server">
    <title>Working with Data Services</title>
</head>
<body>
    <form id="form1" runat="server">
        <asp:GridView ID="GridView1" runat="server" BackColor="White"
            BorderColor="#DEDFDE" BorderStyle="None" BorderWidth="1px"
            CellPadding="4"
            ForeColor="Black" GridLines="Vertical">
            <RowStyle BackColor="#F7F7DE" />
            <FooterStyle BackColor="#CCCC99" />
            <PagerStyle BackColor="#F7F7DE" ForeColor="Black"
                HorizontalAlign="Right" />
            <SelectedRowStyle BackColor="#CE5D5A" Font-Bold="True"
                ForeColor="White" />
            <HeaderStyle BackColor="#6B696B" Font-Bold="True"
                ForeColor="White" />
            <AlternatingRowStyle BackColor="White" />
        </asp:GridView>
    </form>
</body>
</html>
```

Now that you have a basic page ready, right-click your project within the Visual Studio Solution Explorer and select Add Service Reference from the provided menu. The Add Service Reference dialog box appears.

Because a WCF Data Service is a standard .svc file, you can make reference to your AdventureWorksDataService.svc file within the textbox provided and click the Go button. Figure 13-31 shows something similar to what appears.

As you can see from the figure, all the underlying objects are represented in the dialog box. Within the Namespace textbox, you can name the reference **AWServiceReference** and then click OK to accept this configuration.

The next step is to work with this reference as shown in Listing 13-41. (Both files are the Default .aspx.vb and Default.aspx.cs in Chapter13-WcfDSConsumer-VB and Chapter13-WcfDSConsumer, respectively, in the code download for this chapter.)

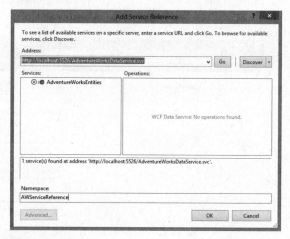

FIGURE 13-31

LISTING 13-41: Working with a WCF Data Service

VB

```
Partial Class _Default
    Inherits System.Web.UI.Page

    Protected Sub Page_Load(ByVal sender As Object,
```

continues

LISTING 13-41 *(continued)*

```
            ByVal e As System.EventArgs) Handles Me.Load

            Dim svc As New AdventureWorksEntities(New _
                Uri("http://localhost:4113/Adventure WorksDataService.svc"))
            GridView1.DataSource = svc.Customers
            GridView1.DataBind()
        End Sub
    End Class
```

C#

```
public partial class _Default : System.Web.UI.Page
{
    protected void Page_Load(object sender, EventArgs e)
    {
        AdventureWorksEntities svc = new AdventureWorksEntities(new
            Uri("http://localhost:5526/AdventureWorksDataService.svc"));
        GridView1.DataSource = svc.Customers;
        GridView1.DataBind();
    }
}
```

In the preceding code, it is simply a matter of making a reference to the Entity Data Model that the service exposes through the URI of the data service. This EDM instantiation will include a list of all the capabilities that interact with the underlying service. In the case of Listing 13-41, the entire `Customers` table is returned through the use of `svc.Customers`. This resultset is then bound to the GridView control. Figure 13-32 shows the results.

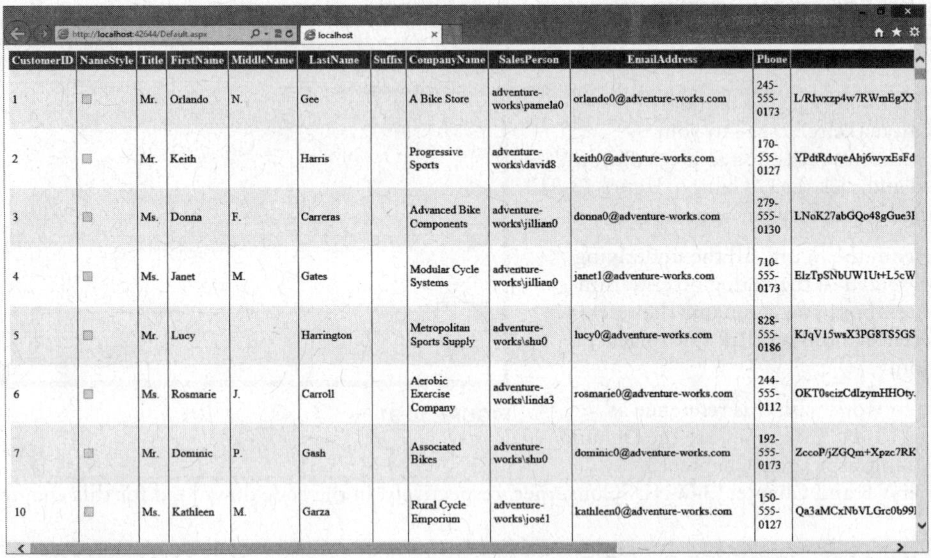

CustomerID	NameStyle	Title	FirstName	MiddleName	LastName	Suffix	CompanyName	SalesPerson	EmailAddress	Phone	
1		Mr.	Orlando	N.	Gee		A Bike Store	adventure-works\pamela0	orlando0@adventure-works.com	245-555-0173	L/Rlwxzp4w7RWmEgX
2		Mr.	Keith		Harris		Progressive Sports	adventure-works\david8	keith0@adventure-works.com	170-555-0127	YPdtRdvqeAhj6wyxEsFd
3		Ms.	Donna	F.	Carreras		Advanced Bike Components	adventure-works\jillian0	donna0@adventure-works.com	279-555-0130	LNoK27abGQo48gGue3I
4		Ms.	Janet	M.	Gates		Modular Cycle Systems	adventure-works\jillian0	janet1@adventure-works.com	710-555-0173	ElzTpSNbUW1Ut+L5cW
5		Mr.	Lucy		Harrington		Metropolitan Sports Supply	adventure-works\shu0	lucy0@adventure-works.com	828-555-0186	KJqV15wsX3PG8TS5GS
6		Ms.	Rosmarie	J.	Carroll		Aerobic Exercise Company	adventure-works\linda3	rosmarie0@adventure-works.com	244-555-0112	OKT0scizCdlzymHHOty.
7		Mr.	Dominic	P.	Gash		Associated Bikes	adventure-works\shu0	dominic0@adventure-works.com	192-555-0173	ZccoP/jZGQm+Xpzc7RK
10		Ms.	Kathleen	M.	Garza		Rural Cycle Emporium	adventure-works\josé1	kathleen0@adventure-works.com	150-555-0127	Qa3aMCxNbVLGrc0b99I

FIGURE 13-32

In addition to a query as simple as the one in the preceding code, you can also start using some of the command logic presented earlier in this chapter when using LINQ within your code. Listing 13-42 shows a query against the `Customers` table in which you are interested only in seeing the customers that have a `CompanyName` that contains the word `Bike` in the name.

LISTING 13-42: Using LINQ

VB

```vb
Dim svc As New AdventureWorksEntities(New _
    Uri("http://localhost:4113/Adventure WorksDataService.svc"))

Dim query = svc.Customers.Where(Function(w) w.CompanyName.Contains("Bike"))

GridView1.DataSource = svc.Customers
GridView1.DataBind()
```

C#

```csharp
AdventureWorksEntities svc = new AdventureWorksEntities(new
    Uri("http://localhost:5526/AdventureWorksDataService.svc"));

var query = svc.Customers.Where(w => w.CompanyName.Contains("Bike"));

GridView1.DataSource = query;
GridView1.DataBind();
```

In this code, a LINQ query is performed and this object is then bound as the `DataSource` value of the GridView control. This produces another list of items in the grid.

ASP.NET WEB API

ASP.NET 4.5 brings many new features to the platform. One of the most useful features is the Web API. Prior to the ASP.NET 4.5 release, many developers would complain that it took more time to configure WCF to create a RESTful service than it did to develop the service. So, to assist in exposing application functionality, better known as a web API, Web API was created.

> **WARNING** *Web API is an ASP.NET MVC application. If you do not have experience with ASP.NET MVC, it is highly recommended that you review Chapter 34 before completing this chapter.*

Because Web API is an ASP.NET MVC application that relies heavily on HTTP, developers can make use of HTTP verbs and meaningful routes to build a solid, representational state transfer (REST) service.

Building Your First Web API

It's quite simple to build a Web API project. Visual Studio 2012 has a great template that helps scaffold Web API projects. You'll use this when building your first Web API project. In some cases, developers can generate a fully functional web API using the Web API project template and without writing a single line of code (meaning that he or she uses drag and drop and configuration only).

To begin, create a new ASP.NET MVC 4 project as shown in Figure 13-33.

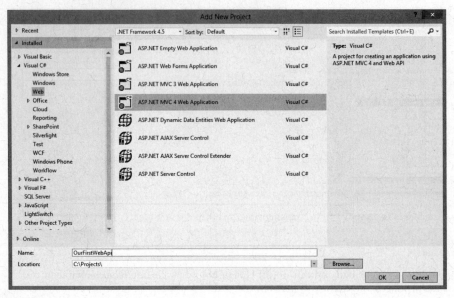

FIGURE 13-33

When you click OK, a prompt for customizing your ASP.NET MVC 4 project appears as shown in Figure 13-34. For this example, choose the Web API template. Because this is your first service and this project is only being used for your API, leave the default Razor view engine for your project.

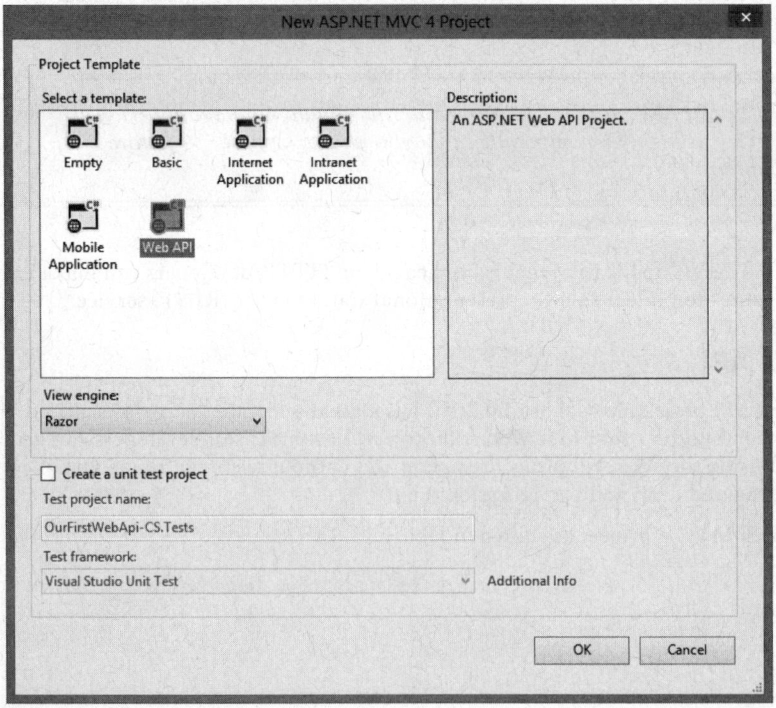

FIGURE 13-34

After you create your project, you are immediately taken to a default controller called ValuesController. Delete this controller because you'll soon build your own.

When you are exposing an API on the web, most likely, you will be interacting with a data source. In this case, use the AdventureWorks database that you used earlier in this chapter. Place the database in the App_Data folder.

Next, create an EF model exactly like the model you built earlier to connect to WCF. However, in this case, you'll add the AdventureWorks.edmx file to the Models folder. Before you continue, build this project. When you build the project, your model is compiled into the project binary and exposed for usage in the Visual Studio IDE.

Next, you must build a new controller. Right-click the Controllers folder and choose Add ⇨ Controller. Name the new controller **ProductsController**. In the controller template, choose "API controller with read/write actions, using Entity Framework," as shown in Figure 13-35.

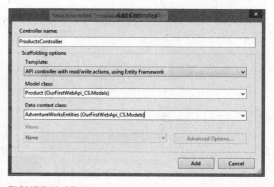

In the Model class drop-down, choose the Product model. This allows your controller to be bound to the products contained within your data source. The Data context class drop-down enables switching between multiple data context objects. In this case, choose AdventureWorkEntities.

FIGURE 13-35

The ProductsController file will appear containing the core functionality of the API, as shown in Listing 13-43. You'll notice that each method has a comment above it informing the developer which HTTP verb should be used for that method and what the proper structure of the URL should be to obtain the desired results.

LISTING 13-43: The generated code of the ProductsController file

VB

```vb
Public Class ProductsController
    Inherits System.Web.Http.ApiController

    Private db As New AdventureWorksEntities

    ' GET api/Products
    Function GetProducts() As IEnumerable(Of Product)
        Dim products = db.Products.Include(Function(p) p.ProductCategory)
            .Include(Function(p) p.ProductModel)
        Return products.AsEnumerable()
    End Function

    ' GET api/Products/5
    Function GetProduct(ByVal id As Integer) As Product
        Dim product As Product = db.Products.Find(id)
        If IsNothing(product) Then
            Throw New HttpResponseException(Request.CreateResponse(HttpStatusCode.NotFound))
        End If
        Return product
    End Function

    ' PUT api/Products/5
    Function PutProduct(ByVal id As Integer, ByVal product As Product) As HttpResponseMessage
```

continues

LISTING 13-43 *(continued)*

```vb
        If ModelState.IsValid And id = product.ProductID Then
            db.Entry(product).State = EntityState.Modified
            Try
                db.SaveChanges()
            Catch ex As DbUpdateConcurrencyException
                Return Request.CreateResponse(HttpStatusCode.NotFound)
            End Try

            Return Request.CreateResponse(HttpStatusCode.OK)
        Else
            Return Request.CreateResponse(HttpStatusCode.BadRequest)
        End If
    End Function

    ' POST api/Products
    Function PostProduct(ByVal product As Product) As HttpResponseMessage
        If ModelState.IsValid Then
            db.Products.Add(product)
            db.SaveChanges()

            Dim response As HttpResponseMessage =
                Request.CreateResponse(HttpStatusCode.Created, product)
            response.Headers.Location = New Uri(Url.Link("DefaultApi",
                New With {.id = product.ProductID}))
            Return response
        Else
            Return Request.CreateResponse(HttpStatusCode.BadRequest)
        End If
    End Function

    ' DELETE api/Products/5
    Function DeleteProduct(ByVal id As Integer) As HttpResponseMessage
        Dim product As Product = db.Products.Find(id)
        If IsNothing(product) Then
            Return Request.CreateResponse(HttpStatusCode.NotFound)
        End If

        db.Products.Remove(product)

        Try
            db.SaveChanges()
        Catch ex As Exception
            Return Request.CreateResponse(HttpStatusCode.NotFound)
        End Try

        Return Request.CreateResponse(HttpStatusCode.OK, product)
    End Function

    Protected Overrides Sub Dispose(ByVal disposing As Boolean)
        db.Dispose()
        MyBase.Dispose(disposing)
    End Sub
End Class
```

C#

```csharp
public class ProductsController : ApiController
{
```

```
    private AdventureWorksEntities db = new AdventureWorksEntities();

    // GET api/Products
    public IEnumerable<Product> GetProducts()
    {
        var products = db.Products.Include(p => p.ProductCategory)
          .Include(p => p.ProductModel);
        return products.AsEnumerable();
    }

    // GET api/Products/5
    public Product GetProduct(int id)
    {
        Product product = db.Products.Find(id);
        if (product == null)
        {
            throw new HttpResponseException(Request.CreateResponse(HttpStatusCode.NotFound));
        }

        return product;
    }

    // PUT api/Products/5
    public HttpResponseMessage PutProduct(int id, Product product)
    {
        if (ModelState.IsValid && id == product.ProductID)
        {
            db.Entry(product).State = EntityState.Modified;

            try
            {
                db.SaveChanges();
            }
            catch (DbUpdateConcurrencyException)
            {
                return Request.CreateResponse(HttpStatusCode.NotFound);
            }

            return Request.CreateResponse(HttpStatusCode.OK);
        }
        else
        {
            return Request.CreateResponse(HttpStatusCode.BadRequest);
        }
    }

    // POST api/Products
    public HttpResponseMessage PostProduct(Product product)
    {
        if (ModelState.IsValid)
        {
            db.Products.Add(product);
            db.SaveChanges();

            HttpResponseMessage response = Request.CreateResponse(HttpStatusCode.Created,
              product);
            response.Headers.Location = new Uri(Url.Link("DefaultApi",
              new { id = product.ProductID }));
            return response;
        }
        else
        {
            return Request.CreateResponse(HttpStatusCode.BadRequest);
        }
```

continues

LISTING 13-43 *(continued)*

```
        }

        // DELETE api/Products/5
        public HttpResponseMessage DeleteProduct(int id)
        {
            Product product = db.Products.Find(id);
            if (product == null)
            {
                return Request.CreateResponse(HttpStatusCode.NotFound);
            }

            db.Products.Remove(product);

            try
            {
                db.SaveChanges();
            }
            catch (DbUpdateConcurrencyException)
            {
                return Request.CreateResponse(HttpStatusCode.NotFound);
            }

            return Request.CreateResponse(HttpStatusCode.OK, product);
        }

        protected override void Dispose(bool disposing)
        {
            db.Dispose();
            base.Dispose(disposing);
        }
    }
}
```

Understanding Web API Routing

You may notice a few things are different with the Web API controllers. Instead of inheriting from `Controller`, the class is inheriting from `ApiController`. Next, you'll notice that the methods do not use an HTTP verb attribute. Rather, the HTTP verbs are placed as the first part in your method names. This enables you to use HTTP verbs in your method names. This is handled through the `ApiController` class.

As mentioned earlier, the methods shown in Listing 13-43 each have a comment above showing the verb and the anticipated URL to be used to reach that method. The URL is generated based on the route in place for the Web API. The default Web API route is shown in Listing 13-44.

LISTING 13-44: The default Web API route

VB

```
    Public Class WebApiConfig
        Public Shared Sub Register(ByVal config As HttpConfiguration)
            config.Routes.MapHttpRoute( _
                name:="DefaultApi", _
                routeTemplate:="api/{controller}/{id}", _
                defaults:=New With {.id = RouteParameter.Optional} _
            )
        End Sub
    End Class
```

C#

```csharp
public static class WebApiConfig
{
    public static void Register(HttpConfiguration config)
    {
        config.Routes.MapHttpRoute(
            name: "DefaultApi",
            routeTemplate: "api/{controller}/{id}",
            defaults: new { id = RouteParameter.Optional }
        );
    }
}
```

Because Web API uses ASP.NET MVC, you can add additional routes or change the route template altogether.

Consuming a Web API

Now that the Web API is built, it will need to be consumed by a client. Because the Web API uses HTTP, the client can be anything from a mobile device such as a Windows Phone to a desktop application to a web application built using another technology. You'll see the results shown in Figure 13-36 if you open up Internet Explorer and access your Web API using `http://localhost:43059/api/products/710`.

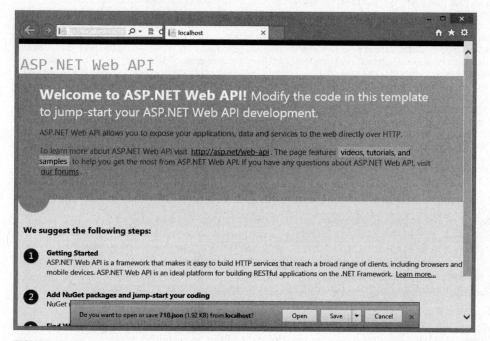

FIGURE 13-36

In this case, the file that is ready to download is a JSON file, as shown in the full HTTP response in Listing 13-45.

LISTING 13-45: The complete HTTP response for the Web API call

```
HTTP/1.1 200 OK
Cache-Control: no-cache
Pragma: no-cache
Content-Type: application/json; charset=utf-8
Expires: -1
Server: Microsoft-IIS/8.0
X-AspNet-Version: 4.0.30319
X-SourceFiles: =?UTF-8?B?QzpcVXNlcnNcSmFzb25HYXlsb3JkXERvY3VtZW50c1xWaXN1Y
WwgU3R1ZGlvIDIwMTJcUHJvamVjdHNcQ2hhcHRlcjEzLUNTXE91ckJpcnN0V2ViQXBpLUNTXGFwaVxwc
m9kWN0c1w3MTA=?=
X-Powered-By: ASP.NET
Date: Wed, 28 Nov 2012 21:48:16 GMT
Content-Length: 1968
```

```
{"ProductID":710,"Name":"Mountain Bike Socks, L","ProductNumber":"SO-B909 -L", "Color":"White","
StandardCost":3.3963,"ListPrice":9.5000,"Size":"L","Weight":null,"ProductCategoryID":27,"Product
ModelID":18, "SellStartDate":"2001-07-01T00:00:00","SellEndDate":"2002-06-30T00:00:00", "Discont
inuedDate":null,"ThumbNailPhoto":"R0lGODlhUAAxAPcAAAAAAIAA AACAAICAAAAAgIAAgACAgICAgMDAwP8AAAD/
AP//AAAA//8A/wD//////wAAAAAAAAAAAAAAAAAAAAAAAAAAAAAAAAAAAAAAAAAAAA AAAAAAAAA
AAAAAAAAAAAAAAAAAAAAAAAAAAAAAAAAAAAAMwAAZgAAmQAAzAAA/wAzAAAzMwAzZgAzmQAzzAAz/
wBmAABmMwBmZgBmmQBmzABm/wCZAACZMwCZZgCZmQCZzACZ /wDMAADMMwDMZgDMmQDMzADM/wD/AAD/MwD/
ZgD/mQD/zAD//z MAADMAMzMAMzjMAmTMAzDMA/zMzADMzMzMzZjMzmTMzzDMz/zNmADNmMzNmZjNmmTNmzDNm/
zOZADOZMzOZZjOZmTOZzDOZ/ z PMADPMMzPMZjPMmTPMzDPM/zP/ADP/MzP/ZjP/mTP/zDP//2YAAGYAM2YAZmYAmWY
AzGYA/2YzAGYzM2YzZmYzmYzzGYz/2ZmAGZmM2ZmZmZmmWZmzGZm/2aZAGaZM2aZZmaZmWaZzGaZ/2bMAGbMM2bMZmb
MmWbMzGbM/2b/AGb/M2b/Zmb/mWb/zGb//5kAAJkAM5kAZpkA mZkAzJkA/5kzAJkzM5kzZpkzmZkzzJkz/5lmAJlmM5
lmZplmmZlmzJlm/5mZAJmZM5mZZpmZmZmZzJmZ/5nMAJnMM5nMZpnMmZnMzJnM/5n/AJn/M5n/Zpn/mZn/zJn//8wAAM
wAM8wAZswAmcwAzMwA/8wzAMwzM8wzZswzmcwzzMwz/8xmAMxmM8xmZsxmmcxmzMxm/8yZAMyZM8yZZsyZmcyZzMyZ/8z
MAMzMM8zMZszMmczMzMzM/8z/AMz/M8z/Zsz/mcz/zMz//8wAAM8wAM/8wzZsz/mcz/zZ v8zmf8z
zP8z//9mAP9mM/9mZ9mmf9mzP9m//+ZAP+ZM/+ZZv+Zmf+ZzP+Z///MAP/MM//MZv/Mmf/MzP/M///AP//M///Zv//
mf//zP///yH5BAEAABAALAAAAABQADEAAAj/AP8JHEiwoMGDCBMqXMiwocOHECNKnEixosWLGDNq3Mi xo8ePIEOKHEm
ypMmTKKFOqXJkRBYqBLhfGZPnQ5ct/MxPmpMnQpsCZNm/CfBnTZ86gQ3HeRMoRadGlQpUQjfoUZ9KnVH9GxVhUK tCoVa
WKnZrVK9SmVMPuVHvWrFFisPjd+LbuW7tmvb8t6nJuXIIFutfbH2lSt07ta/eeOy3clTYuGtjS8yjUy5suXLmDHHdRjWIG
PGIjdDBA3Y3L2SQVY+mvQsVL16yqLOqfuyWtlHZbTv+nY1 76G67H38DTs068GrSkoMSN+62+fKQqrW2Xe6aem7CSaf6f
q7ceevTmcOLEh9Pvrz58+jTq1/Pvr379/DDAgA7","ThumbnailPhotoFileName":"no_image_available_small.
gif","rowguid":"161c035e-21b3-4e14-8e44-af508f35d80a","ModifiedDate":"2004-03-11T10:01:36.827",
"ProductCategory":null,"ProductModel":null,"SalesOrderDetails":[]}
```

> **NOTE** *If you happen to get an exception within the response that reads* The
> 'ObjectContent`1' type failed to serialize the response body for
> content type 'application/json;', *you can update your controller's default
> construct to turn off EF proxy creation by adding the following:* db.Configuration
> .ProxyCreationEnabled = false;.

In most cases, you would consume your Web API using jQuery or another JavaScript library (as discussed further in Chapter 25). However, you can consume the Web API in several other ways.

If you are using ASP.NET Web Forms or ASP.NET MVC and you want to connect to your Web API using server-side code, you can do so by using an HttpClient call. You can do this by using the Web API Client library.

> **NOTE** *If you do not have the Web API Client library referenced in this project, you can either download it from the NuGet Package Manager Console or update the projects that have this package installed if it has already been downloaded as part of your solution. To do the latter, go into the Package Manager, find the package, and choose Manage. NuGet is discussed in more detail in Appendix G.*

To demonstrate, create a new ASP.NET Web Forms project called **ApiConsumer**. Because you are going to consume one of the tables from your model, you need to create a class to cast the JSON result to. For simplicity's sake, you will use two properties as shown in Listing 13-46. If you'd like to get all of the properties from your model, you'll need to add them to your class.

LISTING 13-46: The Product class

VB

```vb
Public Class Product
    Private _Name As String
    Private _Color As String

    Public Property Name() As String
        Get
            Return _Name
        End Get
        Set(value As String)
            _Name = value
        End Set
    End Property

    Public Property Color() As String
        Get
            Return _Color
        End Get
        Set(value As String)
            _Color = value
        End Set
    End Property
End Class
```

C#

```csharp
public class Product
{
    public string Name { get; set; }
    public string Color { get; set; }
}
```

Then, create a new page called **Default.aspx**. Using `HttpClient`, pass the URI for `/api/products/710`. If you get a successful response, parse the result. Otherwise, display an exception in a separate label as shown in Listing 13-47.

LISTING 13-47: The default.aspx page to call your Web API

VB

```vb
<%@ Page Language="VB" %>
<%@ Import Namespace="System.Net.Http" %>
<%@ Import Namespace="System.Net.Http.Headers" %>
```

continues

LISTING 13-47 *(continued)*

```
<!DOCTYPE html>
<script runat="server">
    Protected Sub Page_Load(sender As Object, e As EventArgs)
        Dim client As HttpClient = New HttpClient()
        client.BaseAddress = New Uri("http://localhost:43059/")
        client.DefaultRequestHeaders.Accept.Add( _
            New MediaTypeWithQualityHeaderValue("application/json"))

        Dim response As HttpResponseMessage = client.GetAsync("api/products/710").Result
        If (response.IsSuccessStatusCode) Then
            Dim prod As Product = response.Content.ReadAsAsync(Of Product)().Result
            NameLabel.Text = prod.Name
            ColorLabel.Text = prod.Color
        Else
            ErrorLabel.Text = response.ReasonPhrase
        End If
    End Sub
</script>
<html xmlns="http://www.w3.org/1999/xhtml">
<head id="Head1" runat="server">
    <title>Web API Demo</title>
</head>
<body>
    <form id="form1" runat="server">
    <div>
        Product Name: <asp:Label ID="NameLabel" runat="server" /><br />
        Color: <asp:Label ID="ColorLabel" runat="server" /><br /><br />
        <asp:Label ID="ErrorLabel" runat="server" />
    </div>
    </form>
</body>
</html>
```

C#

```
<%@ Page Language="C#" %>
<%@ Import Namespace="System.Net.Http" %>
<%@ Import Namespace="System.Net.Http.Headers" %>
<!DOCTYPE html>
<script runat="server">
    protected void Page_Load(Object sender, EventArgs e)
    {
        HttpClient client = new HttpClient();
        client.BaseAddress = new Uri("http://localhost:43059/");
        client.DefaultRequestHeaders.Accept.Add(
            new MediaTypeWithQualityHeaderValue("application/json"));

        HttpResponseMessage response = client.GetAsync("api/products/710").Result;
        if (response.IsSuccessStatusCode)
        {
            var product = response.Content.ReadAsAsync<Product>().Result;
            NameLabel.Text = product.Name;
            ColorLabel.Text = product.Color;
        }
        else
        {
            ErrorLabel.Text = response.ReasonPhrase;
        }
    }
</script>
```

Figure 13-37 shows the results when you receive a successful HTTP response code.

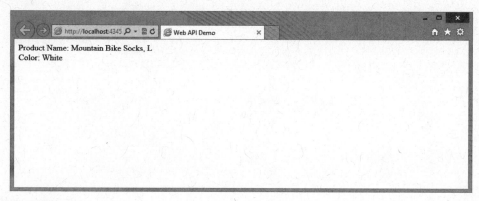

FIGURE 13-37

In some cases, you may not be the developer that will consume the Web API, but you may need to test it. In these cases, you can look to several tools to test your Web API. The most popular tool for testing the Web API is Fiddler. Fiddler is a free utility that inspects traffic that follows HTTP or HTTPS. In the utility, you can create a new HTTP Request Header and send the request to a specific URL.

> **NOTE** *To download Fiddler, perform an Internet search for "Fiddler download." Several online tools for testing REST API service calls are also available, such as hurl.it. To find some of these others, perform an Internet search for "How to test REST API service calls."*

SUMMARY

This chapter was a whirlwind tour of web services in the .NET platform. It is definitely a topic that merits an entire book of its own. The chapter showed you the power of exposing your data and logic as SOAP and also how to consume these SOAP messages directly in the ASP.NET applications you build.

Although not exhaustive, this chapter broadly outlined the basics of the WCF framework. As you start to dig deeper in the technology, you will find capabilities that are strong and extensible.

WCF Data Services is a powerful way to expose your database content. This chapter examined working with commands against the interface to filter out specific content. You can use a number of commands as part of the URI to get at the specific resultsets you are interested in. However, using code, and more specifically LINQ, is also just as possible to get at the results from the interface that you are looking for when working with your ASP.NET pages.

Finally, the chapter wrapped up with a quick overview of the new Web API in ASP.NET 4.5. This is by far the easiest solution to creating RESTful web services.

PART IV
Providers

14

Introduction to the Provider Model

WHAT'S IN THIS CHAPTER?

➤ What providers are

➤ What the provider model comprises for ASP.NET 4.5

➤ Configuring providers

WROX.COM CODE DOWNLOADS FOR THIS CHAPTER

Please note that all the code examples in this chapter are available as a part of this chapter's code download on the book's website at www.wrox.com on the Download Code tab.

The ASP.NET provider model is an important framework to understand as you build your applications. ASP.NET is a way to build applications for the Internet. That means an application's display code travels over HTTP, which is a stateless protocol. ASP.NET works with a disconnected architecture. The simple nature of this model means that requests come in and then responses are sent back. On top of that, ASP.NET does not differentiate one request from another. The server containing an ASP.NET application is simply reacting to any request thrown at it.

This means that a developer building a web application has to put some thought into how users can remain in context between their requests to the server as they work through the application. Keeping a user in context means recording state (the state of the user) to some type of data store. You can do this in multiple ways, and no one way is the perfect way. Rather, you must choose one of the available methods.

> **NOTE** *You can read about maintaining state in an ASP.NET application in Chapter 21.*

State can be stored via multiple methods, some of which include:

➤ Application state

➤ Session state

➤ The Cache object

You use all these methods on the server, but you can also employ your own custom methods—such as simply storing state in a database using your own custom schema. Writing state back to the clients, either directly on their computers or by placing state in the HTML output in the response, is also possible. Some of these methods include:

➤ Cookies

➤ Querystrings

➤ Hidden Fields

➤ ViewState

Whether it is one of the built-in providers that comes with ASP.NET or a custom one you've put together yourself, you will find that using a provider is a nice model for managing your state. The next section takes a look at what a provider is and how you can use it.

> **NOTE** *Unlike other chapters in this book, this chapter includes all of the listings as plaintext files for your convenience. In most cases, the text file includes the listing only and may not be a complete configuration file.*

UNDERSTANDING THE PROVIDER

These previous state mechanisms work rather well, but most of them are rudimentary and have short life spans. ASP.NET 4.5 includes a handful of systems (such as a membership and role management system) that handle state for users between multiple requests/response transactions. In fact, these systems require state management capabilities that go well beyond the limited timeframes that are possible in the previously mentioned state management methods. Therefore, many of these systems must record state in more advanced modes—something that is easy to do in ASP.NET. Recording state to data stores in more advanced modes is accomplished through the use of *providers*.

> **NOTE** *A provider is an object that allows for programmatic access to data stores, processes, and more.*

By default, sessions in ASP.NET are stored InProc, meaning in the same process where ASP.NET is running. In ASP.NET, you can simply change the provider used for the Session object; this will, in turn, change where the session is stored. The available providers for storing session information include:

➤ InProc

➤ StateServer

➤ SQLServer

Besides InProc, you can use StateServer, which enables you to store sessions in a process that is entirely separate from the one in which ASP.NET runs. This protects your sessions if the ASP.NET process shuts down. You can also store your sessions to disk (in a database, for example) using the SQLServer option. This method enables you to store your sessions directly in Microsoft's SQL Server. How do you go about changing the provider that is used for sessions? You can do this in a couple of ways.

One option to change the provider used for sessions is through the Internet Information Services (IIS) Manager, as shown in Figure 14-1.

The other option is to go directly to a system-wide configuration file (such as the machine.config file) or to an application configuration file (such as the web.config). In the file, change the name of the session state provider that is to be used within the <sessionState> section of the configuration document.

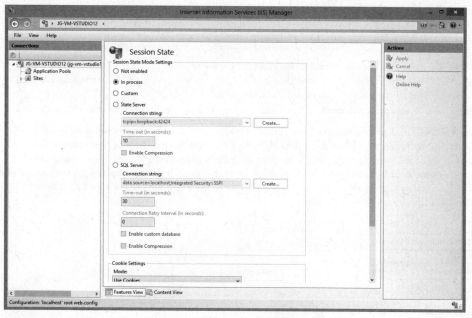

FIGURE 14-1

In later versions of ASP.NET, you have been able to take this provider model one step further than you ever could before. You will discover this next.

THE PROVIDER MODEL IN ASP.NET 4.5

As ASP.NET developed, users wanted to be able to store sessions by means other than the three methods—`InProc`, `StateServer`, and `SQLServer`. For example, one user request was for a provider that could store sessions in an Oracle database. If the team added a provider for Oracle, they would soon get requests to add even more providers for other databases and data storage methods. For this reason, instead of building providers for each and every possible scenario, the developers designed a provider model that enabled them to add any providers they wanted. Thus, the new provider model found in ASP.NET was born.

Today, ASP.NET 4.5 includes a lot of systems that require state storage of some kind. Also, instead of recording state in a fragile mode (the way sessions are stored by default), many of these systems require that their state be stored in more concrete data stores, such as databases or XML files. This also allows a longer-lived state for the users visiting an application—something else that is required by these systems.

The systems based on the provider model found in ASP.NET 4.5 that require advanced state management include the following:

➤ Membership

➤ Role management

➤ Site navigation

➤ Personalization

➤ Health monitoring web events

➤ Configuration file protection

The membership system is a means to allow ASP.NET to work from a user store of some kind to create, delete, or edit application users. Because it is rather apparent that developers want to work with an unlimited amount of different data stores for their user store, they need a means to change the underlying user store for their ASP.NET applications easily. The provider model found in ASP.NET 4.5 is the answer.

> **NOTE** *This chapter covers the built-in, classic providers in ASP.NET. However, it's highly recommended that you download and use the Universal Providers using Package Manager. The Universal Providers are explained more in Chapters 18 and 19.*

Out of the box, ASP.NET 4.5 provides a couple of membership providers that enable you to store user information. The included providers are the SQL Server and the Active Directory membership providers (found at `System.Web.Security.SqlMembershipProvider` and `System.Web.Security.ActiveDirectoryMembershipProvider`, respectively). In fact, for each of the systems (as well as for some of the ASP.NET 1.*x* systems), a series of providers is available to alter the way the state of that system is recorded. Figure 14-2 illustrates these providers.

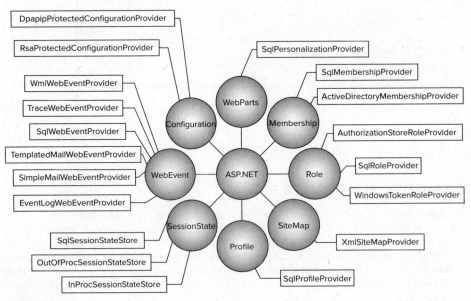

FIGURE 14-2

As you can see from the diagram, ASP.NET provides a large number of providers out of the box. Some systems have only a single provider (such as the profile system that includes only a provider to connect to SQL Server), whereas other systems include multiple providers (such as the WebEvents provider that includes six separate providers). Next, this chapter reviews how to set up SQL Server to work with a number of the providers presented in this chapter. You can use SQL Server 2005, 2008, or 2012 for the backend data store for many of the providers presented (although not all of them). After this explanation, you review each of the available providers built into ASP.NET 4.5.

Setting Up Your Provider to Work with Microsoft SQL Server 2005, 2008, or 2012

Quite a number of providers work with SQL Server. For example, the membership, role management, personalization, and other systems work with SQL Server right out of the box. However, all these systems work with LocalDB by default instead of with one of the full-blown versions of SQL Server such as SQL Server 2005, SQL Server 2008, or SQL Server 2012.

The Provider Model in ASP.NET 4.5 | **533**

To work with any of these databases, you must set up the database using the `aspnet_regsql.exe` tool. Working with `aspnet_regsql.exe` creates the necessary tables, roles, stored procedures, and other items needed by the providers. To get at this tool, open up the Visual Studio 2012 Command Prompt by selecting Start ➪ All Programs ➪ Microsoft Visual Studio 2012 ➪ Visual Studio Tools ➪ Visual Studio 2012 Command Prompt. This gives you access to the ASP.NET SQL Server Setup Wizard. The ASP.NET SQL Server Setup Wizard is an easy-to-use tool that facilitates setup of the SQL Server to work with many of the systems that are built into ASP.NET 4.5, such as the membership, role management, and personalization systems. The Setup Wizard provides two ways for you to set up the database: using a command-line tool or using a GUI tool. First, look at the command-line version of the tool.

The ASP.NET SQL Server Setup Wizard Command-Line Tool

The command-line version of the Setup Wizard gives the developer optimal control over how the database is created. Working from the command line to use this tool is not difficult, so don't be intimidated by it.

You can get at the actual tool, `aspnet_regsql.exe`, from the Visual Studio Command Prompt if you have Visual Studio 2012. At the command prompt, type **`aspnet_regsql.exe -?`** to get a list of all the command-line options at your disposal for working this tool.

Table 14-1 describes some of the available options for setting up your SQL Server instance to work with the personalization framework.

TABLE 14-1

COMMAND OPTION	DESCRIPTION
`-?`	Displays a list of available option commands.
`-W`	Uses the Wizard mode. This uses the default installation if no other parameters are used.
`-S <server>`	Specifies the SQL Server instance to work with.
`-U <login>`	Specifies the username to log in to SQL Server. If you use this, you also use the `-P` command.
`-P <password>`	Specifies the password to use for logging in to SQL Server. If you use this, you also use the `-U` command.
`-E`	Provides instructions to use the current Windows credentials for authentication.
`-C`	Specifies the connection string for connecting to SQL Server. If you use this, you can avoid using the `-U` and `-P` commands because they are specified in the connection string itself.
`-A all`	Adds support for all the available SQL Server operations provided by ASP.NET including membership, role management, profiles, site counters, and page/control personalization.
`-A p`	Adds support for working with profiles.
`-R all`	Removes support for all the available SQL Server operations that have been previously installed. These include membership, role management, profiles, site counters, and page/control personalization.
`-R p`	Removes support for the profile capability from SQL Server.
`-d <database>`	Specifies the database name to use with the application services. If you don't specify a name of a database, `aspnetdb` is used.
`-sqlexportonly <filename>`	Instead of modifying an instance of a SQL Server database, use this command in conjunction with the other commands to generate a SQL script that adds or removes the features specified. This command creates the scripts in a file that has the name specified in the command.

To modify SQL Server to work with the personalization provider using this command-line tool, you enter a command such as the following:

```
aspnet_regsql.exe -A all -E
```

After you enter the preceding command, the command-line tool creates the features required by all the available ASP.NET 4.5 systems. The results are shown in the tool itself, as you see in Figure 14-3.

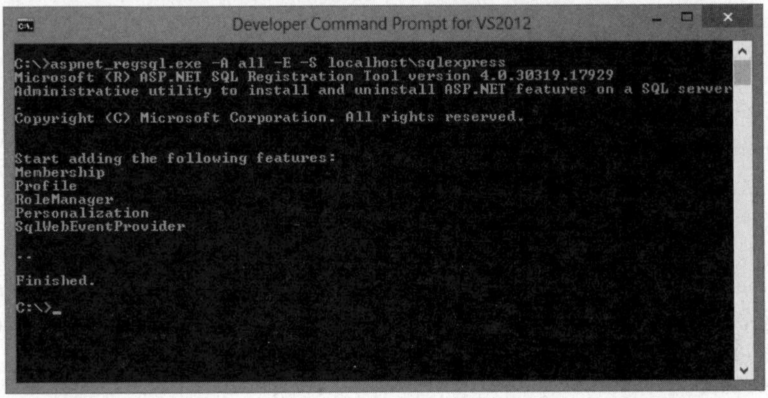

FIGURE 14-3

When this action is completed, you can see that a new database, aspnetdb, has been created in the Microsoft SQL Server Management Studio, which is part of Microsoft SQL Server 2012 (the database used for this example). You now have the appropriate tables for working with all the ASP.NET systems that are able to work with SQL Server (see Figure 14-4).

One advantage of using the command-line tool rather than the GUI-based version of the ASP.NET SQL Server Setup Wizard is that you can install in the database just the features that you are interested in working with instead of installing everything (as the GUI-based version does). For example, if you are going to have only the membership system interact with SQL Server 2012 — not any of the other systems (such as role management and personalization) — you can configure the setup so that only the tables, roles, stored procedures, and other items required by the membership system are established in the database. To set up the database for the membership system only, you use the following command on the command line:

FIGURE 14-4

```
aspnet_regsql.exe -A m -E
```

The ASP.NET SQL Server Setup Wizard GUI Tool

Instead of working with the tool through the command line, you can also work with a GUI version of the same wizard. To get at the GUI version, type the following at the Visual Studio command prompt:

```
aspnet_regsql.exe
```

At this point, the ASP.NET SQL Server Setup Wizard welcome screen appears, as shown in Figure 14-5.

Clicking Next gives you a new screen that offers two options: one to install management features into SQL Server and the other to remove them (see Figure 14-6).

FIGURE 14-5

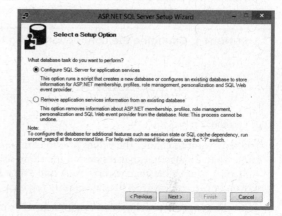

FIGURE 14-6

From here, choose the Configure SQL Server for application services option and click the Next button. The third screen (see Figure 14-7) asks for the login credentials to SQL Server and the name of the database to perform the operations. The Database option is <default>—meaning that the wizard creates a database called aspnetdb. If you want to choose a different folder, such as the application's database, choose the appropriate option.

After you have made your server and database selections, click Next. The screen shown in Figure 14-8 asks you to confirm your settings. If everything looks correct, click Next; otherwise, click Previous and correct your settings.

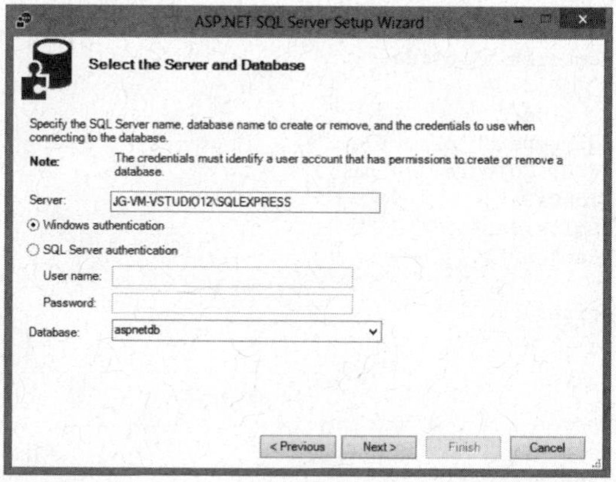

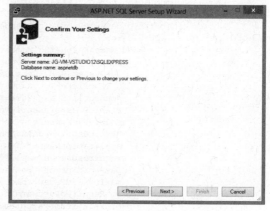

FIGURE 14-7

FIGURE 14-8

When this is complete, a screen appears, notifying you that everything was set up correctly.

Connecting Your Default Provider to a New SQL Server Instance

After you set up the full-blown Microsoft SQL Server to work with the various systems provided by ASP.NET, you create a connection string to the database in your `machine.config` or `web.config` file, as shown in Listing 14-1.

LISTING 14-1: Changing the connection string to work with SQL Server 2012

```
<configuration>
    <connectionStrings>
        <add name="LocalSqlServer"
          connectionString="Data Source=127.0.0.1;Integrated Security=SSPI" />
    </connectionStrings>
</configuration>
```

You may want to change the values provided if you are working with a remote instance of SQL Server rather than an instance that resides on the same server as the application. Changing this value in the `machine.config` file changes how each and every ASP.NET application uses this provider. Applying this setting in the `web.config` file causes only the local application to work with this instance.

After the connection string is set up, look further in the `<providers>` section of the section you are going to work with. For example, if you are using the membership provider, you want to work with the `<membership>` element in the configuration file. The settings to change the SQL Server are shown in Listing 14-2.

LISTING 14-2: Altering the SQL Server used via configuration

```
<?xml version="1.0"?>
<configuration>
    <connectionStrings>
        <add name="LocalSqlServer"
          connectionString=
          "Data Source=127.0.0.1;Integrated Security=SSPI;Initial Catalog=aspnetdb;" />
    </connectionStrings>

    <system.web>
        <compilation debug="false" targetFramework="4.5" />
        <httpRuntime targetFramework="4.5" />
        <membership defaultProvider="AspNetSqlMembershipProvider">
            <providers>
                <add name="AspNetSqlMembershipProvider"
                    type="System.Web.Security.SqlMembershipProvider,
                        System.Web, Version=4.0.0.0, Culture=neutral,
                        PublicKeyToken=b03f5f7f11d50a3a"
                    connectionStringName="LocalSqlServer"
                    enablePasswordRetrieval="false"
                    enablePasswordReset="true"
                    requiresQuestionAndAnswer="true"
                    applicationName="/"
                    requiresUniqueEmail="false"
                    passwordFormat="Hashed"
                    maxInvalidPasswordAttempts="5"
                    minRequiredPasswordLength="7"
                    minRequiredNonalphanumericCharacters="1"
                    passwordAttemptWindow="10"
                    passwordStrengthRegularExpression="" />
            </providers>
        </membership>
    </system.web>
</configuration>
```

With these changes in place, the SQL Server 2012 instance is now one of the providers available for use with your applications. The name of this provider instance is `AspNetSqlMembershipProvider`. You can see that this instance also uses the connection string of `LocalSqlServer`, which was defined in Listing 14-1.

Pay attention to some important attribute declarations from Listing 14-2. The first is that the provider used by the membership system is defined via the `defaultProvider` attribute found in the main `<membership>` node. Using this attribute, you can specify whether the provider is one of the built-in providers or whether it is a custom provider that you have built yourself or received from a third party. With the code from Listing 14-2 in place, the membership provider now works with Microsoft SQL Server 2012 (as shown in this example) instead of the Microsoft SQL Server Express Edition files.

The next section reviews the providers that are built into ASP.NET 4.5, starting with the membership system providers.

Membership Providers

The membership system enables you to easily manage users in your ASP.NET applications. As with most of the systems provided in ASP.NET, it features a series of server controls that interact with a defined provider to either retrieve or record information to and from the data store defined by the provider. Because a provider exists between the server controls and the data stores where the data is retrieved and recorded, having the controls work from an entirely different backend is fairly trivial. You just change the underlying provider of the overall system (in this case, the membership system) by making a simple configuration change in the ASP.NET application. It really makes no difference to the server controls.

As previously stated, ASP.NET 4.5 provides two membership providers out of the box:

➤ `System.Web.Security.SqlMembershipProvider`: Provides you with the capability to use the membership system to connect to Microsoft's SQL Server 2005, 2008, and 2012 as well as with Microsoft SQL Server Express Edition.

➤ `System.Web.Security.ActiveDirectoryMembershipProvider`: Provides you with the capability to use the membership system to connect to Microsoft's Active Directory (available in Microsoft Windows Server).

Both of these membership provider classes inherit from the `MembershipProvider` base class, as illustrated in Figure 14-9.

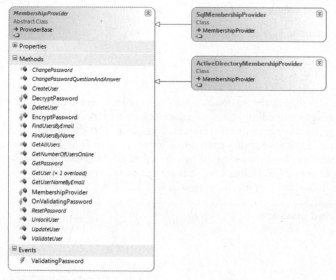

FIGURE 14-9

> **NOTE** *Although ASP.NET 4.5 ships with these two providers, you may hear about two other membership options. The first is* SimpleMembership. *Currently, this is available only in ASP.NET MVC 4 and not available to ASP.NET Web Forms directly. The second is using* DotNetOpenAuth. *This option is bundled with the default templates in ASP.NET 4.5 and is available via NuGet. It is a third-party library. Both of these options are covered in greater detail in Chapter 19.*

Next, you review each of these providers.

System.Web.Security.SqlMembershipProvider

The default provider is the SqlMembershipProvider instance. You find this default declaration for every ASP.NET application that resides on the application server in the machine.config file. You find this file in C:\Windows\Microsoft.NET\Framework\v4.0.30319\Config. Listing 14-3 shows the definition of this provider, which is located in the machine.config file.

LISTING 14-3: A SqlMembershipProvider instance declaration

```
<configuration>
    <system.web>
        <membership defaultProvider="AspNetSqlMembershipProvider">
            <providers>
                <add name="AspNetSqlMembershipProvider"
                    type="System.Web.Security.SqlMembershipProvider,
                        System.Web, Version=4.0.0.0, Culture=neutral,
                        PublicKeyToken=b03f5f7f11d50a3a"
                    connectionStringName="LocalSqlServer"
                    enablePasswordRetrieval="false"
                    enablePasswordReset="true"
                    requiresQuestionAndAnswer="true"
                    applicationName="/"
                    requiresUniqueEmail="false"
                    passwordFormat="Hashed"
                    maxInvalidPasswordAttempts="5"
                    minRequiredPasswordLength="7"
                    minRequiredNonalphanumericCharacters="1"
                    passwordAttemptWindow="10"
                    passwordStrengthRegularExpression="" />
            </providers>
        </membership>
    </system.web>
</configuration>
```

From this listing, you can see that a single instance of the SqlMembershipProvider object is defined in the machine.config file. This single instance is named AspNetSqlMembershipProvider. This is also where you find the default behavior settings for your membership system. By default, this provider is also configured to work with a SQL Server Express instance rather than a full-blown version of SQL Server such as SQL Server 2005, 2008, or 2012. You can see this by looking at the defined connectionStringName property in the provider declaration from Listing 14-3. In this case, it is set to LocalSqlServer. LocalSqlServer is also defined in the machine.config file, as shown in Listing 14-4.

LISTING 14-4: The LocalSqlServer defined instance

```
<configuration>
    <connectionStrings>
        <clear />
        <add name="LocalSqlServer"
```

```
        connectionString=" data source=.\SQLEXPRESS;Integrated
        Security=SSPI;AttachDBFilename=|DataDirectory|aspnetdb.mdf;
        User Instance=true"
        providerName="System.Data.SqlClient" />
    </connectionStrings>
</configuration>
```

You can see that this connection string information is set for a local SQL Server Express Edition file (an `.mdf` file). Of course, you are not required to work with only these file types for the `SqlMembershipProvider` capabilities. Instead, you can also set it up to work with either Microsoft's SQL Server 2005, 2008, or 2012 (as was previously shown).

System.Web.Security.ActiveDirectoryMembershipProvider

It is also possible for the membership system provided from ASP.NET 4.5 to connect this system to a Microsoft Active Directory instance or even Active Directory Application Mode (ADAM), which is a standalone directory product. Because the default membership provider is defined in the `machine.config` files at the `SqlMembershipProvider`, you must override these settings in your application's `web.config` file.

Before creating a defined instance of the `ActiveDirectoryMembershipProvider` in your `web.config` file, you must define the connection string to the Active Directory store, as shown in Listing 14-5.

LISTING 14-5: Defining the connection string to the Active Directory store

```
<configuration>
    <connectionStrings>
        <add name="ADConnectionString"
          connectionString=
          "LDAP://domain.myAdServer.com/CN=Users,DC=domain,DC=testing,DC=com" />
    </connectionStrings>
</configuration>
```

With the connection in place, you can create an instance of the `ActiveDirectoryMembershipProvider` in your `web.config` file that associates itself to this connection string, as illustrated in Listing 14-6.

LISTING 14-6: Defining the ActiveDirectoryMembershipProvider instance

```
<configuration>
    <connectionStrings>
        <add name="ADConnectionString"
            connectionString=
            "LDAP://domain.myAdServer.com/CN=Users,DC=domain,DC=testing,DC=com" />
    </connectionStrings>
    <system.web>
        <membership
            defaultProvider="AspNetActiveDirectoryMembershipProvider">
            <providers>
                <add name="AspNetActiveDirectoryMembershipProvider"
                    type="System.Web.Security.ActiveDirectoryMembershipProvider,
                    System.Web, Version=1.0.3600, Culture=neutral,
                    PublicKeyToken=b03f5f7f11d50a3a"
                    connectionStringName="ADConnectionString"
                    connectionUsername="UserWithAppropriateRights"
                    connectionPassword="PasswordForUser"
                    connectionProtection="Secure"
                    enablePasswordReset="true"
                    enableSearchMethods="true"
                    requiresQuestionAndAnswer="true"
                    applicationName="/"
                    description="Default AD connection"
                    requiresUniqueEmail="false"
```

continues

LISTING 14-6 *(continued)*

```
                        clientSearchTimeout="30"
                        serverSearchTimeout="30"
                        attributeMapPasswordQuestion="department"
                        attributeMapPasswordAnswer="division"
                        attributeMapFailedPasswordAnswerCount="singleIntAttribute"
                        attributeMapFailedPasswordAnswerTime="singleLargeIntAttribute"
                        attributeMapFailedPasswordAnswerLockoutTime="singleLargeIntAttribute"
                        attributeMapEmail = "mail"
                        attributeMapUsername = "userPrincipalName"
                        maxInvalidPasswordAttempts = "5"
                        passwordAttemptWindow = "10"
                        passwordAnswerAttemptLockoutDuration = "30"
                        minRequiredPasswordLength="7"
                        minRequiredNonalphanumericCharacters="1"
                        passwordStrengthRegularExpression=
                          "(?=.{6,})(?=(.*\d){1,})(?=(.*\W){1,})" />
                </providers>
            </membership>
        </system.web>
</configuration>
```

Although not all these attributes are required, this list provides you with the available attributes of the `ActiveDirectoryMembershipProvider`. In fact, you can easily declare the instance in its simplest form, as shown here:

```
<membership
    defaultProvider="AspNetActiveDirectoryMembershipProvider">
    <providers>
        <add name="AspNetActiveDirectoryMembershipProvider"
            type="System.Web.Security.ActiveDirectoryMembershipProvider,
            System.Web, Version=1.0.3600, Culture=neutral,
            PublicKeyToken=b03f5f7f11d50a3a"
            connectionStringName="ADConnectionString" />
    </providers>
</membership>
```

Again, with either the `SqlMembershipProvider` or the `ActiveDirectoryMembershipProvider` in place, the membership system server controls (such as the Login server control) as well as the membership API, once configured, will record and retrieve their information via the provider you have established. That is the power of the provider model that the ASP.NET team has established. You continue to see this power as you learn about the rest of the providers detailed in this chapter.

Role Providers

After a user is logged in to the system (possibly using the ASP.NET membership system), the ASP.NET role management system enables you to work with the role of that user to authorize him for a particular access to the overall application. The role management system in ASP.NET 4.5, as with the other systems, has a set of providers to store and retrieve role information in an easy manner. This, of course, doesn't mean that you are bound to one of the three available providers in the role management system. Instead, you can extend one of the established providers or even create your own custom provider.

By default, ASP.NET 4.5 offers three providers for the role management system. These providers are defined in the following list:

➤ `System.Web.Security.SqlRoleProvider`: Provides you with the capability to use the ASP.NET role management system to connect to Microsoft's SQL Server 2005/2008/2012 as well as to Microsoft SQL Server Express Edition.

➤ `System.Web.Security.WindowsTokenRoleProvider`: Provides you with the capability to connect the ASP.NET role management system to the built-in Windows security group system.

> System.Web.Security
> .Authorization StoreRoleProvider:
> Provides you with the capability to
> connect the ASP.NET role management
> system to either an XML file, Active
> Directory, or in an Active Directory
> Application Mode (ADAM) store.

These three classes for role management inherit
from the `RoleProvider` base class, as illustrated
in Figure 14-10.

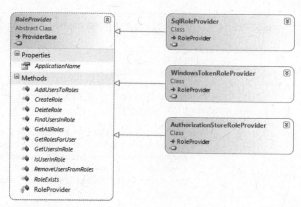

FIGURE 14-10

System.Web.Security.SqlRoleProvider

The role management system in ASP.NET uses
SQL Server Express Edition files by default
(just as the membership system does). The
connection to the SQL Server Express file uses
`SqlRoleProvider`, but you can just as easily configure your SQL Server 2005, 2008, or 2012 server to work
with the role management system through `SqlRoleProvider`. The procedure for setting up your full-blown
SQL Server is described in the beginning of this chapter.

Looking at the `SqlRoleProvider` instance in the `machine.config.comments` file, you will notice the
syntax as defined in Listing 14-7. The `machine.config.comments` file provides documentation on the
`machine.config` and shows you the details of the default settings that are baked into the ASP.NET
Framework.

LISTING 14-7: A SqlRoleProvider instance declaration

```
<configuration>
    <roleManager enabled="false" cacheRolesInCookie="false"
        cookieName=".ASPXROLES" cookieTimeout="30" cookiePath="/"
        cookieRequireSSL="false" cookieSlidingExpiration="true"
        cookieProtection="All" defaultProvider="AspNetSqlRoleProvider"
        createPersistentCookie="false" maxCachedResults="25">
        <providers>
            <clear />
            <add connectionStringName="LocalSqlServer" applicationName="/"
                name="AspNetSqlRoleProvider"
                type="System.Web.Security.SqlRoleProvider, System.Web,
                Version=4.0.0.0, Culture=neutral, PublicKeyToken=b03f5f7f11d50a3a"
                />
            <add applicationName="/" name="AspNetWindowsTokenRoleProvider"
                type="System.Web.Security.WindowsTokenRoleProvider, System.Web,
                Version=4.0.0.0, Culture=neutral, PublicKeyToken=b03f5f7f11d50a3a"
                />
        </providers>
    </roleManager>
</configuration>
```

As stated, this is part of the default `<roleManager>` declaration that is baked into the overall ASP.NET
Framework (note again that you can change any of these defaults by making a new declaration in your
`web.config` file). As you can see, role management is disabled by default through the `enabled` attribute
found in the `<roleManager>` node (it is set to `false` by default). Also, pay attention to the `default`
`Provider` attribute in the `<roleManager>` element. In this case, it is set to `AspNetSqlRoleProvider`. This
provider is defined in the same code example. To connect to the Microsoft SQL Server 2012 instance that
was defined earlier (in the membership system examples), you can use the syntax shown in Listing 14-8.

LISTING 14-8: Connecting the role management system to SQL Server 2012

```
<configuration>
    <connectionStrings>
        <add name="LocalSqlServer"
            connectionString=
            "Data Source=127.0.0.1;Integrated Security=SSPI;Initial Catalog=aspnetdb;" />
    </connectionStrings>
    <system.web>
        <roleManager enabled="true" cacheRolesInCookie="true"
            cookieName=".ASPXROLES" cookieTimeout="30" cookiePath="/"
            cookieRequireSSL="false" cookieSlidingExpiration="true"
            cookieProtection="All" defaultProvider="AspNetSqlRoleProvider"
            createPersistentCookie="false" maxCachedResults="25">
            <providers>
                <clear />
                <add connectionStringName="LocalSqlServer" applicationName="/"
                    name="AspNetSqlRoleProvider"
                    type="System.Web.Security.SqlRoleProvider, System.Web,
                    Version=4.0.0.0, Culture=neutral,
                    PublicKeyToken=b03f5f7f11d50a3a" />
            </providers>
        </roleManager>
    </system.web>
</configuration>
```

With this in place, you can now connect to SQL Server 2012. Next is a review of the second provider available to the role management system.

System.Web.Security.WindowsTokenRoleProvider

The Windows operating system has a role system built into it. This Windows security group system is an ideal system to use when you are working with intranet-based applications where you might have all users already in defined roles. This, of course, works best if you have anonymous authentication turned off for your ASP.NET application, and you have configured your application to use Windows Authentication.

> **NOTE** *Chapter 20 discusses Windows Authentication for ASP.NET applications.*

Some limitations exist when you are using `WindowsTokenRoleProvider`. This is a read-only provider because ASP.NET is not allowed to modify the settings applied in the Windows security group system. This means that not all the methods provided via the `RoleProvider` abstract class are usable when working with this provider. From the `WindowsTokenRoleProvider` class, the only methods you have at your disposal are `IsUserInRole` and `GetUsersInRole`.

To configure your `WindowsTokenRoleProvider` instance, you use the syntax defined in Listing 14-9.

LISTING 14-9: A WindowsTokenRoleProvider instance

```
<configuration>
    <system.web>
        <authentication mode="Windows" />
        <roleManager defaultProvider="WindowsProvider"
            enabled="true" cacheRolesInCookie="false">
            <providers>
                <add name="WindowsProvider"
                    type="System.Web.Security.WindowsTokenRoleProvider" />
            </providers>
        </roleManager>
    </system.web>
</configuration>
```

Remember that you have to declare the default provider using the `defaultProvider` attribute in the `<roleManager>` element to change the assigned provider from the `SqlRoleProvider` association.

System.Web.Security.AuthorizationStoreRoleProvider

The final role provider available to you from a default install of ASP.NET is `AuthorizationStoreRoleProvider`. This role provider class enables you to store roles inside of an Authorization Manager policy store. These types of stores are also referred to as AzMan stores. As with `WindowsTokenRoleProvider`, `AuthorizationStoreRoleProvider` is a bit limited because it is unable to support any AzMan business rules.

To use `AuthorizationStoreRoleProvider`, you must first make a connection in your `web.config` file to the XML data store used by AzMan, as shown in Listing 14-10.

LISTING 14-10: Making a connection to the AzMan policy store

```
<configuration>
    <connectionStrings>
        <add name="LocalPolicyStore"
            connectionString="msxml://~\App_Data\SampleStore.xml" />
    </connectionStrings>
</configuration>
```

Note that when you work with these XML-based policy files, storing them in the App_Data folder is best. Files stored in the App_Data folder cannot be pulled up in the browser.

After the connection string is in place, the next step is to configure your `AuthorizationStoreRoleProvider` instance. This takes the syntax defined in Listing 14-11.

LISTING 14-11: Defining the AuthorizationStoreRoleProvider instance

```
<configuration>
    <connectionStrings>
        <add name="MyLocalPolicyStore"
            connectionString="msxml://~\App_Data\datafilename.xml" />
    </connectionStrings>
    <system.web>
        <authentication mode="Windows" />
        <identity impersonate="true" />
        <roleManager defaultProvider="AuthorizationStoreRoleProvider"
            enabled="true"
            cacheRolesInCookie="true"
            cookieName=".ASPROLES"
            cookieTimeout="30"
            cookiePath="/"
            cookieRequireSSL="false"
            cookieSlidingExpiration="true"
            cookieProtection="All" >
            <providers>
                <clear />
                <add name="AuthorizationStoreRoleProvider"
                    type="System.Web.Security.AuthorizationStoreRoleProvider"
                    connectionStringName="MyLocalPolicyStore"
                    applicationName="SampleApplication"
                    cacheRefreshInterval="60"
                    scopeName="" />
            </providers>
        </roleManager>
    </system.web>
</configuration>
```

Next, this chapter reviews the single personalization provider available in ASP.NET.

The Personalization Provider

As with the membership system found in ASP.NET, the personalization system (also referred to as the profile system) is another system that is based on the provider model. This system makes associations between the end user viewing the application and any data points stored centrally that are specific to that user. As stated, these personalization properties are stored and maintained on a per-user basis. ASP.NET provides a single provider for data storage. This provider enables you to use the ASP.NET personalization system to connect to Microsoft's SQL Server 2005, 2008, and 2012, as well as to Microsoft SQL Server Express Edition.

This single class for the personalization system inherits from the `ProfileProvider` base class, as shown in Figure 14-11.

As with the other providers covered so far, `SqlProfileProvider` connects to a Microsoft SQL Server Express Edition file by default. Although this is the default, you can change the connection to work with SQL Server 2005, 2008, or 2012. For example, if you are connecting to a SQL Server 2012 database, you define your connection in the `web.config` file and then associate your `SqlProfileProvider` declaration to this connection string. Listing 14-12 presents this scenario.

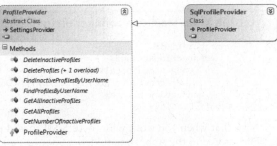

FIGURE 14-11

LISTING 14-12: Connecting the SqlProfileProvider to SQL Server 2012

```
<configuration>
    <connectionStrings>
        <add name="LocalSqlServer"
            connectionString="Data Source=127.0.0.1;Integrated Security=SSPI" />
    </connectionStrings>
    <system.web>
        <profile>
            <providers>
                <clear />
                <add name="AspNetSqlProfileProvider"
                    connectionStringName="LocalSqlServer" applicationName="/"
                    type="System.Web.Profile.SqlProfileProvider, System.Web,
                    Version=4.0.0.0, Culture=neutral,
                    PublicKeyToken=b03f5f7f11d50a3a" />
            </providers>
            <properties>
                <add name="FirstName" />
                <add name="LastName" />
                <add name="LastVisited" />
                <add name="Age" />
                <add name="Member" />
            </properties>
        </profile>
    </system.web>
</configuration>
```

Remember that to store profile information in your SQL Server database, you have to configure this database so the proper tables, stored procedures, and other items are created. This task was discussed earlier in the chapter.

The SiteMap Provider

Similar to the personalization provider just discussed, ASP.NET 4.5 provides a single provider to work with sitemaps. Sitemaps are what ASP.NET uses to provide you with a centralized way of maintaining site navigation. By default, the definition of a web application's navigation is located in a structured XML file. The sitemap provider lets you interact with this XML file, the `.sitemap` file, which you create for your application. The provider available for sitemaps is `System.Web.XmlSiteMapProvider`, which enables you to use the ASP.NET navigation system to connect to an XML-based file.

This single class for the sitemap system inherits from the `StaticSiteMapProvider` base class, which is a partial implementation of the `SiteMapProvider` base class, as shown in Figure 14-12.

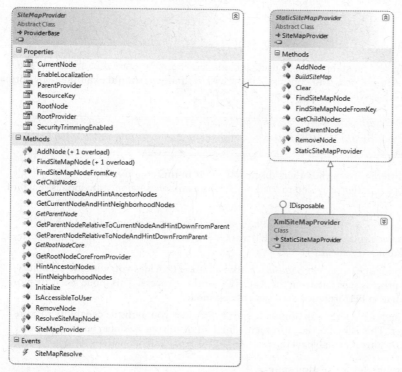

FIGURE 14-12

This is the first provider introduced so far that does not connect to a SQL Server database by default. Instead, this provider is designed to work with a static XML file. This XML file uses a particular schema and is covered in considerable detail in Chapter 17.

Listing 14-13 shows the code required to configure `XmlSiteMapProvider`.

LISTING 14-13: Defining an XmlSiteMapProvider instance in the web.config file

```
<configuration>
    <system.web>
        <siteMap defaultProvider="MyXmlSiteMapProvider" enabled="true">
            <providers>
                <add name="MyXmlSiteMapProvider"
                    description="SiteMap provider that reads in .sitemap files."
```

continues

LISTING 14-13 *(continued)*

```
                type="System.Web.XmlSiteMapProvider, System.Web, Version=4.0.0.0,
                Culture=neutral, PublicKeyToken=b03f5f7f11d50a3a"
                siteMapFile="AnotherWeb.sitemap" />
            </providers>
        </siteMap>
    </system.web>
</configuration>
```

The `XmlSiteMapProvider` allows only a single root element in the strictly designed `web.sitemap` file. The default filename of the XML file it is looking for is `web.sitemap`, although you can change this default setting (as you can see in Listing 14-13) by using the `siteMapFile` attribute within the provider declaration in the `web.config` file.

SessionState Providers

The available modes of storing session state for your users include `InProc`, `StateServer`, `SQLServer`, or even `Custom`. Each mode has definite pros and cons associated with it, and you should examine each option thoroughly when deciding which session state mode to use.

> **NOTE** *More information about session and* `SessionState` *can be found in Chapter 21.*

This provider model is a bit different from the others discussed so far in this chapter. The `SessionStateModule` class is a handler provided to load one of the available session state modes. Each of these modes is defined here:

➤ `System.Web.SessionState.InProcSessionStateStore`: Provides you with the capability to store sessions in the same process as the ASP.NET worker process. This is by far the best-performing method of session state management.

➤ `System.Web.SessionState.OutOfProcSessionStateStore`: Provides you with the capability to store sessions in a process separate from the ASP.NET worker process. This mode is a little more secure, but a little worse in performance than the `InProc` mode.

➤ `System.Web.SessionState.SqlSessionStateStore`: Provides you with the capability to store sessions in SQL Server. This is by far the most secure method of storing sessions, but it is the worst performing mode of the three available methods.

Figure 14-13 shows these three modes for session state management.

Next, this chapter reviews each of the three modes that you can use out of the box in your ASP.NET 4.5 applications.

System.Web.SessionState.InProcSessionStateStore

The `InProcSessionStateStore` mode is the default mode for ASP.NET. In this mode, the sessions generated are held in the same process as that being used by the ASP.NET worker process (`aspnet_wp.exe` or `w3wp.exe`). This mode is the best performing, but some problems exist with this mode as well. Because the sessions are stored in the same process, whenever the worker process is recycled, all the sessions are

FIGURE 14-13

destroyed. Worker processes can be recycled for many reasons (such as a change to the web.config file, the Global.asax file, or a setting in IIS that requires the process to be recycled after a set time period).

Listing 14-14 shows an example of the configuration in the web.config file for working in the InProc mode.

LISTING 14-14: Defining the InProc mode for session state management in the web.config

```
<configuration>
    <system.web>
        <sessionState mode="InProc">
        </sessionState>
    </system.web>
</configuration>
```

As you can see, this mode is rather simple. The next method reviewed is the out-of-process mode—also referred to as the StateServer mode.

System.Web.SessionState.OutOfProcSessionStateStore

In addition to the InProc mode, the StateServer mode is an out-of-process method of storing session state. This method does not perform as well as one that stores the sessions in the same process as the ASP.NET worker process. This makes sense because the method must jump process boundaries to work with the sessions you are employing. Although the performance is poorer than it is in the InProc mode, the OutOfProcSessionStateStore method is more reliable than running the sessions using InProcSessionStateStore. If your application's worker process recycles, the sessions that this application is working with are still maintained. This capability is vital for those applications that are critically dependent upon sessions.

Listing 14-15 shows an example of using OutOfProcSessionStateStore.

LISTING 14-15: Running sessions out of process using OutOfProcSessionStateStore

```
<configuration>
    <system.web>
        <sessionState mode="StateServer"
            stateConnectionString="tcpip=127.0.0.1:42424">
        </sessionState>
    </system.web>
</configuration>
```

When using the StateServer mode, you also must define where the sessions are stored using the stateConnectionString attribute. In this case, the local server is used, meaning that the sessions are stored on the same machine, but in an entirely separate process. You could have just as easily stored the sessions on a different server by providing the appropriate IP address as a value for this attribute. In addition to the IP address, note that port 42424 is used. This port is required when using the StateServer mode for sessions. Chapter 21 covers changing the port for the StateServer.

System.Web.SessionState.SqlSessionStateStore

The final provider for session state management available to you in ASP.NET is the SqlSessionStateStore. This method is definitely the most resilient of the three available modes. With that said, however, it is also the worst performing of the three modes. Setting up your database appropriately is important if you use this method of session state storage. Again, Chapter 21 shows you how to set up your database.

To configure your application to work with SqlSessionStateStore, you must configure the web.config file as detailed in Listing 14-16.

LISTING 14-16: Defining SqlSessionStateStore in the web.config

```
<configuration>
    <system.web>
        <sessionState mode="SQLServer"
            allowCustomSqlDatabase="true"
            sqlConnectionString="Data Source=127.0.0.1;
            database=MyCustomASPStateDatabase;Integrated Security=SSPI">
        </sessionState>
    </system.web>
</configuration>
```

Next, you review the providers available for the web events architecture.

Web Event Providers

Among all the available systems provided in ASP.NET 4.5, more providers are available for the health monitoring system than for any other system. The health monitoring system enables ASP.NET application administrators to evaluate the health of a running ASP.NET application and to capture events (errors and other possible triggers) that can then be stored via one of the available providers. These events are referred to as *web events*. A large list of events can be monitored via the health monitoring system, and this means that you can start recording items such as authentication failures/successes, all errors generated, ASP.NET worker process information, request data, response data, and more. Recording items means using one of the providers available to record to a data store of some kind.

By default, ASP.NET 4.5 offers several possible providers for the health monitoring system. This is more than for any of the other ASP.NET systems. These providers are defined in the following list:

➤ `System.Web.Management.EventLogWebEventProvider`: Provides you with the capability to use the ASP.NET health monitoring system to record security operation errors and all other errors into the Windows event log.

➤ `System.Web.Management.SimpleMailWebEventProvider`: Provides you with the capability to use the ASP.NET health monitoring system to send error information in an e-mail.

➤ `System.Web.Management.TemplatedMailWebEventProvider`: Similar to the `SimpleMailWebEventProvider`, the `TemplatedMailWebEventProvider` class provides you with the capability to send error information in a templated e-mail. Templates are defined using a standard .aspx page.

➤ `System.Web.Management.SqlWebEventProvider`: Provides you with the capability to use the ASP.NET health monitoring system to store error information in SQL Server. As with the other SQL providers for the other systems in ASP.NET, the `SqlWebEventProvider` stores error information in SQL Server Express Edition by default.

➤ `System.Web.Management.TraceWebEventProvider`: Provides you with the capability to use the ASP.NET health monitoring system to send error information to the ASP.NET page tracing system.

➤ `System.Web.Management.IisTraceWebEventProvider`: Provides you with the capability to use the ASP.NET health monitoring system to send error information to the IIS tracing system.

➤ `System.Web.Management.WmiWebEventProvider`: Provides you with the capability to connect the ASP.NET health monitoring system, the Windows Management Instrumentation (WMI) event provider.

These seven providers for the ASP.NET health monitoring system inherit from either the `WebEventProvider` base class, or the `BufferedWebEventProvider` (which, in turn, inherits from the `WebEventProvider`), as shown in Figure 14-14.

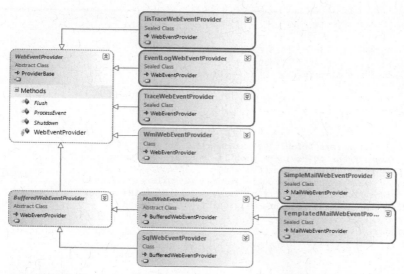

FIGURE 14-14

What is the difference between the `WebEventProvider` class and the `BufferedWebEventProvider`? The big difference is that the `WebEventProvider` writes events as they happen, whereas the `BufferedWebEventProvider` holds web events until a collection of them is made. The collection is then written to the database or sent in an e-mail in a batch. If you use the `SqlWebEventProvider` class, you actually want this batch processing to occur rather than having the provider make a connection to the database and write to it for each web event that occurs.

Next, this chapter looks at each of the seven more prominent available providers for the health monitoring system.

System.Web.Management.EventLogWebEventProvider

Traditionally, administrators and developers are used to reviewing system and application errors in the built-in Windows event log. The items in the event log can be viewed via the Event Viewer. You find this GUI-based tool for viewing events by selecting Administration Tools in the Control Panel and then selecting Event Viewer.

By default, the health monitoring system uses the Windows event log to record the items that are already specified in the server's configuration files or items you have specified in the `web.config` file of your application. If you look in the `web.config.comments` file in the CONFIG folder of the Microsoft .NET Framework installed on your server, you see that the `EventLogWebEventProvider` is detailed in this location. Listing 14-17 presents the code.

LISTING 14-17: The EventLogWebEventProvider declared in the web.config.comments file

```
<configuration>
    <system.web>
        <healthMonitoring heartbeatInterval="0" enabled="true">
            <bufferModes>
                <!-- Removed for clarity -->
            </bufferModes>
            <providers>
                <clear />
                <add name="EventLogProvider"
                    type="System.Web.Management.EventLogWebEventProvider,
```

continues

LISTING 14-17 *(continued)*

```
                        System.Web,Version=4.0.0.0,Culture=neutral,
                        PublicKeyToken=b03f5f7f11d50a3a" />
                <!-- Removed for clarity -->
            </providers>
            <profiles>
                <!-- Removed for clarity -->
            </profiles>
            <rules>
                <add name="All Errors Default" eventName="All Errors"
                    provider="EventLogProvider" profile="Default" minInstances="1"
                    maxLimit="Infinite" minInterval="00:01:00" custom="" />
                <add name="Failure Audits Default" eventName="Failure Audits"
                    provider="EventLogProvider" profile="Default" minInstances="1"
                    maxLimit="Infinite" minInterval="00:01:00" custom="" />
            </rules>
            <eventMappings>
                <!-- Removed for clarity -->
            </eventMappings>
        </healthMonitoring>
    </system.web>
</configuration>
```

As you can see from Listing 14-17, a lot of possible settings can be applied in the health monitoring system. Depending on the rules and event mappings you have defined, these items are logged into the event log of the server that is hosting the application. Looking closely at the `<rules>` section of the listing, you can see that specific error types are assigned to be monitored. In this section, two types of errors are trapped in the health monitoring system—`All Errors Default` and `Failure Audits Default`.

When one of the errors defined in the `<rules>` section is triggered and captured by the health monitoring system, it is recorded. Where it is recorded depends on the specified provider. The provider attribute used in the `<add>` element of the `<rules>` section determines this. In both cases in the example in Listing 14-17, you can see that the `EventLogProvider` is the assigned provider. This means that the Windows error log is used for recording the errors of both types.

> **NOTE** *As you work through the rest of the providers, note that the health monitoring system behaves differently when working with providers than the other systems that have been introduced in this chapter. Using the health monitoring system in ASP.NET 4.5, you are able to assign more than one provider at a time. This means that you are able to specify in the* `web.config` *file that errors are logged not only into the Windows event log, but also into any other data store using any other provider you designate. Even for the same web event type, you can assign the web event to be recorded to the Windows event log and SQL Server at the same time, for example.*

System.Web.Management.SimpleMailWebEventProvider

Sometimes when errors occur in your applications, you as an administrator or a concerned developer want e-mail notification of the problem. In addition to recording events to disk using something such as the `EventLogWebEventProvider`, you can also have the error notification e-mailed to you using the `SimpleMailWebEventProvider`. As it states in the provider name, the e-mail is a simply constructed one. Listing 14-18 shows you how you would go about adding e-mail notification in addition to writing the errors to the Windows event log.

LISTING 14-18: The SimpleMailWebEventProvider definition

```xml
<configuration>
    <system.web>
        <healthMonitoring heartbeatInterval="0" enabled="true">
            <bufferModes>
                <add name="Website Error Notification"
                    maxBufferSize="100"
                    maxFlushSize="20"
                    urgentFlushThreshold="1"
                    regularFlushInterval="00:01:00"
                    urgentFlushInterval="00:01:00"
                    maxBufferThreads="1" />
            </bufferModes>
            <providers>
                <clear />
                <add name="EventLogProvider"
                    type="System.Web.Management.EventLogWebEventProvider,
                    System.Web,Version=4.0.0.0,Culture=neutral,
                    PublicKeyToken=b03f5f7f11d50a3a" />
                <add name="SimpleMailProvider"
                    type="System.Web.Management.SimpleMailWebEventProvider,
                    System.Web, Version=4.0.0.0, Culture=neutral,
                    PublicKeyToken=b03f5f7f11d50a3a"
                    from="website@company.com"
                    to="admin@company.com"
                    cc="adminLevel2@company.com" bcc="director@company.com"
                    bodyHeader="Warning!"
                    bodyFooter="Please investigate ASAP."
                    subjectPrefix="Action required."
                    buffer="true"
                    bufferMode="Website Error Notification"
                    maxEventLength="4096"
                    maxMessagesPerNotification="1" />
            </providers>
            <profiles>
                <!-- Removed for clarity -->
            </profiles>
            <rules>
                <add name="All Errors Default" eventName="All Errors"
                    provider="EventLogProvider" profile="Default" minInstances="1"
                    maxLimit="Infinite" minInterval="00:01:00" custom="" />
                <add name="Failure Audits Default" eventName="Failure Audits"
                    provider="EventLogProvider" profile="Default" minInstances="1"
                    maxLimit="Infinite" minInterval="00:01:00" custom="" />
                <add name="All Errors Simple Mail" eventName="All Errors"
                    provider="SimpleMailProvider" profile="Default" />
                <add name="Failure Audits Default" eventName="Failure Audits"
                    provider="SimpleMailProvider" profile="Default" />
            </rules>
            <eventMappings>
                <!-- Removed for clarity -->
            </eventMappings>
        </healthMonitoring>
    </system.web>
</configuration>
```

In this example, the errors that occur are captured and not only written to the event log, but are also e-mailed to the end users specified in the provider definition. One very interesting point of the `SimpleMailWebEventProvider` is that this class inherits from the `BufferedWebEventProvider` instead of from the `WebEventProvider` as the `EventLogWebEventProvider` does. Inheriting from the

`BufferedWebEventProvider` means that you can have the health monitoring system build a collection of error notifications before sending them on. The `<bufferModes>` section defines how the buffering works.

System.Web.Management.TemplatedMailWebEventProvider

The aforementioned `SimpleMailWebEventProvider` does exactly what its name states—it sends out a simple, text-based e-mail. To send out a more artistically crafted e-mail that contains even more information, you can use the `TemplatedMailWebEventProvider`. Just like the `SimpleMailWebEventProvider`, you simply define the provider appropriately in the `<healthMonitoring>` section. Listing 14-19 presents the model for this definition.

LISTING 14-19: The TemplatedMailWebEventProvider definition

```
<providers>
    <clear />
    <add name="EventLogProvider"
        type="System.Web.Management.EventLogWebEventProvider,
        System.Web,Version=4.0.0.0,Culture=neutral,
        PublicKeyToken=b03f5f7f11d50a3a" />
    <add name="TemplatedMailProvider"
        type="System.Web.Management.TemplatedMailWebEventProvider,
        System.Web, Version=4.0.0.0, Culture=neutral,
        PublicKeyToken=b03f5f7f11d50a3a"
        template="../mailtemplates/errornotification.aspx"
        from="website@company.com"
        to="admin@company.com"
        cc="adminLevel2@company.com" bcc="director@company.com"
        bodyHeader="Warning!"
        bodyFooter="Please investigate ASAP."
        subjectPrefix="Action required."
        buffer="true"
        bufferMode="Website Error Notification"
        maxEventLength="4096"
        maxMessagesPerNotification="1" />
</providers>
```

The big difference between this provider declaration and the `SimpleMailWebEventProvider` appears in bold in Listing 14-19. The `TemplatedMailWebEventProvider` has a `template` attribute that specifies the location of the template to use for the e-mail that is created and sent from the health monitoring system.

System.Web.Management.SqlWebEventProvider

In many instances, you may want to write to disk when you are trapping and recording the web events that occur in your application. The `EventLogWebEventProvider` is an excellent provider because it writes these web events to the Windows event log on your behalf. However, in some instances, you may want to write these web events to disk elsewhere. In this case, a good alternative is to write these web events to SQL Server instead (or even in addition to the writing to an event log).

Writing to SQL Server gives you some benefits over writing to the Windows event log. When your application is running in a web farm, you might want all the errors that occur across the farm to be written to a single location. In this case, writing all web events that are trapped via the health monitoring system to a SQL Server instance to which all the servers in the web farm can connect makes sense.

By default, the `SqlWebEventProvider` (like the other SQL Server-based providers covered so far in this chapter) uses SQL Server Express Edition as its underlying database. To connect to the full-blown version of SQL Server instead, you need a defined connection as shown in Listing 14-20.

LISTING 14-20: The LocalSqlServer defined instance

```
<configuration>
    <connectionStrings>
        <add name="LocalSqlServer"
            allowCustomSqlDatabase="true"
            connectionString="Data Source=127.0.0.1;Integrated Security=SSPI" />
    </connectionStrings>
</configuration>
```

With this connection in place, the next step is to use this connection in your `SqlWebEventProvider` declaration in the `web.config` file, as illustrated in Listing 14-21.

LISTING 14-21: Writing web events to SQL Server 2012 using the SqlWebEventProvider

```
<configuration>
    <system.web>
        <healthMonitoring>
            <!-- Other nodes removed for clarity -->
            <providers>
                <clear />
                <add name="SqlWebEventProvider"
                    type="System.Web.Management.SqlWebEventProvider,System.Web"
                    connectionStringName="LocalSqlServer"
                    maxEventDetailsLength="1073741823"
                    buffer="true"
                    bufferMode="SQL Analysis" />
            </providers>
        </healthMonitoring>
    </system.web>
</configuration>
```

Events are now recorded in SQL Server 2012 on your behalf. The nice thing about the `SqlWebEventProvider` is that, as with the `SimpleMailWebEventProvider` and the `TemplatedMailWebEventProvider`, the `SqlWebEventProvider` inherits from the `BufferedWebEventProvider`. This means that the web events can be written in batches as opposed to one by one. You trigger these batches by using the `buffer` and `bufferMode` attributes in the provider declaration. It works in conjunction with the settings applied in the `<bufferModes>` section of the `<healthMonitoring>` declarations.

System.Web.Management.TraceWebEventProvider

One method of debugging an ASP.NET application is to use the tracing capability built into the system. Tracing enables you to view details on the request, application state, cookies, the control tree, the form collection, and more. You output web events to the trace output via the `TraceWebEventProvider` object. Setting the `TraceWebEventProvider` instance in a configuration file is shown in Listing 14-22.

LISTING 14-22: Writing web events to the trace output using TraceWebEventProvider

```
<configuration>
    <system.web>
        <healthMonitoring>
            <!-- Other nodes removed for clarity -->
            <providers>
                <clear />
                <add name="TraceWebEventProvider"
                    type="System.Web.Management.TraceWebEventProvider,System.Web"
                    maxEventLength="4096"
                    maxMessagesPerNotification="1" />
            </providers>
        </healthMonitoring>
    </system.web>
</configuration>
```

Remember, even with the provider in place, you must assign the provider to the particular errors you want to trap. You do so through the `<rules>` section of the health monitoring system.

The `IisTraceWebEventProvider` is the same, except that the tracing information is sent to IIS rather than to the ASP.NET tracing system.

System.Web.Management.WmiWebEventProvider

The last provider built into the health monitoring system is the `WmiWebEventProvider`. This provider enables you to map any web events that come from the health monitoring system to Windows Management Instrumentation (WMI) events. When you pass events to the WMI subsystem, you can represent the events as objects.

By default, the `WmiWebEventProvider` is already set up for you, and you simply need to map the web events you are interested in to the already declared `WmiWebEventProvider` in the `<rules>` section of the health monitoring declaration. This declaration is documented in the `web.config.comments` file in the CONFIG folder of the Microsoft .NET Framework installed on your server and is shown in Listing 14-23 (the `WmiWebEventProvider` appears in bold).

LISTING 14-23: The WmiWebEventProvider definition in the web.config.comments file

```
<configuration>
    <system.web>
        <healthMonitoring>
            <!-- Other nodes removed for clarity -->
            <providers>
                <clear />
                <add name="EventLogProvider"
                    type="System.Web.Management.EventLogWebEventProvider,
                    System.Web,Version=4.0.0.0,Culture=neutral,
                    PublicKeyToken=b03f5f7f11d50a3a" />
                <add connectionStringName="LocalSqlServer"
                    maxEventDetailsLength="1073741823" buffer="false"
                    bufferMode="Notification" name="SqlWebEventProvider"
                    type="System.Web.Management.SqlWebEventProvider,
                    System.Web,Version=4.0.0.0,Culture=neutral,
                    PublicKeyToken=b03f5f7f11d50a3a" />
                <add name="WmiWebEventProvider"
                    type="System.Web.Management.WmiWebEventProvider,
                    System.Web,Version=4.0.0.0,Culture=neutral,
                    PublicKeyToken=b03f5f7f11d50a3a" />
            </providers>
        </healthMonitoring>
    </system.web>
</configuration>
```

Remember, the wonderful thing about how the health monitoring system uses the provider model is that it permits more than a single provider for the web events that the system traps.

Configuration Providers

A wonderful feature of ASP.NET 4.5 is that it enables you to actually encrypt sections of your configuration files. You are able to encrypt defined ASP.NET sections of the `web.config` file as well as custom sections that you have placed in the file yourself. This is an ideal way of keeping sensitive configuration information away from the eyes of everyone who peruses the file repository of your application.

By default, ASP.NET 4.5 provides two possible configuration providers out of the box. These providers are defined as follows:

➤ System.Configuration.DpapiProtectedConfigurationProvider: Provides you with the capability to encrypt and decrypt configuration sections using the Data Protection API (DPAPI) that is built into the Windows operating system.

➤ System.Configuration.RsaProtectedConfigurationProvider: Provides you with the capability to encrypt and decrypt configuration sections using an RSA public-key encryption algorithm.

These two providers used for encryption and decryption of the configuration sections inherit from the ProtectedConfigurationProvider base class, as illustrated in Figure 14-15.

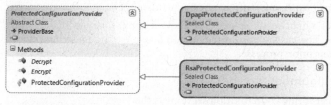

FIGURE 14-15

> **NOTE** *You can find information on how to use these providers to encrypt and decrypt configuration sections in Chapter 28.*

Next, this chapter takes you through each of these providers.

System.Configuration.DpapiProtectedConfigurationProvider

The DpapiProtectedConfigurationProvider class enables you to encrypt and decrypt configuration sections using the Windows Data Protection API (DPAPI). This provider enables you to perform these encryption and decryption tasks on a per-machine basis. This provider is not good to use on a web farm. If you are using protected configuration on your configuration files in a web farm, you might want to turn your attention to the RsaProtectedConfigurationProvider.

If you look in the machine.config on your server, you see a definition in place for both the DpapiProtectedConfigurationProvider and the RsaProtectedConfigurationProvider. The RsaProtectedConfigurationProvider is set as the default configuration provider. To establish the DpapiProtectedConfigurationProvider as the default provider, you might use the web.config file of your application, or you might change the defaultProvider attribute in the machine.config file for the <configProtectedData> node. Changing it in the web.config file is shown in Listing 14-24.

LISTING 14-24: Using the DpapiProtectedConfigurationProvider in the web.config file

```
<configuration>
    <configProtectedData defaultProvider="DataProtectionConfigurationProvider">
        <providers>
            <clear />
            <add name="DataProtectionConfigurationProvider"
                type="System.Configuration.DpapiProtectedConfigurationProvider,
                System.Configuration, Version=4.0.0.0,
                Culture=neutral, PublicKeyToken=b03f5f7f11d50a3a"
                description="Uses CryptProtectData and CryptUnProtectData Windows
                APIs to encrypt and decrypt"
                useMachineProtection="true"
                keyEntropy="RandomStringValue" />
        </providers>
    </configProtectedData>
</configuration>
```

The provider is defined within the `<configProtectedData>` section of the configuration file. Note that this configuration section sits *outside* the `<system.web>` section.

The two main attributes of this provider definition are as follows:

➤ The `useMachineProtection` attribute by default is set to `true`, meaning that all applications in the server share the same means of encrypting and decrypting configuration sections. This also means that applications residing on the same machine can perform encryption and decryption against each other. Setting the `useMachineProtection` attribute to `false` means that the encryption and decryption are done on an application basis only. This setting also means that you must change the account that the application runs against so it is different from the other applications on the server.

➤ The `keyEntropy` attribute provides a lightweight approach to prevent applications from decrypting each other's configuration sections. The `keyEntropy` attribute can take any random string value to take part in the encryption and decryption processes.

System.Configuration.RsaProtectedConfigurationProvider

The default provider for encrypting and decrypting configuration sections is the `RsaProtectedConfigurationProvider`. You can see this setting in the `machine.config` file on your application server. Listing 14-25 presents code from the `machine.config` file.

LISTING 14-25: The RsaProtectedConfigurationProvider declaration in the machine.config file

```
<configuration>
    <configProtectedData defaultProvider="RsaProtectedConfigurationProvider">
        <providers>
            <add name="RsaProtectedConfigurationProvider"
                type="System.Configuration.RsaProtectedConfigurationProvider,
                System.Configuration, Version=4.0.0.0, Culture=neutral,
                PublicKeyToken=b03f5f7f11d50a3a"
                description="Uses RsaCryptoServiceProvider to encrypt and decrypt"
                keyContainerName="NetFrameworkConfigurationKey" cspProviderName=""
                useMachineContainer="true" useOAEP="false" />
            <add name="DataProtectionConfigurationProvider"
                type="System.Configuration.DpapiProtectedConfigurationProvider,
                System.Configuration, Version=4.0.0.0, Culture=neutral,
                PublicKeyToken=b03f5f7f11d50a3a"
                description="Uses CryptProtectData and CryptUnProtectData
                Windows APIs to encrypt and decrypt"
                useMachineProtection="true" keyEntropy="" />
        </providers>
    </configProtectedData>
</configuration>
```

The `RsaProtectedConfigurationProvider` uses Triple-DES encryption to encrypt the specified sections of the configuration file. This provider has only a few attributes available to it.

The `keyContainerName` attribute is the defined key container that is used for the encryption/decryption process. By default, this provider uses the default key container built into the .NET Framework, but you can easily switch an application to another key container via this attribute.

The `cspProviderName` attribute is used only if you have specified a custom cryptographic service provider (CSP) to use with the Windows Cryptographic API (CAPI). If so, you specify the name of the CSP as the value of the `cspProviderName` attribute.

The `useMachineContainer` attribute enables you to specify that you want either a machine-wide or user-specific key container. This attribute is quite similar to the `useMachineProtection` attribute found in the `DpapiProtectedConfigurationProvider`.

The useOAEP attribute specifies whether to turn on the Optional Asymmetric Encryption and Padding (OAEP) capability when performing the encryption/decryption process.

> **CONFIGURING PROVIDERS**
>
> As you have seen in this chapter, you can easily associate these systems in ASP.NET 4.5 to a large base of available providers. From there, you can also configure the behavior of the associated providers through the attributes exposed from the providers. You can easily do this configuring through either the system-wide configuration files (such as the machine.config file) or through more application-specific configuration files (such as the web.config file).

SUMMARY

This chapter covered the basics of the provider model and what providers are available to you as you start working with the various ASP.NET systems at your disposal. Understanding the built-in providers available for each of these systems and how you can fine-tune the behaviors of each provider is important.

This provider model allows for an additional level of abstraction and permits you to decide for yourself on the underlying data stores to be used for the various systems. For example, you have the power to decide whether to store the membership and role management information in SQL Server or in Oracle without making any changes to business or presentation logic!

The next chapter shows you how to take the provider model to the next level.

15

Extending the Provider Model

WHAT'S IN THIS CHAPTER?

➤ Modifying and extending providers

➤ Building your own providers

WROX.COM CODE DOWNLOADS FOR THIS CHAPTER

Please note that all the code examples in this chapter are available as a part of this chapter's code download on the book's website at www.wrox.com on the Download Code tab.

The previous chapter introduced the provider model found in ASP.NET 4.5 and explained how it is used with the membership and role management systems.

As discussed in the previous chapter, these systems in ASP.NET 4.5 require that some type of user state be maintained for long periods of time. Their time-interval and security requirements for state storage are greater than those for earlier systems that simply used the Session object. Out of the box, ASP .NET 4.5 gives you a series of providers to use as the underlying connectors for any data storage needs that arise from state management for these systems.

The providers that come with the default install of the .NET Framework 4.5 include the most common means of state management data storage needed to work with any of the systems. But like most things in .NET, you can customize and extend the providers that are supplied.

This chapter looks at some of the ways to extend the provider model found in ASP.NET 4.5. This chapter also reviews a couple of sample extensions to the provider model. First, however, you look at some of the simpler ways to modify and extend the providers already present in the default install of .NET 4.5.

PROVIDERS ARE ONE TIER IN A LARGER ARCHITECTURE

Remember from the previous chapter that providers enable you to define the data-access tier for many of the systems in ASP.NET 4.5. They also enable you to define your core business logic implementation on how the data is manipulated or handled. They enable you to use the various controls and APIs that compose these systems in a uniform manner regardless of the underlying data storage method of the provider. The provider model also enables you to easily swap one provider for another without affecting the underlying controls and API that are interacting with the provider. Figure 15-1 presents this model.

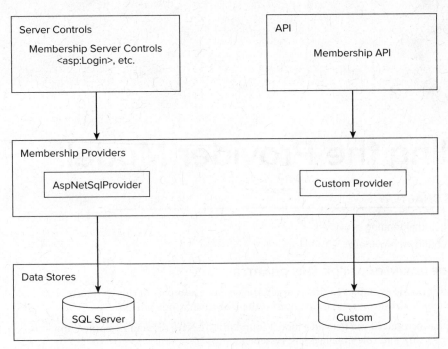

FIGURE 15-1

From this diagram, you can see that both the controls utilized in the membership system, as well as the Membership API, use the defined provider. Changing the underlying provider does not change the controls or the API, but you can definitely modify how these items behave (as you see shortly). You can also simply change the location where the state management required by these items is stored.

> **NOTE** *Besides the samples covered in this chapter, you can use the ASP.NET Universal Providers (by installing the Microsoft.AspNet.Providers package in Package Manager). The Universal Providers do not alter the API, but they do replace the data store mechanism from the built-in providers. As mentioned in the previous chapter, you can find more on this topic in Chapters 18 and 19.*

MODIFYING THROUGH ATTRIBUTE-BASED PROGRAMMING

Probably the easiest way to modify the behaviors of the providers built into the .NET Framework 4.5 is through attribute-based programming. In ASP.NET 4.5, you can apply advanced behavior modification through attribute usage. Using the definitions of the providers found in either the machine.config files or within the root web.config file, you can change the provider behavior. This chapter provides an example of how to modify the SqlMembershipProvider.

Simpler Password Structures through the SqlMembershipProvider

When you create users with the `SqlMembershipProvider` instance, whether you are using SQL Server Express or Microsoft's SQL Server 2005, 2008, or 2012, notice that the password required to create a user is a "semi-strong" password. This is evident when you create a user through the ASP.NET Web Site Administration Tool, as illustrated in Figure 15-2. For more about the ASP.NET Web Site Administration Tool, check out Appendix D.

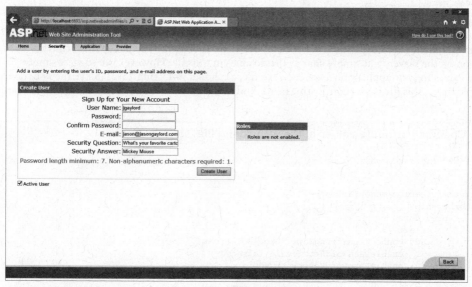

FIGURE 15-2

On this screen, I attempted to enter a password and was notified that the password did not meet the application's requirements. Instead, I was warned that the minimum password length is seven characters and that at least one non-alphanumeric character is required. This means that a password such as *Micro$oft* is what is required. This kind of behavior is specified by the membership provider and not by the controls or the API used in the membership system. You find the definition of the requirements in the `machine.config` `.comments` file located at `C:\WINDOWS\Microsoft.NET\Framework\v4.0.xxxxx\CONFIG`. Listing 15-1 presents this definition.

LISTING 15-1: The SqlMembershipProvider instance declaration

```xml
<?xml version="1.0"?>
<configuration>
    <system.web>
        <membership defaultProvider="AspNetSqlMembershipProvider"
                userIsOnlineTimeWindow="15" hashAlgorithmType="">
            <providers>
                <clear />
                <add connectionStringName="LocalSqlServer"
                    enablePasswordRetrieval="false"
                    enablePasswordReset="true" requiresQuestionAndAnswer="true"
                    applicationName="/" requiresUniqueEmail="false"
                    passwordFormat="Hashed" maxInvalidPasswordAttempts="5"
                    minRequiredPasswordLength="7"
                    minRequiredNonalphanumericCharacters="1"
                    passwordAttemptWindow="10"
                    passwordStrengthRegularExpression=""
```

continues

LISTING 15-1 *(continued)*

```
                name="AspNetSqlMembershipProvider"
                type="System.Web.Security.SqlMembershipProvider, System.Web,
                    Version=4.0.0.0, Culture=neutral,
                    PublicKeyToken=b03f5f7f11d50a3a" />
            </providers>
        </membership>
    </system.web>
</configuration>
```

Looking over the attributes of this provider, notice that the `minRequiredPasswordLength` and the `minRequiredNonalphanumericCharacters` attributes define this behavior. To change this behavior across every application on the server, you simply change these values in this file. However, we suggest simply changing these values in your application's `web.config` file, as shown in Listing 15-2. (Since the `web.config` changes multiple times, this file is saved as Listing15-02.xml in the code download for this chapter for easier downloading.)

LISTING 15-2: Changing attribute values in the web.config file

```
<?xml version="1.0" ?>
<configuration>
    <system.web>
        <authentication mode="Forms" />
        <membership>
            <providers>
                <clear />
                <add connectionStringName="LocalSqlServer"
                    enablePasswordRetrieval="false"
                    enablePasswordReset="true"
                    requiresQuestionAndAnswer="true"
                    applicationName="/" requiresUniqueEmail="false"
                    passwordFormat="Hashed" maxInvalidPasswordAttempts="5"
                    minRequiredPasswordLength="4"
                    minRequiredNonalphanumericCharacters="0"
                    passwordAttemptWindow="10"
                    name="AspNetSqlMembershipProvider"
                    type="System.Web.Security.SqlMembershipProvider,
                        System.Web, Version=4.0.0.0, Culture=neutral,
                        PublicKeyToken=b03f5f7f11d50a3a" />
            </providers>
        </membership>
    </system.web>
</configuration>
```

In this example, the password requirements are changed through the `minRequiredPasswordLength` and `minRequiredNonalphanumericCharacters` attributes. In this case, the minimum length allowed for a password is four characters, and none of those characters is required to be non-alphanumeric (for example, a special character such as !, $, or #).

Redefining a provider in the application's `web.config` file is a fairly simple process. In the example in Listing 15-2, you can see that the `<membership>` element is quite similar to the same element presented in the `machine.config` file.

You have a couple of options when defining your own instance of the `SqlMembershipProvider`. One approach, as presented in Listing 15-2, is to redefine the named instance of the `SqlMembershipProvider` that is defined in the `machine.config` file (`AspNetSqlMembershipProvider`, the value from the name attribute in the provider declaration). If you take this approach, you must *clear* the previous defined instance of `AspNetSqlMembershipProvider`. You must redefine the `AspNetSqlMembershipProvider` using the `<clear />` node within the `<providers>` section. Failure to do so causes an error to be thrown stating that this provider name is already defined.

After you have cleared the previous instance of `AspNetSqlMembershipProvider`, you redefine this provider using the `<add>` element. In the case of Listing 15-2, you can see that the password requirements are redefined with the use of new values for the `minRequiredPasswordLength` and the `minRequiredNonalphanumericCharacters` attributes (shown in bold).

The other approach to defining your own instance of the `SqlMembershipProvider` is to give the provider defined in the `<add>` element a unique value for the `name` attribute. If you take this approach, you must specify this new named instance as the default provider of the membership system using the `defaultProvider` attribute. Listing 15-3 presents this approach. (Since the `web.config` changes multiple times, this file is saved as Listing15-03.xml in the code download for this chapter for easier downloading.)

LISTING 15-3: Defining your own named instance of the SqlMembershipProvider

```xml
<?xml version="1.0"?>
<configuration>
    <system.web>
        <authentication mode="Forms" />
        <membership defaultProvider="JasonsSqlMembershipProvider">
            <providers>
                <add connectionStringName="LocalSqlServer"
                    enablePasswordRetrieval="false"
                    enablePasswordReset="true"
                    requiresQuestionAndAnswer="true"
                    applicationName="/" requiresUniqueEmail="false"
                    passwordFormat="Hashed" maxInvalidPasswordAttempts="5"
                    minRequiredPasswordLength="4"
                    minRequiredNonalphanumericCharacters="0"
                    passwordAttemptWindow="10"
                    name="JasonsSqlMembershipProvider"
                    type="System.Web.Security.SqlMembershipProvider,
                        System.Web, Version=4.0.0.0, Culture=neutral,
                        PublicKeyToken=b03f5f7f11d50a3a" />
            </providers>
        </membership>
    </system.web>
</configuration>
```

In this case, the `SqlMembershipProvider` instance in the `machine.config` file (defined under the `JasonsSqlMembershipProvider` name) is not even redefined. Instead, a completely new named instance (`JasonsSqlMembershipProvider`) is defined here in the `web.config` file.

Stronger Password Structures through the SqlMembershipProvider

Next, let's make the password structure a bit more complicated. You can, of course, accomplish this task in a couple of ways. One approach is to use the same `minRequiredPasswordLength` and `minRequiredNonalphanumericCharacters` attributes (as shown earlier) to make the password meet a required length (longer passwords usually mean more secure passwords) and to make the password contain a certain number of non-alphanumeric characters (which also makes for a more secure password).

Another option is to use the `passwordStrengthRegularExpression` attribute. If the `minRequiredPasswordLength` and the `minRequiredNonalphanumericCharacters` attributes cannot give you the password structure you are searching for, using the `passwordStrengthRegularExpression` attribute is your next best alternative.

For an example of using this attribute, suppose you require that the user's password contains the following:

➤ At least one (1) uppercase letter

➤ At least one (1) lowercase letter

➤ At least one (1) number

➤ At least one (1) special character

➤ At least eight (8) characters in length

You can then define your provider as shown in Listing 15-4. (Since the `web.config` changes multiple times, this file is saved as Listing15-04.xml in the code download for this chapter for easier downloading.)

LISTING 15-4: A provider instance in the web.config file to change the password structure

```xml
<?xml version="1.0"?>
<configuration>
    <system.web>
        <authentication mode="Forms" />
        <membership defaultProvider="JasonsSqlMembershipProvider">
            <providers>
                <add connectionStringName="LocalSqlServer"
                    enablePasswordRetrieval="false"
                    enablePasswordReset="true"
                    requiresQuestionAndAnswer="true"
                    applicationName="/" requiresUniqueEmail="false"
                    passwordFormat="Hashed" maxInvalidPasswordAttempts="5"
                    passwordStrengthRegularExpression=
                        "(?=^.{8,}$)(?=.*\d)(?=.*\W+)(?![.\n])(?=.*[A-Z])(?=.*[a-z]).*$"
                    passwordAttemptWindow="10"
                    name="JasonsSqlMembershipProvider"
                    type="System.Web.Security.SqlMembershipProvider,
                        System.Web, Version=4.0.0.0, Culture=neutral,
                        PublicKeyToken=b03f5f7f11d50a3a" />
            </providers>
        </membership>
    </system.web>
</configuration>
```

Instead of using the `minRequiredPasswordLength` and the `minRequiredNonalphanumericCharacters` attributes, the `passwordStrengthRegularExpression` attribute is used and given a value of `(?=^.{8,}$)(?=.*\d)(?=.*\W+)(?![.\n])(?=.*[A-Z])(?=.*[a-z]).*$`.

> **NOTE** *You can find several online resources for discovering regular expressions. As mentioned in Chapter 6, one of the most popular Internet sites for finding regular expressions is called RegExLib, found at* `www.regexlib.com`.

The lesson here is that you have many ways to modify the behaviors of the providers already available in the .NET Framework 4.5 install. You can adapt a number of providers built into the framework to suit your needs by using attribute-based programming. The `SqlMembershipProvider` example demonstrated this technique, and you can just as easily make similar types of modifications to any of the other providers.

EXAMINING PROVIDERBASE

All the providers derive in some fashion from the `ProviderBase` class, found in the `System.Configuration.Provider` namespace. `ProviderBase` is an abstract class used to define a base template for inheriting providers. Looking at `ProviderBase`, note that there isn't much to this abstract class, as illustrated in Figure 15-3.

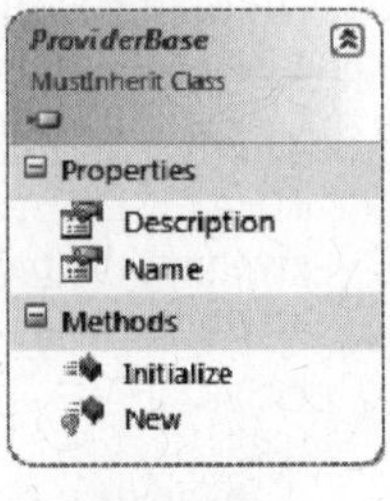

FIGURE 15-3

As stated, there is not much to this class. It is really just a root class for a provider that exists to allow providers to initialize themselves.

The `Name` property is used to provide a friendly name, such as `AspNetSqlRoleProvider`. The `Description` property is used to enable a textual description of the provider, which can then be used later by any administration tools. The main item in the `ProviderBase` class is the `Initialize()` method. Here is the constructor for `Initialize()`:

```
public virtual void Initialize(string name, NameValueCollection config)
```

Note the two parameters to the `Initialize()` method. The first is the `name` parameter, which is simply the value assigned to the `name` attribute in the provider declaration in the configuration file. The `config` parameter is of type `NameValueCollection`, which is a collection of name and value pairs. These name/value pairs are the items that are also defined in the provider declaration in the configuration file as all the various attributes and their associated values.

When looking over the providers that are included in the default install of ASP.NET 4.5, note that each of the providers has defined a class you can derive from that implements the `ProviderBase` abstract class. For example, looking at the model in place for the membership system, you can see a base `MembershipProvider` instance that is inherited in the final `SqlMembershipProvider` declaration. The `MembershipProvider`, however, implements the `ProviderBase` itself. Figure 15-4 presents this model.

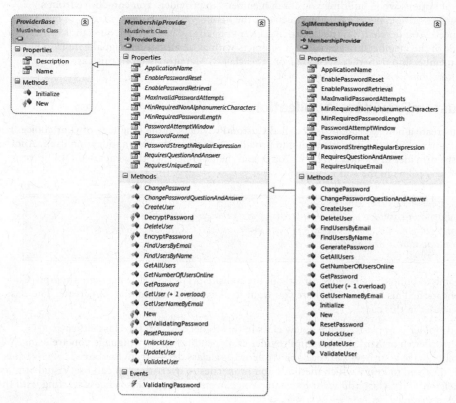

FIGURE 15-4

Notice that each of the various systems has a specific base provider implementation for you to work with. There really cannot be a single provider that addresses the needs of all the available systems. Looking at Figure 15-4, you can see that the `MembershipProvider` instance exposes some very specific functionality required by the ASP.NET membership system. The methods exposed are definitely not needed by the role management system or the Web Parts capability.

With these various base implementations in place, when you are creating your own customizations for working with the ASP.NET membership system, you have several options available to you. First, you can simply create your own provider that implements the `ProviderBase`. We do not recommend this approach, however, because abstract classes are already in place for you to use with the various systems. Therefore, as mentioned, you can implement the `MembershipProvider` instance (a better approach) and work from the model it provides. Finally, if you are working with SQL Server in some capacity and simply want to change the underlying behaviors of this provider, you can inherit from `SqlMembershipProvider` and modify the behavior of the class from this inheritance. The next section evaluates the various means of extending the provider model through examples.

BUILDING YOUR OWN PROVIDERS

You now examine the process of building your own provider to use within your ASP.NET application. Actually, providers are not that difficult to put together (as you see shortly) and can even be created directly in any of your ASP.NET 4.5 projects. The example demonstrates building a membership provider that works from an XML file. For a smaller website, this scenario might be common. For larger websites and web-based applications, you probably want to use a database of some kind, rather than an XML file, for managing users.

You have a couple of options when building your own membership provider. You can derive from a couple of classes—the `SqlMembershipProvider` class or the `MembershipProvider` class—to build the functionality you need. You derive from the `SqlMembershipProvider` class only if you want to extend or change the behavior of the membership system as it interacts with SQL. Because the goal here is to build a read-only XML membership provider, deriving from this class is inappropriate. In this case, basing everything on the `MembershipProvider` class is best.

Creating the CustomProviders Application

In this section, you create a new website project called CustomProviders in the language of your choice. For this example, you want to build the new membership provider directly in the web application itself. Another option is to build the provider in a Class Library project and then to reference the generated DLL in your web project. Either way is fine in the end.

> **NOTE** *For the examples in this chapter, we have created Chapter15-CustomProviders-VB and Chapter15-CustomProviders-CS, respectively, for the code download available at* www.wrox.com.

Because you are going to build this provider directly in the website project itself, you create the App_Code folder in your application. This location is where you want to place the class file that you create. The class file is the actual provider in this case.

After the App_Code folder is in place, create a new class in this folder and call the class either **XmlMembershipProvider.vb** or **XmlMembershipProvider.cs**, depending on the language you are using. With this class now in place, have your new `XmlMembershipProvider` class derive from `MembershipProvider`. To accomplish this task and to know which methods and properties to override, you can use Visual Studio 2012 to build a skeleton of the class you want to create. You can step through this process starting with the code demonstrated in Listing 15-5.

LISTING 15-5: The start of your XmlMembershipProvider class

VB

```
Public Class XmlMembershipProvider
    Inherits MembershipProvider
End Class
```

C#

```
namespace Chapter15_CustomProviders_CS.App_Code
{
    public class XmlMembershipProvider : MembershipProvider
    {
    }
}
```

To start, you'll make one change to this new class, the `XmlMembershipProvider` class. You'll update it to inherit from `MembershipProvider`.

Constructing the Class Skeleton Required

To get Visual Studio 2012 to stub out your class with the appropriate methods and properties, take the following steps (depending on the language you are using). If you are using Visual Basic, all you have to do is press the Enter key. In C#, all you have to do is right-click the `MembershipProvider` statement in your code and simply select Implement Abstract Class from the available options. Another option is to place the cursor on the `MembershipProvider` statement in the document window and then select Edit ⇨ IntelliSense ⇨ Implement Abstract Class from the Visual Studio menu. After you perform one of these operations, you see the full skeleton of the class in the document window of Visual Studio. Listing 15-6 shows the code that is generated if you are creating a C# `XmlMembershipProvider` class (you'll soon see why we are only showing the C# example here).

LISTING 15-6: Code generated for the XmlMembershipProvider class by Visual Studio

C#

```
namespace Chapter15_CustomProviders_CS.App_Code
{
    public class XmlMembershipProvider : MembershipProvider
    {
        public override string ApplicationName
        {
            get
            {
                throw new NotImplementedException();
            }
            set
            {
                throw new NotImplementedException();
            }
        }

        public override bool ChangePassword(string username, string oldPassword,
          string newPassword)
        {
            throw new NotImplementedException();
        }

        public override bool ChangePasswordQuestionAndAnswer(string username, string password,
          string newPasswordQuestion, string newPasswordAnswer)
```

continues

LISTING 15-6 *(continued)*

```
{
    throw new NotImplementedException();
}

public override MembershipUser CreateUser(string username, string password,
  string email, string passwordQuestion, string passwordAnswer, bool isApproved,
  object providerUserKey, out MembershipCreateStatus status)
{
    throw new NotImplementedException();
}

public override bool DeleteUser(string username, bool deleteAllRelatedData)
{
    throw new NotImplementedException();
}

public override bool EnablePasswordReset
{
    get { throw new NotImplementedException(); }
}

public override bool EnablePasswordRetrieval
{
    get { throw new NotImplementedException(); }
}

public override MembershipUserCollection FindUsersByEmail(string emailToMatch,
  int pageIndex, int pageSize, out int totalRecords)
{
    throw new NotImplementedException();
}

public override MembershipUserCollection FindUsersByName(string usernameToMatch,
  int pageIndex, int pageSize, out int totalRecords)
{
    throw new NotImplementedException();
}

public override MembershipUserCollection GetAllUsers(int pageIndex, int pageSize,
  out int totalRecords)
{
    throw new NotImplementedException();
}

public override int GetNumberOfUsersOnline()
{
    throw new NotImplementedException();
}

public override string GetPassword(string username, string answer)
{
    throw new NotImplementedException();
}

public override MembershipUser GetUser(string username, bool userIsOnline)
{
    throw new NotImplementedException();
}

public override MembershipUser GetUser(object providerUserKey, bool userIsOnline)
```

```
    {
        throw new NotImplementedException();
    }

    public override string GetUserNameByEmail(string email)
    {
        throw new NotImplementedException();
    }

    public override int MaxInvalidPasswordAttempts
    {
        get { throw new NotImplementedException(); }
    }

    public override int MinRequiredNonAlphanumericCharacters
    {
        get { throw new NotImplementedException(); }
    }

    public override int MinRequiredPasswordLength
    {
        get { throw new NotImplementedException(); }
    }

    public override int PasswordAttemptWindow
    {
        get { throw new NotImplementedException(); }
    }

    public override MembershipPasswordFormat PasswordFormat
    {
        get { throw new NotImplementedException(); }
    }

    public override string PasswordStrengthRegularExpression
    {
        get { throw new NotImplementedException(); }
    }

    public override bool RequiresQuestionAndAnswer
    {
        get { throw new NotImplementedException(); }
    }

    public override bool RequiresUniqueEmail
    {
        get { throw new NotImplementedException(); }
    }

    public override string ResetPassword(string username, string answer)
    {
        throw new NotImplementedException();
    }

    public override bool UnlockUser(string userName)
    {
        throw new NotImplementedException();
    }

    public override void UpdateUser(MembershipUser user)
    {
        throw new NotImplementedException();
```

continues

LISTING 15-6 *(continued)*

```
        }

        public override bool ValidateUser(string username, string password)
        {
            throw new NotImplementedException();
        }
    }
}
```

Wow, that's a lot of code! Although the skeleton is in place, the next step is to code some of the items that will be utilized by the provider that Visual Studio laid out for you—starting with the XML file that holds all the users allowed to access the application.

Creating the XML User Data Store

Because this provider is an XML membership provider, the intent is to read the user information from an XML file rather than from a database such as SQL Server. For this reason, you must define the XML file structure that the provider can use. Listing 15-7 shows the structure used for this example (App_Data\Users .xml in each of the respective projects).

LISTING 15-7: The XML file used to store usernames and passwords

```xml
<?xml version="1.0" encoding="utf-8" ?>
<Users>
    <User>
        <Username>JasonGaylord</Username>
        <Password>Reindeer</Password>
        <Email>jason@jasongaylord.com</Email>
        <DateCreated>12/10/2012</DateCreated>
    </User>
    <User>
        <Username>ScottHanselman</Username>
        <Password>YabbaDabbaDo</Password>
        <Email>scott@outlook.com</Email>
        <DateCreated>12/02/2012</DateCreated>
    </User>
    <User>
        <Username>ChristianWenz</Username>
        <Password>BamBam</Password>
        <Email>christian@outlook.com</Email>
        <DateCreated>01/11/2013</DateCreated>
    </User>
</Users>
```

This XML file holds three user instances, all of which include the username, password, e-mail address, and the date on which the user is created. Because it is a data file, you should place this file in the App_Data folder of your ASP.NET application. You can name the file anything you want; but in this case, we have named the file Users.xml.

Later, this chapter reviews how to grab these values from the XML file when validating users.

Defining the Provider Instance in the web.config File

As you saw in the previous chapter on providers, you define a provider and its behavior in a configuration file (such as the machine.config or the web.config file). Because this provider is being built for a single application instance, this example defines the provider in the web.config file of the application.

The default provider is the `SqlMembershipProvider`, which is defined in the `machine.config` file on the server. For this example, you must override this setting and establish a new default provider. The XML membership provider declaration in the `web.config` should appear as shown in Listing 15-8.

LISTING 15-8: Defining the XmlMembershipProvider in the web.config file

```xml
<?xml version="1.0"?>
<configuration>
    <system.web>
        <compilation debug="true" targetFramework="4.5" />
        <httpRuntime targetFramework="4.5" />
        <authentication mode="Forms"/>
        <membership defaultProvider="XmlFileProvider">
            <providers>
                <add name="XmlFileProvider" type="XmlMembershipProvider"
                 xmlUserDatabaseFile="/App_Data/Users.xml"/>
            </providers>
        </membership>
    </system.web>
</configuration>
```

In this listing, you can see that the default provider is defined as the `XmlFileProvider`. Because this provider name will not be found in any of the parent configuration files, you must define `XmlFileProvider` in the `web.config` file.

Using the `defaultProvider` attribute, you can define the name of the provider you want to use for the membership system. In this case, it is `XmlFileProvider`. Then you define the `XmlFileProvider` instance using the `<add>` element within the `<providers>` section. The `<add>` element gives a name for the provider — `XmlFileProvider`. It also points to the class (or type) of the provider. In this case, it is the skeleton class you just created — `XmlMembershipProvider`.

> **NOTE** *The provider type may need a fully qualified class name, meaning that the class name is preceded with the appropriate namespace.*

Beyond the attributes already used so far, you can create any attribute in your provider declaration that you want. Whatever type of provider you create, however, you must address the attributes in your provider and act upon the values that are provided with the attributes. In the case of the simple `XmlMembershipProvider`, only a single custom attribute exists — `xmlUserDatabaseFile`. This attribute points to the location of the user database XML file. For this provider, it is an optional attribute. If you do not provide a value for `xmlUserDatabaseFile`, you have a default value. In Listing 15-8, however, you can see that a value is indeed provided for the XML file to use. Note that the `xmlUserDatabaseFile` is simply the filename.

One attribute is not shown in the example, but is an allowable attribute because it is addressed in the `XmlMembershipProvider`'s class. This attribute, the `applicationName` attribute, points to the application that the `XmlMembershipProvider` instance should address. Here is the default value, which you can also place in this provider declaration within the configuration file:

```
applicationName="/"
```

Not Implementing Methods and Properties of the MembershipProvider Class

Now, turn your attention to the `XmlMembershipProvider` class. The next step is to implement any methods or properties needed by the provider. You are not required to make any *real* use of the methods contained in this skeleton; instead, you can simply build-out only the methods you are interested in working with. For example, if you do not allow for programmatic access to change passwords (and, in turn, the controls that use this programmatic access), you either want to not initiate an action or to throw an exception if someone tries to implement this method, as shown in Listing 15-9.

LISTING 15-9: Not implementing one of the available methods by throwing an exception

VB

```
Public Overrides Function ChangePassword(username As String,
    oldPassword As String, newPassword As String) As Boolean
    Throw New NotSupportedException()
End Function
```

C#

```
public override bool ChangePassword(string username, string oldPassword,
    string newPassword)
{
    throw new NotSupportedException();
}
```

In this case, a NotSupportedException is thrown if the ChangePassword() method is invoked. If you do not want to throw an actual exception, you can simply return a false value and not take any other action, as shown in Listing 15-10 (although not throwing an exception may cause annoyance for a developer who is trying to implement this provider).

LISTING 15-10: Not implementing one of the available methods by returning a false value

VB

```
Public Overrides Function ChangePassword(username As String,
    oldPassword As String, newPassword As String) As Boolean
    Return False
End Function
```

C#

```
public override bool ChangePassword(string username, string oldPassword,
    string newPassword)
{
    return false;
}
```

This chapter does not address every possible action you can take with XmlMembershipProvider, and therefore, you may want to work through the available methods and properties of the derived MembershipProvider instance and make the necessary changes to any item that you won't be using.

Implementing Methods and Properties of the MembershipProvider Class

Now it is time to implement some of the methods and properties available from the MembershipProvider class to get the XmlMembershipProvider class to work. The first items are some private variables that multiple methods can utilize throughout the class. Listing 15-11 presents these variable declarations.

LISTING 15-11: Declaring some private variables in the XmlMembershipProvider class

VB

```
Public Class XmlMembershipProvider
    Inherits MembershipProvider

    Private _AppName As String
    Private _MyUsers As Dictionary(Of String, MembershipUser)
```

```
        Private _FileName As String

        ' Code removed for clarity
    End Class
```

C#

```
    public class XmlMembershipProvider : MembershipProvider
    {
        private string _AppName;
        private Dictionary<string, MembershipUser> _MyUsers;
        private string _FileName;

        // Code removed for clarity
    }
```

The variables being declared are items needed by multiple methods in the class. The _AppName variable defined will be set to the application name that uses the XML membership provider. In all cases, it is the local application. You also want to place all the members found in the XML file into a collection of some type. This example uses a dictionary generic type named _MyUsers. Finally, this example points to the file to use with the _FileName variable.

Defining the ApplicationName Property

After the private variables are in place, the next step is to define the ApplicationName property. You now make use of the first private variable—_AppName. Listing 15-12 presents the property definition of ApplicationName.

LISTING 15-12: Defining the ApplicationName property

VB

```
    Public Overrides Property ApplicationName() As String
        Get
            Return _AppName
        End Get
        Set(ByVal value As String)
            _AppName = value
        End Set
    End Property
```

C#

```
    public override string ApplicationName
    {
        get
        {
            return _AppName;
        }
        set
        {
            _AppName = value;
        }
    }
```

Now that the ApplicationName property is defined and in place, the next step is to retrieve the values defined in the web.config file's provider declaration (XmlFileProvider).

Extending the Initialize() Method

You now extend the Initialize() method so that it reads in the custom attribute and its associated values as defined in the provider declaration in the web.config file. Look through the class skeleton of your XmlMembershipProvider class, and note that no Initialize() method is included in the list of available items.

The `Initialize()` method is invoked when the provider is first initialized. Overriding this method is not a requirement, and therefore, you won't see it in the declaration of the class skeleton. To put the `Initialize()` method in place within the `XmlMembershipProvider` class, simply type `Public Overrides` (for Visual Basic) or `public override` (for C#) in the class. IntelliSense then presents you with the `Initialize()` method, as shown in Figure 15-5.

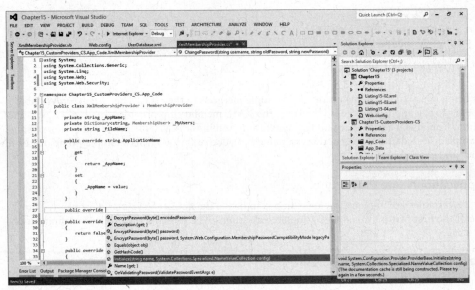

FIGURE 15-5

Placing the `Initialize()` method in your class in this manner is quite easy. Select the `Initialize()` method from the list in IntelliSense and press the Enter key. This method gives you a base construction of the method in your code, as shown in Listing 15-13.

LISTING 15-13: The beginnings of the Initialize() method

VB

```
Public Overrides Sub Initialize(ByVal name As String, _
    ByVal config As System.Collections.Specialized.NameValueCollection)
    MyBase.Initialize(name, config)
End Sub
```

C#

```
public override void Initialize(string name,
    System.Collections.Specialized.NameValueCollection config)
{
    base.Initialize(name, config);
}
```

The `Initialize()` method takes two parameters. The first parameter is the name of the parameter. The second is the name/value collection from the provider declaration in the `web.config` file. This collection includes all the attributes and their values, such as the `xmlUserDatabaseFile` attribute and the value of the name of the XML file that holds the user information. Using `config`, you can gain access to these defined values.

For the `XmlFileProvider` instance, you address the `applicationName` attribute and the `xmlUserDatabaseFile` attribute as shown in Listing 15-14.

LISTING 15-14: Extending the Initialize() method

VB

```vb
Public Overrides Sub Initialize(ByVal name As String, _
    ByVal config As System.Collections.Specialized.NameValueCollection)
    MyBase.Initialize(name, config)

    _AppName = config("applicationName")

    If (String.IsNullOrEmpty(_AppName)) Then
        _AppName = "/"
    End If

    _FileName = config("xmlUserDatabaseFile")

    If (String.IsNullOrEmpty(_FileName)) Then
        _FileName = "/App_Data/Users.xml"
    End If
End Sub
```

C#

```csharp
public override void Initialize(string name,
    System.Collections.Specialized.NameValueCollection config)
{
    base.Initialize(name, config);

    _AppName = config["applicationName"];

    if (String.IsNullOrEmpty(_AppName))
    {
        _AppName = "/";
    }

    _FileName = config["xmlUserDatabaseFile"];

    if (String.IsNullOrEmpty(_FileName))
    {
        _FileName = "/App_Data/Users.xml";
    }
}
```

Besides performing the initialization using MyBase.Initialize(), you retrieve both the applicationName and xmlUserDatabaseFile attributes' values using config. In all cases, you should first check whether the value is either null or empty. You use the String.IsNullOrEmpty() method to assign default values if the attribute is missing for the provider declaration in the web.config file. In the case of the XmlFileProvider instance, this is, in fact, the case. The applicationName attribute in the XmlFileProvider declaration is actually not declared and, for this reason, the default value of / is assigned as the value.

In the case of the xmlUserDatabaseFile attribute, a value is provided. If no value is provided in the web.config file, the provider looks for an XML file named Users.xml found in the App_Data folder.

Validating Users

One of the more important features of the membership provider is that it validates users (it authenticates them). The validation of users is accomplished through the ASP.NET Login server control. This control, in turn, makes use of the Membership.ValidateUser() method that ends up using the ValidateUser() method in the XmlMembershipProvider class.

Now that the Initialize() method and private variables are in place, you can start giving the provider some functionality. Listing 15-15 presents the implementation of the ValidateUser() method.

LISTING 15-15: Implementing the ValidateUser() method

VB

```vb
Public Overrides Function ValidateUser(username As String, password As String) _
    As Boolean
    If (String.IsNullOrEmpty(username) Or String.IsNullOrEmpty(password)) Then
        Return False
    End If

    Try
        ReadUserFile()

        Dim mu As MembershipUser

        If (_MyUsers.TryGetValue(username.ToLower(), mu)) Then
            If (mu.Comment = password) Then
                Return True
            End If
        End If

        Return False
    Catch ex As Exception
        Throw New Exception(ex.Message.ToString())
    End Try
End Function
```

C#

```csharp
public override bool ValidateUser(string username, string password)
{
    if (String.IsNullOrEmpty(username) || String.IsNullOrEmpty(password))
    {
        return false;
    }

    try
    {
        ReadUserFile();

        MembershipUser mu;

        if (_MyUsers.TryGetValue(username.ToLower(), out mu))
        {
            if (mu.Comment == password)
            {
                return true;
            }
        }

        return false;
    }
    catch (Exception ex)
    {
        throw new Exception(ex.Message.ToString());
    }
}
```

Looking over the ValidateUser() method, you can see that it takes two parameters: the username and the password of the user (both of type String). The value returned from ValidateUser() is a Boolean—just a True or False value to inform of the success or failure of the validation process.

One of the first operations performed in the `ValidateUser()` method is a check to determine whether either the username or the password is missing from the invocation. If one of these items is missing in the request, a `False` value is returned.

From there, a `Try...Catch` is done to check whether the user and the user's password are included in the XML file. The process of getting the user information out of the XML file and into the `MyUsers` variable is done by the `ReadUserFile()` method. This method is described shortly, but the important concept is that the `_MyUsers` variable is an instance of the `Dictionary` generic class. The key is a lowercase string value of the username, whereas the value is of type `MembershipUser`, a type provided via the membership system.

After the `_MyUsers` object is populated with all users in the XML file, a `MembershipUser` instance is created. This object is the output of a `TryGetValue` operation. The `MembershipUser` does not contain the password of the user, and for this reason, the `ReadUserFile()` method makes the user's password the value of the `Comment` property of the `MembershipUser` class. If the username is found in the dictionary collection, the password of that particular `MembershipUser` instance is compared to the value in the `Comment` property. The return value from the `ValidateUser()` method is `True` if they are found to be the same.

As you can see, this method really is dependent upon the results that come from the `ReadUserFile()` method, which is covered next.

Building the ReadUserFile() Method

The `ReadUserFile()` method reads the contents of the XML file that contains all the users for the application. This method is a custom method, and its work is done outside of the `ValidateUser()` method. This means you can reuse it in other methods that you might want to implement (such as the `GetAllUsers()` method). The only job of the `ReadUserFile()` method is to read the contents of the XML file and place all the users in the `_MyUsers` variable, as shown in Listing 15-16.

LISTING 15-16: The ReadUserFile() method to get all the users of the application

VB

```
Private Sub ReadUserFile()
    If (_MyUsers Is Nothing) Then
        SyncLock (Me)
            _MyUsers = New Dictionary(Of String, MembershipUser)()
            Dim query = From users In _
                            XElement.Load( _
                                HostingEnvironment.MapPath(_FileName)).Elements("User") _
                            Select users

            For Each user In query
                Dim mu As MembershipUser = New MembershipUser(Name, _
                    user.Element("Username").Value, _
                    Nothing, _
                    user.Element("Email").Value, _
                    String.Empty, _
                    user.Element("Password").Value, _
                    True, _
                    False, _
                    DateTime.Parse(user.Element("DateCreated").Value), _
                    DateTime.Now, _
                    DateTime.Now, _
                    DateTime.Now, _
                    DateTime.Now)

                _MyUsers.Add(mu.UserName.ToLower(), mu)
            Next
        End SyncLock
    End If
End Sub
```

continues

LISTING 15-16 *(continued)*

C#

```csharp
private void ReadUserFile()
{
    if (_MyUsers == null)
    {
        lock (this)
        {
            _MyUsers = new Dictionary<string, MembershipUser>();
            var query = from users in
                            XElement.Load(
                                HostingEnvironment.MapPath(_FileName)).Elements("User")
                        select users;

            foreach (var user in query)
            {
                MembershipUser mu = new MembershipUser(Name,
                    user.Element("Username").Value,
                    null,
                    user.Element("Email").Value,
                    String.Empty,
                    user.Element("Password").Value,
                    true,
                    false,
                    DateTime.Parse(user.Element("DateCreated").Value),
                    DateTime.Now,
                    DateTime.Now,
                    DateTime.Now,
                    DateTime.Now);

                _MyUsers.Add(mu.UserName.ToLower(), mu);
            }
        }
    }
}
```

> **NOTE** *You need to import the* System.Xml, System.Xml.Linq, *and* System.Web .Hosting *namespaces for this code to work.*

The first action of the ReadUserFile() method is to place a lock on the action that is going to occur in the thread being run. This is a unique feature in ASP.NET. When you are writing your own providers, be sure you use thread-safe code. For most items that you write in ASP.NET, such as an HttpModule or an HttpHandler (covered in Chapter 30), you don't need to make them thread-safe. These items may have multiple requests running on multiple threads, and each thread making a request to either the HttpModule or the HttpHandler sees a unique instance of these items.

Unlike an HttpHandler, only one instance of a provider is created and utilized by your ASP.NET application. If multiple requests are being made to your application, all these threads are trying to gain access to the single provider instance contained in the application. Because more than one request might be coming into the provider instance at the same time, you should create the provider in a thread-safe manner. You can do so by using a lock operation when performing tasks such as file I/O operations. To lock the access, use the SyncLock (for Visual Basic) and the lock (for C#) statements in the ReadUserFile() method.

The advantage of this code construction, however, is that a single instance of the provider is running in your application. After the _MyUsers object is populated with the contents of the XML file, you have no need to repopulate the object. The provider instance doesn't just disappear after a response is issued to the requestor. Instead, the provider instance is contained in memory and utilized for multiple requests, which is the reason for checking whether _MyUsers contains any values before reading the XML file.

If you find that _MyUsers is null, use LINQ to XML to get at every <User> element in the document. For each <User> element in the document, you assign the values to a MembershipUser instance. The MembershipUser object takes the following arguments:

```
public MembershipUser (
    string providerName,
    string name,
    Object providerUserKey,
    string email,
    string passwordQuestion,
    string comment,
    bool isApproved,
    bool isLockedOut,
    DateTime creationDate,
    DateTime lastLoginDate,
    DateTime lastActivityDate,
    DateTime lastPasswordChangedDate,
    DateTime lastLockoutDate
)
```

Although you do not provide a value for each and every item in this construction, the values that are really needed are pulled from the XML file using the XElement object. Then, after the MembershipUser object is populated with everything you want, the next job is to add these items to the _MyUsers object using the following:

```
_MyUsers.Add(mu.UserName.ToLower(), mu);
```

With the ReadUserFile() method in place, as stated, you can now use it in more than the ValidateUser() method. Remember that after the _MyUsers collection is populated, you don't need to repopulate the collection again. Instead, it remains in place for the other methods to use. Next, this chapter looks at using what has been demonstrated so far in your ASP.NET application.

Using the XmlMembershipProvider for User Login

If you have made it this far in the example, you do not need to do much more to make use of the XmlMembershipProvider class. At this point, you should have the XML data file in place that is a representation of all the users of your application (this XML file appears earlier in Listing 15-7) and the XmlFileProvider declaration in the web.config file of your application (the changes to the web.config file appear in Listing 15-8). Of course, another necessary item is either the XmlMembershipProvider.vb or .cs class in the App_Code folder of your application. However, if you built the provider using the Class Library project template, you want to just make sure the DLL created is referenced correctly in your ASP.NET application (which means the DLL is in the Bin folder). After you have these items in place, getting started with using the provider is simple.

For a quick example, simply create a Default.aspx page that has only the text You are authenticated!

Next, you create a Login.aspx page, and place a single Login server control on the page. You won't need to make any other changes to the Login.aspx page besides placing the control. Users can now log in to the application.

> **NOTE** *For information on the membership system, which includes detailed explanations of the various server controls it offers, visit Chapter 19.*

When you have those two files in place within your mini-ASP.NET application, the next step is to make some minor changes to the `web.config` file to allow for Forms authentication and to deny all anonymous users to view any of the pages. Listing 15-17 presents this bit of code.

LISTING 15-17: Denying anonymous users to view the application in the web.config file

```xml
<?xml version="1.0"?>
<configuration>
    <system.web>
        <compilation debug="true" targetFramework="4.5" />
        <httpRuntime targetFramework="4.5" />
        <authentication mode="Forms"/>
        <authorization>
            <deny users="?"/>
        </authorization>
        <!-- Other settings removed for clarity -->
    </system.web>
</configuration>
```

Now, run the `Default.aspx` page, and you are immediately directed to the `Login.aspx` page (you should have this file created in your application and it should contain only a single Login server control) where you apply one of the username and password combinations that are present in the XML file. It is as simple as that!

The nice thing with the provider-based model found in ASP.NET 4.5 is that the controls that are working with the providers don't know the difference when these large changes to the underlying provider are made. In this example, you have removed the default `SqlMembershipProvider` and replaced it with a read-only XML provider. When the end user clicks the Log In button within the Login server control, the control is still simply making use of the `Membership.ValidateUser()` method, which is working with the `XmlMembershipProvider` that was just created. As you should see by now, this model is powerful.

EXTENDING PREEXISTING PROVIDERS

In addition to building your own providers from one of the base abstract classes such as `MembershipProvider`, another option is to simply extend one of the preexisting providers that come with ASP.NET.

For example, you might be interested in using the membership and role management systems with SQL Server but want to change how the default providers (`SqlMembershipProvider` or `SqlRoleProvider`) work under the covers. If you are going to work with an underlying data store that is already utilized by one of the providers available out of the box, actually changing the behavior of the available provider makes a lot more sense than building a brand-new provider from the ground up.

The other advantage of working from a preexisting provider is that no need exists to override everything the provider exposes. Instead, if you are interested in changing only a particular behavior of a built-in provider, you might only need to override a couple of the exposed methods and nothing more, making this approach rather simple and quick to achieve in your application.

Next, this chapter looks at extending one of the built-in providers to change the underlying functionality of the provider.

Limiting Role Capabilities with a New LimitedSqlRoleProvider Provider

Suppose you want to utilize the role management system in your ASP.NET application and have every intention of using a SQL Server backend for the system. Suppose you also want to limit what roles developers can create in their applications, and you want to remove their capability to add users to a particular role in the system.

Instead of building a role provider from scratch from the `RoleProvider` abstract class, deriving your provider from `SqlRoleProvider` and simply changing the behavior of a few methods that deal with the creation of roles and adding users to roles makes more sense.

For this example, create the provider in your application within the App_Code folder as before. In reality, however, you probably want to create a Class Library project if you want to use this provider across your company so that your development teams can use a DLL rather than a modifiable class file.

Within the App_Code folder, create a class file called `LimitedSqlRoleProvider.vb` or `.cs`. You want this class to inherit from `SqlRoleProvider`, and this gives you the structure shown in Listing 15-18.

LISTING 15-18: The beginnings of the LimitedSqlRoleProvider class

VB

```
Imports System.Web.Security

Public Class LimitedSqlRoleProvider
    Inherits SqlRoleProvider

End Class
```

C#

```
using System;
using System.Collections.Generic;
using System.Linq;
using System.Web;
using System.Web.Security;

namespace Chapter15_CustomProviders_CS.App_Code
{
    public class LimitedSqlRoleProvider : SqlRoleProvider
    {
    }
}
```

Creating this class is similar to creating the `XmlMembershipProvider` class. When you did that, however, you were able to use Visual Studio to build the entire class skeleton of all the methods and properties you had to override to get the new class up and running. In this case, if you try to do the same thing in Visual Studio, you get an error (if using C#) or, perhaps, no result at all (if using Visual Basic) because you are not working with an abstract class. You do not need to override an enormous number of methods and properties. Instead, because you are deriving from a class that already inherits from one of these abstract classes, you can get by with overriding only the methods and properties that you must work with and nothing more.

To get at this list of methods and properties within Visual Studio, you simply type `Public Overrides` (when using Visual Basic) or `public override` (when using C#). IntelliSense then provides you with a large drop-down list of available methods and properties to work with, as shown in Figure 15-6.

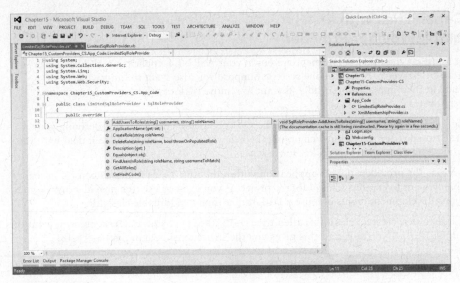

FIGURE 15-6

For this example, you only override the CreateRole(), AddUsersToRoles(), and DeleteRole() methods. They are described next.

The CreateRole() Method

The CreateRole() method in the SqlRoleProvider class enables developers to add any role to the system. The only parameter required for this method is a string value that is the name of the role. For this example, instead of letting developers create any role they want, this provider limits the role creation to only the Administrator and Manager roles. To accomplish this in the CreateRole() method, you code the method as presented in Listing 15-19.

LISTING 15-19: Allowing only the Administrator or Manager role in the CreateRole() method

VB

```vb
Public Overrides Sub CreateRole(ByVal roleName As String)
    If (roleName = "Administrator" Or roleName = "Manager") Then
        MyBase.CreateRole(roleName)
    Else
        Throw New _
            ProviderException("Role creation limited to only Administrator and Manager")
    End If
End Sub
```

C#

```csharp
public override void CreateRole(string roleName)
{
    if (roleName == "Administrator" || roleName == "Manager")
    {
        base.CreateRole(roleName);
    }
    else
    {
        throw new
            ProviderException("Role creation limited to only Administrator and Manager");
    }
}
```

> **NOTE** *You need to import the* `System.Configuration.Provider` *namespace for this code to work.*

In this method, you can see that a check is first done to determine whether the role being created is either Administrator or Manager. If the role being created is not one of these defined roles, a `ProviderException` is thrown informing the developer of which roles he or she is allowed to create.

If Administrator or Manager is one of the roles, the base class (`SqlRoleProvider`) `CreateRole()` method is invoked.

The DeleteRole() Method

If you allow developers using this provider to create only specific roles, you might not want them to delete any role after it is created. If this is the case, you want to override the `DeleteRole()` method of the `SqlRoleProvider` class, as shown in Listing 15-20.

LISTING 15-20: Disallowing the DeleteRole() method

VB

```
Public Overrides Function DeleteRole(ByVal roleName As String, _
    ByVal throwOnPopulatedRole As Boolean) As Boolean
    Return False
End Function
```

C#

```
public override bool DeleteRole(string roleName, bool throwOnPopulatedRole)
{
    return false;
}
```

Looking at the `DeleteRole()` method, you can see that deleting any role is completely disallowed. A `false` value is returned and no action is taken instead of raising the base class's `DeleteRole()` and returning the following:

```
return this.DeleteRole(roleName, throwOnPopulatedRole);
```

Another approach is to throw a `NotSupportedException`, as shown here:

```
throw new NotSupportedException();
```

The AddUsersToRoles() Method

As you look over the methods that can be overridden, notice that only one single method enables you to add any number of users to any number of roles. Multiple methods in the `Roles` class actually map to this method. If you look at the `Roles` class, notice the `AddUserToRole()`, `AddUserToRoles()`, `AddUsersToRole()`, and `AddUsersToRoles()` methods at your disposal. All these actually map to the `AddUsersToRoles()` method that is available in the `RoleProvider` base class.

For example, suppose you want to enable developers to add users only to the Manager role but not to add any users to the Administrator role. You could accomplish something like this by constructing a method, as shown in Listing 15-21.

LISTING 15-21: Disallowing users to be added to a particular role

VB

```vb
Public Overrides Sub AddUsersToRoles(ByVal usernames() As String, _
    ByVal roleNames() As String)

    For Each roleItem As String In roleNames
        If roleItem = "Administrator" Then
            Throw New _
                ProviderException("You are not authorized to add any users" & _
                    " to the Administrator role")
        End If
    Next

    MyBase.AddUsersToRoles(usernames, roleNames)
End Sub
```

C#

```csharp
public override void AddUsersToRoles(string[] usernames, string[] roleNames)
{
    foreach (string roleItem in roleNames)
    {
        if (roleItem == "Administrator")
        {
            throw new ProviderException("You are not authorized to add any users" +
                " to the Administrator role");
        }
    }

    base.AddUsersToRoles(usernames, roleNames);
}
```

This overridden method iterates through all the provided roles, and if one of the roles contained in the string array is the role Administrator, a `ProviderException` instance is thrown informing the developer that he or she is not allowed to add any users to this particular role. Although it is not shown here, you can also take the same approach with the `RemoveUsersFromRoles()` method exposed from the `RoleProvider` base class.

Using the New LimitedSqlRoleProvider Provider

After you have the provider in place and ready to use, you have to make some modifications to the `web.config` file in order to use this provider in your ASP.NET application. You learn how you add what you need to the `web.config` file for this provider in Listing 15-22.

LISTING 15-22: Making the appropriate changes to the web.config file for the provider

```xml
<?xml version="1.0"?>
<configuration>
    <system.web>
        <roleManager defaultProvider="LimitedProvider" enabled="true">
            <providers>
                <add connectionStringName="LocalSqlServer" applicationName="/"
                  name="LimitedProvider"
                  type="LimitedSqlRoleProvider" />
            </providers>
        </roleManager>
    </system.web>
</configuration>
```

Remember that you have to define the provider to use in your application by providing a value for the `defaultProvider` attribute and defining that provider further in the `<providers>` section. You also have to enable the provider by setting the `enabled` attribute to `true`. By default, the role management system is disabled.

Using the `<add>` element, you can add a provider instance that makes use of the `LimitedSqlRoleProvider` class. Because this provider derives from the `SqlRoleProvider` class, you must use some of the same attributes that this provider requires, such as the `connectionStringName` attribute that points to the connection string to use to connect to the specified SQL instance.

After you have the new `LimitedSqlRoleProvider` instance in place and defined in the `web.config` file, you can use the `Roles` class in your application just as you normally would, but notice the behavior of this class is rather different from the normal `SqlRoleProvider`.

To see it in action, construct a simple ASP.NET page that includes a TextBox, Button, and Label server control. The page should appear as shown in Listing 15-23.

LISTING 15-23: Using Roles.CreateRole()

VB

```
<%@ Page Language="VB" %>
<script runat="server">
    Protected Sub Button1_Click(ByVal sender As Object, _
      ByVal e As System.EventArgs)

        Try
            Roles.CreateRole(TextBox1.Text)
            Label1.Text = "Role successfully created."
        Catch ex As Exception
            Label1.Text = ex.Message.ToString()
        End Try
    End Sub
</script>
<!DOCTYPE html>

<html xmlns="http://www.w3.org/1999/xhtml">
<head runat="server">
    <title>>Main Page</title>
</head>
<body>
    <form id="form1" runat="server">
    <div>
        Role Name:<br />
        <asp:TextBox ID="TextBox1" runat="server"></asp:TextBox><br />
        <br />
        <asp:Button ID="Button1" runat="server" Text="Create Role"
            OnClick="Button1_Click" /><br />
        <br />
        <asp:Label ID="Label1" runat="server"></asp:Label>
    </div>
    </form>
</body>
</html>
```

C#

```
<%@ Page Language="C#" %>
<script runat="server">
    protected void Button1_Click(object sender, EventArgs e)
```

continues

LISTING 15-23 *(continued)*

```
    {
        try
        {
            Roles.CreateRole(TextBox1.Text);
            Label1.Text = "Role successfully created.";
        }
        catch (Exception ex)
        {
            Label1.Text = ex.Message.ToString();
        }
    }
</script>
```

This simple ASP.NET page enables you to type in a string value in the textbox and to attempt to create a new role using this value. Note that anything other than the role Administrator and Manager results in an error. So, when the `Roles.CreateRole()` is called, an error is produced if the rules defined by the provider are not followed. In fact, running this page and typing in a role other than the Administrator or Manager role gives you the results presented in Figure 15-7.

FIGURE 15-7

To show this provider in action, create another ASP.NET page that allows you to add users to a particular role. As stated, you can do so with a number of available methods, but in this case, this example uses the `Roles.AddUserToRole()` method, shown in Listing 15-24.

LISTING 15-24: Attempting to add users to a role through the new role provider

VB

```
<%@ Page Language="vb" %>
<script runat="server">
    Protected Sub Button1_Click(ByVal sender As Object, _
      ByVal e As System.EventArgs)

        Try
```

```
            Roles.AddUserToRole(TextBox1.Text, TextBox2.Text)
            Label1.Text = "User successfully added to role"
        Catch ex As Exception
            Label1.Text = ex.Message.ToString()
        End Try
    End Sub
</script>
<!DOCTYPE html>

<html xmlns="http://www.w3.org/1999/xhtml">
<head runat="server">
    <title>Main Page</title>
</head>
<body>
    <form id="form1" runat="server">
    <div>
        Add the following user:<br />
        <asp:TextBox ID="TextBox1" runat="server"></asp:TextBox><br />
        <br />
        To role:<br />
        <asp:TextBox ID="TextBox2" runat="server"></asp:TextBox><br />
        <br />
        <asp:Button ID="Button1" runat="server" Text="Add User to Role"
            OnClick="Button1_Click" /><br />
        <br />
        <asp:Label ID="Label1" runat="server"></asp:Label>
    </div>
    </form>
</body>
</html>
```

C#

```
<%@ Page Language="C#" %>
<script runat="server">
    protected void Button1_Click(object sender, EventArgs e)
    {
        try
        {
            Roles.AddUserToRole(TextBox1.Text, TextBox2.Text);
            Label1.Text = "User successfully added to role";
        }
        catch (Exception ex)
        {
            Label1.Text = ex.Message.ToString();
        }
    }
</script>
```

In this example, two textboxes are provided. The first asks for the username and the second asks for the role to add the user to. The code for the button click event uses the `Roles.AddUserToRole()` method. Because you built the provider, you know that an error is thrown if there is an attempt to add a user to the Administrator role. This attempt is illustrated in Figure 15-8.

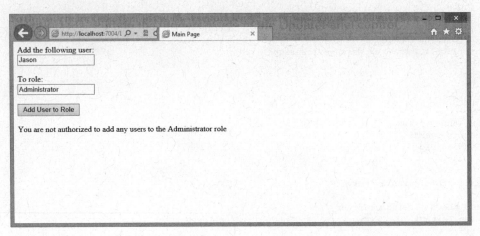

FIGURE 15-8

In this case, an attempt was made to add Jason to the Administrator role. This, of course, throws an error and returns the error message that is defined in the provider.

SUMMARY

In this chapter and the previous chapter, you were provided with an overview of the provider model and what it means to the ASP.NET 4.5 applications you build today. Although a lot of providers are available to you out of the box to use for interacting with one of the many systems provided in ASP.NET, you are not limited to just these providers. You definitely can either build your own providers or extend the functionality of the providers already present in the system.

This chapter looked at both of these scenarios. First, you built your own provider to use the membership system with an XML data store for the user data, and then you worked through an example of extending the `SqlRoleProvider` class (something already present in ASP.NET) to change the underlying behavior of this provider.

PART V
ASP.NET Features

16

Working with Master Pages

WHAT'S IN THIS CHAPTER?

- ➤ Coding master pages and content pages
- ➤ Using master pages to specify default content
- ➤ Assigning master pages programmatically
- ➤ Nesting master pages
- ➤ Master pages for different browsers
- ➤ Understanding the order of events for master pages
- ➤ Using master pages with ASP.NET AJAX

WROX.COM CODE DOWNLOADS FOR THIS CHAPTER

Please note that all the code examples in this chapter are available as a part of this chapter's code download on the book's website at www.wrox.com on the Download Code tab.

Visual inheritance is a great feature provided in ASP.NET that you can use to build your web pages. This feature was first introduced to ASP.NET in version 2.0. In effect, you can create a single template page that you can use as a foundation for any number of ASP.NET content pages in your application. These templates, called *master pages*, increase your productivity by making your applications easier to build and easier to manage after they are built. Visual Studio 2012 includes full designer support for master pages, making the developer experience richer than ever before. For example, even if you have nested master pages, Visual Studio provides you with a quite realistic WYSIWYG view of how the page might actually look in the browser.

This chapter takes a close look at how to utilize master pages to the fullest extent in your applications, and begins by explaining the advantages of master pages.

WHY DO YOU NEED MASTER PAGES?

Most websites today have common elements that are used throughout the entire application or on a majority of the pages within the application. For example, if you look at the main page of the Reuters News website (www.reuters.com), you see common elements that are used throughout the entire website. These common areas are labeled in Figure 16-1.

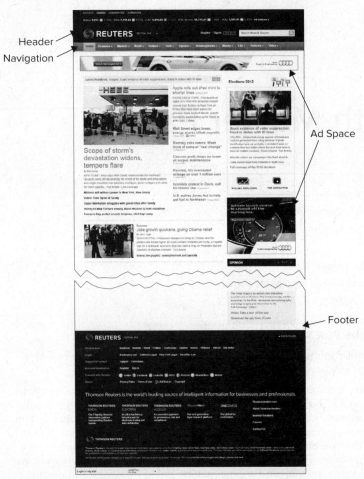

FIGURE 16-1

In this screenshot, notice the header section, the navigation section, and the footer section on the page. In fact, nearly every page within the entire site uses these same elements. Even before master pages, you had ways to put these elements into every page through a variety of means; but in most cases, doing so posed difficulties.

Some developers simply copy and paste the code for these common sections to each and every page that requires them. This works, but it's rather labor intensive—whenever you need to make a change to one of these common sections, you have to go into each and every page and duplicate the change. That's not much fun and an ineffective use of your time!

In the days of Classic Active Server Pages, one popular option was to put all the common sections into what was called an *include file*. You could then place this file within your page like this:

```
<!-- #include virtual="/myIncludes/header.asp" -->
```

The problem with using `include` files was that you had to take into account the newly opened HTML tags in the header `include` file. These tags had to be closed in the main document or in the footer `include` file. Keeping all the HTML tags in order was usually difficult, especially if multiple people worked on a project. Web pages sometimes displayed strange results because of inappropriate or nonexistent tag closings or openings. Working with `include` files in a visual designer was also difficult. Using `include` files didn't allow the developer to see the entire page as it would appear in a browser. The developer ended up developing the page in sections and *hoping* that the pieces would come together as planned. Many hours were wasted "chasing tables" opened in an `include` file and possibly closed later!

With the introduction of ASP.NET 1.0 in 2000, developers started using *user controls* to encapsulate common sections of their web pages. For example, you could build a web page that included header, navigation, and footer sections by simply dragging and dropping these sections of code onto each page that required them.

This technique worked, but it also raised some issues. Before Visual Studio 2005 and ASP.NET 2.0, user controls caused problems similar to those related to `include` files. When you worked in the Design view of your web page, the common areas of the page displayed only as gray boxes in Visual Studio .NET 2002 and 2003. This made building a page harder: You could not visualize what the page you were building actually looked like until you compiled and ran the completed page in a browser. User controls also suffered from the same problem as `include` files—you had to match up the opening and closing of your HTML tags in two separate files. Personally, I prefer user controls over `include` files, but user controls aren't perfect template pieces for use throughout an application. You will find that Visual Studio corrects some of the problems by rendering user-control content in the Design view. User controls are ideal if you are including only small sections on a web page; they are still rather cumbersome, however, when working with larger page templates.

In light of the issues with `include` files and user controls, the ASP.NET team developed the idea of *master pages*—an outstanding way of applying templates to your applications. They inverted the way the developer attacks the problem. Master pages live outside the pages you develop, whereas user controls live within your pages and are doomed to duplication. These master pages draw a more distinct line between the common areas that you carry over from page to page and the content areas that are unique on each page. You will find that working with master pages is easy and fun. The next section of this chapter looks at some of the basics of master pages in ASP.NET.

THE BASICS OF MASTER PAGES

Master pages are an easy way to provide a template that can be used by any number of ASP.NET pages in your application. In working with master pages, you create a master file that is the template referenced by a *subpage* or *content page*. Master pages use a `.master` file extension, whereas content pages use the `.aspx` file extension you're used to; but content pages are declared as such within the file's `Page` directive.

You can place anything you want to include as part of the template in the `.master` file, such as the header, navigation, and footer sections used across the web application. The content page itself would then only contain all the page-specific content but not the master page's elements. At run time, the ASP.NET engine combines these elements into a single page for the end user. Figure 16-2 shows a diagram of how this process works.

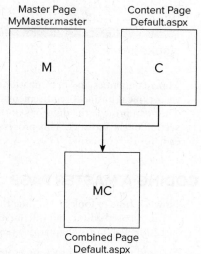

FIGURE 16-2

One of the nice things about working with master pages is that you can see the template in the IDE when you are creating the content pages. Because you can see the entire page while you are working on it, developing content pages that use a template is much easier. While you are working on the content page, all the templated items are shaded gray and are not editable. The only items you can alter are clearly shown in the template. These workable areas, called *content areas*, originally are defined in the master page itself. Within the master page, you specify the areas of the page that the content pages can use. You can have more than one content area in your master page if you want. Figure 16-3 shows the master page with a couple of content areas shown.

If you look at the screenshot from Figure 16-3, you can sort of see two defined areas on the page—these are content areas. Any content areas are represented in the Design view of the page by a light dotted box that represents the ContentPlaceHolder control. Also, if you hover your mouse over the content area, the name of the control appears above the control (although lightly). This hovering is also shown in action in Figure 16-3.

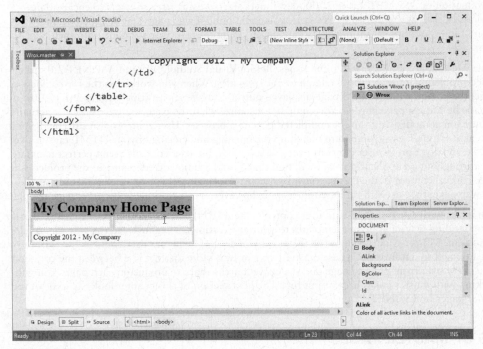

FIGURE 16-3

Many companies and organizations find using master pages ideal, because the technology closely models their typical business requirements. Many companies apply a common look and feel across their intranet. They can provide the divisions of their company with a `.master` file to use when creating a department's section of the intranet. This process makes keeping a consistent look and feel across its entire intranet quite easy for the company.

CODING A MASTER PAGE

Now it's time to look at building the master page shown previously in Figure 16-3. You can create one in any text-based editor, but of course we recommend you use Visual Studio 2012 or Visual Studio Express 2012 for Web. This chapter demonstrates how to do it with Visual Studio 2012.

You add master pages to your projects the same way you add regular `.aspx` pages—choose the Master Page option when you add a new file to your application, as shown in Figure 16-4.

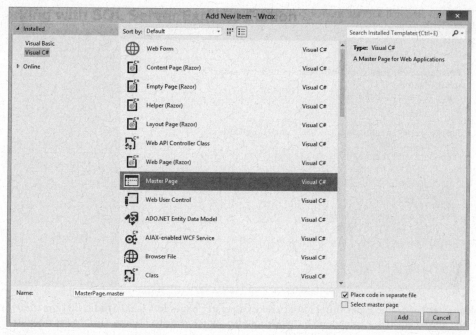

FIGURE 16-4

Because it's quite similar to any other `.aspx` page, the Add New Item dialog box enables you to choose from a master page that uses the inline coding model or a master page that places its code in a separate file. Not placing your server code in a separate file means that you use the inline code model for the page you are creating. This option creates a single `.master` page. Choosing the option to place your code in a separate file means that you use the new code-behind model with the page you are creating. Selecting the "Place code in separate file" check box creates a single `.master` page, along with an associated `.master.vb` or `.master.cs` file. You also have the option of nesting your master page within another master page by selecting the Select master page option, but this is covered later in this chapter.

A sample master page that uses the inline-coding model is shown in Listing 16-1.

LISTING 16-1: A sample master page

```
<%@ Master Language="C#" %>
<script runat="server">
</script>
<html xmlns="http://www.w3.org/1999/xhtml" >
<head runat="server">
  <title>My Company Master Page</title>
  <asp:ContentPlaceHolder id="head" runat="server">
  </asp:ContentPlaceHolder>
</head>
<body>
  <form id="form1" runat="server">
    <table cellpadding="3" border="1">
      <tr style="background:silver">
        <td colspan="2">
          <h1>My Company Home Page</h1>
        </td>
      </tr>
```

continues

LISTING 16-1 *(continued)*

```
      <tr>
        <td>
          <asp:ContentPlaceHolder ID="ContentPlaceHolder1"
           runat="server">
          </asp:ContentPlaceHolder>
        </td>
        <td>
          <asp:ContentPlaceHolder ID="ContentPlaceHolder2"
           runat="server">
          </asp:ContentPlaceHolder>
        </td>
      </tr>
      <tr>
        <td colspan="2">
          Copyright 2012 - My Company
        </td>
      </tr>
    </table>
  </form>
</body>
</html>
```

This is a simple master page. The great thing about creating master pages in Visual Studio 2012 is that you can work with the master page in Code view, but you can also switch over to Design view to create your master pages just as you would any other ASP.NET page.

Start by reviewing the code for the master page. The first line is the directive:

```
<%@ Master Language="C#" %>
```

Instead of using the Page directive, as you would with a typical .aspx page, you use the Master directive for a master page. This master page uses only a single attribute, Language. The Language attribute's value here is C#, but of course, you can also use VB if you are building a Visual Basic master page.

You code the rest of the master page just as you would any other .aspx page. You can use server controls, raw HTML and text, images, events, or anything else you normally would use for any .aspx page. This means that your master page can have a Page_Load event as well or any other event that you deem appropriate.

In the code shown in Listing 16-1, notice the use of the server control—the <asp:ContentPlaceHolder> control. This control defines the areas of the template where the content page can place its content:

```
<tr>
  <td>
    <asp:ContentPlaceHolder ID="ContentPlaceHolder1"
     runat="server">
    </asp:ContentPlaceHolder>
  </td>
  <td>
    <asp:ContentPlaceHolder ID="ContentPlaceHolder2"
     runat="server">
    </asp:ContentPlaceHolder>
  </td>
</tr>
```

In the case of this master page, two defined areas exist where the content page can place content. The master page contains a header and a footer area. It also defines two areas in the page where any inheriting content page can place its own content. You see how a content page uses this master page in the next section.

Coding a Content Page | 597

CODING A CONTENT PAGE

Now that you have a master page in place in your application, you can use this new template for any content pages in your application. Right-click the application in the Solution Explorer and choose Add New Item to create a new content page within your application.

To create a content page or a page that uses this master page as its template, you select a typical Web Form from the list of options in the Add New Item dialog box (see 16-5). Instead of creating a typical Web Form, however, you select the Select master page check box. This gives you the option of associating this Web Form later to some master page.

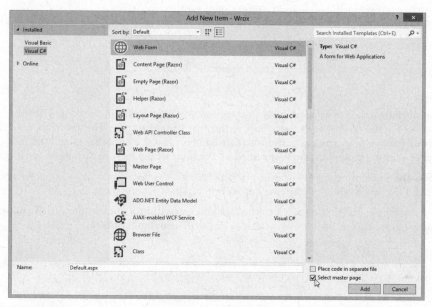

FIGURE 16-5

After you name your content page and click the Add button in the Add New Item dialog box, the Select a Master Page dialog box appears, as shown in Figure 16-6.

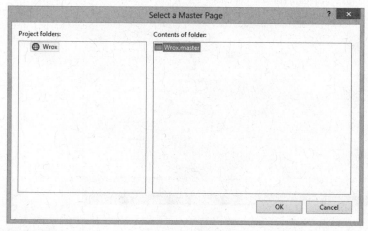

FIGURE 16-6

This dialog box enables you to choose the master page from which you want to build your content page. You choose from the available master pages that are contained within your application. For this example, select the new master page that you created in Listing 16-1 and click OK. This creates the content page. The created page is a simple .aspx page with only a couple of lines of code contained in the file, as shown in Listing 16-2.

LISTING 16-2: The created content page

C#

```
<%@ Page Language="C#" MasterPageFile="~/Wrox.master" Title="" %>
<script runat="server">
</script>
<asp:Content ID="Content1" ContentPlaceHolderID="head" Runat="Server">
</asp:Content>
<asp:Content ID="Content2" ContentPlaceHolderID="ContentPlaceHolder1"
 Runat="Server">
</asp:Content>
```

This content page is not much different from the typical .aspx page you have coded in the past. The big difference is the inclusion of the `MasterPageFile` attribute within the `Page` directive. The use of this attribute indicates that this particular .aspx page constructs its controls based on another page. The location of the master page within the application is specified as the value of the `MasterPageFile` attribute.

The other big difference is that it contains neither the `<form id="form1" runat="server">` tag nor any opening or closing HTML tags that would normally be included in a typical .aspx page.

This content page may seem simple, but if you switch to the Design view within Visual Studio 2012, you see the power of using content pages. Figure 16-7 shows what you get with visual inheritance.

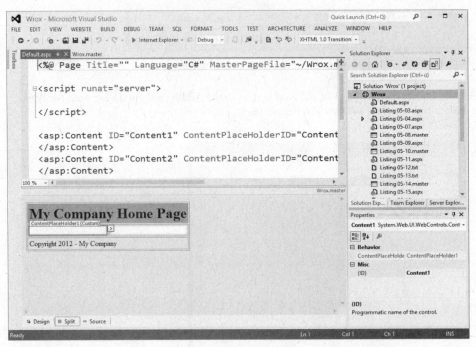

FIGURE 16-7

In this screenshot, you can see that just by using the `MasterPageFile` attribute in the `Page` directive, you are able to visually inherit everything that the `Wrox.master` file exposes. From the Design view within Visual Studio, you can also see what master page you are working with because the name of the referenced master page appears in the upper-right corner of the Design view page. If you try to click into the gray area that represents what is inherited from the master page, your cursor changes to show you are not allowed, as illustrated in Figure 16-8 (the cursor is on the word Page in the title).

All the common areas defined in the master page are shown in gray, whereas the content areas that you specified in the master page using the `<asp:ContentPlaceHolder>` server control are shown clearly and are available for additional content in the content page. You can add any content to these defined content areas as if you were working with a regular `.aspx` page. Listing 16-3 shows an example of using this `.master` page for a content page.

FIGURE 16-8

LISTING 16-3: The content page that uses Wrox.master

VB

```
<%@ Page Language="VB" MasterPageFile="~/Wrox.master" %>
<script runat="server">
  Protected Sub Button1_Click(ByVal sender As Object,
    ByVal e As System.EventArgs)
         Label1.Text = "Hello " & HttpUtility.HtmlEncode(TextBox1.Text) & "!"
  End Sub
</script>
<asp:Content ID="Content1" ContentPlaceHolderId="ContentPlaceHolder1"
 runat="server">
  <b>Enter your name:</b><br />
  <asp:Textbox ID="TextBox1" runat="server" />
  <br />
  <br />
  <asp:Button ID="Button1" runat="server" Text="Submit"
   OnClick="Button1_Click" /><br />
  <br />
  <asp:Label ID="Label1" runat="server" Font-Bold="True" />
</asp:Content>
      <asp:Content ID="Content2" ContentPlaceHolderId="ContentPlaceHolder2"
 runat="server">
    <asp:Image ID="Image1" runat="server" ImageUrl="wrox.gif" />
</asp:Content>
```

C#

```
<%@ Page Language="C#" MasterPageFile="~/Wrox.master" %>
<script runat="server">
  protected void Button1_Click(object sender, System.EventArgs e)
  {
    Label1.Text = "Hello " + HttpUtility.HtmlEncode(TextBox1.Text) + "!";
  }
</script>
```

Right away you see some differences. As stated before, this page has no `<form id="form1" runat="server">` tag nor any opening or closing `<html>` tags. These tags are not included because they are located in the master page. Also notice the server control—the `<asp:Content>` server control:

```
<asp:Content ID="Content1" ContentPlaceHolderId="ContentPlaceHolder1"
 runat="server">
  ...
</asp:Content>
```

The `<asp:Content>` server control is a defined content area that maps to a specific `<asp:ContentPlaceHolder>` server control on the master page. In this example, you can see that the `<asp:Content>` server control maps itself to the `<asp:ContentPlaceHolder>` server control in the master page that has the ID of `ContentPlaceHolder1`. Within the content page, you don't have to worry about specifying the location of the content because it is already defined within the master page. Therefore, your only concern is to place the appropriate content within the provided content sections, allowing the master page to do most of the work for you.

Just as when you work with any typical `.aspx` page, you can create any event handlers for your content page. In this case, you are using just a single event handler—the button click when the end user submits the form. The created `.aspx` page that includes the master page and content page material is shown in Figure 16-9.

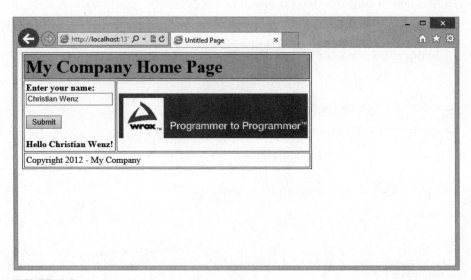

FIGURE 16-9

Mixing Page Types and Languages

One interesting point: When you use master pages, you are not tying yourself to a specific coding model (inline or code-behind), nor are you tying yourself to the use of a specific language. You can mix these elements within your application because they all work well.

You can use the master page created earlier, knowing that it was created using the inline-coding model, and then build your content pages using the code-behind model. Listing 16-4 shows a content page created using a Web Form that uses the code-behind option.

LISTING 16-4: A content page that uses the code-behind model

.ASPX (VB)

```
<%@ Page Language="VB" MasterPageFile="~/Wrox.master" AutoEventWireup="false"
  CodeFile="MyContentPage.aspx.cs" Inherits="MyContentPage" %>
<asp:Content ID="Content1" ContentPlaceHolderID="head" Runat="Server">
</asp:Content>
<asp:Content ID=»Content2» ContentPlaceHolderId="ContentPlaceHolder1"
 runat=»server»>
```

```
        <b>Enter your name:</b><br />
        <asp:Textbox ID="TextBox1" runat="server" />
        <br />
        <br />
        <asp:Button ID="Button1" runat=»server" Text="Submit" /><br />
        <br />
        <asp:Label ID="Label1" runat="server" Font-Bold="True" />
    </asp:Content>
    <asp:Content ID="Content3" ContentPlaceHolderId="ContentPlaceHolder2"
     runat="server">
        <asp:Image ID="Image1" runat="server" ImageUrl="wrox.gif" />
    </asp:Content>
```

VB CODE-BEHIND

```
    Partial Class MyContentPage
      Inherits System.Web.UI.Page
      Protected Sub Button1_Click(ByVal sender As Object, _
       ByVal e As System.EventArgs) Handles Button1.Click
        Label1.Text = "Hello " & HttpUtility.HtmlEncode(TextBox1.Text) & "!"
      End Sub
    End Class
```

C# CODE-BEHIND

```
    public partial class MyContentPage : System.Web.UI.Page
    {
      protected void Button1_Click (object sender, System.EventArgs e)
      {
        Label1.Text = "Hello " + HttpUtility.HtmlEncode(TextBox1.Text) + "!";
      }
    }
```

> **NOTE** *Even though the master page is using the inline-coding model, you can easily create content pages (such as the page shown in Listing 16-4) that use the code-behind model. The pages will still work perfectly.*

Not only can you mix the coding models when using master pages, you can also mix the programming languages you use for the master or content pages. Just because you build a master page in C# doesn't mean that you are required to use C# for all the content pages that use this master page. You can also build content pages in Visual Basic. For a good example, create a master page in C# that uses the `Page_Load` event handler and then create a content page in Visual Basic. When it is complete, run the page. It works perfectly well. This means that even though you might have a master page in one of the available .NET languages, the programming teams that build applications from the master page can use whatever .NET language they want. You have to love the openness that the .NET Framework offers!

Specifying Which Master Page to Use

You just observed that specifying at page level which master page to use is quite easy. In the `Page` directive of the content page, you simply use the `MasterPageFile` attribute:

```
<%@ Page Language="VB" MasterPageFile="~/Wrox.master" %>
```

Besides specifying the master page that you want to use at the page level, you have a second way to specify which master page you want to use in the `web.config` file of the application, as shown in Listing 16-5.

LISTING 16-5: Specifying the master page in the web.config file

```
<configuration>
  <system.web>
   <pages masterPageFile="~/Wrox.master" />
  </system.web>
</configuration>
```

Specifying the master page in the `web.config` file causes every single content page you create in the application to inherit from the specified master page. If you declare your master page in the `web.config` file, you can create any number of content pages that use this master page. Once specified in this manner, you can then construct the content page's `Page` directive like this:

```
<%@ Page Language="C#" %>
```

You can easily override the application-wide master page specification by simply declaring a different master page within your content page:

```
<%@ Page Language="VB" MasterPageFile="~/MyOtherCompany.master" %>
```

By specifying the master page in the `web.config` file, you are not really saying that you want *all* the `.aspx` pages to use this master page. If you create a normal Web Form and run it, ASP.NET will know that the page is not a content page and will run the page as a normal `.aspx` page.

Applying the Master Page Template to a Subset of Pages

If you want to apply the master page template to only a specific subset of pages (such as pages contained within a specific folder of your application), you can use the `<location>` element within the `web.config` file, as shown in Listing 16-6.

LISTING 16-6: Specifying the master page for a specific folder in the web.config file

```
<configuration>
  <location path="AdministrationArea">
    <system.web>
       <pages masterPageFile="~/WroxAdmin.master" />
    </system.web>
  </location>
</configuration>
```

With the addition of this `<location>` section in the `web.config` file, you have now specified that a specific folder (`AdministrationArea`) will use a different master file template. You do so using the `path` attribute of the `<location>` element. The value of the `path` attribute can be a folder name as shown, or it can even be a specific page—such as `AdminPage.aspx`.

Working with the Page Title

When you create content pages in your application, by default all the content pages automatically use the title that is declared in the master page. For example, you have primarily been using a master page with the title `My Company Master Page`. Every content page that is created using this particular master page also uses the same `My Company Master Page` title. You can avoid this by specifying the page's title using the `Title` attribute in the `@Page` directive in the content page. You can also work with the page title programmatically in your content pages. To accomplish this, in the code of the content page, you use the `Master` object. The `Master` object conveniently has a property called `Title`. The value of this property is the page title that is used for the content page. You code it as shown in Listing 16-7.

LISTING 16-7: Coding a custom page title for the content page

VB

```
<%@ Page Language="VB" MasterPageFile="~/Wrox.master" %>
<script runat="server">
  Protected Sub Page_LoadComplete(ByVal sender As Object, _
    ByVal e As System.EventArgs)
          Master.Page.Title = "This page was generated on: " & _
      DateTime.Now.ToString()
  End Sub
</script>
```

C#

```
<%@ Page Language="C#" MasterPageFile="~/Wrox.master" %>
<script runat="server">
  protected void Page_LoadComplete(object sender, EventArgs e)
  {
    Master.Page.Title = "This page was generated on: " +
      DateTime.Now.ToString();
  }
</script>
```

Working with Controls and Properties from the Master Page

When working with master pages from a content page, you actually have access to the controls and the properties that the master page exposes. The master page, when referenced by the content page, exposes a property called `Master`. You use this property to get at control values or custom properties that are contained in the master page itself.

To see an example of this control you have, create a GUID (unique identifier) in the master page that you can retrieve on the content page that is using the master. For this example, use the master page that was created in Listing 16-1, but add a Label server control and the `Page_Load` event (see Listing 16-8).

LISTING 16-8: A master page that creates a GUID on the first request

VB

```
    Protected Sub Page_Load(ByVal sender As Object, ByVal e As System.EventArgs)
      If Not Page.IsPostBack Then
        Label1.Text = System.Guid.NewGuid().ToString()
      End If
    End Sub
<html xmlns="http://www.w3.org/1999/xhtml" >
<head runat="server">
  <title>My Company Master Page</title>
  <asp:ContentPlaceHolder id="head" runat="server">
  </asp:ContentPlaceHolder>
</head>
<body>
  <form id="form1" runat="server">
    <table cellpadding="3" border="1">
      <tr bgcolor="silver">
        <td colspan="2">
          <h1>My Company Home Page</h1>
          <b>User's GUID:  
            <asp:Label ID="Label1" runat="server" /></b>
        </td>
      </tr>
```

continues

LISTING 16-8 *(continued)*

```
        <tr>
          <td>
            <asp:ContentPlaceHolder ID="ContentPlaceHolder1"
             runat="server">
            </asp:ContentPlaceHolder>
          </td>
          <td>
            <asp:ContentPlaceHolder ID="ContentPlaceHolder2"
             runat="server">
            </asp:ContentPlaceHolder>
          </td>
        </tr>
        <tr>
          <td colspan="2">
            Copyright 2012 - My Company
          </td>
        </tr>
      </table>
    </form>
  </body>
</html>
```

C#

```
<%@ Master Language="C#" %>
<script runat="server">
  protected void Page_Load(object sender, EventArgs e)
  {
    if (!Page.IsPostBack)
    {
      Label1.Text = System.Guid.NewGuid().ToString();
    }
  }
</script>
```

Now you have a Label control on the master page that you can access from the content page:

➤   Using `FindControl()`

➤   Using a custom property

You have a couple of ways to accomplish this task. The first way is to use the `FindControl()` method that the master page exposes. Listing 16-9 shows this approach.

LISTING 16-9: Getting at the Label's Text value in the content page

VB

```
<%@ Page Language="VB" MasterPageFile="~/Wrox.master" %>
<script runat="server" language="vb">
  Protected Sub Page_LoadComplete(ByVal sender As Object, _
    ByVal e As System.EventArgs)
    Label1.Text = CType(Master.FindControl("Label1"), Label).Text
  End Sub
  Protected Sub Button1_Click(ByVal sender As Object, _
    ByVal e As System.EventArgs)
    Label2.Text = "Hello " & TextBox1.Text & "!"
  End Sub
</script>
<asp:Content ID="Content1" ContentPlaceHolderID="head" Runat="Server">
</asp:Content>
<asp:Content ID="Content2" ContentPlaceHolderId="ContentPlaceHolder1"
```

```
  runat="server">
  <b>Your GUID number from the master page is:<br />
  <asp:Label ID="Label1" runat="server" /></b><p>
  <b>Enter your name:</b><br />
  <asp:Textbox ID="TextBox1" runat="server" />
  <br />
  <br />
  <asp:Button ID="Button1" runat="server" Text="Submit"
   OnClick="Button1_Click" /><br />
  <br />
  <asp:Label ID="Label2" runat="server" Font-Bold="True" /></p>
</asp:Content>
<asp:Content ID="Content3" ContentPlaceHolderId="ContentPlaceHolder2"
 runat="server">
    <asp:Image ID="Image1" runat="server" ImageUrl="Wrox.gif" />
</asp:Content>
```

C#

```
<%@ Page Language="C#" MasterPageFile="~/Wrox.master" %>
<script runat="server">
  protected void Page_LoadComplete(object sender, EventArgs e)
  {
    Label1.Text = (Master.FindControl("Label1") as Label).Text;
  }
  protected void Button1_Click(object sender, EventArgs e)
  {
    Label2.Text = "<b>Hello " + TextBox1.Text + "!</b>";
  }
</script>
```

In this example, the master page in Listing 16-8 creates a GUID that it stores as a text value in a Label server control on the master page itself. The ID of this Label control is Label1. The master page generates this GUID only on the first request for this particular content page. From here, you then populate one of the content page's controls with this value.

The interesting thing about the content page is that you put code in the Page_LoadComplete event handler so that you can access the GUID value that is on the master page. This event in ASP.NET fires immediately after the Page_Load event fires. Event ordering is covered later in this chapter, but the Page_Load event in the content page always fires before the Page_Load event in the master page. To access the newly created GUID (if it is created in the master page's Page_Load event), you have to get the GUID in an event that comes after the Page_Load event—and that is where Page_LoadComplete comes into play. Therefore, within the content page's Page_LoadComplete event, you populate a Label server control within the content page itself. Note that the Label control in the content page has the same ID as the Label control in the master page, but this doesn't make a difference. You can differentiate between them with the use of the Master property.

As previously mentioned there is also a second option: Not only can you access the server controls in the master page in this way, you can access any custom properties the master page might expose as well. Look at the master page shown in Listing 16-10; it uses a custom property for the <h1> section of the page.

LISTING 16-10: A master page that exposes a custom property

VB

```
<%@ Master Language="VB" %>
<script runat="server">
  Protected Sub Page_Load(ByVal sender As Object, ByVal e As System.EventArgs)
    If Not Page.IsPostBack Then
      Label1.Text = Guid.NewGuid().ToString()
```

continues

LISTING 16-10 *(continued)*

```vbnet
      End If
   End Sub
   Dim m_PageHeadingTitle As String = "My Company"
   Public Property PageHeadingTitle() As String
      Get
         Return m_PageHeadingTitle
      End Get
      Set(ByVal Value As String)
         m_PageHeadingTitle = Value
      End Set
   End Property
</script>
<html xmlns="http://www.w3.org/1999/xhtml" >
<head id="Head1" runat="server">
  <title>My Company Master Page</title>
  <asp:ContentPlaceHolder id="head" runat="server">
  </asp:ContentPlaceHolder>
</head>
<body>
  <form id="Form1" runat="server">
    <table cellpadding="3" border="1">
      <tr bgcolor="silver">
        <td colspan="2">
          <h1><%= PageHeadingTitle %></h1>
          <b>User's GUID:  
            <asp:Label ID="Label1" runat="server" /></b>
        </td>
      </tr>
      <tr>
        <td>
          <asp:ContentPlaceHolder ID="ContentPlaceHolder1"
           runat="server">
          </asp:ContentPlaceHolder>
        </td>
        <td>
          <asp:ContentPlaceHolder ID="ContentPlaceHolder2"
           runat="server">
          </asp:ContentPlaceHolder>
        </td>
      </tr>
      <tr>
        <td colspan="2">
          Copyright 2010 - My Company
        </td>
      </tr>
    </table>
  </form>
</body>
</html>
```

C#

```csharp
<%@ Master Language="C#" %>
<script runat="server">
  protected void Page_Load(object sender, EventArgs e)
  {
    if (!Page.IsPostBack)
    {
      Label1.Text = System.Guid.NewGuid().ToString();
    }
```

```
      }
      string m_PageHeadingTitle = "My Company";
      public string PageHeadingTitle
      {
        get
        {
          return m_PageHeadingTitle;
        }
        set
        {
          m_PageHeadingTitle = value;
        }
      }
    </script>
```

In this master page example, the master page is exposing the property you created called `PageHeadingTitle`. A default value of `"My Company"` is assigned to this property. You then place it within the HTML of the master page file between some `<h1>` elements, which makes the default value become the heading used on the page within the master page template. Although the master page already has a value it uses for the heading, any content page that is using this master page can override the `<h1>` title heading. Listing 16-11 shows the process.

LISTING 16-11: A content page that overrides the property from the master page

VB

```
<%@ Page Language="VB" MasterPageFile="~/Wrox.master" %>
<%@ MasterType VirtualPath="~/Wrox.master" %>
<script runat="server">
  Protected Sub Page_Load(ByVal sender As Object, ByVal e As System.EventArgs)
    Master.PageHeadingTitle = "My Company-Division X"
  End Sub
</script>
```

C#

```
<%@ Page Language="C#" MasterPageFile="~/Wrox.master" %>
<%@ MasterType VirtualPath="~/Wrox.master" %>
<script runat="server">
  protected void Page_Load(object sender, EventArgs e)
  {
    Master.PageHeadingTitle = "My Company-Division X";
  }
</script>
```

From the content page, you can assign a value to the property that is exposed from the master page by the use of the `Master` property. This is quite simple to do. Remember that not only can you access any public properties that the master page might expose, but you can also retrieve any methods that the master page contains as well.

The item that makes this all possible is the `MasterType` page directive. Using the `MasterType` directive enables you to make a strongly typed reference to the master page and access the master page's properties via the `Master` object.

Earlier, you saw how to access the server controls that are on the master page by using the `FindControl()` method. The `FindControl()` method works fine, but it is a late-bound approach, and as such, the method call may fail if the control is removed from markup. Use defensive coding practices and always check for null when returning objects from `FindControl()`. Using the mechanics just illustrated (with the use of public properties shown in Listing 16-10), you can use another approach to expose any server controls on the master page. You may find this approach to be more effective.

To take this different approach, you simply expose the server control as a public property, as shown in Listing 16-12.

LISTING 16-12: Exposing a server control from a master page as a public property

VB

```
<%@ Master Language="VB" %>
<script runat="server">
  Public Property MasterPageLabel1() As Label
    Get
      Return Label1
    End Get
    Set(ByVal Value As Label)
      Label1 = Value
    End Set
  End Property
</script>
```

C#

```
<%@ Master Language="C#" %>
<script runat="server">
  public Label MasterPageLabel1
  {
    get
    {
      return Label1;
    }
    set
    {
      Label1 = value;
    }
  }
</script>
```

In this case, a public property called `MasterPageLabel1` provides access to the Label control that uses the ID of `Label1`. You can now create an instance of the `MasterPageLabel1` property on the content page and override any of the attributes of the Label server control. So if you want to increase the size of the GUID that the master page creates and displays in the `Label1` server control, you can simply override the `Font .Size` attribute of the Label control, as shown in Listing 16-13.

LISTING 16-13: Overriding an attribute from the Label control that is on the master page

VB

```
<%@ Page Language"VB" MasterPageFile"~/Wrox.master" %>
<%@ MasterType VirtualPath"~/Wrox.master" %>
<script runat"server">
  Protected Sub Page_Load(ByVal sender As Object, ByVal e As System.EventArgs)
    Master.MasterPageLabel1.Font.Size = 25
  End Sub
</script>
```

C#

```
<%@ Page Language"C#" MasterPageFile"~/Wrox.master" %>
<%@ MasterType VirtualPath"~/Wrox.master" %>
<script runat"server">
```

```
      protected void Page_Load(object sender, EventArgs e)
      {
        Master.MasterPageLabel1.Font.Size = 25;
      }
    </script>
```

This approach may be the most effective way to access any server controls that the master page exposes to the content pages.

SPECIFYING DEFAULT CONTENT IN THE MASTER PAGE

As you have seen, the master page enables you to specify content areas the content page can use. Master pages can consist of just one content area, or they can have multiple content areas. The nice thing about content areas is that when you create a master page, you can specify default content for the content area. You can leave this default content in place to be utilized by the content page if you choose not to override it. Listing 16-14 shows a master page that specifies some default content within a content area.

LISTING 16-14: Specifying default content in the master page

```
<%@ Master Language="C#" %>
<html xmlns="http://www.w3.org/1999/xhtml" >
<head runat="server">
  <title>My Company</title>
  <asp:ContentPlaceHolder id="head" runat="server">
  </asp:ContentPlaceHolder>
</head>
<body>
  <form id="form1" runat="server">
    <asp:ContentPlaceHolder ID="ContentPlaceHolder1" runat="server">
    Here is some default content.
    </asp:ContentPlaceHolder><p>
    <asp:ContentPlaceHolder ID="ContentPlaceHolder2" runat="server">
    Here is some more default content.
    </asp:ContentPlaceHolder></p>
  </form>
</body>
</html>
```

To place default content within one of the content areas of the master page, you simply put it in the `ContentPlaceHolder` server control on the master page itself. Any content page that inherits this master page also inherits the default content. Listing 16-15 shows a content page that overrides just one of the content areas from this master page.

LISTING 16-15: Overriding some default content in the content page

```
<%@ Page Language="C#" MasterPageFile="~/MasterPage.master" %>
<asp:Content ID="Content3" ContentPlaceHolderId="ContentPlaceHolder2"
 runat="server">
  Here is some new content.
</asp:Content>
```

This code creates a page with one content area that shows content coming from the master page itself in addition to other content that comes from the content page (see Figure 16-10).

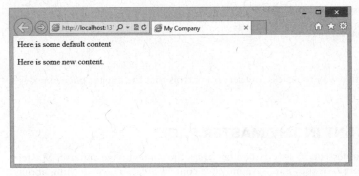

FIGURE 16-10

The other interesting point when you work with content areas in the Design view of Visual Studio 2012 is that the smart tag enables you to work easily with the default content.

When you first start working with the content page, you will notice that all the default content is at first populated in all the Content server controls. You can change the content by clicking the control's smart tag and selecting the Create Custom Content option from the provided menu. This option enables you to override the master page content and insert your own defined content. After you have placed some custom content inside the content area, the smart tag shows a different option—Default to Master's Content. This option enables you to return the default content that the master page exposes to the content area and to erase whatever content you have already placed in the content area—thereby simply returning to the default content. If you choose this option, you will be warned that you are about to delete any custom content you placed within the Content server control (see Figure 16-11).

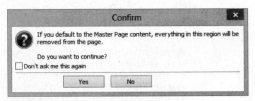

FIGURE 16-11

After changing the default content of one of the Content controls, the WYSIWYG view changes, too, as you can see in Figure 16-12.

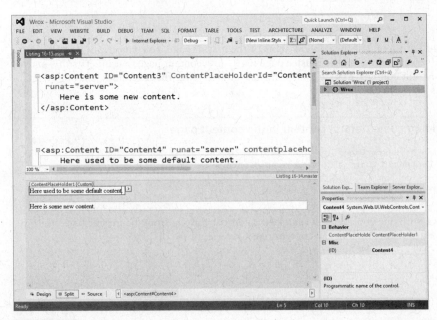

FIGURE 16-12

PROGRAMMATICALLY ASSIGNING THE MASTER PAGE

From any content page, you can easily assign a master page programmatically. You assign the master page to the content page using the `Page.MasterPageFile` property. You can use this property regardless of whether another master page is already assigned in the `@Page` directive.

To assign a master page with the `Page.MasterPageFile` property you use the `PreInit` event. The `PreInit` event is the earliest point in which you can access the page life cycle. For this reason, this event is where you need to assign any master page that is used by any content pages. `PreInit` is an important event to make note of when you are working with master pages, because it is the only point where you can affect both the master and content page before they are combined into a single instance. Listing 16-16 shows how to assign the master page programmatically from the content page.

LISTING 16-16: Using Page_PreInit to assign the master page programmatically

VB

```
<%@ Page Language="VB" %>
<script runat="server">
  Protected Sub Page_PreInit(ByVal sender As Object, ByVal e As System.EventArgs)
    Page.MasterPageFile = "~/MyMasterPage.master"
  End Sub
</script>
```

C#

```
<%@ Page Language="C#" %>
<script runat="server">
  protected void Page_PreInit(object sender, EventArgs e)
  {
    Page.MasterPageFile = "~/MyMasterPage.master";
  }
</script>
```

In this case, when the page is being generated dynamically, the master page is assigned to the content page in the beginning of the page construction process. Note that the content page must have the Content controls defined in the master page; otherwise, an error is thrown.

NESTING MASTER PAGES

So far, you have been creating a single master page that the content page can use. Most companies and organizations, however, are not just two layers. Many divisions and groups exist within the organization that might want to use variations of the master by, in effect, having a master page within a master page. With ASP.NET, this type of page is quite possible.

For example, imagine that Reuters is creating a master page to be used throughout the entire company intranet. Not only does the Reuters enterprise want to implement this master page companywide, but various divisions within Reuters also want to provide templates for the subsections of the intranet directly under their control. For example, Reuters Europe and Reuters America each want their own unique master page, as illustrated in Figure 16-13.

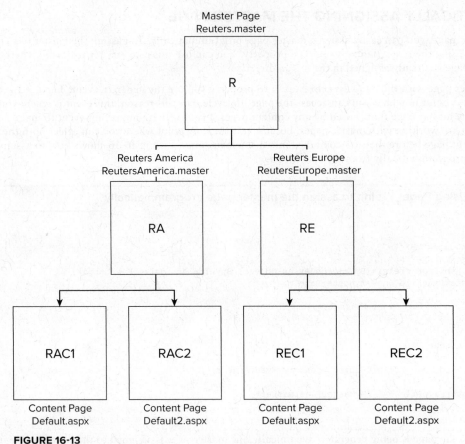

FIGURE 16-13

To get these unique pages, the creators of the Reuters Europe and Reuters America master pages simply create a master page that inherits from the global master page, as shown in Listing 16-17. You can find this file, named `ReutersMain.master`, as part of the Chapter 16 code download for this book.

LISTING 16-17: The main master page

```
<%@ Master Language="C#" %>
<html xmlns="http://www.w3.org/1999/xhtml" >
<head runat="server">
  <title>Reuters</title>
  <asp:ContentPlaceHolder id="head" runat="server">
  </asp:ContentPlaceHolder>
</head>
<body>
  <form id="form1" runat="server">
    <p><asp:Label ID="Label1" runat="server" BackColor="LightGray"
      BorderColor="Black" BorderWidth="1px" BorderStyle="Solid"
      Font-Size="XX-Large"> Reuters Main Master Page </asp:Label></p>
    <asp:ContentPlaceHolder ID=»ContentPlaceHolder1» runat=»server»>
    </asp:ContentPlaceHolder>
  </form>
</body>
</html>
```

This master page is simple, but excellent for showing you how this nesting capability works. The main master page is the master page used globally in the company. It has the ContentPlaceHolder server control with the ID of ContentPlaceHolder1.

You create a submaster or nested master page in the same manner as you would when building any other master page. From the Add New Item dialog box, select the Master Page option and make sure you have the Select master page option selected, as illustrated in Figure 16-14. Again, the Select a Master Page dialog box appears, in which you make a master page selection.

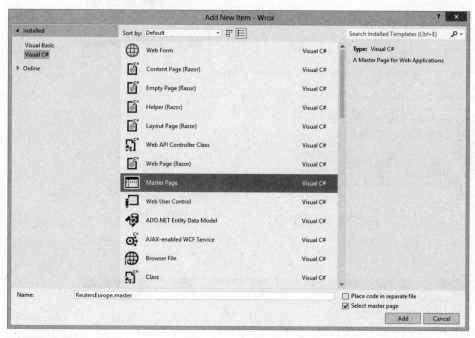

FIGURE 16-14

Listing 16-18 shows how you can work with this main master from a submaster file. You can find this file, named ReutersEurope.master, as part of the Chapter 16 code download for this book.

LISTING 16-18: THE SUBMASTER PAGE

```
<%@ Master Language="C#" MasterPageFile="~/ReutersMain.master" %>
<asp:Content ID="Content1" ContentPlaceHolderID="head" Runat="Server">
</asp:Content>
<asp:Content ID="Content2" ContentPlaceHolderId="ContentPlaceHolder1"
 runat="server">
  <asp:Label ID="Label1" runat="server" BackColor="#E0E0E0" BorderColor="Black"
    BorderStyle="Dotted" BorderWidth="2px" Font-Size="Large">
    Reuters Europe </asp:Label><br /><hr />
    <asp:ContentPlaceHolder ID="ContentPlaceHolder1" runat="server">
    </asp:ContentPlaceHolder>
</asp:Content>
```

Looking this page over, you can see that it isn't much different than a typical .aspx page that makes use of a master page. The MasterPageFile attribute is used just the same, but instead of using the @Page directive, it uses the @Master page directive. Then the Content2 control also uses the

`ContentPlaceHolderId` attribute of the Content control. This attribute ties this content area to the content area `ContentPlaceHolder1`, which is defined in the main master page.

One feature of ASP.NET is the ability to view nested master pages directly in the Design view of Visual Studio 2012. Figure 16-15 shows a nested master page in the Design view of Visual Studio 2012.

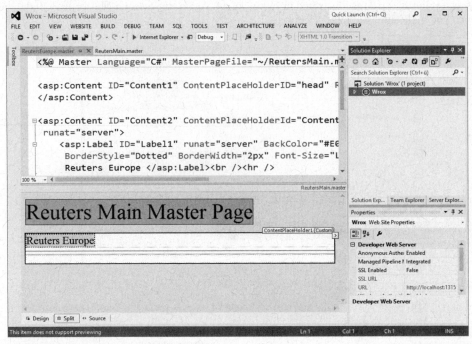

FIGURE 16-15

Within the submaster page presented in Listing 16-18, you can also now use as many ContentPlaceHolder server controls as you want. Any content page that uses this master can use these controls. Listing 16-19 shows a content page that uses the submaster page `ReutersEurope.master`.

LISTING 16-19: The content page

DEFAULT.ASPX

```
<%@ Page Language="C#" MasterPageFile="~/ReutersEurope.master" %>
<asp:Content ID="Content1" ContentPlaceHolderId="ContentPlaceHolder1"
 runat="server">
   Hello World
</asp:Content>
```

As you can see, in this content page the value of the `MasterPageFile` attribute in the `@Page` directive is the submaster page that you created. Inheriting the ReutersEurope master page actually combines both master pages (`ReutersMain.master` and `ReutersEurope.master`) into a single master page. The Content control in this content page points to the content area defined in the submaster page as well. You can see this in the code with the use of the `ContentPlaceHolderId` attribute. In the end, you get a very non-artistic page, as shown in Figure 16-16.

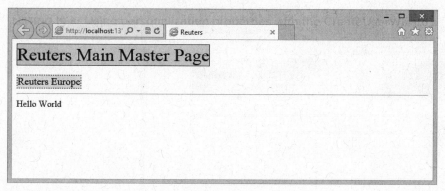

FIGURE 16-16

> **WARNING** *As you can see, creating a content page that uses a submaster page works quite well. However it is not always the right solution, and is sometimes even considered an anti-pattern. The structure of those nested master pages can become very complex, so that in the end you might be overrelying on inheritance. Also, a subtle change on one of the (many) master pages might have a big impact on all derived content pages.*

CONTAINER-SPECIFIC MASTER PAGES

In many cases, developers are building applications that will be viewed in a multitude of different containers. Some viewers may view the application in Microsoft Internet Explorer and some might view it using Firefox or Google Chrome. Still other viewers may call up the application on a tablet or cell phone.

For this reason, ASP.NET enables you to use multiple master pages within your content page. Depending on the viewing container used by the end user, the ASP.NET engine pulls the appropriate master file. Therefore, you want to build container-specific master pages to provide your end users with the best possible viewing experience by taking advantage of the features that a specific container provides. Listing 16-20 demonstrates the capability to use multiple master pages.

LISTING 16-20: A content page that can work with more than one master page

```
<%@ Page Language="C#" MasterPageFile="~/Wrox.master"
      Firefox:MasterPageFile="~/WroxFirefox.master"
      Safari:MasterPageFile="~/WroxSafari.master"
      Opera:MasterPageFile="~/WroxOpera.master"
      Chrome:MasterPageFile="~/WroxChrome.master" %></asp:Content>
      <asp:Content ID="Content2" ContentPlaceHolderId="ContentPlaceHolder1"
runat="server">
   Hello World
</asp:Content>
```

As you can see from this example content page, it can work with three different master page files. The first one uses the attribute `MasterPageFile`. It is the default setting used for any page that doesn't fit the criteria for any of the other options. This means that if the requestor is not a Firefox, Chrome, Safari, or Opera browser, the default master page, `Wrox.master`, is used. However, if the requestor is a Chrome browser, `WroxChrome.master` is used instead, as illustrated in Figure 16-17.

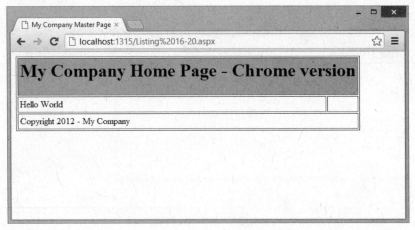

FIGURE 16-17

You can find a list of available browsers on the production server where the application will be hosted at `C:\Windows\Microsoft.NET\Framework\v4.0.xxxxx\CONFIG\Browsers`. Some of the available options include the following:

- Blackberry
- Chrome
- Default
- Firefox
- Gateway
- Generic
- IE
- IEMobile
- iPhone
- Opera
- Safari
- UCBrowser

Of course, you can also add any additional `.browser` files that you deem necessary.

EVENT ORDERING

When you work with master pages and content pages, both can use the same events (such as the `Load` event). Be sure you know which events come before others. This is one of the most important aspects of master pages, since there are differences compared to the event order of regular pages.

You are bringing two classes together to create a single page class, and a specific order is required. When an end user requests a content page in the browser, the event ordering is as follows:

1. **Initialization of master page child controls:** All server controls contained within the master page are first initialized.
2. **Initialization of content page child controls:** All server controls contained in the content page are initialized.
3. **Initialization of the master page:** The master page itself is initialized.

4. **Initialization of the content page:** The content page is initialized.

5. **Loading of the content page:** The content page is loaded (this is the `Page_Load` event followed by the `Page_LoadComplete` event).

6. **Loading of the master page:** The master page is loaded (this is also the `Page_Load` event followed by the `Page_LoadComplete` event).

7. **Loading of the master page's child controls:** The server controls on the master page are loaded onto the page.

8. **Loading of the content page's child controls:** The server controls on the content page are loaded onto the page.

Pay attention to this event ordering when building your applications. If you want to use server control values that are contained on the master page within a specific content page, for example, you can't retrieve the values of these server controls from within the content page's `Page_Load` event. This is because this event is triggered before the master page's `Page_Load` event. This problem prompted the creation of the `Page_LoadComplete` event in the .NET Framework. The content page's `Page_LoadComplete` event follows the master page's `Page_Load` event. You can, therefore, use this ordering to access values from the master page even though it isn't populated when the content page's `Page_Load` event is triggered.

CACHING WITH MASTER PAGES

When working with typical `.aspx` pages, you can apply output caching to the page by using the following construct (or variation thereof):

```
<%@ OutputCache Duration="10" Varybyparam="None" %>
```

This line caches the page in the server's memory for 10 seconds. Many developers use output caching to increase the performance of their ASP.NET pages. Using it on pages with data that doesn't become stale too quickly also makes a lot of sense.

How do you go about applying output caching to ASP.NET pages when working with master pages? You cannot apply caching to just the master page. You cannot put the `OutputCache` directive on the master page itself. If you do so, on the page's second retrieval, you get an error because the application cannot find the cached page.

To work with output caching when using a master page, place the `OutputCache` directive in the content page. Doing so caches both the contents of the content page and the contents of the master page (remember, it is just a single page at this point). Placing the `OutputCache` directive in the master page does not cause the master page to produce an error, but it will not be cached. This directive works in the content page only.

Another new and interesting feature of ASP.NET 4+ in regards to working with any caching capabilities is that ASP.NET now enables you to control view state at the control level. Although you might immediately think of being able to control view state in this manner with controls such as the GridView or something that generally has a lot of view state, you can also use this new capability with the ContentPlaceHolder control.

For example, you can construct something such as the following:

```
<asp:ContentPlaceHolder ID="ContentPlaceHolder1" runat="server"
  ViewStateMode="Disabled">
</asp:ContentPlaceHolder>
```

In this case, `ContentPlaceHolder1` will not use view state even if the rest of the page is using it. The available options for the `ViewStateMode` property include `Disabled`, `Enabled`, and `Inherit`. `Disabled` turns off view state for the control, `Enabled` turns it on, and `Inherit` takes the value that is assigned in the `@Page` directive. Removing view state improves the performance of your pages.

> **NOTE** *Chapter 22 contains more information about the available caching features of ASP.NET.*

ASP.NET AJAX AND MASTER PAGES

Many of the larger ASP.NET applications today make use of master pages and the power this technology provides in building templated websites. ASP.NET includes ASP.NET AJAX as part of the default install, and you will find that master pages and Ajax go together quite well.

> **NOTE** *Chapter 23 covers ASP.NET AJAX.*

Every page that is going to make use of Ajax capabilities must have the ScriptManager control on the page. If the page you want to use Ajax with is a content page making use of a master page, you must place the ScriptManager control on the master page itself.

> **NOTE** *You can have only one ScriptManager on a page.*

It isn't too difficult to set up your master page so that it is Ajax-enabled. To do this, simply add a ScriptManager server control to the master page itself. Listing 16-21 shows an example of this in action.

LISTING 16-21: The Ajax master page

```
<%@ Master Language="C#" %>
<script runat="server">
</script>
<html xmlns="http://www.w3.org/1999/xhtml">
<head runat="server">
  <title></title>
  <asp:ContentPlaceHolder id="head" runat="server">
  </asp:ContentPlaceHolder>
</head>
<body>
  <form id="form1" runat="server">
  <div>
    <asp:ScriptManager ID="ScriptManager1" runat="server" />
    <asp:ContentPlaceHolder id="ContentPlaceHolder1" runat="server">
    </asp:ContentPlaceHolder>
  </div>
  </form>
</body>
</html>
```

As you can see from Listing 16-21, the only real difference between this Ajax master page and the standard master page is the inclusion of the ScriptManager server control. You want to use this technique if your master page includes any Ajax capabilities whatsoever, even if the content page makes no use of Ajax at all.

The ScriptManager control on the master page also is beneficial if you have common JavaScript items to place on all the pages of your web application. For example, Listing 16-22 shows how you could easily include JavaScript on each page through the master page.

LISTING 16-22: Including scripts through your master page

```
<%@ Master Language="C#" %>
<html xmlns"http://www.w3.org/1999/xhtml">
<head runat="server">
  <title></title>
  <asp:ContentPlaceHolder id="head" runat="server">
  </asp:ContentPlaceHolder>
</head>
<body>
  <form id="form1" runat="server">
  <div>
    <asp:ScriptManager ID="ScriptManager1" runat="server">
      <Scripts>
       <asp:ScriptReference Path="myScript.js" />
      </Scripts>
    </asp:ScriptManager>
    <asp:ContentPlaceHolder id="ContentPlaceHolder1" runat="server">
    </asp:ContentPlaceHolder>
  </div>
  </form>
</body>
</html>
```

In this example, the `myScript.js` file is included on every content page that makes use of this Ajax master page. If your content page also needs to make use of Ajax capabilities, you cannot simply add another ScriptManager control to the page. Instead, the content page needs to make use of the ScriptManager control that is already present on the master page.

That said, if your content page needs to add additional items to the ScriptManager control, it is able to access this control on the master page using the ScriptManagerProxy server control. Using the ScriptManagerProxy control enables you to add any items to the ScriptManager that are completely specific to the instance of the content page that makes the inclusions.

For example, Listing 16-23 shows how a content page adds additional scripts to the page through the ScriptManagerProxy control.

LISTING 16-23: Adding additional items using the ScriptManagerProxy control

```
<%@ Page Language="C#" MasterPageFile="~/AjaxMaster.master" %>
<asp:Content ID="Content1" ContentPlaceHolderID="head" runat="Server">
</asp:Content>
<asp:Content ID="Content2" ContentPlaceHolderID="ContentPlaceHolder1"
 runat="Server">
 <asp:ScriptManagerProxy ID="ScriptManagerProxy1" runat="server">
   <Scripts>
     <asp:ScriptReference Path="myOtherScript.js" />
   </Scripts>
 </asp:ScriptManagerProxy>
</asp:Content>
```

In this case, this content page uses the ScriptManagerProxy control to add an additional script to the page. This ScriptManagerProxy control works exactly the same as the main ScriptManager control, except that it is meant for content pages making use of a master page. The ScriptManagerProxy control then interacts with the page's ScriptManager control to perform the necessary actions.

SUMMARY

When you create applications that use a common header, footer, or navigation section on nearly every page of the application, master pages are a great solution. Master pages are easy to implement and enable you to make changes to each and every page of your application by changing a single file. Imagine how much easier this method makes managing large applications that contain thousands of pages.

This chapter described master pages in ASP.NET and explained how you build and use master pages within your web applications. In addition to the basics, the chapter covered master page event ordering, caching, and specific master pages for specific containers. In the end, when you are working with templated applications, master pages should definitely be considered.

17

Site Navigation

WHAT'S IN THIS CHAPTER?

➤ Using `.sitemap` files and the SiteMapPath server control

➤ Using the TreeView and Menu server controls

➤ Taking advantage of URL mapping

➤ Localizing your `Web.sitemap` files and filtering the results of the site navigation contents

WROX.COM CODE DOWNLOADS FOR THIS CHAPTER

Please note that all the code examples in this chapter are available as a part of this chapter's code download on the book's website at www.wrox.com on the Download Code tab.

The web applications that you develop generally have more than a single page to them. Usually, you create a number of web pages that are interconnected in some fashion. If you also build the navigation around your collection of pages, you make it easy for the end user to successfully work through your application in a straightforward manner.

Currently, you must choose from a number of ways to expose the paths through your application to the end user. The difficult task of site navigation is compounded when you continue to add pages to the overall application.

The present method for building navigation within web applications is to sprinkle pages with hyperlinks. Hyperlinks are generally added to web pages by using include files or user controls. They can also be directly hard-coded onto a page so that they appear in the header or the sidebar of the page being viewed. The difficulties in working with navigation become worse when you move pages around or change page names. Sometimes, developers are forced to go to every page in the application just to change some aspect of the navigation.

ASP.NET 4.5 tackles this problem by providing a navigation system that makes managing how end users work through the applications you create quite trivial. This capability in ASP.NET is complex; but the great thing is that it can be as simple as you need it to be, or you can actually get in deep and control every aspect of how it works.

The site navigation system includes the capability to define your entire site in an XML file that is called a *sitemap*. After you define a sitemap, you can work with it programmatically using the `SiteMap` class. Another aspect of the sitemap capability available in ASP.NET is a data provider that is specifically developed to work with sitemap files and to bind them to a series of navigation-based server controls. This chapter looks at all these components in the ASP.NET 4.5 navigation system. The following section introduces sitemaps.

XML-BASED SITEMAPS

Although a sitemap is not a required element (as you see later), one of the common first steps you take in working with the ASP.NET 4.5 navigation system is building a sitemap for your application. A sitemap is an XML description of your site's structure.

You use this sitemap to define the navigational structure of all the pages in your application and how they relate to one another. If you do this according to the ASP.NET sitemap standard, you can then interact with this navigation information using either the `SiteMap` class or the SiteMapDataSource control. By using the SiteMapDataSource control, you can then bind the information in the sitemap file to a variety of data-binding controls, including the navigation server controls provided by ASP.NET.

To create a sitemap file for your application, add a sitemap or an XML file to your application. When asked, you name the XML file **Web.sitemap**; this file is already in place if you select the Sitemap option. The file is named `Web` and has the file extension of `.sitemap`. Take a look at an example of a `.sitemap` file, shown here in Listing 17-1 (Web.sitemap in the code download for this chapter).

LISTING 17-1: An example of a Web.sitemap file

```xml
<?xml version="1.0" encoding="utf-8" ?>

<siteMap xmlns="http://schemas.microsoft.com/AspNet/SiteMap-File-1.0" >
    <siteMapNode title="Home" description="Home Page" url="Default.aspx">
        <siteMapNode title="News" description="The Latest News" url="News.aspx">
            <siteMapNode title="U.S." description="U.S. News"
             url="News.aspx?cat=us" />
            <siteMapNode title="World" description="World News"
             url="News.aspx?cat=world" />
            <siteMapNode title="Technology" description="Technology News"
             url="News.aspx?cat=tech" />
            <siteMapNode title="Sports" description="Sports News"
             url="News.aspx?cat=sport" />
        </siteMapNode>
        <siteMapNode title="Finance" description="The Latest Financial Information"
          url="Finance.aspx">
            <siteMapNode title="Quotes" description="Get the Latest Quotes"
             url="Quotes.aspx" />
            <siteMapNode title="Markets" description="The Latest Market Information"
             url="Markets.aspx">
                <siteMapNode title="U.S. Market Report"
                 description="Looking at the U.S. Market" url="MarketsUS.aspx" />
                <siteMapNode title="NYSE"
                 description="The New York Stock Exchange" url="NYSE.aspx" />
            </siteMapNode>
            <siteMapNode title="Funds" description="Mutual Funds"
             url="Funds.aspx" />
        </siteMapNode>
        <siteMapNode title="Weather" description="The Latest Weather"
         url="Weather.aspx" />
    </siteMapNode>
</siteMap>
```

So what does this file give you? Well, it gives you a logical structure that ASP.NET can now use in the rest of the navigation system it provides. Next, this chapter examines how this file is constructed.

The root node of this XML file is a `<siteMap>` element. Only one `<siteMap>` element can exist in the file. Within the `<siteMap>` element is a single root `<siteMapNode>` element. This is generally the start page of the application. In the case of the file in Listing 17-1, the root `<siteMapNode>` points to the `Default.aspx` page, the start page:

```
<siteMapNode title="Home" description="Home Page" url="Default.aspx">\
```

Table 17-1 describes the most common attributes in the `<siteMapNode>` element.

TABLE 17-1

ATTRIBUTE	DESCRIPTION
Title	Provides a textual description of the link. The `String` value used here is the text used for the link.
Description	Not only reminds you what the link is for, but also is used for the `ToolTip` attribute on the link. The `ToolTip` attribute is the yellow box that shows up next to the link when the end user hovers the cursor over the link for a couple of seconds.
url	Describes where the file is located in the solution. If the file is in the root directory, simply use the filename, such as `Default.aspx`. If the file is located in a subfolder, be sure to include the folders in the String value used in this attribute. For example, `MySubFolder/Markets.aspx`.

After you have the first `<siteMapNode>` in place, you can then nest as many additional `<siteMapNode>` elements as you need within the root `<siteMapNode>` element. You can also create additional link-levels by creating child `<siteMapNode>` elements for any parent `<siteMapNode>` in the structure.

The example in Listing 17-1 gives the application the following navigational structure:

```
Home
    News
        U.S.
        World
        Technology
        Sports
    Finance
        Quotes
        Markets
            U.S. Market Report
            NYSE
        Funds
    Weather
```

You can see that this structure goes down three levels in some places. One of the easiest places to use this file is with the SiteMapPath server control that comes with ASP.NET. The SiteMapPath server control in ASP.NET is built to work specifically with the `.sitemap` files.

SITEMAPPATH SERVER CONTROL

Using the `.sitemap` file you just created with the SiteMapPath server control provided with ASP.NET is quite easy. You can find this control in the Navigation section of the Visual Studio 2012 IDE.

The SiteMapPath control creates navigation functionality that you once might either have created yourself or have seen elsewhere in web pages on the Internet. The SiteMapPath control creates what some refer to as *breadcrumb navigation*. This linear path defines where the end user is in the navigation structure. The newegg.com website, shown in Figure 17-1, uses the breadcrumb navigation.

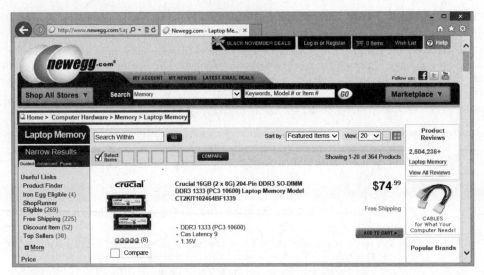

FIGURE 17-1

The purpose of this type of navigation is to show end users where they are in relation to the rest of the site. Traditionally, coding this kind of navigation has been tricky, to say the least; but with the SiteMapPath server control, you should find coding for this type of navigation a breeze. As an example, you'll see a site structure for a (fictitious) news website in this chapter.

You should first create an application that has the `Web.sitemap` file created in Listing 17-1. From there, create a Web Form called `MarketsUS.aspx`. This file is defined in the `Web.sitemap` file as being on the lowest tier of files in the application.

The SiteMapPath control is so easy to work with that it doesn't even require a data source control to hook it up to the `Web.sitemap` file where it infers all its information. All you do is drag and drop a SiteMapPath control onto your `MarketsUS.aspx` page. In the end, you should have a page similar to the one shown in Listing 17-2.

LISTING 17-2: Using the Web.sitemap file with a SiteMapPath server control

```
<%@ Page Language="C#" %>

<html xmlns="http://www.w3.org/1999/xhtml">
<head runat="server">
    <title>Using the SiteMapPath Server Control</title>
</head>
<body>
    <form id="form1" runat="server">
        <asp:SiteMapPath ID="Sitemappath1" runat="server">
        </asp:SiteMapPath>
    </form>
</body>
</html>
```

Not much to it, is there? It really is that easy. Run this page and you see the results shown in Figure 17-2.

FIGURE 17-2

This screenshot shows that you are on the U.S. Market Report page at `MarketsUS.aspx`. As an end user, you can see that this page is part of the Markets section of the site; Markets, in turn, is part of the Finance section of the site. With breadcrumb navigation, end users who understand the structure of the site and their place in it can quickly select the links to navigate to any location in the site.

If you hover your mouse over the Finance link, you see a tooltip appear after a couple of seconds, as shown in Figure 17-3.

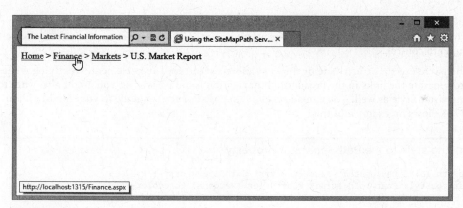

FIGURE 17-3

This tooltip, which reads `The Latest Financial Information`, comes from the description attribute of the `<siteMapNode>` element in the `Web.sitemap` file.

```
<siteMapNode title="Finance" description="The Latest Financial Information"
   url="Finance.aspx">
```

The SiteMapPath control works automatically, requiring very little work on your part. You just add the basic control to your page, and the control automatically creates the breadcrumb navigation you have just seen. However, you can use the properties discussed in the following sections to modify the appearance and behavior of the control.

The PathSeparator Property

One important style property for the SiteMapPath control is the `PathSeparator` property. By default, the SiteMapPath control uses a greater-than sign (>) to separate the link elements. You can change it by reassigning a new value to the `PathSeparator` property. Listing 17-3 illustrates the use of this property.

LISTING 17-3: Changing the PathSeparator value

```
<asp:SiteMapPath ID="Sitemappath1" runat="server" PathSeparator=" | ">
</asp:SiteMapPath>
```

or

```
<asp:SiteMapPath ID="Sitemappath1" runat="server">
   <PathSeparatorTemplate> | </PathSeparatorTemplate>
</asp:SiteMapPath>
```

The SiteMapPath control in this example uses the pipe character (|), which is found above the Enter key. When it is rendered, you get the results shown in Figure 17-4.

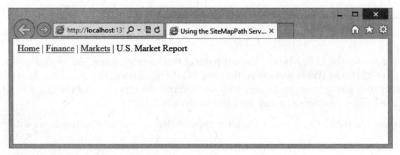

FIGURE 17-4

As you can see, you can use either the `PathSeparator` attribute or the `<PathSeparatorTemplate>` element within the SiteMapPath control.

With the use of the `PathSeparator` attribute or the `<PathSeparatorTemplate>` element, specifying what you want to use to separate the links in the breadcrumb navigation is quite easy, but you might also want to give this pipe some visual style as well. You can add a `<PathSeparatorStyle>` node to your SiteMapPath control. Listing 17-4 shows an example of this.

LISTING 17-4: Adding style to the PathSeparator property

```
<asp:SiteMapPath ID="Sitemappath1" runat="server" PathSeparator=" | ">
   <PathSeparatorStyle Font-Bold="true" Font-Names="Verdana" ForeColor="#663333"
     BackColor="#cccc66"></PathSeparatorStyle>
</asp:SiteMapPath>
```

Okay, it may not be pretty, but by using the `<PathSeparatorStyle>` element with the `SiteMapPath` control, you can change the visual appearance of the separator elements. Figure 17-5 shows the results.

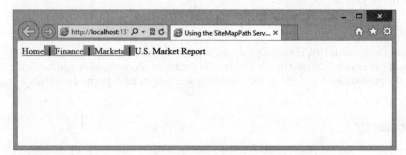

FIGURE 17-5

Using these constructs, you can also add an image as the separator, as shown in Listing 17-5.

LISTING 17-5: Using an image as the separator

```
<%@ Page Language="C#" %>

<html xmlns="http://www.w3.org/1999/xhtml">
<head runat="server">
    <title>Using the SiteMapPath Server Control</title>
</head>
<body>
    <form id="form1" runat="server">
        <asp:SiteMapPath ID="SiteMapPath1" runat="server">
            <PathSeparatorTemplate>
                <asp:Image ID="Image1" runat="server" ImageUrl="divider.gif" />
            </PathSeparatorTemplate>
        </asp:SiteMapPath>
    </form>
</body>
</html>
```

To utilize an image as the separator between the links, you use the `<PathSeparatorTemplate>` element and place an Image control within it. In fact, you can place any type of control between the navigation links that the SiteMapPath control produces.

The PathDirection Property

Another interesting property to use with the SiteMapPath control is `PathDirection`. This property changes the direction of the links generated in the output. Only two settings are possible for this property: `RootToCurrent` and `CurrentToRoot`.

The Root link is the first link in the display and is usually the Home page. The Current link is the link for the page currently being displayed. By default, this property is set to `RootToCurrent`. Changing the example to `CurrentToRoot` produces the results shown in Figure 17-6.

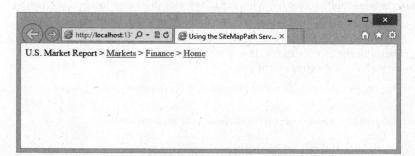

FIGURE 17-6

The ParentLevelsDisplayed Property

In some cases, your navigation may go quite deep. You can see on the sitemap shown in Listing 17-1 that you go three pages deep, which isn't a big deal. Some of you, however, might be dealing with sites that go quite a number of pages deeper. In these cases, using the SiteMapPath control might be a bit silly. Doing so would display a huge list of pages.

In a case like this, you can turn to the `ParentLevelsDisplayed` property that is part of the SiteMapPath control. When set, this property displays pages only as deep as specified. Therefore, if you are using the SiteMapPath control with the `Web.sitemap`, as shown in Listing 17-1, and you give the `ParentLevelsDisplayed` property a value of 3, you don't notice any change to your page. It already displays the path three pages deep. If you change this value to 2, however, the SiteMapPath control is constructed as follows:

```
<asp:SiteMapPath ID="Sitemappath1" runat="server" ParentLevelsDisplayed="2">
</asp:SiteMapPath>
```

Notice the result of this change in Figure 17-7. The SiteMapPath control shows links only two pages deep and doesn't show the Home page link.

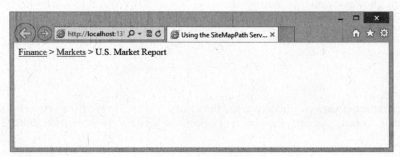

FIGURE 17-7

By default, no limit is set on the number of links shown, so the SiteMapPath control just generates the specified number of links based on what is labeled in the sitemap file.

The ShowToolTips Property

By default, the SiteMapPath control generates tooltips for each link if a description property is used within the `Web.sitemap` file. Remember, a tooltip is the text that appears onscreen when an end user hovers the mouse over one of the links in the SiteMapPath control. This capability was shown earlier in this chapter.

There may be times when you do not want your SiteMapPath control to show any tooltips for the links that it generates. For these situations, you can actually turn off this capability in a couple of ways. The first way is to omit any description attributes in the `.sitemap` file. If you remove these attributes from the file, the SiteMapPath has nothing to display for the tooltips on the page.

The other way to turn off the display of tooltips is to set the `ShowToolTips` property to `False`, as shown here:

```
<asp:SiteMapPath ID="Sitemappath1" runat="server" ShowToolTips="false">
</asp:SiteMapPath>
```

This code turns off the tooltips capability but still enables you to use the description property in the `.sitemap` file. You may still want to use the description attribute because it allows you to keep track of what the links in your file are used for. This feature is quite advantageous when you are dealing with hundreds or even thousands of links in your application.

The SiteMapPath Control's Child Elements

You already saw the use of the `<PathSeparatorStyle>` and the `<PathSeparatorTemplate>` child elements for the SiteMapPath control, but additional child elements exist. Table 17-2 covers each of the available child elements.

TABLE 17-2

CHILD ELEMENT	DESCRIPTION
CurrentNodeStyle	Applies styles to the link in the SiteMapPath navigation for the currently displayed page.
CurrentNodeTemplate	Applies a template construction to the link in the SiteMapPath navigation for the currently displayed page.
NodeStyle	Applies styles to all links in the SiteMapPath navigation. The settings applied in the CurrentNodeStyle or RootNodeStyle elements supersede any settings placed here.
NodeTemplate	Applies a template construction to all links in the SiteMapPath navigation. The settings applied in the CurrentNodeTemplate or RootNodeTemplate elements supersede any settings placed here.
PathSeparatorStyle	Applies styles to the link dividers in the SiteMapPath navigation.
PathSeparatorTemplate	Applies a template construction to the link dividers in the SiteMapPath navigation.
RootNodeStyle	Applies styles to the first link (the root link) in the SiteMapPath navigation.
RootNodeTemplate	Applies a template construction to the first link in the SiteMapPath navigation.

TREEVIEW SERVER CONTROL

The TreeView server control is a rich server control for rendering a hierarchy of data, so it is quite ideal for displaying what is contained in your .sitemap file. Figure 17-8 shows you how it displays the contents of the sitemap (again from Listing 17-1) that you have been working with thus far in this chapter. This figure first shows a completely collapsed TreeView control at the top of the screen; the second TreeView control has been completely expanded.

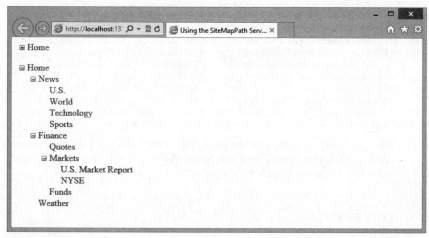

FIGURE 17-8

This control can dynamically load the nodes to be displayed as they are selected by the expandable and collapsible framework of the control. If the control can render the TreeView output along with some client-side script, the control can make a call back to the server if someone expands one of the nodes in the control to get the subnodes of the selected item. This feature is ideal if your site navigation system is large. In this case, loading nodes of the TreeView control dynamically greatly helps performance. One of the great features of this postback capability is that it is done under the covers and does not require the ASP.NET page to be completely refreshed. Of course, this capability is there only if the browser accepts the client-side code that goes along with the TreeView control. If the browser does not, the control knows this and renders only what is appropriate (pulling all the information that is required of the entire TreeView control). It only performs these JavaScript-based postbacks for those clients who can work with this client-side script.

You can definitely see this scenario in action if you run the TreeView control on a page that is being monitored by an HTTP sniffer of some kind to monitor the traffic moving across the wire.

> **NOTE** *Most web browsers come with built-in tools that facilitate sniffing network traffic; users of Firefox should install the Firebug extension from* `getfirebug.com`. *A good external sniffer is Fiddler, available at* `fiddler2.com`.

If your browser allows client-side script and you expand one of the expandable nodes of the TreeView control, your HTTP request will be similar to the following:

```
POST /Navigation/Default.aspx HTTP/1.1
Accept: */*
Accept-Language: en-us
Referrer: http://localhost:1882/Navigation/Default.aspx
Content-Type: application/x-www-form-urlencoded
Accept-Encoding: gzip, deflate
User-Agent: Mozilla/5.0 (compatible; MSIE 10.0; Windows NT 6.2; WOW64; Trident/6.0)

DNT: 1
Host: localhost:1882
Content-Length: 904
Proxy-Connection: Keep-Alive
Pragma: no-cache

__EVENTTARGET=&__EVENTARGUMENT=&TreeView1_ExpandState=c&TreeView1_SelectedNode=Tree
View1t0&TreeView1_PopulateLog=&__VIEWSTATE=%2FwEPDwUKLTY0ODk0OTE2Mg9kFgICBA9kFgICAw
88KwAJAgAPFggeDU5ldmVyRXhwYW5kZWRkHgtfIURhdGFCb3VuZGceDFNlbGVjdGVkTm9kZQULVHJlZVZpZ
XcxdDAeCUxhc3RJbmRleEIBZAgUKwACBQMwOjAUKwACFhAeBFRleHQFBEhvbWUeBVZhbHVlBQRIb21lHgtO
YXZpZ2F0ZVVybAUYL05hdmlnYXRpb24vRGVmYXVsdC5hc3B4HgdUb29sVGlwBQlIb21lIFBhZ2UeCERhdGF
QYXRoBRgvbmF2aWdhdGlvbi9kZWZhdWx0LmFzcHgeCURhdGFCb3VuZGceCFNlbGVjdGVkZx4QUG9wdWxhdG
VPbkRlbWFuZGdkZBgBBR5fX0NvbnRyb2xzUmVxdWlyZVBvc3RCYWNrS2V5X18WAwURTG9naW4xJFJlbWVtY
mVyTWUFF0xvZ2luMSRMb2dpbkltYWdlQnV0dG9uBQlUcmVlVmlldzFtwszVpUMxFTDtpERnNjgEIkWWbg%3
D%3D&Login1$UserName=&Login1$Password=&__CALLBACKID=TreeView1&__CALLBACKPARAM=0%7C1
%7Ctft%7C4%7CHome24%7C2Fnavigation%2Fdefault.aspxHome&__EVENTVALIDATION=%2FwEWBgKg
8Yn8DwKUvNa1DwL666vYDAKC0q%2BkBgKnz4ybCAKn5fLxBaSy6WQwPagNZsHisWRoJfuiopOe
```

The response from your ASP.NET application will *not* be the entire page that holds the TreeView control, but instead, it is a small portion of HTML that is used by a JavaScript method on the page and is loaded into the TreeView control dynamically. Here is a sample response:

```
HTTP/1.1 200 OK
Server: Microsoft-IIS/8.0
Date: Sat, 10 Nov 2012 17:55:03 GMT
X-AspNet-Version: 4.0.30319
Cache-Control: private, no-store
Content-Type: text/html; charset=utf-8
Content-Length: 1756
Connection: Close

112|/wEWCgKg8Yn8DwKUvNa1DwL666vYDAKC0q+kBgKnz4ybCAKn5fLxBQKAgtPaBALEmcbhCgK8nZDfCAL
M/ZK8AR/nFcl4nlPgp6HcFlU6YiFBfoNM14|nn|<div id="TreeView1n6Nodes"
style="display:none;">
```

```
<table cellpadding="0" cellspacing="0" style="border-width:0;">
     <tr>
             <td><div style="width:20px;height:1px"></div></td><td><div
             style="width:20px;height:1px"><img
             src="/Navigation/WebResource.axd?d=GOWKLfnbFU9fYyy
             PCMT8DIfngU4PXeMiAHxJNuXB-tU1&amp;t=632662834831594592" alt="" />
             </div></td><td><div style="width:20px;height:1px"><img
             src="/Navigation/WebResource.axd?d=GOWKLfnbFU9fYyyPCMT8DIfngU
             4PXeMiAHxJNuXB-tU1&amp;t=632662834831594592" alt="" />
             </div></td><td><img
             src="/Navigation/WebResource.axd?d=GOWKLfnbFU9fYyy
             PCMT8DCXmyNCWX5x-n_pSXFIW2qE1&amp;t=632662834831594592"
             alt="" /></td><td style="white-space:nowrap;">
             <a href="/Navigation/MarketsUSasdf.aspx"
             title="Looking at the U.S. Market" id="TreeView1t12"
             style="text-decoration:none;">U.S. Market Report</a></td>
     </tr>
</table><table cellpadding="0" cellspacing="0" style="border-width:0;">
     <tr>
             <td><div style="width:20px;height:1px"></div></td><td><div
             style="width:20px;height:1px"><img
             src="/Navigation/WebResource.axd?d=GOWKLfnbFU9fYyyPCMT8DI
             fngU4PXeMiAHxJNuXB-tU1&amp;t=632662834831594592" alt="" />
             </div></td><td><div style="width:20px;height:1px"><img
             src="/Navigation/WebResource.axd?d=GOWKLfnbFU9fYyyPCMT8DI
             fngU4PXeMiAHxJNuXB-tU1&amp;t=632662834831594592" alt="" />
             </div></td><td><img
             src="/Navigation/WebResource.axd?d=GOWKLfnbFU9fY
             yyPCMT8DGyYai5iS-79vjeYzdeJoiI1&amp;t=632662834831594592"
             alt="" />
             </td><td style="white-space:nowrap;">
             <a href="/Navigation/NYSE.aspx" title="The New York Stock Exchange"
             id="TreeView1t13" style="text-decoration:none;">NYSE</a></td>
     </tr>
</table>
</div>
```

This postback capability is rather powerful, but if you want to disable it (even for browsers that can handle it), you just set the `PopulateNodesFromClient` attribute to `False` in the TreeView control (the default value is `True`).

The TreeView control is quite customizable; but first, take a look at how to create a default version of the control using the `.sitemap` file from Listing 17-1. For this example, continue to use the `MarketsUS.aspx` page you created earlier.

The first step is to create a SiteMapDataSource control on the page. When working with the TreeView control that displays the contents of your `.sitemap` file, you must apply one of these data source controls. The TreeView control doesn't just bind to your sitemap file automatically as the SiteMapPath control does.

After a basic SiteMapDataSource control is in place, position a TreeView control on the page and set the `DataSourceId` property to `SiteMapDataSource1`. When you have finished, your code should look like Listing 17-6.

LISTING 17-6: A basic TreeView control

```
<%@ Page Language="C#" %>

<html xmlns="http://www.w3.org/1999/xhtml">
<head runat="server">
    <title>Using the TreeView Server Control</title>
</head>
```

continues

LISTING 17-6 *(continued)*

```
<body>
    <form id="form1" runat="server">
        <asp:SiteMapPath ID="SiteMapPath1" runat="server">
        </asp:SiteMapPath>
        <br /><p>
        <asp:TreeView ID="TreeView1" runat="server"
         DataSourceID="SiteMapDataSource1">
        </asp:TreeView>
        <asp:SiteMapDataSource ID="SiteMapDataSource1" runat="server" /></p>
    </form>
</body>
</html>
```

After you run the page and expand the TreeView control, the results appear as shown in Figure 17-9.

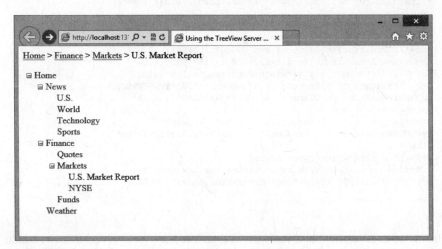

FIGURE 17-9

This TreeView control is very basic. The great thing about this control is that it allows for a high degree of customization and even gives you the capability to use some predefined styles that come prepackaged with ASP.NET 4.5.

Identifying the TreeView Control's Built-In Styles

As stated, the TreeView control does come with a number of pre-built styles right out of the box. The best way to utilize these predefined styles is to do so from the Design view of your page. Click on the arrow located in the upper-right section of the server control in the Design view in Visual Studio 2012 to find the Auto Format option. Click this option and a number of styles become available to you. Selecting one of these styles changes the code of your TreeView control to adapt to that chosen style. For example, if you choose MSDN from the list of options, the simple one-line TreeView control you created is converted to what is shown in Listing 17-7.

LISTING 17-7: A TreeView control with the MSDN style applied to it

```
<asp:TreeView ID="TreeView1" runat="server" DataSourceID="SiteMapDataSource1"
 ImageSet="Msdn" NodeIndent="10">
    <ParentNodeStyle Font-Bold="False" />
    <HoverNodeStyle BackColor="#CCCCCC" BorderColor="#888888" BorderStyle="Solid"
```

```
            Font-Underline="True" />
        <SelectedNodeStyle BackColor="White" BorderColor="#888888" BorderStyle="Solid"
            BorderWidth="1px" Font-Underline="False" HorizontalPadding="3px"
            VerticalPadding="1px" />
        <NodeStyle Font-Names="Verdana" Font-Size="8pt" ForeColor="Black"
            HorizontalPadding="5px" NodeSpacing="1px" VerticalPadding="2px" />
    </asp:TreeView>
```

As you can see, if you use these built-in styles, then completely changing the look-and-feel of the TreeView control is not too difficult. When you run this bit of code, you get the results shown in Figure 17-10.

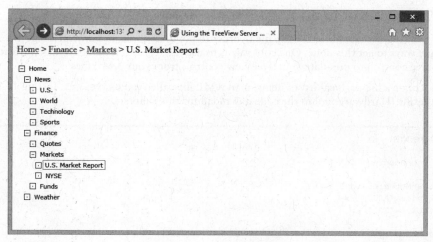

FIGURE 17-10

Examining the Parts of the TreeView Control

To master working with the TreeView control, you must understand the terminology used for each part of the hierarchical tree that is created by the control.

Every element or entry in the TreeView control is called a *node*. The uppermost node in the hierarchy of nodes is the *root node*. A TreeView control can have multiple root nodes. Any node, including the root node, is also considered a *parent node* if it has any nodes that are directly under it in the hierarchy of nodes. The nodes directly under this parent node are referred to as *child nodes*. Each parent node can have one or more child nodes. A node that contains no child nodes is called a *leaf node*.

The following is based on the sitemap shown earlier and details the use of this terminology:

```
    Home - Root node, parent node
      News - Parent node, child node
        U.S. - Child node, leaf node
        World - Child node, leaf node
        Technology - Child node, leaf node
        Sports - Child node, leaf node
      Finance - Parent node, child node
        Quotes - Child node, leaf node
        Markets - Parent node, child node
          U.S. Market Report - Child node, leaf node
          NYSE - Child node, leaf node
        Funds - Child node, leaf node
      Weather - Child node, leaf node
```

From this listing, you can see what each node is and how it is referred to in the hierarchy of nodes. For example, the `U.S. Market Report` node is a leaf node—meaning that it doesn't have any child nodes associated with it. However, it is also a child node to the `Markets` node, which is a parent node to the `U.S. Market Report` node. If you are working with the `Markets` node directly, it is also a child node to the `Finance` node, which is its parent node. The main point to take away from all this is that each node in the sitemap hierarchy has a relationship to the other nodes in the hierarchy. You must understand these relationships because you can programmatically work with these nodes (as is demonstrated later in this chapter), and the methods used for working with them include terms such as `RootNode`, `CurrentNode`, and `ParentNode`.

Binding the TreeView Control to an XML File

You are not limited to working with just a `.sitemap` file in order to populate the nodes of your TreeView controls. You have many ways to get this done. One cool way is to use the XmlDataSource control (instead of the SiteMapDataSource control) to populate your TreeView controls from your XML files.

For an example of this, create a hierarchical list of items in an XML file called `Hardware.xml`. Listing 17-8 shows an example of this file (Hardware.xml in the code download for this chapter).

LISTING 17-8: Hardware.xml

```xml
<?xml version="1.0" encoding="utf-8"?>
<Hardware>
    <Item Category="Motherboards">
        <Option Choice="ASUS" />
        <Option Choice="MSI" />
    </Item>
    <Item Category="Memory">
        <Option Choice="2048mb" />
        <Option Choice="4096mb" />
        <Option Choice="8192mb" />
    </Item>
    <Item Category="HardDrives">
        <Option Choice="250GB" />
        <Option Choice="500GB" />
        <Option Choice="750GB" />
    </Item>
    <Item Category="Drives">
        <Option Choice="DVD Burner" />
        <Option Choice="Blu-ray" />
        <Option Choice="Blu-ray Burner" />
    </Item>
</Hardware>
```

As you can see, this list is not meant to be used for site navigation purposes, but instead for allowing the end user to make a selection from a hierarchical list of options. This XML file is divided into four categories of available options: `Motherboards`, `Memory`, `HardDrives`, and `Drives`. To bind your TreeView control to this XML file, use an XmlDataSource control that specifies the location of the XML file you are going to use. Then, within the TreeView control itself, use the `<asp:TreeNodeBinding>` element to specify which elements to bind in the XML file to populate the nodes of the TreeView control, as shown in Listing 17-9.

LISTING 17-9: Binding a TreeView control to the Hardware.xml file

```
<%@ Page Language="C#" %>

<html xmlns="http://www.w3.org/1999/xhtml">
<head runat="server">
    <title>Latest Hardware</title>
```

```
        </head>
        <body>
            <form id="form1" runat="server">
                <asp:TreeView ID="TreeView1" runat="server" DataSourceID="XmlDataSource1">
                    <DataBindings>
                        <asp:TreeNodeBinding DataMember="Hardware"
                         Text="Computer Hardware" />
                        <asp:TreeNodeBinding DataMember="Item" TextField="Category" />
                        <asp:TreeNodeBinding DataMember="Option" TextField="Choice" />
                    </DataBindings>
                </asp:TreeView>
                <asp:XmlDataSource ID="XmlDataSource1" runat="server"
                 DataFile="Hardware.xml">
                </asp:XmlDataSource>
            </form>
        </body>
        </html>
```

The first item to look at is the `<asp:XmlDataSource>` control. It is just as simple as the previous `<asp:SiteMapDataSource>` control, but it points at the `Hardware.xml` file using the `DataFile` property.

The next step is to create a TreeView control that binds to this particular XML file. You can bind a default TreeView control directly to the XmlDataSource control as follows:

```
<asp:TreeView ID="TreeView1" runat="server" DataSourceId="XmlDataSource1" />
```

When you do this, you get the *incorrect* result shown in Figure 17-11.

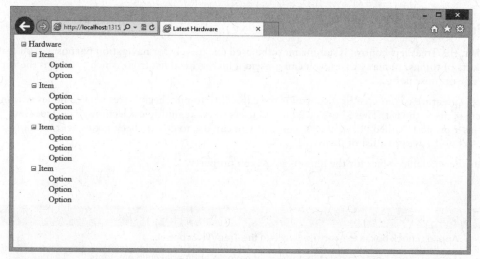

FIGURE 17-11

As you can see, the TreeView control binds just fine to the `Hardware.xml` file, but looking at the nodes within the TreeView control, you can see that it is simply displaying the names of the actual XML elements from the file itself. Because this isn't what you want, you specify how to bind to the XML file with the use of the `<DataBindings>` element within the TreeView control.

The `<DataBindings>` element encapsulates one or more `TreeNodeBinding` objects. Two of the more important available properties of a `TreeNodeBinding` object are the `DataMember` and `TextField` properties. The `DataMember` property points to the name of the XML element that the TreeView control should look for. The `TextField` property specifies the XML attribute that the TreeView should look for in that particular XML element. If you use the `<DataBindings>` element correctly, using the `<DataBindings>` construct, you get the result shown in Figure 17-12.

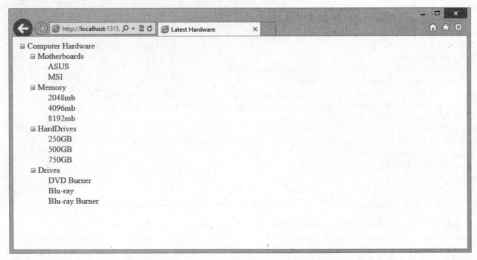

FIGURE 17-12

You can also see from Listing 17-9 that you can override the text value of the root node from the XML file, `<Hardware>`, and have it appear as `Computer Hardware` in the TreeView control, as follows:

```
<asp:TreeNodeBinding DataMember="Hardware" Text="Computer Hardware" />
```

Selecting Multiple Options in a TreeView

As stated earlier, the TreeView control is not meant to be used exclusively for navigation purposes. You can use it for all sorts of things. In many cases, you can present a hierarchical list from which you want the end user to select one or more items.

One great built-in feature of the TreeView control is the capability to put check boxes next to nodes within the hierarchical items in the list. These boxes enable end users to make multiple selections. The TreeView control contains a property called `ShowCheckBoxes` that you can use to create check boxes next to many different types of nodes within a list of items.

Table 17-3 lists the available values for the `ShowCheckBoxes` property.

TABLE 17-3

VALUE	DESCRIPTION
All	Applies check boxes to every node within the TreeView control.
Leaf	Applies check boxes to only the nodes that have no additional child elements.
None	Applies no check boxes to any node within the TreeView control.
Parent	Applies check boxes to only the nodes considered parent nodes within the TreeView control. A parent node has at least one child node associated with it.
Root	Applies a check box to any root node contained within the TreeView control.

When working with the `ShowCheckBoxes` property, you can set it declaratively in the control itself, as follows:

```
<asp:TreeView ID="Treeview1" runat="server" Font-Underline="false"
  DataSourceID="XmlDataSource1" ShowCheckBoxes="Leaf">
   ...
</asp:TreeViewTreeView>
```

Or you can set it programmatically by using the following code:

VB

```
TreeView1.ShowCheckBoxes = TreeNodeTypes.Leaf
```

C#

```
TreeView1.ShowCheckBoxes = TreeNodeTypes.Leaf;
```

For an example of using check boxes with the TreeView control, let's continue to expand on the computer hardware example from Listing 17-9. Create a hierarchical list that enables people to select multiple items from the list in order to receive additional information about them. Listing 17-10 shows an example of this list.

LISTING 17-10: Applying check boxes next to the leaf nodes within the hierarchical list of nodes

VB

```
<%@ Page Language="VB" %>
<script runat="server">
    Protected Sub Button1_Click(ByVal sender As Object, ByVal e As System.EventArgs)
        If TreeView1.CheckedNodes.Count > 0 Then
            Label1.Text = "We are sending you information on:<p>"

            For Each node As TreeNode In TreeView1.CheckedNodes
                Label1.Text += node.Text & " " & node.Parent.Text & "<br>"
            Next
        Else
            Label1.Text = "You didn't select anything. Sorry!"
        End If
    End Sub
</script>
<html xmlns="http://www.w3.org/1999/xhtml">
<head runat="server">
    <title>Latest Hardware</title>
</head>
<body>
    <form runat="server">
        Please select the items you are interested in:
        <p>
        <asp:TreeView ID="TreeView1" runat="server" Font-Underline="False"
         DataSourceID="XmlDataSource1" ShowCheckBoxes="Leaf">
            <DataBindings>
                <asp:TreeNodeBinding DataMember="Hardware"
                 Text="Computer Hardware" />
                <asp:TreeNodeBinding DataMember="Item" TextField="Category" />
                <asp:TreeNodeBinding DataMember="Option" TextField="Choice" />
            </DataBindings>
        </asp:TreeView>
        <p>
        <asp:Button ID="Button1" runat="server" Text="Submit Choices"
         OnClick="Button1_Click" />
        </p>
        <asp:XmlDataSource ID="XmlDataSource1" runat="server"
         DataFile="Hardware.xml">
        </asp:XmlDataSource>
        </p>
```

continues

LISTING 17-10 *(continued)*

```
            <asp:Label ID="Label1" runat="Server" />
        </form>
    </body>
</html>
```

C#

```
<%@ Page Language="C#" %>
<script runat="server">
    protected void Button1_Click(object sender, System.EventArgs e)
    {
        if (TreeView1.CheckedNodes.Count > 0)
        {
            Label1.Text = "We are sending you information on:<p>";
            foreach (TreeNode node in TreeView1.CheckedNodes)
            {
                Label1.Text += node.Text + " " + node.Parent.Text + "<br>";
            }
        }
        else
        {
            Label1.Text = "You didn't select anything. Sorry!";
        }
    }
</script>
```

In this example, you first set the `ShowTextBoxes` property to `Leaf`, meaning that you are interested in having check boxes appear only next to items in the TreeView control that do not contain any child nodes. The items with check boxes next to them should be the last items that can be expanded in the hierarchical list.

After setting this property, you then work with the items that are selected by the end user in the `Button1_Click` event. The first thing you should check is whether any selection was made:

```
if (TreeView1.CheckedNodes.Count > 0) {
    ...
}
```

In this case, the number of checked nodes on the postback needs to be greater than zero, meaning that at least one was selected. If so, you can execute the code within the `If` statement. The `If` statement then proceeds to populate the Label control that is on the page. To populate the Label control with data from the selected nodes, you use a `For Each` statement, as shown here:

```
foreach (TreeNode node in TreeView1.CheckedNodes) {
    ...
}
```

This works with an instance of a `TreeNode` object and checks each `TreeNode` object within the `TreeView1` collection of checked nodes.

For each node that is checked, you grab the node's `Text` value and the `Text` value of this node's parent node to further populate the Label control, as follows:

```
Label1.Text += node.Text + " " + node.Parent.Text + "<br>";
```

In the end, you get a page that produces the results shown in Figure 17-13.

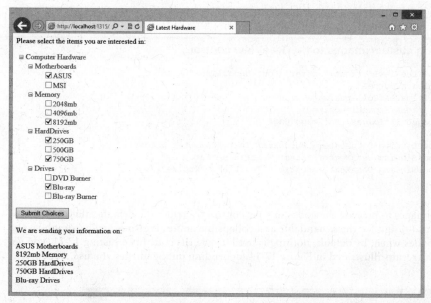

FIGURE 17-13

Specifying Custom Icons in the TreeView Control

The TreeView control allows for a high degree of customization. You saw earlier in the chapter that you can customize the look-and-feel of the TreeView control by specifying one of the built-in styles. Applying one of these styles dramatically changes the appearance of the control. One of the most noticeable changes concerns the icons used for the nodes within the TreeView control. Although it is not as easy as just selecting one of the styles built into the TreeView control, you can apply your own icons to be used for the nodes within the hierarchical list of nodes.

The TreeView control contains the properties discussed in Table 17-4. These properties enable you to specify your own images to use for the nodes of the control.

TABLE 17-4

PROPERTY	DESCRIPTION
CollapseImageUrl	Applies a custom image next to nodes that have been expanded to show any of their child nodes and have the capability of being collapsed.
ExpandImageUrl	Applies a custom image next to nodes that have the capability of being expanded to display their child nodes.
LeafNodeStyle-ImageUrl	Applies a custom image next to a node that has no child nodes and is last in the hierarchical chain of nodes.
NoExpandImageUrl	Applies a custom image to nodes that, for programmatic reasons, cannot be expanded or to nodes that are leaf nodes. This property is primarily used for spacing purposes to align leaf nodes with their parent nodes.
ParentNodeStyle-ImageUrl	Applies a custom image only to the parent nodes within the TreeView control.
RootNodeStyle-ImageUrl	Applies a custom image next to only the root nodes within the TreeView control.

Listing 17-11 shows an example of these properties in use.

LISTING 17-11: Applying custom images to the TreeView control

```
<asp:TreeView ID="TreeView1" runat="server" Font-Underline="False"
 DataSourceId="XmlDataSource1"
 CollapseImageUrl="Images/CollapseImage.png"
 ExpandImageUrl="Images/ExpandImage.png"
 LeafNodeStyle-ImageUrl="Images/LeafImage.png">
    <DataBindings>
        <asp:TreeNodeBinding DataMember="Hardware" Text="Computer Hardware" />
        <asp:TreeNodeBinding DataMember="Item" TextField="Category" />
        <asp:TreeNodeBinding DataMember="Option" TextField="Choice" />
    </DataBindings>
</asp:TreeView>
```

Specifying these three images to precede the nodes in your control overrides the default values of using a plus (+) sign and a minus (–) sign for the expandable and collapsible nodes. It also overrides simply using an image for any leaf nodes when, by default, nothing is used. Using the code from Listing 17-11, you get something similar to the results illustrated in Figure 17-14 (depending on the images you use, of course).

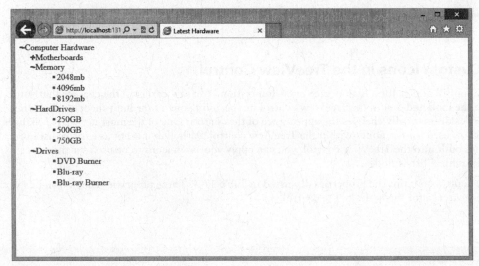

FIGURE 17-14

Specifying Lines Used to Connect Nodes

Because the TreeView control shows a hierarchical list of items to the end user, you sometimes want to show the relationship between these hierarchical items more explicitly than is shown by default with the TreeView control. One possibility is to show line connections between parent and child nodes within the display. Simply set the ShowLines property of the TreeView control to True (by default, this property is set to False):

```
<asp:TreeView ID="TreeView1" runat="server" Font-Underline="False"
 DataSourceId="XmlDataSource1" ShowCheckBoxes="Leaf" ShowLines="True">
    . . .
</asp:TreeViewTreeView>
```

This code gives the result shown in Figure 17-15.

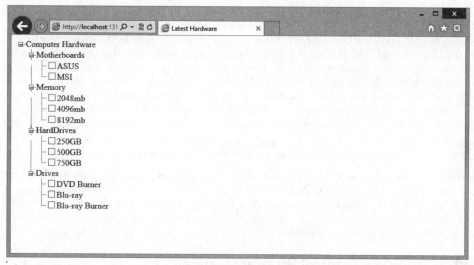

FIGURE 17-15

If the `ShowLines` property is set to `True`, you can also define your own lines and images within the TreeView control. Doing so is quite easy because Visual Studio 2012 provides you with an ASP.NET TreeView Line Image Generator tool. This tool enables you to visually design how you want the lines and corresponding expanding and collapsing images to appear. After you have it set up as you want, the tool then creates all the necessary files for any of your TreeView controls to use.

To get at the tool, move to the Design view of your file and click the smart tag for the TreeView control that is on your page. Here, you find the option Customize Line Images. You will not see this option unless the Show Lines check box is selected. Click it and the ASP.NET TreeView Line Image Generator dialog box appears (shown in Figure 17-16).

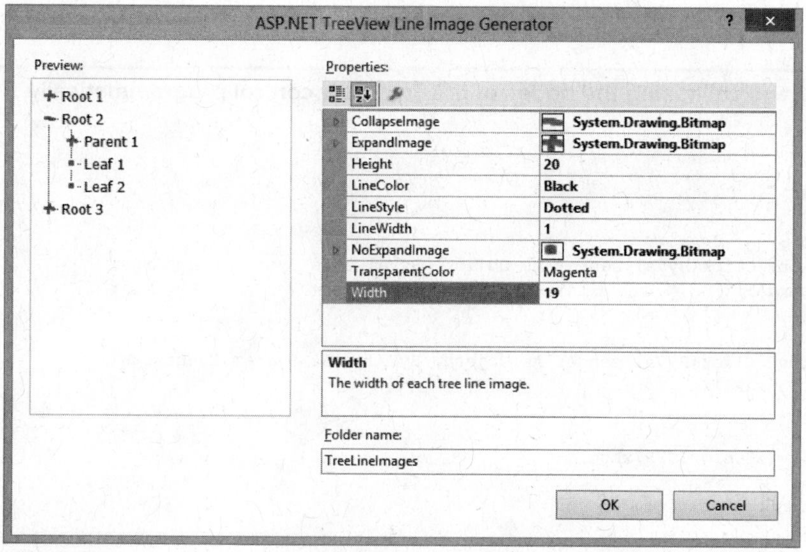

FIGURE 17-16

From within this dialog box, you can select the images used for the nodes that require an Expand, Collapse, or NoCollapse icon. You can also specify the color and style of the lines that connect the nodes. As you create your styles, a sample TreeView control output is displayed for you directly in the dialog box based on how your styles are to be applied. The final step is to choose the output of the files that this dialog box will create. When you have completed this step, click OK. This generates a long list of new files to the folder that you specified in the dialog box. By default, the ASP.NET TreeView Line Image Generator wants you to name the output folder TreeLineImages, but feel free to name it as you want. If the folder does not exist in the project, you are prompted to allow Visual Studio to create the folder for you. After this folder is in place, the TreeView control can use your new images and styles if you set the `LineImagesFolder` property as follows:

```
<asp:TreeView ID="TreeView1" runat="server" ShowLines="True"
    DataSourceId="SiteMapDataSource1" LineImagesFolder="TreeViewLineImages">
```

The important properties are shown in bold. You must set the `ShowLines` property to `True`. After it is set, the property uses the default settings displayed earlier, unless you have specified a location where it can retrieve custom images and styles using the `LineImagesFolder` property. As you can see, this simply points to the new folder, `TreeViewLineImages`, which contains all the new images and styles you created. Look in the folder—seeing what the tool produces is interesting.

Working with the TreeView Control Programmatically

So far, with the TreeView control, you have learned how to work with the control declaratively. The great thing about ASP.NET is that you are not simply required to work with its components declaratively, but you can also manipulate these controls programmatically.

The TreeView control has an associated `TreeView` class that enables you to completely manage the TreeView control and how it functions from within your code. The next section looks at how to use some of the more common ways to control the `TreeView` programmatically.

Expanding and Collapsing Nodes Programmatically

One thing you can do with your TreeView control is to expand or collapse the nodes within the hierarchy programmatically. You can do so by using either the `ExpandAll` or `CollapseAll` methods from the `TreeView` class. Listing 17-12 shows you one of the earlier TreeView controls that you used in Listing 17-6, but with a couple of buttons above it that you can now use to initiate the expanding and collapsing of the nodes.

LISTING 17-12: Expanding and collapsing the nodes of the TreeView control programmatically

VB

```
<%@ Page Language="VB" %>

<script runat="server">
    Protected Sub Button1_Click(ByVal sender As Object, ByVal e As System.EventArgs)
        TreeView1.ExpandAll()
    End Sub

    Protected Sub Button2_Click(ByVal sender As Object, ByVal e As System.EventArgs)
        TreeView1.CollapseAll()
    End Sub
</script>
<html xmlns="http://www.w3.org/1999/xhtml">
<head runat="server">
    <title>TreeView Control</title>
</head>
<body>
    <form id="Form1" runat="server">
```

```
        <p>
            <asp:Button ID="Button1" runat="server" Text="Expand Nodes"
             OnClick="Button1_Click" />
            <asp:Button ID="Button2" runat="server" Text="Collapse Nodes"
             OnClick="Button2_Click" />
            <br />
            <br />
        <asp:TreeView ID="TreeView1" runat="server"
         DataSourceId="SiteMapDataSource1">
        </asp:TreeView>
        <asp:SiteMapDataSource ID="SiteMapDataSource1" runat="server" /></p>
    </form>
</body>
</html>
```

C#

```
<%@ Page Language="C#" %>

<script runat="server">
    protected void Button1_Click(object sender, System.EventArgs e)
    {
        TreeView1.ExpandAll();
    }

    protected void Button2_Click(object sender, System.EventArgs e)
    {
        TreeView1.CollapseAll();
    }
</script>
```

Running this page gives you two buttons above your TreeView control. Clicking the first button invokes the ExpandAll() method and completely expands the entire list of nodes. Clicking the second button invokes the CollapseAll() method and completely collapses the list of nodes (see Figure 17-17).

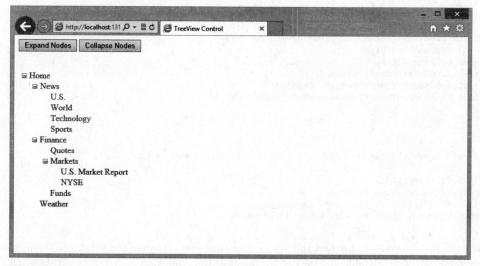

FIGURE 17-17

The example shown in Listing 17-12 is nice, but it expands and collapses the nodes only on end-user actions (when the end user clicks the button). Being able to initiate this action programmatically would be even nicer.

You might want to simply place the `TreeView1.CollapseAll()` command within the `Page_Load` event, but if you try this technique, you'll see that it doesn't work. Instead, you use the `OnDataBound` attribute within the TreeView control:

```
<asp:TreeView ID="TreeView1" runat="server"
 DataSourceId="SiteMapDataSource1" OnDataBound="TreeView1_DataBound">
</asp:TreeView>
```

The value of this attribute points to a method in your code, as shown here:

VB

```
Protected Sub TreeView1_DataBound(ByVal sender As Object, _
  ByVal e As System.EventArgs)
    TreeView1.CollapseAll()
End Sub
```

C#

```
protected void TreeView1_DataBound(object sender, System.EventArgs e)
{
    TreeView1.CollapseAll();
}
```

Now when you run the page, notice that the TreeView control is completely collapsed when the page is first loaded in the browser.

You can also expand or collapse specific nodes within the tree instead of just working the entire list. For this example, use the `TreeView1_DataBound()` method you just created. Using the sitemap from Listing 17-1, change the `TreeView1_DataBound()` method so that it appears as shown in Listing 17-13.

LISTING 17-13: Expanding specific nodes programmatically

VB

```
Protected Sub TreeView1_DataBound(ByVal sender As Object, _
  ByVal e As System.EventArgs)
    TreeView1.CollapseAll()
    TreeView1.FindNode("Home").Expand()
    TreeView1.FindNode("Home/Finance").Expand()
    TreeView1.FindNode("Home/Finance/Markets").Expand()
End Sub
```

C#

```
protected void TreeView1_DataBound(object sender, System.EventArgs e)
{
    TreeView1.CollapseAll();
    TreeView1.FindNode("Home").Expand();
    TreeView1.FindNode("Home/Finance").Expand();
    TreeView1.FindNode("Home/Finance/Markets").Expand();
}
```

In this case, you use the `FindNode()` method and expand the node that is found. The `FindNode()` method takes a `String` value, which is the node and the path of the node that you want to reference. For example, `TreeView1.FindNode("Home/Finance").Expand()` expands the `Finance` node. To find the node, specifying the entire path from the root node to the node you want to work with (in this case, the `Finance` node) is important. You separate the nodes within the sitemap path structure with a forward slash between each of the nodes in the sitemap path.

Note that you had to expand each of the nodes individually until you got to the `Finance` node. If you simply used `TreeView1.FindNode("Home/Finance/Markets").Expand()` in the `TreeView1_DataBound()` method, the `Markets` node would indeed be expanded, but the parent nodes above it (the `Finance` and `Home` nodes) would not have been expanded, and you wouldn't see the expanded `Markets` node when invoking the page. (Try it; it's interesting.)

Instead of using the `Expand` method, you can just as easily set the `Expanded` property to `True`, as shown in Listing 17-14.

LISTING 17-14: Expanding nodes programmatically using the Expanded property

VB

```
Protected Sub TreeView1_DataBound(ByVal sender As Object, _
  ByVal e As System.EventArgs)
    TreeView1.CollapseAll()
    TreeView1.FindNode("Home").Expanded = True
    TreeView1.FindNode("Home/Finance").Expanded = True
    TreeView1.FindNode("Home/Finance/Markets").Expanded = True
End Sub
```

C#

```
protected void TreeView1_DataBound(object sender, System.EventArgs e)
{
    TreeView1.CollapseAll();
    TreeView1.FindNode("Home").Expanded = true;
    TreeView1.FindNode("Home/Finance").Expanded = true;
    TreeView1.FindNode("Home/Finance/Markets").Expanded = true;
}
```

Although you focus on the `Expand` method and the `Expanded` property here, you can just as easily programmatically collapse nodes using the `Collapse()` method. No `Collapsed` property really exists. Instead, you simply set the `Expanded` property to `False`.

Adding Nodes

Another interesting thing you can do with the TreeView control is to add nodes to the overall hierarchy programmatically. The TreeView control is made up of a collection of `TreeNode` objects. Therefore, as you see in previous examples, the `Finance` node is actually a `TreeNode` object that you can work with programmatically. It includes the capability to add other `TreeNode` objects.

A `TreeNode` object typically stores a `Text` and `Value` property. The `Text` property is what is displayed in the TreeView control for the end user. The `Value` property is an additional data item that you can use to associate with this particular `TreeNode` object. Another property that you can use (if your TreeView control is a list of navigational links) is the `NavigateUrl` property. Listing 17-15 demonstrates how to add nodes programmatically to the same sitemap from Listing 17-1 that you have been using.

LISTING 17-15: Adding nodes programmatically to the TreeView control

VB

```
<%@ Page Language="VB" %>

<script runat="server">
    Protected Sub Button1_Click(ByVal sender As Object, ByVal e As System.EventArgs)
        TreeView1.ExpandAll()
    End Sub
    Protected Sub Button2_Click(ByVal sender As Object, ByVal e As System.EventArgs)
        TreeView1.CollapseAll()
```

continues

LISTING 17-15 *(continued)*

```
    End Sub
    Protected Sub Button3_Click(ByVal sender As Object, ByVal e As System.EventArgs)
        Dim myNode As New TreeNode
        myNode.Text = TextBox1.Text
        myNode.NavigateUrl = TextBox2.Text
        TreeView1.FindNode("Home/Finance/Markets").ChildNodes.Add(myNode)
    End Sub
</script>

<html xmlns="http://www.w3.org/1999/xhtml">
<head runat="server">
    <title>TreeView Control</title>
</head>
<body>
    <form id="Form1" runat="server">
        <p>
            <asp:Button ID="Button1" runat="server" Text="Expand Nodes"
             OnClick="Button1_Click" />
            <asp:Button ID="Button2" runat="server" Text="Collapse Nodes"
             OnClick="Button2_Click" /></p>
        <p>
            <strong>Text of new node:</strong>
            <asp:TextBox ID="TextBox1" runat="server">
            </asp:TextBox>
        </p>
        <p>
            <strong>Destination URL of new node:</strong>
            <asp:TextBox ID="TextBox2" runat="server">
            </asp:TextBox>
            <br />
            <br />
            <asp:Button ID="Button3" runat="server" Text="Add New Node"
             OnClick="Button3_Click" />
        </p>
        <p>
        <asp:TreeView ID="TreeView1" runat="server"
         DataSourceId="SiteMapDataSource1">
        </asp:TreeView></p>
        <p>
        <asp:SiteMapDataSource ID="SiteMapDataSource1" runat="server" /></p>
    </form>
</body>
</html>
```

C#

```
<%@ Page Language="C#" %>

<script runat="server">
protected void Button3_Click(object sender, System.EventArgs e)
{
    TreeNode myNode = new TreeNode();
    myNode.Text = TextBox1.Text;
    myNode.NavigateUrl = TextBox2.Text;
    TreeView1.FindNode("Home/Finance/Markets").ChildNodes.Add(myNode);
}
</script>
```

This page contains two textboxes and a new Button control. The first textbox is used to populate the `Text` property of the new node that is created. The second textbox is used to populate the `NavigateUrl` property of the new node.

If you run the page, you can expand the entire hierarchy by clicking the `Expand Nodes` button. Then you can add child nodes to the `Markets` node. To add a new node programmatically, use the `FindNode` method as you did before to find the `Markets` node. When you find it, you can add child nodes by using the `ChildNodes.Add()` method and pass in a `TreeNode` object instance. Submitting `NASDAQ` in the first textbox and `Nasdaq.aspx` in the second textbox changes your TreeView control, as illustrated in Figure 17-18.

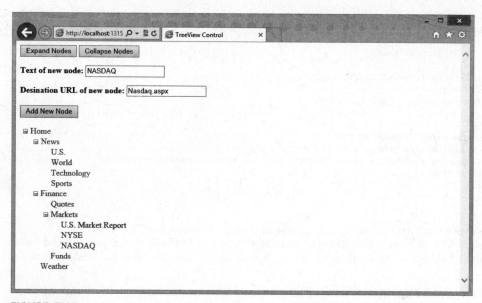

FIGURE 17-18

After it is added, the node stays added even after the hierarchy tree is collapsed and reopened. You can also add as many child nodes as you want to the `Markets` node. Note that, although you are changing nodes programmatically, this in no way alters the contents of the data source (the XML file, or the `.sitemap` file). These sources remain unchanged throughout the entire process.

MENU SERVER CONTROL

One of the cooler navigation controls found in ASP.NET 4.5 is the Menu server control. This control is ideal for allowing the end user to navigate a larger hierarchy of options while utilizing very little browser real estate in the process. Figure 17-19 shows you what the menu control looks like when it is either completely collapsed or completely extended down one of the branches of the hierarchy.

From here, you can see that the first Menu control displayed simply shows the Home link with a small arrow to the right of the display. The arrow means that more options are available that relate to this upmost link in the hierarchy. The second Menu control displayed shows what the default control looks like when the end user works down one of the branches provided by the sitemap.

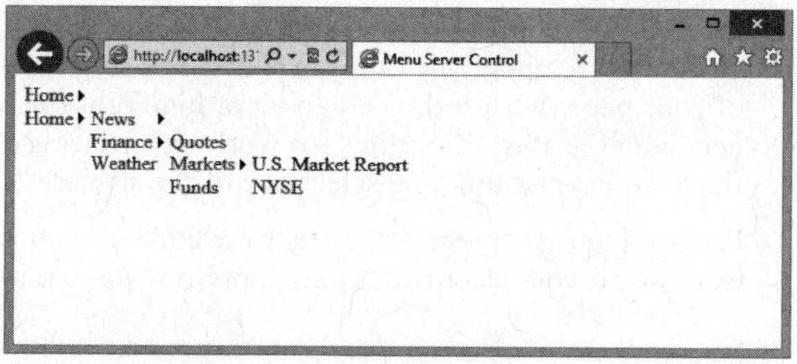

FIGURE 17-19

The Menu control is an ideal control to use when you have lots of options—whether these options are selections the end user can make or navigation points provided by the application in which they are working. The Menu control can provide a multitude of options and consumes little space in the process.

Using the Menu control in your ASP.NET applications is rather simple. The Menu control works with a SiteMapDataSource control. You can drag and drop the SiteMapDataSource control and the Menu control onto the Visual Studio 2012 design surface and connect the two by using the Menu control's `DataSourceId` property. Alternatively, you can create and connect them directly in code. Listing 17-16 shows an example of the Menu control in its simplest form.

LISTING 17-16: A simple use of the Menu control

```
<%@ Page Language="C#" %>

<html xmlns="http://www.w3.org/1999/xhtml">
<head runat="server">
    <title>Menu Server Control</title>
</head>
<body>
    <form id="form1" runat="server">
        <asp:SiteMapDataSource ID="SiteMapDataSource1" runat="server" />
        <asp:Menu ID="Menu1" runat="server" DataSourceID="SiteMapDataSource1">
        </asp:Menu>
    </form>
</body>
</html>
```

This example uses a SiteMapDataSource control that automatically works with the application's `Web.sitemap` file. The only other item included is the Menu control, which uses the typical ID and runat attributes and the `DataSourceID` attribute to connect it with what is retrieved from the SiteMapDataSource control.

Although the default Menu control is rather simple, you can highly customize how it looks and works by redefining its properties. The following sections look at some examples of how you can modify the appearance and change the behavior of this control.

Applying Different Styles to the Menu Control

By default, the Menu control is rather plain. If you want to maintain this appearance, you can use what is provided or simply change the font sizes and styles to make it fit in with your site. You actually have quite a number of ways in which you can modify this control so that it appears unique and fits in with your site. Either you can customize this control's appearance yourself, or you can use one of the predefined styles that come with the control.

Using a Predefined Style

Visual Studio 2012 includes some predefined styles that you can use with the Menu control to quickly apply a look-and-feel to the displayed menu of items. Some of the provided styles include Classic, Professional, and more. To apply one of these predefined styles, you work with the Menu control from the Design view of your page. Within the Design view, highlight the Menu control and expand the control's smart tag. From here, you see a list of options for working with this control. To change the look-and-feel of the control, click the Auto Format link and select one of the styles.

Performing this operation changes the code of your control by applying a set of style properties. For example, if you select the Classic option, you get the results shown in Listing 17-17.

LISTING 17-17: Code changes when you apply a style to the Menu control

```
<asp:Menu ID="Menu1" runat="server" DataSourceID="SiteMapDataSource1"
 BackColor="#B5C7DE" ForeColor="#284E98"
 Font-Names="Verdana" Font-Size="0.8em" StaticSubMenuIndent="10px"
 DynamicHorizontalOffset="2">
   <StaticSelectedStyle BackColor="#507CD1"></StaticSelectedStyle>
   <StaticMenuItemStyle HorizontalPadding="5"
    VerticalPadding="2"></StaticMenuItemStyle>
   <DynamicMenuStyle BackColor="#B5C7DE"></DynamicMenuStyle>
   <DynamicSelectedStyle BackColor="#507CD1"></DynamicSelectedStyle>
   <DynamicMenuItemStyle HorizontalPadding="5"
    VerticalPadding="2"></DynamicMenuItemStyle>
   <DynamicHoverStyle ForeColor="White" Font-Bold="True"
    BackColor="#284E98"></DynamicHoverStyle>
   <StaticHoverStyle ForeColor="White" Font-Bold="True"
    BackColor="#284E98"></StaticHoverStyle>
</asp:Menu>
```

You can see a lot of added styles that change the menu items that appear in the control. Figure 17-20 shows how this style selection appears in the browser.

Changing the Style for Static Items

The Menu control considers items in the hierarchy to be *static* or *dynamic*. The Home link that appears when the page is generated is an example of a static item. Dynamic links are the items that appear dynamically when the user hovers the mouse over the Home link in the menu. Changing the styles for both these types of nodes in the menu is possible.

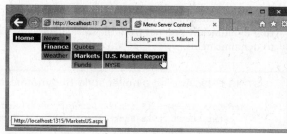

FIGURE 17-20

To apply a specific style to the static links that appear, you must add a static style element to the Menu control. The Menu control includes the following static style elements:

➤   <StaticHoverStyle>
➤   <StaticItemTemplate>
➤   <StaticMenuItemStyle>
➤   <StaticMenuStyle>
➤   <StaticSelectedStyle>

The important options from this list include the <StaticHoverStyle> and the <StaticMenuItemStyle> elements. You use the <StaticHoverStyle> element to define the style of the static item in the menu when the end user hovers the mouse over the option. You use the <StaticMenuItemStyle> element for the style of the static item when the end user is not hovering the mouse over the option.

Listing 17-18 shows how to add a style that is applied when the end user hovers the mouse over static items.

LISTING 17-18: Adding a hover style to static items in the menu control

```
<asp:Menu ID="Menu1" runat="server" DataSourceID="SiteMapDataSource1">
   <StaticHoverStyle BackColor="DarkGray" BorderColor="Black" BorderStyle="Solid"
    BorderWidth="1"></StaticHoverStyle>
</asp:Menu>
```

This little example adds a background color and border to the static items in the menu when the end user hovers the mouse over the item. Figure 17-21 shows the result.

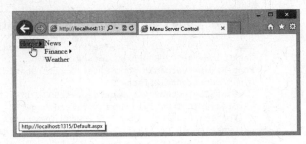

FIGURE 17-21

Adding Styles to Dynamic Items

Adding styles to the dynamic items of the menu control is just as easy as adding them to static items. The Menu control has a number of elements for modifying the appearance of dynamic items, including the following:

➤ `<DynamicHoverStyle>`

➤ `<DynamicItemTemplate>`

➤ `<DynamicMenuItemStyle>`

➤ `<DynamicMenuStyle>`

➤ `<DynamicSelectedStyle>`

These elements change menu items the same way as the static versions do, but they change only the items that dynamically pop out from the static items. Listing 17-19 shows an example of applying the hover style to dynamic items.

LISTING 17-19: Adding a hover style to dynamic items in the menu control

```
<asp:Menu ID="Menu1" runat="server" DataSourceID="Sitemapdatasource1">
   <StaticHoverStyle BackColor="DarkGray" BorderColor="Black" BorderStyle="Solid"
   BorderWidth="1"></StaticHoverStyle>
   <DynamicHoverStyle BackColor="DarkGray" BorderColor="Black" BorderStyle="Solid"
   BorderWidth="1"></DynamicHoverStyle>
</asp:Menu>
```

This code produces the results shown in Figure 17-22.

Changing the Layout of the Menu Items

By default, the dynamic menu items are displayed from left to right. This means that, as the items in the menu expand, they are continually displayed in a vertical fashion. You can actually control this behavior, but another option is available to you.

The other option is to have the first level of menu items appear directly below the first static item (horizontally). You change this behavior by using the `Orientation` attribute of the Menu control, as shown in Listing 17-20.

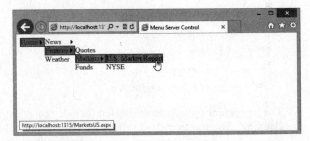

FIGURE 17-22

LISTING 17-20: Forcing the menu items to use a horizontal orientation

```
<asp:Menu ID="Menu1" runat="server" DataSourceID="SiteMapDataSource1"
 Orientation="Horizontal">
</asp:Menu>
```

This code produces the results shown in Figure 17-23.

The `Orientation` attribute can take a value of `Horizontal` or `Vertical` only. The default value is `Vertical`.

Changing the Pop-Out Symbol

As the default, an arrow is used as the pop-out symbol for the menu items generated, whether they are static or dynamic, as shown in Figure 17-24.

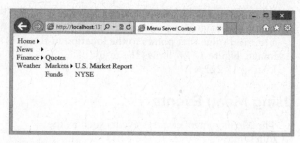

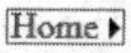

FIGURE 17-23

You are not forced to use this arrow symbol; in fact, you can change it to an image with relatively little work. Listing 17-21 shows how to accomplish this task.

FIGURE 17-24

LISTING 17-21: Using custom images

```
<asp:Menu ID="Menu1" runat="server" DataSourceID="SiteMapDataSource1"
  Orientation="Horizontal" DynamicPopOutImageUrl="Images/myArrow.png"
  StaticPopOutImageUrl="Images/myArrow.png">
</asp:Menu>
```

To change the pop-out symbol to an image of your choice, you use the `DynamicPopOutImageUrl` or `StaticPopOutImageUrl` properties. The `String` value these attributes take is simply the path of the image you want to use. Depending on the image used, it produces something similar to what you see in Figure 17-25.

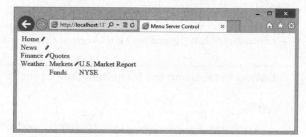

FIGURE 17-25

Separating Menu Items with Images

Another nice styling option of the Menu control is the capability to add a divider image to the menu items. You use the `StaticBottomSeparatorImageUrl`, `StaticTopSeparatorImageUrl`, `DynamicBottomSeparatorImageUrl`, and `DynamicTopSeparatorImageUrl` properties, depending on where you want to place the separator image.

For example, if you wanted to place a divider image under only the dynamic menu items, you use the `DynamicBottomSeparatorImageUrl` property, as shown in Listing 17-22.

LISTING 17-22: Applying divider images to dynamic items

```
<asp:Menu ID="Menu1" runat="server" DataSourceID="SiteMapDataSource1"
  DynamicBottomSeparatorImageUrl="Images/myDivider.png">
</asp:Menu>
```

All the properties of the Menu control that define the image to use for the dividers take a `String` value that points to the location of the image. Figure 17-26 shows the result of Listing 17-22.

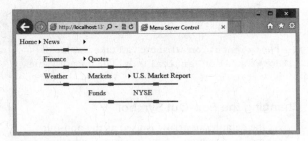

FIGURE 17-26

Using Menu Events

The Menu control exposes events such as the following:

➤ DataBinding

➤ DataBound

➤ Disposed

➤ Init

➤ Load

➤ MenuItemClick

➤ MenuItemDataBound

➤ PreRender

➤ Unload

One nice event to be aware of is `MenuItemClick`. This event, shown in Listing 17-23, enables you to take some action when the end user clicks one of the available menu items.

LISTING 17-23: Using the MenuItemClick event

VB

```
Protected Sub Menu1_MenuItemClick(ByVal sender As Object, _
    ByVal e As System.Web.UI.WebControls.MenuEventArgs)

  ' Code for event here

End Sub
```

C#

```
protected void Menu1_MenuItemClick(object sender, MenuEventArgs e)
{

    // Code for event here

}
```

This delegate uses the `MenuEventArgs` data class and provides you with access to the text and value of the item selected from the menu.

Binding the Menu Control to an XML File

Just as with the TreeView control, binding the Menu control to items that come from other data source controls provided with ASP.NET 4.5 is possible. Although most developers are likely to use the Menu control to enable end users to navigate to URL destinations, you can also use the Menu control to enable users to make selections.

As an example, take the previous XML file, `Hardware.xml`, which was used with the TreeView control from Listing 17-8 earlier in the chapter. For this example, the Menu control works with an XmlDataSource control. When the end user makes a selection from the menu, you populate a listbox on the page with the items selected. Listing 17-24 shows the code for this control.

LISTING 17-24: Using the Menu control with an XML file

VB

```
<%@ Page Language="VB" %>

<script runat="server">
    Protected Sub Menu1_MenuItemClick(ByVal sender As Object, _
        ByVal e As System.Web.UI.WebControls.MenuEventArgs)
            Listbox1.Items.Add(e.Item.Parent.Value & " : " & e.Item.Value)
    End Sub
</script>

<html xmlns="http://www.w3.org/1999/xhtml">
<head runat="server">
    <title>Menu Server Control</title>
</head>
<body>
    <form id="form1" runat="server">
        <asp:Menu ID="Menu1" runat="server" DataSourceID="XmlDataSource1"
         OnMenuItemClick="Menu1_MenuItemClick">
            <DataBindings>
                <asp:MenuItemBinding DataMember="Item"
                 TextField="Category"></asp:MenuItemBinding>
                <asp:MenuItemBinding DataMember="Option"
                 TextField="Choice"></asp:MenuItemBinding>
            </DataBindings>
        </asp:Menu>
        <p>
        <asp:ListBox ID="Listbox1" runat="server">
        </asp:ListBox></p>
        <asp:xmldatasource ID="XmlDataSource1" runat="server"
         datafile="Hardware.xml" />
    </form>
</body>
</html>
```

C#

```
<%@ Page Language="C#" %>

<script runat="server">
    protected void Menu1_MenuItemClick(object sender, MenuEventArgs e)
    {
        Listbox1.Items.Add(e.Item.Parent.Value + " : " + e.Item.Value);
    }
</script>
```

From this example, you can see that instead of using the `<asp:TreeNodeBinding>` elements, as you did with the TreeView control, the Menu control uses the `<asp:MenuItemBinding>` elements to make connections to items listed in the XML file, `Hardware.xml`. In addition, the root element of the Menu control, the `<asp:Menu>` element, now includes the `OnMenuItemClick` attribute, which points to the event delegate `Menu1_MenuItemClick`.

The `Menu1_MenuItemClick` delegate includes the data class `MenuEventArgs`, which enables you to get at both the values of the child and parent elements selected. For this example, both are used and then populated into the Listbox control, as illustrated in Figure 17-27.

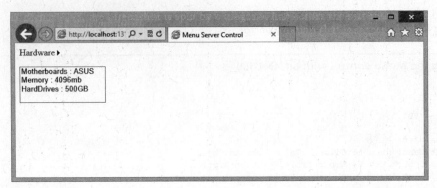

FIGURE 17-27

SITEMAP DATA PROVIDER

A series of data providers in the form of DataSource controls is available in ASP.NET 4.5. One of these DataSource controls now at your disposal, which you looked at earlier in the chapter, is the SiteMapDataSource control. This DataSource control was developed to work with sitemaps and the controls that can bind to them.

Some controls do not need a SiteMapDataSource control in order to bind to the application's sitemap (which is typically stored in the Web.sitemap file). Earlier in the chapter, you saw this in action when using the SiteMapPath control. This control was able to work with the Web.sitemap file directly—without the need for this data provider.

Certain navigation controls, however, such as the TreeView control and the DropDownList control, require an intermediary SiteMapDataSource control to retrieve the site navigation information.

The SiteMapDataSource control is simple to use as demonstrated throughout this chapter. The SiteMapDataSource control in its simplest form is illustrated here:

```
<asp:SiteMapDataSource ID="SiteMapDataSource1" runat="server" />
```

In this form, the SiteMapDataSource control simply grabs the info as a tree hierarchy (as consistently demonstrated so far). Be aware that a number of properties do change how the data is displayed in any control that binds to the data output.

ShowStartingNode

The ShowStartingNode property determines whether the root node of the .sitemap file is retrieved with the retrieved collection of node objects. This property takes a Boolean value and is set to True by default. If you are working with the Web.sitemap file shown in Listing 17-1, you construct your SiteMapDataSource control as shown in Listing 17-25 to remove the root node from the collection.

LISTING 17-25: Removing the root node from the retrieved node collection

```
<%@ Page Language="C#" %>

<html xmlns="http://www.w3.org/1999/xhtml">
<head runat="server">
    <title>Menu Server Control</title>
</head>
<body>
    <form id="form1" runat="server">
        <asp:SiteMapDataSource ID="SiteMapDataSource1" runat="server"
            ShowStartingNode="False" />
```

```
        <asp:Menu ID="Menu1" runat="server" DataSourceID="SiteMapDataSource1">
        </asp:Menu>
    </form>
</body>
</html>
```

This code produces a menu like the one shown in Figure 17-28.

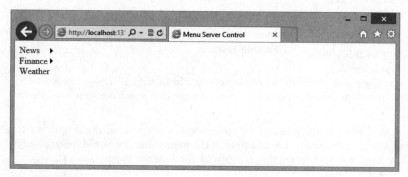

FIGURE 17-28

From this screenshot, you can see that, indeed, the root node has been removed, and the menu shown starts by using all the child nodes of the root node.

StartFromCurrentNode

The StartFromCurrentNode property causes the SiteMapDataProvider to retrieve only a node collection that starts from the current node of the page being viewed. By default, this property is set to False, meaning that the SiteMapDataProvider always retrieves all the available nodes (from the root node to the current node).

For an example of this property, use the .sitemap file from Listing 17-1 and create a page called Markets .aspx. This page in the hierarchy of the node collection is a child node of the Finance node, as well as having two child nodes itself: U.S. Market Report and NYSE. Listing 17-26 shows an example of setting the StartFromCurrentNode property to True.

LISTING 17-26: The Markets.aspx page using the StartFromCurrentNode property

```
<%@ Page Language="C#" %>

<html xmlns="http://www.w3.org/1999/xhtml">
<head runat="server">
    <title>Menu Server Control</title>
</head>
<body>
    <form id="form1" runat="server">
        <asp:SiteMapDataSource ID="SiteMapDataSource1" runat="server"
            StartFromCurrentNode="True" />
        <asp:Menu ID="Menu1" runat="server" DataSourceID="SiteMapDataSource1">
        </asp:Menu>
    </form>
</body>
</html>
```

This simple property addition produces the result shown in Figure 17-29.

StartingNodeOffset

The `StartingNodeOffset` property takes an `Integer` value that determines the starting point of the hierarchy collection. By default, this property is set to `0`, meaning that the node collection retrieved by the SiteMapDataSource control starts at the root node. Any other value provides the offset from the root node and,

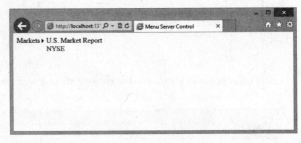

FIGURE 17-29

in turn, makes this the new starting point. From the example provided in Listing 17-1, you know that the collection starts with the Home page found at `Default.aspx`, a page that you have seen in numerous examples in this chapter.

If you set this property's value to `1`, the starting point of the collection is one space off the default starting point (the Home page starting at `Default.aspx`). For example, if the page using the SiteMapDataSource control is the `MarketsUS.aspx` page, the node collection starts with the Finance page (`Finance.aspx`).

```
Home     Offset 0
  News   Offset 1
    U.S.     Offset 2
    World   Offset 2
    Technology     Offset 2
    Sports     Offset 2
  Finance   Offset 1
    Quotes     Offset 2
    Markets   Offset 2
      U.S. Market Report     Offset 3
      NYSE     Offset 3
    Funds     Offset 2
  Weather     Offset 1
```

From this hierarchy, you can see how much each node is offset from the root node. Therefore, if you set the `StartingNodeOffset` property to `1` and you are browsing on the U.S. Market Report page, you can see that the node collection starts with the Finance page (`Finance.aspx`), and the other child nodes of the root node (News and Weather) are not represented in the node collection because the `Finance.aspx` page is on the direct hierarchical path of the requested page.

StartingNodeUrl

The `StartingNodeUrl` property enables you to specify the page found in the `.sitemap` file from which the node collection should start. By default, the value of this property is empty; but when set to something such as `Finance.aspx`, the collection starts with the Finance page as the root node of the node collection. Listing 17-27 shows an example of using the `StartingNodeUrl` property.

LISTING 17-27: Using the StartingNodeUrl property

```
<%@ Page Language="C#" %>

<html xmlns="http://www.w3.org/1999/xhtml">
<head runat="server">
    <title>Menu Server Control</title>
</head>
<body>
    <form id="form1" runat="server">
        <asp:SiteMapDataSource ID="SiteMapDataSource1" runat="server"
            StartingNodeUrl="Finance.aspx" />
```

```
                <asp:Menu ID="Menu1" runat="server" DataSourceID="SiteMapDataSource1">
                </asp:Menu>
          </form>
    </body>
    </html>
```

When the `StartingNodeUrl` property value is encountered, the value is compared against the `url` attributes in the `Web.sitemap` file. When a match is found, the matched page is used as the root node in the node collection retrieved by the SiteMapDataSource control.

SITEMAP API

The `SiteMap` class is an in-memory representation of the site's navigation structure. This class is great for programmatically working around the hierarchical structure of your site. The `SiteMap` class comes with a couple of objects that make working with the navigation structure easy. Table 17-5 describes these objects (or public properties).

TABLE 17-5

PROPERTIES	DESCRIPTION
CurrentNode	Retrieves a `SiteMapNode` object for the current page.
RootNode	Retrieves a `SiteMapNode` object that starts from the root node and the rest of the site's navigation structure.
Provider	Retrieves the default `SiteMapProvider` for the current sitemap.
Providers	Retrieves a collection of available, named `SiteMapProvider` objects.

Listing 17-28 shows an example of working with some `SiteMap` objects by demonstrating how to use the `CurrentNode` object from the `Markets.aspx` page.

LISTING 17-28: Working with the CurrentNode object

VB

```
<%@ Page Language="VB" %>

<script runat="server" language="vb">
    Protected Sub Page_Load(ByVal sender As Object, ByVal e As System.EventArgs)
        Label1.Text = SiteMap.CurrentNode.Description & "<br>" & _
            SiteMap.CurrentNode.HasChildNodes & "<br>" & _
            SiteMap.CurrentNode.NextSibling.ToString() & "<br>" & _
            SiteMap.CurrentNode.ParentNode.ToString() & "<br>" & _
            SiteMap.CurrentNode.PreviousSibling.ToString() & "<br>" & _
            SiteMap.CurrentNode.RootNode.ToString() & "<br>" & _
            SiteMap.CurrentNode.Title & "<br>" & _
            SiteMap.CurrentNode.Url
    End Sub
</script>

<html xmlns="http://www.w3.org/1999/xhtml">
<head runat="server">
    <title>SiteMapDataSource</title>
</head>
<body>
    <form id="form1" runat="server">
        <asp:Label ID="Label1" runat="server"></asp:Label>
    </form>
```

continues

LISTING 17-28 *(continued)*

```
    </body>
    </html>
```

C#

```
<%@ Page Language="C#" %>

<script runat="server">
    protected void Page_Load(object sender, System.EventArgs e)
    {
        Label1.Text = SiteMap.CurrentNode.Description + "<br>" +
            SiteMap.CurrentNode.HasChildNodes + "<br>" +
            SiteMap.CurrentNode.NextSibling.ToString() + "<br>" +
            SiteMap.CurrentNode.ParentNode.ToString() + "<br>" +
            SiteMap.CurrentNode.PreviousSibling.ToString() + "<br>" +
            SiteMap.CurrentNode.RootNode.ToString() + "<br>" +
            SiteMap.CurrentNode.Title + "<br>" +
            SiteMap.CurrentNode.Url;
    }
</script>
```

As you can see from this little bit of code, by using the `SiteMap` class and the `CurrentNode` object, you can work with a plethora of information regarding the current page. Running this page, you get the following results printed to the screen:

```
The Latest Market Information
True
Funds
Finance
Quotes
Home
Markets
/SiteNavigation/Markets.aspx
```

Using the `CurrentNode` property, you can actually create your own style of the SiteMapPath control, as shown in Listing 17-29.

LISTING 17-29: Creating a custom navigation display using the CurrentNode property

VB

```
<%@ Page Language="VB" %>

<script runat="server">
    Protected Sub Page_Load(ByVal sender As Object, ByVal e As System.EventArgs)
        Hyperlink1.Text = SiteMap.CurrentNode.ParentNode.ToString()
        Hyperlink1.NavigateUrl = SiteMap.CurrentNode.ParentNode.Url

        Hyperlink2.Text = SiteMap.CurrentNode.PreviousSibling.ToString()
        Hyperlink2.NavigateUrl = SiteMap.CurrentNode.PreviousSibling.Url

        Hyperlink3.Text = SiteMap.CurrentNode.NextSibling.ToString()
        Hyperlink3.NavigateUrl = SiteMap.CurrentNode.NextSibling.Url
    End Sub
</script>

<html xmlns="http://www.w3.org/1999/xhtml" >
<head runat="server">
    <title>SiteMapDataSource</title>
</head>
<body>
```

```
                <form id="form1" runat="server">
                    Move Up:
                    <asp:Hyperlink ID="Hyperlink1" runat="server"></asp:Hyperlink><br />
                    &lt;-- <asp:Hyperlink ID="Hyperlink2" runat="server"></asp:Hyperlink> |
                    <asp:Hyperlink ID="Hyperlink3" runat="server"></asp:Hyperlink> --&gt;
                </form>
            </body>
        </html>
```

C#

```
    <%@ Page Language="C#" %>

    <script runat="server">
        protected void Page_Load(object sender, System.EventArgs e)
        {
            Hyperlink1.Text = SiteMap.CurrentNode.ParentNode.ToString();
            Hyperlink1.NavigateUrl = SiteMap.CurrentNode.ParentNode.Url;

            Hyperlink2.Text = SiteMap.CurrentNode.PreviousSibling.ToString();
            Hyperlink2.NavigateUrl = SiteMap.CurrentNode.PreviousSibling.Url;

            Hyperlink3.Text = SiteMap.CurrentNode.NextSibling.ToString();
            Hyperlink3.NavigateUrl = SiteMap.CurrentNode.NextSibling.Url;
        }
    </script>
```

When run, this page gives you your own custom navigation structure, as shown in Figure 17-30.

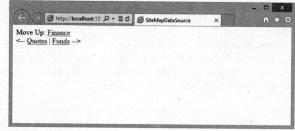

FIGURE 17-30

URL MAPPING

The URLs used by web pages can sometimes get rather complex as your application grows and grows. Sometimes, you could be presenting web pages that change their content based on query strings that are provided via the URL, such as:

```
    http://www.asp.net/forums/view.aspx?forumid=12&categoryid=6
```

In other cases, your web page might be so deep within a hierarchy of folders that the URL has become rather cumbersome for an end user to type or remember when they want to pull up the page later in their browser. There are also moments when you want a collection of pages to look like they are the same page or a single destination.

In cases such as these, you can take advantage of an ASP.NET feature called *URL mapping*. URL mapping enables you to map complex URLs to simpler ones. You accomplish this mapping through settings you apply in the web.config file using the <urlMappings> element (see Listing 17-30).

LISTING 17-30: Mapping URLs using the <urlMappings> element

```
    <configuration>

        <system.web>

            <urlMappings>
                <add url="~/Content.aspx" mappedUrl="~/SystemNews.aspx?categoryid=5" />
            </urlMappings>

        </system.web>

    </configuration>
```

This example uses a fake URL—Content.aspx—that is mapped to a more complicated URL: SystemNews.aspx?categoryid=5. With this construction in place, when the end user types the URL, Content.aspx, the application knows to invoke the more complicated URL SystemNews .aspx?categoryid=5 page. This takes place without the URL even being changed in the browser. Even after the page has completely loaded, the browser will still show the Content.aspx page as the destination—thereby tricking the end user, in a sense.

> **NOTE** *It is important to note that in this situation, the end user is routed to* SystemNews .aspx?categoryid=5 *no matter what—even if a* Content.aspx *page exists! Therefore, mapping to pages that are not actually contained within your application is important.*

SITEMAP LOCALIZATION

The improved resource files (.resx) are a great way to localize ASP.NET applications. Chapter 32 covers this localization of web applications using ASP.NET. However, this introduction focused on applying localization features to the pages of your applications, but didn't demonstrate how to take this localization capability further by applying it to items such as the Web.sitemap file.

Structuring the Web.sitemap File for Localization

Just as applying localization instructions to the pages of your ASP.NET web applications is possible, you can also use the same framework to accomplish your localization tasks in the Web.sitemap file. To show you this technique in action, Listing 17-31 constructs a Web.sitemap file somewhat similar to the one presented in Listing 17-1, but much simpler.

LISTING 17-31: Creating a basic .sitemap file for localization

```xml
<?xml version="1.0" encoding="utf-8" ?>

<siteMap xmlns="http://schemas.microsoft.com/AspNet/SiteMap-File-1.0"
 enableLocalization="true">
 <siteMapNode url="Default.aspx" resourceKey="Home">
        <siteMapNode url="News.aspx" resourceKey="News">
                <siteMapNode url="News.aspx?cat=us" resourceKey="NewsUS" />
                <siteMapNode url="News.aspx?cat=world" resourceKey="NewsWorld" />
                <siteMapNode url="News.aspx?cat=tech" resourceKey="NewsTech" />
                <siteMapNode url="News.aspx?cat=sport" resourceKey="NewsSport" />
        </siteMapNode>
 </siteMapNode>
</siteMap>
```

Listing 17-31 shows a rather simple Web.sitemap file. To enable the localization capability from the Web.sitemap file, you have to turn on this capability by using the enableLocalization attribute in the <siteMap> element and setting it to True. After it is enabled, you can then define each of the navigation nodes as you would normally, using the <siteMapNode> element. In this case, however, because you are going to define the contents of these navigation pieces (most notably, the title and description attributes) in various .resx files, you do not need to repeatedly define these items in this file. That means you need to define only the url attribute for this example. It is important to note, however, that you could also define this attribute through your .resx files, thereby forwarding end users to different pages depending on their defined culture settings.

The next attribute to note is the `resourceKey` attribute used in the `<siteMapNode>` elements. This key is used and defined in the various `.resx` files you will implement. Take the following `<siteMapNode>` element as an example:

```
<siteMapNode url="News.aspx" resourceKey="News">
    . . .
</siteMapNode>
```

In this case, the value of the `resourceKey` (and the key that will be used in the `.resx` file) is `News`. This means that you can define the values of the `title` and `description` attributes in the `.resx` file using the following syntax:

```
News.Title
News.Description
```

Now that the `Web.sitemap` is in place, the next step is to make some minor modifications to the `web.config` file, as shown next.

Making Modifications to the web.config File

Now that the `Web.sitemap` file is in place and ready, the next step is to provide some minor additions to the `web.config` file. In order for your web application to make an automatic detection of the culture of the users visiting the various pages you are providing, you must set the `Culture` and `uiCulture` settings in the `@Page` directive, or set these attributes for automatic detection in the `<globalization>` element of the `web.config` file.

When you are working with navigation and the `Web.sitemap` file, as in this example, making this change in the `web.config` file is actually best so that it automatically takes effect on every page in your application. Adding it to the `web.config` file makes it much simpler because you won't have to make these additions yourself to every page.

To make these changes, open your `web.config` file and add a `<globalization>` element, as shown in Listing 17-32.

LISTING 17-32: Adding culture detection to the web.config file

```
<configuration>
    <system.web>

        <globalization culture="auto" uiCulture="auto" />

    </system.web>
</configuration>
```

For the auto-detection capabilities to occur, you simply set the `culture` and `uiCulture` attributes to `auto`. You also could have defined the values as `auto:en-US`, which means that the automatic culture detection capabilities should occur, but if the culture defined is not found in the various resource files, then use `en-US` (American English) as the default culture. However, because you are going to define a default `Web.sitemap` set of values, there really is no need for you to bring forward this construction.

Next, you create the assembly resource files that define the values used by the `Web.sitemap` file.

Creating Assembly Resource (.resx) Files

To create a set of assembly resource files that you will use with the `Web.sitemap` file, create a folder in your project called `App_GlobalResources`. If you are using Visual Studio 2012 (or Visual Studio Express 2012 for Web), you can add this folder by right-clicking on the project and selecting Add ASP.NET Folder ⇨ App_GlobalResources.

After the folder is in place, add two assembly resource files to this folder. Name the first file **Web.sitemap .resx** and the second one **Web.sitemap.de.resx**. Your goal with these two files is to have a default set of values for the Web.sitemap file that will be defined in the Web.sitemap.resx file, and a version of these values that has been translated to the German language and is contained in the Web.sitemap.de.resx file.

The de value used in the name will be the file used by individuals who have their preferred language set to de-DE (or variants such as de-AT or de-CH). Table 17-6 describes other possible variations of these constructions.

TABLE 17-6

.RESX FILE	CULTURE SERVED
Web.sitemap.resx	The default values used when the end user's culture cannot be identified through another .resx file
Web.sitemap.en.resx	The resource file used for all en (English) users
Web.sitemap.en-gb.resx	The resource file used for the English speakers of Great Britain
Web.sitemap.fr-ca.resx	The resource file used for the French speakers of Canada
Web.sitemap.ru.resx	The resource file used for Russian speakers

Now that the Web.sitemap.resx and Web.sitemap.de.resx files are in place, the next step is to fill these files with values. To accomplish this task, you use the keys defined earlier directly in the Web.sitemap file. Figure 17-31 shows the result of this exercise.

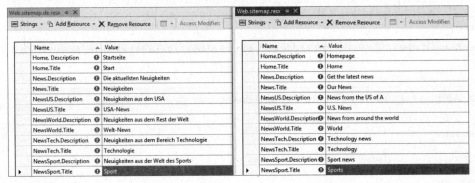

FIGURE 17-31

Although the IDE states that these are not valid identifiers, the application still works with this model. After you have the files in place, you can test how this localization endeavor works, as shown in the following section.

Testing the Results

Create a page in your application and place a TreeView server control on the page. In addition to the TreeView control, you must also include a SiteMapDataSource control to work with the Web.sitemap file you created. Be sure to tie the two controls together by giving the TreeView control the attribute DataSourceID="SiteMapDataSource1", as demonstrated earlier in this chapter.

If you have your language preference in Microsoft's Internet Explorer set to en-us (American English), you will see the results shown in Figure 17-32.

When you pull up the page in the browser, the culture of the request is checked. Because the only finely grained preference defined in the example is for users using the culture of de (German), the default `Web.sitemap.resx` is used instead. Because of this, the `Web.sitemap.resx` file is used to populate the values of the TreeView control, as shown in Figure 17-32. If the requestor has a culture setting of de, however, she gets an entirely different set of results.

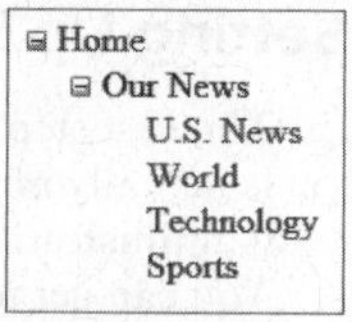

FIGURE 17-32

To test this out, change the preferred language used in IE by selecting Tools ⇨ Internet Options in IE. On the first tab (General), click the Languages button at the bottom of the dialog box. The Language Preferences dialog box appears. Add the German language setting to the list of options. The final step is to use the Move Up button to move the German choice to the top of the list. In the end, you should see something similar to what is shown in Figure 17-33. If you are using the Firefox browser, navigate to Tools ⇨ Options ⇨ Content, and click on the Choose button in the Languages section to change the language settings.

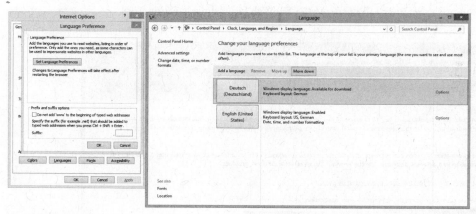

FIGURE 17-33

With this setting in place, running the page with the TreeView control gives you the result shown in Figure 17-34.

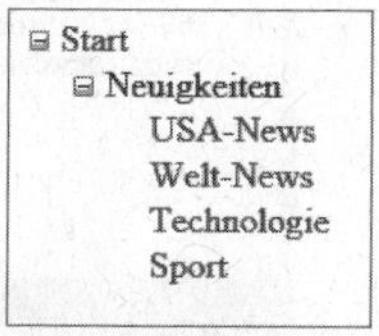

Now, when the page is requested, the culture is set to de and correlates to the `Web.sitemap.de.resx` file instead of to the default `Web.sitemap.resx` file.

FIGURE 17-34

SECURITY TRIMMING

If you have been following the examples so far in this chapter, you might notice that one of the attributes available to a `<siteMapNode>` tag hasn't yet been discussed. The `roles` attribute is a powerful one that allows you to provide an authorization model to the items contained in the navigation system. This really means that you have the capability to display *only* the navigational items that a user is entitled to see and nothing more. The term commonly used for this behavior is *security trimming*. This section looks at how to apply security trimming to the application you are building in ASP.NET 4.5.

This capability is a good example of two ASP.NET 4.5 systems interacting with one another in the site navigation system. Security trimming works only when you have enabled the ASP.NET 4.5 role-management system. Chapter 19 covers this system in more detail. Be sure to check out this chapter because this section does not go into much detail about this system.

As an example of security trimming in your ASP.NET applications, this section shows you how to limit access to the navigation of your application's administration system to only those users who are contained within a specific application role.

Setting Up Role Management for Administrators

The first step in applying security trimming is to set up your application to handle roles. This process is actually rather simple. One easy way to accomplish this task is to open the ASP.NET Web Site Administration Tool for your application and enable role management directly in this web-based tool. You can get to this administration tool by clicking the ASP.NET Configuration button in the menu of the Solution Explorer in Visual Studio. This button has the logo of a hammer and a globe.

After launching the ASP.NET Web Site Administration Tool, select the Security tab; a new page then appears where you can administer the membership and role-management systems for your application.

First, you enable and build up the role-management system, and then, you also enable the membership system. Chapter 19 covers the membership system in detail. After you turn on the membership system, you build some actual users in your application. You want a user to log in to your application and be assigned a specific role. This role assignment changes the site navigation system display.

Figure 17-35 shows the Security tab in the ASP.NET Web Site Administration Tool.

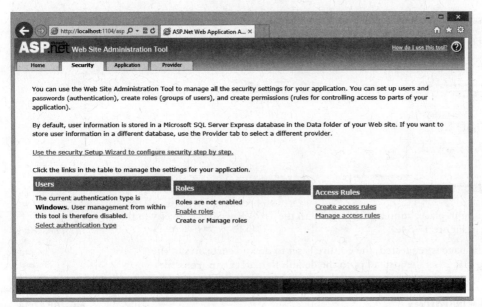

FIGURE 17-35

On this page, you can easily enable the role-management system by selecting the Enable Roles link. After you have done this, you are informed that no roles exist in the system. To create the role that you need for the site navigation system, select the Create or Manage Roles link. A new page then appears where you can create the administrator role. For this example, I named the role **Admin**.

After adding the Admin role, click the Back button and then select the authentication type that is utilized for the application. You want to make sure that you have selected the From the Internet option. This enables you to create a user in the system. By default, these users are stored in the Microsoft SQL Server Express Edition file that ASP.NET creates in your application, so the database server must be installed. You can also provide a custom connection string in the web.config file to configure ASP.NET to use another database server or type.

After you have selected the authentication type, you can then create the new user and place the user in the Admin role by making sure the role is selected (using a check box) on the screen where you are creating the user.

After you are satisfied that a user has been created and placed in the Admin role, you can check whether the settings are appropriately set in the web.config file, as presented in Listing 17-33.

LISTING 17-33: The role-management system enabled in the web.config file

```
<configuration>
   <system.web>
      <authentication mode="Forms" />
      <roleManager enabled="true" />
   </system.web>
</configuration>
```

Setting Up the Administrators' Section

The next step is to set up a page for administrators only. For this example, I named the page **AdminOnly .aspx**, and it contains only a simple string value welcoming administrators to the page. This page is locked down only for users who are contained in the Admin role. This lockdown is done by making the appropriate settings in the web.config file, as shown in Listing 17-34.

LISTING 17-34: Locking down the AdminOnly.aspx page in the web.config

```
<configuration>
  <location path="AdminOnly.aspx">
     <system.web>
        <authorization>
           <allow roles="Admin" />
           <deny users="*" />
        </authorization>
     </system.web>
  </location>
</configuration>
```

Now, because the AdminOnly.aspx page is accessible only to the users who are in the Admin role, the next step is to allow users to log in to the application. The application demo accomplishes this task by creating a Default.aspx page that contains a Login server control as well as a TreeView control bound to a SiteMapDataSource control. Listing 17-35 presents this simple ASP.NET page.

LISTING 17-35: The Default.aspx page

```
<%@ Page Language="C#" %>

<html xmlns="http://www.w3.org/1999/xhtml">
<head runat="server">
    <title>Main Page</title>
</head>
<body>
    <form id="form1" runat="server">
    <div>
        <asp:Login ID="Login1" runat="server">
        </asp:Login>
        <br />
        <asp:TreeView ID="TreeView1" runat="server"
         DataSourceID="SiteMapDataSource1" ShowLines="True">
        </asp:TreeView>
        <br />
        <asp:SiteMapDataSource ID="SiteMapDataSource1" runat="server" />
    </div>
    </form>
</body>
</html>
```

With the `Default.aspx` page in place, you make another change to the `Web.sitemap` file that was originally presented in Listing 17-1. For this example, you add a `<siteMapNode>` element that works with the new `AdminOnly.aspx` page. This node is presented here:

```
<siteMapNode title="Administration" description="The Administrators page"
  url="AdminOnly.aspx" roles="Admin" />
```

Since the Login control uses validation, you need to reference jQuery or disable unobtrusive validation (see also Chapter 6); the latter can be done with the following `web.config` setting:

```
<appSettings>
  <add key="ValidationSettings:UnobtrusiveValidationMode" value="None" />
</appSettings>
```

After all items are in place in your application, the next step is to enable security trimming for the site navigation system.

Enabling Security Trimming

By default, security trimming is disabled. Even if you start applying values to the `roles` attribute for any `<siteMapNode>` element in your `web.config` file, it does not work. To enable security trimming, you must fine-tune the provider declaration for the site navigation system.

To make the necessary changes to the XmlSiteMapProvider, you must make these changes high up in the configuration chain, such as to the `machine.config` file or the default `web.config` file; or you can make the change lower down, such as in your application's `web.config` file. This example makes the change in the `web.config` file.

To alter the XmlSiteMapProvider in the `web.config` file, you first clear out the already declared instance. After it is cleared, you then redeclare a new instance of the XmlSiteMapProvider, but this time, you enable security trimming, as shown in Listing 17-36.

LISTING 17-36: Enabling security trimming in the provider

```
<configuration>
  <system.web>
    <siteMap>
      <providers>
        <clear />
        <add siteMapFile="web.sitemap" name="AspNetXmlSiteMapProvider"
            type="System.Web.XmlSiteMapProvider, System.Web, Version=4.0.0.0,
              Culture=neutral, PublicKeyToken=b03f5f7f11d50a3a"
              securityTrimmingEnabled="true" />
      </providers>
    </siteMap>
  </system.web>
</configuration>
```

From this example, you can see that a new XmlSiteMapProvider is defined, and the `securityTrimmingEnabled` attribute is then set to `True` (shown in bold). With security trimming enabled, the `roles` attribute in the `<siteMapNode>` element is utilized in the site navigation system.

To test it out for yourself, run the `Default.aspx` page. A page appears that does not include the link to the administration portion of the page, as illustrated in Figure 17-36.

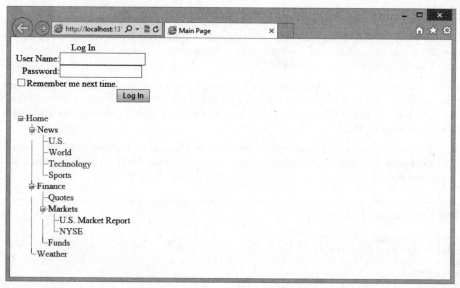

FIGURE 17-36

From this figure, you can see that the Administration link is not present in the TreeView control. Now, however, log in to the application as a user contained in the Admin role. You then see that, indeed, the site navigation has changed to reflect the role of the user, as presented in Figure 17-37.

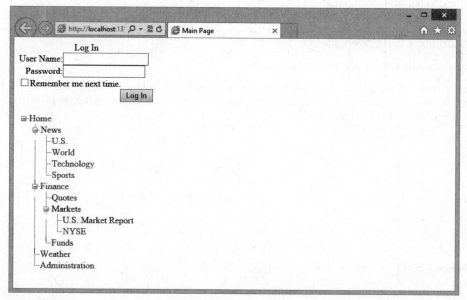

FIGURE 17-37

Security trimming is an ideal way of automatically altering the site navigation that is presented to users based upon the roles they have in the role-management system.

NESTING SITEMAP FILES

You are not required to place all your site navigation within a single `Web.sitemap` file. In fact, you can spread it out into multiple `.sitemap` files if you want and then bring them all together into a single `.sitemap` file—also known as *nesting* `.sitemap` files.

For example, suppose you are using the sitemap file from Listing 17-1 and you have a rather large amount of site navigation to add under the area of *Entertainment*. You could put all this new information in the current `Web.sitemap` file, or you could keep all the Entertainment links in another sitemap file and just reference that in the main sitemap file.

In the simplest case, nesting sitemap files is easily achievable. To see it in action, create a new `.sitemap` file (called **Entertainment.sitemap**) and place this file in your application. Listing 17-37 presents an example `Entertainment.sitemap` file.

LISTING 17-37: The Entertainment.sitemap

```xml
<?xml version="1.0" encoding="utf-8" ?>
<siteMap xmlns="http://schemas.microsoft.com/AspNet/SiteMap-File-1.0" >
    <siteMapNode url="Entertainment.aspx" title="Entertainment"
     description="The Entertainment Page">
        <siteMapNode url="Movies.aspx" title="Movies"
         description="The Latest in Movies" />
        <siteMapNode url="Fashion.aspx" title="Fashion"
         description="The Latest in Fashion" />
    </siteMapNode>
</siteMap>
```

You can place the `Entertainment.sitemap` in the root directory where you also have the main `Web.sitemap` file. Now, working from the sitemap file from the earlier Listing 17-1, you make the following addition to the bottom of the list, as presented in Listing 17-38.

LISTING 17-38: Additions to the Web.sitemap file

```xml
<siteMapNode siteMapFile="Entertainment.sitemap" />
```

Instead of using the standard `url`, `title`, and `description` attributes, you just point to the other sitemap file to be included in this main sitemap file using the `siteMapFile` attribute. Running this page gives you results similar to those presented in Figure 17-38.

FIGURE 17-38

Another approach to nesting sitemap files is to build a second provider in the sitemap provider model definitions, and then to use the `provider` attribute within the `<siteMapNode>` element to reference this declaration. To accomplish this task, you add a new sitemap provider reference in the `web.config` file, as is illustrated in Listing 17-39.

LISTING 17-39: Using another provider in the same Web.sitemap file

```
<configuration>
  <system.web>

    <siteMap>
      <providers>
        <add siteMapFile="Entertainment.sitemap" name="AspNetXmlSiteMapProvider2"
           type="System.Web.XmlSiteMapProvider, System.Web, Version=4.0.0.0,
             Culture=neutral, PublicKeyToken=b03f5f7f11d50a3a" />
      </providers>
    </siteMap>

  </system.web>
</configuration>
```

From this bit of code, you can see that a second provider is defined. Defining a second sitemap provider does not mean that you have to use the `<clear />` element in the `<provider>` section, but instead, you simply define a new provider that has a new name. In this case, the name of the provider is `AspNetXmlSiteMapProvider2`. Also, within this provider definition, the `siteMapFile` attribute is used to point to the name of the sitemap file that should be utilized.

With this in place, you can then reference this declaration by using the `provider` attribute within the `<siteMapNode>` element of the `Web.sitemap` file. To add the `Entertainment.sitemap` file in this manner, your `<siteMapNode>` element should take the form presented in Listing 17-40.

LISTING 17-40: Using a second provider in the Web.sitemap file

```
<siteMapNode provider="AspNetXmlSiteMapProvider2" />
```

This code gives you the same results as those shown in Figure 17-38. Besides providing another way of nesting sitemap files, you gain a lot of power using the `provider` attribute. If you build a new sitemap provider that pulls sitemap navigation information from another source (rather than from an XML file), you can mix those results in the main `Web.sitemap` file. The end result could have items that come from two or more completely different data sources.

SUMMARY

This chapter introduced the navigation mechanics that ASP.NET 4.5 provides. At the core of the navigation capabilities is the power to detail the navigation structure in an XML file, which various navigation controls—such as the new TreeView and SiteMapPath controls—can then utilize.

The powerful functionality that the navigation capabilities provide saves you a tremendous amount of coding time.

In addition to showing you the core infrastructure for navigation in ASP.NET 4.5, this chapter also described both the TreeView and SiteMapPath controls and how to use them throughout your applications. The great thing about these controls is that, right out of the box, they can richly display your navigation hierarchy and enable the end user to work through the site easily. In addition, these controls are easily changeable so that you can go beyond the standard appearance and functionality that they provide.

Along with the TreeView server control, this chapter also looked at the Menu server control. You will find a lot of similarities between these two controls as they both provide a means to look at hierarchical data.

Finally, this chapter looked at how to achieve URL mapping, as well as how to localize your `Web.sitemap` files and filter the results of the site navigation contents based upon a user's role in the role-management system.

18

Personalization

WHAT'S IN THIS CHAPTER?

➤ Exploring ASP.NET's personalization capabilities

➤ Working with personalization properties

➤ Storing data using personalization providers

➤ Working with anonymous users

WROX.COM CODE DOWNLOADS FOR THIS CHAPTER

Please note that all the code examples in this chapter are available as a part of this chapter's code download on the book's website at www.wrox.com on the Download Code tab.

Many web applications must be customized with information that is specific to the end user who is presently viewing the page. In the past, the developer usually provided storage of personalization properties for end users viewing the page by means of cookies, the `Session` object, or the `Application` object. Cookies enabled storage of persistent items so that when the end user returned to a web page, any settings related to him were retrieved to be utilized again by the application. Cookies are not the best way to approach persistent user data storage, because they are not accepted by all computers and because a crafty end user can easily alter them.

As you will see in Chapter 19, ASP.NET membership and role management capabilities are ways that ASP.NET can store information about the user. How can you, as the developer, use the same mechanics to store custom information?

ASP.NET 4.5 provides you with an outstanding feature—*personalization*. The ASP.NET personalization engine provided with this latest release makes an automatic association between the end user viewing the page and any data points stored for that user. The personalization properties that are maintained on a per-user basis are stored on the server and not on the client. These items are conveniently placed in a data store of your choice (such as Microsoft's SQL Server) and, therefore, the end user can then access these personalization properties on later site visits.

This feature is an ideal way to start creating highly customizable and user-specific sites without building any of the plumbing beforehand. In this case, the plumbing has been built for you! This chapter shows you how the personalization feature is yet another way that the ASP.NET team is making developers' jobs easier and more productive.

THE PERSONALIZATION MODEL

The personalization model provided with ASP .NET 4.5 is simple and, as with most items that come with ASP.NET, is an extensible model as well. Figure 18-1 shows a simple diagram that outlines the personalization model.

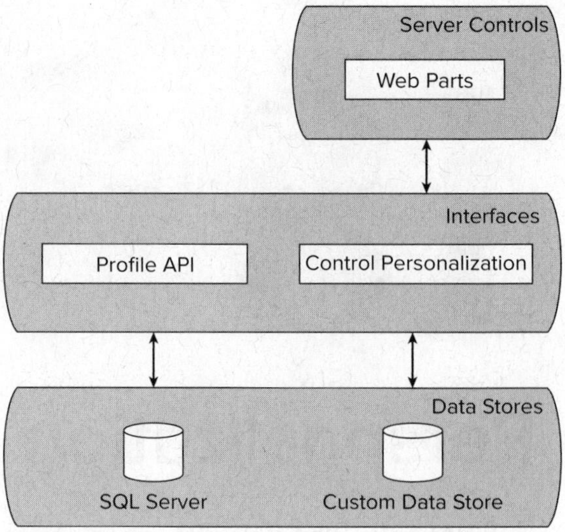

From this diagram, you can see the three layers in this model. Look at the middle layer of the personalization model—the Personalization Services layer. This layer contains the Profile API. This Profile API layer enables you to program your end users' data points into one of the lower-layer data stores.

FIGURE 18-1

Although certain controls built into ASP.NET can utilize the personalization capabilities for storing information about the page settings, you can also use this engine to store your own data points. As with Web Parts, you can use these points within your ASP.NET pages.

Below the Personalization Services layer, you'll find the default personalization data provider for working with Microsoft's SQL Server starting from version 2000, as well as Microsoft's SQL Server Express Edition. You are not limited to just this one data store when applying the personalization features of ASP.NET 4.5; you can also extend the model and create a custom data provider for the personalization engine.

> **NOTE** *You can read about how to create your own providers in Chapter 15.*

Now that you have looked briefly at the personalization model, you can begin using it by creating some stored personalization properties that you can use later within your applications.

CREATING PERSONALIZATION PROPERTIES

The nice thing about creating custom personalization properties is that you can do it so easily. After you create these properties, you gain the capability to have strongly typed access to them. You can create personalization properties that are used only by authenticated users, and also some that anonymous users can utilize. These data points are powerful, mainly because you can start using them immediately in your application without building any underlying infrastructures to support them. As an example of working with the ASP.NET personalization system, this chapter starts by showing you how to create some simple personalization properties. Later, you learn how to use these personalization properties within your application.

Adding a Simple Personalization Property

When adding a personalization property, you must decide what data items from the user you are going to store. For this example, create a few items about the user that you can use within your application; assume that you want to store the following information about the user:

➤ First name

➤ Last name

➤ Last visited

➤ Age

➤ Membership status

ASP.NET has a heavy dependency on storing configurations inside XML files, and the ASP.NET 4.5 personalization engine is no different. You define and store all these customization points concerning the end user within the `web.config` file of the application, as shown in Listing 18-1 (Web.config in the code download for this chapter).

LISTING 18-1: Creating personalization properties in the web.config file

```
<configuration>
  <system.web>
     <profile>
       <properties>
         <add name="FirstName" />
         <add name="LastName" />
         <add name="LastVisited" />
         <add name="Age" />
         <add name="Member" />
       </properties>
     </profile>
     <authentication mode="Windows" />
  </system.web>
</configuration>
```

In the `<system.web>` section of the `web.config` file, you create a `<profile>` section to work with the ASP.NET 4.5 personalization engine. Within this `<profile>` section of the `web.config` file, you create a `<properties>` section, where you can define all the properties you want the personalization engine to store.

From this code example, you can see that defining simple properties using the `<add>` element is rather easy. This element simply takes the `name` attribute, which takes the name of the property you want to persist.

You start out with the assumption that accessing the page you will build with these properties is already authenticated using Windows authentication (you can read more on authentication and authorization in the next chapter). Later in this chapter, you look at how to apply personalization properties to anonymous users as well. The capability to apply personalization properties to anonymous users is disabled by default (for good reasons).

After you have defined these personalization properties, using them is just as easy as defining them. The next section looks at how to use these definitions in an application.

Using Personalization Properties

Now that you have defined the personalization properties in the `web.config` file, you can use these items in code. For example, you can create a simple form that asks for some of this information from the end user. When the user submits the form, the data is stored in the personalization engine.

In order to make this work, you should set up a new website (we will cover web applications and why personalization properties are a bit harder to work with there later in this chapter) and add Listings 18-1 and 18-2 to it. Also go to the site properties and disable Anonymous and enable Windows Authentication (which should be the default setting anyway). This allows ASP.NET to store personalization information for the current user. Anonymous users will also be covered later in this chapter.

As with the Authentication features, ASP.NET uses SQL Server Express by default as a data store, so it needs to be set up.

Listing 18-2 shows how to access the profile information set up in Listing 18-1.

LISTING 18-2: Using the defined personalization properties

VB

```vb
<%@ Page Language="VB" %>
    <script runat="server">
 Protected Sub Button1_Click(ByVal sender As Object, ByVal e As System.EventArgs)
  If Page.User.Identity.IsAuthenticated Then
    Profile.FirstName = TextBox1.Text
    Profile.LastName = TextBox2.Text
    Profile.Age = TextBox3.Text
    Profile.Member = Radiobuttonlist1.SelectedItem.Text
    Profile.LastVisited = DateTime.Now().ToString()
        Label1.Text = "<p>Stored information includes:</p><p>" & _
        "First name: " & Profile.FirstName & _
        "<br />Last name: " & Profile.LastName & _
        "<br />Age: " & Profile.Age & _
        "<br />Member: " & Profile.Member & _
        "<br />Last visited: " & Profile.LastVisited & "</p>"
  Else
    Label1.Text = "You must be authenticated!"
  End If
 End Sub
</script>
<html xmlns="http://www.w3.org/1999/xhtml">
<head runat="server">
  <title>Storing Personalization</title>
</head>
<body>
  <form id="form1" runat="server">
    <p>First Name:
    <asp:TextBox ID="TextBox1" Runat="server"></asp:TextBox></p>
    <p>Last Name:
    <asp:TextBox ID="TextBox2" Runat="server"></asp:TextBox></p>
    <p>Age:
    <asp:TextBox ID="TextBox3" Runat="server" Width="50px"
    MaxLength="3"></asp:TextBox></p>
    <p>Are you a member?
    <asp:RadioButtonList ID="Radiobuttonlist1" Runat="server">
      <asp:ListItem Value="1">Yes</asp:ListItem>
      <asp:ListItem Value="0" Selected="True">No</asp:ListItem>
    </asp:RadioButtonList></p>
    <p><asp:Button ID="Button1" Runat="server" Text="Submit"
    OnClick="Button1_Click" />
    </p>
    <hr /><p>
    <asp:Label ID="Label1" Runat="server"></asp:Label></p>
  </form>
</body>
</html>
```

C#

```csharp
<%@ Page Language="C#" %>
<script runat="server">
  protected void Button1_Click(object sender, EventArgs e)
  {
   if (Page.User.Identity.IsAuthenticated)
   {
    Profile.FirstName = TextBox1.Text;
    Profile.LastName = TextBox2.Text;
```

```
        Profile.Age = TextBox3.Text;
        Profile.Member = Radiobuttonlist1.SelectedItem.Text;
        Profile.LastVisited = DateTime.Now.ToString();
        Label1.Text = "<p>Stored information includes:</p><p>" +
            "First name: " + Profile.FirstName +
            "<br />Last name: " + Profile.LastName +
            "<br />Age: " + Profile.Age +
            "<br />Member: " + Profile.Member +
            "<br />Last visited: " + Profile.LastVisited + "</p>";
    }
    else
    {
      Label1.Text = "You must be authenticated!";
    }
  }
</script>
```

You work with personalization properties similarly to the way you worked with the `Session` object in the past, but note that the personalization properties you are storing and retrieving are not key based. Therefore, when working with them you do not need to remember key names.

All items stored by the personalization system are type cast to a particular .NET data type. By default, these items are stored as type `String`, and you have early-bound access to the items stored. To store an item, you simply populate the personalization property directly using the `Profile` object:

```
Profile.FirstName = TextBox1.Text
```

To retrieve the same information, you simply grab the appropriate property of the `Profile` class as shown here:

```
Label1.Text = Profile.FirstName
```

The great thing about using the `Profile` class and all the personalization properties defined in the Code view is that this method provides IntelliSense as you build your pages. When you are working with the `Profile` class in this view, all the items you define are listed as available options through the IntelliSense feature, as illustrated in Figure 18-2.

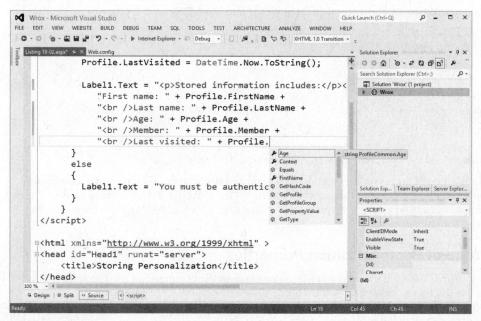

FIGURE 18-2

All these properties are accessible in IntelliSense because the `Profile` class is hidden and compiled dynamically behind the scenes whenever you save the personalization changes made to the `web.config` file. After you save these items in the `web.config` file, these properties are available to you throughout your application in a strongly typed manner.

When run, the page from Listing 18-2 produces the results shown in Figure 18-3. You may need to activate Windows authentication in your website settings and disable anonymous authentication.

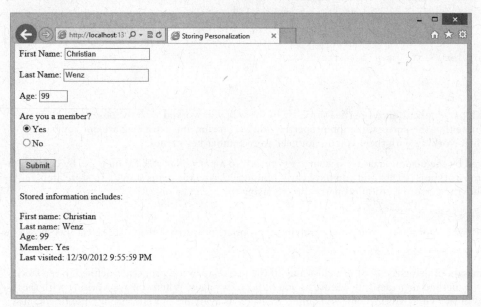

FIGURE 18-3

In addition to using early-bound access techniques, you can also use late-bound access for the items that you store in the personalization engine. Listing 18-3 shows the late-bound access technique.

LISTING 18-3: Using late-bound access

VB

```
Dim myFirstName As String
myFirstName = Profile.GetPropertyValue("FirstName").ToString()
```

C#

```
string myFirstName;
myFirstName = Profile.GetPropertyValue("FirstName").ToString();
```

Whether it is early-bound access or late-bound access, you can easily store and retrieve personalization properties for a particular user using this capability afforded by ASP.NET 4.5. All this storage and retrieval is done in the personalization engine's simplest form—now take a look at how you can customize for specific needs in your applications.

Adding a Group of Personalization Properties

Items you have stored about a particular end user somewhere in the beginning of the application can be retrieved later for use on any other page within the application. Because different sections of your web applications store different personalization properties, you sometimes end up with a large collection of items that you need to store and make accessible.

To make it easier not only to store the items, but also to retrieve them, the personalization engine enables you to store your personalization properties in groups, as shown in Listing 18-4.

LISTING 18-4: Creating personalization groups in the web.config file

```
<configuration>
   <system.web>
      <profile>
         <properties>
            <add name="FirstName" />
            <add name="LastName" />
            <add name="LastVisited" />
            <add name="Age" />
            <group name="MemberDetails">
             <add name="Member" />
             <add name="DateJoined" />
             <add name="PaidDuesStatus" />
             <add name="Location" />
            </group>
            <group name="FamilyDetails">
             <add name="MarriedStatus" />
             <add name="DateMarried" />
             <add name="NumberChildren" />
             <add name="Location" />
            </group>
         </properties>
      </profile>
      <authentication mode="Windows" />
   </system.web>
</configuration>
```

From the code in Listing 18-4, which is placed within the web.config file, you can see that two groups are listed. The first group is the MemberDetails group, which has four specific items defined; the second group — FamilyDetails — has three other related items defined. You define personalization groups using the <group> element within the <properties> definition. You specify the name of the group using the name attribute, just as you specify the <add> element. You can define as many groups as you deem necessary or as have been recommended as good practice to employ.

Using Grouped Personalization Properties

You can also see from Listing 18-4 that some items are not defined in any particular group. Mixing properties defined from within a group with those that are not is possible. The items not defined in a group in Listing 18-4 can still be accessed in the manner illustrated previously:

```
Label1.Text = Profile.FirstName
```

Now, concerning working with personalization groups, you can access your defined items in a logical manner using nested namespaces:

```
Label1.Text = Profile.MemberDetails.DateJoined
Label2.Text = Profile.FamilyDetails.MarriedStatus
```

From this example, you can see that two separate items from each of the defined personalization groups were accessed in a logical manner. When you study the defined properties in the web.config file of your application, you can see that each of the groups in the example has a property with the same name — Location. This is possible because they are defined using personalization groups. With this structure, getting at each of the Location properties by specifying the appropriate group is now possible:

```
Label1.Text = Profile.MemberDetails.Location
Label2.Text = Profile.FamilyDetails.Location
```

Defining Types for Personalization Properties

By default, when you store personalization properties, these properties are created as type System.String. Changing the type to another type altogether through configuration settings within the web.config file is quite easy, however. To define the name of the personalization property along with its appropriate type, you use the type attribute of the <add> element contained within the <properties> section, as shown in Listing 18-5.

LISTING 18-5: Defining types for personalization properties

```
<properties>
  <add name="FirstName" type="System.String" />
  <add name="LastName" type="System.String" />
  <add name="LastVisited" type="System.DateTime" />
  <add name="Age" type="System.Int32" />
  <add name="Member" type="System.Boolean" />
</properties>
```

The first two properties, FirstName and LastName, are cast as type System.String. This is not actually required. Even if you omitted this step, they would still be cast as type String because that is the default type of any property defined in the personalization system (if no other type is defined). The next personalization property is the LastVisited property, which is defined as type System.DateTime and used to store the date and time of the end user's last visit to the page. Beyond that, you can see the rest of the personalization properties are defined using a specific .NET data type.

This approach is preferred because it gives you type-checking capabilities as you code your application and use the personalization properties you have defined.

Using Custom Types

As you can see from the earlier examples that show you how to define types for the personalization properties, defining and type casting properties to particular data types that are available in the .NET Framework are quite simple. You can easily define items such as System.Integer, System.String, System.DateTime, System.Byte, and System.Boolean within the web.config file. But how do you go about defining complex types?

Personalization properties that utilize custom types are just as easy to define as personalization properties that use simple types. Custom types enable you to store complex items such as shopping cart information or other status information from one use of the application to the next. Listing 18-6 first shows a class, ShoppingCart, which you use later in one of the personalization property definitions (ShoppingCart.cs and ShoppingCart.vb in the code download for this chapter).

LISTING 18-6: Creating a class to use as a personalization type

VB

```
<Serializable()> _
Public Class ShoppingCart
  Private PID As String
  Private CompanyProductName As String
  Private Number As Integer
  Private Price As Decimal
  Private DateAdded As DateTime
    Public Property ProductID() As String
  Get
    Return PID
  End Get
  Set(ByVal value As String)
    PID = value
  End Set
End Property
```

```vbnet
      Public Property ProductName() As String
    Get
      Return CompanyProductName
    End Get
    Set(ByVal value As String)
      CompanyProductName = value
    End Set
  End Property
      Public Property NumberSelected() As Integer
    Get
      Return Number
    End Get
    Set(ByVal value As Integer)
      Number = value
    End Set
  End Property
      Public Property ItemPrice() As Decimal
    Get
      Return Price
    End Get
    Set(ByVal value As Decimal)
      Price = value
    End Set
  End Property
      Public Property DateItemAdded() As DateTime
    Get
      Return DateAdded
    End Get
    Set(ByVal value As DateTime)
      DateAdded = value
    End Set
  End Property
End Class
```

C#

```csharp
using System;
[Serializable]
public class ShoppingCart
{
  private string PID;
  private string CompanyProductName;
  private int Number;
  private decimal Price;
  private DateTime DateAdded;
public ShoppingCart() {}
public string ProductID
  {
    get {return PID;}
    set {PID = value;}
  }
public string ProductName
  {
    get { return CompanyProductName; }
    set { CompanyProductName = value; }
  }
public int NumberSelected
  {
    get { return Number; }
    set { Number = value; }
  }
public decimal ItemPrice
  {
    get { return Price; }
    set { Price = value; }
```

continues

LISTING 18-6 *(continued)*

```
   }
   public DateTime DateItemAdded
   {
      get { return DateAdded; }
      set { DateAdded = value; }
   }
}
```

This simple shopping cart construction can now store the end user's shopping cart basket as the user moves around on an e-commerce site. The basket can even be persisted when the end user returns to the site at another time. Be sure to note that the class requires a `Serializable` attribute preceding the class declaration to ensure proper transformation to XML or binary.

Listing 18-7 shows how you would specify from within the `web.config` file that a personalization property is this complex type, such as a `ShoppingCart` type.

LISTING 18-7: Using complex types for personalization properties

```
<properties>
  <add name="FirstName" type="System.String" />
  <add name="LastName" type="System.String" />
  <add name="LastVisited" type="System.DateTime" />
  <add name="Age" type="System.Int32" />
  <add name="Member" type="System.Boolean" />
  <add name="Cart" type="ShoppingCart" serializeAs="Binary" />
</properties>
```

Just as the basic data types are stored in the personalization data stores, this construction enables you to easily store custom types and to have them serialized into the end data store in the format you choose. In this case, the `ShoppingCart` object is serialized as a binary object into the data store. The `serializeAs` attribute can take the values defined in the following list:

➤ `Binary`: Serializes and stores the object as binary data within the chosen data store.

➤ `ProviderSpecific`: Stores the object based upon the direction of the provider. This simply means that instead of the personalization engine determining the serialization of the object, the serialization is simply left up to the personalization provider specified.

➤ `String`: The default setting. Stores the personalization properties as a string inside the chosen data store.

➤ `XML`: Takes the object and serializes it into an XML format before storing it in the chosen data store.

Providing Default Values

In addition to defining the data types of the personalization properties, you can also define their default values directly in the `web.config` file. By default, the personalization properties you create do not have a value, but you can easily change this using the `defaultValue` attribute of the `<add>` element. Listing 18-8 shows how to define default values.

LISTING 18-8: Defining default values for personalization properties

```
<properties>
  <add name="FirstName" type="System.String" />
  <add name="LastName" type="System.String" />
  <add name="LastVisited" type="System.DateTime" />
  <add name="Age" type="System.Int32" />
  <add name="Member" type="System.Boolean" defaultValue="false" />
</properties>
```

From this example, you can see that only one of the personalization properties is provided with a default value. The last personalization property, `Member` in this example, is given a default value of `false`. This means that when you add a new end user to the personalization property database, `Member` is defined instead of remaining a blank value within the system.

Making Personalization Properties Read-Only

Making personalization properties read-only is also possible. To do it, you simply add the `readOnly` attribute to the `<add>` element:

```
<add name="StartDate" type="System.DateTime" readOnly="true" />
```

To make the personalization property a read-only property, you give the `readOnly` attribute a value of `true`. By default, this property is set to `false`.

ANONYMOUS PERSONALIZATION

A great feature in ASP.NET enables anonymous end users to utilize the personalization features it provides. This is important if a site requires registration of some kind. For example, many e-commerce sites allow anonymous end users to shop a site and use the site's shopping cart before the shoppers register with the site.

Enabling Anonymous Identification of the End User

By default, anonymous personalization is turned off because it consumes database resources on popular sites. Therefore, one of the first steps in allowing anonymous personalization is to turn on this feature using the appropriate setting in the `web.config` file. You must also make some changes regarding how the properties are actually defined in the `web.config` file and to determine whether you are going to allow anonymous personalization for your application.

As shown in Listing 18-9, you can turn on anonymous identification using the `<anonymousIdentification>` element to enable the personalization engine to identify the unknown end users.

LISTING 18-9: Allowing anonymous identification

```
<configuration>
    <system.web>
        <anonymousIdentification enabled="true" />
    </system.web>
</configuration>
```

To enable anonymous identification of the end users who might visit your applications, you add an `<anonymousIdentification>` element to the `web.config` file within the `<system.web>` nodes. Then within the `<anonymousIdentification>` element, you use the `enabled` attribute and set its value to `true`. Remember that, by default, this value is set to `false`.

When anonymous identification is turned on, ASP.NET uses a unique identifier for each anonymous user who comes to the application. This identifier is sent with each and every request, although after the end user becomes authenticated by ASP.NET, the identifier is removed from the process.

For an anonymous user, information is stored by default as a cookie on the end user's machine. Additional information (the personalization properties that you enable for anonymous users) is stored in the specified data store on the server.

To see the use of anonymous identification in action, turn off the Windows Authentication for your example application and, instead, use Forms Authentication. Listing 18-10 demonstrates this change.

LISTING 18-10: Turning off Windows Authentication and using Forms Authentication

```
<configuration>
    <system.web>
        <anonymousIdentification enabled="true" />
        <authentication mode="Forms" />
    </system.web>
</configuration>
```

With this code in place, if you run the page from the earlier example in Listing 18-2, you see the header presented in Listing 18-11.

LISTING 18-11: Setting an anonymous cookie in the HTTP header

```
HTTP/1.1 200 OK
Server: Microsoft-IIS/8.0
Date: Sun, 30 Dec 2012 21:02:33 GMT
X-AspNet-Version: 4.0.30319
X-SourceFiles: =?UTF-8?B?QzpcVXNlcnNcQ2hyaXN0aWFuXERvY3VtZW50c1xWaXN1YWwgU3R1ZGlvIDIwMTJcV2ViU2
10ZXNcV3JveFxaXN0aW5nXWebW5IDE4LTAyLmFzcHg=?=
X-Powered-By: ASP.NET
Set-Cookie: .ASPXANONYMOUS=HduG02IdzgEkAAAAMzA4NzIxZDUtZDk4ZC00ODQyLTk3ZDItY2Rh
NzI5N2NiODZjq7SGklbzPMq49DZkIgxpDBBXlk7ZD2mP5lC5e4xcPFY1; expires=Sun, 10-Mar-2013 07:42:33
GMT; path=/; HttpOnly
Cache-Control: private
Content-Type: text/html; charset=utf-8
Content-Length: 1419
Connection: Close
```

From this HTTP header, you can see that a cookie— `.ASPXANONYMOUS`—is set to a hashed value for later retrieval by the ASP.NET personalization system.

Changing the Name of the Cookie for Anonymous Identification

Cookies are used by default under the cookie name `.ASPXANONYMOUS`. You can change the name of this cookie from the `<anonymousIdentification>` element in the `web.config` file by using the `cookieName` attribute, as shown in Listing 18-12.

LISTING 18-12: Changing the name of the cookie

```
<configuration>
    <system.web>
        <anonymousIdentification
            enabled="true"
            cookieName=".ASPXWenzWebApplication" />
    </system.web>
</configuration>
```

Changing the Length of Time the Cookie Is Stored

Also, by default, the cookie stored on the end user's machine is stored for 100,000 minutes (which is almost 70 days). If you want to change this value, you do it within this `<anonymousIdentification>` element using the `cookieTimeout` attribute, as shown in Listing 18-13.

LISTING 18-13: Changing the length of time the cookie is stored

```
<configuration>
    <system.web>
        <anonymousIdentification
```

```
      enabled="true"
      cookieTimeout="1440" />
  </system.web>
</configuration>
```

In this case, the `cookieTimeout` value was changed to `1440`—meaning 1,440 minutes (or one day). This setting would be ideal for something like a shopping cart where you do not want to persist the identification of the end user too long.

Changing How the Identifiers Are Stored

Although anonymous identifiers are stored through the use of cookies, you can also easily change this method. Cookies are, by far, the preferred way to achieve identification, but you can also do it without the use of cookies. Other options include using the URI or device profiles. Listing 18-14 shows an example of using the URI to place the identifiers.

LISTING 18-14: Specifying how cookies are stored

```
<configuration>
  <system.web>
    <anonymousIdentification
      enabled="true"
      cookieless="UseUri" />
  </system.web>
</configuration>
```

Besides `UseUri`, other options include `UseCookies`, `AutoDetect`, and `UseDeviceProfile`. The following list reviews each of the options:

➤ `UseCookies`: This setting is the default. If you set no value, ASP.NET assumes this is the value. `UseCookies` means that a cookie is placed on the end user's machine for identification.

➤ `UseUri`: This value means that a cookie *will not* be stored on the end user's machine, but instead the unique identifier will be munged within the URL of the page. Although this setting is great if developers want to avoid sticking a cookie on an end user's machine, it does create strange-looking URLs and can be an issue when an end user bookmarks pages for later retrieval.

➤ `AutoDetect`: Using this value means that you are letting the ASP.NET engine decide whether to use cookies or use the URL approach for the anonymous identification. It makes this decision on a per-user basis, which does not perform as well as the preceding two options because ASP.NET must check the end user before deciding which approach to use. My suggestion is to use `AutoDetect` instead of `UseUri` *only* if you absolutely must allow for end users who have cookies turned off (which is rare these days).

➤ `UseDeviceProfile`: Configures the identifier for the device or browser that is making the request.

Looking at the Anonymous Identifiers Stored

ASP.NET uses a globally unique identifier (GUID) to make the anonymous identifiers unique. You can also now grab hold of this unique identifier for your own use. To retrieve the GUID, the `Request` object has been enhanced with an `AnonymousID` property. The `AnonymousID` property returns a value of type `String`, which you can use in your code, as shown here:

```
Label1.Text = Request.AnonymousID
```

Working with Anonymous Identification

In working with the creation of anonymous users, be aware of an important event that you can use from your `Global.asax` file for managing the process: `AnonymousIdentification_Creating`.

By using the `AnonymousIdentification_Creating` event, you can work with the identification of the end user as it occurs. For example, if you do not want to use GUIDs for uniquely identifying the end user, you can change the identifying value from this event instead.

To do so, create the event using the event delegate of type `AnonymousIdentificationEventArgs`, as shown in Listing 18-15.

LISTING 18-15: Changing the unique identifier of the anonymous user

VB

```vb
Public Sub AnonymousIdentification_Creating(ByVal sender As Object, _
  ByVal e As AnonymousIDentificationEventArgs)
       e.AnonymousID = "Bubbles " & DateTime.Now()
End Sub
```

C#

```csharp
public void AnonymousIdentification_Creating(object sender,
  AnonymousIDentificationEventArgs e)
{
    e.AnonymousID = "Bubbles " + DateTime.Now;
}
```

The `AnonymousIdentificationEventArgs` event delegate exposes an `AnonymousID` property that assigns the value used to uniquely identify the anonymous user. Now, instead of a GUID to uniquely identify the anonymous user as

```
d13fafec-244a-4d21-9137-b213236ebedb
```

the `AnonymousID` property is changed within the `AnonymousIdentification_Creating` event to

```
Bubbles 12/31/2012 2:07:33 PM
```

Anonymous Options for Personalization Properties

If you have tried to get the anonymous capability working, you might have received the error shown in Figure 18-4.

To get your application to work with anonymous users, you must specify which personalization properties you want to enable for the anonymous users visiting your pages. You can also do this through the `web.config` file by adding the `allowAnonymous` attribute to the `<add>` element of the properties you have defined within the `<properties>` section (see Listing 18-16).

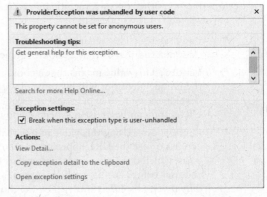

FIGURE 18-4

LISTING 18-16: Turning on anonymous capabilities for personalization properties

```xml
<properties>
  <add name="FirstName" type="System.String" />
  <add name="LastName" type="System.String" />
  <add name="LastVisited" type="System.DateTime" allowAnonymous="true" />
  <add name="Age" type="System.Integer" />
  <add name="Member" type="System.Boolean" />
</properties>
```

In this example, the `LastVisited` property is set to allow anonymous users by setting the `allowAnonymous` attribute to `true`. Because this property is the only one that works with anonymous users, the rest of the defined properties do not store information for these types of users. If you are still checking if the user is authenticated in your code, be sure to comment that out for these examples to work.

Warnings about Anonymous User Profile Storage

Taking into account everything said so far about anonymous users, you should be very careful about how you approach anonymous user profile storage. Storing profile information about anonymous users can dramatically populate the data store you are using. For example, in my examples, I used Microsoft's SQL Server Express Edition, and I stored profile information for one authenticated user and then for a single anonymous user. This puts information for both these users in the aspnet_Profile and the aspnet_Users tables.

Figure 18-5 shows the two users listed in the aspnet_Users table.

dbo.aspnet_Users [Data]						
■ 🔾 ▶	Max Rows: 1000	▾	🗗 🗗			

ApplicationId	UserId	UserName	LoweredUserN...	MobileAlias	IsAnonymous	LastActivityDate
fa1d0c76-f841-...	b3fbadd2-4ac5...	308721d5-d98d...	308721d5-d98d...	NULL	True	12/30/2012 9:08...
fa1d0c76-f841-...	32d18eea-e6d3...	Win8Pro-EN-V...	win8pro-en-vh...	NULL	False	12/30/2012 8:55...
▶* NULL	NULL	NULL	NULL	NULL	NULL	NULL

FIGURE 18-5

In this figure, the anonymous user is the first line in the table, and you can see that this user has a rather cryptic name, which is the `Request.AnonymousID` presented earlier. The other big difference between the two users appears in the `IsAnonymous` column in the table. The anonymous user has a setting of `true` for this column, whereas the authenticated user has a setting of `false`. Because your database can fill up quickly with anonymous user information, you should weigh which information you really must store on these types of users.

PROGRAMMATIC ACCESS TO PERSONALIZATION

When an ASP.NET page is invoked, ASP.NET creates a class (`ProfileCommon`) by inheriting from the `ProfileBase` class, which it uses to strongly type the profile properties that were defined in the `web.config` file. This created class, meant to deal with the user's profile store, gets and sets profile properties through the use of the `GetPropertyValue` and `SetPropertyValue` methods from the `ProfileBase` class.

As you would expect, ASP.NET provides you with the hooks necessary to get at specific `Profile` events using the `ProfileModule` class. The `ProfileModule` class is what ASP.NET itself uses to create and store profile information in the page's `Profile` object.

The `ProfileModule` class exposes three events that you can use to handle your user's profile situations. These events—`MigrateAnonymous`, `Personalize`, and `ProfileAutoSaving`—are focused around the area of authentication. Because you just saw how to work with anonymous users in your applications, this section now looks at how to migrate these users from anonymous users to authenticated users, because you are most likely going to want to move their profile properties as well as change their status.

Migrating Anonymous Users

When working with anonymous users, you must be able to migrate anonymous users to registered users. For example, after an end user fills a shopping cart, he can register on the site to purchase the items. At that moment, the end user switches from being an anonymous user to a registered user.

For this reason, ASP.NET provides a `Profile_MigrateAnonymous` event handler that enables you to migrate anonymous users to registered users. The `Profile_MigrateAnonymous` event requires a data class of type `ProfileMigrateEventArgs`. You place it either in the page that deals with the migration or within the `Global.asax` file (if it can be used from anywhere within the application). Listing 18-17 shows the use of this event.

LISTING 18-17: Migrating anonymous users for particular personalization properties

VB

```
Public Sub Profile_MigrateAnonymous(ByVal sender As Object, _
  ByVal e As ProfileMigrateEventArgs)
    Dim anonymousProfile As ProfileCommon = Profile.GetProfile(e.AnonymousID)
    Profile.LastVisited = anonymousProfile.LastVisited
End Sub
```

C#

```
public void Profile_MigrateAnonymous(object sender,
  ProfileMigrateEventArgs e)
{
    ProfileCommon anonymousProfile = Profile.GetProfile(e.AnonymousID);
    Profile.LastVisited = anonymousProfile.LastVisited;
}
```

In this example, you create an instance of the `ProfileCommon` object and populate it with the profile from the visiting anonymous user. From there, you can use the instance to get at all the profile properties of that anonymous user, which means that you can then populate a profile through a movement from the anonymous user's profile information to the authenticated user's profile system.

Listing 18-17 shows how to migrate a single personalization property from an anonymous user to the new registered user. In addition to migrating single properties, you can also migrate properties that come from personalization groups, as shown in Listing 18-18.

LISTING 18-18: Migrating anonymous users for items in personalization groups

VB

```
Public Sub Profile_MigrateAnonymous(ByVal sender As Object, _
  ByVal e As ProfileMigrateEventArgs)
    Dim au As ProfileCommon = Profile.GetProfile(e.AnonymousID)
    If au.MemberDetails.DateJoined <> "" Then
        Profile.MemberDetails.DateJoined = DateTime.Now().ToString()
        Profile.FamilyDetails.MarriedStatus = au.FamilyDetails.MarriedStatus
    End If
    AnonymousIdentificationModule.ClearAnonymousIdentifier()
End Sub
```

C#

```
public void Profile_MigrateAnonymous(object sender,
  ProfileMigrateEventArgs e)
{
    ProfileCommon au = Profile.GetProfile(e.AnonymousID);
    if (au.MemberDetails.DateJoined != String.Empty) {
      Profile.MemberDetails.DateJoined = DateTime.Now.ToString();
      Profile.FamilyDetails.MarriedStatus = au.FamilyDetails.MarriedStatus;
    }
    AnonymousIdentificationModule.ClearAnonymousIdentifier();
}
```

Using this event in the `Global.asax` file enables you to logically migrate anonymous users as they register themselves with your applications. The migration process also enables you to pick and choose which items you migrate and to change the values as you want.

Personalizing Profiles

Besides working with anonymous users from the `Global.asax` file, you can also programmatically personalize the profiles retrieved from the personalization store. You do so through the use of the `Profile_Personalize` event. Listing 18-19 demonstrates an example use of this event.

LISTING 18-19: Personalizing a retrieved profile

VB

```vb
Public Sub Profile_Personalize(sender As Object, args As ProfileEventArgs)
  Dim checkedProfile As ProfileCommon
  If User Is Nothing Then Return
  checkedProfile = CType(ProfileBase.Create(User.Identity.Name), ProfileCommon)
  If (Date.Now.IsDaylightSavingTime()) Then
    checkedProfile = checkedProfile.GetProfile("TimeDifferenceUser")
  Else
    checkedProfile = checkedProfile.GetProfile("TimeUser")
  End If
  If Not checkedProfile Is Nothing Then
    args.Profile = checkedProfile
  End If
End Sub
```

C#

```csharp
public void Profile_Personalize(object sender, ProfileEventArgs args)
{
  ProfileCommon checkedProfile;
  if (User == null) { return; }
  checkedProfile = (ProfileCommon)ProfileBase.Create(User.Identity.Name);
  if (DateTime.Now.IsDaylightSavingTime()) {
    checkedProfile = checkedProfile.GetProfile("TimeDifferenceUser");
  }
  else {
    checkedProfile = checkedProfile.GetProfile("TimeUser");
  }
  if (checkedProfile != null) {
    args.Profile = checkedProfile;
  }
}
```

In this case, based on a specific parameter (whether it is Daylight Savings Time or something else), you are able to assign a specific profile to the user. You do this by using the `ProfileModule.Personalize` event, which you would usually stick inside the `Global.asax` page.

Determining Whether to Continue with Automatic Saves

When you are working with the profile capabilities provided by ASP.NET, the page automatically saves the profile values to the specified data store at the end of the page's execution. You can set this capability, which is turned on (set to `true`) by default, to `false` through the use of the `automaticSaveEnabled` attribute in the `<profile>` node in the `web.config` file, as shown in Listing 18-20.

LISTING 18-20: Working with the automaticSaveEnabled attribute

```xml
<profile automaticSaveEnabled="false">
  <properties>
    <add name="FirstName" />
    <add name="LastName" />
    <add name="LastVisited" />
```

continues

LISTING 18-20 *(continued)*

```
        <add name="Age" />
        <add name="Member" />
    </properties>
</profile>
```

If you have set the `automaticSaveEnabled` attribute value to `false`, you will have to invoke the `ProfileBase.Save()` method yourself. In most cases, though, you are going to leave this setting on `true`. After a page request has been made and finalized, the `ProfileModule.ProfileAutoSaving` event is raised. You can also work with this event, as shown in Listing 18-21. You would place this event in the `Global .asax` file.

LISTING 18-21: Using the ProfileAutoSaving event to turn off the auto-saving feature

VB

```vb
Public Sub Profile_ProfileAutoSaving(sender As Object,
 args As ProfileAutoSaveEventArgs)
  If Profile.PaidDueStatus.HasChanged Then
    args.ContinueWithProfileAutoSave = True
  Else
    args.ContinueWithProfileAutoSave = False
  End If
End Sub
```

C#

```csharp
public void Profile_ProfileAutoSaving(object sender, ProfileAutoSaveEventArgs args)
{
  if (Profile.PaidDueStatus.HasChanged) {
    args.ContinueWithProfileAutoSave = true;
  } else {
    args.ContinueWithProfileAutoSave = false;
  }
}
```

In this case, when the `Profile_ProfileAutoSaving` event is triggered, you can then work within this event and change some behaviors. Listing 18-21 looks to see whether the `Profile.PaidDueStatus` property has changed. If it has changed, the auto-saving feature of the profile system is continued; if the `Profile .PaidDueStatus` has not changed, the auto-saving feature is turned off.

Using Profile Information in Web Application Projects

As convenient as the access to profile properties is, by default, only ASP.NET Web Site Projects (WSP) support this feature. More common, however, are ASP.NET Web Application Projects (WAP). If you are using one of those, the shortcut access to profile properties is not available. When working with WSP, ASP .NET automatically creates proxy classes that expose all profile properties; this is not the case with WAP.

However, there is a more or less easy way to emulate such a shortcut access: Just create your own profile class. Former ASP.NET team member Jon Galloway has more details in his excellent writeup at `http://weblogs.asp.net/jgalloway/archive/2008/01/19/writing-a-custom-asp-net-profile- class.aspx`, but here are the basic steps.

First, you need to create a class that derives from `ProfileBase`. In here you add properties for the profile options you would like to have. Even support for anonymous access is available by using the `SettingsAllowAnonymous` attribute. Listing 18-22 shows a sample implementation for a shortened version of the profile properties used throughout this chapter.

LISTING 18-22: Using profile properties within Web Application Projects

VB

```vb
Imports System.Web.Profile
Imports System.Web.Security

Namespace Wrox
    Public Class UserProfile
        Inherits ProfileBase

        Public Shared Function GetUserProfile(username As String) As UserProfile
            Return CType(Create(username), UserProfile)
        End Function

        Public Shared Function GetUserProfile() As UserProfile
            Return CType(Create(Membership.GetUser().UserName), UserProfile)
        End Function

        <SettingsAllowAnonymous(False)> _
        Public Property FirstName() As String
            Get
                Return MyBase.GetPropertyValue("FirstName").ToString()
            End Get

            Set(value As String)
                MyBase.SetPropertyValue("FirstName", value)
            End Set
        End Property

        <SettingsAllowAnonymous(False)> _
        Public Property LastName() As String
            Get
                Return MyBase.GetPropertyValue("LastName").ToString()
            End Get

            Set(value As String)
                MyBase.SetPropertyValue("LastName", value)
            End Set
        End Property

        <SettingsAllowAnonymous(True)>
        Public Property LastVisited() As DateTime
            Get
                Return CType(MyBase.GetPropertyValue("LastVisited"), DateTime)
            End Get

            Set(value As DateTime)
                MyBase.SetPropertyValue("LastVisited", value)
            End Set
        End Property

    End Class
End Namespace
```

C#

```csharp
using System.Web.Profile;
using System.Web.Security;

namespace Wrox
{
```

continues

LISTING 18-22 *(continued)*

```
public class UserProfile : ProfileBase
{
    public static UserProfile GetUserProfile(string username)
    {
        return Create(username) as UserProfile;
    }

    public static UserProfile GetUserProfile()
    {
        return Create(Membership.GetUser().UserName) as UserProfile;
    }

    [SettingsAllowAnonymous(false)]
    public string FirstName
    {
        get { return base["FirstName"] as string; }
        set { base["FirstName"] = value; }
    }

    [SettingsAllowAnonymous(false)]
    public string LastName
    {
        get { return base["LastName"] as string; }
        set { base["LastName"] = value; }
    }

    [SettingsAllowAnonymous(true)]
    public DateTime LastVisited
    {
        get { return base["LastVisited"] as DateTime; }
        set { base["LastVisited"] = value; }
    }
}
```

Then, you need to make sure in `web.config` that the profile properties come from the class you just created. The setting shown in Listing 18-23 shows how to do this.

LISTING 18-23: Referencing the profile class in web.config

```
<profile defaultProvider="AspNetSqlProfileProvider" inherits="Wrox.UserProfile">
</profile>
```

Finally, the API shown in Listing 18-19 provides access to the profile properties.

PERSONALIZATION PROVIDERS

As shown in Figure 18-1 earlier in the chapter, the middle tier of the personalization model, the personalization API layer, communicates with a series of default data providers. By default, the personalization model uses Microsoft SQL Server Express Edition files for storing the personalization properties you define. You are not limited to just this type of data store, however. You can also use the Microsoft SQL Server data provider to enable you to work with Microsoft SQL Server 7.0 or higher. Besides the Microsoft SQL Server data provider, the architecture also enables you to create your own data providers if one of these data stores does not fit your requirements.

Working with SQL Server Express Edition

The Microsoft SQL Server data provider does enable you to work with your SQL Server Express Edition files. The SQL Server data provider is the default provider used by the personalization system provided by ASP.NET. When used with Visual Studio 2012, the IDE places the `ASPNETDB.MDF` file within your application's App_Data folder.

As you look through the `machine.config` file, notice the sections that deal with how the personalization engine works with this database. In the first reference to the `LocalSqlServer` file, you find a connection string to this file (shown in Listing 18-24) within the `<connectionStrings>` section of the file.

LISTING 18-24: Adding a connection string to the SQL Server Express file

```
<configuration>
  <connectionStrings>
    <clear />
    <add name="LocalSqlServer"
     connectionString="data source=.\SQLEXPRESS;Integrated Security=SSPI;
     AttachDBFilename=|DataDirectory|aspnetdb.mdf;User Instance=true"
     providerName="System.Data.SqlClient" />
  </connectionStrings>
</configuration>
```

In this example, you see that a connection string with the name `LocalSqlServer` has been defined. The location of the file, specified by the `connectionString` attribute, points to the relative path of the file. This means that in every application you build that utilizes the personalization capabilities, the default SQL Server provider should be located in the application's App_Data folder and have the name of `ASPNETDB.MDF`.

The SQL Server Express file's connection string is specified through the `LocalSqlServer` declaration within this `<connectionStrings>` section. You can see the personalization engine's reference to this in the `<profile>` section within the `machine.config` file. The `<profile>` section includes a subsection listing all the providers available to the personalization engine, as shown in Listing 18-25.

LISTING 18-25: Adding a new SQL Server data provider

```
<configuration>
  <system.web>
    <profile>
      <providers>
        <add name="AspNetSqlProfileProvider"
          connectionStringName="LocalSqlServer" applicationName="/"
          type="System.Web.Profile.SqlProfileProvider, System.Web,
            Version=4.0.0.0, Culture=neutral,
            PublicKeyToken=b03f5f7f11d50a3a" />
      </providers>
    </profile>
  </system.web>
</configuration>
```

From this, you can see that you add a provider by using the `<add>` element. Within this element, the `connectionStringName` attribute points to what was declared in the `<connectionString>` attribute from Listing 18-24.

You can specify an entirely different Microsoft SQL Server Express Edition file other than the one specified in the `machine.config` file. Create a connection string that points to a new SQL Server Express file that is a templated version of the `ASPNETDB.MDF` file. At this point, you can use `<connectionString>` to point to this new file. If you change these values in the `machine.config` file, all the ASP.NET applications that reside on the server will then use this specified file. If you make the changes only to the `web.config` file, however, only the application using this particular `web.config` file uses this new data store. Other applications on the server remain unchanged.

Working with Microsoft SQL Server

You will likely find working with the personalization framework using the SQL Server Express files quite easy. But when you work with larger applications that require the factors of performance and reliability, you should use the SQL Server personalization provider along with SQL Server starting from version 7.0 (and also including 2000, 2005, 2008, and 2012). If this data store is available, you should always try to use this option instead of the default SQL Server Express Edition files.

If you worked with the SQL Server personalization provider using SQL Server Express files as explained earlier, you probably found it easy to use. The personalization provider works right out of the box, without any setup or configuration on your part. Using the SQL Server personalization provider with a full-blown version of SQL Server, however, is a bit of a different story. Although working with it is not difficult, you must set up and configure your SQL Server before using it.

ASP.NET 4.5 provides a couple of ways to set up and configure SQL Server for the personalization framework. One way is through the ASP.NET SQL Server Setup Wizard, and the other is by running some of the SQL Server scripts provided with the .NET Framework 4.5.

> **NOTE** *Chapter 14 covers using the ASP.NET SQL Server Setup Wizard in detail.*

To use the ASP.NET SQL Server Setup Wizard to set up your SQL Server for the ASP.NET 4.5 personalization features, open the aspnet_regsql.exe tool by invoking it from the Visual Studio 2012 Command Prompt. At the prompt, type in **aspnet_regsql.exe** to open the GUI of the ASP.NET SQL Server Setup Wizard. If you step through the wizard, you can set up your SQL Server instance for many of the ASP .NET systems, such as the personalization system.

Using SQL Scripts to Install Personalization Features

Another option for setting up and configuring SQL Server for the personalization framework is to use the same SQL scripts that these tools and wizards use. If you look at `C:\WINDOWS\ Microsoft.NET\Framework\v4.0.xxxxx\`, from this location you can see the install and remove scripts—`InstallPersonalization.sql` and `UninstallPersonalization.sql`. Running these scripts provides your database with the tables needed to run the personalization framework. Be forewarned that you must run the `InstallCommon.sql` script before running the personalization script (or any of the new other ASP.NET system scripts).

Configuring the Provider for SQL Server

After you have set up your SQL Server database for the personalization system, the next step is to redefine the personalization provider so that it works with this instance (instead of with the default Microsoft SQL Server Express Edition files).

You accomplish this step in the `web.config` file of your application. Here, you want to configure the provider and then define this provider instance as the provider to use. Listing 18-26 shows these additions plus the enlarged `<profile>` section of the `web.config` file.

LISTING 18-26: Connecting the SqlProfileProvider to SQL Server

```
<configuration>
  <connectionStrings>
    <add name="LocalSql2012Server"
    connectionString="data source=127.0.0.1;Integrated Security=SSPI" />
  </connectionStrings>
  <profile defaultProvider="AspNetSql2012ProfileProvider">
    <providers>
```

```
            <clear />
            <add name="AspNetSql2012ProfileProvider"
              connectionStringName="LocalSql2012Server" applicationName="/"
              type="System.Web.Profile.SqlProfileProvider, System.Web,
                Version=4.0.0.0, Culture=neutral,
                PublicKeyToken=b03f5f7f11d50a3a" />
        </providers>
        <properties>
            <add name="FirstName" />
            <add name="LastName" />
            <add name="LastVisited" />
            <add name="Age" />
            <add name="Member" />
        </properties>
      </profile>
  </configuration>
```

The big change you make to this profile definition is to use the `defaultProvider` attribute with a value that is the name of the provider you want to use—in this case, the newly created SQL Server provider `AspNetSql2012ProfileProvider`. You can also make this change to the `machine.config` file by changing the `<profile>` element, as shown in Listing 18-27.

LISTING 18-27: Using SQL Server as the provider in the machine.config file

```
<configuration>
  <system.web>
      ...
      <profile enabled="true" defaultProvider="AspNetSql2012ProfileProvider">
      ...
      </profile>
      ...
  </system.web>
</configuration>
```

This change forces each and every application that resides on this server to use this new SQL Server provider instead of the default SQL Server provider (unless this command is overridden in the application's `web.config` file).

Using Multiple Providers

You are not limited to using a single datastore or provider. Instead, you can use any number of providers. You can even specify the personalization provider for each property defined. This means that you can use the default provider for most properties, as well as allowing a few of them to use an entirely different provider (see Listing 18-28).

LISTING 18-28: Using different providers

```
<configuration>
  <system.web>
    <profile
        defaultProvider="AspNetSqlProvider">
        <properties>
            <add name="FirstName" />
            <add name="LastName" />
            <add name="LastVisited" />
            <add name="Age" />
            <add name="Member" provider="AspNetSql2012ProfileProvider" />
        </properties>
    </profile>
  </system.web>
</configuration>
```

From this example, you can see that a default provider is specified—`AspNetSqlProvider`. Unless another provider is specified, this provider is used. The only property that changes this setting is the `Member` property. The `Member` property uses an entirely different personalization provider. In this case, it employs the Access provider (`AspNetSql2012ProfileProvider`) through the use of the `provider` attribute of the `<add>` element. With this attribute, you can define a specific provider for each and every property that is defined.

Using Universal Providers

ASP.NET 4.5's profile feature is tied to Microsoft SQL Server. To be exact, it's the profile provider that has this dependency. To make the API more flexible and easier to use with other database systems, Microsoft provides so-called Universal Providers. Unfortunately, they are not part of the standard distribution of ASP.NET, but are available as a separate package on NuGet. The package name is `Microsoft.AspNet.Providers` (careful: Older versions of the package were called `System.Web.Providers`), and the NuGet package homepage is at `http://nuget.org/packages/Microsoft.AspNet.Providers`. When you start the NuGet Package Manager from within Visual Studio (using the Tools ⇨ Library Package Manager ⇨ Package Manager Console entry), you can install the package to the current project by executing the following command:

```
Install-Package Microsoft.AspNet.Providers
```

Figure 18-6 shows a typical console output of the installation. Afterwards, the `System.Web.Providers.dll` assembly is part of your project.

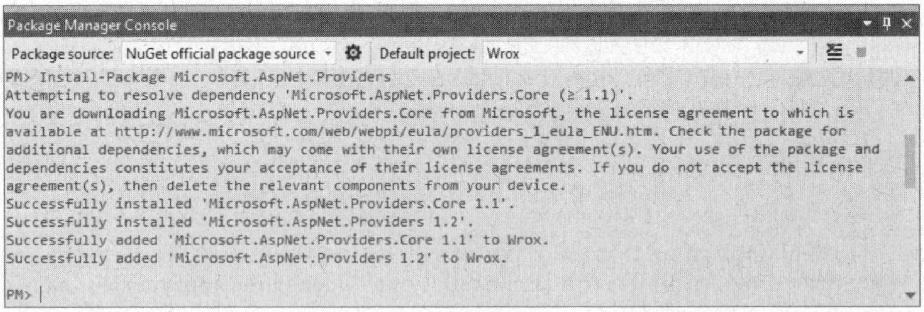

FIGURE 18-6

To actually use the new assembly, you once again need to configure ASP.NET via `web.config`. The trick is to use a provider defined in the `System.Web.Providers` assembly so that ASP.NET can pick up the data and work with any supported database. The list of supported databases is currently focused on Microsoft's Azure cloud offering, but it's possible that more databases will be added at a later point. Listing 18-29 shows a sample configuration.

LISTING 18-29: Using Universal Providers in web.config

```
<configuration>
  <connectionstrings>
    <add connectionstring="..." name="DefaultConnection" />
  </connectionstrings>
  <system.web>
    <profile defaultprovider="DefaultProfileProvider">
      <providers>
        <add name="DefaultProfileProvider" applicationname="/"
             type="System.Web.Providers.DefaultProfileProvider"
             connectionstringname="DefaultConnection" />
      </providers>
    </profile>
  </system.web>
</configuration>
```

MANAGING APPLICATION PROFILES

When you put into production an ASP.NET application that uses profile information, you quickly realize that you need a way to manage all the profile information collected over the life cycle of the application. As you look at the ASP.NET MMC snap-in or the ASP.NET Web Site Administration Tool, note that neither of these tools gives you a way to delete a specific user's profile information or even to cleanse a database of profile information for users who haven't been active in a while.

ASP.NET 4.5 gives you the means to manage the profile information that your application stores, through the use of the `ProfileManager` class available in .NET.

You can use the `ProfileManager` class to build in the administration capabilities to completely manage the profile information that is stored by your application. In addition to being able to access property values, such as the name of the provider being used by the personalization system or the name of the application in question, you also have a large number of methods available in the `ProfileManager` class to retrieve all sorts of other information concerning your user's profile. Through the `ProfileManager` class, you also have the capability to perform actions on this stored profile information including cleansing the database of old profile information.

Properties of the ProfileManager Class

Table 18-1 details the properties of the `ProfileManager` class.

TABLE 18-1

PROPERTIES	DESCRIPTION
`ApplicationName`	Gets or sets the name of the application to work with
`AutomaticSaveEnabled`	Gets or sets a boolean value indicating whether the profile information is stored at the end of the page execution
`Enabled`	Gets or sets a boolean value indicating whether the application is able to use the personalization system
`Provider`	Gets the name of the provider being used for the personalization system
`Providers`	Gets a collection of all the providers available for the ASP.NET application

You can see that these properties include a bit of information about the personalization system and the providers available to it that you can integrate into any management system you build. Next, this chapter looks at the methods available for the `ProfileManager` class.

Methods of the ProfileManager Class

A good number of methods are available to the `ProfileManager` class that help you manage the profiles of the users of your application. Table 18-2 briefly describes these methods.

TABLE 18-2

METHODS	DESCRIPTION
`DeleteInactiveProfiles`	Enables you to delete any profiles that haven't seen any activity for a specified time period
`DeleteProfile`	Enables you to delete a specific profile
`DeleteProfiles`	Enables you to delete a collection of profiles
`FindInactiveProfilesBy UserName`	Provides you with all the inactive profiles under a specific username according to a specified date

continues

TABLE 18-2 *(continued)*

METHODS	DESCRIPTION
FindProfilesByUserName	Provides you with all the profiles from a specific username
GetAllInactiveProfiles	Provides you with all the profiles that have been inactive since a specified date
GetAllProfiles	Provides you with a collection of all the profiles
GetNumberOf InactiveProfiles	Provides you with the number of inactive profiles from a specified date
GetNumberOfProfiles	Provides you with the number of total profiles in the system

As you can see from this list of methods, you can do plenty to manage the profile information that is stored in your database.

Next, this chapter looks at building a profile manager administration page for your ASP.NET application. This example builds it as an ASP.NET page, but you can just as easily build it as a console application.

Building the Profile Manager Page

To create a simple profile manager for your application, create a single ASP.NET page in your application with the code in Listing 18-30. You use this page to manage the profiles that are stored in the database for this particular application.

This page includes a number of controls, but the most important is a DropDownList control that holds all the usernames of entities that have profile information in the database. You might see the same username a couple of times depending on what you are doing with your application. Remember that a single user can have multiple profiles in the database.

Using the DropDownList control, you can select a user and see information about his profile stored in your data store. From this page, you can also delete his profile information. You can actually perform many operations with the `ProfileManager` class, but this is a good example of some basic ones.

Listing 18-30 presents the code for the profile manager.

LISTING 18-30: The Profile Manager page

VB

```
<%@ Page Language="VB" %>
    <script runat="server">
  Protected Sub Page_Load(ByVal sender As Object, ByVal e As System.EventArgs)
    If (DropDownList1.Items.Count = 0) Then
       WriteDropdownList()
       WriteUserOutput()
    End If
  End Sub
  Protected Sub DeleteButton_Click(ByVal sender As Object,
   ByVal e As System.EventArgs)
     ProfileManager.DeleteProfile(DropDownList1.Text.ToString())
     DropDownList1.Items.Clear()
     WriteDropdownList()
     WriteUserOutput()
  End Sub
  Protected Sub SelectButton_Click(ByVal sender As Object,
   ByVal e As System.EventArgs)
     WriteUserOutput()
  End Sub
  Protected Sub WriteUserOutput()
```

```
      Dim outputInt As Integer
      Dim pic As ProfileInfoCollection = New ProfileInfoCollection()
      If DropDownList1.Text <> "" Then
      pic = ProfileManager.FindProfilesByUserName( _
        ProfileAuthenticationOption.All, _
        DropDownList1.Text, 0, 1, outputInt)
      End If
      DetailsView1.DataSource = pic
      DetailsView1.DataBind()
    End Sub
    Protected Sub WriteDropdownList()
      Dim outputInt As Integer
      Dim pic As ProfileInfoCollection = New ProfileInfoCollection()
      pic = ProfileManager.Provider.GetAllProfiles( _
        ProfileAuthenticationOption.All, 0, 10000, outputInt)
      For Each proInfo As ProfileInfo In pic
        Dim li As ListItem = New ListItem()
        li.Text = proInfo.UserName.ToString()
        DropDownList1.Items.Add(li)
      Next
      Label1.Text = outputInt.ToString()
    End Sub
</script>
<html xmlns="http://www.w3.org/1999/xhtml" >
<head id="Head1" runat="server">
  <title>ProfileAdmin Page</title>
</head>
<body>
  <form id="form1" runat="server">
  <div>
    <b>Profile Manager<br />
    </b>
    <br />
    Total number of users in system:
    <asp:Label ID="Label1" runat="server"></asp:Label><br />
     <br />
    <asp:DropDownList ID="DropDownList1" runat="server">
    </asp:DropDownList> 
    <asp:Button ID="SelectButton" runat="server"
     OnClick="SelectButton_Click"
      Text="Get User Profile Information" /><br />
    <br />
    <asp:DetailsView ID="DetailsView1" runat="server" CellPadding="4"
     ForeColor="#333333" GridLines="None"
      Height="50px">
      <FooterStyle BackColor="#1C5E55" Font-Bold="True" ForeColor="White" />
      <EditRowStyle BackColor="#7C6F57" />
      <PagerStyle BackColor="#666666" ForeColor="White"
       HorizontalAlign="Center" />
      <HeaderStyle BackColor="#1C5E55" Font-Bold="True" ForeColor="White" />
      <AlternatingRowStyle BackColor="White" />
      <CommandRowStyle BackColor="#C5BBAF" Font-Bold="True" />
      <RowStyle BackColor="#E3EAEB" />
      <FieldHeaderStyle BackColor="#D0D0D0" Font-Bold="True" />
    </asp:DetailsView>
    <br />
    <asp:Button ID="DeleteButton" runat="server"
     Text="Delete Selected User's Profile Information"
      OnClick="DeleteButton_Click" />
  </div>
  </form>
</body>
</html>
```

continues

LISTING 18-30 *(continued)*

C#

```csharp
<%@ Page Language="C#" %>
<script runat="server">
  protected void Page_Load(object sender, EventArgs e)
  {
    if (DropDownList1.Items.Count == 0)
    {
      WriteDropdownList();
      WriteUserOutput();
    }
  }
  protected void DeleteButton_Click(object sender, EventArgs e)
  {
    ProfileManager.DeleteProfile(DropDownList1.Text.ToString());
    DropDownList1.Items.Clear();
    WriteDropdownList();
    WriteUserOutput();
  }
  protected void SelectButton_Click(object sender, EventArgs e)
  {
    WriteUserOutput();
  }
  protected void WriteUserOutput()
  {
    int outputInt;
    ProfileInfoCollection pic = new ProfileInfoCollection();
    if (DropDownList1.Text != "") {
        pic = ProfileManager.FindProfilesByUserName
          (ProfileAuthenticationOption.All,
          DropDownList1.Text.ToString(), 0, 1, out outputInt);
    }
    DetailsView1.DataSource = pic;
    DetailsView1.DataBind();
  }
  protected void WriteDropdownList()
  {
    int outputInt;
    ProfileInfoCollection pic = ProfileManager.Provider.GetAllProfiles
      (ProfileAuthenticationOption.All, 0, 10000, out outputInt);
    foreach (ProfileInfo proInfo in pic)
    {
      ListItem li = new ListItem();
      li.Text = proInfo.UserName.ToString();
        DropDownList1.Items.Add(li);
    }
    Label1.Text = outputInt.ToString();
  }
</script>
```

Examining the Profile Manager Page's Code

As you look over the code of the profile manager page, note that the `ProfileManager` class is used to perform a couple of different operations.

The `ProfileManager` class's `GetAllProfiles()` method is used to populate the DropDownList control that is on the page. Here is the constructor of this method:

```
GetAllProfiles(
  authenticationOption,
  pageIndex,
  pageSize,
  totalRecords)
```

The `GetAllProfiles()` method takes a number of parameters, the first of which enables you to define whether you are using this method for *all* profiles in the system, or just the anonymous or authenticated users' profiles contained in the system. In this example, all the profiles are retrieved with this method. This is accomplished using the `ProfileAuthenticationOption` enumeration. Then, the other parameters of the `GetAllProfiles()` method require you to specify a page index and the number of records to retrieve from the database. There is not a *get all* option (because of the potential size of the data that might be retrieved); so instead, in this example, you specify the first page of data (using 0) and that this page contains the first 10,000 records (which is basically a *get all* for this application). The last parameter of the `GetAllProfiles()` method enables you to retrieve the count of the records if you want to use that anywhere within your application or if you want to use that number to iterate through the records. The profile manager page uses this number to display within the Label1 server control.

In return from the `GetAllProfiles()` method, you get a `ProfileInfoCollection` object, which is a collection of `ProfileInfo` objects. Iterating through all the `ProfileInfo` objects in the `ProfileInfoCollection` enables you to pull out some of the main properties for a particular user's profile information. In this example, just the `UserName` property of the `ProfileInfo` object is used to populate the DropDownList control on the page.

When the end user selects one of the users from the drop-down list, the `FindProfilesByUserName()` method is used to display the profile of the selected user. Again, a `ProfileInfoCollection` object is returned from this method as well.

To delete the profile of the user selected in the DropDownList control, simply use the `DeleteProfile()` method and pass in the name of the selected user like so:

```
ProfileManager.DeleteProfile(DropDownList1.Text.ToString())
DropDownList1.Items.Clear()
WriteDropdownList()
WriteUserOutput()
```

After you delete the profile from the system, that name will not appear in the drop-down list anymore (because the DropDownList control has been redrawn). If you look in the database, particularly at the aspnet_Profile table, you see that the profile of the selected user is, in fact, deleted. However, also notice that the user (even if the user is anonymous) is still stored in the aspnet_Users table.

If you want to delete not only the profile information of the user but also delete the user from the aspnet_Users table, you invoke the `DeleteUser()` method from the `Membership` class:

```
ProfileManager.DeleteProfile(DropDownList1.Text.ToString())
Membership.DeleteUser(DropDownList1.Text.ToString())
DropDownList1.Items.Clear()
WriteDropdownList()
WriteUserOutput()
```

This use of the `DeleteUser()` method also deletes the selected user from the aspnet_Users table. You could have also achieved the same thing by using the other constructor of the `DeleteUser()` method:

```
Membership.DeleteUser(DropDownList1.Text.ToString(), True)
DropDownList1.Items.Clear()
WriteDropdownList()
WriteUserOutput()
```

The second parameter used in this operation of the `DeleteUser()` method deletes all data related to that user across *all* the tables held in the ASPNETDB.mdf database.

Running the Profile Manager Page

When you compile and run the profile manager page, you see results similar to those shown in Figure 18-7.

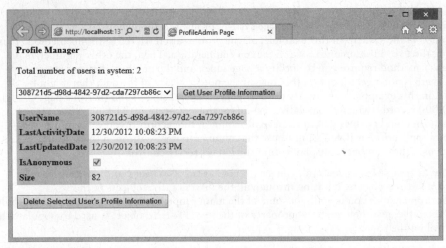

FIGURE 18-7

From this screen, you can see that this page is dealing with an anonymous user (based upon the GUID for the username). You can also see that the IsAnonymous column is indeed checked. You can then delete this user's profile information by selecting the appropriate button on the page.

SUMMARY

The personalization capabilities provided by ASP.NET 4.5 make it incredibly easy to make your web applications unique for all end users, whether they are authenticated or anonymous. This system enables you to store everything from basic data types provided by the .NET Framework to custom types that you create. This system is more versatile and extensible than using the Session or Application objects. The data is stored via a couple of built-in personalization providers that ship with ASP.NET. These providers include ones that connect with either Microsoft's SQL Server Express Edition files or Microsoft SQL Server.

You can also use the ProfileManager class to manage your system's profile information. This includes the capability to monitor and delete profiles as you deem necessary.

19

Membership and Role Management

WHAT'S IN THIS CHAPTER?

➤ Managing ASP.NET 4.5 authentication and authorization

➤ Adding and managing roles

➤ Working with ASP.NET Login server controls

➤ Creating a customized registration process

➤ Reviewing the Membership and Roles APIs and the controls that utilize them

➤ Integrating OAuth/OpenID authentication

WROX.COM CODE DOWNLOADS FOR THIS CHAPTER

Please note that all the code examples in this chapter are available as a part of this chapter's code download on the book's website at www.wrox.com on the Download Code tab.

The authentication and authorization of users are important functions in many websites and browser-based applications. Traditionally, when working with Microsoft's Windows Forms applications (thick-client), you depended on Windows Integrated Authentication; when working with browser-based applications (thin-client), you used forms authentication.

Forms authentication enabled you to take requests that were not yet authenticated and redirect them to an HTML form using HTTP client-side redirection. The user provided his login information and submitted the form. After the application authenticated the request, the user received an HTTP cookie, which was then used on any subsequent requests. This kind of authentication was fine in many ways, but it required developers to build every element and even manage the backend mechanics of the overall system. This task was daunting for many developers and, in most cases, it was rather time-consuming.

ASP.NET 4.5 includes an authentication and authorization management service that takes care of the login, authentication, authorization, and management of users who require access to your web pages or applications. This outstanding *membership and role management service* is an easy-to-implement framework that works out of the box using Microsoft SQL Server as the backend data store.
This framework also includes an API that allows for programmatic access to the capabilities of both the membership and role management services. In addition, a number of membership and role management–focused server controls make it easy to create web applications that incorporate everything these services have to offer.

Before you look at the membership and role management features of ASP.NET 4.5, understanding the basic principles of authentication and authorization is vital. The following provides a quick review:

➤ *Authentication* is a process that determines the identity of a user. After a user has been authenticated, a developer can determine whether the identified user has authorization to proceed. Giving an entity authorization if no authentication process has been applied is impossible. In ASP.NET 4.5, you use the membership service to provide authentication.

➤ *Authorization* is the process of determining whether an authenticated user is allowed access to any part of an application, access to specific points of an application, or access only to specific data sets that the application provides. When you authenticate and authorize users or groups, you can customize a site based on user types or preferences. In ASP.NET 4.5, you use a role management service to provide authorization.

ASP.NET 4.5 AUTHENTICATION

ASP.NET 4.5 provides the membership management service to deal with authenticating users to access a page or an entire site. The ASP.NET management service not only provides an API suite for managing users, but it also gives you some server controls, which in turn work with this API. These server controls work with the end user through the process of authentication. You look at the functionality of these controls shortly.

Setting Up Your Website for Membership

Before you can use the security controls that are provided with ASP.NET 4.5, you first have to set up your application to work with the membership service. How you do this depends on how you approach the security framework provided.

Up to and including Visual Studio 2010, the built-in `SqlMembershipProvider` instance is used for storing details about the registered users of your application. Visual Studio 2012 templates for ASP.NET MVC default to the new `DefaultMembershipProvider`, but ASP.NET Web Forms templates still use `SqlMembershipProvider`. From an API point of view, the kind of provider used will not matter in this chapter.

For the initial demonstrations, the examples in this chapter work with forms-based authentication. You can assume for these examples that the application is on the public Internet and, therefore, is open to the public for registration and viewing. If it were an intranet-based application (meaning that all the users are on a private network), you could use Windows Integrated Authentication for authenticating users.

> **NOTE** *As with the ASP.NET profile support shown in Chapter 18, you can also use Universal Providers to plug in even more functionality.*

ASP.NET 4.5, as you know, offers a data provider model that handles the detailed management required to interact with multiple types of underlying data stores. Figure 19-1 shows a diagram of the ASP.NET 4.5 membership service.

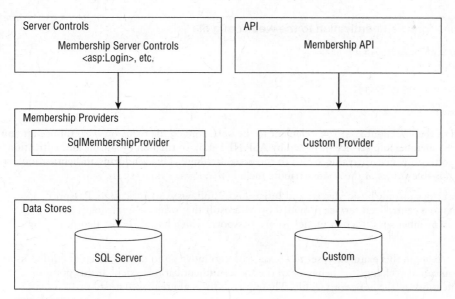

FIGURE 19-1

From the diagram, you can see that, like the rest of the ASP.NET provider models, the membership providers can access a wide variety of underlying data stores. In this diagram, you can see the built-in Microsoft SQL Server data store. You can also build your own membership providers to get at any other custom data stores that work with user credentials. Above the membership providers in the diagram, you can see a collection of security-focused server controls that utilize the access granted by the underlying membership providers to work with the users in the authentication process.

FROM SYSTEM.WEB.SECURITY TO SYSTEM.WEB.APPLICATIONSERVICES

If you are migrating from a previous version of ASP.NET, you might notice that some ASP.NET membership types have been moved from `System.Web.dll` to `System.Web .ApplicationServices.dll`. In the website model you are using, you will not notice this change because the new DLL is automatically used by ASP.NET during compilation. You just need to make sure that ASP.NET 4.5 is used for compilation.

For older web application projects you are migrating to ASP.NET 4.5, you need to add a reference to `System.Web.ApplicationServices.dll` to your project. The "breaking changes" whitepaper from `http://www.asp.net/whitepapers/aspnet4/ breaking-changes#0.1__Toc256770156` has a complete list of types that have been moved.

Adding an <authentication> Element to the web.config File

To have the forms authentication element in your web application work with the membership service, the first step is to turn on forms authentication within the `web.config` file. To do so, create a `web.config` file (if you do not already have one in your application). Next, add the section shown in Listing 19-1 to this file.

LISTING 19-1: Adding forms authentication to the web.config file

```xml
<?xml version="1.0" encoding="utf-8"?>
<configuration>
  <system.web>
    <authentication mode="Forms" />
  </system.web>
</configuration>
```

The simple addition of the `<authentication>` element to the `web.config` file turns on everything that you need to start using the membership service provided by ASP.NET 4.5. To turn on the forms authentication using this element, you simply give the value `Forms` to the `mode` attribute. This is a forms authentication example, but other possible values of the `mode` attribute include `Windows`, `Passport`, or `None`.

IIS authentication schemes include basic, digest, and Integrated Windows Authentication. Passport authentication points to a centralized service provided by Microsoft that offers a single login and core profile service for any member sites. It costs money to use Passport, which has also been deprecated by Microsoft.

Because the `mode` attribute in this example is set to `Forms`, you can move on to the next step of adding users to the data store. You can also change the behavior of the forms authentication system at this point by making some modifications to the `web.config` file. These possibilities are reviewed next.

Adding a <forms> Element to the web.config File

Using forms authentication, you can provide users with access to a site or materials based upon credentials they input into a web-based form. When an end user attempts to access a website, he is entering the site using anonymous authentication, which is the default authentication mode. If he is found to be anonymous, he can be redirected (by ASP.NET) to a specified login page. After the end user inputs the appropriate login information and passes the authentication process, he is provided with an HTTP cookie, which can be used in any subsequent requests.

You can modify the behavior of the forms-based authentication by defining that behavior within a `<forms>` section in the `web.config` file. You can see the possibilities of the forms authentication setting in Listing 19-2, which shows possible changes to the `<forms>` section in the `web.config` file.

LISTING 19-2: Modifying the form's authentication behavior

```xml
<?xml version="1.0" encoding="utf-8"?>
<configuration>
  <system.web>
    <authentication mode="Forms">
      <forms name=".ASPXAUTH"
        loginUrl="Login.aspx"
        protection="All"
        timeout="30"
        path="/"
        requireSSL="false"
        slidingExpiration="true"
        cookieless="UseDeviceProfile" />
    </authentication>
  </system.web>
</configuration>
```

You can set these as you want, and you have plenty of options for values other than the ones that are displayed. Also, as stated earlier, these values are not required. You can use the membership service right away with only the configuration setting that is shown in Listing 19-1.

You can find some interesting settings in Listing 19-2, however. You can really change the behavior of the forms authentication system by adding this `<forms>` element to the `web.config` file. If you do this, however, make sure that you have the `<forms>` element nested within the `<authentication>` elements. The following list describes the possible attributes of the `<forms>` element:

➤ `name`: Defines the name used for the cookie sent to end users after they have been authenticated. By default, this cookie is named `.ASPXAUTH`.

➤ `loginUrl`: Specifies the page location to which the HTTP request is redirected for logging in the user if no valid authentication cookie (`.ASPXAUTH` or otherwise) is found. By default, it is set to `Login.aspx`.

➤ `protection`: Specifies the amount of protection that you want to apply to the cookie that is stored on the end user's machine after he has been authenticated. The possible settings include `All`, `None`, `Encryption`, and `Validation`. You should always attempt to use `All`.

➤ `timeout`: Defines the amount of time (in minutes) after which the cookie expires. The default value is 30 minutes.

➤ `path`: Specifies the path for cookies issued by the application.

➤ `requireSSL`: Defines whether you require that credentials be sent over an encrypted wire (SSL) instead of clear text.

➤ `slidingExpiration`: Specifies whether the timeout of the cookie is on a sliding scale. The default value is `true`. This means that the end user's cookie does not expire until 30 minutes (or the time specified in the `timeout` attribute) after the last request to the application has been made. If the value of the `slidingExpiration` attribute is set to `false`, the cookie expires 30 minutes from the first request.

➤ `cookieless`: Specifies how the cookies are handled by ASP.NET. The possible values include `UseDeviceProfile`, `UseCookies`, `AutoDetect`, and `UseUri`. The default value is `UseDeviceProfile`. This value detects whether to use cookies based on the user agent of the device. `UseCookies` requires that all requests have the credentials stored in a cookie. `AutoDetect` auto-determines whether the details are stored in a cookie on the client or within the URI (it does this by sending a test cookie first). Finally, `UseUri` forces ASP.NET to store the details within the URI on all instances.

Now that forms authentication is turned on, the next step is adding users to the Microsoft SQL Server Express Edition data store, `ASPNETDB.mdf`.

Adding Users

To add users to the membership service, you can register users into the Microsoft SQL Server Express Edition data store. The first question you might ask is, "Where is this data store?"

> **NOTE** *Of course, you can use a number of editions of Microsoft's SQL Server to work through the examples in this book. With that said, this chapter uses the default database the membership system uses in creating users.*

The Microsoft SQL Server provider for the membership system can use a SQL Server Express Edition file that is structured specifically for the membership service (and other ASP.NET systems, such as the role management system). ASP.NET is set to automatically create this particular file for you if the appropriate file does not exist already. To create the `ASPNETDB.mdf` file, you work with the ASP.NET server controls that utilize an aspect of the membership service. When the application requires the `ASPNETDB.mdf` file, ASP.NET creates this file on your behalf in the `App_Data` folder.

After the data store is in place, it is time to start adding users to the data store.

Using the CreateUserWizard Server Control

The CreateUserWizard server control is one that can be used in conjunction with the membership service. You can find this and the other controls mentioned in this chapter under the Login section in the Visual Studio 2012 Toolbox. The CreateUserWizard control enables you to plug registered users into your data store for later retrieval. If a page in your application allows end users to register for your site, you want, at a minimum, to retrieve a login and password from the user and place these values in the data store. This enables the end user to access these items later to log in to the application using the membership system.

To make your life as simple as possible, the CreateUserWizard control takes complete control of registration on your behalf. Listing 19-3 shows a simple use of the control.

LISTING 19-3: Allowing end users to register with the site

```
<%@ Page Language="C#" %>
<html xmlns="http://www.w3.org/1999/xhtml">
<head runat="server">
  <title>Creating Users</title>
</head>
<body>
  <form id="form1" runat="server">
    <asp:CreateUserWizard ID="CreateUserWizard1" Runat="server"
     BorderWidth="1px" BorderColor="#FFDFAD" BorderStyle="Solid"
     BackColor="#FFFBD6" Font-Names="Verdana">
      <TitleTextStyle Font-Bold="True" BackColor="#990000"
       ForeColor="White"></TitleTextStyle>
    </asp:CreateUserWizard>
  </form>
</body>
</html>
```

This page uses the CreateUserWizard control and nothing more. This one control enables you to register end users for your web application. This particular CreateUserWizard control has a little style applied to it, but this control can be as simple as:

```
<asp:CreateUserWizard ID="CreateUserWizard1" Runat="server">
</asp:CreateUserWizard>
```

When this code is run, an end user is presented with the form shown in Figure 19-2.

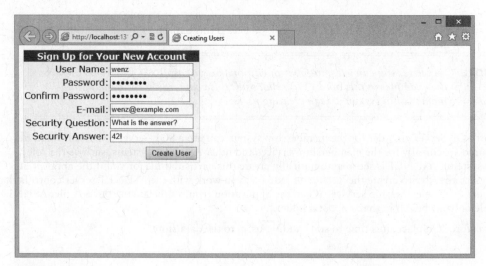

FIGURE 19-2

This screenshot shows the form as it would appear when filled out by the end user and includes information such as the username, password, e-mail address, as well as a security question-and-answer section. Clicking the Create User button places this defined user information into the data store.

The username and password provided via this control enable the end user to log in to the application later through the Login server control. A Confirm Password textbox is also included in the form of the CreateUser server control to ensure that the password provided is spelled correctly. An e-mail address textbox is included (in case end users forget their login credentials and want the credentials e-mailed to them at some later point in time). Finally, the security question and answer are used to verify the identity of the end user before any credentials or user information is changed or later provided via the browser.

After the end user clicks the Create User button on this form, a confirmation of the information being stored appears (see Figure 19-3).

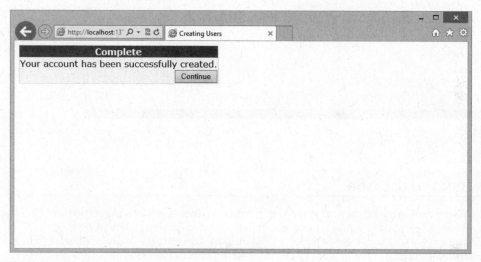

FIGURE 19-3

Seeing Where Users Are Stored

Now that you have used the CreateUserWizard control to add a user to the membership service, look at where this information is stored. If you used Visual Studio to create the Microsoft SQL Server Express Edition file in which you want to store the user information, the file is created when the previous example is run, and you complete the form process as shown in the preceding figures. When the example is run and completed, you can click the Refresh button in the Solution Explorer to find the ASPNETDB.mdf file, which is located in the App_Data folder of your project. Many different tables are included in this file, but you are interested in the aspnet_Membership table only.

When you open the aspnet_Membership table (by right-clicking the table in the Server Explorer and selecting Show Table Data), the users you entered are in the system, as illustrated in Figure 19-4.

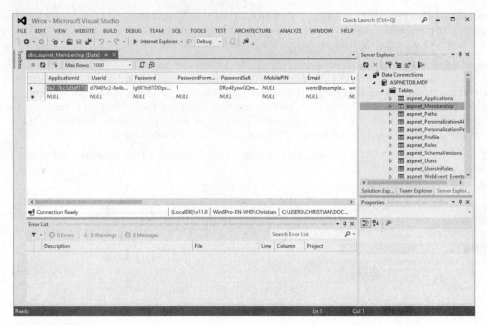

FIGURE 19-4

UPGRADING TO LOCALDB

If SQL Server is not installed on your system, or the version does not match the version of the file, Server Explorer may refuse to open the aforementioned database file, stating that it isn't compatible with the current SQL Server instance. In that case, the Microsoft knowledge base article at http://msdn.microsoft.com/en-us/library/hh873188.aspx provides instructions to upgrade the database file to either a more recent version of SQL Server Express or to the new LocalDB format.

The user password in this table is not stored as clear text; instead, it is hashed, which is a one-way form of encryption that cannot be reversed easily. When a user logs in to an application that is using the ASP.NET 4.5 membership service, his or her password is immediately hashed and then compared to the hashed password stored in the database. If the two hashed strings do not compare, the passwords are not considered a match. Storing clear-text passwords is considered a security risk, so you should never do so without weighing the risk involved.

A note regarding the passwords used in ASP.NET 4.5: If you are having difficulty entering users because of a password error, it might be because ASP.NET requires strong passwords by default. All passwords input into the system must be at least seven characters and contain at least one non-alphanumeric character (such as [,], !, @, #, or $). Whew! An example password of this combination is:

```
$h@rd#2#cr@ck!
```

Although this type of password is a heck of a lot more secure, a password like this is sometimes difficult to remember. You can actually change the behavior of the membership provider so that it doesn't require such difficult passwords by reworking the membership provider in the `web.config` file, as shown in Listing 19-4. Note, however, that this can also facilitate attackers guessing a password.

LISTING 19-4: Modifying the membership provider in web.config

```
<configuration>
  <system.web>
    <membership>
      <providers>
       <clear />
       <add name="AspNetSqlMembershipProvider"
        type="System.Web.Security.SqlMembershipProvider, System.Web,
         Version=4.0.0.0, Culture=neutral, PublicKeyToken=b03f5f7f11d50a3a"
        connectionStringName="LocalSqlServer"
        enablePasswordRetrieval="false"
        enablePasswordReset="true"
        requiresQuestionAndAnswer="false"
        requiresUniqueEmail="true"
        passwordFormat="Hashed"
        minRequiredNonalphanumericCharacters="0"
        minRequiredPasswordLength="3" />
      </providers>
    </membership>
  </system.web>
</configuration>
```

This example shows the membership provider reworked for SQL Server so that it does not require any non-alphanumeric characters and allows passwords as small as three characters in length. You do this by using the `minRequiredNonalphanumericCharacters` and `minRequiredPasswordLength` attributes. With these in place, you can now create users with these password rules as set forth in these configuration settings. Modifying the membership provider is covered in more detail later in this chapter.

Working with the CreateUserWizard Control

When you work with the CreateUserWizard control, be aware of the `ContinueButtonClick()` and the `CreatedUser()` events. The `ContinueButtonClick()` event is triggered when the Continue button on the second page is clicked after the user has been successfully created (see Listing 19-5). (Note Listings 19-5 and 19-6 are exemplary code that cannot run on their own and are therefore not included in the code download for this chapter.)

LISTING 19-5: The ContinueButtonClick event

VB

```
Protected Sub CreateUserWizard1_ContinueButtonClick(ByVal sender As Object, _
  ByVal e As System.EventArgs)
      Response.Redirect("Default.aspx")
End Sub
```

C#

```
protected void CreateUserWizard1_ContinueButtonClick(object sender, EventArgs e)
{
  Response.Redirect("Default.aspx");
}
```

In this example, after the user has been added to the membership service through the form provided by the CreateUserWizard control, he or she can click the Continue button to be redirected to another page in the application. This is done with a simple `Response.Redirect` statement. Remember when you use this event, you must add an `OnContinueButtonClick = "CreateUserWizard1_ContinueButtonClick"` to the `<asp:CreateUserWizard>` control.

The `CreatedUser()` event is triggered when a user is successfully created in the data store. Listing 19-6 shows the use of this event.

LISTING 19-6: The CreatedUser() event

VB

```
Protected Sub CreateUserWizard1_CreatedUser(ByVal sender As Object, _
  ByVal e As System.EventArgs)
        ' Code here
End Sub
```

C#

```
protected void CreateUserWizard1_CreatedUser(object sender, EventArgs e)
{
  // Code here
}
```

Use this event if you want to take any additional actions when a user is registered to the service.

Incorporating Personalization Properties in the Registration Process

As you saw in the previous chapter on personalization, using the personalization management system that comes with ASP.NET 4.5 and storing user-specific details is fairly simple. The registration process provided by the CreateUserWizard control is an ideal spot to retrieve this information from the user to store directly in the personalization system. The retrieval is not too difficult to incorporate into your code.

The first step, as you learned in the previous chapter, is to define some personalization points in the application's `web.config` file, as shown in Listing 19-7.

LISTING 19-7: Creating personalization properties in the web.config file

```
<configuration>
    <system.web>
      <profile>
       <properties>
         <add name="FirstName" />
         <add name="LastName" />
         <add name="LastVisited" />
         <add name="Age" />
         <add name="Member" />
       </properties>
      </profile>
    </system.web>
</configuration>
```

Now that these properties are defined in the `web.config` file, you can use them when you create users in the ASP.NET membership system. Again, using the CreateUserWizard control, you can create a process that requires the user to enter his or her preferred username and password in the first step, and then the second step asks for these custom-defined personalization points. Listing 19-8 shows a CreateUserWizard control that incorporates this idea.

LISTING 19-8: Using personalization properties with the CreateUserWizard control

VB

```vb
<%@ Page Language="VB" %>
<script runat="server">
  Protected Sub CreateUserWizard1_CreatedUser(ByVal sender As Object, _
    ByVal e As System.EventArgs)
    Dim pc As ProfileCommon = New ProfileCommon()
    pc.Initialize(CreateUserWizard1.UserName.ToString(), True)
    pc.FirstName = Firstname.Text
    pc.LastName = Lastname.Text
    pc.Age = Age.Text
    pc.Save()
  End Sub
</script>
<html xmlns="http://www.w3.org/1999/xhtml">
<head id="Head1" runat="server">
  <title>Creating Users with Personalization</title>
</head>
<body>
  <form id="form1" runat="server">
    <asp:CreateUserWizard ID="CreateUserWizard1" Runat="server"
     BorderWidth="1px" BorderColor="#FFDFAD" BorderStyle="Solid"
     BackColor="#FFFBD6" Font-Names="Verdana"
     LoginCreatedUser="true" OnCreatedUser="CreateUserWizard1_CreatedUser" >
      <WizardSteps>
        <asp:WizardStep ID="WizardStep1" Runat="server"
         Title="Additional Information" StepType="Start">
          <table width="100%"><tr><td>
          Firstname: </td><td>
          <asp:TextBox ID="Firstname" Runat="server"></asp:TextBox>
          </td></tr><tr><td>
          Lastname: </td><td>
          <asp:TextBox ID="Lastname" Runat="server"></asp:TextBox>
          </td></tr><tr><td>
          Age: </td><td>
          <asp:TextBox ID="Age" Runat="server"></asp:TextBox>
          </td></tr></table>
        </asp:WizardStep>
        <asp:CreateUserWizardStep Runat="server"
         Title="Sign Up for Your New Account">
        </asp:CreateUserWizardStep>
        <asp:CompleteWizardStep Runat="server" Title="Complete">
        </asp:CompleteWizardStep>
      </WizardSteps>
      <StepStyle BorderColor="#FFDFAD" Font-Names="Verdana"
       BackColor="#FFFBD6" BorderStyle="Solid"
       BorderWidth="1px"></StepStyle>
      <TitleTextStyle Font-Bold="True" BackColor="#990000"
       ForeColor="White"></TitleTextStyle>
    </asp:CreateUserWizard>
  </form>
</body>
</html>
```

C#

```csharp
<%@ Page Language="C#" %>
<script runat="server">
  protected void CreateUserWizard1_CreatedUser(object sender, EventArgs e)
```

continues

LISTING 19-8 *(continued)*

```
    {
      ProfileCommon pc = new ProfileCommon();
      pc.Initialize(CreateUserWizard1.UserName.ToString(), true);
      pc.FirstName = Firstname.Text;
      pc.LastName = Lastname.Text;
      pc.Age = Age.Text;
      pc.Save();
    }
  </script>
```

With this change to the standard registration process as is defined by a default instance of the CreateUserWizard control, your registration system now includes the request for properties stored and retrieved using the `ProfileCommon` object. Then, using the `ProfileCommon.Initialize()` method, you initialize the property values for the current user. Next, you set the property values using the strongly typed access to the profile properties available via the `ProfileCommon` object. After all the values have been set, you use the `Save()` method to finalize the process.

> ### USING PROFILECOMMON
>
> As already discussed in Chapter 18, the direct, convenient access to profile information is available only in the website model, not in the web application model. Therefore, the `ProfileCommon` class is available only when you have a website and if you have defined profile properties in `web.config` as detailed in Listing 19-7. If you are working with the web application model, you have to use a helper class as shown in Chapter 18.

You can define a custom step within the CreateUserWizard control by using the `<WizardSteps>` element. Within this element, you can construct a series of registration steps in whatever fashion you choose. From the `<WizardSteps>` section, shown in Listing 19-8, you can see that three steps are defined. The first is the custom step in which the end user's personalization properties are requested with the `<asp:WizardStep>` control. Within the `<asp:WizardStep>` control, a table is laid out and a custom form is created.

Two additional steps are defined within Listing 19-8: a step to create the user (using the `<asp:CreateUserWizardStep>` control) and a step to confirm the creation of a new user (using the `<asp:CompleteWizardStep>` control). The order in which these steps appear is the order in which they are presented to the end user.

After the steps are created the way you want, you can then store the custom properties using the CreateUserWizard control's `CreatedUser()` event:

```
    protected void CreateUserWizard1_CreatedUser(object sender, EventArgs e)
    {
      ProfileCommon pc = new ProfileCommon();
      pc.Initialize(CreateUserWizard1.UserName.ToString(), true);
      pc.FirstName = Firstname.Text;
      pc.LastName = Lastname.Text;
      pc.Age = Age.Text;
      pc.Save();
    }
```

You are not limited to having a separate step in which you ask for personal bits of information; you can incorporate these items directly into the `<asp:CreateUserWizardStep>` step itself. An easy way to do this is to switch to the Design view of your page and pull up the smart tag for the CreateUserWizard control. Then click the Customize Create User Step link (shown in Figure 19-5).

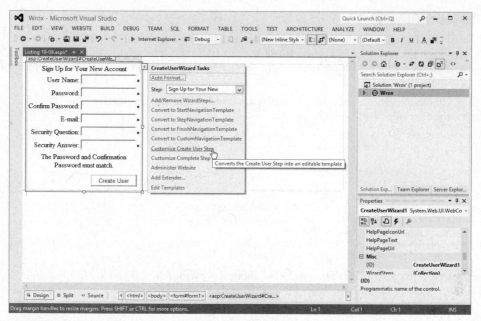

FIGURE 19-5

Clicking the Customize Create User Step link details the contents of this particular step within a new `<ContentTemplate>` section that is now contained within the `<asp:CreateUserWizardStep>` control. Within the `<ContentTemplate>` element, you can see the complete default form used for creating a new user. At this point, you are free to change the form by adding your own sections that request the end user's personal information. You can also remove items from this detailed form. For example, if you are not interested in asking for the security question and answer, you can remove these two items from the form (remember that you must disable the question-and-answer requirement in the membership provider definition). By changing this default form, you can completely customize the registration process for your end users (see Figure 19-6).

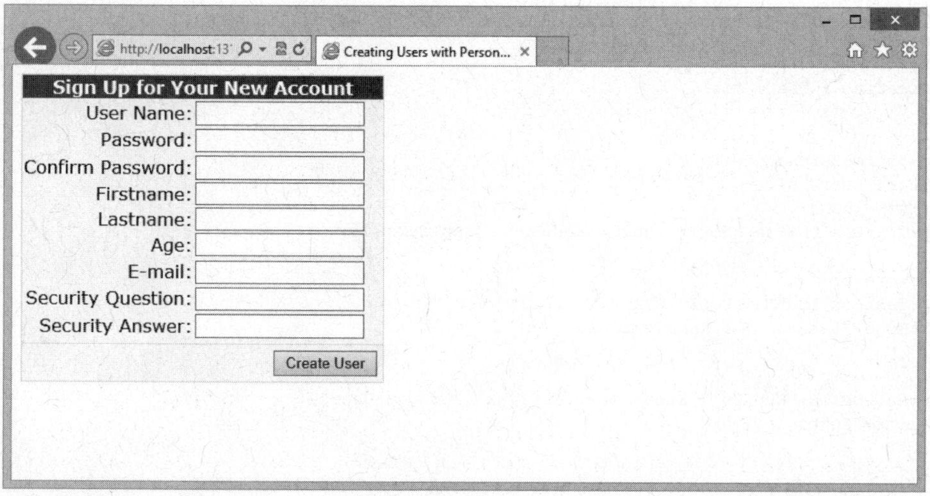

FIGURE 19-6

Adding Users Programmatically

You are not limited to using only server controls to register or add new users to the membership service. ASP.NET 4.5 provides a Membership API for performing this task programmatically. This feature is ideal for creating your own mechanics for adding users to the service—or if you are modifying a web application that was created using ASP.NET 1.0/1.1.

The Membership API includes the CreateUser() method for adding users to the service. The CreateUser() method includes four possible signatures:

```
Membership.CreateUser(username As String, password As String)
    Membership.CreateUser(username As String, password As String,
email As String)
    Membership.CreateUser(username As String, password As String,
email As String, passwordQuestion As String,
passwordAnswer As String, isApproved As Boolean,
  ByRef status As System.Web.Security.MembershipCreateStatus)
    Membership.CreateUser(username As String, password As String,
email As String, passwordQuestion As String,
passwordAnswer As String, isApproved As Boolean, providerUserKey As Object
  ByRef status As System.Web.Security.MembershipCreateStatus)
```

You can use this method to create users. The nice thing about this method is that you are not required to create an instance of the Membership class; you use it directly. Listing 19-9 shows a simple use of the CreateUser() method. (Don't run the listing yet, but read on for more prerequisites.)

LISTING 19-9: Creating users programmatically

VB

```
<%@ Page Language="VB" %>
<script runat="server">
Protected Sub Button1_Click(ByVal sender As Object, _
    ByVal e As System.EventArgs)
  Try
   Membership.CreateUser(TextBox1.Text, TextBox2.Text)
   Label1.Text = "Successfully created user " & TextBox1.Text
  Catch ex As MembershipCreateUserException
   Label1.Text = "Error: " & ex.ToString()
  End Try
End Sub
</script>
<html xmlns="http://www.w3.org/1999/xhtml">
<head runat="server">
  <title>Creating a User</title>
</head>
<body>
  <form id="form1" runat="server">
    <h1>Create User</h1>
    <p>Username<br />
      <asp:TextBox ID="TextBox1" Runat="server"></asp:TextBox>
    </p>
    <p>Password<br />
      <asp:TextBox ID="TextBox2" Runat="server"
      TextMode="Password"></asp:TextBox>
    </p>
    <p>
      <asp:Button ID="Button1" Runat="server" Text="Create User"
      OnClick="Button1_Click" />
    </p>
    <p>
```

```
            <asp:Label ID="Label1" Runat="server"></asp:Label>
        </p>
    </form>
</body>
</html>
```

C#

```csharp
<%@ Page Language="C#" %>
<script runat="server">
  protected void Button1_Click(object sender, EventArgs e)
  {
    try
    {
      Membership.CreateUser(TextBox1.Text.ToString(),
        TextBox2.Text);
      Label1.Text = "Successfully created user " + TextBox1.Text;
    }
    catch (MembershipCreateUserException ex)
    {
      Label1.Text = "Error: " + ex.ToString();
    }
  }
</script>
```

So, use either the CreateUserWizard control or the `CreateUser()` method found in the Membership API to create users for your web applications with relative ease.

From this bit of code, you can see that if a problem occurs when creating the user with the `CreateUser()` method, a `MembershipCreateUserException` is thrown. In this example, we intentionally trigger an exception (since the configuration requires us to have a security question and answer), and this exception is written to the screen within a Label server control. Here is an example of an exception written to the screen:

```
Error: System.Web.Security.MembershipCreateUserException: The password-answer
supplied is invalid. at System.Web.Security.Membership.CreateUser(String username,
String password, String email) at System.Web.Security.Membership.CreateUser(String
username, String password) at ASP.default_aspx.Button1_Click(Object sender,
EventArgs e) in c:\Documents and Settings\Christian\My Documents\Visual Studio
2012\WebSites\Wrox\Default.aspx:line 10
```

You might not want such details sent to the end user. You might prefer to return a simpler message to the end user with something like the following construct:

```
Label1.Text = "Error: " + ex.Message.ToString();
```

This gives you results as simple as the following:

```
Error: The password-answer supplied is invalid.
```

You can also capture the specific error using the `MembershipCreateUserException` and return something that might be a little more appropriate. Listing 19-10 presents an example of this usage.

LISTING 19-10: Capturing the specific MembershipCreateUserException value

VB

```vb
<%@ Page Language="VB" %>
    <script runat="server">
      Protected Sub Button1_Click(ByVal sender As Object, _
    ByVal e As System.EventArgs)
      Try
        Membership.CreateUser(TextBox1.Text, TextBox2.Text)
        Label1.Text = "Successfully created user " & TextBox1.Text
      Catch ex As MembershipCreateUserException
```

continues

LISTING 19-10 *(continued)*

```
      Select Case ex.StatusCode
        Case MembershipCreateStatus.DuplicateEmail
          Label1.Text = "You have supplied a duplicate email address."
        Case MembershipCreateStatus.DuplicateUserName
          Label1.Text = "You have supplied a duplicate username."
        Case MembershipCreateStatus.InvalidEmail
          Label1.Text = "You have not supplied a proper email address."
        Case Else
          Label1.Text = "ERROR: " & ex.Message.ToString()
      End Select
    End Try
  End Sub
</script>
<html xmlns="http://www.w3.org/1999/xhtml">
<head id="Head1" runat="server">
  <title>Creating a User</title>
</head>
<body>
  <form id="form1" runat="server">
    <h1>Create User</h1>
    <p>Username<br />
      <asp:TextBox ID="TextBox1" Runat="server"></asp:TextBox>
    </p>
    <p>Password<br />
      <asp:TextBox ID="TextBox2" Runat="server"
       TextMode="Password"></asp:TextBox>
    </p>
    <p>
      <asp:Button ID="Button1" Runat="server" Text="Create User"
       OnClick="Button1_Click" />
    </p>
    <p>
      <asp:Label ID="Label1" Runat="server"></asp:Label>
    </p>
  </form>
</body>
</html>
```

C#

```
<%@ Page Language="C#" %>
<script runat="server">
  protected void Button1_Click(object sender, EventArgs e)
  {
    try
    {
      Membership.CreateUser(TextBox1.Text, TextBox2.Text);
      Label1.Text = "Successfully created user " + TextBox1.Text;
    }
    catch (MembershipCreateUserException ex)
    {
      switch(ex.StatusCode)
      {
        case MembershipCreateStatus.DuplicateEmail:
          Label1.Text = "You have supplied a duplicate email address.";
          break;
        case MembershipCreateStatus.DuplicateUserName:
          Label1.Text = "You have supplied a duplicate username.";
          break;
        case MembershipCreateStatus.InvalidEmail:
          Label1.Text = "You have not supplied a proper email address.";
```

```
            break;
        default:
            Label1.Text = "ERROR: " + ex.Message.ToString();
            break;
        }
      }
    }
  }
</script>
```

In this case, you are able to look for the specific error that occurred in the `CreateUser` process. Here, this code is looking for only three specific items, but the list of available error codes includes the following:

- `MembershipCreateStatus.DuplicateEmail`
- `MembershipCreateStatus.DuplicateProviderUserKey`
- `MembershipCreateStatus.DuplicateUserName`
- `MembershipCreateStatus.InvalidAnswer`
- `MembershipCreateStatus.InvalidEmail`
- `MembershipCreateStatus.InvalidPassword`
- `MembershipCreateStatus.InvalidProviderUserKey`
- `MembershipCreateStatus.InvalidQuestion`
- `MembershipCreateStatus.InvalidUserName`
- `MembershipCreateStatus.ProviderError`
- `MembershipCreateStatus.Success`
- `MembershipCreateStatus.UserRejected`

In addition to giving better error reports to your users by defining what is going on, you can use these events to take any actions that might be required.

Changing How Users Register with Your Application

You determine how users register with your applications and what is required of them by the membership provider you choose. You will find a default membership provider and its applied settings are established within the `machine.config` file. If you dig down in the `machine.config` file on your server, you find the code shown in Listing 19-11.

LISTING 19-11: Membership provider settings in the machine.config file

```
<membership>
  <providers>
   <add name="AspNetSqlMembershipProvider"
    type="System.Web.Security.SqlMembershipProvider, System.Web,
     Version=4.0.0.0, Culture=neutral, PublicKeyToken=b03f5f7f11d50a3a"
    connectionStringName="LocalSqlServer"
    enablePasswordRetrieval="false"
    enablePasswordReset="true"
    requiresQuestionAndAnswer="true"
    applicationName="/"
    requiresUniqueEmail="false"
    passwordFormat="Hashed"
    maxInvalidPasswordAttempts="5"
    minRequiredPasswordLength="7"
    minRequiredNonalphanumericCharacters="1"
    passwordAttemptWindow="10"
    passwordStrengthRegularExpression="" />
  </providers>
</membership>
```

This section of the `machine.config` file shows the default membership provider that comes with ASP.NET 4.5—named `AspNetSqlProvider`. If you are adding membership providers for server-wide use, add them to this `<membership>` section of the `machine.config` file; if you intend to use them for only a specific application instance, you can add them to your application's `web.config` file.

The important attributes of the SqlMembershipProvider definition include the `enablePasswordRetrieval`, `enablePasswordReset`, `requiresQuestionAndAnswer`, `requiresUniqueEmail`, and `PasswordFormat` attributes. Table 19-1 defines these attributes.

TABLE 19-1

ATTRIBUTE	DESCRIPTION
`enablePasswordRetrieval`	Defines whether the provider supports password retrievals. This attribute takes a `Boolean` value. The default value is `False`. When it is set to `False`, passwords cannot be retrieved although they can be changed with a new random password.
`enablePasswordReset`	Defines whether the provider supports password resets. This attribute takes a `Boolean` value. The default value is `True`.
`requiresQuestionAndAnswer`	Specifies whether the provider should require a question-and-answer combination when a user is created. This attribute takes a `Boolean` value, and the default value is `False`.
`requiresUniqueEmail`	Defines whether the provider should require a unique e-mail to be specified when the user is created. This attribute takes a `Boolean` value, and the default value is `False`. When set to `True`, only unique e-mail addresses can be entered into the data store.
`passwordFormat`	Defines the format in which the password is stored in the data store. The possible values include `Hashed`, `Clear`, and `Encrypted`. The default value is `Hashed`. Hashed passwords use SHA1, whereas encrypted passwords use Triple-DES encryption.

In addition to having these items defined in the `machine.config` file, you can also redefine them again (thus overriding the settings in the `machine.config`) in the `web.config` file.

Asking for Credentials

After you have users who can access your web application using the membership service provided by ASP.NET, you can then give these users the means to log in to the site. This requires little work on your part. Before you learn about the controls that enable users to access your applications, you should make a few more modifications to the `web.config` file.

Turning Off Access with the <authorization> Element

After you make the changes to the `web.config` file by adding the `<authentication>` and `<forms>` elements (Listings 19-1 and 19-2), your web application is accessible to each and every user that browses to any page your application contains. To prevent open access, you have to deny unauthenticated users access to the pages of your site.

Listing 19-12 shows the code for denying unauthenticated users access to your site.

LISTING 19-12: Denying unauthenticated users

```xml
<?xml version="1.0" encoding="utf-8"?>
<configuration>
  <system.web>
    <authentication mode="Forms" />
    <authorization>
      <deny users="?" />
    </authorization>
  </system.web>
</configuration>
```

Using the `<authorization>` and `<deny>` elements, you can deny specific users access to your web application—or (as in this case) simply deny every unauthenticated user (this is what the question mark signifies).

Now that everyone but authenticated users has been denied access to the site, you want to make it easy for viewers of your application to become authenticated users. To do so, use the Login server control.

Using the Login Server Control

The Login server control enables you to turn unauthenticated users into authenticated users by allowing them to provide login credentials that can be verified in a data store of some kind. In the examples so far, you have used Microsoft SQL Server Express Edition as the data store, but you can just as easily use the full-blown version of Microsoft's SQL Server.

The first step in using the Login control is to create a new web page titled `Login.aspx`. This is the default page to which unauthenticated users are redirected to obtain their credentials. Remember that you can change this behavior by changing the value of the `<forms>` element's `loginUrl` attribute in the `web.config` file.

The `Login.aspx` page needs an `<asp:Login>` control to give the end user everything he or she needs to become authenticated, as shown in Listing 19-13 (Login.aspx in the code download for the chapter).

LISTING 19-13: Providing a login for the end user using the Login control

```
<%@ Page Language="C#" %>

<html xmlns="http://www.w3.org/1999/xhtml">
<head runat="server">
  <title>Login Page</title>
</head>
<body>
  <form id="form1" runat="server">
    <asp:Login ID="Login1" Runat="server">
    </asp:Login>
  </form>
</body>
</html>
```

In the situation established here, if the unauthenticated user hits a different page in the application, he or she is redirected to the `Login.aspx` page. You can see how ASP.NET tracks the location in the URL from the address bar in the browser:

```
http://localhost:1315/Membership/Login.aspx?ReturnUrl=%2fMembership%2fDefault.aspx
```

The login page, using the Login control, is shown in Figure 19-7.

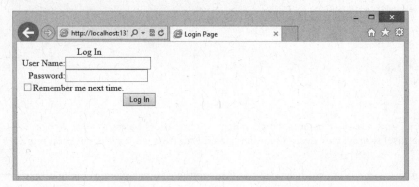

FIGURE 19-7

From this figure, you can see that the Login control asks the user for a username and password. A check box allows a cookie to be stored on the client machine. This cookie enables the end user to bypass future logins. You can remove the check box and related text created to remember the user by setting the Login control's `DisplayRememberMe` property to `False`.

In addition to the `DisplayRememberMe` property, you can work with this aspect of the Login control by using the `RememberMeText` and the `RememberMeSet` properties. The `RememberMeText` property is rather self-explanatory because its value simply defines the text set next to the check box. The `RememberMeSet` property, however, is fairly interesting. The `RememberMeSet` property takes a `Boolean` value (by default, it is set to `False`) that specifies whether to set a persistent cookie on the client's machine after a user has logged in using the Login control. If set to `True` when the `DisplayRememberMe` property is also set to `True`, the check box is checked by default when the Login control is generated in the browser. If the `DisplayRememberMe` property is set to `False` (meaning the end user does not see the check box or cannot select the option of persisting the login cookie) and `RememberMeSet` is set to `True`, a cookie is set on the user's machine automatically without the user's knowledge or choice in the matter. You should think carefully about taking this approach because end users sometimes use public computers, and this method would mean you are setting authorization cookies on public machines.

This cookie remains on the client's machine until the user logs out of the application (if this option is provided). With the persisted cookie, and assuming the end user has not logged out of the application, the user never needs to log in again when he returns to the application because his credentials are provided by the contents found in the cookie. After the end user has logged in to the application, he is returned to the page he originally intended to access.

You can also modify the look-and-feel of the Login control just as you can for the other controls. One way to do this is by clicking the Auto Format link in the control's smart tag. There you find a list of options for modifying the look-and-feel of the control (see Figure 19-8).

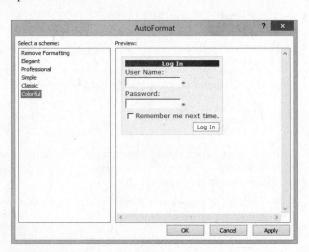

FIGURE 19-8

Select the Colorful option, for example, and the code is modified. Listing 19-14 shows the code generated for this selection.

LISTING 19-14: A formatted Login control

```
<asp:Login ID="Login1" Runat="server" BackColor="#FFFBD6"
 BorderColor="#FFDFAD" BorderPadding="4" BorderStyle="Solid"
 BorderWidth="1px" Font-Names="Verdana" Font-Size="0.8em"
 ForeColor="#333333" TextLayout="TextOnTop">
  <TextBoxStyle Font-Size="0.8em" />
  <LoginButtonStyle BackColor="White" BorderColor="#CC9966"
  BorderStyle="Solid" BorderWidth="1px" Font-Names="Verdana"
  Font-Size="0.8em" ForeColor="#990000" />
  <InstructionTextStyle Font-Italic="True" ForeColor="Black" />
  <TitleTextStyle BackColor="#990000" Font-Bold="True" Font-Size="0.9em"
  ForeColor="White" />
</asp:Login>
```

From this listing, you can see that a number of subelements are used to modify particular items displayed by the control. The available styling elements for the Login control include the following:

- `<CheckboxStyle>`
- `<FailureTextStyle>`
- `<HyperLinkStyle>`
- `<InstructionTextStyle>`
- `<LabelStyle>`
- `<LoginButtonStyle>`
- `<TextBoxStyle>`
- `<TitleTextStyle>`
- `<ValidatorTextStyle>`

The Login control has numerous properties that enable you to alter how the control appears and behaves. An interesting change you can make is to add some links at the bottom of the control to provide access to additional resources. With these links, you can give users the capability to get help or register for the application so that they can be provided with any login credentials.

You can provide links to do the following:

- Redirect users to a help page using the `HelpPageText`, `HelpPageUrl`, and `HelpPageIconUrl` properties.
- Redirect users to a registration page using the `CreateUserText`, `CreateUserUrl`, and `CreateUserIconUrl` properties.
- Redirect users to a page that allows them to recover their forgotten passwords using the `PasswordRecoveryText`, `PasswordRecoveryUrl`, and `PasswordRecoveryIconUrl` properties.

When these links are used, the Login control looks like what is shown in Figure 19-9.

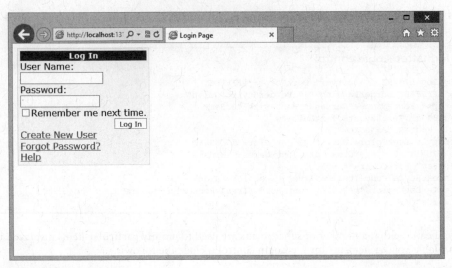

FIGURE 19-9

Logging In Users Programmatically

Besides using the prebuilt mechanics of the Login control, you can also perform this task programmatically using the Membership class. To validate credentials that you receive, you use the ValidateUser() method of this class. The ValidateUser() method takes a single signature:

```
Membership.ValidateUser(username As String, password As String)
```

Listing 19-15 presents this method.

LISTING 19-15: Validating a user's credentials programmatically

VB

```
If Membership.ValidateUser(TextBox1.Text, TextBox2.Text) Then
   FormsAuthentication.RedirectFromLoginPage(TextBox1.Text, False)
Else
   Label1.Text = "You are not registered with the site."
End If
```

C#

```
if (Membership.ValidateUser(TextBox1.Text, TextBox2.Text)) {
   FormsAuthentication.RedirectFromLoginPage(TextBox1.Text, false);
}
else {
   Label1.Text = "You are not registered with the site.";
}
```

The ValidateUser() method returns a Boolean value of True if the user credentials pass the test and False if they do not. From the code snippet in Listing 19-15, you can see that end users whose credentials are verified as correct are redirected from the login page using the RedirectFromLoginPage() method. This method takes the username and a Boolean value that specifies whether the credentials are persisted through a cookie setting.

Locking Out Users Who Provide Bad Passwords

When providing a user login form in any application you build, always guard against repeated bogus password attempts. If you have a malicious end user who knows a username, he may try to access the application by repeatedly trying different passwords. You want to guard against this kind of activity. You don't want to allow this person to try hundreds of possible passwords with this username.

ASP.NET has built-in protection against this type of activity. If you look in the aspnet_Membership table, you see two columns focused on protecting against this activity. These columns are `FailedPasswordAttemptCount` and `FailedPasswordAttemptWindowStart`.

By default, a username can be used with an incorrect password in a login attempt only five times within a 10-minute window. On the fifth failed attempt, the account is locked down. You do this in ASP.NET by setting the `IsLockedOut` column to `True`.

You can actually control the number of password attempts that are allowed and the length of the attempt window for your application. These two items are defined in the SqlMembershipProvider declaration in the `machine.config` file. You can change the values either in the server-wide configuration files or in your application's `web.config` file. Listing 19-16 presents code for changing these values in your `web.config` file.

LISTING 19-16: Changing the values for password attempts in the provider declaration

```
<configuration>
  <system.web>
   <membership defaultProvider="AspNetSqlMembershipProvider">
    <providers>
     <clear />
     <add connectionStringName="LocalSqlServer"
      applicationName="/"
      maxInvalidPasswordAttempts="3"
      passwordAttemptWindow="15"
      name="AspNetSqlMembershipProvider"
      type="System.Web.Security.SqlMembershipProvider, System.Web,
        Version=4.0.0.0, Culture=neutral, PublicKeyToken=b03f5f7f11d50a3a" />
    </providers>
   </membership>
  </system.web>
</configuration>
```

To determine the number of password attempts that are allowed, use `maxInvalidPasswordAttempts`. This example changes the value to 3, meaning that users are allowed to enter an incorrect password three times before being locked out (within the time window defined). The default value of the `maxInvalidPasswordAttempts` attribute is 5. You can set the time allowed for bad password attempts to 15 minutes using the `passwordAttemptWindow` attribute. The default value of this attribute is 10, so an extra five minutes is added.

Now that these items are in place, the next step is to test it. Listing 19-17 provides you with an example of the test. It assumes you have an application established with a user already in place.

LISTING 19-17: A sample page to test password attempts

VB

```
<%@ Page Language="VB" %>
<script runat="server">
  Protected Sub Button1_Click(ByVal sender As Object, _
   ByVal e As System.EventArgs)
      If CheckBox1.Checked = True Then
     Dim user As MembershipUser = Membership.GetUser(TextBox1.Text)
     user.UnlockUser()
    End If
    If Membership.ValidateUser(TextBox1.Text, TextBox2.Text) Then
     Label1.Text = "You are logged on!"
```

continues

LISTING 19-17 *(continued)*

```
      Else
        Dim user As MembershipUser = Membership.GetUser(TextBox1.Text)
        Label1.Text = "Locked out value: " & user.IsLockedOut.ToString()
      End If
    End Sub
  </script>
  <html xmlns="http://www.w3.org/1999/xhtml">
  <head runat="server">
    <title>Login Page</title>
  </head>
  <body>
    <form id="form1" runat="server">
    <div>
      <h1>Login User</h1>
      <p>
        <asp:CheckBox ID="CheckBox1" runat="server" Text="Unlock User" />
      </p>
      <p>
        Username<br />
        <asp:TextBox ID="TextBox1" Runat="server"></asp:TextBox>
      </p>
      <p>Password<br />
        <asp:TextBox ID="TextBox2" Runat="server"
         TextMode="Password"></asp:TextBox>
      </p>
      <p>
        <asp:Button ID="Button1" Runat="server" Text="Login"
         OnClick="Button1_Click" />
      </p>
      <p>
        <asp:Label ID="Label1" Runat="server"></asp:Label>
      </p>
    </div>
    </form>
  </body>
  </html>
```

C#

```
<%@ Page Language="C#" %>
<script runat="server">
  protected void Button1_Click(object sender, EventArgs e)
  {
    if (CheckBox1.Checked == true)
    {
      MembershipUser user = Membership.GetUser(TextBox1.Text);
      user.UnlockUser();
    }
      if (Membership.ValidateUser(TextBox1.Text, TextBox2.Text))
    {
      Label1.Text = "You are logged on!";
    }
    else
    {
      MembershipUser user = Membership.GetUser(TextBox1.Text);
      Label1.Text = "Locked out value: " + user.IsLockedOut.ToString();
    }
  }
</script>
```

This page contains two textboxes: one for the username and another for the password. Above these, however, is a check box that you can use to unlock a user after you have locked down the account because of bad password attempts.

If you run this page and enter three consecutive bad passwords for your user, you get the results presented in Figure 19-10.

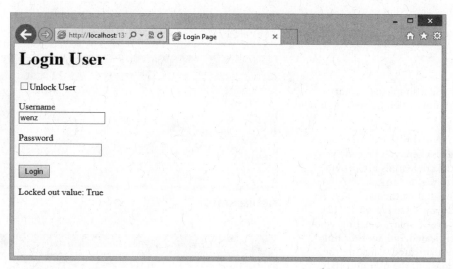

FIGURE 19-10

The IsLockedOut property is read through an instantiation of the MembershipUser object. This object gives you programmatic access to the user data points contained in the aspnet_Membership table. In this case, the IsLockedOut property is retrieved and displayed to the screen. The MembershipUser object also exposes a lot of available methods—one of which is the UnlockUser() method. This method is invoked if the check box is selected in the button-click event.

> **WARNING** *Make sure you unlock the user again before you proceed, otherwise you cannot log into the application any longer.*

Working with Authenticated Users

After users are authenticated, ASP.NET 4.5 provides a number of different server controls and methods that you can use to work with the user details. Included in this collection of tools are the LoginStatus and the LoginName controls.

The LoginStatus Server Control

The LoginStatus server control enables users to click a link to log in or log out of a site. For a good example of this control, remove the <deny> element from the web.config file so that the pages of your site are accessible to unauthenticated users. Then code your Default.aspx page so that it is similar to the code shown in Listing 19-18.

LISTING 19-18: Login and logout features of the LoginStatus control

```
<%@ Page Language="VB" %>
<html xmlns="http://www.w3.org/1999/xhtml">
<head runat="server">
  <title>Login or Logout</title>
</head>
<body>
  <form id="form1" runat="server">
    <asp:LoginStatus ID="LoginStatus1" Runat="server" />
  </form>
</body>
</html>
```

Running this gives you a simple page that contains only a hyperlink titled Login, as shown in Figure 19-11.

Clicking the Login hyperlink forwards you to the Login.aspx page where you provide your credentials. After the credentials are provided, you are redirected to the Default .aspx page—although now the page includes a hyperlink titled Logout (see Figure 19-12). The LinkStatus control displays one link when the user is unauthenticated and another link when the user is authenticated. Clicking the Logout hyperlink logs out the user and redraws the Default.aspx page—but with the Login hyperlink in place.

FIGURE 19-11

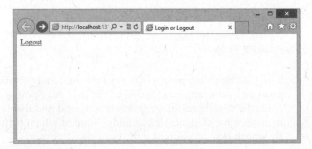

FIGURE 19-12

The LoginName Server Control

The LoginName server control enables you to display the username of the authenticated user. This practice is common today. For an example of it, change the Default.aspx page so that it now includes the authenticated user's login name when that user is logged in, as illustrated in Listing 19-19.

LISTING 19-19: Displaying the username of the authenticated user

```
<%@ Page Language="VB" %>
<html xmlns="http://www.w3.org/1999/xhtml">
<head runat="server">
  <title>Login or Logout</title>
</head>
<body>
  <form id="form1" runat="server">
    <asp:LoginStatus ID="LoginStatus1" Runat="server" />
    <p><asp:LoginName ID="LoginName1" Runat="server"
      Font-Bold="True" Font-Size="XX-Large" /></p>
  </form>
</body>
</html>
```

When the user logs in to the application and is returned to the Default.aspx page, he sees his username displayed, as well as the hyperlink generated by the LoginStatus control (see Figure 19-13).

In addition to just showing the username of the logged-in user, you can also add text by using the LoginName control's FormatString property. For example, to provide a welcome message along with the username, you construct the LoginName control as follows:

FIGURE 19-13

```
<asp:LoginName ID="LoginName1" Runat="Server"
  FormatString="Welcome to our Website {0}!" />
```

You can also use the following construction in one of the page events. (This is shown in C#; if you are using VB, remove the semicolon at the end of the line.)

```
LoginName1.FormatString = "Welcome to the site {0}!";
```

When the page is generated, ASP.NET replaces the {0} part of the string with the username of the logged-in user. This provides you with a result similar to the following:

```
Welcome to the site Christian!
```

If you do not want to show the username when using the LoginName control, simply omit the {0} aspect of the string. The control then places the FormatString property's value on the page.

Showing the Number of Users Online

One cool feature of the membership service is that you can display how many users are online at a given moment. This option is an especially popular one for a portal or a forum that wants to impress visitors to the site with its popularity.

To show the number of users online, you use the GetNumberOfUsersOnline method provided by the Membership class. You can add to the Default.aspx page shown in Figure 19-11 with the code provided in Listing 19-20.

LISTING 19-20: Displaying the number of users online

VB

```
<%@ Page Language="VB" %>
<script runat="server">
  Protected Sub Page_Load(ByVal sender As Object, ByVal e As System.EventArgs)
    Label1.Text = Membership.GetNumberOfUsersOnline().ToString()
  End Sub
</script>
<html xmlns="http://www.w3.org/1999/xhtml">
<head runat="server">
  <title>Login or Logout</title>
</head>
<body>
  <form id="form1" runat="server">
    <asp:LoginStatus ID="LoginStatus1" Runat="server" />
    <p><asp:LoginName ID="LoginName1" Runat="server"
      Font-Bold="True" Font-Size="XX-Large" /></p>
    <p>There are <asp:Label ID="Label1" Runat="server" Text="0" />
     users online.</p>
```

continues

LISTING 19-20 *(continued)*

```
      </form>
   </body>
   </html>
```

C#

```
<%@ Page Language="C#" %>
<script runat="server">
  protected void Page_Load(object sender, EventArgs e)
  {
    Label1.Text = Membership.GetNumberOfUsersOnline().ToString();
  }
</script>
```

When the page is generated, it displays the number of users who have logged on in the last 15 minutes. Figure 19-14 shows an example of what is generated.

You can see that two users have logged on in the last 15 minutes. This 15-minute period is determined in the `machine.config` file from within the `<membership>` element:

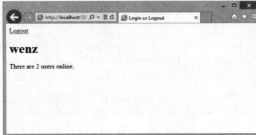

```
<membership userIsOnlineTimeWindow="15" >
</membership>
```

FIGURE 19-14

By default, the `userIsOnlineTimeWindow` is set to `15`. The number is specified here in minutes. To increase the time window, you simply increase this number. In addition to specifying this number from within the `machine.config` file, you can also set this number in the `web.config` file.

Dealing with Passwords

Many of us seem to spend our lives online and have username/password combinations for many different websites on the Internet. For this reason, end users forget passwords or want to change them every so often. ASP.NET provides a couple of server controls that work with the membership service so that end users can either change their passwords or retrieve forgotten passwords.

The ChangePassword Server Control

The ChangePassword server control enables end users to change their passwords directly in the browser. Listing 19-21 shows a use of the ChangePassword control.

LISTING 19-21: Allowing users to change passwords

```
<%@ Page Language="C#" %>
<html xmlns="http://www.w3.org/1999/xhtml">
<head runat="server">
  <title>Change Your Password</title>
</head>
<body>
  <form id="form1" runat="server">
    <asp:LoginStatus ID="LoginStatus1" Runat="server" />
    <p><asp:ChangePassword ID="ChangePassword1" Runat="server">
      </asp:ChangePassword><p>
  </form>
</body>
</html>
```

This example is a rather simple use of the <asp:ChangePassword> control. Running this page produces the results shown in Figure 19-15.

The ChangePassword control produces a form that asks for the previous password. It also requires the end user to type the new password twice. Clicking the Change Password button launches an attempt to change the password if the user is logged in. If the end user is not logged in to the application yet, he or she is redirected to the login page. Only a logged-in user can change a password. After the password is changed, the end user is notified (see Figure 19-16).

Remember that end users are allowed to change their passwords because the enablePasswordReset attribute of the membership provider is set to true. To deny this capability, set the enablePasswordReset attribute to false.

You can also specify rules on how the passwords must be constructed when an end user attempts to change her password. For instance, you might want to require that the password contain more than a certain number of characters or that it use numbers and/or special characters in addition to alphabetic characters. Using the NewPasswordRegularExpression attribute, you can specify the construction required for the new password, as shown here:

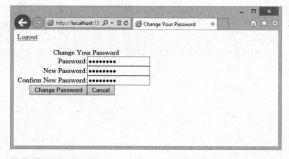

FIGURE 19-15

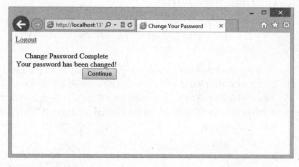

FIGURE 19-16

```
NewPasswordRegularExpression='@\"(?=.{6,})(?=(.*\d){1,})(?=(.*\W){1,})'
```

Any new passwords created by the end user are checked against this regular expression. If there isn't a match, you can use the NewPasswordRegularExpressionErrorMessage attribute (one of the lengthier names for an attribute in ASP.NET) to cause an error message to appear within the control output.

The PasswordRecovery Server Control

People simply forget their passwords. For this reason, you should provide the means to retrieve passwords from your data store. The PasswordRecovery server control provides an easy way to accomplish this task.

Password recovery usually means sending the end user's password to that user in an e-mail. Therefore, you need to set up an SMTP server (it might be the same as the application server). You configure for SMTP in the web.config file, as illustrated in Listing 19-22.

LISTING 19-22: Configuring passwords to be sent via e-mail in the web.config file

```
<configuration>
  <system.web>
   <!-- Removed for clarity -->
  </system.web>
  <system.net>
   <mailSettings>
     <smtp from="wenz@example.com">
      <network host="localhost" port="25"
      defaultCredentials="true" />
     </smtp>
   </mailSettings>
  </system.net>
</configuration>
```

After you have the `<mailSettings>` element set up correctly, you can start to use the PasswordRecovery control. Listing 19-23 shows a simple use of the PasswordRecovery control.

LISTING 19-23: Using the PasswordRecovery control

```
<%@ Page Language="C#" %>
<html xmlns="http://www.w3.org/1999/xhtml">
<head runat="server">
  <title>Getting Your Password</title>
</head>
<body>
  <form id="form1" runat="server">
    <asp:PasswordRecovery ID="PasswordRecovery1" Runat="server">
      <MailDefinition From="wenz@example.com">
      </MailDefinition>
    </asp:PasswordRecovery>
  </form>
</body>
</html>
```

The `<asp:PasswordRecovery>` element needs a `<MailDefinition>` subelement. The `<MailDefinition>` element contains details about the e-mail to be sent to the end user. The minimum requirement is that the `From` attribute is used, which provides the e-mail address for the From part of the e-mail. The `String` value of this attribute should be an e-mail address. Other attributes for the `<MailDefinition>` element include the following:

- ➤ `BodyFileName`
- ➤ `CC`
- ➤ `From`
- ➤ `IsBodyHtml`
- ➤ `Priority`
- ➤ `Subject`

When you run this page, the PasswordRecovery control asks for the user's username, as shown in Figure 19-17.

When it has the username, the membership service retrieves the question and answer that was earlier entered by the end user and generates the view shown in Figure 19-18.

FIGURE 19-17

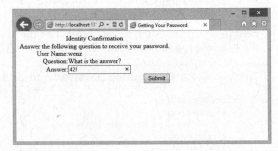

FIGURE 19-18

If the question is answered correctly (notice that the answer is case sensitive), an e-mail containing the password is generated and mailed to the end user. If the question is answered incorrectly, an error message is displayed. Of course, a question will not be used if you have the question/answer feature of the membership system disabled.

> **NOTE** *If you do not have a mail server available, we recommend using the open source mail server simulator from* `http://smtp4dev.codeplex.com/` *which does not actually send an e-mail, but displays them. This makes debugging this feature so much easier.*

By default, the membership service data store is not storing the actual password—just a hashed version of it. Therefore you do not get the original password, but a new one that was generated by ASP.NET for you.

For you to be able to send back an actual password to the user, you must change how the passwords are stored in the membership service data store. You do this (as stated earlier in the chapter) by changing the `PasswordFormat` attribute of your membership data provider. The other possible values (besides `Hashed`) are `Clear` and `Encrypted`. Changing the value to either `Clear` or `Encrypted` makes it possible for the passwords to be sent back to the end user in a readable format.

Generating Random Passwords

Certain applications must generate a random password when you create a user. ASP.NET includes a helper method that enables you to retrieve random passwords. Listing 19-24 shows an example of creating a helper method to pull a random password.

LISTING 19-24: Generating a random password

VB

```vb
Protected Function GeneratePassword() As String
   Dim returnPassword As String
   returnPassword = Membership.GeneratePassword(10, 3)
   Return returnPassword
End Function
```

C#

```csharp
protected string GeneratePassword()
{
   string returnPassword;
   returnPassword = Membership.GeneratePassword(10, 3);
   return returnPassword;
}
```

To generate a password randomly in ASP.NET, you can use the `GeneratePassword()` helper method. This method enables you to generate a random password of a specified length, and you can specify how many non-alphanumeric characters the password should contain (at minimum). This example utilizes this method five times to produce the results shown here (of course, your results will be different):

- ➤   D](KQg6s2[
- ➤ $X.M9]*x2-
- ➤   Q+lIy2#zD%
- ➤   %kWZL@zy&f
- ➤   o]&IhL#iU1

With your helper method in place, you can create users with random passwords, as shown in Listing 19-25.

LISTING 19-25: Creating users with a random password

VB

```
Membership.CreateUser(TextBox1.Text, GeneratePassword())
```

C#

```
Membership.CreateUser(TextBox1.Text, GeneratePassword());
```

ASP.NET 4.5 AUTHORIZATION

Now that you can deal with the registration and authentication of users who want to access your web applications, the next step is authorization. What are they allowed to see and what roles do they take? These questions are important for any web application. The following section explains how to show only certain items to authenticated users while you show different items to unauthenticated users.

Using the LoginView Server Control

The LoginView server control enables you to control who views what information on a particular part of a page. Using the LoginView control, you can dictate which parts of the pages are for authenticated users and which parts of the pages are for unauthenticated users. Listing 19-26 shows an example of this control.

LISTING 19-26: Controlling information viewed via the LoginView control

```
<%@ Page Language="C#" %>
<html xmlns="http://www.w3.org/1999/xhtml">
<head runat="server">
  <title>Changing the View</title>
</head>
<body>
  <form id="form1" runat="server">
    <asp:LoginStatus ID="LoginStatus1" Runat="server" />
    <p>
    <asp:LoginView ID="LoginView1" Runat="server">
      <LoggedInTemplate>
        Here is some REALLY important information that you should know
        about all those people that are not authenticated!
      </LoggedInTemplate>
      <AnonymousTemplate>
        Here is some basic information for you.
      </AnonymousTemplate>
    </asp:LoginView></p>
  </form>
</body>
</html>
```

The `<asp:LoginView>` control is a templated control that takes two possible subelements—the `<LoggedInTemplate>` and `<AnonymousTemplate>` elements. In this case, the information defined in the `<AnonymousTemplate>` section (see Figure 19-19) is for unauthenticated users.

It is quite different from what authenticated users see defined in the `<LoggedInTemplate>` section (see Figure 19-20).

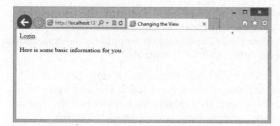

FIGURE 19-19

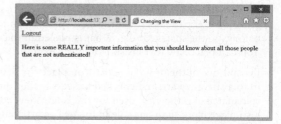

FIGURE 19-20

Only simple ASCII text is placed inside both of these templates, but you can actually place anything else within the template including additional server controls. This means that you can show entire sections of pages, including forms, from within the templated sections.

Besides using just the `<LoggedInTemplate>` and the `<AnonymousTemplate>` of the LoginView control, you can also enable sections of a page or specific content for entities that are part of a particular role—such as someone who is part of the `Admin` group. You can accomplish this by using the `<RoleGroups>` section of the LoginView control, as shown in Listing 19-27.

LISTING 19-27: Providing a view for a particular group

```
<%@ Page Language="C#" %>
<html xmlns="http://www.w3.org/1999/xhtml">
<head runat="server">
  <title>Changing the View</title>
</head>
<body>
  <form id="form1" runat="server">
    <asp:LoginStatus ID="LoginStatus1" Runat="server" />
    <p>
    <asp:LoginView ID="LoginView1" Runat="server">
      <LoggedInTemplate>
        Here is some REALLY important information that you should know
        about all those people that are not authenticated!
      </LoggedInTemplate>
      <AnonymousTemplate>
        Here is some basic information for you.
      </AnonymousTemplate>
      <RoleGroups>
        <asp:RoleGroup Roles="Admins">
          <ContentTemplate>
            You are an Admin!
          </ContentTemplate>
        </asp:RoleGroup>
        <asp:RoleGroup Roles="CoolPeople">
          <ContentTemplate>
            You are cool!
          </ContentTemplate>
        </asp:RoleGroup>
      </RoleGroups>
    </asp:LoginView><p>
  </form>
</body>
</html>
```

To show content for a particular group of users, you add a `<RoleGroups>` element to the LoginView control. The `<RoleGroups>` section can take one or more RoleGroup controls (you will not find this control in Visual Studio's Toolbox). To provide content to display using the RoleGroup control, you provide a `<ContentTemplate>` element, which enables you to define the content to be displayed for an entity that belongs to the specified role. What is placed in the `<ContentTemplate>` section completely depends on you. You can place raw text (as shown in the example) or even other ASP.NET controls.

Be cautious of the order in which you place the defined roles in the `<RoleGroups>` section. When users log in to a site, they are first checked to see whether they match one of the defined roles. The first (uppermost) role matched is the view used for the LoginView control—even if they match more than one role. You can also place more than one role in the `Roles` attribute of the `<asp:RoleGroups>` control, like this:

```
<asp:RoleGroup Roles="CoolPeople, HappyPeople">
  <ContentTemplate>
   You are cool or happy (or both)!
  </ContentTemplate>
</asp:RoleGroup>
```

Setting Up Your Website for Role Management

In addition to the membership service just reviewed, ASP.NET provides you with the other side of the end-user management service—the ASP.NET role management service. The membership service covers all the details of authentication for your applications, whereas the role management service covers authorization. Just as the membership service can use any of the data providers listed earlier, the role management service can also use a provider that is focused on SQL Server (SqlRoleProvider) or any custom providers. In fact, this service is comparable to the membership service in many ways. Figure 19-21 shows you a simple diagram that details some particulars of the role management service.

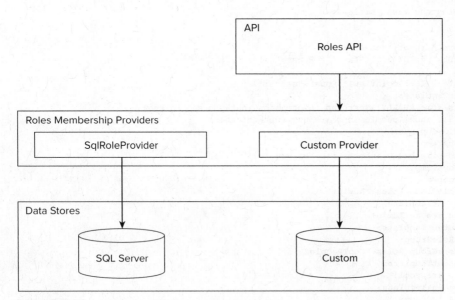

FIGURE 19-21

Making Changes to the <roleManager> Section

The first step in working with the role management service is to change any of the role management provider's behaviors either in the machine.config or from the web.config files. If you look in the machine.config.comments file, you will see an entire section that deals with the role management service (see Listing 19-28).

LISTING 19-28: Role management provider settings in the machine.config.comments file

```
<roleManager
 enabled="false"
 cacheRolesInCookie="false"
 cookieName=".ASPXROLES"
 cookieTimeout="30"
 cookiePath="/"
 cookieRequireSSL="false"
 cookieSlidingExpiration="true"
 cookieProtection="All"
 defaultProvider="AspNetSqlRoleProvider"
 createPersistentCookie="false"
 maxCachedResults="25">
  <providers>
   <clear />
   <add connectionStringName="LocalSqlServer" applicationName="/"
    name="AspNetSqlRoleProvider" type="System.Web.Security.SqlRoleProvider,
    System.Web, Version=4.0.0.0, Culture=neutral,
    PublicKeyToken=b03f5f7f11d50a3a" />
   <add applicationName="/" name="AspNetWindowsTokenRoleProvider"
    type="System.Web.Security.WindowsTokenRoleProvider, System.Web,
    Version=4.0.0.0, Culture=neutral, PublicKeyToken=b03f5f7f11d50a3a" />
  </providers>
</roleManager>
```

The role management service documents its settings from within the `machine.config.comments` file, as shown in the previous code listing. You can make changes to these settings either directly in the `machine.config` file or by overriding any of the higher-level settings you might have by making changes in the `web.config` file itself (thereby making changes only to the application at hand).

The main settings are defined in the `<roleManager>` element. Table 19-2 defines some of the attributes of the `<roleManager>` element.

TABLE 19-2

ATTRIBUTE	DESCRIPTION
enabled	Defines whether the role management service is enabled for the application. This attribute takes a Boolean value and is set to False by default. This means that the role management service is disabled by default. This is done to avoid breaking changes that would occur for users migrating from ASP.NET 1.0/1.1 to ASP.NET 2.0, 3.5, 4, or 4.5. Therefore, you must first change this value to True in either the machine.config or the web.config file.
cacheRolesInCookie	Defines whether the roles of the user can be stored within a cookie on the client machine. This attribute takes a Boolean value and is set to True by default. This situation is ideal because retrieving the roles from the cookie prevents ASP.NET from looking up the roles of the user via the role management provider. Set it to False if you want the roles to be retrieved via the provider for all instances.
cookieName	Defines the name used for the cookie sent to the end user for role management information storage. By default, this cookie is named .ASPXROLES, and you probably will not change this.
cookieTimeout	Defines the amount of time (in minutes) after which the cookie expires. The default value is 30 minutes.

continues

TABLE 19-2 *(continued)*

ATTRIBUTE	DESCRIPTION
cookieRequireSSL	Defines whether you require that the role management information be sent over an encrypted wire (SSL) instead of being sent as clear text. The default value is False.
cookieSlidingExpiration	Specifies whether the timeout of the cookie is on a sliding scale. The default value is True. This means that the end user's cookie does not expire until 30 minutes (or the time specified in the cookieTimeout attribute) after the last request to the application has been made. If the value of the cookieSlidingExpiration attribute is set to False, the cookie expires 30 minutes from the first request.
createPersistentCookie	Specifies whether a cookie expires or whether it remains alive indefinitely. The default setting is False because a persistent cookie is not always advisable for security reasons.
cookieProtection	Specifies the amount of protection you want to apply to the cookie stored on the end user's machine for management information. The possible settings include All, None, Encryption, and Validation. You should always attempt to use All.
defaultProvider	Defines the provider used for the role management service. By default, it is set to AspNetSqlRoleProvider up to ASP.NET 4.0, and to DefaultRoleProvider starting with ASP.NET 4.5.

Making Changes to the web.config File

The next step is to configure your web.config file so that it can work with the role management service. Certain pages or subsections of your application may be accessible only to people with specific roles. To manage this access, you define the access rights in the web.config file. Listing 19-29 shows the necessary changes.

LISTING 19-29: CHANGING THE WEB.CONFIG FILE

```
<?xml version="1.0" encoding="utf-8"?>
<configuration>
  <system.web>
    <compilation targetFramework="4.5" />
    <roleManager enabled="true"/>
    <authentication mode="Forms" />
    <authorization>
      <deny users="?" />
    </authorization>
  </system.web>
  <location path="AdminPage.aspx">
    <system.web>
      <authorization>
        <allow roles="AdminPageRights" />
        <deny users="*" />
      </authorization>
    </system.web>
  </location>
</configuration>
```

This web.config file is doing a couple of things. First, the function of the first <system.web> section is no different from that of the membership service shown earlier in the chapter. The <deny> element is denying all unauthenticated users across the board.

The second section of this `web.config` file is rather interesting. The `<location>` element is used to define the access rights of a particular page in the application (`AdminPage.aspx`). In this case, only users contained in the `AdminPageRights` role are allowed to view the page, but all other users—regardless of whether they are authenticated—are not allowed to view the page. When using the asterisk (*) as a value of the `users` attribute of the `<deny>` element, you are saying that all users (regardless of whether they are authenticated) are not allowed to access the resource being defined. This overriding denial of access, however, is broken open a bit via the use of the `<allow>` element, which allows users contained within a specific role.

Adding and Retrieving Application Roles

Now that the `machine.config` or the `web.config` file is in place, you can add roles to the role management service. The role management service, just like the membership service, uses data stores to store information about the users. These examples focus primarily on using Microsoft SQL Server Express Edition as the provider because it is the default provider.

One big difference between the role management service and the membership service is that no server controls are used for the role management service. You manage the application's roles and the user's role details through a Roles API or through the Web Site Administration Tool provided with ASP.NET 4.5. Listing 19-30 shows how to use some of the new methods to add roles to the service.

LISTING 19-30: Adding roles to the application

VB

```
<%@ Page Language="VB" %>
<script runat="server">
   Protected Sub Page_Load(ByVal sender As Object, ByVal e As System.EventArgs)
     If Not Page.IsPostBack Then
       ListBoxDataBind()
     End If
   End Sub
   Protected Sub Button1_Click(ByVal sender As Object, _
     ByVal e As System.EventArgs)
     Roles.CreateRole(TextBox1.Text)
     ListBoxDataBind()
   End Sub
   Protected Sub ListBoxDataBind()
     ListBox1.DataSource = Roles.GetAllRoles()
     ListBox1.DataBind()
   End Sub
</script>
<html xmlns="http://www.w3.org/1999/xhtml">
<head runat="server">
   <title>Role Manager</title>
</head>
<body>
   <form id="form1" runat="server">
     <h1>Role Manager</h1>
     Add Role:<br />
     <asp:TextBox ID="TextBox1" Runat="server"></asp:TextBox>
     <p><asp:Button ID="Button1" Runat="server" Text="Add Role to Application"
       OnClick="Button1_Click" /></p>
     Roles Defined:<br />
     <asp:ListBox ID="ListBox1" Runat="server">
     </asp:ListBox>
   </form>
</body>
</html>
```

continues

LISTING 19-30 *(continued)*

C#

```csharp
<%@ Page Language="C#" %>
<script runat="server">
  protected void Page_Load(object sender, EventArgs e)
  {
    if (!Page.IsPostBack)
    {
      ListBoxDataBind();
    }
  }

  protected void Button1_Click(object sender, EventArgs e)
  {
    Roles.CreateRole(TextBox1.Text);
    ListBoxDataBind();
  }

  protected void ListBoxDataBind()
  {
    ListBox1.DataSource = Roles.GetAllRoles();
    ListBox1.DataBind();
  }
</script>
```

This example enables you to enter roles into the textbox and then to submit them to the role management service. The roles contained in the role management service then appear in the list box, as illustrated in Figure 19-22.

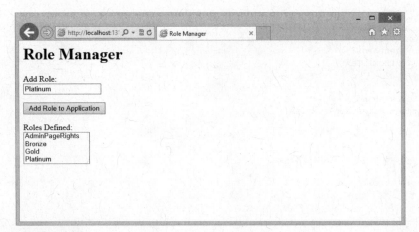

FIGURE 19-22

To enter the roles into the management service, you use the `CreateRole()` method of the `Roles` class. As with the `Membership` class, you do not instantiate the `Roles` class. To add roles to the role management service, use the `CreateRole()` method that takes only a single parameter—the name of the role as a `String` value:

```
Roles.CreateRole(rolename As String)
```

With this method, you can create as many roles as you want, but each role must be unique; otherwise, an exception is thrown.

To retrieve the roles that are in the application's role management service (such as the list of roles displayed in the list box from the earlier example), you use the `GetAllRoles()` method of the `Roles` class. This method returns a `String` collection of all the available roles in the service:

```
Roles.GetAllRoles()
```

Deleting Roles

It would be just great to sit and add roles to the service all day long. Every now and then, however, you might want to delete roles from the service as well. Deleting roles is just as easy as adding roles to the role management service. To delete a role, you use one of the `DeleteRole()` method signatures. The first option of the `DeleteRole()` method takes a single parameter—the name of the role as a `String` value. The second option takes the name of the role plus a `Boolean` value that determines whether to throw an exception when one or more members are contained within that particular role (so that you don't accidentally delete a role with users in it when you don't mean to):

```
Roles.DeleteRole(rolename As String)
Roles.DeleteRole(rolename As String, throwOnPopulatedRole As Boolean)
```

Listing 19-31 is a partial code example that builds on Listing 19-30. For this example, you add an additional button that initiates a second button-click event that deletes the role from the service.

LISTING 19-31: Deleting roles from the application

VB

```
Protected Sub DeleteButton_Click(ByVal sender As Object,
  ByVal e As System.EventArgs)
  For Each li As ListItem In ListBox1.Items
    If li.Selected = True Then
      Roles.DeleteRole(li.ToString())
    End If
  Next
  ListBoxDataBind()
End Sub
```

C#

```
protected void DeleteButton_Click(object sender, EventArgs e)
{
  foreach (ListItem li in ListBox1.Items) {
  if (li.Selected == true) {
    Roles.DeleteRole(li.ToString());
  }
  }
  ListBoxDataBind();
}
```

This example deletes the selected items from the ListBox control. If more than one selection is made (meaning that you have placed the attribute `SelectionMode="Multiple"` in the ListBox control), each of the roles is deleted from the service, in turn, in the `For Each` loop. Although `Roles.DeleteRole(li .ToString())` is used to delete the role, `Roles.DeleteRole(li.ToString(), True)` could also be used to make sure that no roles are deleted if that role contains any members.

Adding Users to Roles

Now that the roles are in place and it is possible to delete these roles if required, the next step is adding users to the roles created. A role does not do much good if no users are associated with it. To add a single user to a single role, you use the following construct:

```
Roles.AddUserToRole(username As String, rolename As String)
```

To add a single user to multiple roles at the same time, you use this construct:

```
Roles.AddUserToRoles(username As String, rolenames() As String)
```

To add multiple users to a single role, you use the following construct:

```
Roles.AddUsersToRole(usernames() As String, rolename As String)
```

Finally, to add multiple users to multiple roles, you use the following construct:

```
Roles.AddUsersToRoles(usernames() As String, rolenames() As String)
```

The parameters that can take collections, whether they are `usernames()` or `rolenames()`, are presented to the method as `String` arrays.

Getting All the Users of a Particular Role

Looking up information is easy in the role management service, whether you are determining which users are contained within a particular role or whether you want to know the roles to which a particular user belongs.

Methods are available for either of these scenarios. First, look at how to determine all the users contained in a particular role, as illustrated in Listing 19-32.

LISTING 19-32: Looking up users in a particular role

VB

```
<%@ Page Language="VB" %>
<script runat="server">
  Protected Sub Page_Load(ByVal sender As Object, ByVal e As System.EventArgs)
    If Not Page.IsPostBack Then
     DropDownDataBind()
    End If
  End Sub

  Protected Sub Button1_Click(ByVal sender As Object, _
    ByVal e As System.EventArgs)
    GridView1.DataSource = Roles.GetUsersInRole(DropDownList1.SelectedValue)
    GridView1.DataBind()
    DropDownDataBind()
  End Sub

  Protected Sub DropDownDataBind()
   DropDownList1.DataSource = Roles.GetAllRoles()
   DropDownList1.DataBind()
  End Sub
</script>
<html xmlns="http://www.w3.org/1999/xhtml">
<head runat="server">
  <title>Role Manager</title>
</head>
<body>
  <form id="form1" runat="server">
    Roles:
    <asp:DropDownList ID="DropDownList1" Runat="server">
    </asp:DropDownList>
    <asp:Button ID="Button1" Runat="server" Text="Get Users In Role"
     OnClick="Button1_Click" />
    <br />
    <br />
    <asp:GridView ID="GridView1" Runat="server">
```

```
        </asp:GridView>
      </form>
  </body>
  </html>
```

C#

```csharp
<%@ Page Language="C#" %>
<script runat="server">
  protected void Page_Load(object sender, EventArgs e)
  {
    if (!Page.IsPostBack)
    {
      DropDownDataBind();
    }
  }

  protected void Button1_Click(object sender, EventArgs e)
  {
    GridView1.DataSource = Roles.GetUsersInRole(DropDownList1.SelectedValue);
    GridView1.DataBind();
    DropDownDataBind();
  }

  protected void DropDownDataBind()
  {
    DropDownList1.DataSource = Roles.GetAllRoles();
    DropDownList1.DataBind();
  }
</script>
```

This page creates a drop-down list that contains all the roles for the application. Clicking the button displays all the users for the selected role. Users of a particular role are determined using the GetUsersInRole() method. This method takes a single parameter—a String value representing the name of the role:

```
Roles.GetUsersInRole(rolename As String)
```

When run, the page looks similar to the page shown in Figure 19-23.

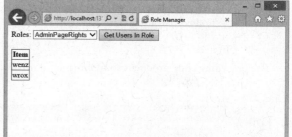

FIGURE 19-23

Getting All the Roles of a Particular User

To determine all the roles for a particular user, create a page with a single textbox and a button. In the textbox, you type the name of the user; a button click initiates the retrieval and populates a GridView control. Listing 19-33 presents the button-click event (where all the action is).

LISTING 19-33: Getting all the roles of a specific user

VB

```vb
<%@ Page Language="VB" %>
<script runat="server">
  Protected Sub Button1_Click(ByVal sender As Object, _
    ByVal e As System.EventArgs)
    GridView1.DataSource = Roles.GetRolesForUser(TextBox1.Text)
    GridView1.DataBind()
```

continues

LISTING 19-33 *(continued)*

```
    End Sub
</script>

<html xmlns="http://www.w3.org/1999/xhtml">
<head id="Head1" runat="server">
    <title>Role Manager</title>
</head>
<body>
    <form id="form1" runat="server">
        User:
        <asp:TextBox ID="TextBox1" runat="server" />
        <asp:Button ID="Button1" runat="server" Text="Get Roles of User"
            OnClick="Button1_Click" />
        <br />
        <br />
        <asp:GridView ID="GridView1" runat="server">
        </asp:GridView>
    </form>
</body>
</html>
```

C#

```
<%@ Page Language="C#" %>

<script runat="server">
  protected void Button1_Click(object sender, EventArgs e)
  {
      GridView1.DataSource = Roles.GetRolesForUser(TextBox1.Text);
      GridView1.DataBind();
  }
</script>
```

The preceding code produces something similar to what is shown in Figure 19-24.

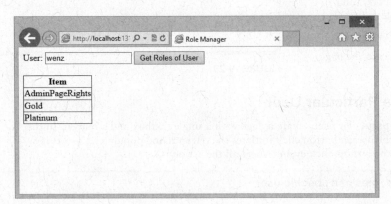

FIGURE 19-24

To get the roles of a particular user, you use the `GetRolesForUser()` method. This method has two possible signatures. The first is shown in the preceding example—a `String` value that represents the name of the user. The other option is an invocation of the method without any parameters listed. This returns the roles of the user who has logged in to the membership service.

Removing Users from Roles

In addition to adding users to roles, you can also easily remove users from roles. To delete or remove a single user from a single role, you use the following construct:

```
Roles.RemoveUserFromRole(username As String, rolename As String)
```

To remove a single user from multiple roles at the same time, you use this construct:

```
Roles.RemoveUserFromRoles(username As String, rolenames() As String)
```

To remove multiple users from a single role, you use the following construct:

```
Roles.RemoveUsersFromRole(usernames() As String, rolename As String)
```

Finally, to remove multiple users from multiple roles, you use the following construct:

```
Roles.RemoveUsersFromRoles(usernames() As String, rolenames() As String)
```

The parameters shown as collections, whether they are usernames() or rolenames(), are presented to the method as String arrays.

Checking Users in Roles

One final action you can take is checking whether a particular user is in a role. You can go about this in a couple of ways. The first is using the IsUserInRole() method.

The IsUserInRole() method takes two parameters—the username and the name of the role:

```
Roles.IsUserInRole(username As String, rolename As String)
```

This method returns a Boolean value on the status of the user, and you can use it as shown in Listing 19-34.

LISTING 19-34: Checking a user's role status

VB

```
If (Roles.IsUserInRole(TextBox1.Text, "AdminPageRights")) Then
  ' perform action here
End If
```

C#

```
if (Roles.IsUserInRole(TextBox1.Text, "AdminPageRights"))
{
  // perform action here
}
```

The other option, in addition to the IsUserInRole() method, is to use FindUsersInRole(). This method enables you make a name search against all the users in a particular role. The FindUsersInRole() method takes two parameters—the name of the role and the username, both as String values:

```
Roles.FindUsersInRole(rolename As String, username As String)
```

Listing 19-35 shows an example of this method.

LISTING 19-35: Checking for a specific user in a particular role

VB

```
<%@ Page Language="VB" %>
<script runat="server">
  Protected Sub Button1_Click(ByVal sender As Object, _
    ByVal e As System.EventArgs)
    GridView1.DataSource = _
```

continues

LISTING 19-35 *(continued)*

```
      Roles.FindUsersInRole("AdminPageRights", TextBox1.Text)
    GridView1.DataBind()
  End Sub
</script>
<html xmlns="http://www.w3.org/1999/xhtml" >
<head runat="server">
  <title>Role Manager</title>
</head>
<body>
  <form id="form1" runat="server">
    <asp:TextBox ID="TextBox1" Runat="server"></asp:TextBox>
    <asp:Button ID="Button1" Runat="server" Text="Button"
     OnClick="Button1_Click" />
    <p><asp:GridView ID="GridView1" Runat="server">
    </asp:GridView></p>
  </form>
</body>
</html>
```

C#

```
<%@ Page Language="C#" %>
<script runat="server">
  protected void Button1_Click(object sender, EventArgs e)
  {
    GridView1.DataSource =
      Roles.FindUsersInRole("AdminPageRights", TextBox1.Text);
    GridView1.DataBind();
  }
</script>
```

Understanding How Roles Are Cached

By default, after you retrieve a user's roles from the data store underlying the role management service, you can store these roles as a cookie on the client machine. You do this so you do not have to access the data store each and every time the application needs a user's role status. A bit of risk always exists when working with cookies because the end user can manipulate the cookie and thereby gain access to information or parts of an application that normally would be forbidden to that particular user.

Although roles are cached in a cookie, the default is that they are cached for only 30 minutes at a time. You can deal with this role cookie in several ways—some of which might help to protect your application better.

One protection for your application is to delete this role cookie, using the DeleteCookie() method of the Roles API, when the end user logs on to the site, as illustrated in Listing 19-36.

LISTING 19-36: Deleting the end user's role cookie upon authentication

VB

```
If Membership.ValidateUser(TextBox1.Text, TextBox2.Text) Then
  Roles.DeleteCookie()
  FormsAuthentication.RedirectFromLoginPage(TextBox1.Text, False)
Else
  Label1.Text = "You are not registered with the site."
End If
```

C#

```
if (Membership.ValidateUser(TextBox1.Text, TextBox2.Text)
{
  Roles.DeleteCookie();
  FormsAuthentication.RedirectFromLoginPage(TextBox1.Text, false);
}
else {
  Label1.Text = "You are not registered with the site.";
}
```

Using `Roles.DeleteCookie()` does exactly what you would think — it deletes from the client machine any cookie that is used to define the user's roles. If the end user is re-logging in to the site, no problem should arise with re-authenticating his exact roles within the application. There is no need to rely on the contents of the cookie. This step provides a little more protection for your site.

USING THE SIMPLEMEMBERSHIP API

To be honest, the Membership API is liked by few, loathed by many. It was conceived more than ten years ago, but is too complicated for simple tasks and not prepared for some of the authentication mechanisms that are common in today's web. You look at modern authentication mechanisms shortly, but first, you learn a simpler way of doing authentication in ASP.NET.

With WebMatrix, Microsoft provides a quite powerful IDE for "beginners and students," as the official PR calls it. What that supposedly means is that you probably should not work on commercial projects with WebMatrix (although you are allowed to), but can get fast results for simpler kinds of applications.

The membership and roles part that ships with the ASP.NET Web Pages technology is an integral part of WebMatrix. Chapter 35 goes into much more detail on the features available there, but this chapter briefly discusses one specific bit of API that is also available for ASP.NET Web Forms applications.

The SimpleMembership and SimpleRoles APIs give you programmatic access to membership and roles information, however with a much simpler interface than the "regular" Membership and Roles APIs. Here is a list of some of the methods in SimpleMembership:

➤ `WebSecurity.ChangePassword()`

➤ `WebSecurity.CreateUserAndAccount()`

➤ `WebSecurity.Login()`

➤ `WebSecurity.Logout()`

➤ `WebSecurity.RequireAuthenticatedUser()`

The basic functionality is nothing new in comparison to what you have worked with until now, but the wording alone is simpler and much more to the point — `RequireAuthenticatedUser()` automatically redirects to the login page if the user is not authenticated, for instance.

Matthew M. Osborn wrote one of the first blog posts on this subject (http://blog.osbornm .com/archive/2010/07/21/using-simplemembership-with-asp.net-webpages.aspx), and Jon Galloway provides more details and a technical background at http://weblogs.asp.net/jgalloway/ archive/2012/08/29/simplemembership-membership-providers-universal-providers-and-the-new-asp-net-4-5-web-forms-and-asp-net-mvc-4-templates.aspx.

In the corporate projects we are working with we have very rarely seen the simpler APIs yet, but they are still interesting to look at and might be well suited for your specific project, so we didn't want to miss the opportunity to mention them here.

USING THE WEB SITE ADMINISTRATION TOOL

You can also perform many of the actions shown in this chapter through the Web Site Administration Tool shown in Figure 19-25. You can get at the ASP.NET Web Site Administration Tool by selecting Website ⇨ ASP.NET Configuration from the Visual Studio 2012 menu.

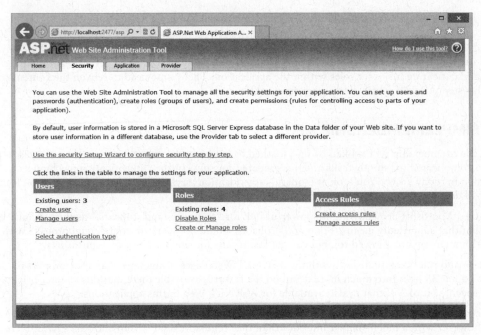

FIGURE 19-25

Although you can easily use this tool to perform all the actions for you, often you perform these actions through your own applications as well. Knowing all the possibilities when programming an ASP.NET application is important.

Appendix D provides details on the Web Site Administration Tool.

PUBLIC METHODS OF THE MEMBERSHIP API

Table 19-3 presents the public methods of the Membership API. You would use this API when working with the authentication process of your application.

TABLE 19-3

MEMBERSHIP METHODS	DESCRIPTION
CreateUser	Adds a new user to the appointed data store.
DeleteUser	Deletes a specified user from the data store.
FindUsersByEmail	Returns a collection of users who have an e-mail address to match the one provided.
FindUsersByName	Returns a collection of users who have a username to match the one provided.

`GeneratePassword`	Generates a random password of a length that you specify.
`GetAllUsers`	Returns a collection of all the users contained in the data store.
`GetNumberOfUsersOnline`	Returns an `Integer` that specifies the number of users who have logged in to the application. The time window during which users are counted is specified in the `machine.config` or the `web.config` files.
`GetUser`	Returns information about a particular user from the data store.
`GetUserNameByEmail`	Retrieves a username of a specific record from the data store based on an e-mail address search.
`UpdateUser`	Updates a particular user's information in the data store.
`ValidateUser`	Returns a `Boolean` value indicating whether a specified set of credentials is valid.

PUBLIC METHODS OF THE ROLES API

Table 19-4 provides the public methods of the Roles API. You would use this API when working with the authorization process of your application.

TABLE 19-4

ROLES METHODS	DESCRIPTION
`AddUsersToRole`	Adds a collection of users to a specific role.
`AddUsersToRoles`	Adds a collection of users to a collection of roles.
`AddUserToRole`	Adds a specific user to a specific role.
`AddUserToRoles`	Adds a specific user to a collection of roles.
`CreateRole`	Adds a new role to the appointed data store.
`DeleteCookie`	Deletes the cookie on the client used to store the roles to which the user belongs.
`DeleteRole`	Deletes a specific role in the data store. Using the proper parameters for this method, you can also control whether roles are deleted or kept intact whether or not that particular role contains users.
`FindUsersInRole`	Returns a collection of users who have a username to match the one provided.
`GetAllRoles`	Returns a collection of all the roles stored in the data store.
`GetRolesForUser`	Returns a collection of roles for a specific user.
`IsUserInRole`	Returns a `Boolean` value that specifies whether a user is contained in a particular role.
`RemoveUserFromRole`	Removes a specific user from a specific role.
`RemoveUserFromRoles`	Removes a specific user from a collection of roles.
`RemoveUsersFromRole`	Removes a collection of users from a specific role.
`RemoveUsersFromRoles`	Removes a collection of users from a collection of roles.
`RoleExists`	Returns a `Boolean` value indicating whether a role exists in the data store.

INTEGRATING OAUTH AND OPENID AUTHENTICATION

So far you have seen that the authentication system of ASP.NET is very powerful and—thanks to the provider model and approaches like Universal Providers (which was mentioned in Chapter 18)—very flexible. However, it gets even better. Many websites are resorting to open standards when it comes to authentication. For this purpose, two approaches are most commonly used:

➤ OpenID was created by the OpenID Foundation (`http://openid.net/foundation`). The general approach is that users register with one of many identity providers, for instance Google's, or Yahoo!'s. Then, when these users want to log in to any OpenID-enabled third-party website, they are redirected to the provider's site, log in there, and receive a token that can then be used to authenticate with the third-party website.

➤ OAuth is controlled by the Internet Engineering Task Force (IETF, `http://ietf.org/`). The authentication process is similar to the one OpenID uses, though OAuth does not really do authentication; instead, OAuth provides the user with an access token, but not a proof of its identity.

> **NOTE** *The OAuth Wikipedia article has a nice visualization of the difference between OpenID and OAuth at* `http://en.wikipedia.org/wiki/OAuth#OpenID_vs` `._pseudo-authentication_using_OAuth.`

Luckily, the details of the standards are not of much concern, because you will discover a very convenient way of plugging these standards into your trusted and true ASP.NET authentication system.

Using OpenID

The bad news first: There is no built-in OpenID or OAuth support in ASP.NET. However, external packages coming from Microsoft make implementing these standards very easy. This section discusses OpenID, not that it is (from an ASP.NET API point of view) that much different from OpenAuth. Google's OpenID service is simple to implement. The most convenient way to use OpenID and OAuth is to use the ASP.NET Web Forms Application template that ships with Visual Studio 2012 and is shown in Figure 19-26.

FIGURE 19-26

Create a new web application with that template and have a look at the `App_Start/AuthConfig.cs` or `App_Start/AuthConfig.vb` file. You will find there several commented lines of code that hint at what is possible with the template. Uncomment the line with the call to `OpenAuth.AuthenticationClients .AddGoogle()`. Listing 19-37 shows the relevant parts.

LISTING 19-37: Activating OpenID and OAuth in AuthConfig.cs/.vb

VB

```
'OpenAuth.AuthenticationClients.AddTwitter(
'    consumerKey:= "your Twitter consumer key",
'    consumerSecret:= "your Twitter consumer secret")

'OpenAuth.AuthenticationClients.AddFacebook(
'    appId:= "your Facebook app id",
'    appSecret:= "your Facebook app secret")

'OpenAuth.AuthenticationClients.AddMicrosoft(
'    clientId:= "your Microsoft account client id",
'    clientSecret:= "your Microsoft account client secret")

OpenAuth.AuthenticationClients.AddGoogle()
```

C#

```
//OpenAuth.AuthenticationClients.AddTwitter(
//    consumerKey: "your Twitter consumer key",
//    consumerSecret: "your Twitter consumer secret");

//OpenAuth.AuthenticationClients.AddFacebook(
//    appId: "your Facebook app id",
//    appSecret: "your Facebook app secret");

//OpenAuth.AuthenticationClients.AddMicrosoft(
//    clientId: "your Microsoft account client id",
//    clientSecret: "your Microsoft account client secret");

OpenAuth.AuthenticationClients.AddGoogle();
```

Then, run the application and click the login link in the top-right corner. You will see a login screen similar to the one in Figure 19-27. In this figure, several login mechanisms are made available in the form of buttons (Facebook, Twitter, Microsoft, Google), whereas on your system only Google is available (which is fine, because it is the only provider that works without further configuration).

Click the Google button, and you are redirected to a Google site (have a look at the URL in Figure 19-28!) where you are asked for your Google credentials.

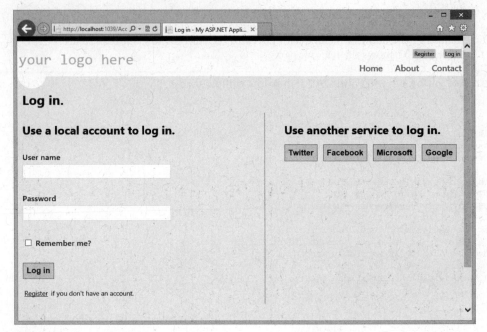

FIGURE 19-27

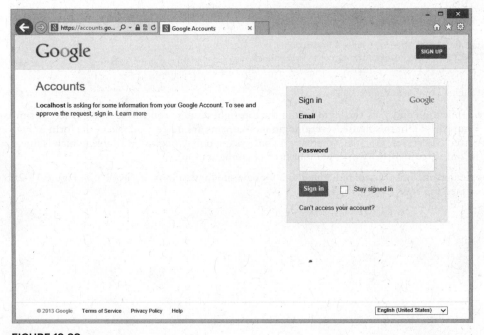

FIGURE 19-28

After logging in to Google, the Google site—not the ASP.NET site!—asks you if it is really okay whether the "Localhost" application may access your data, especially your Google e-mail address (see Figure 19-29). After agreeing with this, you are redirected back to the ASP.NET application where your Google address is shown, and you are asked to pick a username (see Figure 19-30).

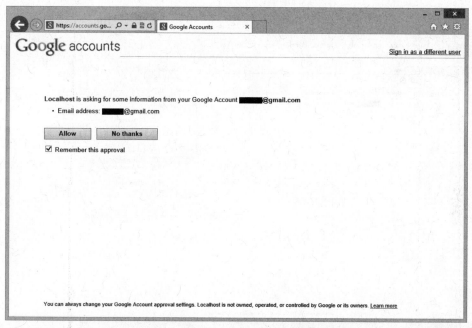

FIGURE 19-29

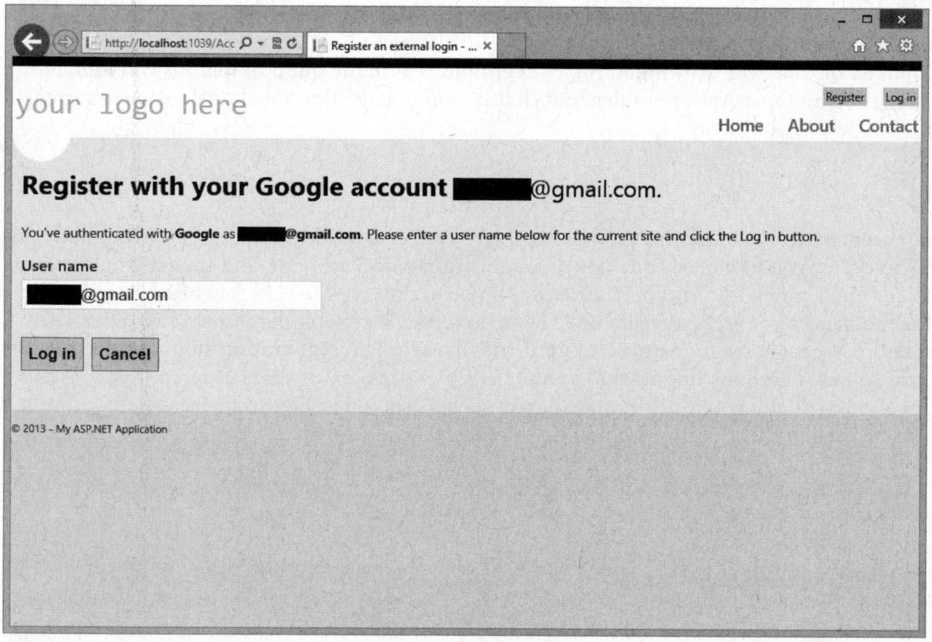

FIGURE 19-30

Choose a username, and then have a look at the database the application uses by default. You will see two new tables, UsersOpenAuthAccounts and UsersOpenAuthData. The former is used to store which OpenID or OAuth provider was used for which user, and the latter links the OpenID/OAuth data to ASP.NET's membership system. In Figure 19-31 you see the result after one user has logged in using Google's OpenID service.

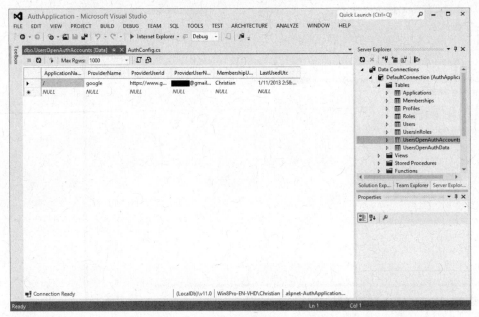

FIGURE 19-31

If you are basing an application on the template shipping with Visual Studio, you have Google OpenID support already baked in. The API working in the background is actually quite simple, so you look at it next, but this time using an OpenAuth provider (not that it would make that much difference in terms of the ASP.NET API).

Using OAuth

You want to use Facebook to log in to the ASP.NET website you have been working with throughout this chapter. In order to do so, you first need to create an application with Facebook and then configure your ASP.NET site to communicate with this application. So if you are one of the very few brave people who do not have a Facebook account yet, do create one. Then go to the Facebook developers site (`https://developers.facebook.com/`), see if you need to go through additional registration steps before you can access it, and create a new Facebook application at `https://developers.facebook.com/apps`. Pick a unique name (Facebook will tell you if it is not available) such as shown in Figure 19-32—note. though, that the application name used in this chapter is obviously already taken.

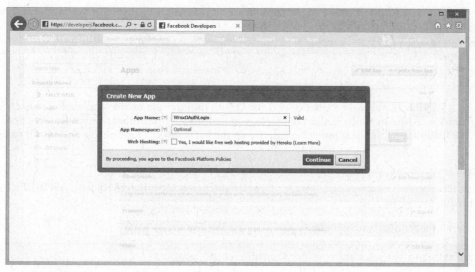

FIGURE 19-32

On top of the resulting page you will receive two important pieces of information, which you should now share with others (the code downloads for this chapter do not contain these pieces of information): the application ID and the application secret. Write them down for later.

Now look for the "Select how your app integrates with Facebook" section and choose the Website with Facebook Login option. You need to provide the URL of the page that is loaded after the user authenticates with Facebook. In this chapter this will be Listing 19-41.aspx in the code download, but of course your mileage may vary. Also note that the port number used by ASP.NET is random, so if the port changes, you need to change the Facebook application's settings, too. Figure 19-33 shows the settings screen.

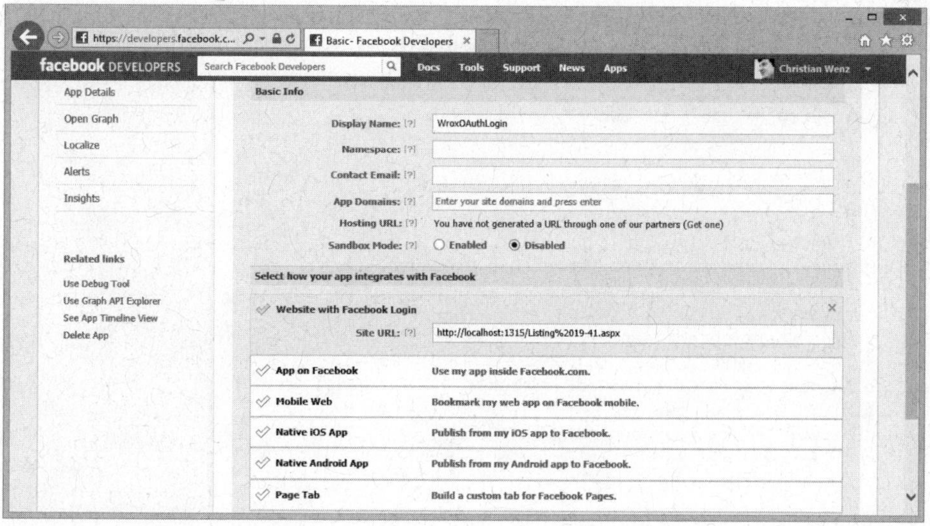

FIGURE 19-33

> **NOTE** *Sometimes it is difficult to use localhost as the server name; some OAuth services even forbid using it. A simple yet effective workaround is to use a special domain name that actually points to the local machine. The service at localtest.me provides this feature; go to* `http://readme.localtest.me/` *for more information.*

But now back to ASP.NET: If you want to use OpenID or OAuth in a website or web application that does not originate from Visual Studio's fully fledged template, you have to add the authentication features first. When an ASP.NET website (or application) is loaded, fire up the Packet Manager Console and install two packages:

➤ `DotNetOpenAuth.AspNet` (which implements the OpenID/OAuth standards)

➤ `Microsoft.AspNet.Membership.OpenAuth` (which integrates OpenID/OAuth with ASP.NET's membership providers)

Listing 19-38 shows the required commands.

LISTING 19-38: Installing NuGet packages for OpenID/OAuth support

```
Install-Package DotNetOpenAuth.AspNet
Install-Package Microsoft.AspNet.Membership.OpenAuth
```

After installation, you need to set up the application or website so that one or more OpenID or OAuth providers are activated. The best way to do this is when the application starts. Create a `Global.asax` file and include the code shown in Listing 19-39. Make sure that you are entering the application ID and application secret of the Facebook app you just set up.

LISTING 19-39: Activating Facebook OAuth in Global.asax

VB

```
<%@ Application Language="VB" %>
<%@ Import Namespace="Microsoft.AspNet.Membership.OpenAuth"  %>

<script runat="server">
    Sub Application_Start(ByVal sender As Object, ByVal e As EventArgs)
        OpenAuth.AuthenticationClients.AddFacebook( _
            appId:= "* use your own *", _
            appSecret:= "* use your own *")
    End Sub
</script>
```

C#

```
<%@ Application Language="C#" %>
<%@ Import Namespace="Microsoft.AspNet.Membership.OpenAuth"  %>

<script runat="server">
    void Application_Start(object sender, EventArgs e)
    {
        OpenAuth.AuthenticationClients.AddFacebook(
            appId: "* use your own *",
            appSecret: "* use your own *");
    }

</script>
```

Before continuing, it is important to briefly discuss the process that follows. If you want to be able to log in with Facebook, you first have to redirect the user to a Facebook authentication page, which will then redirect you to the URL provided in the Facebook application settings (in this case Listing 19-41.aspx on the server). Of course, you do not have to find out the Facebook URL all by yourself; the NuGet packages you installed do most of the work. Listing 19-40 shows the new login page (which must eventually replace Login.aspx in your project, because Login.aspx is your site's only page that an unauthenticated user can access). Note that you add a button, which, when clicked, calls the OpenAuth.RequestAuthentication() method, asking for Facebook authentication with redirection to Listing 19-41.aspx.

LISTING 19-40: Adding a Facebook login to your site

VB

```
<%@ Page Language="VB" %>
<%@ Import Namespace="Microsoft.AspNet.Membership.OpenAuth" %>

<script runat="server">

    Protected Sub Button1_Click(sender As Object, e As EventArgs)
        OpenAuth.RequestAuthentication("facebook", "~/Listing 19-41.aspx")
    End Sub
</script>

<html xmlns="http://www.w3.org/1999/xhtml" >
<head id="Head1" runat="server">
    <title>Login Page</title>
</head>
<body>
    <form id="form1" runat="server">
        <asp:Login ID="Login1" Runat="server">
        </asp:Login>
        <asp:Button ID="Button1" Text="Login with Facebook"
            runat="server" OnClick="Button1_Click" />
    </form>
</body>
</html>
```

C#

```
<%@ Page Language="C#" %>
<%@ Import Namespace="Microsoft.AspNet.Membership.OpenAuth" %>

<script runat="server">

    protected void Button1_Click(object sender, EventArgs e)
    {
        OpenAuth.RequestAuthentication("facebook", "~/Listing 19-41.aspx");
    }
</script>
```

Figure 19-34 shows the new login screen, and Figure 19-35 displays what happens after clicking the new button: The browser is redirected to Facebook where the user needs to approve that your application can access his or her e-mail address.

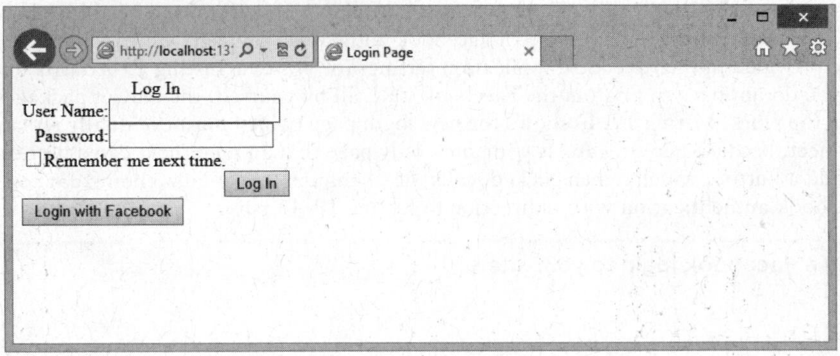

FIGURE 19-34

FIGURE 19-35

All that is left to do is to implement that page that is called when the user returns from the Facebook OAuth authentication site. The `Microsoft.AspNet.Membership.OpenAuth` package you installed provides a number of interesting features, but probably the most suitable API call now is `OpenAuth.VerifyAuthentication()`, where you need to provide the URL of the (current) callback page as an argument. The return value of that call is of type `AuthenticationResult`. Its `IsSuccessful` property tells you whether the authentication succeeded, and if so, the `UserName` property contains the username from the OAuth provider, in this case the e-mail address your Facebook account runs under.

Listing 19-41 puts these pieces together and displays the user's name if authentication worked, or redirects back to the login page if not. Figure 19-36 shows the result in the former case.

LISTING 19-41: Processing the authentication result

VB

```
<%@ Page Language="VB" %>
<%@ Import Namespace="Microsoft.AspNet.Membership.OpenAuth" %>

<script runat="server">
```

```vb
    Protected Sub Page_Load()
        Dim result = OpenAuth.VerifyAuthentication("~/Listing%2019-41.aspx")
        If result.IsSuccessful Then
            Label1.Text = HttpUtility.HtmlEncode(result.UserName)
        Else
            FormsAuthentication.RedirectToLoginPage()
        End If
    End Sub
</script>

<!DOCTYPE html>

<html xmlns="http://www.w3.org/1999/xhtml">
<head runat="server">
    <title></title>
</head>
<body>
    <form id="form1" runat="server">
    <div>
        Welcome, <asp:Label ID="Label1" runat="server" />
    </div>
    </form>
</body>
</html>
```

C#

```csharp
<%@ Page Language="C#" %>
<%@ Import Namespace="Microsoft.AspNet.Membership.OpenAuth" %>

<script runat="server">
    void Page_Load()
    {
        var result = OpenAuth.VerifyAuthentication("~/Listing%2019-41.aspx");
        if (result.IsSuccessful)
        {
            Label1.Text = HttpUtility.HtmlEncode(result.UserName);
        }
        else
        {
            FormsAuthentication.RedirectToLoginPage();
        }
    }
</script>
```

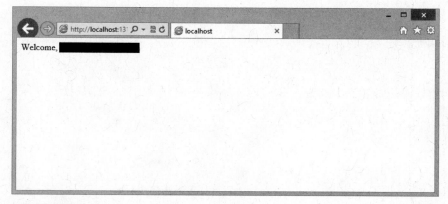

FIGURE 19-36

> **NOTE** *Pranav Rastogi, a coauthor on this book, has blogged extensively on OpenID and OAuth support in ASP.NET, so you should definitely have a look at his articles on that topic. The best entry point is this blog post:* `http://blogs.msdn.com/b/webdev/archive/2012/08/15/oauth-openid-support-for-webforms-mvc-and-webpages.aspx`. *At the end of the article you will find links to other relevant posts. One of the other highlights is the blog entry at* `http://blogs.msdn.com/b/webdev/archive/2012/09/12/integrate-openauth-openid-with-your-existing-asp-net-application-using-universal-providers.aspx`, *which brings together OpenID, OAuth, and Universal Providers.*

SUMMARY

This chapter covered two outstanding features available to ASP.NET 4.5. The membership and role management services that are a part of ASP.NET make managing users and their roles almost trivial.

This chapter reviewed both the Membership and Roles APIs and the controls that also utilize these APIs. These controls and APIs follow the same data provider models as the rest of ASP.NET. The examples were presented using Microsoft SQL Server Express Edition for the backend storage, but you can easily configure these systems to work with another type of data store.

Using standards like OAuth and OpenID it is also possible to connect to external authentication services like those offered by Facebook, Twitter, and Google.

20

Security

WHAT'S IN THIS CHAPTER?

➤ Using Windows-based and forms-based authentication

➤ Managing programmatic authorization

➤ Securing through IIS

WROX.COM CODE DOWNLOADS FOR THIS CHAPTER

Please note that all the code examples in this chapter are available as a part of this chapter's code download on the book's website at www.wrox.com on the Download Code tab.

Not every page that you build with ASP.NET is meant to be open and accessible to everyone on the Internet. Sometimes, you want to build pages or sections of an application that are accessible to only a select group of your choosing. For this reason, you need the security measures explained in this chapter. They can help protect the data behind your applications and the applications themselves from fraudulent use.

Security is a very wide-reaching term. During every step of the application-building process, you must, without a doubt, be aware of how mischievous end users might attempt to bypass your lockout measures. You must take steps to ensure that no one can take over the application or gain access to its resources. Whether it involves working with basic server controls or accessing databases, you should be thinking through the level of security you want to employ to protect yourself.

How security is applied to your applications is a measured process. For instance, a single ASP.NET page on the Internet, open to public access, has different security requirements than does an ASP.NET application that is available only to selected individuals because it deals with confidential information, such as credit card numbers or medical information.

The first step is to apply the appropriate level of security for the task at hand. Because you can take so many different actions to protect your applications and the resources, you have to decide for yourself which of these measures to employ. This chapter looks at some of the possibilities for protecting your applications.

Notice that security is discussed throughout this book. In addition, a couple of chapters focus on specific security frameworks provided by ASP.NET that are not discussed in this chapter. Chapters 18 and 19 discuss ASP.NET's membership and role management frameworks, as well as the personalization features in this version. These topics are aspects of security that can make building safe applications even easier for you. Although these security frameworks are provided with this latest release of ASP.NET, you can still build your own measures as you did in the previous versions of ASP.NET. This chapter discusses how to do so.

An important aspect of security is how you handle the authentication and authorization for accessing resources in your applications. Before you begin working through some of the authentication/authorization possibilities in ASP.NET, which is what this chapter covers, you should know exactly what we mean by those two terms:

➤ As discussed in Chapter 19, *authentication* is the process that determines the identity of a user. After a user has been authenticated, a developer can determine whether the identified user has authorization to proceed. Giving an entity authorization is impossible if no authentication process has been applied.

➤ *Authorization* is the process of determining whether an authenticated user is permitted access to any part of an application, access to specific points of an application, or access only to specified data sets that the application provides. Authenticating and authorizing users and groups enable you to customize a site based on user types or preferences.

APPLYING AUTHENTICATION MEASURES

ASP.NET provides many different types of authentication measures to use within your applications, including basic authentication, digest authentication, forms authentication, and Integrated Windows authentication. You also can develop your own authentication methods. You should never authorize access to resources you mean to be secure if you have not applied an authentication process to the requests for the resources.

The different authentication modes are established through settings that can be applied to the application's `web.config` file or in conjunction with the application server's Internet Information Services (IIS) instance.

ASP.NET is configured through a series of `.config` files on the application server. These XML-based files enable you to easily change how ASP.NET behaves. Having these settings sit within an XML-based file is an ideal way to work with the configuration settings you require. ASP.NET configuration files are applied in a hierarchical manner. The .NET Framework provides a server-level configuration file called the `machine .config` file, which you can find at `C:\Windows\Microsoft.NET\Framework\v4.0.xxxxx\CONFIG`. The folder contains the `machine.config` file. This file provides ASP.NET application settings at a server level, meaning that the settings are applied to every ASP.NET application that resides on the particular server.

A `web.config` file is another XML-based configuration file that resides in the root directory of the web application. The settings applied in the `web.config` file override the same settings applied in the higher-level `machine.config` file.

You can even nest the `web.config` files so that the main application `web.config` file is located in the root directory of your application, but additional `web.config` files reside in some of the application's subdirectories (see Figure 20-1). The `web.config` files contained in any of the subdirectories supersede the root directory's `web.config` file. Therefore, any settings applied through a subdirectory's `web.config` file change whatever was set in the application's main `web.config` file.

In many of the examples in this chapter, you use the `web.config` file to apply the authentication and authorization mechanics you want in your applications. You also can work with IIS to apply settings directly to your applications.

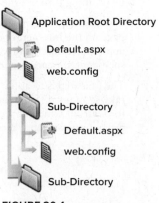

FIGURE 20-1

IIS is the web server that handles all the incoming HTTP requests that come into the server. You must modify IIS to perform as you want. IIS hands a request to the ASP.NET engine only if the page has a specific file extension (for example, `.aspx`). In this chapter, you will work with IIS 7.x and 8, as well.

The <authentication> Node

You use the `<authentication>` node in the application's `web.config` file to set the type of authentication your ASP.NET application requires:

```
<system.web>
    <authentication mode="Windows|Forms|Passport|None">

    </authentication>
</system.web>
```

The `<authentication>` node uses the `mode` attribute to set the form of authentication that is to be used. Options include `Windows`, `Forms`, `Passport`, and `None`. Each option is explained in Table 20-1.

TABLE 20-1

PROVIDER	DESCRIPTION
Windows	Windows authentication is used together with IIS authentication. Authentication is performed by IIS in the following ways: basic, digest, or Integrated Windows Authentication. When IIS authentication is complete, ASP.NET uses the authenticated identity to authorize access. This is the default setting.
Forms	Requests that are not authenticated are redirected to an HTML form using HTTP client-side redirection. The user provides his login information and submits the form. If the application authenticates the request, the system issues a form that contains the credentials or a key for reacquiring the identity.
Passport	A centralized authentication service provided by Microsoft that offers single login and core profile services for member sites. This mode of authentication was "de-emphasized" (in other words, deprecated) by Microsoft at the end of 2005.
None	No authentication mode is in place with this setting.

As you can see, a couple of methods are at your disposal for building an authentication/authorization model for your ASP.NET applications. The next section examines the Windows mode of authentication.

Windows-Based Authentication

Windows-based authentication is handled between the Windows server where the ASP.NET application resides and the client machine. In a Windows-based authentication model, the requests go directly to IIS to provide the authentication process. This type of authentication is quite useful in an intranet environment, where you can let the server deal completely with the authentication process—especially in environments where users are already logged on to a network. In this scenario, you simply grab and utilize the credentials that are already in place for the authorization process.

IIS first takes the user's credentials from the domain login. If this process fails, IIS displays a pop-up dialog box so the user can enter or re-enter his login information. To set up your ASP.NET application to work with Windows-based authentication, begin by creating some users and groups.

Creating Users

You use aspects of Windows-based authentication to allow specific users who have provided a domain login to access your application or parts of your application. Because it can use this type of authentication,

ASP.NET makes working with applications that are deployed in an intranet environment quite easy. If a user has logged on to a local computer as a domain user, she will not need to be authenticated again when accessing a network computer in that domain.

The following steps show you how to create a user. It is important to note that you must have sufficient rights to be authorized to create users on a server. If you are authorized, the steps to create users are as follows:

1. Within Windows 7 or 8, choose Start ⇨ Control Panel ⇨ System and Security ⇨ Administrative Tools ⇨ Computer Management. If you are using Windows Server 2003 or 2008 or 2012, choose Start ⇨ Control Panel ⇨ Administrative Tools ⇨ Computer Management. Either one opens the Computer Management utility. It manages and controls resources on the local web server. You can accomplish many things using this utility, but the focus here is on the creation of users.

2. Expand the System Tools node.

3. Expand the Local Users and Groups node.

4. Select the Users folder. You see something similar to the results shown in Figure 20-2.

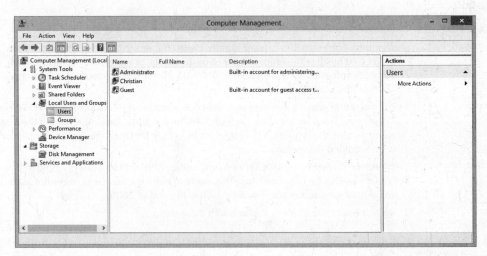

FIGURE 20-2

5. Right-click the Users folder and select New User. The New User window appears, as shown in Figure 20-3.

6. Give the user a name, password, and description stating that this is a test user. In this example, the user is called Bubbles.

7. Clear the check box that requires the user to change his password at the next login.

8. Click the Create button. Your test user is created and presented in the Users folder of the Computer Management utility, as shown in Figure 20-4.

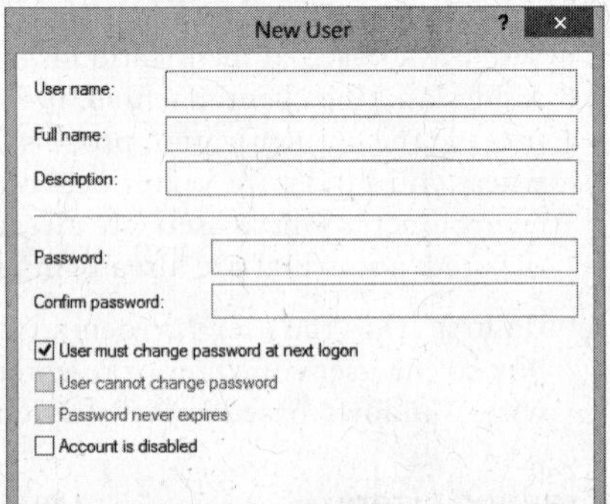

FIGURE 20-3

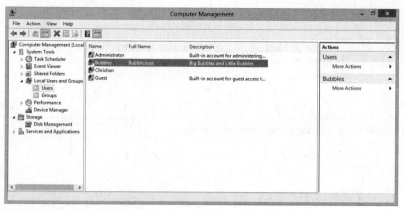

FIGURE 20-4

Now create a page to work with this user.

Authenticating and Authorizing a User

Now create an application that enables the user to enter it. You work with the application's `web.config` file to control whicth users are allowed to access the site and which users are not allowed.

Add the section presented in Listing 20-1 to your `web.config` file.

LISTING 20-1: Denying all users through the web.config file

```
<system.web>
   <authentication mode="Windows" />
   <authorization>
      <deny users="*" />
   </authorization>
</system.web>
```

In this example, the `web.config` file is configuring the application to employ Windows-based authentication using the `<authentication>` element's `mode` attribute. In addition, the `<authorization>` element is used to define specifics about the users or groups who are permitted access to the application. In this case, the `<deny>` element specifies that all users (even if they are authenticated) are denied access to the application. Not permitting specific users with the `<allow>` element does not make much sense, but for this example, leave it as it is. Figure 20-5 shows the results.

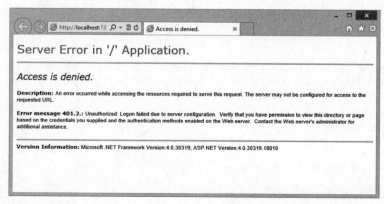

FIGURE 20-5

Any end user—authenticated or not—who tries to access the site sees a large "Access is denied" statement in her browser window, which is just what you want for those not allowed to access your application!

In most instances, however, you want to allow at least some users to access your application. Use the `<allow>` element in the `web.config` file to allow a specific user. Here is the syntax:

```
<allow users="Domain\Username" />
```

Listing 20-2 shows how the user is permitted access.

LISTING 20-2: Allowing a single user through the web.config file

```
<system.web>
    <authentication mode="Windows" />
    <authorization>
        <allow users="Win8Pro-En\Bubbles"/>
        <deny users="*"/>
    </authorization>
</system.web>
```

Even though all users (even authenticated ones) are denied access through the use of the `<deny>` element, the definitions defined in the `<allow>` element take precedence. In this example, a single user—Bubbles—is allowed.

Now, if you are logged on to the client machine as the user Bubbles and run the page in the browser, you get access to the application.

Looking Closely at the <allow> and <deny> Nodes

The `<allow>` and `<deny>` nodes enable you to work not only with specific users, but also with groups. The elements support the attributes defined in Table 20-2.

TABLE 20-2

ATTRIBUTE	DESCRIPTION
Users	Enables you to specify users by their domains and/or names
Roles	Enables you to specify access groups that are allowed or denied access
Verbs	Enables you to specify the HTTP transmission method that is allowed or denied access

When using any of these attributes, you can specify all users with the use of the asterisk (*):

```
<allow roles="*" />
```

In this example, all roles are allowed access to the application. Another symbol you can use with these attributes is the question mark (?), which represents all anonymous users. For example, if you want to block all anonymous users from your application, use the following construction:

```
<deny users="?" />
```

When using `users`, `roles`, or `verbs` attributes with the `<allow>` or `<deny>` elements, you can specify multiple entries by separating the values with a comma. If you are going to allow more than one user, you can either separate these users into different elements, as shown here:

```
<allow users="MyDomain\User1" />
<allow users="MyDomain\User2" />
```

or you can use the following:

```
<allow users="MyDomain\User1, MyDomain\User2" />
```

Use the same construction when defining multiple roles and verbs.

Authenticating and Authorizing a Group

You can define groups of individuals allowed or denied access to your application or the application's resources. Your server can contain a number of different groups, each of which can have any number of users belonging to it. The possibility also exists for a single user to belong to multiple groups. Pull up the Computer Management utility to access the list of the groups defined on the server you are working with. Simply click the Groups folder in the Computer Management utility, and the list of groups appears, as illustrated in Figure 20-6.

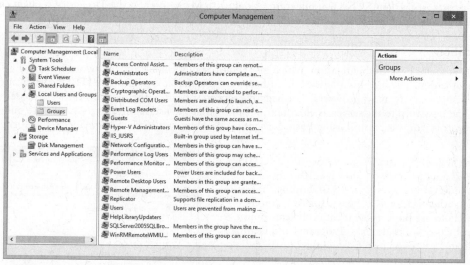

FIGURE 20-6

Right-click the Groups folder to select New Group. The New Group window appears (see Figure 20-7).

To create a group, give it a name and description; then click the Add button and select the users whom you want to be a part of the group. After a group is created, you can allow it access to your application like this:

```
<allow roles="MyGroup" />
```

You can use the `roles` attribute in either the `<allow>` or `<deny>` element to work with a group that you have created or with a specific group that already exists.

Authenticating and Authorizing an HTTP Transmission Method

In addition to authenticating and authorizing specific users or groups of users, you can also authorize or deny requests that come via a specific HTTP transmission protocol. You do so using the `verbs` attribute in the `<allow>` and `<deny>` elements:

```
<deny verbs="GET, DEBUG" />
```

In this example, requests that come in using the HTTP `GET` or HTTP `DEBUG` protocols are denied access to the site. Possible values for the `verbs` attribute include `POST`, `GET`, `HEAD`, and `DEBUG`.

FIGURE 20-7

Integrated Windows Authentication

So far, you have been using the default Integrated Windows authentication mode for the authentication/ authorization process. This is fine if you are working with an intranet application and each of the clients is using Windows, the only system that the authentication method supports. This system of authentication also requires the client to be using Microsoft's Internet Explorer for straight-through processing (if you don't want your end users to be challenged), which might not always be possible.

Integrated Windows authentication was previously known as NTLM or Windows NT Challenge/Response authentication. This authentication model has the client prove its identity by sending a hash of its credentials to the server that is hosting the ASP.NET application. Along with Microsoft's Active Directory, a client can also use Kerberos if it is using Microsoft's Internet Explorer.

Basic Authentication

Another option is to use Basic authentication, which also requires a username and password from the client for authentication. The big plus about Basic authentication is that it is part of the HTTP specification and therefore is supported by most browsers. The negative aspect of Basic authentication is that it passes the username and password to the server as clear text, meaning that the username and password are quite visible to prying eyes. For this reason, using Basic authentication along with SSL (*Secure Sockets Layer*) is important.

If you are using Windows Vista/Windows Server 2008 (IIS 7.0), Windows 7/Windows Server 2008 R2 (IIS 7.5), or Windows 8/Windows Server 2012 (IIS 8.0), finding the option to enable Basic authentication is not easy. Instead, you first have to enable IIS to use Basic authentication by choosing Start ⇨ Control Panel ⇨ Programs ⇨ Programs and Features ⇨ Turn Windows features on or off. From the provided dialog box, navigate to the Internet Information Services section and expand until you arrive at World Wide Web Services ⇨ Security. From here, select the Basic Authentication option and click OK to install. Figure 20-8 shows this option.

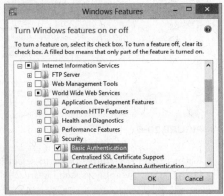

FIGURE 20-8

After this option is installed, you can then return to the Internet Information Services (IIS) Manager and select the Authentication option in the IIS section for the virtual directory you are focusing on. From there, highlight the Basic Authentication option and select Enable from the Actions pane, as illustrated in Figure 20-9 after enabling this feature.

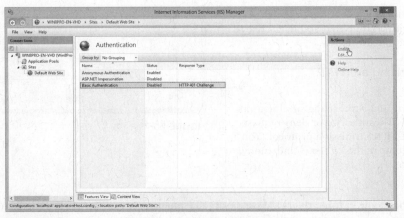

FIGURE 20-9

If you are using IIS 6 (or even an earlier version) to implement Basic authentication for your application, you must pull up IIS and open the Properties window for the website you are working with. Select the Directory Security tab and click the Edit button in the Anonymous Access and Authentication Control box. The Authentication Methods dialog box opens.

Uncheck the Integrated Windows Authentication check box at the bottom and select the Basic Authentication check box above it (see Figure 20-10). When you do, you are warned that this method transmits usernames and passwords as clear text.

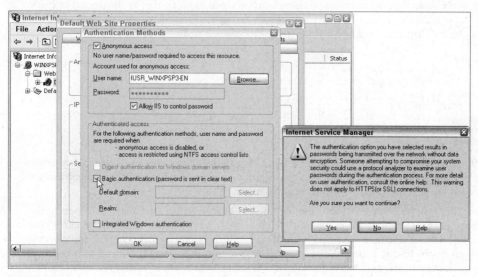

FIGURE 20-10

End by clicking OK in the dialog box. Now your application uses Basic authentication instead of Integrated Windows authentication.

Digest Authentication

Digest authentication is the final mode you are going to explore in this chapter. This model alleviates the Basic authentication problem of passing the client's credentials as clear text. Instead, Digest authentication uses an algorithm to encrypt the client's credentials before they are sent to the application server.

To use Digest authentication, you are required to have a Windows domain controller. One of the main issues that arises with Digest authentication is that it is not supported on all platforms and requires browsers that conform to the HTTP 1.1 specification. Digest authentication, however, not only works well with firewalls, but is also compatible with proxy servers.

If you are using IIS 7 or higher, you need to install Digest Authentication just as you installed Basic Authentication. After you install it, you can find this option and are able to enable it from the Authentication section within the IIS Manager.

For IIS 6 or earlier, you can select Digest authentication as the choice for your application in the same Authentication Methods window—simply select the Digest Authentication check box from the properties window.

Forms-Based Authentication

Forms-based authentication is a popular mode of authenticating users to access an entire application or specific resources within an application. Using it enables you to put the login form directly in the application so that the end user simply enters his username and password into an HTML form contained within the browser itself. One negative aspect of forms-based authentication is that the usernames and passwords are sent as clear text unless you are using SSL.

Implementing forms-based authentication in your web application is easy and relatively straightforward. To begin, you make some modifications to your application's `web.config` file, as illustrated in Listing 20-3.

LISTING 20-3: Modifying the web.config file for forms-based authentication

```
<system.web>
    <authentication mode="Forms">
        <forms name="Wrox" loginUrl="Login.aspx" path="/" />
    </authentication>
    <authorization>
        <deny users="?" />
    </authorization>
</system.web>
```

You must apply this structure to the `web.config` file. Using the `<authorization>` element described earlier, you are denying access to the application to all anonymous users. Only authenticated users are allowed to access any page contained within the application.

If the requestor is not authenticated, what is defined in the `<authentication>` element is put into action. The value of the `mode` attribute is set to `Forms` to employ forms-based authentication for your web application. The next attribute specified is `loginUrl`, which points to the page that contains the application's login form. In this example, `login.aspx` is specified as a value. If the end user trying to access the application is not authenticated, his request is redirected to `login.aspx` so that the user can be authenticated and authorized to proceed. After valid credentials have been provided, the user is returned to the location in the application where he originally made the request. The final attribute used here is `path`. It simply specifies the location in which to save the cookie used to persist the authorized user's access token. In most cases, you want to leave the value as `/`. Table 20-3 describes each of the possible attributes for the `<forms>` element.

TABLE 20-3

ATTRIBUTE	DESCRIPTION
name	This name is assigned to the cookie saved in order to remember the user from request to request. The default value is `.ASPXAUTH`.
loginUrl	Specifies the URL to which the request is redirected for login if no valid authentication cookie is found. The default value is `login.aspx`.
protection	Specifies the amount of protection you want to apply to the authentication cookie. The four available settings are: ➤ `All`: The application uses both data validation and encryption to protect the cookie. This is the default setting. ➤ `None`: Applies no encryption to the cookie. ➤ `Encryption`: The cookie is encrypted but data validation is not performed on it. Cookies used in this manner might be subject to plaintext attacks. ➤ `Validation`: The opposite of the `Encryption` setting. Data validation is performed, but the cookie is not encrypted.

path	Specifies the path for cookies issued by the application. In most cases, you want to use /, which is the default setting.
timeout	Specifies the amount of time, in minutes, after which the cookie expires. The default value is 30.
cookieless	Specifies whether the forms-based authentication process should use cookies when working with the authentication/authorization process.
defaultUrl	Specifies the default URL.
domain	Specifies the domain name to be sent with forms authentication cookies.
slidingExpiration	Specifies whether to apply a sliding expiration to the cookie. If set to True, the expiration of the cookie is reset with each request made to the server. The default value is False.
enableCrossAppsRedirect	Specifies whether to allow for cross-application redirection.
requireSSL	Specifies whether a Secure Sockets Layer (SSL) connection is required when transmitting authentication information.

After the `web.config` file is in place, the next step is to create a typical page for your application that people can access. Listing 20-4 (Default.aspx in the code download for this chapter) presents a simple page.

LISTING 20-4: A simple page

```
<%@ Page Language="VB" %>

<html xmlns="http://www.w3.org/1999/xhtml">
<head runat="server">
    <title>The Application</title>
</head>
<body>
    <form id="form1" runat="server">
    <div>
       Hello World
    </div>
    </form>
</body>
</html>
```

As you can see, this page simply writes `Hello World` to the browser. The real power of forms authentication is shown in the `login.aspx` page presented in Listing 20-5 (Login.aspx in the code download for this chapter).

LISTING 20-5: The login.aspx page

VB

```
<%@ Page Language="VB" %>

<script runat="server">
    Protected Sub Button1_Click(ByVal sender As Object, _
      ByVal e As System.EventArgs)
        If (tbUsername.Text = "Christian" And tbPassword.Text = "Bubbles") Then
            FormsAuthentication.RedirectFromLoginPage(tbUsername.Text, True)
        Else
            Response.Write("Invalid credentials")
        End If
    End Sub
```

continues

LISTING 20-5 *(continued)*

```
</script>

<html xmlns="http://www.w3.org/1999/xhtml">
<head runat="server">
    <title>Login Page</title>
</head>
<body>
    <form id="form1" runat="server">
    <div>
        Username<br />
        <asp:TextBox ID="tbUsername" runat="server"></asp:TextBox><br />
        <br />
        Password<br />
        <asp:TextBox ID="tbPassword" runat="server"
         TextMode="Password"></asp:TextBox><br />
        <br />
        <asp:Button ID="Button1" OnClick="Button1_Click" runat="server"
         Text="Submit" />
    </div>
    </form>
</body>
</html>
```

C#

```
<%@ Page Language="C#"%>

<script runat="server">
    protected void Button1_Click(object sender, EventArgs e)
    {
        if (tbUsername.Text == "Christian" && tbPassword.Text == "Bubbles") {
            FormsAuthentication.RedirectFromLoginPage(tbUsername.Text, true);
        }
        else {
            Response.Write("Invalid credentials");
        }
    }
</script>
```

Login.aspx has two simple TextBox controls and a Button control that asks the user to submit his username and password. The Button1_Click event uses the RedirectFromLoginPage method of the FormsAuthentication class. This method does exactly what its name implies—it redirects the request from Login.aspx to the original requested resource.

RedirectFromLoginPage takes two arguments. The first is the name of the user, used for cookie authentication purposes. This argument does not actually map to an account name and is used by ASP.NET's URL authorization capabilities. The second argument specifies whether a durable cookie should be issued. If this is set to True, the end user does not need to log in again to the application from one browser session to the next.

Using the three pages you have constructed, each request for the Default.aspx page from Listing 20-4 causes ASP.NET to check that the proper authentication token is in place. If the proper token is not found, the request is directed to the specified login page (in this example, Login.aspx). Looking at the URL in the browser, you can see that ASP.NET is using a query string value to remember where to return the user after he has been authorized to proceed:

```
http://localhost:35089/Security/Login.aspx?ReturnUrl=%2fSecurity%2fDefault.aspx
```

Here, the query string `ReturnUrl` is used with a value of the folder and page that was the initial request.

Look more closely at the `Login.aspx` page from Listing 20-5, and note that the values placed in the two textboxes are checked to make sure they abide by a specific username and password. If they do, the `RedirectFromLoginPage` method is invoked; otherwise, the `Response.Write()` statement is used. In most cases, you do not want to hardcode a username and password in your code. Many other options exist for checking whether usernames and passwords come from authorized users. Some of the other options follow.

Authenticating against Values Contained in the web.config File

The previous example is not the best approach for dealing with usernames and passwords offered for authentication. Hardcoding them directly into your applications is never a good idea. Take a quick look at storing these values in the `web.config` file itself.

The `<forms>` element in the `web.config` file that you worked with in Listing 20-3 can also take a sub-element. The sub-element, `<credentials>`, allows you to specify username and password combinations directly in the `web.config` file. You can choose from a couple of ways to add these values. Listing 20-6 shows the simplest method.

LISTING 20-6: Modifying the web.config file to add username/password values

```
<system.web>
   <authentication mode="Forms">
      <forms name="Wrox" loginUrl="Login.aspx" path="/">
         <credentials passwordFormat="Clear">
            <user name="Christian" password="Bubbles" />
         </credentials>
      </forms>
   </authentication>
   <authorization>
      <deny users="?" />
   </authorization>
</system.web>
```

The `<credentials>` element has been included to add users and their passwords to the configuration file. `<credentials>` takes a single attribute—`passwordFormat`. The possible values of `passwordFormat` are `Clear`, `MD5`, and `SHA1`. The following list describes each of these options:

➤ `Clear`: Passwords are stored in clear text. The user password is compared directly to this value without further transformation.

➤ `MD5`: Passwords are stored using a Message Digest 5 (MD5) hash digest. When credentials are validated, the user password is hashed using the MD5 algorithm and compared for equality with this value. The clear-text password is never stored or compared. This algorithm produces better performance than SHA1, but less security.

➤ `SHA1`: Passwords are stored using the SHA1 hash digest. When credentials are validated, the user password is hashed using the SHA1 algorithm and compared for equality with this value. The clear-text password is never stored or compared. Use this algorithm for best security.

In the example from Listing 20-6, you use a setting of `Clear`. This method is not the most secure, but it is used for demonstration purposes. A sub-element of `<credentials>` is `<user>`; that is where you define the username and password for the authorized user with the attributes `name` and `password`.

The next step is to change the `Button1_Click` event on the `login.aspx` page shown earlier, as illustrated in Listing 20-7.

LISTING 20-7: Changing the login.aspx page to work with the web.config file

VB

```
<%@ Page Language="VB" %>

<script runat="server">
    Protected Sub Button1_Click(ByVal sender As Object, _
      ByVal e As System.EventArgs)
        If FormsAuthentication.Authenticate(tbUsername.Text, tbPassword.Text) Then
            FormsAuthentication.RedirectFromLoginPage(tbUsername.Text, True)
        Else
            Response.Write("Invalid credentials")
        End If
    End Sub
</script>
```

C#

```
<%@ Page Language="C#"%>

<script runat="server">
    protected void Button1_Click(object sender, EventArgs e)
    {
        if (FormsAuthentication.Authenticate(tbUsername.Text, tbPassword.Text)) {
            FormsAuthentication.RedirectFromLoginPage(tbUsername.Text, true);
        }
        else {
            Response.Write("Invalid credentials");
        }
    }
</script>
```

In this example, you simply use the Authenticate() method to get your ASP.NET page to look at the credentials stored in the web.config file for verification. The Authenticate() method takes two parameters—the username and the password that you are passing in to be checked. If the credential lookup is successful, the RedirectFromLoginPage method is invoked.

> **NOTE** *Of course, an even better approach is to store user information in a database for performance and maintenance reasons, as outlined in Chapter 19.*

It is best not to store your users' passwords in the web.config file as clear text, as the preceding example did. Instead, use one of the available hashing capabilities so you can keep the end user's password out of sight of prying eyes. To do this, simply store the hashed password in the configuration file, as shown in Listing 20-8.

LISTING 20-8: Using encrypted passwords

```
<forms name="Wrox" loginUrl="Login.aspx" path="/">
    <credentials passwordFormat="SHA1">
        <user name="Christian" password="58356FB4CAC0B801F011B397F9DFF45ADB863892" />
    </credentials>
</forms>
```

Using this kind of construct makes it impossible for even the developer to discover a password, because the clear-text password is never used. The Authenticate() method in the login.aspx page hashes the password using SHA1 (because it is the method specified in the `web.config` file's `<credentials>` node) and compares the two hashes for a match. If a match is found, the user is authorized to proceed.

When using SHA1 or MD5, the only changes you make are in the `web.config` file and nowhere else. You do not have to make any changes to the login page or to any other page in the application. To store hashed passwords, however, you use the `FormsAuthentication.HashPasswordForStoringInConfigFile()` method (one of the longer method names in the .NET Framework). You use this method in the following manner:

```
FormsAuthentication.HashPasswordForStoringInConfigFile(TextBox2.Text, "SHA1")
```

Authenticating against Values in a Database

Another common way to retrieve username/password combinations is by getting them directly from a datastore of some kind. This enables you, for example, to check the credentials input by a user against values stored in Microsoft's SQL Server. Listing 20-9 presents exemplary code for this credentials check.

LISTING 20-9: Checking credentials in SQL Server

VB

```
<%@ Page Language="VB" %>
<%@ Import Namespace="System.Data" %>
<%@ Import Namespace="System.Data.SqlClient" %>
<script runat="server">
    Protected Sub Button1_Click(ByVal sender As Object, _
      ByVal e As System.EventArgs)
        Dim conn As SqlConnection
        Dim cmd As SqlCommand
        Dim cmdString As String = "SELECT [Password] FROM [AccessTable] WHERE" &
            " (([Username] = @Username) AND ([Password] = @Password))"
        conn = New SqlConnection("Data Source=localhost;Initial " &
            "Catalog=Northwind;Persist Security Info=True;User ID=sa")
        cmd = New SqlCommand(cmdString, conn)
        cmd.Parameters.Add("@Username", SqlDbType.VarChar, 50)
        cmd.Parameters("@Username").Value = TextBox1.Text
        cmd.Parameters.Add("@Password", SqlDbType.VarChar, 50)
        cmd.Parameters("@Password").Value = TextBox2.Text
        conn.Open()
        Dim myReader As SqlDataReader
        myReader = cmd.ExecuteReader(CommandBehavior.CloseConnection)
        If myReader.Read() Then
            FormsAuthentication.RedirectFromLoginPage(TextBox1.Text, False)
        Else
            Response.Write("Invalid credentials")
        End If
        myReader.Close()
    End Sub
</script>
```

C#

```
<%@ Page Language="C#"%>
<%@ Import Namespace="System.Data" %>
<%@ Import Namespace="System.Data.SqlClient" %>
<script runat="server">
    protected void Button1_Click(object sender, EventArgs e)
    {
        SqlConnection conn;
        SqlCommand cmd;
```

continues

LISTING 20-9 *(continued)*

```
            string cmdString = @"SELECT [Password] FROM [AccessTable] WHERE
                (([Username] = @Username) AND ([Password] = @Password))";

            conn = new SqlConnection(@"Data Source=localhost;Initial
                Catalog=Northwind;Persist Security Info=True;User ID=sa");
            cmd = new SqlCommand(cmdString, conn);
            cmd.Parameters.Add("@Username", SqlDbType.VarChar, 50);
            cmd.Parameters["@Username"].Value = tbUsername.Text;
            cmd.Parameters.Add("@Password", SqlDbType.VarChar, 50);
            cmd.Parameters["@Password"].Value = tbPassword.Text;
            conn.Open();
            SqlDataReader myReader;
            myReader = cmd.ExecuteReader(CommandBehavior.CloseConnection);
            if (myReader.Read()) {
                FormsAuthentication.RedirectFromLoginPage(tbUsername.Text, false);
            }
            else {
                Response.Write("Invalid credentials");
            }
            myReader.Close();
        }
    </script>
```

Leave everything else from the previous examples the same, except for the Login.aspx page. You can now authenticate usernames and passwords against data stored in SQL Server. In the Button1_Click event, a connection is made to SQL Server. (For security reasons, you should store your connection string in the web.config file.) Two parameters are passed in—the inputs from tbUsername and tbPassword. If a result is returned, the RedirectFromLoginPage() method is invoked.

Using the Login Control with Forms Authentication

You have seen how to use ASP.NET forms authentication with standard ASP.NET server controls, such as simple TextBox and Button controls. You can also use the ASP.NET server controls—such as the Login server control—with your custom-developed forms-authentication framework instead of using other controls. This really shows the power of ASP.NET—you can combine so many pieces to construct the solution you want.

Listing 20-10 shows a modified Login.aspx page using the Login server control.

LISTING 20-10: Using the Login server control on the login.aspx page

VB

```
<%@ Page Language="VB" %>

<script runat="server">
    Protected Sub Login1_Authenticate(ByVal sender As Object, _
        ByVal e As System.Web.UI.WebControls.AuthenticateEventArgs)
        If (Login1.UserName = "Christian" And Login1.Password = "Bubbles") Then
            FormsAuthentication.RedirectFromLoginPage(Login1.UserName, _
                Login1.RememberMeSet)
        Else
            Response.Write("Invalid credentials")
        End If
    End Sub
```

```
    </script>

    <html xmlns="http://www.w3.org/1999/xhtml" >
    <head runat="server">
        <title>Login Page</title>
    </head>
    <body>
        <form id="form1" runat="server">
        <div>
            <asp:Login ID="Login1" runat="server" OnAuthenticate="Login1_Authenticate">
            </asp:Login>
        </div>
        </form>
    </body>
    </html>
```

C#

```
<%@ Page Language="C#" %>

<script runat="server">
    protected void Login1_Authenticate(object sender, AuthenticateEventArgs e)
    {
        if (Login1.UserName == "Christian" && Login1.Password == "Bubbles") {
            FormsAuthentication.RedirectFromLoginPage(Login1.UserName,
                Login1.RememberMeSet);
        }
        else {
            Response.Write("Invalid credentials");
        }
    }
</script>
```

Because no Button server control is on the page, you use the Login control's `OnAuthenticate` attribute to point to the authentication server-side event—`Login1_Authenticate()`. The event takes care of the authorization lookup (although the values are hardcoded in this example). The username textbox of the Login control can be accessed via the `Login1.UserName` declaration, and the password can be accessed using `Login1.Password`. You use the `Login1.RememberMeSet` property to specify whether to persist the authentication cookie for the user so that he is remembered on his next visit.

This example is a bit simpler than creating your own login form using TextBox and Button controls. You can give the Login control a predefined look-and-feel that is provided for you. You can also get at the subcontrol properties of the Login control a bit more easily. In the end, which methods you employ in your ASP.NET applications is really up to you.

Looking Closely at the FormsAuthentication Class

As you can tell from the various examples in the forms authentication part of this chapter, a lot of what goes on depends on the `FormsAuthentication` class. For this reason, you should learn what that class is all about.

`FormsAuthentication` provides a number of methods and properties that enable you to read and control the authentication cookie as well as other information (such as the return URL of the request). Table 20-4 details some of the methods and properties available in the `FormsAuthentictation` class.

TABLE 20-4

METHOD/PROPERTY	DESCRIPTION
`Authenticate`	This method is used to authenticate credentials that are stored in a configuration file (such as the `web.config` file).
`Decrypt`	Returns an instance of a valid, encrypted authentication ticket retrieved from an HTTP cookie as an instance of a `FormsAuthenticationTicket` class.
`Encrypt`	Creates a string that contains a valid encrypted authentication ticket that can be used in an HTTP cookie.
`FormsCookieName`	Returns the name of the cookie for the current application.
`FormsCookiePath`	Returns the cookie path (the location of the cookie) for the current application.
`GetAuthCookie`	Provides an authentication cookie for a specified user.
`GetRedirectUrl`	Returns the URL to which the user is redirected after being authorized by the login page.
`HashPasswordFor Storing InConfigFile`	Creates a hash of a provided string password. This method takes two parameters—one is the password and the other is the type of hash to perform on the string. Possible hash values include `SHA1` and `MD5`.
`Initialize`	Performs an initialization of the `FormsAuthentication` class by reading the configuration settings in the `web.config` file, as well as getting the cookies and encryption keys used in the given instance of the application.
`RedirectFromLogin Page`	Performs a redirection of the HTTP request back to the original requested page. This should be performed only after the user has been authorized to proceed.
`RenewTicketIfOld`	Conditionally updates the sliding expiration on a `FormsAuthenticationTicket` instance.
`RequireSSL`	Specifies whether the cookie should be transported via SSL only (HTTPS).
`SetAuthCookie`	Creates an authentication ticket and attaches it to a cookie that is contained in the outgoing response.
`SignOut`	Removes the authentication ticket.
`SlidingExpiration`	Provides a `Boolean` value indicating whether sliding expiration is enabled.

AUTHENTICATING SPECIFIC FILES AND FOLDERS

You may not want to require credentials for every page or resource in your application. For example, you might have a public Internet site with pages anyone can access without credentials, although you might have an administration section as part of your application that might require authentication/authorization measures.

URL authorization enables you to use the `web.config` file to apply the settings you need. Using URL authorization, you can apply any of the authentication measures to only specific files or folders. Listing 20-11 shows an example of locking down a single file.

LISTING 20-11: Applying authorization requirements to a single file

```
<configuration>
    <system.web>
        <authentication mode="None" />

        <!-- The rest of your web.config file settings go here -->

    </system.web>

    <location path="AdminPage.aspx">
        <system.web>
            <authentication mode="Windows" />

            <authorization>
                <allow users="Win8Pro-En\Christian" />
                <deny users="*" />
            </authorization>
        </system.web>
    </location>
</configuration>
```

This web.config file construction keeps the web application open to the general public while, at the same time, it locks down a single file contained within the application—the AdminPage.aspx page. You accomplish this lockdown through the <location> element. <location> takes a single attribute (path) to specify the resource defined within the <system.web> section of the web.config file.

In the example, the <authentication> and <authorization> elements are used to provide the authentication and authorization details for the AdminPage.aspx page. For this page, Windows authentication is applied, and the only user allowed access is Christian in the Win8Pro-En domain. You can have as many <location> sections in your web.config file as you want.

PROGRAMMATIC AUTHORIZATION

So far, you have seen a lot of authentication examples that simply provide a general authorization to a specific page or folder within the application. Yet, you may want to provide more granular authorization measures for certain items on a page. For example, you might provide a link to a specific document only for users who have an explicit Windows role. Other users may see something else. You also might want additional commentary or information for specified users, while other users see a condensed version of the information. Whatever your reason, this role-based authorization practice is possible in ASP.NET by working with certain objects.

You can use the Page object's User property, which provides an instance of the IPrincipal object. The User property provides a single method and a single property:

➤ Identity: This property provides an instance of the System.Security.Principal.IIdentity object for you to get at specific properties of the authenticated user.

➤ IsInRole: This method takes a single parameter, a string representation of the system role. It returns a Boolean value that indicates whether the user is in the role specified.

Working with User.Identity

The User.Identity property enables you to work with some specific contextual information about the authorized user. Using the property within your ASP.NET applications enables you to make resource-access decisions based on the information the object provides.

With User.Identity, you can gain access to the user's name, her authentication type, and whether she is authenticated. Table 20-5 details the properties provided through User.Identity.

TABLE 20-5

ATTRIBUTE	DESCRIPTION
AuthenticationType	Provides the authentication type of the current user. Example values include Basic, NTLM, Forms, and Passport.
IsAuthenticated	Returns a Boolean value specifying whether the user has been authenticated.
Name	Provides the username of the user as well as the domain of the user (only if he logged on with a Windows account).

For some examples of working with the User object, take a look at checking the user's login name. To do this, you use code similar to that shown in Listing 20-12.

LISTING 20-12: Getting the username of the logged-in user

VB

```
Dim UserName As String
UserName = User.Identity.Name
```

C#

```
string userName;
userName = User.Identity.Name;
```

Another task you can accomplish with the User.Identity object is checking whether the user has been authenticated through your application's authentication methods, as illustrated in Listing 20-13.

LISTING 20-13: Checking whether the user is authenticated

VB

```
Dim AuthUser As Boolean
AuthUser = User.Identity.IsAuthenticated
```

C#

```
bool authUser;
authUser = User.Identity.IsAuthenticated;
```

This example provides you with a Boolean value indicating whether the user has been authenticated. You can also use the IsAuthenticated method in an if/then statement, as shown in Listing 20-14.

LISTING 20-14: Using an if/then statement that checks authentication

VB

```
If (User.Identity.IsAuthenticated) Then
' Do some actions here for authenticated users
Else
' Do other actions here for unauthenticated users
End If
```

C#

```
if (User.Identity.IsAuthenticated) {
    // Do some actions here for authenticated users
}
else {
    // Do other actions here for unauthenticated users
}
```

You can also use the User object to check the authentication type of the user. You do so with the AuthenticationType property, illustrated in Listing 20-15.

LISTING 20-15: Using the AuthenticationType property

VB

```
Dim AuthType As String
AuthType = User.Identity.AuthenticationType
```

C#

```
string authType;
authType = User.Identity.AuthenticationType;
```

Again, the result usually is Basic, NTLM, or Forms.

Working with User.IsInRole()

If you are using Windows-based authentication, you can check to make sure that an authenticated user is in a specific Windows role. For example, you might want to show specific information only for users in the Subscribers group in the Computer Management Utility. To accomplish that, you can use the User object's IsInRole method, as shown in Listing 20-16.

LISTING 20-16: Checking whether the user is part of a specific role

VB

```
If (User.IsInRole("Win8Pro-En\Subscribers")) Then
   ' Private information for subscribers
Else
   ' Public information
End If
```

C#

```
if (User.IsInRole("Win8Pro-En\\Subscribers")) {
   // Private information for subscribers
}
else {
   // Public information
}
```

The IsInRole method's parameter provides a string value that represents the domain and the group (Windows role). In this case, you specify that any user in the Subscribers Windows role from the Win8Pro-En domain is permitted to see some information not available to users who don't belong to that specific role.

Another possibility is to specify some of the built-in groups available to you. Windows includes a series of built-in accounts such as Administrator, Guest, and User. You can access these built-in accounts in a couple of ways. One is to specify the built-in account with the domain directly:

```
User.IsInRole("Win8Pro-En\Administrator")
```

The other possibility is to use the BUILTIN keyword:

```
User.IsInRole("BUILTIN\Administrator")
```

Pulling More Information with WindowsIdentity

So far, in working with the user's identity information, you have used the standard Identity object that is part of ASP.NET by default. If you are working with Windows-based authentication, you also have the option of using the `WindowsIdentity` object and other objects. To gain access to these richer objects, create a reference to the `System.Security.Principal` object in your application.

Used in combination with the `Identity` object from the preceding examples, these additional objects make certain tasks even easier. For example, if you are working with roles, `System.Security.Principal` provides access to the `WindowsBuiltInRole` enumeration.

Listing 20-17 is an example of using the `WindowsBuiltInRole` enumeration.

LISTING 20-17: Using the WindowsBuiltInRole enumeration

VB

```vb
Dim AdminUser As Boolean
AdminUser = User.IsInRole(WindowsBuiltInRole.Administrator.ToString())
```

C#

```csharp
bool adminUser;
adminUser = User.IsInRole(WindowsBuiltInRole.Administrator.ToString());
```

Instead of specifying a string value of the domain and the role, you can use the `WindowsBuiltInRole` enumeration to easily access specific roles on the application server. When working with this and other enumerations, you also have IntelliSense (see Figure 20-11) to help you make your selections easily.

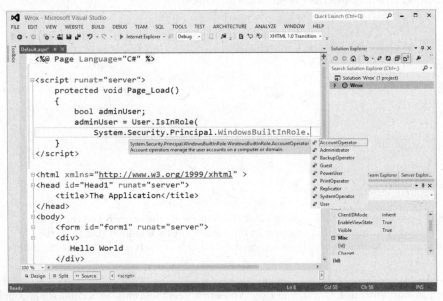

FIGURE 20-11

The roles in the `WindowsBuiltInRole` enumeration include the following:

➤ AccountOperator

➤ Administrator

➤ BackupOperator

➤ Guest

➤ PowerUser

➤ PrintOperator

➤ Replicator

➤ SystemOperator

➤ User

Using `System.Security.Principal`, you have access to the `WindowsIdentity` object, which is much richer than working with the default `Identity` object. Listing 20-18 lists some of the additional information you can get through the `WindowsIdentity` object.

LISTING 20-18: Using the WindowsIdentity object

VB

```
<%@ Page Language="VB" %>
<%@ Import Namespace="System.Security.Principal" %>

<script runat="server">
    Protected Sub Page_Load(ByVal sender As Object, _
      ByVal e As System.EventArgs)

        Dim AuthUser As WindowsIdentity = WindowsIdentity.GetCurrent()
        Response.Write(AuthUser.AuthenticationType.ToString() & "<br>" &
            AuthUser.ImpersonationLevel.ToString() & "<br>" &
            AuthUser.IsAnonymous.ToString() & "<br>" &
            AuthUser.IsAuthenticated.ToString() & "<br>" &
            AuthUser.IsGuest.ToString() & "<br>" &
            AuthUser.IsSystem.ToString() & "<br>" &
            AuthUser.Name.ToString())
    End Sub
</script>
```

C#

```
<%@ Page Language="C#" %>
<%@ Import Namespace="System.Security.Principal" %>

<script runat="server">
    protected void Page_Load(object sender, EventArgs e)
    {
        WindowsIdentity AuthUser = WindowsIdentity.GetCurrent();
        Response.Write(AuthUser.AuthenticationType.ToString() + "<br>" +
            AuthUser.ImpersonationLevel.ToString() + "<br>" +
            AuthUser.IsAnonymous.ToString() + "<br>" +
            AuthUser.IsAuthenticated.ToString() + "<br>" +
            AuthUser.IsGuest.ToString() + "<br>" +
            AuthUser.IsSystem.ToString() + "<br>" +
            AuthUser.Name.ToString());
    }
</script>
```

In this example, an instance of the `WindowsIdentity` object is created and populated with the current identity of the user accessing the application. Then you have access to a number of properties that are written to the browser using a `Response.Write()` statement. The displayed listing shows information about the current user's credentials, such as whether the user is authenticated, anonymous, or running under a guest account or a system account (like the one for the application pool used). It also gives you the user's authentication type and login name. Figure 20-12 shows a result.

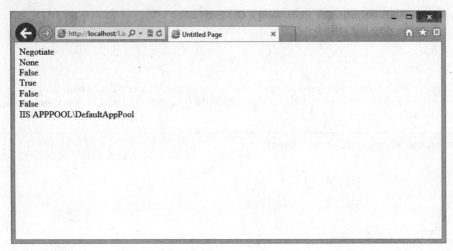

FIGURE 20-12

IDENTITY AND IMPERSONATION

By default, ASP.NET runs under an account that has limited privileges. For example, you might find that although the account can gain access to a network, it cannot be authenticated to any other computer on the network.

The account setting is provided in the machine.config file:

```
<processModel
  enable="true"
  userName="machine"
  password="AutoGenerate" />
```

These settings force ASP.NET to run under the system account (ASP.NET or Network Service). This is really specified through the userName attribute that contains a value of machine. The other possible value you can have for this attribute is system. Here's what each entails:

➤ machine: The most secure setting. You should have good reasons to change this value. It's the ideal choice mainly because it forces the ASP.NET account to run under the fewest number of privileges possible.

➤ system: Forces ASP.NET to run under the local SYSTEM account, which has considerably more privileges to access networking and files.

Specifying an account of your choosing using the <processModel> element in either the machine.config or web.config files is also possible:

```
<processModel
  enable="true"
  userName="MySpecifiedUser"
  password="MyPassword" />
```

In this example, ASP.NET runs under a specified administrator or user account instead of the default ASP.NET or Network Service account. It inherits all the privileges this account offers. You should consider encrypting this section of the file. Chapter 28 covers encrypting sections of a configuration file.

You can also change how ASP.NET behaves in whatever account it is specified to run under through the <identity> element in the web.config file. The <identity> element in the web.config file allows you to turn on *impersonation*. Impersonation provides ASP.NET with the capability to run as a process using the privileges of another user for a specific session. In more detail, impersonation allows ASP.NET to run under the account of the entity making the request to the application. To turn on this impersonation capability, you use the impersonate attribute in the <identity> element, as shown here:

```
<configuration>
   <system.web>
      <identity impersonate="true" />
   </system.web>
</configuration>
```

By default, the `impersonate` attribute is set to `False`. Setting this property to `True` ensures that ASP.NET runs under the account of the person making the request to the application. If the requestor is an anonymous user, ASP.NET runs under the `IUSR_MachineName` account. To see this in action, run the example shown in Listing 20-18, but this time with impersonation turned on (`True`). Instead of getting a username of `IIS APPPOOL\DefaultAppPool` as the user, you get the name of the user who is requesting the page—`Win8Pro-EN\Christian` in this example—as shown in Figure 20-13. Of course, this requires that the user has permissions to access the ASP.NET file.

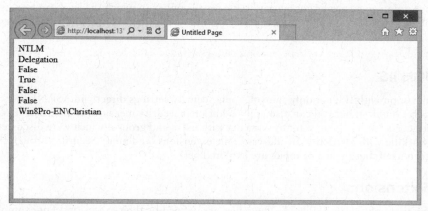

FIGURE 20-13

> **NOTE** *You may need to use the following* `web.config` *setting so that the web server accepts the new impersonation setting:*

```
<system.webServer>
   <validation validateIntegratedModeConfiguration="false" />
</system.webServer>
```

You also have the option of running ASP.NET under a specified account that you declare using the `<identity>` element in the `web.config` file:

```
<identity impersonate="true" userName="MySpecifiedUser" password="MyPassword"/>
```

As shown, you can run the ASP.NET process under an account that you specify through the `userName` and `password` attributes. These values are stored as clear text in the `web.config` file.

Look at the root `web.config` file, and you can see that ASP.NET runs under full trust, meaning that it has some rather high-level capabilities to run and access resources. Here is the setting:

```
<system.web>

   <location allowOverride="true">
      <system.web>
         <securityPolicy>
            <trustLevel name="Full" policyFile="internal"/>
```

```
                    <trustLevel name="High" policyFile="web_hightrust.config"/>
                    <trustLevel name="Medium" policyFile="web_mediumtrust.config"/>
                    <trustLevel name="Low" policyFile="web_lowtrust.config"/>
                    <trustLevel name="Minimal" policyFile="web_minimaltrust.config"/>
                </securityPolicy>
                <trust level="Full" originUrl=""/>
                <fullTrustAssemblies />
                <partialTrustVisibleAssemblies />
            </system.web>
        </location>

    </system.web>
```

Five possible settings exist for the level of trust that you give ASP.NET—`Full`, `High`, `Medium`, `Low`, and `Minimal`. You specify the level of trust applied through the `<trust>` element's `level` attribute. By default, it is set to `Full`. Each one points to a specific configuration file for the policy in which the level can find its trust level settings. The `Full` setting does not include a policy file because it simply skips all the code access security checks.

SECURING THROUGH IIS

ASP.NET works in conjunction with IIS; not only can you apply security settings directly in ASP.NET (through code or configuration files), but you can also apply additional security measures in IIS itself. IIS enables you to apply the access methods you want by working with users and groups (which were discussed earlier in the chapter), working with restricting IP addresses, file extensions, and more. Security through IIS is deserving of a chapter in itself, but the major topics are explored here.

Working with File Extensions

You can work with many types of files in ASP.NET. These files are defined by their extensions. For example, you know that `.aspx` is a typical ASP.NET page, and `.asmx` is an ASP.NET web service file extension. These files are mapped by IIS to the ASP.NET DLL, `aspnet_isapi.dll`.

If you are working with Windows 7 or higher, you can map file extensions to handlers through the IIS Manager. In this tool, select Handler Mappings in the IIS section. You will find a large list of mappings that have already been provided, as illustrated in Figure 20-14.

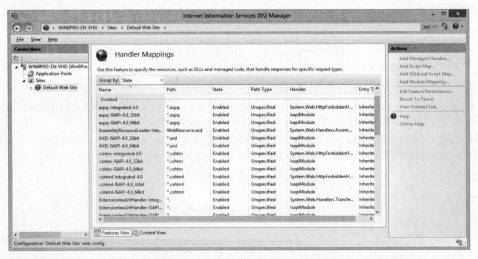

FIGURE 20-14

By highlighting the first `*.aspx` option and clicking the Edit button, you see that this extension is mapped to the handler `System.Web.UI.PageHandlerFactory`, as shown in Figure 20-15.

Clicking the Request Restrictions button provides a window that enables you to select the verbs allowed (as shown in Figure 20-16).

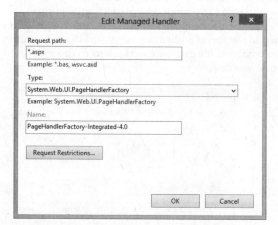

FIGURE 20-15

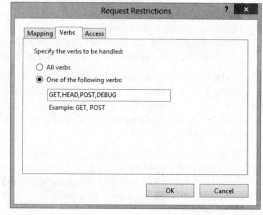

FIGURE 20-16

To achieve a similar result in IIS 6.0, pull up the Properties window of your web application in IIS or pull up the default website properties. In a specific web application, you must work from the Directory tab; but if you are working with the Default Web Site Properties window, you can instead use the Home Directory tab. From these tabs, click the Configuration button in the Application Settings box. The Application Configuration window includes a Mappings tab, where the mappings are configured. Highlight `.aspx` in the list of mappings and click the Edit button. Figure 20-17 shows the result.

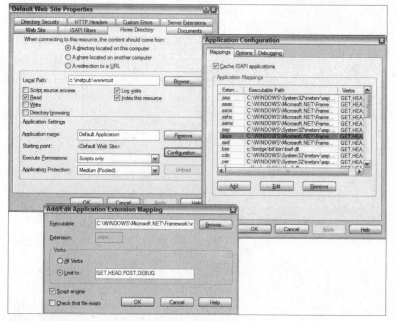

FIGURE 20-17

In the Executable textbox, you can see that all .aspx pages map to the aspnet_isapi.dll from ASP.NET, and that you can also specify which types of requests are allowed in the application. You can either allow all verbs (for example, GET or POST) or specify which verbs are allowed access to the application.

One important point regarding these mappings is that you do not see .html, .htm, .jpg, or other file extensions such as .txt in the list. Your application will not be passing requests for these files to ASP.NET. That might not be a big deal, but in working through the various security examples in this chapter, you might want to have the same type of security measures applied to these files as to .aspx pages. If, for example, you want all .html pages to be included in the forms authentication model that you require for your ASP.NET application, you must add .html (or whatever file extension you want) to the list. To do so, click the Add button in the Application Configuration window.

In the next window, you can add the ASP.NET DLL to the Executable textbox, and the appropriate file extension and verbs to the list, before adding the mapping to your application's mapping table. Figure 20-18 illustrates this example.

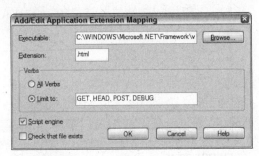

When dealing with the security of your site, you have to remember all the files that might not be included in the default mapping list and add the ones you think should fall under the same security structure.

FIGURE 20-18

Using the IIS 7.x/8 Manager

The tool to make the same site modifications in IIS 7, 7.5, and 8, is the Internet Information Services (IIS) Manager, as shown in Figure 20-19.

After making any changes through this window, you can select the Apply Changes link in the Actions pane, and it will notify you if the changes made have been saved. When you are successful, the changes made are applied to the site's web.config file.

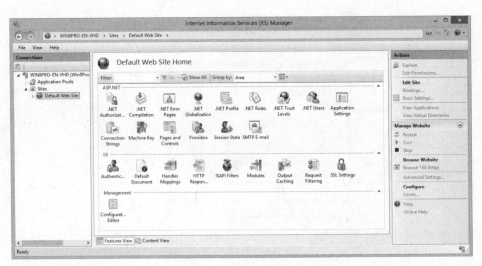

FIGURE 20-19

Using the ASP.NET MMC Snap-In

In older versions of IIS than 7, there was no IIS Manager yet; however the ASP.NET MMC console enables you to edit the `web.config` and `machine.config` files using an easy-to-use GUI instead of having to dig through the text of those files yourself to make the necessary changes. You can also modify and change most of the items examined in this book using this window. The plug-in is available on the ASP.NET tab (see Figure 20-20) of your web application running under IIS.

When you make the changes directly in the window, you are also making the hardcoded changes to the actual configuration files.

Click the Edit Configuration button on the ASP.NET tab, and the ASP.NET Configuration Settings window opens. There, you can modify how your forms authentication model works in the GUI without going to the application's `web.config` file directly. Figure 20-21 shows an example of working with forms authentication in the GUI.

FIGURE 20-20

SUMMARY

This chapter covered some of the foundation items of ASP.NET security and showed you how to apply both authentication and authorization to your web applications. It reviewed some of the various authentication and authorization models at your disposal, such as Basic, Digest, and Windows Integrated Authentication. Other topics included forms-based authentication and how to construct your own forms-based authentication models outside of the ones provided via ASP.NET 4.5 by using the membership and role management capabilities it provides. The chapter also discussed how to use authentication properties within your applications and how to authorize users and groups based on those properties. This chapter also took a look at securing your applications through IIS.

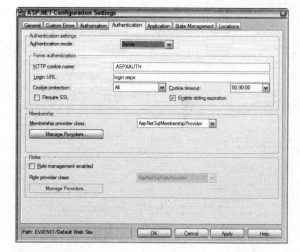

FIGURE 20-21

PART VI
Application State

21

State Management

WHAT'S IN THIS CHAPTER?

➤ Using the Session object

➤ Utilizing other options for controlling state

WROX.COM CODE DOWNLOADS FOR THIS CHAPTER

Please note that all the code examples in this chapter are available as a part of this chapter's code download on the book's website at www.wrox.com.

HTTP is a stateless protocol, so it cannot remember things. Many current web applications have to maintain state, though: They need to remember the logged-in user, the contents of the shopping cart, and more.

Before the web became popular, standard client-server architecture meant using a fat client and a fat server. Perhaps your desktop application could talk to a database. The state was held either on the client-side in memory, or in the server-side database. Typically, you could count on a client having a little bit of memory and a hard drive of its own to manage state. The most important aspect of traditional client/server design, however, was that the client was *always* connected to the server. It's easy to forget, but HTTP is a stateless protocol. For the most part, a connection is built up and torn down each time a call is made to a remote server. Yes, HTTP 1.1 includes a keep-alive technique that provides optimizations at the TCP level. Even with these optimizations, the server has no way to determine that subsequent connections came from the same client.

ASP.NET's session management support provides an easy API to store data during a session; the whole "heavy lifting" is done by the framework, so we do not have to worry about it. But there is more — this chapter will present several state management techniques so that you can pick the one that suits your needs best.

YOUR SESSION STATE CHOICES

Given a stateless protocol such as HTTP, and ASP.NET on the server side, how do you manage state on the web? Figure 21-1 is a generalized diagram that identifies the primary means available for managing state. The problem is huge, and the solution range is even larger. This chapter assumes that you are not using Java applets or ActiveX controls to manage state, because these techniques do not work on all systems.

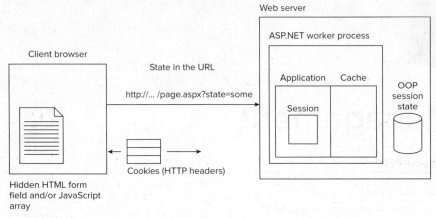

FIGURE 21-1

If you remember one thing about state management, remember this: There is no right answer. Some answers are more right than others, certainly; but many, many ways exist for managing state. Think about your last project. How many days did you spend trying to decide where you should manage state? The trick is to truly understand the pros and cons of each method.

To make an educated decision about a method, you should understand the lifecycle of a request and the opportunities for state management at each point in the process:

1. A web browser makes an `HTTP GET` request for a page on your server, `http://myserver/myapp/ mypage.aspx`. This client web browser has *never* visited your site before.

2. IIS and your ASP.NET application respond by returning HTML rendered by `mypage.aspx`. Additionally, `mypage.aspx` returns a cookie with a unique ID to track this web browser. Remember that a cookie is actually a slightly abstract concept. The cookie is set by returning a Set-Cookie HTTP header to the client. The client then promises to return the values of the cookie in every subsequent HTTP call in the HTTP header. The *state* in this example is an agreement between the client and server to bounce the cookie back and forth on every request in response.

3. The HTML that is returned may contain hidden textboxes such as `<input type="hidden" value="somestate" />`. These textboxes are similar to cookies because they are passed back to the server if the form on this page is submitted. Cookies are set per domain; hidden form fields are set per page.

4. Upon the next request, the previously set cookies are returned to the server. If this request was the submission of the form as an `HTTP POST`, all fields in the form are returned—hidden or otherwise.

5. The unique identifier that was set earlier as a cookie can now be used as a key into any kind of server-side state mechanism. That state might be as simple as an in-memory hashtable, or as complicated as a SQL database.

One of the repeating themes you might notice is the agreement between the client and the server to pass information back and forth. That information can be in the URL, in HTTP headers, or even in the submitted form as an input field.

On the server side, you have a few options. You will want to weigh the options based on the amount of storage you have available, the amount of data you want to store, and how often and how fast you will require access to the data.

Tables 21-1 and 21-2 express each of the server-side and client-side options and list a few pros and cons for each.

TABLE 21-1

SERVER-SIDE OPTION	PROS	CONS
Application State	Fast. Shared among all users.	State is stored once per server.
Cache Object (Application Scope)	Like the Application State but includes expiration via dependencies (see Chapter 22 on caching).	State is stored once per server in multiple server configurations.
Session State	Three choices: in process, out of process, and DB-backed. Can be configured as cookieless.	Can be abused. You pay a serialization cost when objects leave the process. In process requires web server affinity. Cookieless configuration makes hijacking easier.
Custom Database	State can be accessed by any server in a web farm.	Pay a serialization and persistence cost when objects leave the process.

On the client side, every option costs you in bandwidth. Each option involves passing data back and forth from client to server. Every byte of data you store will be paid for twice: once when it is passed to the server and once when it is passed back.

TABLE 21-2

CLIENT-SIDE OPTION	PROS	CONS
Cookie	Simple	Can be rejected by browser. Not appropriate for large amounts of data. Inappropriate for sensitive data. Size cost is paid on every HTTP request and response.
Hidden Field	Simple for page-scoped data	Not appropriate for large amounts of data. Inappropriate for sensitive data.
ViewState	Simple for page-scoped data	Encoding of serialized object as binary Base64-encoded data adds approximately 30 percent overhead. Small serialization cost. Has a negative reputation, particularly with DataGrids.
ControlState	Simple for page-scoped control-specific data	Like ViewState, but used for controls that require ViewState even if the developer has turned it off.
QueryString (URL)	Incredibly simple and often convenient if you want your URLs to be modified directly by the end user	Comparatively complex. Can't hold a lot of information. Inappropriate for sensitive data. Easily modified by the end user.
HTML5 Web Storage	Simple API to store name-value pairs	Data is never automatically sent to the server, so mostly used for client logic only.

These tables provide you with some of the server-side and client-side options. Chapter 22 covers the improvements to caching in ASP.NET 4.x.

UNDERSTANDING THE SESSION OBJECT IN ASP.NET

In classic ASP, the `Session` object was held in-process (as was everything) to the IIS process. The user received a cookie with a unique key in the form of a GUID. The session key was an index into a dictionary where object references could be stored.

In all versions of ASP.NET the `Session` object offers an in-process option, but also includes an out-of-process and a database-backed option. Additionally, the developer has the option to enable a *cookieless* session state where the session key appears in the URL rather than being sent as a cookie.

Sessions and the Event Model

The `HttpApplication` object raises a series of events during the life of the HTTP protocol request; this section mentions all of them, but only provides more details on those events that are related to sessions:

➤   `BeginRequest`

➤   `AuthenticateRequest`

➤   `AuthorizeRequest`

➤   `ResolveRequestCache`

➤   `AcquireRequestState`: This event indicates that all session state associated with this HTTP request is about to be acquired.

> **NOTE** *Session state is available to you, the developer, after the* `AcquireRequestState` *event fires. The session state key that is unique to each user is retrieved either from a cookie or from the URL.*

➤   `PreRequestHandlerExecute`

➤   `PostRequestHandlerExecute`

➤   `ReleaseRequestState`: Indicates that the session state should be stored. Session state is persisted at this point, using whatever session-state module is configured in `web.config`.

➤   `UpdateRequestCache`

➤   `EndRequest`

By the time your application code executes, the `Session` object has been populated using the session key that was present in the cookie or, as you see later, from the URL. If you want to handle some processing at the time the session begins, rather than handling it in `AcquireRequestState`, you can define an event handler for the `Start` event of a session state HttpModule.

```
void Session_OnStart() {
    'this fires after session state has been acquired by the SessionStateModule.
}
```

> **WARNING** *The* `Session` *object includes both* `Start` *and* `End` *events that you can hook event handlers to for your own needs. However, the* `Session_OnEnd` *event is supported only in the in-process session state mode. This event will not be raised if you use out-of-process state server or SQL Server modes. The session ends, but your handlers will never hear about it.*

The `HttpSessionState` object can be used within any event in a subclass of the `Page` object. The pages you create in ASP.NET derive from `System.Web.UI.Page`, and you can access session state as a collection because `System.Web.SessionState.HttpSessionState` implements `ICollection`.

The `Page` has a public property aptly named `Session` that automatically retrieves the `Session` from the current `HttpContext`. Even though it seems as if the `Session` object lives inside the page, it actually lives in the `HttpContext`, and the page's public `Session` property actually retrieves the reference to the session state. This convenience not only makes it more comfortable for the classic ASP programmer, but saves you a little typing as well.

The `Session` object can be referred to within a page in this way:

```
Session["SomeSessionState"] = "Here is some data";
```

or

```
HttpContext.Current.Session["SomeSessionState"] = "Here is some data";
```

The fact that the `Session` object actually lives in the current HTTP context is more than just a piece of trivia. This knowledge enables you to access the `Session` object in contexts other than the page (such as in your own `HttpHandler`).

Configuring Session State Management

All the code within a page refers to the `Session` object using the dictionary-style syntax seen previously, but the `HttpSessionState` object uses a provider pattern to extract possible choices for session state storage. You can choose between the included providers by changing the `sessionState` element in the `web.config` file. ASP.NET ships with the following three storage providers:

➤ **In-Process Session State Store:** Stores sessions in the ASP.NET in-memory cache

➤ **Out-of-Process Session State Store:** Stores sessions in the ASP.NET state server service `aspnet_state.exe`

➤ **Sql Session State Store:** Stores sessions in Microsoft SQL Server database and is configured with `aspnet_regsql.exe`

The format of the `web.config` file's `sessionState` element is shown in the following code:

```
<configuration>
    <system.web>
        <sessionState mode="Off|InProc|StateServer|SQLServer|Custom" ../>
    </system.web>
```

Begin configuring session state by setting the `mode="InProc"` attribute of the `sessionState` element in the `web.config` file of a new website. This is the most common configuration for session state within ASP.NET and is also the fastest, as you see next.

In-Process Session State

When the configuration is set to `InProc`, session data is stored in the `HttpRuntime`'s internal cache in an implementation of `ISessionStateItemCollection` that implements `ICollection`. The session state key is a 120-bit value string that indexes this global dictionary of object references. When session state is in process, objects are stored as live references. This mechanism is incredibly fast because no serialization occurs, nor do objects leave the process space. Certainly, your objects are not garbage-collected if they exist in the `In-Process Session` object because a reference is still being held.

Additionally, because the objects are stored (held) in memory, they use up memory until that session times out. If a user visits your site and hits one page, he might cause you to store a 50MB `XmlDocument` object in an in-process session. If that user never comes back, you are left sitting on that large chunk of memory for the next 20 minutes or so (a configurable value) until the session ends.

InProc Gotchas

Although the InProc session model is the fastest, the default, and the most common, it does have a significant limitation. If the worker process or application domain recycles, all session state data is lost. In addition, the ASP.NET application may restart for a number of reasons, such as the following:

➤ You have changed the `web.config` or `Global.asax` file or "touched" it by changing its modified date.

➤ You have modified files in the `\bin` or `\App_Code` directory.

➤ The `processModel` element has been set in the `web.config` or `machine.config` file indicating when the application should restart. Conditions that could generate a restart might be a memory limit or request-queue limit.

➤ Antivirus software modifies any of the previously mentioned files. This is particularly common with antivirus software that *inoculates* files.

This said, in-process session state works great for smaller applications that require only a single web server, or in situations where IP load balancing is returning each user to the server where his original session was created.

Now imagine that a user already has a session key, but is returned to a different machine than the one on which his session was created. In that case the target machine does not know the session key, therefore a new session is created. The basis for this new session is the session ID supplied by the user. While the session key may be the same, the target machine did not know this session before and so does not have any data associated with the session key. The new session is empty and unexpected results may occur. There is a solution, however: If `regenerateExpiredSessionId` is set to `True` in the `web.config` file, a new session ID is created and assigned to the user.

Web Gardening

Web gardening is a technique for multiprocessor systems wherein multiple instances of the ASP.NET worker process are started and assigned with processor affinity. On a larger web server with as many as four CPUs, you can have anywhere from one to four worker processes hosting ASP.NET. *Processor affinity* means literally that an ASP.NET worker process has an affinity for a particular CPU. It's "pinned" to that CPU. This technique is usually enabled only in very large web farms.

Do not forget that in-process session state is just that—in-process. Even if your web application consists of only a single web server and all IP traffic is routed to that single server, you have no guarantee that each subsequent request will be served on the same processor. A web garden must follow many of the same rules that a web farm follows.

> **WARNING** *If you are using web gardening on a multiprocessor system, you must not use in-process session state or you lose sessions. In-process session state is appropriate only where there is a 1:1 ratio of applications to application domains.*

Storing Data in the Session Object

In the following simple example, in a `Button_Click` event, the content of the textbox is added to the `Session` object with a specific key. The user then clicks to go to another page within the same application, and the data from the `Session` object is retrieved and presented in the browser.

Note the use of the `<asp:HyperLink>` control. Certainly, that markup could have been hard-coded as HTML, but this small distinction will serve you well later. Additionally, the URL is relative to this site, not absolute. Watch for it to help you later in this chapter.

Listing 21-1 illustrates how simple using the `Session` object is. It behaves like any other `IDictionary` collection and allows you to store keys of type `String` associated with any kind of object. The retrieval file that's referenced is added in Listing 21-2.

LISTING 21-1: Setting values in session state

VB

```
Protected Sub Button1_Click(ByVal sender As Object, ByVal e As System.EventArgs) _
    Handles Button1.Click
    Session("mykey") = TextBox1.Text
End Sub

<html>
<head id="Head1" runat="server">
    <title>Session State</title>
</head>
<body>
    <form id="form1" runat="server">
    <div>
        <asp:TextBox ID="TextBox1" Runat="server"></asp:TextBox>
        <asp:Button ID="Button1" Runat="server" Text="Store in Session"
         OnClick="Button1_Click" />
        <br />
        <asp:HyperLink ID="HyperLink1" Runat="server"
         NavigateUrl="Listing 21-02.aspx">Next Page</asp:HyperLink>
    </div>
    </form>
</body>
</html>
```

C#

```
<%@ Page Language="C#" %>

<!DOCTYPE html>

<script runat="server">
    protected void Button1_Click(object sender, EventArgs e)
    {
        Session["mykey"] = TextBox1.Text;
    }
</script>
```

The page from Listing 21-1 renders in the browser as shown in Figure 21-2. The `Session` object is accessed as any dictionary indexed by a string key. You can also use methods like `Add()`, `Count()` and others, yet the syntax above is the most common one.

More details about the page and the `Session` object can be displayed to the developer if page tracing is enabled. You add this element to your application's `web.config` file inside the `<system.web>` element, as follows:

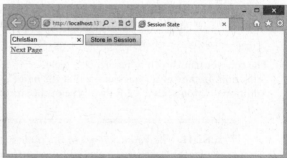

FIGURE 21-2

```
<trace enabled="true" pageOutput="true" />
```

Now tracing is enabled, and the tracing output is sent directly to the page. More details on tracing and debugging are given in Chapter 29. For now, make this change and refresh your browser.

In Figure 21-3, the screenshot is split by a diagonal line across the screenshot to show both the top and roughly the middle of the large amount of trace information that is returned when trace is enabled. Session state is very much baked into the fabric of ASP.NET. You can see in the Request Details section of the trace that not only was this page the result of an HTTP GET but the session ID was as well—elevated to the status of first-class citizen. However, the ASP.NET session ID lives as a cookie by default, as you can see in the Cookies collection at the bottom of the figure.

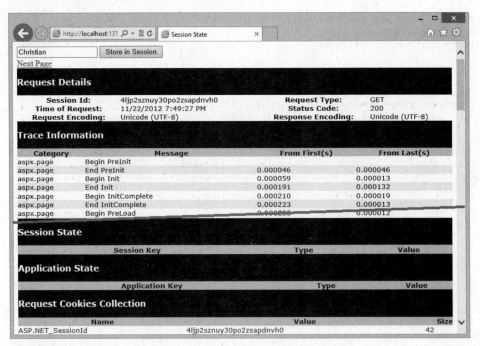

FIGURE 21-3

The default name for that cookie is ASP.NET_SessionId, but its name can be configured via the cookieName attribute of the <sessionState> element in the web.config file. Some large enterprises allow only certain named cookies past their proxies, so you might need to change this value when working on an extranet or a network with a gateway server; but this would be a very rare occurrence. The cookieName is changed to use the name "Foo" in the following example:

```
<sessionState cookieName="Foo" mode="InProc" />
```

The trace output shown in Figure 21-3 includes a section listing the contents of the Session State collection. In the figure, you can see that the name mykey and the value Hanselman are currently stored. Additionally, you see the CLR data type of the stored value; in this case, it's System.String.

> **NOTE** *The Value column of the trace output comes from a call to the contained object's* ToString() *method. If you store your own objects in the session, you can override* ToString() *to provide a text-friendly representation of your object that might make the trace results more useful.*

Now add the next page, which pulls this value out of the session. Create a new ASP.NET page, add a label, and then add a Page_Load event handler, as shown in Listing 21-2.

LISTING 21-2: Retrieving values from the session

VB

```
Protected Sub Page_Load(ByVal sender As Object, ByVal e As System.EventArgs) _
    Handles Me.Load
    Dim myValue As String = CType(Session("mykey"), String)
    Label1.Text = myValue
End Sub

<!DOCTYPE html>

<html>
<head id="Head1" runat="server">
    <title>Untitled Page</title>
</head>
<body>
    <form id="form1" runat="server">
    <div>
        <asp:Label ID="Label1" runat="server" />
    </div>
    </form>
</body>
</html>
```

C#

```
<%@ Page Language="C#" %>

<script runat="server">
    protected void Page_Load(object sender, EventArgs e)
    {
        string myValue = (string)Session["mykey"];
        Label1.Text = myValue;
    }
</script>
```

Because the session contains object references, the resulting object is converted to a string by way of a cast in C# or the `CType` or `CStr` function in VB.

Making Sessions Transparent

It is unfortunate that you can't store and retrieve values of a specific data type in the Session object without using any type casting syntax, since everything is getting stored as an object. Combined with the string key used as an index, it makes for a fairly weak contract between the page and the `Session` object. You can create a session helper that is specific to your application to hide these details, or you can add properties to a base `Page` class that presents these objects to your pages in a friendlier way. Because the generic `Session` object is available as a property on `System.Web.UI.Page`, add a new class derived from `Page` that exposes a new property named `MyKey`.

Start by right-clicking your project and selecting Add New Item from the context menu to create a new class. Name it `SmartSessionPage` and click OK. The IDE may tell you that it would like to put this new class in the `App_Code` folder to make it available to the whole application. Click Yes.

Your new base page is very simple. Via derivation, it does everything that `System.Web.UI.Page` does, plus it has a new property, as shown in Listing 21-3 (code file `SmartSessionPage.cs` and `SmartSessionPage.vb`).

LISTING 21-3: A more session-aware base page

VB

```vb
Imports Microsoft.VisualBasic
Imports System
Imports System.Web

Public Class SmartSessionPage
    Inherits System.Web.UI.Page

    Private Const MYSESSIONKEY As String = "mykey"
    Public Property MyKey() As String
        Get
            Return CType(Session(MYSESSIONKEY), String)
        End Get
        Set(ByVal value As String)
            Session(MYSESSIONKEY) = value
        End Set
    End Property
End Class
```

C#

```csharp
using System;
using System.Web;

public class SmartSessionPage : System.Web.UI.Page
{
    private const string MYKEY = "mykey";
    public string MyKey
    {
        get
        {
            return (string)Session[MYKEY];
        }
        set
        {
            Session[MYKEY] = value;
        }
    }
}
```

Now, return to your code from Listing 21-1 and derive your pages from this new base class. To do this, change the base class to inherit from SmartSessionPage. Listing 21-4 shows how the page derives from the SmartSessionPage, which in turn derives from System.Web.UI.Page. Listing 21-4 outlines the changes to make to Listing 21-1.

LISTING 21-4: Deriving from the new base page

VB

```vb
<%@ Page Language="VB" Inherits="SmartSessionPage" %>

Partial Class _Default
    Inherits SmartSessionPage

    Protected Sub Button1_Click(ByVal sender As Object, ByVal e As System.EventArgs)

        ' Session("mykey") = TextBox1.Text
        MyKey = TextBox1.Text
```

```
        End Sub
    End Class
```

C#

```
<%@ Page Language="C#" Inherits="SmartSessionPage" %>

<script runat="server">
    protected void Button1_Click(object sender, EventArgs e)
    {
        //Session["mykey"] = TextBox1.Text;
        MyKey = TextBox1.Text;
    }
</script>
```

In this code, you change the access to the Session object so it uses the new public property. After the changes in Listing 21-3, all derived pages have a public property called MyKey. This property can be used without any concern about casting or session key indexes. Additional specific properties can be added as other objects are included in the session.

> **NOTE** *Here is an interesting language note: In Listing 21-3 the name of the private string value collides with the public property in VB because they differ only in case. In C#, a private variable named* MYKEY *and a public property named* MyKey *are both acceptable. Be aware of things like this when creating APIs that will be used with multiple languages. Aim for CLS compliance.*

Advanced Techniques for Optimizing Session Performance

By default, all pages have write access to the Session. Because it's possible that more than one page from the same browser client might be requested at the same time (using frames, more than one browser window on the same machine, and so on), a page holds a reader/writer lock on the same session for the duration of the page request. If a page has a writer lock on the same session, all other pages requested in the same session must wait until the first request finishes. To be clear, the session is locked only for that session ID. These locks do not affect other users with different sessions.

In order to get the best performance out of your pages that use session, ASP.NET allows you to declare exactly what your page requires of the Session object via the EnableSessionState @Page attribute. The options are True, False, or ReadOnly:

➤ EnableSessionState="True": The page requires read and write access to the session. The session with that session ID will be locked during each request.

➤ EnableSessionState="False": The page does not require access to the Session. If the code uses the Session object anyway, an HttpException is thrown, stopping page execution.

➤ EnableSessionState="ReadOnly": The page requires read-only access to the session. A reader lock is held on the session for each request, but concurrent reads from other pages can occur. The order in which locks are requested is essential. As soon as a writer lock is requested, even before a thread is granted access, all subsequent reader lock requests are blocked, regardless of whether a reader lock is currently held. Although ASP.NET can obviously handle multiple requests, only one request at a time gets write access to a session. By setting the session state to ReadOnly, multiple requests may access the session at the same time.

By modifying the @Page direction to reflect each page's actual need, you affect performance when the site is under load. Add the EnableSessionState attribute to the pages, as shown in the following code:

```
<%@ Page Language="VB" EnableSessionState="True" %>
<%@ Page Language="C#" EnableSessionState="ReadOnly" %>
```

Under the covers, ASP.NET is using marker interfaces from the `System.Web.SessionState` namespace to keep track of each page's needs. When the partial class for `Default.aspx` is generated, it implements the `IRequiresSessionState` interface, whereas `Retrieve.aspx` implements `IReadOnlySessionState`. All `HttpRequests` are handled by objects that implement `IHttpHandler`. Pages are handled by a `PageHandlerFactory`. You can find more on `HttpHandlers` in Chapter 30. Internally, the `SessionStateModule` is executing code similar to the pseudo-code that follows:

```
If TypeOf HttpContext.Current.Handler Is IReadOnlySessionState Then
    Return SessionStateStore.GetItem(itemKey)
ElseIf TypeOf HttpContext.Current.Handler Is IRequiresSessionState
    Return SessionStateStore.GetItemExclusive(itemKey)
End If
```

As the programmer, you know things about the intent of your pages at compile time that ASP.NET cannot figure out at run time. By including the `EnableSessionState` attribute in your pages, you allow ASP.NET to operate more efficiently. Remember, ASP.NET always makes the most conservative decision unless you give it more information to act upon.

> **NOTE** *Performance Tip: If you are coding a page that doesn't require anything of the session, by all means, set* `EnableSessionState="False"`. *This causes ASP.NET to schedule that page ahead of pages that require* `Session` *and helps with the overall scalability of your app. Additionally, if your application doesn't use* `Session` *at all, set* `Mode="Off"` *in your* `web.config` *file to reduce overhead for the entire application.*

Out-of-Process Session State

Out-of-process session state is held in a process called `aspnet_state.exe` that runs as a Windows Service. You can start the ASP.NET state service by using the Services MMC snap-in or by running the following `net` command from an administrative command line:

```
net start aspnet_state
```

By default, the state service listens on TCP port 42424, but this port can be changed at the registry key for the service, as shown in the following code. The state service is not started by default.

```
HKEY_LOCAL_MACHINE\SYSTEM\CurrentControlSet\Services\aspnet_state\Parameters\Port
```

Change the `web.config` file's settings from `InProc` to `StateServer`, as shown in the following code. Additionally, you must include the `stateConnectionString` attribute with the IP address and port on which the session state service is running. In a web farm (a group of more than one web server), you could run the state service on any single server or on a separate machine entirely. In this example, the state server is running on the local machine, so the IP address is the localhost IP 127.0.0.1. If you run the state server on another machine, make sure the appropriate port is open—in this case, TCP port 42424.

```
<configuration>
    <system.web>
        <sessionState mode="StateServer"
            stateConnectionString="tcpip=127.0.0.1:42424"/>
    </system.web>
</configuration>
```

The state service used is always the most recent one installed with ASP.NET. That means that if you are running ASP.NET 2.0/3.5/4 or 4.5 and 1.1 on the same machine, all the states stored in `Session` objects for any and all versions of ASP.NET are kept together in a single instance of the ASP.NET state service, and the service used for handling sessions belongs to the latest version of ASP.NET.

Because your application's code runs in the ASP.NET worker process (`aspnet_wp.exe`, or `w3wp.exe`) and the state service runs in the separate `aspnet_state.exe` process, objects stored in the session cannot be stored as references. Your objects must physically leave the worker process via binary serialization.

> **NOTE** *For a world-class, highly available, and scalable website, consider using a session model other than InProc. Even if you can guarantee via your load-balancing appliance that your sessions will be sticky, you still have application-recycling issues to contend with. The out-of-process state service's data is persisted across application pool recycles but not computer reboots. However, if your state is stored on a different machine entirely, it will survive web server recycles and reboots.*

Only classes that have been marked with the `[Serializable]` attribute may be serialized. In the context of the `Session` object, think of the `[Serializable]` attribute as a permission slip for instances of your class to leave the worker process. This is especially important if you have used InProc sessions before, since they do not have this requirement. So you might change your code, if you change your session state mode.

Update your `App_Code` directory to include a new class called `Person`, as shown in Listing 21-5. Be sure to mark it as `[Serializable]` or you will see the error shown in Figure 21-4.

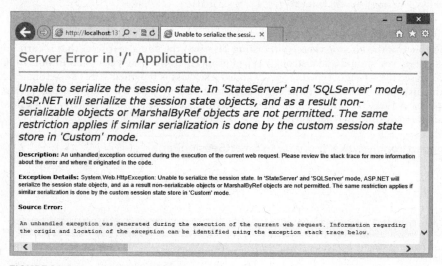

FIGURE 21-4

As long as you have marked your objects as `[Serializable]`, they will be allowed out of the ASP.NET process. Notice that the objects in Listing 21-5 (code files `Person.cs` and `Person.vb`) are marked `[Serializable]`.

LISTING 21-5: A serializable object that can be used in the out-of-process session

VB

```
Imports Microsoft.VisualBasic
Imports System
Imports System.Web

<Serializable()> _
Public Class Person
```

continues

LISTING 21-5 *(continued)*

```
      Public firstName As String
      Public lastName As String

      Public Overrides Function ToString() As String
          Return String.Format("Person Object: {0} {1}", firstName, lastName)
      End Function
  End Class
```

C#

```
using System;
using System.Web;

[Serializable]
public class Person
{
   public string firstName;
   public string lastName;

   public override string ToString()
   {
       return String.Format("Person Object: {0} {1}", firstName, lastName);
   }
}
```

Because you put an instance of the `Person` class from Listing 21-5 into the `Session` object that is currently configured as `StateServer`, you should add a strongly typed property to the base `Page` class from Listing 21-3. In Listing 21-6 you see the strongly typed property added (the class is renamed `SmartSessionPage2` to make it easily distinguishable). You can find the code for Listing 21-6 in code files `SmartSessionPage2` `.cs` and `SmartSessionPage2.vb`. Note the cast on the property `Get`, and the strongly typed return value indicating that this property deals only with objects of type `Person`.

LISTING 21-6: Adding a strongly typed property to SmartSessionPage

VB

```
Imports Microsoft.VisualBasic
Imports System
Imports System.Web

Public Class SmartSessionPage2
    Inherits System.Web.UI.Page

    Private Const MYSESSIONPERSONKEY As String = "myperson"

    Public Property MyPerson() As Person
        Get
            Return CType(Session(MYSESSIONPERSONKEY), Person)
        End Get
        Set(ByVal value As Person)
            Session(MYSESSIONPERSONKEY) = value
        End Set
    End Property
End Class
```

C#

```
using System;
using System.Web;

public class SmartSessionPage2 : System.Web.UI.Page
```

```
{
    private const string MYPERSON = "myperson";

    public Person MyPerson
    {
        get
        {
            return (Person)Session[MYPERSON];
        }
        set
        {
            Session[MYPERSON] = value;
        }
    }
}
```

Now, add code to create a new `Person`, populate its fields from the textbox, and put the instance into the now out-of-process session state service. Then, retrieve the `Person` and write its values out to the browser using the overloaded `ToString()` method from Listing 21-5.

> **WARNING** *Certain classes in the Framework Class Library are not marked as serializable. If you use objects of this type within your own objects, these objects are not serializable at all. For example, if you include a DataRow field in a class and add your object to the state service, you receive a message telling you it "... is not marked as serializable" because the DataRow includes objects that are not serializable.*

In Listing 21-7, the value of the `TextBox` is split into a string array and the first two strings are put into a `Person` instance. For example, if you entered `"Christian Wenz"` as a value, `"Christian"` is put into `Person .firstName` and `"Wenz"` is put into `Person.lastName`. The values you enter should appear when they are retrieved later in Listing 21-8 and written out to the browser.

LISTING 21-7: Setting objects from the session using state service and a base page

VB

```
Protected Sub Button1_Click(ByVal sender As Object, ByVal e As System.EventArgs) _
    Handles Button1.Click
    Dim names As String()
    names = TextBox1.Text.Split(" "c) ' " "c creates a char
    Dim p As New Person() With {
        .firstName = names(0),
        .lastName = names(1)
    }
    MyPerson = p
End Sub

<!DOCTYPE html>

<html>
<head id="Head1" runat="server">
    <title>Session State</title>
</head>
<body>
    <form id="form1" runat="server">
    <div>
        <asp:TextBox ID="TextBox1" Runat="server"></asp:TextBox>
```

continues

LISTING 21-7 *(continued)*

```
            <asp:Button ID="Button1" Runat="server" Text="Store in Session"
            OnClick="Button1_Click" />
            <br />
            <asp:HyperLink ID="HyperLink1" Runat="server"
            NavigateUrl="Listing 21-08.aspx">Next Page</asp:HyperLink>
        </div>
        </form>
    </body>
    </html>
```

C#

```
<%@ Page Language="C#" Inherits="SmartSessionPage2" %>

<script runat="server">
    protected void Button1_Click(object sender, EventArgs e)
    {
        string[] names = TextBox1.Text.Split(' ');
        Person p = new Person()
        {
            firstName = names[0],
            lastName = names[1]
        };
        MyPerson = p;
    }
</script>
```

LISTING 21-8: Retrieving objects from the session using state service and a base page

VB

```
<%@ Page Language="C#" Inherits="SmartSessionPage2" %>

<script runat="server">
Protected Sub Page_Load(ByVal sender As Object, ByVal e As System.EventArgs) _
    Handles Me.Load
    Dim p As Person = MyPerson
    Label1.Text = p.ToString()
End Sub
</script>

<!DOCTYPE html>

<html>
<head id="Head1" runat="server">
    <title>Untitled Page</title>
</head>
<body>
    <form id="form1" runat="server">
    <div>
        <asp:Label ID="Label1" runat="server" />
    </div>
    </form>
</body>
</html>
```

C#

```
<script runat="server">
    protected void Page_Load(object sender, EventArgs e)
    {
        Person p = MyPerson;
        Label1.Text = p.ToString();
    }
</script>
```

Now, launch the browser with Listing 21-7, enter your name, click the button to store it in the Session object, and then visit Listing 21-8 via the hyperlink. You see a result, as shown in Figure 21-5.

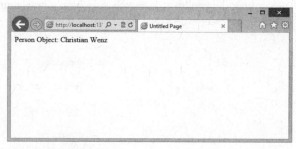

FIGURE 21-5

The completed code and techniques shown in Listings 21-7 and 21-8 illustrate a number of best practices for session management:

➤ Mark your objects as Serializable if you might ever use non-In-Proc session state.

➤ Even better, do all your development with a local session state server. This forces you to discover non-serializable objects early, gives you a sense of the performance and memory usages of aspnet_state.exe, and allows you to choose from any of the session options at deployment time.

➤ Use a base Page class or helper object with strongly typed properties to simplify your code. It enables you to hide the casts made to session keys otherwise referenced throughout your code.

These best practices apply to all state storage methods, including SQL session state (covered shortly). When using out-of-process session state, whether as described previously or using the SQL-backed session state, the objects that are stored within this state are serialized and deserialized back and forth in order for your applications to work with this type of state. Some of the objects that you are moving to be serialized into memory can be quite large.

ASP.NET 4.x includes a capability to compress the objects that are stored in an out-of-process state. This is illustrated in the following snippet of code:

```
<sessionState
  mode="SqlServer"
  sqlConnectionString="data source=dbserver;Initial Catalog=aspnetstate"
  allowCustomSqlDatabase="true"
  compressionEnabled="true"
/>
```

When compression is enabled through the use of the compressionEnabled attribute, the System.IO.Compression.GZipStream class is used for compressing the object. By default, the compressionEnabled attribute is set to False. By doing this compression, you will notice a significant difference in the amount of memory used to store your state.

SQL-Backed Session State

ASP.NET sessions can also be stored in a SQL Server database. InProc offers speed, state server offers a resilience/speed balance, and storing sessions in SQL Server offers resilience that can serve sessions to a large web farm that persists across IIS restarts, if necessary.

SQL-backed session state is configured with `aspnet_regsql.exe`. This tool adds and removes support for a number of ASP.NET features such as cache dependency (see Chapter 22) and personalization/membership (see Chapters 18 and 19), as well as session support. When you run `aspnet_regsql.exe` from the command line without any options, surprisingly, it pops up a GUI, as shown in Figure 21-6. This utility is located in the .NET Framework's installed directory, usually something like `C:\Windows\Microsoft.NET\Framework\v4.0.30319`.

The text of the dialog box shown in Figure 21-6 contains instructions to run `aspnet_regsql` from the command line with a `-?` switch. You have a huge number of options, so you will want to pipe it through in a form like `aspnet_regsql -? | more`. Here are the session state–specific options:

```
                    -- SESSION STATE OPTIONS --

    -ssadd              Add support for SQLServer mode session state.

    -ssremove           Remove support for SQLServer mode session state.

    -sstype t|p|c       Type of session state support:

                        t: temporary. Session state data is stored in the
                        "tempdb" database. Stored procedures for managing
                        session are installed in the "ASPState" database.
                        Data is not persisted if you restart SQL. (Default)

                        p: persisted. Both session state data and the stored
                        procedures are stored in the "ASPState" database.

                        c: custom. Both session state data and the stored
                        procedures are stored in a custom database. The
                        database name must be specified.

    -d <database>       The name of the custom database to use if -sstype is "c"
```

Three options exist for session state support: `t`, `p`, and `c`. The most significant difference is that the `-sstype t` option does not persist session state data across SQL Server restarts, whereas the `-sstype p` option does. Alternatively, you can specify a custom database with the `-c` option and give the database name with `-d database`.

The following command-line example configures your system for SQL session support with the SQL Server on `localhost` with an `sa` password of `wrox` and a persistent store in the ASPState database. (Certainly, you know not to deploy your system using `sa` and a weak password, but this simplifies the example. Ideally, you would use Windows Integration Authentication and give the Worker Process identity access to the ASPState database.) If you are using SQL Express, replace `localhost` with `.\SQLEXPRESS`. If you are not using Windows Authentication, you may need to explicitly enable the `sa` account from the Management Studio, run this tool, and then disable the `sa` account for security reasons.

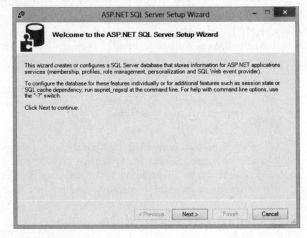

FIGURE 21-6

```
C:\>aspnet_regsql -S localhost -U sa -P wrox -ssadd -sstype p
Microsoft (R) ASP.NET SQL Registration Tool version 4.0.30319.17929
Administrative utility to install and uninstall ASP.NET features on a SQL server.
Copyright (C) Microsoft Corporation. All rights reserved.

Start adding session state.

...........

Finished.
```

When using a trusted connection (and Windows authentication), use the -E switch:

```
C:\>aspnet_regsql -S localhost -E -ssadd -sstype p
```

Next, open SQL Management Studio (or its Express version) and look at the newly created database. Two tables are created—ASPStateTempApplications and ASPStateTempSessions—as well as a series of stored procedures to support moving the session back and forth from SQL to memory.

If your SQL Server has its security locked down tight, you might get an error 15501 after executing aspnet_regsql.exe that says, "An error occurred during the execution of the SQL file 'InstallSqlState.sql'." The SQL error number is 15501 and the SqlException message is

```
This module has been marked OFF. Turn on 'Agent XPs' in order to be able to access
the module. If the job does not exist, an error from msdb.dbo.sp_delete_job
is expected.
```

This message is rather obscure, but aspnet_regsql.exe is trying to tell you that the extended stored procedures it needs to enable session state are not enabled for security reasons. You have to allow them explicitly. To do so, execute the following commands within the SQL Server Management Studio Express:

```
USE master
EXECUTE sp_configure 'show advanced options', 1
RECONFIGURE WITH OVERRIDE
GO
EXECUTE sp_configure 'Agent XPs', 1
RECONFIGURE WITH OVERRIDE
GO
EXECUTE sp_configure 'show advanced options', 0
RECONFIGURE WITH OVERRIDE
GO
```

Now, change the web.config <sessionState> element to use SQL Server, as well as the new connection string:

```
<sessionState mode="SQLServer" sqlConnectionString="data source=127.0.0.1;user
id=sa;password=Wrox"/ >
```

For a trusted connection, the connection string could look like this:

```
<sessionState mode="SQLServer"
  sqlConnectionString="data source=127.0.0.1;trusted_connection=yes"/ >
```

The session code shown in Listings 21-7 and 21-8 continues to work as before. However, if you open the ASPStateTempSessions table, you see the serialized objects. Notice in Figure 21-7 that the session ID from the trace appears as a primary key in a row in the ASPStateTempSessions table.

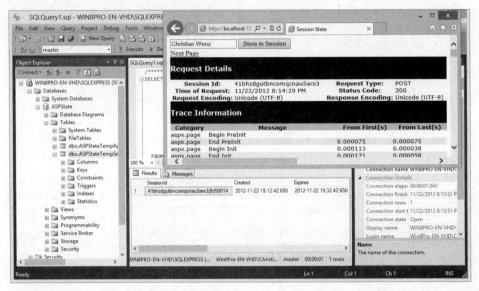

FIGURE 21-7

Figure 21-7 shows the `SessionId` as seen in the Request Details of ASP.NET tracing. That `SessionId` appears in the `SessionId` column of the `ASPStateTempSessions` table in the `ASPState` database just created. Notice also the `ASPStateTempApplications` table keeps track of each IIS application that may be using the same database to manage sessions.

If you want to use your own database to store session state, you specify the database name with the `-d <database>` switch of `aspnet_regsql.exe` and include the `allowCustomSqlDatabase="true"` attribute and the name of the database in the connection string:

```
<sessionState allowCustomSqlDatabase="true" mode="SQLServer"
    sqlConnectionString="data source=127.0.0.1; database=MyCustomASPStateDatabase;" />
```

The user ID and password can be included in the connection string; or Windows Integrated Security can be used if the ASP.NET Worker Process's identity is configured with access in SQL Server.

Extending Session State with Other Providers

ASP.NET session state is built on an extensible, provider-based storage model. You can implement custom providers that store session data in other storage mechanisms simply by deriving from `SessionStateStoreProviderBase`. This extensibility feature also allows you to generate session IDs via your own algorithms by implementing `ISessionIDManager`.

You start by creating a class that inherits from `SessionStateStoreProviderBase`. The session module will call methods on any session provider as long as it derives from `SessionStateStoreProviderBase`. Register your custom provider in your application's `web.config` file, as in the following example:

```
<sessionState mode ="Custom" customProvider ="WroxProvider">
    <providers >
        <add name="WroxProvider" type="Wrox.WroxStore, WroxSessionSupplier"/>
    </providers>
< /sessionState >
```

ASP.NET initializes the `SessionStateModule`, and these methods are called on any custom implementation:

➤ `Initialize`: This method is inherited ultimately from `System.Configuration.Provider` `.ProviderBase` and is called immediately after the constructor. With this method, you set your provider name and call up to the base implementation of `Initialize`.

➤ `SetItemExpireCallback`: With this method, you can register any methods to be called when a session item expires.

➤ `InitializeRequest`: This method is called by the `SessionStateModule` for each request. This is an early opportunity to get ready for any requests for data that are coming.

➤ `CreateNewStoreData`: With this method, you create a new instance of `SessionStateStoreData`, the data structure that holds session items, the session timeout values, and any static items.

When a session item is requested, ASP.NET calls your implementation to retrieve it. Implement the following methods to retrieve items:

➤ `GetItemExclusive`: This method enables you to get `SessionStateStoreData` from your chosen store. You may have created an Oracle provider, stored data in XML, or stored data elsewhere.

➤ `GetItem`: This is your opportunity to retrieve it as you did in `GetItemExclusive`, except without exclusive locking. You might not care, depending on what backing store you have chosen.

When it's time to store an item, the following method is called:

➤ `SetAndReleaseItemExculsive`: Here you should save the `SessionStateStoreData` object to your custom store.

> **NOTE** *ScaleOut Software released the first third-party ASP.NET State Provider in the form of their StateServer product. It fills a niche between the ASP.NET included singleton StateServer and the SQL Server Database State Provider. ScaleOut Software's StateServer is an out-of-process service that runs on each machine in the web farm and ensures that session state is stored in a transparent and distributed manner among machines in the farm. You can learn more about StateServer and its ASP.NET Session Provider at* `www.scaleoutsoftware.com`*.*

Cookieless Session State

In the previous example, the ASP.NET session state ID was stored in a cookie. Some devices do not support cookies, or a user may have turned off cookie support in her browser. Cookies are convenient because the values are passed back and forth with every request and response. That means every `HttpRequest` contains cookie values, and every `HttpResponse` contains cookie values. What is the only other thing that is passed back and forth with every `Request` and `Response`? The answer is the URL.

If you include the `cookieless="UseUri"` attribute in the `web.config` file, ASP.NET does not send the ASP.NET session ID back as a cookie. Instead, it modifies every URL to include the session ID just before the requested page:

```
<sessionState mode="SQLServer" cookieless="UseUri" sqlConnectionString="data
source=127.0.0.1;user id=sa;password=Wrox" />
```

Notice that the session ID appears in the URL as if it were a directory of its own situated between the actual website virtual directory and the page. With this change, server-side user controls such as the `HyperLink` control, used in Listing 21-1, have their properties automatically modified. The link in Listing 21-1 could have been hard-coded as HTML directly in the Designer, but then ASP.NET could not modify the target URL shown in Figure 21-8.

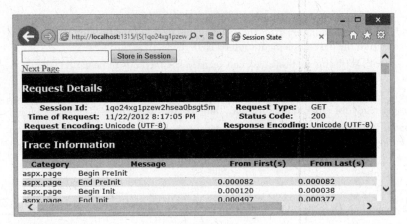

FIGURE 21-8

The session ID is a string that contains only the ASCII characters allowed in a URL. That makes sense when you realize that moving from a cookie-based session state system to a cookieless system requires putting that session state value in the URL.

Notice in Figure 21-8 that the request URL contains a session ID within parentheses. One disadvantage to cookieless sessions is how easily they can be tampered with. Certainly, cookies can be tampered with using HTTP sniffers, but URLs can be edited by anyone. The only way session state is maintained is if *every* URL includes the session ID in this way.

Additionally, all URLs *must* be relative. Remember that the session ID appears as if it were a directory. The session is lost if an absolute URL, such as `/myapp/my/file.aspx`, is invoked. If you are generating URLs on the server side, use `HttpResponse.ApplyAppPathModifier()`. It changes a URL when the session ID is embedded, as shown here:

```
Response.Write(Response.ApplyAppPathModifier("my/file.aspx"));
```

The previous line generates a URL similar to the following:

```
/myapp/(S(avkbnbml4n1n5mi5dmfqnu45))/my/file.aspx
```

Notice that not only was session information added to the URL, but it was also converted from a relative URL to an absolute URL, including the application's virtual directory. This method can be useful when you need to use `Response.Redirect` or build a URL manually to redirect from an HTTP page to an HTTPS page while still maintaining a cookieless session state.

Choosing the Correct Way to Maintain State

Now that you are familiar with the variety of options available for maintaining state in ASP.NET, here's some real-world advice from production systems. The in-process (InProc) session provider is the fastest method, of course, because everything held in memory is a live object reference. This provider is held in the `HttpApplication`'s cache and, as such, it is susceptible to application recycles. If you use Windows 2000 Server or Windows XP, the `aspnet_wp.exe` process manages the ASP.NET HTTP pipeline. If you are running a more recent version like Windows Server 2008, or 2012, or Windows 7 or 8, `w3wp.exe` is the default process that hosts the run time.

You must find a balance between the robustness of the out-of-process state service and the speed of the in-process provider. In the authors' experience, the out-of-process state service is usually about 15 percent slower than the in-process provider because of the serialization overhead and the marshaling that needs to occur. SQL session state is about 25 percent slower than InProc. Of course, your mileage will likely vary.

Do not let these numbers concern you too much. Be sure to do scalability testing on your applications before you panic and make inappropriate decisions.

> **NOTE** *It is worth saying again: We recommend that all developers use out-of-process session state during development, even if this is not the way your application will be deployed. Forcing yourself to use the out-of-process provider enables you to catch any potential problems with custom objects that do not carry the* Serializable *attribute. If you design your entire site using the in-process provider and then discover, late in the project, that requirements force you to switch to the SQL or out-of-process providers, you have no guarantee that your site will work as you wrote it. Developing with the out-of-process provider gives you the best of both worlds and does not affect your final deployment method. Think of it as an insurance policy that costs you nothing up front.*

THE APPLICATION OBJECT

The Application object is the equivalent of a bag of global variables for your ASP.NET application. Global variables have been considered harmful for many years in other programming environments, and ASP.NET is no different. You should give some thought to what you want to put in the Application object and why. Often, the more flexible Cache object that helps you control an object's lifetime is the more useful. Caching is discussed in depth in Chapter 22.

The Application object is not global to the machine; it is global to the HttpApplication. If you are running in the context of a web farm, each ASP.NET application on each web server has its own Application object. Because ASP.NET applications are multithreaded and are receiving requests that are being handled by your code on multiple threads, access to the Application object should be managed using the Application.Lock and Application.Unlock methods. If your code does not call Unlock directly (which it should, shame on you) the lock is removed implicitly at the end of the HttpRequest that called Lock originally.

This small example shows you how to lock the Application object just before inserting an object. Other threads that might be attempting to write to the Application will wait until it is unlocked. This example assumes there is an integer already stored in Application under the key GlobalCount.

VB

```
Application.Lock()
Application("GlobalCount") = CType(Application("GlobalCount"), Integer) + 1
Application.UnLock()
```

C#

```
Application.Lock();
Application["GlobalCount"] = (int)Application["GlobalCount"] + 1;
Application.UnLock();
```

Object references can be stored in the Application, as in the Session, but they must be cast back to their known types when retrieved (as shown in the preceding sample code).

QUERYSTRINGS

The URL, or QueryString, is the ideal place for navigation-specific—not user-specific—data. The QueryString is the most hackable element on a website, and that fact can work for you or against you. For example, if your navigation scheme uses your own page IDs at the end of a query string (such as /mysite/mypage.aspx?id=54) be prepared for a user to play with that URL in his browser, and try every value for id under the sun. Do not blindly cast `id` to an `int`, and if you do, have a plan if it fails. A good idea is to return `Response.StatusCode=404` when someone changes a URL to an unreasonable value. Another fine idea that `Amazon.com` implemented was the *Smart 404*. Perhaps you have seen these: They say "Sorry you didn't find what you're looking for. Did you mean _____?"

Remember, your URLs are the first thing your users may see, even before they see your HTML. *Hackable* URLs—hackable even by my mom—make your site more accessible. Which of these URLs is friendlier and more hackable (for the *right* reason)?

```
http://reviews.cnet.com/Philips_42PF9996/4505-6482_7-31081946.html?tag=cnetfd.sd
```

or

```
http://www.hanselman.com/blog/CategoryView.aspx?category=Movies
```

COOKIES

Remember when cookies were first introduced. Most users were not quite sure just what a cookie was, but they were all convinced that cookies were evil and were storing their personal information. Back then, it *was* likely that personal information was stored in the cookie! Never, ever store sensitive information, such as a user ID or password, in a cookie. Cookies should be used to store only non-sensitive information, or information that can be retrieved from an authoritative source. Cookies should not be trusted, and their contents should be able to be validated. For example, if a Forms Authentication cookie has been tampered with, the user is logged out and an exception is thrown. If an invalid session ID cookie is passed in for an expired session, a new cookie can be assigned.

When you store information in cookies (using `Response.Cookies`—reading is done using `Request.Cookies`), remember that it is quite different from storing data in the `Session` object:

➤ Cookies are passed back and forth on *every* request. That means you are paying for the size of your cookie during *every* `HTTP GET` and `HTTP POST`. If you have ten 1-pixel spacer GIFs on your page used for table layouts, the user's browser is sending the same cookie *eleven* times—once for the page itself, and once for each spacer GIF, even if the GIF is already cached.

➤ Cookies can be stolen, sniffed, and faked. If your code counts on a cookie's value, have a plan in your code for the inevitability that the cookie will be corrupted or tampered with.

➤ What is the expected behavior of your application if a cookie does not show? What if it is 4096 bytes? Be prepared. You should design your application around the "principle of least surprise." Your application should attempt to heal itself if cookies are found missing or if they are larger than expected.

➤ Think twice before Base64 encoding anything large and placing it in a cookie. If your design depends on this kind of technique, rethink using either the session or another backing-store.

POSTBACKS AND CROSS-PAGE POSTBACKS

ASP.NET uses the concept of the postback, wherein a server-side event is raised to alert the developer of a client-side action. If a button is clicked on the browser, the Form collection is POSTed back to the server, but now ASP.NET allows the developer to write code in events such as `Button1_Click()` and `TextBox1_Changed()`.

However, this technique of posting *back* to the same page is counterintuitive, especially when you are designing user interfaces that aim to create wizards to give the user the sense of forward motion.

This chapter is about all aspects of state management. Postbacks and cross-page postbacks, however, are covered extensively in Chapter 3, so this chapter touches on them only in the context of state management. Postbacks were introduced in ASP.NET 1.*x* to provide an eventing subsystem for web development. Having only single-page postbacks in 1.*x* was inconvenient, however, and that caused many developers to store small objects in the session on a postback and then redirect to the next page to pick up the stored data. With cross-page postbacks, data can be posted "forward" to a different page, often obviating the need for storing small bits of data that could otherwise be passed directly.

ASP.NET 2.0 and above includes the notion of a `PostBackUrl` to all the Button controls including LinkButton and ImageButton. The `PostBackUrl` property is both part of the markup when a control is presented as part of the ASPX page, as shown in the following code snippet, and is a property on the server-side component that is available in the code-behind:

```
<asp:Button PostBackUrl="url" ...>
```

When a button control with the `PostBackUrl` property set is clicked, the page does not post back to itself; instead, the page is posted to the URL assigned to the button control's `PostBackUrl` property. When a cross-page request occurs, the `PreviousPage` property of the current `Page` class holds a reference to the page that caused the postback. To get a control reference from the `PreviousPage`, use the `Controls` property, or use the `FindControl()` method (which requires casting), or the `@PreviousPageType` attribute.

Create a new page (as shown in Listing 21-9). Put a `TextBox` and a `Button` on it, and set the `Button` `PostBackUrl` property to `Listing 21-10.aspx`. Then create a `Listing 21-10.aspx` page with a single `Label` and add a `Page_Load` handler by double-clicking the HTML Designer. Listing 21-10 then contains the code to receive and process the postback.

LISTING 21-9: Cross-page postbacks: The sender

```
<%@ Page Language="C#" %>

<!DOCTYPE html>

<script runat="server">

</script>

<html>
<head id="Head1" runat="server">
    <title>Cross-page PostBacks</title>
</head>
<body>
    <form id="form1" runat="server">
    <div>
        <asp:TextBox ID="TextBox1" Runat="server"></asp:TextBox>
        <asp:Button ID="Button1" Runat="server" Text="Button"
            PostBackUrl="~/Listing 21-10.aspx" />
    </div>
    </form>
</body>
</html>
```

LISTING 21-10: Cross-page postbacks: The receiver

VB

```
<%@ Page Language="C#" %>

<script runat="server">
Protected Sub Page_Load(ByVal sender As Object, ByVal e As System.EventArgs) _
```

continues

LISTING 21-10 *(continued)*

```
            Handles Me.Load

        If PreviousPage IsNot Nothing AndAlso PreviousPage.IsCrossPagePostBack Then
            Dim text As TextBox = _
                    CType(PreviousPage.FindControl("TextBox1"), TextBox)
            If text IsNot Nothing Then
                Label1.Text = text.Text
            End If
        End If

    End Sub
    </script>

    <html>
    <head id="Head1" runat="server">
        <title>Step 2</title>
    </head>
    <body>
        <form id="form1" runat="server">
        <div>
            <asp:Label ID="Label1" runat="server" Text="Label"></asp:Label></div>
        </form>
    </body>
    </html>
```

C#

```
    <%@ Page Language="C#" %>

    <script runat="server">
        protected void Page_Load(object sender, EventArgs e)
        {
            if (PreviousPage != null && PreviousPage.IsCrossPagePostBack)
            {
                TextBox text = PreviousPage.FindControl("TextBox1") as TextBox;
                if (text != null)
                {
                    Label1.Text = text.Text;
                }
            }
        }
    }
    </script>
```

In Listing 21-9, the page posts *forward* to Listing 21-10, which can then access the Page.PreviousPage property and retrieve a populated instance of the Page, which caused the postback. A call to FindControl and a cast retrieves the TextBox from the previous page and copies its value into the label of Listing 21-10.

HIDDEN FIELDS, VIEWSTATE, AND CONTROLSTATE

Hidden input fields such as <input type="hidden" name="myName" /> are sent back as name/value pairs in a form POST exactly like any other control, except that they are not rendered. Think of them as hidden textboxes. Figure 21-9 shows a HiddenField control on the Visual Studio Designer with its available properties. Hidden fields are available in all versions of ASP.NET.

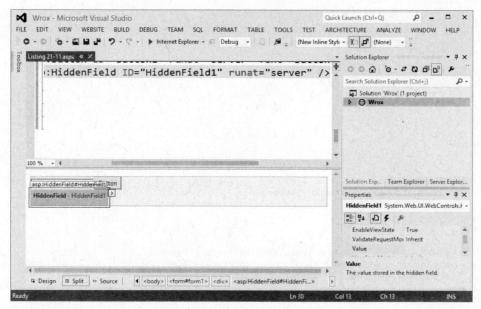

FIGURE 21-9

ViewState, on the other hand, exposes itself as a collection of key/value pairs like the `Session` object, but renders itself as a hidden field with the name "`__VIEWSTATE`" like this:

```
<input type="hidden" name="__VIEWSTATE" value="/AAASSDAS ... Y/lOI=" />
```

Any objects put into the ViewState must be marked `Serializable`. ViewState serializes the objects with a special binary formatter called the LosFormatter. LOS stands for *limited object serialization*. It serializes any kind of object, but it is optimized to contain strings, arrays, and hashtables.

To see this at work, create a new page and drag a `TextBox`, `Button`, and `HiddenField` onto it. Double-click in the Designer to create a `Page_Load` and include the code from Listing 21-11. This example adds a string to `HiddenField.Value`, but adds an instance of a `Person` to the `ViewState` collection. This listing illustrates that while ViewState is persisted in a single HTML `TextBox` on the client, it can contain both simple types such as strings, and complex types such as `Person`. This technique has been around since ASP .NET 1.*x* and continues to be a powerful and simple way to persist small pieces of data without utilizing server resources.

LISTING 21-11: Hidden fields and ViewState

VB

```
<%@ Page Language="C#" %>

<script runat="server">
Protected Sub Page_Load(ByVal sender As Object, ByVal e As System.EventArgs) _
        Handles Me.Load

    If Not Page.IsPostBack Then
        HiddenField1.Value = "value 1"
        ViewState("AnotherHiddenValue") = "value 2"

        Dim p As New Person() With {
            .firstName = "Christian",
```

continues

LISTING 21-11 *(continued)*

```
                    .lastName = "Wenz"
                }
            ViewState("HiddenPerson") = p
    End If

End Sub
</script>

<!DOCTYPE html>

<html>
<head id="Head1" runat="server">
    <title>Hidden Fields and ViewState</title>
</head>
<body>
    <form id="form1" runat="server">
        <div>
            <asp:TextBox ID="TextBox1" runat="server"></asp:TextBox>
            <asp:Button ID="Button1" runat="server" Text="Button" />
            <asp:HiddenField ID="HiddenField1" runat="server" />
        </div>
    </form>
</body>
</html>
```

C#

```
<%@ Page Language="C#" %>

<script runat="server">
    protected void Page_Load(object sender, EventArgs e)
    {
        if (!Page.IsPostBack)
        {
            HiddenField1.Value = "value 1";
            ViewState["AnotherHiddenValue"] = "value 2";

            Person p = new Person()
            {
                firstName = "Christian",
                lastName = "Wenz"
            };
            ViewState["HiddenPerson"] = p;
        }
    }
</script>
```

In Listing 21-11, a string is added to a `HiddenField` and to the `ViewState` collection. Then, a `Person` instance is added to the `ViewState` collection with another key. A fragment of the rendered HTML is shown in the following code:

```
<form method="post" action="Listing 21-11.aspx" id="form1">
<div>
<input type="hidden" name="__VIEWSTATE" id="__VIEWSTATE" value="U77CNOTJ/2LWlBwWh4u
hvq+FGDtavwu+NmR3cqXa9patotBdiioisxrbCrqe3FQqBk/rvwgCnNC2VzdUcXN+bUx3+M0wZ1oqAMCTRvZ
QqnYyc/KG+YoMTo+4httTnyCfNKYBzDwZtQQhLCOJUzRPlduaS/YYFgze3t+ORW6fnRZ/ai8Pfn4LPS+ejoV
woY71mkCO2iIHLzWjU0g7lsemPJpjVl1KN+asG8IF2rb5vvGP6RPckWZ1P6e0EMWlWKZcZaaJ9j0toeEcCYZ
SU/GwGvab1SPUSV39onQ3a+UzEG0dzmg6jqaW/tQUahBkudZpZ7dbirUqaul642Q3FIjkadibrS9zUQn/KAP
898X+lQvvYgL0IOwpf1G5Jk6Xe6++" />
```

```
        </div>
        <div>
            <input name="TextBox1" type="text" id="TextBox1" />
            <input type="submit" name="Button1" value="Button" id="Button1" />
            <input type="hidden" name="HiddenField1" id="HiddenField1" value="foo" />
        </div>
    </form>
```

Notice that the `ViewState` value uses only valid ASCII characters to represent all its contents. Do not let the sheer mass of it fool you. It is big and it appears to be opaque. However, it is just a hidden textbox and is automatically POSTed back to the server. The entire `ViewState` collection is available to you in the `Page_Load`. The value of the `HiddenField` is stored as plaintext.

Neither ViewState nor hidden fields are acceptable for any kind of sensitive data.

By default, the `ViewState` field is sent to the client with a *salted hash* to prevent tampering. Salting means that the ViewState's data has a unique value appended to it before it is encoded. As Keith Brown says, "Salt is just one ingredient to a good stew." The technique used is called HMAC, or hashed message authentication code. As shown in the following code, you can use the `<machineKey>` element of the web `.config` file to specify the `validationKey`, as well as the algorithm used to protect ViewState. This section of the file and the `decryptionKey` attribute also affect how forms authentication cookies are encrypted (see Chapter 20 for more on forms authentication).

```
<machineKey validationKey="AutoGenerate,IsolateApps"
decryptionKey="AutoGenerate,IsolateApps" validation="SHA1" / >
```

If you are running your application in a web farm, `<validationKey>` and `<decryptionKey>` have to be manually set to the same value. Otherwise, ViewState generated from one machine could be POSTed back to a machine in the farm with a different key! The keys should be 128 characters long (the maximum) and generated by random means. If you add `IsolateApps` to these values, ASP.NET generates a unique encrypted key for each application using each application's application ID.

The `validation` attribute can be set to SHA1 or MD5 to provide tamper proofing, but you can include added protection by encrypting ViewState as well. ASP.NET offers a decryption attribute that is used exclusively for specifying the encryption and decryption mechanisms for forms authentication tickets; the `validation` attribute is used exclusively for ViewState, which can now be encrypted using 3DES or AES with the key stored in the `validationKey` attribute.

With ASP.NET 4.*x*, you can also add the `ViewStateEncryptionMode` attribute to the `<pages>` configuration element with two possible values, `Auto` or `Always`. Setting the attribute to `Always` forces encryption of ViewState, whereas setting it to `Auto` encrypts ViewState only if a control requested encryption uses the new `Page.RegisterRequiresViewStateEncryption` method.

Added protection can be applied to ViewState by setting `Page.ViewStateUserKey` in the `Page_Init` to a unique value, such as the user's ID. This must be set in `Page_Init` because the key should be provided to ASP.NET before ViewState is loaded or generated. For example:

```
protected void Page_Init (Object sender, EventArgs e)
{
    if (User.Identity.IsAuthenticated) {
        ViewStateUserKey = User.Identity.Name;
    }
}
```

When optimizing their pages, ASP.NET programmers often disable ViewState for many controls when that extra bit of state is not absolutely necessary. So that controls that require state information will still work, ASP.NET includes a second, parallel ViewState-like collection called `ControlState`. This dictionary can be used for round-tripping crucial information of limited size that should not be disabled even when ViewState is. You should only store data in the `ControlState` collection that is absolutely critical to the functioning of the control.

Recognize that ViewState, and also ControlState, although not secure, are a good place to store small bits of a data and state that don't quite belong in a cookie or in the `Session` object. If the data that must be stored is relatively small and local to that specific instance of your page, ViewState is a much better solution than littering the `Session` object with lots of transient data.

USING HTTPCONTEXT.CURRENT.ITEMS FOR VERY SHORT-TERM STORAGE

The `Items` collection of `HttpContext` is one of ASP.NET's best-kept secrets. It is an `IDictionary` key/value collection of objects that's shared across the life of a single `HttpRequest`. That's a *single* `HttpRequest`. Why would you want to store state for such a short period of time? Consider these reasons:

➤ **When you share content between IHttpModules and IHttpHandlers:** If you write a custom `IHttpModule`, you can store context about the user for use later in a page.

➤ **When you communicate between two instances of the same UserControl on the same page:** Imagine you are writing a UserControl that serves banner ads. Two instances of the same control could select their ads from `HttpContext.Items` to prevent showing duplicates on the same page.

➤ **When you store the results of expensive calls that might otherwise happen twice or more on a page:** If you have multiple UserControls that each show a piece of data from a large, more expensive database retrieval, those UserControls can retrieve the necessary data from `HttpContext.Items`. The database is hit only once.

➤ **When individual units within a single HttpRequest need to act on the same or similar data:** If the lifetime of your data is just one request, consider using `HttpContext.Items` as a short-term cache.

The `Items` collection holds objects, just like many of the collections that have been used in this chapter. You need to cast those objects back to their specific type when they are retrieved.

Within a web-aware database access layer, per-request caching can be quickly implemented with the simple coding pattern shown here. Note that this sample code is a design pattern, and there is no `MyData` class; it is for illustration.

VB

```
Public Shared Function GetExpensiveData(ID As Integer) As MyData
  Dim key as string = "data" & ID.ToString()
  Dim d as MyData = _
      CType(HttpContext.Current.Items(key), MyData)
  If d Is Nothing Then
    d = New Data()
    'Go to the Database, do whatever...
    HttpContext.Current.Items(key) = d
  End If
  Return d
End Function
```

C#

```
public static MyData GetExpensiveData(int ID)
{
  string key = "data" + ID.ToString();
  MyData d = (MyData) HttpContext.Current.Items[key];
  if (d == null)
  {
    d = new Data();
    //Go to the Database, do whatever...
    HttpContext.Current.Items[key] = d;
  }
  return d;
```

This code checks the Items collection of the current HttpContext to see whether the data is already there. If it's not, the data is retrieved from the appropriate backing store and then stored in the Items collection. Subsequent calls to this function within the same HttpRequest receive the already-cached object.

As with all optimizations and caching, premature optimization is the root of all evil. Measure your need for caching and measure your improvements. Do not cache just because it *feels right*; cache because it makes sense.

SUMMARY

This chapter explored the many ways to manage state within your ASP.NET application. The Session object and its providers offer many choices. Each has its own pros and cons for managing state in the form of object references and serialized objects in a way that can be made largely transparent to the application. Server-side session state data can have its unique identifying key stored in a cookie, or the key can be carried along in the URL. Cookies can also be used independently to store small amounts of data and persist it between visits, albeit in much smaller amounts and with simpler types. Hidden fields, ViewState, ControlState, postbacks, and cross-page postbacks offer possibilities for managing small bits of state within a multi-page user experience. HttpContext.Current.Items offers a perfect place to hold transient state, living the life of only a single HttpRequest. QueryStrings are an old standby for holding non-private state that is appropriate for navigation.

Subsequent versions of ASP.NET have improved on ASP.NET 1.*x*'s state management options with a flexible Session State Provider module, the addition of ControlState for user controls, and cross-page postbacks for a more mature programming model.

22

Caching

WHAT'S IN THIS CHAPTER?

➤ Dealing with caching in ASP.NET

➤ Working with caching programmatically

➤ Understanding SQL cache dependency

➤ Using and testing SQL cache invalidation

WROX.COM CODE DOWNLOADS FOR THIS CHAPTER

Please note that all the code examples in this chapter are available as a part of this chapter's code download on the book's website at www.wrox.com on the Download Code tab.

Performance is a key requirement for any application or piece of code that you develop. The browser helps with client-side caching of text and images, whereas the server-side caching you choose to implement is vital for creating the best possible performance. *Caching* is the process of storing frequently used data on the server to fulfill subsequent requests. You will discover that grabbing objects from memory is much faster than re-creating the web pages or items contained in them from scratch each time they are requested. Caching increases your application's performance, scalability, and availability. The more you fine-tune your application's caching approach, the better it performs.

This chapter focuses on caching, including the SQL cache-invalidation capabilities that ASP.NET provides. This chapter takes a close look at this unique aspect of caching. When you are using SQL cache invalidation, if the resultset from SQL Server changes, the output cache can be triggered to change automatically. This ensures that the end user always sees the latest resultset, and the data presented is never stale. After introducing SQL cache invalidation, this chapter also covers other performance enhancements. It discusses the post-cache substitution feature, which caches entire pages while dynamically replacing specified bits of content. Lastly, this chapter covers a capability that enables a developer to create custom dependencies.

CACHING

You have several ways to deal with caching in ASP.NET, one of which being that you can cache an entire HTTP response (the entire web page) using a mechanism called output caching. Two other methods are partial page caching and data caching. The following sections describe these methods.

Output Caching

Output caching is a way to keep the dynamically generated page content in the server's memory or disk for later retrieval. This type of cache saves post-rendered content so it will not have to be regenerated again the next time it is requested. After a page is cached, it can be served up again when any subsequent requests are made to the server. You apply output caching by inserting an `OutputCache` page directive at the top of an `.aspx` page, as follows:

```
<%@ OutputCache Duration="60" VaryByParam="None" %>
```

The `Duration` attribute defines the number of seconds a page is stored in the cache. The `VaryByParam` attribute determines which versions of the page output are actually cached. You can generate different responses based on whether an HTTP-POST or HTTP-GET response is required. Other than the attributes for the `OutputCache` directive, ASP.NET includes the `VaryByHeader`, `VaryByCustom`, `VaryByControl`, and `Location` attributes. Additionally, the `Shared` attribute can affect user controls, as you will see later.

Caching in ASP.NET is implemented as an `HttpModule` that listens to all `HttpRequests` that come through the ASP.NET worker process. The `OutputCacheModule` listens to the application's `ResolveRequestCache` and `UpdateRequestCache` events, handles cache hits and misses, and returns the cached HTML, bypassing the page handler if need be.

VaryByParam

The `VaryByParam` attribute can specify which `QueryString` parameters cause a new version of the page to be cached:

```
<%@ OutputCache Duration="90" VaryByParam="pageId;subPageId" %>
```

For example, if you have a page called `navigation.aspx` that includes navigation information in the `QueryString`, such as `pageId` and `subPageId`, the `OutputCache` directive shown here caches the page for every different value of `pageId` and `subPageId`. In this example, the number of pages is best expressed with an equation:

```
cacheItems = (num of pageIds) * (num of subPageIds)
```

where `cacheItems` is the number of rendered HTML pages that would be stored in the cache. Pages are cached only after they are requested and pass through the `OutputCacheModule`. The maximum amount of cache memory in this case is used only after every possible combination is visited at least once. Although these are just *potential* maximums, creating an equation that represents your system's potential maximum is an important exercise.

If you want to cache a new version of the page based on any differences in the `QueryString` parameters, use `VaryByParam="*"`, as in the following code:

```
<%@ OutputCache Duration="90" VaryByParam="*" %>
```

"Doing the math" when using the `VaryBy` attributes is important. For example, you could add `VaryByHeader` and cache a different version of the page based on the browser's reported `User-Agent` HTTP header.

```
<%@ OutputCache Duration="90" VaryByParam="*" VaryByHeader="User-Agent"%>
```

The `User-Agent` identifies the user's browser type. ASP.NET can automatically generate different renderings of a given page that are customized to specific browsers, so in many cases saving these various renderings in the cache makes sense. A Firefox user might have slightly different HTML than an IE user, so you do not want to send all users the same post-rendered HTML. Literally dozens, if not hundreds, of User-Agent strings exist in the wild because they identify more than just the browser type; this OutputCache directive could multiply into thousands of versions of this page being cached, depending on server load. In this case, you should measure the cost of the caching against the cost of re-creating the page dynamically.

> **WARNING** *Always cache what will give you the biggest performance gain, and prove that assumption with testing. Don't "cache by coincidence" using attributes like* VaryByParam="*"*. A common general rule is to cache the least possible amount of data at first and add more caching later if you determine a need for it. Remember that the server memory is a limited resource, so you may want configure the use of disk caching in some cases. Be sure to balance your limited resources with security as a primary concern; do not put sensitive data on the disk.*

VaryByControl

VaryByControl can be a very easy way to get some serious performance gains from complicated user controls that render a lot of HTML that does not change often. For example, imagine a user control that renders a ComboBox showing the names of all the countries in the world. Perhaps those names are retrieved from a database and rendered in the combo box as follows:

```
<%@ OutputCache Duration="2592000" VaryByControl="comboBoxOfCountries" %>
```

Certainly, the names of the world's countries do not change that often, so the Duration might be set to a month (in seconds). The rendered output of the UserControl is cached, allowing a page using that control to reap performance benefits of caching the control while the page itself remains dynamic.

VaryByCustom

Although the VaryBy attributes offer a great deal of power, sometimes you need more flexibility. If you want to take the OutputCache directive from the previous navigation example and cache by a value stored in a cookie, you can add VaryByCustom. The value of VaryByCustom is passed into the GetVaryByCustomString method that can be added to the Global.asax.cs. This method is called every time the page is requested, and it is the function's responsibility to return a value.

A different version of the page is cached for each unique value returned. For example, suppose your users have a cookie called Language that has three potential values: en, es, and fr. You want to allow users to specify their preferred language, regardless of their language reported by their browser. Language also has a fourth potential value—it may not exist! Therefore, the OutputCache directive in the following example caches many versions of the page, as described in this equation:

```
cacheItems = (num of pageIds) * (num of subPageIds) * (4 possible Language values)
```

To summarize, suppose there were ten potential values for pageId, five potential subPageId values for each pageId, and four possible values for Language. That adds up to 200 different potential cached versions of this single navigation page. This math is not meant to scare you away from caching, but you should realize that with great (caching) power comes great responsibility.

The following OutputCache directive includes pageId and subPageId as values for VaryByParam, and VaryByCustom passes in the value of "prefs" to the GetVaryByCustomString callback function in Listing 22-1:

```
<%@ OutputCache Duration="90" VaryByParam="pageId;subPageId" VaryByCustom="prefs"%>
```

Caching in ASP.NET involves a tradeoff between CPU and memory: how hard is it to make this page, versus whether you can afford to hold 200 versions of it. If it is only 5KB of HTML, a potential megabyte of memory could pay off handsomely versus thousands and thousands of database accesses. Because most pages will hit the database at least once during a page cycle, every page request served from the cache saves you a trip to the database. Efficient use of caching can translate into cost savings if fewer database servers and licenses are needed.

The code in Listing 22-1 (code file Global.asax) returns the value stored in the Language cookie. The arg parameter to the GetVaryByCustomString method contains the string "prefs", as specified in VaryByCustom.

LISTING 22-1: GetVaryByCustomString callback method in the HttpApplication

VB

```vb
Overrides Function GetVaryByCustomString(ByVal context As HttpContext,
       ByVal arg As String) As String
    If arg.ToLower() = "prefs" Then
        Dim cookie As HttpCookie = context.Request.Cookies("Language")
        If cookie IsNot Nothing Then
            Return cookie.Value
        End If
    End If
    Return MyBase.GetVaryByCustomString(context, arg)
End Function
```

C#

```csharp
public override string GetVaryByCustomString(HttpContext context, string arg)
{
    if (arg.ToLower() == "prefs")
    {
      HttpCookie cookie = context.Request.Cookies["Language"];
      if (cookie != null)
      {
          return cookie.Value;
      }
    }
    return base.GetVaryByCustomString(context, arg);
}
```

The GetVaryByCustomString method in Listing 22-1 is used by the HttpApplication in Global.asax and will be called for every page that uses the VaryByCustom OutputCache directive. If your application has many pages that use VaryByCustom, you can create a switch statement and a series of helper functions to retrieve whatever information you want from the user's HttpContext and to generate unique values for cache keys.

Extending <outputCache>

Starting with the release of ASP.NET 4, you can extend how the OutputCache directive works and have it work off your own custom means to caching. This means that you can wire the OutputCache directive to any type of caching means including distributed caches, cloud caches, disc, XML, or anything else you can dream up.

To accomplish this, you are required to create a custom output-cache provider as a class and this class will need to inherit from the new System.Web.Caching.OutputCacheProvider class. To inherit from OutputCacheProvider, you must override the Add(), Get(), Remove(), and Set() methods to implement your custom version of output caching.

After you have your custom implementation in place, the next step is to configure this in a configuration file: the machine.config or the web.config file. Some changes have been made to the <outputCache> element in the configuration file to allow you to apply your custom cache extensions.

The `<outputCache>` element is found within the `<caching>` section of the configuration file and it now includes a new `<providers>` subelement.

```
<caching>
    <outputCache>
        <providers>
        </providers>
    </outputCache>
</caching>
```

Within the new `<providers>` subelement, you can nest an `<add>` element to make the appropriate references to your new output cache capability, which you built by deriving from the `OutputCacheProvider` class.

```
<caching>
    <outputCache defaultProvider="AspNetInternalProvider">
        <providers>
            <add name="myDistributedCacheExtension"
             type="Wrox.OutputCacheExtension.DistributedCacheProvider,
                     DistributedCacheProvider" />
        </providers>
    </outputCache>
</caching>
```

With this new `<add>` element in place, your new extended output cache is available to use. One new addition here to also pay attention to is the new `defaultProvider` attribute within the `<outputCache>` element. In this case, it is set to `AspNetInternalProvider`, which is the default setting in the configuration file. This means that by default the output cache works as it always has done and stores its cache in the memory of the computer that the program is running.

With your own output cache provider in place, you can now point to this provider through the `OutputCache` directive on the page as defined here:

```
<%@ OutputCache Duration="90" VaryByParam="*"
    providerName="myDistributedCacheExtension" %>
```

If the provider name isn't defined, then the provider that is defined in the configuration's `defaultProvider` attribute is utilized.

Partial Page (UserControl) Caching

Similar to output caching, *partial page caching* (also called *donut caching*) enables you to cache only specific blocks of a web page. You can, for example, cache only the center of the page the user sees. Partial page caching is achieved with the caching of user controls so you can build your ASP.NET pages to utilize numerous user controls and then apply output caching to the selected user controls. This, in essence, caches only the parts of the page that you want, leaving other parts of the page outside the reach of caching. This feature is nice, and, if done correctly, can lead to pages that perform better. This requires a modular design to be planned up front so you can partition the components of the page into logical units composed of user controls.

Typically, user controls are designed to be placed on multiple pages to maximize reuse of common functionality. However, when these user controls (`.ascx` files) are cached with the `@OutputCache` directive's default attributes, they are cached on a per-page basis. That means that even if a user control outputs the identical HTML when placed on `pageA.aspx`, as it does when placed on `pageB.aspx`, its output is cached twice. By enabling the `Shared="true"` attribute, the UserControl's output can be shared among multiple pages and on sites that make heavy use of shared UserControls:

```
<%@ OutputCache Duration="300" VaryByParam="*" Shared="true" %>
```

The resulting memory savings can be surprisingly large because you only cache one copy of the post-rendered user control instead of caching a copy for each page. As with all optimizations, you need to test both for correctness of output as well as for memory usage.

> **WARNING** *If you have an ASCX UserControl using the* OutputCache *directive, remember that the UserControl exists only for the first request. If a UserControl has its HTML retrieved from the* OutputCache*, the control does not really exist on the ASPX page. Instead, a PartialCachingControl is created that acts as a proxy or ghost of that control.*

Any code in the ASPX page that requires a UserControl to be constantly available will fail if that control is reconstituted from the OutputCache. So be sure to always check for this type of caching before using any control. The following code fragment illustrates the kind of logic required when accessing a potentially cached UserControl:

VB

```
Protected Sub Page_Load()
    If Not PossiblyCachedUserControl is Nothing Then
        ' Place code manipulating PossiblyCachedUserControl here.
    End If
End Sub
```

C#

```
protected void Page_Load()
{
    if (PossiblyCachedUserControl != null)
    {
        // Place code manipulating PossiblyCachedUserControl here.
    }
}
```

Post-Cache Substitution

Output caching has typically been an all-or-nothing proposition. The output of the entire page is cached for later use. However, often you want the benefits of output caching, but you also want to keep a small bit of dynamic content on the page. It would be a shame to cache a page but be unable to output a dynamic "Welcome, Scott!"

Ever since ASP.NET 2.0, a means has existed of using a post-cache substitution as an opportunity to affect the about-to-be-rendered page. A control is added to the page that acts as a placeholder. It calls a method that you specify after the cached content has been returned. The method returns any string output you like, but you should be careful not to abuse the feature. If your post-cache substitution code calls an expensive stored procedure, you could easily lose any performance benefits you might have expected.

Post-cache substitution is an easy feature to use. It gives you two ways to control the substitution:

➤ Call the Response.WriteSubstitution method, passing it a reference to the desired substitution method callback.

➤ Add an <asp:Substitution> control to the page at the desired location, and set its methodName attribute to the name of the callback method.

To try this feature, create a new website with a Default.aspx page. Drag a label control and a substitution control to the design surface. The code in Listing 22-2 updates the label to display the current time, but the page is cached immediately and future requests return that cached value. Set the methodName property in the substitution control to GetUpdatedTime, meaning the name of the static method that is called after the page is retrieved from the cache.

The callback function must be static because the page that is rendered does not really exist at this point (an instance of it does not). Because you do not have a page instance to work with, this method is limited in its scope. However, the current `HttpContext` is passed into the method, so you have access to the `Session`, `Request`, and `Response`. The string returned from this method is injected into the `Response` in place of the substitution control.

LISTING 22-2: Using the substitution control

VB

```vb
<%@ Page Language="VB" %>
<%@ OutputCache Duration="30" VaryByParam="None" %>

<script runat="server">
Public Shared Function GetUpdatedTime(ByVal context As HttpContext) As String
    Return DateTime.Now.ToLongTimeString() + " by " + _
            context.User.Identity.Name
End Function

Protected Sub Page_Load(ByVal sender As Object, ByVal e As System.EventArgs) _
        Handles Me.Load
    Label1.Text = DateTime.Now.ToLongTimeString()
End Sub
</script>

<!DOCTYPE html>

<html>
<head>
    <title>Substitution Control</title>
</head>
<body>
    <form id="form1" runat="server">
    <div>
        <asp:Label ID="Label1" Runat="server" Text="Label"></asp:Label>
        <br />
        <asp:Substitution ID="Substitution1" runat="server"
            MethodName="GetUpdatedTime" />
        <br />
    </div>
    </form>
</body>
</html>
```

C#

```csharp
<%@ Page Language="C#" %>
<%@ OutputCache Duration="30" VaryByParam="None" %>

<script runat="server">
    public static string GetUpdatedTime(HttpContext context)
    {
        return DateTime.Now.ToLongTimeString() + " by " +
                context.User.Identity.Name;
    }
    protected void Page_Load(object sender, EventArgs e)
    {
        Label1.Text = DateTime.Now.ToLongTimeString();
    }
</script>
```

The ASPX page in Listing 22-2 has a label and a post-cache substitution control. The control acts as a placeholder in the spot where you want fresh content injected after the page is returned from the cache. The first time the page is visited only the label is updated because no cached content is returned. The second time the page is visited, however, the entire page is retrieved from the cache—the page handler is not called and, consequently, none of the page-level events fire. However, the `GetUpdatedTime` method is called after the cache module completes its work. Figure 22-1 shows the result if the first line is cached and the second line is created dynamically.

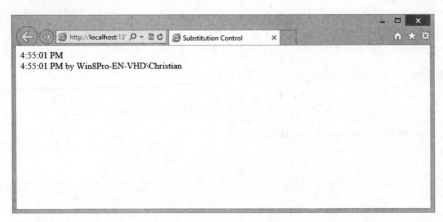

FIGURE 22-1

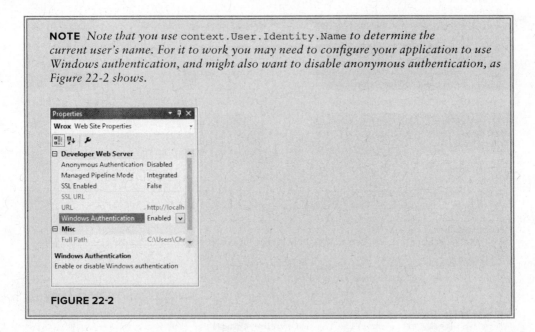

NOTE *Note that you use* `context.User.Identity.Name` *to determine the current user's name. For it to work you may need to configure your application to use Windows authentication, and might also want to disable anonymous authentication, as Figure 22-2 shows.*

FIGURE 22-2

HttpCachePolicy and Client-Side Caching

Caching is more than just holding data in memory on the server-side. A good caching strategy should also include the browser and its client-side caches, controlled by the Cache-Control HTTP header. HTTP headers are hints and directives to the browser on how to handle a request.

Some people recommend using HTML <meta> tags to control caching behavior. Be aware that neither the browsers nor routers along the way are obligated to pay attention to these directives. You might have more success using HTTP headers to control caching.

Because HTTP headers travel outside the body of the HTTP message, you have several options for viewing them. You can enable tracing (see Chapter 29) and view the headers from the tracing output. You can also use additional software, like your browsers' web developer plug-ins (usually activated by F12), or the popular Firefox extension Firebug from getfirebug.com.

> **NOTE** *For background information on HTTP headers and controlling caching, see the document RFC 2616: Hypertext Transfer Protocol - HTTP/1.1, available on the World Wide Web Consortium's site at www.w3c.org. You might also check out Fiddler at www.fiddler2.com. Commercial tools such as HttpWatch from www.httpwatch.com add more features.*

To set up caching, create a file that writes the current time in its Load event. Now, view the default HTTP headers used by ASP.NET. Note that one header, Cache-Control: private, indicates to routers and other intermediates that this response is intended only for you (private).

The HttpCachePolicy class gives you an object model for managing client-side state that insulates you from adding HTTP headers yourself. Add the lines from Listing 22-3 to your Page_Load to influence the response's headers and the caching behavior of the browser. This listing tells the browser not to cache this response in memory nor store it on disk. It also directs the response to expire immediately.

LISTING 22-3: Using HTTP headers to force the browser not to cache on the client side

VB
```
Protected Sub Page_Load(ByVal sender As Object, _
  ByVal e As System.EventArgs) Handles Me.Load
    Response.Cache.SetCacheability(HttpCacheability.NoCache)
    Response.Cache.SetNoStore()
    Response.Cache.SetExpires(DateTime.MinValue)

    Response.Write(DateTime.Now.ToLongTimeString())
End Sub
```

C#
```
protected void Page_Load(object sender, EventArgs e)
{
    Response.Cache.SetCacheability(HttpCacheability.NoCache);
    Response.Cache.SetNoStore();
    Response.Cache.SetExpires(DateTime.MinValue);

    Response.Write(DateTime.Now.ToLongTimeString());
}
```

Compare the results of running the page before adding the code from Listing 22-3 (top part of Figure 22-3) and then after adding the code (bottom part of Figure 22-3). Two new HTTP headers have been injected directing the client's browser and the Cache-Control header has changed to no-cache, no-store. The output caching HttpModule will respect these HTTP headers, so sending no-cache, no-store to the browser also advises the HttpModule to record the response as a cache miss. Figure 22-3 shows the difference.

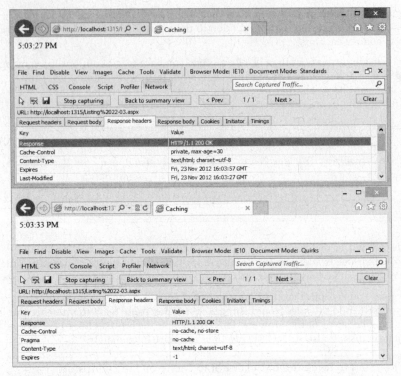

FIGURE 22-3

If your ASP.NET application contains a considerable number of relatively static or non–time-sensitive pages, consider what your client-side caching strategy is. Taking advantage of the disk space and the memory of your users' powerful client machines is better than burdening your server's limited resources.

CACHING PROGRAMMATICALLY

Output caching is a very declarative business. UserControls and pages can be marked up with OutputCache directives and dramatically change the behavior of your site. Declarative caching controls the lifecycle of HTML markup, but ASP.NET also includes deep imperative programmatic support for caching objects.

Data Caching Using the Cache Object

Another method of caching is to use the System.Web.Caching.Cache object to start caching specific data items for later use on a particular page or group of pages. The Cache object enables you to store everything from simple name/value pairs to more complex objects, such as data sets and entire .aspx pages.

> **WARNING** *Although it is quite similar to session state, the* Cache *object is shared by all users of the particular web server's app domain that is hosting this application. Therefore, if you put a particular item in the cache, all users will be able to see that object. This may not work as expected in a server farm scenario because you cannot be assured of which server the user will hit next, and even if there is only one server involved, more than one app domain may be running this application. In addition, the server is free to invalidate any cached item at any time if it needs to reclaim some of the memory.*

You use the `Cache` object in the following fashion:

VB

```
Cache("WhatINeedToStore") = myDataSet
```

C#

```
Cache["WhatINeedToStore"] = myDataSet;
```

After an item is in the cache, you can retrieve it later as shown here:

VB

```
Dim ds As New DataSet
ds = CType(Cache("WhatINeedToStore"), DataSet)
```

C#

```
DataSet ds = new DataSet();
ds = (DataSet)Cache["WhatINeedToStore"];
```

Using the `Cache` object is an outstanding way to cache your pages and is, in fact, what the `OutputCache` directive uses under the covers. This small fragment shows the simplest use of the `Cache` object. Simply put an object reference in it. However, the real power of the `Cache` object comes with its capability to invalidate itself. That is where cache dependencies come in.

> **WARNING** *You must always follow the pattern of testing to see whether an item is in the cache, and if not, you need to do whatever processing is necessary to re-create the object. After it's re-created, you can insert it back into the cache to become available for the next request.*

Controlling the ASP.NET Cache

Ordinarily the default parameters set by ASP.NET for the caching subsystem are appropriate for general use. They are configurable, however, within the `machine.config` or `web.config` files. These options let you make changes like preventing cached items from expiring when the system is under memory pressure, or turning off item expiration completely. You can set the maximum size of the application's private bytes before the cache begins to flush items:

```
<system.web>
  <cache disableMemoryCollection="false"
  disableExpiration="false" privateBytesLimit="0"
  percentagePhysicalMemoryUsedLimit="90"
  privateBytesPollTime="00:02:00" />
...snip...
```

> **NOTE** *It's best to leave the default values as they are unless you have done formal pro-filing of your application and understand how it utilizes the cache. You can find more detail on this section on MSDN at* `http://msdn.microsoft.com/en-us/library/vstudio/ms228248(v=vs.100).aspx`*.*

Cache Dependencies

Using the `Cache` object, you can store and invalidate items in the cache based on several different dependencies. Way back in ASP.NET 1.0/1.1, the only possible dependencies were the following:

➤   File-based dependencies

➤   Key-based dependencies

➤   Time-based dependencies

When inserting items into the cache using the `Cache` object, you set the dependencies with the `Insert` method, as shown in the following example:

```
Cache.Insert("DSN", connectionString,
    New CacheDependency(Server.MapPath("~/myconfig.xml")))
```

By using a *dependency* when the item being referenced changes, you remove the cache for that item from memory.

Cache dependencies have been improved ever since ASP.NET 2.0 with the addition of the `AggregateCacheDependency` class, the extendable `CacheDependency` class, and the capability to create your own custom `CacheDependency` classes. These three things are discussed in the following sections.

The AggregateCacheDependency Class

The `AggregateCacheDependency` class is like the `CacheDependency` class but it enables you to create an association connecting an item in the cache with many disparate dependencies of *different types*. For example, if you have a cached data item that is built from XML from a file and you have information from a SQL database table, you can create an `AggregateCacheDependency` with inserted `CacheDependency` objects for each subdependency. To do this, you call `Cache.Insert()` and add the `AggregateCacheDependency` instance. For example:

```
var agg = new AggregateCacheDependency();
agg.Insert(new CacheDependency(Server.MapPath("~/myconfig.xml")));
agg.Insert(new SqlCacheDependency("Northwind", "Customers"));
Cache.Insert("DSN", connectionString, agg);
```

Note that `AggregateCacheDependency` is meant to be used with *different* kinds of `CacheDependency` classes. If you simply want to associate one cached item with multiple files, use an overload of `CacheDependency`, as in this example:

VB

```
Cache.Insert("DSN", yourObject, _
    New System.Web.Caching.CacheDependency( _
        New String() _
      { _
        Server.MapPath("~/file1.xml"), _
        Server.MapPath("~/file2.xml") _
      } _
    ) _
  )
```

C#

```
Cache.Insert("DSN", yourObject,
    new System.Web.Caching.CacheDependency(
        new string[]
        {
            Server.MapPath("~/file1.xml"),
            Server.MapPath("~/file2.xml")
        }
    )
);
```

The AggregateCacheDependency class is made possible by the support for extending the previously sealed CacheDependency class. You can use this innovation to create your own custom CacheDependency.

The Unsealed CacheDependency Class

A big change in caching ever since ASP.NET 2.0 was released was that the CacheDependency class had been refactored and unsealed (or made overrideable). This allowed you to create classes that inherit from the CacheDependency class and create more elaborate dependencies that are not limited to the Time, Key, or File dependencies.

When you create your own cache dependencies, you have the option to add procedures for such things as web services data, only-at-midnight dependencies, or textual string changes within a file. The dependencies you create are limited only by your imagination. The unsealing of the CacheDependency class puts you in the driver's seat to let you decide when items in the cache need to be invalidated.

Along with the unsealing of the CacheDependency class, the ASP.NET team also built a SQL Server cache dependency—SqlCacheDependency. When a cache becomes invalid because a table changes within the underlying SQL Server, you now know it immediately in your ASP.NET application.

Because CacheDependency is unsealed, you can derive your own custom cache dependencies; that's what you do in the next section.

Creating Custom Cache Dependencies

ASP.NET has time-based, file-based, and SQL-based CacheDependency support. You might ask yourself why you would write your own CacheDependency. Here are a few ideas:

➤ Invalidate the cache from the results of an Active Directory lookup query.

➤ Invalidate the cache upon arrival of an MSMQ or MQSeries message.

➤ Create an Oracle-specific CacheDependency.

➤ Invalidate the cache using data reported from an XML web service.

➤ Update the cache with new data from a Stock Price service.

The CacheDependency class exposes three members and a constructor overload that developers can use to do this work:

➤ GetUniqueID: When overridden, enables you to return a unique identifier for a custom cache dependency to the caller.

➤ DependencyDispose: Used for disposing of resources used by the custom cache dependency class. When you create a custom cache dependency, you are required to implement this method.

➤ NotifyDependencyChanged: Called to cause expiration of the cache item dependent on the custom cache dependency instance.

➤ The CacheDependency public constructor.

Listing 22-4 (code files RssCacheDependency.cs and RssCacheDependency.vb in the download for this chapter) creates a new RssCacheDependency that invalidates a cache key if an RSS (Rich Site Summary) XML document has changed.

LISTING 22-4: Creating an RssCacheDependency class

VB

```
Imports System
Imports System.Web
Imports System.Threading
Imports System.Web.Caching
```

continues

LISTING 22-4 *(continued)*

```vbnet
Imports System.Xml

Public Class RssCacheDependency
        Inherits CacheDependency

    Dim backgroundThread As Timer
    Dim howOften As Integer = 900
    Dim RSS As XmlDocument
    Dim RSSUrl As String

    Public Sub New(ByVal URL As String, ByVal polling As Integer)
        howOften = polling
        RSSUrl = URL
        RSS = RetrieveRSS(RSSUrl)

        If backgroundThread Is Nothing Then
            backgroundThread = New Timer(
                New TimerCallback(AddressOf CheckDependencyCallback),
                Me, (howOften * 1000), (howOften * 1000))
        End If
    End Sub

    Function RetrieveRSS(ByVal URL As String) As XmlDocument
        Dim retVal As New XmlDocument
        retVal.Load(URL)
        Return retVal
    End Function

    Public Sub CheckDependencyCallback(ByVal Sender As Object)
        Dim CacheDepends As RssCacheDependency = _
            CType(Sender, RssCacheDependency)
        Dim NewRSS As XmlDocument = RetrieveRSS(RSSUrl)
        If Not NewRSS.OuterXml = RSS.OuterXml Then
            CacheDepends.NotifyDependencyChanged(CacheDepends, EventArgs.Empty)
        End If
        End Sub

    Protected Overrides Sub DependencyDispose()
        backgroundThread = Nothing
        MyBase.DependencyDispose()
    End Sub

    Public ReadOnly Property Document() As XmlDocument
        Get
            Return RSS
        End Get
    End Property
End Class
```

C#

```csharp
using System;
using System.Web;
using System.Threading;
using System.Web.Caching;
using System.Xml;

public class RssCacheDependency : CacheDependency
{
    Timer backgroundThread;
```

```
        int howOften = 900;
        XmlDocument RSS;
        string RSSUrl;

        public RssCacheDependency(string URL, int polling)
        {
            howOften = polling;
            RSSUrl = URL;
            RSS = RetrieveRSS(RSSUrl);

            if (backgroundThread == null)
            {
                backgroundThread = new Timer(
                        new TimerCallback(CheckDependencyCallback),
                        this, (howOften * 1000), (howOften * 1000));
            }
        }

        public XmlDocument RetrieveRSS(string URL)
        {
            XmlDocument retVal = new XmlDocument();
            retVal.Load(URL);
            return retVal;
        }

        public void CheckDependencyCallback(object sender)
        {
            RssCacheDependency CacheDepends = sender as RssCacheDependency;
            XmlDocument NewRSS = RetrieveRSS(RSSUrl);
            if (NewRSS.OuterXml != RSS.OuterXml)
            {
                CacheDepends.NotifyDependencyChanged(CacheDepends, EventArgs.Empty);
            }
        }

        override protected void DependencyDispose()
        {
            backgroundThread = null;
            base.DependencyDispose();
        }

        public XmlDocument Document
        {
            get
            {
                return RSS;
            }
        }
    }
}
```

To use the new code, open a new website and put the `RssCacheDependency` class in the `App_Code` folder. Create a new file and add two textboxes, a label, and a button onto the page. Execute the website and enter an RSS URL for a blog (like the MSDN feed at http://sxp.microsoft.com/feeds/3.0/msdnnews/msdnnews), and click the button. The program checks the `Cache` object using the URL itself as a key. If the `XmlDocument` containing RSS does not exist in the cache, a new `RssCacheDependency` is created with a 10-minute (600-second) timeout. The `XmlDocument` is then cached, and all future requests within the next 10 minutes to this page retrieve the RSS `XmlDocument` from the cache.

Next, your new `RssCacheDependency` class from Listing 22-4 is illustrated in Listing 22-5. The `RssCacheDependency` is created and passed into the call to `Cache.Insert()`. The `Cache` object handles the lifetime and calling of the methods of the `RssCacheDependency` instance.

LISTING 22-5: Using the RssCacheDependency class

VB

```
<%@ Page Language="VB" ValidateRequest="false" %>

<script runat="server">
Sub Button1_Click(ByVal sender As Object, ByVal e As System.EventArgs)
    Dim RSSUrl As String = TextBox1.Text
    Label2.Text = "Loaded From Cache"
    If Cache(TextBox1.Text) Is Nothing Then
        Label2.Text = "Loaded Fresh"
        Dim itDepends As New RssCacheDependency(RSSUrl, 600)
        Cache.Insert(RSSUrl, itDepends.Document, itDepends)
    End If
    TextBox2.Text = CType(Cache(TextBox1.Text), _
        System.Xml.XmlDocument).OuterXml
End Sub
</script>

<!DOCTYPE html>

<html>
<head id="Head1" runat="server">
    <title>Custom Cache Dependency Example</title>
</head>
<body>
    <form id="Form1" runat="server"> RSS URL:
        <asp:TextBox ID="TextBox1" Runat="server"/>
        <asp:Button ID="Button1" onclick="Button1_Click" Runat="server"
        Text="Get RSS" />
        Cached:<asp:Label ID="Label2" Runat="server"></asp:Label><br />
        RSS:<br />
        <asp:TextBox ID="TextBox2" Runat="server" TextMode="MultiLine"
         Width="800px" Height="300px"></asp:TextBox>
    </form>
</body>
</html>
```

C#

```
<script runat="server">
    void Button1_Click(object sender, System.EventArgs e)
    {
        string RSSUrl = TextBox1.Text;
        Label2.Text = "Loaded From Cache";
        if (Cache[TextBox1.Text] == null)
        {
            Label2.Text = "Loaded Fresh";
            RssCacheDependency itDepends = new RssCacheDependency(RSSUrl, 30);
            Cache.Insert(RSSUrl, itDepends.Document, itDepends);
        }
        TextBox2.Text = ((System.Xml.XmlDocument)Cache[TextBox1.Text]).OuterXml;
    }
</script>
```

The RssCacheDependency class creates a Timer background thread to poll for changes in the RSS feed. If it detects changes, the RssCacheDependency notifies the caching subsystem with the NotifyDependencyChanged event. The cached value with that key clears, and the next page view forces a reload of the requested RSS from the specified feed.

.NET 4.x's New Object Caching Option

From what you have seen so far with the `System.Web.Caching.Cache` object, you can see that it is quite powerful and allows for you to even create a custom cache. This extensibility and power has changed under the hood of the `Cache` object, though.

Driving this is the `System.Runtime.Caching.dll`, as what was in the `System.Web` version has been refactored out and everything was rebuilt into the new namespace of `System.Runtime.Caching`.

The reason for this change wasn't so much for the ASP.NET developer, but instead for other application types such as Windows Forms, Windows Presentation Foundation, and more. The reason for this is that the `System.Web.Caching.Cache` object was so useful that other application developers were bringing over the `System.Web` namespace into their projects to make use of this object. So, to get away from a Windows Forms developer needing to bring the `System.Web.dll` into their project just to use the `Cache` object it provided, this was all extracted out and extended with the `System.Runtime.Caching` namespace.

As an ASP.NET developer, you can still make use of the `System.Web.Caching.Cache` object just as you did in all the prior versions of ASP.NET. It isn't going away. However, it is important to note that as the .NET Framework evolves, the .NET team will be making its investments into the `System.Runtime.Caching` namespace rather than `System.Web.Caching`. This means that over time, you will most likely see additional enhancements in the `System.Runtime.Caching` version that don't appear in the `System.Web.Caching` namespace as you might expect. With that said, it doesn't also mean that you need to move everything over to the new `System.Runtime.Caching` namespace to make sure you are following the strategic path of Microsoft, because the two caches are managed together under the covers.

This section runs through an example of using the cache from the `System.Runtime.Caching` namespace. For this example, the ASP.NET page simply uses a Label control that shows the name of a user that is stored in an XML file. The first step is to create an XML file in the `App_Data` folder and name it **Username.xml**. This simple file is presented in Listing 22-6 (code file Username.xml).

LISTING 22-6: The contents of the Username.xml file

```xml
<?xml version="1.0" encoding="utf-8" ?>
<usernames>
  <user>Christian Wenz</user>
</usernames>
```

With this XML file sitting in the root of your drive, now turn your attention to the `Default.aspx` code-behind page to use the name in the file and present it into a single Label control on the page. The code-behind for the `Default.aspx` page is presented in Listing 22-7.

LISTING 22-7: Using the System.Runtime.Caching namespace

VB

```vb
<%@ Page Language="C#" %>
<%@ Import Namespace="System.Runtime.Caching" %>

<script runat="server">
Protected Sub Page_Load(ByVal sender As Object, _
  ByVal e As EventArgs)

    Dim cache As ObjectCache = MemoryCache.Default

    Dim usernameFromXml As String = _
      TryCast(cache("userFromXml"), String)

    If usernameFromXml Is Nothing Then
        Dim userFilePath As New List(Of String)()
```

continues

LISTING 22-7 *(continued)*

```vb
        userFilePath.Add(Server.MapPath("~/App_Data/Username.xml"))

        Dim policy As New CacheItemPolicy()
        policy.ChangeMonitors.Add(New HostFileChangeMonitor(userFilePath))

        Dim xdoc As XDocument = _
          XDocument.Load(Server.MapPath("~/App_Data/Username.xml"))
        Dim query = From u In xdoc.Elements("usernames")
            Select u.Value

        usernameFromXml = query.First().ToString()

        cache.Set("userFromXml", usernameFromXml, policy)
    End If

    Label1.Text = usernameFromXml
End Sub
</script>

<!DOCTYPE html>

<html>
<head runat="server">
    <title>Using System.Runtime.Caching</title>
</head>
<body>
    <form id="form1" runat="server">
        <div>
            <asp:Label ID="Label1" runat="server"></asp:Label>
        </div>
    </form>
</body>
</html>
```

C#

```csharp
<script runat="server">
    protected void Page_Load(object sender, EventArgs e)
    {
        ObjectCache cache = MemoryCache.Default;

        string usernameFromXml = cache["userFromXml"] as string;

        if (usernameFromXml == null)
        {
            List<string> userFilePath = new List<string>();
            userFilePath.Add(Server.MapPath("~/App_Data/Username.xml"));

            CacheItemPolicy policy = new CacheItemPolicy();
            policy.ChangeMonitors.Add(new HostFileChangeMonitor(userFilePath));

            XDocument xdoc = XDocument.Load(Server.MapPath(
                "~/App_Data/Username.xml"));
            var query = from u in xdoc.Elements("usernames")
                        select u.Value;

            usernameFromXml = query.First().ToString();

            cache.Set("userFromXml", usernameFromXml, policy);
```

```
        }

            Label1.Text = usernameFromXml;
    }
</script>
```

This example from Listing 22-7 makes use of the new cache at `System.Runtime.Caching`. You need to reference this namespace in your ASP.NET project for this to work (see Figure 22-4).

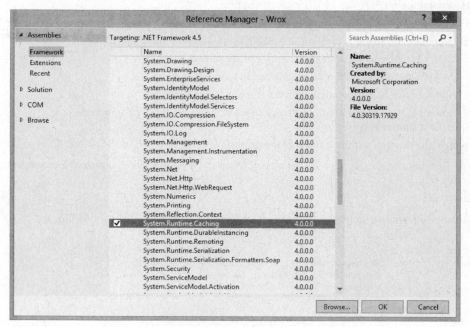

FIGURE 22-4

To start, you create a default instance of the cache object:

```
ObjectCache cache = MemoryCache.Default;
```

You then can work with this cache as you would with the traditional ASP.NET cache object:

```
string usernameFromXml = cache["userFromXml"] as string;
```

To get the cache started, you need to create an object that defines what type of cache you are dealing with. You can build a custom implementation, or you can use one of the default implementations provided with .NET 4.x:

```
CacheItemPolicy policy = new CacheItemPolicy();
policy.ChangeMonitors.Add(new HostFileChangeMonitor(userFilePath));
```

The `HostFileChangeMonitor` is a means to look at directories and file paths and monitor for change. So, for instance, when the XML file changes, that triggers an invalidation of the cache. Other implementations of the `ChangeMonitor` object include the `FileChangeMonitor` and the `SqlChangeMonitor`.

Running this example, notice that the text *Christian Wenz* is loaded into the cache on the first run, and this text appears in the Label1 control. Keep your application running and then you can go back to the XML file and change the value, and you will then notice that this causes the cache to be invalidated on the page's refresh.

USING THE SQL SERVER CACHE DEPENDENCY

To utilize the SQL Server Cache Dependency feature in ASP.NET, you must perform a one-time setup of your SQL Server database. To set up your SQL Server, use the `aspnet_regsql.exe` tool found at `C:\Windows\MicroSoft.NET\Framework\v4.0.xxxxx\`. This tool makes the necessary modifications to SQL Server so that you can start working with the SQL cache-invalidation features.

Follow these steps when using the SQL Server Cache Dependency features:

1. Enable your database for SQL Cache Dependency support.
2. Enable a table or tables for SQL Cache Dependency support.
3. Include SQL connection string details in the ASP.NET application's `web.config` file.
4. Utilize the SQL Cache Dependency features in one of the following ways:
   - ➤ Programmatically create a `SqlCacheDependency` object in code.
   - ➤ Add a `SqlDependency` attribute to an `OutputCache` directive.
   - ➤ Add a `SqlCacheDependency` instance to the `Response` object via `Response.AddCacheDependency`.

This section explains all the steps required and the operations available to you.

To start, you need to get at the `aspnet_regsql.exe` tool. Open the Visual Studio Command Prompt, and then type this command:

```
aspnet_regsql.exe -?
```

This code outputs the help command list for this command-line tool, as shown in the following:

```
                        -- SQL CACHE DEPENDENCY OPTIONS --

    -d <database>           Database name for use with SQL cache dependency. The
                            database can optionally be specified using the
                            connection string with the -c option instead.
                            (Required)

    -ed                     Enable a database for SQL cache dependency.

    -dd                     Disable a database for SQL cache dependency.

    -et                     Enable a table for SQL cache dependency. Requires -t
                            option.

    -dt                     Disable a table for SQL cache dependency. Requires -t
                            option.

    -t <table>              Name of the table to enable or disable for SQL cache
                            dependency. Requires -et or -dt option.

    -lt                     List all tables enabled for SQL cache dependency.
```

The following sections show you how to use some of these commands.

> **NOTE** *Microsoft's trusted Northwind database is used as an example in this chapter, and it's not part of the chapter code downloads. It needs to be retrieved and installed separately. You can download the Northwind database used for this chapter at* www.wrox.com/go/SQLServer2012DataSets. *Chapter 24 contains more information on retrieving this sample database. Of course, the techniques covered also work with other databases.*

Enabling Databases for SQL Server Cache Invalidation

To use SQL Server cache invalidation with a SQL Server database, begin with two steps. The first step enables the appropriate database. In the second step, you enable the tables that you want to work with. You must perform both steps for this process to work. If you want to enable your databases for SQL cache invalidation and you are working on the computer where the SQL Server instance is located, you can use the following construct. If your SQL instance is on another computer, change `localhost` in this example to the name of the remote machine.

```
aspnet_regsql.exe -S localhost -U username -P password -d Northwind -ed
```

The syntax for using the `SQLEXPRESS` instance on the local machine, using Windows authentication, looks like this:

```
aspnet_regsql.exe -S .\SQLEXPRESS -E -d Northwind -ed
```

This produces something similar to the following output:

```
Enabling the database for SQL cache dependency.


.


Finished.
```

From this command prompt, you can see that you simply enabled the Northwind database (a sample database for SQL Server) for SQL cache invalidation. The name of the SQL machine was passed in with `-S`, the username with `-U`, the database with `-d`, and most importantly, the command to enable SQL cache invalidation was `-ed`.

Now that you have enabled the database for SQL cache invalidation, you can enable one or more tables contained within the Northwind database.

Enabling Tables for SQL Server Cache Invalidation

You enable more tables by using the following command:

```
aspnet_regsql.exe -S localhost -U username -P password -d Northwind -t Customers
-et

aspnet_regsql.exe -S localhost -U username -P password -d Northwind -t Products -et
```

You can see that this command is not much different from the one for enabling the database, except for the extra `-t Customers` entry and the use of `-et` to enable the table rather than `-ed` to enable a database. `Customers` is the name of the table that is enabled in this case.

Go ahead and enable both the `Customers` and `Products` tables. You run the command once per table. After a table is successfully enabled, you receive the following response:

```
Enabling the table for SQL cache dependency.


.


Finished.
```

After the table is enabled, you can begin using the SQL cache-invalidation features. However, before you do, the following section shows you what happens to SQL Server when you enable these features.

Looking at SQL Server

Now that the Northwind database and the `Customers` and `Products` tables have all been enabled for SQL cache invalidation, look at what has happened in SQL Server. If you open the SQL Server Management

Studio (or its Express edition), you see a new table contained within the Northwind database — `AspNet_SqlCacheTablesForChangeNotification` (whew, that's a long one!). Your screen should look like Figure 22-5.

At the top of the list of tables in the left pane, you see the `AspNet_SqlCacheTablesForChangeNotification` table. ASP.NET uses this table to learn which tables are being monitored for change notification and also to make note of any changes to the tables being monitored. The new table is actually quite simple when you look at its columns, also shown in Figure 22-5.

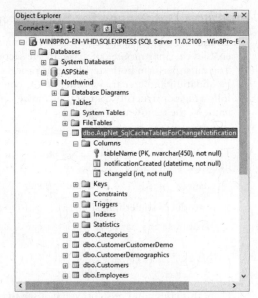

FIGURE 22-5

➤ `tableName`: This column simply shows a `String` reference to the names of the tables contained in the same database. Any table named here is enabled for SQL cache invalidation.

➤ `notificationCreated`: This shows the date and time when the table was enabled for SQL cache invalidation.

➤ `changeId`: Communicates any changes to the included tables to ASP.NET. ASP.NET monitors this column for changes and, depending on the value, either uses what is stored in memory or makes a new database query.

Looking at the Tables That Are Enabled

Using the `aspnet_regsql.exe` tool, you can see (by using a simple command) which tables are enabled in a particular database. If you are working through the preceding examples, you see that so far you have enabled the `Customers` and `Products` tables of the Northwind database. To get a list of the tables that are enabled, use something similar to the following command:

```
aspnet_regsql.exe -S localhost -U username -P password -d Northwind -lt
```

The `-lt` command produces a simple list of tables enabled for SQL cache invalidation. Inputting this command produces the following results:

```
Listing all tables enabled for SQL cache dependency:
Customers
Products
```

Disabling a Table for SQL Server Cache Invalidation

Now that you know how to enable your SQL Server database for SQL Server cache invalidation, look at how you remove the capability for a specific table to be monitored for this process. To remove a table from the SQL Server cache-invalidation process, you use the `-dt` command.

In the preceding example, using the `-lt` command showed that you have both the `Customers` and `Products` tables enabled. Next, you remove the `Products` table from the process using the following command:

```
aspnet_regsql.exe -S localhost -U username -P password -d Northwind -t Products -dt
```

You can see that all you do is specify the name of the table using the `-t` command followed by a `-dt` command (disable table). The command line for disabling table caching will again list the tables that are enabled for SQL Server cache invalidation; this time, the `Products` table is not listed — instead, `Customers`, the only enabled table, is listed.

Disabling a Database for SQL Server Cache Invalidation

Not only can you pick and choose the tables that you want to remove from the process, but you can also disable the entire database for SQL Server cache invalidation. To disable an entire database, you use the `-dd` command (disable database).

> **NOTE** *Note that disabling an entire database for SQL Server cache invalidation also means that every single table contained within this database is also disabled.*

This example shows the Northwind database being disabled on my computer:

```
C:\>aspnet_regsql -S localhost -U username -P password -d Northwind -dd

Disabling the database for SQL cache dependency.
.
Finished.
```

To ensure that the table is no longer enabled for SQL Server cache invalidation, I attempted to list the tables that were enabled for cache invalidation using the `-lt` command. I received the following error:

```
C:\ >aspnet_regsql -S localhost -U username -P password -d Northwind -lt
An error has happened. Details of the exception:
The database 'Northwind' is not enabled for SQL cache notification, please
 use the System.Web.Caching.SqlCacheDependencyAdmin.EnableNotifications method,
 or the command line tool aspnet_regsql. To use the tool, please run
 'aspnet_regsql.exe -?' for more information.
```

If you now open the Northwind database in the SQL Server Management Studio, you can see that the `AspNet_SqlCacheTablesForChangeNotification` table has been removed from the database.

SQL Server Cache Invalidation

SQL Server supports a more granular series of notification that doesn't require polling. Direct notification of changes is a built-in feature of SQL Server and is presented via the ADO.NET `SqlCommand`. Listing 22-8 shows this.

LISTING 22-8: Using SQL Server cache invalidation

VB

```
<%@ Page Language="C#" %>
<%@ Import Namespace="System.Data.SqlClient" %>

<script runat="server">
Protected Sub Page_Load(ByVal sender As Object, ByVal e As System.EventArgs) _
  Handles Me.Load
    Response.Write("Page created: " + DateTime.Now.ToLongTimeString())
    Dim connStr As String = ConfigurationManager.ConnectionStrings( _
      "AppConnectionString1").ConnectionString
    SqlDependency.Start(connStr)
    Dim connection As New SqlConnection(connStr)
    Dim command As New SqlCommand("Select * FROM Customers", connection)
    Dim depends As New SqlCacheDependency(command)

    connection.Open()
    GridView1.DataSource = command.ExecuteReader()
```

continues

LISTING 22-8 *(continued)*

```
        GridView1.DataBind()

        connection.Close()

        'Now, do what you want with the sqlDependency object like:
        Response.AddCacheDependency(depends)
    End Sub
</script>

<!DOCTYPE html>

<html>
<head runat="server">
    <title></title>
</head>
<body>
    <form id="form1" runat="server">
        <asp:GridView ID="GridView1" runat="server" Height="400px" Width="400px">
        </asp:GridView>
    </form>
</body>
</html>
```

C#

```
<script runat="server">
    protected void Page_Load(object sender, EventArgs e)
    {
        Response.Write("Page created: " + DateTime.Now.ToLongTimeString());
        string connStr = ConfigurationManager.ConnectionStrings[
            "AppConnectionString1"].ConnectionString;
        SqlDependency.Start(connStr);
        SqlConnection connection = new SqlConnection(connStr);
        SqlCommand command = new SqlCommand("Select * FROM Customers", connection);
        SqlCacheDependency depends = new SqlCacheDependency(command);

        connection.Open();
        GridView1.DataSource = command.ExecuteReader();
        GridView1.DataBind();

        connection.Close();

        Response.AddCacheDependency(depends);
    }
</script>
```

SQL Server supports both programmatic and declarative techniques when caching. Use the string `"CommandNotification"` in the `OutputCache` directive to enable notification-based caching for a page as in this example. You can specify SQL caching options either programmatically or declaratively, but not both. Note that you must first call `System.Data.SqlClient.SqlDependency.Start`, passing in the connection string, to start the SQL notification engine:

```
<%@ OutputCache Duration="3600" VaryByParam="none"
    SqlDependency="CommandNotification"%>
```

Alternatively, if you're using a SqlDataSource control from within your ASP.NET page, you would do the following:

```
<asp:SqlDataSource EnableCaching="true" SqlCacheDependency="CommandNotification"
    CacheDuration="2600" />
```

As data changes within SQL Server, SQL and ADO.NET automatically invalidate data cached on the web server.

CONFIGURING YOUR ASP.NET APPLICATION

After you enable a database for SQL Server cache invalidation and enable a couple of tables within this database, the next step is to configure your application for SQL Server cache invalidation.

To configure your application to work with SQL Server cache invalidation, the first step is to make some changes to the `web.config` file. In the `web.config` file, specify that you want to work with the Northwind database, and you want ASP.NET connected to it.

Listing 22-9 (code file web.config) shows an example of how you should change your `web.config` file to work with SQL Server cache invalidation. The `pollTime` attribute is not needed if you are using a recent version of SQL Server (2005 or higher) notification because it uses database events instead of the polling needed for earlier versions.

LISTING 22-9: Configuring the web.config file

```
<configuration>

  <connectionStrings>
    <add name="AppConnectionString1" connectionString="Data Source=localhost;
      User ID=username;Password=password;Database=Northwind;Persist Security Info=False"
      providerName="System.Data.SqlClient" />
  </connectionStrings>

  <system.web>

    <caching>
      <sqlCacheDependency enabled="true">
        <databases>
          <add name="Northwind" connectionStringName="AppConnectionString1"
            pollTime="500" />
        </databases>
      </sqlCacheDependency>
    </caching>

  </system.web>
</configuration>
```

From this listing, you can see that the first thing established is the connection string to the Northwind database using the `<connectionStrings>` element in the `web.config` file. Note the name of the connection string because it is utilized later in the configuration settings for SQL Server cache invalidation.

The SQL Server cache invalidation is configured using the `<caching>` element. This element must be nested within the `<system.web>` elements. Because you are working with a SQL Server cache dependency, you must use a `<sqlCacheDependency>` child node. You enable the entire process by using the `enabled="true"` attribute. After this attribute is enabled, you work with the `<databases>` section. You use the `<add>` element, nested within the `<databases>` nodes, to reference the Northwind database. Table 22-1 explains the attributes of the `<add>` element.

TABLE 22-1

ATTRIBUTE	DESCRIPTION
Name	Provides an identifier to the SQL Server database.
connectionStringName	Specifies the name of the connection. Because the connection string in the preceding example is called `AppConnectionString1`, you use this value for the `connectionStringName` attribute as well.
pollTime	Specifies the time interval from one SQL Server poll to the next. The default is .5 seconds or 500 milliseconds (as shown in Listing 22-9). This is not needed for SQL Server 2005, 2008, and 2012 notification.

Now that the `web.config` file is set up correctly, you can start using SQL Server cache invalidation on your pages. ASP.NET makes a separate SQL Server request on a completely different thread to the `AspNet_SqlCacheTablesForChangeNotification` table to see whether the `changeId` number has been incremented. If the number is changed, ASP.NET knows that an underlying change has been made to the SQL Server table and that a new resultset should be retrieved. When it checks to see whether it should make a SQL Server call, the request to the small `AspNet_SqlCacheTablesForChangeNotification` table has a single result. With SQL Server cache invalidation enabled, this is done so quickly that you really notice the difference.

TESTING SQL SERVER CACHE INVALIDATION

Now that the `web.config` file is set up and ready to go, the next step is to actually apply these capabilities to a page. Listing 22-10 is an example of a page using the SQL Server cache-invalidation process.

LISTING 22-10: An ASP.NET page utilizing SQL Server cache invalidation

VB

```
<%@ Page Language="C#" %>
<%@ OutputCache Duration="30" VaryByParam="none"
    SqlDependency="Northwind:Customers"%>

<script runat="server">
Protected Sub Page_Load(ByVal sender As Object, ByVal e As System.EventArgs)
    Label1.Text = "Page created at " & DateTime.Now.ToString()
End Sub
</script>

<!DOCTYPE html>

<html>
<head id="Head1" runat="server">
    <title>Sql Cache Invalidation</title>
</head>
<body>
    <form id="form1" runat="server">
        <asp:Label ID="Label1" runat="server"></asp:Label><br />
        <br />
        <asp:GridView ID="GridView1" Runat="server" DataSourceID="SqlDataSource1">
        </asp:GridView>
        <asp:SqlDataSource ID="SqlDataSource1" Runat="server"
         SelectCommand="Select * From Customers"
         ConnectionString="<%$ ConnectionStrings:AppConnectionString1 %>"
         ProviderName="<%$ ConnectionStrings:AppConnectionString1.providername %>">
        </asp:SqlDataSource>
```

```
            </form>
        </body>
    </html>
```

C#

```
<%@ Page Language="VB" %>
<%@ OutputCache Duration="30" VaryByParam="none"
    SqlDependency="Northwind:Customers"%>

<script runat="server">
    protected void Page_Load(object sender, System.EventArgs e)
    {
        Label1.Text = "Page created at " + DateTime.Now.ToShortTimeString();
    }
</script>
```

The first and most important part of this page is the OutputCache page directive that is specified at the top of the file. Typically, the OutputCache directive specifies how long the page output is held in the cache using the Duration attribute. Next is the VaryByParam attribute. An addition here is the SqlDependency attribute. This enables a particular page to use SQL Server cache invalidation. The following line shows the format of the value for the SqlDependency attribute:

```
SqlDependency="database:table"
```

The value of Northwind:Customers specifies that you want the SQL Server cache invalidation enabled for the Customers table within the Northwind database. The Duration attribute of the OutputCache directive shows you that, typically, the output of this page is stored in the cache for a long time—but this cache is invalidated immediately if the Customers table has any underlying changes made to the data that it contains.

A change to any of the cells in the Customers table of the Northwind database invalidates the cache, and a new cache is generated from the result, which now contains a new SQL Server database request. Figure 22-6 shows an example of the page generated the first time it is run.

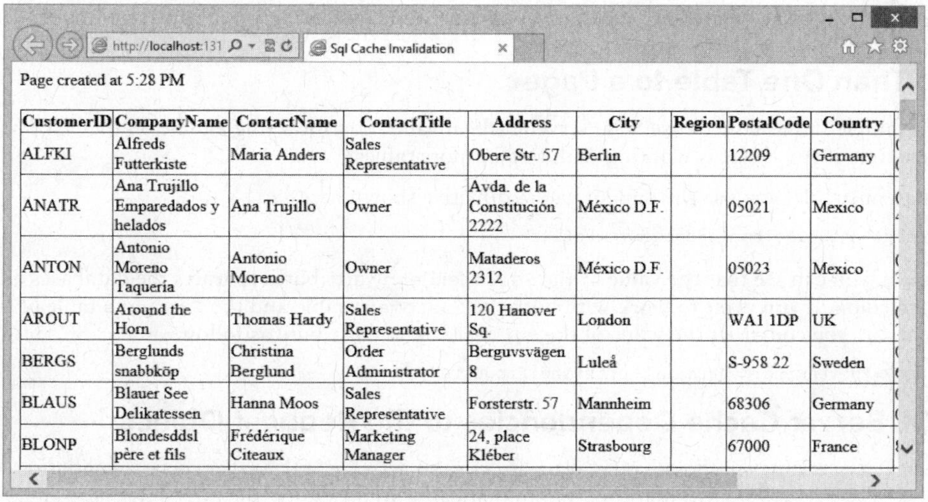

FIGURE 22-6

From this figure, you can see the contents of the customer with the CustomerID of ALFKI. For this entry, go to SQL Server and change the value of the ContactName from Maria Anders to Mary Anders. If you were not using SQL Server cache invalidation, this change would have done nothing to the output cache. The original page output in the cache would still be present and the end user would still see the Maria Anders entry for the duration specified in the page's OutputCache directive. However, because you are using SQL Server cache invalidation, after the underlying information in the table is changed, the output cache is invalidated, a new resultset is retrieved, and the new resultset is cached. When a change has been made, you see the results as shown in Figure 22-7.

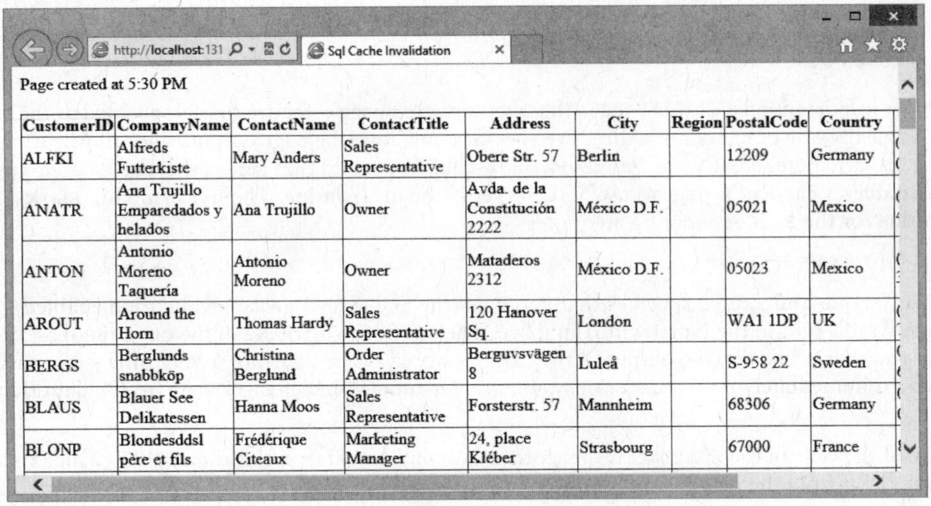

Page created at 5:30 PM

CustomerID	CompanyName	ContactName	ContactTitle	Address	City	Region	PostalCode	Country
ALFKI	Alfreds Futterkiste	Mary Anders	Sales Representative	Obere Str. 57	Berlin		12209	Germany
ANATR	Ana Trujillo Emparedados y helados	Ana Trujillo	Owner	Avda. de la Constitución 2222	México D.F.		05021	Mexico
ANTON	Antonio Moreno Taquería	Antonio Moreno	Owner	Mataderos 2312	México D.F.		05023	Mexico
AROUT	Around the Horn	Thomas Hardy	Sales Representative	120 Hanover Sq.	London		WA1 1DP	UK
BERGS	Berglunds snabbköp	Christina Berglund	Order Administrator	Berguvsvägen 8	Luleå		S-958 22	Sweden
BLAUS	Blauer See Delikatessen	Hanna Moos	Sales Representative	Forsterstr. 57	Mannheim		68306	Germany
BLONP	Blondesddsl père et fils	Frédérique Citeaux	Marketing Manager	24, place Kléber	Strasbourg		67000	France

FIGURE 22-7

Notice also that the text "Page created at" includes an updated time indicating when this page was rendered.

Adding More Than One Table to a Page

The preceding example shows how to use SQL Server cache invalidation for a single table on the ASP.NET page. What do you do if your page is working with two or more tables?

To add more than one table, you use the OutputCache directive shown here:

```
SqlDependency="database:table;database:table"
```

From this example, you can see that the value of the SqlDependency attribute separates the databases and tables with a semicolon. If you want to work with both the Customers table and the Products table of the Northwind database, you construct the value of the SqlDependency attribute as follows:

```
SqlDependency="Northwind:Customers;Northwind:Products"
```

Attaching SQL Server Cache Dependencies to the Request Object

In addition to changing settings in the OutputCache directive to activate SQL Server cache invalidation, you can also set the SQL Server cache invalidation programmatically. To do so, use the SqlCacheDependency class, which is illustrated in Listing 22-11.

LISTING 22-11: Working with SQL Server cache invalidation programmatically

VB

```vb
Dim myDependency As SqlCacheDependency = _
    New SqlCacheDependency("Northwind", "Customers")
Response.AddCacheDependency(myDependency)
Response.Cache.SetValidUntilExpires(true)
Response.Cache.SetExpires(DateTime.Now.AddMinutes(60))
Response.Cache.SetCacheability(HttpCacheability.Public)
```

C#

```csharp
SqlCacheDependency myDependency = new SqlCacheDependency("Northwind", "Customers");
Response.AddCacheDependency(myDependency);
Response.Cache.SetValidUntilExpires(true);
Response.Cache.SetExpires(DateTime.Now.AddMinutes(60));
Response.Cache.SetCacheability(HttpCacheability.Public);
```

You first create an instance of the `SqlCacheDependency` object, assigning it the value of the database and the table at the same time. The `SqlCacheDependency` class takes the following argument:

```
SqlCacheDependency(System.Data.SqlClient.SqlCommand sqlCmd)
```

After the `SqlCacheDependency` class is in place, you add the dependency to the `Cache` object and set some of the properties of the `Cache` object as well. You can do this either programmatically or through the `OutputCache` directive.

Attaching SQL Server Cache Dependencies to the Cache Object

In addition to attaching SQL Server cache dependencies to the `Request` object, you can attach them to the `Cache` object for data that can be cached much longer. The `Cache` object is contained within the `System.Web.Caching` namespace, and it enables you to work programmatically with the caching of any type of object. Listing 22-12 shows a page that utilizes the `Cache` object with the `SqlDependency` object.

LISTING 22-12: Using the Cache object with the SqlDependency object

VB

```vb
<%@ Page Language="VB" %>
<%@ Import Namespace="System.Data" %>
<%@ Import Namespace="System.Data.SqlClient" %>

<!DOCTYPE html>

<script runat="server">
Protected Sub Page_Load(ByVal sender As Object, ByVal e As System.EventArgs)
    Dim myCustomers As DataSet
    myCustomers = CType(Cache("firmCustomers"), DataSet)

    If myCustomers Is Nothing Then
        Dim conn As SqlConnection =
          New SqlConnection(ConfigurationManager.ConnectionStrings( _
          "AppConnectionString1").ConnectionString)
        Dim da As SqlDataAdapter = _
         New SqlDataAdapter("Select * From Customers", conn)

        myCustomers = New DataSet
```

continues

LISTING 22-12 *(continued)*

```
        da.Fill(myCustomers)

        Dim myDependency As SqlCacheDependency = _
            New SqlCacheDependency("Northwind", "Customers")
        Cache.Insert("firmCustomers", myCustomers, myDependency)

        Label1.Text = "Produced from database."
    Else
        Label1.Text = "Produced from Cache object."
    End If

    GridView1.DataSource = myCustomers
    GridView1.DataBind()
End Sub
</script>

<html>
<head runat="server">
    <title>Sql Cache Invalidation</title>
</head>
<body>
    <form id="form1" runat="server">
    <div>
        <asp:Label ID="Label1" Runat="server"></asp:Label><br />
        <br />
        <asp:GridView ID="GridView1" Runat="server"></asp:GridView>
    </div>
    </form>
</body>
</html>
```

C#

```
<%@ Page Language="C#" %>
<%@ Import Namespace="System.Data" %>
<%@ Import Namespace="System.Data.SqlClient" %>

<script runat="server">
    protected void Page_Load(object sender, System.EventArgs e)
    {
        DataSet myCustomers;
        myCustomers = (DataSet)Cache["firmCustomers"];

        if (myCustomers == null)
        {
            SqlConnection conn = new SqlConnection(
              ConfigurationManager.ConnectionStrings[
                "AppConnectionString1"].ConnectionString);
            SqlDataAdapter da = new SqlDataAdapter("Select * from Customers", conn);

            myCustomers = new DataSet();
            da.Fill(myCustomers);

            SqlCacheDependency myDependency = new SqlCacheDependency(
              "Northwind", "Customers");
            Cache.Insert("firmCustomers", myCustomers, myDependency);

            Label1.Text = "Produced from database.";
        }
        else
```

```
        {
            Label1.Text = "Produced from Cache object.";
        }

        GridView1.DataSource = myCustomers;
        GridView1.DataBind();
    }
</script>
```

In this example, the `SqlCacheDependency` class associated itself to the `Customers` table in the Northwind database as before. This time, however, you use the `Cache` object to insert the retrieved data set along with a reference to the `SqlCacheDependency` object. The `Insert()` method of the `Cache` class is constructed as follows:

```
Cache.Insert(String key, Object value,
System.Web.Caching.CacheDependency dependencies)
```

You can also insert more information about the dependency using the following construct:

```
Cache.Insert(String key, Object value,
System.Web.Caching.CacheDependency dependencies
Date absoluteExpiration, System.TimeSpan slidingExpiration)
```

And finally:

```
Cache.Insert(String key, Object value,
System.Web.Caching.CacheDependency dependencies,
Date absoluteExpiration, System.TimeSpan slidingExpiration,
System.Web.Caching.CacheItemPriority priority,
System.Web.Caching.CacheItemRemovedCallback onRemoveCallback)
```

The SQL Server cache dependency created comes into action and does the same polling as it would have done otherwise. If any of the data in the `Customers` table has changed, the `SqlCacheDependency` class invalidates what is stored in the cache. When the next request is made, the `Cache["firmCustomers"]` is found to be empty and a new request is made to SQL Server. The `Cache` object again repopulates the cache with the new results generated.

Figure 22-8 shows the results generated when the ASP.NET page from Listing 22-12 is called for the first time.

Produced from database.

CustomerID	CompanyName	ContactName	ContactTitle	Address	City	Region	PostalCode	Country
ALFKI	Alfreds Futterkiste	Mary Anders	Sales Representative	Obere Str. 57	Berlin		12209	Germany
ANATR	Ana Trujillo Emparedados y helados	Ana Trujillo	Owner	Avda. de la Constitución 2222	México D.F.		05021	Mexico
ANTON	Antonio Moreno Taquería	Antonio Moreno	Owner	Mataderos 2312	México D.F.		05023	Mexico
AROUT	Around the Horn	Thomas Hardy	Sales Representative	120 Hanover Sq.	London		WA1 1DP	UK
BERGS	Berglunds snabbköp	Christina Berglund	Order Administrator	Berguvsvägen 8	Luleå		S-958 22	Sweden
BLAUS	Blauer See Delikatessen	Hanna Moos	Sales Representative	Forsterstr. 57	Mannheim		68306	Germany
BLONP	Blondesddsl père et fils	Frédérique Citeaux	Marketing Manager	24, place Kléber	Strasbourg		67000	France

FIGURE 22-8

Because this is the first time that the page is generated, nothing is in the cache. The `Cache` object is then placed in the resultset along with the association to the SQL Server cache dependency. Figure 22-9 shows the result of the second request. Notice that the HTML table is identical because it was generated from the identical `DataSet`, but the first line of the page has changed to indicate that this output was produced from cache.

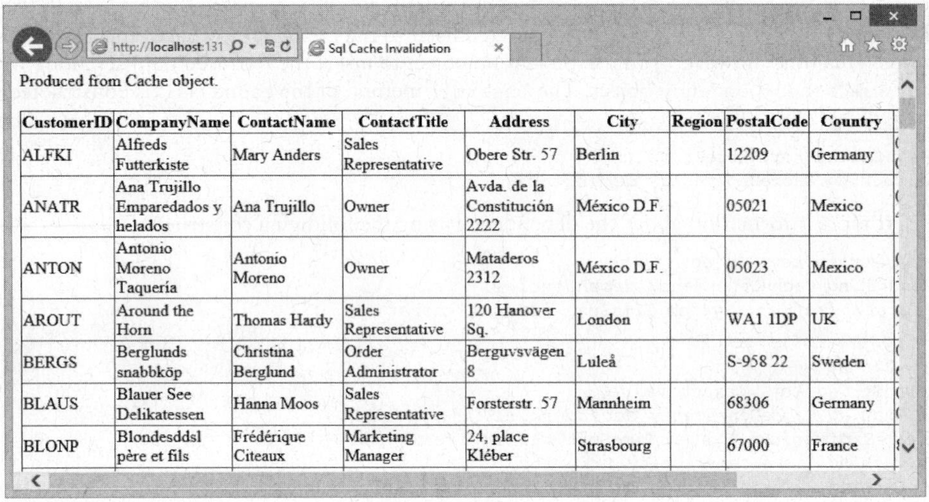

FIGURE 22-9

On the second request, the data set is already contained within the cache; therefore, it is retrievable. You are not required to hit SQL Server to get the full results again. If any of the information has changed within SQL Server itself, however, the `Cache` object returns nothing; a new resultset is retrieved.

SUMMARY

ASP.NET provides several built-in mechanisms for caching. Most of these features can be achieved using attributes, so no actual coding is required. It is important that you understand the different types of caching, including partial page caching and post-cache substitution.

When working with a database, SQL Server cache invalidation is an outstanding feature of ASP.NET that enables you to invalidate items stored in the cache when underlying changes occur to the data in the tables being monitored. Post-cache substitution fills in an important gap in ASP.NET's technology, enabling you to have both the best highly dynamic content and a high-performance website with caching.

When you are monitoring changes to the database, you can configure these procedures easily in the `web.config` file, or you can work programmatically with cache invalidation directly in your code. These changes are possible because the `CacheDependency` object has been unsealed. You can now inherit from this object and create your own cache dependencies. The SQL Server cache-invalidation process is the first example of this capability.

PART VII
Client-Side Development

23

ASP.NET AJAX

WHAT'S IN THIS CHAPTER?

➤ Developing applications with ASP.NET AJAX

➤ Using ASP.NET AJAX's server-side controls

WROX.COM CODE DOWNLOADS FOR THIS CHAPTER

Please note that all the code examples in this chapter are available as a part of this chapter's code download on the book's website at www.wrox.com on the Download Code tab.

In web application development, Ajax signifies the capability to build applications that make use of the XMLHttpRequest object, an object responsible for making HTTP requests.

The creation and the inclusion of the XMLHttpRequest object in JavaScript and the fact that all modern browsers support it led to the creation of the Ajax model. Ajax applications initially gained popularity after Google released a number of notable, Ajax-enabled applications, such as Google Maps. These and other applications demonstrated the value of Ajax and were noticed by the world at large. The original inventor of XMLHttpRequest was actually Microsoft; they implemented this functionality as an ActiveX component for Internet Explorer, and all other browsers ported it to their browsers. Nowadays, Internet Explorer supports XMLHttpRequest as a native JavaScript object (as all other browsers do).

Shortly thereafter, Microsoft released a beta for a toolkit that enabled developers to incorporate Ajax features in their web applications. This toolkit, code-named *Atlas* and later renamed ASP.NET AJAX, makes using Ajax features in your applications extremely simple.

If you are using ASP.NET 3.5 or 4 or 4.5, then you don't even have to worry about installing the ASP.NET AJAX framework because everything you need is already in place for you.

UNDERSTANDING THE NEED FOR AJAX

ASP.NET AJAX makes your web applications seem more fluid. Ajax-enabled applications are responsive and give the end user immediate feedback and direction through the workflows that you provide.

Before Ajax

So, what is Ajax doing to your web application? Take a look at what a web page does when it does *not* use Ajax. Figure 23-1 shows a typical request-and-response activity for a web application.

In this figure, an end user makes a request from his browser to the application that is stored on your web server. The server processes the request and ASP.NET renders a page, which is then sent to the requestor as a response. The response, when received by the end user, is displayed within the end user's browser.

From here, many events that take place within the application instance as it sits within the end user's browser cause the complete request-and-response process to reoccur. For instance, the end user might click a radio button, a check box, a button, a calendar, or anything else, and this action causes the entire web page to be refreshed or a new page to be provided.

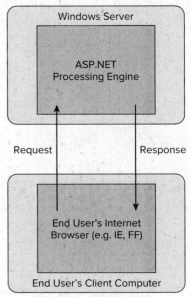

FIGURE 23-1

Ajax Changes the Story

In contrast, an Ajax-enabled web page includes a JavaScript library on the client that takes care of issuing requests to the web server. It does this when it is possible to send a request and get a response for just part of the page and when using script; the client library updates that part of the page without updating the entire page. An entire page requires a lot of bandwidth to be sent down to the browser to process each and every time. By processing just part of the page, the end user experiences what some people term "fluidity" in the page, which makes the page seem more responsive. The amount of code of the portion of a page that is updated is less and produces the responsiveness the end user expects. Figure 23-2 shows a diagram of how this works.

Figure 23-2 demonstrates that the first thing that happens is that the entire page is delivered in the initial request and response. From there, any partial updates required by the page are done using the client script library. This library can make asynchronous page requests and update just the portion of the page that needs updating. One major advantage to this is that a minimal amount of data is transferred for the updates to occur. Updating a partial page is better than recalling the entire page for what is just a small change to the page.

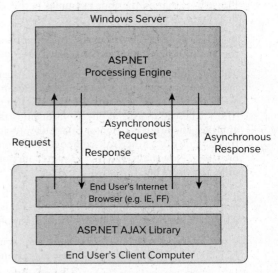

FIGURE 23-2

Ajax is dependent on a few technologies for it to work. The first is the XMLHttpRequest object. This object allows the browser to communicate to a backend server and has been available in the Microsoft world since Internet Explorer 5 through the MSXML ActiveX component. Of course, the other major component is JavaScript. This technology provides the client-side initiation to communication with the backend services and takes care of packaging a message to send to any server-side services. Another aspect of Ajax is support for the Document Object Model (DOM). These pieces change the page when the asynchronous response is received from the server. Finally, the last piece is the data that is being transferred from the client to the server. This transfer is done in XML, or more importantly in the effective JavaScript Object Notation (JSON).

Support for the XMLHttpRequest object gives JavaScript functions within the client script library the capability to call server-side code. As stated, HTTP requests are typically issued by a browser. The browser also takes care of processing the response that comes from the server and then usually regenerates the entire web page in the browser after a response is issued. Figure 23-3 details this process.

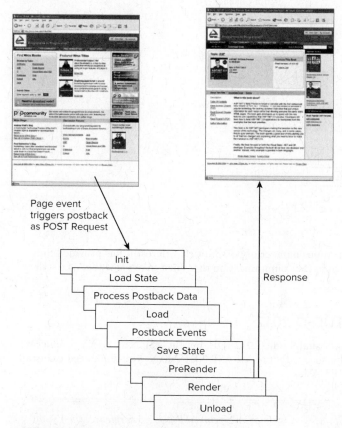

FIGURE 23-3

If you use the XMLHttpRequest object from your JavaScript library, then you do not actually issue full-page requests from the browser. Instead, you use a client-side script engine (which is basically a JavaScript function) to initiate the request and also to receive the response. Because you are also not issuing a request and response to deal with the entire web page, you can skip a lot of the page processing because it is not needed. This is the essence of an Ajax web request. It is illustrated in Figure 23-4.

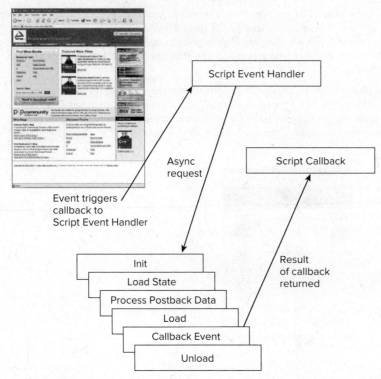

FIGURE 23-4

As stated, Ajax opens the door to a tremendous number of possibilities. Microsoft has provided the necessary script engines to automate much of the communication that must take place for Ajax-style functionality to occur.

ASP.NET AJAX AND VISUAL STUDIO 2012

Not only is ASP.NET AJAX a part of the Visual Studio 2012 IDE, but the ASP.NET AJAX product is also baked into the .NET Framework 4.5. This means that to use ASP.NET AJAX, you don't need to install anything if you are working with ASP.NET 4.5.

> **NOTE** *If you are using an ASP.NET version prior to the ASP.NET 3.5 release, then you need to visit* www.asp.net/ajax *to get the components required to work with Ajax.*

Overall, Microsoft has fully integrated the entire ASP.NET AJAX experience so you can easily use Visual Studio and its visual designers to work with your Ajax-enabled pages and even have the full debugging story that you would want to have with your applications. Using Visual Studio 2012, you can also debug the JavaScript that you are using in the pages.

In addition, it is important to note that Microsoft focused a lot of attention on cross-platform compatibility with ASP.NET AJAX. You will find that the Ajax-enabled applications that you build on the .NET Framework 4.5 can work within all the major browsers out there (such as Firefox and Chrome).

Client-Side Technologies

The ASP.NET AJAX story really has two parts. The first is a client-side framework and a set of services that are completely on the client-side. The other part of the story is a server-side framework. Remember that the client-side of ASP.NET AJAX is all about the client communicating asynchronous requests to the server-side of the offering.

For this reason, Microsoft offers a Client Script Library, which is a JavaScript library that takes care of the required communications. Figure 23-5 shows the Client Script Library.

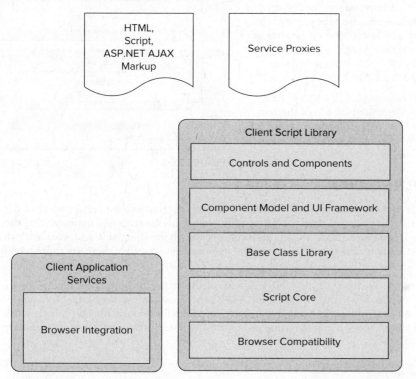

FIGURE 23-5

The Client Script Library provides a JavaScript, object-oriented interface that is reasonably consistent with aspects of the .NET Framework. Because browser compatibility components are built in, any work that you build in this layer or (in most cases) work that you let ASP.NET AJAX perform for you here will function with a multitude of different browsers. Also, several components support a rich UI infrastructure that produces many things that would take some serious time to build yourself.

The interesting thing about the client-side technologies that are provided by ASP.NET AJAX is that they are completely independent of ASP.NET. In fact, any developer can freely download the Microsoft AJAX Library (again from `asp.net/ajax`) and use it with other web technologies such as PHP (`php.net`) and Java Server Pages (JSP) — even though admittedly almost no one does that. With that said, the entire web story is a lot more complete with the server-side technologies that are provided with ASP.NET AJAX.

And even though Microsoft now embraces the jQuery JavaScript library (which is covered in Chapter 25), there are some unique and convenient features exclusive to ASP.NET AJAX.

Server-Side Technologies

As an ASP.NET developer, you will likely spend most of your time on the server-side aspect of ASP.NET AJAX. Remember that ASP.NET AJAX is all about the client-side technologies talking back to the server-side technologies. You can actually perform quite a bit on the server-side of ASP.NET AJAX.

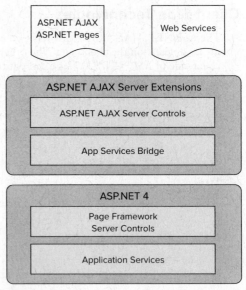

The server-side framework knows how to deal with client requests (such as putting responses in the correct format). The server-side framework also takes care of the marshalling of objects back and forth between JavaScript objects and the .NET objects that you are using in your server-side code. Figure 23-6 illustrates the server-side framework provided by ASP.NET AJAX.

When you have the .NET Framework 4.5, you will have the ASP.NET AJAX Server Extensions on top of the core ASP.NET Framework, the Windows Communication Foundation, as well as ASP.NET-based web services (.asmx).

FIGURE 23-6

Developing with ASP.NET AJAX

A couple of types of web developers exist out there. There are the web developers who are accustomed to working with ASP.NET and who have experience working with server-side controls and manipulating these controls on the server-side. Then there are developers who concentrate on the client-side and work with the DOM and JavaScript to manipulate and control the page and its behaviors (and then there are those who fit in both types, of course).

With that said, it is important to realize that ASP.NET AJAX was designed for both types of developers. If you want to work more on the server-side of ASP.NET AJAX, then you can use the ScriptManager control and the UpdatePanel control to Ajax-enable your current ASP.NET applications with little work on your part. You can do all this work using the same programming models that you are quite familiar with in ASP.NET.

> **NOTE** *You find out more about both the ScriptManager and the UpdatePanel controls later in this chapter.*

In turn, you can also use the Client Script Library directly and gain greater control over what is happening on the client's machine. Next, this chapter looks at building a simple web application that makes use of Ajax.

BUILDING ASP.NET AJAX APPLICATIONS

Now that you understand the reasons for Ajax, the next step is to build a basic sample using this framework. Create a new empty ASP.NET website application using the New Web Site dialog box (as shown in Figure 23-7) and choose an arbitrary name.

After you create the application, you are presented with what is now a standard website project. If you were building this application with ASP.NET 3.5, you would have noticed some additional settings in the web.config file. In this case, at the top of the web.config file, you would find some configuration sections

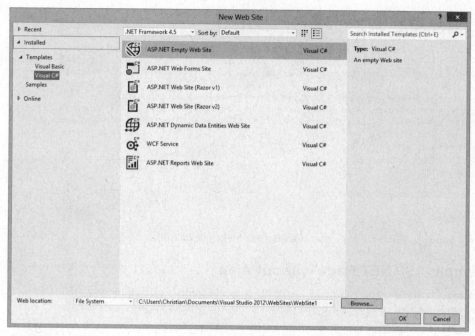

FIGURE 23-7

that are registered that deal with AJAX in particular. In the case of ASP.NET 4.5, this same section of configuration previously found in the web.config file is now found back in the machine.config file. Listing 23-1 presents this section from the machine.config.

LISTING 23-1: The <configSections> element found in the machine.config

```
<?xml version="1.0"?>

<configuration>
  <configSections>
    <sectionGroup name="system.web.extensions" type="System.Web.Configuration.
SystemWebExtensionsSectionGroup, System.Web.Extensions, Version=4.0.0.0, Culture=neutral, Publi
cKeyToken=31bf3856ad364e35">
      <sectionGroup name="scripting" type="System.Web.Configuration.ScriptingSectionGroup,
System.Web.Extensions, Version=4.0.0.0, Culture=neutral, PublicKeyToken=31bf3856ad364e35">
        <section name="scriptResourceHandler" type="System.Web.Configuration.
ScriptingScriptResourceHandlerSection, System.Web.Extensions, Version=4.0.0.0, Culture=neutral,
PublicKeyToken=31bf3856ad364e35" requirePermission="false" allowDefinition="MachineToApplicat
ion"/>
        <sectionGroup name="webServices" type="System.Web.Configuration.
ScriptingWebServicesSectionGroup, System.Web.Extensions, Version=4.0.0.0, Culture=neutral, Publ
icKeyToken=31bf3856ad364e35">
          <section name="jsonSerialization" type="System.Web.Configuration.
ScriptingJsonSerializationSection, System.Web.Extensions, Version=4.0.0.0, Culture=neutral, Pub
licKeyToken=31bf3856ad364e35" requirePermission="false" allowDefinition="Everywhere"/>
          <section name="profileService" type="System.Web.Configuration.
ScriptingProfileServiceSection, System.Web.Extensions, Version=4.0.0.0, Culture=neutral, Public
KeyToken=31bf3856ad364e35" requirePermission="false" allowDefinition="MachineToApplication"/>
```

continues

LISTING 23-1 *(continued)*

```
                <section name="authenticationService" type="System.Web.Configuration.
ScriptingAuthenticationServiceSection, System.Web.Extensions, Version=4.0.0.0, Culture=neutral,
PublicKeyToken=31bf3856ad364e35" requirePermission="false" allowDefinition="MachineToApplicat
ion"/>
                <section name="roleService" type="System.Web.Configuration.
ScriptingRoleServiceSection, System.Web.Extensions, Version=4.0.0.0, Culture=neutral, PublicKey
Token=31bf3856ad364e35" requirePermission="false" allowDefinition="MachineToApplication"/>
            </sectionGroup>
        </sectionGroup>
      </sectionGroup>
    </configSections>

    <!-- Configuration removed for clarity -->

    </configuration>
```

Next, you build a simple ASP.NET page that does not yet make use of Ajax.

Building a Simple ASP.NET Page without Ajax

To build a simple page that does not yet make use of the Ajax capabilities offered by ASP.NET 4.5, your page needs only a Label control and Button server control. Listing 23-2 presents the code for the page.

LISTING 23-2: A simple ASP.NET 4.5 page that does not use Ajax

VB

```
<%@ Page Language="VB" %>

<script runat="server">
    Protected Sub Button1_Click(ByVal sender As Object, ByVal e As System.EventArgs)
        Label1.Text = DateTime.Now.ToString()
    End Sub
</script>

<!DOCTYPE html>
<html>
<head runat="server">
    <title>My Normal ASP.NET Page</title>
</head>
<body>
    <form id="form1" runat="server">
    <div>
        <asp:Label ID="Label1" runat="server"></asp:Label>
        <br />
        <br />
        <asp:Button ID="Button1" runat="server" Text="Click to get machine time"
            onclick="Button1_Click" />
    </div>
    </form>
</body>
</html>
```

C#

```
<%@ Page Language="C#" %>

<script runat="server">
    protected void Button1_Click(object sender, EventArgs e)
    {
        Label1.Text = DateTime.Now.ToString();
    }
</script>
```

When you open this page in the browser, it contains only a single button. When the button is clicked, the Label control that is on the page is populated with the time from the server machine. Before the button is clicked, the page's markup is similar to the code presented in Listing 23-3.

LISTING 23-3: The page output for a page that is not using Ajax

```
<!DOCTYPE html>
<html>
<head><title>
    My Normal ASP.NET Page
</title></head>
<body>
    <form method="post" action="Listing 23-02.aspx" id="form1">
<div class="aspNetHidden">
<input type="hidden" name="__VIEWSTATE" id="__VIEWSTATE" value="pVEIMzKuHfHM8A10duc6kbGylGmyb0H
8CjA0LI9dKlVRyylcUJXhQRd/p3cvsGTRor7wtWsUZGgu8uEWGnFcx3/tLVfqhgqN8aAP4Jxb9M0=" />
</div>

<div class="aspNetHidden">

    <input type="hidden" name="__EVENTVALIDATION" id="__EVENTVALIDATION" value="/
QH9EPcAvi4a4BLc182HKfMOBKUpxA+2dZkl9KS33lgGgRBza5bYURjDLLkyCwA6OKzqthVHfjDFy
9aW9il4V4EYWRlN974paiCVSFbfEa8jprjN5bAl2MbXFMtIVBZu" />
</div>
    <div>
        <span id="Label1"></span>
        <br />
        <br />
        <input type="submit" name="Button1" value="Click to get machine time" id="Button1" />
    </div>
    </form>
</body>
</html>
```

There is not much in this code. There is a little ViewState and a typical form that will be posted back to the `Default.aspx` page. When the end user clicks the button on the page, a full postback to the server occurs, and the entire page is reprocessed and returned to the client's browser. Really, the only change made to the page is that the `<span id="Lable1"></span>` element is populated with a value, but in this case, the entire page is returned.

Building a Simple ASP.NET Page with Ajax

The next step is to build on the page from Listing 23-2 and add Ajax capabilities to it. In this example, you add some additional controls. Two of the controls are typical ASP.NET server controls—another Label and Button server control. In addition to these controls, you must add some ASP.NET AJAX controls.

In the Visual Studio 2012 toolbox is a section entitled AJAX Extensions. This section is shown in Figure 23-8.

FIGURE 23-8

From AJAX Extensions, add a ScriptManager server control to the top of the page and include the second Label and Button control inside the UpdatePanel control. The UpdatePanel control is a template server control and allows you to include any number of items within it (just as other templated ASP.NET server controls). When you have your page set up, it should look something like Figure 23-9.

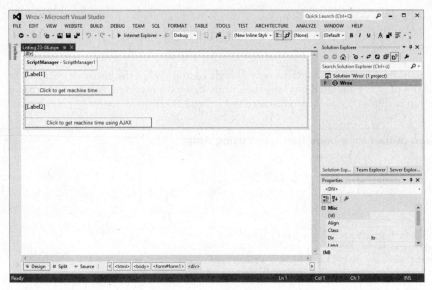

FIGURE 23-9

Listing 23-4 shows the code for this page.

LISTING 23-4: A simple ASP.NET AJAX page

VB

```vb
<%@ Page Language="VB" %>

<script runat="server">
    Protected Sub Button1_Click(ByVal sender As Object, _
        ByVal e As System.EventArgs)
        Label1.Text = DateTime.Now.ToString()
    End Sub

    Protected Sub Button2_Click(ByVal sender As Object, _
        ByVal e As System.EventArgs)
        Label2.Text = DateTime.Now.ToString()
    End Sub
</script>

<!DOCTYPE html>
<html>
<head runat="server">
    <title>My ASP.NET AJAX Page</title>
</head>
<body>
    <form id="form1" runat="server">
    <div>
        <asp:ScriptManager ID="ScriptManager1" runat="server">
```

```
            </asp:ScriptManager>
            <asp:Label ID="Label1" runat="server"></asp:Label>
            <br />
            <br />
            <asp:Button ID="Button1" runat="server" Text="Click to get machine time"
                onclick="Button1_Click" />
            <br />
            <br />
            <asp:UpdatePanel ID="UpdatePanel1" runat="server">
                <ContentTemplate>
                    <asp:Label ID="Label2" runat="server" Text=""></asp:Label>
                    <br />
                    <br />
                    <asp:Button ID="Button2" runat="server"
                     Text="Click to get machine time using Ajax"
                     onclick="Button2_Click" />
                </ContentTemplate>
            </asp:UpdatePanel>
        </div>
        </form>
    </body>
    </html>
```

C#

```
<%@ Page Language="C#" %>

<script runat="server">
    protected void Button1_Click(object sender, EventArgs e)
    {
        Label1.Text = DateTime.Now.ToString();
    }

    protected void Button2_Click(object sender, EventArgs e)
    {
        Label2.Text = DateTime.Now.ToString();
    }
</script>
```

When you open this page in the browser, it has two buttons. The first button causes a complete page postback and updates the current time in the Label1 server control. Clicking on the second button causes a partial Ajax asynchronous postback. Clicking this second button updates the current server time in the Label2 server control. When you click the Ajax button, the time in Label1 will not change at all, as it is outside of the UpdatePanel. Figure 23-10 presents a screenshot of the final result.

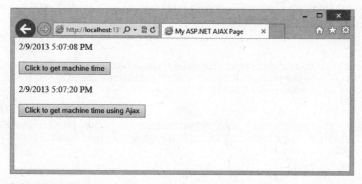

FIGURE 23-10

When you first open the page from Listing 23-4, the code of the page is quite different from the page that you built without using Ajax. Listing 23-5 shows the page results that you will see.

LISTING 23-5: The page output for a page that is using Ajax

```
<!DOCTYPE html>
<html>
<head><title>
     My ASP.NET AJAX Page
</title></head>
<body>
    <form method="post" action="Listing 23-04.aspx" id="form1">
<div class="aspNetHidden">
<input type="hidden" name="__EVENTTARGET" id="__EVENTTARGET" value="" />
<input type="hidden" name="__EVENTARGUMENT" id="__EVENTARGUMENT" value="" />
<input type="hidden" name="__VIEWSTATE" id="__VIEWSTATE" value="WWtnNoYlMaNb9VaXbk6Zu8WKDrp6d2h
tzRxkrRGD7jPvrZP2WPLX0FA7YUBF4pYZRlQogz6EK+PuFjiYhwMDKAFkqBFCct1EC2uWNZzT+xI=" />
</div>

<script type="text/javascript">
//<![CDATA[
var theForm = document.forms['form1'];
if (!theForm) {
    theForm = document.form1;
}
function __doPostBack(eventTarget, eventArgument) {
    if (!theForm.onsubmit || (theForm.onsubmit() != false)) {
        theForm.__EVENTTARGET.value = eventTarget;
        theForm.__EVENTARGUMENT.value = eventArgument;
        theForm.submit();
    }
}
//]]>
</script>


<script src="/WebResource.axd?d=pynGkmcFUV13He1Qd6_TZOfsGAliiRzhbNCK-_Bbdm5qc7-I-DHw9-
fyqR7RqDfDXC3Wksp3fzYjv78lBXTZtA2&amp;t=634776625276709129" type="text/javascript"></script>


<script src="/ScriptResource.axd?d=D9drwtSJ4hBA6O8UhT6CQhrg7DRKGxEuvpwpedj7vopaTC0bITXA9Dx
80QJ3ecSfbXi4t2bNWufm4ED2tyMQPnb6IIgfUv2Z17WvQn25Nc6r2Il_j0Z1DvnIupc15FHAgUL6JsUsSt_CcKQ
NorkPXUgaBAhSYXnodIyqbwTUy3Y1&amp;t=6119e399" type="text/javascript"></script>
<script type="text/javascript">
//<![CDATA[
if (typeof(Sys) === 'undefined') throw new Error('ASP.NET Ajax client-side framework failed to
load.');
//]]>
</script>


<script src="/ScriptResource.axd?d=JnUc-DEDOM5KzzVKtsL1tbPwOqzhED1dD8elz4bygtpKPKhJiqq0b_O9X56
JcIGvkszfugIvdyvz3Efx8suOaifmIwTH_7frKsQOuAjd6Fm3WaKZGEdw75nIgO80ypkfh2PCNd7QinNN1Xyd7uh6dROI
OZ6HqaAT27wpkGD-lfYDELDKBMimdCxNgTRLQi6M0&amp;t=6119e399" type="text/javascript"></script>
<div class="aspNetHidden">

    <input type="hidden" name="__EVENTVALIDATION" id="__EVENTVALIDATION" value="RGmI1vtxaurgS
A6tbndg3zXfgDOK9D+pWkEkUg4X/kJbGksDfFNL5ML2hEEetD+00phBDkOCzf97bxcGQcog/Bk/jsv574AGkbqT26VM8
KsxUvIFRSJWeA3b6vs/4gGwQMU4fPn2SlR1v5kfVEwOdQ==" />
</div>
    <div>
        <script type="text/javascript">
//<![CDATA[
```

```
Sys.WebForms.PageRequestManager._initialize('ScriptManager1', 'form1', ['tUpdatePanel1','Update
Panel1'], [], [], 90, '');
//]]>
</script>

        <span id="Label1"></span>
        <br />
        <br />
        <input type="submit" name="Button1" value="Click to get machine time" id="Button1" />
        <br />
        <br />
        <div id="UpdatePanel1">

                <span id="Label2"></span>
                <br />
                <br />
                <input type="submit" name="Button2" value="Click to get machine time using
Ajax" id="Button2" />

        </div>
    </div>
    </form>
</body>
</html>
```

From there, if you click Button1 and perform the full-page postback, you get this entire bit of code back in a response—even though you are interested in updating only a small portion of the page! However, if you click Button2—the Ajax button—you send the request shown in Listing 23-6.

LISTING 23-6: The asynchronous request from the ASP.NET AJAX page

```
POST /Listing%2023-04.aspx HTTP/1.1
Accept: */*
X-Requested-With: XMLHttpRequest
X-MicrosoftAjax: Delta=true
Cache-Control: no-cache
Content-Type: application/x-www-form-urlencoded; charset=utf-8
Referer: http://localhost:1315/Listing%2023-04.aspx
Accept-Language: en-US,en;q=0.8,de-DE;q=0.5,de;q=0.3
Accept-Encoding: gzip, deflate
User-Agent: Mozilla/5.0 (compatible; MSIE 10.0; Windows NT 6.2; WOW64; Trident/6.0)
Host: localhost:1315
Content-Length: 457
DNT: 1
Connection: Keep-Alive

ScriptManager1=UpdatePanel1%7CButton2&__EVENTTARGET=&__EVENTARGUMENT=&__VIEWSTATE=AGUaegmKl6uk
Z0igyXSeqIUW1YM%2F56cB9CvQ%2BKmbx6wzbEtmJZ3b5wehOayVnxS1fia6%2BEH9ZF98axT8I7yvNNWGS5qzl%2BlxW
xTFNqFTb%2FSb0lYWeXwW31q%2BnqvTOxzO12aGjtZOv9oKuWW2qFU%2F%2B7J%2B4e2HDAkJTKdlH6dlVAc%3D&__EVE
NTVALIDATION=sKpjfJEGzCQ6ObwXMOi1u%2BSAz2Of341uW4OCIOfTPbUgYxWzz9G6nJLAh1r3NzY7Fa4vcU0p4Ft783
W%2BP5KzZGu4HkiUROxRR1trx3hE%2FtkFy%2B%2B9%2Bx0lmRQsnaDK%2FljYNW52e438i4wQ5SyqOAadWA%3D%3D&__
ASYNCPOST=true&Button2=Click%20to%20get%20machine%20time%20using%20AJAX
```

Listing 23-7 shows the response for this asynchronous request.

LISTING 23-7: The asynchronous response from the ASP.NET AJAX page

```
HTTP/1.1 200 OK
Cache-Control: private
Content-Type: text/plain; charset=utf-8
Server: Microsoft-IIS/8.0
```

continues

LISTING 23-7 *(continued)*

```
X-AspNet-Version: 4.0.30319
X-SourceFiles: =?UTF-8?B?QzpcVXNlcnNcQ2hyaXN0aW5uXERvY3VtZW50c1xWaXN1YWwgU3R1ZGlvIDIwMTJcV2
ViU2l0ZXNcV3JveFxMaXN0aW5nNIDE4LTA0LmFzcHg=?=
X-Powered-By: ASP.NET
Date: Fri, 07 Dec 2012 21:09:56 GMT

1|#||4|240|updatePanel|UpdatePanel1|
                <span id="Label2">12/7/2012 10:09:56 PM</span>
                <br />
                <br />
                <input type="submit" name="Button2" value="Click to get machine time using
Ajax" id="Button2" />
        |172|hiddenField|__VIEWSTATE|zhb9R4rHc1avl1CCq/
gAoOeF7XPxtQaoiv64pBVojEhaVevAbRJq6e9rDJe5fC0thgxo51Ls55qg42/6uEUys1ld1h1zM0t0JmLv55CIhsyD5me
Wk6kxHkYO4X0jxdIVj8YbphKp+CB485z/cPAzZk1LkQs7J96ZtzLGfg11cv4=|152|hiddenField|__EVENTVALIDATION
|sCJzmPa+sVbkZ2zvON/kvEn6/7qjGZKpheMuCF34am8ZaaHtdk+Zdepz+uf97h+RZWWAv5/is+Mwig6DEPEOOI+oAwOMqf
PwnUOF1Dt3G5L/6KwE3EPyK1XLmd9Xm/29BKYhM0RGxwO31H2/wuBRXQ==|0|asyncPostBackControlIDs|||0|post
BackControlIDs|||26|updatePanelIDs||tUpdatePanel1,UpdatePanel1|0|childUpdatePanelIDs|||25|pane
lsToRefreshIDs||UpdatePanel1,UpdatePanel1|2|asyncPostBackTimeout||90|18|formAction||Listing
23-04.aspx|20|pageTitle||My ASP.NET AJAX Page|
```

From Listing 23-7, you can see that the response is much smaller than an entire web page! In fact, the main part of the response is only the code that is contained within the UpdatePanel server control and nothing more. The items at the bottom of the output deal with the ViewState of the page (as it has now changed) and some other small page changes.

ASP.NET AJAX'S SERVER-SIDE CONTROLS

When you look at the AJAX Extensions section in the Visual Studio 2012 toolbox, you will notice that not many controls are at your disposal. The controls there are focused on allowing you to Ajax-enable your ASP.NET applications. They are enabling controls. If you are looking for more specific server controls that take advantage of the Ajax model, then look at the Ajax Control Toolkit—a separate download that is covered in Chapter 24.

Table 23-1 describes the ASP.NET AJAX server controls that come with ASP.NET 4.5.

TABLE 23-1

ASP.NET AJAX SERVER CONTROL	DESCRIPTION
ScriptManager	A component control that manages the marshalling of messages to the Ajax-enabled server for the parts of the page requiring partial updates. Every ASP.NET page requires a ScriptManager control in order to work. Note that you can have only a single ScriptManager control on a page.
ScriptManager Proxy	A component control that acts as a ScriptManager control for a content page. The ScriptManagerProxy control, which sits on the content page (or sub-page), works in conjunction with a required ScriptManager control that resides on the master page.
Timer	The Timer control executes client-side events at specific intervals and allows specific parts of your page to update or refresh at these moments.
UpdatePanel	A container control that allows you to define specific areas of the page that are enabled to work with the ScriptManager. These areas can then, in turn, make the partial page postbacks and update themselves outside the normal ASP.NET page postback process.
UpdateProgress	A control that allows you to display a visual element to the end user to show that a partial-page postback is occurring to the part of the page making the update. This control is ideal to use when you have long-running Ajax updates.

The next few sections of this chapter look at these controls and explain how to use them within your ASP.NET pages.

The ScriptManager Control

Probably the most important control in your ASP.NET AJAX arsenal is the ScriptManager server control, which works with the page to allow for partial page rendering. You use a single ScriptManager control on each page for which you want to use the Ajax capabilities provided by ASP.NET 4.5. When placed in conjunction with the UpdatePanel server control, Ajax-enabling your ASP.NET applications can be as simple as adding two server controls to the page, and then you are ready to go!

The ScriptManager control takes care of managing the JavaScript libraries that are used on your page as well as marshalling the messages back and forth between the server and the client for the partial page rendering process. The marshalling of the messages can be done using either SOAP or JSON through the ScriptManager control.

If you place only a single ScriptManager control on your ASP.NET page, it takes care of loading the JavaScript libraries needed by ASP.NET AJAX. Listing 23-8 presents the page for this task.

LISTING 23-8: An ASP.NET page that includes only the ScriptManager control

```
<%@ Page Language="C#" %>

<!DOCTYPE html>
<html>
<head runat="server">
    <title>The ScriptManager Control</title>
</head>
<body>
    <form id="form1" runat="server">
    <div>
        <asp:ScriptManager ID="ScriptManager1" runat="server">
        </asp:ScriptManager>
    </div>
    </form>
</body>
</html>
```

From Listing 23-8, you can see that this control is like all other ASP.NET controls and needs only an ID and a runat attribute to do its work. Listing 23-9 shows the page output from this bit of ASP.NET code.

LISTING 23-9: The page output from the ScriptManager control

```
<!DOCTYPE html>
<html>
<head><title>
    The ScriptManager Control
</title></head>
<body>
    <form method="post" action="Listing 23-08.aspx" id="form1">
<div class="aspNetHidden">
<input type="hidden" name="__EVENTTARGET" id="__EVENTTARGET" value="" />
<input type="hidden" name="__EVENTARGUMENT" id="__EVENTARGUMENT" value="" />
<input type="hidden" name="__VIEWSTATE" id="__VIEWSTATE" value="zpV5crkAwVuhffQapeLOpcyY7E3sDEm
epTrY/bsvgCn/drFkzuIEIbGMZSnm8fkgNjzDGQ29rapFR3M/2jUcMfMh6z291dYhyQUzLL0wLQA=" />
</div>

<script type="text/javascript">
```

continues

LISTING 23-9 *(continued)*

```
//<![CDATA[
var theForm = document.forms['form1'];
if (!theForm) {
    theForm = document.form1;
}
function __doPostBack(eventTarget, eventArgument) {
    if (!theForm.onsubmit || (theForm.onsubmit() != false)) {
        theForm.__EVENTTARGET.value = eventTarget;
        theForm.__EVENTARGUMENT.value = eventArgument;
        theForm.submit();
    }
}
//]]>
</script>


<script src="/WebResource.axd?d=pynGkmcFUV13He1Qd6_TZOfsGAliiRzhbNCK-_Bbdm5qc7-I-DHw9-fyqR7RqDf
DXC3Wksp3fzYjv78lBXTZtA2&amp;t=634776625276709129" type="text/javascript"></script>


<script src="/ScriptResource.axd?d=D9drwtSJ4hBA6O8UhT6CQhrg7DRKGxEuvpwpedj7vopaTC0bITXA9Dx80
QJ3ecSfbXi4t2bNWufm4ED2tyMQPnb6IIgfUv2Z17WvQn25Nc6r2Il_j0Z1DvnIupc15FHAgUL6JsUsSt_CcKQNorkPXUga
BAhSYXnodIyqbwTUy3Y1&amp;t=6119e399" type="text/javascript"></script>
<script type="text/javascript">
//<![CDATA[
if (typeof(Sys) === 'undefined') throw new Error('ASP.NET Ajax client-side framework failed to
load.');
//]]>
</script>


<script src="/ScriptResource.axd?d=JnUc-DEDOM5KzzVKtsL1tbPwOqzhED1dD8elz4bygtpKPKhJiqq0b_
O9X56Jc
IGvkszfugIvdyvz3Efx8suOaifmIwTH_7frKsQOuAjd6Fm3WaKZGEdw75nIgO80ypkfh2PCNd7QinNN1Xyd7uh6dROIOZ6
HqaAT27wpkGD-1fYDELDKBMimdCxNgTRLQi6M0&amp;t=6119e399" type="text/javascript"></script>
    <div>
        <script type="text/javascript">
//<![CDATA[
Sys.WebForms.PageRequestManager._initialize('ScriptManager1', 'form1', [], [], [], 90, '');
//]]>
</script>

    </div>
    </form>
</body>
</html>
```

The page output shows that a number of JavaScript libraries load with the page. Also notice that the scripts' sources are dynamically registered and available through the HTTP handler provided through the `ScriptResource.axd` handler.

> **NOTE** *If you are interested in seeing the contents of the JavaScript libraries, you can use the* `src` *attribute's URL in the address bar of your browser, and you will be prompted to download the JavaScript file that is referenced. You will be prompted to save the* `ScriptResource.axd` *file, but you can rename it with a* `.txt` *or* `.js` *extension if you want.*

An interesting point about the ScriptManager is that it deals with the scripts that are sent to the client by taking the extra step to compress them.

The ScriptManagerProxy Control

The ScriptManagerProxy control was actually introduced in Chapter 16, as this control deals specifically with master pages and user controls. As with the ScriptManager control covered in the previous section, you need a single ScriptManager control on each page that is going to be working with ASP.NET AJAX. However, with that said, the big question is what do you do when you are using master pages? Do you need to put the ScriptManager control on the master page, and how does this work with the content pages that use the master page?

When you create a new master page from the Add New Item dialog box, you simply just select the typical master page option and just change the code a bit in order to deal with Ajax. This is demonstrated in Listing 23-10.

LISTING 23-10: The Ajax master page

```
<%@ Master Language="C#" %>

<script runat="server">

</script>

<!DOCTYPE html>
<html>
<head runat="server">
    <title>Untitled Page</title>
    <asp:ContentPlaceHolder id="head" runat="server">
    </asp:ContentPlaceHolder>
</head>
<body>
    <form id="form1" runat="server">
    <div>
        <asp:ScriptManager ID="ScriptManager1" runat="server" />
        <asp:ContentPlaceHolder id="ContentPlaceHolder1"
         runat="server">

        </asp:ContentPlaceHolder>
    </div>
    </form>
</body>
</html>
```

This code shows that, indeed, a ScriptManager control is on the page and that this page will be added to each and every content page that uses this master page. You do not need to do anything special to a content page to use the ASP.NET AJAX capabilities provided by the master page. Instead, you can create a content page that is no different from any other content page that you might be used to creating.

However, if you want to modify the ScriptManager control that is on the master page in any way, then you must add a ScriptManagerProxy control to the content page, as shown in Listing 23-11.

LISTING 23-11: Adding to the ScriptManager control from the content page

```
<%@ Page Language="C#" MasterPageFile="~/AJAXMaster.master" %>

<asp:Content ID="Content1" ContentPlaceHolderID="head" Runat="Server">
</asp:Content>
<asp:Content ID="Content2" ContentPlaceHolderID="ContentPlaceHolder1"
 Runat="Server">
 <asp:ScriptManagerProxy ID="ScriptManagerProxy1" runat="server">
    <Scripts>
        <asp:ScriptReference Path="myOtherScript.js" />
    </Scripts>
 </asp:ScriptManagerProxy>
</asp:Content>
```

In this case, the content page adds to the ScriptManager control that is on the master page by interjecting a script reference from the content page. If you use a ScriptManagerProxy control on a content page and a ScriptManager control does not happen to be on the master page, you will get an error.

The Timer Control

One common task when working with asynchronous postbacks from your ASP.NET pages is that you might want these asynchronous postbacks to occur at specific intervals in time. To accomplish this, you use the Timer control available from the AJAX Extensions part of the toolbox. A simple example to demonstrate how this control works involves putting some timestamps on your page and setting postbacks to occur at timed intervals, as illustrated in Listing 23-12.

LISTING 23-12: Using the Timer control

VB

```
<%@ Page Language="VB" %>

<script runat="server">
    Protected Sub Page_Load(ByVal sender As Object, ByVal e As System.EventArgs)
        If Not Page.IsPostBack Then
            Label1.Text = DateTime.Now.ToString()
        End If
    End Sub

    Protected Sub Timer1_Tick(ByVal sender As Object, ByVal e As System.EventArgs)
        Label1.Text = DateTime.Now.ToString()
    End Sub
</script>

<!DOCTYPE html>
<html>
<head id="Head1" runat="server">
    <title>Timer Example</title>
</head>
<body>
    <form id="form1" runat="server">
        <div>
            <asp:ScriptManager ID="ScriptManager1" runat="server" />
            <asp:UpdatePanel ID="UpdatePanel1" runat="server">
                <ContentTemplate>
                    <asp:Label ID="Label1" runat="server" Text="Label"></asp:Label>
```

```
                    <asp:Timer ID="Timer1" runat="server" OnTick="Timer1_Tick"
                       Interval="10000">
                    </asp:Timer>
                </ContentTemplate>
            </asp:UpdatePanel>
        </div>
    </form>
</body>
</html>
```

C#

```
<%@ Page Language="C#" %>

<script runat="server">
    protected void Page_Load(object sender, EventArgs e)
    {
        if (!Page.IsPostBack)
        {
            Label1.Text = DateTime.Now.ToString();
        }
    }

    protected void Timer1_Tick(object sender, EventArgs e)
    {
        Label1.Text = DateTime.Now.ToString();
    }
</script>
```

In this case, only three controls are on the page. The first is the ScriptManager control, followed by a Label and the Timer control. When this page loads for the first time, the Label control is populated with the `DateTime` value through the invocation of the `Page_Load` event handler. After this initial load of the `DateTime` value to the Label control, the Timer control takes care of changing this value.

The `OnTick` attribute from the Timer control enables you to accomplish this task. It points to the function triggered when the time span specified in the `Interval` attribute is reached.

The `Interval` attribute is set to `10000`, which is 10,000 milliseconds (remember that there are 1,000 milliseconds to every second). This means that every 10 seconds an asynchronous postback is performed and the `Timer1_Tick()` function is called.

When you run this page, you see the time change on the page every 10 seconds.

The UpdatePanel Control

The UpdatePanel server control is an Ajax-specific control that is part of ASP.NET 4.5. The UpdatePanel control is the control that you are likely to use the most when dealing with Ajax. This control preserves the postback model and allows you to perform a partial page render.

The UpdatePanel control is a container control, which means that it does not actually have UI-specific items associated with it. It is a way to trigger a partial page postback and update only the portion of the page that the UpdatePanel specifies.

The <ContentTemplate> Element

You have a couple of ways to deal with the controls on the page that initiate the asynchronous page postbacks. The first is by far the simplest and is shown in Listing 23-13.

LISTING 23-13: Putting the triggers inside of the UpdatePanel control

VB

```
<%@ Page Language="VB" %>

<script runat="server">
    Protected Sub Button1_Click(ByVal sender As Object, _
        ByVal e As System.EventArgs)

            Label1.Text = "This button was clicked on " & DateTime.Now.ToString()
    End Sub
</script>

<!DOCTYPE html>
<html>
<head id="Head1" runat="server">
    <title>UpdatePanel Control</title>
</head>
<body>
    <form id="form1" runat="server">
        <div>
            <asp:ScriptManager ID="ScriptManager1" runat="server">
            </asp:ScriptManager>
            <asp:UpdatePanel ID="UpdatePanel1" runat="server">
                <ContentTemplate>
                    <asp:Label ID="Label1" runat="server"></asp:Label>
                    <br />
                    <br />
                    <asp:Button ID="Button1" runat="server"
                        Text="Click to initiate async request"
                        OnClick="Button1_Click" />
                </ContentTemplate>
            </asp:UpdatePanel>
        </div>
    </form>
</body>
</html>
```

C#

```
<%@ Page Language="C#" %>

<script runat="server">
    protected void Button1_Click(object sender, EventArgs e)
    {
        Label1.Text = "This button was clicked on " + DateTime.Now.ToString();
    }
</script>
```

In this case, the Label and Button server controls are contained within the UpdatePanel server control. The `<asp:UpdatePanel>` element has two possible sub-elements: `<ContentTemplate>` and `<Triggers>`. Any content that needs to be changed with the asynchronous page postbacks should be contained within the `<ContentTemplate>` section of the UpdatePanel control.

By default, any type of control trigger (something that would normally trigger a page postback) that is contained within the `<ContentTemplate>` section instead causes the asynchronous page postback. That means, in the case of Listing 23-13, that the button on the page will trigger an asynchronous page postback instead of a full-page postback. Each click on the button changes the time displayed in the Label control.

The <Triggers> Element

Listing 23-13 demonstrates one of the big issues with this model—when the asynchronous postback occurs, you are not only sending the date/time value for the Label control, but also sending back the entire code for the button that is on the page—as presented here:

```
1|#||4|282|updatePanel|UpdatePanel1|
                    <span id="Label1">This button was clicked on 12/7/2012 10:15:13 PM</span>
                    <br />
                    <br />
                    <input type="submit" name="Button1" value="Click to initiate async request"
id="Button1" />
                |216|hiddenField|__VIEWSTATE|9SRD65c4+HKABtyXj1cwTSdqRx5djmaw4UM/
pnsbaV6BW9Yp3Jt0dMEUO49qM6bpcgVY7ZGaizibE3WuKeC39UPCgR3ivwhh+47AYvrBWPoKY7YpNww7zr7mo5HoMqgY
JeUnJIPlXQml2/gFiOl8CmEbk/9u0t156Bjjw/rEWOYJdNSXHBxsWJgGe2cA+JZstvkNnOaJtGBjlOHfkkhqCg==|128
|hiddenField|__EVENTVALIDATION|rcyhqzLnEyzijEQwniWhKYVo9K47PWymKxRO+QMdU2BwNSArt0P8hu3
3J7bgc+80rIB2IUeWXrR3YLsPZyDoFl2BoHyJ7gCCmjzhPUyUrSH4c0xR3c9EjVqL2BlZQYvK|0|asyncPostBackCont
rol
IDs|||0|postBackControlIDs|||26|updatePanelIDs||tUpdatePanel1,UpdatePanel1|0|childUpdatePanel
IDs
|||25|panelsToRefreshIDs||UpdatePanel1,UpdatePanel1|2|asyncPostBackTimeout||90|18|formAction|
|Listing 23-13.aspx|19|pageTitle||UpdatePanel Control|
```

This bit of code that is sent back to the client via the asynchronous postback shows that the entire section contained within the UpdatePanel control is reissued. You can slim down your pages by including only the portions of the page that are actually updating. If you take the button outside of the `<ContentTemplate>` section of the UpdatePanel control, then you must include a `<Triggers>` section within the control.

The reason for this is that although the content that you want to change with the asynchronous postback is all contained within the `<ContentTemplate>` section, you need to tie up a page event to cause the postback to occur. This is how the `<Triggers>` section of the UpdatePanel control is used. You use this section of the control to specify the various triggers that initiate an asynchronous page postback. Using the `<Triggers>` element within the UpdatePanel control, you can rewrite Listing 23-13, as shown in Listing 23-14.

LISTING 23-14: Using a trigger to cause the asynchronous page postback

VB

```
<%@ Page Language="VB" %>

<script runat="server">
    Protected Sub Button1_Click(ByVal sender As Object, _
        ByVal e As System.EventArgs)
        Label1.Text = "This button was clicked on " & DateTime.Now.ToString()
    End Sub
</script>

<!DOCTYPE html>
<html>
<head id="Head1" runat="server">
    <title>UpdatePanel</title>
</head>
<body>
    <form id="form1" runat="server">
        <div>
            <asp:ScriptManager ID="ScriptManager1" runat="server">
            </asp:ScriptManager>
            <asp:UpdatePanel ID="UpdatePanel1" runat="server">
```

continues

LISTING 23-14 *(continued)*

```
                    <ContentTemplate>
                        <asp:Label ID="Label1" runat="server"></asp:Label>
                    </ContentTemplate>
                    <Triggers>
                        <asp:AsyncPostBackTrigger ControlID="Button1" EventName="Click" />
                    </Triggers>
                </asp:UpdatePanel>
                <br />
                <br />
                <asp:Button ID="Button1" runat="server"
                    Text="Click to initiate async request"
                    OnClick="Button1_Click" />
        </div>
    </form>
</body>
</html>
```

C#

```
<%@ Page Language="C#" %>

<script runat="server">
    protected void Button1_Click(object sender, EventArgs e)
    {
        Label1.Text = "This button was clicked on " + DateTime.Now.ToString();
    }
</script>
```

In this case, the Button control and the HTML elements are outside of the `<ContentTemplate>` section of the UpdatePanel control and, therefore, will not be sent back to the client for each asynchronous page postback. The only item contained in the `<ContentTemplate>` section is the only item on the page that needs to change with the postbacks—the Label control. Tying this all together is the `<Triggers>` section.

The `<Triggers>` section can contain two possible controls: AsyncPostBackTrigger and PostBackTrigger. In this case, the AsyncPostBackTrigger is used. The PostBackTrigger control will cause a full-page postback, whereas the AsyncPostBackTrigger control will cause only an asynchronous page postback (obviously, as described by the names of the controls).

As you can see from the example in Listing 23-14, which uses the AsyncPostBackTrigger element, only two attributes are used to tie the Button control to the trigger for the asynchronous postback: the `ControlID` and the `EventName` attributes. The control you want to act as the initiator of the asynchronous page postback is put here (the control's name as specified by the control's `ID` attribute). The `EventName` attribute's value is the name of the event for the control that is specified in the `ControlID` that you want to be called in the asynchronous request from the client. In this case, the Button control's `Click()` event is called, and this is the event that changes the value of the control that resides within the `<ContentTemplate>` section of the UpdatePanel control.

Running this page and clicking on the button gives you a smaller asynchronous response back to the client:

```
1|#||4|113|updatePanel|UpdatePanel1|
                    <span id="Label1">This button was clicked on 12/7/2012 10:16:00 PM</span>
            |216|hiddenField|__VIEWSTATE|exYy/K/aPNML3q+zrqHMWbTkzeycwcLnuu
HX4mfKnCfPJggjY8k7//liUwxhyUEg2eJU/QLD4Cgr4E/B/V7ossp0Rcn2zO5s17I/0oK2mw0MKM0/
OQ3F2NtqeCR5rwic9FiqbVx8G8V52uW0CL1pdnLArj9pi/NSyYpeeVmEAXapYQklsDPvcSKpHmjhIWIhfJ0QmSvO6Yv7LUS
k4OFETg==|128|hiddenField|__EVENTVALIDATION|MdQFKILTdqEbZgfpPoEQwHNM/A1icFRG9iE9Qy+b6wB4LQZQXWf
```

```
e9OK1Y6nNzLoFtTFX/hOdRHxv1Fci3EZNZSfpap+bu5DHqP+wDA6qL85imfWkquq8you1y59ztNKU|15|asyncPostBackC
ontrolIDs||Button1,Button1|0|postBackControlIDs|||26|updatePanelIDs||tUpdatePanel1,UpdatePanel1
|0|childUpdatePanelIDs|||25|panelsToRefreshIDs||UpdatePanel1,UpdatePanel1|2|asyncPostBackTimeou
t||90|18|formAction||Listing 23-14.aspx|11|pageTitle||UpdatePanel|
```

Although not considerably smaller than the previous example, it is, in fact, just a bit smaller—the size similarity is really due to the size of the page used in this example (pages that are more voluminous would show more dramatic improvements). Pages with heavy content associated with them can show some dramatic size reductions, depending on how you structure your pages with the UpdatePanel control.

Building Triggers Using Visual Studio 2012

If you like to work on the design surface of Visual Studio when building your ASP.NET pages, then you will find that there is good support for building your ASP.NET AJAX pages, including the creation of triggers in the UpdatePanel control. To see this in action, place a single UpdatePanel server control on your page and view the control in the Properties dialog box within Visual Studio. The Triggers item in the list has a button next to it that allows you to modify the items associated with it, as illustrated in Figure 23-11.

Clicking on this button in the Properties dialog box launches the UpdatePanelTrigger Collection Editor, as shown in Figure 23-12. This editor allows you to add any number of triggers and to associate them to a control and a control event very easily.

FIGURE 23-11

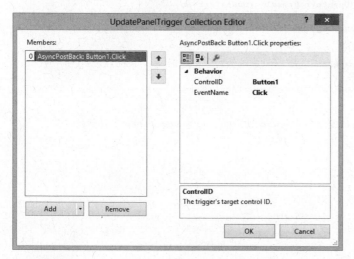

FIGURE 23-12

Clicking OK adds the trigger to the `<Triggers>` section of your UpdatePanel control.

The UpdateProgress Control

The final server control in the AJAX Extensions section of Visual Studio 2012 is the UpdateProgress control. Some asynchronous postbacks take some time to execute because of the size of the response or because of the computing time required to get a result together to send back to the client. The UpdateProgress control allows you to provide a visual signifier to the clients to show that, indeed, work is being done and that they will get results soon (and that the browser didn't just lock up).

Listing 23-15 shows a textual implementation of the UpdateProgress control.

LISTING 23-15: Using the UpdateProgress control to show a text message to the client

VB

```
<%@ Page Language="VB" %>

<script runat="server">
    Protected Sub Button1_Click(ByVal sender As Object, _
        ByVal e As System.EventArgs)
            System.Threading.Thread.Sleep(10000)
            Label1.Text = "This button was clicked on " & DateTime.Now.ToString()
    End Sub
</script>

<!DOCTYPE html>
<html>
<head id="Head1" runat="server">
    <title>UpdatePanel</title>
</head>
<body>
    <form id="form1" runat="server">
    <div>
        <asp:ScriptManager ID="ScriptManager1" runat="server">
        </asp:ScriptManager>
        <asp:UpdateProgress ID="UpdateProgress1" runat="server">
            <ProgressTemplate>
                An update is occurring...
            </ProgressTemplate>
        </asp:UpdateProgress>
        <asp:UpdatePanel ID="UpdatePanel1" runat="server" UpdateMode="Conditional">
            <ContentTemplate>
                <asp:Label ID="Label1" runat="server"></asp:Label>
            </ContentTemplate>
            <Triggers>
                <asp:AsyncPostBackTrigger ControlID="Button1" EventName="Click" />
            </Triggers>
        </asp:UpdatePanel>
        <br />
        <br />
        <asp:Button ID="Button1" runat="server"
         Text="Click to initiate async request"
         OnClick="Button1_Click" />
    </div>
    </form>
</body>
</html>
```

C#

```
<%@ Page Language="C#" %>

<script runat="server">
    protected void Button1_Click(object sender, EventArgs e)
    {
        System.Threading.Thread.Sleep(10000);
        Label1.Text = "This button was clicked on " + DateTime.Now.ToString();
    }
</script>
```

To add some delay to the response (to simulate a long-running computer process), the `Thread.Sleep()` method is called. From here, you add an UpdateProgress control to the part of the page where you want the update message to be presented. In this case, the UpdateProgress control was added above the UpdatePanel server control. This control does not go inside the UpdatePanel control; instead, it sits outside of the control. However, like the UpdatePanel control, the UpdateProgress control is a template control.

The UpdateProgress control has only a single sub-element: the `<ProgressTemplate>` element. Whatever you place in this section of the control will appear when the UpdateProgress control is triggered. In this case, the only item present in this section of the control is some text. When you run this page, the update shown in Figure 23-13 appears.

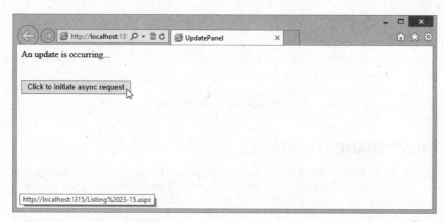

FIGURE 23-13

The text appears immediately in this case and will not disappear until the asynchronous postback has finished. The code you put in the `<ProgressTemplate>` section is actually contained in the page, but its display is turned off through CSS.

```
<div id="UpdateProgress1" style="display:none;">
    An update is occurring...
</div>
```

Controlling When the Message Appears

Right now, the UpdateProgress appears as soon as the button is clicked. However, some of your processes might not take that long, and you might not always want a progress notification going out to the client. The UpdateProgress control includes a `DisplayAfter` attribute, which allows you to control when the progress update message appears. Listing 23-16 shows the use of the `DisplayAfter` attribute.

LISTING 23-16: Using the DisplayAfter attribute

```
<asp:UpdateProgress ID="UpdateProgress1" runat="server" DisplayAfter="5000">
    <ProgressTemplate>
        An update is occurring...
    </ProgressTemplate>
</asp:UpdateProgress>
```

The value of the `DisplayAfter` property is a number that represents the number of milliseconds that the UpdateProgress control will wait until it displays what is contained within the `<ProgressTemplate>` section. The code in Listing 23-16 specifies that the text found in the `<ProgressTemplate>` section will not be displayed for 5,000 milliseconds (5 seconds).

Adding an Image to the <ProcessTemplate>

The previous examples, which use the UpdateProgress control, use this control with text, but you can put anything you want within this template control. For instance, you can put a spinning wheel image that will show the end user that the request is being processed. Listing 23-17 shows the use of the image.

LISTING 23-17: Using an image in the <ProcessTemplate> section

```
<asp:UpdateProgress ID="UpdateProgress1" runat="server"
 DisplayAfter="5000">
    <ProgressTemplate>
        <asp:Image ID="Image1" runat="server"
         ImageUrl="~/spinningwheel.gif" />
    </ProgressTemplate>
</asp:UpdateProgress>
```

Just as in the text approach, the code for the image is already placed on the client's page instance and is just turned off via CSS.

```
<div id="UpdateProgress1" style="display:none;">
    <img id="Image1" src="spinningwheel.gif" style="border-width:0px;" />
</div>
```

USING MULTIPLE UPDATEPANEL CONTROLS

So far, this chapter has showed you how to work with a single UpdatePanel control, but it is important to realize that you can have multiple UpdatePanel controls on a single page. This, in the end, gives you the ability to control the output to specific regions of the page when you want.

Listing 23-18 presents an example of using more than a single UpdatePanel control.

LISTING 23-18: Using more than one UpdatePanel control

VB

```
<%@ Page Language="VB" %>

<script runat="server">
    Protected Sub Button1_Click(ByVal sender As Object, _
        ByVal e As System.EventArgs)
        Label1.Text = "Label1 was populated on " & DateTime.Now.ToString()
        Label2.Text = "Label2 was populated on " & DateTime.Now.ToString()
    End Sub
</script>

<!DOCTYPE html>
<html>
<head id="Head1" runat="server">
    <title>Multiple UpdatePanel Controls</title>
</head>
<body>
    <form id="form1" runat="server">
        <div>
            <asp:ScriptManager ID="ScriptManager1" runat="server">
            </asp:ScriptManager>
            <asp:UpdatePanel ID="UpdatePanel1" runat="server">
                <ContentTemplate>
```

```
                    <asp:Label ID="Label1" runat="server"></asp:Label>
                </ContentTemplate>
                <Triggers>
                    <asp:AsyncPostBackTrigger ControlID="Button1" EventName="Click" />
                </Triggers>
            </asp:UpdatePanel>
            <asp:UpdatePanel ID="UpdatePanel2" runat="server">
                <ContentTemplate>
                    <asp:Label ID="Label2" runat="server"></asp:Label>
                </ContentTemplate>
            </asp:UpdatePanel>
            <br />
            <br />
            <asp:Button ID="Button1" runat="server"
                Text="Click to initiate async request"
                OnClick="Button1_Click" />
        </div>
    </form>
</body>
</html>
```

C#

```
<%@ Page Language="C#" %>

<script runat="server">
    protected void Button1_Click(object sender, EventArgs e)
    {
        Label1.Text = "Label1 was populated on " + DateTime.Now;
        Label2.Text = "Label2 was populated on " + DateTime.Now;
    }
</script>
```

This page is interesting. It has two UpdatePanel controls: UpdatePanel1 and UpdatePanel2. Both of these controls contain a single Label control that at one point can take a date/time value from a server response.

The UpdatePanel1 control has an associated trigger: the Button control on the page. When this button is clicked, the Button1_Click() event triggers and does its job. If you run this page, both of the UpdatePanel controls are updated according to the Button1_Click() event, as illustrated in Figure 23-14.

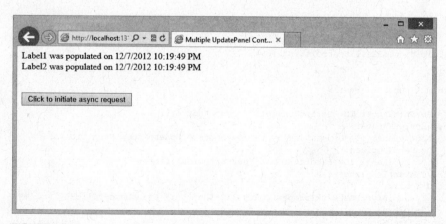

FIGURE 23-14

Both UpdatePanel sections were updated with the `Button1_Click()` event because, by default, all UpdatePanel controls on a single page update with *each* asynchronous postback that occurs. This means that the postback that occurred with the `Button1` button control also causes a postback to occur with the `UpdatePanel2` control.

You can actually control this behavior through the UpdatePanel's `UpdateMode` property. The `UpdateMode` property can take two possible enumerations—`Always` and `Conditional`. If you do not set this property, then it uses the value of `Always`, meaning that each UpdatePanel control always updates with each asynchronous request.

The other option is to set the property to `Conditional`. This means that the UpdatePanel updates only if one of the trigger conditions is met. For an example of this, change the UpdatePanel controls on the page so that they are now using an `UpdateMode` of `Conditional`, as shown in Listing 23-19.

LISTING 23-19: Using more than one (conditional) UpdatePanel control

VB

```
<%@ Page Language="VB" %>

<script runat="server">
    Protected Sub Button1_Click(ByVal sender As Object, _
        ByVal e As System.EventArgs)
        Label1.Text = "Label1 was populated on " & DateTime.Now.ToString()
        Label2.Text = "Label2 was populated on " & DateTime.Now.ToString()
    End Sub
</script>
```

C#

```
<%@ Page Language="C#" %>

<script runat="server">
    protected void Button1_Click(object sender, EventArgs e)
    {
        Label1.Text = "Label1 was populated on " + DateTime.Now;
        Label2.Text = "Label2 was populated on " + DateTime.Now;
    }
</script>

<!DOCTYPE html>
<html>
<head id="Head1" runat="server">
    <title>Multiple UpdatePanel Controls</title>
</head>
<body>
    <form id="form1" runat="server">
        <div>
            <asp:ScriptManager ID="ScriptManager1" runat="server">
            </asp:ScriptManager>
            <asp:UpdatePanel ID="UpdatePanel1" runat="server" UpdateMode="Conditional">
                <ContentTemplate>
                    <asp:Label ID="Label1" runat="server"></asp:Label>
                </ContentTemplate>
                <Triggers>
                    <asp:AsyncPostBackTrigger ControlID="Button1" EventName="Click" />
                </Triggers>
            </asp:UpdatePanel>
            <asp:UpdatePanel ID="UpdatePanel2" runat="server" UpdateMode="Conditional">
                <ContentTemplate>
```

```
                    <asp:Label ID="Label2" runat="server"></asp:Label>
                </ContentTemplate>
            </asp:UpdatePanel>
            <br />
            <br />
            <asp:Button ID="Button1" runat="server"
                Text="Click to initiate async request"
                OnClick="Button1_Click" />
        </div>
    </form>
</body>
</html>
```

Now that both of the UpdatePanel controls are set to have an `UpdateMode` of `Conditional`, when running this page, you will see the results presented in Figure 23-15.

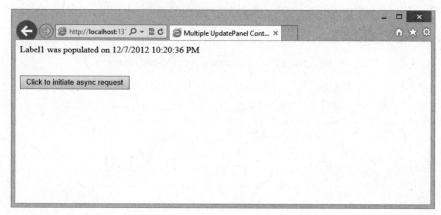

FIGURE 23-15

In this case, only the right Label control, `Label1`, was updated with the asynchronous request even though the `Button1_Click()` event tries to change the values of both `Label1` and `Label2`. The reason for this is that the `UpdatePanel2` control had no trigger that was met.

WORKING WITH PAGE HISTORY

One issue when working with any Ajax page is that when the end user clicks the browser's Back button, it destroys the asynchronous requests that are occurring between the current page and the server and any kind of state that you might be managing between these requests.

If you have a process of working with Ajax in the page and you clicked the Back button within the browser, you would go to the page that was just prior to the Ajax-enabled page, regardless of the asynchronous page requests that occurred prior to this action.

Also, if your first page in navigation is a series of asynchronous page requests, as an end user, you will never see the option to click on the Back button of the page, even if you work your way quite far into the navigation that the page provides.

With ASP.NET AJAX, you have the capability to work with the back history of your application. It isn't as simple as just activating something; it will take a little bit of coding to accomplish what you want. You need to work through a process of telling the ASP.NET page what state you are going to keep track of as you allow end users to navigate with the Back and Forward buttons on the browser.

To see this scenario in action, create a simple page that uses Ajax. This page is presented in Listing 23-20.

LISTING 23-20: Building a basic ASP.NET AJAX page

VB

```
<%@ Page Language="VB" %>

<script runat="server">
    Protected Sub Button1_Click(ByVal sender As Object, _
        ByVal e As System.EventArgs)

        PopulateFields(TextBox1.Text)

    End Sub

    Private Sub PopulateFields(ByVal InputName As String)
        If InputName Is Nothing Then
            Label1.Text = "Hello there. What is your name?"
        Else
            Label1.Text = "Hello there " & HttpUtility.HtmlEncode(InputName)
        End If
    End Sub
</script>

<!DOCTYPE html>
<html>
<head runat="server">
    <title>Ajax Page</title>
</head>
<body>
    <form id="form1" runat="server">
        <div>
            <asp:ScriptManager ID="ScriptManager1" runat="server">
            </asp:ScriptManager>
            <asp:UpdatePanel ID="UpdatePanel1" runat="server">
                <ContentTemplate>
                    <asp:Label ID="Label1" runat="server"
                        Text="Hello there. What is your name?"></asp:Label><br />
                    <br />
                    <asp:TextBox ID="TextBox1" runat="server"></asp:TextBox><br />
                    <asp:Button ID="Button1" runat="server" Text="Submit Name"
                        OnClick="Button1_Click" />
                </ContentTemplate>
            </asp:UpdatePanel>
        </div>
    </form>
</body>
</html>
```

C#

```
<%@ Page Language="C#" %>

<script runat="server">

    protected void Button1_Click(object sender, EventArgs e)
    {
        PopulateFields(TextBox1.Text);
    }

    private void PopulateFields(string InputName)
```

```
        {
            if (InputName == null)
            {
                Label1.Text = "Hello there. What is your name?";
            }
            else
            {
                Label1.Text = "Hello there " + HttpUtility.HtmlEncode(InputName);
            }
        }

    </script>
```

This is a standard ASP.NET AJAX page, and nothing tricky is going on here. In this case, you use Ajax to enter your name into the textbox, and then this name is put into the Label control that is on the page. However, if you enter more than one name, you will find that it *seems* as if you are working through multiple pages, but the browser's navigation buttons (the Back and Forward buttons) are not enabled, and you do not have the option to work back to the previous items you entered into the textbox. Also, browser bookmarks do not work, since they only store the (never changing) URL of the page, not its state.

Unfortunately, end users expect this type of behavior, so the new capability adds the back history to these types of pages.

If you are using ASP.NET 3.5 SP1 or higher and you look at the ScriptManager control that is on the page, you will notice a property called EnableHistory. It is set to False by default, but for this example, you want to set this property to True.

The changes made to the EnableHistory property are not the only changes you must put into place when working with the back history on ASP.NET AJAX pages. You need to instruct ASP.NET on how to remember the previous page and what to do when a user navigates to a previous page (or even a later page if the user has clicked the Back button a few times).

You can specify easily the history points to remember and the indexes to use when you are on the page. Listing 23-21 shows a complete instance of a page that remembers the state for users working with the Back and Forward buttons on the browser.

LISTING 23-21: Adding history capabilities

VB

```
<%@ Page Language="VB" %>

<script runat="server">

    Protected Sub Button1_Click(ByVal sender As Object, ByVal e As EventArgs)
        PopulateFields(TextBox1.Text)
    End Sub

    Private Sub PopulateFields(ByVal InputName As String)
        If InputName Is Nothing Then
            Label1.Text = "Hello there. What is your name?"
        Else
            Label1.Text = "Hello there " & InputName
        End If

        If ScriptManager1.IsInAsyncPostBack AndAlso _
          (Not ScriptManager1.IsNavigating) Then
```

continues

LISTING 23-21 *(continued)*

```
            ScriptManager1.AddHistoryPoint("myIndexPoint", InputName, _
                String.Format("Entering name: {0}", InputName))
        Else
            TextBox1.Text = InputName
            Page.Title = String.Format("Entering name: {0}", InputName)
        End If
    End Sub

    Protected Sub ScriptManager1_Navigate(ByVal sender As Object, _
      ByVal e As HistoryEventArgs)
        PopulateFields(e.State("myIndexPoint"))
    End Sub
</script>

<!DOCTYPE html>
<html>
<head runat="server">
    <title>Ajax Page</title>
</head>
<body>
    <form id="form1" runat="server">
        <div>
            <asp:ScriptManager ID="ScriptManager1" runat="server" EnableHistory="True"
                OnNavigate="ScriptManager1_Navigate">
            </asp:ScriptManager>
            <asp:UpdatePanel ID="UpdatePanel1" runat="server">
                <ContentTemplate>
                    <asp:Label ID="Label1" runat="server"
                        Text="Hello there. What is your name?"></asp:Label><br />
                    <br />
                    <asp:TextBox ID="TextBox1" runat="server"></asp:TextBox><br />
                    <asp:Button ID="Button1" runat="server" Text="Submit Name"
                        OnClick="Button1_Click" />
                </ContentTemplate>
            </asp:UpdatePanel>
        </div>
    </form>
</body>
</html>
```

C#

```
<%@ Page Language="C#" %>

<script runat="server">

    protected void Button1_Click(object sender, EventArgs e)
    {
        PopulateFields(TextBox1.Text);
    }

    private void PopulateFields(string InputName)
    {
        if (InputName == null)
        {
            Label1.Text = "Hello there. What is your name?";
        }
        else
        {
            Label1.Text = "Hello there " + InputName;
```

```
        }

        if (ScriptManager1.IsInAsyncPostBack && !ScriptManager1.IsNavigating)
        {
            ScriptManager1.AddHistoryPoint("myIndexPoint", InputName,
              string.Format("Entering name: {0}", InputName));
        }
        else
        {
            TextBox1.Text = InputName;
            Page.Title = string.Format("Entering name: {0}", InputName);
        }
    }

    protected void ScriptManager1_Navigate(object sender, HistoryEventArgs e)
    {
        PopulateFields(e.State["myIndexPoint"]);
    }

</script>
```

Now, looking at the event that occurs when the button on the page is clicked, you can see there are some changes to it to deal with the registration of the history point:

```
if (ScriptManager1.IsInAsyncPostBack && !ScriptManager1.IsNavigating)
{
    ScriptManager1.AddHistoryPoint("myIndexPoint", InputName,
      string.Format("Entering name: {0}", InputName));
}
else
{
    TextBox1.Text = InputName;
    Page.Title = string.Format("Entering name: {0}", InputName);
}
```

A check occurs to see whether the ScriptManager control on the page is performing an asynchronous postback or is not navigating. If either of these is the case, then a history point is registered using the AddHistoryPoint() event. The idea of the AddHistoryPoint() call is that you are able to add a key/value pair to define the state of the index that you want the page to remember. In this case, the key is the string myIndexPoint and the value is what was provided from the Textbox server control that is on the page. The last option in the list of input parameters is the title to use for the page. This page title will appear in the browser on the page tab (if you have page tabs) as well as in the list of navigation items in the list of option items for the Back and Forward buttons.

In addition to calling AddHistoryPoint() with a single key/value pair, you can also pass in an entire set of them using the NameValueCollection object.

So, in the case of this example, the key myIndexPoint is used along with the value of what was placed in the TextBox1 server control, and this name is also used in the page title.

After you have this code in place, you must also create a Navigate() method off the ScriptManager control that instructs what should be done when one of the buttons is used. You use this method to provide the index of the item that you are working with:

```
protected void ScriptManager1_Navigate(object sender, HistoryEventArgs e)
{
    PopulateFields(e.State["myIndexPoint"]);
}
```

Here, you can see that `HistoryEventArgs` provides you with the access to the items that you have registered.

Running this page now, sequentially entering in names, and clicking on the page's button control provides you with a history of items in the Back button list of options. You are able also to navigate back to this item (or forward, if that's what is needed), and you will be returned to the page that you were working with. This list from the Back button is illustrated in Figure 23-16.

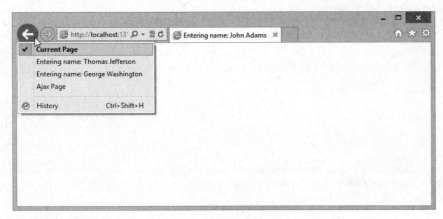

FIGURE 23-16

From the URL on the page, you are able to see how the state is stored. In this case, you end up with something similar to the following:

```
http://localhost:1315/Listing%2023-21.aspx#&&wqMi/gEg0K2EhqXXhZ/
AnMrZ5icHgZTHIkB2OLoKnWV/+5utJPEUUtMfqp9c3dYDB89CnH5SlUPmDYfcy2Q9V91S5tAKv9ulfKHf2h30dkw=
```

Notice that the index point is encrypted in the URL. This is the default behavior, although, as with most things in ASP.NET, you can change this behavior. To change it, from the ScriptManager control, you set the `EnableSecureHistoryState` property to `False`.

```
<asp:ScriptManager ID="ScriptManager1" runat="server" EnableHistory="True"
    OnNavigate="ScriptManager1_Navigate" EnableSecureHistoryState="False">
```

With this code in place, you get a URL something like the following:

```
http://localhost:1315/Listing%2023-21.aspx#&&myIndexPoint=John+Adams
```

> **NOTE** *There even is an ASP.NET JavaScript API that can accomplish the same effects with purely client-side code only. HTML5 also introduces a history API; however, only recent browsers support it.*

SCRIPT COMBINING

By default, ASP.NET AJAX pages sometimes download a number of different scripts for the page that is being viewed. When they are being downloaded separately, the performance is worse overall for the page.

The reason for this is that the browser must make a separate request for each of the scripts on the page. This means that the time to get all the scripts is longer than if it were done in one larger batch. Also, calling the scripts separately means that the overall load to the page that is being delivered is larger than it would otherwise be.

ASP.NET 4.5 includes the capability to combine the scripts into a single request and response. This is termed *script combining* or *bundling*. This feature is covered in more depth in Chapter 28.

Apart from that, you can specify to ASP.NET the scripts that you want combined via the ScriptManager server control on your page. The trick is figuring out what scripts need to be combined, as it isn't always that apparent.

For this reason, there is a CodePlex project on the Internet that provides you with a server control that you can place on the page to help you figure this out. The server control, ScriptReferenceProfiler, provides you with a list of the scripts that are required for the page. You can find this control at the following address:

```
http://aspnet.codeplex.com/releases/view/13356
```

The project hasn't been updated in a few years and you will get an error message when you click on one of the links shown in Figure 23-17, but apart from that, the project is still very convenient for determining the scripts needed for script combining with ASP.NET AJAX.

This project comes as a simple `.dll` file. Right-click within the toolbox of Visual Studio and select Choose Items from the provided menu. A dialog box of new controls that you can add to the toolbox then appears. Click the Browse button and navigate to the `.dll` file that you just downloaded. After selecting it, click OK to add it to your collection of controls. After this is done, you are ready to create an example page that will be used to combine the scripts for better overall performance. Listing 23-22 presents this new page.

LISTING 23-22: Using the ScriptReferenceProfiler control

VB

```
<%@ Page Language="VB" %>

<%@ Register Assembly="ScriptReferenceProfiler"
            Namespace="ScriptReferenceProfiler" TagPrefix="cc1" %>
<%@ Register Assembly="AjaxControlToolkit" Namespace="AjaxControlToolkit" TagPrefix="asp" %>

<script runat="server">

    Protected Sub Button1_Click(ByVal sender As Object, ByVal e As EventArgs)
        Label1.Text = "Hello " & TextBox1.Text & ".<br />" & "Today is " & TextBox2.Text
    End Sub

</script>

<!DOCTYPE html>
<html>
<head runat="server">
    <title>Script Combining</title>
</head>
<body>
    <form id="form1" runat="server">
        <div>
            <asp:ScriptManager ID="ScriptManager1" runat="server">
            </asp:ScriptManager>
            <asp:UpdatePanel ID="UpdatePanel1" runat="server">
                <ContentTemplate>
                    What is your name?<br />
                    <asp:TextBox ID="TextBox1" runat="server"></asp:TextBox>
                    <br />
                    <br />
                    What is today&#39;s date?<br />
                    <asp:TextBox ID="TextBox2" runat="server"></asp:TextBox>
                    <asp:CalendarExtender ID="TextBox2_CalendarExtender" runat="server"
                        Enabled="True" TargetControlID="TextBox2">
```

continues

LISTING 23-22 *(continued)*

```
                    </asp:CalendarExtender>
                    <br />
                    <br />
                    <asp:Button ID="Button1" runat="server" Text="Submit"
                        OnClick="Button1_Click" />
                    <br />
                    <br />
                    <asp:Label ID="Label1" runat="server"></asp:Label>
                </ContentTemplate>
            </asp:UpdatePanel>
            <cc1:ScriptReferenceProfiler ID="ScriptReferenceProfiler1" runat="server" />
        </div>
    </form>
</body>
</html>
```

C#

```
<%@ Page Language="C#" %>

<%@ Register Assembly="ScriptReferenceProfiler"
            Namespace="ScriptReferenceProfiler" TagPrefix="cc1" %>
<%@ Register Assembly="AjaxControlToolkit" Namespace="AjaxControlToolkit" TagPrefix="asp" %>

<script runat="server">
    protected void Button1_Click(object sender, EventArgs e)
    {
        Label1.Text = "Hello " + TextBox1.Text + ".<br />"
            + "Today is " + TextBox2.Text;
    }

</script>
```

This simple page uses Ajax to update a Label server control on the page based on some end user input into your page. The two textbox controls that are on the page ask for the end user's name and the current date. Adding the ScriptReferenceProfiler control will add a couple of @Register page directives at the top of the page.

FIGURE 23-17

Running the page, you see the following results, as illustrated in Figure 23-17.

This page provides you with a list of scripts that are being called for on the page. You are now able to use the ScriptManager control on the page and specify that these are scripts that you are interested in loading with the script-combining feature of ASP.NET.

To accomplish this task, copy the provided configuration script from the page in the browser and paste this text into your ScriptManager control within the `<CompositeScript>` section (see Listing 23-23).

LISTING 23-23: Combining scripts using the ScriptManager server control

```
<%@ Page Language="C#" %>

<%@ Register Assembly="AjaxControlToolkit" Namespace="AjaxControlToolkit" TagPrefix="asp" %>

<script runat="server">

...

</script>

<!DOCTYPE html>
<html>
<head runat="server">
    <title>Script Combining</title>
</head>
<body>
    <form id="form1" runat="server">
    <div>
        <asp:ScriptManager ID="ScriptManager1" runat="server">
            <CompositeScript>
                <Scripts>
                    <asp:ScriptReference name="MicrosoftAjax.js"/>
                        <asp:ScriptReference name="MicrosoftAjaxWebForms.js"/>
                        <asp:ScriptReference name="Common.Common.js"
assembly="AjaxControlToolkit, Version=4.1.60919.0, Culture=neutral, PublicKeyToken=28f01b0e84b6
d53e"/>
                        <asp:ScriptReference name="Common.DateTime.js"
assembly="AjaxControlToolkit, Version=4.1.60919.0, Culture=neutral, PublicKeyToken=28f01b0e84b6
d53e"/>
                        <asp:ScriptReference name="Compat.Timer.Timer.js"
assembly="AjaxControlToolkit, Version=4.1.60919.0, Culture=neutral, PublicKeyToken=28f01b0e84b6
d53e"/>
                        <asp:ScriptReference name="Animation.Animations.js"
assembly="AjaxControlToolkit, Version=4.1.60919.0, Culture=neutral, PublicKeyToken=28f01b0e84b6
d53e"/>
                        <asp:ScriptReference name="ExtenderBase.BaseScripts.js"
assembly="AjaxControlToolkit, Version=4.1.60919.0, Culture=neutral, PublicKeyToken=28f01b0e84b6
d53e"/>
                        <asp:ScriptReference name="Animation.AnimationBehavior.js"
assembly="AjaxControlToolkit, Version=4.1.60919.0, Culture=neutral, PublicKeyToken=28f01b0e84b6
d53e"/>
                        <asp:ScriptReference name="PopupExtender.PopupBehavior.js"
assembly="AjaxControlToolkit, Version=4.1.60919.0, Culture=neutral, PublicKeyToken=28f01b0e84b6
d53e"/>
                        <asp:ScriptReference name="Common.Threading.js"
assembly="AjaxControlToolkit, Version=4.1.60919.0, Culture=neutral, PublicKeyToken=28f01b0e84b6
d53e"/>
                        <asp:ScriptReference name="Calendar.CalendarBehavior.js"
assembly="AjaxControlToolkit, Version=4.1.60919.0, Culture=neutral, PublicKeyToken=28f01b0e84b6
d53e"/>
```

continues

LISTING 23-23 *(continued)*

```
              </Scripts>
          </CompositeScript>
      </asp:ScriptManager>
      <asp:UpdatePanel ID="UpdatePanel1" runat="server">
          <ContentTemplate>
              What is your name?<br />
              <asp:TextBox ID="TextBox1" runat="server"></asp:TextBox>
              <br /><br />
              What is today&#39;s date?<br />
              <asp:TextBox ID="TextBox2" runat="server"></asp:TextBox>
              <asp:CalendarExtender ID="TextBox2_CalendarExtender" runat="server"
                  Enabled="True" TargetControlID="TextBox2">
              </asp:CalendarExtender>
              <br /><br />
              <asp:Button ID="Button1" runat="server" Text="Submit"
               OnClick="Button1_Click" />
              <br /><br />
              <asp:Label ID="Label1" runat="server"></asp:Label>
          </ContentTemplate>
      </asp:UpdatePanel>
    </div>
    </form>
</body>
</html>
```

Having all of these defined scripts in the `<CompositeScript>` section will now signify that all these scripts are to be combined and sent to the page collectively, thereby improving the overall performance of your ASP.NET application.

THE FUTURE OF ASP.NET AJAX

With Microsoft's embrace of the jQuery JavaScript library (which is covered in Chapter 25), ASP.NET AJAX will probably not get any new features, but it still enjoys Microsoft's support since it is a part of ASP.NET. So code that uses ASP.NET AJAX features will be supported as long as ASP.NET is supported. However, it is quite unlikely that Microsoft will make fundamental upgrades to the code or functionality. Especially for legacy applications, we do not believe that ASP.NET AJAX needs to be discarded; however, for new applications, we recommend to at least evaluate if jQuery fits your needs.

SUMMARY

Ajax has fundamentally changed the way web application development is approached. ASP.NET AJAX is a fine framework that facilitates several Ajax features within the context of an ASP.NET site, including partial page updates. You do not need to completely tear down a page and rebuild it for each and every request. Instead, you are able to rebuild the pages slowly in sections as the end user requests them. Note, however, that Microsoft will further support ASP.NET AJAX, but probably not add any new features to it.

This chapter explored the core foundation of ASP.NET AJAX that is available with the default install of Visual Studio 2012. Beyond that, Ajax offers much more, including the Ajax Control Toolkit, the focus of the next chapter.

24

Ajax Control Toolkit

WHAT'S IN THIS CHAPTER?

➤ Installing the Ajax Control Toolkit

➤ Adding interactivity and animation to your web pages

WROX.COM CODE DOWNLOADS FOR THIS CHAPTER

Please note that all the code examples in this chapter are available as a part of this chapter's code download on the book's website at www.wrox.com on the Download Code tab.

ASP.NET AJAX applications were introduced in the previous chapter. You might be wondering why there were so few server controls for ASP.NET AJAX, given that ASP.NET Web Forms heavily rely on this way of modularizing code. The reason is that Microsoft has treated them as an open source project instead of just blending them into Visual Studio 2012.

Developers at Microsoft and in the community have developed a series of Ajax-capable server controls that you can use in your ASP.NET applications. Originally, these controls were collectively called the ASP.NET AJAX Control Toolkit. However, Microsoft eventually rebranded the library a bit, making it sound less like a part of ASP.NET. It is now called the Ajax Control Toolkit and is hosted at CodePlex at http://ajaxcontroltoolkit.codeplex.com/. Figure 24-1 shows the download page for the Ajax Control Toolkit.

As you may remember from the previous chapter, ASP.NET AJAX is the foundation on which to build richer web applications that leverage the browser more fully, but it does not have the rich UI elements that really blur the distinction between web and desktop applications. ASP.NET AJAX includes several powerful ASP.NET controls that make adding Ajax functionality to an existing application or building better user experiences into a new application easy. The Ajax Control Toolkit, however, was developed to provide rich ASP.NET AJAX controls that you can use to make your web applications really come to life. The toolkit makes pushing the user interface of an application beyond what users expect from a web application easy.

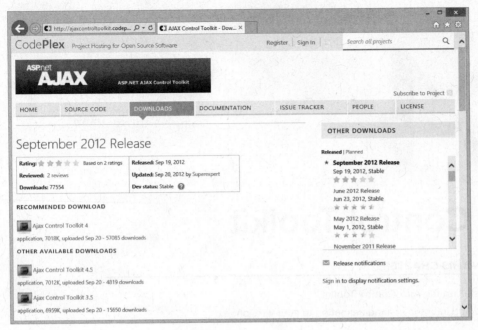

FIGURE 24-1

The toolkit is a shared source project with code contributions from developers from Microsoft and elsewhere. Most developers who work with ASP.NET AJAX should also download the toolkit for the additional set of controls it contains. The Ajax Control Toolkit download mentioned earlier enables you to download a compiled DLL with the controls and extenders, or you can download the source code and project files and compile it yourself. Either way, make sure you add the DLL to your toolbox in Visual Studio, as described shortly.

The toolkit contains some controls that have Ajax functionality and many control extenders. The control extenders attach to another control to enhance or "extend" the control's functionality. Because the controls cover such a wide variety of application-development areas, the ones we chose to cover are listed alphabetically and the control names are self-explanatory to make locating the information you need when using this chapter for later reference easy.

Also, note that the toolkit project is ongoing and will continue to evolve as developers contribute to it. This chapter is up-to-date as of the time of this writing, but the expectation is that more will be added to the toolkit regularly. Chapter 25 covers a truly open source project that provides similar functionality, but is completely independent of Microsoft technologies. So whereas the Ajax Control Toolkit is closely tied to ASP.NET and therefore a bit easier to use at first, you should not miss the following chapter to see a well-maintained alternative, jQuery.

DOWNLOADING AND INSTALLING THE AJAX CONTROL TOOLKIT

Because the Ajax Control Toolkit is not part of the default install of Visual Studio 2012, you must set up the controls yourself. Again, the Control Toolkit's site offers a couple of options.

The CodePlex site offers versions of the Ajax Control Toolkit for .NET 3.5, 4.0, and 4.5. This chapter focuses on using the control toolkit with Visual Studio 2012 and the .NET Framework 4.5. You can also completely omit the project homepage and use NuGet to add the Ajax Control Toolkit to a project:

```
Install-Package AjaxControlToolkit
```

If you would like to see prior to the installation what you are actually adding to the project, we recommend the manual installation. To get set up, download the `.zip` file from the aforementioned site at `http://ajaxcontroltoolkit.codeplex.com/` and unzip it where you want it on your machine. Then follow these steps:

1. Install the controls into Visual Studio. Adding the controls to your Visual Studio 2012 toolbox is very easy. Right-click in the toolbox and select Add Tab from the provided menu. Name the tab as you want—for this example, the tab is called Ajax Controls.

2. With the new tab in your toolbox, right-click the tab and select Choose Items from the provided menu, as illustrated in Figure 24-2. The Choose Toolbox Items dialog box appears.

3. Select the `AjaxControlToolkit.dll` from the download. When you find the DLL and click Open, Visual Studio 2012 first asks you if you really want to install something from the Internet (see Figure 24-3). If you agree, the Choose Toolbox Items dialog box changes to include the controls that are contained within this DLL. The controls are highlighted in the dialog box and are already selected for you (as shown in Figure 24-4).

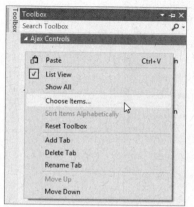

FIGURE 24-2

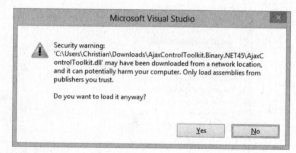

FIGURE 24-3

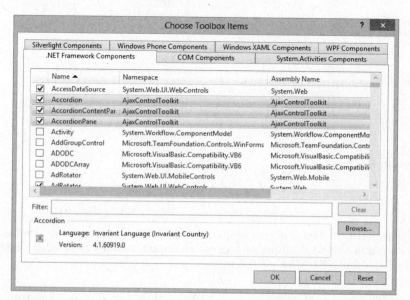

FIGURE 24-4

4. Click OK, and the Ajax Control Toolkit's controls are added to your Visual Studio toolbox. Figure 24-5 presents the end result.

More than 40 controls and extenders have been added to the toolbox for use in your ASP.NET applications.

THE ASP.NET AJAX CONTROLS

The number of controls and extenders available from the control toolkit is large. As stated, more than 40 controls and extenders are at your disposal. This section looks at these items and how you can use them in your ASP.NET applications.

When you add an ASP.NET AJAX server control to your page, you may notice that a number of DLLs focused on localization into a number of languages have been added to the Bin folder of your solution. All the resource files have been organized into language folders within the folder. Figure 24-6 presents an example of what you will find.

FIGURE 24-6

FIGURE 24-5

In addition to the localization DLLs added to your project, the ASP.NET AJAX control is added just as any other custom server control in ASP.NET. Listing 24-1 shows what your ASP.NET page should look like after the addition of a single ASP.NET AJAX control to it.

LISTING 24-1: Changes to the ASP.NET page after adding an Ajax Control Toolkit control

```
<%@ Page Language="C#" AutoEventWireup="true"
    CodeFile="Default.aspx.cs" Inherits="_Default" %>

<%@ Register Assembly="AjaxControlToolkit"
    Namespace="AjaxControlToolkit" TagPrefix="asp" %>

<!DOCTYPE html>

<html>
<head runat="server">
    <title>First Page</title>
</head>
<body>
    <form id="form1" runat="server">
    <div>
        <asp:ToolkitScriptManager ID="ToolkitScriptManager1" runat="server" />

        <asp:AlwaysVisibleControlExtender
         ID="AlwaysVisibleControlExtender1" runat="server"
         TargetControlID="TextBox1">
        </asp:AlwaysVisibleControlExtender>

        <asp:TextBox ID="TextBox1" runat="server"></asp:TextBox>
    </div>
    </form>
</body>
</html>
```

In this example, you can see that the ASP.NET AJAX control is registered on the page using the `@Register` directive. This directive points to the `AJAXControlToolkit` assembly and gives all controls that use this assembly reference a tag prefix of `asp`. Visual Studio 2012 by default adds the reference to `web.config`, but in order to make our code as self-contained as possible, we moved these references to the top using `@Register` for this chapter.

Another interesting aspect to the controls that are provided through the Ajax Control Toolkit is the ToolkitScriptManager control (which you need to add manually; Visual Studio does not do that for you automatically). This control derives from the base ScriptManager control and extends it to handle script combining for you by default, thus making your pages more expedient than before. The examples provided in this chapter make use of this newer version of the ScriptManager control.

Ajax Control Toolkit Extenders

The first set of items you look at includes the extenders that are part of the Ajax Control Toolkit. Extenders are basically controls that reach out and extend other controls. For example, you can think of the ASP.NET Validation Controls (covered in Chapter 6 of this book) as extender controls themselves. For instance, you can add a RequiredFieldValidator server control to a page and associate it to a TextBox control. This extends the TextBox control and changes its behavior. Normally it would just accept text. Now, if nothing is entered into the control, then the control will trigger an event back to the RequiredFieldValidator control whose client-side behavior is controlled by JavaScript.

The Ajax Control Toolkit's extenders accomplish the same thing. The controls extend the behavior of the ASP.NET server controls with additional JavaScript on the client as well as some server-side communications.

AlwaysVisibleControlExtender

When presenting information in the browser, you may want to keep a piece of information fixed in the user's view. Screen space is a limited commodity, and sometimes a screen element should always be available without the user ever having to scroll. The AlwaysVisibleControlExtender lets you designate any ASP.NET control as having this distinction. You specify a position for the control using the AlwaysVisibleControlExtender, and while the user scrolls the page to view other information, the control you designate is always kept in view. It seems to move around as the user scrolls the screen or resizes the window, so that it stays in the same relative position in the viewable portion of the browser window.

The AlwaysVisibleControlExtender has only six properties. Listing 24-2 presents an example of using this control.

LISTING 24-2: Using the AlwaysVisibleControlExtender

VB

```
<%@ Page Language="VB" %>

<%@ Register Assembly="AjaxControlToolkit"
    Namespace="AjaxControlToolkit" TagPrefix="asp" %>

<script runat="server">
    Protected Sub Button1_Click(ByVal sender As Object, _
        ByVal e As System.EventArgs)
          Response.Write("The page has been submitted!")
    End Sub
</script>

<!DOCTYPE html>
<html>
<head runat="server">
    <title>AlwaysVisibleControlExtender</title>
</head>
<body>
    <form id="form1" runat="server">
    <div>
        <asp:ToolkitScriptManager ID="ToolkitScriptManager1" runat="server" />
        <asp:AlwaysVisibleControlExtender
         ID="AlwaysVisibleControlExtender1"
            runat="server" TargetControlID="Panel1"
            HorizontalOffset="10"
            HorizontalSide="Right" VerticalOffset="10">
        </asp:AlwaysVisibleControlExtender>
        Form Element :
        <asp:TextBox ID="TextBox1" runat="server"></asp:TextBox>
        <br />
        Form Element :
        <asp:TextBox ID="TextBox2" runat="server"></asp:TextBox>
        <br />

        <!-- Excessive code removed for clarity -->

        Form Element :
        <asp:TextBox ID="TextBox29" runat="server"></asp:TextBox>
        <br />
        Form Element :
        <asp:TextBox ID="TextBox30" runat="server"></asp:TextBox>
        <br />
```

```
            <br />
            <asp:Panel ID="Panel1" runat="server">
                <asp:Button ID="Button1" runat="server" Text="Submit"
                 OnClick="Button1_Click" />
                <asp:Button ID="Button2" runat="server" Text="Clear" />
            </asp:Panel>
        </div>
        </form>
    </body>
    </html>
```

C#

```
<%@ Page Language="C#" %>

<%@ Register Assembly="AjaxControlToolkit"
    Namespace="AjaxControlToolkit" TagPrefix="asp" %>

<script runat="server">
    protected void Button1_Click(object sender, EventArgs e)
    {
        Response.Write("The page has been submitted!");
    }
</script>
```

This code presents a very long form that requires end users to scroll the page in their browser. The AlwaysVisibleControlExtender control is present, and its presence requires that you also have a ScriptManager control on the page (this is the same requirement for all ASP.NET AJAX controls).

The AlwaysVisibleControlExtender1 control extends the Panel1 control through the use of the `TargetControlID` attribute. In this case, the value of the `TargetControlID` attribute points to the Panel1 control. The Panel1 control contains the form's Submit button. The result of the code from Listing 24-2 is shown in Figure 24-7.

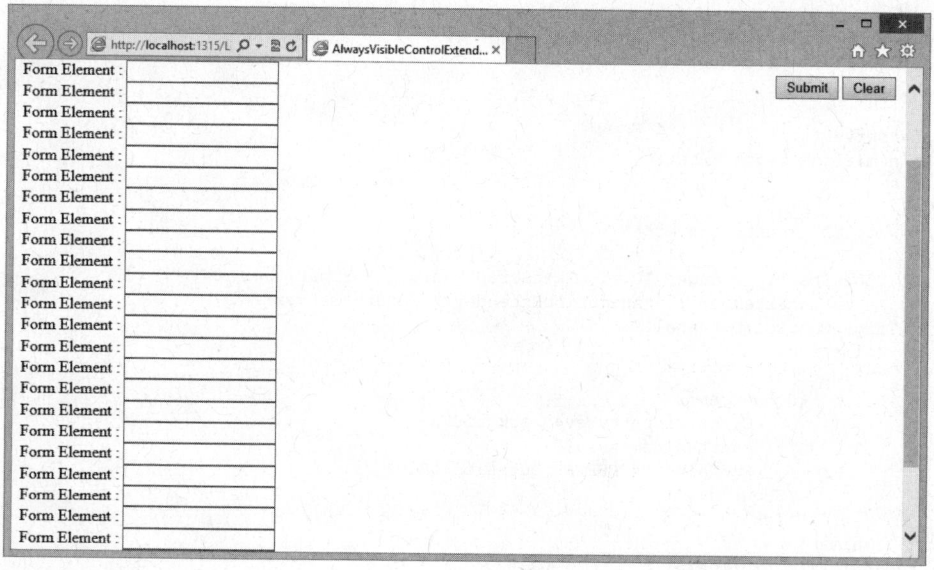

FIGURE 24-7

The location of the Submit and Clear buttons on the page is controlled via a combination of several control attributes. The location on the page is determined by the `HorizontalSide` (possible values include `Center`, `Left`, and `Right`) and `VerticalSide` properties (possible values include `Bottom`, `Middle`, and `Top`). A padding is also placed around the control using the `HorizontalOffset` and `VerticalOffset` properties, both of which are set to `10` pixels in this example.

AnimationExtender

The AnimationExtender server control provides a tremendous amount of capabilities. It enables you to program fluid animations to the controls that you put on the page. You can do a lot with this control—much more than can be shown in this chapter.

This control enables you to program elements that can move around the page based on specific end-user triggers (such as a button click). Specific events are available for you to program your animations against. These events are as follows:

- ➤ OnClick
- ➤ OnHoverOver
- ➤ OnHoverOut
- ➤ OnLoad
- ➤ OnMouseOver
- ➤ OnMouseOut

Creating animations is not as straightforward as many would like because it has little Visual Studio support, such as wizards or even IntelliSense. For an example of creating your first animation, Listing 24-3 shows how you can fade an element in and out of the page based on an end-user action.

LISTING 24-3: Using the AnimationExtender to fade a background color

```
<%@ Page Language="C#" %>

<%@ Register Assembly="AjaxControlToolkit"
    Namespace="AjaxControlToolkit" TagPrefix="asp" %>

<!DOCTYPE html>
<html>
<head runat="server">
    <title>AnimationExtender</title>
</head>
<body>
    <form id="form1" runat="server">
    <div>
        <asp:ToolkitScriptManager ID="ToolkitScriptManager1" runat="server" />
        <asp:AnimationExtender ID="AnimationExtender1" runat="server"
            TargetControlID="Panel1">
            <Animations>
                <OnClick>
                    <Sequence>
                        <Color PropertyKey="background"
                            StartValue="#999966"
                            EndValue="#FFFFFF" Duration="5.0" />
                    </Sequence>
                </OnClick>
            </Animations>
        </asp:AnimationExtender>
        <asp:Panel ID="Panel1" runat="server" BorderColor="Black"
            BorderWidth="3px" Font-Bold="True" Width="600px">
            Lorem ipsum dolor sit amet, consectetuer adipiscing elit.
```

```
                    Donec accumsan lorem. Ut consectetuer tempus metus.
                    Aenean tincidunt venenatis tellus. Suspendisse molestie
                    cursus ipsum. Curabitur ut lectus. Nulla ac dolor nec elit
                    convallis vulputate. Nullam pharetra pulvinar nunc. Duis
                    orci. Phasellus a tortor at nunc mattis congue.
                    Vestibulum porta tellus eu orci. Suspendisse quis massa.
                    Maecenas varius, erat non ullamcorper nonummy, mauris erat
                    eleifend odio, ut gravida nisl neque a ipsum. Vivamus
                    facilisis. Cras viverra. Curabitur ut augue eget dolor
                    semper posuere. Aenean at magna eu eros tempor
                    pharetra. Aenean mauris.
                </asp:Panel>
        </div>
        </form>
    </body>
    </html>
```

In this case, when you open the page from Listing 24-3, you will see that it uses a single AnimationExtender control that is working off the Panel1 control. This connection is made using the `TargetControlID` property.

As stated, IntelliSense is not enabled when you are typing the code that is contained within the AnimationExtender control, so you need to look in the documentation for the animations that you want to create. In the case of the previous example, the `<OnClick>` element is utilized to define a sequence of events that needs to occur when the control is clicked. For this example, only one animation is defined within the `<Sequence>` element—a color change to the background of the element. Here, the `<Color>` element states that the background CSS property will need to start at the color #999966 and change completely to color #FFFFFF within 5 seconds (defined using the `Duration` property).

When you open this page and click the Panel element, you will see the color change in a 5-second duration from the described start color to the end color.

AutoCompleteExtender

The AutoCompleteExtender control enables you to help end users find what they might be looking for when they need to type in search terms within a textbox. This feature, used on a lot of search sites today, helps in that when you start typing characters in the textbox, you get results from a datastore as a drop-down list directly below the textbox you are working with that match what you have typed so far.

To establish something similar for yourself, create a new page that contains only a ScriptManager control, an AutoCompleteExtender control, and a TextBox control. The ASP.NET portion of the page should appear as presented in Listing 24-4 (AutoCompleteExtender.aspx in the code download for this chapter).

LISTING 24-4: The ASP.NET page

```
<%@ Page Language="C#" AutoEventWireup="true"
    CodeFile="AutoComplete.aspx.cs" Inherits="AutoComplete" %>

<%@ Register Assembly="AjaxControlToolkit"
    Namespace="AjaxControlToolkit" TagPrefix="asp" %>

<!DOCTYPE html>
<html>
<head runat="server">
    <title>AutoComplete</title>
</head>
<body>
    <form id="form1" runat="server">
    <div>
        <asp:ToolkitScriptManager ID="ToolkitScriptManager1" runat="server">
```

continues

LISTING 24-4 *(continued)*

```
        </asp:ToolkitScriptManager>
        <asp:AutoCompleteExtender ID="AutoCompleteExtender1"
         runat="server" TargetControlID="TextBox1"
         ServiceMethod="GetCompletionList" UseContextKey="True">
        </asp:AutoCompleteExtender>
        <asp:TextBox ID="TextBox1" runat="server"></asp:TextBox>
    </div>
    </form>
</body>
</html>
```

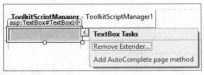

FIGURE 24-8

Again, like the other ASP.NET AJAX controls, you extend the TextBox control using the `TargetControlID` property. When you first add these controls to the page, you will not have the `ServiceMethod` property defined in the AutoCompleteExtender control. Using Visual Studio 2012, you can make the framework for a service method and tie the extender control to this method all from the design surface. After expanding the TextBox control's smart tag, select the Add AutoComplete page method option from the provided menu, shown in Figure 24-8.

This action creates a service method in the code-behind for your page. Listing 24-5 (AutoCompleteExtender .aspx.vb and AutoCompleteExtender.aspx.cs in the code download for this chapter) shows the steps necessary to complete this method to call the company names from Microsoft's classic Northwind database.

> **NOTE** *You can find instructions on downloading and using the Northwind database with Visual Studio 2012 at* `http://msdn.microsoft.com/en-us/ library/8b6y4c7s.aspx`*. The version of the Northwind database that we used for this book is available for download at* `www.wrox.com/go/SQLServer2012DataSets`*.*

LISTING 24-5: The code-behind that sets up the service method for auto-complete

VB

```
Imports System.Data
Imports System.Data.SqlClient

Partial Class AutoComplete
    Inherits System.Web.UI.Page

    <System.Web.Services.WebMethodAttribute(),
     System.Web.Script.Services.ScriptMethodAttribute()>
    Public Shared Function GetCompletionList(ByVal _
      prefixText As String, ByVal count As Integer) As String()
        Dim conn As SqlConnection
        Dim cmd As SqlCommand
        Dim cmdString As String =
        "Select CompanyName from Customers WHERE CompanyName LIKE " & _
            "@prefixText"
        conn = New SqlConnection("Data Source=.\SQLEXPRESS;
            AttachDbFilename=|DataDirectory|\NORTHWND.MDF;
            Integrated Security=True;User Instance=True")
        ' Put this string on one line in your code
        cmd = New SqlCommand(cmdString, conn)
```

```vbnet
        cmd.Parameters.AddWithValue("@prefixText", prefixText & "%")
        conn.Open()

        Dim myReader As SqlDataReader
        Dim returnData As List(Of String) = New List(Of String)
        myReader = cmd.ExecuteReader(CommandBehavior.CloseConnection)

        While myReader.Read()
            returnData.Add(myReader("CompanyName").ToString())
        End While

        Return returnData.ToArray()
    End Function
End Class
```

C#

```csharp
using System.Collections.Generic;
using System.Data;
using System.Data.SqlClient;
public partial class AutoComplete : System.Web.UI.Page
{
    [System.Web.Services.WebMethodAttribute(),
     System.Web.Script.Services.ScriptMethodAttribute()]
    public static string[] GetCompletionList(string prefixText,
        int count, string contextKey)
    {
        SqlConnection conn;
        SqlCommand cmd;
        string cmdString =
          "Select CompanyName from Customers WHERE CompanyName LIKE " +
            "@prefixText";
        conn = new
            SqlConnection(@"Data Source=.\SQLEXPRESS;
            AttachDbFilename=|DataDirectory|\NORTHWND.MDF;
            Integrated Security=True;User Instance=True");
        // Put this string on one line in your code
        cmd = new SqlCommand(cmdString, conn);
        cmd.Parameters.AddWithValue("@prefixText", prefixText + "%");
        conn.Open();

        SqlDataReader myReader;
        List<string> returnData = new List<string>();

        myReader = cmd.ExecuteReader(CommandBehavior.CloseConnection);

        while (myReader.Read())
        {
            returnData.Add(myReader["CompanyName"].ToString());
        }

        return returnData.ToArray();
    }
}
```

When you run this page and type the characters **ant** into the textbox, the `GetCompletionList()` method is called, passing in these characters. These characters are retrievable through the `prefixText` parameter (you can also use the `count` parameter, which is defaulted at 10). The Northwind database is called using the `prefixText` value and this is what is returned back to the TextBox1 control. In the end, you get a drop-down list of the items that match the first three characters that were entered into the textbox. This is illustrated in Figure 24-9.

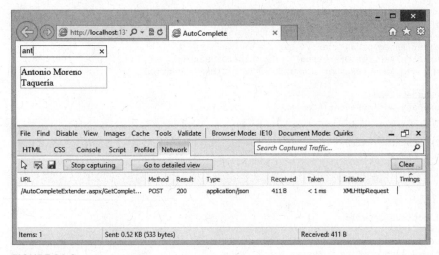

FIGURE 24-9

It is good to know that the results, once called the first time, are cached. This caching is controlled via the `EnableCaching` property (it is defaulted to `true`). You can also change the style of the drop-down auto-complete list, configure how many elements appear, and much more with this feature. One more important point is that you are not required to call out a method that is exposed on the same page as the control, as the example in this book demonstrates, but you can also call out another server-side method on another page, or a web method.

BalloonPopupExtender

One of the most requested additions to the Ajax Control Toolkit has always been a control that provides a balloon-like UI added to an element. Finally, starting with the November 2011 edition of the Ajax Control Toolkit, the team gave in and added such a control.

The BalloonPopupExtender adds a "balloon" to the element referenced in the `TargetControlID`. The actual content of the balloon resides in an arbitrary control on the page; the extender's `BalloonPopupControlID` property contains the ID of that control.

The extender supports several built-in styles (`BalloonStyle` property) and sizes (`BalloonSize` property), and also custom styling. Listing 24-6 shows an example of providing a cloud-like balloon for a TextBox control.

LISTING 24-6: Adding a balloon to a TextBox control

```
<%@ Page Language="C#" %>

<%@ Register Assembly="AjaxControlToolkit" Namespace="AjaxControlToolkit" TagPrefix="asp" %>

<!DOCTYPE html>

<script runat="server">

</script>

<!DOCTYPE html>
<html>
<head runat="server">
    <title>BalloonPopupExtender</title>
</head>
```

```
<body>
    <form id="form1" runat="server">
    <div>
        <asp:ToolkitScriptManager ID="ToolkitScriptManager1" runat="server">
        </asp:ToolkitScriptManager>

        <asp:TextBox ID="TextBox1" runat="server" />
        <asp:Panel ID="Panel1" runat="server">
            Please enter your country.
        </asp:Panel>

        <asp:BalloonPopupExtender ID="BalloonPopupExtender1" runat="server"
            TargetControlID="TextBox1"
            BalloonPopupControlID="Panel1"
            BalloonStyle="Cloud" BalloonSize="Small" />

    </div>
    </form>
</body>
</html>
```

When you click in the textbox, the balloon appears, as shown in Figure 24-10.

FIGURE 24-10

CalendarExtender

Selecting a date is a common requirement of many applications. It is also one of the most common points in a form that can hinder form submission. End users are often slowed down by trying to figure out the format of the date that the form requires. The CalendarExtender control enables you to make it simple for your end users to select a date within a form. The CalendarExtender attaches to a textbox and pops up a calendar for selecting a date. By default, the calendar is shown when the textbox gets focus, but if you set the `PopupButtonID` to the ID of another control, the calendar becomes visible when that control is clicked.

The best way to set up fast date selection in a form is to provide a calendar that can be navigated and allow a date to quickly be selected, which will then be translated to a textual date format in the textbox. The CalendarExtender is very easy to use with just a few key properties. The `TargetControlID` points to the textbox that receives the selected date. The `Format` property specifies the string format for the date input of the textbox. The CalendarExtender control gives you all the client-side code required for this kind of action. Listing 24-7 shows you an example of providing a calendar control off your textbox controls.

LISTING 24-7: Using a calendar control from a TextBox control

```
<%@ Page Language="C#" %>

<%@ Register Assembly="AjaxControlToolkit"
    Namespace="AjaxControlToolkit" TagPrefix="asp" %>

<!DOCTYPE html>
<html>
<head runat="server">
    <title>CalendarExtender</title>
</head>
<body>
    <form id="form1" runat="server">
    <div>
        <asp:ToolkitScriptManager ID="ToolkitScriptManager1" runat="server">
        </asp:ToolkitScriptManager>
        <asp:CalendarExtender ID="CalendarExtender1" runat="server"
         TargetControlID="TextBox1">
        </asp:CalendarExtender>
        <asp:TextBox ID="TextBox1" runat="server"></asp:TextBox>
    </div>
    </form>
</body>
</html>
```

When you run this page, the result is a single textbox on the page, appearing no different from any other textbox. However, when the end user clicks inside the textbox, a calendar appears directly below it, as shown in Figure 24-11.

Then, when the end user selects a date from the calendar, the date is placed as text within the textbox.

Some of the properties exposed from this control are `FirstDayOfWeek` and `PopupPosition` (which has the options `BottomLeft`,

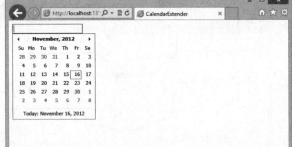

FIGURE 24-11

`BottomRight`, `TopLeft`, and `TopRight`). You can also change how the calendar is initiated on the client. Some sites offer a calendar button next to the textbox and only pop up the calendar option when the end user clicks the button. If this is something that you want to do on your pages, use the `PopupButtonID` property, which you must point to the ID of the image or button that you are using.

CollapsiblePanelExtender

The CollapsiblePanelExtender server control enables you to collapse one control into another. When working with two Panel server controls, you can provide a nice way to control any real estate issues that you might be experiencing on your ASP.NET page.

The CollapsiblePanelExtender is similar to the Accordion control (presented later in this chapter), but it does not target multiple content areas. An ASP.NET panel control is shown or hidden from view based on the user's interaction with a given control. This enables you to hide something the user does not always need to see. The `TargetControlID` is shown when the `ExpandControlID` is clicked or hidden when the `CollapseControlID` is clicked. Alternatively, it can be shown or hidden based on a mouse hover if the `AutoCollapse` and `AutoExpand` properties are set to True.

Listing 24-8 demonstrates the use of a CollapsiblePanelExtender to set the panel size to 0 when it is collapsed and to 300 pixels when it is expanded. Another panel is used as the selector for expanding and collapsing the panel. In addition, a label is included that is designated as the TextLabelID. The value of the Label control is changed between the ExpandedText and CollapsedText values based on the current state.

LISTING 24-8: Using CollapsiblePanelExtender with two Panel controls

```
<%@ Page Language="C#" %>

<%@ Register Assembly="AjaxControlToolkit"
    Namespace="AjaxControlToolkit" TagPrefix="asp" %>

<!DOCTYPE html>
<html>
<head id="Head1" runat="server">
    <title>CollapsiblePanelExtender</title>
</head>
<body>
    <form id="form1" runat="server">
    <div>
        <asp:ToolkitScriptManager ID="ToolkitScriptManager1" runat="server">
        </asp:ToolkitScriptManager>
        <asp:Panel ID="Panel1" runat="server" BackColor="#000066"
          ForeColor="White">
            <asp:Label ID="Label2" runat="server"
             Text="This is my title"></asp:Label>
            <asp:Label ID="Label1" runat="server"></asp:Label>
        </asp:Panel>
        <asp:Panel ID="Panel2" runat="server" Style="overflow: hidden;"
          Height="0">
          Lorem ipsum dolor sit amet, consectetuer adipiscing elit.
          Donec accumsan lorem. Ut consectetuer tempus metus.
          Aenean tincidunt venenatis tellus. Suspendisse molestie
          cursus ipsum. Curabitur ut lectus. Nulla ac dolor nec elit
          convallis vulputate. Nullam pharetra pulvinar nunc. Duis
          orci. Phasellus a tortor at nunc mattis congue. Vestibulum
          porta tellus eu orci. Suspendisse quis massa.
          Maecenas varius, erat non ullamcorper nonummy, mauris erat
          eleifend odio, ut gravida nisl neque a ipsum. Vivamus
          facilisis. Cras viverra. Curabitur ut augue eget dolor
          semper posuere. Aenean at magna eu eros tempor pharetra.
          Aenean mauris.
        </asp:Panel>
        <asp:CollapsiblePanelExtender ID="CollapsiblePanelExtender1"
          runat="server"
          TargetControlID="Panel2" Collapsed="true"
          ExpandControlID="Panel1"
          CollapseControlID="Panel1"
          CollapsedSize="1"
          ExpandedSize="300" CollapsedText="[Click to expand]"
          ExpandedText="[Click to collapse]" TextLabelID="Label1"
          SuppressPostBack="true">
        </asp:CollapsiblePanelExtender>
    </div>
    </form>
</body>

</html>
```

In this case, when the page opens for the first time you will see only the contents of Panel1—the title panel. By default, you would usually see both controls, but because the `Collapsed` property is set to `True` in the control, you will see only Panel1. Clicking the Panel control will then expose the contents of Panel2. In fact, the contents will slide out from the Panel1 control. Tying these two controls together to perform this action is accomplished through the use of the CollapsiblePanelExtender control. This control's `TargetControlID` is assigned to the second Panel control—Panel2, because this is the control that needs to expand onto the page. The `ExpandControlID` property is the control that initiates the expansion.

Once expanded, it is when the end user clicks Panel2 that the contents will disappear by sliding back into Panel1. This is accomplished through the use of the `CollapseControlID` property being assigned to Panel2.

The CollapsiblePanelExtender control has a number of properties that enable you to fine-tune how the expanding and collapsing occur. For instance, you could have also set the Label1 control to be the initiator of this process and even change the text of the Label control depending on the whether Panel2 is collapsed or expanded.

ColorPickerExtender

One of the difficult data points to retrieve from an end user is color. This particular data point is tough to define if you are using just text. If you have an open selection of colors, how does the end user define a darker shade of blue? For this reason, you have the ColorPickerExtender to quickly and easily extend something like a TextBox control to a tool that makes this selection process a breeze. Listing 24-9 shows a quick and easy way to do this task.

LISTING 24-9: Using the ColorPickerExtender control to allow for color selection

```
<%@ Page Language="C#" %>

<%@ Register Assembly="AjaxControlToolkit"
    Namespace="AjaxControlToolkit" TagPrefix="asp" %>

<!DOCTYPE html>
<html>
<head runat="server">
    <title>ColorPickerExtender</title>
</head>
<body>
    <form id="form1" runat="server">
    <div>
        <asp:ToolkitScriptManager ID="ToolkitScriptManager1" runat="server">
        </asp:ToolkitScriptManager>
        <br />
        Pick your favorite color:<br />
        <asp:TextBox ID="TextBox1" runat="server"></asp:TextBox>
        <asp:ColorPickerExtender ID="ColorPickerExtender1"
         runat="server" TargetControlID="TextBox1">
        </asp:ColorPickerExtender>
    </div>
    </form>
</body>
</html>
```

When this page opens, you simply have a single TextBox server control on the page. Applying focus to this TextBox control pops up the color selector, as illustrated here in black and white in Figure 24-12.

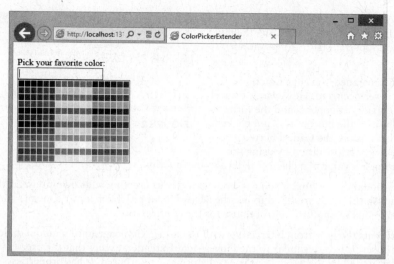

FIGURE 24-12

The end user then can scroll across the color options and after the user selects one of these colors, the pop-up disappears and the hexadecimal color code is shown in the TextBox. This end result is presented here in Figure 24-13.

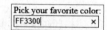

FIGURE 24-13

ConfirmButtonExtender and ModalPopupExtender

Usually before allowing your end users to make deletions of data via a browser application, you want to confirm such actions with the end user. ConfirmButtonExtender enables you to question the end user's action and reconfirm that he wants the action to occur. Listing 24-10 shows how to use this control.

LISTING 24-10: Using the ConfirmButtonExtender control to reconfirm a user action

```
<%@ Page Language="C#" %>

<%@ Register Assembly="AjaxControlToolkit"
    Namespace="AjaxControlToolkit" TagPrefix="asp" %>

<!DOCTYPE html>
<html>
<head runat="server">
    <title>ConfirmButtonExtender</title>
</head>
<body>
    <form id="form1" runat="server">
    <div>
        <asp:ToolkitScriptManager ID="ToolkitScriptManager1" runat="server">
        </asp:ToolkitScriptManager>
        <asp:ConfirmButtonExtender ID="ConfirmButtonExtender1"
         runat="server" TargetControlID="Button1"
         ConfirmText="Are you sure you wanted to click this button?">
        </asp:ConfirmButtonExtender>
        <asp:Button ID="Button1" runat="server" Text="Button" />
    </div>
    </form>
</body>
</html>
```

In this case, the ConfirmButtonExtender extends the Button1 server control and adds a confirmation dialog box using the text defined with the `ConfirmText` property. Figure 24-14 shows this page.

FIGURE 24-14

If the end user clicks OK in this instance, the page functions normally as if the dialog box never occurred. However, if Cancel is clicked, the dialog box, by default, disappears and the form will not be submitted (it will be as if the button were not clicked at all). In this case, you can also capture the Cancel button being clicked and perform a client-side operation by using the `OnClientClick` event and giving it a value of a client-side JavaScript function.

Instead of using the browser's modal dialog boxes, you can even go as far as creating your own to use as the confirmation form. To accomplish this task, you need to use the ModalPopupExtender server control. The ModalPopupExtender control points to another control to use for the confirmation.

The ModalPopupExtender prevents the user from interacting with the underlying page until a modal dialog box has been addressed by the user. It is very similar to the HoverMenuExtender, except that the user must work with the control designated by the `PopupControlID` before he can proceed. It has properties for specifying the `OkControlID` and the `CancelControlID`, along with `OnOkScript` and `OnCancelScript` properties that will run based on the user's selection. Listing 24-11 shows how to use this control.

LISTING 24-11: Using the ModalPopupExtender control to create your own confirmation form

```
<%@ Page Language="C#" %>

<%@ Register Assembly="AjaxControlToolkit"
    Namespace="AjaxControlToolkit" TagPrefix="asp" %>

<!DOCTYPE html>
<html>
<head runat="server">
    <title>ConfirmButtonExtender</title>
</head>
<body>
    <form id="form1" runat="server">
    <div>
        <asp:ToolkitScriptManager ID="ToolkitScriptManager1" runat="server">
        </asp:ToolkitScriptManager>
        <asp:ConfirmButtonExtender ID="ConfirmButtonExtender1"
         runat="server" TargetControlID="Button1"
         DisplayModalPopupID="ModalPopupExtender1">
        </asp:ConfirmButtonExtender>
        <asp:ModalPopupExtender ID="ModalPopupExtender1" runat="server"
            CancelControlID="ButtonNo" OkControlID="ButtonYes"
            PopupControlID="Panel1"
            TargetControlID="Button1">
        </asp:ModalPopupExtender>
        <asp:Button ID="Button1" runat="server" Text="Button" />
        <asp:Panel ID="Panel1" runat="server"
         style="display:none; background-color:White; width:200;
         border-width:2px; border-color:Black; border-style:solid;
         padding:20px;">
         Are you sure you wanted to click this button?<br />
         <asp:Button ID="ButtonYes" runat="server" Text="Yes" />
         <asp:Button ID="ButtonNo" runat="server" Text="No" />
        </asp:Panel>
    </div>
    </form>
</body>
</html>
```

In this example, the ConfirmButtonExtender still points to the Button1 control on the page, meaning that when the button is clicked, the ConfirmButtonExtender takes action. Instead of using the `ConfirmText` property, the `DisplayModalPopupID` property is used. In this case, it points to the ModalPopupExtender1 control—another extender control.

The ModalPopupExtender control, in turn, references the Panel1 control on the page through the use of the `PopupControlID` property. The contents of this Panel control are used for the confirmation on the button click. For this to work, the ModalPopupExtender control must have a value for the `OkControlID` and the `CancelControlID` properties. In this case, these two properties point to the two Button controls that are contained within the Panel control. When you run this page, you get the results shown in Figure 24-15.

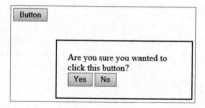

FIGURE 24-15

DragPanelExtender

The DragPanelExtender enables you to define areas where end users can move elements around the page as they want. The end user actually has the ability to drag and drop the element anywhere on the browser page.

To enable this feature, you must do a few things. The first suggestion is to create a `<div>` area on the page that is large enough to drag the item around in. From here, you need to specify what will be used as the drag handle and another control that will follow the drag handle around. In the example in Listing 24-12, the Label control is used as the drag handle, and the Panel2 control is the content that is dragged around the screen.

LISTING 24-12: Dragging a Panel control around the page

```
<%@ Page Language="C#" %>

<%@ Register Assembly="AjaxControlToolkit"
    Namespace="AjaxControlToolkit" TagPrefix="asp" %>

<!DOCTYPE html>
<html>
<head runat="server">
    <title>DragPanel control</title>
</head>
<body>
    <form id="form1" runat="server">
    <div>
        <asp:ToolkitScriptManager ID="ToolkitScriptManager1" runat="server">
        </asp:ToolkitScriptManager>
        <div style="height: 600px;">
            <asp:DragPanelExtender ID="DragPanelExtender1"
             runat="server"
             DragHandleID="Label1" TargetControlID="Panel1">
            </asp:DragPanelExtender>
            <asp:Panel ID="Panel1" runat="server" Width="450px">
                <asp:Label ID="Label1" runat="server"
                 Text="Drag this Label control to move the control"
                 BackColor="DarkBlue" ForeColor="White"></asp:Label>
                <asp:Panel ID="Panel2" runat="server" Width="450px">
        Lorem ipsum dolor sit amet, consectetuer adipiscing elit.
        Donec accumsan lorem. Ut consectetuer tempus metus.
        Aenean tincidunt venenatis tellus. Suspendisse molestie
        cursus ipsum. Curabitur ut lectus. Nulla ac dolor nec elit
        convallis vulputate. Nullam pharetra pulvinar nunc. Duis
        orci. Phasellus a tortor at nunc mattis congue.
```

continues

LISTING 24-12 *(continued)*

```
                Vestibulum porta tellus eu orci. Suspendisse quis massa.
                Maecenas varius, erat non ullamcorper nonummy, mauris erat
                eleifend odio, ut gravida nisl neque a ipsum. Vivamus
                facilisis. Cras viverra. Curabitur
                ut augue eget dolor semper posuere. Aenean at magna eu eros
                tempor pharetra. Aenean mauris.
                   </asp:Panel>
                </asp:Panel>
            </div>
        </div>
        </form>
    </body>
    </html>
```

This example creates a `<div>` element that has a height of 600 pixels. Within this defined area, the example uses a DragPanelExtender control and targets the Panel1 control through the use of the `TargetControlID` property being assigned to this control.

Within the Panel1 control are two other server controls—a Label and another Panel control. The Label control is assigned to be the drag handle using the `DragHandleID` property of the DragPanelExtender control. With this little bit of code in place, you are now able to drag the Panel1 control around on your browser window. Figure 24-16 shows the Label control being used as a handle to drag around the Panel control.

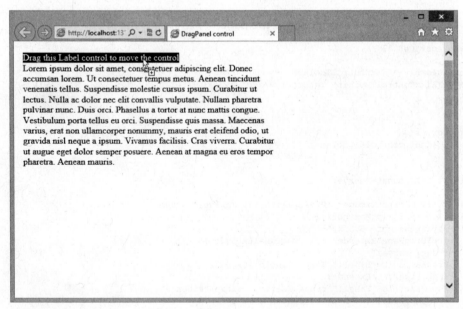

FIGURE 24-16

DropDownExtender

The DropDownExtender control enables you to take any control and provide a drop-down list of options below it for selection. It provides a different framework from a typical drop-down list control because it allows for an extreme level of customization. Listing 24-13 shows how you can even use an image as the initiator of a drop-down list of options.

LISTING 24-13: Using an Image control as an initiator of a drop-down list

VB

```
<%@ Page Language="VB" %>

<%@ Register Assembly="AjaxControlToolkit"
    Namespace="AjaxControlToolkit" TagPrefix="asp" %>

<script runat="server">
    Protected Sub Page_Load(ByVal sender As Object, _
      ByVal e As System.EventArgs)
        Image1.ImageUrl = "Images/Creek.jpg"
    End Sub

    Protected Sub Option_Click(ByVal sender As Object, _
      ByVal e As System.EventArgs)
        Image1.ImageUrl = "Images/" & DirectCast(sender, _
          LinkButton).Text & ".jpg"
    End Sub
</script>


<!DOCTYPE html>
<html>
<head runat="server">
    <title>DropDownExtender Control</title>
</head>
<body>
    <form id="form1" runat="server">
    <div>
        <asp:ToolkitScriptManager ID="ToolkitScriptManager1" runat="server">
        </asp:ToolkitScriptManager>
        <asp:UpdatePanel ID="UpdatePanel1" runat="server">
            <ContentTemplate>
                <asp:DropDownExtender ID="DropDownExtender1"
                 runat="server"
                 DropDownControlID="Panel1" TargetControlID="Image1">
                </asp:DropDownExtender>
                <asp:Image ID="Image1" runat="server">
                </asp:Image>
            <asp:Panel ID="Panel1" runat="server" Height="50px"
            Width="125px">
                <asp:LinkButton ID="Option1" runat="server"
                 OnClick="Option_Click">ToolkitLogo</asp:LinkButton>
                <asp:LinkButton ID="Option2" runat="server"
                 OnClick="Option_Click">ToolkitLogo1</asp:LinkButton>
                <asp:LinkButton ID="Option3" runat="server"
                 OnClick="Option_Click">ToolkitLogo2</asp:LinkButton>
            </asp:Panel>
            </ContentTemplate>
        </asp:UpdatePanel>
    </div>
    </form>
</body>
</html>
```

C#

```
<%@ Page Language="C#" %>

<%@ Register Assembly="AjaxControlToolkit"
```

continues

LISTING 24-13 *(continued)*

```
        Namespace="AjaxControlToolkit" TagPrefix="asp" %>

    <script runat="server">
        protected void Page_Load(object sender, EventArgs e)
        {
            Image1.ImageUrl = "Images/ToolkitLogo.jpg";
        }

        protected void Option_Click(object sender, EventArgs e)
        {
            Image1.ImageUrl = "Images/" + ((LinkButton)sender).Text
              + ".jpg";
        }
    </script>
```

In this case, a DropDownExtender control is tied to an Image control that displays a specific image on the `Page_Load()` event. The DropDownExtender control has two specific properties that need to be filled. The first is the `TargetControlID` property that defines the control that becomes the initiator of the drop-down list. The second property is the `DropDownControlID` property, which defines the element on the page that will be used for the drop-down items that appear below the control. In this case, it is a Panel control with three LinkButton controls.

Each of the LinkButton controls designates a specific image that should appear on the page. Selecting one of the options changes the image through the `Option_Click()` method. Running this page gives you the results illustrated in Figure 24-17.

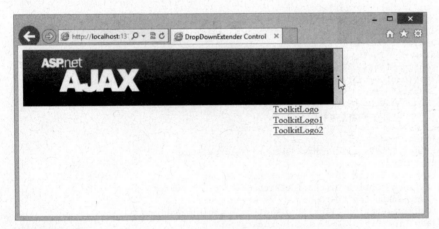

FIGURE 24-17

DropShadowExtender

The DropShadowExtender enables you to add a DropShadow effect to an ASP.NET panel or image on the page. You set the `TargetControlID`, and you can then control the `Width` and `Opacity`, and whether the corners should be `Rounded`. If the panel can be moved or resized, you can also set the `TrackPosition` property to `True` to indicate that JavaScript should run to track the panel and update the DropShadow as needed.

Your first thought for where to use this might be an image (as shown in Listing 24-14), but you can use it for any control that you want.

LISTING 24-14: Using DropShadowExtender with an Image control

```
<%@ Page Language="C#" %>

<%@ Register Assembly="AjaxControlToolkit"
    Namespace="AjaxControlToolkit" TagPrefix="asp" %>

<!DOCTYPE html>
<html>
<head runat="server">
    <title>DropShadowExtender Control</title>
</head>
<body>
    <form id="form1" runat="server"> <div>
        <asp:ToolkitScriptManager ID="ToolkitScriptManager1" runat="server">
        </asp:ToolkitScriptManager>
        <asp:DropShadowExtender ID="DropShadowExtender1" runat="server"
         TargetControlID="Image1">
        </asp:DropShadowExtender>
        <asp:Image ID="Image1" runat="server"
         ImageUrl="Images/ToolkitLogo.jpg" />
    </div>
    </form>
</body>
</html>
```

In this example, accomplishing this is as simple as using the DropShadowExtender control with a `TargetControlID` of `Image1`. With this in place, the image appears in the browser, as shown in Figure 24-18.

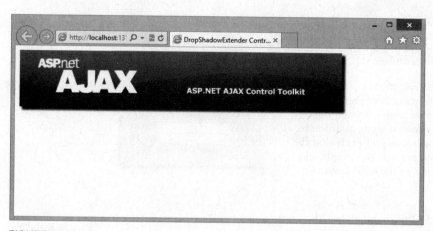

FIGURE 24-18

As stated, in addition to images, you can use DropShadowExtender for almost anything. Listing 24-15 shows how to use it with a Panel control.

LISTING 24-15: Using the DropShadowExtender with a Panel control

```
<%@ Page Language="C#" %>

<%@ Register Assembly="AjaxControlToolkit"
    Namespace="AjaxControlToolkit" TagPrefix="asp" %>

<!DOCTYPE html>
<html>
<head runat="server">
    <title>DropShadowExtender Control</title>
</head>
<body>
    <form id="form1" runat="server"> <div>
        <asp:ToolkitScriptManager ID="ToolkitScriptManager1" runat="server">
        </asp:ToolkitScriptManager>
        <asp:DropShadowExtender ID="DropShadowExtender1" runat="server"
         TargetControlID="Panel1" Rounded="True">
        </asp:DropShadowExtender>
        <asp:Panel ID="Panel1" runat="server" BackColor="Orange"
         Width="300" HorizontalAlign="Center">
            <asp:Login ID="Login1" runat="server">
            </asp:Login>
        </asp:Panel>
    </div>
    </form>
</body>
</html>
```

> **NOTE** *If you get an error stating that "WebForms UnobtrusiveValidationMode requires a ScriptResourceMapping for 'jquery'," just use the following setting in web.config:*
>
> ```
> <appSettings>
>     <add key="ValidationSettings:UnobtrusiveValidationMode" value="None" />
>     </appSettings>
> ```

In this case, a Panel control with a Login control is extended with the DropShadowExtender control. The result is quite similar to that of the Image control's result. However, one addition to the DropShadowExtender control here is that the Rounded property is set to True (by default, it is set to False). This produces the look shown in Figure 24-19.

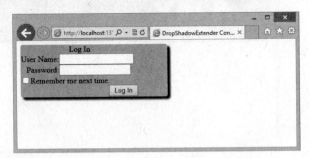

As you can see from Figure 24-19, not only are the edges of the drop shadow rounded, but also the entire Panel control has rounded edges. Other style properties that you can work with include the Opacity property, which controls the opacity

FIGURE 24-19

of the drop shadow only, and the Radius property, which controls the radius used in rounding the edges and obviously works only if the Rounded property is set to True. By default, the Opacity setting is set at 1, which means 100 percent visible. To set it at, say, 50 percent opacity, you need to set the Opacity value to .5.

DynamicPopulateExtender

The DynamicPopulateExtender control enables you to send dynamic HTML output to a Panel control. For this to work, you need one control or event that triggers a callback to the server to get the HTML that, in turn, gets pushed into the Panel control, thereby making a dynamic change on the client.

As with the AutoCompleteExtender control, you need a server-side event that returns something to the client asynchronously. Listing 24-16 shows the code required to use this control on the .aspx page (DynamicPopulateExtender.aspx in the code download for the chapter).

LISTING 24-16: Using the DynamicPopulateExtender control to populate a Panel control

.ASPX

```
<%@ Page Language="C#" AutoEventWireup="true" CodeFile="DynamicPopulateExtender.aspx.cs"
    Inherits="DynamicPopulateExtender" %>

<%@ Register Assembly="AjaxControlToolkit" Namespace="AjaxControlToolkit" TagPrefix="asp" %>

<!DOCTYPE html>
<html>
<head id="Head1" runat="server">
    <title>DynamicPopulateExtender Control</title>
    <script type="text/javascript">
      function updateGrid(value) {
        var behavior = $find('DynamicPopulateExtender1');
        if (behavior) {
            behavior.populate(value);
        }
      }
    </script>
</head>
<body>
    <form id="form1" runat="server">
    <div>
        <asp:ToolkitScriptManager ID="ToolkitScriptManager1" runat="server" />
        <asp:DynamicPopulateExtender ID="DynamicPopulateExtender1" runat="server"
            TargetControlID="Panel1" ServiceMethod="GetDynamicContent">
        </asp:DynamicPopulateExtender>
        <div onclick="updateGrid(0);">
        <asp:LinkButton ID="LinkButton1" runat="server"
         OnClientClick="return false;">Customers</asp:LinkButton></div>
        <div onclick="updateGrid(1);">
        <asp:LinkButton ID="LinkButton2" runat="server"
         OnClientClick="return false;">Employees</asp:LinkButton></div>
        <div onclick="updateGrid(2);">
        <asp:LinkButton ID="LinkButton3" runat="server"
         OnClientClick="return false;">Products</asp:LinkButton></div>
        <asp:Panel ID="Panel1" runat="server">
        </asp:Panel>
    </div>
    </form>
</body>
</html>
```

This .aspx page is doing a lot, one thing being that a client-side JavaScript function called `updateGrid()` calls the DynamicPopulateExtender control that is on the page. You will also find three LinkButton server controls, each of which is encased within a `<div>` element that calls the `updateGrid()` function and provides a value that is passed into the function. Because you want the `<div>` element's `onclick` event to be triggered with a click and not the LinkButton control's click event, each LinkButton contains an `OnClientClick` attribute that simply does nothing. This is accomplished using `return false;`.

The DynamicPopulateExtender control on the page targets the Panel1 control as the container that will take the HTML that comes from the server on an asynchronous request. The DynamicPopulateExtender control knows where to go to get the HTML using the `ServiceMethod` attribute. The value of this attribute calls the `GetDynamicContent()` method, which is in the page's code-behind file.

After the `.aspx` page is in place, the next step is to create the code-behind page. This page will contain the server-side method that is called by the DynamicPopulateExtender control. This is presented in Listing 24-17 (DynamicPopulateExtender.aspx.cs and DynamicPopulateExtender.aspx.vb in the code download for the chapter).

LISTING 24-17: The code-behind page of the DynamicPopulateExtender.aspx page

VB

```
Imports System.Data
Imports System.Data.SqlClient
Imports System.IO

Partial Class DynamicPopulateExtender
    Inherits System.Web.UI.Page

    <System.Web.Services.WebMethodAttribute()>
    <System.Web.Script.Services.ScriptMethodAttribute()>
    Public Shared Function GetDynamicContent(ByVal contextKey As _
        System.String) As System.String
        Dim conn As SqlConnection
        Dim cmd As SqlCommand
        Dim cmdString As String = "Select * from Customers"

        Select Case contextKey
            Case "1"
                cmdString = "Select * from Employees"
            Case "2"
                cmdString = "Select * from Products"
        End Select

        conn = New SqlConnection("Data Source=.\SQLEXPRESS;
            AttachDbFilename=|DataDirectory|\NORTHWND.MDF;
            Integrated Security=True;User Instance=True")
            ' Put this string on one line in your code
        cmd = New SqlCommand(cmdString, conn)
        conn.Open()

        Dim myReader As SqlDataReader
        myReader = cmd.ExecuteReader(CommandBehavior.CloseConnection)

        Dim dt As New DataTable
        dt.Load(myReader)
        myReader.Close()

        Dim myGrid As New GridView
        myGrid.ID = "GridView1"
        myGrid.DataSource = dt
        myGrid.DataBind()

        Dim sw As New StringWriter
        Dim htw As HtmlTextWriter = New HtmlTextWriter(sw)

        myGrid.RenderControl(htw)
```

```
            htw.Close()

        Return sw.ToString()
    End Function
End Class
```

C#

```csharp
using System.Data;
using System.Data.SqlClient;
using System.IO;
using System.Web.UI;
using System.Web.UI.WebControls;

public partial class DynamicPopulateExtender : System.Web.UI.Page
{
    [System.Web.Services.WebMethodAttribute(),
     System.Web.Script.Services.ScriptMethodAttribute()]
    public static string GetDynamicContent(string contextKey)
    {
        SqlConnection conn;
        SqlCommand cmd;
        string cmdString = "Select * from Customers";

        switch (contextKey)
        {
            case ("1"):
                cmdString = "Select * from Employees";
                break;
            case ("2"):
                cmdString = "Select * from Products";
                break;
        }

        conn = new
            SqlConnection(@"Data Source=.\SQLEXPRESS;
                AttachDbFilename=|DataDirectory|\NORTHWND.MDF;
                Integrated Security=True;User Instance=True");
                // Put this string on one line in your code
        cmd = new SqlCommand(cmdString, conn);
        conn.Open();

        SqlDataReader myReader;
        myReader = cmd.ExecuteReader(CommandBehavior.CloseConnection);

        DataTable dt = new DataTable();
        dt.Load(myReader);
        myReader.Close();

        GridView myGrid = new GridView();
        myGrid.ID = "GridView1";
        myGrid.DataSource = dt;
        myGrid.DataBind();

        StringWriter sw = new StringWriter();
        HtmlTextWriter htw = new HtmlTextWriter(sw);

        myGrid.RenderControl(htw);
        htw.Close();

        return sw.ToString();
    }
}
```

This code is the code-behind page for the `DynamicPopulateExtender.aspx` page and contains a single method that is callable asynchronously. The `GetDynamicContent()` method takes a single parameter, `contextKey`, a string value that can be used to determine what link the end user clicked.

Based on the selection, a specific command string is used to populate a `DataTable` object. From here, the `DataTable` object is used as the data source for a programmatic GridView control that is rendered and returned as a string to the client. The client will take the large string and use the text to populate the Panel1 control that is on the page. Figure 24-20 shows the result of clicking one of the links.

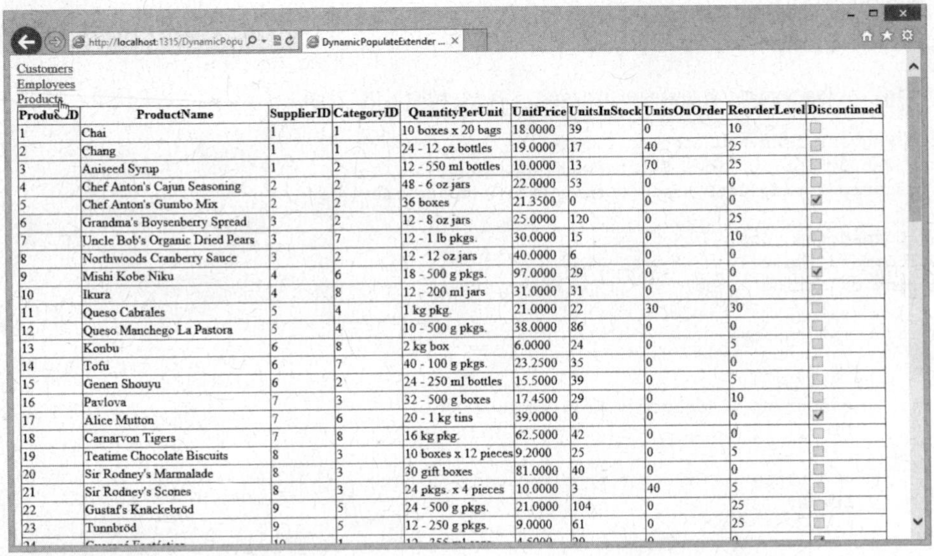

ProductID	ProductName	SupplierID	CategoryID	QuantityPerUnit	UnitPrice	UnitsInStock	UnitsOnOrder	ReorderLevel	Discontinued
1	Chai	1	1	10 boxes x 20 bags	18.0000	39	0	10	
2	Chang	1	1	24 - 12 oz bottles	19.0000	17	40	25	
3	Aniseed Syrup	1	2	12 - 550 ml bottles	10.0000	13	70	25	
4	Chef Anton's Cajun Seasoning	2	2	48 - 6 oz jars	22.0000	53	0	0	
5	Chef Anton's Gumbo Mix	2	2	36 boxes	21.3500	0	0	0	✓
6	Grandma's Boysenberry Spread	3	2	12 - 8 oz jars	25.0000	120	0	25	
7	Uncle Bob's Organic Dried Pears	3	7	12 - 1 lb pkgs.	30.0000	15	0	10	
8	Northwoods Cranberry Sauce	3	2	12 - 12 oz jars	40.0000	6	0	0	
9	Mishi Kobe Niku	4	6	18 - 500 g pkgs.	97.0000	29	0	0	✓
10	Ikura	4	8	12 - 200 ml jars	31.0000	31	0	0	
11	Queso Cabrales	5	4	1 kg pkg.	21.0000	22	30	30	
12	Queso Manchego La Pastora	5	4	10 - 500 g pkgs.	38.0000	86	0	0	
13	Konbu	6	8	2 kg box	6.0000	24	0	5	
14	Tofu	6	7	40 - 100 g pkgs.	23.2500	35	0	0	
15	Genen Shouyu	6	2	24 - 250 ml bottles	15.5000	39	0	5	
16	Pavlova	7	3	32 - 500 g boxes	17.4500	29	0	10	
17	Alice Mutton	7	6	20 - 1 kg tins	39.0000	0	0	0	✓
18	Carnarvon Tigers	7	8	16 kg pkg.	62.5000	42	0	0	
19	Teatime Chocolate Biscuits	8	3	10 boxes x 12 pieces	9.2000	25	0	5	
20	Sir Rodney's Marmalade	8	3	30 gift boxes	81.0000	40	0	0	
21	Sir Rodney's Scones	8	3	24 pkgs. x 4 pieces	10.0000	3	40	5	
22	Gustaf's Knäckebröd	9	5	24 - 500 g pkgs.	21.0000	104	0	25	
23	Tunnbröd	9	5	12 - 250 g pkgs.	9.0000	61	0	25	

FIGURE 24-20

FilteredTextBoxExtender

The FilteredTextBoxExtender control, actually originally contributed by the author of this chapter, works off a TextBox control to specify the types of characters the end user can input into the control. For instance, if you want the end user to be able to enter only numbers into the textbox, you can associate a FilteredTextBoxExtender to the TextBox control and specify such behavior. Listing 24-18 presents an example of this.

LISTING 24-18: Filtering a textbox to use only numbers

```
<%@ Page Language="C#" %>

<%@ Register Assembly="AjaxControlToolkit"
    Namespace="AjaxControlToolkit" TagPrefix="asp" %>

<!DOCTYPE html>
<html>
<head runat="server">
    <title>FilteredTextBoxExtender Control</title>
</head>
<body>
    <form id="form1" runat="server">
    <div>
        <asp:ToolkitScriptManager ID="ToolkitScriptManager1" runat="server">
```

```
            </asp:ToolkitScriptManager>
            <asp:FilteredTextBoxExtender ID="FilteredTextBoxExtender1"
             runat="server"
             TargetControlID="TextBox1" FilterType="Numbers">
            </asp:FilteredTextBoxExtender>
            <asp:TextBox ID="TextBox1" runat="server"></asp:TextBox>
        </div>
        </form>
    </body>
</html>
```

In this case, a FilteredTextBoxExtender control is attached to the TextBox1 control through the use of the `TargetControlID` property. The FilteredTextBoxExtender control has a property called `FilterType` that has the possible values of `Custom`, `LowercaseLetters`, `Numbers`, and `UppercaseLetters`.

This example uses a `FilterType` value of `Numbers`, meaning that only numbers can be entered into the textbox. If the end user tries to enter any other type of information, nothing happens—it will seem to the end user as if the key doesn't even function.

The FilteredTextBoxExtender control also exposes the `FilterMode` and the `InvalidChars` properties. Here is an example of using these two properties:

```
<asp:FilteredTextBoxExtender ID="FilteredTextBoxExtender1" runat="server"
  TargetControlID="TextBox1" InvalidChars="*" FilterMode="InvalidChars">
</asp:FilteredTextBoxExtender>
```

The default value of the `FilterMode` property is `ValidChars`. When set to `ValidChars`, the control works from the `FilterType` property and allows only what this property defines. When set to `InvalidChars`, you then use the `InvalidChars` property and put the characters here (multiple characters all go together with no space or item between them).

HoverMenuExtender

The HoverMenuExtender control enables you to make a hidden control appear on the screen when the end user hovers on another control. This means that you can either build elaborate tooltips or provide extra functionality when an end user hovers somewhere in your application.

One example is to change a ListView control so that when the end user hovers over a product name, the Edit button for that row of data appears on the screen. The complete code, which adds the extender to the `<ItemTemplate>` in the ListView control, is shown in Listing 24-19.

LISTING 24-19: Adding a hover button to the ListView control's ItemTemplate

```
<%@ Page Language="C#" %>

<%@ Register Assembly="AjaxControlToolkit" Namespace="AjaxControlToolkit" TagPrefix="asp" %>

<!DOCTYPE html>
<html>
<head id="Head1" runat="server">
    <title>HoverMenuExtender Control</title>
</head>
<body>
    <form id="form1" runat="server">
        <div>
            <asp:ToolkitScriptManager ID="ToolkitScriptManager1" runat="server">
            </asp:ToolkitScriptManager>
            <asp:ListView ID="ListView1" runat="server" DataSourceID="SqlDataSource1">
                <LayoutTemplate>
                    <table>
                        <tr>
```

continues

LISTING 24-19 *(continued)*

```
                                <th></th>
                                <th>ProductID</th>
                                <th>ProductName</th>
                                <th>SupplierID</th>
                                <th>CategoryID</th>
                                <th>QuantityPerUnit</th>
                        </tr>
                        <asp:PlaceHolder ID="itemPlaceholder" runat="server" />
                    </table>
            </LayoutTemplate>
            <ItemTemplate>
                <tr style="background-color: #DCDCDC; color: #000000;">
                    <td>
                        <asp:HoverMenuExtender ID="HoverMenuExtender1" runat="server"
                            TargetControlID="ProductNameLabel" PopupControlID="Panel1"
                            PopDelay="25" OffsetX="-50">
                        </asp:HoverMenuExtender>
                        <asp:Panel ID="Panel1" runat="server" Height="50px"
                            Width="125px">
                            <asp:Button ID="EditButton" runat="server"
                                CommandName="Edit" Text="Edit" />
                        </asp:Panel>
                    </td>
                    <td>
                        <asp:Label ID="ProductIDLabel" runat="server"
                            Text='<%# Eval("ProductID") %>' />
                    </td>
                    <td>
                        <asp:Label ID="ProductNameLabel" runat="server"
                            Text='<%# Eval("ProductName") %>' />
                    </td>
                    <td>
                        <asp:Label ID="SuppliedIDLabel" runat="server"
                            Text='<%# Eval("SupplierID") %>' />
                    </td>
                    <td>
                        <asp:Label ID="CategoryIDLabel" runat="server"
                            Text='<%# Eval("CategoryID") %>' />
                    </td>
                    <td>
                        <asp:Label ID="QuantityPerUnitLabel" runat="server"
                            Text='<%# Eval("QuantityPerUnit") %>' />
                    </td>
                </tr>
            </ItemTemplate>
        </asp:ListView>
            <asp:SqlDataSource ID="SqlDataSource1" runat="server" ConnectionString="Data
Source=.\SQLEXPRESS;AttachDbFilename=|DataDirectory|\NORTHWND.MDF;Integrated Security=True;User
Instance=True" ProviderName="System.Data.SqlClient" SelectCommand="SELECT * FROM [Products]"></
asp:SqlDataSource>
        </div>
    </form>
</body>
</html>
```

Here, a HoverMenuExtender control is attached to the Label control with the ID of ProductNameLabel, which appears in each row of the ListView control. This is done using the TargetControlID property, whereas the PopupControlID property is used to assign the control that appears dynamically when a user hovers the mouse over the targeted control.

The HoverMenuExtender control exposes several properties that control the style and behaviors of the pop-up. The `PopDelay` property is used in this example and provides a means to delay the pop-up from occurring (in milliseconds). The `OffsetX` and `OffsetY` properties specify the location of the pop-up based on the targeted control. In this case, the offset is set to `-50` (pixels). Figure 24-21 shows the results of the operation.

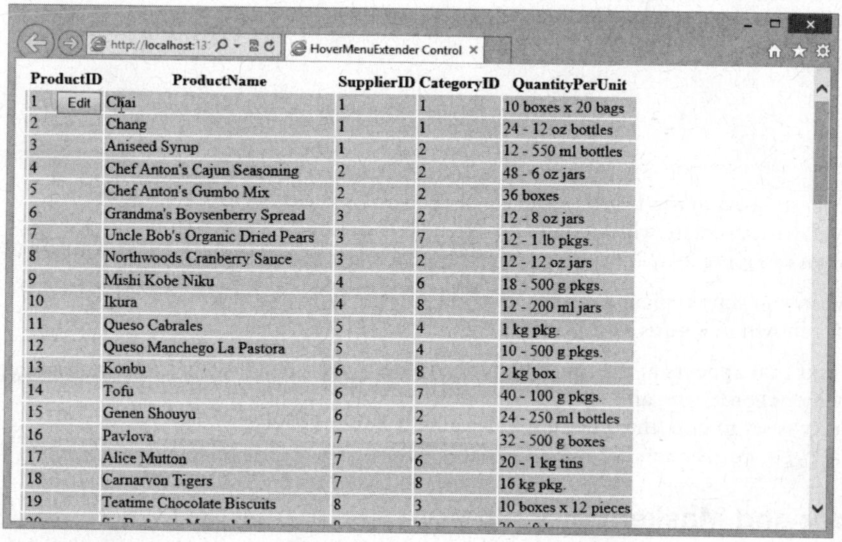

FIGURE 24-21

ListSearchExtender

The ListSearchExtender control extends either a ListBox or a DropDownList control, although not always with the best results in browsers such as Opera and Safari. This extender enables you to provide search capabilities through large collections that are located in either of these controls. This alleviates the need for the end users to search through the collection to find the item they are looking for.

When utilized, the extender adds a search text that shows the characters the end user types for the search in the area above the control. Listing 24-20 shows the use of this extender.

LISTING 24-20: Extending a ListBox control with the ListSearchExtender control

```
<%@ Page Language="C#" %>

<%@ Register Assembly="AjaxControlToolkit"
    Namespace="AjaxControlToolkit" TagPrefix="asp" %>

<!DOCTYPE html>
<html>
<head runat="server">
    <title>ListSearchExtender Control</title>
</head>
<body>
    <form id="form1" runat="server">
    <div>
        <asp:ToolkitScriptManager ID="ToolkitScriptManager1" runat="server">
        </asp:ToolkitScriptManager>
        <asp:ListSearchExtender ID="ListSearchExtender1" runat="server"
         TargetControlID="ListBox1">
        </asp:ListSearchExtender>
        <asp:ListBox ID="ListBox1" runat="server" Width="150">
```

continues

LISTING 24-20 *(continued)*

```
                <asp:ListItem>Aardvark</asp:ListItem>
                <asp:ListItem>Bee</asp:ListItem>
                <asp:ListItem>Camel</asp:ListItem>
                <asp:ListItem>Dog</asp:ListItem>
                <asp:ListItem>Elephant</asp:ListItem>
            </asp:ListBox>
        </div>
        </form>
    </body>
    </html>
```

In this case, the only property used in the ListSearchExtender control is the
TargetControlID property to associate which control it extends. Running this page
produces the results shown in Figure 24-22.

FIGURE 24-22

Then, as an end user, when you start typing, you will see what you are typing in the
text below the control (as shown in Figure 24-23).

You can customize the text that appears at the top of the control with
the PromptCssClass, PromptPosition, and PromptText properties. By default, the
PromptPosition property is set to Top (the other possible value is Bottom) and
the PromptText value is Type to search.

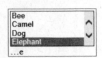

FIGURE 24-23

MaskedEditExtender and MaskedEditValidator

The MaskedEditExtender control is similar to the FilteredTextBoxExtender control in that it restricts the
end user from entering specific text within a TextBox control. This control takes the process one step further
by providing end users with a template within the textbox for them to follow. If the end users do not follow
the template, then they will be unable to proceed and might receive a validation warning from the control
using the MaskedEditValidator control.

Listing 24-21 provides an example of using both of these controls.

LISTING 24-21: Using both the MaskedEditExtender and the MaskedEditValidator controls

```
<%@ Page Language="C#" %>

<%@ Register Assembly="AjaxControlToolkit"
    Namespace="AjaxControlToolkit" TagPrefix="asp" %>

<!DOCTYPE html>
<html>
<head runat="server">
    <title>MaskedEditExtender Control</title>
</head>
<body>
    <form id="form1" runat="server">
    <div>
        <asp:ToolkitScriptManager ID="ToolkitScriptManager1" runat="server">
        </asp:ToolkitScriptManager>
        <asp:MaskedEditExtender ID="MaskedEditExtender1" runat="server"
         TargetControlID="TextBox1" MaskType="Number" Mask="999">
        </asp:MaskedEditExtender>
        <asp:TextBox ID="TextBox1" runat="server"></asp:TextBox>
        <asp:MaskedEditValidator ID="MaskedEditValidator1"
         runat="server" ControlExtender="MaskedEditExtender1"
         ControlToValidate="TextBox1" IsValidEmpty="False"
         EmptyValueMessage="A three digit number is required!"
```

```
        Display="Dynamic"></asp:MaskedEditValidator>
      </div>
      </form>
  </body>
  </html>
```

In this case, the MaskedEditExtender control uses the TargetControlID to associate itself with the TextBox1 control. The MaskType property supplies the type of mask or filter to place on the textbox. The possible values include:

➤ None: No validation will be performed.

➤ Date: Date validation will occur.

➤ DateTime: Date and time validation will occur.

➤ Number: A number validation will occur.

➤ Time: A time validation will occur

Listing 24-21 uses Number and then specifies the mask or template the numbers need to take. This is done through the use of the Mask property. In this case, the Mask property is set to 999. This means that all numbers can be only three digits in length.

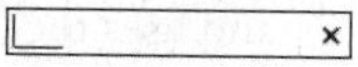

Using 999 as a value to the Mask property means that when an end user enters a value in the textbox, he will be presented with three underscores inside the textbox. Figure 24-24 shows the template for entering items.

FIGURE 24-24

If the Mask property is changed to 99,999.99 as follows:

```
<asp:MaskedEditExtender ID="MaskedEditExtender1" runat="server"
  TargetControlID="TextBox1" MaskType="Number" Mask="99,999.99">
</asp:MaskedEditExtender>
```

the textbox template appears, as illustrated in Figure 24-25.

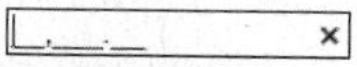

From Figure 24-25, you can see that the comma and the period are present in the template. As the end users type, they do not need to retype these values. The cursor simply moves to the next section of numbers required.

FIGURE 24-25

As you can see from the Mask property value, numbers are represented by the number 9. When working with other MaskType values, you also need to be aware of the other mask characters:

➤ 9: Only a numeric character

➤ L: Only a letter

➤ $: Only a letter or a space

➤ C: Only a custom character (case sensitive)

➤ A: Only a letter or a custom character

➤ N: Only a numeric or custom character

➤ ?: Any character

In addition to the character specifications, the template uses delimiters, which are detailed in the following list:

➤ / is a date separator.

➤ : is a time separator.

➤ . is a decimal separator.

➤ , is a thousand separator.

➤ \ is the escape character.

➤ { is the initial delimiter for repetition of masks.

➤ } is the final delimiter for repetition of masks.

Using some of these items, you can easily change MaskedEditExtender to deal with a `DateTime` value:

```
<asp:MaskedEditExtender ID="MaskedEditExtender1" runat="server"
 TargetControlID="TextBox1" MaskType="DateTime" Mask="99/99/9999 99:99:99">
</asp:MaskedEditExtender>
```

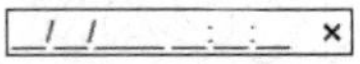

The template created in the textbox for this is shown in Figure 24-26.

FIGURE 24-26

The MaskedEditExtender control has many properties that are exposed to control and manipulate the behavior and style of the textbox. The MaskedEditExtender control can work in conjunction with the MaskedEditValidator control, which provides validation against the textbox controls.

In the earlier example, the validation was accomplished through an instance of the MaskedEditValidator control:

```
<asp:MaskedEditValidator ID="MaskedEditValidator1" runat="server"
 ControlExtender="MaskedEditExtender1" ControlToValidate="TextBox1"
 IsValidEmpty="False" EmptyValueMessage="A three digit number is required!"
 Display="Dynamic"></asp:MaskedEditValidator>
```

This control uses the `ControlExtender` property to associate itself with the MaskedEditExtender control and uses the `ControlToValidate` property to watch a specific control on the form. By default, the `IsValidEmpty` property is set to `True`. Changing it to `False` means that the end user will be required to enter some value in the textbox to pass validation and not receive the error message that is presented in the `EmptyValueMessage` property.

Triggering the MaskedEditValidator control gives you something like the message shown in Figure 24-27. It is important to remember that you can style the control in many ways to produce the validation message appearance that you are looking for.

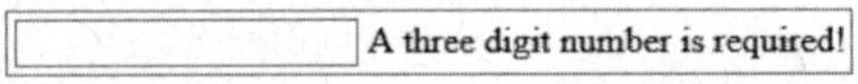

MutuallyExclusiveCheckBoxExtender

FIGURE 24-27

Often, you want to offer a list of check boxes that behave as if they are radio buttons. That is, when you have a collection of check boxes, you want the end user to make only a single selection from the provided list of items.

Using the MutuallyExclusiveCheckBoxExtender control, you can perform such an action. Listing 24-22 shows you how to accomplish this task.

LISTING 24-22: Using the MutuallyExclusiveCheckBoxExtender control with check boxes

```
<%@ Page Language="C#" %>

<%@ Register Assembly="AjaxControlToolkit"
    Namespace="AjaxControlToolkit" TagPrefix="asp" %>

<!DOCTYPE html>
<html>
<head runat="server">
    <title>MutuallyExclusiveCheckBoxExtender Control</title>
</head>
<body>
    <form id="form1" runat="server">
    <div>
        <asp:ToolkitScriptManager ID="ToolkitScriptManager1" runat="server">
        </asp:ToolkitScriptManager>
        <asp:MutuallyExclusiveCheckBoxExtender
         ID="MutuallyExclusiveCheckBoxExtender1" runat="server"
         TargetControlID="CheckBox1" Key="MyCheckboxes" />
        <asp:CheckBox ID="CheckBox1" runat="server" Text="Blue" />
        <br />
        <asp:MutuallyExclusiveCheckBoxExtender
         ID="MutuallyExclusiveCheckBoxExtender2" runat="server"
```

```
            TargetControlID="CheckBox2" Key="MyCheckboxes" />
            <asp:CheckBox ID="CheckBox2" runat="server" Text="Brown" />
            <br />
            <asp:MutuallyExclusiveCheckBoxExtender
             ID="MutuallyExclusiveCheckBoxExtender3" runat="server"
             TargetControlID="CheckBox3" Key="MyCheckboxes" />
            <asp:CheckBox ID="CheckBox3" runat="server" Text="Green" />
            <br />
            <asp:MutuallyExclusiveCheckBoxExtender
             ID="MutuallyExclusiveCheckBoxExtender4" runat="server"
             TargetControlID="CheckBox4" Key="MyCheckboxes" />
            <asp:CheckBox ID="CheckBox4" runat="server" Text="Orange" />
            <br />
        </div>
        </form>
    </body>
    </html>
```

Associating a MutuallyExclusiveCheckBoxExtender control with a CheckBoxList control is impossible; therefore, each of the check boxes needs to be laid out with CheckBox controls as the previous code demonstrates. You need to have one MutuallyExclusiveCheckBoxExtender control for each CheckBox control on the page.

You form a group of CheckBox controls by using the Key property. All the check boxes that you want in one group need to have the same Key value. In the example in Listing 24-22, all the check boxes share a Key value of MyCheckboxes.

Running this page results in a list of four check boxes. When you select one of the check boxes, a check mark appears. Then, when you select another check box, the first check box you selected gets deselected. The best part is that you can even deselect what you have selected in the group, thereby selecting nothing in the check box group.

NumericUpDownExtender

The NumericUpDownExtender control enables you to put some up/down indicators next to a TextBox control that allow the end user to more easily control a selection (which is similar to HTML5's `<input type="number">` element).

A simple example of this is illustrated in Listing 24-23.

LISTING 24-23: Using the NumericUpDownExtender control

```
<%@ Page Language="C#" %>

<%@ Register Assembly="AjaxControlToolkit"
    Namespace="AjaxControlToolkit" TagPrefix="asp" %>

<!DOCTYPE html>
<html>
<head runat="server">
    <title>NumericUpDownExtender Control</title>
</head>
<body>
    <form id="form1" runat="server">
    <div>
        <asp:ToolkitScriptManager ID="ToolkitScriptManager1" runat="server">
        </asp:ToolkitScriptManager>
        <asp:NumericUpDownExtender ID="NumericUpDownExtender1"
         runat="server" TargetControlID="TextBox1" Width="150"
         Maximum="10" Minimum="1">
        </asp:NumericUpDownExtender>
```

continues

LISTING 24-23 *(continued)*

```
            <asp:TextBox ID="TextBox1" runat="server"></asp:TextBox>
        </div>
        </form>
    </body>
</html>
```

The NumericUpDownExtender control here extends the TextBox control on the page. When using the NumericUpDownExtender control, you must specify the width of the control with the Width property. Otherwise, you will see only the up and down arrow keys and not the textbox area. In this case, the Width property is set to 150 (pixels). The Maximum and Minimum properties provide the range used by the up and down indicators.

With a Maximum value setting of 10 and a Minimum value of 1, the only range in the control will be 1 through 10. Running this page produces the results shown in Figure 24-28.

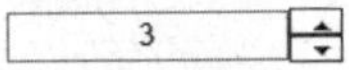

FIGURE 24-28

In addition to numbers, as shown in Listing 24-23, you can use text, as illustrated in Listing 24-24.

LISTING 24-24: Using characters instead of numbers with NumericUpDownExtender

```
<asp:NumericUpDownExtender ID="NumericUpDownExtender1" runat="server"
 TargetControlID="TextBox1" Width="150"
 RefValues="Blue;Brown;Green;Orange;Black;White">
</asp:NumericUpDownExtender>
```

In this case, the words are defined within the RefValues property (all separated with a semicolon). This gives you the results presented in Figure 24-29.

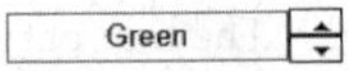

FIGURE 24-29

PagingBulletedListExtender

The PagingBulletedListExtender control enables you to take long bulleted lists and easily apply alphabetic paging to the list. For an example of this, Listing 24-25 works off the Customers table within the Northwind database.

LISTING 24-25: Paging a bulleted list from the Northwind database

```
<%@ Page Language="C#" %>

<%@ Register Assembly="AjaxControlToolkit"
    Namespace="AjaxControlToolkit" TagPrefix="ajaxToolkit" %>

<!DOCTYPE html>
<html>
<head runat="server">
    <title>PagingBulletedListExtender Control</title>
</head>
<body>
    <form id="form1" runat="server">
    <div>
        <ajaxToolkit:ToolkitScriptManager ID="ToolkitScriptManager1" runat="server">
        </ajaxToolkit:ToolkitScriptManager>
        <ajaxToolkit:PagingBulletedListExtender
         ID="PagingBulletedListExtender1"
         runat="server" TargetControlID="BulletedList1">
        </ajaxToolkit:PagingBulletedListExtender>
        <asp:SqlDataSource ID="SqlDataSource1" runat="server"
            ConnectionString="Data Source=.\SQLEXPRESS;
                AttachDbFilename=|DataDirectory|\NORTHWND.MDF;
```

```
                 Integrated Security=True;User Instance=True"
             ProviderName="System.Data.SqlClient"
             SelectCommand="SELECT [CompanyName] FROM [Customers]">
        </asp:SqlDataSource>
        <asp:BulletedList ID="BulletedList1" runat="server"
             DataSourceID="SqlDataSource1" DataTextField="CompanyName"
             DataValueField="CompanyName">
        </asp:BulletedList>
     </div>
     </form>
  </body>
  </html>
```

This code pulls all the `CompanyName` values from the `Customers` table of the Northwind database and binds those values to the BulletList control on the page. Running this page gives you the results illustrated in Figure 24-30.

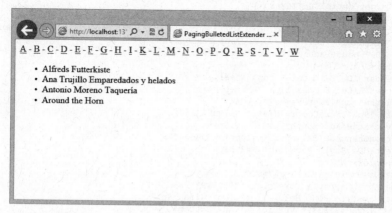

FIGURE 24-30

From this figure, you can see that the paging is organized alphabetically on the client side. Only the letters for which there are values appear in the linked list of letters. Clicking any of the letters gives you the items from the bulleted list that start with that character.

PopupControlExtender

The PopupControlExtender control enables you to create a pop-up for any control on your page. For instance, you can completely mimic the CalendarExtender control that was presented earlier by creating a pop-up containing a Calendar control off a TextBox control. Listing 24-26 mimics this behavior.

LISTING 24-26: Creating a CalendarExtender control with PopupControlExtender

VB

```
<%@ Page Language="VB" %>

<%@ Register Assembly="AjaxControlToolkit"
    Namespace="AjaxControlToolkit" TagPrefix="asp" %>

<script runat="server">
    Protected Sub Calendar1_SelectionChanged(ByVal sender As Object, _
      ByVal e As System.EventArgs)
        PopupControlExtender1.Commit( _
          Calendar1.SelectedDate.ToShortDateString())
```

continues

LISTING 24-26 *(continued)*

```
    End Sub
</script>

<!DOCTYPE html>
<html>
<head runat="server">
    <title>PopupControlExtender Control</title>
</head>
<body>
    <form id="form1" runat="server">
    <div>
        <asp:ToolkitScriptManager ID="ToolkitScriptManager1" runat="server">
        </asp:ToolkitScriptManager>
        <asp:PopupControlExtender ID="PopupControlExtender1"
         runat="server" TargetControlID="TextBox1"
         PopupControlID="UpdatePanel1" OffsetY="25">
        </asp:PopupControlExtender>
        <asp:TextBox ID="TextBox1" runat="server"></asp:TextBox>
        <asp:UpdatePanel ID="UpdatePanel1" runat="server">
            <ContentTemplate>
                <asp:Calendar ID="Calendar1" runat="server"
                 BackColor="White" BorderColor="White"
                 BorderWidth="1px" Font-Names="Verdana"
                 Font-Size="9pt" ForeColor="Black" Height="190px"
                 NextPrevFormat="FullMonth" Width="350px"
                 OnSelectionChanged="Calendar1_SelectionChanged">
                    <SelectedDayStyle BackColor="#333399"
                     ForeColor="White" />
                    <TodayDayStyle BackColor="#CCCCCC" />
                    <OtherMonthDayStyle ForeColor="#999999" />
                    <NextPrevStyle Font-Bold="True" Font-Size="8pt"
                     ForeColor="#333333" VerticalAlign="Bottom" />
                    <DayHeaderStyle Font-Bold="True" Font-Size="8pt" />
                    <TitleStyle BackColor="White" BorderColor="Black"
                     BorderWidth="4px" Font-Bold="True"
                     Font-Size="12pt" ForeColor="#333399" />
                </asp:Calendar>
            </ContentTemplate>
        </asp:UpdatePanel>
    </div>
    </form>
</body>
</html>
```

C#

```
<%@ Page Language="C#" %>

<%@ Register Assembly="AjaxControlToolkit"
Namespace="AjaxControlToolkit"
    TagPrefix="asp" %>

<script runat="server">
    protected void Calendar1_SelectionChanged(object sender,
        EventArgs e)
    {
        PopupControlExtender1.Commit(
            Calendar1.SelectedDate.ToShortDateString());
    }
</script>
```

When you run this page, you get a single textbox on the page. Click within the textbox and a pop-up calendar appears so you can select a date that will be populated back into the textbox (as illustrated in Figure 24-31).

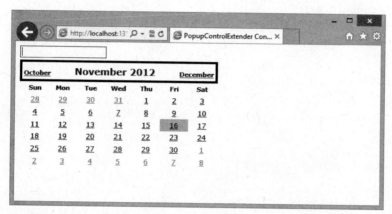

FIGURE 24-31

You will want to place your pop-up control within an ASP.NET AJAX UpdatePanel control and to pass the value from the pop-up control back to the target control (the TextBox1 control), so you use the Commit() method:

```
PopupControlExtender1.Commit(Calendar1.SelectedDate.ToShortDateString())
```

ResizableControlExtender

In many situations, you may want to limit the size of an element when it is initially displayed but allow users to grow or shrink the element as they see fit. The ResizableControlExtender makes this easy. Place the ResizableControl on the page and point it to an ASP.NET Panel control using the TargetControlID property.

The ResizableControlExtender control enables you to take a Panel control and give end users the ability to grab a handle and change the size of the element. Anything you put inside the Panel control will then change in size depending on how the end user extends the item. For this to work, you also need to create a handle for the end user to work from in pulling or contracting the item.

Use the HandleCssClass property to specify the style information about the appearance of the handle the user selects to begin resizing the panel. The ResizableCssClass property refers to style information shown while the panel is being altered.

The control also exposes events that are raised that you can attach code to react to the panel being resized: OnClientResizeBegin, OnClientResizing, and finally OnClientResize. These are very useful for actions such as altering text size or retrieving additional data if the panel is enlarged or hiding elements if the panel is shrunk. Listing 24-27 is an example of using the ResizableControlExtender with the CSS information inline in the page. The example shows you how to use the ResizableControlExtender with an image.

LISTING 24-27: Using the ResizableControlExtender control with an image

```
<%@ Page Language="C#" %>

<%@ Register Assembly="AjaxControlToolkit"
    Namespace="AjaxControlToolkit" TagPrefix="asp" %>

<!DOCTYPE html>
<html>
<head runat="server">
    <title>ResizableControlExtender Control</title>
    <style type="text/css">
        .handle
        {
            width:10px;
            height:10px;
            background-color:Black;
            cursor: se-resize;
        }
        .resizable
        {
            border-style:solid;
            border-width:2px;
            border-color:Black;
        }
    </style>
</head>
<body>
    <form id="form1" runat="server">
    <div>
        <asp:ToolkitScriptManager ID="ToolkitScriptManager1" runat="server">
        </asp:ToolkitScriptManager>
        <asp:ResizableControlExtender ID="ResizableControlExtender1"
         runat="server"
         TargetControlID="Panel1" HandleCssClass="handle"
         ResizableCssClass="resizable">
        </asp:ResizableControlExtender>
        <asp:Panel ID="Panel1" runat="server" Width="300" Height="225">
            <asp:Image ID="Image1" runat="server"
             ImageUrl="Images/ToolkitLogo.jpg"
             style="width:100%; height:100%"/>
        </asp:Panel>
    </div>
    </form>
</body>
</html>
```

In this example, the ResizableControlExtender control depends on CSS to create the handle for the end user to grab to resize the Panel control. The TargetControlID property points to the control to be resized.

Two CSS references are in the ResizableControlExtender control. One deals with the control as it sits on the screen with no end user interaction. This is really to show the end user that there is an ability to resize the element. This is done through the HandleCssClass property. The value of this property points to the CSS class handle contained within the same file. The second CSS reference deals with the control as it is clicked and held (when the end user does not let up with the mouse click performed). This one is done with the ResizableCssClass property. The value of this property points to the CSS class resizable.

When compiled and run, the code should generate the same page presented in Figure 24-32.

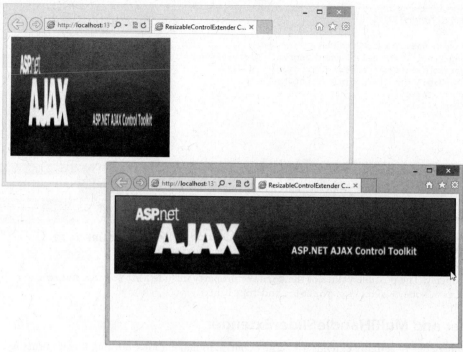

FIGURE 24-32

You can see in the top screenshot how the image looks when there is no end user interaction. In this case, there is a black square (as defined by the CSS) in the lower-right corner of the image. The screenshot on the bottom shows what happens when the end user grabs the handle and starts changing the shape of the image.

RoundedCornersExtender

The RoundedCornersExtender control enables you to put rounded corners on the elements on your page. As with the ResizableControlExtender control, you put the element you are interested in working with inside a Panel control. Listing 24-28 shows this done with a Login server control.

LISTING 24-28: Rounding the corners of the Panel control containing a Login server control

```
<%@ Page Language="C#" %>

<%@ Register Assembly="AjaxControlToolkit" Namespace="AjaxControlToolkit" TagPrefix="asp" %>

<!DOCTYPE html>
<html>
<head runat="server">
    <title>RoundedCornersExtender Control</title>
</head>
<body>
    <form id="form1" runat="server">
    <div>
        <asp:ToolkitScriptManager ID="ToolkitScriptManager1" runat="server">
        </asp:ToolkitScriptManager>
        <asp:RoundedCornersExtender ID="RoundedCornersExtender1"
         runat="server" TargetControlID="Panel1">
```

continues

LISTING 24-28 *(continued)*

```
        </asp:RoundedCornersExtender>
        <asp:Panel ID="Panel1" runat="server" Width="250px"
         HorizontalAlign="Center" BackColor="Orange">
            <asp:Login ID="Login1" runat="server">
            </asp:Login>
        </asp:Panel>
    </div>
    </form>
</body>
</html>
```

Here, the RoundedCornersExtender control simply points to the Panel control with the `TargetControlID` property. This Panel control has a background color of orange to show that the corners are indeed rounded. The result of this bit of code is illustrated in Figure 24-33.

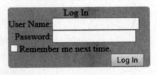

FIGURE 24-33

You can control the degree of the rounded corners using the `Radius` property of the RoundedCornersExtender control. By default, this property is set to a value of 5. You can even choose the corners that you want to round using the `Corners` property. The possible values of the `Corners` property include `All`, `Bottom`, `BottomLeft`, `BottomRight`, `Left`, `None`, `Right`, `Top`, `TopLeft`, and `TopRight`.

SliderExtender and MultiHandleSliderExtender

The SliderExtender control actually extends a TextBox control to make it look nothing like it normally does. This Ajax Control Toolkit control enables you to create a true slider control that allows the end user to select a range of numbers using a mouse instead of typing in the number. Listing 24-29 shows a simple example of using the slider.

LISTING 24-29: Using the SliderExtender control

```
<%@ Page Language="C#" %>

<%@ Register Assembly="AjaxControlToolkit"
    Namespace="AjaxControlToolkit" TagPrefix="asp" %>

<!DOCTYPE html>
<html>
<head runat="server">
    <title>SliderExtender Control</title>
</head>
<body>
    <form id="form1" runat="server">
    <div>
        <asp:ToolkitScriptManager ID="ToolkitScriptManager1" runat="server">
        </asp:ToolkitScriptManager>
        <asp:SliderExtender ID="SliderExtender1" runat="server"
         TargetControlID="TextBox1">
        </asp:SliderExtender>
        <asp:TextBox ID="TextBox1" runat="server"></asp:TextBox>
    </div>
    </form>
</body>
</html>
```

This little bit of code to tie a SliderExtender control to a typical TextBox control is simple and produces the result presented in Figure 24-34.

FIGURE 24-34

This is fine, but it is hard for the end users to tell what number they are selecting. Therefore, you might find it better to give a signifier to the end user. Adding a Label control to the page (called Label1) and changing the SliderExtender control to include a `BoundControlID` property gives you the signifier that you are looking for. Here is the code for this change:

```
<asp:SliderExtender ID="SliderExtender1" runat="server" TargetControlID="TextBox1"
  BoundControlID="Label1">
</asp:SliderExtender>
```

This small change produces the result (with the appropriate Label control on the page) shown in Figure 24-35.

FIGURE 24-35

Now when the end users slide the handle on the slider, they see the number that they are working with quite easily. Some of the following properties are available to the SliderExtender control:

➤ `Decimal`: Enables you to specify the number of decimals the result should take. The more decimals you have, the more unlikely the end user will be able to pick an exact number.

➤ `HandleCssClass`: The CSS class that you are using to design the handle.

➤ `HandleImageUrl`: The image file you are using to represent the handle.

➤ `Length`: The length of the slider in pixels. The default value is 150.

➤ `Maximum`: The maximum number represented in the slider. The default value is 100.

➤ `Minimum`: The minimum number represented in the slider. The default value is 0.

➤ `Orientation`: The orientation of the slider. The possible values include `Horizontal` and `Vertical`. The default value is `Horizontal`.

➤ `RailCssClass`: The CSS class that you are using to design the rail of the slider.

➤ `ToolTipText`: The tooltip when the end user hovers over the slider. Using 0 within the text enables you to show the end user the current position of the slider.

The MultiHandleSliderExtender is basically the same thing, but this particular extender enables you to have more than one handle for the end user to work with. This works great if you need a slider that needs to do things like allow the end user to select a range or a minimum/maximum value.

SlideShowExtender

The SlideShowExtender control enables you to put an image slideshow in the browser. The slideshow controls enable the end user to move to the next or previous images as well as to simply play the images as a slideshow with a defined wait between each image. Listing 24-30 (SlideShowExtender.aspx in the code download for this chapter) shows an example of creating a slideshow.

LISTING 24-30: Creating a slideshow with three images

.ASPX

```
<%@ Page Language="C#" AutoEventWireup="true"
        CodeFile="SlideShowExtender.aspx.cs" Inherits="SlideShowExtender" %>

<%@ Register Assembly="AjaxControlToolkit" Namespace="AjaxControlToolkit" TagPrefix="asp" %>

<!DOCTYPE html>
<html>
<head id="Head1" runat="server">
    <title>SlideShowExtender Control</title>
</head>
<body>
    <form id="form1" runat="server">
```

continues

LISTING 24-30 *(continued)*

```
    <div>
        <asp:ToolkitScriptManager ID="ToolkitScriptManager1" runat="server">
        </asp:ToolkitScriptManager>
        <asp:Panel ID="Panel1" runat="server" Width="300px"
         HorizontalAlign="Center">
            <asp:SlideShowExtender ID="SlideShowExtender1" runat="server"
                ImageTitleLabelID="LabelTitle" TargetControlID="Image1"
                UseContextKey="True" NextButtonID="ButtonNext"
                PlayButtonID="ButtonPlay"
                PreviousButtonID="ButtonPrevious"
                SlideShowServiceMethod="GetSlides"
                ImageDescriptionLabelID="LabelDescription">
            </asp:SlideShowExtender>
            <asp:Label ID="LabelTitle" runat="server" Text="Label"
             Font-Bold="True"></asp:Label><br /><br />
            <asp:Image ID="Image1" runat="server"
             ImageUrl="Images/ToolkitLogo.jpg" /><br />
            <asp:Label ID="LabelDescription" runat="server"
             Text="Label"></asp:Label><br /><br />
            <asp:Button ID="ButtonPrevious" runat="server" Text="Previous" />
            <asp:Button ID="ButtonNext" runat="server" Text="Next" />
            <asp:Button ID="ButtonPlay" runat="server" />
        </asp:Panel>
    </div>
    </form>
</body>
</html>
```

The SlideShowExtender control has a lot of properties available. You can specify the location where you are defining the image title and description using the `ImageTitleLabelID` and the `ImageDescriptionLabelID` properties. In addition, this page contains three Button controls: one to act as the Previous button, another for the Next button, and the final one as the Play button. However, it is important to note that when the Play button is clicked (to start the slideshow), it turns into the Stop button.

The `SlideShowServiceMethod` property is important because it points to the server-side method that returns the images that are part of the slideshow. In this case, it is referring to a method called `GetSlides`, which is represented in Listing 24-31 (SlideShowExtender.aspx.cs and SlideShowExtender.aspx.vb in the code download for this chapter).

LISTING 24-31: The GetSlides method implementation

VB

```
Partial Class SlideShowExtender
    Inherits System.Web.UI.Page

    <System.Web.Services.WebMethodAttribute()>
    <System.Web.Script.Services.ScriptMethodAttribute()>
    Public Shared Function GetSlides(ByVal _
     contextKey As System.String) As AjaxControlToolkit.Slide()

        Return New AjaxControlToolkit.Slide() {
            New AjaxControlToolkit.Slide("Images/ToolkitLogo.jpg", _
                "The Logo", "This is the Ajax Control Toolkit Logo."),
            New AjaxControlToolkit.Slide("Images/ToolkitLogo1.jpg", _
                "The 2nd Logo", "This is the modified Ajax Control Toolkit Logo."),
            New AjaxControlToolkit.Slide("Images/ToolkitLogo2.jpg", _
```

```
                    "The 3rd Logo", "This is another modified Ajax Control Toolkit Logo.")}
        End Function
    End Class
```

C#

```
public partial class SlideShowExtender : System.Web.UI.Page
{
    [System.Web.Services.WebMethodAttribute(),
     System.Web.Script.Services.ScriptMethodAttribute()]
    public static AjaxControlToolkit.Slide[]
      GetSlides(string contextKey)
    {
        return new AjaxControlToolkit.Slide[] {
            new AjaxControlToolkit.Slide("Images/ToolkitLogo.jpg",
              "The Logo", "This is the Ajax Control Toolkit Logo."),
            new AjaxControlToolkit.Slide("Images/ToolkitLogo1.jpg",
              "The 2nd Logo", "This is the modified Ajax Control Toolkit Logo."),
            new AjaxControlToolkit.Slide("Images/ToolkitLogo2.jpg",
              "The 3rd Logo", "This is another modified Ajax Control Toolkit Logo.") };
    }
}
```

With the code-behind in place, the SlideShowExtender has a server-side method to call for the photos. This method, called `GetSlides()`, returns an array of `Slide` objects that require the location of the object (the path), the title, and the description. When running this page, you get something similar to the results shown in Figure 24-36.

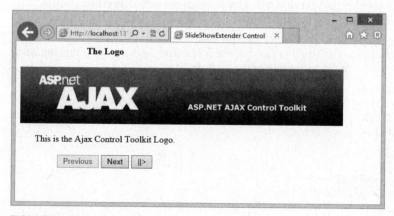

FIGURE 24-36

Clicking the Play button on the page rotates the images until they are done. They will not repeat in a loop unless you have the SlideShowExtender control's `Loop` property set to `True`. (It is set to `False` by default.)

The other important property to pay attention to is the `PlayInterval` property. The value of this property is an integer that represents the number of milliseconds that the browser will take to change to the next photo in the series of images. By default, this is set to `3000` milliseconds.

TextBoxWatermarkExtender

The TextBoxWatermarkExtender control enables you to put instructions within controls for the end users, which gives them a better understanding of what to use the control for. This can be text or even images (when using CSS). Listing 24-32 shows an example of using this control with a TextBox server control.

LISTING 24-32: Using the TextBoxWatermarkExtender control with a TextBox control

```
<%@ Page Language="C#" %>

<%@ Register Assembly="AjaxControlToolkit"
    Namespace="AjaxControlToolkit" TagPrefix="asp" %>

<!DOCTYPE html>
<html>
<head runat="server">
    <title>TextBoxWatermarkExtender Control</title>
</head>
<body>
    <form id="form1" runat="server">
    <div>
        <asp:ToolkitScriptManager ID="ToolkitScriptManager1" runat="server">
        </asp:ToolkitScriptManager>
        <asp:TextBoxWatermarkExtender ID="TextBoxWatermarkExtender1"
         runat="server" WatermarkText="Enter in something here!"
         TargetControlID="TextBox1">
        </asp:TextBoxWatermarkExtender>
        <asp:TextBox ID="TextBox1" runat="server"></asp:TextBox>
    </div>
    </form>
</body>
</html>
```

In this case, the TextBoxWatermarkExtender control is associated with a simple TextBox control and uses the `WatermarkText` property to provide the text that will appear inside the actual TextBox control. Figure 24-37 shows the results of the code from this listing.

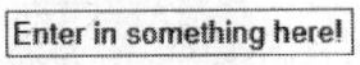

The text in the image from Figure 24-37 is straight text with no style inside the TextBox control. When the end user clicks inside the TextBox control, the text will disappear and the cursor will be properly placed at the beginning of the textbox.

Enter in something here!

FIGURE 24-37

To apply some style to the content that you use as a watermark, you can use the `WatermarkCssClass` property. You can change the code to include a bit of style, as shown in Listing 24-33.

LISTING 24-33: Applying style to the watermark

```
<%@ Page Language="C#" %>

<%@ Register Assembly="AjaxControlToolkit"
    Namespace="AjaxControlToolkit" TagPrefix="asp" %>

<!DOCTYPE html>
<html>
<head runat="server">
    <title>TextBoxWatermarkExtender Control</title>
    <style type="text/css">
        .watermark
        {
        width:150px;
        font:Verdana;
        font-style:italic;
        color:GrayText;
        }

    </style>
</head>
```

```
<body>
    <form id="form1" runat="server">
    <div>
        <asp:ToolkitScriptManager ID="ToolkitScriptManager1" runat="server">
        </asp:ToolkitScriptManager>
        <asp:TextBoxWatermarkExtender ID="TextBoxWatermarkExtender1"
         runat="server" WatermarkText="Enter in something here!"
         TargetControlID="TextBox1"
         WatermarkCssClass="watermark">
        </asp:TextBoxWatermarkExtender>
        <asp:TextBox ID="TextBox1" runat="server"></asp:TextBox>
    </div>
    </form>
</body>
</html>
```

This time, the `WatermarkCssClass` property is used and points to the inline CSS class, `watermark`, which is on the page. When you run this page, you will see the style applied as shown in Figure 24-38.

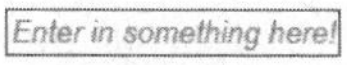

Enter in something here!

FIGURE 24-38

ToggleButtonExtender

The ToggleButtonExtender control works with CheckBox controls and enables you to use an image of your own instead of the standard check box images that the CheckBox controls typically use. Using the ToggleButtonExtender control, you are able to specify images for checked, unchecked, and disabled statuses. Listing 24-34 shows an example of using this control.

LISTING 24-34: Using the ToggleButtonExtender control

```
<%@ Page Language="C#" %>

<%@ Register Assembly="AjaxControlToolkit"
    Namespace="AjaxControlToolkit" TagPrefix="asp" %>

<!DOCTYPE html>
<html>
<head runat="server">
    <title>ToggleButtonExtender Control</title>
</head>
<body>
    <form id="form1" runat="server">
    <div>
        <asp:ToolkitScriptManager ID="ToolkitScriptManager1" runat="server">
        </asp:ToolkitScriptManager>
        <asp:MutuallyExclusiveCheckBoxExtender
         ID="MutuallyExclusiveCheckBoxExtender1" runat="server"
         Key="MyCheckBoxes" TargetControlID="CheckBox1">
        </asp:MutuallyExclusiveCheckBoxExtender>
        <asp:MutuallyExclusiveCheckBoxExtender
         ID="MutuallyExclusiveCheckBoxExtender2" runat="server"
         Key="MyCheckBoxes" TargetControlID="CheckBox2">
        </asp:MutuallyExclusiveCheckBoxExtender>
        <asp:ToggleButtonExtender ID="ToggleButtonExtender1"
         runat="server" TargetControlID="CheckBox1"
         UncheckedImageUrl="Images/Unchecked.gif"
         CheckedImageUrl="Images/Checked.gif"
         CheckedImageAlternateText="Checked"
         UncheckedImageAlternateText="Not Checked" ImageWidth="25"
         ImageHeight="25">
```

continues

LISTING 24-34 *(continued)*

```
            </asp:ToggleButtonExtender>
            <asp:CheckBox ID="CheckBox1" runat="server"
             Text=" Option One" />
            <asp:ToggleButtonExtender ID="ToggleButtonExtender2"
             runat="server" TargetControlID="CheckBox2"
             UncheckedImageUrl="Images/Unchecked.gif"
             CheckedImageUrl="Images/Checked.gif"
             CheckedImageAlternateText="Checked"
             UncheckedImageAlternateText="Not Checked" ImageWidth="25"
             ImageHeight="25">
            </asp:ToggleButtonExtender>
            <asp:CheckBox ID="CheckBox2" runat="server"
             Text=" Option Two" />
        </div>
        </form>
    </body>
    </html>
```

This page has two CheckBox controls. Each check box has an associated ToggleButtonExtender control along with a MutuallyExclusiveCheckBoxExtender control to tie the two check boxes together. The ToggleButtonExtender control uses the `CheckedImageUrl` and the `UncheckedImageUrl` properties to specify the appropriate images to use. Then, if images are disabled by the end user's browser instance, the text that is provided in the `CheckedImageAlternateText` and `UncheckedImageAlternateText` properties is used instead. You will also need to specify values for the `ImageWidth` and `ImageHeight` properties for the page to run.

Running this page gives you results similar to those presented in Figure 24-39.

FIGURE 24-39

UpdatePanelAnimationExtender

Animating an UpdatePanel as its content is being refreshed is a common scenario. The UpdatePanelAnimationExtender enables you to use the broad set of animations available in the toolkit and automatically coordinates playing them when the specified UpdatePanel is being updated or when the update has completed.

The UpdatePanelAnimationExtender control enables you to apply an animation to a Panel control for two specific events. The first is the `OnUpdating` event and the second is the `OnUpdated` event. You can then use the animation framework provided by the Ajax Control Toolkit to change the page's style based on these two events. Listing 24-35 shows an example of using the `OnUpdated` event when the end user clicks a specific date within a Calendar control contained within the UpdatePanel control on the page.

LISTING 24-35: Using animations on the OnUpdated event

VB

```
<%@ Page Language="VB" %>

<%@ Register Assembly="AjaxControlToolkit"
    Namespace="AjaxControlToolkit" TagPrefix="asp" %>

<script runat="server">
    Protected  Sub Calendar1_SelectionChanged(ByVal sender As Object, _
       ByVal e As EventArgs)
        Label1.Text = "The date selected is " & _
           Calendar1.SelectedDate.ToLongDateString()
```

```
            End Sub
        </script>

        <!DOCTYPE html>
        <html>
        <head runat="server">
            <title>UpdatePanelAnimationExtender Control</title>
        </head>
        <body>
            <form id="form1" runat="server">
            <div>
                <asp:ToolkitScriptManager ID="ToolkitScriptManager1" runat="server">
                </asp:ToolkitScriptManager>
                <asp:UpdatePanelAnimationExtender
                 ID="UpdatePanelAnimationExtender1"
                 runat="server" TargetControlID="UpdatePanel1">
                    <Animations>
                        <OnUpdated>
                            <Sequence>
                                <Color PropertyKey="background"
                                 StartValue="#999966"
                                 EndValue="#FFFFFF" Duration="5.0" />
                            </Sequence>
                        </OnUpdated>
                    </Animations>
                </asp:UpdatePanelAnimationExtender>
                <asp:UpdatePanel ID="UpdatePanel1" runat="server">
                    <ContentTemplate>
                        <asp:Label ID="Label1" runat="server"></asp:Label>
                        <br />
                        <asp:Calendar ID="Calendar1" runat="server"
                            onselectionchanged="Calendar1_SelectionChanged">
                        </asp:Calendar>
                    </ContentTemplate>
                </asp:UpdatePanel>
            </div>
            </form>
        </body>
        </html>
```

C#

```
<%@ Page Language="C#" %>

<%@ Register Assembly="AjaxControlToolkit"
Namespace="AjaxControlToolkit"
    TagPrefix="asp" %>

<script runat="server">
    protected void Calendar1_SelectionChanged(object sender,
      EventArgs e)
    {
        Label1.Text = "The date selected is " +
            Calendar1.SelectedDate.ToLongDateString();
    }
</script>
```

With this bit of code, when you click a date within the Calendar control, the entire background of the UpdatePanel holding the calendar changes from one color to another for a 5-second duration as specified in the animation you built. The animations you define can get complex, and building deluxe animations is beyond the scope of this chapter.

ValidatorCalloutExtender

The last extender control covered is the ValidatorCalloutExtender control. This control enables you to add a more noticeable validation message to end users working with a form. You associate this control not with the control that is being validated, but instead with the validation control itself. An example of associating the ValidatorCalloutExtender control with a RegularExpressionValidator control is presented in Listing 24-36.

LISTING 24-36: Creating validation callouts with the ValidatorCalloutExtender

```
<%@ Page Language="C#" %>

<%@ Register Assembly="AjaxControlToolkit"
    Namespace="AjaxControlToolkit" TagPrefix="asp" %>

<!DOCTYPE html>
<html>
<head runat="server">
    <title>ValidatorCalloutExtender Control</title>
</head>
<body>
    <form id="form1" runat="server">
    <div>
        <asp:ToolkitScriptManager ID="ToolkitScriptManager1" runat="server">
        </asp:ToolkitScriptManager>
        <asp:ValidatorCalloutExtender ID="ValidatorCalloutExtender1"
         runat="server" TargetControlID="RegularExpressionValidator1">
        </asp:ValidatorCalloutExtender>
        Email Address: 
        <asp:TextBox ID="TextBox1" runat="server"></asp:TextBox>
        <asp:RegularExpressionValidator
         ID="RegularExpressionValidator1" runat="server"
         ErrorMessage="You must enter an email address" Display="None"
         ControlToValidate="TextBox1"
         ValidationExpression=
            "\w+([-+.']\w+)*@\w+([-.]\w+)*\.\w+([-.]\w+)*">
        </asp:RegularExpressionValidator><br />
        <asp:Button ID="Button1" runat="server" Text="Submit" />
    </div>
    </form>
</body>
</html>
```

This page has a single textbox for the form, a Submit button, and a RegularExpressionValidator control. You build the RegularExpressionValidator control as you would normally, except you make use of the `Display` property and set it to `None`. You do not want the normal ASP.NET validation control to also display its message, because it will collide with the one displayed with the ValidatorCalloutExtender control. Although the `Display` property is set to `None`, you still use the `ErrorMessage` property to provide the error message. Running this page produces the results presented in Figure 24-40.

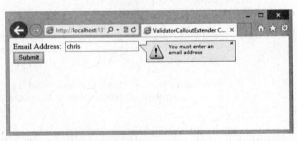

FIGURE 24-40

AJAX CONTROL TOOLKIT SERVER CONTROLS

The following ASP.NET AJAX controls actually do not always extend other ASP.NET controls, but instead, are controls themselves. The following sections detail some of these controls.

Accordion Control

The Accordion control is used to specify a set of panes, similar to the famous navigation menu in Microsoft Outlook. Each pane is made up of a header template and a content template. The header templates of all panes are always visible, whereas only one content template is visible. The user selects which pane to view by clicking the header. The content from the previously active pane is hidden from view, and the content of the newly selected pane is displayed instead.

The Accordion control can provide a fade transition when switching among active panes. Set the FadeTransitions property to True and then you can set the TransitionDuration and FramesPerSecond values. The default values are 250 milliseconds and 40 frames per second, respectively.

The SelectedIndex property lets you declaratively and programmatically control which pane to show. Other important properties are the AutoSize and Height properties. The AutoSize property is None by default, meaning that the size of the Accordion control changes based on the active pane. Other content on the screen may be shifted to accommodate the changing size. However, when the AutoSize property is set to Limit, the size is restricted to the Height value. The active pane displays scrollbars if the content is larger than the space available. The other possible value is Fill, which results in expanding a pane if the content is not large enough to satisfy the Height value provided. Listing 24-37 shows the Accordion control in action. The Accordion control is used with two panes.

LISTING 24-37: An Accordion control with two AccordionPane controls

```
<%@ Page Language="C#" %>

<%@ Register Assembly="AjaxControlToolkit"
    Namespace="AjaxControlToolkit" TagPrefix="asp" %>

<!DOCTYPE html>
<html>
<head runat="server">
    <title>Accordion Control</title>
    <style type="text/css">
        .titlebar
        {
            background-color:Blue;
            color:White;
            font-size:large;
            font-family:Verdana;
            border:solid 3px Black;
        }
    </style>
</head>
<body>
    <form id="form1" runat="server">
    <div>
        <asp:ToolkitScriptManager ID="ToolkitScriptManager1" runat="server">
        </asp:ToolkitScriptManager>
        <asp:Accordion ID="Accordion1" runat="server" HeaderCssClass="titlebar"
         HeaderSelectedCssClass="titlebar"
         FadeTransitions="true"
         TransitionDuration="333"
         FramesPerSecond="30">
            <Panes>
```

continues

LISTING 24-37 *(continued)*

```
                <asp:AccordionPane runat="server" ID="AccordionPane1">
                    <Header>
                        This is the first pane
                    </Header>
                    <Content>
            Lorem ipsum dolor sit amet, consectetuer adipiscing elit.
            Donec accumsan lorem. Ut consectetuer tempus metus.
            Aenean tincidunt venenatis tellus. Suspendisse molestie
            cursus ipsum. Curabitur ut lectus. Nulla ac dolor nec elit
            convallis vulputate. Nullam pharetra pulvinar nunc. Duis
            orci. Phasellus a tortor at nunc mattis congue.
            Vestibulum porta tellus eu orci. Suspendisse quis massa.
            Maecenas varius, erat non ullamcorper nonummy, mauris erat
            eleifend odio, ut gravida nisl neque a ipsum. Vivamus
            facilisis. Cras viverra. Curabitur
            ut augue eget dolor semper posuere. Aenean at magna eu eros
            tempor pharetra. Aenean mauris.
                    </Content>
                </asp:AccordionPane>
                <asp:AccordionPane runat="server" ID="AccordionPane2">
                    <Header>
                        This is the second pane
                    </Header>
                    <Content>
            Lorem ipsum dolor sit amet, consectetuer adipiscing elit.
            Donec accumsan lorem. Ut consectetuer tempus metus.
            Aenean tincidunt venenatis tellus. Suspendisse molestie
            cursus ipsum. Curabitur ut lectus. Nulla ac dolor nec elit
            convallis vulputate. Nullam pharetra pulvinar nunc. Duis
            orci. Phasellus a tortor at nunc mattis congue.
            Vestibulum porta tellus eu orci. Suspendisse quis massa.
            Maecenas varius, erat non ullamcorper nonummy, mauris erat
            eleifend odio, ut gravida nisl neque a ipsum. Vivamus
            facilisis. Cras viverra. Curabitur
            ut augue eget dolor semper posuere. Aenean at magna eu eros
            tempor pharetra. Aenean mauris.
                    </Content>
                </asp:AccordionPane>
                </Panes>
            </asp:Accordion>
        </div>
        </form>
    </body>
    </html>
```

A single CSS class is defined in the document, and this class, titlebar, is used as the value of the HeaderCssClass and the HeaderSelectedCssClass properties. The Accordion control here contains two AccordionPane controls. The sub-elements of the AccordionPane control are the <Header> and the <Content> elements. The items placed in the <Header> section will be in the clickable pane title, whereas the items contained within the <Content> section will slide out and appear when the associated header is selected.

You will notice that there is also a transition effect in place when the panes are switched. Running this page produces the results illustrated in Figure 24-41.

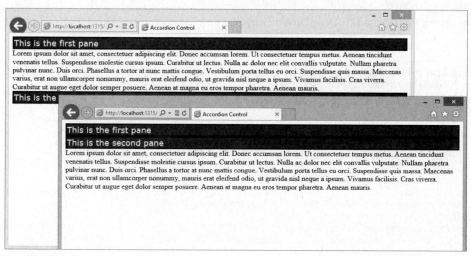

FIGURE 24-41

This figure shows a screenshot of each of the panes selected. Some of the more important properties are described in the following list:

➤ `AutoSize`: Defines how the control deals with its size expansion and shrinkage. The possible values include `None`, `Fill`, and `Limit`. The default is `None`, and when used, items below the control may move to make room for the control expansion. A value of `Fill` works with the `Height` property and the control will fill to the required `Height`. This means that some of the panes may need to grow to accommodate the space, whereas other panes might need to shrink and include a scrollbar to handle the limited space from the height restriction. A value of `Limit` also works with the `Height` property and will never grow larger than this value. It is possible that the pane might be smaller than the specified height.

➤ `TransitionDuration`: The number of milliseconds it takes to transition to another pane.

➤ `FramesPerSecond`: The number of frames per second to use to transition to another pane.

➤ `RequireOpenedPane`: Specifies that at least one pane is required to be open at all times. The default setting of this property is `True`. A value of `False` means that all panes can be collapsed.

Finally, the properties of `DataSource`, `DataSourceID`, and `DataMember` enable you to bind to this control from your code.

CascadingDropDown

The available options for one DropDownList can be a function of the selection made in another DropDownList. The CascadingDropDown control makes enabling this in your application easy. You set the `TargetControlID` to the DropDownList that should be populated by a callback to the server. You also assign a category to classify the DropDownList.

Before the DropDownList is populated, the value of the `PromptText` property is presented. Moreover, while the call to the server is underway, the value of the `LoadingText` property is displayed. You can set the `ServicePath` property to call a `ServiceMethod` on a separate web service, or you can just set the `ServiceMethod` name to a static `ScriptMethod` located directly in the page, as illustrated in Listing 24-38.

The first DropDownList in this example lets the user pick a state. This example includes only Missouri and Oregon. When a state is selected, a second DropDownList is populated based on the value selected by the user in the first DropDownList. The way to specify that one DropDownList is dependent on the value of another is to set the `ParentControlID` of the CascadingDropDown control.

LISTING 24-38: Using the CascadingDropDown control

VB

```vb
<%@ Import Namespace="System.Web.Services" %>
<%@ Import Namespace="AjaxControlToolkit" %>
<%@ Register Assembly="AjaxControlToolkit"
    Namespace="AjaxControlToolkit" TagPrefix="asp" %>

<!DOCTYPE html>
<html>
<head id="Head1" runat="server">

    <script runat="server" language="vb">

        <WebMethod, System.Web.Script.Services.ScriptMethod> _
         Public Shared Function GetStates(ByVal _
           knownCategoryValues As String, _
           ByVal category As String) As CascadingDropDownNameValue()

             Return New CascadingDropDownNameValue() { New _
               CascadingDropDownNameValue("Missouri", "Missouri"), _
               New CascadingDropDownNameValue("Oregon", "Oregon") }
         End Function

        <WebMethod, System.Web.Script.Services.ScriptMethod> _
         Public Shared Function GetCounties(ByVal _
           knownCategoryValues As String, _
           ByVal category As String) As CascadingDropDownNameValue()

           If knownCategoryValues.Contains("Missouri") Then
               Return New CascadingDropDownNameValue() { New _
                 CascadingDropDownNameValue("St. Charles", _
                  "St. Charles"), _
                 New CascadingDropDownNameValue("St. Louis", _
                  "St. Louis"), _
                 New CascadingDropDownNameValue("Jefferson", _
                  "Jefferson"), _
                 New CascadingDropDownNameValue("Warren", "Warren"), _
                 New CascadingDropDownNameValue("Franklin", "Franklin") }
           End If


           If knownCategoryValues.Contains("Oregon") Then
             Return New CascadingDropDownNameValue() { New _
               CascadingDropDownNameValue("Baker", "Baker"), _
               New CascadingDropDownNameValue("Benton", "Benton"), _
               New CascadingDropDownNameValue("Clackamas", "Clackamas"),
               New CascadingDropDownNameValue("Clatsop", "Clatsop"), _
               New CascadingDropDownNameValue("Columbia", "Columbia") }
           End If

           Return Nothing
         End Function

    </script>

<!DOCTYPE html>
<html>
<head id="Head1" runat="server">
    <title>CascadingDropDown</title>
```

```
    </head>
    <body>
        <form id="form1" runat="server">
        <asp:ToolkitScriptManager runat="server" ID="scriptManager" />
        <div>
            <asp:DropDownList runat="server" ID="ddl1" Width="200" />
            <br />
            <asp:DropDownList runat="server" ID="ddl2" Width="200" />
            <br />
            <asp:CascadingDropDown runat="server" ID="cdd1"
                TargetControlID="ddl1"
                PromptText="Select a State"
                Category="state" LoadingText="[Loading States]"
                ServiceMethod="GetStates" />
            <asp:CascadingDropDown runat="server" ID="cdd2"
                TargetControlID="ddl2"
                ParentControlID="ddl1"
                PromptText="Select County" Category="county"
                LoadingText="[Loading Counties]"
                ServiceMethod="GetCounties" />
        </div>
        </form>
    </body>
    </html>
```

C#

```
<%@ Import Namespace="System.Web.Services" %>
<%@ Import Namespace="AjaxControlToolkit" %>
<%@ Register Assembly="AjaxControlToolkit"
    Namespace="AjaxControlToolkit" TagPrefix="asp" %>

    <script runat="server" language="C#">

        [WebMethod]
        [System.Web.Script.Services.ScriptMethod]
        public static CascadingDropDownNameValue[]
            GetStates(string knownCategoryValues, string category)
        {
            return new[] {
        new CascadingDropDownNameValue("Missouri", "Missouri"),
        new CascadingDropDownNameValue("Oregon", "Oregon") };
        }

        [WebMethod]
        [System.Web.Script.Services.ScriptMethod]
        public static CascadingDropDownNameValue[]
            GetCounties(string knownCategoryValues, string category)
        {
            if (knownCategoryValues.Contains("Missouri"))
            {
                return new[] {
                    new CascadingDropDownNameValue("St. Charles",
                        "St. Charles"),
                    new CascadingDropDownNameValue("St. Louis",
                        "St. Louis"),
                    new CascadingDropDownNameValue("Jefferson",
                        "Jefferson"),
                    new CascadingDropDownNameValue("Warren", "Warren"),
                    new CascadingDropDownNameValue("Franklin",
                        "Franklin") };
            }
```

continues

LISTING 24-38 *(continued)*

```
            if (knownCategoryValues.Contains("Oregon"))
            {
                return new[] {
                    new CascadingDropDownNameValue("Baker", "Baker"),
                    new CascadingDropDownNameValue("Benton", "Benton"),
                    new CascadingDropDownNameValue("Clackamas",
                        "Clackamas"),
                    new CascadingDropDownNameValue("Clatsop",
                        "Clatsop"),
                    new CascadingDropDownNameValue("Columbia",
                        "Columbia") };
            }
            return null;
        }

    </script>
```

NoBot Control

The NoBot control works to determine how entities interact with your forms. It helps you ensure that actual humans are working with your forms and some automated code isn't working through your application.

The NoBot control is illustrated in Listing 24-39 (NoBot.aspx in the code download for this chapter).

LISTING 24-39: Using the NoBot control to limit a login form

.ASPX

```
<%@ Page Language="C#" AutoEventWireup="true" CodeFile="NoBot.aspx.cs" Inherits="NoBot" %>

<%@ Register Assembly="AjaxControlToolkit" Namespace="AjaxControlToolkit" TagPrefix="asp" %>

<!DOCTYPE html>
<html>
<head id="Head1" runat="server">
    <title>NoBot Control</title>
</head>
<body>
    <form id="form1" runat="server">
    <div>
        <asp:ToolkitScriptManager ID="ToolkitScriptManager1" runat="server">
        </asp:ToolkitScriptManager>
        <asp:NoBot ID="NoBot1" runat="server" CutoffMaximumInstances="3"
            CutoffWindowSeconds="15" ResponseMinimumDelaySeconds="10"
            OnGenerateChallengeAndResponse="NoBot1_GenerateChallengeAndResponse" />
        <asp:Login ID="Login1" runat="server">
        </asp:Login>
        <asp:Label ID="Label1" runat="server"></asp:Label>
    </div>
    </form>
</body>
</html>
```

The NoBot control has three important properties to be aware of when controlling how your forms are submitted. These properties include `CutoffMaximumInstances`, `CutoffWindowSeconds`, and `ResponseMinimumDelaySeconds`.

`CutoffMaximumInstances` is the number of times the end user is allowed to try to submit the form within the number of seconds specified by the `CutoffWindowSeconds` property. The `ResponseMinimumDelaySeconds` property defines the minimum number of seconds the end user has to submit the form. If you know the form you are working with will take some time, setting this property to a value (even if it is 5 seconds) will help stop submissions that are not made by humans.

The `OnGenerateChallengeAndResponse` property enables you to define the server-side method that works with the challenge and enables you to provide a response based on the challenge. This property is used in Listing 24-39 and posts the status of the form submission back to the user.

The code-behind for this page is represented in Listing 24-40 (NoBot.aspx.vb and NoBot.aspx.cs in the code download for this chapter).

LISTING 24-40: The code-behind for the NoBot control's OnGenerateChallengeAndResponse

VB

```vb
Imports System
Imports AjaxControlToolkit

Public partial Class NoBot
  Inherits System.Web.UI.Page
    Protected Sub NoBot1_GenerateChallengeAndResponse(ByVal _
        sender As Object, _
        ByVal void As AjaxControlToolkit.NoBotEventArgs)
        Handles NoBot1.GenerateChallengeAndResponse

        Dim state As NoBotState
        NoBot1.IsValid(state)

        Label1.Text = state.ToString()
    End Sub
End Class
```

C#

```csharp
using System;
using AjaxControlToolkit;

public partial class NoBot : System.Web.UI.Page
{
    protected void NoBot1_GenerateChallengeAndResponse(object sender,
        AjaxControlToolkit.NoBotEventArgs e)
    {
        NoBotState state;
        NoBot1.IsValid(out state);

        Label1.Text = state.ToString();
    }
}
```

Running this page and trying to submit the form before the ten-second minimum time results in an invalid submission. In addition, trying to submit the form more than three times within 15 seconds results in an invalid submission.

PasswordStrength Control

The PasswordStrength control enables you to check the contents of a password in a TextBox control and validate its strength. It will also then give a message to the end user about whether the strength is reasonable. Listing 24-41 presents a simple example of the PasswordStrength control.

LISTING 24-41: Using the PasswordStrength control with a TextBox control

```
<%@ Page Language="C#" %>

<%@ Register Assembly="AjaxControlToolkit"
    Namespace="AjaxControlToolkit" TagPrefix="asp" %>

<!DOCTYPE html>
<html>
<head runat="server">
    <title>Password Strength Control</title>
</head>
<body>
    <form id="form1" runat="server">
    <div>
        <asp:ToolkitScriptManager ID="ToolkitScriptManager1" runat="server">
        </asp:ToolkitScriptManager>
        <asp:PasswordStrength ID="PasswordStrength1" runat="server"
         TargetControlID="TextBox1">
        </asp:PasswordStrength>
        <asp:TextBox ID="TextBox1" runat="server"></asp:TextBox>
    </div>
    </form>
</body>
</html>
```

This simple page produces a single textbox, and when end users start typing in the textbox, they are notified on the strength of the submission as they type. This is illustrated in Figure 24-42.

Some of the important properties to work with here include MinimumLowerCaseCharacters, MinimumNumericCharacters, MinimumSymbolCharacters, MinimumUpperCaseCharacters, and PreferredPasswordLength.

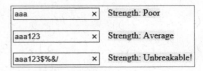

FIGURE 24-42

Rating Control

The Rating control gives your end users the ability to view and set ratings (such as star ratings). You have control over the number of ratings, the look of the filled ratings, the look of the empty ratings, and more. Listing 24-42 shows you a page that shows a five-star rating system that enables end users to set the rating themselves.

LISTING 24-42: A rating control that the end user can manipulate

```
<%@ Page Language="C#" %>

<%@ Register Assembly="AjaxControlToolkit"
    Namespace="AjaxControlToolkit" TagPrefix="asp" %>

<!DOCTYPE html>
<html>
<head runat="server">
    <title>Rating Control</title>
    <style type="text/css">
        .ratingStar {
            font-size: 0pt;
            width: 13px;
            height: 12px;
            margin: 0px;
            padding: 0px;
            cursor: pointer;
            display: block;
            background-repeat: no-repeat;
        }

        .filledRatingStar {
            background-image: url(Images/FilledStar.png);
        }

        .emptyRatingStar {
            background-image: url(Images/EmptyStar.png);
        }

        .savedRatingStar {
            background-image: url(Images/SavedStar.png);
        }
    </style>
</head>
<body>
    <form id="form1" runat="server">
    <div>
        <asp:ToolkitScriptManager ID="ToolkitScriptManager1" runat="server">
        </asp:ToolkitScriptManager>
        <asp:Rating ID="Rating1" runat="server"
         StarCssClass="ratingStar"
         WaitingStarCssClass="savedRatingStar"
         FilledStarCssClass="filledRatingStar"
         EmptyStarCssClass="emptyRatingStar">
        </asp:Rating>
    </div>
    </form>
</body>
</html>
```

Here, the Rating control uses a number of CSS classes to define its look-and-feel in various states. In addition to the CSS class properties (StarCssClass, WaitingStarCssClass, FilledStarCssClass, and EmptyCssClass), you can also specify rating alignments, the number of rating items (the default is 5), the width, the current rating, and more. The code presented in Listing 24-42 produces the results shown in Figure 24-43.

FIGURE 24-43

TabContainer Control

The TabContainer and TabPanel controls make presenting the familiar tabbed UI easy. The user is presented with a set of tabs across the top of a single pane of content displayed for the active tab. When the user selects a different tab, the content is changed. Tabs are a great way to control a page that has a lot of content to present. The TabContainer control can contain one or more TabPanel controls that provide you with a set of tabs that show content one tab at a time.

The TabContainer enables you to attach a server event called the `ActiveTabChanged` event, which is fired during a postback if the active tab has changed. You can also use the `OnClientActiveTabChanged` event to have your JavaScript event triggered in the browser when the user selects a different tab. The `ScrollBars` property lets you designate whether scrollbars should be `Horizontal`, `Vertical`, `Both`, `None`, or set to `Auto`, in which case the control makes the determination.

The TabPanel control has a `<HeaderTemplate>` for the tab and a `<ContentTemplate>` for the body. You can forego using the `<HeaderTemplate>` and specify the `HeaderText` property instead. It also has an event that is triggered when the tab is selected called `OnClientClick`. One particularly interesting feature of the Tabs feature is the ability to disable tabs programmatically in JavaScript in the browser by setting the `Enabled` property to `False`.

Listing 24-43 shows an example of a TabContainer control with three TabPanel controls.

LISTING 24-43: Showing three tabs in a TabContainer control

```
<%@ Page Language="C#" %>

<%@ Register Assembly="AjaxControlToolkit"
    Namespace="AjaxControlToolkit" TagPrefix="asp" %>

<!DOCTYPE html>
<html>
<head runat="server">
    <title>TabContainer Control</title>
</head>
<body>
    <form id="form1" runat="server">
    <div>
        <asp:ToolkitScriptManager ID="ToolkitScriptManager1" runat="server">
        </asp:ToolkitScriptManager>
        <asp:TabContainer ID="TabContainer1" runat="server"
         Height="300px">
            <asp:TabPanel runat="server">
                <HeaderTemplate>Tab 1</HeaderTemplate>
                <ContentTemplate>
                 Here is some tab one content.
                </ContentTemplate>
            </asp:TabPanel>
            <asp:TabPanel runat="server">
                <HeaderTemplate>Tab 2</HeaderTemplate>
                <ContentTemplate>
                 Here is some tab two content.
                </ContentTemplate>
            </asp:TabPanel>
            <asp:TabPanel runat="server">
                <HeaderTemplate>Tab 3</HeaderTemplate>
                <ContentTemplate>
                 Here is some tab three content.
                </ContentTemplate>
```

```
            </asp:TabPanel>
          </asp:TabContainer>
      </div>
      </form>
  </body>
  </html>
```

Figure 24-44 presents the result of this simple page.

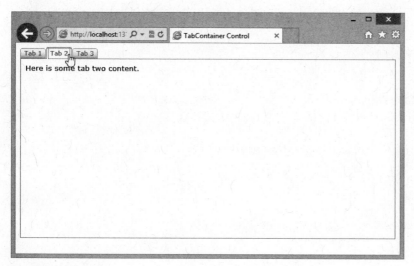

FIGURE 24-44

SUMMARY

The Ajax Control Toolkit makes adding rich animations and interactivity to a web application easy. In addition to being able to use the UpdatePanel control to enable asynchronous updates of page content, you can use the UpdatePanelAnimation to show the user that background processing is occurring. The toolkit helps blur the distinction between desktop applications and web applications. Modal dialog boxes and pop-up dialog boxes start to push the web application beyond what the user expects from working in the browser.

As you can see, a myriad of these controls are at your disposal. The best thing about this is that this is a community effort along with Microsoft and the list of available controls is only going to grow over time.

This chapter explored a lot of the Ajax Control Toolkit controls and how to use them in your ASP.NET applications. Remember to visit the Microsoft Ajax page and the Ajax Control Toolkit site for these controls often and take advantage of the newest offerings out there.

25

jQuery

WROX.COM CODE DOWNLOADS FOR THIS CHAPTER

Please note that all the code examples in this chapter are available as a part of this chapter's code download on the book's website at www.wrox.com on the Download Code tab.

The open source JavaScript library jQuery is the de facto standard for today's modern JavaScript development. According to a statistic from http://trends.builtwith.com/javascript (as of January 2013), more than 40 percent of the top 1,000,000 websites that use a well-known JavaScript library have picked jQuery. So, it comes as no surprise that Microsoft has also embraced jQuery.

Previously, Microsoft worked on its own JavaScript project: the Microsoft Ajax Library. It is still part of ASP.NET Web Forms (and is loaded automatically if the ScriptManager control is added to a page, as discussed in Chapter 23), but never caught on with non-Microsoft developers. Therefore, Microsoft decided to favor the market leader instead. Many of the web templates that ship with Visual Studio 2010 and later come with jQuery.

jQuery is a very powerful library and makes countless common JavaScript tasks really easy. Entire books have been written about jQuery, including Wrox's 336-page *Professional jQuery* by Cesar Otero and Rob Larsen (John Wiley & Sons, 2012). Obviously, this chapter can only scratch the surface and guide you through the most common tasks when working with the JavaScript library. For more in-depth information, refer to the aforementioned book, or the rich documentation on the jQuery site at http://api.jquery.com/.

> **NOTE** *The code in this chapter was written and tested with jQuery 1.9, but should also run in all jQuery versions after 1.7 (some of the listings will run with even older versions).*

INTRODUCTION TO JQUERY

The jQuery homepage is `http://jquery.com/` (see Figure 25-1) and was redesigned in January 2013. It prominently features the three main selling points of the library:

➤ **It is light weight:** The whole library clocks in at approximately 32KB, if HTTP's Gzip compression is used.

➤ **It is compliant with CSS3:** Most of the CSS3 standard is supported, even in those browsers that do not support CSS3 (for example, Internet Explorer down to version 6).

➤ **It is cross-browser:** jQuery is thoroughly tested with the most common browsers, including Internet Explorer, Firefox, Chrome, Opera, and Safari.

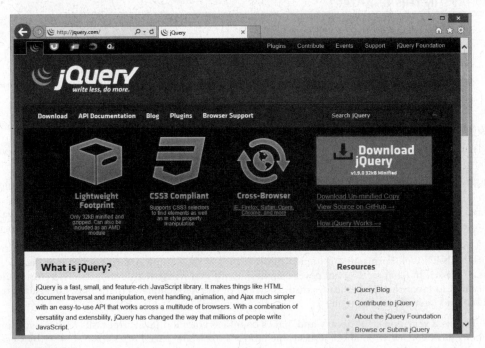

FIGURE 25-1

To use jQuery in an ASP.NET application, you need to add the library to the current website or project. If you want to download the library manually, just click the download link on the jQuery homepage; however, the code looks quite illegible (see Figure 25-2). The reason is that the code has been optimized for performance: Whitespace was removed, and identifiers have been renamed so that they are shorter.

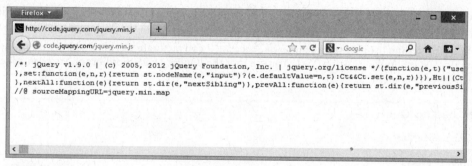

FIGURE 25-2

You can download a more readable, and commented, version of the code if you click the Download Un-minified Copy link. Figure 25-3 shows part of the JavaScript within that file.

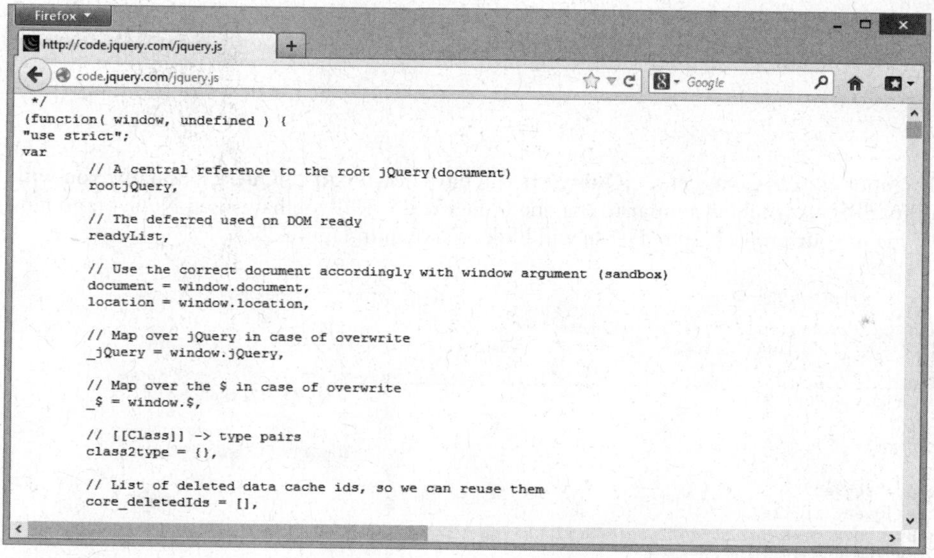

FIGURE 25-3

Pick whichever version of the file you want (hint: usually, the smaller version is good enough for development, and it's the one you should deploy anyway), and add it to your site or web project.

A more convenient way to add the most current version of jQuery to your project is to use the NuGet package manager. In the Package Manager Console, execute the command from Listing 25-1.

LISTING 25-1: Installing jQuery via NuGet

```
Install-Package jQuery
```

After a short while, your website contains a new Script folder with at least the following files in it (assuming that jQuery 1.9.0 is the most current version—the latest version at the time you are trying this may vary):

➤ `jquery-1.9.0.js`: The commented, readable version of jQuery

➤ `jquery-1.9.0.min.js`: The compressed version of jQuery

➤ `jquery-1.9.0-vsdoc.js`: Hints for Visual Studio's IntelliSense

Depending on how you are installing jQuery and which version is current, the path and the name of the file might be a bit different than what is used in this chapter. Make sure you adapt the filenames to your system.

The third file in the preceding list is of specific interest, because it can facilitate working with jQuery a bit. To demonstrate this, have a look at Listing 25-2. You see that the jQuery JavaScript library has been added to a page with a `<script>` tag.

LISTING 25-2: Loading jQuery

```
<%@ Page Language="C#" %>

<!DOCTYPE html>
<html>
<head runat="server">
    <title>jQuery</title>
    <script type="text/javascript" src="Scripts/jquery.js"></script>
    <script type="text/javascript">

    </script>
</head>
<body>
    <div>
    </div>
</body>
</html>
```

In the currently empty `<script>` tag, enter **jQuery(**. If you have downloaded jQuery manually, you will probably get an IntelliSense window similar to the one in Figure 25-4. If you have used NuGet (and have the jQuery VSDOC file in your project), IntelliSense will look as shown in Figure 25-5.

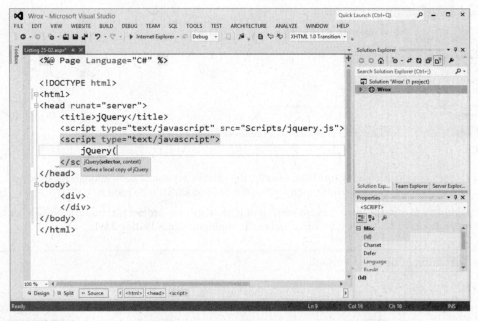

FIGURE 25-4

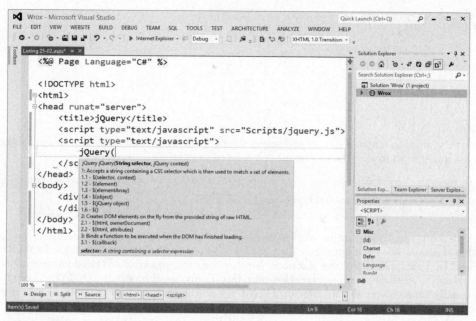

FIGURE 25-5

The reason for the different IntelliSense: The VSDOC file contains the additional type hints and comments shown in Figure 25-5. But even if you downloaded jQuery manually, there is no reason to despair: You can also download the VSDOC file separately. Microsoft's content delivery network (CDN) usually carries the VSDOC version shortly after a new jQuery version has been released. `http://www.asp.net/ajaxlibrary/cdn .ashx#jQuery_Releases_on_the_CDN_0` shows you an up-to-date list.

Before diving deeper into using jQuery, this section presents a common pattern that is used in most jQuery-powered sites. Listing 25-3 shows the usual setup: first, you load jQuery; you might just want to change the version number if you are using a different one than used here. In the next `<script>` block, you start using jQuery code. The first line looks a bit strange:

```
$(function() {
```

It starts with the dollar sign—are you suddenly using PHP? To the contrary—in JavaScript it's perfectly fine to use `$` as an identifier. Because no one would actually call one of their functions `$()`, many JavaScript libraries use `$()` instead so that there is no name clash.

LISTING 25-3: A Common pattern for using jQuery

```
<%@ Page Language="C#" %>

<!DOCTYPE html>
<html>
<head runat="server">
    <title>jQuery</title>
    <script type="text/javascript" src="Scripts/jquery.js"></script>
    <script type="text/javascript">
        $(function () {
            // DOM is ready
        });
```

continues

LISTING 25-3 *(continued)*

```
        </script>
    </head>
    <body>
        <div>
        </div>
    </body>
</html>
```

Actually, `$()` is the central function of jQuery and serves several purposes. If you think that this makes code hard to read, you might want to use `jQuery` instead of `$`—its equivalent.

> **NOTE** *Most code written with jQuery uses the short form.*

If you have a look at the IntelliSense output of `$()`/`jQuery()` in Figure 25-5, you will see several of the overloads of that function. The third option is called "Binds a function to be executed when the DOM has finished loading." In Ajax applications, this is crucial. Most of the time, you are using the document object model (DOM) to access an element on the page. However, this is only possible once the DOM has been fully loaded—this usually happens very shortly after the HTML document has been fully transmitted from the server to the browser.

So if you are providing a function as an argument to `$()` —isn't JavaScript a fascinating language!—this very function is executed once the DOM is ready. Most of the time, this is exactly what you want. Therefore, you use this pattern throughout this chapter.

> **NOTE** *Some time ago, a more common—but more verbose—way of achieving the same effect (code being executed once the DOM is ready) looked like this:*
>
> ```
> $(document).ready(function() {
>     //...
> });
> ```
>
> *Today this is a sign of old code. It still works, though.*

SELECTING ELEMENTS

The common order of actions when working with any JavaScript library is as follows: you wait for an event (for example, the DOM has finished loading, the user clicks a button, and so on), then you select an element on the page, and, finally, you read from or write to that HTML element. Because you already know how one of those events works (the DOM has finished loading), you can move on to selecting elements. Luckily, the jQuery team did not invent a completely new syntax for this task; instead, it was reusing an established standard that serves the same purpose: cascading style sheets (CSS) selectors.

This World Wide Web Consortium (W3C) standard, part of CSS, describes how specific elements on a page are selected. In the context of CSS, the purpose of this selection process is to style or position elements. In the context of jQuery, you can do anything you want with those objects.

> **NOTE** *The current version of the specification (*`http://www.w3.org/TR/`*
> *`css3-selectors/`*) contains a complete list of the standard, and jQuery supports most
> of it. Actually, jQuery is very clever: In older browsers, the JavaScript library has its
> own selector engine called Sizzle, which is also available as a separate project
> (*`http://sizzlejs.com/`*). This selector engine parses a CSS selector and returns
> a set of elements.*

More modern browsers have built-in JavaScript APIs to do CSS selection. If such a client is encountered, jQuery delegates the complex parsing and selection task to the browser.

Like jQuery, CSS is a very complex topic. Wrox's *Beginning CSS* by Richard York (John Wiley & Sons, 2004) had 648 pages! However, in most scenarios one of the common CSS selectors just does the job. Three general kinds of CSS element selectors exist:

➤ **Tag selectors:** For instance, the selector p matches all <p> elements on the page; p a matches all <a> elements within a <p> elements. Note that the resulting HTML matters, not the ASP.NET Web Controls used. A selector Calendar, for instance, would not work.

➤ **Class selectors:** These are prefixed by a dot. For instance, the selector .myClass would select all elements that have the HTML attribute class="myClass". You can also mix and match: a.myClass would match all <a> tags with class myClass, but not <p> tags. When using ASP.NET, remember that a web control's CssClass attribute turns into the class attribute in the resulting HTML.

➤ **ID selectors:** If an HTML element has an ID, such as id="myID", the selector #myID would match this element.

> **WARNING** *When working with ASP.NET Web Forms, this approach is usually danger-
> ous, because ASP.NET by default rewrites some IDs. Using* `ClientIDMode="Static"`
> *might help, or dynamically determining a client ID with a control's* `ClientID` *property.
> In most cases, however, a combination of tag and class selectors is the best way to go.*

If you call the $() function with a CSS selector as an argument, you will get back a list of those elements on the page that match this selector. To be exact, you will receive a jQuery object, representing the selected elements. The difference is that a jQuery object can have methods, so you could process those selected elements further. You use this feature quite a bit later in this chapter.

For now, you just use one of the methods of the jQuery object: size() returns the number of elements. Listing 25-4 shows a simple page that contains a few elements. The JavaScript code then selects a few elements and uses JavaScript's alert() to output the result, which is also shown in Figure 25-6.

LISTING 25-4: Selecting elements with jQuery

```
<%@ Page Language="C#" %>

<!DOCTYPE html>
<html>
<head runat="server">
    <title>jQuery</title>
    <script type="text/javascript" src="Scripts/jquery.js"></script>
    <script type="text/javascript">
        $(function () {
            var divs = $("div").size();
```

continues

LISTING 25-4 *(continued)*

```
            var spans = $("span").size();
            alert(divs + " <div> elements\n" +
                    spans + " <span> elements");
        });
    </script>
</head>
<body>
    <form runat="server">
        <div>
            <span>First label</span>
        </div>
        <asp:Panel ID="Panel1" runat="server">
            <asp:Label ID="Label1" runat="server"
                Text="Second label" />
        </asp:Panel>
    </form>
</body>
</html>
```

FIGURE 25-6

The result in Figure 25-6 might be a bit surprising. However, consider that `<asp:Panel>` is rendered as a `<div>` element by default, and `<asp:Label>` turns into a `<span>` element. Also, a look at the resulting HTML markup reveals that the hidden ViewState field is enclosed in yet another `<div>` element, so the result is correct. Remember: It's the HTML that matters, not the ASP.NET markup.

MODIFYING ELEMENTS

Just counting how many elements you have selected is rare; usually you know exactly how many elements you are getting. What matters is what you do with them afterwards. You have full Create, Read, Update, Delete (CRUD) functionality with jQuery, but most of the time you either read from or write/into an element, or you add new elements to your page.

Modifying Content

jQuery offers four methods to read information from a selected element, depending on the type of element:

➤   `attr("name of attribute")`: Value of an HTML attribute of the selected element

➤   `html()`: Inner HTML content of the selected element

➤   `text()`: Inner content of the selected element, text only (HTML stripped)

➤   `val()`: Value of most form elements, corresponding to the element's value HTML attribute

Changing those values is possible, too. The following four methods are provided:

➤   `attr("name of attribute", "value of attribute")`

➤   `html("new HTML content")`

➤   `text("new text content")`

➤   `val("new value")`

As you can see, the getter and setter methods are the same—just the number of arguments helps jQuery determine what to do. From an API point of view, this may look weird at first, but it also helps to keep the list of methods short and concise.

Listing 25-5 shows the two purposes of the `html()` method in action: Once the DOM is ready, the current HTML content of the selected element is retrieved; then, the current time is appended. See Figure 25-7 for the result.

LISTING 25-5: Reading and writing HTML content with jQuery

```
<%@ Page Language="C#" %>

<!DOCTYPE html>
<html>
<head runat="server">
    <title>jQuery</title>
    <script type="text/javascript" src="Scripts/jquery.js"></script>
    <script type="text/javascript">
        $(function () {
            var oldvalue = $("div").html();
            $("div").html(oldvalue + " " + new Date().toLocaleTimeString());
        });
    </script>
</head>
<body>
    <div>
        <i>jQuery</i>
    </div>
</body>
</html>
```

If you are using `html()` (or `text()`, `val()`, or `attr()`), as a setter, the return value of such a method call is still a jQuery object representing the selected elements. Therefore, you can use chaining—just chain method call after method call. Cynics may claim that most jQuery code is actually just one line of JavaScript—a very long line.

To demonstrate chaining, take a look at another jQuery method that you can use to modify

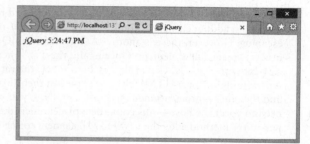

FIGURE 25-7

elements: `css()`. As the name suggests, you can use it to get or set CSS properties. This method has three uses:

➤ `css("property")`: Reads a CSS property

➤ `css("property", "value")`: Writes a CSS property

➤ `css({"property1": "value1", "property2":"value2", . . .])`: Writes several CSS properties

Listing 25-6 builds upon Listing 25-5 and adds a background and foreground color to the text that has been changed by jQuery before. The calls to `css()` are chained after the call to `html()`. Figure 25-8 depicts the result in the browser.

LISTING 25-6: Changing CSS styles with jQuery

```
<%@ Page Language="C#" %>

<!DOCTYPE html>
<html>
<head runat="server">
    <title>jQuery</title>
    <script type="text/javascript" src="Scripts/jquery.js"></script>
    <script type="text/javascript">
        $(function () {
            var oldvalue = $("div").html();
            $("div").html(oldvalue + " " + new Date().toLocaleTimeString())
                    .css("color", "orange")
                    .css("background-color", "black");
        });
    </script>
</head>
<body>
    <div>
        <i>jQuery</i>
    </div>
</body>
</html>
```

Adding and Removing Elements

The techniques demonstrated in the previous section are very well suited for displaying text and HTML on a page. However, when you want to add several HTML elements to the page, this

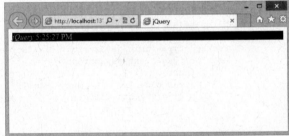

FIGURE 25-8

approach becomes cumbersome: You need to assemble HTML markup, be careful about special characters, and, in the end, everything is added with the `html()` method.

However, jQuery has a very powerful API to add (and remove) new elements to an HTML page, as well. Start with adding elements. You could use the `html()` method, but then would need to take care about escaping. However, there is another API available in jQuery. Several steps are required to use it. First you need to create a new element. Once again, the `$()` function can help here. If the first argument is an HTML element with angle brackets (such as `$("<a>")`), the return value of the function call is a jQuery object representing the new HTML element. You can then further modify this element using `html()`, `css()`, and the other aforementioned methods. Finally, if you want to add the new element to the page, you first need to select the host—this could be a placeholder like a `<div>` element or the `<body>` element. Then, the `append()` method adds the new HTML element to the selected one.

Listing 25-7 creates a new `<a>` element and then sets its `href` attribute to make it a proper link. Finally, the new link is then appended to the page's `<body>` element.

LISTING 25-7: Adding an element with append()

```
<%@ Page Language="C#" %>

<!DOCTYPE html>
<html>
<head runat="server">
    <title>jQuery</title>
    <script type="text/javascript" src="Scripts/jquery.js"></script>
    <script type="text/javascript">
        $(function () {
            $("body").append(
                $("<a>").attr("href", "http://jquery.com/").html("jQuery")
            );
        });
    </script>
</head>
<body>
</body>
</html>
```

In Listing 25-8, a similar approach is used. This time, you use the `appendTo()` method of the newly created element. As an argument you once again have to pick a CSS selector, this time one for the existing element(s) you would like to append the new HTML element *to*.

LISTING 25-8: Adding an element with appendTo()

```
<%@ Page Language="C#" %>

<!DOCTYPE html>
<html>
<head runat="server">
    <title>jQuery</title>
    <script type="text/javascript" src="Scripts/jquery.js"></script>
    <script type="text/javascript">
        $(function () {
            $("<a>").attr("href", "http://jquery.com/")
                    .html("jQuery")
                    .appendTo("body");
        });
    </script>
</head>
<body>
</body>
</html>
```

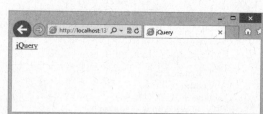

FIGURE 25-9

Both Listings 25-7 and 25-8 lead to the result shown in Figure 25-9.

If you want to get rid of elements, it is quite easy to delete them. A rather hacky way is to select a surrounding element and then execute `html("")`. A cleaner approach is to select the element you want to delete, and then call the `remove()` method, as Listing 25-9 shows.

LISTING 25-9: Removing an element with remove()

```
$(function() {
    $("p.myClass").remove();
});
```

EVENT HANDLING

So far, all code has been executed once the DOM is fully loaded. This is an important step, because availability of the DOM is paramount for most JavaScript applications. However, there are more events, for instance the user clicking a button, or hitting a key.

For most of those events, jQuery provides a specific method. The following list shows some of the most common ones:

➤ `blur()`: An element loses the focus.

➤ `change()`: The content of a form element changes.

➤ `click()`: An element is clicked.

➤ `dblclick()`: An element receives a double-click.

➤ `focus()`: An element receives the focus.

➤ `submit()`: A form is submitted.

These methods are jQuery object methods: You first use `$()` to select one or more elements, and can then subscribe to events fired for those elements. As an argument for aforementioned methods, you provide a JavaScript function. This function is then executed should the element actually receive the given event.

Listing 25-10 adds text to the page when the user clicks a button. Note that the event handling is (and can only be) set up once the DOM has finished loading. Figure 25-10 shows the result.

LISTING 25-10: Event handling with a specific method

```
<%@ Page Language="C#" %>

<!DOCTYPE html>
<html>
<head runat="server">
    <title>jQuery</title>
    <script type="text/javascript" src="Scripts/jquery.js"></script>
    <script type="text/javascript">
        $(function () {
            $("#button1").click(
                function () {
                    $("#label1").html("clicked at: " +
                                    new Date().toLocaleTimeString());
                }
            );
        });
    </script>
</head>
<body>
    <form runat="server">
        <span id="label1"></span>
        <input type="button" id="button1" value="Click!" />
    </form>
</body>
</html>
```

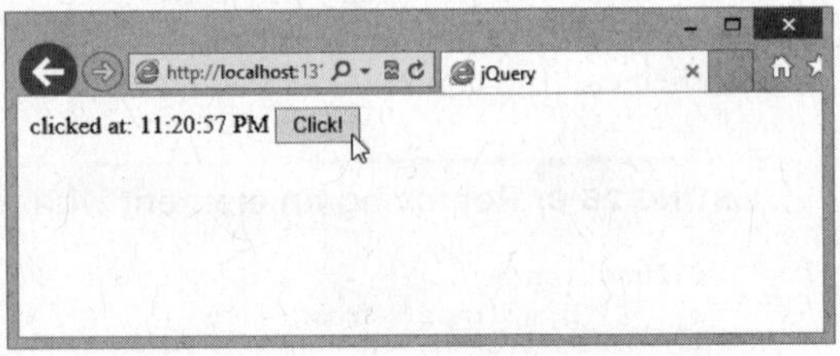

Not all DOM events are represented by those specific jQuery methods; for instance, gestures available on mobile devices. For this purpose, jQuery offers a generic event handler setup method called `on()`. You provide the name of the event and the event handler function, and you are set. See Listing 25-11 for a port of Listing 25-10 to use the `on()` method.

FIGURE 25-10

LISTING 25-11: Event handling with the on() method

```
<%@ Page Language="C#" %>

<!DOCTYPE html>
<html>
<head runat="server">
    <title>jQuery</title>
    <script type="text/javascript" src="Scripts/jquery.js"></script>
    <script type="text/javascript">
        $(function () {
            $("#button1").on(
                "click",
                function () {
                    $("#label1").html("clicked at: " +
                                new Date().toLocaleTimeString());
                }
            );
        });
    </script>
</head>
<body>
    <form runat="server">
        <span id="label1"></span>
        <input type="button" id="button1" value="Click!" />
    </form>
</body>
</html>
```

USING BIND(), LIVE(), DELEGATE()

The `on()` method (and also its counterpart to remove event handlers, `off()`) was intro-duced in jQuery 1.7. It includes additional features, like adding event handlers to HTML elements added later to the page. Previous versions of the JavaScript library had other methods to set up event handlers, usually `bind()`, and for binding event handlers later, `delegate()` and `live()`. Using `on()` is preferred over using these methods, although you will still find them in older code. The jQuery documentation has great information on how to port older code to the new `on()` syntax; see http://api.jquery.com/bind/, http://api.jquery.com/delegate/, and http://api.jquery.com/live/.

In some cases, you want your event handler to be fired only once; for instance, when submitting an order. (I've learned the hard way that not all websites take this into account, and impatiently clicking twice is a bad thing.) For this scenario, the `one()` method will be your friend: The event handler will be executed once and then be removed.

Have a look at Listing 25-12, which uses `one()`. When you click the button the first time, the current time is shown. All subsequent clicks show no result.

LISTING 25-12: Event handling with the one() method

```
$(function () {
    $("#button1").one(
        "click",
        function () {
            $("#label1").html("clicked at: " + new Date().toLocaleTimeString());
        }
    );
});
```

AJAX

The last missing "big" ingredient for your jQuery recipes is, of course, Ajax in its true sense: making HTTP requests to the server. To facilitate testing this feature, you first create an ASHX handler (see Listing 25-13) that accepts GET and POST requests and returns some data depending on the input. Actually, there are three behaviors of this handler:

1. The browser sends a simple GET request. Then the handler returns the current time as a string.

2. The browser sends a GET request with the URL info `json=true`. Then the handler returns the current time as a string in JSON format (enclosed in double quotes).

3. The browser sends a POST request. Then the handler returns a text stating exactly that this is a POST request.

LISTING 25-13: The generic handler for your Ajax calls

VB

```
<%@ WebHandler Language="VB" Class="Listing_25_13" %>

Imports System
Imports System.Web
Imports System.Web.Script.Serialization

Public Class Listing_25_13 : Implements IHttpHandler

    Public Sub ProcessRequest(ByVal context As HttpContext) _
        Implements IHttpHandler.ProcessRequest
        Select context.Request.RequestType
            Case "GET"
                If context.Request("json") Is Nothing OrElse _
                    context.Request("json") <> "true" Then
                    context.Response.ContentType = "text/plain"
                    context.Response.Write(DateTime.Now.ToLongTimeString())
                Else
                    Dim json = New JavaScriptSerializer().Serialize(
                        DateTime.Now.ToLongTimeString())
                    context.Response.ContentType = "application/json"
                    context.Response.Write(json)
                End If
            Case "POST"
                context.Response.ContentType = "text/plain"
                context.Response.Write("POST at " + _
                                    DateTime.Now.ToLongTimeString())
        End Select
    End Sub

    Public ReadOnly Property IsReusable() As Boolean Implements IHttpHandler.IsReusable
```

```
        Get
            Return False
        End Get
    End Property

End Class
```

C#

```csharp
<%@ WebHandler Language="C#" Class="Listing_25_13" %>

using System;
using System.Web;
using System.Web.Script.Serialization;

public class Listing_25_13 : IHttpHandler {

    public void ProcessRequest(HttpContext context)
    {
        switch (context.Request.RequestType)
        {
            case "GET":
                if (context.Request["json"] == null ||
                    context.Request["json"] != "true")
                {
                    context.Response.ContentType = "text/plain";
                    context.Response.Write(DateTime.Now.ToLongTimeString());
                }
                else
                {
                    var json = new JavaScriptSerializer().Serialize(
                        DateTime.Now.ToLongTimeString());
                    context.Response.ContentType = "application/json";
                    context.Response.Write(json);
                }
                break;
            case "POST":
                context.Response.ContentType = "text/plain";
                context.Response.Write("POST at " +
                                        DateTime.Now.ToLongTimeString());
                break;
        }
    }

    public bool IsReusable
    {
        get
        {
            return false;
        }
    }

}
```

jQuery offers a number of ways to do the actual Ajax requests. Let's first start with the simple GET request. The method `$.get()` (note the dot between `$` and `get`!) prompts the browser to send an HTTP GET request to a URL (first argument). Once the server sends data back, the callback function (second argument) is executed, with the data from the server automatically passed as an argument. Listing 25-14 shows this.

LISTING 25-14: Sending a simple GET request

```
<%@ Page Language="C#" %>

<!DOCTYPE html>
<html>
<head runat="server">
    <title>jQuery</title>
    <script type="text/javascript" src="Scripts/jquery.js"></script>
    <script type="text/javascript">
        $(function () {
            $.get("Listing%2025-13.ashx", function (result) {
                $("div").text(result);
            });
        });
    </script>
</head>
<body>
    <div></div>
</body>
</html>
```

If you are using a browser add-in like the Internet Explorer F12 Developer Tools or Firebug for Firefox, you can watch the HTTP request being made and the data being sent back to the browser before it is displayed (see Figure 25-11).

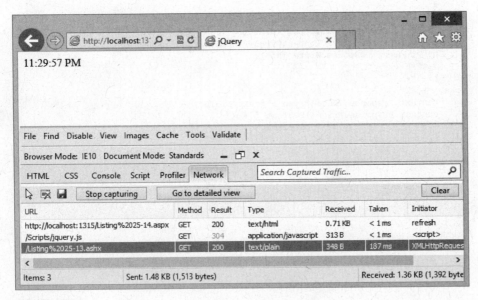

FIGURE 25-11

> **WARNING** *The Same Origin Policy is a JavaScript security feature which dictates that HTTP requests are only possible if the request target (the URL that is requested) has the same origin (domain, port, protocol) as the HTML page that hosts the JavaScript code doing the Ajax request. Modern browsers provide mechanisms to circumvent this restriction; however, for the sake of backward compatibility you should try to use the same origin for your Ajax call targets and for your HTML pages. To make the code examples in this section work, it is best to use a website that hosts both the HTML files and the services (ASHX, ASMX).*

If you want to send data along with your GET request, you can provide it as the second argument; the callback function then moves back to the third place. Note that it is best to provide an object; jQuery takes care of URL-encoding this properly. Listing 25-15 sends a GET request with some additional data.

LISTING 25-15: Sending a GET request with data

```
<%@ Page Language="C#" %>

<!DOCTYPE html>
<html>
<head runat="server">
    <title>jQuery</title>
    <script type="text/javascript" src="Scripts/jquery.js"></script>
    <script type="text/javascript">
        $(function () {
            $.get("Listing%2025-13.ashx",
                { a: 1, b: 2 },
                function (result) {
                    $("div").text(result);
                });
        });
    </script>
</head>
<body>
    <div></div>
</body>
</html>
```

So far, the data being returned by the GET request was a simple string. For more complex data, the de facto standard is to use JavaScript Object Notation (JSON, http://json.org/). Of course, it would be possible to load the JSON from the server as a string and then write user-land code to convert it to a JavaScript object, for instance with JavaScript's built-in `JSON.parse()` method. However, it is even more convenient to use jQuery's `$.getJSON()` method—it both does the HTTP request and parses the JSON result, as Listing 25-16 shows.

> **NOTE** *The `$.get()` method also supports parsing JSON. By default, jQuery tries to be clever: If it looks like JSON was returned, the data is parsed as JSON. If you want to explicitly state which data is expected to come back, you can provide the data type (for example, `"json"`) as the last argument to the method call.*

LISTING 25-16: Sending a GET request and parsing the returned JSON data

```
<%@ Page Language="C#" %>

<!DOCTYPE html>
<html>
<head runat="server">
    <title>jQuery</title>
    <script type="text/javascript" src="Scripts/jquery.js"></script>
    <script type="text/javascript">
        $(function () {
            $.getJSON("Listing%2025-13.ashx",
                { json: "true" },
                function (result) {
                    $("div").text(result);
                });
        });
    </script>
</head>
<body>
    <div></div>
</body>
</html>
```

Sending a POST request seems to be very similar, but underneath the surface you will find out that the browser needs to send an additional HTTP header so that the server can parse the input data. Of course, jQuery can take care of all of this, if you are using the $.post() method. It works exactly as $.get(), except that POST is used instead of GET. Listing 25-17 sends a POST request to the server and displays the result; Figure 25-12 proves that POST was indeed used.

LISTING 25-17: Sending a POST request

```
<%@ Page Language="C#" %>

<!DOCTYPE html>
<html>
<head runat="server">
    <title>jQuery</title>
    <script type="text/javascript" src="Scripts/jquery.js"></script>
    <script type="text/javascript">
        $(function () {
            $.post("Listing%2025-13.ashx",
                { a: 1, b: 2 },
                function (result) {
                    $("div").text(result);
                });
        });
    </script>
</head>
<body>
    <div></div>
</body>
</html>
```

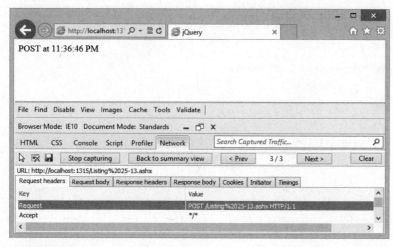

FIGURE 25-12

`$.get()`,`$.getJSON()`, and `$.post()` are actually short-hand methods that internally just delegate the work to the generic Ajax method of jQuery: `$.ajax()`. This method expects two arguments: the URL to send the HTTP request to, and a hashtable containing additional options, like the HTTP verb to use, the callback function, and much more. As of jQuery 1.9.0, 33 different options are possible, so a complete list would be out of the scope of this chapter. However, Table 25-1 shows the most important ones.

TABLE 25-1

OPTION	DESCRIPTION
`contentType`	The content type HTTP header to be sent to the server.
`Data`	Data to be sent to the server.
`dataType`	Format of data expected back from the server (for example, `"json"` or `"xml"`).
`error`	Handler function in case the HTTP request fails.
`success`	Handler function in case the HTTP request succeeds.
`timeout`	Timeout value in milliseconds. After this amount of time has passed after sending the HTTP request without a result coming back from the server, the error handler function is executed.
`type`	Request type like GET or POST.
`url`	The URL to send the request to.

With this, it is possible to execute more complex HTTP requests. For instance, if an ASMX Web Service is used, the HTTP request to call it from Ajax (see also Chapter 23) needs to be very specific: An additional header must be set, and the return data has a specific format.

Listing 25-18 implements a simple ASMX service. Note how the `System.Web.Script.Services` `.ScriptService` attribute is used to make it callable via JavaScript. The ASMX service creates a list of "Link" objects. Each of those objects contains a link URL and a link text. Finally, the list is returned. The ASMX service automatically converts this data to JSON and returns it to the browser.

Listing 25-19 then calls this service using `$.ajax()` and parses the JSON object (which has actually been encapsulated in another JSON object, where the value of the `"d"` property contains the actual data returned). Then you create one list item (`<li>` HTML element) per link and append it to the page. Figure 25-13 shows the result in the browser.

LISTING 25-18: An ASMX service to be consumed via Ajax

VB

```
<%@ WebService Language="VB" Class="Listing_25_18" %>

Imports System.Web
Imports System.Web.Services
Imports System.Web.Services.Protocols

<System.Web.Script.Services.ScriptService()> _
<WebService(Namespace:="http://tempuri.org/")> _
<WebServiceBinding(ConformsTo:=WsiProfiles.BasicProfile1_1)> _
Public Class Listing_25_18
    Inherits System.Web.Services.WebService

    <WebMethod()> _
    Public Function getLinks() As List(Of Link)
        Dim links = New List(Of Link)()
        links.Add(New Link With {.Url = "http://jquery.com/", .Text = "jQuery"})
        links.Add(New Link With {.Url = "http://jqueryui.com/", .Text = "jQuery UI"})
        links.Add(New Link With {.Url = "http://juiceui.com/", .Text = "Juice UI"})
        Return links
    End Function

End Class

Public Class Link
    Private _url As String
    Public Property Url() As String
        Get
            Return _url
        End Get
        Set(ByVal value As String)
            _url = value
        End Set
    End Property

    Private _text As String
    Public Property Text() As String
        Get
            Return _text
        End Get
        Set(ByVal value As String)
            _text = value
        End Set
    End Property
End Class
```

C#

```
<%@ WebService Language="C#" Class="Listing_25_18" %>

using System;
using System.Web;
using System.Web.Services;
using System.Web.Services.Protocols;
using System.Collections.Generic;

[WebService(Namespace = "http://tempuri.org/")]
[WebServiceBinding(ConformsTo = WsiProfiles.BasicProfile1_1)]
```

```csharp
[System.Web.Script.Services.ScriptService]
public class Listing_25_18  : System.Web.Services.WebService {

    [WebMethod]
    public List<Link> getLinks() {
        var links = new List<Link>() {
            new Link() { Url="http://jquery.com/", Text="jQuery"},
            new Link() { Url="http://jqueryui.com/", Text="jQuery UI"},
            new Link() { Url="http://juiceui.com/", Text="Juice UI"}
        };
        return links;
    }

}

public class Link
{
    public string Url { get; set; }
    public string Text { get; set; }
}
```

LISTING 25-19: Sending a POST request

```asp
<%@ Page Language="C#" %>

<!DOCTYPE html>
<html>
<head runat="server">
    <title>jQuery</title>
    <script type="text/javascript" src="Scripts/jquery.js"></script>
    <script type="text/javascript">
        $(function () {
            $.ajax({
                url: "Listing%2025-18.asmx/getLinks",
                contentType: "application/json",
                dataType: "json",
                type: "POST",
                success: function (result) {
                    var links = result.d;
                    $.each(links, function (key, value) {
                        $("<li>").append(
                            $("<a>").attr("href", value.Url).text(value.Text)
                        ).appendTo("ul");
                    });
                }
            });
        });
    </script>
</head>
<body>
    <ul></ul>
</body>
</html>
```

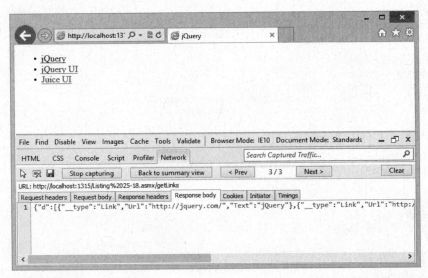

FIGURE 25-13

JQUERY UI

So far you have "just" worked with JavaScript features of jQuery, but you still have to actually code behaviors and the user interface. However, there is a sister project of jQuery called jQuery UI, with its homepage at `http://jqueryui.com/`. It describes itself as "a curated set of user interface interactions, effects, widgets, and themes." And indeed: The feature set of jQuery UI is not huge, but the quality is very high. Think of jQuery UI to jQuery as ASP.NET Web Controls to ASP.NET: The latter is the framework, and the former builds upon that framework to provide UI controls. This section briefly demonstrates one of the widgets to show the general approach for using the library.

When you look at the top-right corner of the jQuery UI homepage (see Figure 25-14), you see that you can download the full jQuery UI package (we usually recommend the "stable" version), or you can click Custom Download and then pick only those components you need (Figure 25-15). For the sake of simplicity, this example uses the full package. You can also use the package manager to install jQuery UI. Listing 25-20 installs the complete package.

LISTING 25-20: Installing jQuery UI using NuGet

```
Install-Package jQuery.UI.Combined
```

> **WARNING** *The jQuery UI NuGet package also installs jQuery. Shortly after a new jQuery release, the jQuery UI package might reference an outdated jQuery version, so installation might fail. In that case, we recommend a manual installation.*

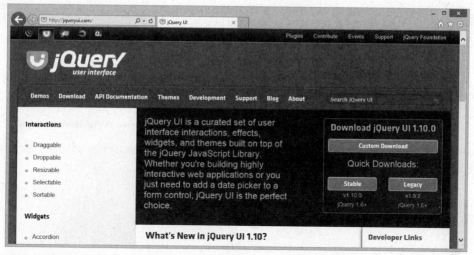

FIGURE 25-14

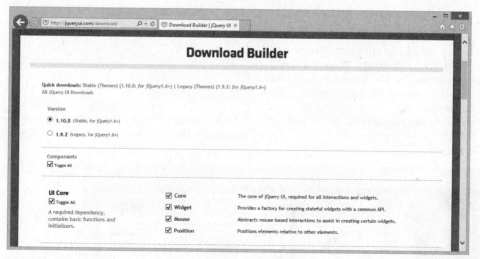

FIGURE 25-15

Depending on how you install jQuery, some of the paths used later in this section may be different, so make sure you adapt the code to your local system. We assume that the jQuery and jQuery UI JavaScript files are residing in the Scripts folder, and the css folder of the jQuery UI distribution was placed in the website's Content folder.

Using jQuery UI is really simple, because the widgets are completely integrated into the jQuery API. Essentially, you are first loading the jQuery library, then the jQuery UI library, and also the jQuery CSS file that is shipped with the package.

This is demonstrated in Listing 25-21 by using the datepicker control of jQuery UI. To do so, you place a simple textbox on the page. Then, you use `$()` to select this textbox. The returned `jQuery` object supports the `datepicker()` method, which you execute. And as Figure 25-16 shows, once you click into the textbox, the datepicker appears.

LISTING 25-21: Using the jQuery UI datepicker

```
<%@ Page Language="C#" %>

<!DOCTYPE html>

<html xmlns="http://www.w3.org/1999/xhtml">
<head runat="server">
    <title></title>
    <link href="Content/css/smoothness/jquery-ui-1.10.0.custom.css" rel="stylesheet" />
    <script type="text/javascript" src="Scripts/jquery.js"></script>
    <script type="text/javascript" src="Scripts/jquery-ui-1.10.0.custom.js"></script>
    <script type="text/javascript">
        $(function () {
            $(".dp").datepicker();
        });
    </script>
</head>
<body>
    <form id="form1" runat="server">
    <div>
        <input type="text" class="dp" />
    </div>
    </form>
</body>
</html>
```

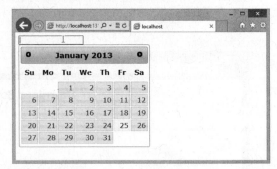

As mentioned before, jQuery UI tries to achieve a similar thing as ASP.NET Web Controls. There is a way to combine both technologies. The Juice UI project has created web controls for each jQuery UI element. The project homepage is http://juiceui.com/ (Figure 25-17), and the installation is done via NuGet (see Listing 25-22).

FIGURE 25-16

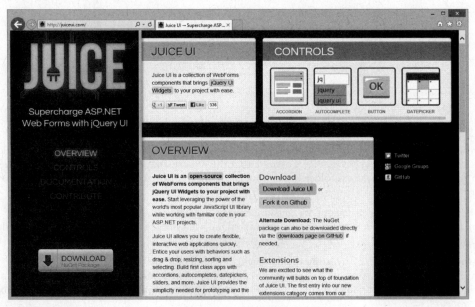

FIGURE 25-17

LISTING 25-22: Installing Juice UI

```
Install-Package JuiceUI
```

Afterwards it's quite easy to port Listing 25-21 to Juice UI: The `<Juice:Datepicker>` control represents the datepicker widget. Similar to the API of the Ajax Control Toolkit (see Chapter 24), the `TargetControlID` property is used to reference the textbox that receives the datepicker. Listing 25-23 shows the (short) code.

LISTING 25-23: Using the jQuery UI datepicker, with Juice UI

```
<asp:TextBox ID="TextBox1" runat="server" />

<Juice:Datepicker TargetControlID="TextBox1" runat="server" />
```

SUMMARY

This concludes your whirlwind tour through jQuery. This chapter discussed adding jQuery to a website or web application, and you then worked your way through the common approach for most Ajax applications: selecting elements, modifying them, listening to events, and doing Ajax requests. jQuery UI is jQuery's widget library, which can be used as web controls thanks to the third-party Juice UI project.

There is a good reason why jQuery currently is the number one JavaScript library: It is compact, concise, easy to learn, yet powerful. Thanks to the good integration into Visual Studio (including the VSDOC files provided), no one really misses the Microsoft Ajax Library. Maybe, one day, its remains—currently still in heavy use by the controls introduced in Chapter 23—will be replaced, too.

26

Real-Time Communication

WHAT'S IN THIS CHAPTER?

➤ Understanding the real-time web technologies

➤ Implementing HTML5 WebSockets

➤ Understanding SignalR

WROX.COM CODE DOWNLOADS FOR THIS CHAPTER

Please note that all the code examples in this chapter are available as a part of this chapter's code download on the book's website at www.wrox.com on the Download Code tab.

The World Wide Web has matured quite a lot in the last decade. It has transformed from the days where most web applications consisted of static pages to more dynamic content. In the last few years WWW is moving to Web 2.0, which allows users to interact and collaborate with each other. All these collaborations and interactions happen in real time on the social networking sites such as Facebook, Twitter and many more. For example when someone pokes you on Facebook or tweets something, you are notified immediately about this action so you can interact in real time with the other person.

Real-time web is a set of technologies and practices that enable users to receive information as soon as it is published by its authors rather than requiring them to check periodically for updates. Examples of real-time applications include social applications such as Facebook or Twitter; multiuser games such as Scrabble or Tic-Tac-Toe; business collaboration such as multi-user collaboration over a drawing board; and news, weather, or financial update applications such as stock tickers. This chapter looks at how you can write ASP.NET applications to enhance the real-time user experience by reducing the latency between the client and the server.

TRADITIONAL REAL-TIME COMMUNICATION OPTIONS

This chapter begins by looking at the prevailing options for writing real-time applications in .NET. The most common requirement in such an application is to maintain a persistent connection between the client and the server so data can be pushed from the server to the client as soon as the server receives it. Consider an example of IRC (Internet Relay Chat)—you want this connection to be open for the entire duration of the chat. There are times when no data is being transferred during the chat session, since users could be idle. In such situations, you still want the connection between the server and the client to be open.

Although HTTP is great at maintaining a persistent connection by using the Keep-Alive flag, it cannot maintain a long running persistent connection if no data is being transferred. Either the browser or the server will kill the connection; if new data comes in, the connection needs to be reestablished. This process of reconnecting increases latency and provides a sluggish user experience. Most browsers allow only two connections to be open from a browser to a server. If one of the connections is held up doing real-time communication, then it will slow down the website, which needs to download other resources such as JavaScript, CSS files, and so on. HTTP is a request/response protocol whereby a client makes a request to a server and the server sends the response back to the client. There is no way for the server to send a response to the client without the client initiating a request. Figure 26-1 shows a simple representation of this protocol.

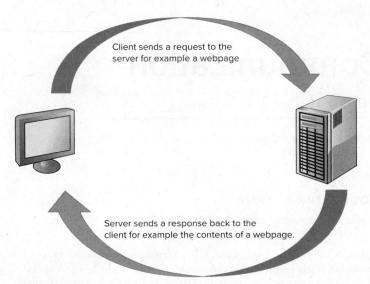

Client sends a request to the server for example a webpage

Server sends a response back to the client for example the contents of a webpage.

FIGURE 26-1

This section looks at some of the ways in which you can have a long-running persistent connection between a client and server so that the server can push data to the client without requiring that the client request it. Another way of achieving real-time functionality is when the client can explicitly pull data from the server, but this leads to a less performant application.

Using Comet

Comet is a web application model in which a client and server can have a long-running HTTP connection and the server can push data to the browser without requiring that the browser request the data. Since browsers and proxies are not designed with server events in mind, several techniques to achieve this have been developed, each with different benefits and drawbacks. The biggest hurdle is the HTTP 1.1 specification, which states that a browser should not have more than two simultaneous connections with a web server. Following are the two methods for implementing Comet. These rely on features that are commonly available in all browsers, such as JavaScript rather than a plug-in model.

Streaming

An application that implements Comet streaming opens a persistent connection between a server and client and listens for events. These events are handled in the browser each time the server sends a new event. Streaming can be implemented using a hidden `iframe` or by using `XMLHttpRequest` API.

The application can have a hidden `iframe` element. Each time the server sends a new message, the message is sent in chunked blocks as an `iframe` element. As events occur the `iframe` is filled with script tags containing JavaScript, which needs to be executed in the browser. Since all browsers process the page sequentially, each script tag is processed as it is received.

Ajax with Long Polling

Long polling is a technique whereby the client polls the server to check if there is any new data the server wants to send. The browser makes an Ajax-style request to the server and the request is kept open until the server sends data to the client in the response. As soon as the client gets the response, it immediately sends another request to the server so that the connection can be kept open. That way, the server can send new data as soon as an event happens on the server.

Polling

Polling is the method whereby the client makes a request to the server and the server responds immediately, regardless of whether it has data. The client then waits for some time (a few seconds) and makes another request to the server. The server sends new data if it has any; otherwise, it sends an empty response back to the client. Figure 26-2 shows how polling works.

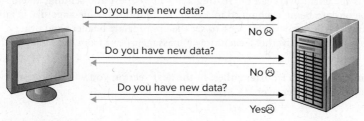

FIGURE 26-2

Server-Sent Events

Server-sent events (SSE) is a technology for sending push notifications from a server to a client. The notifications are sent in the form of DOM events, which the client can handle via a JavaScript API called Event Source. SSE is useful when you don't need bi-directional data transfer (like you would need with chat applications) because the server just needs to send data. For example, if you are building a stock ticker application, SSE is a good option. Figure 26-3 shows a simple workflow of server-sent events.

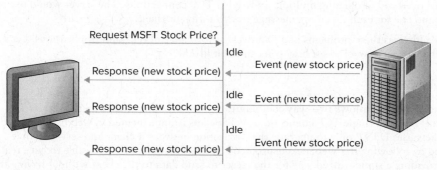

FIGURE 26-3

There are numerous implementations of these approaches that exist today, and developers can use them to build real-time web applications. The next section looks at some of the drawbacks of these approaches, many of which were the motivation of building WebSockets as a protocol.

Drawbacks of the Existing Approaches

All of the above push technologies try to maintain long-running persistent connections between the client and the server so that the server can push data to the client.

Comet streaming is fairly simple to implement, but is difficult to make work across different browsers. Not all of the browsers support all the streaming methods, so developers need to implement complex streaming transports to support all browsers and need to switch based on the browser. There is no way to implement reliable error handling or track the state of the connection since the connection and data transfer is handled through the HTML tags.

Long polling with Ajax does a step better than streaming in terms of reliable error handling and connection management, but it has the overhead of keeping the connection open on the server until there is data to be sent. The server implementation of this method becomes difficult because the request is left hanging until there is a response to send. That means a server thread is being utilized until there is data to be sent.

Traditional polling keeps the client and server implementation really simple. However, each time a client makes a request to the server, there is the extra overhead of creating a HTTP request and sending an empty response. If you think about the type of data being exchanged in a chat application, the message size is fairly small. However, when you construct a HTTP request you need to set the appropriate headers and other metadata about a request. This amounts to huge overhead each time a message is sent from the server to the client, which increases the latency.

SSE is not good for supporting bi-directional data transfer either. In the next section you will look at a new standard of performing bi-directional data transfer over HTTP.

HTML5 WEBSOCKETS

The last section looked briefly at some of the traditional patterns used to implement real-time communication and some of the advantages and disadvantages of using them.

Apart from the issues mentioned earlier in the chapter, all of the existing traditional approaches to real-time communication rely on transferring data over HTTP, which means that there is an overhead in the data transfer due to the HTTP headers needed with each request. Imagine if you were writing a chat application and were sending chat data. Each time you send a message (which is usually small, maybe a few bytes) because your message is sent over HTTP there is the added overhead of sending the HTTP headers. This increases the payload of the message being transferred.

There is also the added overhead of opening multiple underlying TCP connections. The server would use one for sending messages and one for each incoming message from a different client.

HTML5 WebSockets addresses these problems and improves performance of real-time applications. Let's take a look at the WebSockets protocol to see how you can use it in ASP.NET.

What Is WebSockets?

WebSockets is a specification that allows two-way communication between the client and the server. The communication channel is over a single TCP connection. WebSockets is implemented in web browsers and web servers. WebSockets uses HTTP only to upgrade the connection between a client and server so that data can be exchanged by following the WebSockets protocol. This protocol makes it possible to have real-time interaction by providing a standardized way for the server to send data to the client without having the client request the data.

One of the key implementations of WebSockets is that all communications are done over port 80 or 443. This was particularly important since there are lots of environments that block nonstandard HTTP connections not on port 80. So because WebSockets is implemented in this manner, the technology can run in existing environments without the problems some other HTTP connections might encounter.

WebSockets needs to be implemented in the browser clients and also on the server. All the modern desktop browsers support the WebSockets protocol. If you are using ASP.NET 4.5 on Windows 8, you will have WebSockets support on the server side. Before you look at the WebSockets protocol, let's take a brief historical tour of the existing transport layers. Figure 26-4 shows the different OSI layers.

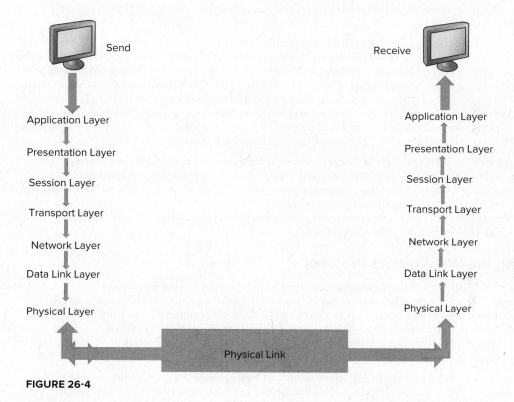

FIGURE 26-4

TCP/IP

TCP (Transmission Control Protocol)/IP (Internet Protocol) is a collection of interrelated protocols used for the Internet and similar networks. These were the first networking protocols defined. The Internet has evolved quite a lot over time and so has the kind of communication that happens on it. TCP/IP is modeled after OSI (Open System Interconnection), which defines a number of layers that make up TCP/IP. Separating TCP/IP into layers has helped it evolve over time and adjust to hardware and technology changes and has allowed developers to work on different layers to build the protocol stack or applications on top of the protocol.

At the bottom of the OSI model is the physical layer. It is implemented by protocols such as wired media access control. This layer provides physical connectivity. Moving up the OSI layers, there is the networking layer, which is implemented by IP. The networking layer allows TCP/IP to interoperate with different physical layers and route packages from one machine to another.

TCP/HTTP

TCP and UDP (User Datagram Protocol) are the most well-known transport protocols found in the transport layer. These protocols have a concept of *port*, which they use to multiplex and de-multiplex messages when they are sent. UDP has been widely adopted in private network applications, but hasn't been adopted much on the web. TCP, on the other hand, is widely used on the web, due to HTTP.

TCP provides a reliable transfer of data between computers. It manages with complex situations such as packet ordering, constructing messages properly from incoming data packets, error detection, flow control, timeouts, and many more. The application developer gets a seamless experience of getting bi-directional data transfer without having to go through the hassle of managing the lower-level complexities.

The HTTP protocol brings support for a reliable connection-oriented request-response protocol. When a client needs to send a request to the server, a TCP port is opened, over which the request/response happens. If a client sends another request, it happens over a different TCP port. This simplicity in the HTTP protocol made it very popular and is why it is used so widely on the web. HTTP is also a stateless protocol, which allows it to scale much better. However, HTTP does not utilize the bi-directional data transfer support in TCP. TCP allows the client and the server to send data simultaneously. This means that a server can send a message to the client without a request from the client. This simplification of HTTP resulted in the server caching the response until the communication channel was clear. This meant that this model was not highly scalable.

As use of the web has matured, there is a richer collaborative medium comprising instant sharing, messaging, and many more real-time interactions. Although there have been many techniques to improve the response time of loading applications by using compression or CDN (Content Delivery Networks), they all still use HTTP. The lack of significant progress in HTTP to support such real-time applications so that users can have smooth real-time web experiences is what has led to the implementation of the WebSockets protocol, which enables bi-directional data transfer over TCP.

Introducing the WebSockets Protocol

One of the main challenges of the WebSockets protocol was to get it to work with existing web environments. This meant that the protocol had to work with existing proxies, routers, and firewalls. In these environments, port 80 or port 443 is opened for HTTP/HTTPS connections and any data can be exchanged. When the client wants to send data over a WebSockets connection, it makes a call to the server to connect using HTTP. Since it is still using HTTP, the intermediate proxy or routers don't have to be updated to allow the connection.

The protocol starts with a handshake between a client and a server, where a client indicates to the server that it wants to send data over WebSockets. This handshake again happens over HTTP so that any intermediate routers do not reject this handshake. Listing 26-1 shows the headers that the client needs to send to the server to indicate that it wants to establish a WebSockets connection.

LISTING 26-1: WebSockets handshake

```
GET /chat HTTP/1.1
        Host: server.example.com
        Upgrade: websocket
        Connection: Upgrade
        Sec-WebSocket-Key: dGhlIHNhbXBsZSBub25jZQ==
        Origin: http://example.com
        Sec-WebSocket-Protocol: chat, superchat
        Sec-WebSocket-Version: 13
```

Nothing in these headers is different from any normal HTTP header. This handshake is a normal HTTP GET request. The client includes the hostname in the Host header so that the client and server can verify that they agree on which host is in use. The `Upgrade` and `Connection` headers are also specified in HTTP and are used by clients to upgrade the protocol being used. The `Upgrade` header is required by the WebSockets protocol. It indicates that the client wants to upgrade the connection to the WebSockets protocol. Figure 26-5 shows how a HTTP request is upgraded to a WebSockets connection.

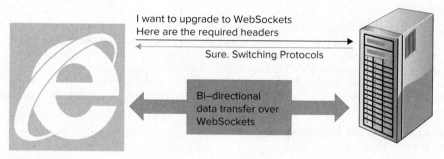

I want to upgrade to WebSockets
Here are the required headers

Sure. Switching Protocols

Bi–directional data transfer over WebSockets

FIGURE 26-5

The `Origin` header field is used to protect against unauthorized cross-origin use of WebSockets by scripts using WebSockets API in the browser. If the server does not want to accept incoming connections from this host, it can reject the connection and send an error code back.

The `Sec-WebSocket-Version` header tells the server which version of the WebSockets protocol the client supports. This should be set to 13 if you are building applications on Windows 8. If a server supports WebSockets but does not support this version of the protocol, the server can abort this request. This is important because, as the WebSockets specification is evolving, different clients (such as IE, Chrome, Firefox, and so on) and servers support different versions of the specification. Clients and servers can upgrade to the latest version of the specification in their own time. In an ideal world, all clients and servers are using the latest version. However, given how much time software implementations take across different companies, there can be situations when the version support varies across clients and servers. This header ensures that the client and server can verify which version of the protocol each supports and can accept or reject a WebSockets request when they are not compatible.

The `Sec-WebSocket-Key` header protects servers from accepting connections from clients that are not WebSockets clients. This prevents an attacker from tricking a WebSockets server by sending it packets using `XMLHttpRequest` or a form submission. This header proves to the client and server that a legitimate connection is being established. The value must be a randomly selected—ideally cryptographically random—16-byte number, known as a *nonce* in security parlance, which is then base-64encoded for this header value.

Additional header fields are used to select options in the WebSockets protocol. Typical options available in this version are the sub-protocol selector (`Sec-WebSocket-Protocol`), which is a list of extensions supported by the client (`Sec-WebSocket-Extensions`). The `Sec-WebSocket-Protocol` request-header field can be used to indicate which sub-protocols (application-level protocols layered over the WebSockets protocol) are acceptable to the server. The server selects one or none of the acceptable protocols and echoes that value in its handshake to indicate that it has selected that sub-protocol.

Once the client sends the handshake and the server understands WebSockets, the server switches the protocol to WebSockets. The server sends an HTTP 101 response to the client indicating that the WebSockets protocol handshake was completed and the connection is now upgraded to use the WebSockets protocol. Listing 26-2 shows the response headers that the server sends back to the client.

LISTING 26-2: WebSockets handshake response

```
HTTP/1.1 101 Switching Protocols
        Upgrade: websocket
        Connection: Upgrade
        Sec-WebSocket-Accept: s3pPLMBiTxaQ9kYGzzhZRbK+xOo=
        Sec-WebSocket-Protocol: chat
```

These are again valid HTTP headers, thus making it a normal HTTP response. The client needs to validate the response as well to ensure it is coming from the server it sent the handshake to. The client does this by using the `Sec-WebSocket-Accept` header. When the server gets the `Sec-WebSocket-Key` value, it does not decode it. It concatenates the string with a well-known GUID (Globally Unique Identifier) and hashes the combination with SHA1 to produce a value that's base-64-encoded and sent back to the client in this header. The client can perform the same and validate the result. If the validation is successful, the client can accept the handshake response and establish a WebSockets connection.

The client and server can now send and receive data over this WebSockets connection. The next section looks at how this data transfer happens.

WebSockets Data Transfer

The WebSockets protocol was designed to provide high scalability and low overhead for bi-directional communication between the server and the client. Once the connection is upgraded, communication happens over TCP. The protocol provides a packet-framing mechanism on top of TCP but without the limitations such as packet size. Whereas TCP is stream-based, WebSockets is a message-based data transfer. This means when data is transferred over WebSockets, it is transferred as a sequence of frames. The framing protocol requires only a few additional bytes of framing overhead, and since the transfer happens over TCP, it has the benefits of reliability and sequential delivery over TCP. There are two kinds of frames—control and data frames. Control frames are used to communicate state about the WebSockets whereas data frames are used to transfer data.

Each frame has an `opcode` that indicates the type of frame as well as the size of the payload. The payload has the actual data that the client and server send to each other. WebSockets protocol supports fragmentation of frames. This means that the message can be broken into different frames of varying lengths. This provides the convenience of packets without having to deal with the complexities of size limits. If the sender/receiver does not know the exact length of the data being sent or received, WebSockets will fragment the message into frames. Then, each frame can indicate how much data it has and whether it is the last frame in the message, indicating that the entire message has been transferred. The data frames can carry binary or text data, which is indicated in the frames by the `opcode` value of the frame. Figure 26-6 shows how a typical data frame for WebSockets looks like.

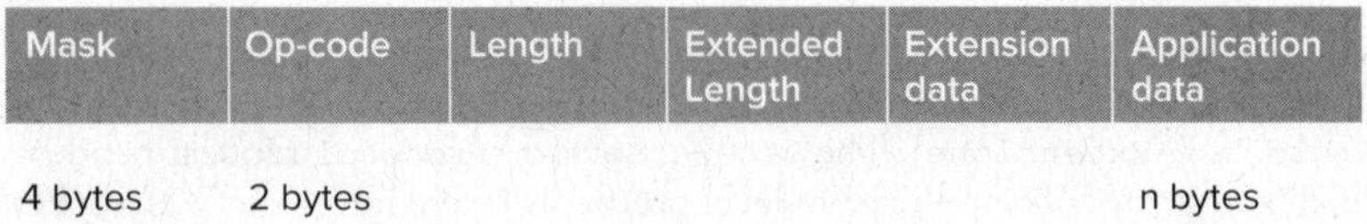

Mask	Op-code	Length	Extended Length	Extension data	Application data

4 bytes   2 bytes   n bytes

FIGURE 26-6

Control frames are primarily used to close a connection but can also be used to ping the client or server to ensure that the end points are still alive and to keep the TCP connection open. If one side of the connection sends a ping, the other side can send a pong to confirm that the connection is alive. This is useful in keeping the connection alive in case of overzealous proxies or firewalls, which might kill a connection if the connection is idle. The client or server can construct a control frame by specifying the appropriate `opcode`.

A key aspect of data framing is masking. *Masking* is a simple algorithm whereby the payload is XORed with a key that's contained within the frame. The masking key needs to be unpredictable to prevent authors of malicious applications from selecting the bytes that appear on the wire.

WebSockets API

The WebSockets protocol has been standardized by the IETF (Internet Engineering Task Force) standards body. This means that anyone can follow this standard and implement it in his or her own clients or servers.

All of the commonly used browsers—such as Internet Explorer, Chrome, FireFox, Safari, Opera, and others—have added support for the WebSockets API.

Table 26-1 shows some of the common JavaScript event listeners you can use to do basic operations over a WebSockets connection with a web browser.

TABLE 26-1

EVENT LISTENERS	DESCRIPTION
Onopen	This event is fired when a WebSockets connection is opened.
onclose	This event is fired when the WebSockets connection is closed.
onmessage	This event is fired when the client receives data sent from the server over a WebSockets connection.
Send	This method is used to send data from the client to the server.
close	This method closes the WebSockets connection between the server and the client.

WebSockets in ASP.NET 4.5

Now that you've seen the WebSockets protocol in action, in this section you'll take a look at how you can build applications using WebSockets in ASP.NET.

Since the WebSockets protocol needs to be implemented both by the client and server, you'll look at both of these cases. On the web server, there is a new module called the WebSockets module. It was introduced in IIS 8 on Windows Server 2012. The module implements the WebSockets protocol and is responsible for handling the data transfer.

Figure 26-7 shows how you can enable the WebSockets protocol in IIS 8. You have to enable IIS Web Server role in Windows. Once you have enabled this, you need to select the WebSocket Protocol option in the IIS Application Development Features area.

ASP.NET provides nice APIs, which an application developer can use to handle WebSockets requests. These APIs allow developers to accept a WebSockets connection and communicate over the connection. You will write ASP.NET HTTP handlers, which can interact with any kind of WebSockets request and can send and receive data.

When a client sends a WebSockets handshake, ASP.NET checks to see if the server supports WebSockets and upgrades the request if all the protocol requirements are met. On a successful upgrade of the connection between a server and the client, ASP.NET and IIS receive incoming data over the connection and send data over the connection.

When the application needs to send data, the module constructs appropriate frames as per the WebSockets specification and sends the frames over the WebSockets connection. The module also looks at incoming frames from clients and can construct a message from these frames so that the application can receive the message.

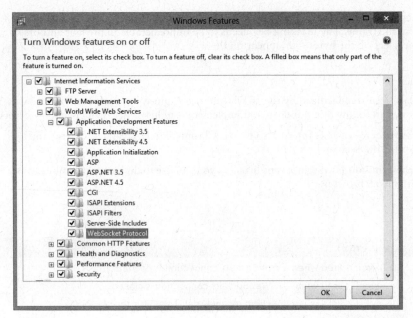

FIGURE 26-7

Examining Server-Side WebSockets Echo Handler

Listing 26-3 shows a simple WebSockets echo handler. It accepts a WebSockets request, receives a message from the client, and sends the same message back to the client.

LISTING 26-3: Typical WebSockets echo handler in ASP.NET

VB

```
Public Class Handler
    Implements IHttpHandler

    Public Async Function MyWebSocket (context As AspNetWebSocketContext) As Task
        Dim socket As WebSocket = context.WebSocket
        While True
            Dim buffer As New ArraySegment(Of Byte)(New Byte(1023) {})

            ' Asynchronously wait for a message to arrive from a client

Dim result As WebSocketReceiveResult = Await socket.ReceiveAsync(buffer, CancellationToken.None)

            ' If the socket is still open, echo the message back to the client
            If socket.State = WebSocketState.Open Then

Dim userMessage As String = Encoding.UTF8.GetString(buffer.Array, 0, result.Count)

userMessage = "You sent: " & userMessage & " at " & DateTime.Now.ToLongTimeString()
                buffer = New ArraySegment(Of Byte)(Encoding.UTF8.GetBytes(userMessage))

                ' Asynchronously send a message to the client
```

```
Await socket.SendAsync(buffer, WebSocketMessageType.Text, True, CancellationToken.None)
                Else
                    Exit While
                End If
            End While
        End Function

        Public ReadOnly Property IsReusable() As Boolean Implements IHttpHandler.IsReusable
            Get
                Throw New NotImplementedException()
            End Get
        End Property
        Public Sub ProcessRequest(context As HttpContext) Implements IHttpHandler.ProcessRequest
            If context.IsWebSocketRequest Then
                context.AcceptWebSocketRequest(AddressOf MyWebSocket)
            End If
        End Sub
    End Class
```

C#

```csharp
public class Handler : IHttpHandler {

    public async Task MyWebSocket(AspNetWebSocketContext context)
    {
        WebSocket socket = context.WebSocket;
        while (true)
        {
            ArraySegment<byte> buffer = new ArraySegment<byte>(new byte[1024]);

            // Asynchronously wait for a message to arrive from a client
            WebSocketReceiveResult result =
                    await socket.ReceiveAsync(buffer, CancellationToken.None);

            // If the socket is still open, echo the message back to the client
            if (socket.State == WebSocketState.Open)
            {
                string userMessage = Encoding.UTF8.GetString(buffer.Array, 0,
                        result.Count);
                userMessage = "You sent: " + userMessage + " at " +
                        DateTime.Now.ToLongTimeString();
                buffer = new ArraySegment<byte>(Encoding.UTF8.GetBytes(userMessage));

                // Asynchronously send a message to the client
                await socket.SendAsync(buffer, WebSocketMessageType.Text,
                        true, CancellationToken.None);
            }
            else { break; }
        }
    }

    public bool IsReusable
    {
        get { throw new NotImplementedException(); }
    }

    public void ProcessRequest(HttpContext context)
    {
        if (context.IsWebSocketRequest)
        {
            context.AcceptWebSocketRequest(MyWebSocket);
        }
    }
}
```

When a request comes to this echo handler, the handler first checks whether the request is a WebSockets request or not in the `ProcessRequest` function. If it is then the Echo Handler reads the message sent over the WebSockets connection in the `MyWebSocket` task which was called in `ProcessRequest`. The echo handler uses the WebSockets APIs to receive and send messages.

Examining Client-Side WebSockets Code

Now that you have looked at the server side implementation of WebSockets in an ASP.NET handler, it's time to see how you can create a WebSockets connection from inside a web page.

To connect to an endpoint, you just create a new WebSockets instance, providing the new object with a URL that represents the endpoint to which you want to connect.

> **NOTE** *A* ws:// *and* wss:// *prefix are typically used to indicate a WebSockets and a secure WebSockets connection, respectively.*

Once a connection is established, you can use the `send` and `onmessage` event listeners to send and receive messages over the connection. You can use the other event listeners shown in Table 26-1 to close the connection and perform any other functions supported by the WebSockets API.

Listing 26-4 shows a typical web page that uses the WebSockets API implementation in JavaScript to connect to the WebSockets echo handler.

LISTING 26-4: Typical WebSockets JavaScript client

```
<%@ Page AutoEventWireup="true" %>
<!doctype html>
<html>
<head>
<meta content="text/html; charset=utf-8" http-equiv="Content-Type">
<title>Web Socket Test</title>
<script type="text/javascript">
        var socket;
        function initializeWebSocket() {
          var host = "ws://localhost:33610 /CS/Handler.ashx";
            try {
                socket = new WebSocket(host);

                socket.onopen = function (msg) {
                    var s = 'Socket open';
                    document.getElementById("serverStatus").innerHTML = s;
                };

                socket.onmessage = function (msg) {
                    var serverData = document.getElementById("serverData");
                    var newElem = document.createElement("p");
                    newElem.appendChild(document.createTextNode(msg.data));
                    serverData.insertBefore(newElem, serverData.firstChild);
                };

                socket.onclose = function (msg) {
                    var s = 'Socket closed';
                    document.getElementById("serverStatus").innerHTML = s;
                };

        }
```

```
                    catch (ex) { alert(ex); }
            }

            function send() {
                var e = document.getElementById("msgText");
                socket.send(e.value);
            }
            initializeWebSocket();
    </script>
    </head>
    <body>
    <h1>Web Socket Echo Demo</h1>
    <p id="serverStatus"></p>
    <p>
            This text will be sent on the socket:<br />
    <input id="msgText" type="text" size="30">
    <input type="button" value="Send" onclick="send()">

    </p>
    <div id="serverData"></div>
    </body>
    </html>
```

When you browse to this page, the JavaScript code gets executed. Initially in the JavaScript, the page tries to make a WebSockets request to the echo handler that you just saw in Listing 26-3. When you click the Send button on the page, the page sends the data over a WebSockets connection to the echo handler. The echo handler sends a response back to the browser and when the browser receives the data, then the `onmessage()` JavaScript function is called which displays the received data on the page. Figure 26-8 shows how this sample echo demo would look like.

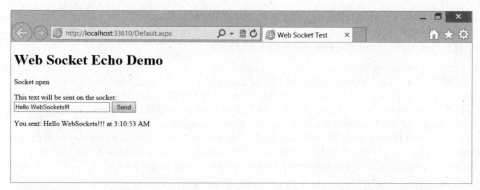

FIGURE 26-8

Benefits of Using WebSockets

HTML5 WebSockets is not just an incremental advance in HTTP communication. It goes above and beyond everything else to make real-time applications much more powerful. The improvements related to reducing the payload overhead and latency are so great that most of the big names in the web immediately switched to using WebSockets in their web applications.

WebSockets provides a native support in HTTP for writing real-time applications. By upgrading the connection from HTTP to WebSockets and transferring data over the WebSockets channel, there is tremendous reduction in the payload size. This is because the HTTP headers do not need to be sent with each message transfer. Also, because the WebSockets communication happens over a single TCP connection, there is no longer the need to open multiple ports on the server to send and receive data from multiple clients. The application becomes very simple when implementing real-time scenarios because the easy to use WebSockets APIs make it easier to maintain connections from client to server and track replies coming in from the server.

The WebSockets protocol handshake happens over HTTP. This means it can be used in environments where HTTP/HTTPS is already being used. This was done to ensure easy adoption of WebSockets since these ports and all the intermediaries can transfer data over HTTP.

WebSockets is secure. One of the many challenges that existed for the designers of this protocol was security. WebSockets has a URI specification called `wss` that uses the same encryption as HTTPS with TLS/SSL. When the WebSockets handshake happens, the client and server validate the connection using the `Sec-WebSocket-Protocol` headers. Masking is used when transferring data as frames, which prevents attacks on the network infrastructure.

SIGNALR

WebSockets is a great step forward in supporting highly scalable real-time applications. With the investment in the WebSockets protocol, it is now possible to perform bi-directional data transfer over HTTP. Because WebSockets is a modern standard and was introduced recently as part of the HTML5 specification, it has not yet been widely adopted. This section looks at a more realistic alternative for some who can't adopt WebSockets: SignalR, which may be the best of both worlds.

WebSockets, being a modern standard, has its share of advantages and drawbacks. Although the modern standard paves the way for a better and powerful future, it does take time for the standard to be adopted widely by the masses. On the server side, WebSockets is supported only on Windows 8 or Windows Server 2012 and in the .NET Framework 4.5. This limits the reach of the WebSockets applications.

If you write an application using WebSockets, users who are on older platforms will not be able to use your application unless you provide them with a fallback behavior. This fallback behavior could involve defaulting to Comet or other push technologies. It's daunting to need two implementations of your application and will eventually result in a maintenance nightmare.

The whole idea behind developing WebSockets was to address the fundamental issue of bi-directional data transfer over HTTP. As you learned earlier, HTTP is a simple protocol that's best suited for request-response scenarios. As the web has grown richer in terms of the applications people are using to communicate, HTTP has become a bottleneck. The main motivation for the WebSockets protocol was to solve this problem. A part of the WebSockets specification also focused on the WebSockets API, which provided very basic support for creating WebSockets connections—sending and receiving data over the connection. These APIs do not provide any higher level programming constructs for writing real-time applications, such as managing multiple connections, error recovery, and many more.

The biggest change in web access over the last decade has been in how the web is accessed. Desktop browsers are no longer the only way people are browsing the web. There has been an explosion of devices with different form factors, ranging from smartphones to tablets and anything in between. Apart from the browsers, these form factors expose applications that people can use to interact with an application. As part of this change, users interact with these applications using touch devices rather than traditional mice and keyboards.

These changes present challenges to application developers. They must write real-time applications that work on different environments and devices. There is a need for a library that addresses these problems and makes it easier for developers to write applications rather than having to worry about the lower-level details of environments and devices. This is where SignalR comes in. It makes the experience of developing real-time applications much easier and more fun.

What Is SignalR?

SignalR is a library which is built on ASP.NET. It makes adding real-time functionality to your web applications incredibly simple. SignalR uses WebSockets under the covers when it's available, and gracefully falls back to other techniques and technologies when it isn't. All the while, your application code stays the same.

SignalR also provides a very simple, high-level API for writing real-time applications and adds useful hooks for connection management. It also enables completely new types of applications that require high-frequency updates from the server (such as real-time gaming). Figure 26-9 shows the high-level features of SignalR.

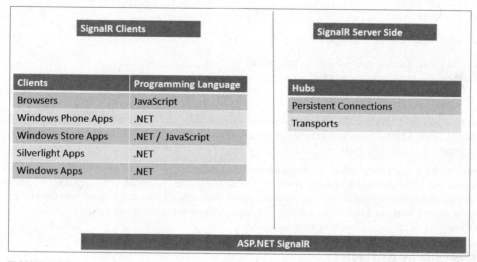

FIGURE 26-9

SignalR supports different environments and devices as well. It will determine what the client and server support and choose the best approach to set up a real-time connection. If the client and server both support WebSockets, it will use WebSockets or else it will use the next best option. This means that your application will continue to work seamlessly across various browsers on different Windows versions, without you having to change your application code. The other beauty of SignalR is that it exposes APIs so you can build real-time applications for mobile devices and tablets. This enables you to have the same server-side code for the client's connection from different devices.

Server-Side SignalR in ASP.NET

Using SignalR in your ASP.NET application is similar to using WebSockets. There is a server-side piece that's responsible for accepting connections from clients and transmitting data among all clients. The difference between SignalR and WebSockets APIs is that SignalR provides the extra functionality of managing connections and making sure all the clients can exchange data seamlessly. As you saw a HTTP handler that handles WebSockets connections in Listing 26-3, a hub is a server-side end point which clients can call. It also manages all the connections and sends or receives data from various clients. Listing 26-5 shows an example of a hub that can be used for chat applications.

Unlike the WebSockets echo handler, hubs do not need any code to accept connections. The lower-level details of negotiating a connection and choosing the best protocol are hidden from the developers so that they can focus on the application code rather than on protocol negotiation.

LISTING 26-5: Typical ASP.NET SignalR Chat hub

VB

```vb
Public Class VBChat
    Inherits Hub
    Public Sub Send(message As String)
        ' Call the addMessage method on all clients
        Clients.All.addMessage(message)
    End Sub
End Class
```

C#

```csharp
public class CSChat : Hub
{
    public void Send(string message)
    {
        // Call the addMessage method on all clients
        Clients.All.addMessage(message);
    }
}
```

SignalR does server-to-client RPCs (calls functions in your clients from the server-side .NET code). For example, in Listing 26-5, addMessage is a JavaScript function on the web page, as shown in Listing 26-6, which is called from the server-side hub.

Hubs provide lots of high-level functionality on the server side, including a level of security. They can check whether the clients are authenticated and authorized to talk to the server. Hubs can broadcast messages in a variety of ways to all the connected clients, to only the client that sent the message, or to specific clients. Hubs also provide events that are fired when a client connects, disconnects, or reconnects. These features make it easy to keep track of clients and transmit messages.

Client-Side SignalR in ASP.NET

The other aspect of using SignalR in your application is the client. SignalR can be used with different kinds of clients. This section looks at how you can use it in a web page that can be accessed by a browser. This experience will look similar to Listing 26-4, which shows how you use the WebSockets API in JavaScript to make a WebSockets connection to the echo handler in Listing 26-3.

When you run your application, SignalR generates a proxy on the client side so that the client can call functions on the server through the proxy. As shown in Listing 26-6, the client calls a function called Send, which is defined on the server, as shown back in Listing 26-5.

Listing 26-6 uses a SignalR JavaScript library in a web page.

LISTING 26-6: Typical ASP.NET SignalR JavaScript client

```html
<!DOCTYPE html>
<script src="Scripts/jquery-1.6.4.js"></script>
<script src="Scripts/jquery.signalR-1.0.1.js" type="text/javascript"></script>
<script src="<%= ResolveClientUrl("~/signalr/hubs") %>" type="text/javascript"></script>
<script type="text/javascript">
    $(function () {
        // Proxy created on the fly
        var chat = $.connection.cSChat;

        // Declare a function on the chat hub so the server can invoke it
        chat.client.addMessage = function (message) {
```

```
                 $('#messages').append('<li>' + message + '</li>');
            };

            // Start the connection
            $.connection.hub.start().done(function () {
                $("#broadcast").click(function () {
                    // Call the chat method on the server
                    chat.server.send($('#msg').val());
                });
            });
        });
    </script>

    <html xmlns="http://www.w3.org/1999/xhtml">
    <head runat="server">
    <title></title>
    </head>
    <body>
    <form id="form1" runat="server">
    <div>
    <input type="text" id="msg" />
    <input type="button" id="broadcast" value="send" />

    <ul id="messages">
    </ul>
    </div>
    </form>
    </body>
    </html>
```

As shown in Listing 26-6, to make a connection to a hub, you call into the proxy /signalr/hubs generated by SignalR. Once the connection is started you can send and receive data over the connection. Figure 26-10 shows a chat sample based on code from Listing 26-5 and Listing 26-6. All you have to write in your application to implement a basic chat scenario was the code shown in the preceding two listings. Once you run the applications, you can browse to this application using different browsers, and when you send text from one browser, SignalR will automatically send the message to all the other connected clients.

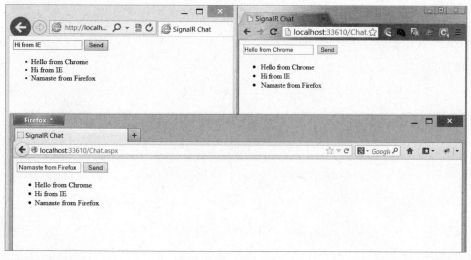

FIGURE 26-10

The biggest advantage to using SignalR is the "write once, work everywhere" approach. As a developer you simply write your application using SignalR and it will choose the best transport to communicate with based on the platform the user is using.

Since SignalR is built on top of ASP.NET, you can utilize all the familiar ASP.NET concepts such as routing, authentication, and authorization, and you can use them while building a SignalR application.

SUMMARY

The web has come a long way in different kinds of interaction and communication models for users. As users are gravitating toward more social applications, the need for real-time communication has increased immensely. The use of social interaction has also raised user expectations in terms of providing a real-time collaborative environment. This has pushed the World Wide Web Consortium to think of creative ways to upgrade common communication protocols so that they support real-time communications.

This chapter looked at a variety of approaches that have existed to support real-time applications. Some of the drawbacks of these older approaches makes them perform poorly in modern web situations. To address these drawbacks, the WebSockets protocol was introduced as part of the HTML5 specification. WebSockets has taken a quantum leap in ensuring that real-time applications perform and scale well.

Finally, the chapter took a short look at how SignalR takes the developer experience of writing real-time applications to the next level by making it easier to achieve the "write once, run anywhere" model.

27

Developing Websites with Mobile in Mind

WHAT'S IN THIS CHAPTER?

➤   What is responsive web design?

➤   How to detect a mobile device

➤   All about ASP.NET mobile features

➤   Understanding ASP.NET MVC 4 mobile features

➤   How to test the rendering of your mobile site

WROX.COM CODE DOWNLOADS FOR THIS CHAPTER

Please note that all the code examples in this chapter are available as a part of this chapter's code download on the book's website at www.wrox.com on the Download Code tab.

Today, having a successful website means making it accessible to mobile devices. The number of mobile phones that are capable of browsing the Internet continues to grow, as does the number of people using them to do just that. It is no longer safe to assume that a particular website won't be browsed with a mobile device. For many businesses, having a mobile website is the source of an increasing percentage of their revenue. Even for businesses that don't rely on mobile traffic for income, their customers are beginning to expect the ability to browse their site on a mobile device. As mobile usage continues to rise, mobile web design becomes more important than ever.

This chapter looks at various techniques and technologies that make it easier to accommodate mobile devices. While ASP.NET provides tools to help, not all solutions depend on a particular technology.

THE ORIGINS OF WIRELESS MARKUP LANGUAGE

Although mobile design has changed considerably over the years, the concept of developing a mobile website is nothing new. As a matter of fact, *Wireless Markup Language* (WML), an XML-based language designed specifically for developing websites for mobile devices, was developed in 1998. Microsoft created a set of mobile controls for ASP.NET as early as version 2 of the .NET Framework. The controls in the `System.Web.UI.MobileControls` namespace produced WML, CHTML, or HTML based on the browser. The namespace was marked obsolete in version 4 of the .NET Framework in favor of more current mobile web development standards. Visual Studio 2010 and ASP.NET MVC introduced a set of tools to make developing mobile websites much easier. Visual Studio 2012 and the latest version of ASP.NET MVC continue to enhance the tools available for mobile web development and make it easier than ever to build mobile sites.

FACING MOBILE WEB DESIGN CHALLENGES

Although the tools and technology for developing mobile websites has changed, the challenges remain the same and they are as follows:

➤ **Screen size:** This is the most obvious of challenges. Working with a smaller screen size often means that the choices you would make for laying out a website are very different on a mobile device. You may have to change multiple horizontal columns on a desktop browser to a single stacked column in order to fit on a smaller screen. You may need to flatten complex horizontal navigation menus and display them vertically.

➤ **Bandwidth:** This is often overlooked. Using a desktop browser, a user is likely to have a high-availability, high-bandwidth connection to the Internet. A mobile device will typically have a lower bandwidth connection and may, at times, be disconnected. Not to mention that bandwidth on a mobile device is usually more expensive. It is important to make effective use of bandwidth when serving content to a mobile device. Though you may rely on many large client script libraries and large CSS files when building rich desktop websites, it may not be practical when designing for smaller mobile browsers.

➤ **Image size:** It is not just client script libraries and CSS files that are a concern in mobile websites. You must also take image size into account, not just because of the increase in bandwidth, but also because of physical size. Ideally, images for use on a mobile device would be significantly smaller in both pixel size and file size.

➤ **User interaction:** Interacting with a mobile device is significantly different than interacting with a desktop device. A mobile device uses touch and gestures, whereas a desktop uses a mouse and a keyboard. Selecting an element on a desktop screen using the mouse is much different than touching an element on a mobile screen. Touch is much less precise and elements must be larger for a user to select them. Keyboard input is not only more difficult on a mobile device due to the size of the keys, but it can be different on different devices. Some devices may use a virtual keyboard, whereas others have physical ones.

The challenges facing mobile web developers don't end with these. But they are representative of the kinds of challenges presented when developing websites for mobile devices. Overcoming these challenges often comes from experience, both good and bad. Tools like those in Visual Studio 2012, version 4.5 of the .NET Framework, and the latest version of ASP.NET MVC definitely make it easier.

RESPONSIVE DESIGN AND ADAPTIVE DESIGN

Designing sites for mobile browsers is no longer the exception. It is the rule. Most successful websites now have explicit support for mobile browsers. As with most technologies or techniques that become a mainstream, the amount of terminology surrounding them can become confusing. Perhaps you have heard terms such as responsive design, progressive enhancement, and adaptive design. What is the difference between them?

➤ *Adaptive design* is term that typically encompasses various techniques for allowing a single web page to "adapt" to the size and orientation of the device that is viewing it. There is no single technique that is called adaptive design. Adaptive design comes about through the use of multiple techniques that work in conjunction. *Progressive enhancement* refers to a practice of designing initially for the lowest common denominator and then "progressively" adding features or styles based on a client's support for them.

➤ *Responsive design* is a type of adaptive design. It incorporates techniques that allow a website to stretch and rearrange based on the browser that is rendering it. It also allows a site to respond to real-time changes in the size and orientation of the browser.

These terms are often used in conjunction with one another. A technique that is an example of responsive design may also be an example of progressive enhancement and vice versa. Two of the techniques used in responsive design involve including the `viewport` meta tag and utilizing CSS media queries. Utilizing CSS media queries can also be used in progressive enhancement.

Modifying the Viewport

When a browser renders a website, it does so in a viewport. A *viewport* is simply the area available for viewing a website. When you browse a website using a mobile browser, the browser, by default, assumes that you're viewing the website on a desktop. The browser assumes you want to see the entire site and not just one corner of it. It therefore sets the viewport width much larger than the physical screen width, causing the viewport displaying the entire site to be stuffed into the small display. To demonstrate this, create a new ASP.NET Empty Web Application project called `HTMLMobile`. Then create a new HTML page by right-clicking the project and selecting Add ➪ New Item. Select Html Page and name it `default.html`. The content of the `default.html` page is shown in Listing 27-1 (file defaultbasic.html in the code download for this chapter).

LISTING 27-1: The default.html page

```html
<!DOCTYPE html>
<html xmlns="http://www.w3.org/1999/xhtml">
<head>
    <title>Responsive Design Example</title>
    <style>
        header{ background-color: #808080; }
        footer{
            background-color: #808080;
            text-align: left;
            height: 50px;
            clear: both;
        }
        nav{ text-align:left; }
        nav a{
            padding-left: 10px;
            padding-right: 10px;
            color: black;
        }
        #content{
            padding-left: 10px;
            border-right: 1px solid black;
            width: 45%;
            float: left;
        }
        #news{
```

continues

LISTING 27-1 *(continued)*

```
                padding-left: 10px;
                width: 45%;
                float: left;
            }
        </style>
    </head>
    <body>
        <header>
            <nav>
                <a href="#">Home</a>
                <a href="#">Page 1</a>
                <a href="#">Page 2</a>
                <a href="#">About</a>
            </nav>
        </header>
        <div id="content">
            <h1>Welcome!</h1>
            Welcome to responsive design example.
        </div>
        <div id="news">
            <h2>News</h2>
            Breaking news!
        </div>
        <footer>
            Copyright &copy; Examples By U
        </footer>
    </body>
</html>
```

It is easy to see the effect of the viewport by browsing to the page using a mobile browser. Figure 27-1 shows the `default.html` page viewed in a mobile browser.

You can see that the browser has rendered the page as though it were on a larger screen and then shrunk it to fit in the mobile browser screen. Many of the elements on the screen are too small to read, much less interact with. To fix the problem, you need to tell the browser to use a viewport that is the same size as the device screen width. You do this by adding the Viewport Meta tag between the opening and closing `head` tag. Listing 27-2 (file defaultviewport.html in the code download for this chapter) shows a part of the `default.html` file after adding the Viewport Meta tag.

FIGURE 27-1

LISTING 27-2: Default page with Viewport Meta tag

```
<!DOCTYPE html>
<html xmlns="http://www.w3.org/1999/xhtml">
<head>
    <title>Responsive Design Example</title>
    <meta name="viewport" content="width=device-width" />
    <style>
        header
        {
            background-color: #808080;
        }
```

Figure 27-2 shows the page displayed in a mobile browser after adding the Viewport Meta tag.

It is easy to see that the Viewport Meta tag has done the job. Now the content of the site is more readable. But you can see a new problem starting to present itself. Although the content is not too small, the layout of the page does not really suit the smaller screen. Elements on the page are beginning to overlap. The scale of the site is correct, but now the layout needs to be made more responsive to screen size.

Using CSS Media Queries

Forcing the browser to scale its contents based on the size of the screen is a first step. But most of the time, a layout designed for a larger screen may not be appropriate for a smaller one. If the layout of the page has been designed to use CSS, the layout can be changed using different CSS. The question is how you tell the browser to use different CSS for different sizes of screens. The answer is by using CSS media queries.

CSS media queries enable you to target CSS rules at particular display features. Targeting media types such as "screen" and "print" with CSS rules has been available since HTML4 and CSS2. However, media queries extend this functionality to include other conditions. A media query consists of a media type and zero or more expressions that check for the conditions of particular media features. Some of the media features that you can use are "width," "height," and "color." When targeting different screen sizes, the most common is "width." Though you can use other conditions, typical conditions are `min-width` and `max-width`.

FIGURE 27-2

It is possible to implement progressive enhancement using CSS media queries. It may not always be possible to adopt the practice of progressive enhancement. At times, especially when adding mobile capabilities to an existing website, your starting point is already set. However, in this example you can modify the layout of the site to target, by default, the lowest common denominator, which is a mobile browser. Then, using CSS media queries, you can add additional style rules to provide a different layout for more accommodating screen sizes. Listing 27-3, shown in file defaultqueries.html in the code download for this chapter, shows the style block after making changes to target, by default, a mobile browser, and then progressively larger screens.

LISTING 27-3: The style block after adding CSS Media Queries

```
<style>
    header{ background-color: #808080; }
    footer{
        background-color: #808080;
        text-align: center;
        height: 50px;
    }
    nav{ text-align:center; }
    nav a{
        display: block;
        padding-left: 10px;
        padding-right: 10px;
        color: black;
    }
    #content{ padding-left: 10px; }
    #news{ padding-left: 10px; }
    @media screen and (min-width: 601px)
    {
        footer{ clear: both; }
        nav a{ display: inline; }
        #content{
            border-right: 1px solid black;
            width: 45%;
            float: left;
        }
```

continues

LISTING 27-3 *(continued)*

```
            #news{
                width: 45%;
                float: left;
            }
        }
        @media screen and (min-width: 901px)
        {
            footer{ text-align: left; }
            nav{ text-align: left; }
        }
    </style>
```

For the preceding code, the first set of style rules are applied as the base set of rules targeting a mobile browser. Notice the `nav` and `footer` elements have been changed to specify the text to be centered and the anchor elements have a display value of `block`. The `content` and `news` divs have also had their float values removed, thus stacking them vertically instead of horizontally. Elements presented vertically are often more appropriate in a mobile browser than horizontally because horizontal space is limited.

A media query defines a block of style rules that are applied only if the media type is `screen` and the minimum width of the screen is `601px`. A screen width of 601px to 900px will accommodate many tablet devices. Notice the style rules in this block replace many of the layout styles that were removed from those targeting the lowest common denominator, the mobile browser:

```
@media screen and (min-width: 601px)
```

Another media query defines a block of style rules that are applied only if the media type is `screen` and the minimum width of the screen is `901px`. Because many tablet devices utilize a screen width up to 900px, the rules defined in this block accommodate larger screen sizes, such as a desktop. When the following media query is applied, you just left justify the menu items and the footer text. Although this may seem trivial, it demonstrates multiple levels of progressive enhancement.

```
@media screen and (min-width: 901px)
```

FIGURE 27-3

Figure 27-3 shows the page displayed in a mobile browser. For contrast, Figure 27-4 shows the same page displayed in a desktop browser.

FIGURE 27-4

ASP.NET MOBILE APPLICATIONS

Targeting your ASP.NET applications to mobile devices involves changes on both the client and the server. Choosing to do just one or the other does not provide a complete solution. This is an area of much debate in mobile web development. Some believe that the content in an application should be the same, whether viewed from a desktop or a mobile device. In these cases, the only things that change when users view content from a mobile device is simply the layout of the content and perhaps the styling of the elements used to present it. This is a responsive web design approach. Still others believe that the mobile user may not need to see the same content, or at least not as much of it. In these cases, the differences between viewing on a desktop and a mobile device are more extensive.

Only making client changes, such as those for responsive design, allows your application to scale better to the size of the mobile device screen. Your application can then respond to changes in orientation. It can provide layout and styling options more suited to the size of the device on which it's viewed. However, attempting to accommodate all potential devices with a single page may mean including unnecessary markup, CSS, and JavaScript, thus increasing required bandwidth.

Making the changes on the server involves providing dedicated pages to be served to mobile devices. This may cause some duplication of effort and code, but it also allows for ultimate control of what the user sees in both a desktop browser and a mobile browser. When taking a more server-centric approach, you must take care to encapsulate common logic and functionality into libraries that can be shared between the two different versions of a page.

If you have read this chapter from the beginning, you're already familiar with the kinds of changes you can make in the client code to create more mobile-friendly pages. This section focuses on a server-centric approach to building mobile applications.

You can start by creating a new ASP.NET Web Forms Application and calling it `WebFormsMobile`.

Detecting Mobile Browsers and Devices

The first hurdle to overcome is determining how to detect the characteristics of the browser that views your application. Knowing information about the browser is necessary if you are going to make decisions on the server based on this information. Luckily, ASP.NET provides the `Request.Browser` object, which retrieves information about the characteristics of the browser in use. Although the `Request.Browser` object has many interesting and helpful properties, three are specifically targeted toward mobile browsers:

➤ `MobileDeviceManufacturer`: Returns the name of the manufacturer of the device, if available.

➤ `MobileDeviceModel`: Returns the model of the device, if available.

➤ `IsMobileDevice`: Though it might be interesting to target certain mobile manufacturers and models, these approaches are impractical because so many different mobile devices exist. The more useful property is `IsMobileDevice`, which simply returns a value indicating whether or not the request is coming from a mobile device.

Serving Mobile Master Pages

Now that you have the means to detect the capabilities of the browser requesting a page, you can use that to serve mobile-specific pages to mobile browsers. It may be possible to handle the differences between mobile pages and standard pages simply through the use of a mobile-specific master page. Create a new master page in the root of your application by right-clicking the project and selecting Add ➪ New Item. Choose Master Page from the Add New Item dialog box and name it `MobileSite.Master`. You'll create a simplified version of the standard master file for use with mobile devices. Listing 27-4 presents the code for the C# version of the `MobileSite.Master` file. You can find this code in file MobileSite.Master located in the root of the WebFormsMobileCS or WebFormsMobileVB projects in the code download for this chapter.

LISTING 27-4: MobileSite.Master file

```
<%@ Master Language="C#" AutoEventWireup="true" CodeBehind="MobileSite.master.cs"
    Inherits="WebFormMobile.MobileSite" %>

<!DOCTYPE html>

<html xmlns="http://www.w3.org/1999/xhtml">
<head id="Head1" runat="server">
    <title></title>
    <asp:ContentPlaceHolder ID="head" runat="server">
    </asp:ContentPlaceHolder>
    <meta name="viewport" content="width=device-width" />
</head>
<body>
    <form id="form1" runat="server">
    <div>
        This is a mobile browser!

        <asp:ContentPlaceHolder ID="FeaturedContent" runat="server">
        </asp:ContentPlaceHolder>

        <asp:ContentPlaceHolder ID="MainContent" runat="server">
        </asp:ContentPlaceHolder>
    </div>
    </form>
</body>
</html>
```

Having created a simplified mobile version of the master page, you have to instruct any page displaying in a mobile browser to use the `MobileSite.Master` master page. To do this, override the `Page_PreInit` handler of each page and change the master page that it is set to use. You can start by modifying the default page in the project to use the `MobileSite.Master` when users view it in a mobile browser. Listing 27-5 shows the default page code-behind after you override the `Page_PreInit` handler to change the master page if it's viewed on a mobile device. You can find the code for this listing in files Default.aspx.cs and Default.aspx. vb located in the root of the WebFormsMobileCS or WebFormsMobileVB projects in the code download for this chapter.

LISTING 27-5: Default code-behind with overridden Page_PreInit

VB

```
Public Class _Default
    Inherits Page

    Protected Overrides Sub OnPreInit(e As EventArgs)
        If Request.Browser.IsMobileDevice Then
            MasterPageFile = "~/MobileSite.Master"
        End If

        MyBase.OnPreInit(e)
    End Sub

    Protected Sub Page_Load(ByVal sender As Object, ByVal e As EventArgs) Handles
        Me.Load

    End Sub
End Class
```

C#

```csharp
using System;
using System.Web.UI;

namespace WebFormMobile
{
    public partial class _Default : Page
    {
        protected void Page_PreInit(object sender, EventArgs e)
        {
            if (Request.Browser.IsMobileDevice)
                MasterPageFile = "~/MobileSite.Master";
        }

        protected void Page_Load(object sender, EventArgs e)
        {

        }
    }
}
```

Executing the application and viewing it in a mobile browser produces the results shown in Figure 27-5.

Creating Mobile Web Forms

You may have a need for more changes than modifying the master page can provide. For example, you may need to more dramatically alter the content that is provided to a mobile browser. If that is the case, you can provide a parallel set of pages that are designed specifically for viewing in mobile browsers. Although this does introduce some duplication of code, it also supplies a dedicated set of pages that only mobile browsers can target. For each standard page in the application that would be available to a mobile browser, you build a mobile-specific version. To do this, create a folder at the root of the application named `Mobile`. Then create a new Web Form in this folder named `Default.aspx`. This Web Form will be the mobile-specific version of the standard default web form located in the root folder. To keep the example fairly manageable, you won't include any styles or scripts, just some simple content. The content for the C# version of the new `Default.aspx` file is shown in Listing 27-6 (file /Mobile/Default.aspx in the code download for this chapter).

FIGURE 27-5

LISTING 27-6: Mobile-specific Default.aspx

```aspnet
<%@ Page Language="C#" MasterPageFile="~/MobileSite.Master" AutoEventWireup="true"
    CodeBehind="Default.aspx.cs" Inherits="WebFormMobile.Mobile.Default" %>

<asp:Content runat="server" ID="FeaturedContent"
    ContentPlaceHolderID="FeaturedContent">
    <p>
        Welcome to the Mobile version of the site!
    </p>
</asp:Content>

<asp:Content runat="server" ID="BodyContent" ContentPlaceHolderID="MainContent">
    <p>
        This is a mobile version of the site!
    </p>
</asp:Content>
```

If you replicate all the standard web forms including their relative folders in the `Mobile` folder you created, it makes redirecting mobile browsers much easier. You only have to redirect the first request for a standard web form to the equivalent web form in the `Mobile` folder. Subsequent requests utilize relative paths in the `Mobile` folder and do not need further redirection. Additionally, if you want to give the users the capability to switch to the standard desktop version of the application on their mobile browser, you simply provide a link back to the standard version of the web form. Again, relative paths keep subsequent requests all in the standard web form folder structure.

The initial redirect for a mobile browser to the `Mobile` folder structure can occur upon the start of the browsing session. Add a handler for the `Session_Start` event in the `Global.asax.cs` or `Global.asax.vb` file depending on the application language. Listing 27-7 shows the code for the `Session_Start` handler. You can find the code for this listing in code file Global.asax.cs and Global.asax.vb located in the root of the WebFormsMobileCS or WebFormsMobileVB projects in the code download for this chapter.

LISTING 27-7: Session_Start handler in the Global.asax file

VB

```vb
Sub Session_Start(sender As Object, e As EventArgs)
    Dim httpRequest As HttpRequest = HttpContext.Current.Request
    If httpRequest.Browser.IsMobileDevice Then
        Dim path As String = httpRequest.Url.PathAndQuery
        Dim isOnMobilePage As Boolean = path.StartsWith("/Mobile/",
            StringComparison.OrdinalIgnoreCase)
        If Not isOnMobilePage Then
            Dim redirectTo As String = "~/Mobile/"
            HttpContext.Current.Response.Redirect(redirectTo)
        End If
    End If
End Sub
```

C#

```csharp
void Session_Start(object sender, EventArgs e)
{
    HttpRequest httpRequest = HttpContext.Current.Request;
    if (httpRequest.Browser.IsMobileDevice)
    {
        string path = httpRequest.Url.PathAndQuery;
        bool isOnMobilePage = path.StartsWith("/Mobile/",
                            StringComparison.OrdinalIgnoreCase);
        if (!isOnMobilePage)
        {
            string redirectTo = "~/Mobile/";

            HttpContext.Current.Response.Redirect(redirectTo);
        }
    }
}
```

If you execute the application and browse to the root of the site you will see the new default page in the `Mobile` folder instead of the standard default page. Figure 27-6 shows the mobile browser being forwarded to the mobile-specific default page.

FIGURE 27-6

Friendly URLs in ASP.NET Web Forms

Routing in ASP.NET Web Applications provides a way to give the user a URL that is easier to remember and understand. However creating routes and managing route tables can take some time to understand. A new ASP.NET feature called FriendlyUrls makes routing easier and URLs cleaner.

FriendlyUrls is included in the Visual Studio 2012.2 update. But it is also available for C# projects as a NuGet package. The name of the NuGet package is `Microsoft.AspNet.FriendlyUrls`. To install the NuGet package in our WebFormsMobileCS project, you can use the NuGet Package Manager, which is installed by default in Visual Studio 2012. Open the Package Manager Console by clicking on Tools ⇨ Library Package Manager ⇨ Package Manager Console from the Visual Studio menu. At the console prompt, run the command:

```
Install-Package Microsoft.AspNet.FriendlyUrls
```

When you install the FriendlyUrls NuGet package, a `RouteConfig.cs` file will be added to the `App_Start` folder in the root of the Web application. You will need to add one line of code to the `Application_Start` handler in the `Global.asax` file located in the root of the web application. Add the following line to the `Application_Start` handler:

```
RouteConfig.RegisterRoutes(RouteTable.Routes);
```

Now if you execute the application, you can browse to any `.aspx` page without specifying the extension. For example, in order to browse to the `Contact.aspx` page, you can simply specify `Contact` in the URL without the extension and FriendlyUrls will look for a file called `Contact.aspx`. Figure 27-7 shows the `Contact.aspx` page rendered in a mobile browser by only specifying `Contact` in the URL.

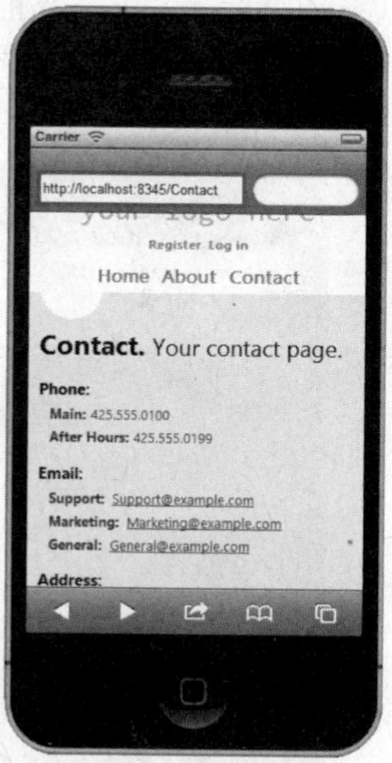

Using the `FriendlyUrlSettings` object, you can also instruct ASP.NET to automatically strip the extensions from pages in the URL. When you are working with an existing project like the WebFormsMobileCS project, you don't want to have to go through every Web Form in the project and modify every link and URL to remove the `.aspx` extension. You can have ASP.NET FriendlyUrls do it for you. Open the `RouteConfig.cs` file in the App_Start folder. This is the file that was added by the FriendlyUrls Nuget package. Change

FIGURE 27-7

```
routes.EnableFriendlyUrls();
```
to
```
FriendlyUrlSettings settings = new FriendlyUrlSettings();
         settings.AutoRedirectMode = RedirectMode.Permanent;
       routes.EnableFriendlyUrls(settings);
```

After making this change, execute the application and browse to the `Contact.aspx` Web Form. ASP.NET turns the GET request for /`Contact.aspx` into a 301 redirect to /`Contact`.

ASP.NET MVC 4 MOBILE APPLICATIONS

ASP.NET MVC (MVC) is a framework for building standards-based web applications that are easily scalable and testable. It uses the well-established Model-View-Controller design pattern. In MVC 3, a set of features were introduced to make mobile web development easier. Even with these features, it is increasingly difficult to provide a consistent experience on so many different mobile browsers and platforms. MVC 4 enhances and adds to the features originally introduced in version 3. These additions aim to make it even easier to develop a consistent mobile experience across more devices and browsers.

Adaptive Rendering in ASP.NET MVC 4

The Visual Studio project templates in version 4 of the MVC framework include many changes from version 3, not the least of which is the overall visual design. Even if you are going to use the design that the new templates offer, the more interesting change is the inclusion elements that provide adaptive rendering. The use of the viewport meta tag and CSS Media Queries allow these new templates to provide better scaling of your pages and a modified layout for smaller screen sizes. Figure 27-8 shows the default MVC 3 template in a mobile browser and Figure 27-9 shows the default MVC 4 template in a mobile browser. Ignoring the fact that the template design is different, the scaling difference in the two templates is obvious. The MVC 3 template attempts to render the page as though it were in a desktop browser scaled to the size of the Windows Phone screen. The MVC 4 template uses adaptive rendering to render the page at a scale more appropriate for the screen size. What you can't see from these two figures is that the MVC 4 template also modifies the page layout to better present the page material on a smaller screen.

FIGURE 27-8

FIGURE 27-9

To see the new adaptive rendering elements provided in these new templates, you can create an MVC project. Begin by creating a new project in Visual Studio called MvcMobile. Select .NET 4.5 Framework as the target framework and the ASP.NET MVC 4 Web Application project type. Due to the number of templates available when creating a new MVC Web Application, this is a two-step process. Selecting an ASP.NET MVC 4 Web Application doesn't immediately create the web application. You must select the particular type of MVC 4 application template you would like to use. After you select the ASP.NET MVC 4 Web Application, a template selection dialog box is displayed. Select the Internet Application template. Figure 27-10 shows the New ASP.NET MVC 4 Project dialog box with the correct selections made.

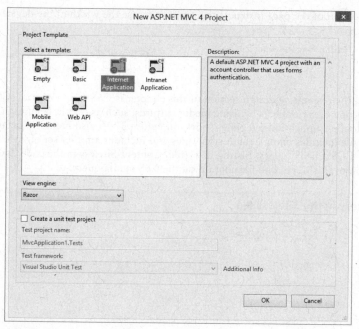

FIGURE 27-10

Working with Viewport Meta Tags

If you read the earlier section of this chapter on responsive design, you will be familiar with the viewport meta tag used to instruct the browser to take into account the physical size of the browser viewing area when displaying a web page. The Internet, Intranet, and Mobile Application templates shown in Figure 27-10 include a default Layout file. The Layout file already contains the viewport Meta tag. Listing 27-8 shows part of the C# version of the layout file that is included in the project when using the Internet Application template. The layout file is located in the \Views\Shared folder off of the root of the project. You can find the code for this listing in files _Layout.cshtml and _Layout.vbhtml in the code download for this chapter.

LISTING 27-8: The default Layout file in an MVC 4 application

```
<!DOCTYPE html>
<html lang="en">
    <head>
        <meta charset="utf-8" />
        <title>@ViewBag.Title - My ASP.NET MVC Application</title>
        <link href="~/favicon.ico" rel="shortcut icon" type="image/x-icon" />
        <meta name="viewport" content="width=device-width" />
        @Styles.Render("~/Content/css")
        @Scripts.Render("~/bundles/modernizr")
    </head>
    <body>
        <header>
            <div class="content-wrapper">
                <div class="float-left">
                    <p class="site-title">
                    @Html.ActionLink("your logo here", "Index" "Home")
                    </p>
                </div>
```

The viewport meta tag in the head section of the page instructs the browser to use the width of the device screen as the page layout width:

```
<meta name="viewport" content="width=device-width" />
```

Working with CSS Media Queries

One of the other concepts covered in the responsive design section of this chapter is CSS media queries. CSS media queries are used to limit the scope of style sheets by using media features, such as width, height, and color. The Internet, Intranet, and Mobile Application templates shown in Figure 27-10 also include a default CSS file named `Site.css`. The CSS file includes many default style rules and includes another set of style rules that are filtered, or limited, by a CSS media query. Listing 27-9 (file \Content\Site.css in the code download for this chapter) shows a portion of this `Site.css` file containing the CSS media query.

LISTING 27-9: The CSS media query in the Site.css file

```
/*********************
 *   Mobile Styles   *
 *********************/
@media only screen and (max-width: 850px) {

    /* header
    ---------------------------------------------------------*/
    header .float-left,
    header .float-right {
        float: none;
    }

    /* logo */
    header .site-title {
        margin: 10px;
        text-align: center;
    }
}
```

You use a CSS media query to provide a set of style rules that alter the layout of the page based on the width of the browser screen. The media query dictates that the style rules included in the Mobile Styles section of the CSS file are not used unless the media type is `only screen` and the width is less than or equal to 850px:

```
@media only screen and (max-width: 850px)
```

Creating Mobile-Specific Views

Adaptive rendering enables you to modify the scaling and layout of CSS-styled elements on a page when it is viewed in various conditions, including smaller screens. However, you may want a more radical change to a page when it is viewed in a mobile browser. To do this, you provide one view for use by non-mobile browsers and one for use by mobile browsers only. Prior to MVC 4, you had to use browser-sniffing and ViewEngine overrides to determine which view to serve to the browser.

MVC 4 provides new functionality to enable you to override views served to mobile devices using a convention over configuration approach. This functionality is available to all views including Layouts. To provide a mobile-specific version of a view, you simply create a file using the naming convention `[viewname].mobile.cshtml` or `[viewname].mobile.vbhtml`. When ASP.NET MVC 4 services a request from a mobile browser, it first looks for a file following this alternate mobile naming convention. If it does not find one, it falls back to the standard view.

To build a mobile view, you can create a new view in the `Views/Home` folder by right-clicking the folder and choosing Add ➪ View. Name the view `Index.mobile`. Now you can create content in the view that is displayed only when the page is requested from a mobile browser. The `Index.mobile` view is presented in Listing 27-10 (files Views/Home/Index.mobile.cshtml and Views/Home/Index.mobile.vbhtml in the code download for this chapter).

LISTING 27-10: The Index mobile view

VB

```
@Code
    ViewData("Title") = "Index.mobile"
End Code

<h2>Index Mobile View</h2>
This page is being viewed in a mobile browser
```

C#

```
@{
    ViewBag.Title = "Index Mobile";
}

<h2>Index Mobile View</h2>
This page is being viewed in a mobile browser
```

Running the application and viewing it in a mobile browser displays the content from the mobile version of the Index view, whereas viewing the application in a desktop browser displays the content from the standard Index view. Figure 27-11 shows the Index view displayed in a desktop browser. Figure 27-12 shows the same view in a mobile browser. You can see that both browsers are pointed to the same URL, but the displayed content is different.

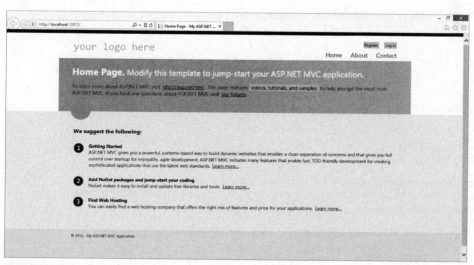

FIGURE 27-11

Providing Display Modes

Using mobile-specific views, you can provide specific views and layouts for use when any mobile browser makes a request. But you may need another level of customization such as providing a specific view to a particular browser or device. For example, if someone using an iPhone or an iPad views your site, you may want to provide a view that is styled more like a native application on that device.

If you have been building applications for the web for any length of time, you have probably had to write styles or script to make something work in a particular browser. If so, you know how painful it is to target multiple specific browsers or platforms in a single page. ASP.NET MVC 4 introduces a new feature called Display Modes, which makes targeting a specific browser or platform easier. And, like many new features in MVC 4, it uses a convention over configuration approach.

Creating a new display mode involves using a particular naming convention for your views and browser sniffing for particular trigger conditions. To see this in action, create a particular view that displays when an iPhone browses the site. To do so, create a new view in the `Views\Home` folder and name the view `Index.iphone`. Then create content in the view that displays only when the page is requested from an iPhone. The `Index.iphone` view is presented in Listing 27-11 (files Views\Home\Index.iphone.cshtml and Views\Home\Index.iphone.vbhtml in the code download for this chapter).

FIGURE 27-12

LISTING 27-11: The Index view for an iPhone

VB

```
@Code
    ViewData("Title") = "Index.iphone"
End Code

<h2>Index iPhone View</h2>
This page is being viewed on an iPhone
```

C#

```
@{
    ViewBag.Title = "Index iPhone";
}

<h2>Index iPhone View</h2>
This page is being viewed on an iPhone
```

Now, you need to register a display mode for the `iphone` suffix. You need to register the display mode only once, so you typically do this in the `Global.asax` in the `Application_Start` event handler. In the `Global.asax` file, include a reference to the `System.Web.WebPages` namespace:

VB

```
Imports System.Web.WebPages
```

C#

```
using System.Web.WebPages;
```

Now you need to register the display mode with the `DisplayModeProvider`. In the case of the iPhone, you want to specify that the condition for the display mode is that the user agent contains the word "iPhone." Listing 27-12 shows the `Global.asax` file after adding the display mode registration. You can find the code in files Global.asax.cs and Global.asax.vb in the root of the MvcMobileCS and MvcMobileVB projects in the code download for this chapter.

LISTING 27-12: Global.asax file showing the Display Mode registration

VB

```vb
' Note: For instructions on enabling IIS6 or IIS7 classic mode,
' visit http://go.microsoft.com/?LinkId=9394802
Imports System.Web.Http
Imports System.Web.Optimization
Imports System.Web.WebPages

Public Class MvcApplication
    Inherits System.Web.HttpApplication

    Sub Application_Start()
        AreaRegistration.RegisterAllAreas()

        WebApiConfig.Register(GlobalConfiguration.Configuration)
        FilterConfig.RegisterGlobalFilters(GlobalFilters.Filters)
        RouteConfig.RegisterRoutes(RouteTable.Routes)
        BundleConfig.RegisterBundles(BundleTable.Bundles)
        AuthConfig.RegisterAuth()

        DisplayModeProvider.Instance.Modes.Insert(0, _
            New DefaultDisplayMode("iphone")
            With {.ContextCondition = Function(context As HttpContextBase)
            context.GetOverriddenUserAgent().IndexOf("iPhone",
            StringComparison.OrdinalIgnoreCase) >= 0})

    End Sub
End Class
```

C#

```csharp
using System;
using System.Web.Http;
using System.Web.Mvc;
using System.Web.Optimization;
using System.Web.Routing;
using System.Web.WebPages;

namespace MvcMobile
{
    // Note: For instructions on enabling IIS6 or IIS7 classic mode,
    // visit http://go.microsoft.com/?LinkId=9394801

    public class MvcApplication : System.Web.HttpApplication
    {
        protected void Application_Start()
        {
            AreaRegistration.RegisterAllAreas();

            WebApiConfig.Register(GlobalConfiguration.Configuration);
            FilterConfig.RegisterGlobalFilters(GlobalFilters.Filters);
```

continues

LISTING 27-12 *(continued)*

```
        RouteConfig.RegisterRoutes(RouteTable.Routes);
        BundleConfig.RegisterBundles(BundleTable.Bundles);
        AuthConfig.RegisterAuth();

        DisplayModeProvider.Instance.Modes.Insert(0, new
            DefaultDisplayMode("iphone")
        {
            ContextCondition = (context =>
              context.GetOverriddenUserAgent().IndexOf
              ("iPhone", StringComparison.OrdinalIgnoreCase) >= 0)
        });
    }
  }
}
```

The new display mode is inserted at the top of the Modes collection:

```
DisplayModeProvider.Instance.Modes.Insert
```

The new display mode is also given a name. In this case, it is called "iphone":

```
new DefaultDisplayMode("iphone")
```

The name of the display mode is what you use as the suffix of the view naming convention Index.iphone. You could have used whatever name you'd liked here. Just make sure that the name of the display mode matches the suffix used in the name of the view.

Finally, you specify the condition that must be met to invoke the display mode. In this case, the word "iPhone" must exist in the user agent string:

```
context.GetOverriddenUserAgent()
    .IndexOf("iPhone", StringComparison.OrdinalIgnoreCase) >= 0)
```

> **NOTE** *Note that you use the* GetOverriddenUserAgent *method to get the user agent string.* GetOverriddenUserAgent *returns the overridden user agent value or the actual user agent string if no override has been specified. The technique of overriding the user agent string is often used to provide users with the capability to see the desktop view of a page even though they are using a mobile device.*

Now when viewing the page using an iPhone, you will see the iPhone version of the page specified by the iPhone-specific view. Figure 27-13 shows the Index view as seen on an iPhone.

Including jQuery Mobile and the ViewSwitcher

Once you begin to develop views that are designed specifically for mobile browsers, you may want to include mobile-specific functionality and client libraries in those views. One of the common mobile JavaScript libraries is jQuery Mobile. jQuery Mobile is an open source library for building UIs for mobile devices based on jQuery Core. Although ASP.NET MVC 4 includes many features to aid with mobile web application development, the ASP.NET MVC project templates don't include jQuery Mobile by default (with the exception of the Mobile Application project template).

If you want to install jQuery Mobile in your project, you can do so using NuGet. There is a NuGet package for installing jQuery Mobile in an ASP.NET MVC project. The NuGet Package Manager is installed by default in Visual Studio 2012. Open the Package Manager Console by clicking Tools ⇨ Library Package Manager ⇨ Package Manager Console from the Visual Studio menu. At the console prompt, run the command `Install-Package jQuery.Mobile.MVC`.

The `jQuery.Mobile.MVC` Nuget package adds a handful of files to the project, including the CSS and JavaScript files needed for jQuery Mobile. It also adds a mobile-specific Layout named `_Layout.Mobile.cshtml` or `_Layout.Mobile.vbhtml` depending on your choice of language. This mobile-specific Layout includes references to the added CSS and JavaScript files as bundles. To create these bundles, you need to include a line of code in the `Global.asax` file. A readme file is included with the Nuget package that provides the line of code. You must add the line of code to the `Application_Start` handler. Listing 27-13 provides the `Application_Start` handler after adding the necessary line of code (shown in bold). You can find the code for this listing in files Global.asax.cs and Global.asax.vb located in the root of the MvcMobileCS or MvcMobileVB projects in the code download for this chapter.

FIGURE 27-13

LISTING 27-13: Application_Start with necessary jQuery Mobile bundle

VB

```vb
Sub Application_Start()
    AreaRegistration.RegisterAllAreas()

    WebApiConfig.Register(GlobalConfiguration.Configuration)
    FilterConfig.RegisterGlobalFilters(GlobalFilters.Filters)
    RouteConfig.RegisterRoutes(RouteTable.Routes)
    BundleConfig.RegisterBundles(BundleTable.Bundles)
    AuthConfig.RegisterAuth()

    DisplayModeProvider.Instance.Modes.Insert(0, _
        New DefaultDisplayMode("iphone")
        With {.ContextCondition = Function(context As HttpContextBase)
        context.GetOverriddenUserAgent().IndexOf("iPhone",
        StringComparison.OrdinalIgnoreCase) >= 0})

    BundleMobileConfig.RegisterBundles(BundleTable.Bundles)
End Sub
```

C#

```csharp
protected void Application_Start()
{
    AreaRegistration.RegisterAllAreas();

    WebApiConfig.Register(GlobalConfiguration.Configuration);
    FilterConfig.RegisterGlobalFilters(GlobalFilters.Filters);
    RouteConfig.RegisterRoutes(RouteTable.Routes);
    BundleConfig.RegisterBundles(BundleTable.Bundles);
    AuthConfig.RegisterAuth();

    DisplayModeProvider.Instance.Modes.Insert(0, new
        DefaultDisplayMode("iphone")
    {
```

continues

LISTING 27-13 *(continued)*

```
                ContextCondition = (context =>
                  context.GetOverriddenUserAgent().IndexOf
                  ("iPhone", StringComparison.OrdinalIgnoreCase) >= 0)
          });

          BundleMobileConfig.RegisterBundles(BundleTable.Bundles);
      }
```

Besides the files that support jQuery Mobile, the Nuget package also adds a controller and partial view for a ViewSwitcher. The ViewSwitcher allows a user to switch between the mobile browser view and the standard desktop browser view. You may have seen other mobile websites that provide a way to view the desktop version of the site on a mobile device. That is what the ViewSwitcher does for you. The ViewSwitcher partial view is included in the mobile Layout file:

```
@Html.Partial("_ViewSwitcher")
```

The ViewSwitcher partial view renders a link that allows the user to switch to the desktop view of your application. If you want your users to be able to switch back to the mobile view, you can add this partial view to your standard Layout file as well. Listing 27-14 (code files Views\Shared_ViewSwitcher.cshtml and Views\Shared_ViewSwitcher.vbhtml) shows the ViewSwitcher partial view.

LISTING 27-14: ViewSwitcher partial view

VB

```
@If Request.Browser.IsMobileDevice And Request.HttpMethod = "GET" Then
    @:<div class="view-switcher ui-bar-a">
        @If ViewContext.HttpContext.GetOverriddenBrowser().IsMobileDevice Then
            @: Displaying mobile view
            @Html.ActionLink("Desktop view", "SwitchView", "ViewSwitcher", New With
                {.mobile = False, .returnUrl = Request.Url.PathAndQuery}, New With
                {.rel = "external"})
        Else
            @: Displaying desktop view
            @Html.ActionLink("Mobile view", "SwitchView", "ViewSwitcher", New With
                {.mobile = True, .returnUrl = Request.Url.PathAndQuery}, New With
                {.rel = "external"})
        End If
    @:</div>
End If
```

C#

```
@if (Request.Browser.IsMobileDevice && Request.HttpMethod == "GET")
{
    <div class="view-switcher ui-bar-a">
        @if (ViewContext.HttpContext.GetOverriddenBrowser().IsMobileDevice)
        {
            @: Displaying mobile view
            @Html.ActionLink("Desktop view", "SwitchView", "ViewSwitcher", new {
                mobile = false, returnUrl = Request.Url.PathAndQuery }, new { rel =
                "external" })
        }
        else
        {
            @: Displaying desktop view
            @Html.ActionLink("Mobile view", "SwitchView", "ViewSwitcher",
```

```
                    new { mobile= true,
                    returnUrl = Request.Url.PathAndQuery },
                    new { rel = "external"
                    })
            }
        </div>
    }
```

The ViewSwitcher is visible only if the request is coming from a mobile browser:

```
@if (Request.Browser.IsMobileDevice && Request.HttpMethod == "GET")
```

If the request is coming from a mobile browser, the GetOverriddenBrowser method is called to determine if the browser type has been overridden. Based on the response, a link is displayed to switch the view between the mobile and standard views:

```
@if (ViewContext.HttpContext.GetOverriddenBrowser().IsMobileDevice)
```

The ActionLinks reference the SwitchView action of the ViewSwitcher controller that was added by the jQuery.Mobile.MVC Nuget package. Listing 27-15 (files Controllers\ViewSwitcherController.cs and Controllers\ViewSwitcherController.vb in the code download for this chapter) shows the ViewSwitcher controller.

LISTING 27-15: ViewSwitcher controller

VB

```vb
Imports System.Web.WebPages

Namespace MvcMobileVB
    Public Class ViewSwitcherController
        Inherits System.Web.Mvc.Controller

        Public Function SwitchView(mobile As Boolean, returnUrl As String) As
            RedirectResult
            If Request.Browser.IsMobileDevice = mobile Then
                HttpContext.ClearOverriddenBrowser()
            Else
                HttpContext.SetOverriddenBrowser(DirectCast(IIf(mobile,
                    BrowserOverride.Mobile, BrowserOverride.Desktop),
                    BrowserOverride))
            End If
            Return Redirect(returnUrl)
        End Function

    End Class
End Namespace
```

C#

```csharp
using System.Web.Mvc;
using System.Web.WebPages;

namespace MvcMobile.Controllers
{
    public class ViewSwitcherController : Controller
    {
        public RedirectResult SwitchView(bool mobile, string returnUrl) {
            if (Request.Browser.IsMobileDevice == mobile)
                HttpContext.ClearOverriddenBrowser();
            else
                HttpContext.SetOverriddenBrowser(mobile ? BrowserOverride.Mobile :
```

continues

LISTING 27-15 *(continued)*

```
                    BrowserOverride.Desktop);

            return Redirect(returnUrl);
        }
    }
}
```

Figure 27-14 shows the application viewed in a mobile browser after the addition of the `jQuery.Mobile.MVC` Nuget package.

Using the Mobile Application Project Template

So far all the MVC 4 features presented involve supporting both desktop and mobile browsers in one way or another. What if you just want to build a purely mobile web application? What if you are not interested in having to provide a desktop browsing experience? ASP.NET MVC 4 provides a project template that is targeted directly at mobile devices—vvthe Mobile Application project template. You can see the Mobile Application project template in the New ASP.NET MVC 4 Project dialog box, shown in Figure 27-10.

When you create a project with the Mobile Application project template, you'll notice that the overall structure of the project is the same as the other project templates. You still have the same views, controllers, and models. If you look at the content of the views, though, you'll see that they are built specifically for mobile browsers. jQuery Mobile is included by default and is implemented in all the views. All the default page elements are designed specifically for mobile devices specifying the `data-` attributes used by jQuery Mobile. Figure 27-15 shows an application built using the Mobile Application project template viewed in a mobile browser.

FIGURE 27-14

TESTING YOUR MOBILE APPLICATIONS

It is possible to test some aspects of a mobile website by browsing it on a desktop and decreasing the size of the browser window. However, to truly test a mobile website, you need to view it on a mobile device. Unless you have one of each device you want to test on, you will need to find other ways to test your mobile site. Two of the more common ways to test without an actual device are with browsers that let you change the HTTP Header information and emulators.

Browsers, such as Mozilla Firefox and Google Chrome, have multiple extensions available that you can use to modify HTTP Header information in a request. By modifying this information in a browser request, you can trick a web server into thinking the request is coming from a mobile device.

The other way to test a mobile site is with an emulator for the particular device you are trying to test on. You can install the Windows Phone emulator by installing the Windows Phone SDK. As of this writing, the Windows Phone 8 SDK requires Hyper-V and a 64-bit version of Windows 8 Pro. If you don't have hardware to support running the Windows Phone 8 emulator, you can still install the Windows Phone SDK 7.1. Although it is not the latest version of the emulator, it still enables you to test your site on IE9 running on Windows Phone 7 or 7.5.

FIGURE 27-15

Two other popular devices used for testing mobile websites are Apple's iPhone and iPad devices. Electric Plum offers an iPhone and iPad simulator as part of its Electric Mobile Studio. It has partnered with Microsoft to provide the iPhone and iPad simulators as extensions to version 2 of WebMatrix, a free lightweight web development tool developed by Microsoft. The simulators are also available as a Visual Studio 2012 extension. By installing the Electric Mobile Studio extension in Visual Studio 2012, the iPad and iPhone simulators become available in the "Browse With..." option of Visual Studio. Figure 27-16 shows the "Browse With..." drop-down, which displays after you install the Electric Mobile Studio extension.

FIGURE 27-16

SUMMARY

Developers have been building mobile websites since the late 1990s. But as the popularity and use of mobile devices continues to increase, the demand for sites that are compatible with mobile devices is also increasing.

Despite the amount of time developers have been building mobile websites, the challenges remain the same. Building a mobile website requires different design decisions and considerations. Plenty of options are available, ranging from adaptive design of a single website to parallel websites or pages targeted directly at mobile devices.

Tools like Visual Studio 2012 and features like those available in the latest version of ASP.NET MVC make the task of developing mobile sites much easier. Testing these mobile sites has also become easier through the use of browser extensions, emulators, and simulators.

You no longer have any excuse to avoid building sites designed to be viewed on both a desktop and a mobile device.

PART VIII
Application Configuration and Deployment

28

Configuration

WROX.COM CODE DOWNLOADS FOR THIS CHAPTER

Please note that all the code examples in this chapter are available as a part of this chapter's code download on the book's website at www.wrox.com on the Download Code tab.

ASP.NET uses an XML file-based configuration system that is flexible, accessible, and easy to use. The XML configuration file allows an administrator, the person who takes care of the web applications after they are built and deployed, to configure ASP.NET applications quite easily by working either directly with the various configuration files or by using GUI tools that, in turn, interact with configuration files. Before examining the various GUI-based tools in detail in Appendix D, this chapter will first take an in-depth look at how to work directly with the XML configuration files to change the behavior of your ASP.NET applications.

The journey examining ASP.NET configuration in depth starts with an overview of configuration in ASP.NET.

CONFIGURATION OVERVIEW

ASP.NET configuration is stored in two primary XML-based files in a hierarchal fashion. XML is used to describe the properties and behaviors of various aspects of ASP.NET applications.

The ASP.NET configuration system supports two kinds of configuration files:

➤ Server or machine-wide configuration files such as the `machine.config` file

➤ Application configuration files such as the `web.config` file

Because the configuration files are based upon XML, the elements that describe the configuration are, therefore, case-sensitive. Moreover, the ASP.NET configuration system follows camel-casing naming conventions. If you look at the session state configuration example shown in Listing 28-1, for example, you can see that the XML element that deals with session state is presented as `<sessionState>`.

LISTING 28-1: Session state configuration

```xml
<?xml version="1.0" encoding="UTF-8" ?>
<configuration>
<system.web>
    <sessionState
        mode="InProc"
        stateConnectionString="tcpip=127.0.0.1:42424"
        stateNetworkTimeout="10"
        sqlConnectionString="data source=127.0.0.1; user id=sa; password=P@55worD"
        cookieless="false"
        timeout="20" />
    </system.web>
</configuration>
```

The benefits of having an XML configuration file instead of a binary metabase include the following:

➤ The configuration information is human-readable and can be modified using a plaintext editor such as Notepad, although using Visual Studio 2012 or another XML-aware editor is recommended. Unlike a binary metabase, the XML-based configuration file can be easily copied from one server to another, as with any simple file. This feature is extremely helpful when working in a web farm scenario.

➤ When some settings are changed in the configuration file, ASP.NET automatically detects the changes and applies them to the running ASP.NET application. ASP.NET accomplishes this by creating a new instance of the ASP.NET application instance and sending all future requests by end users to this new application instance.

➤ The configuration changes are applied to the ASP.NET application without the need for the administrator to stop and start the web server. Changes are completely transparent to the end user.

➤ The ASP.NET configuration system is extensible.

➤ Application-specific information can be stored and retrieved very easily.

➤ The sensitive information stored in the ASP.NET configuration system can optionally be encrypted to keep it from prying eyes.

Server Configuration Files

Every ASP.NET server installation includes a series of configuration files, such as the `machine.config` file. This file is installed as a part of the default .NET Framework installation. You can find `machine.config` and the other server-specific configuration files in `C:\Windows\Microsoft.NET\Framework\v4.0.30319\CONFIG`. They represent the default settings used by all ASP.NET web applications installed on the server.

Some of the server-wide configuration files include the following:

➤ `legacy.web_hightrust.config`

➤ `legacy.web_hightrust.config.default`

➤ `legacy.web_lowtrust.config`

➤ `legacy.web_lowtrust.config.default`

➤ `legacy.web_mediumtrust.config`

➤ `legacy.web_mediumtrust.config.default`

➤ `legacy.web_minimaltrust.config`

➤ `legacy.web_minimaltrust.config.default`

➤ `machine.config`

➤ `machine.config.comments`

➤ `machine.config.default`

➤ `web.config`

➤ `web.config.comments`

➤ `web.config.default`

➤ `web_hightrust.config`

➤ `web_hightrust.config.default`

➤ `web_lowtrust.config`

➤ `web_lowtrust.config.default`

➤ `web_mediumtrust.config`

➤ `web_mediumtrust.config.default`

➤ `web_minimaltrust.config`

➤ `web_minimaltrust.config.default`

The system-wide configuration file, `machine.config`, is used to configure common .NET Framework settings for all applications on the machine. As a rule, editing or manipulating the `machine.config` file is not a good idea unless you know what you are doing. Changes to this file can affect all applications on your computer (Windows, web, and so on).

> **NOTE** *Because the .NET Framework supports side-by-side execution mode, you might find more than one installation of the* `machine.config` *file if you have multiple versions of the .NET Framework installed on the server. If you have .NET Framework versions 1.0, 1.1, 2.0, and 4 running on the server, for example, each .NET Framework installation has its own* `machine.config` *file. This means that you will find four* `machine.config` *file installations on that particular server. It is interesting to note that the .NET Framework 3 and 3.5 are actually more of a bolt-on to the .NET Framework 2.0. (It includes extra DLLs, which are sometimes referred to as extensions.) Thus, the .NET Framework 3 and 3.5 use the same* `machine.config` *file as the .NET Framework 2.0. It is important to note that the .NET Framework 4 is a completely new CLR and doesn't have the same 2.0 dependency that the .NET Framework 3 or 3.5 does. The .NET 4 version of the framework includes its own* `machine.config` *file. .NET Framework 4.5 is different as it's more of an enhancement to .NET Framework 4. The original .NET Framework 4 libraries are replaced by .NET Framework 4.5.*

In addition to the `machine.config` file, the .NET Framework installer also installs two more files called `machine.config.default` and `machine.config.comments`. The `machine.config.default` file acts as a backup for the `machine.config` file. If you want to revert to the factory setting for `machine.config`, simply copy the settings from the `machine.config.default` to the `machine.config` file.

The machine.config.comments file contains a description for each configuration section and explicit settings for the most commonly used values. The machine.config.default and machine.config.comments files are not used by the .NET Framework run time; they're installed in case you want to revert to default factory settings and default values.

You will also find a root-level web.config file in place within the same CONFIG folder as the machine.config. When making changes to settings on a server-wide basis, you should always attempt to make these changes in the root web.config file rather than in the machine.config file. You will find that files like the machine.config.comments and the machine.config.default files also exist for the web.config files (web.config.comments and web.config.default).

By default, your ASP.NET web applications run under a *full trust* setting. You can see this setting by looking at the <securityPolicy> and <trust> sections in the root-level web.config file. Listing 28-2 presents these sections.

LISTING 28-2: The root web.config file showing the trust level

```
<configuration>
    <location allowOverride="true">
        <system.web>
            <securityPolicy>
                <trustLevel name="Full" policyFile="internal" />
                <trustLevel name="High" policyFile="web_hightrust.config" />
                <trustLevel name="Medium" policyFile="web_mediumtrust.config" />
                <trustLevel name="Low"  policyFile="web_lowtrust.config" />
                <trustLevel name="Minimal" policyFile="web_minimaltrust.config" />
            </securityPolicy>
            <trust level="Full" originUrl="" />
        </system.web>
    </location>
</configuration>
```

The other policy files are defined at specific trust levels. These levels determine the code-access security (CAS) allowed for ASP.NET. To change the trust level in which ASP.NET applications can run on the server, you simply change the <trust> element within the document or within your application's instance of the web.config file. For example, you can change to a medium trust level using the code shown in Listing 28-3.

LISTING 28-3: Changing the trust level to medium trust

```
<configuration>
    <location allowOverride="false">
        <system.web>
            <securityPolicy>
                <trustLevel name="Full" policyFile="internal" />
                <trustLevel name="High" policyFile="web_hightrust.config" />
                <trustLevel name="Medium" policyFile="web_mediumtrust.config" />
                <trustLevel name="Low" policyFile="web_lowtrust.config" />
                <trustLevel name="Minimal" policyFile="web_minimaltrust.config" />
            </securityPolicy>
            <trust level="Medium" originUrl="" />
        </system.web>
    </location>
</configuration>
```

In this case, not only does this code mandate use of the web_mediumtrust.config file, but also (by setting the allowOverride attribute to false) it forces this trust level upon every ASP.NET application on the server. Individual application instances are unable to change this setting by overriding it in their local web.config files because this setting is in the root-level web.config file.

If you look through the various trust level configuration files (such as the `web_mediumtrust.config` file), notice that they define what kinds of actions you can perform through your code operations. For example, the `web_hightrust.config` file allows for open FileIO access to any point on the server as illustrated in Listing 28-4.

LISTING 28-4: The web_hightrust.config file's definition of FileIO CAS

```
<IPermission
    class="FileIOPermission"
    version="1"
    Unrestricted="true"
/>
```

If, however, you look at the medium trust `web.config` file (`web_mediumtrust.config`), you see that this configuration file restricts ASP.NET to *only* those FileIO operations within the application directory. Listing 28-5 presents this definition.

LISTING 28-5: FileIO restrictions in the web_mediumtrust.config file

```
<IPermission
    class="FileIOPermission"
    version="1"
    Read="\$AppDir\$"
    Write="\$AppDir\$"
    Append="\$AppDir\$"
    PathDiscovery="\$AppDir\$"
/>
```

Seeing in which trust level you can run your ASP.NET applications and changing the `<trust>` section to enable the appropriate level of CAS is always a good idea.

Application Configuration File

Unlike the `machine.config` file, nearly all ASP.NET applications have their own copy of configuration settings stored in a file called `web.config`. If the web application spans multiple subfolders, each subfolder can have its own `web.config` file that inherits or overrides the parent's file settings.

To update servers in your farm with these new settings, you simply copy this `web.config` file to the appropriate application directory. ASP.NET takes care of the rest — no server restarts and no local server access is required—and your application continues to function normally, except that it now uses the new settings applied in the configuration file.

Applying Configuration Settings

When the ASP.NET run time applies configuration settings for a given web request, `machine.config` (as well as any of the `web.config` files' configuration information) is merged into a single unit, and that information is then applied to the given application. Configuration settings are inherited from any parent `web.config` file or `machine.config`, which is the root configuration file or the ultimate parent. Figure 28-1 presents an example of this.

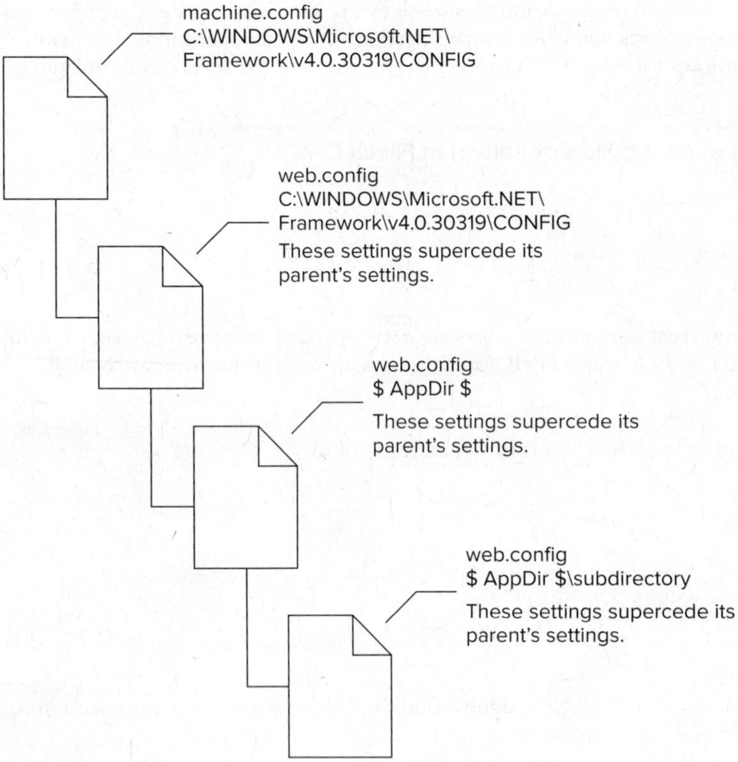

machine.config
C:\WINDOWS\Microsoft.NET\
Framework\v4.0.30319\CONFIG

web.config
C:\WINDOWS\Microsoft.NET\
Framework\v4.0.30319\CONFIG
These settings supercede its
parent's settings.

web.config
$ AppDir $
These settings supercede its
parent's settings.

web.config
$ AppDir $\subdirectory
These settings supercede its
parent's settings.

FIGURE 28-1

The configuration for each web application is unique; however, settings are inherited from the parent. For example, if the web.config file in the root of your website defines a session timeout of 10 minutes, then that particular setting overrides the default ASP.NET setting inherited from the machine.config or the root web.config file. The web.config files in the subdirectories or subfolders can override these settings or inherit the settings (such as the 10-minute session timeout).

> **NOTE** *The configuration settings for virtual directories are independent of the physical directory structure. Unless the manner in which the virtual directories are organized is exclusively specified, configuration problems can result.*

Note that these inheritance/override rules can be blocked in most cases by using the allowOverride="false" mechanism shown earlier in Listing 28-3.

Detecting Configuration File Changes

ASP.NET automatically detects when configuration files, such as machine.config or web.config, are changed. This logic is implemented based on listening for file-change notification events provided by the operating system.

When an ASP.NET application is started, the configuration settings are read and stored in the ASP.NET cache. A file dependency is then placed on the entry within the cache in the machine.config and/or web.config configuration file. When the configuration file update is detected in the machine.config,

ASP.NET creates a new application domain to service new requests. The old application domain is destroyed as soon as it completes servicing all its outstanding requests.

Configuration File Format

The main difference between `machine.config` and `web.config` is the filename. Other than that, their schemas are the same. Configuration files are divided into multiple groups. The root-level XML element in a configuration file is named `<configuration>`. This pseudo-`web.config` file has a section to control ASP.NET, as shown in Listing 28-6.

LISTING 28-6: A pseudo-web.config file

```
<?xml version="1.0" encoding="UTF-8"?>
<configuration>
    <configSections>
        <section name="[sectionSettings]" type="[Class]"/>
        <sectionGroup name="[sectionGroup]">
            <section name="[sectionSettings]" type="[Class]"/>
        </sectionGroup>
    </configSections>
</configuration>
```

> **NOTE** *Values within brackets [ ] have unique values within the real configuration file.*

The root element in the XML configuration file is always `<configuration>`. Each of the section handlers and settings are optionally wrapped in a `<sectionGroup>`. A `<sectionGroup>` provides an organizational function within the configuration file. It allows you to organize configuration into unique groups—for instance, the `<system.web>` section group is used to identify areas within the configuration file specific to ASP.NET.

The `<configSections>` section is the mechanism to group the configuration section handlers associated with each configuration section. When you want to create your own section handlers, you must declare them in the `<configSections>` section. The `<httpModules>` section has a configuration handler that is set to `System.Web.Caching.HttpModulesSection`, and the `<sessionState>` section has a configuration handler that is set to the `System.Web.SessionState.SessionStateSection` classes, as shown in Listing 28-7.

LISTING 28-7: HTTP module configuration setting from the machine.config file

```
<configSections>
    <sectionGroup>
        <section name="httpModules"
            type="System.Web.Configuration.HttpModulesSection,
            System.Web, Version=4.0.0.0, Culture=neutral,
            PublicKeyToken=b03f5f7f11d50a3a"/>
    </sectionGroup>
</configSections>
```

COMMON CONFIGURATION SETTINGS

The ASP.NET applications depend on a few common configuration settings. These settings are common to both the `web.config` and `machine.config` files. In this section, you look at some of these common configuration settings.

Connection Strings

In very early ASP.NET releases, all the connection string information was stored in the <appSettings> section. The latest versions of ASP.NET include a section called <connectionStrings> that stores a variety of connection-string information. Even though storing connection strings in the <appSettings> element works fine, it poses the following challenges:

➤ When connection strings are stored in the appSettings section, it is impossible for a data-aware control such as SqlCacheDependency or MembershipProvider to discover the information.

➤ Securing connection strings using cryptographic algorithms is a challenge.

➤ Last, but not least, this feature does not apply to ASP.NET only; rather, it applies to all the .NET application types including Windows Forms, web services, and so on.

Because the connection-string information is stored independently of the appSettings section, it can be retrieved using the strongly typed collection method ConnectionStrings. Listing 28-8 gives an example of how to store connection strings.

LISTING 28-8: Storing a connection string

```
<configuration>
    <connectionStrings>
        <add
            name="ExampleConnection"
            connectionString="server=401kServer;database=401kDB;
            uid=WebUser;pwd=P@$$worD9" />
    </connectionStrings>
</configuration>
```

Listing 28-9 shows how to retrieve the connection string (ExampleConnection) in your code.

LISTING 28-9: Retrieving a connection string

VB
```
Protected Sub Page_Load(sender As Object, e As EventArgs)
    . . .
    Dim dbConnection As New SqlConnection( _
        ConfigurationManager.ConnectionStrings("ExampleApplication") _
        .ConnectionString)
    . . .
End Sub
```

C#
```
protected void Page_Load(Object sender, EventArgs e)
{
    . . .
    SqlConnection dbConnection = new
        SqlConnection(ConfigurationManager.ConnectionStrings["ExampleApplication"]
        .ConnectionString);
    . . .
}
```

This type of construction has a lot of power. Instead of hard-coding your connection strings into every page within your ASP.NET application, you can store one instance of the connection string centrally (in the web .config file, for example). Now, if you have to make a change to this connection string, you can make this change in only *one* place rather than in multiple places.

Configuring Session State

Because web-based applications utilize the stateless HTTP protocol, you must store the application-specific state or user-specific state where it can persist. The `Session` object is the common store where user-specific information is persisted. Session store is implemented as a `Hashtable` and stores data based on key-value pair combinations.

ASP.NET has the capability to persist the session store data in `InProc`, `StateServer`, `SqlServer`, or `Custom`. The `Custom` setting gives the developer a lot more control regarding how the session state is persisted in a permanent store. For example, out-of-the-box ASP.NET does not support storing session data on non-Microsoft databases such as Oracle or NoSQL databases such as MongoDB. If you want to store the session data in any of these databases or in a custom store such as an XML file, you can implement that by writing a custom provider class. (See the section "Custom State Store" later in this chapter or Chapter 21 to learn more about the session state features in ASP.NET 4.5.)

You can configure the session information using the `<sessionState>` element presented in Listing 28-10.

LISTING 28-10: Configuring session state

```
<sessionState
 mode="StateServer"
 cookieless="false"
 timeout="20"
 stateConnectionString="tcpip=ExampleSessionStore:42424"
 stateNetworkTimeout="60"
 sqlConnectionString=""
/>
```

The following list describes some of the attributes for the `<sessionState>` element shown in the preceding code:

➤   `mode`: Specifies whether the session information should be persisted. The mode setting supports five options: `Off`, `InProc`, `StateServer`, `SQLServer`, and `Custom`. The default option is `InProc`.

➤   `cookieless`: Specifies whether HTTP cookieless Session key management is supported.

➤   `timeout`: Specifies the `Session` lifecycle time. The `timeout` value is a sliding value; at each request, the timeout period is reset to the current time plus the timeout value. For example, if the `timeout` value is 20 minutes and a request is received at 10:10 am, the timeout occurs at 10:30 am.

➤   `stateConnectionString`: When `mode` is set to `StateServer`, this setting is used to identify the TCP/IP address and port to communicate with the Windows Service providing state management.

➤   `stateNetworkTimeout`: Specifies the timeout value (in seconds) while attempting to store state in an out-of-process session store such as `StateServer`.

➤   `sqlConnectionString`: When `mode` is set to `SQLServer`, this setting is used to connect to the SQL Server database to store and retrieve session data.

Web Farm Support

Multiple web servers working as a group are called a *web farm*. If you would like to scale out your ASP.NET application into multiple servers inside a web farm, ASP.NET supports this kind of deployment out of the box. However, the session data needs to be persisted in an out-of-process session state such as `StateServer` or `SQLServer`.

State Server

Both `StateServer` and `SQLServer` support the out-of-process session state. However, the `StateServer` stores all the session information in a Windows Service, which stores the session data in memory. Using this option, if the server that hosts the session state service goes down in the web farm, all the ASP.NET clients that are accessing the website fail; there is no way to recover the session data.

You can configure the session state service using the Services window available by choosing Start ➪ Control Panel ➪ System and Security ➪ Administrative Tools ➪ Services if you are using Windows 7. In Windows 8, you enter and choose View Local Services in the Settings tab of the Search charm (as shown in Figure 28-2).

FIGURE 28-2

Alternatively, you can start the session state service by using the command prompt and entering the `net start` command, like this:

```
C:\Windows\Microsoft.NET\Framework\v4.0.30319\> net start aspnet_state
```

> **NOTE** *All compatible versions of ASP.NET share a single state service instance, which is the service installed with the highest version of ASP.NET. For example, if you have installed ASP.NET 4.5 on a server where ASP.NET 2.0 and 1.1 are already running, the ASP.NET 4.5 installation replaces the ASP.NET 2.0's state server instance. The ASP.NET 4.5 service is guaranteed to work for all previous compatible versions of ASP.NET. In addition, you must run the command prompt with elevated privileges to use* `net start`.

SQL Server

When you choose the `SQLServer` option, session data is stored in a Microsoft SQL Server database. Even if SQL Server goes down, the built-in SQL Server recovery features enable you to recover all the session data. Configuring ASP.NET to support SQL Server for session state is just as simple as configuring the Windows Service. The only difference is that you run a T-SQL script that ships with ASP.NET, `InstallSqlState.sql`. The T-SQL script that uninstalls ASP.NET SQL Server support, called `UninstallSqlState.sql`, is also included. The install and uninstall scripts are available in the Framework folder. Listing 28-11 shows an example of using the SQL Server option.

LISTING 28-11: Using the SQLServer option for session state

```
<configuration>
    <system.web>
        <sessionState
            mode="SQLServer"
            sqlConnectionString="data source=ExampleSessionServer;
            user id=ExampleWebUser;password=P@55worD"
            cookieless="false"
            timeout="20"
        />
    </system.web>
</configuration>
```

ASP.NET accesses the session data stored in SQL Server via stored procedures. By default, all the session data is stored in the Temp DB database. However, you can modify the stored procedures so they are stored in tables in a full-fledged database other than Temp DB.

> **NOTE** *Even though the SQL Server–based session state provides a scalable use of session state, it could become the single point of failure. This is because SQL Server session state uses the same SQL Server database for all applications in the same ASP.NET process. This problem has been fixed ever since ASP.NET 2.0, and you can configure different databases for each application. Now you can use the* `aspnet_regsql.exe` *utility to configure the SQL Server-based session state for all your applications. However, if you are looking for a solution for older .NET Frameworks, a fix is available at* `http://support.microsoft.com/kb/836680`*.*

Because the connection strings are stored in the strongly typed mode, the connection string information can be referenced in other parts of the configuration file. For example, when configuring session state to be stored in SQL Server, you can specify the connection string in the `<connectionStrings>` section, and then you can specify the name of the connection string in the `<sessionState>` element, as shown in Listing 28-12.

LISTING 28-12: Configuring session state with a connection string

```
<configuration>
    <connectionStrings>
        <add name = "ExampleSqlSessionState"
            connectionString = "data source=ExampleSessionServer;
            user id=ExampleWebUser;password=P@55worD" />
    </connectionStrings>
    <system.web>
        <sessionState
            mode="SQLServer"
            sqlConnectionString="ExampleSqlSessionState"
            cookieless="false"
            timeout="20"
        />
    </system.web>
</configuration>
```

Custom State Store

The session state in ASP.NET 4.5 is based on a pluggable architecture with different providers that inherit the `SessionStateStoreProviderBase` class. If you want to create your own custom provider or use a third-party provider, you must set the mode to `Custom`.

You specify the custom provider assembly that inherits the `SessionStateStoreProviderBase` class, as shown in Listing 28-13.

LISTING 28-13: Working with your own session state provider

```
<configuration>
    <system.web>
        <sessionState mode="Custom" customProvider="CustomStateProvider">
            <providers>
                <add name="CustomStateProvider"
                    type="CustomStateProviderAssembly,
                    CustomStateProviderNamespace.CustomStateProvider"/>
            </providers>
        </sessionState>
    </system.web>
</configuration>
```

In the previous example, you have configured the session state mode as `Custom` because you have specified the provider name as `CustomStateProvider`. From there, you add the provider element and include the type of the provider with namespace and class name.

> **NOTE** *You can read more about the provider model and custom providers in Chapters 14 and 15.*

Compilation Configuration

ASP.NET supports the dynamic compilation of ASP.NET pages, web services, HttpHandlers, ASP.NET application files (such as the `Global.asax` file), source files, and so on. These files are automatically compiled on demand when they are first required by an ASP.NET application.

Any changes to a dynamically compiled file causes all affected resources to become automatically invalidated and recompiled. This system enables developers to quickly develop applications with a minimum of process overhead because they can just click Save to immediately cause code changes to take effect within their applications.

You can configure the ASP.NET compilation settings using the `<compilation>` section in the `web.config` or `machine.config` files. The ASP.NET engine compiles the page when necessary and saves the generated code in code cache. This cached code is used when executing the ASP.NET pages. Listing 28-14 shows the syntax for the `<compilation>` section.

LISTING 28-14: The <compilation> section

```
<!-- compilation Attributes -->
<compilation
    tempDirectory="" [String]
    debug="false" [true|false]
    strict="false" [true|false]
    explicit="true" [true|false]
    batch="true" [true|false]
    optimizeCompilations="false" [true|false]
    urlLinePragmas="false" [true|false]
    batchTimeout="900" [in Seconds][number]
    maxBatchSize="1000" [number]
    maxBatchGeneratedFileSize="1000" [number]
    numRecompilesBeforeAppRestart="15" [number]
    defaultLanguage="vb" [String]
    targetFramework="" [String]
```

```
        assemblyPostProcessorType="" [String]
    >
      <assemblies>
          <add assembly="" [String, Required, Collection Key] />
      </assemblies>
      <buildproviders>
          <add extension="" [String, Required, Collection Key]
            type="" [String, Required] />
      </buildproviders>
      <folderLevelBuildProviders>
          <add name="" [String, Required, Collection Key]
            type="" [String, Required] />
      </folderLevelBuildProviders>
      <expressionBuilders>
          <add expressionPrefix="" [String, Required, Collection Key]
            type="" [String, Required] />
      </expressionBuilders>
      <codeSubDirectories>
          <add directoryName="" [String, Required, Collection Key] />
      </codeSubDirectories>
    </compilation>
```

Now take a more detailed look at these `<compilation>` attributes:

➤ batch: Specifies whether the batch compilation is supported. The default value is true.

➤ maxBatchSize: Specifies the maximum number of pages/classes that can be compiled into a single batch. The default value is 1000.

➤ maxBatchGeneratedFileSize: Specifies the maximum output size of a batch assembly compilation. The default value is 1000KB.

➤ batchTimeout: Specifies the amount of time (minutes) granted for batch compilation to occur. If this timeout elapses without compilation being completed, an exception is thrown. The default value is 15 minutes.

➤ optimizeCompilations: Specifies whether dynamic compilation compiles the entire site or only the items that have changed. When set to false (the default), the entire site will recompile when top-level files are changed; a setting of true will recompile only the changed files.

➤ debug: Specifies whether to compile production assemblies or debug assemblies. The default is false.

➤ defaultLanguage: Specifies the default programming language, such as VB or C#, to use in dynamic compilation files. Language names are defined using the `<compiler>` child element. The default value is VB.

➤ explicit: Specifies whether the Microsoft Visual Basic code compile option is explicit. The default is true.

➤ numRecompilesBeforeAppRestart: Specifies the number of dynamic recompiles of resources that can occur before the application restarts.

➤ strict: Specifies the setting of the Visual Basic strict compile option.

➤ urlLinePragmas: Instructs the compiler if it should use URLs rather than physical paths (which is the default behavior).

➤ tempDirectory: Specifies the directory to use for temporary file storage during compilation. By default, ASP.NET creates the temp file in the [WinNT\Windows] \Microsoft .NET\Framework\ [version]\Temporary ASP.NET Files folder.

➤ assemblies: Specifies assemblies that are used during the compilation process.

➤ codeSubDirectories: Specifies an ordered collection of subdirectories containing files compiled at run time. Adding the codeSubDirectories section creates separate assemblies.

➤ `buildproviders`: Specifies a collection of build providers used to compile custom resource files.

➤ `folderLevelBuildProviders`: Specifies a collection of build providers used to compile custom resource files in specific folders.

➤ `expressionBuilders`: Specifies a collection of resource strings to be utilized during the compilation process.

Custom Errors

When the ASP.NET application fails, the ASP.NET page can show the default error page with the source code and line number of the error. However, this approach has a few problems:

➤ The source code and error message might not make any sense to a less-experienced end user.

➤ If the same source code and the error messages are displayed to a hacker, subsequent damage could result.

Displaying too much error information could provide important implementation details that in most cases you want to keep from the public. Figure 28-3 shows an example.

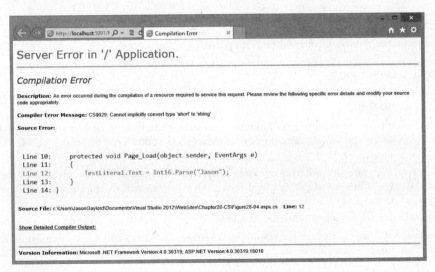

FIGURE 28-3

However, ASP.NET provides excellent infrastructure to prevent this kind of error information. The `<customErrors>` section provides a means for defining custom error messages in an ASP.NET application. The syntax is as follows:

```
<customErrors defaultRedirect="[url]" mode="[on/off/remote]">
    <error statusCode="[statuscode]" redirect="[url]" />
</customErrors>
```

➤ `defaultRedirect`: Specifies the default URL to which the client browser should be redirected if an error occurs. This setting is optional.

➤ `mode`: Specifies whether the status of the custom errors is enabled, disabled, or shown only to remote machines. The possible values are `On`, `Off`, and `RemoteOnly`. `On` indicates that the custom errors are enabled. `Off` indicates that the custom errors are disabled. `RemoteOnly` indicates that the custom errors are shown only to remote clients.

➤ `customErrors`: The `<customErrors>` section supports multiple `<error>` sub-elements that are used to define custom errors. Each `<error>` sub-element can include a `statusCode` attribute and a URL.

Authentication

In Chapter 20, you see the authentication process in detail. In this section, you can review configuration-specific information. Authentication is a process that verifies the identity of the user and establishes the identity between the server and a request. Because HTTP is a stateless protocol, the authentication information is persisted somewhere in the client or the server; ASP.NET supports both of these.

You can store the server-side information in `Session` objects. When it comes to the client side, you have many options:

➤ Cookies

➤ ViewState

➤ URL

➤ Hidden fields

ASP.NET supports following authentication methods out of the box:

➤ Windows authentication

➤ Forms authentication

> **NOTE** *Before ASP.NET 4, a third provider, the passport authentication provider, was available. However, this provider was marked as deprecated and is no longer considered to be a valid mode type.*

If you want to disable authentication, you can use the setting `mode = "None"`:

```
<authentication mode="None" />
```

Windows Authentication

ASP.NET relies on IIS's infrastructure to implement Windows authentication, and Windows authentication enables you to authenticate requests using Windows Challenge/Response semantics. When the web server receives a request, it initially denies access to the request (which is a challenge). This triggers the browser to pop up a window to collect the credentials; the request responds with a hashed value of the Windows credentials, which the server can then choose to authenticate.

To implement Windows authentication, you configure the appropriate website or virtual directory using IIS. You can then use the `<authentication>` element to mark the web application or virtual directory with Windows authentication. Listing 28-15 illustrates this process.

LISTING 28-15: Setting authentication to Windows authentication

```
<configuration>
    <system.web>
        <authentication mode="Windows" />
    </system.web>
</configuration>
```

> **NOTE** *You can declare the* `<authentication>` *element only at the machine, site, or application level. Any attempt to declare it in a configuration file at the subdirectory or page level results in a parser error message.*

Forms Authentication

Forms authentication is the widely used authentication mechanism. To configure forms authentication you use the <authentication> section along with the <forms> subsection. Listing 28-16 shows the structure of an <authentication> section that deals with forms authentication in the configuration file.

LISTING 28-16: The <authentication> section working with forms authentication

```
<configuration>
    <system.web>
        <authentication mode="Forms">
            <forms
                name=".ASPXAUTH" [String]
                loginUrl="login.aspx" [String]
                defaultUrl="default.aspx" [String]
                protection="All" [All|None|Encryption|Validation]
                timeout="30" [in Minutes] [number]
                path="/" [String]
                requireSSL="false" [true|false]
                slidingExpiration="true" [true|false]
                enableCrossAppRedirects="false" [true|false]
                cookieless="UseDeviceProfile"
                   [UseUri|UseCookies|AutoDetect|UseDeviceProfile]
                domain="" [String]
                ticketCompatibilityMode="Framework20" [Framework20|Framework40] >
                <credentials passwordFormat="SHA1" [Clear|SHA1|MD5] >
                    <user name="" [String, Required, CollectionKey]
                        password="" [String, Required] />
                </credentials>
            </forms>
        </authentication>
    </system.web>
</configuration>
```

Each attribute is shown in detail in the following list:

➤ name: Specifies the name of the HTTP authentication ticket. The default value is .ASPXAUTH.

➤ loginUrl: Specifies the URL to which the request is redirected if the current request doesn't have a valid authentication ticket.

➤ protection: Specifies the method used to protect cookie data. Valid values are All, None, Encryption, and Validation.

  ➤ Encryption: Specifies that content of the cookie is encrypted using TripleDES or DES cryptography algorithms in the configuration file. However, the data validation is not done on the cookie.

  ➤ Validation: Specifies that the content of the cookie is not encrypted, but validates that the cookie data has not been altered in transit.

  ➤ All: Specifies that that content of the cookie is protected using both data validation and encryption. The configured data validation algorithm is used based on the <machineKey> element, and Triple DES is used for encryption. The default value is All, and it indicates the highest protection available.

  ➤ None: Specifies no protection mechanism is applied on the cookie. Web applications that do not store any sensitive information and potentially use cookies for personalization can look at this option. When None is specified, both encryption and validation are disabled.

➤ timeout: Specifies cookie expiration time in terms of minutes. The timeout attribute is a sliding value, which expires n minutes from the time the last request was received. The default value is 30 minutes.

➤ path: Specifies the path to use for the issued cookie. The default value is / to avoid difficulties with mismatched case in paths because browsers are strictly case-sensitive when returning cookies.

➤ requireSSL: Specifies whether forms authentication should happen in a secure HTTPS connection.

➤ slidingExpiration: Specifies whether valid cookies should be updated periodically when used. When this option is set to false, a ticket is good for only the duration of the period for which it is issued, and a user must re-authenticate even during an active session.

➤ cookieless: Specifies whether cookieless authentication is supported. Supported values are UseCookies, UseUri, Auto, and UseDeviceProfile. The default value is UseDeviceProfile.

➤ defaultUrl: Specifies the default URL used by the login control to control redirection after authentication.

➤ enableCrossAppRedirects: When set to true, this allows for redirection to URLs that are not in the current application.

➤ domain: Specifies the domain name string to be attached in the authentication cookie. This attribute is particularly useful when the same authentication cookie is shared among multiple sites across the domain.

➤ ticketCompatibilityMode: By default, the Framework20 setting uses local time for the ticket expiration date, whereas setting it to Framework40 will use UTC.

> **NOTE** *Having the* loginUrl *be an SSL URL (*https://*) is strongly recommended to keep secure credentials secure from prying eyes.*

Anonymous Identity

Many application types require the capability to work with anonymous users, although this is especially true for e-commerce web applications. In these cases, your site must support *both* anonymous and authenticated users. When anonymous users are browsing the site and adding items to a shopping cart, the web application needs a way to uniquely identify these users. For example, if you look at busy e-commerce websites such as Amazon.com or BN.com, they do not have a concept called anonymous users. Rather these sites assign a unique identity to each user.

In early versions of ASP.NET, no out-of-the box feature existed to enable a developer to achieve this identification of users. Most developers used SessionID to identify users uniquely. They experienced a few pitfalls inherent in this method. Later, ASP.NET included anonymous identity support using the <anonymousIdentification> section in the configuration file. Listing 28-17 shows the <anonymousIdentification> configuration section settings.

LISTING 28-17: Working with anonymous identification in the configuration file

```
<configuration>
    <system.web>
        <anonymousIdentification
            enabled="false" [true|false]
            cookieName=".ASPXANONYMOUS" [String]
            cookieTimeout="100000" [in Minutes] [number]
            cookiePath="/" [String]
            cookieRequireSSL="false" [true|false]
            cookieSlidingExpiration="true" [true|false]
            cookieProtection="Validation" [None|Validation|Encryption|All]
            cookieless="UseCookies"
                [UseUri|UseCookies|AutoDetect|UseDeviceProfile]
            domain="" [String]
            />
    </system.web>
</configuration>
```

The `enabled` attribute within the `<anonymousIdentification>` section specifies whether the anonymous access capabilities of ASP.NET are enabled. The other attributes are comparable to those in the `<authentication>` section from Listing 28-16. When you are working with anonymous identification, the possibility exists that the end users will have cookies disabled in their environments. When the end users don't enable cookies, their identities are stored in the URL strings within their browsers.

Authorization

The authorization process verifies whether a user has the privilege to access the resource he is trying to request. ASP.NET supports both file and URL authorization. The authorization process dictated by an application can be controlled by using the `<authorization>` section within the configuration file. The `<authorization>` section, as presented in Listing 28-18, can contain subsections that either allow or deny permission to a user, a group of users contained within a specific role in the system, or a request that is coming to the server in a particular fashion (such as an HTTP GET request). Optionally, you can also use the `<location>` section to grant special authorization permission to only a particular folder or file within the application.

LISTING 28-18: Authorization capabilities from the configuration file

```
<authorization>
    <allow users="" roles="" verbs="" />
    <deny users="" roles="" verbs="" />
</authorization>
```

URL Authorization

The URL authorization is a service provided by `URLAuthorizationModule` (inherited from `HttpModule`) to control the access to resources such as `.aspx` files. The URL authorization is very useful if you want to allow or deny certain parts of your ASP.NET application to certain people or roles.

For example, you might want to restrict the administration part of your ASP.NET application only to administrators and deny access to others. You can achieve this task very easily with URL authorization. URL authorization can be configurable based on the user, the role, or HTTP verbs such as the HTTP GET request or the HTTP POST request.

You can configure URL authorization in the `web.config` file with `<allow>` and `<deny>` attributes. For example, the code in Listing 28-19 shows how you can allow the user `Jason` and deny the groups `Sales` and `Marketing` access to the application.

LISTING 28-19: Allowing and denying entities from the `<authorization>` section

```
<system.web>
    <authorization>
        <allow users="Jason" />
        <deny roles="Sales, Marketing" />
    </authorization>
</system.web>
```

The `<allow>` and `<deny>` elements support `users`, `roles`, and `verbs` values. As you can see from the previous code example, you can add multiple users and groups by separating them with commas.

Two special characters, an asterisk (`*`) and a question mark (`?`), are supported by `URLAuthorizationModule`. The asterisk symbol represents all users (anonymous and registered) and the question mark represents only anonymous users. The following code example in Listing 28-20 denies access to all anonymous users and grants access to anyone contained within the `Admin` role.

LISTING 28-20: Denying anonymous users

```
<system.web>
    <authorization>
        <allow roles="Admin" />
        <deny users="?" />
    </authorization>
</system.web>
```

You can also grant or deny users or groups access to certain HTTP methods. In the example in Listing 28-21, access to the HTTP GET method is denied to the users contained within the Admin role, whereas access to the HTTP POST method is denied to all users.

LISTING 28-21: Denying users and roles by verb

```
<system.web>
    <authorization>
        <deny verbs="GET" roles="Admin" />
        <deny verbs="POST" users="*" />
    </authorization>
</system.web>
```

File Authorization

It's possible to construct the authorization section within the configuration file so that what is specified can be applied to a specific file or directory using the <location> element. For example, suppose you have a root directory called Home within your application, and nested within that root directory you have a subdirectory called Documents. Suppose you want to allow access to the Documents subdirectory only to those users contained within the Admin role. Listing 28-22 illustrates this scenario.

LISTING 28-22: Granting access to the Documents subdirectory for the Admin role

```
<configuration>
    <location path="Documents">
        <system.web>
            <authorization>
                <allow roles="Admin" />
                <deny users="*" />
            </authorization>
        </system.web>
    </location>
</configuration>
```

> **NOTE** *The ASP.NET application does not verify the path specified in the* path *attribute. If the given path is invalid, ASP.NET does not apply the security setting.*

You can also set the security for a single file as presented in Listing 28-23.

LISTING 28-23: Granting access to a specific file for the Admin role

```
<configuration>
    <location path="Documents/Default.aspx">
        <system.web>
            <authorization>
                <allow roles="Admin" />
                <deny users="*" />
            </authorization>
        </system.web>
    </location>
</configuration>
```

Locking-Down Configuration Settings

ASP.NET's configuration system is quite flexible in terms of applying configuration information to a specific application or folder. Even though the configuration system is flexible, in some cases you may want to limit the configuration options that a particular application on the server can control. For example, you could decide to change the way in which the ASP.NET session information is stored. This lock-down process can be achieved using the <location> attributes allowOverride and allowDefinition, as well as the path attribute.

Listing 28-24 illustrates this approach. A <location> section in this machine.config file identifies the path "Default Web Site/ExampleApplication" and allows that application to override the <trace> setting through the use of the allowOverride attribute.

LISTING 28-24: Allowing a <trace> section to be overridden in a lower configuration file

```
<configuration>
    <location path="Default Web Site/ExampleApplication" allowOverride="true">
        <trace enabled="false"/>
    </location>
</configuration>
```

The trace attribute can be overridden because the allowOverride attribute is set to true. You are able to override the tracing setting in the ExampleApplication's web.config file and enable the local <trace> element, thereby overriding the settings presented in Listing 28-24.

However, if you had written the attribute as allowOverride="false" in the <location> section of the machine.config file, the web.config file for ExampleApplication is unable to override that specific setting.

ASP.NET Page Configuration

When an ASP.NET application has been deployed, the <pages> section of the configuration file enables you to control some of the default behaviors for each ASP.NET page. These behaviors include options such as whether you should buffer the output before sending it or whether session state should be enabled for the entire application. Listing 28-25 shows an example of using the <pages> section.

LISTING 28-25: Configuring the <pages> section

```
<configuration>
    <system.web>
        <pages
            buffer="true" [true]|false]
            enableSessionState="true" [False|ReadOnly|True]
            enableViewState="true" [true]|false]
            enableViewStateMac="true" [true]|false]
            enableEventValidation="true" [true]|false]
            smartNavigation="false" [true]|false]
            autoEventWireup="true" [true]|false]
            maintainScrollPositionOnPostBack="false" [true]|false]
            pageBaseType="System.Web.UI.Page" [String]
            userControlBaseType="System.Web.UI.UserControl" [String]
            pageParserFilterType="" [String]
            validateRequest="true" [true]|false]
            masterPageFile="" [String]
            theme="" [String]
            styleSheetTheme="" [String]
            maxPageStateFieldLength="-1" [number]
            compilationMode="Always" [Auto|Never|Always]
            viewStateEncryptionMode="Auto" [Auto|Always|Never]
```

```
                   asyncTimeout="45" [in Seconds][number]
                   renderAllHiddenFieldsAtTopOfForm="true" [true]|false]
                   clientIDMode="Predictable" [Inherit|AutoID|Predictable|Static]
                   controlRenderingCompatibilityVersion="4.0" [Version] >
                   <namespaces autoImportVBNamespace="true" [true|false] >
                       <add namespace="" [String, Required, CollectionKey] />
                   </namespaces>
                   <controls />
                   <tagMapping />
                   <ignoreDeviceFilters />
               </pages>
           </system.web>
       </configuration>
```

The following list gives you some of the ASP.NET page configuration information elements in detail:

➤ buffer: Specifies whether the requests must be buffered on the server before they are sent to the client.

➤ enableSessionState: Specifies whether the session state for the current ASP.NET application should be enabled. The possible values are true, false, or readonly. The readonly value means that the application can read the session values but cannot modify them.

➤ enableViewState: Specifies whether the ViewState is enabled for all the controls. If the application does not use ViewState, you can set the value to false in the application's web.config file.

➤ autoEventWireup: Specifies whether ASP.NET can automatically wire-up common page events such as Load or Error.

➤ smartNavigation: Smart navigation is a feature that takes advantage of IE as a client's browser to prevent the redrawing that occurs when a page is posted back to itself. Using smart navigation, the request is sent through an IFRAME on the client, and IE redraws only the sections of the page that have changed. By default, this option is set to false. When it is enabled, it is available only to Internet Explorer browsers; all other browsers get the standard behavior.

➤ maintainScrollPositionOnPostback: Specifies whether to return the user to the same position on the page after the postback occurs. If set to false (the default), the user is returned to the top of the page.

➤ masterPageFile: Identifies the master page for the current ASP.NET application. If you want to apply the master page template to only a specific subset of pages (such as pages contained within a specific folder of your application), you can use the <location> element within the web.config file:

```
           <configuration>
               <location path="ExampleApplicationAdmin">
                   <system.web>
                       <pages
                           masterPageFile="~/ExampleApplicationAdminMasterPage.master"
                           />
                   </system.web>
               </location>
           </configuration>
```

➤ theme: Specifies the name of the theme to use for the page.

➤ styleSheetTheme: Defines the theme to use after control declaration.

➤ maxPageStateFieldLength: If set to a positive number, ASP.NET will separate the ViewState into chucks that are smaller than the defined size. The default value is -1, meaning all the ViewState comes down in one piece.

➤ pageBaseType: Specifies the base class for all the ASP.NET pages in the current ASP.NET application. By default, this option is set to System.Web.UI.Page. However, if you want all ASP.NET pages to inherit from some other base class, you can change the default via this setting.

➤ userControlBaseType: Specifies the base class for all the ASP.NET user controls in the current ASP.NET application. The default is System.Web.UI.UserControl. You can override the default option using this element.

➤ `validateRequest`: Specifies whether ASP.NET should validate all the incoming requests that are potentially dangerous, such as the cross-site script attack and the script injection attack. This feature provides out-of-the-box protection against cross-site scripting and script injection attacks by automatically checking all parameters in the request, ensuring that their content does not include HTML elements. For more information about this setting, visit `www.asp.net/faq/RequestValidation.aspx`.

➤ `namespaces`: Optionally, you can import a collection of assemblies that can be included in the precompilation process.

➤ `compilationMode`: Specifies how ASP.NET should compile the current web application. Supported values are `Never`, `Always`, and `Auto`. A setting of `compilationMode="Never"` means that the pages should never be compiled. A part error occurs if the page has constructs that require compilation. Setting `compilationMode="Always"` means that the pages are always compiled. When you set `compilationMode="Auto"`, ASP.NET does not compile the pages if that is possible.

➤ `viewStateEncryptionMode`: Specifies whether to encrypt the ViewState.

➤ `asyncTimeout`: Specifies the number of seconds that the page should wait for an asynchronous handler to finish during an asynchronous operation.

➤ `clientIDMode`: Specifies the algorithm that should be used to create the `ClientID` values for server controls on your page. The default setting is `AutoID`, while the default value for the server controls is `Inherit`.

➤ `controlRenderingCompatibilityVersion`: Specifies the version of ASP.NET to use when controls render their HTML.

Include Files

ASP.NET supports *include* files in both the `machine.config` and the `web.config` files. When configuration content is to be included in multiple places or inside the location elements, an include file is an excellent way to encapsulate the content.

Any section in a configuration file can include content from a different file using the `configSource` attribute in the `<pages>` section. The value of the attribute indicates a virtual relative filename to the include file. Listing 28-26 is an example of such a directive.

LISTING 28-26: Adding content to the web.config file

```
<configuration>
    <system.web>
        <pages configSource="SystemWeb.config" />
    </system.web>
</configuration>
```

The configuration include files can contain information that applies to a single section, and a single include file cannot contain more than one configuration section or a portion of a section. If the `configSource` attribute is present, the section element in the source file should not contain any other attribute or any child element.

Nevertheless, the include file is not a full configuration file. It should contain only the include section, as presented in Listing 28-27.

LISTING 28-27: The SystemWeb.config file

```
<pages authentication mode="Forms" />
```

The `configSource` attribute cannot be nested. An include file cannot nest another file inside it using the `configSource` attribute.

> **NOTE** *When an ASP.NET configuration file is changed, the application is restarted at run time. When an external include file is used within the configuration file, the configuration reload happens without restarting the application.*

Configuring ASP.NET Runtime Settings

The general configuration settings specify how long a given ASP.NET resource, such as a page, is allowed to execute before being considered timed-out. The other settings specify the maximum size of a request (in kilobytes) or whether to use fully qualified URLs in redirects. To specify these settings you use the `<httpRuntime>` section within a configuration file. The `<httpRuntime>` element is applied at the ASP.NET application at the folder level. Listing 28-28 shows the default values used in the `<httpRuntime>` section.

LISTING 28-28: The <httpRuntime> section

```
<configuration>
    <system.web>
        <httpRuntime
            useFullyQualifiedRedirectUrl="false"
            enable="true"
            executionTimeout="90"
            maxRequestLength="4096"
            requestLengthDiskThreshold="512"
            appRequestQueueLimit="5000"
            minFreeThreads="8"
            minLocalRequestFreeThreads="4"
            enableKernelOutputCache="true" />
    </system.web>
</configuration>
```

Enabling and Disabling ASP.NET Applications

The `enable` attribute specifies whether the current ASP.NET application is enabled. When set to `false`, the current ASP.NET application is disabled, and all the clients trying to connect to this site receive the HTTP 404—File Not Found exception. This value should be set only at the machine or application level. If you set this value in any other level (such as subfolder level), it is ignored. This great feature enables the administrators to bring down the application for whatever reason without starting or stopping IIS. The default value is `true`.

> **NOTE** *Outside of this setting, you can also take applications offline quickly by simply placing an* App_Offline.htm *file in the root of your application. This* .htm *file does not need to actually contain anything (it will not make any difference). However, if this file's file size does not exceed 512 bytes, all requests to the application get a Page Not Found error.*

Fully Qualified Redirect URLs

The `useFullyQualifiedRedirectUrl` attribute specifies whether the client-side redirects should include the fully qualified URL. When you are programming against the mobile devices, some devices require specifying fully qualified URLs. The default value is `false`.

Request Time-Out

The `executionTimeout` setting specifies the timeout option for an ASP.NET request time-out. The value of this attribute is the amount of time in seconds during which a resource can execute before ASP.NET times out the request. The default setting is 110 seconds. If you have a particular ASP.NET page or web service that takes longer than 110 seconds to execute, you can extend the time limit in the configuration.

Maximum Request Length

The maxRequestLength attribute specifies the maximum upload size accepted by ASP.NET run time. For example, if the ASP.NET application is required to process huge files, then this setting is the one you will want to change. The default is 4096. This number represents kilobytes (KB or around 4MB).

Web applications are prone to attacks these days. The attacks range from a script injection attack to a denial of service (DoS) attack. The DoS is a typical attack that bombards the web server with requests for large files. This huge number of requests ultimately brings down the web server. The maxRequestLength attribute could save you from a DoS attack by setting a restriction on the size of requests.

Buffer Uploads

ASP.NET 4.5 includes a setting called requestLengthDiskThreshold. This setting enables an administrator to configure the file upload buffering behavior without affecting the programming model. Administrators can configure a threshold below which requests will be buffered into memory. After a request exceeds the limit, it is transparently buffered on disk and consumed from there by whatever mechanism is used to consume the data. The valid values for this setting are numbers between 1 and Int32.MaxSize in KB.

When file buffering is enabled, the files are uploaded to the codegen folder. The default path for the codegen folder is the following:

```
[WinNT\Windows]\Microsoft.NET\Framework\[version]\Temporary ASP.NET Files\
[ApplicationName]
```

The files are buffered using a random name in a subfolder within the codegen folder called Uploads. The location of the codegen folder can be configured on a per-application basis using the tempDirectory attribute of the <compilation> section.

Thread Management

ASP.NET run time uses free threads available in its thread pool to fulfill requests. The minFreeThreads attribute indicates the number of threads that ASP.NET guarantees is available within the thread pool. The default number of threads is eight. For complex applications that require additional threads to complete processing, this attribute simply ensures that the threads are available and that the application will not be blocked while waiting for a free thread to schedule more work. The minLocalRequestFreeThreads attribute controls the number of free threads dedicated for local request processing; the default is four.

Application Queue Length

The appRequestQueueLimit attribute specifies the maximum number of requests that ASP.NET queues for the current ASP.NET application. ASP.NET queues requests when it does not have enough free threads to process them. The minFreeThreads attribute specifies the number of free threads the ASP.NET application should maintain, and this setting affects the number of items stored in the queue.

> **NOTE** *When the number of requests queued exceeds the limit set in the* appRequestQueueLimit *setting, all the incoming requests are rejected and an* HTTP 503 - Server Too Busy *error is thrown back to the browser.*

Output Caching

The enableKernelOutputCache specifies whether the output caching is enabled at the IIS kernel level (Http.sys). At present, this setting applies only to web servers IIS6 and higher.

Configuring the ASP.NET Worker Process

When a request for an ASP.NET page is received by IIS, it passes the request to an unmanaged DLL called `aspnet_isapi.dll`. The `aspnet_isapi.dll` further passes the request to a separate worker process—`aspnet_wp.exe` if you are working with IIS5—which runs all the ASP.NET applications. With IIS6 and higher, however, all the ASP.NET applications are run by the `w3wp.exe` process. The ASP.NET worker process can be configured using the `<processModel>` section in the `machine.config` file.

> **NOTE** *All the configuration sections talked about so far are read by managed code. On the other hand, the `<processModel>` section is read by the `aspnet_isapi.dll` unmanaged DLL. Because the configuration information is read by an unmanaged DLL, the changed process model information is applied to all ASP.NET applications only after an IIS restart.*

The code example in Listing 28-29 shows the default format for the `<processModel>` section.

LISTING 28-29: The structure of the `<processModel>` element

```
<processModel
  enable="true|false"
  timeout="hrs:mins:secs|Infinite"
  idleTimeout="hrs:mins:secs|Infinite"
  shutdownTimeout="hrs:mins:secs|Infinite"
  requestLimit="num|Infinite"
  requestQueueLimit="num|Infinite"
  restartQueueLimit="num|Infinite"
  memoryLimit="percent"
  cpuMask="num"
  webGarden="true|false"
  userName="username"
  password="password"
  logLevel="All|None|Errors"
  clientConnectedCheck="hrs:mins:secs|Infinite"
  responseDeadlockInterval="hrs:mins:secs|Infinite"
  responseRestartDeadlockInterval="hrs:mins:secs|Infinite"
  comAuthenticationLevel="Default|None|Connect|Call|
Pkt|PktIntegrity|PktPrivacy"
  comImpersonationLevel="Default|Anonymous|Identify|
Impersonate|Delegate"
  maxWorkerThreads="num"
  maxIoThreads="num"
  autoConfig="true|false"
  minWorkerThreads="num"
  minIoThreads="num"
  serverErrorMessageFile=""
  pingFrequency="hrs:mins:secs|Infinite"
  pingTimeout="hrs:mins:secs|Infinite"
  maxAppDomains="number"
/>
```

The following section looks at each of these attributes in more detail:

➤ `enable`: Specifies whether the process model is enabled. When set to `false`, the ASP.NET applications run under IIS's process model.

> **NOTE** *When ASP.NET is running under IIS6 or higher in native mode, the IIS6 or higher process model is used and most of the* <processModel> *section within the configuration file is simply ignored. The* autoConfig *and* requestQueueLimit *attributes are still applied in this case.*

➤ timeout: Specifies how long the worker process lives before a new worker process is created to replace the current worker process. This value can be extremely useful if a scenario exists where the application's performance starts to degrade slightly after running for several weeks, as in the case of a memory leak. Rather than your having to manually start and stop the process, ASP.NET can restart automatically. The default value is Infinite.

➤ idleTimeout: Specifies how long the worker process should wait before it is shut down. You can shut down the ASP.NET worker process automatically using the idleTimeout option. The default value is Infinite. You can also set this value to a time using the format, HH:MM:SS.

➤ shutdownTimeout: Specifies how long the worker process is given to shut itself down gracefully before ASP.NET calls the Kill command on the process. Kill is a low-level command that forcefully removes the process. The default value is 5 seconds.

➤ requestLimit: Specifies when the ASP.NET worker process should be recycled after a certain number of requests are served. The default value is Infinite.

➤ requestQueueLimit: Instructs ASP.NET to recycle the worker process if the limit for queued requests is exceeded. The default setting is 5000.

➤ memoryLimit: Specifies how much physical memory the worker process is allowed to consume before it is considered to be misbehaving or leaking memory. The default value is 60 percent of the available physical memory.

➤ username and password: By default, all ASP.NET applications are executed using the ASPNET identity. If you want an ASP.NET application to run with a different account, you can provide the username and the password pair using these attributes.

➤ logLevel: Specifies how the ASP.NET worker process logs events. The default setting is to log errors only. However, you can also disable logging by specifying None or you can log everything using All. All the log items are written to the Windows Application Event Log.

➤ clientConnectedCheck: Enables you to check whether the client is still connected at timed intervals before performing work. The default setting is 5 seconds.

➤ responseDeadlockInterval: Specifies how frequently the deadlock check should occur. A deadlock is considered to exist when requests are queued and no responses have been sent during this interval. After a deadlock, the process is restarted. The default value is 3 minutes.

➤ responseRestartDeadlockInterval: Specifies, when a deadlock is detected by the run time, how long the run time should wait before restarting the process. The default value is 9 minutes.

➤ comAuthenticationLevel: Controls the level of authentication for DCOM security. The default is set to Connect. Other values are Default, None, Call, Pkt, PktIntegrity, and PktPrivacy.

➤ comImpersonationLevel: Controls the authentication level for COM security. The default is set to Impersonate. Other values are Default, Anonymous, Identify, and Delegate.

➤ webGarden: Specifies whether Web Garden mode is enabled. The default setting is false. A web garden lets you host multiple ASP.NET worker processes on a single server, thus providing the application with better hardware scalability. Web Garden mode is supported only on multiprocessor servers.

➤ cpuMask: Specifies which processors should be affinities to ASP.NET worker processes when webGarden="true". The cpuMask is a hexadecimal value. The default value is all processors, shown as 0xFFFFFFFF.

➤ `maxWorkerThreads`: Specifies the maximum number of threads that exist within the ASP.NET worker process thread pool. The default is 20.

➤ `maxIoThreads`: Specifies the maximum number of I/O threads that exist within the ASP.NET worker process. The default is 20.

➤ `autoConfig`: Specifies whether to configure the ASP.NET application's performance settings.

➤ `minWorkerThreads`: Specifies the minimum number of threads that exist within the ASP.NET worker process thread pool. The default is 1.

➤ `minIoThreads`: Specifies the minimum number of I/O threads that exist within the ASP.NET worker process. The default is 1.

➤ `serverErrorMessageFile`: Specifies the page to use for content for the error message rather than the default "Server Unavailable" message.

➤ `pingFrequency`: Specifies the time interval at which the ISAPI extension pings the worker process to determine whether it is running.

➤ `pingTimeout`: Specifies the time interval at which a worker process is restarted after not responding.

➤ `maxAppDomains`: Sets the absolute maximum number of application domains for one process.

Running Multiple Websites with Multiple Versions of the .NET Framework

In the same context as the ASP.NET worker process, multiple websites within the given web server can host multiple websites, and each of these sites can be bound to a particular version of a .NET Framework. This is typically done using the `aspnet_regiis.exe` utility. The `aspnet_regiis.exe` utility ships with each version of the framework.

This utility has multiple switches. Using the `-s` switch allows you to install the current version of the .NET Framework run time on a given website. Listing 28-30 shows how to install .NET Framework version 2.0 on the ExampleApplication website.

LISTING 28-30: Installing .NET Framework version 2.0 on the ExampleApplication website

```
C:\WINDOWS\Microsoft.NET\Framework\v2.0.50727>
    aspnet_regiis -s W3SVC/1ROOT/ExampleApplication
```

Storing Application-Specific Settings

Every web application must store some application-specific information for its runtime use. The `<appSettings>` section of the `web.config` file provides a way to define custom application settings for an ASP.NET application. The section can have multiple `<add>` sub-elements. Its syntax is as follows:

```
<appSettings>
    <add key="[key]" value="[value]"/>
</appSettings>
```

The `<add>` sub-element supports two attributes:

➤ `key`: Specifies the key value in an `appSettings` hash table

➤ `value`: Specifies the value in an `appSettings` hash table

Listing 28-31 shows how to store an application-specific connection string. The `key` value is set to `ApplicationInstanceID`, and the `value` is set to the ASP.NET application instance and the name of the server on which the application is running.

LISTING 28-31: Application instance information

```
<appSettings>
    <add key="ApplicationInstanceID" value="Instance1onServerOprta"/>
</appSettings>
```

Programming Configuration Files

ASP.NET includes APIs (ASP.NET Management Objects) to manipulate the configuration information settings in machine.config and web.config files. ASP.NET Management Objects provide a strongly typed programming model that addresses targeted administrative aspects of a .NET Web Application Server. They also govern the creation and maintenance of the ASP.NET web configuration. Using the ASP.NET Management Objects, you can manipulate the configuration information stored in the configuration files in the local or remote computer. These can be used to script any common administrative tasks or to write installation scripts.

All the ASP.NET Management Objects are stored in the System.Configuration and System.Web .Configuration namespaces. You can access the configuration using the WebConfigurationManager class. The System.Configuration.Configuration class represents a merged view of the configuration settings from the machine.config and hierarchical web.config files. The System.Configuration and System .Web.Configuration namespaces have multiple classes that enable you to access nearly all the settings available in the configuration file. The main difference between the System.Configuration and System .Web.Configuration namespaces is that the System.Configuration namespace contains all the classes that apply to all the .NET applications. On the other hand, the System.Web.Configuration namespace contains the classes that are applicable only to ASP.NET web applications. Table 28-1 shows the important classes in System.Configuration and their uses.

TABLE 28-1

CLASS NAME	PURPOSE
Configuration	Enables you to manipulate the configuration stored in the local computer or a remote one
ConfigurationElementCollection	Enables you to enumerate the child elements stored inside the configuration file
AppSettingsSection	Enables you to manipulate the <appSettings> section of the configuration file
ConnectionStringsSettings	Enables you to manipulate the <connectionStrings> section of the configuration file
ProtectedConfigurationSection	Enables you to manipulate the <protectedConfiguration> section of the configuration file
ProtectedDataSection	Enables you to manipulate the <protectedData> section of the configuration file

Table 28-2 shows some of the classes from the System.Web.Configuration namespace and their uses.

TABLE 28-2

CLASS NAME	PURPOSE
AuthenticationSection	Enables you to manipulate the <authentication> section of the configuration file
AuthorizationSection	Enables you to manipulate the <authorization> section of the configuration file

CompilationSection	Enables you to manipulate the `<compilation>` section of the configuration file
CustomErrorsSection	Enables you to manipulate the `<customErrors>` section of the configuration file
FormsAuthenticationConfiguration	Enables you to manipulate the `<forms>` section of the configuration file
GlobalizationSection	Enables you to manipulate the `<globalization>` section of the configuration file
HttpHandlersSection	Enables you to manipulate the `<httpHandlers>` section of the configuration file
HttpModulesSection	Enables you to manipulate the `<httpModules>` section of the configuration file
HttpRuntimeSection	Enables you to manipulate the `<httpRuntime>` section of the configuration file
MachineKeySection	Enables you to manipulate the `<machineKey>` section of the configuration file
MembershipSection	Enables you to manipulate the `<membership>` section of the configuration file
PagesSection	Enables you to manipulate the `<pages>` section of the configuration file
ProcessModelSection	Enables you to manipulate the `<processModel>` section of the configuration file
WebPartsSection	Enables you to manipulate the `<webParts>` section of the configuration file

All the configuration classes are implemented based on simple object-oriented based architecture that has an entity class that holds all the data and a collection class that has methods to add, remove, enumerate, and so on. You start your configuration file programming with a simple connection string enumeration, as shown in the following section.

Enumerating Connection Strings

In a web application, you can store multiple connection strings. Some of them are used by the system and the others may be application-specific. You can write a very simple ASP.NET application that enumerates all the connection strings stored in the `web.config` file, as shown in Listing 28-32.

LISTING 28-32: The web.config file

```
<?xml version="1.0" ?>
<configuration>
    <appSettings>
        <add key="symbolServer" value="192.168.1.1" />
    </appSettings>
    <connectionStrings>
        <add name="ExampleApplication"
          connectionString="server=ExampleApplicationServer;
```

continues

LISTING 28-32 *(continued)*

```
                database=ExampleApplicationDB;uid=WebUser;pwd=P@$$worD9"
            providerName="System.Data.SqlClient" />
    </connectionStrings>
    <system.web>
        <compilation debug="false" targetFramework="4.5" />
        <authentication mode="None" />
    </system.web>
</configuration>
```

As shown in Listing 28-32, one application setting points to the symbol server, and one connection string is stored in the `web.config` file. Use the `ConnectionStrings` collection of the `System.Web.Configuration .WebConfigurationManager` class to read the connection strings, as shown in Listing 28-33.

LISTING 28-33: Binding the ConnectionStrings collection properties to a GridView control

VB

```vb
Protected Sub Page_Load(sender As Object, e As EventArgs)
    GridView1.DataSource =
        System.Web.Configuration.WebConfigurationManager.ConnectionStrings
    GridView1.DataBind()
End Sub
```

C#

```csharp
protected void Page_Load(object sender, EventArgs e)
{
    GridView1.DataSource =
        System.Web.Configuration.WebConfigurationManager.ConnectionStrings;
    GridView1.DataBind();
}
```

As shown in Listing 28-33, you've bound the `ConnectionStrings` property collection of the `WebConfigurationManager` class into the GridView control. The `WebConfigurationManager` class returns an instance of the `Configuration` class and the `ConnectionStrings` property is a static (shared in Visual Basic) property. Therefore, you are just binding the property collection into the GridView control. Figure 28-4 shows the list of connection strings stored in the ASP.NET application.

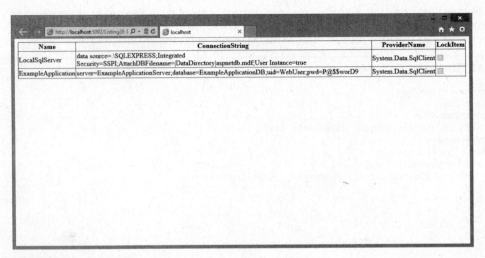

FIGURE 28-4

Adding a connection string at run time is also a very easy task. If you do it as shown in Listing 28-34, you get an instance of the configuration object. Then you create a new `connectionStringSettings` class. You add the new class to the collection and call the `update` method. Listing 28-34 shows examples of this in both VB and C#.

LISTING 28-34: Adding a connection string

VB

```
Protected Sub Button1_Click(ByVal sender As Object, ByVal e As System.EventArgs)
    ' Get the file path for the current web request
    Dim webPath As String = Request.ApplicationPath

    Try
        ' Get configuration object of the current web request
        Dim config As Configuration = _
          System.Web.Configuration.WebConfigurationManager.OpenWebConfiguration(webPath)

        ' Create new connection setting from text boxes
        Dim newConnSetting As New _
          ConnectionStringSettings(txtName.Text, txtValue.Text, txtProvider.Text)

        ' Add the connection string to the collection
        config.ConnectionStrings.ConnectionStrings.Add(newConnSetting)

        ' Save the changes
        config.Save()
    Catch cEx As ConfigurationErrorsException
        lblStatus.Text = "Status: " & cEx.ToString()
    Catch ex As System.UnauthorizedAccessException
        ' The ASP.NET process account must have read/write access to the directory
        lblStatus.Text = "Status: " & "The ASP.NET process account must have" & _
            "read/write access to the directory"
    Catch eEx As Exception
        lblStatus.Text = "Status: " & eEx.ToString()
    End Try

    ShowConnectionStrings()
End Sub

Protected Sub ShowConnectionStrings()
    GridView1.DataSource = System.Web.Configuration.WebConfigurationManager.ConnectionStrings
    GridView1.DataBind()
End Sub
```

C#

```
protected void Button1_Click(object sender, EventArgs e)
{
    // Get the file path for the current web request
    string webPath = Request.ApplicationPath;

    // Get configuration object of the current web request
    Configuration config =
    System.Web.Configuration.WebConfigurationManager.OpenWebConfiguration(webPath);

    // Create new connection setting from text boxes
    ConnectionStringSettings newConnSetting = new
    ConnectionStringSettings(txtName.Text, txtValue.Text, txtProvider.Text);

    try
    {
```

LISTING 28-34 *(continued)*

```
            // Add the connection string to the collection
            config.ConnectionStrings.ConnectionStrings.Add(newConnSetting);

            // Save the changes
            config.Save();
        }
        catch (ConfigurationErrorsException cEx)
        {
            lblStatus.Text = "Status: " + cEx.ToString();
        }
        catch (System.UnauthorizedAccessException uEx)
        {
            // The ASP.NET process account must have read/write
            // access to the directory
            lblStatus.Text = "Status: " + "The ASP.NET process account must have" +
                "read/write access to the directory";
        }
        catch (Exception eEx)
        {
            lblStatus.Text = "Status: " + eEx.ToString();
        }

        // Reload the connection strings in the list box
        ShowConnectionStrings();
    }

    protected void ShowConnectionStrings()
    {
        GridView1.DataSource = System.Web.Configuration.WebConfigurationManager.ConnectionStrings;
        GridView1.DataBind();
    }
```

Manipulating a machine.config File

The `OpenMachineConfiguration` method of the `System.Configuration.ConfigurationManager` class provides a way to manipulate the `machine.config` file. The `OpenMachineConfiguration` method is a static method.

Listing 28-35 shows a simple example that enumerates all the section groups stored in the `machine .config` file. As shown in this listing, you're getting an instance of the configuration object using the `OpenMachineConfiguration` method. Then you are binding the `SectionGroups` collection with the GridView control.

LISTING 28-35: Configuration groups from machine.config

VB

```
Protected Sub Page_Load(sender As Object, e As EventArgs)
    ' List all the SectionGroups in machine.config file
    Dim configSetting As Configuration =
        System.Configuration.ConfigurationManager.OpenMachineConfiguration()
    GridView1.DataSource = configSetting.SectionGroups
    GridView1.DataBind()
End Sub
```

C#

```
protected void Page_Load(Object sender, EventArgs e)
{
    // List all the SectionGroups in machine.config file
```

```
            Configuration configSetting =
                System.Configuration.ConfigurationManager.OpenMachineConfiguration();
            GridView1.DataSource = configSetting.SectionGroups;
            GridView1.DataBind();
    }
```

Protecting Configuration Settings

ASP.NET stores configuration information inside the registry using the Data Protection API (or DPAPI). For example, Listing 28-36 shows how you can store a process model section's username and password information inside the registry.

LISTING 28-36: Storing the username and password in the registry and then referencing these settings in the machine.config file

```
<processModel
    userName="registry:HKLM\SOFTWARE\ExampleApp\Identity\ASPNET_SETREG,userName"
    password="registry:HKLM\SOFTWARE\ExampleApp\Identity\ASPNET_SETREG,password"
/>
```

ASP.NET 4.5 includes a system for protecting sensitive data stored in the configuration system. It uses industry-standard XML encryption to encrypt specified sections of configuration that contain any sensitive data.

Developers often feel apprehensive about sticking sensitive items such as connection strings, passwords, and more in the web.config file. For this reason, ASP.NET makes possible the storing of these items in a format that is not readable by any human or machine process without intimate knowledge of the encryption techniques and keys used in the encryption process.

One of the most encrypted items in the web.config file is the <connectionStrings> section. Listing 28-37 shows an example of a web.config file with an exposed connection string.

LISTING 28-37: A standard connection string exposed in the web.config file

```
<?xml version="1.0"?>
<configuration>
    <appSettings/>
    <connectionStrings>
        <add name="AdventureWorks"
          connectionString="Server=localhost;Integrated Security=True;Database=AdventureWorks"
          providerName="System.Data.SqlClient" />
    </connectionStrings>
    <system.web>
        <compilation debug="false" />
        <authentication mode="Forms">
            <forms name="Wrox" loginUrl="Login.aspx" path="/">
                <credentials passwordFormat="Clear">
                    <user name="JasonGaylord" password="Reindeer" />
                </credentials>
            </forms>
        </authentication>
    </system.web>
</configuration>
```

In this case, you might want to encrypt this connection string to the database. To accomplish this, the install of ASP.NET provides a tool called *aspnet_regiis.exe*. You find this tool at C:\WINDOWS\Microsoft .NET\Framework\v4.0.30319. To use this tool to encrypt the <connectionStrings> section, open a command prompt and navigate to the specified folder using cd C:\WINDOWS\Microsoft.NET\Framework\ v4.0.30319. Another option is to open the Visual Studio 2012 command prompt as an administrator. After you are in one of these environments, you use the syntax presented in Listing 28-38 to encrypt the <connectionStrings> section.

LISTING 28-38: Encrypting the <connectionStrings> section

```
aspnet_regiis -pe "connectionStrings" -app "/EncryptionExample"
```

Running this bit of script produces the results presented in Figure 28-5.

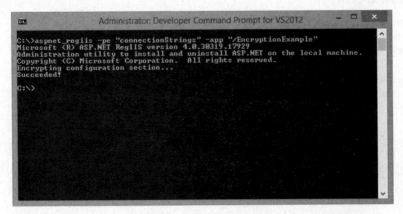

FIGURE 28-5

Looking over the script used in the encryption process, you can see that the -pe command specifies the section in the web.config file to encrypt, whereas the -app command specifies which application to actually work with. If you look back at the web.config file and examine the encryption that occurred, you see something similar to the code in Listing 28-39.

LISTING 28-39: The encrypted <connectionStrings> section of the web.config file

```
<?xml version="1.0"?>
<configuration>
    <connectionStrings configProtectionProvider="RsaProtectedConfigurationProvider">
        <EncryptedData Type="http://www.w3.org/2001/04/xmlenc#Element"
            xmlns="http://www.w3.org/2001/04/xmlenc#">
        <EncryptionMethod
            Algorithm="http://www.w3.org/2001/04/xmlenc#tripledes-cbc" />
        <KeyInfo xmlns="http://www.w3.org/2000/09/xmldsig#">
            <EncryptedKey xmlns="http://www.w3.org/2001/04/xmlenc#">
                <EncryptionMethod
                    Algorithm="http://www.w3.org/2001/04/xmlenc#rsa-1_5" />
                <KeyInfo xmlns="http://www.w3.org/2000/09/xmldsig#">
                    <KeyName>Rsa Key</KeyName>
                </KeyInfo>
                <CipherData>
                    <CipherValue>UAqurj7pvS7WLwt4CSXJN2Fe2yYcrXA1K
                    Go33DVzec0nOhUy6FYO751MARiaJvqSepvkuRPSU3ZRP
                    xESmc7p4t3N6i9OGT3q3xHIzSJV7rzSSpDZcd+DxQkwPp
                    oXeGx7x7H22DSWrxDEyn4EJQf3ZeTY2tcTcDcvH4UNLTD
                    wIW2ACM56s/OOZOCOVUq4nKdRC0q4W8enBoNIvhDdL2E5
                    ZpTUAsJl4MvrWOMqlVX8F0P6Osn+apX5Zh9QhvPLXz7G8
                    nbwNzSc8tLuCW1M419dmM6r97vID6qxNgBz3bJbM03BjT
                    WUBQEXSN5HBmuAVFl1QjzBDZbqFrBl+Mgu7TpQMw==</CipherValue>
                </CipherData>
            </EncryptedKey>
        </KeyInfo>
        <CipherData>
```

```
                  <CipherValue>OEr7uMFQU7736eCharUocrRs442uD3Ivi2woGfon
                     SnpiReILGlkSfMdfdF7CLzfUIt8KIARZeKkAswJrOVDjinM75840
                     QLmwFnQhtSqKqphM92kbudTsmVrQkKJFN6Y2PElTpa9BG+nEf0HX
                     Y7cERhj2Yv1Hua7B+oYhM5TtfPUTEP3fpqROPNSlWvRmJN2XwDyj
                     mjTGON2Lk0pbAAf8rLwVB0IGT3lF6CKsK0YCPuiMAcFAHzcgzEXP
                     UFXOqJqXBFjoEL0jx/sWV4DHOFJq5p2+DPxHKoI4ZTWo1p1oxFWF
                     roleLimzygvjnsUmbHyP</CipherValue>
               </CipherData>
            </EncryptedData>
         </connectionStrings>
         <system.web>
            <compilation debug="true" targetFramework="4.5"/>
            <httpRuntime targetFramework="4.5"/>
         </system.web>
      </configuration>
```

Now when you work with a connection string in your ASP.NET application, ASP.NET itself automatically decrypts this section to utilize the values stored. Looking at the `web.config` file, you can see a subsection within the `<system.web>` section that exposes a username and password as clear text. This is also something that you might want to encrypt in order to keep it away from prying eyes. Because it is a subsection, you use the script presented in Listing 28-40.

LISTING 28-40: Encrypting the <authentication> section

```
aspnet_regiis -pe "system.web/authentication" -app "/EncryptionExample"
```

This code gives you the partial results presented in Listing 28-41.

LISTING 28-41: The encrypted <authentication> section of the web.config file

```
<?xml version="1.0"?>
<configuration>
   <connectionStrings>
      <add name="ExampleApplication"
        connectionString="server=ExampleApplicationServer;
        database=ExampleApplicationDB;uid=WebUser;pwd=P@$$worD9"
        providerName="System.Data.SqlClient" />
   </connectionStrings>
   <system.web>
      <compilation debug="true" targetFramework="4.5"/>
      <httpRuntime targetFramework="4.5"/>
      <authentication
        configProtectionProvider="RsaProtectedConfigurationProvider">
         <EncryptedData Type="http://www.w3.org/2001/04/xmlenc#Element"
            xmlns="http://www.w3.org/2001/04/xmlenc#">
            <EncryptionMethod
              Algorithm="http://www.w3.org/2001/04/xmlenc#tripledes-cbc" />
            <KeyInfo xmlns="http://www.w3.org/2000/09/xmldsig#">
               <EncryptedKey xmlns="http://www.w3.org/2001/04/xmlenc#">
                  <EncryptionMethod
                    Algorithm="http://www.w3.org/2001/04/xmlenc#rsa-1_5" />
                  <KeyInfo xmlns="http://www.w3.org/2000/09/xmldsig#">
                     <KeyName>Rsa Key</KeyName>
                  </KeyInfo>
                  <CipherData>
                     <CipherValue>P4mqGAlV4Nmdsa+c3nARXx5OQeeOyo6JrKFJ/
                        DYYGFomQwq3tvErbaHQhffRr9S3UkeNcloFM/zg0Oxvdfq9X
                        tkR/dOb0o8LOKAnlBwoJ9+sKAdsd2U6tv+Of+k7h1Qwi3jM4
                        guTiBAudpZXr9TnjouwN9KI3xmebagYTkR2NSPFoFMcH5RQb
                        +iIRLeiGecVMpz17qz72acd3KWzabYHW2W+zbVA9lm2aATUb
                        kDrdk3BahxzdOID62+svSDqzSgyibaAjc4WSN1nTRsNvPKLo
                        aIUJiliTxn7APaunH8afdeqMmvOEGI3jVt733Pcz2rljMjUQ
```

LISTING 28-41 *(continued)*

```
                                    yPkxfow1OMyhGKfAg==</CipherValue>
                        </CipherData>
                    </EncryptedKey>
                </KeyInfo>
                <CipherData>
                    <CipherValue>kqNlrAcWy2ZHK+cRSpWQUOX4OPfjl2x3wqu
                        f9cXNFU+TuleXF3EUwCb/SQCYgdJz</CipherValue>
                </CipherData>
            </EncryptedData>
        </authentication>
    </system.web>
</configuration>
```

After you have sections of your web.config file encrypted, you need a process to decrypt these sections to their original unencrypted values. To accomplish this task, you use the aspnet_regiis tool illustrated in Listing 28-42.

LISTING 28-42: Decrypting the <connectionStrings> section in the web.config file

```
aspnet_regiis -pd "connectionStrings" -app "/EncryptionExample"
```

Running this script returns the encrypted values to original values.

Editing Configuration Files

So far in this chapter, you have learned about configuration files and what each configuration entry means. Even though the configuration entries are in an easy, human-readable XML format, editing these entries can be cumbersome. To help with editing, Microsoft ships three tools:

➤ Visual Studio 2012 IDE
➤ Web Site Administration Tool
➤ Internet Information Services (IIS) Manager

One of the nice capabilities of the Visual Studio 2012 IDE is that it supports IntelliSense-based editing for configuration files, as shown in Figure 28-6.

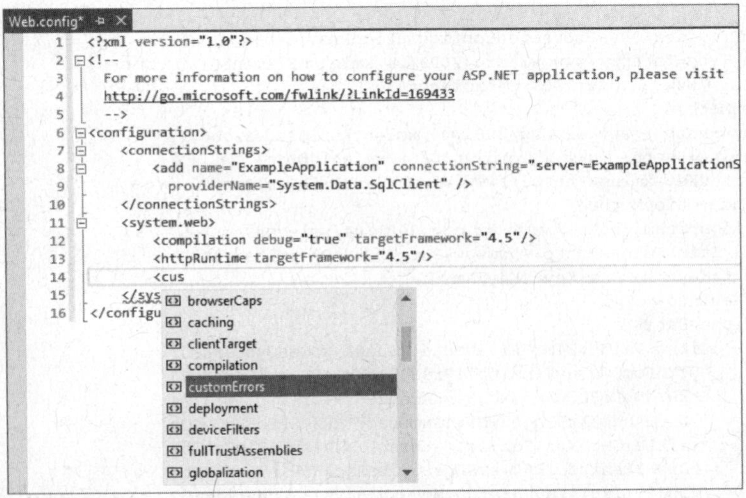

FIGURE 28-6

The Visual Studio 2012 IDE also supports XML element syntax checking, as shown in Figure 28-7.

> **NOTE** *XML element syntax checking and IntelliSense for XML elements are accomplished using the XSD-based XML validation feature available for all the XML files inside Visual Studio 2012. The configuration XSD file is located at* `<drive>:\Program Files\Microsoft Visual Studio 11.0\Xml\Schemas\DotNetConfig40.xsd`.

```
Web.config*  ☐ ✕
   1     <?xml version="1.0"?>
   2   ⊟ <!--
   3         For more information on how to configure your ASP.NET application, please visit
   4         http://go.microsoft.com/fwlink/?LinkId=169433
   5         -->
   6   ⊟ <configuration>
   7   ⊟     <connectionStrings>
   8   ⊟         <add name="ExampleApplication" connectionString="server=ExampleApplicationS
   9               providerName="System.Data.SqlClient" />
  10         </connectionStrings>
  11   ⊟     <system.web>
  12             <compilation debug="true" targetFramework="4.5"/>
  13             <httpRuntime targetFramework="4.5"/>
  14             <customErrors
  15         </system.web>
  16     </configuration>
```

FIGURE 28-7

The Visual Studio 2012 IDE includes two new useful features via the XML toolbar options that can help you with formatting the configuration settings:

➤ **Reformat selection:** This option reformats the current XML notes content.

➤ **Format the whole document:** This option formats the entire XML document.

The Web Site Administration Tool and IIS Manager allow you to edit the configuration entries without knowing the XML element names and their corresponding values. Appendix D covers these tools in more detail.

CREATING CUSTOM SECTIONS

In addition to using the web.config file as discussed, you can also extend it and add your own custom sections to the file that you can make use of just as with the other sections.

One way of creating custom sections is to use some built-in handlers that enable you to read key-value pairs from the .config file. All three of the following handlers are from the System.Configuration namespace:

➤ `NameValueFileSectionHandler`: This handler works with the current `<appSettings>` section of the web.config file. You are able to use this handler to create new sections of the configuration file that behave in the same manner as the `<appSettings>` section.

➤ `DictionarySectionHandler`: This handler works with a dictionary collection of key-value pairs.

➤ `SingleTagSectionHandler`: This handler works from a single element in the configuration file and allows you to read key-value pairs that are contained as attributes and values.

Next, this chapter looks at each of these handlers and some programmatic ways to customize the configuration file.

Using the NameValueFileSectionHandler Object

If you are looking to create a custom section that behaves like the `<appSettings>` section of the web `.config` file, then using this handler is the way to go. Above the `<system.web>` section of the `web.config` file, make a reference to the `NameValueFileSectionHandler` object, along with the other default references you will find in an ASP.NET 4.5 application. Listing 28-43 shows this additional reference.

LISTING 28-43: Creating your own custom section of key-value pairs in the web.config file

```
<configSections>
    <section name="MyCompanyAppSettings"
      type="System.Configuration.NameValueFileSectionHandler, System,
      Version=4.0.0.0, Culture=neutral, PublicKeyToken=b77a5c561934e089"
      restartOnExternalChanges="false" />
</configSections>
```

After you have made this reference to the `System.Configuration.NameValueFileSectionHandler` object and have given it a name (in this case, `MyCompanyAppSettings`), you can create a section in your web `.config` file that makes use of this reference, as illustrated in Listing 28-44.

LISTING 28-44: Creating your own custom key-value pair section in the web.config

```
<configuration>
    <MyCompanyAppSettings>
        <add key="Key1" value="This is value 1" />
        <add key="Key2" value="This is value 2" />
    </MyCompanyAppSettings>
    <system.web>
        <!-- Removed for clarity -->
    </system.web>
</configuration>
```

After you have this code in place within your `web.config` file, you can programmatically get access to this section, as illustrated in Listing 28-45.

LISTING 28-45: Getting access to your custom section in the web.config file

VB
```
Dim nvc As NameValueCollection = New NameValueCollection()
nvc = System.Configuration.ConfigurationManager.GetSection("MyCompanyAppSettings")
Response.Write(nvc("Key1") + "<br />")
Response.Write(nvc("Key2"))
```

C#
```
NameValueCollection nvc = new NameValueCollection();
nvc = ConfigurationManager.GetSection("MyCompanyAppSettings") as
    NameValueCollection;
Response.Write(nvc["Key1"] + "<br />");
Response.Write(nvc["Key2"]);
```

For this to work, you must import the `System.Collections.Specialized` namespace into the file, because this is where you will find the `NameValueCollection` object.

Using the DictionarySectionHandler Object

The `DictionarySectionHandler` works nearly the same as the `NameValueFileSectionHandler`. The difference, however, is that the `DictionarySectionHandler` returns a `HashTable` object instead of returning an `Object`. Listing 28-46 presents this handler.

```
<configSections>
    <section name="MyCompanyAppSettings"
        type="System.Configuration.DictionarySectionHandler, System,
        Version=4.0.0.0, Culture=neutral, PublicKeyToken=b77a5c561934e089"
        restartOnExternalChanges="false" />
</configSections>
```

With this configuration setting in place, you can then make the same `MyCompanyAppSettings` section in the `web.config` file, as shown in Listing 28-47.

```
<configuration>
    <MyCompanyAppSettings>
        <add key="Key1" value="This is value 1" />
        <add key="Key2" value="This is value 2" />
    </MyCompanyAppSettings>
    <system.web>
        <!-- Removed for clarity -->
    </system.web>
</configuration>
```

Now that the `web.config` file is ready, you can call the items from code using the `Configuration` API, as illustrated in Listing 28-48.

VB

```
Dim nv As NameValueCollection = New NameValueCollection()
nv = System.Configuration.ConfigurationManager.GetSection("MyCompanyAppSettings")
Response.Write(nv("Key1") + "<br />")
Response.Write(nv("Key2"))
```

C#.

```
NameValueCollection nv = new NameValueCollection();
nv = ConfigurationManager.GetSection("MyCompanyAppSettings") as NameValueCollection;
Response.Write(nv["Key1"] + "<br />");
Response.Write(nv["Key2"]);
```

Using the SingleTagSectionHandler Object

The `SingleTagSectionHandler` works almost the same as the previous `NameValueFileSectionHandler` and `DictionarySectionHandler`. However, this object looks to work with a single element that contains the key-value pairs as attributes.

Listing 28-49 presents this handler.

```
<configSections>
    <section name="MyCompanyAppSettings"
        type="System.Configuration.SingleTagSectionHandler, System,
        Version=4.0.0.0, Culture=neutral, PublicKeyToken=b77a5c561934e089"
        restartOnExternalChanges="false" />
</configSections>
```

With this configuration setting in place, you can make a different `MyCompanyAppSettings` section in the `web.config` file, as presented in Listing 28-50.

LISTING 28-50: Creating a custom key-value pair section in the web.config file

```
<configuration>
    <MyCompanyAppSettings Key1="This is value 1" Key2="This is value 2" />
    <system.web>
        <!-- Removed for clarity -->
    </system.web>
</configuration>
```

Now that the `web.config` file is complete, you can call the items from code using the `Configuration` API, as illustrated in Listing 28-51.

LISTING 28-51: Getting access to your custom section in the web.config file

VB

```
Dim ht As Hashtable = New Hashtable()
ht = System.Configuration.ConfigurationManager.GetSection("MyCompanyAppSettings")
Response.Write(ht("Key1") + "<br />")
Response.Write(ht("Key2"))

Dim ht As Hashtable = New Hashtable()
ht = System.Configuration.ConfigurationManager.GetSection("MyCompanyAppSettings")
Response.Write(ht("Key1") + "<br />")
Response.Write(ht("Key2"))
```

C#

```
Hashtable ht = new Hashtable();
ht = ConfigurationManager.GetSection("MyCompanyAppSettings") as Hashtable;
Response.Write(ht["Key1"] + "<br />");
Response.Write(ht["Key2"]);
```

Using Your Own Custom Configuration Handler

You can also create your own custom configuration handler. To do this, you first must create a class that represents your section in the `web.config` file. In your `App_Code` folder, create a class called `MyCompanySettings`. Listing 28-52 shows this class.

LISTING 28-52: The MyCompanySettings class

VB

```
Public Class MyCompanySettings
    Inherits ConfigurationSection

    <ConfigurationProperty("Key1", DefaultValue:="This is the value of Key 1", _
        IsRequired:=False)> _
    Public ReadOnly Property Key1() As String
        Get
            Return MyBase.Item("Key1").ToString()
        End Get
    End Property

    <ConfigurationProperty("Key2", IsRequired:=True)> _
    Public ReadOnly Property Key2() As String
        Get
```

```
                    Return MyBase.Item("Key2").ToString()
            End Get
        End Property
    End Class
```

C#

```
using System.Configuration;

public class MyCompanySettings : ConfigurationSection
{
    [ConfigurationProperty("Key1", DefaultValue = "This is the value of Key 1",
     IsRequired = false)]
    public string Key1
    {
        get
        {
            return this["Key1"] as string;
        }
    }

    [ConfigurationProperty("Key2", IsRequired = true)]
    public string Key2
    {
        get
        {
            return this["Key2"] as string;
        }
    }
}
```

You can see that this class inherits from the ConfigurationSection and the two properties that are created using the ConfigurationProperty attribute. You can use a couple of attributes here, such as the DefaultValue, IsRequired, IsKey, and IsDefaultCollection.

After you have this class in place, you can configure your application to use this handler, as illustrated in Listing 28-53.

LISTING 28-53: Making a reference to the MyCompanySettings object

```
<configSections>
    <section name="MyCompanySettings" type="MyCompanySettings" />
</configSections>
```

You can now use this section in your web.config file, as illustrated in Listing 28-54.

LISTING 28-54: Creating your own custom key-value pair section in the web.config file

```
<configuration>
    <configSections>
        <!-- Removed for clarity -->
    </configSections>
    <MyCompanySettings Key2="Here is a value for Key2" />
    <system.web>
        <!-- Removed for clarity -->
    </system.web>
</configuration>
```

Using this configuration you can programmatically access this key-value pair from code, as illustrated in Listing 28-55.

LISTING 28-55: Accessing a custom section in the web.config file

VB

```
Dim cs As MyCompanySettings = New MyCompanySettings()
cs = ConfigurationManager.GetSection("MyCompanySettings")
Response.Write(cs.Key1 + "<br />")
Response.Write(cs.Key2)
```

C#

```
MyCompanySettings cs = ConfigurationManager.GetSection("MyCompanySettings") as
    MyCompanySettings;
Response.Write(cs.Key1 + "<br />");
Response.Write(cs.Key2);
```

USING CONFIGURATION TRANSFORMS

By now, you should see how powerful the XML configuration system is. However, you may also be thinking of how many settings you'll need to change or about the manual process of changing the `config` files upon deployment. Although there have been several solutions in the past besides these two manual processes, the ASP.NET team realized that something needed to change.

With ASP.NET 4 and Visual Studio 2010, `web.config` transforms were introduced. ASP.NET 4.5 continues to use this behavior. The transforms can be used with any configuration element or attribute, including the custom `config` sections covered in this chapter.

> **NOTE** *The configuration transforms work with web applications and not websites.*

Adding web.config Transforms

`Web.config` transforms are used with ASP.NET web applications. After creating a new ASP.NET web application, you'll notice that the `web.config` file can be expanded and will include a `web.Debug` `.config` and `web.Release.config` file. Both of these files are the `config` transform files for the related configuration mode. Since each ASP.NET web application starts with the Debug and Release configuration mode, these files are created for you, as shown in Figure 28-8.

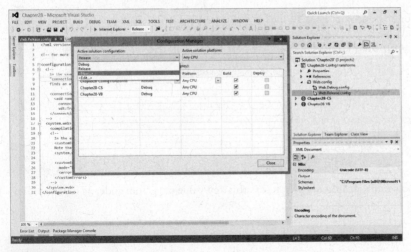

FIGURE 28-8

In Figure 28-8, you can see that there are two configuration modes. You can also see in the Solution Explorer that there are two additional `web.config` files, as mentioned a moment ago.

However, assume for a moment that you have another custom configuration process that corresponds with the new Publish features in Visual Studio 2012. This configuration process includes deploying to a staging server. You can add a new configuration mode called Staging by choosing the New option in the Configuration Manager window, as shown in Figure 28-8. Next, you can enter the new configuration mode name and copy any settings from another build configuration, as shown in Figure 28-9.

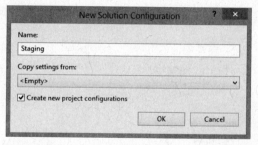

FIGURE 28-9

After you add the new configuration mode, the mode will be available in the Configuration Manager window, as shown in Figure 28-10.

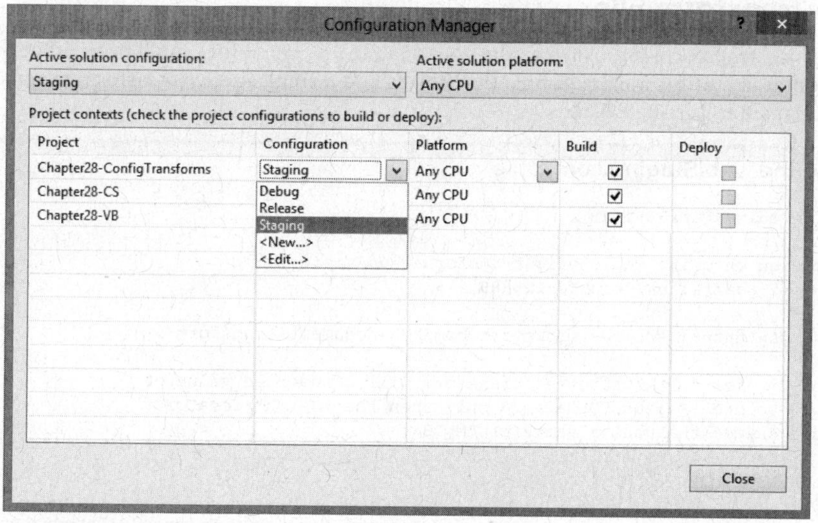

FIGURE 28-10

At this point, you've added the new configuration mode. However, the transform has not yet been added. Visual Studio 2012 has a built-in method to assist you with adding the transform. If you right-click on the `web.config` file in Solution Explorer, you'll see an option called Add Config Transform (shown in Figure 28-11).

After you add the config transform, you can see the corresponding file in Solution Explorer, as shown in Figure 28-12.

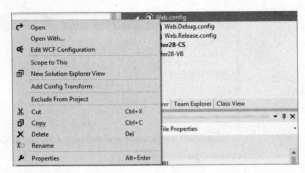

FIGURE 28-11

FIGURE 28-12

Updating the Config Transform File

After opening one of the config transform files, such as the `web.Staging.config` file, you'll notice that the file is essentially empty. Contained in this file are sample transforms and a single, active transform to remove the `debug` attribute, as illustrated in Listing 28-56.

LISTING 28-56: Browsing the web.Staging.config file

```xml
<?xml version="1.0" encoding="utf-8"?>

<!-- For more information on using web.config transformation visit
     http://go.microsoft.com/fwlink/?LinkId=125889 -->

<configuration xmlns:xdt="http://schemas.microsoft.com/XML-Document-Transform">
    <!--
    In the example below, the "SetAttributes" transform will change the value of
    "connectionString" to use "ReleaseSQLServer" only when the "Match" locator
    finds an attribute "name" that has a value of "MyDB".

    <connectionStrings>
      <add name="MyDB"
        connectionString="Data Source=ReleaseSQLServer;Initial Catalog=MyReleaseDB;Integrated
        Security=True"
        xdt:Transform="SetAttributes" xdt:Locator="Match(name)"/>
    </connectionStrings>
  -->
    <system.web>
        <compilation xdt:Transform="RemoveAttributes(debug)" />
        <!--
    In the example below, the "Replace" transform will replace the entire
    <customErrors> section of your web.config file.
    Note that because there is only one customErrors section under the
    <system.web> node, there is no need to use the "xdt:Locator" attribute.

        <customErrors defaultRedirect="GenericError.htm"
          mode="RemoteOnly" xdt:Transform="Replace">
          <error statusCode="500" redirect="InternalError.htm"/>
        </customErrors>
      -->
    </system.web>
</configuration>
```

> **NOTE** *As suggested in the comments of the files, a full listing of the transformation commands for* web.config *transforms can be found at* http://go.microsoft.com/fwlink/?LinkId=125889.

The compilation configuration element contains a transform. This transform is possible because of the XML Document Transform namespace that has been added to the configuration root element. You'll notice that the value for the transform attribute is RemoveAttributes(debug). The RemoveAttributes name is the transform method that will be used. In this case, this method will remove attributes from the configuration element. The value passed into the method is debug. This means that the attribute named debug will be removed from the configuration.

There are two attributes for the XML Document Transform namespace. The first, transform, is demonstrated in the transformation of the compilation configuration element. The possible methods for the transform attribute are:

➤ Insert: Inserts the defined element as a child to the selected element

➤ InsertAfter: Inserts the element after the specified path (XPath expression)

➤ InsertBefore: Inserts the element before the specified path (XPath expression)

➤ Remove: Removes the selected element

➤ RemoveAll: Removes all of the selected elements

➤ RemoveAttributes: Removes the specified attributes of the current element

➤ Replace: Replaces the entire element with the one specified in the transform file

➤ SetAttributes: Sets the specified values of the specified attributes of the current element

The second attribute, location, is used to select a particular element. The possible methods for the location attribute are:

➤ Condition: An XPath expression that is evaluated on the current element to determine when the transform should occur

➤ Match: Specifies one or more elements that have a matching value

➤ XPath: An XPath expression that navigates to another element and then evaluates a condition to determine whether the transform should occur

Using both the location and transform attributes can be necessary. For instance, you created a custom configuration section earlier in this chapter called MyCompanyAppSettings as a NameValueFileSectionHandler. When you are transforming the configuration file, you may need to replace a value for only one of the items in the collection. As an example, add the following to the MyCompanyAppSettings configuration section:

```
<add key="Key2" value="The is value 2 in staging"
    xdt:Transform="SetAttributes(value)" xdt:Locator="Match(key)" />
```

After publishing to your staging server using the staging configuration mode, you should notice that your web.config file will look similar to Listing 28-57.

> **NOTE** *Chapter 33 details the various publish methods.*

LISTING 28-57: The result of the config transform

```xml
<?xml version="1.0"?>
<configuration>
    <configSections>
        <section name="MyCompanyAppSettings"
            type="System.Configuration.NameValueFileSectionHandler, System,
                Version=4.0.0.0, Culture=neutral, PublicKeyToken=b77a5c561934e089"
            restartOnExternalChanges="false" />
    </configSections>
    <MyCompanyAppSettings>
        <add key="Key1" value="This is value 1" />
        <add key="Key2" value="The is value 2 in staging" />
    </MyCompanyAppSettings>
    <system.web>
      <compilation targetFramework="4.5" />
      <httpRuntime targetFramework="4.5" />
    </system.web>
</configuration>
```

This practice is used frequently to replace the connectionString value for specific connections during a release deployment.

> **NOTE** *There are many options when using configuration transforms that I simply cannot cover in this chapter. It is highly recommended that you continue to search online for more examples of configuration transformations. You can also search MSDN for Web.config Transformation Syntax.*

BUNDLING AND MINIFICATION

ASP.NET 4.5 includes a new feature to minify and bundle CSS and JavaScript within your web application. If you use any of the default project templates in Visual Studio 2012, this new feature is turned on.

What Is Bundling and Minification?

Most static content files, such as CSS and JavaScript, contain a lot of whitespace and comments. Although the whitespace and comments do not necessarily take up significant space, depending on the client's Internet speed, the additional space can noticeably slow the page load of the site. Figure 28-13 shows the network traffic before minification.

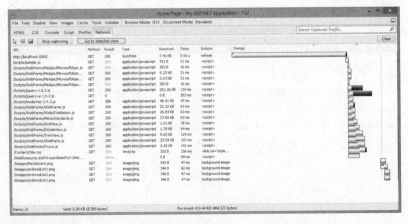

FIGURE 28-13

An example of a JavaScript snippet before minification can be found is as follows:

```
function helloWorld(firstName) {
    // Declare variables
    var message = "Hello, " + firstName;

    // Display an alert message
    alert(message);
}
```

In the past, one of the best techniques for compressing static content was to enable HTTP compression on the web server, such as IIS. The most common compression method was to gzip the static files. The issue with this process is that it is very difficult to customize which files to minify. In larger organizations, you may need to get an administrator involved to update the web server for you. In ASP.NET, you now have the ability to have complete control over the minification process without the need for an administrator.

To take the minification process a step further, you can also bundle a group of files, such as all CSS files, into a single minified path.

Enabling Bundling and Minification

There are numerous ways to bundle and minify scripts and styles. One way to handle the bundling is to add a bundle.config file to the project and add the appropriate file listing in the file. However, you can also add the files to the bundle manually during the application start method.

To enable this feature in your projects, download the Microsoft ASP.NET Web Optimization Framework package from the package manager. After it's downloaded and enabled, head right to the Global.asax file. Then, in the Global.asax file, include the namespace System.Web.Optimization. Finally, to bundle and minify CSS files located in the styles folder of your web, for example, add the following to the Application_Start method:

```
var cssBundle = new Bundle("~/styles/css");
cssBundle.IncludeDirectory("~/styles", "*.css");
BundleTable.Bundles.Add(cssBundle);
```

Like everything else in ASP.NET, developers can have complete control over the way CSS and JavaScript are bundled. This includes creating custom transforms, including and excluding specific files, and creating multiple bundles. It is important to note that the files are minified and added in the order they are listed. If a script file is dependent upon another file, it's best to move the dependent file to a bundle above.

Figure 28-14 shows the network traffic after minification.

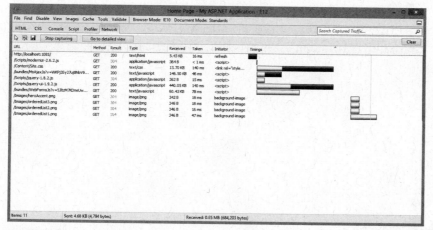

FIGURE 28-14

The JavaScript snippet from earlier, when compressed, will render like so:

```
function helloWorld(n){var t="Hello, "+n;alert(t)}
```

> **NOTE** *For more about customizing bundling, search online for ASP.NET 4.5 Bundling and Minification. Also note that since this feature is released out-of-band on NuGet (package manager in Visual Studio), additional enhancements will likely be made before the next version of Visual Studio is released.*

SUMMARY

In this chapter, you have seen the ASP.NET configuration system and learned how it does not rely on the IIS metabase. Instead, ASP.NET uses an XML configuration system that is human-readable.

You also looked at the two different ASP.NET XML configuration files:

➤ `machine.config`
➤ `web.config`

The `machine.config` file applies default settings to all web applications on the server. However, if the server has multiple versions of the framework installed, the `machine.config` file applies to a particular framework version. On the other hand, a particular web application can customize or override its own configuration information using `web.config` files. Using a `web.config` file, you can also configure the applications on an application-by-application or folder-by-folder basis.

Next, you looked at some typical configuration settings that you can apply to an ASP.NET application, such as configuring connection strings, session state, browser capabilities, and so on. Then you looked at protecting the configuration section using cryptographic algorithms. You also reviewed replacing configuration values upon deployment. Finally, you looked at minifying your scripts and CSS files and placing those files into a bundle.

29

Debugging and Error Handling

WHAT'S IN THIS CHAPTER?

➤ Tracing your ASP.NET applications

➤ Exploring ASP.NET debugging options

➤ Handling exceptions and errors efficiently

➤ Debugging with Page Inspector

WROX.COM CODE DOWNLOADS FOR THIS CHAPTER

Please note that all the code examples in this chapter are available as a part of this chapter's code download on the book's website at www.wrox.com on the Download Code tab.

Your code always runs exactly as you wrote it, and you will *never* get it right the first time. So, expect to spend about 30 percent of your time debugging, and to be a successful debugger, you should learn to use the available tools effectively. Visual Studio has upped the ante, giving you a host of features that greatly improve your debugging experience. Having so many features, however, can be overwhelming at first. This chapter breaks down all the techniques available to you, one at a time, while presenting a holistic view of Visual Studio, the Common Language Runtime (CLR), and the Base Class Library (BCL).

Additionally, because debugging is more than stepping through code, this chapter discusses efficient error and exception handling, tracing and logging, and cross-language (C#, Visual Basic, client-side JavaScript, XSLT, and SQL Stored Procedure) debugging.

DESIGN-TIME SUPPORT

Visual Studio has always done a good job of warning you of potential errors at design time. *Syntax notifications* or *squiggles* underline code that won't compile or that might cause an error before you have compiled the project. A new *error notification* pops up when an exception occurs during a debugging session and recommends a course of action that prevents the exception. At every step, Visual Studio tries to be smarter, anticipating your needs and catching common mistakes.

Rico Mariani, the Chief Architect of Visual Studio, has used the term "The Pit of Success" to describe the experience Microsoft wants you to have with Visual Studio. When Microsoft designed these features, it wanted the customer to simply fall into winning practices. The company tried to achieve this by making it more difficult for you to write buggy code or make common mistakes. Microsoft's developers put a great deal of thought into building APIs that point you in the right direction.

Syntax Notifications

Both the Visual Basic and C# editors show squiggles and tooltips for many syntax errors well before compilation, as illustrated in Figure 29-1.

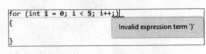

FIGURE 29-1

Syntax notifications aren't just for CLR programming languages; Visual Studio works just as well through the XML Editor and includes capabilities like the following:

➤ Full XML 1.0 syntax checking

➤ Support for XSD and DTD validation and IntelliSense

➤ Support for XSLT 1.0 syntax checking

Figure 29-2 shows a detailed tooltip indicating that the element `<junk>` does not have any business being in the `web.config` file. The editor knows this because of a combination of the XSD validation support in the XML Editor and the addition of schemas for configuration files such as `web.config`. This change is welcome for anyone who, when manually editing a `web.config` file, has wondered whether he guessed the right elements.

```
Web.config
        <?xml version="1.0"?>

    <!--
          For more information on how to configure your ASP.NET application, please visit
          http://go.microsoft.com/fwlink/?LinkId=169433
          -->

    <configuration>
      <connectionStrings>
        <junk></junk>
      </c
         The element 'connectionStrings' has invalid child element 'junk'. List of possible elements expected: 'add, remove, clear'.
```

FIGURE 29-2

The ASPX/HTML Editor benefits from these capabilities as well; for example, Figure 29-3 shows a warning that the `<badElement/>` element is not available in the active schema. Code that appears in `<script runat="Server"/>` blocks in ASP.NET pages is also parsed and marked with squiggles. This makes including code in your pages considerably easier. Notice also that the ASP.NET page in Figure 29-3 has an XHTML DOCTYPE declaration on the first line, and the HTML element has a default XHTML namespace. This HTML page is treated as XML because XHTML has been targeted.

```
Default.aspx
    <%@ Page Language="C#" AutoEventWireup="true" CodeFile="Default.aspx.cs"

    <!DOCTYPE html>

    <html xmlns="http://www.w3.org/1999/xhtml">
    <head runat="server">
        <title></title>
    </head>
    <body>
        <form id="form1" runat="server">
        <div>
        <badelement></badelement>
        <
            Validation (XHTML5): Element 'badelement' is not supported.
```

FIGURE 29-3

The Visual Basic Editor takes assistance to the next level with a *smart tag* like the pull-down/button that appears when you hover your mouse cursor over a squiggle. A very nicely rendered modeless window appears with your code in a box along with some suggested changes to make your code compile. Figure 29-4 shows a recommendation to insert a missing `End If`; making the correction is simple—just click `Insert the missing 'End If'`.

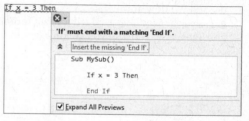

All these design-time features exist to help you ensure better code while it's being written, before it's been compiled and run. Two related features—the Immediate and Command windows—help you run arbitrary code within the development environment as well as organize the tasks still to be performed.

FIGURE 29-4

Immediate and Command Window

The Immediate window lets you run arbitrary bits of code in design mode without compiling your application. You can evaluate code at design time or while you are debugging. It can be a great way to test a line of code or a static method quickly. The Immediate mode of this window is used primarily for debugging.

Access the Immediate window from Debug ➪ Windows ➪ Immediate. To evaluate a variable or run a method, simply click in the Immediate window and type a question mark (?) followed by the expression, variable, or method you want to evaluate.

The Immediate window can also be switched into the Command window by prefacing commands with a greater-than sign (>). When you enter a greater-than sign in the Immediate or Command window, an IntelliSense drop-down appears exposing the complete Visual Studio object model as well as any macros that you may have recorded. Command mode of this window is used for executing Visual Studio commands without using the menus. You can also execute commands that may not have a menu item.

If you type `>alias` into the Command window, you receive a complete list of all current aliases and their definitions. Some useful command aliases include the following:

➤ `>Log filename /overwrite /on|off`: The `Log` command starts logging all output from the Command window to a file. If no filename is included for logging, go to `cmdline.log`. This is one of the more useful and least-used features of the debugger, and reason enough to learn a few things about the Immediate and Command windows.

➤ `>Shell args /command /output /dir:folder`: The `Shell` command enables you to launch executable programs from within the Visual Studio Command window such as utilities, command shells, batch files, and so on.

Task List

The Task List in Visual Studio is more useful than you might think. People who have not given it much attention are missing out on a great feature. The Task list supports two views: User Tasks and Comments.

The User Tasks view enables you to add and modify tasks, which can include anything from "Remember to Test" to "Buy Milk." These tasks are stored in the `.suo` (solution user options) file that is a parallel partner to the `.sln` files.

The Comments view shows text from the comments in your code where those lines are prefixed with a specific token. Visual Studio comes configured to look for the `TODO:` token, but you can add your own in Tools ➪ Options ➪ Environment ➪ Task List.

In Figure 29-5, the comment token `HACK` has been added in the Options dialog box. A comment appears in the source with `HACK:` preceding it, so that comment line automatically appears in the Task List in the docked window at the bottom of Visual Studio. The three circles in Figure 29-5 illustrate the connection between the word HACK added to the Options dialog box and its subsequent appearance in the source code and Task List. You and your team can add as many of these tokens as you want.

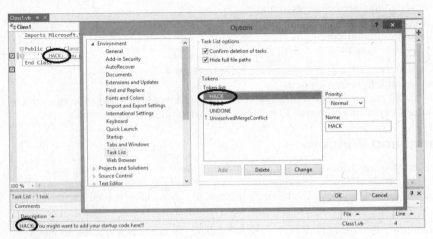

FIGURE 29-5

TRACING

Tracing is a way to monitor the execution of your ASP.NET application. You can record exception details and program flow in a way that does not affect the program's output. In classic ASP, tracing and debugging facilities were nearly nonexistent, forcing developers to use "got here" debugging in the form of many `Response.Write` statements that litter the resulting HTML with informal trace statements announcing to the programmer that the program "got here" and "got there" with each new line executed. This kind of intrusive tracing was very inconvenient to clean up, and many programmers ended up creating their own informal trace libraries to get around these classic ASP limitations.

In ASP.NET, there is rich support for tracing. The destination for trace output can be configured with `TraceListeners`, such as the `EventLogTraceListener`. Configuration of `TraceListeners` is covered later in this section. ASP.NET allows for trace forwarding between the ASP.NET page-specific `Trace` class and the standard Base Class Library's (BCL) `System.Diagnostics.Trace` used by non-web developers. Additionally, the resolution of the timing output by ASP.NET tracing has a precision of 18 digits for highly accurate profiling.

System.Diagnostics.Trace and ASP.NET's Page.Trace

Multiple things are named *Trace* in the whole of the .NET Framework, so it may appear that tracing isn't unified between web and non-web applications. Don't be confused because there is a class called `System.Diagnostics.Trace` and there is also a public property on `System.Web.UI.Page` called `Trace`. The `Trace` property on the `Page` class gives you access to the `System.Web.TraceContext` and the ASP.NET-specific tracing mechanism. The `TraceContext` class collects all the details and timing of a web request. It contains a number of methods, but the one you will use the most is `Write`. It also includes `Warn`, which simply calls `Write()`, and also ensures that the output generated by `Warn` is colored red.

If you're writing an ASP.NET application that has no supporting components or other assemblies that may be used in a non-web context, you can usually get a great deal of utility using only the ASP.NET `TraceContext`. However, ASP.NET support tracing is different from the rest of the Base Class Library's tracing. You explore ASP.NET's tracing facilities first, and then learn how to bridge the gap and see some features that make debugging even easier.

Page-Level Tracing

You can enable ASP.NET tracing on a page-by-page basis by adding `Trace="true"` to the `Page` directive in any ASP.NET page:

```
<%@ Page Language="C#" Inherits="System.Web.UI.Page" Trace="true" %>
```

Additionally, you can add the `TraceMode` attribute that sets `SortByCategory` or the default, `SortByTime`. You might include a number of categories, one per subsystem, and use `SortByCategory` to group them, or you might use `SortByTime` to see the methods that take up the most CPU time for your application. You can enable tracing programmatically as well, using the `Trace.IsEnabled` property. The capability to enable tracing programmatically means you can enable tracing via a query string, cookie, or IP address; it's up to you.

Application Tracing

Alternatively, you can enable tracing for the entire application by adding tracing settings in the `web.config` file. In the following example, `pageOutput="false"` and `requestLimit="20"` are used, so trace information is stored for 20 requests, but not displayed on the page:

```
<configuration>
   <system.web>
      <trace enabled="true" pageOutput="false" requestLimit="20"
         traceMode="SortByTime" localOnly="true" />
   </system.web>
</configuration>
```

The page-level settings take precedence over settings in the `web.config` file, so if `enabled="false"` is set in the `web.config` file but `trace="true"` is set on the page, tracing occurs.

Viewing Trace Data

You can view tracing for multiple page requests at the application level by requesting a special page handler called `trace.axd`. Note that `trace.axd` doesn't actually exist; it is provided by `System.Web.Handlers.TraceHandler`, a special `IHttpHandler` to which `trace.axd` is bound. When ASP.NET detects an HTTP request for `trace.axd`, that request is handled by the `TraceHandler` rather than by a page.

Create a website and a page, and in the `Page_Load` event, call `Trace.Write()`. Enable tracing in the `web.config` file as shown in Listing 29-1.

LISTING 29-1: Tracing using Page.Trace

```
<configuration>
   <system.web>
      <trace enabled="true" pageOutput="true" />
   </system.web>
</configuration>
```

VB

```
Protected Sub Page_Load(ByVal sender As Object,
   ByVal e As System.EventArgs)
   Handles Me.Load'All on one line!
      Trace.Write("This message is from the START OF the Page_Load method!")
End Sub
```

C#

```
protected void Page_Load(object sender, EventArgs e)
{
   Trace.Write("This message is from the START of the Page_Load method!");
}
```

Open the page in the browser a few times and notice that, although this page doesn't create any HTML to speak of, a great deal of trace information is presented in the browser, as shown in Figure 29-6, because the setting is pageOutput="true".

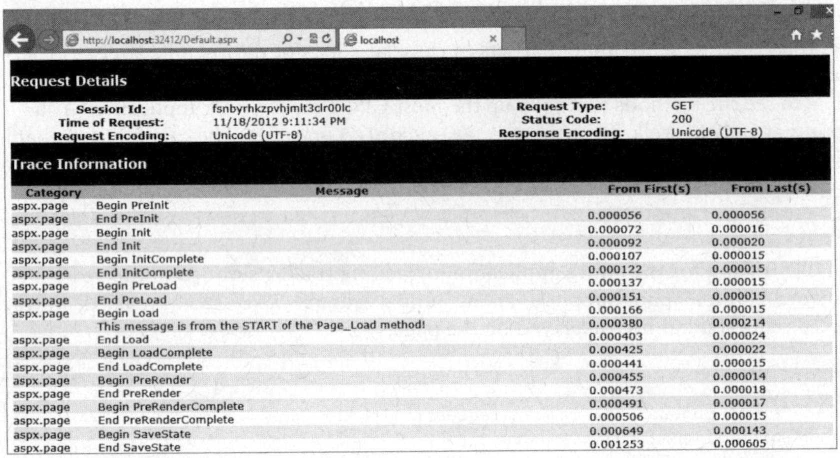

FIGURE 29-6

The message from Trace.Write appears after Begin Load and before End Load—it's right in the middle of the Page_Load method where you put it. The page was automatically JIT-compiled as you ran it, and that initial performance hit is over. Now that it's been compiled into native code, a subsequent run of this same page, performed by clicking Refresh in the browser, took only 0.000167 seconds on my laptop because the page had already compiled. Collecting this kind of very valuable performance timing data between trace statements is very easy and extremely useful.

Eleven different sections of tracing information provide a great deal of detail and specific insight into the ASP.NET page-rendering process, as described in Table 29-1.

TABLE 29-1

SECTION	DESCRIPTION
Request Details	Includes the ASP.NET session ID, the character encoding of the request and response, and the HTTP conversation's returned status code. Be aware of the request and response encoding, especially if you are using any non-Latin character sets. If you are returning languages other than English, you'll want your encoding to be UTF-8. Fortunately, that is the default.
Trace Information	Includes all the Trace.Write methods called during the lifetime of the HTTP request and a great deal of information about timing. This is probably the most useful section for debugging. The timing information located here is valuable when profiling and searching for methods in your application that take too long to execute.
Control Tree	Presents an HTML representation of the ASP.NET Control Tree. Shows each control's unique ID, runtime type, the number of bytes it took to be rendered, and the bytes it requires in ViewState and ControlState. Do not undervalue the usefulness of these two sections, particularly of the three columns showing the weight of each control. The weight of the control indicates the number of bytes occupied in ViewState and/or ControlState by that particular control. Be aware of the number of bytes that each of your controls uses, especially if you write your own custom controls, because you want your controls to return as few bytes as possible to keep overall page weight down.

Session State	Lists all the keys for a particular user's session, their types, and their values. Shows only the current user's session state.
Application State	Lists all the keys in the current application's `Application` object and their types and values.
Request Cookies	Lists all the cookies passed in during the page's request.
Response Cookies	Lists all the cookies that were passed back during the page's response.
Headers Collection	Shows all the headers that might be passed in during the request from the browser, including `Accept-Encoding`, indicating whether the browser supports compressed HTTP responses; `Accept-Languages`, a list of ISO language codes that indicate the order of the user's language preferences; and `User-Agent`, the identifying string for the user's browser. The string also contains information about the user's operating system and the version or versions of the .NET Framework he is running (on IE).
Form Collection	Displays a complete dump of the Form collection and all its keys and values.
Querystring Collection	Displays a dump of the Querystring collection and all its contained keys and values.
Server Variables	A complete dump of name-value pairs of everything that the web server knows about the application and the requesting browser.

Page output of tracing shows only the data collected for the current page request. However, when visiting `http://localhost/yoursite/trace.axd` you will see detailed data collected for all requests to the site thus far. If you're using the built-in ASP.NET Development Server, remove the current page from the URL and replace it with `trace.axd`. Do not change the automatically selected port or path.

Again, `trace.axd` is an internal handler, not a real page. When it's requested from a local browser, as shown in Figure 29-7, it displays all tracing information for all requests up to a preset limit.

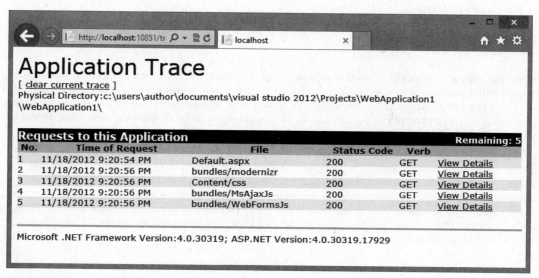

FIGURE 29-7

Figure 29-7 shows that five requests have been made to this application and the right side of the header indicates "Remaining: 5." That means that there are five more requests remaining before tracing stops for this application. After the final request, tracing data is not saved until an application recycle or until you click "Clear current trace" from the `trace.axd` page. The request limit can be raised in the `web.config` file at the expense of memory:

```
<trace requestLimit="100" pageOutput="true" enabled="true"/>
```

The maximum request limit value is 10000. If you try to use any greater value, ASP.NET uses 10000 anyway and gives you no error. However, you can add a property called `mostRecent` to the trace section in ASP.NET. When set to `true`, it shows the most recent requests that are stored in the trace log up to the request limit—instead of showing tracing in the order it occurs (the default)—without using up a lot of memory. Setting `mostRecent` to true causes memory to be used only for the trace information it stores and automatically throws away tracing information over the `requestLimit`.

Clicking View Details from `Trace.axd` on any of these requests takes you to a request-specific page with the same details shown in Figure 29-6.

Tracing from Components

The tracing facilities of ASP.NET are very powerful and can stand alone. However, you saw a previous mention of `System.Diagnostics.Trace`, the tracing framework in the Base Class Library that is not web-specific and that receives consistent and complete tracing information when an ASP.NET application calls a non-web-aware component. This can be confusing. Which should you use?

`System.Diagnostics.Trace` is the core .NET Framework tracing library. Along with `System.Diagnostics.Debug`, this class provides flexible, non-invasive tracing and debug output for any application. However, as mentioned earlier, rich tracing is built into the `System.Web` namespace. As a web developer, you will find yourself using ASP.NET's tracing facilities. You may need to have ASP.NET-specific tracing forwarded to the base framework's `System.Diagnostics.Trace`, or more likely, you will want to have your non-web-aware components output their trace calls to ASP.NET so you can take advantage of `trace.axd` and other ASP.NET-specific features.

Additionally, some confusion surrounds `Trace.Write` and `Debug.Write` functions. Look at the source code for `Debug.Write`, and you see something like this:

```
[Conditional("DEBUG")]
public static void Write(string message)
{
        TraceInternal.Write(message);
}
```

Notice that `Debug.Write` calls a function named `TraceInternal.Write`, which has a conditional attribute indicating that `Debug.Write` is compiled only if the debug preprocessor directive was set. In other words, you can put as many calls to `Debug.Write` as you want in your application without affecting your performance when you compile in Release mode. This enables you to be as verbose as you want during the debugging phase of development.

`TraceInternal` cycles through all attached trace listeners, meaning all classes that derive from the `TraceListener` base class and are configured in that application's configuration file. The default `TraceListener` lives in the aptly named `DefaultTraceListener` class and calls the Win32 API `OutputDebugString`. `OutputDebugString` sends your string into the abyss and, if a debugger is listening, it is displayed. If no debugger is listening, `OutputDebugString` does nothing. Everyone knows the debugger listens for output from `OutputDebugString`, so this can be a very effective way to listen in on debug versions of your application.

> **NOTE** *For quick-and-dirty no-touch debugging, try using DebugView from SysInternals at* `http://technet.microsoft.com/en-us/sysinternals/bb896647` `.aspx`. *DebugView requires no installation, works great with all your calls to* `Debug` `.Write`, *and has many cool features, such as highlighting and logging to a file.*

Now, if you look at the source code for `Trace.Write` (that's TRACE not DEBUG), you see something like this:

```
[Conditional("TRACE")]
public static void Write(string message)
{
    TraceInternal.Write(message);
}
```

The only difference between `Debug.Write` and `Trace.Write` given these two source snippets is the conditional attribute indicating the preprocessor directive TRACE. You can conditionally compile your assemblies to include tracing statements, debug statements, both, or neither. Most people keep TRACE defined even for release builds and use the configuration file to turn tracing on and off. More than likely, the benefits you gain from making tracing available to your users far outweigh any performance issues that might arise.

Because `Trace.Write` calls the `DefaultTraceListener` just like `Debug.Write`, you can use any debugger to tap into tracing information. So, what's the difference?

When designing your application, think about your deployment model. Are you going to ship debug builds or release builds? Do you want a way for end users or systems engineers to debug your application using log files or the event viewer? Are there things you want only the developer to see?

Typically, you want to use tracing and `Trace.Write` for any formal information that could be useful in debugging your application in a production environment. `Trace.Write` gives you everything that `Debug` `.Write` does, except it uses the TRACE preprocessor directive and is not affected by debug or release builds.

This means you have four possibilities for builds: Debug On, Trace On, Both On, or Neither On. You choose what is right for you. Typically, use Both On for debug builds and Trace On for production builds. You can specify these conditional attributes in the property pages or the command line of the compiler, as well as with the C# #define keyword or #CONST keyword for Visual Basic.

Trace Forwarding

You often find existing ASP.NET applications that have been highly instrumented and make extensive use of the ASP.NET `TraceContext` class. ASP.NET includes an attribute to the `web.config` `<trace>` element that enables you to route messages emitted by ASP.NET tracing to `System.Diagnostics` `.Trace: writeToDiagnosticsTrace`:

```
<trace writeToDiagnosticsTrace="true" pageOutput="true" enabled="true"/>
```

When you set `writeToDiagnosticsTrace` to true, all calls to `System.Web.UI.Page.Trace.Write` (the ASP.NET `TraceContext`) also go to `System.Diagnostics.Trace.Write`, enabling you to use all the standard `TraceListeners` and tracing options that are covered later in this chapter. The simple `writeToDiagnoticsTrace` setting connects the ASP.NET tracing functionality with the rest of the Base Class Library. I use this feature when I am deep in debugging my pages, and it is easily turned off using this configuration switch. I believe that more information is better than less, but you may find the exact page event information too verbose. Try it and form your own opinion.

TraceListeners

Output from `System.Diagnostics.Trace` methods is routable by a `TraceListener` to a text file, to ASP.NET, to an external monitoring system, even to a database. This powerful facility is a woefully underused tool in many ASP.NET developers' tool belts. In the early days of ASP.NET, some component developers who knew their components were being used within ASP.NET would introduce a direct reference to System. Web and call HttpContext.Current.Trace. They did this so that their tracing information would appear in the developer-friendly ASP.NET format. All components called within the context of an HttpRequest automatically receive access to that request's current context, enabling the components to talk directly to the request and retrieve cookies or collect information about the user.

However, assuming an HttpContext will always be available is dangerous for a number of reasons. First, you are making a big assumption when you declare that your component can be used only within the context of an HttpRequest. Notice that this is said within the context of *a request*, not within the context of *an application*. If you access HttpContext.Current even from within the Application_Start, you will be surprised to find that HttpContext.Current is null. Second, marrying your component's functionality to HttpContext makes using your application in any non-web context tricky if not impossible, and unit testing becomes particularly difficult.

If you have a component that is being used by a web page, but it also needs to be unit tested outside of web context or must be called from any other context, do not call HttpContext.Current.Trace. Instead, use the standard System.Diagnostics.Trace and redirect output to the ASP.NET tracing facilities using the WebPageTraceListener described in the next section. Using the standard trace mechanism means your component can be used in any context, web or otherwise. You will still be able to view the component's trace output with a TraceListener.

The framework comes with a number of very useful TraceListeners; you can add them programmatically or via a .config file. For example, you can programmatically add a TraceListener log to a file, as shown in Listing 29-2. These snippets required the System.Diagnostics and System.IO namespaces.

LISTING 29-2: Configuring TraceListeners

VB

```
Dim myTextListener As New
    TextWriterTraceListener(File.Create("c:\myListener.log"))
Trace.Listeners.Add(myTextListener)
```

C#

```
TextWriterTraceListener myTextListener = new
    TextWriterTraceListener(File.Create(@"c:\myListener.log"));
Trace.Listeners.Add(myTextListener);
```

You can do the same thing declaratively in the web.config file via an add element that passes in the type of TraceListener to use, along with any initializing data it might need. TraceListeners already configured in machine.config or a parent web.config file can also be removed using the remove tag, along with their name:

```
<configuration>
  <system.diagnostics>
    <trace autoflush="false" indentsize="4">
      <listeners>
        <add name="myListener"
            type="System.Diagnostics.TextWriterTraceListener"
            initializeData="c:\myListener.log" />
        <remove name="Default" />
      </listeners>
    </trace>
  </system.diagnostics>
</configuration>
```

TraceListeners, such as TextWriterTraceListener, that access a resource (such as a file, event log, or database) require that the ASP.NET worker process be run as a user who has sufficient access. To write to c:\foo\example.log, for example, the ASP.NET worker process requires explicit write access in the *access control list* (ACL) of that file.

Notice the preceding example also optionally removes the default TraceListener. If you write your own TraceListener, you must provide a fully qualified assembly name in the type attribute.

Using the ASP.NET WebPageTraceListener

The ASP.NET WebPageTraceListener derives from System.Diagnostics.TraceListener and automatically forwards tracing information from any component calls to System.Diagnostics.Trace.Write. This enables you to write your components using the most generic trace provider and to see its tracing output in the context of your ASP.NET application.

The WebPageTraceListener is added to the web.config file as shown in the following example. Note that this code uses the fully qualified assembly name for System.Web:

```
<configuration>
  <system.diagnostics>
      <trace autoflush="false" indentsize="4">
          <listeners>
              <add name="webListener"
                  type="System.Web.WebPageTraceListener, System.Web, Version=4.0.0.0,
                      Culture=neutral, PublicKeyToken=b03f5f7f11d50a3a"/>
          </listeners>
      </trace>
  </system.diagnostics>
  <system.web>
          <trace enabled="true" pageOutput="false" localOnly="true" />
  </system.web>
</configuration>
```

Figure 29-8 shows output from a call to System.Diagnostics.Trace.Write from a referenced library. It appears within ASP.NET's page tracing. The line generated from the referenced library is circled in this figure.

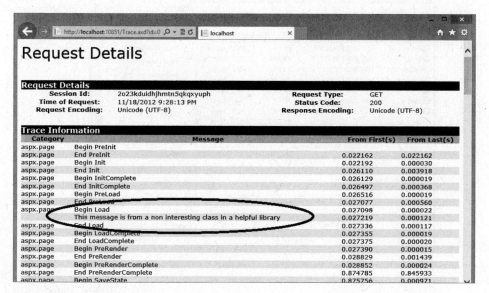

FIGURE 29-8

EventLogTraceListener

Tracing information can also be sent to the event log using the `EventLogTraceListener`. Doing this can be a little tricky because ASP.NET requires explicit write access to the event log:

```
<configuration>
  <system.diagnostics>
    <trace autoflush="false" indentsize="4">
      <listeners>
        <add name="EventLogTraceListener"
             type="System.Diagnostics.EventLogTraceListener"
             initializeData="Wrox"/>
      </listeners>
    </trace>
  </system.diagnostics>
</configuration>
```

Notice that `"Wrox"` is passed in as a string to the `initializeData` attribute as the `TraceListener` is added. The string `"Wrox"` appears as the application or *source* for this event. This works fine when debugging your application; most likely, the debugging user has the appropriate access. However, when your application is deployed, it will probably run under a less privileged account, so you must give explicit write access to a registry key such as `HKLM\System\CurrentControlSet\Services\EventLog\Application\Wrox`, where `"Wrox"` is the same string passed in to `initializeData`. Remember that registry keys have ACLs (access control lists) just as files do. Use `RegEdit.exe` to change the permissions on a registry key by right-clicking the key and selecting Properties, and setting the ACL just like you would for a file.

Be careful when using the `EventLogTraceListener` because your event log can fill up fairly quickly if you have a particularly chatty application. Figure 29-9 shows a sample tracing output in the event log.

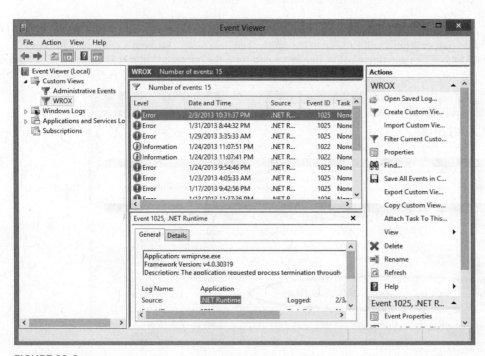

FIGURE 29-9

Other Useful Listeners

The .NET Framework 4 includes two additional `TraceListeners` in addition to the `WebPageTraceListener`:

➤ `XmlWriterTraceListener`: Derives from `TextWriterTraceListener` and writes out a strongly typed XML file.

➤ `DelimitedListTraceListener`: Also derives from `TextWriterTraceListener`; writes out comma-separated values (CSV) files.

One of the interesting things to note about the XML created by the `XmlWriterTraceListener`—it is not well-formed XML! Specifically, it doesn't have a root node; it's just a collection of peer nodes, as shown in the following code. This may seem like it goes against many of the ideas you have been told about XML, but think of each event as a document. Each stands alone and can be consumed alone. They just happen to be next to each other in one file. Certainly, the absence of an ultimate closing tag cleverly dodges the issue of well-formedness and allows easy appending to a file.

```
<E2ETraceEvent xmlns=\"http://schemas.microsoft.com/2012/06/E2ETraceEvent\">
    <System xmlns=\"http://schemas.microsoft.com/2012/06/windows/eventlog/system\">
        <EventID>0</EventID>
        <Type>3</Type>
        <SubType Name="Information">0</SubType>
        <Level>8</Level>
        <TimeCreated SystemTime="2012-11-05T12:43:44.4234234Z">
        <Source Name="WroxChapter29.exe"/>
        <Correlation ActivityID="{00000000-0000-0000-0000-000000000000>
        <Execution ProcessName="WroxChapter29.exe" ProcessID="4234" ThreadID="1"/>
        <Channel/>
        <Computer>SCOTTPC</Computer>
    </System>
    <ApplicationData>Your Text Here</ApplicationData>
</E2ETraceEvent>
<E2ETraceEvent xmlns=\"http://schemas.microsoft.com/2012/06/E2ETraceEvent\">
    <System xmlns=\"http://schemas.microsoft.com/2012/06/windows/eventlog/system\">
        <EventID>0</EventID>
        <Type>3</Type>
... the XML continues ...
```

The "E2E" in `E2ETraceEvent` stands for end-to-end. Notice that it includes information such as your computer name and a "correlation id."

Ever since the .NET Framework 3.5, there has been one additional `TraceListener` added to the list: the `IisTraceListener`. Much like the `WebPageTraceListener` bridges Diagnostics Tracing with ASP.NET tracing, the `IisTraceListener` bridges the tracing mechanism of ASP.NET with IIS 7.0. This listener lets you raise events to the IIS 7.0 infrastructure.

Diagnostic Switches

Recompiling your application just because you want to change tracing characteristics is often not convenient. Sometimes you may want to change your configuration file to add and remove `TraceListeners`. At other times, you may want to change a configuration parameter or "flip a switch" to adjust the amount of detail the tracing produces. That is where `Switch` comes in. `Switch` is an abstract base class that supports a series of diagnostic switches that you can control by using the application's configuration file.

BooleanSwitch

To use a `BooleanSwitch`, create an instance and pass in the switch name that appears in the application's `config` file (see Listing 29-3).

LISTING 29-3: Using diagnostic switches

```
<configuration>
 <system.diagnostics>
  <switches>
   <add name="ImportantSwitch" value="1" /> <!-- This is for the BooleanSwitch -->
   <add name="LevelSwitch" value="3" />     <!-- This is for the TraceSwitch -->
   <add name="SourceSwitch" value="4" />    <!-- This is for the SourceSwitch -->
  </switches>
 </system.diagnostics>
</configuration>
```

Switches can be used in an `if` statement for any purpose, but they are most useful in the context of tracing along with `System.Diagnostics.Trace.WriteIf`:

VB

```
Dim aSwitch As New BooleanSwitch("ImportantSwitch", "Show errors")
System.Diagnostics.Trace.WriteIf(aSwitch.Enabled, "The Switch is enabled!")
```

C#

```
BooleanSwitch aSwitch = new BooleanSwitch("ImportantSwitch", "Show errors");
System.Diagnostics.Trace.WriteIf(aSwitch.Enabled, "The Switch is enabled!");
```

If `ImportantSwitch` is set to 1, or a non-zero value, in the `config` file, the call to `WriteIf` sends a string to trace output.

TraceSwitch

`TraceSwitch` offers five levels of tracing from 0 to 4, implying an increasing order: Off, Error, Warning, Info, and Verbose. You construct a `TraceSwitch` exactly as you create a `BooleanSwitch`:

VB

```
Dim tSwitch As New TraceSwitch("LevelSwitch", "Trace Levels")
System.Diagnostics.Trace.WriteIf(tSwitch.TraceInfo, "The Switch is 3 or more!")
```

C#

```
TraceSwitch tSwitch = new TraceSwitch("LevelSwitch", "Trace Levels");
System.Diagnostics.Trace.WriteIf(tSwitch.TraceInfo, "The Switch is 3 or more!");
```

A number of properties on the `TraceSwitch` class return `true` if the switch is at the same level or at a higher level than the property's value. For example, the `TraceInfo` property returns `true` if the switch's value is set to 3 or more.

SourceSwitch

Since the release of the .NET Framework 2.0, you have been able to use `SourceSwitch`, which is similar to `TraceSwitch` but provides a greater level of granularity. You call `SourceSwitch.ShouldTrace` with an `EventType` as the parameter:

VB

```
Dim sSwitch As New SourceSwitch("SourceSwitch", "Even More Levels")
System.Diagnostics.Trace.WriteIf(sSwitch.ShouldTrace(TraceEventType.Warning),
                        "The Switch is 3 or more!")
```

C#

```
SourceSwitch sSwitch = new SourceSwitch("SourceSwitch", " Even More Levels");
System.Diagnostics.Trace.WriteIf(sSwitch.ShouldTrace(TraceEventType.Warning),
                        "The Switch is 4 or more!");
```

Web Events

It does not exactly qualify as debugging, but you will find a series of application-monitoring and health-monitoring tools in ASP.NET's `System.Web.Management` namespace in ASP.NET. These tools can be as valuable as tracing information in helping you monitor, maintain, and diagnose the health of your application. The system has an event model and event engine that can update your application with runtime details. It has a number of built-in events, including application lifetime events such as start and stop and a heartbeat event. You can take these base classes and events and build on them to create events of your own. For example, you might want to create an event that tells you when a user downloads a particularly large file or when a new user is created in your personalization database. You can have your application send an e-mail to you once a day with statistics.

For instance, you can create your own event by deriving from `System.Web.Management.WebBaseEvent`, as shown in Listing 29-4.

LISTING 29-4 Web events

```
Imports System
Imports System.Web.Management
```

VB

```
Namespace Wrox
    Public Class WroxEvent
        Inherits WebBaseEvent

            Public Const WroxEventCode As Integer = WebEventCodes.WebExtendedBase + 1
            Public Sub New(ByVal message As String, ByVal eventSource As Object)
                MyBase.New(message, eventSource, WroxEventCode)
            End Sub
    End Class
End Namespace
```

C#

```
namespace Wrox
{
    using System;
    using System.Web.Management;

    public class WroxEvent: WebBaseEvent
    {
        public const int WroxEventCode = WebEventCodes.WebExtendedBase + 1;
        public WroxEvent(string message, object eventSource) :
            base(message, eventSource, WroxEventCode){}
    }
}
```

Later, in a sample `Page_Load`, you raise this event to the management subsystem:

VB

```vb
Protected Sub Page_Load(sender As Object, e As EventArgs)
    ' Raise a custom event
    Dim anEvent As Wrox.WroxEvent = New Wrox.WroxEvent("Someone visited here", Me)
    anEvent.Raise()
End Sub
```

C#

```csharp
protected void Page_Load(Object sender, EventArgs e)
{
    // Raise a custom event
    Wrox.WroxEvent anEvent = new Wrox.WroxEvent("Someone visited here!", this);
    anEvent.Raise();
}
```

The event is caught by the management subsystem and can be dispatched to different providers based on a number of rules. This is a much more formal kind of tracing than a call to `Trace.WriteLine`, so you create a strongly typed event class for events specific to your application:

WEB.CONFIG

```xml
<?xml version="1.0"?>
<configuration>
    <system.web>
        <healthMonitoring enabled="true">
            <providers>
                <add name="WroxDatabaseLoggingProvider"
                    type="System.Web.Management.SqlWebEventProvider"
                    connectionStringName="QuickStartSqlServer"
                    maxEventDetailsLength="1073741823"
                    buffer="false"/>
            </providers>
            <rules>
                <add
                    name="Application Lifetime Events Rule"
                    eventName="All Events"
                    provider="WroxDatabaseLoggingProvider"
                    profile="Critical" />
            </rules>
        </healthMonitoring>
    </system.web>
</configuration>
```

DEBUGGING

Visual Studio includes two configurations by default: *debug* and *release*. The debug configuration automatically defines the debug and trace constants, enabling your application to provide context to a troubleshooter. The option to generate debugging information is turned on by default, causing a program database (or debug) file (PDB) to be generated for each assembly and your solution. They appear in the same bin folder as your assemblies. Remember, however, that the actual compilation to native code does not occur in Visual Studio, but rather at run time using Just-In-Time compilation (JIT). The JIT will automatically optimize your code for speed. Optimized code, however, is considerably harder to debug because the operations that are generated may not correspond directly to lines in your source code. For debug purposes, this option is set to `False`.

What's Required

The PDBs are created when either the C# compiler (`csc.exe`) or Visual Basic compiler (`vbc.exe`) is invoked with the `/debug:full` command-line switch. As an option, if you use `/debug:pdbonly`, you will generate PDBs but still direct the compiler to produce release-mode code.

Debug versus Release

The debug and release configurations that come with Visual Studio are generally sufficient for your needs. However, these configurations control only the compilation options of the code-behind files. Remember that, depending on how you have chosen to design your ASP.NET application, the ASP.NET `.aspx` files may be compiled the first time they are hit, or the entire application may compile the first time a page is hit. You can control these compilation settings via the compilation elements within the `<system.web>` section of your application's `web.config` file. Set `<compilation debug="true">` to produce binaries as you do when using the `/debug:full` switches. PDBs are also produced.

The average developer is most concerned with the existence of PDB files. When these files exist in your ASP.NET application's bin folder, the run time provides you with line numbers. Of course, line numbers greatly assist in debugging. You cannot step through source code during an interactive debugging session without these files.

> **NOTE** *An interesting CLR Internals trick: Call* `System.Diagnostics.Debugger` `.Launch` *within your assembly, even if the assembly was compiled via* `/debug:pdbonly`, *and the debugger pops up. The JIT compiler compiles code on the first call to a method, and the code that it generates is debuggable because JIT knows that a debugger is attached.*

Debugging and the JIT Dialog Box

When an unhandled error occurs in an ASP.NET application, the default error handler for the ASP.NET worker process catches it and tries to output some HTML that expresses what happened. However, when you are debugging components outside of ASP.NET, perhaps within the context of unit testing, the debug dialog box appears when the .NET application throws an unhandled exception.

If something has gone horribly wrong with an ASP.NET application, it is conceivable that you may find a web server with the dialog box popped up waiting for your input. This can be especially inconvenient if the machine has no keyboard or monitor hooked up. The day may come when you want to turn off the debug dialog box that appears, and you have two options to do this:

➤ You can disable JIT debugging from the registry. The proper registry key is `HKLM\Software\ Microsoft\.NETFramework\DbgJITDebugLaunchSetting`. The option has three possible values:

  ➤ `0`: Prompts the user by means of a message box. The choices presented include Continue, which results in a stack dump and process termination; and Attach a Debugger, which means the run time spawns the debugger listed in the `DbgManagedDebugger` registry key. If no key exists, the debugger releases control and the process is terminated.

  ➤ `1`: Does not display a dialog box. This results in a stack dump and then process termination.

  ➤ `2`: Launches the debugger listed in the `DbgManagedDebugger` registry key.

> **NOTE** *For this option, the registry entry must be set to 0 for the dialog box to show up.*

➤ To disable the JIT debug dialog box and still present an error dialog box, within Visual Studio.NET, choose Tools ➪ Options ➪ Debugging ➪ Just-In-Time and deselect the provided options. Instead of the Select a Debugger dialog box, an OK/Cancel dialog box will appear during an unhandled exception.

Starting a Debugging Session

You have a number of ways to enter an interactive debugging session with ASP.NET. Visual Studio can fire up the ASP.NET worker process, load your newly compiled website, and attach the debugging to the worker process automatically. Alternatively, you can attach a debugger to a site that is already running. Visual Studio also includes a new simpler remote debugging tool for cross-machine debugging.

F5 Debugging

When you start debugging an ASP.NET application, Visual Studio takes into consideration all the Start options within your project properties. It enables you to start debugging using the currently selected page. The specific page has been selected so that the Visual Studio debugger can automatically attach the correct process, which might be the Visual Studio web server, the ASP.NET worker process, or a remote debug monitor.

Attaching to a Process

Jumping into an interactive debugging session of a website that is already running, and at known state, is often more convenient than starting an application from scratch each time you debug. To begin debugging a site that is already running, from Visual Studio's Debug menu, select Attach to Process. The dialog box has been improved from previous versions of Visual Studio and includes a Refresh button and simplifies most common debugging use cases by showing only those processes that belong to the user and that are in the currently running session.

Also included is a transport drop-down with the default transport selected. The default enables you to select processes on your computer or on a remote computer that's running the Remote Debugging Monitor. Other options are there for smart client or unmanaged debugging.

> **NOTE** *The only difference between starting a debug session via F5 and attaching to a process manually is that when you debug via F5, Visual Studio automatically starts up a browser or external application for you. Remember that if you use Attach to Process, it is assumed that you have already done the work of starting up the process. The ASP.NET worker processes under IIS will start up when the site has been hit with an* HttpRequest *at least once. The debugger can now attach to the running worker process.*

Simpler Remote Debugging

Remote debugging has gotten simpler over the years. However, in the interest of security, you must have the appropriate credentials to perform remote debugging. You will find a Remote Debugger folder in `C:\ Program Files\Microsoft Visual Studio 10.0\Common7\IDE`.

To begin, you must set up remote debugging on the machine that contains the application you want to debug. Rather than performing a complicated installation, you can now use the Remote Debug Monitor, and an application that can simply be run off a file share. The easiest scenario has you sharing these components directly from your Visual Studio machine and then running `msvsmon.exe` off the share.

Simply running the Remote Debug Monitor executable off the file share can make remote ASP.NET debugging of an already-deployed application much simpler, although you still need to attach to the ASP.NET worker process manually because automatic attaching is not supported. Do note that two versions of the debugger now exist, one for x86 processes and one for x64 processes, so make sure you are using the right debugger for your process.

You are allowed to debug a process that is running under your account and password without any special permissions. If you need to debug a process running under another account name, such as an ASP.NET worker process running as a user who is not you, you must be an administrator on the machine running the process.

The most important thing to remember when debugging remotely is this: You need to get the user account that is running as Visual Studio to map somehow to a legitimate user account on the machine running the Remote Debug Monitor (`msvsmon.exe`) machine and vice versa. The easiest way to do this is to create a local user account on both computers with the same username and password. To run `msvsmon` as a user other than Visual Studio, you must create two user accounts on each computer.

If one of the machines is located on a domain, be aware that domain accounts can be mapped to a local account. You create a local user account on both computers. However, if you pick the same username and password as your domain account, Visual Studio can be run as a domain account.

Tools to Help You with Debugging

Visual Studio's debugging experience offers a number of tools — some obvious, some more subtle — to assist you in every step of the debug session.

Debugger DataTips

Visual Studio offers *DataTips*, allowing complex types to be explored using a modeless tree-style view that acts like a tooltip and provides much more information. After you traverse the tree to the node that you are interested in, you can view that simple type using a visualizer by clicking the small magnifying glass icon, as shown in Figure 29-10.

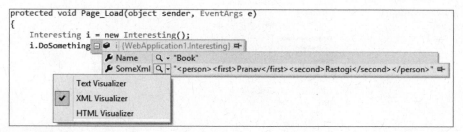

FIGURE 29-10

Floating the DataTips is also possible by clicking once again on the pin of an already pinned DataTip. Doing so enables you to move the DataTip anywhere you want on the screen. Now if you scroll your code, the DataTip remains in place on the screen regardless of what you are doing in Visual Studio. The nice thing with floating your DataTips is that you can move them outside of the code window, and you can even move them to a second monitor if you want.

In a pinned DataTips toolbar, notice a button that enables you to put a comment in the DataTip that stays with it as you move it around. Figure 29-11 shows a DataTip with a comment.

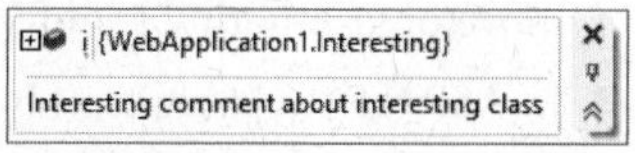

FIGURE 29-11

Data Visualizers

As you saw earlier, you can view a simple type using any number of data visualizers. For example, if a simple variable such as a string contains a fragment of XML, you might want to visualize that data in a style that is more appropriate for the data's native format, as shown in Figure 29-12.

The visualizers are straightforward to write and, although Visual Studio ships with default visualizers for text, HTML, XML, and DataSets, look on the Internet for additional visualizers that might include support for images, collection classes, and more. The result is a rich, unparalleled debugging experience.

FIGURE 29-12

Error Notifications

During an interactive debugging session, Visual Studio assists you with informative error notifications. These notifications not only report on events such as unhandled exceptions, but also offer context-sensitive troubleshooting tips and next steps for dealing with the situation. Figure 29-13 shows an unhandled `NullReferenceException` along with the good advice that you might try using the "new" keyword to create an object instance before using it. Oops!

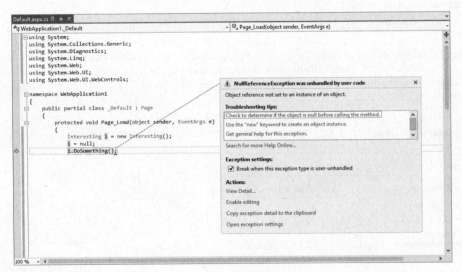

FIGURE 29-13

Edit and Continue (Lack of) Support, or Edit and Refresh

Though Visual Basic offers the Edit and Continue feature, which gives you the capability to change code during a debugging session without restarting the session (in break mode, you can modify code fix bugs and move on) for both C# and VB, unfortunately this feature is not available to ASP.NET developers.

In ASP.NET, your assembly is compiled not by Visual Studio, but by the ASP.NET run time using the same technique it does during a normal web page request by a browser. To cooperate with the debugger and support Edit and Continue within ASP.NET, a number of fantastically complex modifications to the ASP.NET run time would have been required by the development team. Rather than including support for this feature, ASP.NET developers can use *page recycling*.

This means that code changes are made during a debugging session, and then the whole page is refreshed via F5, automatically recompiled, and re-executed. Basically, ASP.NET includes support for Edit and Refresh, but not for Edit and Continue.

Just My Code Debugging

Another concept in the .NET Framework is called *Just My Code* debugging. Any method in code can be explicitly marked with the attribute [DebuggerNonUserCode]. Using this explicit technique and a number of other heuristic methods internal to the CLR, the debugger silently skips over code that is not important to the code at hand. You can find the preference Enable Just My Code in Tools ➪ Options ➪ Debugging.

The [DebuggerHidden] attribute is still available in .NET and hides methods from the debugger, regardless of the user's Just My Code preference. The .NET Framework 1.1 attribute [DebuggerStepThrough] tells the debugger to step through, rather than into, any method to which it is applied; the [DebuggerNonUserCode] attribute is a much more pervasive and complete implementation that works at run time on delegates, virtual functions, and any arbitrarily complex code.

Be aware that these attributes and this user option exist to help you debug code effectively and not be fooled by any confusing call stacks. Although these can be very useful, be sure not to use them on your components until you are sure you will not accidentally hide the very error you are trying to debug. Typically, these attributes are used for components such as proxies or thin shim layers.

Tracepoints

Breakpoints by themselves are useful for stopping execution either conditionally or unconditionally. Standard breakpoints break always. Conditional breakpoints cause you to enter an interactive debugging session based on a condition. Tracing is useful to output the value of a variable or assertion to the debugger or to another location. If you combine all these features, what do you get? *Tracepoints*, a powerful Visual Studio feature. Tracepoints can save you from hitting breakpoints dozens of times just to catch an edge case variable value. They can save you from covering your code with breakpoints to catch a strange case.

To insert a tracepoint, right-click in the code editor and select Breakpoint ➪ Insert Tracepoint. You get the dialog box shown in Figure 29-14. The icon that indicates a breakpoint is a red circle, and the icon for a tracepoint is a red diamond. Arbitrary strings can be created from the dialog box using pseudo-variables in the form of keywords such as $CALLSTACK or $FUNCTION, as well as the values of variables in scope placed in curly braces. In Figure 29-14, the value of i.Name (placed in curly braces) is shown in the complete string with the Debug output of Visual Studio.

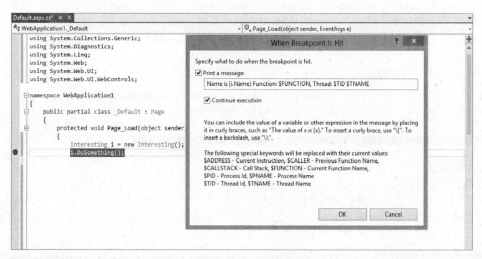

FIGURE 29-14

Breakpoint Options

Right-click a breakpoint in your code to access a number of options that enable you to manage some of the identifiers and behaviors of your breakpoints.

One option is to set a condition for your breakpoint. To get to the Breakpoint Condition dialog box, right-click the breakpoint and select Condition from the provided menu. Here you are presented with a textbox that enables you to create conditions that trigger the breakpoint.

Just as you could with DataTips, Visual Studio 2012 enables you to export your breakpoints. To export all the breakpoints, right-click any breakpoint and select Export from the provided menu. This export enables you to save all the breakpoints in an XML file that then can be loaded by someone else. It is a convenient way to distribute these items.

Historical Debugging with IntelliTrace

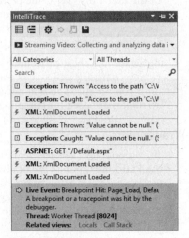

One of the more exciting improvements of Visual Studio 2012 is *IntelliTrace*. IntelliTrace provides you with a historical debugger that enables you to look back in the history of your application running and allows you to jump at previous points in time to see what was occurring.

This feature could only be used in development environments with Visual Studio 2010, but with Visual Studio 2012 it can be used in production environments as well. IntelliTrace supports a lot more features in Visual Studio 2012. You have access to rich debugging information that can show you past events along with call information of your application. You can use IntelliTrace along with Test Manager support in Visual Studio, which collects Diagnostics Trace Data that can be used to find bugs that are difficult to reproduce.

When stopping at a breakpoint within your application, you will now be able to see this history in the IntelliTrace dialog box directly, as illustrated in Figure 29-15.

FIGURE 29-15

From here, you can jump to any point in the past and view the Locals dialog box values and the Call Stack dialog box values for that moment in time. The IntelliTrace capability is configurable as well. You can get to these settings by either clicking Open IntelliTrace Settings from the IntelliTrace toolbar or by selecting Tools ⇨ Options and selecting IntelliTrace from the items in the left side of the dialog box.

From the IntelliTrace Events tab, you can select the events that you want to work with. You can choose from a large series of technologies and situations by making the appropriate selections.

Finally, the Modules tab enables you to specify particular modules that IntelliTrace should work with.

Debugging Multiple Threads

Visual Studio 2012 includes a dialog box that enables you to see what is going on in each of the threads your application is using. You do this through the Threads dialog box shown in Figure 29-16.

FIGURE 29-16

You can double-click a thread and go to where that thread is in the code when debugging. You can also get a visual family tree view of the threads at work by opening up the Parallel Stacks dialog box.

Client-Side JavaScript Debugging

Excellent client-side JavaScript debugging is available in Visual Studio 2012. If you run an ASP.NET application in a debugging session in Internet Explorer, you will need to enable script debugging.

After you have turned on script debugging, try a simple ASP.NET page with some JavaScript that changes the text in a textbox to UPPERCASE when the button is clicked (Listing 29-5).

LISTING 29-5: Simple JavaScript debugging test

ASPX

```
<!DOCTYPE html PUBLIC "-//W3C//DTD XHTML 1.0 Transitional//EN"
"http://www.w3.org/TR/xhtml1/DTD/xhtml1-transitional.dtd">
<html xmlns="http://www.w3.org/1999/xhtml" >
<head runat="server">
    <script type="text/javascript">
        function MakeItUpper()
        {
            newText = document.getElementById("TextBox1").value.toUpperCase();
            document.getElementById("TextBox1").value = newText;
        }
    </script>
</head>
<body>
    <form id="form1" runat="server">
        <div>
            <input type="button" id="Button1" value="Upper"
                onclick="javascript:MakeItUpper()" />
            <input type="text" id="TextBox1" runat="server"/>
        </div>
    </form>
</body>
</html>
```

Put a breakpoint on one of the lines of *client-side* JavaScript. Note that this is code that runs in the browser, not on the web server. Start a debugging session with the page from Listing 29-5. Visual Studio will break at that point, as shown in Figure 29-17.

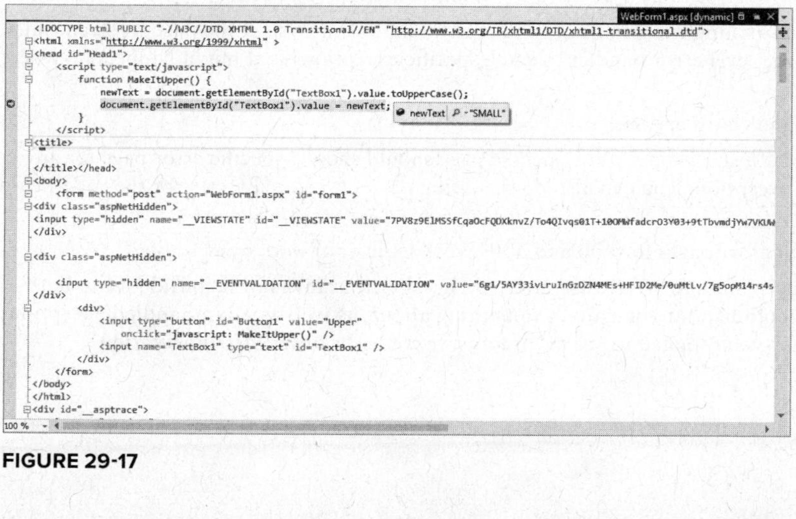

FIGURE 29-17

The JavaScript debugger in Visual Studio supports variable tooltips, visualizers, call stacks, locals, watches, and all the features you're used to when debugging .NET-based languages.

SQL Stored Proc Debugging

Database projects are file-based projects that enable you to manage and execute database queries. You can add your existing SQL scripts to the project or create new ones and edit them within Visual Studio. Database projects and SQL debugging are not available in the Express or Standard versions of Visual Studio. They are available only in the Professional or Team Edition Visual Studio SKUs/versions.

When debugging database applications, you cannot use Step Into (F11) to step between code in the application tier into the code in SQL Server (be it T-SQL or CLR SQL). However, you can set a breakpoint in the stored procedure code and use Continue (F5) to execute code to that set breakpoint.

When debugging SQL on SQL Server 2012, be aware of any software or hardware firewalls you may be running. Sometimes your software firewall will warn you what you are trying to do. Be sure to select "unblock" in any warning dialog boxes to ensure that SQL Server 2012 and Visual Studio can communicate.

If you are using a SQL account to connect to SQL Server, make sure the Windows User Account you run Visual Studio under is also an administrator on the SQL Server machine. You can add accounts to SQL Server's `sysadmin` privilege using the SQL command `sp_addsrvrolemember 'Domain\Name', 'sysadmin'`. Of course, never do this in production; and better yet, do your debugging on a machine with everything installed locally.

If you are using the NT Authentication model on SQL Server 2012, make sure that account has permissions to run the `sp_enable_sql_debug` stored procedure. You can give account access to this stored procedure by using the SQL commands `CREATE USER UserName FOR LOGIN 'Domain\Name'` followed by `GRANT EXECUTE ON sp_enable_sql_debug TO UserName`. This creates a SQL user who is associated directly with a specific Windows User and then explicitly grants permissions to debug T-SQL to that user. On SQL Server 2000, the user must have access to the extended stored procedure `sp_sdidebug`.

EXCEPTION AND ERROR HANDLING

When an exception occurs in your ASP.NET application code, you can handle it in a number of ways, but the best approach is a multi-pronged one:

- ➤ Catch what you expect:
  - ➤ Use a `try/catch` around error-prone code. This can always catch specific exceptions that you can deal with, such as `System.IO.FileNotFoundException`.
  - ➤ Rather than catching exceptions around specific chunks of code at the page level, consider using the page-level error handler to catch specific exceptions that might happen anywhere on the page.
- ➤ But prepare for unhandled exceptions:
  - ➤ Set the `Page.Error` property if a specific page should show a specific error page for any unhandled exception. You can also do this using the `<%@Page>` directive or the code-behind the property.
  - ➤ Have default error pages for 400 and 500 errors set in your `web.config` file.
  - ➤ Have a boilerplate `Application_OnError` handler that takes into consideration both specific exceptions that you can do something about, as well as all unhandled exceptions that you may want logged to the event log, a text file, or other instrumentation mechanism.

The phrase *unhandled exception* may be alarming, but remember that you don't do anyone any good catching an exception that you can't recover from. Unhandled exceptions are okay if they are just that—exceptional. For these situations, rely on global exception handlers for logging and friendly error pages that you can present to the user.

> **NOTE** *Why try to catch an exception by adding code everywhere if you can catch and log exceptions all in one place? A common mistake is creating a* try/catch *block around some arbitrary code and catching the least-specific exception type—* System .Exception. *A general rule is to not catch any exception that you cannot do anything about. Just because an exception can be thrown by a particular method doesn't mean you have to catch it. It is exceptional, remember? In addition, exception handlers are at both the page and the application level. Catch exceptions in these two centralized locations rather than all over.*

Handling Exceptions on a Page

To handle exceptions at a page level, override the OnError method that System.Web.UI.Page inherits from the TemplateControl class (see Listing 29-6). Calling Server.GetLastError gives you access to the exception that just occurred. Be aware that a chain of exceptions may have occurred, and you can use the ExceptionGetBaseException method to return the root exception.

LISTING 29-6: Page-level error handling

VB

```
Protected Overrides Sub OnError(ByVal e As System.EventArgs)
    Dim AnError As System.Exception = Server.GetLastError()
    If (TypeOf AnError.GetBaseException() Is SomeSpecificException) Then
        Response.Write("Something bad happened!")
        Response.StatusCode = 200
        Server.ClearError()
        Response.End()
    End If
End Sub
```

C#

```
protected override void OnError(EventArgs e)
{
    System.Exception anError = Server.GetLastError();
    if (anError.GetBaseException() is SomeSpecificException)
    {
        Response.Write("Something bad happened!");
        Response.StatusCode = 200;
        Server.ClearError();
        Response.End();
    }
}
```

Handling Application Exceptions

The technique of catching exceptions in a centralized location can be applied to error handling at the application level in Global.asax, as shown in Listing 29-7. If an exception is not caught on the page, the web.config file is checked for an alternate error page; if there is not one, the exception bubbles up to the application and your user sees a complete call stack.

LISTING 29-7: Application-level error handling

VB

```
Protected Sub Application_Error(sender as Object, ByVal e As System.EventArgs)
    Dim bigError As System.Exception = Server.GetLastError()
    'Example checking for HttpRequestValidationException
    If (TypeOf bigError.GetBaseException() Is HttpRequestValidationException) Then
        System.Diagnostics.Trace.WriteLine(bigError.ToString)
        Server.ClearError()
    End If
End Sub
```

C#

```
protected void Application_Error(Object sender, EventArgs e)
{
    System.Exception bigError = Server.GetLastError();
    //Example checking for HttpRequestValidationException
    if(bigError.GetBaseException() is HttpRequestValidationException )
    {
        System.Diagnostics.Trace.WriteLine(bigError.ToString());
        Server.ClearError();
    }
}
```

Unhandled application errors turn into HTTP Status Code 500 and display errors in the browser. These errors, including the complete call stack and other technical details, may be useful during development, but are hardly useful at production time. Most often, you want to create an error handler (as shown previously) to log your error and to give the user a friendlier page to view.

> **NOTE** *If you ever find yourself trying to catch exceptions of type* System.Exception, *look at the code to see whether you can avoid it. There is almost never a reason to catch such a non-specific exception, and you are more likely to swallow exceptions that can provide valuable debugging. Check the API documentation for the framework method you are calling—a section specifically lists what exceptions an API call might throw. Never rely on an exception occurring to get a standard code path to work.*

Http Status Codes

Every HttpRequest results in an HttpResponse, and every HttpResponse includes a status code. Table 29-2 describes 11 particularly interesting HTTP status codes.

TABLE 29-2

STATUS CODE	EXPLANATION
200 OK	Everything went well.
301 Moved Permanently	Reminds the caller to use a new, permanent URL rather than the one he used to get here.
302 Found	Returned during a Response.Redirect. This is the way to say "No, no, look over here right now."
304 Not Modified	Returned as the result of a conditional GET when a requested document has not been modified. It is the basis of all browser-based caching. An HTTP message-body must not be returned when using a 304.

307 Temporary Redirect	Redirects calls to ASMX Web Services to alternate URLs. Rarely used with ASP.NET.
400 Bad Request	Request was malformed.
401 Unauthorized	Request requires authentication from the user.
403 Forbidden	Authentication has failed, indicating that the server understood the request but cannot fulfill it.
404 Not Found	The server has not found an appropriate file or handler to handle this request. The implication is that this may be a temporary state. This happens in ASP.NET not only because a file cannot be found, but also because it may be inappropriately mapped to an `IHttpHandler` that was not available to service the request.
410 Gone	The equivalent of a permanent 404 indicating to the client that it should delete any references to this link if possible. 404s usually indicate that the server does not know whether the condition is permanent.
500 Internal Server Error	The official text for this error is "The server encountered an unexpected condition which prevented it from fulfilling the request," but this error can occur when any unhandled exception bubbles all the way up to the user from ASP.NET.

Any status code greater than or equal to 400 is considered an error and, unless you configure otherwise, the user will likely see an unfriendly message in his or her browser. If you have not already handled these errors inside of the ASP.NET run time by checking their exception types, or if the error occurred outside of ASP.NET and you want to show the user a friendly message, you can assign pages to any status code within the web.config file, as the following example shows:

```
<customErrors mode ="On" >
    <error statusCode ="500" redirect ="FriendlyMassiveError.aspx" />
</customErrors>
```

After making a change to the customer errors section of your web.config file, make sure a page is available to be shown to the user. A classic mistake in error redirection is redirecting the user to a page that will cause an error, thereby getting him stuck in a loop. Use a great deal of care if you have complicated headers or footers in your application that might cause an error if they appear on an error page. Avoid hitting the database or performing any other backend operation that requires either user authorization or that the user's session be in any specific state. In other words, make sure that the error page is a reliable standalone.

> **NOTE** *Any status code greater than or equal to 400 increments the ASP.NET Requests Failed performance counter. 401 increments Requests Failed and Requests Not Authorized. 404 and 414 increment both Requests Failed and Requests Not Found. Requests that result in a 500 status code increment Requests Failed and Requests Timed Out. If you are going to return status codes, you must realize their effects and their implications.*

DEBUGGING WITH PAGE INSPECTOR

Page Inspector is a new tool option in Visual Studio 2012 that brings the diagnostics tools experience found in browsers to Visual Studio. This means that by using Page Inspector you can inspect the elements and see which file and line of source code generated the markup. Page Inspector also lets you inspect the DOM elements as well as CSS elements so that you can modify these properties and see the changes in real time.

Figure 29-18 shows what an application looks like when loaded in Page Inspector.

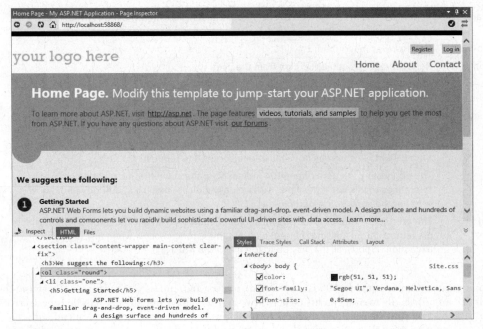

FIGURE 29-18

If you want to load an application in Page Inspector then you can right-click your project and select the "View in Page Inspector" option. Figure 29-19 shows this option in Visual Studio 2012. When you click this option, Visual Studio compiles your project and loads the application in Page Inspector.

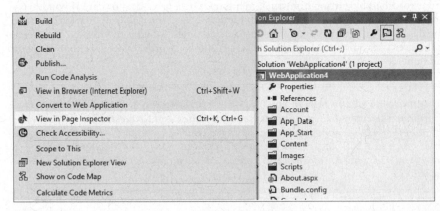

FIGURE 29-19

The primary function of Page Inspector is Source Mapping. When you inspect a certain element on the page, Page Inspector will open the appropriate file in the preview mode in Visual Studio and highlight the line of source code which generated that element. For example, Figure 29-20 shows the Default.aspx in preview mode and highlights the Page Title property when you inspect the title on the page in Page Inspector.

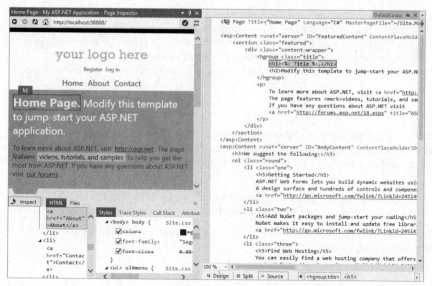

FIGURE 29-20

Page Inspector also supports JavaScript mapping. This means that Page Inspector can be used to figure out which file or line of source code in the JavaScript files is being used on the page that you are browsing in your application. For example, Figure 29-21 shows an SPA application that uses Knockout. When you inspect an element, then the Call Stack tab of Page Inspector shows you the JavaScript call stack that resulted in this element being created. You can click any one of the call stack functions, and Page Inspector will take you to the exact line of JavaScript code. This is very useful when you are building applications that use a lot of JavaScript and the JavaScript code is modifying the DOM elements.

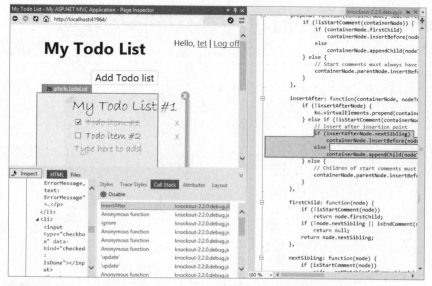

FIGURE 29-21

As you learned earlier, Page Inspector can be used to interact with the DOM and CSS tools to modify the CSS properties and see the changes in real time. For example, to modify the CSS properties, you can select the "Styles" tab in Page Inspector and see all the CSS styles that are used on the web page. Suppose you wanted to change the background color of the web page; then you can select the `background-color` property, change the color, save the CSS file, and refresh the page in Page Inspector to see the changes.

SUMMARY

This chapter examined the debugging tools available to you for creating robust ASP.NET applications. A successful debugging experience includes not only interactive debugging with features such as DataTips, data visualizers, and error notifications, but also powerful options around configurable tracing and logging of information.

Remote debugging is easier than ever with ASP.NET, and the capability to write and debug ASP.NET pages without installing IIS removes yet another layer of complexity from the development process.

Visual Studio and its extensible debugging mechanisms continue to be expanded by intrepid bloggers and enthusiasts, which makes debugging easier every day.

30

Modules and Handlers

WHAT'S IN THIS CHAPTER?

➤ Interacting with the ASP.NET request processing pipeline

➤ Working with HttpModules and HttpHandlers

WROX.COM CODE DOWNLOADS FOR THIS CHAPTER

Please note that all the code examples in this chapter are available as a part of this chapter's code download on the book's website at www.wrox.com on the Download Code tab.

Sometimes, just creating dynamic web pages with the latest languages and databases does not give you, the developer, enough control over an application. At times, you need to be able to dig deeper and create applications that can interact with the web server itself. You want to be able to interact with the low-level processes, such as how the web server processes incoming and outgoing HTTP requests.

Before ASP.NET, to get this level of control using IIS, you were forced to create ISAPI extensions or filters. This task was quite daunting and painful for many developers because creating ISAPI extensions and filters required knowledge of C/C++ and knowledge of how to create native Win32 DLLs. Thankfully, in the .NET world, creating these types of low-level applications is really no more difficult than most other applications you might build. This chapter looks at two methods of manipulating how ASP.NET processes HTTP requests, the HttpModule and the HttpHandler. Each method provides a unique level of access to the underlying processing of ASP.NET and can be a powerful tool for creating web applications.

PROCESSING HTTP REQUESTS

Before starting to write handlers or modules, knowing how IIS and ASP.NET normally process incoming HTTP requests and what options you have for plugging custom logic into those requests is helpful. IIS is the basic endpoint for incoming HTTP requests. At a very high level, its job is to listen for and validate incoming HTTP requests. Then it routes them to the appropriate module for processing and returns any results to the original requestor. ASP.NET is one of the modules that IIS may pass requests to for processing. However, exactly how that processing happens and how you can integrate your own logic into the pipeline differs based on the version of IIS you are using.

IIS 6 and ASP.NET

If you are using IIS 6, the HTTP request processing pipeline is fairly black box to a managed code developer. IIS basically treats ASP.NET as one of the modules to which it can pass requests for processing rather than as an integrated part of the IIS request processing pipeline. Figure 30-1 shows the basic request processing pipeline of IIS 6 and ASP.NET.

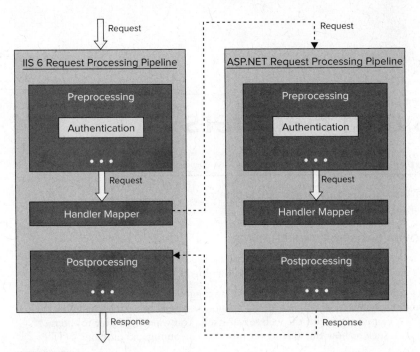

FIGURE 30-1

As you can see, the IIS and ASP.NET request pipelines are very similar and several tasks, such as authentication, are even duplicated between the two pipelines. Furthermore, although you can write handlers and modules using managed code, they are still processed in the isolated context of the ASP.NET process. If you want to integrate deeper into the IIS pipeline you are forced to create modules using native code.

IIS 7 and IIS 8 and ASP.NET

Starting with IIS 7, the request processing pipeline in IIS was completely re-architected using an open and highly extensible module-based system. This change still exists in IIS 8. Instead of IIS seeing ASP.NET as a separate entity, ASP.NET was deeply integrated into the IIS request processing pipeline. As shown in Figure 30-2, the request processing pipeline was streamlined to eliminate duplicate processes and to allow you to integrate managed modules in the pipeline.

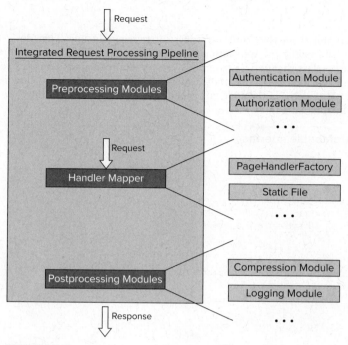

FIGURE 30-2

Because ASP.NET modules are first-class citizens, you can place them at any point in the pipeline, or even completely replace existing modules with your own custom functionality. Features that previously required you to write custom ISAPI modules in unmanaged code can simply be replaced by managed code modules containing your logic.

ASP.NET Request Processing

Regardless of the IIS version, the basic HTTP request pipeline model has two core mechanisms for handling requests: HttpModules and HttpHandlers. ASP.NET uses those two mechanisms to process incoming ASP.NET requests, generate a response, and return that response to the client. In fact, you are probably already familiar with HttpModules and HttpHandlers—although you might not know it. If you have ever used the inbox caching or the authentication features of ASP.NET, you have used several different HttpModules. Additionally, if you have ever served up an ASP.NET application, even something as simple as a *Hello World* web page and viewed it in a browser, you have used an HttpHandler. ASP.NET uses handlers to process and render ASPX pages and other file extensions. Modules and handlers allow you to plug into the request-processing pipeline at different points and interact with the actual requests being processed by IIS.

As you can see in both Figures 30-1 and 30-2, ASP.NET passes each incoming request through a layer of preprocessing HttpModules in the pipeline. ASP.NET allows multiple modules to exist in the pipeline for each request. After the incoming request has passed through each module, it is passed to the HttpHandler, which serves the request. Notice that although a single request may pass through many different modules, it can be processed by one handler only. The handler is generally responsible for creating a response to the incoming HTTP request. After the handler has completed execution and generated a response, the response is passed back through a series of post-processing modules, before it is returned to the client.

You should now have a basic understanding of the IIS and ASP.NET request pipeline—and how you can use HttpModules and HttpHandlers to interact with the pipeline. The following sections take an in-depth look at each of these.

HTTPMODULES

HttpModules are simple classes that can plug themselves into the request-processing pipeline. They do this by hooking into a handful of events thrown by the application as it processes the HTTP request. To create an HttpModule, you simply create a class that derives from the `System.Web.IHttpModule` interface. This interface requires you to implement two methods: `Init` and `Dispose`. Listing 30-1 (files App_Code\SimpleModule.cs and App_Code\SimpleModule.vb in the code download for this chapter) shows the class stub created after you implement the `IHttpModule` interface.

LISTING 30-1: Implementing the IHttpModule interface

VB

```
Public Class SimpleModule
    Implements IHttpModule

    Public Sub Dispose() Implements IHttpModule.Dispose

    End Sub

    Public Sub Init(context As HttpApplication) Implements IHttpModule.Init

    End Sub
End Class
```

C#

```
using System;
using System.Web;

public class SimpleModule : IHttpModule
{

    public void Dispose()
    {
        throw new NotImplementedException();
    }

    public void Init(HttpApplication context)
    {
        throw new NotImplementedException();
    }
}
```

The `Init` method is the primary method you use to implement HttpModule functionality. Notice that it has a single method parameter—an `HttpApplication` object named `context`. This parameter gives you access to the current `HttpApplication` context, and it is what you use to wire up the different events that fire during the request processing. Table 30-1 shows the events that you can register in the `Init` method. The Order column indicates the order in which they are fired for the first time. Some events are fired more than once during the processing of a request.

TABLE 30-1

EVENT NAME	ORDER	DESCRIPTION
AcquireRequestState	9	Raised when ASP.NET run time is ready to acquire the session state of the current HTTP request.
AuthenticateRequest	2	Raised when ASP.NET run time is ready to authenticate the identity of the user.
AuthorizeRequest	4	Raised when ASP.NET run time is ready to authorize the user for the resources that the user is trying to access.
BeginRequest	1	Raised when ASP.NET run time receives a new HTTP request.
Disposed	23	Raised when ASP.NET completes the processing of an HTTP request.
EndRequest	20	Raised just before sending the response content to the client.
Error	N/A	Raised when an unhandled exception occurs during the processing of the HTTP request.
LogRequest	18	Occurs just before ASP.NET performs any logging for the current request.
PostAcquireRequestState	10	Occurs when the request state (for example, session state) that is associated with the current request has been obtained.
PostAuthenticateRequest	3	Occurs when a security module has established the identity of the user.
PostAuthorizeRequest	5	Occurs when the user for the current request has been authorized.
PostLogRequest	19	Occurs when ASP.NET has completed processing all the event handlers for the `LogRequest` event.
PostMapRequestHandler	8	Occurs when ASP.NET has mapped the current request to the appropriate event handler.
PostReleaseRequestState	15	Occurs when ASP.NET has completed executing all request event handlers and the request state data has been stored.
PostRequestHandlerExecute	12	Raised just after the HTTP handler finishes execution.
PostResolveRequestCache	7	Occurs when ASP.NET bypasses execution of the current event handler and allows a caching module to serve a request from the cache.
PostUpdateRequestCache	17	Occurs when ASP.NET finishes updating caching modules and storing responses that are used to serve subsequent requests from the cache.
PreRequestHandlerExecute	11	Raised just before ASP.NET begins executing a handler for the HTTP request. After this event, ASP.NET forwards the request to the appropriate HTTP handler.
PreSendRequestContent	14	Raised just before ASP.NET sends the response contents to the client. This event allows you to change the contents before it gets delivered to the client. You can use this event to add the contents, which are common in all pages, to the page output—for example, a common menu, header, or footer.

continues

TABLE 30-1 *(continued)*

EVENT NAME	ORDER	DESCRIPTION
PreSendRequestHeaders	21	Raised just before ASP.NET sends the HTTP response headers to the client. This event allows you to change the headers before they are delivered to the client. You can use this event to add cookies and custom data into headers.
ReleaseRequestState	13	Occurs after ASP.NET finishes executing all request event handlers. This event causes state modules to save the current state data.
RequestCompleted	22	Occurs when the managed objects that are associated with the request have been released.
ResolveRequestCache	6	Occurs when ASP.NET finishes an authorization event to let the caching modules serve requests from the cache, bypassing execution of the event handler (for example, a page or an XML web service).
UpdateRequestCache	16	Occurs when ASP.NET finishes executing an event handler in order to let caching modules store responses that will be used to serve subsequent requests from the cache.

To see how you can create and use an HttpModule, you can use a simple example involving modifying the HTTP output stream before it is sent to the client. This can be a simple and useful tool if you want to add text to each page served from your website, such as a date/time stamp or the server that processed the request, but do not want to modify each page in your application. To get started creating this HttpModule, create a web application project in Visual Studio and add a class file that inherits from IHttpModule to the App_Code directory. Listing 30-2 (files App_Code\AppendMessage.cs and App_Code\AppendMessage.vb in the code download for this chapter) shows the code for the HttpModule.

LISTING 30-2: Altering the output of an **ASP.NET** web page

VB

```
Public Class AppendMessage
    Implements IHttpModule

    Dim WithEvents _application As HttpApplication = Nothing

    Public Sub Dispose() Implements IHttpModule.Dispose

    End Sub

    Public Sub Init(context As HttpApplication) Implements IHttpModule.Init
        _application = context
    End Sub

    Public Sub context_EndRequest(ByVal sender As Object, ByVal e As EventArgs) _
            Handles _application.EndRequest

        Dim message As String = String.Format("processed on {0}",_
            System.DateTime.Now.ToString())

        _application.Context.Response.Write(message)
    End Sub

End Class
```

C#

```csharp
using System;
using System.Web;

public class AppendMessage : IHttpModule
{
    private HttpApplication _application = null;

    public void Dispose()
    {

    }

    public void Init(HttpApplication context)
    {
        _application = context;
        context.EndRequest += context_EndRequest;
    }

    void context_EndRequest(object sender, EventArgs e)
    {
        string message = string.Format("processed on {0}",
            System.DateTime.Now.ToString());
        _application.Context.Response.Write(message);
    }
}
```

You can see that the class stub from Listing 30-1 has been expanded by handling the `EndRequest` event. This event fires right before the content created by the HttpHandler is sent to the client, and gives you one final opportunity to modify it.

To modify the content of the request, in the `EndRequest` handler method you simply write your modification to the `HttpResponse` object's output stream, which appends the content to the end of the existing content. This sample gets the current date and time and writes it to the output stream. The HTTP request is then sent back to the client.

To use this module, you must let ASP.NET know that you want to include the module in the request-processing pipeline. You do this by modifying the `web.config` file to contain a reference to the module. Listing 30-3 shows how you can add a `<modules>` section to your `web.config` file.

LISTING 30-3: Adding the modules configuration to web.config

```xml
<configuration>
  <system.web>
    <compilation debug="true" targetFramework="4.5" />
    <httpRuntime targetFramework="4.5" />
  </system.web>
  <system.webServer>
    <modules>
      <add name="AppendMessage" type="AppendMessage, App_Code" />
    </modules>
  </system.webServer>
</configuration>
```

The generic format of the `<modules>` section is

```xml
<modules>
    <add name="[modulename]" type="[namespace.classname, assemblyname]" />
</modules>
```

If you are deploying your application to an IIS 6 server, you must also add the module configuration to the `<system.web>` configuration section.

```
<httpModules>
    <add name="AppendMessage" type=" AppendMessage, App_Code"/>
</httpModules>
```

If you add the `<httpModules>` section to a `web.config` file that will potentially be deployed to a server running IIS 7 or IIS 8, you should also add the following validation entry to the `<system.webServer>` configuration section.

```
<validation validateIntegratedModeConfiguration="false"/>
```

Listing 30-4 (file web.config in the code download for this chapter) shows the `web.config` file after registering the modules in the `<system.web>` and `<system.webServer>` configurations sections.

LISTING 30-4: The web.config file after registering the HttpModule

```
<?xml version="1.0"?>

<!--
  For more information on how to configure your ASP.NET application, please visit
  http://go.microsoft.com/fwlink/?LinkId=169433
  -->

<configuration>
  <system.web>
    <compilation debug="true" targetFramework="4.5" />
    <httpRuntime targetFramework="4.5" />
    <httpModules>
      <add name="AppendMessage" type="AppendMessage, App_Code" />
    </httpModules>
  </system.web>
  <system.webServer>
    <validation validateIntegratedModeConfiguration="false"/>
    <modules>
      <add name="AppendMessage" type="AppendMessage, App_Code" />
    </modules>
  </system.webServer>
</configuration>
```

If you have created your HttpModule in the `App_Code` directory of an ASP.NET website, you might wonder how you know what the `assemblyname` value should be, considering ASP.NET now dynamically compiles this code at run time. The solution is to use the text "App_Code" as the assembly name, which tells ASP.NET that your module is located in the dynamically created assembly.

You can also create HttpModules as a separate class library, in which case you simply use the assembly name of the library.

After you have added this section to your `web.config` file, simply view one of the web pages from your project in the browser. A sample page, `Basic.aspx`, has been included in the example project. When you view the page in the browser you will see the message added to the very bottom of the page. If you view the source of the page, you will notice the message has been added at the end of the HTML.

Figure 30-3 shows what you should see when you view the page source.

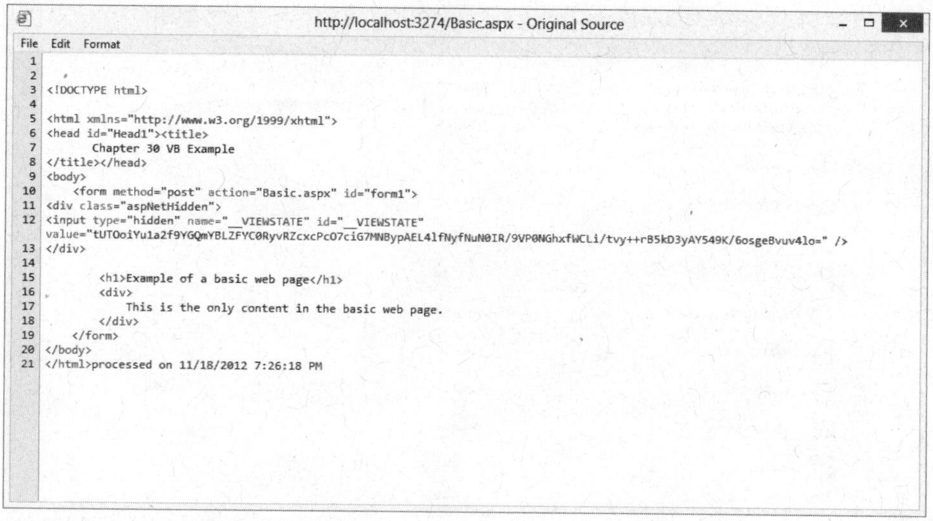

```
1
2        '
3    <!DOCTYPE html>
4
5    <html xmlns="http://www.w3.org/1999/xhtml">
6    <head id="Head1"><title>
7            Chapter 30 VB Example
8    </title></head>
9    <body>
10       <form method="post" action="Basic.aspx" id="form1">
11   <div class="aspNetHidden">
12   <input type="hidden" name="__VIEWSTATE" id="__VIEWSTATE"
     value="tUTOoiYu1a2f9YGQmYBLZFYC0RyvRZcxcPcO7ciG7MNBypAEL4lfNyfNuN0IR/9VP0NGhxfWCLi/tvy++rB5kD3yAY549K/6osgeBvuv4lo=" />
13   </div>
14
15           <h1>Example of a basic web page</h1>
16       <div>
17           This is the only content in the basic web page.
18       </div>
19       </form>
20   </body>
21   </html>processed on 11/18/2012 7:26:18 PM
```

FIGURE 30-3

HTTPHANDLERS

HttpHandlers differ from HttpModules, not only because of their positions in the request-processing pipeline (refer to Figures 30-1 and 30-2), but also because they must be mapped to a specific file extension. Handlers are the last stop for incoming HTTP requests and are ultimately the point in the request-processing pipeline that is responsible for serving up the requested content, be it an ASPX page, HTML, plaintext, or an image.

Using HttpHandlers to serve up content you might normally serve using a standard ASP.NET page (such as a dynamic file download request) can be a good idea because it allows you to write a specialized handler that eliminates some of the overhead of a standard ASP.NET handler.

This section demonstrates two ways to create a simple HttpHandler that you can use to serve up images based on dynamic query-string data:

➤ First, you look at creating an HttpHandler using an .ashx file extension that allows you to get started quickly and requires no server configuration.

➤ Next, you learn how to create even more customized handlers by mapping your HttpHandler to a custom file extension using IIS.

Generic Handlers

Visual Studio provides a standard template for HttpHandlers to help you get started. To add an HttpHandler to your project, you simply select the Generic Handler file type from the Add New Item dialog box. Figure 30-4 shows this dialog box with the file type selected.

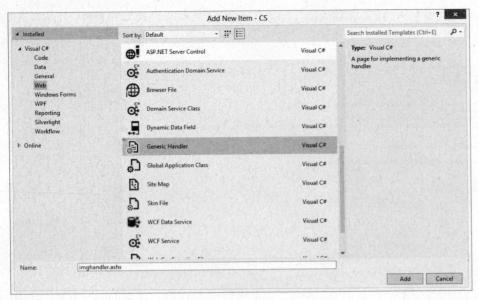

FIGURE 30-4

You can see that when you add the Generic Handler file to your project, it adds a file with an `.ashx` extension. The `.ashx` file extension is the default HttpHandler file extension set up by ASP.NET. Remember that HttpHandlers must be mapped to a unique file extension, so by default ASP.NET uses the `.ashx` extension. This feature is convenient because, otherwise, you would be responsible for adding the file extension yourself. This task is obviously not always possible, nor is it practical. Using the Custom Handler file type helps you avoid any extra configuration.

Notice the class stub that the file type automatically creates for you. Listing 30-5 shows the class (files txthandler.ashx.cs and txthandler.ashx.vb in the code download for this chapter).

LISTING 30-5: The HttpHandler page template

VB

```vb
Imports System.Web
Imports System.Web.Services

Public Class imghandler
    Implements System.Web.IHttpHandler

    Sub ProcessRequest(ByVal context As HttpContext) Implements _
        IHttpHandler.ProcessRequest

        context.Response.ContentType = "text/plain"
        context.Response.Write("Hello World!")

    End Sub

    ReadOnly Property IsReusable() As Boolean Implements IHttpHandler.IsReusable
        Get
            Return False
        End Get
```

```
        End Property

    End Class
```

C#

```csharp
using System;
using System.Collections.Generic;
using System.Linq;
using System.Web;

namespace CS
{
    /// <summary>
    /// Summary description for imghandler
    /// </summary>
    public class imghandler : IHttpHandler
    {

        public void ProcessRequest(HttpContext context)
        {
            context.Response.ContentType = "text/plain";
            context.Response.Write("Hello World");
        }

        public bool IsReusable
        {
            get
            {
                return false;
            }
        }
    }
}
```

Notice that the stub implements the IHttpHandler interface, which requires you to implement the ProcessRequest method and IsReusable property.

➤ You use the ProcessRequest method to process the incoming HTTP request. By default, the class stub changes the content type to plain and then writes the "Hello World" string to the output stream.

➤ The IsReusable property simply lets ASP.NET know whether incoming HTTP requests can reuse the sample instance of this HttpHandler.

The handler generated in the template is ready to run right away. Try executing the handler in your browser and see what happens. The interesting thing to note about this handler is that because it changes the content to text/plain, browsers react to the responses from this handler in potentially very different ways depending on a number of factors:

➤ Browser type and version

➤ Applications loaded on the system that may map to the MIME type

➤ Operating system and service pack level

Based on these factors, you might see the text returned in the browser, you might see Notepad open and display the text, or you might receive the Open/Save/Cancel prompt from Internet Explorer. Make sure you understand the potential consequences of changing the ContentType header.

You can continue the example by modifying it to return an actual file. In this case, you use the handler to return an image. An image file, Garden.jpg, has been included in the example download. To do this, you simply modify the code in the ProcessRequest method, as shown in Listing 30-6 (files imghandler.ashx.cs and imghandler.ashx.vb in the code download for this chapter).

LISTING 30-6: Outputting an image from an HttpHandler

VB

```vb
Imports System.Web
Imports System.Web.Services

Public Class imghandler
    Implements System.Web.IHttpHandler

    Sub ProcessRequest(ByVal context As HttpContext)
        Implements IHttpHandler.ProcessRequest
        'Logic to retrieve the image file
        context.Response.ContentType = "image/jpeg"
        context.Response.WriteFile("Garden.jpg")
    End Sub

    ReadOnly Property IsReusable() As Boolean Implements IHttpHandler.IsReusable
        Get
            Return False
        End Get
    End Property

End Class
```

C#

```csharp
using System;
using System.Collections.Generic;
using System.Linq;
using System.Web;

namespace CS
{
    /// <summary>
    /// Summary description for imghandler
    /// </summary>
    public class imghandler : IHttpHandler
    {

        public void ProcessRequest(HttpContext context)
        {
            //Logic to retrieve the image file
            context.Response.ContentType = "image/jpeg";
            context.Response.WriteFile("Garden.jpg");
        }

        public bool IsReusable
        {
            get
            {
                return false;
            }
        }
    }
}
```

As you can see, you simply change the ContentType to image/jpeg to indicate that you are returning a JPEG image; then you use the WriteFile() method to write an image file to the output stream. Load the handler into a browser, and you see that the handler displays the image. Figure 30-5 shows the resulting web page.

FIGURE 30-5

Now, you create a simple web page to display the image handler. Listing 30-7 (file ShowImage.aspx in the code download for this chapter) shows code for the C# version of the web page.

LISTING 30-7: A sample web page using the HttpHandler for the image source

```
<%@ Page Language="C#" AutoEventWireup="true" CodeBehind="ShowImage.aspx.cs"
    Inherits="CS.ShowImage" %>

<!DOCTYPE html>

<html xmlns="http://www.w3.org/1999/xhtml">
<head runat="server">
    <title>Generic Image Viewer</title>
</head>
<body>
    <form id="form1" runat="server">
    <div>
        <img src="imghandler.ashx" alt="Dynamic Image" />
    </div>
    </form>
</body>
</html>
```

Although this is simple, you can enhance the sample by passing query string parameters to your handler and using them to perform additional logic in the handler:

```
<img src="imghandler.ashx?imageid=123" />
```

Using the query string data you could, for example, dynamically retrieve an image from a SQL database and return it to the client or perform some type of authentication to ensure the requestor is allowed to access this image.

Mapping a File Extension in IIS

Although using the `.ashx` file extension is convenient, you might want to create an HTTP handler for a custom file extension or even for a commonly used extension. You can use the code from the image handler to demonstrate this method.

Create a new class in the `App_Code` directory of your web project. You can simply copy the code from the existing image handler control into this class, as shown in Listing 30-8 (files App_Code\ImgHandler.cs and App_Code\ImgHandler.vb in the code download for this chapter).

LISTING 30-8: The class-based image HttpHandler

VB

```vb
Public Class ImgHandler
    Implements System.Web.IHttpHandler

    Sub ProcessRequest(ByVal context As HttpContext) Implements _
        IHttpHandler.ProcessRequest
        'Logic to retrieve the image file
        context.Response.ContentType = "image/jpeg"
        context.Response.WriteFile("Garden.jpg")
    End Sub

    ReadOnly Property IsReusable() As Boolean Implements IHttpHandler.IsReusable
        Get
            Return False
        End Get
    End Property
End Class
```

C#

```csharp
using System.Web;

public class ImgHandler : IHttpHandler
{
    public void ProcessRequest(HttpContext context)
    {
        //Logic to retrieve the image file
        context.Response.ContentType = "image/jpeg";
        context.Response.WriteFile("Garden.jpg");
    }

    public bool IsReusable
    {
        get
        {
            return false;
        }
    }
}
```

After adding your class, configure the application to show which file extension this handler serves. You do this by adding a `<handlers>` section to the `web.config` file. Listing 30-9 shows the section to add for the image handler.

LISTING 30-9: Adding the handlers' configuration information to the web.config file

```xml
<handlers>
    <add name="ImageHandler" verb="*" path="ImageHandler.img" type="ImgHandler,
        App_Code" />
</handlers>
```

In the configuration section, you direct the application to use the `ImgHandler` class to process incoming requests for `ImageHandler.img`. You can also specify wildcards for the path. Specifying `*.img` for the path indicates that you want the application to use the `ImgHandler` class to process any request with the `.img` file extension. Specifying `*` for `verb` indicates that you want all requests to the application to be processed using the handler.

As with HttpModules, if you are running your web application using IIS 6, then you also must add the `<httpHandlers>` configuration section to the `<system.web>` configuration section of your application's `config` file. When adding the handler configuration in this section, you should not include the `name` attribute.

```
<add verb="*" path="ImageHandler.img" type="ImgHandler, App_Code" />
```

Load the `ImageHandler.img` file into a browser and, again, you should see that it serves up the image. Figure 30-6 shows the results. Notice the path in the browser's address bar leads directly to the `ImageHandler.img` file.

FIGURE 30-6

SUMMARY

This chapter presented a number of ways you can create modules that allow you to interact with the ASP.NET request-processing pipeline. You worked with HttpModules, which give you the power to plug yourself directly into the ASP.NET page-processing pipeline. The events provided to an HttpModule give you great power and flexibility to customize your applications.

You also looked at HttpHandlers. Handlers allow you to skip the ASP.NET page-processing pipeline completely and have complete control over how the framework serves up requested data. You learned how to create your own image handler and then map the handler to any file or file extension you want. Using these features of ASP.NET can help you create features in your application that exercise great control over the standard page processing that ASP.NET uses.

31

Asynchronous Communication

WHAT'S IN THIS CHAPTER?

➤ What is async and why should you use it?

➤ Using the async/await pattern in ASP.NET

WROX.COM CODE DOWNLOADS FOR THIS CHAPTER

Please note that all the code examples in this chapter are available as a part of this chapter's code download on the book's website at www.wrox.com on the Download Code tab.

One of the most important considerations when building a web application is how well the application scales as it starts to get more traffic. Applications that consume lots of server resources do not tend to scale well, which leads to an unresponsive site and a bad user experience. In a lot of cases, precious server resources such as threads are waiting to perform some I/O-based call or are waiting for the result of a database call. This operation blocks the thread from processing any other requests that might come in.

You can solve most of these problems by following an asynchronous programming paradigm, which ensures that you are utilizing your resources effectively. The .NET Framework has had support for writing asynchronous code since .NET 1.0. The async features in the framework have evolved quite a lot during these years.

This chapter explores these asynchronous paradigms and describes how you can use them in your web application. It shows you how you can use the async/await pattern that was introduced in .NET 4.5 and talks about some pitfalls of writing bad asynchronous code. In the end, you look at some tweaks you can make to your web server for increasing concurrency of your web application.

ASYNCHRONOUS PROGRAMMING

This chapter begins with a quick look at why you need to write async code and the challenges it involves. It then looks at how and where you can write async code in ASP.NET. It also goes into some of the pitfalls of writing async code in web applications, which is different from writing async code in traditional desktop applications.

Why Async?

The web server has a finite number of threads to process requests. The need for writing async code arises from this limitation so that the application can use these resources effectively. Whenever a request comes to ASP.NET, a new thread from the CLR thread pool is allocated to process the request. If the application is written in a synchronous way, the thread will be busy processing this request. If part of the processing requires waiting for a result from a database call, this thread is waiting for the result and cannot be used to process any other requests. Now if all the threads from the thread pool are held up, any further request to this website will not be processed, and the user will be waiting. This would ultimately lead to an unresponsive site.

This is where the benefits of writing applications in an asynchronous pattern come into play. If the same application were written using async, when the thread is waiting on the results of the database call, the thread is given back to the thread pool by ASP.NET while the database call happens on a different thread. The thread that is given back to the thread pool is now available to process any other incoming requests to the application. When the database call finishes, the application is notified and the request is completed.

When to Write Async Code

The considerations of when to write async code in web applications are quite different compared to traditional desktop applications.

➤ When writing desktop applications, the goal for writing async code is to not block the UI thread (so the application is always responsive to the user) and to perform any background operations such as computation or database calls on a different thread. Desktop applications are not restricted by the number of threads that are available to the application.

➤ When it comes to writing asynchronous code for web applications, the limiting factor is the number of threads in the thread pool. The goal of writing async code in web applications is to maximize the number of requests the threads can process.

A good rule of thumb of when to write async code for web applications is anytime your application needs to do an I/O-based network call. This includes anytime you need to access files on disk, or you need to make a call to a web service, or you need to make a call to a database server. In each of these cases, making I/O calls is highly optimized in Windows and lets ASP.NET reclaim your thread to process other requests while your application is waiting on the result of this call.

A more modern case of writing async code is when your application depends on a long-running request. In this scenario you have a long-running connection between a server and client, and the data is transferred between them when some event takes place. This is typically used in long polling and HTTP streaming. In the case when no data is being exchanged, you do not want a thread to be processing this request because there is no data, but as soon as some event happens, you want a thread to do to the work. You can look at these cases more in Chapter 26.

History of Async

Since the inception of the .NET Framework programming for async, dealing with server resources has always been challenging. When it comes to writing async code, developers have had to grapple with an added complexity—namely, the conceptual overhead of writing async code. This makes writing and debugging async code difficult, because you have to deal with threads, callbacks, and synchronization state when the request is switched to different threads. The .NET Framework has introduced several patterns that have tried to solve these problems for the developer. In .NET Framework 4.5, a new pattern called async/await was released, which does the best at making it easier to write and debug async code. You take a brief look at all of these patterns in the following sections.

Early Async

In .NET 1.0, the framework introduced a pattern called the *Asynchronous Programming Model* (APM), also called the *IAsyncResult* pattern. In this model, asynchronous operations require `Begin` and `End` methods (for example, `BeginWrite` and `EndWrite` for asynchronous write operations).

In .NET 2.0, the *Event-based Asynchronous Pattern* (EAP) was introduced. This pattern requires a method that has the `Async` suffix, and also requires one or more events, event handler delegate types, and `EventArg`-derived types. Listing 31-1 shows some synchronous code which makes an outbound call to download contents and calculates total bytes downloaded.

LISTING 31-1: Synchronous code

VB

```
Public Function RSSFeedLength(uris As IList(Of Uri)) As Integer
    Dim total As Integer = 0
    For Each uri In uris
        Dim data = New WebClient().DownloadData(uri)
        total += data.Length
    Next
    Return total
End Function
```

C#

```
public int RSSFeedLength(IList<Uri> uris)
{
int total = 0;
foreach (var uri in uris)
{
    var data = new WebClient().DownloadData(uri);
    total += data.Length;
}
    return total;
}
```

Listing 31-2 shows how the same code looks in the EAP async pattern. As you can see from Listing 31-2, the code has become a lot more complicated. The `foreach` loop had to be broken up to manually get an enumerator. The code also looks recursive instead of iterative. This makes understanding and debugging hard as well.

LISTING 31-2: Asynchronous code using EAP

VB

```
Public Sub RSSFeedLengthAsync(uris As IList(Of Uri))
    RSSFeedLengthAsyncHelper(uris.GetEnumerator(), 0)
End Sub

Private Sub RSSFeedLengthAsyncHelper(enumerator As IEnumerator(Of Uri), total As Integer)
    If enumerator.MoveNext() Then
        Dim client = New WebClient()
        AddHandler client.DownloadDataCompleted,
            Sub(sender, e)
                RSSFeedLengthAsyncHelper(enumerator, total + e.Result.Length)
            End Sub
        client.DownloadDataAsync(enumerator.Current)
    Else
```

continues

LISTING 31-2 *(continued)*

```
            enumerator.Dispose()
        End If
   End Sub
```

C#

```csharp
public void RSSFeedLengthAsync(IList<Uri> uris)
{
    RSSFeedLengthAsyncHelper(uris.GetEnumerator(), 0);
}

private void RSSFeedLengthAsyncHelper(IEnumerator<Uri> enumerator, int total)
{
    if (enumerator.MoveNext())
    {
        var client = new WebClient();
        client.DownloadDataCompleted += (sender, e) =>
        {
            RSSFeedLengthAsyncHelper(enumerator, total + e.Result.Length);
        };
        client.DownloadDataAsync(enumerator.Current);
    }
    else
    {
        enumerator.Dispose();
    }
}
```

> **NOTE** *Neither EAP nor APM are recommended for writing any asynchronous applications if you are building applications on .NET Framework v4.0 or v4.5.*

Task and TAP

In .NET Framework v4.0, *Task-based Asynchronous Pattern* (TAP) was introduced. This pattern uses a single method to represent the start and finish of the async operation. The TAP method returns either a `Task` or a `Task<TResult>`, based on whether the corresponding synchronous method returns void or a type `TResult`. A task is an action that can be executed independently of the rest of the program. In that sense, it is semantically equivalent to a thread, except that it is a more lightweight object and comes without the overhead of creating an OS thread. Along with TAP, .NET v4.0 also introduced `Task` as the basic unit of parallelism and provided rich support for managing tasks based on the Task Parallel library. You look at task in more detail later in the chapter.

Async/Await

The .NET Framework v4.5 introduced the async/await pattern. The `async` and `await` keywords are the heart of async programming. By using those two keywords, you can write async code as if you were writing synchronous code. This pattern is based on TAP and provides a nice programming paradigm to write asynchronous code.

Listing 31-3 shows how the synchronous code from Listing 31-1 would look using async/await.

LISTING 31-3: Async code using async/await

VB

```vb
Public Async Function RSSFeedLengthAsync(uris As IList(Of Uri)) As Task(Of Integer)
        Dim total As Integer = 0
        For Each uri In uris
            Dim data = Await New WebClient().DownloadDataTaskAsync(uri)
            total += data.Length
        Next
        Return total
End Function
```

C#

```csharp
public async Task<int> RSSFeedLengthAsync(IList<Uri> uris)
    {
        int total = 0;
        foreach (var uri in uris)
        {
            var data = await new WebClient().DownloadDataTaskAsync(uri);
            total += data.Length;
        }
        return total;
    }
```

The first thing you will notice about Listing 31-3 is how similar it looks to the synchronous code back in Listing 31-1. The control flow is not altered and there are no callbacks. Asynchrony is achieved here by returning `Task<int>`. Task represents a unit of ongoing work. The caller of this method can use the returned task to check if the task has completed and get the result from the task.

The method is also marked as async, which tells the compiler to compile the method in a special way, allowing parts of the code to be turned into callbacks and automatically creating a `Task<int>` in which to return the result. `DownloadTaskAsync` returns a `Task<byte[]>`, which will complete once the data is available. In this case you do not want to do anything until you have data, so you await the task.

It might appear that `await` does a blocking call, but in fact what happens is that `await` puts the rest of the method as a callback and returns immediately. When the awaited task returns, it invokes the callback and resumes the execution of the method from where it left off.

By the time it reaches the return statement, the code has suspended and resumed several times (due to the await call) and returned a `Task<int>` to the caller. The caller can wait on the task and get the result.

ASYNC IN ASP.NET

As you saw in the preceding section, the .NET Framework has evolved to support asynchronous programming. The async support in ASP.NET has also evolved at the same pace.

Asynchrony can be achieved in two places—namely, the page life cycle and the application life cycle. A developer can write async code when a page is being processed or when the request is being processed in the ASP.NET pipeline.

In .NET v4.5 the ASP.NET async pipeline has undergone a major change to support async/await and TAP. The new pipeline is task-based and has new base classes that you can derive from when writing async pages, handlers, or modules. Before you look into how to use the async/await pattern in ASP.NET, the following section looks at how threads are managed in ASP.NET.

Thread Pools

Threads are precious limited resources on a web server, so you should use them wisely when architecting your applications. When a request comes to a web server, it goes through the following flow in Integrated Mode in IIS. HTTP.sys is the first point of entry. HTTP.sys is a kernel-level driver that posts requests on an I/O completion port on which IIS listens. IIS picks up this request on one of its own thread pool threads and calls ASP.NET. ASP.NET starts to process this thread from the CLR thread pool. Once the request has finished processing and a response needs to be sent back to the client, the response is switched from a CLR thread pool to one from an IIS thread pool.

The reason the flow is designed in such a way is to make the system more scalable and resilient. For example, the request switches from kernel mode (HTTP.sys) to user mode (IIS) so that HTTP.sys can process more requests and hand them over to other listeners, which could be non IIS. If the request were to be processed on one thread, a deadlock or error on that request could bring down HTTP on the entire server. Thus, even though you are paying a penalty for context switching, the benefits of having the kernel be more reliable far outweigh the cost of thread switching.

The other reason for switching the request from the IIS thread pool to the ASP.NET thread pool is improving performance for scenarios where IIS is serving a mixture of static and dynamic requests. This is the most common case for a web server. Static files are cached locally and are served by the IIS static file handler (the request does not enter ASP.NET at all). This also allows IIS to process other requests and hand off to other listeners (non ASP.NET), as in the case of HTTP.sys.

Once the request is processed and the response is ready to be sent, the response is switched from a thread in the CLR thread pool to one in the IIS thread pool. This is done because if the client is on a low bandwidth network, you do not want a CLR thread to be blocked while the response is being sent. You want the CLR thread to return back and process more requests.

These thread pools contain a finite number of threads as well. The IIS thread pool has a thread count of 256, and the CLR thread pool has 100 threads per processor. So you can imagine if your application is running synchronously and is holding up threads by waiting on results of database calls, you will soon run out of threads to process more requests from the users and your website will become sluggish, which will lead to a bad user experience. The following section looks at a few ways to write asynchronous code in ASP.NET. Figure 31-1 shows a flow on how a request is processed by the two thread pools.

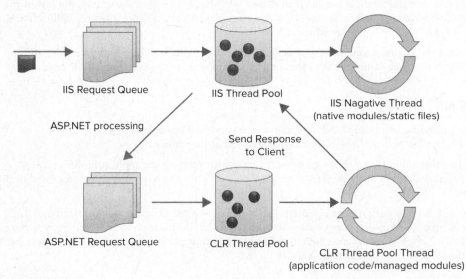

FIGURE 31-1

Writing Async Code

As you saw earlier, in .NET Framework 4.5 async/await was introduced as a pattern to write async applications. To support this pattern in ASP.NET, the existing async pipeline has gone through a radical change. The whole of the async pipeline is now task-based. What has not changed, however, is where you can write async code. You can still use async pages, handlers, and modules to write async code. In Chapter 26, you learned about HTTP handlers and modules. This chapter looks at how you can write asynchronous handlers and modules using async/await.

Async Pages

You should write async pages when your page is accessing data from a database or a web service. In this case you do not want to stop the page life cycle and wait on the results of the database or web service call. You can tell ASP.NET to process this page as async by setting a page directive as shown in Listing 31-4. When you set this attribute, ASP.NET switches the processing of the page from a synchronous pipeline to an asynchronous pipeline.

LISTING 31-4: Marking pages as async

```
<%@ Page Async="true" %>
```

If you do not use this attribute and use async code in your page, ASP.NET throws an error indicating that you need to mark your page as async. It does this to prevent race conditions from happening because the code is async and if you do not mark it as async, the code will get executed in a synchronous manner and can cause deadlock or race conditions.

Once you have done this, you can write async methods in the page. In ASP.NET 4.5 you can now write async Page_Load events, which was not possible earlier. Listing 31-5 shows how you can call a web service asynchronously from Page_Load.

LISTING 31-5: Asynchronous Page_Load

VB

```vb
Protected Async Sub Page_Load(sender As Object, e As EventArgs) Handles Me.Load
    Using client = New HttpClient()
        Dim customersJson = Await client.GetStringAsync(url)

Dim customers = JsonConvert.DeserializeObject(Of IEnumerable(Of Customer))(customersJson)
        results.DataSource = customers
        results.DataBind()
    End Using
End Sub
```

C#

```csharp
protected async void Page_Load(object sender, EventArgs e)
{
    using (var client = new HttpClient())
    {
        var customersJson = await client.GetStringAsync(url);

var customers = JsonConvert.DeserializeObject<IEnumerable<Customer>>(customersJson);
        results.DataSource = customers;
        results.DataBind();
    }
}
```

Although you can do this, this approach is not recommended for most cases. This is because when you execute Page_Load asynchronously, the page life cycle does not proceed further until the async Page_Load finishes execution. This means that the call to GetStringAsync() will happen asynchronously, but the page life cycle will wait until the await portion of the method finishes executing. In Listing 31-5 the code is simulating a call to an external web service by calling an ASP.NET generic handler. Notice also that the code is using HttpClient, which is a new type in .NET Framework 4.5. HttpClient is a modern HTTP client for .NET and supersedes WebClient.

A recommended approach is to use RegisterAsyncTask to register and execute async operations in a page. The benefit of using this approach is that ASP.NET will not halt the page life cycle execution to wait for async Page_Load to finish, but it will continue with the page life cycle until it reaches the PreRender event of the page. At this point ASP.NET will execute all tasks that were registered using RegisterAsyncTask. PreRender is an event in the life cycle where all the controls are created but the content has not been rendered, so it gives you a chance to do data binding if needed. Listing 31-6 shows how you can define Task with ASP.NET using PageAsyncTask, which is a new type introduced in ASP.NET 4.5.

LISTING 31-6: RegisterAsyncTask using PageAsyncTask

VB

```vb
Protected Sub Page_Load(sender As Object, e As EventArgs) Handles Me.Load
        RegisterAsyncTask(New PageAsyncTask(Function() GetCustomersAsync()))
    End Sub

Public Async Function GetCustomersAsync() As Task
        Using client = New HttpClient()

            Dim customersJson =
              Await client.GetStringAsync("http://localhost:64927/Customers.ashx")
            Dim customers =
              JsonConvert.DeserializeObject(Of IEnumerable(Of Customer))(customersJson)
            results.DataSource = customers
            results.DataBind()
        End Using
End Function
```

C#

```csharp
protected void Page_Load(object sender, EventArgs e)
    {
        RegisterAsyncTask(new PageAsyncTask(GetCustomersAsync));
    }
private async Task GetCustomersAsync()
    {
        using (var client = new HttpClient())
        {

var customersJson = await client.GetStringAsync("http://localhost:64927/Customers.ashx");

var customers = JsonConvert.DeserializeObject<IEnumerable<Customer>>(customersJson);
        results.DataSource = customers;
        results.DataBind();
    }
    }
```

Async Handlers

As you saw with writing async pages, there is also a new base type (HttpTaskAsyncHandler) for writing async http handlers using async/await. Listing 31-7 shows how you can write async handlers. This sample downloads the contents from a website and renders them on the page.

LISTING 31-7: Async handlers using HttpTaskAsyncHandler

VB

```vb
Public Class Listing31_7 : Inherits HttpTaskAsyncHandler

    Public Overrides Async Function ProcessRequestAsync(context As HttpContext) As Task
        Using client = New HttpClient()
            Dim bingTask = Await client.GetStringAsync("http://bing.com")
            context.Response.Write(bingTask)
        End Using
    End Function
End Class
```

C#

```csharp
public class Listing31_7 : HttpTaskAsyncHandler
{
    public async override Task ProcessRequestAsync(HttpContext context)
    {
        using (var client = new HttpClient())
        {
            var bingTask = await client.GetStringAsync("http://bing.com");
            context.Response.Write(bingTask);
        }
    }
}
```

Async Modules

One of the differences you will see when writing async modules in ASP.NET 4.5 is how the tasks are registered in ASP.NET modules. There is a new type, `EventHandlerTaskAsyncHelper`, in ASP.NET 4.5. This is a helper that takes in a task as an input and unwraps the beginning and end portions of the async task and passes them as begin and end handlers to the async events that you want to subscribe to in the module. Listing 31-8 shows how you can write async modules using this helper.

LISTING 31-8: Async modules using EventHandlerTaskAsyncHelper

VB

```vb
Public Sub Init(context As HttpApplication) Implements IHttpModule.Init
    Dim helper As New EventHandlerTaskAsyncHelper(AddressOf DownloadWeb)
    context.AddOnBeginRequestAsync(helper.BeginEventHandler, helper.EndEventHandler)
End Sub
Public Async Function DownloadWeb(caller As Object, e As EventArgs) As Task
    Using client = New HttpClient()
        Dim result = Await client.GetStringAsync("http://bing.com")
    End Using
End Function
```

C#

```csharp
public void Init(HttpApplication context)
{
    EventHandlerTaskAsyncHelper helper =
        new EventHandlerTaskAsyncHelper(DownloadWeb);

    context.AddOnBeginRequestAsync(
            helper.BeginEventHandler, helper.EndEventHandler);
}
public async Task DownloadWeb(object caller, EventArgs e)
```

continues

LISTING 31-8 *(continued)*

```
    {
        using (var client = new HttpClient())
        {
            var result = await client.GetStringAsync("http://bing.com");
        }
    }
}
```

Canceling Async Tasks

Hopefully, you have a good idea of how you can write asynchronous code in an ASP.NET application. One of the most common scenarios when dealing with external resources such as web service and database servers is the time it takes to get the response. Because both these calls depend on how slow or fast the network access is, the response time varies a lot, and in some cases you might not get the response if the server is down. In these cases you want your application to be resilient to these occurrences, and you should be able to handle such cases easily. A common operation that you will have to do is to check on the status of an existing task and, if it is canceled (due to server unavailability, for example), to take some custom action.

The object that invokes a cancelable operation, for example by creating a new task, passes the token to the caller doing some operation on the task. That operation can, in turn, pass copies of the token to other operations if needed. Listing 31-9 shows how you can specify a timeout for your async task running on the page. In this case if the async operation takes more than the AsyncTimeout value, you get a TimeOutException, which you can handle in your page. Listing 31-10 shows how you can handle this exception in your async code.

LISTING 31-9: Setting a timeout for async processing on a page

```
<%@ Page Async="true" AsyncTimeout="1" %>
```

LISTING 31-10: Handling a TimeOutException due to AsyncTimeOut

VB

```
Protected Sub Page_Load(sender As Object, e As EventArgs) Handles Me.Load
    RegisterAsyncTask(New PageAsyncTask
        (Function() GetCustomersAsync(Context.Request.TimedOutToken)))
End Sub

Public Async Function GetCustomersAsync(ByVal cancelToken As CancellationToken) As Task
    Using client = New HttpClient()

    Dim response =
        Await client.GetAsync("http://localhost:64927/Common/SlowCustomers.ashx", cancelToken)
        Dim customersJson = Await response.Content.ReadAsStringAsync()
        Dim customers =
            sonConvert.DeserializeObject(Of IEnumerable(Of Customer))(customersJson)
        results.DataSource = customers
        results.DataBind()
    End Using
End Function
Protected Sub Page_Error(sender As Object, e As EventArgs) Handles Me.Error
    Dim exc As Exception = Server.GetLastError()
    If TypeOf exc Is TimeoutException Then
        Throw exc
    End If
End Sub
```

C#

```csharp
protected void Page_Load(object sender, EventArgs e)
{
    RegisterAsyncTask(new PageAsyncTask(GetCustomersAsync));
}
private async Task GetCustomersAsync(CancellationToken cancelToken)
{
    using (var client = new HttpClient())
    {
        var response = await
            client.GetAsync("http://localhost:64927/Common/SlowCustomers.ashx", cancelToken);
        var customersJson = await response.Content.ReadAsStringAsync();

var customers = JsonConvert.DeserializeObject<IEnumerable<Customer>>(customersJson);
        results.DataSource = customers;
        results.DataBind();
    }
}
private void Page_Error(object sender, EventArgs e)
{
    Exception exc = Server.GetLastError();
    if (exc is TimeoutException)
    {
        throw exc;
    }
}
```

In the preceding listing, if the call to the external web service takes more than 1 second, then the call to `GetAsync()` will get timed out. There will be a `TimeOutException` that will be thrown by this code, which can be handled in the application to display a more meaningful error message or perform some customized error handling.

Parallelism

So far you have looked at the benefits of writing asynchronous applications and how you can write asynchronous code in ASP.NET. By writing asynchronous code, you can efficiently utilize threads to make your applications more scalable and responsive. There is another aspect to the asynchronous pattern that can increase the execution time of the application. This is called *parallelism*. With the advancements being made in the hardware, many computers and workstations have multiple cores that enable multiple threads to be executed simultaneously. Since the inception of .NET Framework, this was achieved by low-level manipulation of threads and locks, which made parallelizing and debugging your application very hard.

In .NET Framework 4.0, tasks were introduced to simplify parallel application development so you could write efficient and scalable parallel code without having to deal with low-level threads. The framework introduced various kinds of libraries to make it easier to write parallel code in your applications. These ranged from the Task Parallel Library, which makes it easier to parallelize basic for loops, to Parallel LINQ.

This section looks at some basic techniques for parallelizing your ASP.NET applications with the use of tasks. A task represents a unit of work that can be executed as an atomic unit independently. You can combine tasks, compose tasks, wait on tasks to finish, and many more such operations. This section looks at an example of how you can compose tasks to achieve parallelism.

Listing 31-7 showed an example of waiting on a task to download the contents of a website. Now suppose you have three such running tasks and you want to run them in parallel. Listing 31-11 shows how you can do so. `Task.WhenAll` will execute all the tasks in parallel and will wait until all the tasks have finished executing.

LISTING 31-11: Task.WhenAll to perform tasks in parallel

VB

```
Public Overrides Async Function ProcessRequestAsync(context As HttpContext) As Task
    Using client = New HttpClient()
        Dim bingTask = client.GetStringAsync(uri)
        Dim microsoftTask = client.GetStringAsync(uri)
        Dim twitterTask = client.GetStringAsync(uri)

        Await Task.WhenAll(bingTask, microsoftTask, twitterTask)
    End Using
End Function
```

C#

```
public async override Task ProcessRequestAsync(HttpContext context)
{
    using (var client = new HttpClient())
    {
        var bingTask =  client.GetStringAsync(uri);
        var microsoftTask =  client.GetStringAsync(uri);
        var twitterTask =  client.GetStringAsync(uri);

        await Task.WhenAll(bingTask,microsoftTask,twitterTask);
    }
}
```

Server Configuration

One of the most important aspects of making your application more scalable is tuning your web server to get the most out of it. When you install ASP.NET on IIS, the default configuration of thread pools and concurrency is set to support most of the common cases, so it might or might not meet the needs of your application. It is very important to understand what these default limits are and what kinds of applications they target. It is equally important to understand what your application needs. For example, the default configuration of IIS and ASP.NET is not suited for building real-time applications, which need to maintain a long-running server connection, and the server needs to be optimized for high concurrency and high-latency calls. This section looks at some of the tweaks you can make on your web server to optimize performance for your application.

➤ Whenever you are benchmarking your application for scalability, use the server operating systems instead of a client OS such as Windows 8 or Windows 7, because the client operating systems have a maximum of 10 concurrent requests.

➤ As you saw earlier, when a request reaches the web server, it is processed first by HTTP.sys. The default limit of the HTTP.sys queue is 1000. If this limit is exceeded, the server will start responding with an HTTP status code 503. You can increase this limit to 5000 if you find the default limit of 1000 to be too low. You can configure this setting per application pool in IIS using the IIS Manager.

➤ If your application is using web services over HTTP, you may need to change the connectionManagement/maxconnection element. For ASP.NET applications, this is limited to 12 times the number of CPUs .That means that on a quad-proc, you can have at most 12 * 4 = 48 concurrent connections to an end point. You can change this setting by changing the maxconnection of the System.Net.ServicePointManager.DefaultConnectionLimit property in your application start event.

➤ You also know that there is the CLR thread pool that ASP.NET uses to process managed requests. There is a limit on the concurrency of this thread pool. This means that if the application is executing in an asynchronous manner, the number of requests could exceed the number of threads available.

You can control this concurrency limit by setting `MaxConcurrentRequestsPerCPU` in the `web.config`. The default limit for this setting is 5000 and should be good for most applications, but if you are building an application that has extensive asynchronous processing or long-running requests, you should consider increasing this limit so your application performs optimally.

Pitfalls of Using Async

So far you have seen the benefits of using asynchronous processing in your application. It does make your application more scalable and responsive. However, there is a wise saying: "With great power comes great responsibility." Although async processing does increase your application performance, it can create havoc if not used wisely. Poorly written async code can lead to race conditions, thread deadlock, and synchronization problems. All of these problems are difficult to debug and fix, and can waste hours of precious developer time in investigations. In this section, you learn some of the common pitfalls when writing asynchronous code and how you can avoid them.

➤ If you are writing async applications for the web, it is important to remember when to write async code. If parts of your application are making a network call to a web service or database and a thread is blocked waiting on the response of this call, you should use async so the thread is not blocked. However, if part of your application is doing a computation-intensive task, running it asynchronously will not give you much benefit because the application will just use another thread from the thread pool to do the same operation. In fact, you might pay a price for thread context switching in this case. Async programming for the web is thus quite different from traditional desktop applications where the number of threads is not limited as compared to the web server. So whereas in a desktop application you would run computation-intensive operations on a background task so that the UI is responsive, the same does not apply for a web application.

➤ When it comes to creating new tasks/threads, it is best to let the framework create them and manage the thread life cycle. The application developer should use the task APIs to manage and compose tasks.

➤ It is not unusual for you to access ASP.NET intrinsic objects such as Request, Context, and so on. When you are writing asynchronous code you do not really know which thread you are on. So, when you try to access the intrinsic objects, you might access them on the wrong thread. If you use async/await, the framework takes care of synchronizing these objects across threads.

➤ Because the request can be processed by multiple threads in asynchronous processing, if you are using thread local storage, you might not get the right value for your variables if the request is being processed by different threads during the various parts of the processing. If you do need to store local thread-specific information, you can use `HttpContext.Current`.

SUMMARY

In this chapter you looked at asynchronous processing and why you need it. As your applications become more popular and attract more traffic, you need to make sure that they scale well. You should write your applications in a way that enables them to effectively utilize the server resources and perform well.

The .NET Framework and ASP.NET have come a long way in supporting asynchronous processing. You saw the different patterns of writing async code. .NET Framework 4.5 introduced the async/await pattern, which makes writing async code similar to writing synchronous code. The code flows look similar in both approaches.

ASP.NET supports async/await when you want to write async pages, handlers, and modules. In ASP.NET 4.5, the pipeline has undergone a huge change to support async/await. You also looked at some tweaking that you can do on your web server to make your application scale well under load.

Finally, you looked at some of the pitfalls of writing bad asynchronous code and some of the ways by which you can avoid these pitfalls.

32

Building Global Applications

WHAT'S IN THIS CHAPTER?

➤ Globalizing your applications

➤ Defining culture, both server-side and client-side

➤ Working with local and global resources

WROX.COM CODE DOWNLOADS FOR THIS CHAPTER

Please note that all the code examples in this chapter are available as a part of this chapter's code download on the book's website at www.wrox.com on the Download Code tab.

Developers often build web applications in their native language, and then, as the audience for the application grows, they realize the need to globalize the application. Of course, the ideal is to build the web application to handle an international audience right from the start. In many cases, this may not be possible because of the extra work it requires.

Globalization and localization are both important processes which are used to build a global application, but the terms are not interchangeable. They are not the same thing.

➤ *Globalization* is defined as the process of developing an application so that it functions across multiple cultures and regions.

➤ *Localization*, on the other hand, is customizing the application for a particular culture and locale.

It is good to note that with the ASP.NET Framework, a considerable effort has been made to address the globalization of web applications. You quickly realize that changes to the API, the addition of capabilities to the server controls, and even Visual Studio itself equip you to do the extra work required more easily in order to bring your application to an international audience. This chapter looks at some of the important items to consider when building your web applications for the world.

CULTURES AND REGIONS

The ASP.NET page that is pulled up in an end user's browser runs under a specific culture and region setting. When building an ASP.NET application or page, the defined culture in which it runs is dependent upon both a culture and region setting coming from the server in which the application is run or from a setting applied by the client (the end user). By default, ASP.NET runs under a culture setting defined by various factors on the server.

The world is made up of a multitude of cultures, each of which has a language and a set of defined ways in which it views and consumes numbers, uses currencies, formats dates, sorts alphabetically, and so on. The .NET Framework defines cultures and regions using the Request for Comments (RFC) *1766* standard definition (tags for identification of languages) that specifies a language and region using two-letter codes separated by a dash. Table 32-1 provides examples of some culture definitions.

TABLE 32-1

CULTURE CODE	DESCRIPTION
en-US	English language; United States
en-GB	English language; United Kingdom (Great Britain)
en-AU	English language; Australia
en-CA	English language; Canada
fr-CA	French language; Canada

Looking at the examples in this table, you can see that four distinct cultures are defined. These four cultures have some similarities and some differences. All four cultures speak the same language (English). For this reason, the language code of en is used in each culture setting. After the language setting comes the region setting. Even though these cultures speak the same language, distinguishing them further by setting their region (such as US for the United States, GB for the United Kingdom, AU for Australia, and CA for Canada) is important. As you are probably well aware, the English language in the United States is slightly different from the English language that is used in the United Kingdom, and so forth. Beyond language, differences exist in how dates and numerical values are represented. This is why a culture's language and region are presented together.

The differences do not break down by the country only. Many times, countries contain more than a single language, and each area has its own preference for notation of dates and other items. For example, en-CA specifies English speakers in Canada. Because Canada is not only an English-speaking country, it also includes the culture setting of fr-CA for French-speaking Canadians.

Understanding Culture Types

The culture definition you have just seen is called a *specific culture* definition. This definition is as detailed as you can possibly get—defining both the language and the region. The other type of culture definition is a *neutral culture* definition. Each specific culture has a specified neutral culture with which it is associated. For example, the English language cultures shown in the previous table are separate, but they also all belong to one neutral culture, EN (English). The diagram presented in Figure 32-1 displays how these culture types relate to one another.

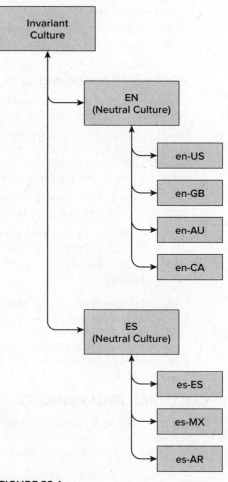

FIGURE 32-1

From this diagram, you can see that many specific cultures belong to a neutral culture. Higher in the hierarchy than the neutral culture is an *invariant culture*, which is an agnostic culture setting that should be utilized when passing items (such as dates and numbers) between physical machines on a network or when storing data. When performing these kinds of operations, make your backend data flows devoid of user-specific culture settings. Instead, apply these settings in the business and presentation layers of your applications.

Also, pay attention to the neutral culture when working with your applications. Invariably, you are going to build applications with web pages that are more dependent on a neutral culture than on a specific culture. For example, if you have a Spanish version of your application, you probably make this version available to all Spanish speakers regardless of their regions. In many applications, it will not matter if the Spanish speaker is from Spain, Mexico, or Argentina. In a case where it does make a difference, use the specific culture settings.

The ASP.NET Threads

When the end user requests an ASP.NET page, this web page is executed on a thread from the thread pool. The thread has a culture associated with it. You can get information about the culture of the thread programmatically and then check for particular details about that culture, as shown in Listing 32-1 (ViewCultureInfo.aspx.cs and ViewCultureInfo.aspx.vb in the code download for this chapter).

LISTING 32-1: Checking the culture of the ASP.NET thread

VB

```vb
Protected Sub Page_Load(ByVal sender As Object, ByVal e As System.EventArgs) Handles Me.Load
    Dim ci As CultureInfo = System.Threading.Thread.CurrentThread.CurrentCulture
    Response.Write("<b><u>CURRENT CULTURE'S INFO</u></b>")
    Response.Write("<p><b>Culture's Name:</b> " & ci.Name.ToString() & "<br>")
    Response.Write("<b>Culture's Parent Name:</b> " & ci.Parent.Name.ToString() & _
        "<br>")
    Response.Write("<b>Culture's Display Name:</b> " & ci.DisplayName.ToString() & _
        "<br>")
    Response.Write("<b>Culture's English Name:</b> " & ci.EnglishName.ToString() & _
        "<br>")
    Response.Write("<b>Culture's Native Name:</b> " & ci.NativeName.ToString() & _
        "<br>")
    Response.Write("<b>Culture's Three Letter ISO Name:</b> " &
        ci.Parent.ThreeLetterISOLanguageName.ToString() & "<br>")
    Response.Write("<b>Calendar Type:</b> " & ci.Calendar.ToString() & "</p >")
End Sub
```

C#

```csharp
protected void Page_Load(object sender, EventArgs e)
{
    CultureInfo ci = System.Threading.Thread.CurrentThread.CurrentCulture;
    Response.Write("<b><u>CURRENT CULTURE'S INFO</u></b>");
    Response.Write("<p><b>Culture's Name:</b> " + ci.Name.ToString() + "<br>");
    Response.Write("<b>Culture's Parent Name:</b> " + ci.Parent.Name.ToString() +
        "<br>");
    Response.Write("<b>Culture's Display Name:</b> " + ci.DisplayName.ToString() +
        "<br>");
    Response.Write("<b>Culture's English Name:</b> " + ci.EnglishName.ToString() +
        "<br>");
    Response.Write("<b>Culture's Native Name:</b> " + ci.NativeName.ToString() +
        "<br>");
    Response.Write("<b>Culture's Three Letter ISO Name:</b> " +
        ci.Parent.ThreeLetterISOLanguageName.ToString() + "<br>");
    Response.Write("<b>Calendar Type:</b> " + ci.Calendar.ToString() + "</p >");
}
```

This bit of code in the `Page_Load` event checks the `CurrentCulture` property. You can place the result of this value in a `CultureInfo` object. To get at this object, you import the `System.Globalization` namespace into your web page. The `CultureInfo` object contains a number of properties that provide you with specific culture information. The following items, which are displayed in a series of simple `Response.Write` statements, are only a small sampling of what is actually available. Running this page produces results similar to what is shown in Figure 32-2.

From this figure, you can see that the en-US culture is the default setting in which the ASP.NET thread executes. In addition to this information, you can use the `CultureInfo` object to get at a lot of other descriptive information about the culture.

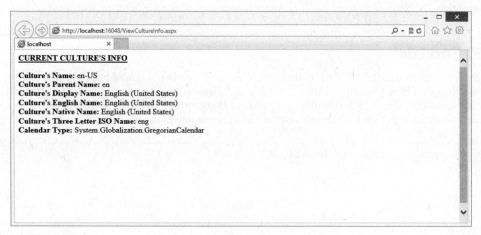

FIGURE 32-2

You can always change a thread's culture on the overloads provided via a new instantiation of the `CultureInfo` object, as presented in Listing 32-2 (ChangeCulture.aspx.cs and ChangeCulture.aspx.vb in the code download for this chapter).

LISTING 32-2: Changing the culture of the thread using the CultureInfo object

VB

```
Protected Sub Page_Load(ByVal sender As Object, ByVal e As System.EventArgs) Handles Me.Load

    System.Threading.Thread.CurrentThread.CurrentCulture = New CultureInfo("th-TH")
    Dim ci As CultureInfo = System.Threading.Thread.CurrentThread.CurrentCulture
    Response.Write("<b><u>CURRENT CULTURE'S INFO</u></b>")
    Response.Write("<p><b>Culture's Name:</b> " & ci.Name.ToString() & "<br>")
    Response.Write("<b>Culture's Parent Name:</b> " & ci.Parent.Name.ToString() & _
        "<br>")
    Response.Write("<b>Culture's Display Name:</b> " & ci.DisplayName.ToString() & _
        "<br>")
    Response.Write("<b>Culture's English Name:</b> " & ci.EnglishName.ToString() & _
        "<br>")
    Response.Write("<b>Culture's Native Name:</b> " & ci.NativeName.ToString() & _
        "<br>")
    Response.Write("<b>Culture's Three Letter ISO Name:</b> " & _
        ci.Parent.ThreeLetterISOLanguageName.ToString() & "<br>")
```

```
      Response.Write("<b>Calendar Type:</b> " & ci.Calendar.ToString() & "</p >")
   End Sub
```

C#

```
protected void Page_Load(object sender, EventArgs e)
{
    System.Threading.Thread.CurrentThread.CurrentCulture = new CultureInfo("th-TH");
    CultureInfo ci = System.Threading.Thread.CurrentThread.CurrentCulture;
    Response.Write("<b><u>CURRENT CULTURE'S INFO</u></b>");
    Response.Write("<p><b>Culture's Name:</b> " + ci.Name.ToString() + "<br>");
    Response.Write("<b>Culture's Parent Name:</b> " + ci.Parent.Name.ToString() +
        "<br>");
    Response.Write("<b>Culture's Display Name:</b> " + ci.DisplayName.ToString() +
        "<br>");
    Response.Write("<b>Culture's English Name:</b> " + ci.EnglishName.ToString() +
        "<br>");
    Response.Write("<b>Culture's Native Name:</b> " + ci.NativeName.ToString() +
        "<br>");
    Response.Write("<b>Culture's Three Letter ISO Name:</b> " +
        ci.Parent.ThreeLetterISOLanguageName.ToString() + "<br>");
    Response.Write("<b>Calendar Type:</b> " + ci.Calendar.ToString() + "</p>");
}
```

In this example, only a single line of code is added to assign a new instance of the CultureInfo object to the CurrentCulture property of the thread being executed by ASP.NET:

```
System.Threading.Thread.CurrentThread.CurrentCulture = new CultureInfo("th-TH")
```

The culture setting enables the CultureInfo object to define the culture you want to utilize. In this case, the Thai language of Thailand is assigned, producing the results shown in Figure 32-3.

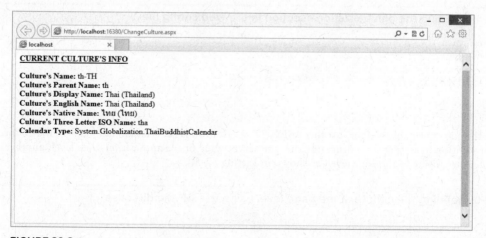

FIGURE 32-3

From this figure, you can see that the .NET Framework goes so far as to provide the native name of the language used even if it is not a Latin-based letter style. In this case, the results are presented for the Thai language in Thailand, as well as some of the properties that are associated with this culture (such as an entirely different calendar from the one used in Western Europe and the United States). Remember that you use the System.Globalization namespace to get at the CultureInfo object.

Server-Side Culture Declarations

ASP.NET enables you to easily define the culture that is used either by your entire ASP.NET application or by a specific page within your application. You can specify the culture for any of your ASP.NET applications by means of the appropriate configuration files. In the default install of ASP.NET, no culture is specified, as is evident when you look at the global `web.config.comments` file (meant for documentation purposes) found in the ASP.NET 4.5 CONFIG folder (`C:\WINDOWS\Microsoft.NET\Framework\ v4.0.30319\ CONFIG`). In the `web.config.comments` file, you find a `<globalization>` section of the configuration document, shown in Listing 32-3.

LISTING 32-3: The <globalization> section in the web.config.comments file

```
<globalization requestEncoding="utf-8" responseEncoding="utf-8" fileEncoding=""
culture="" uiCulture="" enableClientBasedCulture="false"
responseHeaderEncoding="utf-8" resourceProviderFactoryType=""
enableBestFitResponseEncoding="false" />
```

Note the two attributes represented in bold, `culture` and `uiCulture`. The `culture` attribute enables you to define the culture to use for processing incoming requests, whereas the `uiCulture` attribute enables you define the default culture needed to process any resource files in the application. (The use of these attributes is covered later in this chapter.)

As you look at the configuration declaration in Listing 32-3, you can see that nothing is specified for the culture settings. One option you have when specifying a culture on the server is to define this culture in the server version of the `web.config` file found in the CONFIG folder mentioned earlier. This causes every ASP.NET 4.5 application on this server to adopt this particular culture setting. The other option is to specify these settings in the `web.config` file of the application, as shown in Listing 32-4.

LISTING 32-4: Defining the <globalization> section in the web.config file

```
<configuration>
  <system.web>

    <globalization culture="ru-RU" uiCulture="ru-RU" />

  </system.web>
</configuration>
```

In this case, the culture established for just this ASP.NET application is the Russian language in the country of Russia. In addition to setting the culture at either the server-wide or the application-wide level, another option is to set the culture at the page level, as shown in Listing 32-5.

LISTING 32-5: Defining the culture at the page level using the @Page directive

```
<%@ Page Language="vb" UICulture="ru-RU" Culture="ru-RU" %>
```

This example determines that the Russian language and culture settings are used for everything on the page. You can see this in action by using this `@Page` directive and a simple calendar control on the page. A page called `Calendar.aspx` has been included in the project demonstrating modifying the page-level culture information. Figure 32-4 shows the calendar output.

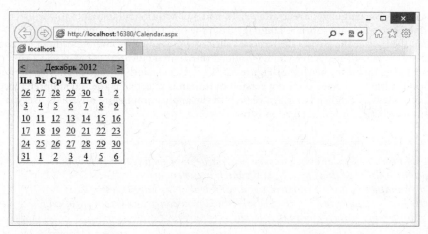

FIGURE 32-4

Client-Side Culture Declarations

In addition to using server-side settings to define the culture for your ASP.NET pages, you also have the option of defining the culture with what the client has set as his preference in a browser instance.

When end users install Microsoft's Internet Explorer and some of the other browsers, they have the option to select their preferred cultures in a particular order (if they have selected more than a single culture preference). To see this in action on Windows 8 in IE, select Tools ⇨ Internet Options from the IE menu. On the General tab, you see a Languages button at the bottom of the dialog box. Click this button and the Language Preference dialog box appears. On the Language Preference dialog box, click the Set Language Preferences button. This opens the Language Preferences section in the Control Panel, as shown in Figure 32-5.

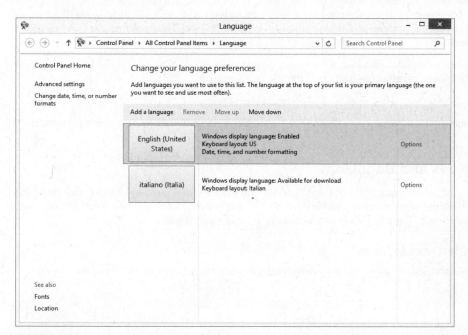

FIGURE 32-5

In this figure, you can see that two languages are available. To add any additional languages to the list, select Add a Language and choose the appropriate language from the list. If that language has multiple regional variants, you can then select the particular regional variant you want. The combination of language and regional variant makes up the culture. After you have added the desired cultures, you can select the order in which you prefer to use them. In the case of Figure 32-5, the U.S version of English culture is established as the most preferred culture, whereas the Italy version of Italian is selected as the second preference. A user with this setting gets the U.S. English language version of the application before anything else; if a U.S. English version is not available, an Italian version is presented.

> **NOTE** *Note that the display language experience has been re-engineered in Windows 8, making it easier for users to find, install, and switch between different languages. When working with Windows 7, the list of currently available display languages in IE is displayed directly in the Language Preference dialog box. You can select the cultures and their order of preference directly from the Language Preference dialog box.*

After the end user selects a culture, you can use the auto feature provided in ASP.NET 4.5. Instead of specifying a distinct culture in any of the configuration files or from the @Page directive, you can also state that ASP.NET should automatically select the culture provided by the end user requesting the page. You do this using the auto keyword, as shown in Listing 32-6.

LISTING 32-6: Changing the culture to the end user's selection

```
<%@ Page Language="vb" UICulture="auto" Culture="auto" %>
```

With this directive in your page, the dates, calendars, and numbers now appear in the preferred culture of the requestor. This presents a complication, however, when you provide resource files with your application that have been translated to other cultures' specifications. What if you have only specific translations, and so cannot handle every possible culture that might be returned to your ASP.NET page? In cases like this, you can specify the auto option with an additional fallback option if ASP.NET cannot find the culture-specific settings of the user. Listing 32-7 shows the usage of this fallback option.

LISTING 32-7: Providing a fallback culture from the auto option

```
<%@ Page Language="vb" UICulture="auto:en-US" Culture="auto:en-US" %>
```

In this case, the automatic detection is utilized, but if the culture the end user prefers is not present, then en-US is used.

Translating Values and Behaviors

In the process of globalizing your ASP.NET application, you may notice a number of items that are done differently from building an application that is devoid of globalization, including how dates are represented and currencies are shown. This next section touches on some of these topics.

Understanding Differences in Dates

Different cultures specify dates and time very differently. For instance, take the following date as an example:

```
08/11/2013
```

What is this date exactly? Depending on your particular culture, it might be August 11, 2013, or it could be November 8, 2013. Due to situations like this, when storing values such as date/time stamps in a database or other storage system, you should always use the same culture, or invariant culture, for these items so that you avoid any mistakes in conversion. Converting these items for use by the end user should be the job of the business logic layer or the presentation layer.

Setting the culture at the server level or in the @Page directive enables ASP.NET to make these conversions for you. You can also simply assign a new culture to the thread in which ASP.NET is running. Listing 32-8 shows the code for a page that changes the culture of the current thread to display date/time data in different cultures (DateAndTime.aspx.cs and DateAndTime.aspx.vb in the code download for the chapter).

LISTING 32-8: Working with date/time values in different cultures

VB

```vb
Imports System.Globalization

Public Class DateAndTime
    Inherits System.Web.UI.Page

    Protected Sub Page_Load(ByVal sender As Object, ByVal e As System.EventArgs)
        Handles Me.Load
        Dim dt As DateTime = New DateTime(2013, 8, 11, 11, 12, 10, 10)
        System.Threading.Thread.CurrentThread.CurrentCulture = _
            New CultureInfo("en-US")
        Response.Write("<b><u>en-US</u></b><br>")
        Response.Write(dt.ToString() & "<br>")

        System.Threading.Thread.CurrentThread.CurrentCulture = _
            New CultureInfo("ru-RU")
        Response.Write("<b><u>ru-RU</u></b><br>")
        Response.Write(dt.ToString() & "<br>")

        System.Threading.Thread.CurrentThread.CurrentCulture = _
            New CultureInfo("fi-FI")
        Response.Write("<b><u>fi-FI</u></b><br>")
        Response.Write(dt.ToString() & "<br>")

        System.Threading.Thread.CurrentThread.CurrentCulture = _
            New CultureInfo("th-TH")
        Response.Write("<b><u>th-TH</u></b><br>")
        Response.Write(dt.ToString())
    End Sub

End Class
```

C#

```csharp
using System;
using System.Globalization;

namespace Chapter32CS
{
    public partial class DateAndTime : System.Web.UI.Page
    {
        protected void Page_Load(object sender, EventArgs e)
        {
            DateTime dt = new DateTime(2013, 8, 11, 11, 12, 10, 10);
            System.Threading.Thread.CurrentThread.CurrentCulture =
                new CultureInfo("en-US");
            Response.Write("<b><u>en-US</u></b><br>");
```

continues

LISTING 32-8 *(continued)*

```
        Response.Write(dt.ToString() + "<br>");

        System.Threading.Thread.CurrentThread.CurrentCulture =
            new CultureInfo("ru-RU");
        Response.Write("<b><u>ru-RU</u></b><br>");
        Response.Write(dt.ToString() + "<br>");

        System.Threading.Thread.CurrentThread.CurrentCulture =
            new CultureInfo("fi-FI");
        Response.Write("<b><u>fi-FI</u></b><br>");
        Response.Write(dt.ToString() + "<br>");

        System.Threading.Thread.CurrentThread.CurrentCulture =
            new CultureInfo("th-TH");
        Response.Write("<b><u>th-TH</u></b><br>");
        Response.Write(dt.ToString());
    }
  }
}
```

This code builds a `DateTime` variable and utilizes four different cultures to display the value to the browser. Figure 32-6 shows the result from executing this code.

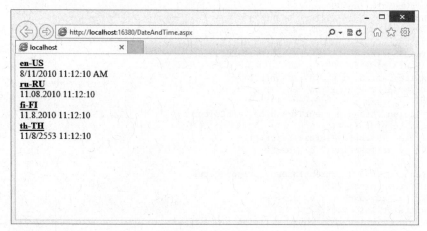

FIGURE 32-6

As you can see, the formats used to represent a date/time value are dramatically different from one another and one of the cultures, the Thai culture (th-TH), even uses an entirely different calendar that displays the year 2012 as 2553.

Understanding Differences in Numbers and Currencies

In addition to date/time values, numbers are constructed quite differently from one culture to the next. How can a number be represented differently in different cultures? Well, it has less to do with the actual number, although certain cultures use different number symbols, and more to do with how the number separators are used for decimals or for showing amounts such as thousands, millions, and more. For example, in the English culture of the United States (en-US), you see numbers represented in the following fashion:

```
5,123,456.00
```

From this example, you can see that the en-US culture uses a comma as a separator for thousands and a period for signifying the start of any decimals. This number appears quite differently when working with other cultures. Listing 32-9 shows an example of representing numbers in other cultures (Numbers.aspx.vb and Numbers.aspx.cs in the code download for the chapter).

LISTING 32-9: Working with numbers in different cultures

VB

```vb
Imports System.Globalization

Public Class Numbers
    Inherits System.Web.UI.Page

    Protected Sub Page_Load(ByVal sender As Object, ByVal e As System.EventArgs)
        Handles Me.Load
        Dim myNumber As Double = 5123456.0
        System.Threading.Thread.CurrentThread.CurrentCulture = _
            New CultureInfo("en-US")
        Response.Write("<b><u>en-US</u></b><br>")
        Response.Write(myNumber.ToString("n") & "<br>")

        System.Threading.Thread.CurrentThread.CurrentCulture = _
            New CultureInfo("vi-VN")
        Response.Write("<b><u>vi-VN</u></b><br>")
        Response.Write(myNumber.ToString("n") & "<br>")

        System.Threading.Thread.CurrentThread.CurrentCulture = _
            New CultureInfo("fi-FI")
        Response.Write("<b><u>fi-FI</u></b><br>")
        Response.Write(myNumber.ToString("n") & "<br>")

        System.Threading.Thread.CurrentThread.CurrentCulture = _
            New CultureInfo("de-CH")
        Response.Write("<b><u>de-CH</u></b><br>")
        Response.Write(myNumber.ToString("n"))
    End Sub

End Class
```

C#

```csharp
using System;
using System.Globalization;

namespace Chapter32CS
{
    public partial class Numbers : System.Web.UI.Page
    {
        protected void Page_Load(object sender, EventArgs e)
        {
            double myNumber = 5123456.00;
            System.Threading.Thread.CurrentThread.CurrentCulture =
                new CultureInfo("en-US");
            Response.Write("<b><u>en-US</u></b><br>");
            Response.Write(myNumber.ToString("n") + "<br>");

            System.Threading.Thread.CurrentThread.CurrentCulture =
                new CultureInfo("vi-VN");
            Response.Write("<b><u>vi-VN</u></b><br>");
```

continues

LISTING 32-9 *(continued)*

```
        Response.Write(myNumber.ToString("n") + "<br>");

        System.Threading.Thread.CurrentThread.CurrentCulture =
            new CultureInfo("fi-FI");
        Response.Write("<b><u>fi-FI</u></b><br>");
        Response.Write(myNumber.ToString("n") + "<br>");

        System.Threading.Thread.CurrentThread.CurrentCulture =
            new CultureInfo("de-CH");
        Response.Write("<b><u>de-CH</u></b><br>");
        Response.Write(myNumber.ToString("n"));
    }
  }
}
```

Running this example produces the results shown in Figure 32-7.

From this example, you can see that the other cultures represented here show numbers in quite a different format than that of the en-US culture. The second culture listed in the figure, vi-VN (Vietnamese in Vietnam), constructs a number exactly the opposite from the way it is constructed in en-US. The Vietnamese culture uses periods for the thousand separators and a comma for signifying decimals. Finnish, on the other hand, uses spaces for the thousand separators and a comma for the decimal separator. Finally, the German-speaking Swiss use a high comma for separating thousands and a period for the decimal separator. As you can see, "translating" numbers to the proper construction so that users of your application can properly understand the numbers represented is important.

FIGURE 32-7

Currencies are represented using numbers as well. In the case of money, making sure that a number is presented correctly for different cultures is not only a matter of visual presentation, but also of making sure the proper value is represented.

Each culture has a distinct currency symbol used to signify that a number represented is an actual currency value. For example, the en-US culture represents a currency in the following format:

```
$5,123,456.00
```

The en-US culture uses a U.S. dollar symbol ($), and the location of this symbol is just as important as the symbol itself. For en-US, the $ symbol directly precedes the currency value with no space in between the symbol and the first character of the number. Other cultures use different symbols to represent a currency and often place those currency symbols in different locations. Change the previous Listing 32-9 so that it now represents the number as a currency. Listing 32-10 presents the necessary changes (Currency.aspx.vb and Currency.aspx.cs in the code download for the chapter).

LISTING 32-10: Working with currencies in different cultures

VB

```
Imports System.Globalization

Public Class Currency
```

```
    Inherits System.Web.UI.Page

Protected Sub Page_Load(ByVal sender As Object, ByVal e As System.EventArgs)
    Handles Me.Load
    Dim myNumber As Double = 5123456.0
    System.Threading.Thread.CurrentThread.CurrentCulture = _
        New CultureInfo("en-US")
    Response.Write("<b><u>en-US</u></b><br>")
    Response.Write(myNumber.ToString("c") & "<br>")

    System.Threading.Thread.CurrentThread.CurrentCulture = _
        New CultureInfo("vi-VN")
    Response.Write("<b><u>vi-VN</u></b><br>")
    Response.Write(myNumber.ToString("c") & "<br>")

    System.Threading.Thread.CurrentThread.CurrentCulture = _
        New CultureInfo("fi-FI")
    Response.Write("<b><u>fi-FI</u></b><br>")
    Response.Write(myNumber.ToString("c") & "<br>")

    System.Threading.Thread.CurrentThread.CurrentCulture = _
        New CultureInfo("de-CH")
    Response.Write("<b><u>de-CH</u></b><br>")
    Response.Write(myNumber.ToString("c"))
End Sub

End Class
```

C#

```
using System;
using System.Globalization;

namespace Chapter32CS
{
    public partial class Currency : System.Web.UI.Page
    {
        protected void Page_Load(object sender, EventArgs e)
        {
            double myNumber = 5123456.00;
            System.Threading.Thread.CurrentThread.CurrentCulture =
                new CultureInfo("en-US");
            Response.Write("<b><u>en-US</u></b><br>");
            Response.Write(myNumber.ToString("c") + "<br>");

            System.Threading.Thread.CurrentThread.CurrentCulture =
                new CultureInfo("vi-VN");
            Response.Write("<b><u>vi-VN</u></b><br>");
            Response.Write(myNumber.ToString("c") + "<br>");

            System.Threading.Thread.CurrentThread.CurrentCulture =
                new CultureInfo("fi-FI");
            Response.Write("<b><u>fi-FI</u></b><br>");
            Response.Write(myNumber.ToString("c") + "<br>");

            System.Threading.Thread.CurrentThread.CurrentCulture =
                new CultureInfo("de-CH");
            Response.Write("<b><u>de-CH</u></b><br>");
            Response.Write(myNumber.ToString("c"));
        }
    }
}
```

Execute the page to see how these cultures represent currency values. The result is shown in Figure 32-8.

From this figure, you can see that not only are the numbers constructed quite differently from one another, but the currency symbol and the location of the symbol in regard to the number are quite different as well.

Because currencies represent actual money, you have an added responsibility when presenting them in a globalized application. Modifying the culture used to display a currency value does not convert the value. It simply displays the same number differently. Take, for example, a page

FIGURE 32-8

in which you have specified the culture to be auto, thus displaying a culture specified by the user. If you are displaying a currency value on the page that is in U.S. dollars and the culture of your page, as specified by the user, is Finnish, the currency value will be incorrect. The value will be displayed as euros but the actual value will not have been converted from U.S. dollars to euros. To avoid any confusion, you can override the culture of the displayed currency. Listing 32-11 shows how you can specify the culture used when displaying a currency value.

LISTING 32-11: Specifying a specific culture when displaying currencies

VB

```
Dim myNumber As Double = 5123456.00
Dim usCurr As CultureInfo = New CultureInfo("en-US")
Response.Write(myNumber.ToString("c", usCurr))
```

C#

```
double myNumber = 5123456.00;
CultureInfo usCurr = new CultureInfo("en-US");
Response.Write(myNumber.ToString("c", usCurr));
```

Understanding Differences in Sorting Strings

Globalization affects more than just the display of numbers, currencies, and date and time values. It can also affect various programming behaviors. Culture settings can be applied to operations such as sorting strings. Generally, most cultures sort strings in the same way, but some differences exist in how sorting occurs. Listing 32-12 shows the code for a page that sorts some string data (SortingEN.aspx.vb and SortingEN .aspx.cs in the code download for the chapter). The sorting operation occurs in the en-US culture.

LISTING 32-12: Working with sorting in different cultures

VB

```
Imports System.Globalization

Public Class SortingEN
    Inherits System.Web.UI.Page

    Protected Sub Page_Load(ByVal sender As Object, ByVal e As System.EventArgs)
        Handles Me.Load
```

```vb
System.Threading.Thread.CurrentThread.CurrentCulture = _
    New CultureInfo("en-US")

Dim myList As List(Of String) = New List(Of String)

myList.Add("Washington D.C.")
myList.Add("Helsinki")
myList.Add("Moscow")
myList.Add("Warsaw")
myList.Add("Vienna")
myList.Add("Tokyo")

myList.Sort()

For Each item As String In myList
    Response.Write(item.ToString() + "<br>")
Next
    End Sub

End Class
```

C#

```csharp
using System;
using System.Collections.Generic;
using System.Globalization;

namespace Chapter32CS
{
    public partial class SortingEN : System.Web.UI.Page
    {
        protected void Page_Load(object sender, EventArgs e)
        {
            System.Threading.Thread.CurrentThread.CurrentCulture =
                new CultureInfo("en-US");

            List<string> myList = new List<string>();

            myList.Add("Washington D.C.");
            myList.Add("Helsinki");
            myList.Add("Moscow");
            myList.Add("Warsaw");
            myList.Add("Vienna");
            myList.Add("Tokyo");

            myList.Sort();

            foreach (string item in myList)
            {
                Response.Write(item.ToString() + "<br>");
            }
        }
    }
}
```

In this example, a generic list of capitals from various countries of the world is created in random order. Then the Sort() method of the generic List(Of String) object is invoked. This sorting operation sorts the strings based on how sorting is done for the defined culture in which the ASP.NET thread is running. Listing 32-12 shows the sorting as it is done for the en-US culture. Figure 32-9 shows the result of this operation.

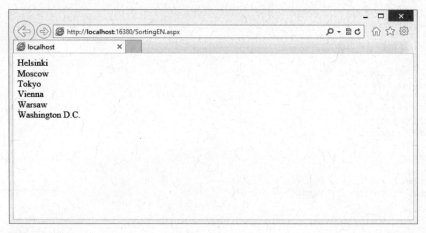

FIGURE 32-9

Based on your particular culture, the result might be what you would expect. However, some differences exist in how string data is sorted in some other cultures. To see this, modify the code in Listing 32-12 so that the culture is set to Finnish. The new modified code is shown in Listing 32-13 (SortingFI.aspx.vb and SortingFI.aspx.cs in the code download for the chapter).

LISTING 32-13: Changing the culture to Finnish

VB

```vb
Imports System.Globalization

Public Class SortingFI
    Inherits System.Web.UI.Page

    Protected Sub Page_Load(ByVal sender As Object, ByVal e As System.EventArgs)
        Handles Me.Load
        System.Threading.Thread.CurrentThread.CurrentCulture = _
            New CultureInfo("fi-FI")

        Dim myList As List(Of String) = New List(Of String)

        myList.Add("Washington D.C.")
        myList.Add("Helsinki")
        myList.Add("Moscow")
        myList.Add("Warsaw")
        myList.Add("Vienna")
        myList.Add("Tokyo")

        myList.Sort()

        For Each item As String In myList
            Response.Write(item.ToString() + "<br>")
        Next
    End Sub

End Class
```

C#

```
using System;
using System.Collections.Generic;
using System.Globalization;

namespace Chapter32CS
{
    public partial class SortingFI : System.Web.UI.Page
    {
        protected void Page_Load(object sender, EventArgs e)
        {
            System.Threading.Thread.CurrentThread.CurrentCulture =
                new CultureInfo("fi-FI");

            List<string> myList = new List<string>();

            myList.Add("Washington D.C.");
            myList.Add("Helsinki");
            myList.Add("Moscow");
            myList.Add("Warsaw");
            myList.Add("Vienna");
            myList.Add("Tokyo");

            myList.Sort();

            foreach (string item in myList)
            {
                Response.Write(item.ToString() + "<br>");
            }
        }
    }
}
```

When you execute this new code with the culture changed to the Finnish culture setting, you get the results presented in Figure 32-10.

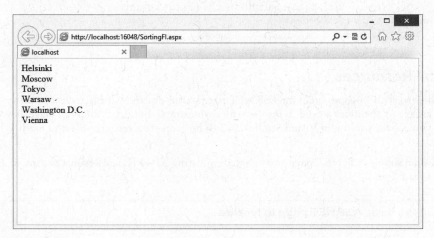

FIGURE 32-10

If you examine the difference between the sorting results with the Finnish culture in Figure 32-10 and the U.S. English culture in Figure 32-9, you see that the city of Vienna is in a different place in the sort order. In the Finnish language, no difference exists between the letter *V* and the letter *W*. Because no difference exists, if you are sorting using the Finnish culture setting, then Vi comes after Wa and, thus, Vienna comes last in the list of strings in the sorting operation.

ASP.NET 4.5 RESOURCE FILES

When working with ASP.NET, one of the most effective ways to create localized web pages is to use resources for the text on your page that are based on the user's language and culture. You can create properties that are stored in resource objects, like resource files. Then ASP.NET can select the correct property at run time according to the user's language and culture. The properties don't have to be only text. Resource files can store other types of elements as well, such as images. Resource files are XML files with a .resx extension. Visual Studio 2012 provides tooling for working with resource files. Resource files can be stored as both local and global resources. Global resource files are placed in the reserved folder App_GlobalResources at the root of an application. A resource file that is in the App_GlobalResources folder has global scope, and its properties can be used by multiple ASP.NET pages. Local resource files are placed in one or more folders with the reserved name App_LocalResources. Unlike the root App_GlobalResources folder, App_LocalResources folders can be in any folder in the application. A local resource file is associated to only one ASP.NET page, by using a particular naming convention.

> ### WHAT ARE SATELLITE ASSEMBLIES
>
> Resource files in ASP.NET have a .resx extension. At run time, .resx files are compiled into assemblies, which are sometimes referred to as satellite assemblies. Because the .resx files are compiled dynamically, like ASP.NET Web pages, you do not have to create these satellite assemblies.
>
> However it is possible to create satellite assemblies manually. In order to create satellite assemblies you use two tools that are installed with Visual Studio and with the Windows SDK. You use Resource File Generator (Resgen.exe) to compile text files or .resx files that contain resources to binary .resources files. You then use Assembly Linker (Al.exe) to compile .resources files into satellite assemblies. Al.exe creates a satellite assembly from the .resources files that you specify. Satellite assemblies can contain only resources; they cannot contain any executable code.

Making Use of Local Resources

You would be surprised how easily you can build an ASP.NET page so that it can be localized into other languages. To take advantage of resources stored in resource files, you simply build an ASP.NET page as you normally would. Then you use the tooling in Visual Studio 2012 to both create a resource file and modify your page to utilize it.

To see this in action, build a simple ASP.NET page as presented in Listing 32-14 (LocalResources.aspx in the code download for this chapter).

LISTING 32-14: Building the basic ASP.NET page to localize

VB

```
<%@ Page Language="VB" %>

<script runat="server">
    Protected Sub Button1_Click(ByVal sender As Object, ByVal e As _
```

```
            System.EventArgs) Handles Button1.Click
            Label2.Text = TextBox1.Text
        End Sub
    </script>

    <!DOCTYPE html>

    <html xmlns="http://www.w3.org/1999/xhtml">
    <head runat="server">
        <title>Local Resources</title>
    </head>
    <body>
        <form id="form1" runat="server">
        <div>
            <asp:Label ID="Label1" runat="server"
             Text="What is your name?"></asp:Label>
            <br />
            <br />
            <asp:TextBox ID="TextBox1" runat="server"></asp:TextBox>
            <asp:Button ID="Button1" runat="server" Text="Submit Name" />
            <br />
            <br />
            <asp:Label ID="Label2" runat="server"></asp:Label>
        </div>
        </form>
    </body>
    </html>
```

C#

```
    <%@ Page Language="C#"%>

    <script runat="server">
        protected void Button1_Click(object sender, System.EventArgs e)
        {
            Label2.Text = TextBox1.Text;
        }
    </script>

    <!DOCTYPE html>

    <html xmlns="http://www.w3.org/1999/xhtml">
    <head id="Head1" runat="server">
        <title>Local Resources</title>
    </head>
    <body>
        <form id="form1" runat="server">
        <div>
            <asp:Label ID="Label1" runat="server"
                Text="What is your name?"></asp:Label>
            <br />
            <br />
            <asp:TextBox ID="TextBox1" runat="server"></asp:TextBox>
            <asp:Button ID="Button1" runat="server" Text="Submit Name"
                OnClick="Button1_Click" />
            <br />
            <br />
            <asp:Label ID="Label2" runat="server"></asp:Label>
        </div>
        </form>
    </body>
    </html>
```

This page is a small ASP.NET page that contains a couple of Label controls, as well as a TextBox and Button control. The key things to pay attention to on the page are the elements that generate text. The first label, the button, and even the title of the page all contain text that is displayed to the user. It would be nice if this text would change based on the culture in which the page is being viewed. That is where resource files can be helpful.

You can use the tooling in Visual Studio 2012 to do all of the initial work to convert your web page to use resource files for localization. Be sure your page is currently being viewed in Design view and then select Tools ➪ Generate Local Resource from the Visual Studio menu. Note that this menu option is available only when you are in the Design view of your page. It will not work in the Split view or the Code view of the page.

After selecting the Generate Local Resource menu, Visual Studio makes several changes to your project. An App_LocalResources folder is created in your project if you do not have one already. A resource file is placed in this new folder. The name of this local resource file is based on the name of the ASP.NET page and follows the pattern *pageOrControlName.extension.language.resx* or *pageOrControlName.extension.language-culture.resx*. If the resource file is for an invariant culture, the *language and culture* part of the file is excluded. For instance, if you are working with the `LocalResources.aspx` page, the resource file is named `LocalResources.aspx.resx`. Notice this resource file is for an invariant culture. Figure 32-11 shows these changes to the project.

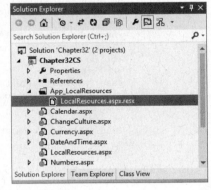

FIGURE 32-11

If you open the resource file, you will see the Resource Editor. You can see that each property has a `Name`, `Value`, and `Comment` field. Figure 32-12 shows the resource file Visual Studio created for you opened in the Resource Editor.

Name	Value	Comment
Button1Resource1.Text	Submit Name	
Button1Resource1.ToolTip		
Label1Resource1.Text	What is your name?	
Label1Resource1.ToolTip		
Label2Resource1.Text		
Label2Resource1.ToolTip		
PageResource1.Title	Local Resources	
TextBox1Resource1.Text		
TextBox1Resource1.ToolTip		

FIGURE 32-12

Visual Studio searched through the page for each control that had translatable properties and created an entry in the resource file for each of those properties. It even contains entries for a few properties you had not populated in the page. Notice that each of the text values from the page controls, including the `title` element, have been added to the resource file as shown in Figure 32-12. Each of these entries has been given a name that can be referenced in the page.

In addition to creating and adding the resource file to the local resources folder, Visual Studio also made some modifications to the page. Listing 32-15 shows the page after the changes made by Visual Studio (LocalResourcesAfter.aspx in the code download for this chapter).

LISTING 32-15: Looking at how Visual Studio altered the page code

VB

```
<%@ Page Language="vb" culture="auto" meta:resourcekey="PageResource1" uiculture="auto" %>

<script runat="server">
    Protected Sub Button1_Click(ByVal sender As Object, ByVal e As _
        System.EventArgs) Handles Button1.Click
        Label2.Text = TextBox1.Text
    End Sub
</script>

<!DOCTYPE html>

<html xmlns="http://www.w3.org/1999/xhtml">
<head runat="server">
    <title>Local Resources</title>
</head>
<body>
    <form id="form1" runat="server">
    <div>
        <asp:Label ID="Label1" runat="server" Text="What is your name?"
            meta:resourcekey="Label1Resource1"></asp:Label>
        <br />
        <br />
        <asp:TextBox ID="TextBox1" runat="server"
            meta:resourcekey="TextBox1Resource1"></asp:TextBox>
        <asp:Button ID="Button1" runat="server" Text="Submit Name"
            meta:resourcekey="Button1Resource1" />
        <br />
        <br />
        <asp:Label ID="Label2" runat="server"
            meta:resourcekey="Label2Resource1"></asp:Label>
    </div>
    </form>
</body>
</html>
```

C#

```
<%@ Page Language="C#" culture="auto" meta:resourcekey="PageResource1"
    uiculture="auto"%>

<script runat="server">
    protected void Button1_Click(object sender, System.EventArgs e)
    {
        Label2.Text = TextBox1.Text;
    }
</script>

<!DOCTYPE html>

<html xmlns="http://www.w3.org/1999/xhtml">
<head id="Head1" runat="server">
    <title>Local Resources</title>
</head>
```

continues

LISTING 32-15 *(continued)*

```
<body>
    <form id="form1" runat="server">
    <div>
        <asp:Label ID="Label1" runat="server" Text="What is your name?"
            meta:resourcekey="Label1Resource1"></asp:Label>
        <br />
        <br />
        <asp:TextBox ID="TextBox1" runat="server"
            meta:resourcekey="TextBox1Resource1"></asp:TextBox>
        <asp:Button ID="Button1" runat="server" Text="Submit Name"
            OnClick="Button1_Click" meta:resourcekey="Button1Resource1" />
        <br />
        <br />
        <asp:Label ID="Label2" runat="server"
            meta:resourcekey="Label2Resource1"></asp:Label>
    </div>
    </form>
</body>
</html>
```

You can see from the modified code that the `Culture` and `UICulture` attributes have been added to the `@Page` directive with a value of `auto`, thus enabling this application to be localized. The attribute `meta:resourcekey`, along with an associated value, has been added to the `Page` directive and each of the controls mentioned earlier with translatable values. The value assigned to each of the `meta:resourcekey` attributes is the name from the resource file that was created for you. In Figure 32-12, the `Button1` control has two properties that have been defined in the resource file, `Text` and `ToolTip`. The value of the `Text` property has been pulled from the page. The names of these two entries in the resource file begin with `Button1Resource1` and end with the name of the original property. Look at the `Button` control in the page after the changes made by Visual Studio. The value of the `meta:resourcekey` for the button control has been set to the `Button1Resource1` prefix:

```
<asp:Button ID="Button1"
    runat="server" Text="Submit Name"
    meta:resourcekey="Button1Resource1" />
```

All the properties using this prefix in the resource file, like the `Text` and `ToolTip` properties, are automatically applied to this button control at run time.

Adding Another Language Resource File

The `LocalResources.aspx.resx` file is used for an invariant culture. If the culture of the page cannot be determined, the invariant culture resources are used. You can add as many resource files as cultures you would like to support. To add another resource file for the `LocalResources.aspx` page that handles another language, you can copy and paste the `LocalResources.aspx.resx` file into the same App_LocalResources folder. Rename it to specify the language and culture you are targeting. Assuming you want to create a resource file to target the Finnish culture, you would name the file `LocalResources .aspx.fi-FI.resx`. Modify the following values in the resource file to support the Finnish language:

```
Button1Resource1.Text     Lähetä Nimi
Label1Resource1.Text      Mikä sinun nimi on?
PageResource1.Title       Näytesivu
```

Add a new entry in both the invariant and the Finnish resource files. This entry will be used later when demonstrating how to access a resource entry programmatically. Name the entry **Label2Answer**. The value of the entry varies based on culture. The value of the entry in the invariant file will be:

```
Hello
```

The value of the entry in the Finnish file will be:

```
Hei
```

Accessing Resource Properties Programmatically

Not only can you apply certain resources to your page automatically using the property naming convention described previously, but you can also reference resources programmatically. Listing 32-16 shows the server script block after adding code to reference the `Label2Answer` resource entry (LocalResourcesCustom.aspx in the code download for this chapter).

LISTING 32-16: Programmatically referencing a resource

VB

```
<script runat="server">
    Protected Sub Button1_Click(ByVal sender As Object, ByVal e As _
        System.EventArgs) Handles Button1.Click
        Label2.Text = GetLocalResourceObject("Label2Answer").ToString() & _
            " " & TextBox1.Text
    End Sub
</script>
```

C#

```
<script runat="server">
    protected void Button1_Click(object sender, System.EventArgs e)
    {
        Label2.Text = GetLocalResourceObject("Label2Answer").ToString() + " " +
            TextBox1.Text;
    }
</script>
```

You can use the `GetLocalResourceObject` method to access a property in a resource file. `GetLocalResourceObject` is a method on the `HttpContext` class. When using `GetLocalResourceObject`, you simply use the name of the entry as a parameter:

```
GetLocalResourceObject("Label2Answer")
```

You could just as easily get at any control's property values from the resource file programmatically using the same method:

```
GetLocalResourceObject("Button1Resource1.Text")
```

With the new script blocks from Listing 32-16 in place and the resource files completed, you can run the page, entering a name in the textbox and then clicking the button to get a response. The result is shown in Figure 32-13.

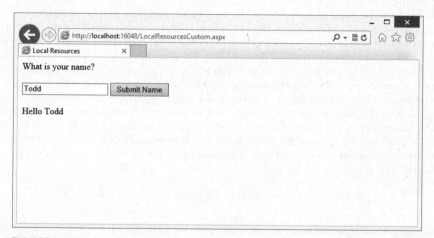

FIGURE 32-13

When executing the `LocalResourcesCustom.aspx` page, the browser was set to the en-US culture. Because there is no en-US culture resource file, ASP.NET looked for an EN neutral culture file. Because there is no EN neutral culture file, ASP.NET defaulted to use the invariant culture resource file. The invariant culture resource file had a value of "Hello" for the `Label2Answer` entry.

If you set your language preference to fi-FI either in IE or in the page directive, you can execute the page again and you will see a Finnish version of the page. Figure 32-14 shows the same page as viewed using a Finnish culture.

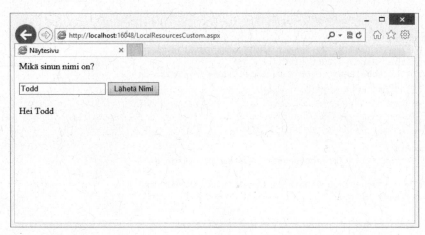

FIGURE 32-14

You can see that all the control properties that were translated and placed within the Finnish resource file are utilized automatically by ASP.NET, including the page title presented in the title bar of IE. Furthermore, the programmatically accessed entry for the `Label2Answer` was also accessed from the Finnish culture resource file.

Neutral Cultures Are Generally More Preferred

So far you have only used invariant resource files or resource files specifying a language and a culture. The `LocalResourcesCustom.aspx.fi-FI.resx` file in the sample code specifies both the language and the culture, the Finnish language as spoken in Finland. Another option would be to make this file work not for a specific culture but, instead, for a neutral culture. To accomplish this, you simply rename the file `LocalResourcesCustom.aspx.fi.resx` eliminating the -FI culture. In this example, having a specific culture declared really does not make that much difference because no other countries speak Finnish. It would make sense for languages such as German, Spanish, or French. These languages are spoken in multiple countries. For instance, if you are going to have a Spanish version of the `LocalResources.aspx` page, you could definitely build it for a specific culture, such as `LocalResources.aspx.es-MX.resx`. This file would be used for the Spanish language as spoken in Mexico. However, if a user requests the page with a culture of es-ES, ASP.NET will fall back to the invariant culture resource file. In this case, it would be better to create a culture-neutral resource file so that any user using the Spanish language, regardless of country, will utilize the Spanish resource file. If you have the resource file `LocalResources.aspx.es.resx`, it won't matter if the end user's preferred setting is set to es-MX, es-ES, or even es-AR; the user gets the appropriate ES neutral culture version of the page.

Making Use of Global Resources

Local resources are utilized by particular pages in your ASP.NET application. You also have the option of creating global resources that can be used across multiple pages. To create a resource file that can be utilized across the entire application, you must first create a folder for global resources. Right-click the project in the Solution Explorer of Visual Studio and select Add ➪ Add ASP.NET Folder ➪ App_GlobalResources. Now you can add global resource files directly to this new folder. Right-click the App_GlobalResources folder and select Add ➪ Resources File. Name the file **Resources.resx**. Similar to the local resource files, this file is the invariant culture global resource file. Open the `Resources.resx` file in the Resource Editor and add a single string entry. Give the entry a name of **PrivacyStatement**. Create some arbitrary long string as the value of the entry. Because this is the invariant culture version of the file, create a Finnish culture version. Name the file **Resources.fi-FI.aspx**. Add the same `PrivacyStatement` entry but give it a different arbitrary value.

The idea of a global resource file is that you have access to these resources across your entire application. You can gain access to the values that you place in these files in several ways. The first is to access the value declaratively in the property of a server control. This is similar to the method of accessing the local resources you saw earlier in the chapter. Add a new Web Form to the project called `GlobalResources.aspx`. Add a Label control to the form. The code in Listing 32-17 (GlobalResources.aspx in the code download for the chapter) shows the VB version of the complete file with the declaration in the label to access the resource.

LISTING 32-17: Using a global resource directly in a server control

```
<%@ Page Language="VB" %>

<!DOCTYPE html>
<html xmlns="http://www.w3.org/1999/xhtml">
<head>
    <title>Global Resources</title>
</head>
<body>
    <asp:Label ID="Label1" runat="server" Text='<%$ Resources: Resource,
        PrivacyStatement %>'></asp:Label>
</body>
</html>
```

To access the global resource entry for `PrivacyStatement`, you use the keyword `Resources` followed by a colon. Then, you specify the name of the resource file. In this case, the name of the resource file is `Resource`, which refers to the `Resource.resx` and `Resource.fi-FI.resx` files. After specifying the particular resource file to use, you specify the particular entry, in this case `PrivacyStatement`.

Another way of achieving the same result is to use a built-in dialog box within Visual Studio 2012. Add another Label control to `GlobalResources.aspx`. Highlight this new label control in Design view so that the control appears within the Properties window. From the Properties window, click the button within the Expressions property within the Data section. This launches the Expressions dialog box and enables you to bind the `PrivacyStatement` value to the `Text` property of the label control. Highlight the `Text` property in the Bindable properties list. Select the Resources expression option from the Expression type drop-down list on the right side of the dialog box. Once you have selected the Resources option, you will need to enter the `ClassKey` and `ResourceKey` properties. The `ClassKey` is the name of the file that should be used. In this example, the file is `Resource.resx`, so the `ClassKey` will be `Resource`. The `ResourceKey` is the name of the entry in the resource file. Enter **PrivacyStatement** as the value of the `ResourceKey`. Figure 32-15 shows the Expressions dialog box with the correct entries.

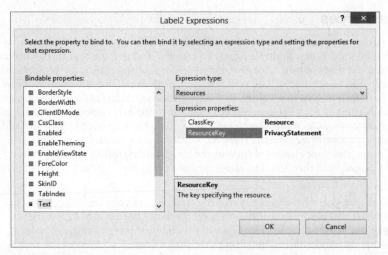

FIGURE 32-15

One nice feature of Visual Studio is that the resources provided via global resources are available in a strongly typed manner. For instance, you can access a global resource value programmatically by using the code presented in Listing 32-18 (GlobalResources.aspx.vb and GlobalResources.aspx.cs in the code download for the chapter).

LISTING 32-18: Programmatically getting at global resources

VB

```
Public Class GlobalResources
    Inherits System.Web.UI.Page

    Protected Sub Page_Load(ByVal sender As Object, ByVal e As System.EventArgs)
        Handles Me.Load
        Label3.Text = Resources.Resource.PrivacyStatement
    End Sub

End Class
```

C#

```
using System;

namespace Chapter32CS
{
    public partial class GlobalResources : System.Web.UI.Page
    {
        protected void Page_Load(object sender, EventArgs e)
        {
            Label3.Text = Resources.Resource.PrivacyStatement;
        }
    }
}
```

In Figure 32-16, you can see that you have full IntelliSense for these resource values.

```
namespace Chapter32CS
{
    public partial class GlobalResources : System.Web.UI.Page
    {
        protected void Page_Load(object sender, EventArgs e)
        {
            Label3.Text = Resources.Resource.
        }
    }
}
```

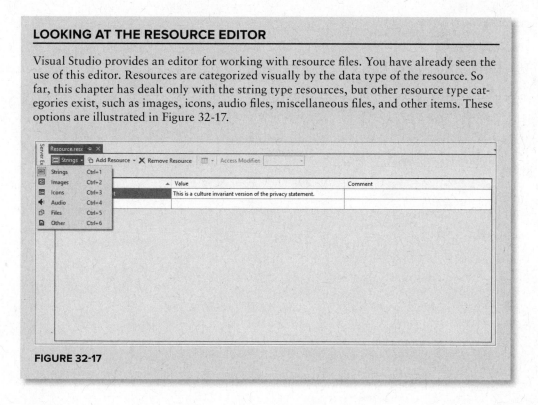

FIGURE 32-16

LOOKING AT THE RESOURCE EDITOR

Visual Studio provides an editor for working with resource files. You have already seen the use of this editor. Resources are categorized visually by the data type of the resource. So far, this chapter has dealt only with the string type resources, but other resource type categories exist, such as images, icons, audio files, miscellaneous files, and other items. These options are illustrated in Figure 32-17.

FIGURE 32-17

SUMMARY

There is a lot of value in globalizing your ASP.NET applications so that they can handle multiple cultures. As more web applications are being accessed by users in multiple countries and using multiple languages, it is increasingly important to add multi-cultural support. This chapter looked at some of the issues you face when globalizing your applications and some of the built-in tools provided both by Visual Studio 2012 and the .NET Framework to make this process easier.

At the very least, globalizing your applications is as easy as taking existing ASP.NET pages and running the tools provided by Visual Studio to modify them to be more receptive to multiple translations.

33

Packaging and Deploying ASP.NET Applications

WHAT'S IN THIS CHAPTER?

➤ Understanding packaging and deploying fundamentals

➤ Selecting a deployment method

➤ Using publish profiles

➤ Deploying to Windows Azure

WROX.COM CODE DOWNLOADS FOR THIS CHAPTER

Please note that this chapter because of its focus on packaging and deploying ASP.NET applications has no corresponding code download.

Packaging and deploying ASP.NET applications are topics that usually receive little attention. This chapter takes a more in-depth look at how you can package and deploy your ASP.NET applications after they are built. After you have developed your ASP.NET application on a development computer, you will need to deploy the finished product to a quality assurance or staging server, and eventually onto a production server.

An important reason to consider the proper packaging and deploying of your ASP.NET applications is that many applications are built as saleable products, starter kits, or solutions. In this case, you may have to allow complete strangers to download and install these products in their own environments that you have absolutely no control over. If this is the case, giving the consumer a single installer file that ensures proper installation of the application in any environment is ideal.

Nevertheless, regardless of whether you will distribute your web application outside your company you still need a way to deploy it to another server where it can be tested before production deployment. You should never assume that it would be perfect just because it worked on your computer. Most of the time you just develop using IIS Express in Visual Studio, so you will need a full test using IIS before you assume all is well. Even if you do test with IIS on your computer, deployment-related factors still need to be ironed out and fully tested before the application goes to production.

> **NOTE** *Web deployment projects are no longer supported in Visual Studio 2012. Using publish profiles is the recommended way for deploying applications to a server. If you want to deploy your application using Windows Installer, you should use WiX (Windows Installer XML) or InstallShield.*

DEPLOYMENT PIECES

So what are you actually deploying? ASP.NET contains a lot of pieces that are all possible parts of the overall application and need to be deployed with the application for it to run properly. The following list details some of the items that are potentially part of your ASP.NET application and need deployment consideration when you are moving your application:

- `.aspx` pages
- The code-behind pages for the `.aspx` pages (`.aspx.vb` or `.aspx.cs` files)
- User controls (`.ascx`)
- Web service files (`.asmx` and `.wsdl` files)
- `.htm` or `.html` files
- Image files such as `.jpg` or `.gif`
- ASP.NET system folders such as `App_Code` and `App_Themes`
- JavaScript files (`.js`)
- Cascading Style Sheets (`.css`)
- Configuration files such as the `web.config` file
- .NET components and compiled assemblies
- Data files such as `.mdf` files
- IIS settings
- HTTP handlers and modules

STEPS TO TAKE BEFORE DEPLOYING

Before deploying your ASP.NET web applications, you should take some basic steps to ensure that your application is *ready* for deployment. These steps are often forgotten and are mentioned here to remind you of how you can ensure that your deployed application performs at its best.

Before you begin, *turn off* debugging in the `web.config` file. You do this by setting the `debug` attribute in the `<compilation>` element to `False`, as shown in Listing 33-1.

LISTING 33-1: Setting debug to False before application deployment

```
<configuration>
  <system.web>
      <compilation debug="false" targetFramework="4.5" />
     </system.web>
</configuration>
```

By default, most developers set the `debug` attribute to `True` when developing their applications. Doing this inserts debug symbols into the compiled ASP.NET pages. These symbols degrade the performance of any application. After the application is built and ready to be deployed, keeping these debug symbols in place is unnecessary.

For those who have been coding ASP.NET for some time now, it is important to note that the Debug option in the drop-down list in the Visual Studio menu does not accomplish much in changing the configuration file or anything similar (shown in Figure 33-1). In the ASP.NET 1.0 and 1.1 days, Visual Studio .NET (as it was called at that time) actually controlled the compilation of the ASP.NET project to a DLL. Now, and ever since ASP.NET 2.0, it is actually ASP.NET itself that controls the compilation process at run time.

FIGURE 33-1

Therefore, although the drop-down with the Debug designation is present, it really has no meaning in the context of building an ASP.NET project. You completely control the compilation designation through what is set in the `web.config` file, as shown earlier in Listing 33-1.

You will find that you can provide `Web.Debug.config` and `Web.Release.config` files in your application as well. Using `Web.Debug.config` allows you to put settings in the configuration file that will be utilized when you do a deployment or run of the application while in the debug mode. You can use the same approach with the `Web.Release.config` file when publishing the application in the Release mode. This approach with the configuration files allows you to use different database connection strings, change the authentication mode, and more. You will find using these varied configuration files beneficial if you are working with more than one environment (for example, testing, staging, and production).

METHODS OF DEPLOYING WEB APPLICATIONS

Remember that deployment is the last step in a process. The first is setting up the program—packaging the program into a component that is best suited for the deployment that follows. You can actually deploy a web application in a number of ways. You can use the XCopy capability that simply wows audiences when demonstrated (because of its simplicity). A second method is to use Visual Studio 2012's capability to copy a website from one location to another using the Copy Web Site feature, as well as an alternative method that uses Visual Studio to deploy a precompiled web application. The final method uses Visual Studio publish profiles to publish an application on a server. After reviewing each of the available methods, you can decide which is best for what you are trying to achieve.

Using XCopy

Applications in .NET compile down to assemblies, and these assemblies contain code that is executed by the Common Language Runtime (CLR). One great thing about assemblies is that they are self-describing. All the details about the assembly are stored within the assembly itself. Because a .NET assembly stores this information within itself, XCopy deployment is possible and no registry settings are needed. Installing an assembly is as simple as copying it to another server and you do not need to stop or start IIS while this is going on.

XCopy is mentioned here because it is the command-line way of basically doing a copy-and-paste of all the files and folders you want to copy. XCopy, however, provides a bit more functionality than just a copy-and-paste, as you will see shortly. XCopy enables you to move files, directories, and even entire drives from one point to another.

The default syntax of the XCopy command is as follows:

```
xcopy [source] [destination] [/w] [/p] [/c] [/v] [/q] [/f] [/l] [/g]
   [/d[:mm-dd-yyyy]] [/u] [/i] [/s [/e]] [/t] [/k] [/r] [/h] [{/a|/m}] [/n] [/o]
   [/x] [/exclude:file1[+[file2]][+file3]] [{/y|/-y}] [/z]
```

To see an example of using the XCopy feature, suppose you are working from your developer machine (C:\) and want to copy your ASP.NET application to a production server (Y:\). In its simplest form, the following command would do the job:

```
xcopy c:\Websites\Website1 Y:\Websites\ /f /e /k /h
```

This command copies the files and folders from the source drive to the destination drive. Figure 33-2 shows an example of this use on the command line.

FIGURE 33-2

When you copy files using XCopy, be aware that this method does not allow for the automatic creation of any virtual directories in IIS. When copying a new web application, you also need to create a virtual directory in the destination server and associate this virtual directory with the application you are copying. It is a simple process, but you must take these extra steps to finalize the site copy actions.

You can provide a number of parameters to this XCopy command to get it to behave as you want it to. Table 33-1 details these parameters.

TABLE 33-1

PARAMETER	DESCRIPTION
/w	Displays the message: Press any key to begin copying file(s). It waits for your response to start the copying process.
/p	Asks for a confirmation on each file being copied. This is done in a file-by-file manner.
/c	Ignores errors that might occur in the copying process.
/v	Performs a verification on the files being copied to make sure they are identical to the source files.
/q	Suppresses any display of the XCopy messages.
/f	Displays the filenames for the source and destination files while the copying process is occurring.
/l	Displays a list of the files to be copied to the destination drive.
/g	Builds decrypted files for the destination drive.
/d	When used as simply /d, the only files copied are those newer than the existing files located in the destination location. Another alternative is to use /d[:mm-dd-yyyy], which copies files that have been modified either on or after the specified date.

`/u`	Copies only source files that already exist in the destination location.
`/I`	If what is being copied is a directory or a file that contains wildcards and the same item does not exist in the destination location, a new directory is created. The XCopy process also copies all the associated files into this directory.
`/s`	Copies all directories and their subdirectories only if they contain files. All empty directories or subdirectories are not copied in the process.
`/e`	Copies all subdirectories regardless of whether these directories contain files.
`/t`	Copies the subdirectories only and not the files they might contain.
`/k`	By default, the XCopy process removes any read-only settings that might be contained in the source files. Using `/k` ensures that these read-only settings remain in place during the copying process.
`/r`	Copies only the read-only files to the destination location.
`/h`	Specifies that the hidden and system files, which are usually excluded by default, are included.
`/a`	Copies only files that have their archive file attributes set, and leaves the archive file attributes in place at the XCopy destination.
`/m`	Copies only files that have their archive file attributes set, and turns off the archive file attributes.
`/n`	Copies using the NTFS short file and short directory names.
`/o`	Copies the discretionary access control list (DACL) in addition to the files.
`/x`	Copies the audit settings and the system access control list (SACL) in addition to the files.
`/exclude`	Allows you to exclude specific files. The construction used for this is `exclude:File1 .aspx + File2.aspx + File3.aspx`.
`/y`	Suppresses any prompts from the XCopy process that ask whether to overwrite the destination file.
`/-y`	Adds prompts to confirm an overwrite of any existing files in the destination location.
`/z`	Copies files and directories over a network in restartable mode.
`/?`	Displays help for the XCopy command.

Using XCopy is an easy way to move your applications from one server to another with little work on your part. If you have no problem setting up your own virtual directories, this mode of deployment should work just fine for you.

When the web application is copied (and if placed in a proper virtual directory), it is ready to be called from a browser.

Using the VS Copy Web Site Option

The next option for copying a website is to use a GUI provided by Visual Studio 2012. This Copy Web Site GUI enables you to copy websites from your development server to either the same server or a remote server (as you can when you use the XCopy command). This option is useful if you are using Web Site projects rather than Web Application projects.

You can open this Copy Web Site window in Visual Studio in two ways. The first way is to click in the Copy Web Site icon in the Visual Studio Solution Explorer. The other way to open the Copy Web Site GUI is to choose Website ⇨ Copy Web Site from the Visual Studio menu. Using either method opens the Copy Web Site GUI in the Document window, as illustrated in Figure 33-3.

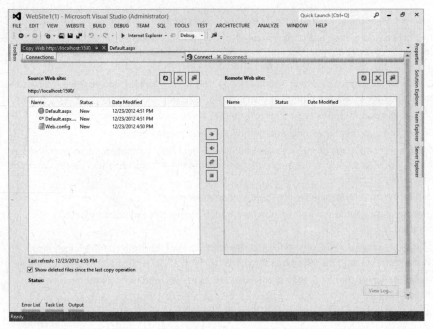

FIGURE 33-3

From this GUI, you can click the Connect To a Remote Server button (next to the Connections textbox and labeled "Connect"). This action opens the Open Web Site window shown in Figure 33-4.

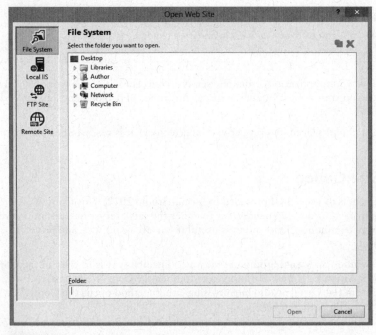

FIGURE 33-4

As you can see from this window, you have a couple of options to connect to and copy your web application. These options include the following:

➤ **File System:** This option allows you to navigate through a file explorer view of the computer. If you are going to install on a remote server from this view, you must have already mapped a drive to the installation location.

➤ **Local IIS:** This option enables you to use your local IIS in the installation of your web application. From this part of the window, you can create new applications as well as new virtual directories directly. You can also delete applications and virtual directories from the same window. The Local IIS option does not permit you to work with IIS installations on any remote servers.

➤ **FTP Site:** This option enables you to connect to a remote server using FTP capabilities. From this window, you can specify the server that you want to contact using a URL or IP address, the port you are going to use, and the directory on the server that you will work with. From this window, you can also specify the username and password that may be required to access the server via FTP. Note that if you access this server with this window via FTP and provide a username and password, the items are transmitted in plaintext.

➤ **Remote Site:** This option enables you to connect to a remote site using FrontPage Server Extensions. From this option in the window, you can also choose to connect to the remote server using Secure Sockets Layer (SSL).

After being connected to a server, you can copy the contents of your web application to it by selecting all or some of the files from the Source Web Site text area. After you select these files in the window, some of the movement arrows become enabled. Clicking the right-pointing arrow copies the selected files to the destination server. In Figure 33-5 you can see that, indeed, the files have been copied to the remote destination.

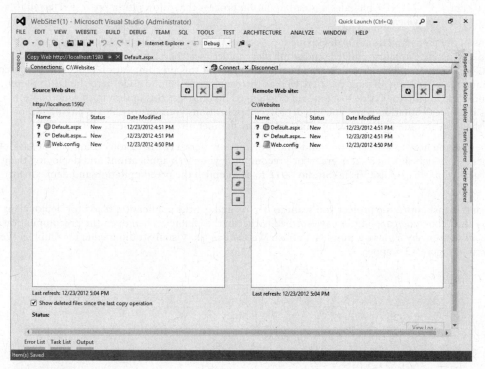

FIGURE 33-5

If you open the same copy window later, after working on the files, you see an arrow next to the files that have been changed in the interim and are, therefore, newer than those on the destination server (see Figure 33-6).

These arrows enable you to select only the files that must be copied again and nothing more. All the copying actions are recorded in a log file. You can view the contents of this log file from the Copy Web Site window by clicking the View Log button at the bottom of the window. This opens the CopyWebSite.log text file. From the copy that you made previously, you can see the transaction that was done. Here is an example log entry:

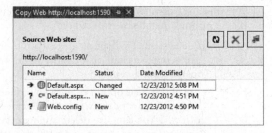

FIGURE 33-6

```
Copy from 'C:\Websites\Website1' to 'E:\Website1' started at 10/6/2009 7:52:31 AM.
    Create folder App_Data in the remote Web site.
            Copy file Default.aspx from source to remote Web site.
    Copy file Default.aspx.cs from source to remote Web site.
    Copy file About.aspx from source to remote Web site.
    Copy file About.aspx.cs from source to remote Web site.
    Copy file web.config from source to remote Web site.
Copy from 'C:\Websites\Website1' to 'E:\Website1' is finished.
            Completed at 10/6/2009 7:52:33 AM.
```

Deploying a Precompiled Web Application

In addition to using Visual Studio to copy a web application from one location to another, using this IDE to deploy a precompiled application is also possible. The process of precompiling a web application is explained in Chapter 3. ASP.NET includes a precompilation process that allows for a process referred to as *precompilation for deployment*.

What happens in the precompilation for deployment process is that each page in the web application is built and compiled into a single application DLL and some placeholder files. These files can then be deployed together to another server and run from there. The nice thing about this precompilation process is that it can obfuscate your code by placing all page code (as well as the page's code-behind code) into the DLL, thereby making it more difficult for your code to be stolen or changed if you select this option in the compilation process. This is an ideal situation when you are deploying applications your customers are paying for, or applications that you absolutely do not want changed in any manner after deployment.

Chapter 3 showed you how to use the command-line tool aspnet_compiler.exe to accomplish the task of precompilation. Although this method is great for precompiling your web applications and deploying them to remote servers, you can also use Visual Studio 2012 to accomplish the precompilation and deployment process.

To accomplish this task, open the project you want to deploy and get the application ready for deployment by turning off the debugging capabilities as described earlier in the chapter. Then open the precompilation and deployment window by choosing Build ⇨ Publish Web Site in the Visual Studio menu. The Publish Web window shown in Figure 33-7 appears.

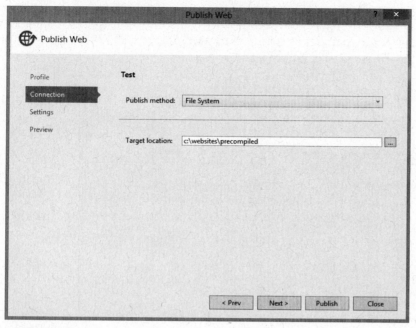

FIGURE 33-7

Using the Browse (. . .) button in this window, you can choose any location (either on your local or remote machine) to which you want to deploy the application. As in earlier examples, your options are a file system location, a place in the local IIS, a location accessed using FTP, or a location accessed via FrontPage Server Extensions.

Figure 33-16 later in the chapter shows the Advanced Precompile settings window where you can find other options in this window such as the Allow (see Fig.33-16) Precompiled Site to Be Updateable check box. When this option is selected, the site will be compiled and copied without any changes to the .aspx pages. This means that after the precompilation process, you can still make minor changes such as modifying the markup of the web pages, and the application will work and function as normal. If this check box is not selected, all the code from the pages is stripped out and placed inside one or more DLLs. In this state, the application is not updateable because updating any of the placeholder files from this compilation process is impossible.

Another option in this window is to assign a strong name to the DLL that is created in this process. You can select the appropriate check box and assign a key to use in the signing process. The created DLL from the precompilation will then be a strong assembly—signed with the key of your choice. Strong names guarantee name uniqueness by relying on unique key pairs and also provide a strong integrity check. Passing the .NET Framework security checks guarantees that the contents of the assembly have not been changed since it was built.

When you are ready to deploy, click OK in the window and then the open application is built and published. *Published* means that the application is deployed to the specified location. Looking at this location, you can see that a `bin` directory has now been added that contains some precompiled DLLs, which is your web application. This is illustrated in Figure 33-8.

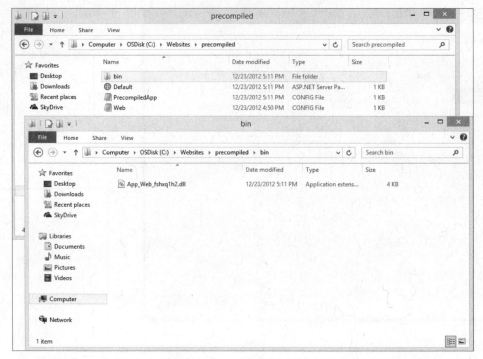

FIGURE 33-8

In this state, the code contained in any of the ASP.NET-specific pages is stripped out and placed inside the DLL. The files that you see are actually just placeholders that the DLL needs for reference.

Building an ASP.NET Web Package

One of the easiest ways to deploy your web application is to use the new built-in publishing features from Visual Studio 2012. Behind the scenes, this capability uses Microsoft's web deployment tool, also known as Web Deploy, which means that if you want to deploy this tool to your server, this server must have Web Deploy on the machine for the hydration of your application to work.

The package that is created and passed around is an actual physical file—a `.zip` file. This `.zip` file contains everything you need to redeploy your web application with all of its settings into the new environment. In addition to the `.zip` file, it also includes a manifest file and a command file that are used to initiate the installation of the package on the host machine.

The first way in which this application can be deployed is to use the One-Click Publishing capability found in Visual Studio 2012. To do this, right-click on the project within the Visual Studio Solution Explorer and select the Publish option from the provided menu. This option is available for both Web Site projects as well as Web Application projects.. The Publish Web window appears, as shown in Figure 33-9.

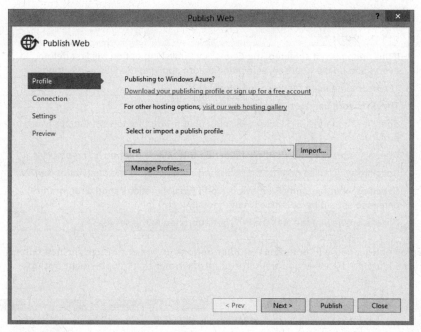

FIGURE 33-9

Because many developers are continually deploying their web applications to their testing, staging, and production environments, there is a capability to store your deployment options in a profile that you can use again and again. This setting comes from what you have set in the toolbar of Visual Studio 2012 before you select the Publish option.

You can configure the settings shown in Table 33-2 when publishing an application using the Publish wizard.

TABLE 33-2

SETTING	DESCRIPTION
Profile Name	The name of your saved profile. This provides you with the ability to reuse your settings as a default for repeated deployments.
Build Configuration	Specifies whether the build compilation will be done in either the Debug or Release mode. This option is not limited to just Debug/Release but works with any build configuration file for the project.
Publish Method	The method you want to employ for the deployment. The possible options include Web Deploy Publish, FTP, File System, and FPSE (FrontPage Server Extensions).
Service URL	Specifies the location of the Web Deploy on the host server. This URL points to the actual IIS handler that has the Web Deploy capability and will be constructed similar to `http://myhostserver:8172/MsDeploy.axd`.
Site/Application	Specifies the location where your application will be deployed. Here you can specify the site as well as the virtual directory to place the application. An example of this is `MyDomain.com/MyApplication`.

continues

TABLE 33-2 *(continued)*

SETTING	DESCRIPTION
Remove additional files at the destination	If this option is not selected, the One-Click Publishing option will first delete everything on the host server location before applying the files and settings.
User Name	The username used for IIS connections.
Password	The password used for IIS connections.
Save password	Specifies to the Visual Studio publishing feature whether to save the password in the profile.
Destination URL	After a successful publish, the destination URL will be opened in the browser.
File Publish Options	Specifies which files need to be published or removed at the destination server.
Databases	Specifies whether Entity Framework Code First Migrations should run or the database should be published incrementally.
Preview	Gives a preview of the files that will get published to the server.

Besides using the Web Deploy option, you will find that the other options provided through the newPublish Web dialog are even simpler. Figure 33-10 show you the settings for the other three deployment options provided.

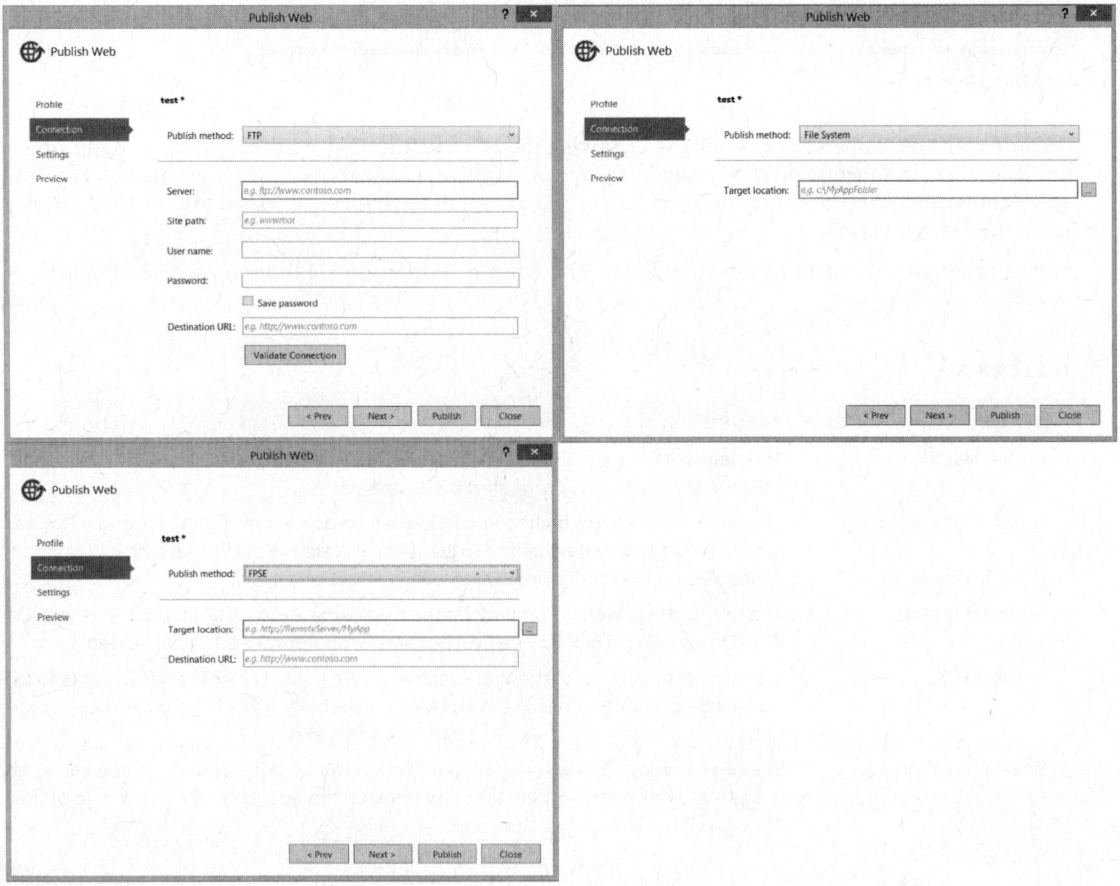

FIGURE 33-10

In this figure you can see some standard settings for doing deployments using FTP, the file system, or FrontPage Server Extensions (FPSE).

The interesting thing with the Web Deploy capabilities that Visual Studio 2012 has is that instead of just connecting to a remote Web Deploy handler and running your deployment real-time, you can also create a Web Deploy package that can be run at any time.

Visual Studio 2012 includes the ability to create these packages that can then be e-mailed or by other means provided to someone else to run on their systems. To create a web deployment package, you can select the Web Deploy package option from the Publish method. When you select this option and specify a location where the package will be created, the progress of the package creation appears in the Visual Studio status bar. After you're notified that the Publish succeeded, you can find the entire package in the location that you specified in the publish window.

Within this folder are all the files that constitute the package. Figure 33-11 presents these files.

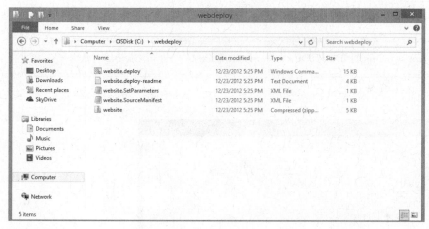

FIGURE 33-11

All of these files constitute the package that you can use in the deployment process.

➤ The website.deploy.cmd file is what your infrastructure team would use to run on the host machine (which has Web Deploy) to install the application and all the settings that are required for the application.

➤ The other files—website.SetParameters.xml and website.SourceManifest.xml—are used to define the settings used in the installation process.

➤ The final file, website.zip, contains the contents of the application.

With this package, passing another team the installation required for your application is easy. A nice example of this usage is if you are deploying to a web farm because multiple deployments need to occur and you want these deployments to all be the same. Running your installations from this single package ensures this similarity.

The other nice advantage to this package system is that it allows you to save your previous deployments, and if you need to go back and verify deployments, you can easily grab hold of a saved package. It also makes rollbacks easy for your deployment process.

Looking More Closely at Publish Profiles

The process of deploying an application to a server has undergone lots of changes in Visual Studio 2012. These changes are also available to developers using Visual Studio 2010. The improvements in the deployment area have been focused on making the commonly used operations easier to do while also making it easier to extend them. This section looks at some of these advanced features.

Database Deployment

Almost all of the applications use a database. As you incrementally deploy your application, you want to make sure that the production database is not destroyed and is updated with the latest schema changes that happened when you were deploying your application on development machine.

Entity Framework Code First

Entity Framework introduced Code First Migrations. Code First Migrations help you to incrementally update the database rather than having to re-create the database each time you deploy your application. You can customize Code First Migrations on how you want to incrementally update the schema and data of your existing database. When you are deploying your application using Visual Studio, you can determine if you want to execute Code First Migrations when the application is deployed. Figure 33-12 shows the Settings tab of the Publish Web window. As you can see in this figure, the "Execute Code First Migrations" option is selected, which means that when the application is deployed on the server, the Code First Migrations will be executed.

> **NOTE** *You can learn more about Entity Framework Code First in Chapter 11.*

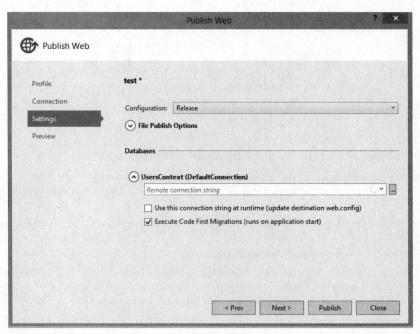

FIGURE 33-12

When you deploy your application, Visual Studio does not do anything to the database during the deployment process. When the application is accessed for the first time, Code First automatically creates the database or updates the schema as needed. If the application implements a Seed method, the Seed method is executed after the database is created or updated.

Incremental Database Update

If your application is not using Entity Framework Code First, you can still update your database using the dbDacFx Web Deploy Provider. This provider uses the new Data-Tier Applications Framework (Dacpac Framework) for syncing databases. The dbDacFx provider is an improvement over the dbFullSql provider, which was used in Visual Studio 2010. The dbFullSql provider used to do a full sync of the database each time you deployed your application. This meant that if you had made changes to your existing tables, an error would result when the provider did a full sync of the database. dbDacFx is an improvement since this provider will compare the two databases and will calculate the changes that need to be applied to the destination database to make is similar to the source database.

Figure 33-13 shows how you can use dbDacFx provider. This option is shown for SQL Server databases that the application accesses without using the Entity Framework Code First `Context` class. This option also allows you to specify custom SQL scripts that should be run on the destination database during deployment. Custom SQL scripts are useful when you want to provide some initial seeding data for any tables.

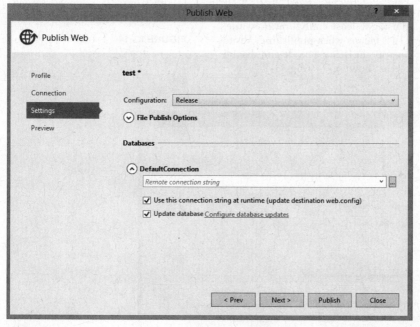

FIGURE 33-13

The dbDacFx Web Deploy Provider is recommended over dbFullSql for database deployment. If you want to use the dbFullSql provider, you can configure the database deployment settings in the Package/Publish SQL tab of your project properties.

web.Config Transforms

Two of the most common operations you do when publishing an application is transform some of the properties of `web.config` and publish a specific `web.config` based on whether you are publishing to a production or test server. For example, if you are publishing to a production server, you'll want to turn off the debugging option for your application.

When you create a web application in Visual Studio, you get a `web.config` file. If you expand the `web.config` file you will see that it has two subfiles called `web.debug.config` and `web.release.config`. Figure 33-14 shows these two files.

When you are deploying your application using Visual Studio you can select which build configuration will be used to build your project, and if there are any associated transforms with that configuration they will be applied. Figure 33-15 shows how you can configure this option in the Settings tab of the Publish Web window. In this figure, I am using Release configuration while publishing my application. This means when publishing, Visual Studio will publish my application in Release mode and disable the debug flag in `web.config` as shown in Listing 33-1.

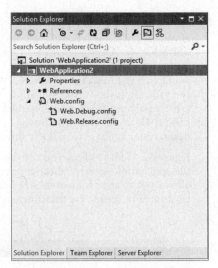

FIGURE 33-14

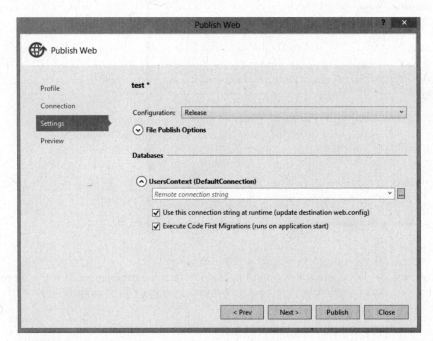

FIGURE 33-15

One of the most important features of these files is how Visual Studio transforms these files while deploying your application. Transformation is a key feature whereby you can change different settings of your `web.config` file. Listing 33-2 shows a common `web.config` where the `debug` option is turned on and Listing 33-3 shows how you can apply a transform to turn off debugging in a release `web.config`.

LISTING 33-2: Typical web.config

```
<system.web>
    <compilation debug="true" />
</system.web>
```

LISTING 33-3: web.release.config transform to turn off debugging

```
<system.web>
    <compilation xdt:Transform="RemoveAttributes(debug)" />
</system.web>
```

Transformation actions are specified by using XML attributes that are defined in the XML-Document-Transform namespace, which is mapped to the `xdt` prefix. The XML-Document-Transform namespace defines two attributes: `Locator` and `Transform`.

➤ The `Locator` attribute specifies the `web.config` element or set of elements that you want to change in some way.

➤ The `Transform` attribute specifies what you want to do to the elements that the `Locator` attribute finds.

You can use the transformation feature to perform other transforms such as enabling logging or setting custom errors.

Other Publish Options

Apart from supporting most of the common operations while deploying, the Publish Web window has advanced settings that enable you to perform more advanced actions.

Editing the Publish Profile Settings File

The Publish Web window only scratches the surface of most of the common operations of deployment. There may be cases where you want to configure advanced operations that aren't covered in the UI. Publish profile files are named `<profilename>.pubxml` and are located in the `PublishProfiles` folder inside your application. For website projects these files are located in `App_Data` folder and are named as `<profilename>.pubxml`. Each `pubxml` file contains settings that apply to one publish profile, so you can store multiple publish profile settings files here, each of which can contain information about different publishing targets for your application. Listing 33-4 shows a sample of a publish profile settings file.

LISTING 33-4: Sample publish profile settings file

```
<Project ToolsVersion="4.0" xmlns="http://schemas.microsoft.com/developer/msbuild/2003">
  <PropertyGroup>
    <IncludeSetACLProviderOnDestination>False</IncludeSetACLProviderOnDestination>
    <WebPublishMethod>Package</WebPublishMethod>
    <LaunchASiteUrlAfterPublish>True</LaunchASiteUrlAfterPublish>
    <SiteUrlToLaunchAfterPublish />
    <MSDeployServiceURL />
    <DeployIisAppPath />
    <RemoteSitePhysicalPath />
    <AllowUntrustedCertificate>False</AllowUntrustedCertificate>
    <SkipExtraFilesOnServer>True</SkipExtraFilesOnServer>
    <DeployAsIisApp>True</DeployAsIisApp>
    <MSDeployPublishMethod>WMSVC</MSDeployPublishMethod>
    <UserName />
    <SavePWD>True</SavePWD>
    <PublishDatabaseSettings>
      <!-- this section omitted to keep the example short -->
    </PublishDatabaseSettings>
  </PropertyGroup>
</Project>
```

The publish profile settings files are MSBuild files, and you can edit this file to configure some options. For example, if you control the ACLs on the server and want to disable the default ACL behavior on deployment, you can remove the `IncludeSetACLProviderOnDestination` element. Visual Studio will not set the default ACLs (which are read-only on the application root and write permissions on the `App_Data` folder).

Advanced Precompile Settings

If you are precompiling your web application, you configure the advanced settings in the precompilation window. You can launch this window by expanding the File Publish Options in the Settings tab of the Publish Web window. Figure 33-16 shows the Advanced Precompile Settings window.

Package/Publish Web

Although the Publish Web window has most of the common settings needed for web deployment, there are certain settings that can be configured in the Package/

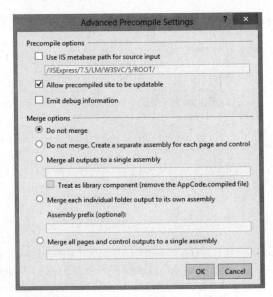

FIGURE 33-16

Publish Web tab of the project properties. Figure 33-17 shows the Package/Publish Web tab. You can use this tab to configure IIS settings that should be transferred, such as application pool settings.

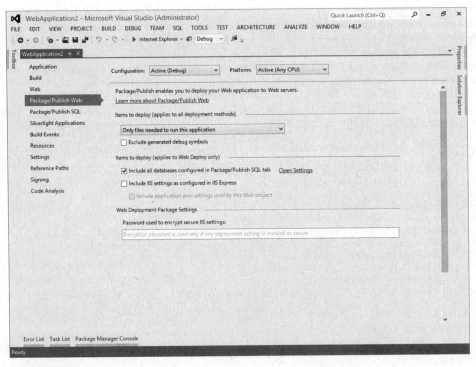

FIGURE 33-17

DEPLOYING TO WINDOWS AZURE WEB SITES

As more and more hosting platforms are moving to the Cloud, there have been substantial improvements in making it easier to deploy your web applications to the Cloud. This section shows how easy it is for developers to make an application on their development machines available to users by deploying the application to Windows Azure.

Windows Azure Web Sites is a model in Windows Azure that allows you to quickly and easily deploy sites to a highly-scalable Cloud environment. That environment allows you to start small and scale as traffic grows. This model provides capabilities that can be found in a shared hosting environment, where you start with sharing resources with other websites on the server, and you can gradually scale up to have more instances of your website once you start getting more load on it.

> **NOTE** *The publishing improvements are available for developers using either Visual Studio 2010 or 2012. You can get the latest update by downloading the latest Azure SDK at* http://www.windowsazure.com/en-us/develop/net/.

You need to create an account on Windows Azure before you can create any new website. To create an account you can go to the Windows Azure management portal at http://www.windowsazure.com/ and sign up to create an account.

To deploy an application as a Windows Azure Web Site, you have to provision a website in Windows Azure. Figure 33-18 shows how you can create a website using the Quick Create option in the Windows Azure management portal. You have the option to create the website in a geographical location that's the closest to you. You can also choose the Quick Create with Database option, which will provision a database for your application as well.

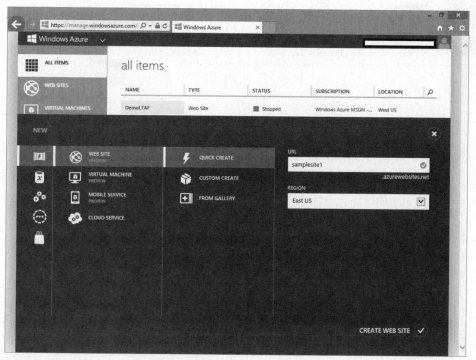

FIGURE 33-18

Once you have created the website, you can download the publish profile to your development machine. You can select your website from the management portal and select the Dashboard tab. This tab gives you an overview of the usage statistics for your website and all the configuration options available. You can download your publish profile from this section. You can download and save your publish setting file anywhere on your computer. Figure 33-19 shows the "Download Publish Profile" option in the Windows Azure management portal that you can use to download the publish profile. This publish profile contains the connection settings needed to connect to your website and the database that was provisioned.

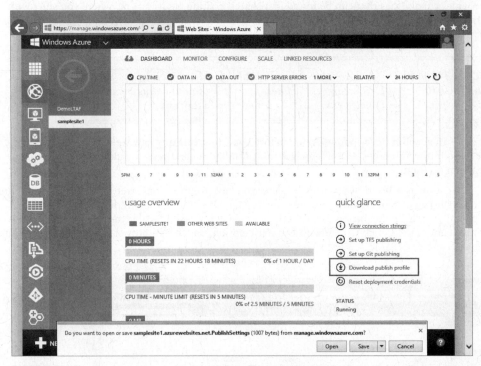

FIGURE 33-19

After you have downloaded this publish profile, you can go to your application and import these settings. Once you launch the Publish Web window, you can import the publish profile settings file that you just downloaded to your machine. Once you import this file, Visual Studio will read this file to get connection values to your website and database in Windows Azure. Once you have imported this file, Visual Studio will store your publish profile settings file as part of your project. This means that your publish profile settings file is added to your project, and you can check this file along with your project into any source control system. This is useful since you do not have to download the publish profile settings file if you copy your project to a different machine and want to republish your application. You can launch the Publish Web window by right-clicking your website. From there you can import the profile (Figure 33-20).

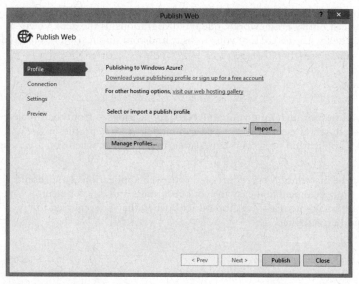

FIGURE 33-20

In the publish profile you can look at the Connection tab and can validate the publish profile settings by clicking the Validate Connection button. The program will try to connect to the Azure Web Site that you provisioned and determine whether the connections supplied in the publish profile settings file are valid.

If your application is using a database, you can set the connection string to use when your application is deployed in the Settings tab. If you are using Entity Framework Code First, you can configure whether Code First Migrations should run when the application is deployed to Azure Web Sites.

The last step of deploying the application to Windows Azure is the Preview tab. This tab shows which files will be deployed. You can use this step to check if all the files that you wanted to publish are there. You can also unselect any file which you do not want to be published. Figure 33-23 shows the Preview tab.

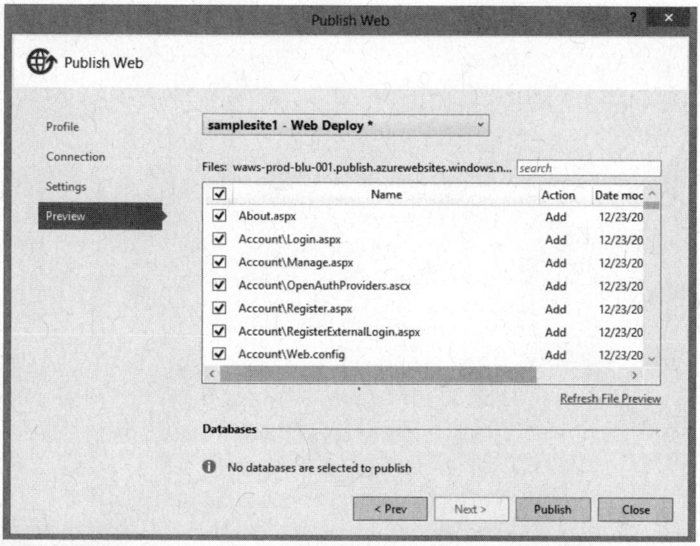

FIGURE 33-21

Once you click Publish, all the files are copied to the server and the database is updated with the schema that you had in your local database or via Entity Framework Code First Migrations. If the deployment is successful, the default browser is launched with the URL of your website and your application is deployed in the Cloud.

SUMMARY

As you can see, you have many possibilities for installing your ASP.NET applications—from the simplest mode of just copying the files to a remote server (sort of a save-and-run mode). Publish profiles make it really easy to publish a website or web application projects to any server, in particular, when you are using Windows Azure.

Just remember that when working on the installation procedures for your web applications, you should be thinking about making the entire process logical and easy for your customers and development team to understand. You do not want to make people's lives too difficult when they are required to programmatically install items on another machine.

PART IX
Additional ASP.NET Technologies

Package Mgr to mng the dependencies of application
(nuGet) also updates

RESTful 496, 505

34

ASP.NET MVC   *Model View Controller*

WHAT'S IN THIS CHAPTER?

➤ Understanding MVC and ASP.NET

➤ Working with routes and URLs

➤ Understanding controllers and views

WROX.COM CODE DOWNLOADS FOR THIS CHAPTER

Please note that all the code examples in this chapter are available as a part of this chapter's code download on the book's website at www.wrox.com on the Download Code tab.

Model-View-Controller (MVC) has been an important architectural pattern in computer science for many years. Originally named Thing-Model-View-Editor in 1979, it was later simplified to Model-View-Controller. It is a powerful and elegant means of separating concerns within an application and applies itself extremely well to web applications. Its explicit separation of concerns does add a small amount of extra complexity to an application's design, but the extraordinary benefits outweigh the extra effort. It's been used in dozens of frameworks since its introduction. You can find MVC in Java and C++, on Mac and on Windows, and inside literally dozens of frameworks.

Understanding the core concepts of MVC is critical to using it effectively. This chapter discusses the history of the MVC pattern, as well as how it is used in web programming today.

ASP.NET MVC 1.0 shipped as a downloadable add-on to Visual Studio 2008. ASP.NET MVC 2 shipped built-in with Visual Studio 2010. ASP.NET MVC 3 shipped as a downloadable add-on to Visual Studio 2010. Now in Visual Studio 2012, ASP.NET MVC 4 ships built-in. This chapter also covers some of the limitations of ASP.NET Web Forms and how ASP.NET MVC attempts to release the developer from those limitations.

Final release 5.2.7   Nov. 28, 2018

ReSharper

DEFINING MODEL-VIEW-CONTROLLER

Model-View-Controller (MVC) is an architectural pattern used to separate an application into three main aspects:

➤ **The Model:** A set of classes that describes the data you're working with as well as the business rules for how the data can be changed and manipulated

➤ **The View:** The application's user interface (UI)

➤ **The Controller:** A set of classes that handles communication from the user, overall application flow, and application-specific logic

This pattern is used frequently in web programming. With ASP.NET MVC, it's translated roughly to the following:

➤ The models are the classes that represent the domain in which you are interested. These domain objects often encapsulate data stored in a database as well as code used to manipulate the data and enforce domain-specific business logic. With ASP.NET MVC, this is most likely a data-access layer of some kind using a tool like LINQ to SQL, Entity Framework, or NHibernate, combined with custom code containing domain-specific logic.

➤ The view is a dynamically generated page. In ASP.NET MVC, you implement it via the `System.Web.Mvc.ViewPage` class, which inherits from `System.Web.UI.Page`.

➤ The controller is a special class that manages the relationship between the view and model. It talks to the model, and it decides which view to render (if any). In ASP.NET MVC, this class is conventionally denoted by the suffix "`Controller`."

MVC ON THE WEB TODAY

For many, the web didn't really become prominent until the first graphical browsers began to flood the market, starting with Mosaic in 1993. Shortly after, dynamic web pages began showing up using languages such as Perl and enabled by technologies like the Common Gateway Interface (CGI). The technology available in the early stages of the web was focused more around the concept of scripting HTML to do light content-driven work, as opposed to deep application logic, which just wasn't needed back then.

As the web grew and HTML standards began to allow for richer interactions, the notion of the web as an application platform began to take off. In terms of Microsoft, the focus was on quick and simple. In line with that, Active Server Pages (ASP) was born in 1996.

ASP used VBScript, a very simple, lightweight language that gave developers a lot of "un-prescribed freedom" in terms of the applications they could create. A request for an ASP page would be handled by a file with the `.asp` extension, which consisted of a server-side script intermixed with HTML markup. Written in a procedural language, many ASP pages often devolved into "spaghetti code," in which the markup was intertwined with code in ways that were difficult to manage and maintain. Although writing clean ASP code was possible, it took a lot of work, and the language and tools were not sufficiently helpful. Even so, although it took a lot of work, ASP did provide full control over the markup produced.

In January of 2002, Microsoft released version 1.0 of the .NET platform, which included the original version of ASP.NET, and thus Web Forms was born. Its birth provided access to more advanced tools and object-oriented languages for building a website.

ASP.NET has grown tremendously over the past 10 years and has made developing web pages very productive and simple by abstracting the repetitive tasks of web development into simple drag-and-drop controls. This abstraction can be a tremendous help, but some developers have found that they want more control over the generated HTML and browser scripting. As the focus on testing has grown, they also want to be able to easily test their web page logic.

As languages matured and web server software grew in capability, MVC soon found its way into web application architectures. But MVC didn't hit its mainstream stride until July of 2004, when a 24-year-old developer at 37Signals in Chicago, Illinois, named David Heinemeier Hansson, introduced the world to his fresh way of thinking about MVC.

David, or DHH as he's known in the community, created Ruby on Rails, a web development framework that used the Ruby language and the MVC pattern to create something special.

Now let's further delve into ASP.NET MVC and answer the question, "Why not Web Forms?"

In February of 2007, Scott Guthrie of Microsoft sketched out the core of ASP.NET MVC while flying on a plane to a conference on the east coast of the United States. It was a simple application, containing a few hundred lines of code, but the promise and potential it offered for parts of the Microsoft web developer audience was huge.

MODEL-VIEW-CONTROLLER AND ASP.NET

ASP.NET MVC relies on many of the same core strategies that the other MVC platforms use, plus it offers the benefits of compiled and managed code and exploits any new language features in the latest version of the .NET Framework. Each of the MVC frameworks used on the web usually share in some fundamental tenets:

➤ Convention over Configuration

➤ Don't repeat yourself (also known as the DRY principle)

➤ Plugability whenever possible

➤ Try to be helpful, but if necessary, get out of the developer's way

Serving Methods, Not Files

Web servers initially served up HTML stored in static files on disk. As dynamic web pages gained prominence, web servers served HTML generated on the fly from dynamic scripts that were also located on disk. With MVC, serving up HTML is a little different. The URL tells the routing mechanism which controller to instantiate and which action method to call and supplies the required arguments to that method. The controller's method then decides which view to use, and that view then does the rendering.

Rather than having a direct relationship between the URL and a file living on the web server's hard drive, a relationship exists between the URL and a method on a controller object. ASP.NET MVC implements the "front controller" variant of the MVC pattern, and the controller sits in front of everything except the routing subsystem.

A good way to conceive of the way that MVC works in a web scenario is that MVC serves up the results of method calls, not dynamically generated (also known as scripted) pages. In fact, a speaker once called this "RPC for the Web," which is particularly apt, although quite a bit narrower in scope.

Is This the Future of Web Forms?

One of the major concerns that we've heard when talking to people about ASP.NET MVC is that its release means the death of Web Forms. This just isn't true. ASP.NET MVC is not ASP.NET Web Forms 4.5. It's an alternative to Web Forms, and it's a fully supported part of the framework. While Web Forms continues to march on with new innovations and new developments, ASP.NET MVC will continue as a parallel alternative that's totally supported by Microsoft.

One interesting way to look at this is to refer to the namespaces in which these technologies live. If you could point to a namespace and say, "That's where ASP.NET lives," it would be the `System.Web` namespace. ASP.NET MVC lives in the `System.Web.Mvc` namespace. It's not `System.Mvc`, and it's not `System.Web2`.

ASP.NET MVC has been folded into .NET since version 4 of the framework, and it's built into Visual Studio 2012 out of the box. This cements ASP.NET MVC's place as a fundamental part of ASP.NET itself.

Why Not Web Forms?

In ASP.NET Web Forms, you create an instance of `System.Web.UI.Page` and put "server controls" on it (for example, a calendar and some buttons) so that the user can enter or view information. You then wire these controls to events on the `System.Web.UI.Page` to allow for interactivity. This page is then compiled, and when it's called by the ASP.NET run time, a server-side control tree is created, each control in the tree goes through an event life cycle, it renders itself, and the result is served back as HTML. As a result, a new web aesthetic started to emerge, Web Forms layers eventing and state management on top of HTTP, a truly stateless protocol.

Why was this abstraction necessary? Remember that Web Forms was introduced to a Microsoft development community that was very accustomed to Visual Basic 6. Developers using VB6 would drag a button onto the design surface, double-click the button, and a `Button_Click` event handler method was instantly created for them. This was an incredibly powerful way to create business applications and had everyone excited about Rapid Application Development (RAD) tools. When developers started using classic ASP, it was quite a step backward from the rich environment they were used to in Visual Basic. For better or worse, Web Forms brought that Rapid Application Development experience to the web.

However, as the web matured and more and more people came to terms with their own understanding of HTML as well as the introduction of cascading style sheets (CSS) and XHTML, a new web aesthetic started to emerge. Web Forms is still incredibly productive for developers, enabling them to create a web-based line of business applications very quickly. However, the HTML it generates looks, well, generated, and can sometimes offend the sensibilities of those who handcraft their XHTML and CSS sites. This is especially true with HTML5 and a renewed focus on more semantic markup. Web Forms concepts like ViewState and the Postback event model have their place, but many developers want a lower-level alternative that embraces not only HTML, but also HTTP itself.

Additionally, the architecture of Web Forms also makes testing via the current unit testing tools such as NUnit, MbUnit, and xUnit.NET difficult. ASP.NET Web Forms wasn't designed with unit testing in mind, and although a number of hacks can be found on the web, it's fair to say that Web Forms does not lend itself well to test-driven development. ASP.NET MVC offers absolute control over HTML, doesn't deny the existence of HTTP, and was designed from the ground up with an eye toward testability.

ASP.NET MVC Is Totally Different!

Yes, ASP.NET MVC is totally different. That's the whole point. It's built on top of a system of values and architectural principles that is very different from those in Web Forms. ASP.NET MVC values extensibility, testability, and flexibility. It's very lightweight and doesn't make a lot of assumptions on how you will use it—aside from the fact that it assumes you appreciate the Model-View-Controller pattern.

Why "(ASP.NET > ASP.NET MVC) == True"

Creating your first MVC application is fairly straightforward. You can use any version of Visual Studio 2012 to create the basic application. Just follow these steps:

1. Open Visual Studio 2012 and select File ⇨ New Project.

2. From the New Project dialog box, shown in Figure 34-1, select ASP.NET MVC 4 Web Application.

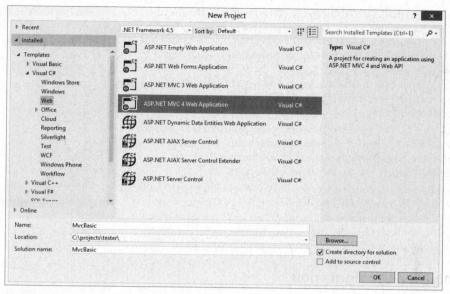

FIGURE 34-1

3. Pick your project name and where it's going to live on disk, and click OK. The New ASP.NET MVC 4 Project dialog box appears, as shown in Figure 34-2. The New ASP.NET MVC 4 Project dialog box enables you to select the specific MVC template you would like to use to create your project. Select the Internet Application project template.

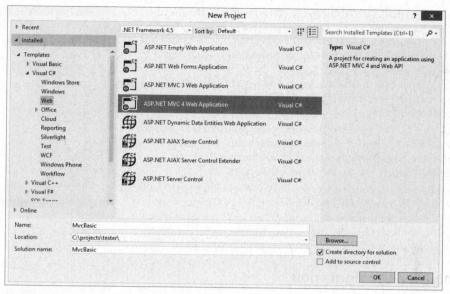

FIGURE 34-2

4. The New ASP.NET MVC 4 Project dialog box also contains the settings for creating a Unit Test project. Check the box labeled "Create a unit test project" to create a solution that includes both the basic ASP.NET MVC project and an additional Unit Test project. By default, the Test framework drop-down list includes Visual Studio Unit Test as an option. If you've installed a third-party unit-testing framework like MbUnit or NUnit, additional options appear in this drop-down.

5. Click OK, and a solution with projects that look like that shown in Figure 34-3 appears. Note that, although this is an ASP.NET application, along with a standard class library, it has some additional folders you haven't seen before.

In fact, the application has quite a few more directories than you might be used to; this is by design. ASP.NET MVC, like other MVC frameworks, relies heavily on the idea that you can reduce effort and code by relying on some basic structural rules in your application. Ruby on Rails expresses this powerful idea very succinctly: *Convention over Configuration*.

FIGURE 34-3

Convention over Configuration

The concept of "Convention over Configuration" was made popular by Ruby on Rails and essentially means the following: We know, by now, how to build a web application. Let's roll that experience into the framework so we don't have to configure absolutely everything again.

You can see this concept at work in ASP.NET MVC by taking a look at the three core directories that make the application work:

➤ Controllers

➤ Models

➤ Views

You don't have to set these folder names in the `web.config` file, they are just expected to be there by convention.

This saves you the work of having to edit an XML file such as your `web.config` file, for example, to explicitly tell the MVC engine "you can find my controllers in the Controllers directory." It already knows. It's *convention*.

ASP.NET MVC's conventions are straightforward. This is what is expected of your application's structure:

➤ It has a single Controllers directory that holds your controller classes.

➤ Each controller's class name ends with `Controller`—`ProductController`, `HomeController`, and so on—and exists in the Controllers directory.

➤ It has a single Views directory for all the Views of your application.

➤ Views that controllers use are located in a subdirectory of the Views main directory, and are named according to the controller name (minus "`Controller`"). For example, the views for the `ProductController` discussed earlier would be in `/Views/Product`.

➤ All reusable UI elements live in a subdirectory of the Views main directory named "Shared".

If you take a deeper, expanded look at the initial structure of the sample application, shown in Figure 34-4, you can see these conventions at work.

FIGURE 34-4

Two controllers, `HomeController` and `AccountController`, are in the Controllers directory, and a number of views are in the Views directory. The following discussion focuses on the views under `/Views/Home` named About and Index.

Although no convention is expected of you with respect to what you name your views, you can lean on the ASP.NET MVC convention that you give your view the same name as your action. Using this convention also makes reviewing and understanding your application easier for other developers.

You can see this convention in action in the way that the template creates the Index and About views. These are also the names of the controller actions that are called, and the code, shown in C#, to render these views is simply:

```
return View();
```

That can be a little confusing. You can see a clear example by changing the application a little and then digging in:

1. Open `HomeController.cs` or `HomeController.vb`, copy and paste the `About` method, and create a duplication called `Foo`, as shown here:

   VB

   ```
   Function Foo() As ActionResult
       ViewData("Message") = "Foo page."

       Return View()
   End Function
   ```

   C#

   ```
   public ActionResult Foo()
   {
       ViewBag.Message = "Foo page.";

       return View();
   }
   ```

2. Having made this one small addition, start debugging your application. The ASP.NET Development Server automatically selects a high port number and your browser launches. Your browser ends up navigating to an address like `http://localhost:3098`, as shown in Figure 34-5.

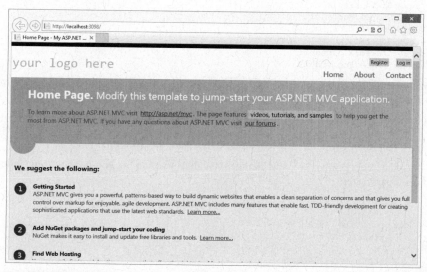

FIGURE 34-5

3. See how there's no .aspx extension? ASP.NET MVC puts you in full control. Now, change the relative URL in your browser's address bar from / to /Home/Foo. Things get interesting, as shown in Figure 34-6. Remember that you're just returning the result of the call to View in your Foo method. Because you're in the Foo method of HomeController, the system is looking for a View called Foo in a number of locations. ASP.NET MVC is smart enough to give you an error message that you can actually do something useful with. It's really quite refreshing!

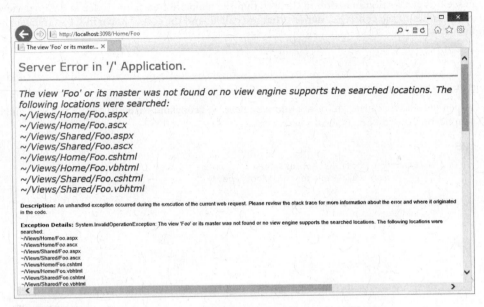

FIGURE 34-6

```
System.InvalidOperationException: The view 'Foo' or its master was not found or no view
engine supports the searched locations. The following locations were searched:
~/Views/Home/Foo.aspx
~/Views/Home/Foo.ascx
~/Views/Shared/Foo.aspx
~/Views/Shared/Foo.ascx
~/Views/Home/Foo.cshtml
~/Views/Home/Foo.vbhtml
~/Views/Shared/Foo.cshtml
~/Views/Shared/Foo.vbhtml
```

The error message lists (see Figure 34-6) the locations where the system looked for Views, in the order searched. It gives you enough information to infer the naming convention for Views.

First, it looks in a directory under /Views with the name of the current controller, in this case Home, then it looks in /Views/Shared. The RazorViewEngine that ASP.NET MVC 4 uses by default looks for .aspx pages, then .ascx files, then .cshtml and .vbhtml files.

4. Go back into the HomeController and change the call to View in the Foo method to include the name of a View as a parameter:

VB

```
Function Foo() As ActionResult
    ViewData("Message") = "Foo page."

    Return View("Index")
End Function
```

C#

```
public ActionResult Foo()
{
    ViewBag.Message = "Foo page.";

    return View("Index");
}
```

5. Start your application again, and visit /Home/Foo again. The Index view is rendered, and the Message string from the Foo action appears in the header of the page.

6. Switch back over to Visual Studio and set a breakpoint on the line that returns the result of View. Refresh your browser, confirming that you're still at /Home/Foo, and get ready to dig in.

The Third Request Is the Charm

Take a moment and think about what's happening here. What's the state of affairs within your application? Your instance of Visual Studio should look more or less like Figure 34-7.

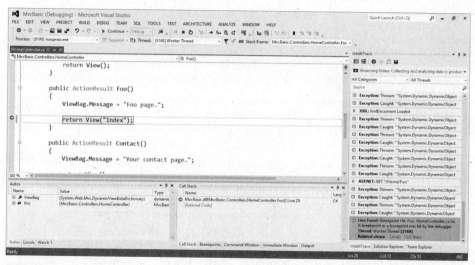

FIGURE 34-7

Spend a moment looking at Visual Studio (or the figure, if you like) and try to determine what it is telling you. How did you get here? Where are you?

You visited /Home/Foo in the browser, and now you're magically sitting on a breakpoint inside of the Foo action method. The Call Stack tool window confirms this, but doesn't tell you enough. How *did* you get here? Right-click the whitespace of the call stack, and select Show External Code. You might also drag the Call Stack tool window and "tear it off" Visual Studio to better analyze the crush of information that's going to be revealed. If you have multiple monitors, remember that Visual Studio 2012 supports that, so you can fill one whole monitor with the Call Stack tool window if you like.

The Call Stack tool window contains so much information, in fact, that some of the important bits and objects have been highlighted, as shown in the snippet in Figure 34-8. Remember that call stacks are read from bottom to top, where the bottom is where you started and the top is the line you are currently debugging. In this call stack, some parts are more significant than others.

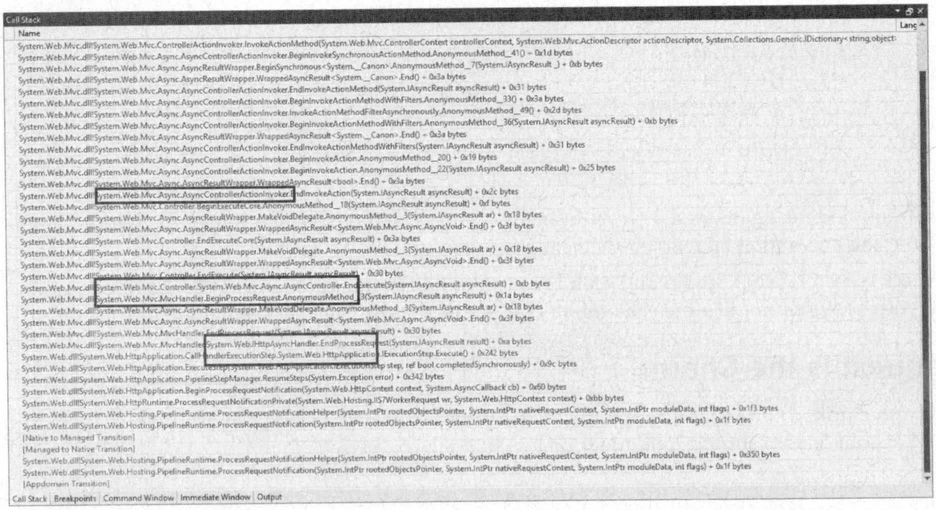

FIGURE 34-8

Starting at the bottom, you can see that the request is being handled by ASP.NET—specifically, by `System.Web.HttpRuntime`. This is the "beginning" of ASP.NET. Note that this is `System.Web`, and you're inside `System.Web.dll`—nothing MVC specific has happened yet. If you're already familiar with Web Forms, you might find it useful to remember what ASP.NET proper is, where it ends, and where ASP.NET MVC starts.

The first significant thing happens (remember, you're reading from bottom to top) in the bottom callout shown in Figure 34-8. What can you learn from the highlighted transition from ASP.NET to ASP.NET MVC? ASP.NET MVC is built on ASP.NET with `HttpHandlers` and `HttpModules`. That's where MVC gets its hooks in.

The fact that ASP.NET MVC is implemented as an `HttpHandler` is comforting because you know that the team "played by the rules" when writing it. No internal knowledge or secrets exist in the design of ASP.NET MVC. It's written using the same public constructs and APIs that are available to all developers.

> **NOTE** *We find great comfort in the discovery that ASP.NET MVC has no secrets in its design. Less magic in ASP.NET MVC means we can understand it more easily. If ASP.NET MVC is an* `HttpHandler`*, and you've written lots of those, then it's less magical than you thought! It's also nice to see that ASP.NET itself was flexible and extensible enough to allow something like ASP.NET MVC to be created.*

Another thing you can glean from these discoveries is that because ASP.NET MVC uses `HttpHandlers` (and `HttpModules`) to do its work, MVC is built on ASP.NET. This might seem like an obvious statement to some, but a very common question is "Is ASP.NET MVC a whole new ASP.NET?" You can see from Figure 34-8 that it's not. It's built on the same infrastructure, the same "core" ASP.NET, that you've used for years.

Glance back at Figure 34-8 and look at that call stack. Remember that you're currently sitting on a breakpoint in the `Foo` method inside `HomeController`. Who created `HomeController`? Someone had to "new it up." Who called `Foo` for you?

Inside the `MvcHandler`'s `ProcessRequest` method an instance of a controller is created by the `DefaultControllerFactory`. `DefaultControllerFactory` is the built-in factory created and used by ASP.NET MVC to search and create controllers. ASP.NET MVC creates an instance of the `HomeController` and then calls the `Execute` method on the controller. This method, in turn, relies on the controller's action invoker (by default a `ControllerActionInvoker`) to actually call the method.

Remember that you opened a browser and requested /Home/Foo. The ASP.NET MVC application routed the request to an MvcHandler. That Handler created an instance of the HomeController and called the Foo method. ASP.NET MVC handled both object activation and method invocation for you.

The /Home/Foo URL was intercepted by the UrlRoutingModule. That module is responsible for making sure the right URLs go to the right controllers by parsing the URLs and creating some routing data. The MVC pipeline uses a ControllerFactory and a ControllerActionInvoker to create your controller and call its method, respectively.

Controllers exist to "do stuff." What that stuff is, is up to you. They talk to a model, do calculations, whatever. However, they don't render HTML, and they don't talk to databases. That's separation of concerns. Controllers are concerned with controlling.

The controller passes ViewData to a view, which is concerned with rendering HTML (or whatever you want). That HTML contains links to other URLs, and the cycle continues.

UNDERSTANDING ROUTES AND URLS

Software developers are well known for paying close attention to the little details, especially when it comes to the quality and structure of their source code. They often fight long battles over code indentation styles and where curly braces should go. So it comes as a bit of a surprise when you approach a majority of sites built using ASP.NET and encounter a URL that looks like this:

```
http://example.com/products/list.aspx?id=17313&catid=33723&page=3
```

For all the attention developers pay to code, why not pay the same amount of attention to the URL? It may not seem all that important, but the URL is a legitimate and widely used web user interface.

Usability expert Jakob Nielsen (www.nngroup.com) urges developers to pay attention to URLs and provides the following guidelines for high-quality URLs:

- A domain name that is easy to remember and easy to spell
- Short URLs
- Easy-to-type URLs
- URLs that reflect the site structure
- URLs that are "hackable" to allow users to move to higher levels of the information architecture by hacking off the end of the URL
- Persistent URLs, which don't change

Traditionally, in many web frameworks such as classic ASP, JSP, PHP, ASP.NET, and the like, the URL represents a physical file on disk. For example, when you see a request for

```
http://example.com/products/list.aspx
```

you could bet your kid's tuition that the website has a directory structure that contains a Products folder and a List.aspx file within that folder. In this case, a direct relationship exists between the URL and what physically exists on disk. When such a request is received by the web server, the web framework executes code associated with this file to respond to the request. In many cases, this code contains or is associated with a template that intermixes server-side declarations with HTML markup to generate the resulting markup sent back to the browser via the response.

Routing within the ASP.NET MVC Framework serves two main purposes:

- It matches incoming requests and maps them to a controller action.
- It constructs outgoing URLs that correspond to controller actions.

Now that you understand something of URLs and routing, it's time to take a closer look at routing and how it's different from URL rewriting.

Routing Compared to URL Rewriting

To better understand routing, many developers compare it to URL rewriting. After all, both approaches are useful in creating a separation between the URL and the code that handles the URL, which can help create "pretty" URLs for search engine optimization (SEO) purposes. One key difference, though, is that URL rewriting represents a "page-centric" view of URLs. Most rewriting schemes with ASP.NET rewrite a URL for one page to be handled by another. For example, you might see

```
/product/bolts.aspx
```

rewritten as

```
/product/display.aspx?productid=111
```

Routing, on the other hand, takes a "resource-centric" view of URLs. In this case, the URL represents a resource (not necessarily a page) on the web. With ASP.NET routing, this resource is a piece of code that executes when the incoming request matches the route. The route determines how the request is dispatched based on the characteristics of the URL—it doesn't rewrite the URL.

Another key difference is that routing also helps generate URLs using the same mapping rules that it uses to match incoming URLs. Another way to look at it is that ASP.NET routing is more like *bidirectional* URL rewriting. Where this comparison falls short is that ASP.NET routing never actually rewrites your URL. The request URL that the user makes in the browser is the same URL your application sees throughout the entire request life cycle.

Defining Routes

Every ASP.NET MVC application needs at least one route to define how the application should handle requests, but usually ends up with at least a handful. Conceivably, a very complex application could have dozens of routes or more.

In this section, you look at how to define routes. Route definitions start with the URL, which specifies a pattern that the route will match. Along with the route URL, routes can also specify default values and constraints for the various parts of the URL, providing tight control over how the route matches incoming request URLs.

You start with an extremely simple route and build up from there.

Setting Route URLs

After you create a new ASP.NET MVC Web Application project, take a quick look at the code in `Global.asax.cs`. You'll notice that the `Application_Start` method contains a call to a static method named `RegisterRoutes` in the `RouteConfig` class. This method is where all routes for the application are registered.

> **NOTE** *Instead of calling the configuration and setup methods directly in the* `Global` `.asax`*, they have been placed in static methods in classes located in the App_Start ASP.NET folder. This not only keeps the* `Global.asax` *cleaner, but enforces separation of concerns.*

Clear out the routes in the `RegisterRoutes` method of the `RouteConfig` class for now and replace them with this very simple route (shown in C#):

```
routes.MapRoute("simple", "{first}/{second}/{third}");
```

The simplest form of the `MapRoute` method takes in a name for the route and the URL pattern for the route. The name is discussed a bit later in this section. For now, focus on the URL pattern.

Notice that the route URL consists of several URL segments (a segment is everything between slashes but not including the slashes), each of which contains a placeholder delimited using curly braces. These placeholders are referred to as URL parameters. This structure is a pattern-matching rule used to determine whether this route applies to an incoming request. In this example, this rule will match any URL with three segments because a URL parameter, by default, matches *any* nonempty value. When it matches a URL with three segments, the text in the first segment of that URL corresponds to the {first} URL parameter, the value in the second segment of that URL corresponds to the {second} URL parameter, and the value in the third segment corresponds to the {third} parameter.

You can name these parameters anything you want, as in this case. When a request comes in, routing parses the request URL into a dictionary (specifically a RouteValueDictionary accessible via the RouteData in the RequestContext), using the URL parameter names as the keys and subsections of the URL in the corresponding position as the values. When using routes in the context of an MVC application, certain parameter names carry a special purpose. Table 34-1 displays how the route just defined converts certain URLs into a RouteValueDictionary.

TABLE 34-1

URL	URL PARAMETER VALUES
/products/display/123	{first} = products
	{second} = display
	{third} = 123
/foo/bar/baz	{first} = foo
	{second} = bar
	{third} = baz
/a.b/c-d/e-f	{first} = "a.b"
	{second} = "c-d"
	{third} = "e-f"

If you actually make a request to the URLs listed in the preceding table, you may notice that your ASP.NET MVC application appears to be broken. Although you can define a route with any parameter names you want, certain special parameter names are required by ASP.NET MVC for the route to function correctly: {controller} and {action}.

The value of the {controller} parameter is used to instantiate a controller class to handle the request. By convention, MVC appends the suffix Controller to the {controller} value and attempts to locate a type of that name (case insensitively) that also inherits from the System.Web.Mvc.IController interface.

Going back to the simple route example (VB example shown), change it from

```
routes.MapRoute("simple", "{first}/{second}/{third}")
```

to

```
routes.MapRoute("simple", "{controller}/{action}/{id}")
```

so that it contains the special URL parameter names.

Now looking again at the first example in Table 34-1, you see that the request for /products/display/123 is a request for a {controller} named "Products". ASP.NET MVC takes that value and appends the Controller suffix to get a type name, ProductsController. If a type of that name that implements the IController interface exists, it is instantiated and used to handle the request.

The {action} parameter value is used to indicate which method of the controller to call to handle the current request. Note that this method invocation applies only to controller classes that inherit from the System.Web.Mvc.Controller base class. Continuing with the example of /products/display/123, the method of ProductsController that MVC will invoke is Display or display, because it is case insensitive.

Note that the third URL in Table 34-1, although it is a valid route URL, will probably not match any real controller and action, because it would attempt to instantiate a controller named a.bController and call the method named c-d, which is not a valid method name.

Any route parameters other than {controller} and {action} are passed as parameters to the action method, if they exist. Listing 34-1 demonstrates a products controller with a single action (Controllers/ProductsController.cs and Controllers/ProductsController.vb in the code download for this chapter).

LISTING 34-1: A products controller with a single action

VB

```vb
Public Class ProductsController
    Inherits System.Web.Mvc.Controller

    Function Display(id As Integer) As ActionResult
        'Do something
        Return View()
    End Function
End Class
```

C#

```csharp
using System.Web.Mvc;

public class ProductsController : Controller
{
    public ActionResult Display(int id)
    {
        //Do something
        return View();
    }
}
```

A request for /products/display/123 would cause MVC to instantiate this class and call the Display method, passing in 123 for the id.

In the previous example with the route URL {controller}/{action}/{id}, each segment contains a URL parameter that takes up the entire segment. This doesn't have to be the case. Route URLs do allow for literal values within the segments. For example, if you are integrating MVC into an existing site and want all your MVC requests to be prefaced with the word *site*, you could do it as follows:

```
site/{controller}/{action}/{id}
```

This indicates that the first segment of a URL must start with site to match this request. Thus, /site/products/display/123 matches this route, but /products/display/123 does not match.

Having URL segments that intermix literals with parameters is even possible. The only restriction is that two consecutive URL parameters are not allowed. Thus

```
{language}-{country}/{controller}/{action}
{controller}.{action}.{id}
```

are valid route URLs, but

```
{controller}{action}/{id}
```

is not a valid route. No way exists for the route to know when the controller part of the incoming request URL ends and when the action part should begin.

Looking at some other samples (shown in Table 34-2) can help you see how the URL pattern corresponds to matching URLs.

TABLE 34-2

ROUTE URL PATTERN	EXAMPLES OF URLS THAT MATCH
{controller}/{action}/{category}	/products/list/beverages/blog/posts/123
service/{action}-{format}	/service/display-xml
{reporttype}/{year}/{month}/{date}	/sales/2008/1/23

Under the Hood: How Routes Tie Your URL to an Action

You have walked through how routes map to controller actions within the MVC Framework. Now you take a look under the hood to get a better look at how this happens and get a better picture of where the dividing line is between routing and MVC.

One common misconception is that routing is just a feature of ASP.NET MVC. During the early stages of ASP.NET MVC implementation, this was true, but after a while, it became apparent that this was a more generally useful feature. The ASP.NET Dynamic Data team in particular was also interested in using routing inside Dynamic Data itself. At that point, routing became a more general-purpose feature that has neither internal knowledge of nor dependency on MVC.

One very outward bit of proof that routing is separate is not just that it's a separate assembly, but that it lives in the `System.Web.Routing` namespace, and not a theoretical `System.Web.Mvc.Routing`. You can glean a lot of information from reading into namespaces.

> **NOTE** *The discussion here focuses on routing for IIS 7 integrated mode and IIS 8. Some slight differences exist when using routing with IIS 7 classic mode or IIS 6. When you are using the Visual Studio 2012 built-in web server, the behavior is very similar to IIS 8.*

The High-Level Request Routing Pipeline

All this talk about routing might be a lot of information for you to process. However, it's important to understand because routing really is your most powerful tool to control your application's URLs.

Broken down into its component parts, the routing pipeline consists of the following five high-level steps:

1. `UrlRoutingModule` attempts to match the current request with the routes registered in the `RouteTable`.

2. If a route matches, the routing module grabs the `IRouteHandler` from that route.

3. The routing module calls `GetHandler` from the `IRouteHandler`, which returns an `IHttpHandler`. Recall that a typical ASP.NET page (also known as `System.Web.UI.Page`) is nothing more than an `IHttpHandler`.

4. `ProcessRequest` is called on the `HttpHandler`, thus handing off the request to be handled.

5. In the case of MVC, the `IRouteHandler` is by default an instance of `MvcRouteHandler`, which in turn returns an `MvcHandler` (implement `IHttpHandler`). The `MvcHandler` is responsible for instantiating the correct controller and calling the action method on that controller.

Route Matching

At its core, routing is simply matching requests and extracting route data from that request and passing it to an `IRouteHandler`. The algorithm for route matching is very simple from a high-level perspective.

When a request comes in, the `UrlRoutingModule` iterates through each route in the `RouteCollection` accessed via `RouteTable.Routes` in order. It then asks each route, "Can you handle this request?" If the route answers "Yes I can!", then the route lookup is done and that route gets to handle the request.

The question of whether a route can handle a request is asked by calling the method `GetRouteData`. The method returns null if the current request is not a match for the route (in other words, no real conversation is going on between the module and routes).

RouteData

Recall that when you call `GetRouteData`, it returns an instance of `RouteData`. What exactly is `RouteData`? `RouteData` contains information about the route that matched a particular request, including context information for the specific request that matched.

Recall that the previous section showed a route with the following URL: `{foo}/{bar}/{baz}`. When a request for `/products/display/123` comes in, the route attempts to match the request. If it does match, it then creates a dictionary that contains information parsed from the URL. Specifically, it adds a key to the dictionary for each url parameter in the route URL.

So, in the case of `{foo}/{bar}/{baz}`, you would expect the dictionary to contain at least three keys: `"foo"`, `"bar"`, and `"baz"`. In the case of `/products/display/123`, the URL is used to supply values for these dictionary keys. In this case, `foo = products`, `bar = list`, and `baz = 123`.

Parameter Defaults and Optional Parameters

In some cases, you may want to specify a default value for a parameter. You can specify default values for parameters when you register your route. You can even specify defaults for the special parameter names `{controller}` and `{action}`. To set default values for a route, you use an override of the `MapRoute` method, assigning the `Defaults` property of the `Route` class. The default route when you create a new MVC app specifies default values for both the controller and the action.

> **NOTE** *If you changed the default route earlier in the chapter, you should change it back to this default route value that is used in the remaining examples.*

VB

```vb
routes.MapRoute( _
    name:="Default", _
    url:="{controller}/{action}/{id}", _
    defaults:=New With {.controller = "Home", .action = "Index", _
        .id = UrlParameter.Optional} _
)
```

C#

```csharp
routes.MapRoute(
    name: "Default",
    url: "{controller}/{action}/{id}",
    defaults: new { controller = "Home", action = "Index",
        id = UrlParameter.Optional }
);
```

You may also notice in the default mapping the use of `UrlParameter.Optional` for the `id` parameter. In certain situations, you may want to specify that a parameter does not have a default and that it is optional. You do this by specifying the default value for the parameter using a special value, `UrlParameter .Optional`. If you want to access this parameter in your action, declare the parameter as a `Nullable` type. Listing 34-2 shows the result of modifying Listing 34-1 to accept an optional parameter (Controllers/ ProductsController.cs and Controllers/ProductsController.vb in the code download for this chapter).

LISTING 34-2: A products controller action with an optional parameter

VB

```vb
Public Class ProductsController
    Inherits System.Web.Mvc.Controller

    Function Display(id As Integer?) As ActionResult
        'Do something
        Return View()
    End Function
End Class
```

C#

```csharp
using System.Web.Mvc;

public class ProductsController : Controller
{
  public ActionResult Display(int? id)
  {
    //Do something
    return View();
  }
}
```

CONTROLLERS

You might want to remember a quick definition: Controllers within the MVC pattern are responsible for responding to user input, often making changes to the model in response to user input.

In this way, controllers in the MVC pattern are concerned with the flow of the application, working with data coming in, and providing data going out to the relevant view.

Defining the Controller: The IController Interface

Among the core focuses of ASP.NET MVC are extensibility and flexibility. When building software with these goals in mind, leveraging abstraction as much as possible by using interfaces is important.

For a class to be a controller in ASP.NET MVC, it must at minimum implement the `IController` interface, and by convention the name of the class must end with the suffix `Controller`. The naming convention is actually quite important—and you'll find that many of these small rules are in play with ASP.NET MVC, which will make your life just a little bit easier by not making you define configuration settings and attributes. Ironically, the `IController` interface is quite simple given the power it is abstracting:

```csharp
public interface IController
{
  void Execute(RequestContext requestContext);
}
```

Creating an `IController` is a simple process, really. When a request comes in, the routing system identifies a controller, and it calls the `Execute` method.

The `ControllerBase` class is an abstract base class that layers a bit more API surface on top of the `IController` interface. It provides the `TempData`, `ViewData`, and `ViewBag` properties. The `Execute` method of `ControllerBase` is responsible for creating the `ControllerContext`, which provides the MVC-specific context for the current request much the same way that an instance of `HttpContext` provides the context for ASP.NET in general (providing request and response, URL, and server information, among other elements).

This base class is still very lightweight and enables developers to provide extremely customized implementations for their own controllers, while benefiting from the action filter infrastructure in ASP.NET MVC. What it doesn't provide is the ability to convert actions into method calls. That's where the `Controller` class comes in.

The Controller Class and Actions

In theory, you could build an entire site with classes that simply implement `ControllerBase` or `IController`, and it would work. Routing would look for an `IController` by name and then call `Execute`, and you would have yourself a very, very basic website.

This approach, however, is akin to working with ASP.NET using raw `HttpHandlers`—it would work, but you're left to reinvent the wheel and plumb the core framework logic yourself. Interestingly, ASP.NET MVC itself is layered on top of HTTP handlers, and overall there was no need to make internal plumbing changes to ASP.NET to implement MVC. Instead, the ASP.NET MVC team simply layered this framework on top of existing ASP.NET extensibility points. The standard approach to writing a controller is to have it inherit from the `System.Web.Mvc.Controller` abstract base class, which implements the `ControllerBase` base class. The `Controller` class is intended to serve as the base class for all controllers, because it provides a lot of nice behaviors to controllers that derive from it.

Now walk through another simple controller example, but this time, add a public method. Using the same project you have been working with previously, create a new controller by right-clicking the Controllers folder and selecting Add ➪ Controller and then name it **Simple2Controller**. Listing 34-3 shows the `Simple2Controller` after adding the necessary code (Controllers/Simple2Controller.vb and Controllers/Simple2Controller.cs in the code download for this chapter).

LISTING 34-3: Simple2Controller class

VB

```vb
Public Class Simple2Controller
    Inherits System.Web.Mvc.Controller

    Sub Hello()
        Response.Write("<h1>Hello World Again!</h1>")
    End Sub

End Class
```

C#

```csharp
using System.Web.Mvc;

public class Simple2Controller : Controller
{
    public void Hello()
    {
        Response.Write("<h1>Hello World Again!</h1>");
    }
}
```

Press Ctrl+F5 (or Debug ⇨ Run) and navigate to /Simple2/Hello in the browser. Figure 34-9 shows the result.

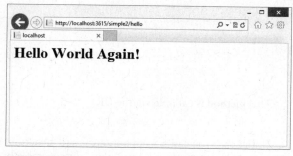

As before, this is not exactly breathtaking, but it is a bit more interesting. Notice that the URL in the address bar directly correlates to the action method of your controller. If you recall from earlier, the default route for MVC breaks URLs into three main components: /{controller}/ {action}/{id}.

FIGURE 34-9

Take a look at how that applies to this example. The Simple2 portion of the URL corresponds to the controller name. The MVC Framework appends the Controller suffix to the controller name and locates your controller class, Simple2Controller:

```
/Simple2/Hello
```

The last portion of the URL corresponds to the action. The framework locates a public method with this name and attempts to call the method.

Working with Parameters

You can add any number of public methods (which are called actions from here on out to keep with convention) to a controller class, which will all be callable via this pattern. Actions may also contain parameters. Going back to the Simple2Controller, add a new action method that takes in a parameter. Listing 34-4 shows the Simple2Controller after adding a Goodbye action (Controllers/Simple2Controller .vb and Controllers/Simple2Controller.cs in the code download for this chapter).

LISTING 34-4: Simple2Controller with added action

VB

```vb
Public Class Simple2Controller
    Inherits System.Web.Mvc.Controller

    Sub Hello()
        Response.Write("<h1>Hello World Again!</h1>")
    End Sub

    Sub Goodbye(name As String)
        Response.Write("Goodbye " + HttpUtility.HtmlEncode(name))
    End Sub

End Class
```

C#

```csharp
using System.Web;
using System.Web.Mvc;

    public class Simple2Controller : Controller
    {
        public void Hello()
        {
            Response.Write("<h1>Hello World Again!</h1>");
        }

        public void Goodbye(string name)
```

continues

LISTING 34-4 *(continued)*

```
        {
            Response.Write("Goodbye " + HttpUtility.HtmlEncode(name));
        }
    }
```

This method is callable via the URL:

```
/Simple2/Goodbye?name=World
```

Notice that you can pass in parameters to an action method by name via the query string. You can also pass in parameters via the URL segments, discoverable by position as defined in your routes. For example, the following URL is more aesthetically pleasing to many developers and Internet users:

```
/Simple2/Goodbye/World
```

Working with parameters passed by URL segment requires you to define how routing will identify these parameters in the URL. Fortunately, the default route (created for you when you click File ⇨ New) is already set up for you and contains a common URL pattern:

```
{controller}/{action}/{id}.
```

Changing the action method signature in the Simple2Controller a little bit (by renaming the parameter "name" to "id") as shown in C#:

```
public void Goodbye(string id)
{
    Response.Write("Goodbye " + HttpUtility.HtmlEncode(id));
}
```

enables you to call that method using the "cleaner" URL, and routing will pass the parameter by structured URL instead of a query string parameter:

```
/Simple2/Goodbye/World
```

Working with Multiple Parameters

What if you have a method with more than one parameter? This scenario is very common, and rest assured that you can still use query strings, but if you want to pass both parameters via the URL segments, you must define a new route specifically for this situation.

For example, suppose that you have an action method in C# that calculates the distance between two points:

```
public void Distance(int x1, int y1, int x2, int y2)
{
    double xSquared = Math.Pow(x2 - x1, 2);
    double ySquared = Math.Pow(y2 - y1, 2);
    Response.Write(Math.Sqrt(xSquared + ySquared));
}
```

Using only the default route, the request would need to look like this:

```
/Simple2/Distance?x2=1&y2=2&x1=0&y1=0
```

You can improve on this situation a bit by defining a route that enables you to specify the parameters in a cleaner format. If you remember from the section in this chapter on routing, it was mentioned that you could specify multiple parameters in a segment if you separated them with a constant. This is a good time for an example of that! In the RegisterRoutes static method within the RouteConfig.cs or RouteConfig.vb file, you can use the MapRoute method to define the new route:

```
routes.MapRoute("distance",
    "Simple2/Distance/{x1},{y1}/{x2},{y2}",
    new { Controller = "Simple2", action = "Distance" }
);
```

Notice that you are using the comma character to separate x and y coordinates. Now this action method is callable via the URL:

```
/Simple2/Distance/0,0/1,2
```

The presence of commas in a URL might look strange, but routing is quite powerful!

So far you've used `Response.Write` in these little example methods, but this violates the principle of separation of concerns. It's really not the business of a controller to be managing the "views" of your data. That's something better handled by the "V" in MVC; that is, views.

VIEWS

The view is responsible for providing the user interface (UI) to the user. It is given a reference to the model, and it transforms that model into a format ready to be presented to the user. In ASP.NET MVC, this consists of examining the `ViewDataDictionary` handed off to it by the controller (accessed via the `ViewData` or `ViewBag` property) and transforming that to HTML. Note that `ViewBag` is a wrapper around the `ViewData` object that enables you to create dynamic properties for the `ViewBag` instead of using "magic" strings as keys in the `ViewData` object.

In the strongly typed view case, which is covered in more depth in the section "Strongly Typed Views" later in the chapter, the `ViewDataDictionary` has a strongly typed `Model` object that the view renders. This model might represent the actual domain object, such as a `Product` instance, or it might be a presentation model object specific to the view, such as a `ProductEditViewData` instance.

Take a quick look at an example of a view. The following code sample shows the Index view within the C# version of the default ASP.NET MVC project template:

```
@{
    ViewBag.Title = "Home Page";
}
@section featured {
    <section class="featured">
        <div class="content-wrapper">
            <hgroup class="title">
                <h1>@ViewBag.Title.</h1>
                <h2>@ViewBag.Message</h2>
            </hgroup>
            <p>
                To learn more about ASP.NET MVC visit
                <a href="http://asp.net/mvc" title="ASP.NET MVC
                    Website">http://asp.net/mvc</a>.
                The page features <mark>videos, tutorials, and samples</mark> to
                    help you get the most from ASP.NET MVC.
                If you have any questions about ASP.NET MVC visit
                <a href="http://forums.asp.net/1146.aspx/1?MVC"
                    title="ASP.NET MVC Forum">our forums</a>.
            </p>
        </div>
    </section>
}
<h3>We suggest the following:</h3>
<ol class="round">
    <li class="one">
        <h5>Getting Started</h5>
        ASP.NET MVC gives you a powerful, patterns-based way to build dynamic
        websites that enables a clean separation of concerns and that gives you
        full control over markup for enjoyable, agile development. ASP.NET MVC
        includes many features that enable fast, TDD-friendly development for
        creating sophisticated applications that usethe latest web standards.
        <a href="http://go.microsoft.com/fwlink/?LinkId=245151">Learn more . . . </a>
```

```
        </li>

        <li class="two">
            <h5>Add NuGet packages and jump-start your coding</h5>
            NuGet makes it easy to install and update free libraries and tools.
            <a href="http://go.microsoft.com/fwlink/?LinkId=245153">Learn more . . . </a>
        </li>

        <li class="three">
            <h5>Find Web Hosting</h5>
            You can easily find a web hosting company that offers the right mix of
            Features and price for your applications.
            <a href="http://go.microsoft.com/fwlink/?LinkId=245157">Learn more . . . </a>
        </li>
    </ol>
```

This is an extremely simple example of a view, but it's useful for pointing out some of the key details of views in ASP.NET MVC. One of the first things you may notice is the use of @{ and } used to delimit certain blocks of text. These characters are used to define a code block to the Razor view engine, which is the default view engine used to render ASP.NET MVC views. You will see more of this Razor syntax later in the chapter. One of the additional things you'll notice is that some of the standard HTML page elements are missing. There are no doctype, html, head, or body elements. Much like master pages in Web Forms, Layouts in ASP.NET MVC enables you to define a common template for the site that can be inherited by all of the views on your site. Layouts are covered a little later in this chapter.

If you are familiar with the page directive on Web Forms, you will also notice there is no page directive. That is because this is not a Web Form. In fact, this view is not even rendered using the `WebFormViewEngine`. ASP.NET MVC enables you to swap out different view engines, but the default view Engine is `RazorViewEngine`.

Views in ASP.NET MVC derive from either the `System.Web.Mvc.ViewPage`, which itself derives from `System.Web.UI.Page` (in the case of the `WebFormViewEngine`) or the `System.Web.Mvc.WebViewPage`, which derives from `System.Web.WebPages.WebPageBase` (in the case of the `RazorViewEngine`). Strongly typed views derive from the generic `ViewPage<T>` or `WebViewPage<T>`, again depending on the view engine.

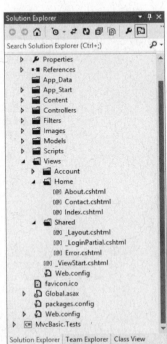

In keeping with the principle of separation of concerns, views should not contain application and business logic. In fact, they should contain as little code as possible. Although it's perfectly acceptable for a view to contain view logic, views are generally the most difficult part of the application to test in an automated fashion, and they, therefore, benefit from having very little code.

Specifying a View

So far, this chapter has discussed what a view does and doesn't do, but it hasn't addressed how to specify the view that should render the output for a specific action. It turns out that this task is very easy when you follow the conventions implicit in the framework.

When you create a new project template, notice that the project contains a Views directory structured in a very specific manner (see Figure 34-10).

By convention, the Views directory contains a folder per controller, with the same name as the controller, sans the `Controller` suffix. Within each Controller folder, there's a view file for each action method, named the same as the action method. This provides the basis for how views are associated to an action method.

FIGURE 34-10

For example, an action method can return a `ViewResult` via the `View` method like so:

```
public class HomeController : Controller
{
    public ActionResult Index()
    {
        ViewBag.Title = "Home Page";
        ViewBag.Message = "Welcome to ASP.NET MVC!";
        return View();
    }
}
```

This method ought to look familiar; it's the `Index` action method of `HomeController` in the default project template. Because the view name was not specified, the `ViewResult` returned by this method looks for a view named the same as the action name in the `/Views/ControllerName` directory. The view selected in this case would be `/Views/Home/Index.cshtml` or `/Views/Home/Index.vbhtml`.

As with most things in ASP.NET MVC, this convention can be overridden. Suppose that you want the `Index` action to render a different view. You could supply a different view name like so:

```
public ActionResult Index()
{
    ViewBag.Title = "Home Page";
    ViewBag.Message = "Welcome to ASP.NET MVC!";
    return View("NotIndex");
}
```

In this case, it will still look in the `/Views/Home` directory, but choose `NotIndex.cshtml` or `NotIndex.vbhtml` as the view. In some situations, you might even want to specify a view in a completely different directory structure.

You can use the tilde syntax to provide the full path to the view like so:

```
public ActionResult Index()
{
    ViewBag.Title = "Home Page";
    ViewBag.Message = "Welcome to ASP.NET MVC!";
    return View("~/Some/Other/View.cshtml");
}
```

When using the tilde syntax, you must supply the file extension of the view because this bypasses the view engine's internal lookup mechanism for finding views.

ASP.NET MVC Layouts

You typically want to create a similar look and feel to your entire site, or at least to various sections of your site. ASP.NET 2.0 introduced the concept of "master pages" to accomplish this when using `.aspx` pages in a typical Web Forms application. Razor supports a feature called Layouts that supports this same concept in Razor views.

The easiest way to explore layouts in Razor views is to look at the default project created earlier in the chapter. If you review Figure 34-10, you will see a folder located under the Views folder that has no corresponding controller, the Shared folder. While most of the views are located in folders corresponding to the controller that provides the data to them, the views in the Shared folder are meant to be "shared" by more than one view. You will also note that many of the views in the Shared folder follow a naming convention having a leading underscore. This convention is carried over from ASP.NET Web Pages, which doesn't have the same sort of protection built in regarding Views folders and routing that you get within MVC. Layout pages are not intended to be served and browsed directly. The Web Pages framework has been configured not to allow a file with a leading underscore in its name to be requested directly. The following code sample shows the C# version of the layout file:

```
<!DOCTYPE html>
<html lang="en">
    <head>
        <meta charset="utf-8" />
        <title>@ViewBag.Title - My ASP.NET MVC Application</title>
        <link href="~/favicon.ico" rel="shortcut icon" type="image/x-icon" />
        <meta name="viewport" content="width=device-width" />
        @Styles.Render("~/Content/css")
        @Scripts.Render("~/bundles/modernizr")
    </head>
    <body>
        <header>
            <div class="content-wrapper">
                <div class="float-left">
                    <p class="site-title">
                        @Html.ActionLink("your logo here", "Index", "Home")
                    </p>
                </div>
                <div class="float-right">
                    <section id="login">
                        @Html.Partial("_LoginPartial")
                    </section>
                    <nav>
                        <ul id="menu">
                            <li>@Html.ActionLink("Home", "Index", "Home")</li>
                            <li>@Html.ActionLink("About", "About", "Home")</li>
                            <li>@Html.ActionLink("Contact", "Contact",
                                "Home")</li>
                        </ul>
                    </nav>
                </div>
            </div>
        </header>
        <div id="body">
            @RenderSection("featured", required: false)
            <section class="content-wrapper main-content clear-fix">
                @RenderBody()
            </section>
        </div>
        <footer>
            <div class="content-wrapper">
                <div class="float-left">
                    <p>&copy; @DateTime.Now.Year - My ASP.NET MVC Application</p>
                </div>
            </div>
        </footer>

        @Scripts.Render("~/bundles/jquery")
        @RenderSection("scripts", required: false)
    </body>
</html>
```

The first thing you should notice is the doctype, html, head, and body tags that were mentioned as missing when first looking at the Index view. This layout file is inherited, by default, by all the views in the site. The next important thing to note is the call to @RenderBody(). The views that are based on this layout file insert their content where this call is made.

A view can specify that it should use a layout page by setting the Layout property on the WebPageBase class. You can do this in the view itself using a Razor code block as shown here:

```
@{
    Layout = "~/Views/Shared/_Layout.cshtml";
}
```

This property must be set on all views that want to use a layout. You can have multiple layout files for a site and specify the particular layout file to be used on each view by simply changing the name of the layout file in that view. Setting the Layout property on all of your views would require a lot of duplicated code. To prevent so much duplication, you can use another feature of Razor that enables you to define layout logic for all views in a single location. This not only cuts down on duplication, but makes your code more maintainable. You can add a file called _ViewStart.cshtml or _ViewStart.vbhtml to the Views folder. The _ViewStart file can be used to define common view code that will execute at the start of the rendering of each view. You can move the setting of the Layout property from the view to the _ViewStart file and it will be applied to all views. You can override this in any view simply by setting the Layout property to a different layout in that view. In the default template, the _ViewStart file contains the code block shown in the preceding code setting the Layout property. You can specify the layout to be used in a view when creating the view using the Add View dialog box in Visual Studio. Figure 34-11 shows the Add View dialog box with the "Use a layout or master page" option checked. Notice that you can leave the layout filename field blank if you are using the _ViewStart file.

FIGURE 34-11

Another important thing you will see in the layout file are calls to the @RenderSection method. So far you have only looked at the main body section of the layout file rendered using the @RenderBody method. Razor also supports created multiple "named sections" that can be used to render dynamic content to multiple, non-contiguous, regions of the final response. The first parameter to the @RenderSection method is the name of the section. This name is used to specify the content of the section in the view. You can specify a section as required or optional by setting the required parameter. Look again at the layout file code snippet shown earlier. You will see a named section called "featured" rendered by the call to @RenderSection:

```
@RenderSection("featured", required: false)
```

Now look at the Index view in the Views/Home folder. The view contains a section called "featured." No matter where the "featured" section is in the view file, it will be displayed at the point in the layout where the corresponding @RenderSection is called. The following code sample shows the section block in the Index view:

```
@section featured {
    <section class="featured">
        <div class="content-wrapper">
            <hgroup class="title">
                <h1>@ViewBag.Title.</h1>
                <h2>@ViewBag.Message</h2>
            </hgroup>
            <p>
                To learn more about ASP.NET MVC visit
                <a href="http://asp.net/mvc" title="ASP.NET MVC
                    Website">http://asp.net/mvc</a>.
```

```
        The page features <mark>videos, tutorials, and samples</mark> to
        help you get the most from ASP.NET MVC.
        If you have any questions about ASP.NET MVC visit
        <a href="http://forums.asp.net/1146.aspx/1?MVC" title="ASP.NET MVC
            Forum">our forums</a>.
      </p>
    </div>
  </section>
}
```

Notice that sections in views can contain both static and dynamic content. Using sections enables you to organize the content in a view file without regard to the order in which it will be finally rendered. Sections also allow a layout file to specify multiple locations for dynamic content from the view being rendered.

Strongly Typed Views

Suppose that you have a list of Product instances you want to display in a view. One means of doing this is to simply add the products to the view data dictionary and iterate them over the view.

For example, the code in your controller action might look like this:

```
public ActionResult List()
{
    var products = new List<Product>();
        for(int i = 0; i < 10; i++)
        {
            products.Add(new Product {ProductName = "Product " + i});
        }
    ViewBag.Products = products;
    return View();
}
```

In your view, you can then iterate and display the products like so using Razor syntax:

```
<ul>
@foreach (Product p in ViewBag.Products){
    <li>@p.ProductName</li>
}
</ul>
```

The ViewBag contains dynamic properties and is not strongly typed, therefore a conversion is required in the foreach loop. The code would be cleaner if you could provide the view with the type for the model being sent in. This is where strongly typed views come in.

In the controller method, you can specify the model via an overload of the View method whereby you pass in the model:

```
public ActionResult List()
{
    var products = new List<Product>();
    for(int i = 0; i < 10; i++)
        {
            products.Add(new Product {ProductName = "Product " + i});
        }
    return View(products);
}
```

Behind the scenes, this sets the value of the ViewData.Model property to the value passed into the View method. The next step is to change the type of the view to inherit from WebViewPage<T>. The view really has no business having a code-behind file in the MVC model. In fact, by default, no code-behind files exist for views in ASP.NET MVC. If you want strongly typed views, just add the type to the @Model directive in the View like this:

```
@Model System.Collections.Generic.List<MvcBasic.Models.Product>
```

This is the preferred way to have strongly typed views. Now within the markup for the view, you can access the strongly typed `ViewData.Model` property, with full IntelliSense support:

```
<ul>
@foreach (Product p in Model){
    <li>@p.ProductName</li>
}
</ul>
```

Using HTML Helper Methods

One of the traits of the ASP.NET MVC Framework often touted is that it puts you in full control of your application, including the HTML markup. Many announce this as a benefit of the framework. After all, full control is good, right? But it's really a characteristic of the framework that's only good or bad depending on the circumstance.

At times you don't want to have control over the markup. You would rather drop a control and have it figure out the markup because you don't care how it looks. Other times, you want to have absolute control over the markup. Being in control is great, but it also means more responsibility. You are now responsible for outputting markup that would have otherwise been handled by a server control in the Web Forms world.

HTML helpers provide a middle ground. These are methods included with the framework that help with rendering markup for very common cases. In most cases, they handle common mistakes such as forgetting to encode attribute values and so on.

HtmlHelper Class and Extension Methods

The `WebViewPage` class has an `HtmlHelper` property named `Html`. When you look at the methods of `HtmlHelper`, you'll notice they are rather sparse. This property is really an anchor point for attaching extension methods. When you import the `System.Web.Mvc.Html` namespace (imported by default in the default template), the `Html` property suddenly lights up with a bunch of helper methods.

In the screenshot in Figure 34-12, the extension methods are denoted by the gray down arrow.

One benefit of the `HtmlHelper`-style approach is that, because they are just regular extension methods, if you don't like the helper methods included with the framework, you can remove this namespace and attach your own HTML helper extension methods. Likewise, it provides a convenient conventional place to add your own helper methods by simply writing extension methods of the `HtmlHelper` class.

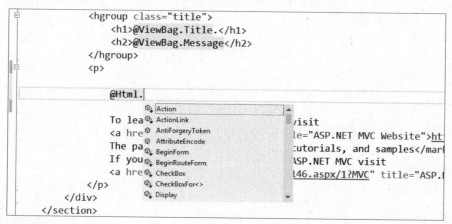

FIGURE 34-12

All helpers share a few common patterns that are worth calling out now:

➤ All helpers' attributes encode attribute values.

➤ All helpers HTML encode values they display, such as link text.

➤ Helpers that accept a `RouteValueDictionary` have a corresponding overload that enables you to specify an anonymous object as the dictionary.

➤ Likewise, helpers that accept an `IDictionary<string, object>` used to specify HTML attributes, have a corresponding overload that enables you to specify an anonymous object as the dictionary.

➤ Helpers used to render form fields will automatically look up their current value in the `ModelState` dictionary. The name argument to the helper is used as the key to the dictionary.

➤ If the `ModelState` contains an error, the form helper associated with that error will render a CSS class of `input-validation-error` in addition to any explicitly specified CSS classes. The default style sheet, `style.css`, included in the project template contains styling for this class.

Views and their `ViewEngines` have a very specific, constrained purpose. They exist to take data passed to them from the controller, and they generate formatted output, usually HTML. Other than those simple responsibilities, or "concerns," as the developer, you are empowered to achieve the goals of your view in any way that makes you happy.

SUMMARY

The ASP.NET Web Forms developer will need to get used to many differences when working with ASP.NET MVC versus Web Forms. In many ways, working with ASP.NET MVC will feel like "taking a step back 10 years" to classic ASP—especially when working with the UI and views.

For some, this is a welcome change and a breath of fresh air; for others, it just doesn't work. It does take some getting used to, but in the end, the core ASP.NET functionality and the .NET Framework in general are there to support you.

Ultimately, the most important thing to remember is that ASP.NET Web Forms and ASP.NET MVC sit on top of ASP.NET proper. Think of it as ASP.NET > Web Forms and ASP.NET > ASP.NET MVC. There's so much underneath both techniques that you can use either or both without fear. Many people find a hybrid model works for them, or they use a hybrid as they move from one model to the other. Pick the model that makes you feel most productive and run with it.

35

ASP.NET Web Pages and Razor

WHAT'S IN THIS CHAPTER?

➤ Introduction to ASP.NET Web Pages
➤ An overview of Razor syntax
➤ Displaying data using Razor
➤ Using Helper functions

WROX.COM CODE DOWNLOADS FOR THIS CHAPTER

Please note that all the code examples in this chapter are available as a part of this chapter's code download on the book's website at www.wrox.com on the Download Code tab.

Throughout this book, we've mentioned "Classic" ASP. You may not have had the privilege of using this great technology. However, if you have, developing ASP.NET Web Pages using the Razor syntax may bring back some of those fond memories. But this technology is much different. Throughout this chapter, you get a chance to see how using Web Pages with Razor can offer a more powerful solution than "Classic" ASP.

The previous chapter discussed ASP.NET MVC. At that point, you had the chance to use the ASP.NET WebForm view engine. You also had a few peeks at using another view engine option, the Razor view engine. The Razor view engine uses the same Razor syntax that Web Pages uses. If your application becomes too complex for ASP.NET Web Pages, it makes the most sense to begin moving pieces to ASP.NET MVC with the Razor view engine.

> **NOTE** *Razor is more than a view engine. Rather, its primary purpose is to be a templating engine.*

Although the ASP.NET MVC Razor view engine is not covered in this chapter, you'll get a good feel for how the Razor syntax works. You'll be able to use the syntax with the MVC principles you learned in the previous chapter.

> **NOTE** *The purpose of this chapter is to provide an overview of Web Pages, the Razor syntax, and ASP.NET WebMatrix. Unfortunately, there is not enough room to cover every possible topic about Web Pages and Razor in this book. If you're interested in learning more about Web Pages and Razor, be sure to check out Professional ASP.NET MVC 4 (also from Wrox) by Jon Galloway, Phil Haack, Brad Wilson, and K. Scott Allen or search online for more details about Web Pages, Razor, or WebMatrix.*

OVERVIEW OF ASP.NET WEB PAGES

ASP.NET Web Pages are a fairly new technology that Microsoft introduced to develop dynamic web applications using ASP.NET, but not necessarily needing Microsoft Visual Studio 2012. Instead, you can develop ASP.NET Web Pages using a basic text editor like Notepad or the preferred method, using an IDE such as ASP.NET WebMatrix.

> **NOTE** *ASP.NET WebMatrix has many capabilities beyond ASP.NET Web Pages. From within WebMatrix, developers can connect to NuGet; access sites remotely; run sites locally using IISExpress; capture request and response traffic from IISExpress; and even develop PHP, node.js, and other applications from within the IDE. Similarly to other ASP.NET technologies, the ASP.NET WebMatrix team is looking to compress the release schedule. Be sure to search online to find the latest version.*

Unlike a static HTML page, a dynamic page allows the end user to interact with web forms, manipulate and save data, and interact with third-party services such as social media services.

> **NOTE** *Web Pages 2 offers several new features and benefits over the first version of the technology. This chapter focuses entirely on using Web Pages 2, and introduces ASP.NET WebMatrix 2, which is a free IDE. However, you could use Visual Studio 2012 to develop the same pages.*

Similar to ASP.NET MVC, Web Pages allows extensibility in several areas. One way to extend Web Pages is to create and consume *helpers*. Helpers are very similar to ASP.NET Server Controls in that most helpers encapsulate reusable markup. As you see throughout this chapter, several helpers are built into Web Pages. You can include others by using NuGet (discussed further in Appendix G) or through custom development.

CREATING AN HTML FORM USING RAZOR

Before you begin building a web page using Razor, you need to know more about using the Razor syntax. In ASP.NET Web Forms, you define inline code by using a script block such as:

```
<script runat="server">
    // Insert code here
</script>
```

The Razor syntax is slightly different. You can still define inline code. However, rather than using a script block in the preceding format, you can define script blocks as shown in Listing 35-1.

LISTING 35-1: The Razor script block for VB and C#

VB

```
@Code
    'Place Code Here
End Code
```

C#

```
@{
    <!-- Insert code here -->
}
```

Before jumping into specific features and helpers within Web Pages, create an HTML page that you can begin using. To do this, use WebMatrix. When you open WebMatrix, you are prompted for an action as shown in Figure 35-1.

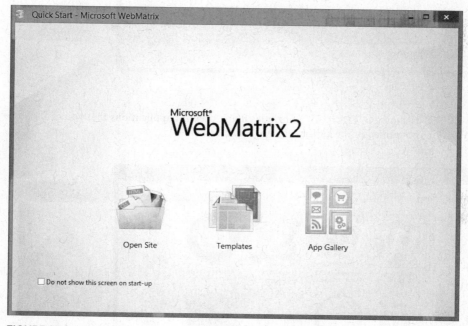

FIGURE 35-1

From this screen, you can see that you have four options. You can open an existing site, use a site template, or load an application using the application gallery. You can also choose to never show this quick menu again and instead load WebMatrix with file browser capabilities. You can also open an existing site, use a site template, or load an application using the application gallery.

The site template list, as shown in Figure 35-2, includes several web templates for ASP.NET, PHP, node.js, and HTML. The ASP.NET templates are for sample applications using Web Pages.

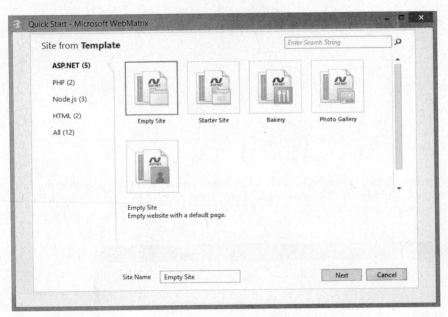

FIGURE 35-2

The application gallery, as shown in Figure 35-3, includes many prebuilt applications that you can load. Most of the applications contained in the gallery use ASP.NET or PHP.

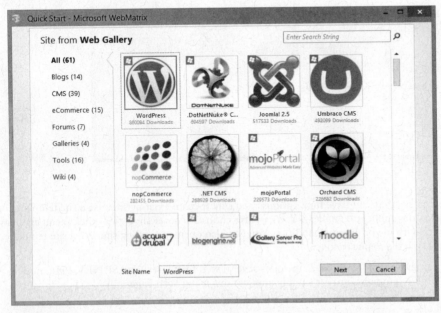

FIGURE 35-3

For this exercise, choose to use an existing site. When you do, you are faced with three options as shown in Figure 35-4.

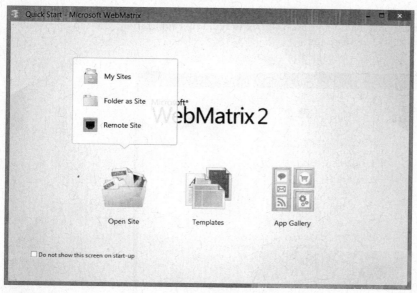

FIGURE 35-4

> ➤ The top option is to choose from My Sites. This enables you to see each website that you've set up to use your local version of IIS or IIS Express.

> ➤ The bottom option enables you to connect to a remote server.

> ➤ Because you are going to create a brand new Web Pages application, choose the Folder as Site option. This enables you to browse to a folder on the machine (or network) and create an application binding with a random port number.

The application spins up within WebMatrix and an empty robots.txt file is added, as shown in Figure 35-5.

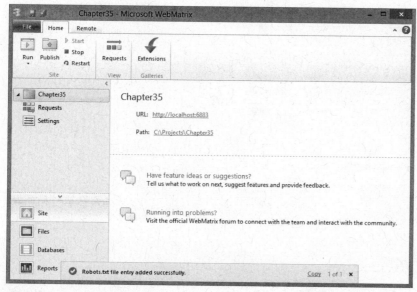

FIGURE 35-5

The next step in building your Web Pages application is to switch over to the Files view. You'll notice in Figure 35-6 that even though you are using WebMatrix to build this application, you can open your application in Visual Studio 2012 at any point.

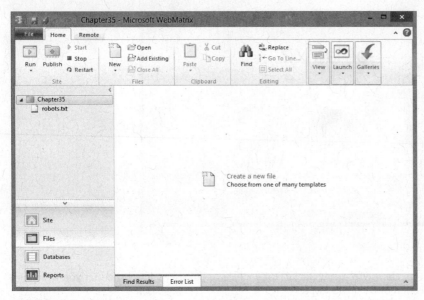

FIGURE 35-6

So, at this point you've created your Web Pages application, you're in WebMatrix, and you're about to add a file to your application. As you can see in Figure 35-6, it's very easy to add a file. Choose the option to create a new file. You are then asked to choose a particular file type, as shown in Figure 35-7. Although you'll be creating HTML in the next step, choose one of the two Razor formats for Web Pages—.cshtml for a C# Web Page or .vbhtml for a VB Web Page.

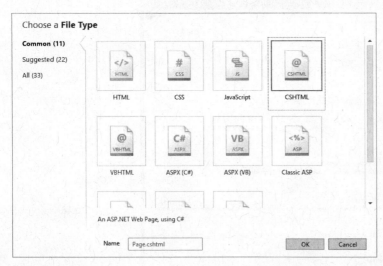

FIGURE 35-7

Name your file **addtask.cshtml** for C# or **addtask.vbhtml** for VB. This creates a file very similar to the following snippet:

```
@{

}
<!DOCTYPE html>
<html lang="en">
    <head>
        <meta charset="utf-8" />
        <title></title>
    </head>
    <body>
    </body>
</html>
```

DISPLAYING DATA

As you can see in the previous code snippet, a basic Razor code block is included at the top of your page. The rest of the page contains HTML for a basic page.

Much like ASP.NET Web Forms, Razor has the capability of connecting to a database and interacting with data. Furthermore, WebMatrix has capabilities to create a database from within the application. If you look back to Figure 35-6, you'll see a Databases tab in the lower left-hand corner of WebMatrix. When the Databases tab is opened, you'll be able to create a database in a similar fashion as when you added the addtask file earlier in this chapter. WebMatrix offers three built-in options for a database. The default option is SQL Server CE (Compact Edition). This database extension ends in `.sdf`. You can also create a SQL Server database or a MySQL database. For your application, leave the default option and create your database as shown in Figure 35-8.

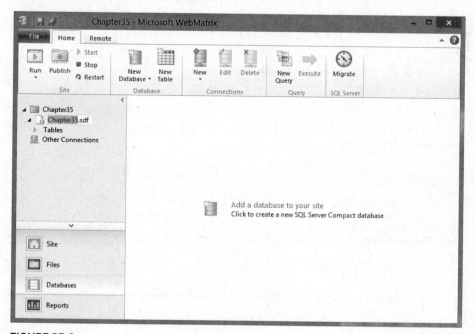

FIGURE 35-8

After the database is created, add a table to store your tasks. The table is going to be fairly straightforward—define the table as shown in Figure 35-9.

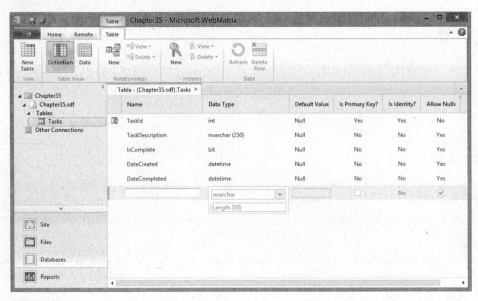

FIGURE 35-9

So, now that your data structure is in place, it's time to go back to your addtask Web Page. You'll add the form elements you'll need to add a task. In this case, you only need a textbox and submit button to add tasks. The HTML for addtask looks like Listing 35-2 (`addtask.vbhtml` or `addtask.cshtml` in the code download for this chapter).

LISTING 35-2: The body of the addtask page of your application

```
<!DOCTYPE html>
<html lang="en">
    <head>
        <meta charset="utf-8" />
        <title>Add a Task</title>
    </head>
    <body>
        <form action="" method="post">
            <p>
                <label for="taskDescription">Task:</label>
                <input type="text" id="taskDescription" name="taskDescription" />
            </p>
            <input type="submit" value="Add Task" />
        </form>
    </body>
</html>
```

The next step in is to add in the connection to the database and add the tasks to the database, as shown in Listing 35-3.

LISTING 35-3: Adding data into the database using the addtask page

VB

```vb
@Code
    Dim taskDescription = ""

    If (IsPost) Then
        taskDescription = Request.Form("taskDescription")

        Dim db = Database.Open("Chapter35-VB")
        Dim insertCommand = "INSERT INTO Tasks (TaskDescription, DateCreated) Values(@0, @1)"
        db.Execute(insertCommand, taskDescription, DateTime.Now)
        db.Close()
        Response.Redirect("~/")
    End If
End Code

<!DOCTYPE html>
<html lang="en">
    <head>
        <meta charset="utf-8" />
        <title>Add a Task</title>
    </head>
    <body>
        <form action="" method="post">
            <p>
                <label for="taskDescription">Task:</label>
                <input type="text" id="taskDescription" name="taskDescription" />
            </p>
            <input type="submit" value="Add Task" />
        </form>
    </body>
</html>
```

C#

```csharp
@{
    var taskDescription = "";

    if(IsPost){
        taskDescription = Request.Form["taskDescription"];

        var db = Database.Open("Chapter35");
        var insertCommand = "INSERT INTO Tasks (TaskDescription, DateCreated) Values(@0, @1)";
        db.Execute(insertCommand, taskDescription, DateTime.Now);
        db.Close();
        Response.Redirect("~/");
    }
}
```

You're not completely done with this page. You'll revisit the page in just a little bit to add last-minute tweaks.

Your next step in the project is to list all of the tasks. Because this is the primary purpose of the application, the task listing will appear on your default page. Add the default.cshtml or default.vbhtml file to your application so you can begin adding the necessary code to display the tasks. You're not expecting that your data will grow to a size where you'll need data paging, so you'll add two items to your default page. The first item is the output generated from a WebGrid helper, and the second item is a hyperlink to allow the user to add additional tasks to the list. The completed default page's source code is shown in Listing 35-4.

LISTING 35-4: Listing the tasks entered on the default page

VB

```vb
@Code
    Dim db = Database.Open("Chapter35-VB")
    Dim tasks = db.Query("SELECT * FROM Tasks WHERE IsComplete = 0 or IsComplete IS NULL")
    Dim grid = New WebGrid(tasks)
End Code
<!DOCTYPE html>
<html lang="en">
    <head>
        <meta charset="utf-8" />
        <title></title>
        <style type="text/css">
            .grid { margin: 4px; padding: 2px; border: 1px solid #666; }
            .grid td, th { border: 1px solid #fff; padding: 5px; }
            .head { background-color: #36648B; }
            .head a { color: #FFF; text-decoration-style: none; }
            .alt { background-color: #F0F8FF; }
        </style>
    </head>
    <body>
        <h1>Open Tasks</h1>
        <div>
            @grid.GetHtml(
                tableStyle:= "grid",
                headerStyle:= "head",
                alternatingRowStyle:= "alt",
                columns:= grid.Columns(
                    grid.Column("TaskDescription","Task")
                )
            )
        </div>
        <p>
            <a href="addtask.vbhtml">Add More Tasks</a>
        </p>
    </body>
</html>
```

C#

```csharp
@{
    var db = Database.Open("Chapter35");
    var tasks = db.Query("SELECT * FROM Tasks WHERE IsComplete = 0 or IsComplete IS NULL");
    var grid = new WebGrid(source: tasks);
}
<!DOCTYPE html>
<html lang="en">
    <head>
        <meta charset="utf-8" />
        <title></title>
        <style type="text/css">
            .grid { margin: 4px; padding: 2px; border: 1px solid #666; }
            .grid td, th { border: 1px solid #fff; padding: 5px; }
            .head { background-color: #36648B; }
            .head a { color: #FFF; text-decoration-style: none; }
            .alt { background-color: #F0F8FF; }
        </style>
    </head>
```

```
<body>
    <h1>Open Tasks</h1>
    <div>
        @grid.GetHtml(
            tableStyle: "grid",
            headerStyle: "head",
            alternatingRowStyle: "alt",
            columns: grid.Columns(
                grid.Column("TaskDescription","Task")
            )
        )
    </div>
    <p>
        <a href="addtask.cshtml">Add More Tasks</a>
    </p>
</body>
</html>
```

Like most helpers in the Razor syntax, the WebGrid helper enables you to set a custom set of properties within code. In this case, you're setting three style properties and adding a custom list of columns. The list of columns contains only the task description itself. The first parameter of the column is the SQL column name. The second is the friendly column header to be added to the rendered HTML.

Validation

Let's revisit the addtask page. Currently, you have no restrictions on the data that you're allowing to be inserted into your database table. So, you can have someone type in more than 250 characters or leave the field blank. Obviously, this isn't going to give you the experience you're anticipating. So, you have to update the AddTask page to include validation. The validation you're going to add includes a ValidationSummary helper, which is very similar to the ValidationSummary Web Form control discussed in Chapter 6. You're also going to add validation to the taskDescription element.

In your source code, you'll need to define your validation rules. In this case, set the task as being required and force a length of 250 characters or less. Use Validation.RequireField and Validation.Add to accomplish these tasks. Validation.Add accepts the element name in the first parameter and a validation type in the second parameter. The validation types that are available include:

➤ Validator.DateTime ([error message])

➤ Validator.Decimal([error message])

➤ Validator.EqualsTo([other element],[error message])

➤ Validator.Float([error message])

➤ Validator.Integer([error message])

➤ Validator.Range([min],[max],[error message])

➤ Validator.RegEx([regex pattern],[error message])

➤ Validator.Required([error message])

➤ Validator.StringLength([maximum length])

➤ Validator.Url([error message])

Much like Web Forms, you'll also need to check to see if the page is valid. Call Validation.IsValid to ensure this. Also, to show that you can use individual errors rather than just supplying the summary, you'll display the user-friendly error message by using the ValidationMessage helper. Listing 35-5 shows the addtask page with the validation implemented.

LISTING 35-5: Updating the addtask page with validation

VB

```vb
@Code
    ' Variables
    Dim taskDescription = ""

    ' Validation
    Validation.RequireField("taskDescription", "A task is required.")
    Validation.Add("taskDescription", Validator.StringLength(250))

    ' If the page has been posted back and if it's valid, insert the data and redirect
    If (IsPost) Then
        If (Validation.IsValid()) Then
            taskDescription = Request.Form("taskDescription")

            Dim db = Database.Open("Chapter35-VB")
            Dim insertCommand = _
              "INSERT INTO Tasks (TaskDescription, DateCreated) Values(@0, @1)"
            db.Execute(insertCommand, taskDescription, DateTime.Now)
            Response.Redirect("~/")
        End If
    End If
End Code

<!DOCTYPE html>
<html lang="en">
    <head>
        <meta charset="utf-8" />
        <title>Add a Task</title>
    </head>
    <body>
        <form action="" method="post">
            <div>
                @Html.ValidationSummary()
            </div>
            <p>
                <label for="taskDescription">Task:</label>
                <input type="text" id="taskDescription" name="taskDescription" />
                @Html.ValidationMessage("taskDescription")
            </p>
            <input type="submit" value="Add Task" />
        </form>
    </body>
</html>
```

C#

```csharp
@{
    // Variables
    var taskDescription = "";

    // Validation
    Validation.RequireField("taskDescription", "A task is required.");
    Validation.Add("taskDescription", Validator.StringLength(250));

    // If the page has been posted back and if it's valid, insert the data and redirect
    if(IsPost){
        if (Validation.IsValid()) {
```

```
            taskDescription = Request.Form["taskDescription"];

            var db = Database.Open("Chapter35");
            var insertCommand =
              "INSERT INTO Tasks (TaskDescription, DateCreated) Values(@0, @1)";
            db.Execute(insertCommand, taskDescription, DateTime.Now);
            Response.Redirect("~/");
        }
    }
}
```

Using Layouts

One of the most useful features on Razor is the template capabilities that it has. Usually this is referring to the data templates that we can create. However, Razor also includes website templates in the form of layouts. Layouts are very similar to the master page found in ASP.NET Web Forms. You can use RenderBody to render everything from one file inside of the layout container. You can also use RenderSection to specify the content to be rendered inside of a certain area. Listing 35-6 shows an example of both of these helpers in the _layout.cshtml or _layout.vbhtml page.

LISTING 35-6: An example layout page derived from the _layout.cshtml file

```
@{
    var sidebarStyle = "#Sidebar { float: right; margin: 0; width: 15%; " +
                       "padding: 5px; background-color: #f2f2f2; border: 1px solid #999; } " +
                       "#MainContent { float: left; width: 80%; }";
}
<!DOCTYPE html>
<html lang="en">
    <head>
        <meta charset="utf-8" />
        <title>@Page.Title</title>
        <style>
            body { font-family: Arial; font-size: 11pt; }
            header { background-color: #3E5CA2; color: #fff; }
            footer { clear: both; text-align: center; font-size: 9pt; }
            @if (IsSectionDefined("Sidebar")) {
                @sidebarStyle
            }
        </style>
    </head>
<body>
        <header>
            <h1>My Honey-Do List</h1>
        </header>
        @if (IsSectionDefined("Sidebar")) {
        <aside id="Sidebar">
            @RenderSection("Sidebar")
        </aside>
        }
        <section id="MainContent">
            @RenderBody()
        </section>
        <footer>
            Copyright 2013. All Rights Reserved.
        </footer>
    </body>
</html>
```

Now that the layout page is created, you'll update both the addtask page, as shown in Listing 35-7, and the default page, as shown in Listing 35-8, so that they use the new layout page. Notice that if the `Sidebar` section is not defined within the content page, the section of markup within the `if` statement shown in Listing 35-6 is ignored.

LISTING 35-7: The updated addtask page using the new layout template

VB

```
@Code
    Layout = "~/_layout.vbhtml"
    Page.Title = "Add a task"

    ' Removed the code below to simplify this example
    ' . . .
End Code
```

C#

```
@{
    Layout = "~/_layout.cshtml";
    Page.Title = "Add a task";
    // Removed the code below to simplify this example
    // . . .
}
```

LISTING 35-8: The updated default page using the new layout template

VB

```
@Code
    Layout = "~/_layout.vbhtml"
    Page.Title = "My Tasks"

    Dim db = Database.Open("Chapter35-VB")
    Dim tasks = db.Query("SELECT * FROM Tasks WHERE IsComplete = 0 or IsComplete IS NULL")
    Dim grid = New WebGrid(tasks)
End Code

<style type="text/css">
    .grid { margin: 4px; padding: 2px; border: 1px solid #666; }
    .grid td, th { border: 1px solid #fff; padding: 5px; }
    .head { background-color: #36648B; }
    .head a { color: #FFF; text-decoration-style: none; }
    .alt { background-color: #F0F8FF; }
</style>
<h1>Open Tasks</h1>
<div>
    @grid.GetHtml(
        tableStyle:= "grid",
        headerStyle:= "head",
        alternatingRowStyle:= "alt",
        columns:= grid.Columns(
            grid.Column("TaskDescription","Task")
        )
    )
</div>
@Section Sidebar
<p>
```

```
        <a href="addtask.vbhtml">Add More Tasks</a>
    </p>
    End Section
```

C#

```
@{
    Layout = "~/_layout.cshtml";
    Page.Title = "My Tasks";
    // Removed the code below to simplify this example
    // . . .
}
```

An example of the page using the new layout is shown in Figure 35-10.

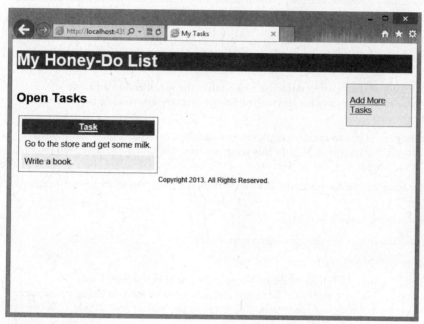

FIGURE 35-10

USING HELPERS

The previous Web Page sample used several built-in helpers. You used `WebGrid` to display data and you used `ValidationSummary` and `ValidationMessage` to display data exception information. You also used `RenderBody` and `RenderSection` to display information from other Web Page files. This is just the beginning. Several helpers are built into Web Pages that you can use.

Core Helpers

You can use several core helpers to add base functionality to your application. These include:

- ➤ `WebSecurity`
- ➤ `OAuthWebSecurity`
- ➤ `ReCaptcha`
- ➤ `WebMail`
- ➤ `WebCache`

WebSecurity Helper

The `WebSecurity` helper allows users to authenticate within your application. It also enables you to define roles and assign them to users. This is very similar to the way that ASP.NET handles membership and role management.

> **NOTE** *We cannot cover all of the functionality the `WebSecurity` helper has to offer. It is recommended that you review the Starter Site template in WebMatrix to get a better understanding of the `WebSecurity` helper. If you use the Starter Site template, you'll notice a folder called Account that contains most of the necessary pages to handle membership and role management.*

You can initiate the use of `WebSecurity` by adding a file called `_AppStart.cshtml` or `_AppStart.vbhtml`. Within the code block in the file, add the following:

```
WebSecurity.InitializeDatabaseConnection("Chapter35", "UserProfile", "UserId",
    "Username", true);
```

The first parameter is the name of the existing database to initialize the membership and role management. The next three parameters are for the user table, the primary key field of the user table, and the username field of the user table.

The next step to using `WebSecurity` is to create a registration page. You can find a great example of a registration page in the Starter Site template. Within this template, you find other example web pages including, but not limited to, a login and logout web page.

You can also create a user from within source code. Before creating the user, you want to ensure that the user doesn't exist:

```
WebSecurity.UserExists("username") == false
```

After verifying that the user doesn't exist, you can create a new user:

```
WebSecurity.CreateUserAndAccount("username","password")
```

So, at this point you have set up your database to create users and created a new user using the `CreateUserAccount` method. Now that your user has been created, it's time for you to log in the user. Again, it's a good idea to see how the login page was implemented in the Starter Site template. When you're ready to log in the user, you can check the credentials by using:

```
WebSecurity.Login("username","password")
```

After the user logs in to the site, you'll likely want to say hello to the user. You can display the username of the user by using:

```
if (WebSecurity.IsAuthenticated())
{
    @WebSecurity.CurrentUserName;
}
```

This code snippet first checks to see if the user is authenticated. If the user is authenticated, the current username is displayed.

The final method that you'll explore is logging your users off the site. You can accomplish that by using:

```
WebSecurity.Logout()
```

OAuthWebSecurity Helper

The `OAuthWebSecurity` helper allows the use of both OAuth and OpenID authentication within your site. In other words, if you've ever visited a website that asks you to log in using Facebook, Google, Microsoft, Twitter, or Yahoo! before continuing, that site is using either OAuth or OpenID. Google and Yahoo! use

OpenID and so their implementation is fairly simple. The other three require an application or client ID and an application or client secret to complete the authentication. These three use the OAuth standard.

As shown previously, you'll need to initialize the database. Immediately after the `InitializeDatabaseConnection`, you can add one or more of the following:

```
OAuthWebSecurity.RegisterGoogleClient("displayName");
OAuthWebSecurity.RegisterYahooClient("displayName");
OAuthWebSecurity.RegisterFacebookClient("appId","appSecret");
OAuthWebSecurity.RegisterMicrosoftClient("clientId","clientSecret");
OAuthWebSecurity.RegisterTwitterClient("consumerKey","consumerSecret");
```

ReCaptcha Helper

The `ReCaptcha` helper makes use of the popular `ReCaptcha` images to help secure web forms and to ensure that the user submitting the form is a human and not an automated system. The `ReCaptcha` helper is part of the Web Page Helpers library that you can download from NuGet.

You can set up the `ReCaptcha` for usage by including the `Microsoft.Web.Helpers` in the `_AppStart.cshtml` or `_AppStart.vbhtml` page. In a code block on that page, add the following:

```
ReCaptcha.PublicKey = "your-public-key";
ReCaptcha.PrivateKey = "your-private-key";
```

In the page that you'd like to use the CAPTCHA image, you can add the following in your HTML markup:

```
@ReCaptcha.GetHtml()
```

In the same page, within a code block, you'll also need to add:

```
if (ReCaptcha.Validate()) {
    // Do something because the ReCaptcha was validated
}
```

WebMail Helper

The `WebMail` helper allows e-mail to be sent in an HTML format. Unlike several other helpers, the `WebMail` helper does not render markup. Instead, it's used to simplify the process to send an e-mail message through source. An example of using the `WebMail` helper is shown in Listing 35-9.

LISTING 35-9: Sample usage of the WebMail helper

```
@{
    // . . .
    // Set the common WebMail properties
    WebMail.SmtpServer = "SMTP Server";
    WebMail.SmtpPort = 25;
    WebMail.UserName = "Username";
    WebMail.Password = "Password";
    WebMail.From = "From Email Address";

    // Send the email
    WebMail.Send(to: "To Email Address",
            subject: "Subject",
            body: "<strong>Body</strong>");
    // . . .
}
```

WebCache Helper

Caching is an extremely important part of ASP.NET. So, it's no surprise that Web Pages also has a caching mechanism. The `WebCache` helper does just that. It's very, very similar to the way items are cached in ASP.NET Web Forms. Listing 35-10 demonstrates the `WebCache` helper.

LISTING 35-10: Using the WebCache helper to cache the current time

VB

```
@Code
    Dim toCache = WebCache.Get("cacheTimestamp")

    If (toCache = Nothing) Then
        toCache = DateTime.Now
        WebCache.Set("cacheTimestamp",toCache,1,False)
    End If
End Code
```

C#

```
@{
    var toCache = WebCache.Get("cacheTimestamp");

    if (toCache == null) {
        toCache = DateTime.Now;
        WebCache.Set("cacheTimestamp",toCache,1,false);
    }
}
```

Adding Functionality Using Helpers

Besides the helpers already covered, several others add functionality to Web Pages. The more popular ones include `WebImage`, `FileUpload`, `Video`, `Bing`, `Maps`, and various social helpers.

WebImage Helper

The `WebImage` helper enables you to manipulate an image by passing in a stream or path. The `WebImage` helper has several methods to resize the image and manipulate it in other ways. To obtain an image that is posted from a form, you can use something similar to:

```
WebImage photo = WebImage.GetImageFromRequest();
```

FileUpload Helper

The `FileUpload` helper allows file upload capabilities on a web page. The helper has several properties that change the rendered markup based on the values. For instance, if you wanted to show three upload boxes and allow more boxes to be shown if the visitor so chooses, you can add the control to the page like the following:

```
@FileUpload.GetHtml(initialNumberOfFiles:3, allowMoreFilesToBeAdded:true,
    includeFormTag:true, uploadText:"Upload")
```

Video Helper

As HTML5 becomes more and more popular, there will be less of a use for the `Video` helper. However, a lot of web applications still use Windows Media, Flash, or Silverlight to display videos. The `Video` helper allows markup to be rendered based on the properties specified. For instance, if you wanted to show a Welcome video using Silverlight in a 600×400 frame, you could use something like the following:

```
@Video.Silverlight(
    path: "Videos/Welcome.xap",
    width: "600",
    height: "400",
    bgColor: "black",
    autoUpgrade: true)
```

Bing Helper

Another common feature that several web applications have is to contain a search box to allow the site, as well as the Internet, to be searched. Of course, for the site search to work, your web application must be publicly accessible and Bing must have indexed your site at least once. If those two conditions have been met, you can configure the site search functions by adding the following to the `_AppStart.cshtml` or `_AppStart.vbhtml` file:

```
Bing.SiteUrl = "your-site.com";
Bing.SiteTitle = "Search This Site";
```

Then, to render a search box on a page, add the following in the desired location in your markup:

```
@Bing.SearchBox()
```

Maps Helper

The `Maps` helper enables you to display a map from Bing, Google, MapQuest, or Yahoo! To display a map of 1 Redmond Way, Redmond, Washington, on Google, you would add the following to the desired location in your markup:

```
@Maps.GetGoogleHtml("1 Redmond Way, Redmond, WA", width: "600", height: "400")
```

Social Networking Helpers

The ability to integrate with social media is crucial for today's web applications. To ease the pain of this task, several helpers have been added to accomplish many common tasks. These include:

➤ Facebook

➤ Twitter

➤ LinkShare

➤ Gravatar

➤ GamerCard

The `Facebook` helper currently has a single purpose. That purpose is to display a like button on a web page. It can be as simple as using `@Facebook.LikeButton()` or as complex as directing the user to like a page other than the current one:

```
@Facebook.LikeButton(href: "http://wrox.com", action: "recommend",
    buttonLayout: "button_count", showFaces: true, colorScheme: "dark")
```

The `Twitter` helper has two methods. One is to help link to a user's Twitter profile and display the results inside of a standard Twitter widget. The second is to obtain Twitter search results and display them inside of a standard Twitter widget. You can use both by doing the following:

```
@Twitter.Profile("jgaylord")
@Twitter.Search("Razor Syntax")
```

The `LinkShare` helper renders social media icons and allows a page to be shared with a custom page heading. The helper renders icons for Delicious, Digg, Facebook, Reddit, StumbleUpon, and Twitter. An example of its usage is:

```
@LinkShare.GetHtml("Social Sharing Example")
```

The `Gravatar` helper connects to the Gravatar website and shows a gravatar based on a username. A gravatar is an image representation for a username. These are commonly used on forums, chat rooms, and comment forms. To display author Jason Gaylord's Gravatar, for example, you use:

```
@Gravatar.GetHtml("jason@jasongaylord.com")
```

The `GamerCard` helper displays a copy of an Xbox gamer card. The gamer card includes your player icon, recently played games, and your reputation score. An example of displaying a gamer card is shown here:

```
@GamerCard.GetHtml("Major Nelson")
```

Creating Custom Helpers

Creating custom helpers is actually much easier than you would think. You can use the task application you started earlier in this chapter or create a new Web Pages application. Start by adding a new folder to the application called `App_Code`.

Within the `App_Code` folder, create a new file named **AmazonBooks.cshtml** (within your C# application) or **AmazonBooks.vbhtml** (within your VB application). This single file will host three different helper methods. The name of this file is crucial because this will be your helper name. So, you want to be sure that if you're using a name such as AmazonBooks that an AmazonBooks helper doesn't already exist.

In your Amazon file, add the code as shown in Listing 35-11.

LISTING 35-11: The Amazon helper for your Web Page application

VB

```
@Helper TextAndImage(isbn As String)
    Dim src = "http://rcm.amazon.com/e/cm?lt1=_blank&bc1=000000&" & _
        "IS2=1&bg1=FFFFFF&fc1=000000&lc1=0000FF&o=1&p=8&l=as4&" & _
        "m=amazon&f=ifr&ref=ss_til&asins=" & isbn

@<iframe src="@src" style="width:120px;height:240px;" scrolling="no"
    marginwidth="0" marginheight="0" frameborder="0"></iframe>
End Helper


@Helper TextOnly(isbn As String, title As String)
    Dim src = "http://www.amazon.com/gp/product/" & isbn & "/" & _
        "ref=as_li_ss_tl?ie=UTF8&linkCode=as2&camp=1789&" & _
        "creative=390957&creativeASIN=" & isbn
    Dim img = "http://www.assoc-amazon.com/e/ir?l=as2&o=1&a=" & isbn

@<a href="@src">@title</a>@<img src="@img" width="1" height="1"
    border="0" alt="" style="border:none !important; margin:0px !important;" />
End Helper


@Helper ImageOnly(isbn As String)
    Dim src = "http://www.amazon.com/gp/product/" & isbn & "/" & _
        "ref=as_li_ss_il?ie=UTF8&linkCode=as2&camp=1789&" & _
        "creative=390957&creativeASIN=" & isbn
    Dim img = "http://ws.assoc-amazon.com/widgets/q?_encoding=UTF8&" & _
        "Format=_SL110_&ASIN=" & isbn & "&MarketPlace=US&" & _
        "ID=AsinImage&WS=1&ServiceVersion=20070822"

@<a href="@src"><img border="0" src="@img"></a>@<img
    src="http://www.assoc-amazon.com/e/ir?l=as2&o=1&a=@isbn" width="1"
    height="1" border="0" alt=""
    style="border:none !important; margin:0px !important;" />
End Helper
```

C#

```
@helper TextAndImage(string isbn) {
var src = "http://rcm.amazon.com/e/cm?lt1=_blank&bc1=000000&" +
    "IS2=1&bg1=FFFFFF&fc1=000000&lc1=0000FF&o=1&p=8&l=as4&" +
    "m=amazon&f=ifr&ref=ss_til&asins=" + isbn;

<iframe src='@src' style="width:120px;height:240px;" scrolling="no"
    marginwidth="0" marginheight="0" frameborder="0"></iframe>
}

@helper TextOnly(string isbn, string title) {
```

```
    var src = "http://www.amazon.com/gp/product/" + isbn + "/" +
        "ref=as_li_ss_tl?ie=UTF8&linkCode=as2&camp=1789&" +
        "creative=390957&creativeASIN=" + isbn;
    var img = "http://www.assoc-amazon.com/e/ir?l=as2&o=1&a=" + @isbn;

    <a href='@src'>@title</a><img src='@img' width="1" height="1"
        border="0" alt="" style="border:none !important; margin:0px !important;" />
    }

    @helper ImageOnly(string isbn) {
    var src = "http://www.amazon.com/gp/product/" + isbn + "/" +
        "ref=as_li_ss_il?ie=UTF8&linkCode=as2&camp=1789&" +
        "creative=390957&creativeASIN=" + isbn;
    var img = "http://ws.assoc-amazon.com/widgets/q?_encoding=UTF8&" +
        "Format=_SL110_&ASIN=" + isbn + "&MarketPlace=US&" +
        "ID=AsinImage&WS=1&ServiceVersion=20070822";

    <a href='@src'><img border="0" src='@img'></a><img
        src="http://www.assoc-amazon.com/e/ir?l=as2&o=1&a=@isbn" width="1"
        height="1" border="0" alt=""
        style="border:none !important; margin:0px !important;" />
    }
```

As you can see in Listing 35-11, you have three helper methods in your `AmazonBooks` helper. Each method renders a different format of a book listing with a link to the page on Amazon. You can now consume this by using it in any page as shown here:

```
@AmazonBooks.ImageOnly("1118311825")
```

The ISBN that has been passed in for this example is the 10-digit ISBN number for this book.

SUMMARY

In this chapter, you have received a taste of Razor syntax and ASP.NET Web Pages. You started by learning about ASP.NET WebMatrix. You reviewed the different ways to create a web application in WebMatrix, including from a folder, template, or application from the application gallery. Then, you learned how to jump between the configuration for your application, files, and databases. You created a SQL Server CE database and table within that database.

Next, you saw the power of Razor syntax. You learned how to connect to a data source using Razor and how to interact with the data from the source. The web pages that you created were moved around to use a layout page. You also used several built-in helpers for Razor including the following:

- ➤ `WebGrid`
- ➤ `ValidationSummary` and `ValidationMessage`
- ➤ `RenderBody` and `RenderSection`
- ➤ `WebSecurity`, `OAuthWebSecurity`, and `ReCaptcha`
- ➤ `WebMail`
- ➤ `WebCache`
- ➤ `WebImage`, `FileUpload`, and `Video`
- ➤ `Bing` and `Maps`
- ➤ `Facebook`, `Twitter`, `LinkShare`, and `Gravatar`

Finally, you learned how to create a custom helper and build upon Razor. Though this chapter didn't cover everything that Razor, Web Pages, or WebMatrix have to offer, you should have a good understanding of how Razor works and how ASP.NET Web Pages uses Razor. You should also have a good idea of how Razor could be useful when using the `RazorViewEngine` for ASP.NET MVC.

PART X
Appendixes

Migrating Older
ASP.NET Projects

In some cases, you will build your ASP.NET 4.5 applications from scratch—starting everything new. In many instances, however, this is not an option. You need to take an ASP.NET application that was previously built on the 1.0, 1.1, 2.0, 3.5, or 4.0 versions of the .NET Framework and migrate the application so that it can run on the .NET Framework 4.5.

This appendix focuses on migrating ASP.NET 1.*x*, 2.0, 3.5, or 4.0 applications to the 4.5 Framework.

MIGRATING IS NOT DIFFICULT

Be aware that Microsoft has done a lot of work to ensure that the migration process from ASP.NET 1.*x* is as painless as possible. In most cases, your applications run with no changes needed.

When moving a 1.*x*, 2.0, 3.5, or 4.0 application to 4.5, you don't have to put the ASP.NET application on a new server or make any changes to your present server beyond installing the .NET Framework 4.5.

After you install the .NET Framework 4.5, you see the framework versions on your server at `C:\WINDOWS\Microsoft.NET\Framework`, as illustrated in Figure A-1. There is also the 64-bit version at `C:\Windows\Microsoft.Net\Framework64` as well if your server is a 64-bit machine.

In this case, you can see that all the official versions of the .NET Framework installed, including v1.0.3705, v1.1.4322, v2.0.50727, v3.0, v3.5, v4.0, and v4.5

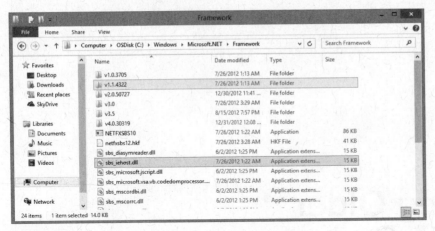

FIGURE A-1

Running Multiple Versions of the Framework Side by Side

From Figure A-1, you can see that running multiple versions of the .NET Framework side by side is possible. ASP.NET 1.0, ASP.NET 1.1, ASP.NET 2.0, ASP.NET 3.5, ASP.NET 4, and ASP.NET 4.5 applications can all run from the same server. Different versions of ASP.NET applications that are running on the same server run in their own worker processes and are isolated from one another.

In-Place Upgrade

The .NET Framework 4.5 is an in-place upgrade that replaces the .NET Framework 4. When you install the .NET Framework 4.5, the installer replaces the existing files that were installed by the .NET Framework 4 and upgrades them to the .NET Framework 4.5. You will not see a folder called v4.5, as you saw similar folders for each of the previous frameworks in Figure A-1.

So if you had ASP.NET 4 applications running on a server that had the .NET Framework 4 installed, after installing the .NET Framework 4.5 all ASP.NET 4 applications will start running on the .NET Framework 4.5. When you install the .NET Framework 4.5, all application pools that were running ASP.NET 4 will now be running as ASP.NET 4.5.

Because the .NET 4.5 Framework is an in-place upgrade, Microsoft has done a considerable amount of work to ensure that there is backward compatibility between the .NET 4.0 Framework and the .NET 4.5 Framework. This means that ASP.NET 4 applications should continue to work without any errors after installing the .NET Framework 4.5.

Upgrading Your ASP.NET Applications

When you install the .NET Framework 4.5, it does not remap all your ASP.NET applications so that they now run off the new framework instance. Instead, you selectively remap applications to run off of the ASP.NET 4.5 Framework.

> **NOTE** *You should always test your older ASP.NET application by first running it on the newer version of ASP.NET in a developer or staging environment. Do not change the version to a newer version on a production system without first testing for any failures.*

If you are not ready to upgrade your entire application to a newer version of ASP.NET, one option is to create additional virtual directories in the root virtual directory of your application and target the portions of the application to the versions of the .NET Framework that you want them to run on. This enables you to take a stepped approach in your upgrade process.

If you are upgrading from ASP.NET 2.0 to ASP.NET 3.5, there really is very little that you have to do. Upgrading to version 4.0 is a bit different than it was when upgrading from version 2.0 to 3.5 because the 3.5 version of the .NET Framework was built upon the .NET Framework 2.0. In this case, the `System.Web` DLL in both versions of the framework was the same. Now, though, the .NET Framework 4 is a complete recompilation of the framework. .NET Framework 4.5 is built on top of .NET Framework 4 so when you install .NET Framework 4.5 on a server with .NET Framework 4, then your server will be running on .NET Framework 4.5

The differences are even more evident when working with the IIS Manager on Windows 8. From this management tool, you can see that the DefaultAppPool is running off version 4.0.*xxxxx* of the .NET Framework, as shown in Figure A-2.

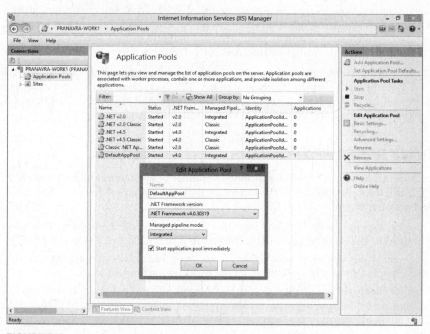

FIGURE A-2

Upgrading your application to ASP.NET 4.5 using Visual Studio 2012 causes the IDE to make all the necessary changes to the application's configuration file. This is illustrated later in this appendix.

WHEN MIXING VERSIONS—FORMS AUTHENTICATION

If you have an ASP.NET application that utilizes multiple versions of the .NET Framework, as was previously mentioned, you must be aware of how forms authentication works in ASP.NET 2.0, 3.5, 4.0, and 4.5.

In ASP.NET 1.x, the forms authentication process uses Triple DES encryption (3DES) for the encryption and decryption process of the authentication cookies. Ever since ASP.NET 2.0, though, it has now been changed to use the Advanced Encryption Standard (AES) encryption technique.

AES is faster and more secure. However, because the two encryption techniques are different, you must change how ASP.NET 4.5 generates these keys. You do this by changing the `<machineKey>` section of the `web.config` file in your ASP.NET 4.5 application so that it works with Triple DES encryption instead (as presented in Listing A-1).

LISTING A-1: Changing your ASP.NET 4.5 application to use Triple DES encryption

```
<configuration>
  <system.web>
      <machineKey validation="3DES" decryption="3DES"
  validationKey="1234567890123456789012345678901234567890"
  decryptionKey="1234567890123456789012345678901234567890" />
      </system.web>
</configuration>
```

By changing the machine key encryption/decryption process to utilize Triple DES, you enable the forms authentication to work across an ASP.NET application that is using both the .NET Framework 1.x and 4. Also, this example shows the `validationKey` and `decryptionKey` attributes using a specific set of keys. These keys should be the same as those you utilize in your ASP.NET 1.x application.

You should understand that you are not required to make these changes when upgrading an ASP.NET 2.0 or 3.5 application to ASP.NET 4.5 because they are all enabled to use AES encryption and are not using Triple DES encryption. If you are mixing an ASP.NET 1.x application along with ASP.NET 2.0, 3.5, 4.0, or 4.5, you must move everything to use Triple DES encryption, as shown in Listing A-1.

UPGRADING—ASP.NET RESERVED FOLDERS

As described in Chapter 3 of this book, ASP.NET 4.5 includes a number of application folders that are specific to the ASP.NET Framework. In addition to the Bin folder that was a reserved folder in ASP.NET 1.x, the following folders are all reserved in ASP.NET 2.0, 3.5, 4.0, and 4.5:

➤ **Bin:** This folder stores the application DLL and any other DLLs used by the application. This folder was present in both ASP.NET 1.0 and 1.1. It is also present in ASP.NET 2.0, 3.5, 4.0 and 4.5.

➤ **App_Code:** This folder is meant to store your classes, `.wsdl` files, and typed data sets. Any items stored in this folder are automatically available to all the pages within your solution.

➤ **App_Data:** This folder holds the data stores utilized by the application. It is a good, central spot to store all the data stores used by your application. The App_Data folder can contain Microsoft SQL Express files (`.mdf` files), Microsoft Access files (`.mdb` files), XML files, and more.

➤ **App_Themes:** Themes are a way of providing a common look-and-feel to your site across every page. You implement a theme by using a `.skin` file, CSS files, and images used by the server controls of your site. All these elements can make a theme, which is then stored in the App_Themes folder of your solution.

➤ **App_GlobalResources:** This folder enables you to store resource files that can serve as data dictionaries for your applications if these applications require changes in their content (based on things such as changes in culture). You can add Assembly Resource Files (`.resx`) to the App_GlobalResources folder, and they are dynamically compiled and made part of the solution for use by all the `.aspx` pages in the application.

➤ **App_LocalResources:** Quite similar to the App_GlobalResources folder, the App_LocalResources folder is a simple method to incorporate resources that can be used for a specific page in your application.

➤ **App_WebReferences:** You can use the App_WebReferences folder and have automatic access to the remote web services referenced from your application.

➤ **App_Browsers:** This folder holds .browser files, which are XML files used to identify the browsers making requests to the application and to elucidate the capabilities these browsers have.

The addition of the App_ prefix to the folder names ensures that you do not already have a folder with a similar name in your ASP.NET 1.*x* applications. If, by chance, you do have a folder with one of the names you plan to use, you should change the name of your previous folder to something else because these ASP.NET 4.5 application folder names are unchangeable.

ASP.NET 4.5 PAGES COME AS HTML5

ASP.NET 4.5, by default, constructs its pages to be HTML5-compliant. You can see the setting for HTML5 in the Visual Studio 2012 IDE, as shown in Figure A-3.

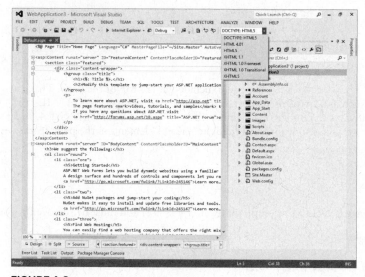

FIGURE A-3

In this case, you can see a list of options for determining how the ASP.NET application outputs the code for the pages. By default, it is set to HTML5. You can also make a change to the web.config file so that the output is not XHTML-specific (as illustrated in Listing A-2).

LISTING A-2: Reversing the XHTML capabilities of your ASP.NET 4.5 application

```
<configuration>
  <system.web>
     <xhtmlConformance mode="Legacy" />
     </system.web>
</configuration>
```

Setting the mode attribute to Legacy ensures that XHTML is not used, but instead, ASP.NET 4.5 will use what was used in ASP.NET 1.*x*.

Note that using the Legacy setting as a value for the mode attribute will sometimes cause problems for your application if you are utilizing Ajax. One of the symptoms that you might experience is that, instead of doing a partial-page update (as Ajax does), you will get a full-page postback. This is because the page is not

XHTML-compliant. The solution is to set the mode property to Traditional or Strict and to make your pages XHTML-compliant.

If you take this approach, you also have to make some additional changes to any new ASP.NET 4.5 pages that you create in Visual Studio 2012. Creating a new ASP.NET 4.5 page in Visual Studio 2012 produces the results illustrated in Listing A-3.

LISTING A-3: A typical ASP.NET 4.5 page

```
<%@ Page Language="VB" %>
<!DOCTYPE HTML>
<html xmlns="http://www.w3.org/1999/xhtml">
<head runat="server">
    <title></title>
</head>
<body>
    <form id="form1" runat="server">
    <div>

    </div>
    </form>
</body>
</html>
```

From this listing, you can see that a <!DOCTYPE ...> element is included at the top of the page. This element signifies to some browsers (such as Microsoft's Internet Explorer) that the page is XHTML-compliant. If this is not the case, you want to remove this element altogether from your ASP.NET 4.5 page. In addition to the <!DOCTYPE> element, you also want to change the <html> element on the page from:

```
<html xmlns="http://www.w3.org/1999/xhtml">
```

to the following:

```
<html>
```

The original also signifies that the page is XHTML-compliant (even if it is not) and must be removed if your pages are not XHTML-compliant.

NO HARD-CODED .JS FILES IN ASP.NET 4.5

ASP.NET 1.x provides some required JavaScript files as hard-coded .js files. For instance, in ASP.NET a JavaScript requirement was necessary for the validation server controls and the smart navigation capabilities to work. If you are utilizing either of these features in your ASP.NET 1.x applications, ASP.NET could pick up the installed .js files and use them directly.

These .js files are found at C:\WINDOWS\Microsoft.NET\Framework\v1.1.4322\ASP.NETClientFiles. Looking at this folder, you see three .js files—two of which deal with the smart navigation feature (SmartNav.js and SmartNavIE5.js) and one that deals with the validation server controls (WebUIValidation.js). Because they are hard-coded .js files, opening them and changing or altering the code in these files to better suit your needs is possible. In some cases, developers have done just that.

If you have altered these JavaScript files in any manner, you must change some code when migrating your ASP.NET application to ASP.NET 2.0, 3.5, or 4.5. ASP.NET 4.5 dynamically includes .js files from the System.Web.dll instead of hard-coding them on the server. In ASP.NET 4.5, the files are included via a handler—WebResource.axd.

VISUAL STUDIO 2012 PROJECT COMPATIBILITY

As previously mentioned, if you have a preexisting ASP.NET 1.*x* application, you can run the application on the ASP.NET 4 run time by simply making the appropriate changes in IIS to the application pool. Using the IIS manager or the MMC Snap-In, you can select the appropriate framework on which to run your application from the provided drop-down list.

ASP.NET 4.5 applications work with the Visual Studio 2012 IDE. If you still intend to work with ASP.NET 1.0 or 1.1 applications, you should keep Visual Studio .NET 2002 or 2003, respectively, installed on your machine. Installing Visual Studio 2012 gives you a complete, new copy of Visual Studio and does not upgrade the previous Visual Studio .NET 2002 or 2003 IDEs. All copies of Visual Studio can run side by side.

If you want to run ASP.NET 4.*x* applications on the .NET Framework 4.5, but you also want to convert the entire ASP.NET project for the application to ASP.NET 4.5, you can use Visual Studio 2012 to help you with the conversion process. After the project is converted, you can build and run the application from Visual Studio 2012. The application is now built and run on the ASP.NET 4 run time.

Visual Studio 2012 has solution- and project-level compatibility with Visual Studio 2010. This means that if you created an ASP.NET application using Visual Studio 2010, you can open this application in Visual Studio 2012, make changes, and open the same application in Visual Studio 2010. All the artifacts of the application will be preserved. This is a very useful feature that supports mixed-mode development, where now you can use Visual Studio 2012 to target applications for ASP.NET 4.0 and ASP.NET 4.5.

> **WARNING** *Remember: Do not upgrade production solutions without testing your programs first in a staging environment to ensure that your application is not affected by the changes between versions of the .NET Framework.*

MIGRATING FROM ASP.NET 2.0/3.5/4.0 TO 4.5

Visual Studio 2012 enables you to build applications that can target more than one framework. For instance, Visual Studio .NET 2002 would only let you build 1.0 applications. If you wanted to build .NET Framework 1.1 applications, you were required to install and use Visual Studio .NET 2003. At the same time, Visual Studio .NET 2003 would not enable you to build .NET Framework 1.0 applications, meaning that if you were dealing with applications that made use of either framework, you were required to have both IDEs on your computer.

When you create a new project in Visual Studio 2012, you have the option of targeting the project at any of the following frameworks:

- ➤ .NET Framework 2.0
- ➤ .NET Framework 3.0
- ➤ .NET Framework 3.5
- ➤ .NET Framework 4
- ➤ .NET Framework 4.5

If you open an ASP.NET application that is built upon the .NET Framework 2.0, you can retarget the application to a newer version of the framework quite easily from the IDE. To do this, right-click the project in the Solution Explorer and select Property Pages from the provided menu. This gives you a form that enables you to change the target framework of the application. In this case, you can see the default options on a Microsoft Windows 8 computer (as shown in Figure A-4).

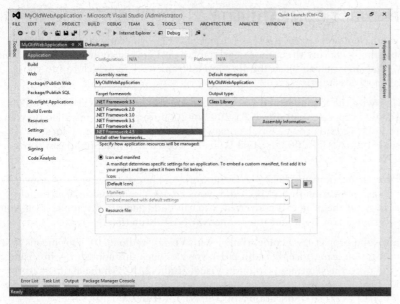

FIGURE A-4

Changing the target framework as illustrated in Figure A-4 requires Visual Studio 2012 to close and reopen your solution. After this is complete, you will see that even the `web.config` file was changed to account for working with the newer version of the framework. You might have to address some issues that deal with any breaking changes that have been presented between the releases of ASP.NET, but you can get a quick list of those problems by building the solution within Visual Studio.

SUMMARY

The nice thing with the Visual Studio 2012 IDE is that you are able to upgrade just your ASP.NET solution and not upgrade the framework version to which your solution is targeted. However, in upgrading your ASP.NET solution to the .NET Framework 4.5, you might find that Visual Studio makes this an easy task to achieve.

This appendix looked at upgrading using the IDE as well as some important changes between the releases that are aimed at making your migration as easy as possible.

B

COM Integration

One of the best practices in programming is to separate your application into workable and separate components—also known as *business objects*. This makes your applications far easier to manage and enables you to achieve the goal of code reuse because you can share these components among different parts of the same application or between entirely separate applications.

Before the introduction of .NET, many applications were using COM as a way to write business objects. If you are moving any legacy applications or aspects of these applications to an ASP.NET environment, you might find that you need to utilize various COM components. This appendix shows you how to use both .NET and COM components in your ASP.NET pages and code.

This appendix gives you an overview of how COM components can be used in ASP.NET.

COM INTEROP: USING COM WITHIN .NET

When .NET came out for the first time, Microsoft knew that every one of its legions of developers out there would be quite disappointed if they couldn't use the thousands of COM controls that it has built, maintained, and improved over the years.

To this end, Microsoft has provided us with COM Interoperability. *COM Interop* (for short) is a technology that enables .NET to wrap the functionality of a COM object with the interface of a .NET component so that your .NET code can communicate with the COM object without having to use COM techniques and interfaces in your code.

Figure B-1 illustrates the Runtime Callable Wrapper (RCW), the middle component that directs traffic between the .NET code and the COM component.

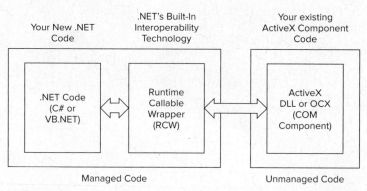

FIGURE B-1

The Runtime Callable Wrapper

The Runtime Callable Wrapper, or RCW, is the magic piece of code that enables interaction to occur between .NET and COM. You create one RCW for each COM component in your project, and to do that, you can use Visual Studio 2012.

To add an ActiveX DLL to the References section of your project, choose Website ⇨ Add Reference or choose the Add Reference menu item that appears when you right-click the root node of your project in the Solution Explorer.

Your Interop library is created for you automatically from the ActiveX DLL that you told Visual Studio 2012 to use. This Interop library is the RCW component customized for your ActiveX control, as shown previously in Figure B-1. The name of the Interop file is simply `Interop.OriginalName.DLL`.

You can also create the RCW files manually instead of doing it through Visual Studio 2012. In the .NET Framework, you will find a method to create RCW Interop files for controls manually through a command-line tool called the Type Library Importer. You invoke the Type Library Importer by using the `tlbimp.exe` executable.

For example, to create the Interop library for the SQLDMO object, start up a Visual Studio 2012 Command Prompt from the Microsoft Visual Studio 2012 ⇨ Visual Studio Tools group within your Start menu. From the comment prompt, type the following:

```
tlbimp sqldmo.dll /out:sqldmoex.dll
```

In this example, the `/out:` parameter specifies the name of the RCW Interop library to be created. If you omit this parameter, you get the same name that Visual Studio would generate for you.

The Type Library Importer is useful when you are not using Visual Studio 2012 as your development environment, if you want to have more control over the assemblies that get created for you, or if you are automating the process of connecting to COM components.

The Type Library Importer is a wrapper application around the `TypeLibConverter` class of the `System.Runtime.InteropServices` namespace.

Using COM Objects in ASP.NET Code

To continue working through some additional examples, you next take a look at a simple example of using a COM object written in Visual Basic 6 within an ASP.NET page.

In the first step, you create an ActiveX DLL that you can use for the upcoming examples. Add the Visual Basic 6 code shown in Listing B-1 to a class called `NameFunctionsClass` and compile it as an ActiveX DLL called `NameComponent.dll`.

LISTING B-1: VB6 code for ActiveX DLL, NameComponent.DLL

VB

```vb
Option Explicit

Private m_sFirstName As String
Private m_sLastName As String

Public Property Let FirstName(Value As String)
  m_sFirstName = Value
End Property

Public Property Get FirstName() As String
  FirstName = m_sFirstName
End Property

Public Property Let LastName(Value As String)
  m_sLastName = Value
End Property

Public Property Get LastName() As String
  LastName = m_sLastName
End Property

Public Property Let FullName(Value As String)
  m_sFirstName = Split(Value, " ")(0)
  If (InStr(Value, " ") > 0) Then
    m_sLastName = Split(Value, " ")(1)
  Else
    m_sLastName = ""
  End If
End Property

Public Property Get FullName() As String
  FullName = m_sFirstName + " " + m_sLastName
End Property

Public Property Get FullNameLength() As Long
  FullNameLength = Len(Me.FullName)
End Property
```

Now that you have created an ActiveX DLL to use in your ASP.NET pages, the next step is to create a new ASP.NET project using Visual Studio 2012. Replace the HTML code in the `Default.aspx` file with the HTML code shown in Listing B-2. This code adds a number of textboxes and labels to the HTML page, as well as the Visual Basic or C# code for the functionality.

LISTING B-2: Using NameComponent.dll

VB

```vb
<%@ Page Language="VB" %>

<script runat="server">
  Protected Sub AnalyzeName_Click(ByVal sender As Object,
```

continues

LISTING B-2 *(continued)*

```
      ByVal e As System.EventArgs)

    Dim Name As New NameComponent.NameFunctionsClass()
    If (FirstName.Text.Length > 0) Then
      Name.FirstName = FirstName.Text
    End If

    If (LastName.Text.Length > 0) Then
      Name.LastName = LastName.Text
    End If

    If (FullName.Text.Length > 0) Then
      Name.FullName = FullName.Text
    End If

    FirstName.Text = Name.FirstName
    LastName.Text = Name.LastName
    FullName.Text = Name.FullName
    FullNameLength.Text = Name.FullNameLength.ToString

  End Sub
</script>

<html xmlns="http://www.w3.org/1999/xhtml" >
  <head runat="server">
    <title>Using COM Components</title>
  </head>
  <body>
    <form id="form1" runat="server">
      <p>
        <asp:Label ID="Label1" runat="server">First Name:</asp:Label>
         
        <asp:TextBox ID="FirstName" runat="server"></asp:TextBox>
      </p>
      <p>
        <asp:Label ID="Label2" runat="server">Last Name:</asp:Label>
         
        <asp:TextBox ID="LastName" runat="server"></asp:TextBox>
      </p>
      <p>
        <asp:Label ID="Label3" runat="server">Full Name:</asp:Label>
         
        <asp:TextBox ID="FullName" runat="server"></asp:TextBox>
      </p>
      <p>
        <asp:Label ID="Label4" runat="server">Full Name Length:</asp:Label>
         
        <asp:Label ID="FullNameLength" runat="server"
         Font-Bold="True">0</asp:Label>
      </p>
      <p>
        <asp:Button ID="AnalyzeName" runat="server"
         OnClick="AnalyzeName_Click" Text="Analyze Name"></asp:Button>
      </p>
    </form>
  </body>
</html>
```

C#

```
<%@ Page Language="C#" %>

<script runat="server">
  protected void AnalyzeName_Click(object sender, System.EventArgs e)
  {
    NameComponent.NameFunctionsClass Name =
      new NameComponent.NameFunctionsClass();

    if (FirstName.Text.Length > 0)
    {
      string firstName = FirstName.Text.ToString();
      Name.set_FirstName(ref firstName);
    }

    if (LastName.Text.Length > 0)
    {
      string lastName = LastName.Text.ToString();
      Name.set_LastName(ref lastName);
    }

    if (FullName.Text.Length > 0)
    {
      string fullName = FullName.Text.ToString();
      Name.set_FullName(ref fullName);
    }

    FirstName.Text = Name.get_FirstName();
    LastName.Text = Name.get_LastName();
    FullName.Text = Name.get_FullName();
    FullNameLength.Text = Name.FullNameLength.ToString();
  }
</script>
```

Next you add the reference to the ActiveX DLL that you created in the previous step. To do so, follow these steps:

1. Right-click your project in the Solution Explorer dialog box.
2. Select the Add Reference menu item.
3. In the Add Reference dialog box, select the Browse tab.
4. Locate the `NameComponent.dll` object by browsing to its location.
5. Click OK to add `NameComponent.dll` to the list of selected components and close the dialog box.

> **NOTE** *If you are not using Visual Studio 2012 or code-behind pages, you can still add a reference to your COM control by creating the RCW manually using the Type Library Converter and then placing an* `Imports` *statement (VB) or* `using` *statement (C#) in the page.*

After you have selected your component using the Add Reference dialog box, an RCW file is created for the component and added to your application.

That's all there is to it! Simply run the application to see the COM Interoperability layer in action.

When the Analyze Name button is clicked, the fields in the First Name, Last Name, and Full Name textboxes are sent to the RCW to be passed to the `NameComponent.DLL` ActiveX component. Data is retrieved in the same manner to repopulate the textboxes and to indicate the length of the full name.

Accessing Tricky COM Members in C#

Sometimes, some members of COM objects do not expose themselves properly to C#. In the preceding examples, the `String` properties did not expose themselves, but the `Long` property (`FullNameLength`) did.

You know when there is a problem because, although you can see the property, you cannot compile the application. For example, instead of the code shown in Listing B-2 for C#, use the following piece of code to set the `FirstName` property of the `NameComponent.dll` ActiveX component:

```
if (FirstName.Text.Length > 0)
   Name.FirstName = FirstName.Text.ToString();
```

When you try to compile this code, you get the following error:

```
c:\inetpub\wwwroot\wrox\Default.aspx.cs(67): Property, indexer, or event
'FirstName' is not supported by the language; try directly calling accessor methods
'NameComponent.NameFunctionsClass.get_FirstName()' or
'NameComponent.NameFunctionsClass.set_FirstName(ref string)'
```

The `FirstName` property seems to be fine. It shows up in IntelliSense, but you can't use it. Instead, you must use `set_FirstName` (and `get_FirstName` to read). These methods do not show up in IntelliSense, but rest assured, they exist.

Furthermore, these methods expect a `ref string` parameter rather than a `String`. In the example from Listing B-2, two steps are used to do this properly. First, `String` is assigned to a local variable, and then the variable is passed to the method using `ref`.

Releasing COM Objects Manually

One of the great things about .NET is that it has its own garbage collection—it can clean up after itself. This is not always the case when using COM Interoperability, however. Because a COM object does not have the built-in garbage collection mechanism that .NET relies on, .NET has no way of knowing when to release a COM object from memory.

Because of this limitation, you should release COM objects from memory as soon as possible using the `ReleaseComObject` class of the `System.Runtime.InteropServices.Marshal` class:

```
System.Runtime.InteropServices.Marshal.ReleaseComObject(Object);
```

Note that if you attempt to use this object again before it goes out of scope, you would raise an exception.

ERROR HANDLING

Error handling in .NET uses exceptions instead of the HRESULT values used by Visual Basic 6 applications. Luckily, the RCW does most of the work to convert between the two.

Take, for example, the code shown in Listing B-3. In this example, a user-defined error is raised if the numerator or the denominator is greater than 1000. Also notice that it is not capturing a divide-by-zero error. Notice what happens when the ActiveX component raises the error on its own.

Begin this example by compiling the code in Listing B-3 into a class named `DivideClass` within an ActiveX component called `DivideComponent.dll`.

LISTING B-3: Raising errors in VB6

VB

```
Public Function DivideNumber(Numerator As Double, _
                       Denominator As Double) As Double

    If ((Numerator > 1000) Or (Denominator > 1000)) Then
```

```
        Err.Raise vbObjectError + 1, _
                "DivideComponent:Divide.DivideNumber", _
                "Numerator and denominator both have to " + _
                "be less than or equal to 1000."

    End If

    DivideNumber = Numerator / Denominator

End Function
```

Next, create a new ASP.NET project; add a reference to the `DivideComponent.dll` (invoking Visual Studio 2012 to create its own copy of the RCW). Remember, you can also do this manually by using the `tlbimp` executable.

Now add the code shown in Listing B-4 to an ASP.NET page.

LISTING B-4: Error handling in .NET

VB

```
<%@ Page Language="VB" %>

<script runat="server">
  Protected Sub Calculate_Click(ByVal sender As Object,
      ByVal e As System.EventArgs)

    Dim Divide As New DivideComponent.DivideClass()

    Try
        Answer.Text = Divide.DivideNumber(Numerator.Text, Denominator.Text)
    Catch ex As Exception
        Answer.Text = ex.Message.ToString()
    End Try

    System.Runtime.InteropServices.Marshal.ReleaseComObject(Divide)

  End Sub
</script>

<html xmlns="http://www.w3.org/1999/xhtml">
  <head runat="server">
    <title>Using COM Components</title>
  </head>
  <body>
    <form id="form1" runat="server">
      <p>
        <asp:Label ID="Label1" runat="server">Numerator:</asp:Label>
         
        <asp:TextBox ID="Numerator" runat="server"></asp:TextBox>
      </p>
      <p>
        <asp:Label ID="Label2" runat="server">Denominator:</asp:Label>
         
        <asp:TextBox ID="Denominator" runat="server"></asp:TextBox>
      </p>
      <p>
        <asp:Label ID="Label3" runat="server">
         Numerator divided by Denominator:</asp:Label>
```

continues

LISTING B-4 *(continued)*

```
         
        <asp:Label ID="Answer" runat="server" Font-Bold="True">0</asp:Label>
      </p>
      <p>
        <asp:Button ID="Calculate"
         runat="server"
         OnClick="Calculate_Click"
         Text="Calculate">
        </asp:Button>
      </p>
    </form>
  </body>
</html>
```

C#

```
<%@ Page Language="C#" %>

<script runat="server">
  protected void Calculate_Click(object sender, System.EventArgs e)
  {

    DivideComponent.DivideClass myDivide = new DivideComponent.DivideClass();

    try
    {
      double numerator = double.Parse(Numerator.Text);
      double denominator = double.Parse(Denominator.Text);
      Answer.Text = myDivide.DivideNumber(ref numerator,
         ref denominator).ToString();
    }

    catch (Exception ex)
    {
      Answer.Text = ex.Message.ToString();
    }

    System.Runtime.InteropServices.Marshal.ReleaseComObject(myDivide);

  }
</script>
```

The code in Listing B-4 passes the user-entered values for the `Numerator` and `Denominator` to the `DivideComponent.dll` ActiveX component for it to divide. Running the application with invalid data gives an exception message as shown in Listing B-4.

Depending on the language that you are using to run the ASP.NET application, you will see different values for different sets of data. For valid inputs, you will always see the correct result, of course, and for any input that is over 1000, you see the Visual Basic 6–appointed error description of `Numerator` and denominator both have to be less than or equal to 1000.

However, for invalid strings, Visual Basic 2012 reports `Cast from string "abc" to type 'Double' is not valid`, whereas C# reports `Input string was not in a correct format`. For a divide by zero, they both report `Divide by Zero` because the error is coming directly from the Visual Basic 6 run time.

DEPLOYING COM COMPONENTS WITH .NET APPLICATIONS

Deploying COM components with your .NET applications is very easy, especially when compared to just deploying ActiveX controls. Two scenarios are possible when deploying .NET applications with COM components:

➤ Using private assemblies

➤ Using shared or public assemblies

Private Assemblies

Installing all or parts of the ActiveX component local to the .NET application is considered installing private assemblies. In this scenario, each installation of your .NET application on the same machine has, at least, its own copy of the Interop library for the ActiveX component you are referencing, as shown in Figure B-2.

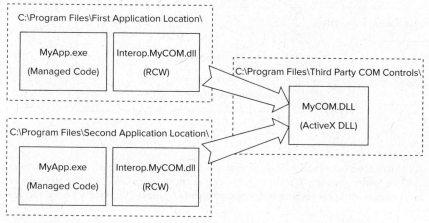

FIGURE B-2

Whether you decide to install the ActiveX component as local to the application or in a shared directory for all calling applications is up to you.

> **NOTE** *It was once considered proper practice to separate ActiveX components into their own directory so that if these components were referenced again by other applications, you did not have to register or install the file for a second time. Using this method meant that when you upgraded a component, you automatically upgraded all the applications using this component. However, this practice didn't work out so well. In fact, it became a very big contributor to DLL hell and the main reason why Microsoft began promoting the practice of installing private .NET component assemblies.*

After you have your components physically in place, the only remaining task is to register the ActiveX component using `regsvr32`, just as you would when deploying an ActiveX-enabled application.

Public Assemblies

The opposite of a private assembly is a public assembly. Public assemblies share the RCW Interop DLL for other applications. To create a public assembly, you must put the RCW file into the *Global Assembly Cache* (GAC), as shown in Figure B-3.

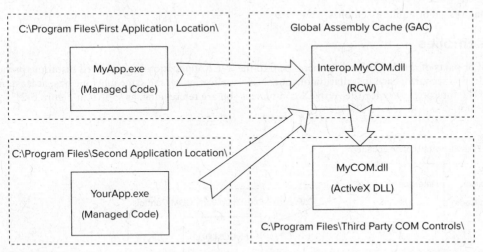

FIGURE B-3

You can find the GAC at `C:\Windows\assembly`. Installing items in the GAC can be as simple as dragging-and-dropping an item into this folder through Windows Explorer. Although the GAC is open to everyone, blindly installing your components into this section is not recommended unless you have a very good reason to do so.

You can also add items to the GAC from the command line using the Global Assembly Cache Tool (`Gacutil.exe`). It enables you to view and manipulate the contents of the GAC and download cache. Although the Explorer view of the GAC provides similar functionality, you can use `Gacutil.exe` from build scripts, makefile files, and batch files.

Finding a very good reason to install your ActiveX Interop assemblies into the GAC is hard. If we had to pick a time to do this, it would be if and when we had a highly shared ActiveX component that many .NET applications would be utilizing on the same machine. In a corporate environment, this might occur when you are upgrading existing business logic from ActiveX to .NET enablement on a server that many applications use. In a commercial setting, we avoid using the GAC.

SUMMARY

In this appendix you learned how COM Interop provided access to existing COM components so you could use .NET and COM components in ASP.NET.

ASP.NET Ultimate Tools

I've always believed that I'm only as good as my tools. I've spent years combing the Internet for excellent tools to help me be a more effective developer. Thousands of tools are out there to be sure, many overlapping in functionality with others. Some tools do one thing incredibly well and others aim to be a Swiss Army knife with dozens of small conveniences packed into their tiny toolbars. Here is a short, exclusive list of some of the ASP.NET tools that I keep turning back to. These are tools that I find myself using consistently while developing ASP.NET-based websites. I recommend that you give them a try if they sound useful. Many are free; some are not. In my opinion, each is worth at least a trial on your part, and many are worth your hard-earned money because they'll save you precious time.

DEBUGGING MADE EASIER

> There has never been an unexpectedly short debugging period in the history of computers.
>
> —STEVEN LEVY

Firebug

There are so many great things about this application one could write a book about it. Firebug is actually a Firefox plug-in, so you'll need to download and install Firefox to use it.

Figure C-1 shows Firebug analyzing all the network traffic required to download the web page. This shows a very detailed graph of when each asset is downloaded and how long it took from first byte to last byte.

It has a wealth of interesting features that enable you to inspect HTML and deeply analyze your CSS, including visualization of some more complicated CSS techniques such as offsets, margins, borders, and padding. Firebug also includes a powerful JavaScript debugger that enables you to debug JavaScript within Firefox. Even more interesting is its JavaScript profiler and a very detailed error handler that helps you chase down even the most obscure bugs.

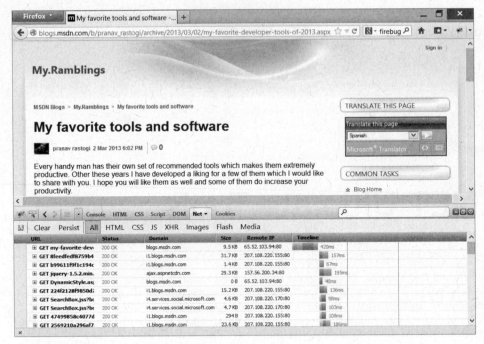

FIGURE C-1

Finally, Firebug includes an interactive console feature similar to the Visual Studio Immediate window that lets you execute JavaScript on the fly, as well as console debugging that enables classic "got here" debugging. Firebug is indispensable for the web developer and it's highly recommended.

> **NOTE** *There is also Firebug Lite in the form of a JavaScript file. You can add it to the pages in which you want a console debugger to work in Internet Explorer, Opera, or Safari. This file enables you to do "got here" debugging using the Firebug JavaScript* `console.log` *method.*

YSlow

YSlow is an add-on to an add-on. Brought to you by Yahoo!, YSlow extends Firebug and analyzes your web pages using Yahoo!'s 13 rules for fast websites. In Figure C-2, you can see Yahoo!'s YSlow analyzing the website.

YSlow is free and is an excellent resource to help you get a clear understanding about how hard the client's browser must work in order to view your website.

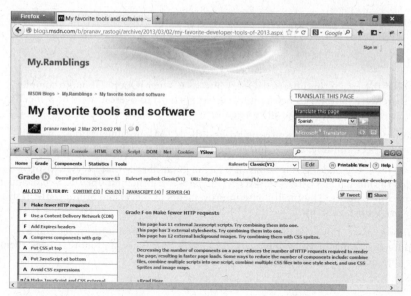

FIGURE C-2

IE10 Developer Tools

The IE10 Developer Tools are from Microsoft and come built-in with IE10. They are free and absolutely essential for web development. You just activate them by pressing F12. They extend Internet Explorer 10 with features such as DOM inspection, JavaScript profiling, and element outlining. You can even visualize the box-model as shown in Figure C-3.

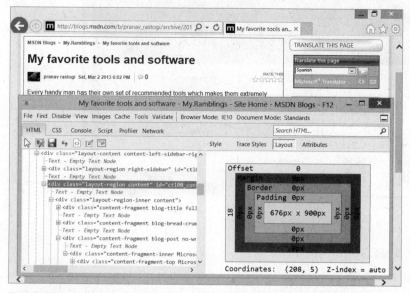

FIGURE C-3

ASP.NET developers today need their sites to look great. This toolbar puts a host of usefulness at your fingertips and is highly recommended.

jQuery and jQuery UI

Although not explicitly "tools," the JavaScript libraries jQuery and its partner jQuery UI make complex JavaScript tasks a joy. Yes, there were JS libraries before jQuery, but it's hard to overestimate how much jQuery not only changed the web, but made JavaScript fun again.

JQuery includes a clean selector engine that makes moving around the HTML document object model (DOM) trivial, allowing you to select and filter nodes and easily apply events and animations to them.

jQuery also includes methods for easily making Ajax calls. It's such a great library that the Microsoft ASP.NET MVC team decided to ship jQuery with ASP.NET MVC, making it the first open source product to ship with .NET along with full support. The IntelliSense improvements in the Visual Studio 2012 IDE also make it really easy to work with JavaScript.

JQuery UI is an additional library that adds even more animation support on top of jQuery, but more importantly adds a scaffold for themeable high-level widgets like sliders, calendars, and more. Check them out at `http://jquery.com` and `http://jqueryui.com` as shown in Figure C-4.

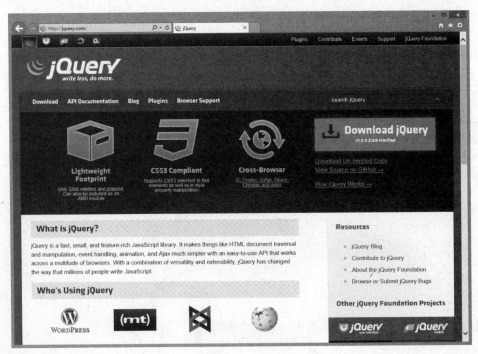

FIGURE C-4

Profilers: dotTrace or ANTS

If you're not measuring your code with a good profiler, you really don't realize what you're missing out on. Only a profiler can give you extensive metrics and a clear understanding of what your code is doing.

Some SKUs of Visual Studio 2012 include a profiler in the top-level Analyze menu. In addition, excellent third-party profilers are available, such as JetBrains' dotTrace and Red Gate Software's ANTS, that are worth your time.

.NET profilers instrument a runtime session of your code and measure how many times each line is hit and how much time is spent executing that line, as shown in Figure C-5. They create a hierarchical series of reports that enable you to analyze time spent not only within a method, but within child methods executed through the stack. You can save reports and analyze multiple versions as you improve your applications, revision after revision.

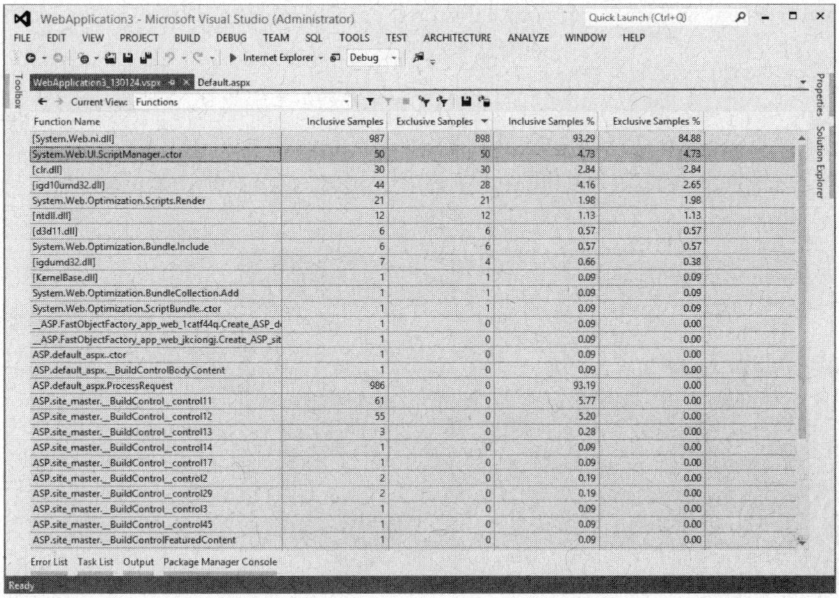

FIGURE C-5

If you haven't already done so, consider adding profiling of your ASP.NET application to your software development life cycle. You'd be surprised to learn how few developers formally analyze and profile their applications. Set aside some time to profile an application that you've never looked at before, and you'll be surprised how much faster it can be made using analysis from a tool such as ANTS or dotTrace.

REFERENCES

> *He who lends a book is an idiot. He who returns the book is more of an idiot.*
>
> —Anonymous, Arabic Proverb

QuirksMode.org and HTMLDog.com

When you're creating websites that need to look nice on all browsers, you're bound to bump into bugs, "features," and general differences in the popular browsers. Web pages are composed of a large combination of standards (HTML, CSS, JS). These standards are not only open to interpretation, but their implementations can differ in subtle ways, especially when they interact.

Reference websites, such as QuirksMode, collect hundreds of these hacks and workarounds. Then they catalog them for your benefit. Many of these features aren't designed, but rather discovered or stumbled upon.

HTML Dog is a fantastic web designer's resource for HTML and CSS. It's full of tutorials, articles, and a large reference section specific to XHTML. QuirksMode includes many resources for learning JavaScript and CSS and includes many test and demo pages demonstrating the quirks.

Visibone

Visibone is known for its amazing reference cards and charts that showcase Color, Fonts, HTML, JavaScript, and CSS. Visibone reference cards and booklets are available online and are very reasonably priced. The best value is the Browser Book available at www.visibone.com/products/browserbook.html. I recommend the laminated version. Be sure to put your name on it because your co-workers will make it disappear.

www.asp.net

www.asp.net is a huge resource for learning about ASP.NET and the various technologies around it. Figure C-6 shows the website, where you can find links to blogs and other community resources.

FIGURE C-6

www.webdevchecklist.com

www.webdevchecklist.com is known for having a comprehensive checklist of tools to run to ensure that your website is in compliance with the best practices for web developers.

SlowCheetah

This is a Visual Studio Extension that you can download from http://visualstudiogallery.msdn .microsoft.com/69023d00-a4f9-4a34-a6cd-7e854ba318b5. You can use this tool to transform your app.config (or any file) using different transformation files based on your build configuration. For example, you can have different database and application settings when you are debugging versus running your application.

TIDYING UP YOUR CODE

After every war someone has to tidy up.

—Wislawa Szymborska

Refactor! for ASP.NET from DevExpress

Refactoring support in Visual Studio 2012 continues to get better. The third-party utilities continue to push the envelope, adding value to the IDE. Refactor! for ASP.NET adds refactoring to the ASP.NET source view.

Refactor can be downloaded from `www.devexpress.com/Products/NET/IDETools/RefactorASP/`. It includes refactorings that make it easier to simplify your code and your ASP.NET markup.

Microsoft Ajax Minifier—JavaScript Minimizer

When creating an ASP.NET website, you often find yourself creating custom JavaScript files. During development, you want these files to be commented and easy to read. During production, however, every byte counts and it's nice to reduce the size of your JavaScript files with a JavaScript "minimizer."

Microsoft Ajax Minifier is a C# application that offers compression of JavaScript or simple "minification" by stripping comments and white space. It's been released on CodePlex at `http://ajaxmin.codeplex.com/`.

You'd be surprised how well these techniques work. For example, Steve Kallestad once reported that a copy of the JavaScript library Prototype 1.50 was 70K before JavaScript-specific compression. It became 30K after the process, and then reached only 14K when gzip HTTP compression was applied. From 70K to 14K is a pretty significant savings.

JavaScript-specific compression does things such as renaming variables to single letters, being aware of global variable renaming vs. local variable renaming, as well as stripping unnecessary white space and comments.

Microsoft Ajax Minifier includes utilities for compression at both the command line and within MSBuild projects. The MSBuild targets can be added to your build process. Consequently, your integration server is continuous so you receive these benefits automatically and unobtrusively.

As an example, a JavaScript library might start out looking like this:

```
var Prototype = {
 Version: '1.5.0',
 BrowserFeatures: {
   XPath: !!document.evaluate
 },

 ScriptFragment: '(?:<script.*?>)((\n|\r|.)*?)(?:<\/script>)',
 emptyFunction: function() {},
 K: function(x) { return x }
}
```

Minified, the JavaScript might end up looking like this (as an example), but it will still work!

```
(c(){f 7.2q(/<\\/?["']+>/5a,"")}),2C:(c(){f 7.2q(P 5d(1m.5s,"9n"),"")}),9j:(c(){k 9m=P
5d(1m.5s,"9n");k 9k=P 5d(1m.5s,"ce");f(7.E(9m)||[]).1F((c(91){f(91.E(9k)||["",""])
[1]}))}),3P:(c(){f7.9j().1F((c(4s){f 6A(4s)}))}),cd:(c(){k 1h=N.4f("1h");k 2V=N.
cc(7);1h.63(2V);f 1h.2P}),cb:(c(){k 1h=N.4f("1h");1h.2P=7.9i();f 1h.20[0]?(1h.20.
o>1?$A(1h.20).2A("",(c(3Y,1G){f 3Y+1G.4j})):1h.20[0].4j):""}),6J:(c(9h){k E=7.4d().E(/([^"?#]*)
(#.*)?$/);h(!E){f{}}f E[1].3m(9h||"&").2A({},(c(2E,Q){h((Q=Q.3m("="))[0]){k v=9g(Q[0]);k
l=Q[1]?9g(Q[1]):1b;h(2E[v]!==1b){h(2E[v].3k!=1M){2E[v]=[2E[v>}h(l){2E[v].M(l)}}1k{2E[v]=l}}f
2E}))}),2F:(c(){f 7.3m("")})
```

Many JavaScript minimizing libraries are available; this is just one of them. However, its options, completeness, and integration with MSBuild make Microsoft Ajax Minifier worth trying out.

EXTENDING ASP.NET

Oh man! :-) I have shoot into my foot myself ;-) Sorry!

—MATZ

Ajax Control Toolkit

The Ajax Control Toolkit is a collaboration between Microsoft and the larger ASP.NET community. Its goal was to provide the largest collection of web client components available. It includes excellent examples if you want to learn how to write ASP.NET AJAX yourself, and then it gives you the opportunity to give back and have your code shared within the community.

Literally dozens of controls build on and extend the ASP.NET AJAX Framework. Some of the controls are simple and provide those nice "little touches" such as drop shadows, rounded corners, watermarks, and animations. Others provide highly functional controls such as calendars, popups, and sliders.

Complete source is available for all the controls so that you can extend and improve them. These controls are more than just samples; they are complete and ready to be used in your applications.

The toolkit is available at `http://www.asp.net/ajax/` (see Figure C-7) There's even a Content Delivery Network (CDN) so you can let Microsoft pay the bandwidth for hosting these JavaScript libraries. They'll be faster and closer to the user as well!

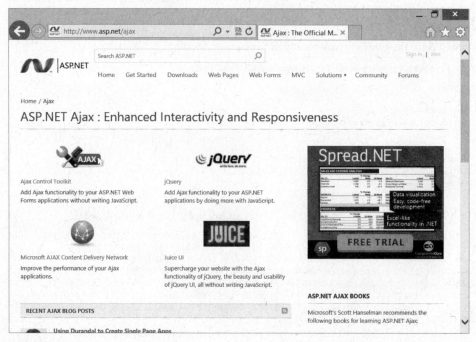

FIGURE C-7

Atif Aziz's ELMAH—Error Logging Modules and Handlers

Troubleshooting errors and unhandled exceptions in your applications can be a full-time job. Rather than writing your own custom global exception handlers every time, consider looking at the ELMAH (Error Logging Modules and Handlers) from Atif Aziz. It's a very flexible application-wide error logging facility with pluggable extension points to the interfaces at nearly every location. You can even configure it in your application without recompilation or even redeployment. Simply modify your `web.config` to include the error logging modules and handlers, and then you'll receive a single web page to remotely review the entire log of unhandled exceptions.

ELMAH captures so much information about exceptions that it can reconstitute the original "yellow screen of death" that ASP.NET would have generated given an exception, even if customErrors was turned off. It's almost like TiVo for your exceptions! Figure C-8 shows ELMAH providing a developer's view, including all the details you might need to debug this error.

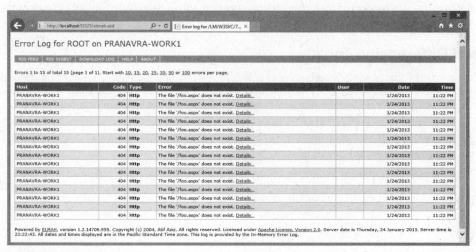

FIGURE C-8

Another clever feature is an RSS feed that shows the last 15 years from your log. This flexible tool is open source and the recent beta includes support for medium trust environments. You can plug in SQL Server or use an XML file to manage your error logs. I highly recommend you take the time to learn about ELMAH.

Helicon's ISAPI_Rewrite and IIS7 URLRewrite

Users of the Apache web server sing the praises of the power of `mod_rewrite`, its URL rewriting mechanism. IIS6 users have this available to them in the form of the ISAPI_Rewrite module from Helicon. It's incredibly fast because it's written in pure C. It integrates nicely with ASP.NET in the IIS "Classic" pipeline because URLs are rewritten before ASP.NET realizes anything has happened. IIS7 users can use the URL Rewriting Module discussed in a moment.

Because it uses regular expressions, ISAPI_Rewrite can initially be very frustrating due to its terse syntax. However, if you are patient, it can be an incredibly powerful tool for your tool belt.

There's also an IIS7-specific URL Rewrite Module available at `http://www.iis.net/extensions/URLRewrite`. It is easier to use than ISAPI_Rewrite because it includes a complete UI for managing and creating rewrites and an import tool for bringing your existing Apache-style rewrites into IIS7.

An extra bonus is that the IIS7 rewrite tool runs inside the managed pipeline for an extra performance boost when you're using it on ASP.NET applications.

GENERAL-PURPOSE DEVELOPER TOOLS

If you get the dirty end of the stick, sharpen it and turn it into a useful tool.

—COLIN POWELL

Telerik's Online Code Converter

Creating samples that should appear in both C# and Visual Basic can be very tedious without the assistance of something like Telerik's CodeChanger.com.'

Although it's not an officially supported tool, this little application will definitely get you 80 percent of the way when converting between Visual Basic and C#.

WinMerge and Differencing Tools

Everyone has their favorite merge tool. Whether yours is WinMerge, or Beyond Compare, or the old standby WinDiff, just make sure that you have one in your list of tools that you're very familiar with. When managing large numbers of changes across large numbers of individuals on software development teams, a good merge tool can help you untangle even the most complicated conflicting checkins.

A number of different plugins are available for WinMerge that extend its functionality to include comparison of Word and Excel documents and XML files.

Other highly recommended merge tools include Beyond Compare from Scooter Software and DiffMerge from SourceGear. Each of these tools integrates with Windows Explorer, so the comparing files are as easy as a right-click.

.NET Reflector

If you're not using .NET Reflector, your .NET developer experience is lesser for it. Reflector is an object browser, decompiler, help system, powerful plug-in host, and incredible learning tool. This tiny utility, originally from Microsoft developer Lutz Roeder and now maintained by Red Gate, is consistently listed as the number-one most indispensable tool available to the .NET developer after Visual Studio.

Reflector is amazing because it not only gives you a representation of the programmer's intent by transforming IL back into C# or VB, but it includes analysis tools that help you visualize dependencies between methods in the .NET Base Class Library and within your code or any third-party code.

Process Explorer

Last, but unquestionably not least, is Process Explorer from Mark Russinovich. To call it "Task Manager on steroids" would not even begin to do it justice. Process Explorer puts Windows itself under a microscope by allowing you to peer inside your active processes, their threads, and the environment to get a clearer understanding about what is actually going on. Advanced and detailed use of this tool, along with the entire SysInternals Suite of Tools, should be required for all developers.

In Figure C-9, I'm looking at all the processes running on my machine. I can use this tool to find which process has a lock on a dll.

Process Explorer - Sysinternals: www.sysinternals.com [PRANAVRA-WORK1\Author]

File Options View Process Find Users Help

Process	PID	CPU	Private Bytes	Working Set	Description	Company Name
System Idle Process	0	75.17	0 K	20 K		
System	4	1.27	132 K	6,180 K		
Interrupts	n/a	2.57	0 K	0 K	Hardware Interrupts and DPCs	
smss.exe	384		284 K	948 K		
csrss.exe	540	< 0.01	1,864 K	4,276 K		
wininit.exe	612		860 K	3,428 K		
services.exe	664	0.01	4,920 K	9,484 K		
svchost.exe	824	0.02	20,376 K	25,660 K	Host Process for Windows S...	Microsoft Corporation
BTStackServer.exe	4964	0.01	9,800 K	16,364 K	Bluetooth Stack COM Server	Broadcom Corporation.
unsecapp.exe	5708		984 K	4,304 K		
WmiPrvSE.exe	5128	0.54	9,712 K	19,904 K		
WmiPrvSE.exe	5848	< 0.01	16,840 K	25,204 K		
WmiPrvSE.exe	1648		4,160 K	9,536 K		
WmiPrvSE.exe	4676		2,124 K	5,972 K		
WmiPrvSE.exe	4512		3,944 K	9,656 K		
WmiPrvSE.exe	4356		2,948 K	10,152 K		
FlashUtil_ActiveX.exe	6660		2,432 K	7,156 K	Adobe® Flash® Player Utility	Adobe Systems Incorporated
WmiPrvSE.exe	6448		4,316 K	7,160 K		
ibmpmsvc.exe	856		788 K	2,564 K	ThinkPad Power Manageme...	Lenovo
svchost.exe	916		19,292 K	23,884 K	Host Process for Windows S...	Microsoft Corporation
MsMpEng.exe	960	0.08	76,652 K	57,076 K	Antimalware Service Execut...	Microsoft Corporation
svchost.exe	120	0.01	31,296 K	38,584 K	Host Process for Windows S...	Microsoft Corporation
audiodg.exe	6688		7,216 K	9,600 K		
svchost.exe	900		16,876 K	27,964 K	Host Process for Windows S...	Microsoft Corporation
svchost.exe	568		6,732 K	14,684 K	Host Process for Windows S...	Microsoft Corporation
svchost.exe	1048	0.48	85,340 K	94,088 K	Host Process for Windows S...	Microsoft Corporation
svchost.exe	1096	0.02	12,008 K	22,852 K	Host Process for Windows S...	Microsoft Corporation
svchost.exe	1144	0.03	81,300 K	82,584 K	Host Process for Windows S...	Microsoft Corporation
WUDFHost.exe	1420		1,432 K	5,512 K		

CPU Usage: 24.83% Commit Charge: 43.13% Processes: 99 Physical Usage: 70.68%

FIGURE C-9

SUMMARY

Having the right tools can mean the difference between a week of time spent with your head against the wall versus 5 minutes of quick analysis in debugging. The right tool can mean the difference between a tedious and keyboard-heavy code slogging or a refactoring session that is actually pleasant. I encourage you to try each of the tools listed here, as well as to explore the ecosystem of available tools to find those that make your development experience not just more productive, but more enjoyable.

Administration and Management

You have almost reached the end of this book. At this point, you have been introduced to ASP .NET 4.5. However, with all advancement comes complexity, as is the case in the areas of ASP.NET configuration and management. The good news is that the ASP.NET development team realized this and provided tools and APIs that enable developers to configure and manage ASP.NET–based applications with reliability and comfort.

This appendix covers these tools in great detail in an effort to educate you about some of the options available to you. It explores two powerful configuration tools: the ASP.NET Web Site Administration Tool, a web-based application, and the IIS Manager, which is used to configure your ASP.NET applications.

THE ASP.NET WEB SITE ADMINISTRATION TOOL

When ASP.NET was first released, it introduced the concept of an XML-based configuration file for its web applications. This `web.config` file is located in the same directory as the application itself. It is used to store a number of configuration settings, some of which can override configuration settings defined in the `machine.config` file or in the root server's `web.config` file. Versions of ASP.NET before ASP.NET 2.0, however, did not provide an administration tool to make it easy to configure the settings. Because of this, a large number of developers ended up creating their own configuration tools to avoid having to work with the XML file manually.

> **NOTE** *If you are starting with the Empty project template for ASP.NET, you must use NuGet to install the Universal Providers and LocalDB (because SQLExpress is not installed by default with Visual Studio 2012). You can find the correct package in NuGet, which is discussed in Appendix G, by installing Microsoft ASP.NET Universal Providers for LocalDB.*

The ASP.NET Web Site Administration Tool enables you to manage website configuration through a simple, easy-to-use web interface. It eliminates some of the need for manually editing the web.config file. If no web.config file exists when you use the administration tool for the first time, it creates one. By default, the ASP.NET Web Site Administration Tool also creates a LocalDB file in the App_Data folder of your website to store application data. The changes made to most settings in the ASP.NET Web Site Administration Tool take effect immediately. You find them reflected in the web.config file.

The default settings are inherited automatically from any configuration files that exist in the root folder of a web server. The ASP.NET Web Site Administration Tool enables you to create or update your own settings for your web application. You can also override the settings inherited from up-level configuration files, if an override for those settings is allowed. If overriding is not permitted, the setting appears dimmed in the administration tool.

The ASP.NET Web Site Administration Tool is installed automatically during installation of the .NET Framework version 4.5. To use the administration tool to administer your own website, you must be logged in as a registered user of your site and have read and write permissions to the web.config file.

You cannot access the ASP.NET Web Site Administration Tool remotely or even locally through IIS. Instead, you access it with Visual Studio 2012, which, in turn, uses its integrated web server (IISExpress) to access the administration tool.

To access this tool through Visual Studio 2012, open the website or web application and click the ASP.NET Configuration menu option found under the top menu named Website or Project, respectively. Another way to launch this tool is to select ASP.NET Configuration from the Website option in the main Visual Studio menu. Figure D-1 shows the ASP.NET Web Site Administration Tool's welcome page.

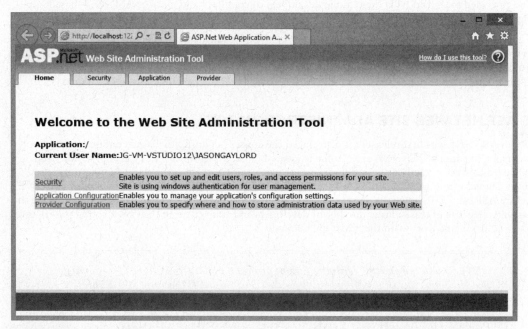

FIGURE D-1

The ASP.NET Web Site Administration Tool (WSAT) features a tabbed interface that groups related configuration settings. The following sections describe the tabs and the configuration settings that they manage.

> **NOTE** *The ASP.NET Web Site Administration Tool requires that SQL Server or SQL Express be used as the default SQL connection string. The WSAT does not currently support LocalDB as the database or Simple Membership as the authentication or role provider.*

The Home Tab

The Home tab (shown previously in Figure D-1) is a summary that supplies some basic information about the application you are monitoring or modifying. It provides the name of the application and the current user context in which you are accessing the application. In addition, you see links to the other administration tool tabs that provide you with summaries of their settings. To make any changes to your web application, you simply click the appropriate tab or link.

Remember that most changes to configuration settings made using this administration tool take effect immediately, causing the web application to be restarted and currently active sessions to be lost if you are using an InProc session. The best practice for administrating ASP.NET is to make configuration changes to a development version of your application and later publish these changes to your production application. That's why this tool can't be used outside of Visual Studio.

Some settings (those in which the administration tool interface has a dedicated Save button) do not save automatically. You can lose the information typed in these windows if you do not click the Save button to propagate the changes you made to the web.config file. The ASP.NET Web Site Administration Tool also times out after a period of inactivity. Any settings that do not take effect immediately and are not saved will be lost if this occurs.

As extensive as the ASP.NET Web Site Administration Tool is, it manages only a few of the basic configuration settings that are available for your web application. All other settings require modification of configuration files manually, by using Visual Studio to manually edit the files, by using the Internet Information Services (IIS) Manager, or by using the Configuration API.

The Security Tab

You use the Security tab to manage access permissions to secure sections of your web application, user accounts, and roles. From this tab, you can select whether your web application is accessed on an intranet or from the Internet. If you specify the intranet, Windows-based authentication is used; otherwise, forms-based authentication is configured. The latter mechanism relies on you to manage users in a custom data store, such as SQL Server database tables. The Windows-based authentication employs the user's Windows logon for identification.

> **NOTE** *This section discusses several ways to use the WSAT to configure security. For more information on this topic, refer to Chapter 19.*

User information is stored in a database by default. The database is created automatically in the App_Data folder of the web application. Storing such sensitive information in a more secure location, such as using a database on a separate server, is recommended. Changing the data store might mean that you also need to change the underlying data provider. To accomplish this, you simply use the Provider tab to select a different data provider. The Provider tab is covered later in this appendix.

You can configure security settings on this tab in two ways: Select the Setup Wizard, or simply use the links provided for the Users, Roles, and Access Management sections. Figure D-2 shows the Security tab.

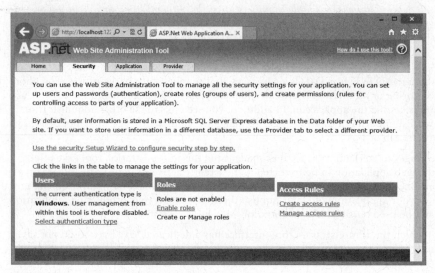

FIGURE D-2

You can use the wizard to configure initial settings. Later, you learn other ways to create and modify security settings.

The Security Setup Wizard

The Security Setup Wizard provides a seven-step process ranging from selecting the way the user will be authenticated to selecting a data source for storing user information. This is followed by definitions of roles, users, and access rules.

> **NOTE** *Be sure to create all folders that need special permissions before you engage the wizard.*

Follow these steps to use the Security Setup Wizard:

1. **Welcome:** On the Security tab, click the "Use the Security Setup Wizard to configure security step by step" link. The wizard welcome screen (shown in Figure D-3) appears and is informational only. It educates you on the basics of security management in ASP.NET. When you finish reading the screen, click Next.

2. **Select Access Method:** From the Select Access Method screen, shown in Figure D-4, select your access method (authentication mechanism). You have two options:

    ➤ **From the Internet:** Indicates you want forms-based authentication. You must use your own database of user information. This option works well in scenarios where non-employees need to access the web application.

    ➤ **From a Local Area Network:** Indicates that users of this application are already authenticated on the domain. You do not have to use your own user information database. Instead, you can use the Windows web server domain user information.

Select From the Internet, and click the Next button.

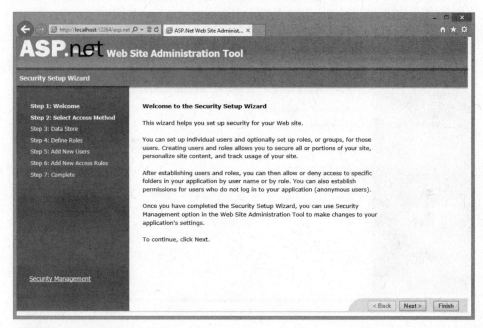

FIGURE D-3

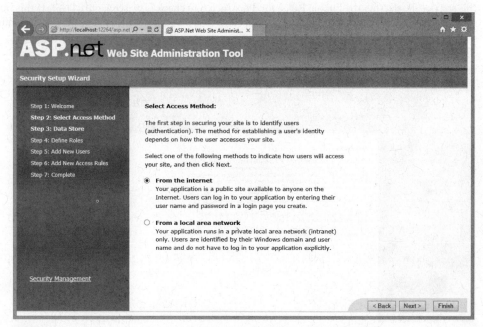

FIGURE D-4

3. **Data Store:** As mentioned earlier, the ASP.NET Web Site Administration Tool uses a database by default. You can configure additional providers on the Providers tab. In the Step 3 screen shown in Figure D-5, only an advanced provider is displayed because no other providers have been configured yet. Click Next.

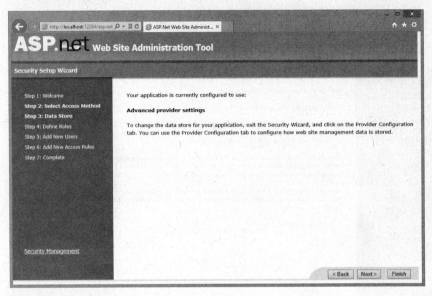

FIGURE D-5

4. **Define Roles:** If you are happy with all users having the same access permission, you can simply skip this step by deselecting the Enable Roles for This Web Site check box (see Figure D-6). If this box is not selected, clicking the Next button takes you directly to the User Management screens. Select this box to see how to define roles using this wizard. When you are ready, click Next.

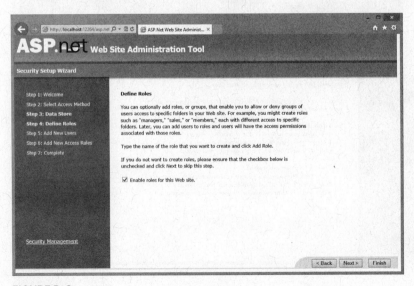

FIGURE D-6

The next screen (see Figure D-7) in the wizard enables you to create and delete roles. The roles simply define categories of users. Later, you can provide users and access rules based on these roles. Go ahead and create roles for Administrators, Human Resources, Interns, and Sales. Click Next.

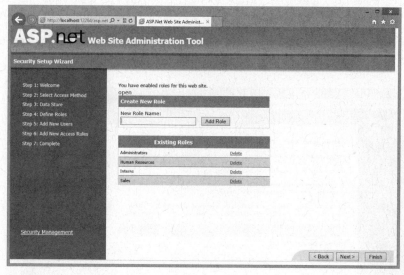

FIGURE D-7

5. **Add New Users:** Earlier, you selected the From the Internet option, so the wizard assumes that you want to use forms authentication and provides you with the option of creating and managing users. The From a Local Area Network option, remember, uses Windows-based authentication.

    The Add New Users screen (see Figure D-8) enables you to enter the username, password, e-mail address, and a security question and answer.

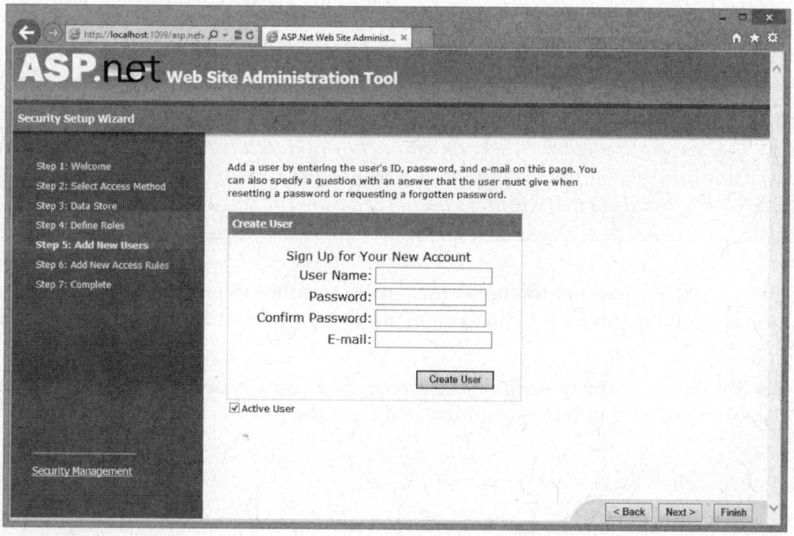

FIGURE D-8

You can create as many users as you like; but to delete or update information for users, you must leave the wizard and manage the users separately. As mentioned earlier, the wizard is simply for creating the initial configuration for future management. Click Next.

6. **Add New Access Rules** (see Figure D-9): First, select the folder in the web application that needs special security settings. Then choose the role or user(s) to whom the rule will apply. Select the permission (Allow or Deny) and click the Add This Rule button. For example, if you had a folder named Secure, you could select it and the Administrators role, and then click the Allow radio button to permit all users in the Administrators role to access the Secure folder.

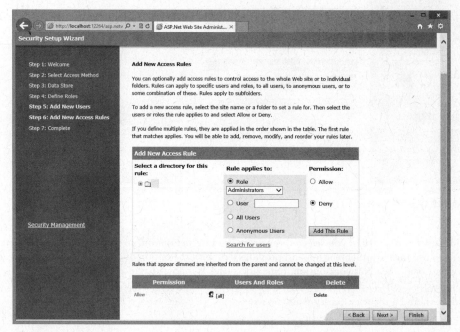

FIGURE D-9

> **NOTE** *All folders that need special permissions must be created ahead of time. The information shown in the wizard is cached and is not updated if you decide to create a new folder inside your web application while you are already on this screen, so remember to create your special security folders before starting the wizard.*

The wizard gives you the capability to apply access rules to either roles or specific users. The Search for Users option is handy if you have defined many users for your website and want to search for a specific user.

All access rules are shown at the bottom on the screen, and you can delete a specific rule and start again. Rules are shown dimmed if they are inherited from the parent configuration and cannot be changed here.

When you are ready, click Next.

7. **Complete:** The last screen in the Security Setup Wizard is an information page. Click the Finish button to exit the wizard.

Creating New Users

The ASP.NET Web Site Administration Tool's Security tab provides ways to manage users without using the wizard and is very helpful for ongoing maintenance of users, roles, and access permissions.

To create a new user, simply click the Create New User link on the main page of the Security tab (shown in Figure D-10). The Create User screen, shown in Figure D-11, appears, enabling you to provide username, password, confirmation of password, e-mail, and the security question and answer. You can assign a new user to any number of roles in the Roles list; these are roles currently defined for your web application. Use this tool to create users named Admin, HRUser, and SalesUser and assign them the corresponding roles.

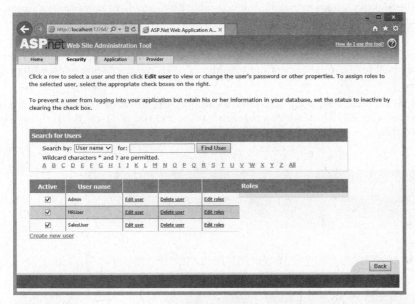

FIGURE D-10

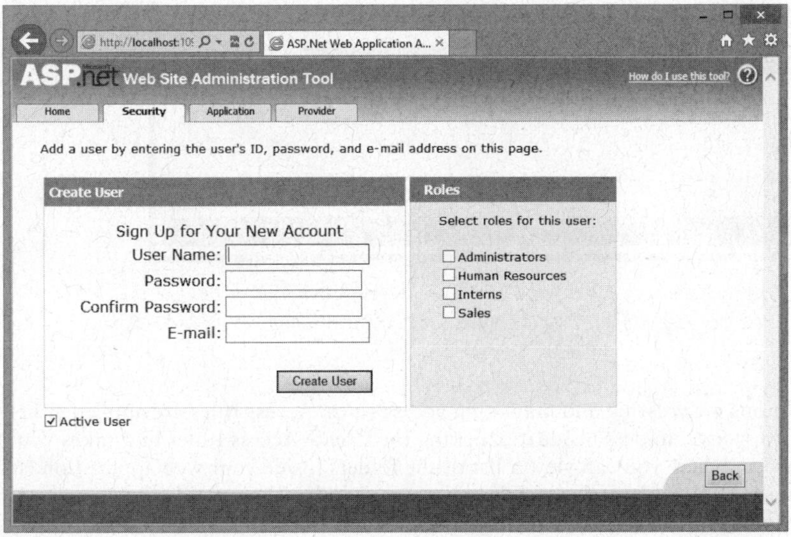

FIGURE D-11

Managing Users

You can manage existing users by clicking the Manage Users link on the Security tab. A new screen displays a list of all existing users (see Figure D-10). A search option is available, which makes finding a specific user easier if the list is long.

Find the user you want to manage, and then you can update his information, delete the user, reassign roles, or set the user to active or inactive.

Managing Roles

Two links are provided in the Security tab for managing roles: Disable Roles and Create or Manage Roles. Clicking Disable Roles does just that—disables role management in the web application; it also dims the other link.

Click the Create or Manage Roles link to start managing roles and assigning users to specific roles. A screen displays all roles you have defined so far. You have options to add new roles, delete existing roles, or manage specific roles.

Click the Manage link next to a specific role, and a screen shows all the users currently assigned to that role (see Figure D-12). You can find other users by searching for their names, and you can then assign them to or remove them from a selected role.

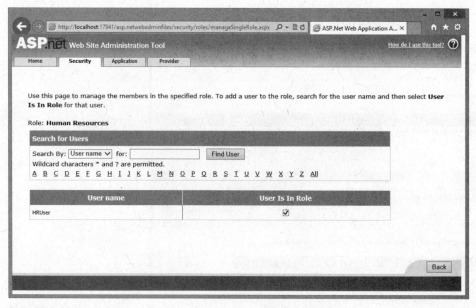

FIGURE D-12

Managing Access Rules

The Security tab provides options for creating and managing access rules. Access rules are applied either to an entire web application or to specific folders inside it. Clicking the Create Access Rules link takes you to the Add New Access Rule screen, where you can view a list of the folders inside your web application (see Figure D-13). You can select a specific folder, select a role or a user, and then choose whether you want to enable access to the selected folder.

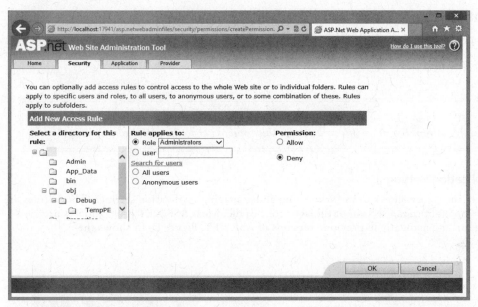

FIGURE D-13

Clicking Manage Access Rules on the Security tab takes you to the Manage Access Rules screen, which shows all existing access rules (see Figure D-14).You can remove any of these rules and add new ones. You can also readjust the list of access rules if you want to apply them in a specific order.

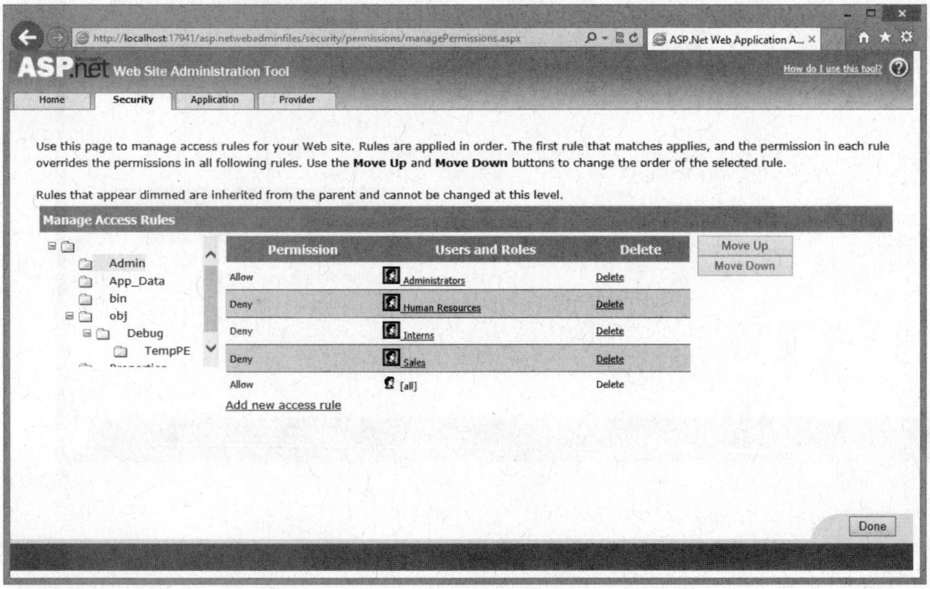

FIGURE D-14

The Application Tab

The Application tab provides a number of application-specific configurations, including the configuration of `<appSettings>`, SMTP mail server settings, debugging and trace settings, and starting/stopping the entire web application.

> **NOTE** *This section discusses several ways to use the WSAT to update the application configuration. For more information on this topic, refer to Part VIII of this book.*

Managing Application Settings

The left side of the screen shows links for creating and managing application settings. The settings are stored in the `<appSettings>` section of the web.config file. Most ASP.NET programmers are used to modifying this tag manually in previous versions of ASP.NET. Figure D-15 shows the Application tab.

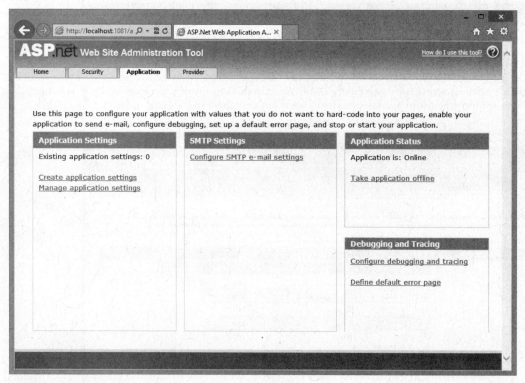

FIGURE D-15

Clicking the Create Application Settings link takes you to a screen where you can provide the name and the value information. Clicking Manage Application Settings takes you to a screen where you can view existing settings and edit or delete them. You can also create a new setting from this screen.

Managing SMTP Configuration

Click the Configure SMTP E-Mail Settings link to view a screen like the one shown in Figure D-16. The configure SMTP mail settings feature is useful if your web application can send auto-generated e-mails. Instead of denoting SMTP server configuration in the code, you can spell it out in the configuration file by entering values here in the administration tool.

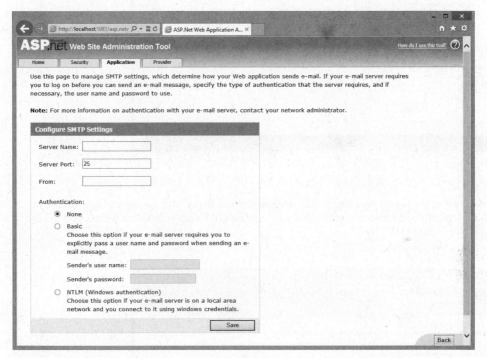

FIGURE D-16

Specify the server name, port, sender e-mail address, and authentication type.

Managing Tracing and Debugging Information

Clicking the Application tab's Configure Debugging and Tracing link takes you to a screen (see Figure D-17) where you can enable or disable tracing and debugging. Select whether you want to display trace information on each page. You can also specify whether to track just local requests or all requests, as well as trace sorting and caching configuration.

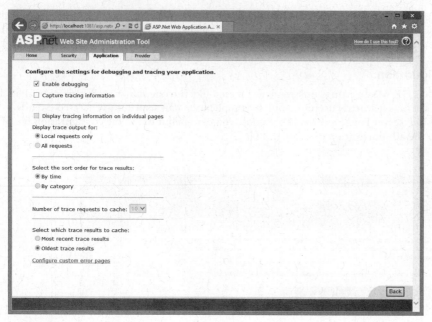

FIGURE D-17

To configure default error pages, you simply click Define Default Error Page on the screen you saw in Figure D-15. This takes you to a screen where you can select a URL that is used for redirection in case of an error condition (see Figure D-18).

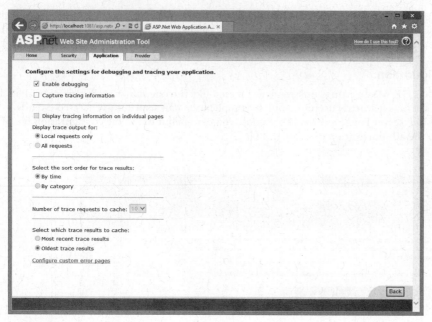

FIGURE D-18

Taking an Application Offline

You can take your entire web application offline simply by clicking the Take Application Offline link (again, refer to Figure D-15). The link stops the app domain for your web application. This feature is useful if you want to perform a scheduled maintenance for an application.

The Provider Tab

The final tab in the ASP.NET Web Site Administration Tool is Provider, shown in Figure D-19. You use it to set up additional providers and to determine the providers your application will use.

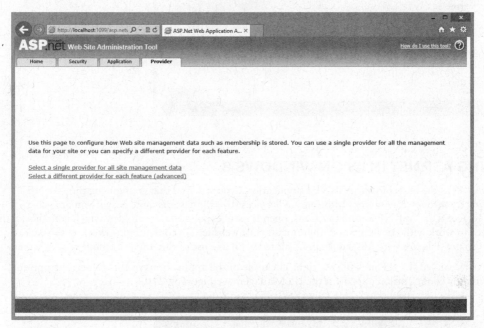

FIGURE D-19

The Provider page is simple, but it contains an important piece of information: the default data provider with which your application is geared to work. In Figure D-19, the application is set up to work with the default data provider.

The two links on this tab let you set up either a single data provider or a specific data provider for each feature in ASP.NET that requires a data provider. If you click the latter, the screen shown in Figure D-20 appears. It enables you to pick the available providers separately for Membership and Role management.

As you can see from the screenshots and brief explanations provided here, you could now handle a large portion of the necessary configurations through a GUI. You no longer have to figure out which setting must be placed in the web.config file. This functionality becomes even more important as the web.config file grows. In ASP.NET 1.0/1.1, the web.config file was a reasonable size, but with all the features provided by ASP.NET 2.0 or 3.5, the web.config file became very large. Again, like ASP.NET 1.0/1.1, the web.config file in ASP.NET 4.5 is now quite small by default. These GUI-based tools are an outstanding way to configure some of the most commonly needed settings. However, many settings cannot be modified with the Web Server Administration Tool, so you will still need to edit the web.config file in many cases.

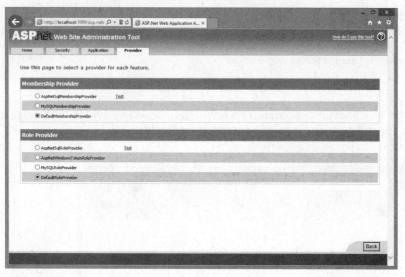

FIGURE D-20

CONFIGURING ASP.NET IN IIS ON WINDOWS 8

If you are using IIS as the basis of your ASP.NET applications, you will find that configuring the ASP.NET application directly through the Internet Information Services (IIS) Manager is quite easy if you are using Windows 8. To access the ASP.NET configurations, open IIS and expand the Sites folder, which contains all the sites configured to work with IIS. Remember that not all your websites are configured to work in this manner because it is also possible to create ASP.NET applications that make use of the ASP.NET built-in web server.

After you have expanded the IIS Sites folder, right-click one of the applications in this folder; the options available to you for configuration appear in the IIS Manager (see Figure D-21).

FIGURE D-21

The options available to you enable you to completely configure ASP.NET or even configure IIS itself. The focus of this appendix is on the ASP.NET section of the options. In addition to the options you can select from one of the available icons, you can also configure some basic settings of the application by clicking the Basic Settings link in the Actions pane on the right side of the IIS Manager. When you click the Basic Settings link, the Edit Site dialog box appears, as shown in Figure D-22.

> **NOTE** *Changes you are making in the IIS Manager are actually being applied to the* web.config *file of your application.*

This dialog box enables you to change the following items:

➤ **Site name:** The name of the website. In the case of Figure D-22, naming the website ProASPNET45 means that the URL will be http://[IP address or domain name]/ProASPNET45.

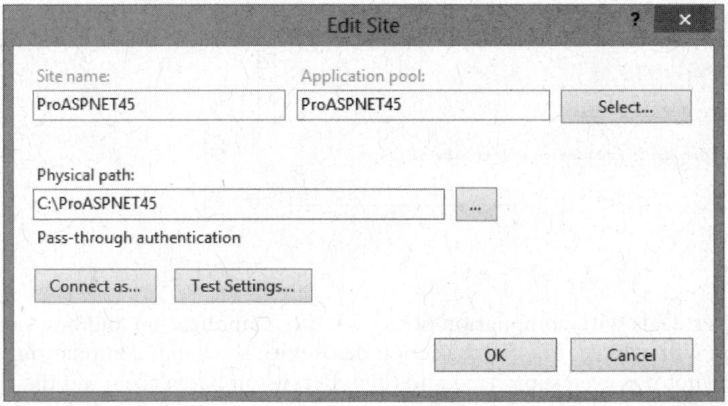

FIGURE D-22

➤ **Application pool:** The application pool you are going to use for the application. You will notice that you have two options by default: DefaultAppPool (which uses the .NET Framework 4 and an integrated pipeline mode) and Classic .NET AppPool (which uses the .NET Framework 4 and a classic pipeline mode). This example uses a new application pool called ProASPNET45.

➤ **Physical path:** The folder location where the ASP.NET application can be found. In this case, it is C:\ProASPNET45.

The sections that follow review some of the options available to you through the icons in the IIS Manager.

.NET Compilation

You use the Application tab to make changes that are more specific to the pages in the context of your application. From the .NET Compilation dialog box (accessible via the IIS Manager) shown in Figure D-23, you can change how your pages are compiled and run. You can also make changes to global settings in your application.

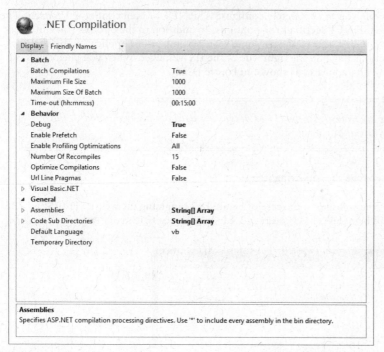

FIGURE D-23

This section of the IIS Manager deals with compilation of the ASP.NET application and how some of the pages of the application will behave. The Batch section deals with the batch compilation of the application — first, whether or not it is even supported and then, details on batch sizes and the time it takes to incur the compilation.

The Behavior section deals with whether or not the compilation produces a release or debug build; you will also find some Visual Basic–specific compilation instructions on whether Option Explicit or Option Script are enabled across the entire application.

The General section focuses on the assemblies that are referenced as well as your code subdirectories if you are going to break up your App_Code folder into separate compiled instances (required for when you want to incorporate Visual Basic and C# code in the same application). You can also specify the default language that is used in the compilation process, such as VB or C#.

.NET Globalization

The .NET Globalization option in the IIS Manager enables you to customize how your ASP.NET application deals with culture and the encoding of the requests and responses. Figure D-24 shows the options available in this dialog box.

In addition to picking a specific Culture or UI Culture setting, you can also select Auto Detect, which will pick up the culture of the client if it is available. By default, you can also see that the encoding of the requests and the responses are set to utf-8, which will work fine for most Latin-based languages.

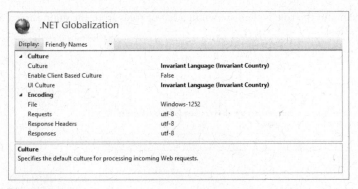

FIGURE D-24

.NET Profile

The IIS Manager.NET Profile options enable you to customize how your ASP.NET application deals with the ASP.NET personalization system. This system was discussed earlier in Chapter 18. Figure D-25 shows the dialog box that is provided when you add a new profile to the personalization system.

In this case, as presented in Figure D-25, you can specify the name of the personalization property, the data type used, its default value, how it is serialized, and whether it is read-only or available for anonymous users. To better understand these settings, it is important to review Chapter 18.

In addition to building properties to use in the personalization system, you can also specify the provider that is used by the system as a whole. By default, it uses the AspNetSqlProfileProvider, as illustrated in Figure D-26. You can get to this dialog box by selecting the Set Default Provider link from the .NET Profile section.

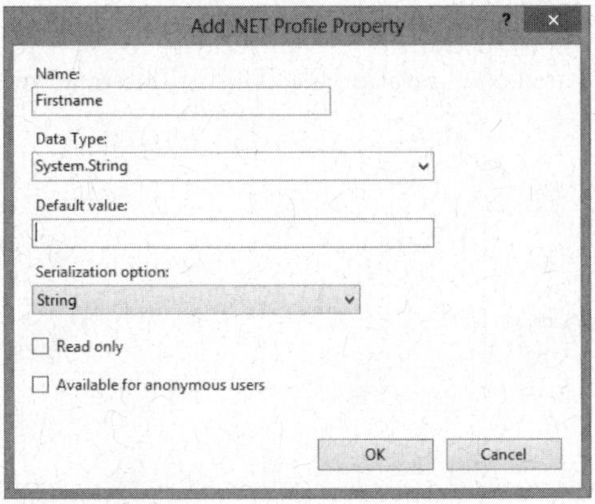

FIGURE D-25

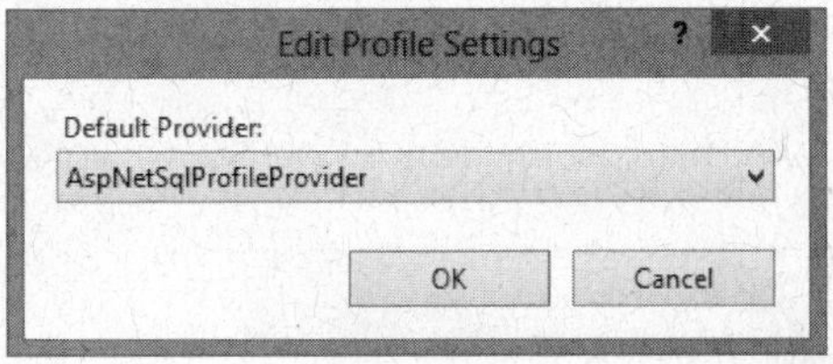

FIGURE D-26

.NET Roles

You can enable role-based management by adding roles to your application from the .NET Roles section of the IIS Manager. Figure D-27 shows an example of adding a role called Administrators to the application after clicking the Add link from the Actions section.

FIGURE D-27

Clicking OK adds the role to the system and the role is then shown in a list of roles from the main screen of the section, as illustrated in Figure D-28.

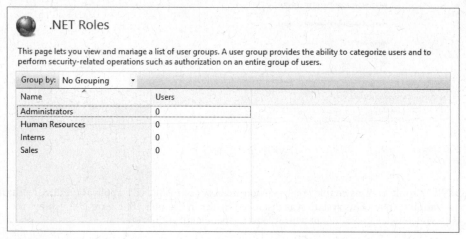

FIGURE D-28

By default, no users are added to the role. You can add users to roles through the .NET Users section, discussed shortly.

.NET Trust Levels

The .NET Trust Levels section of the IIS Manager enables you to specify the level of security to apply to your application through the selection of a specific pre-generated configuration file. This is illustrated in the list of options presented in Figure D-29.

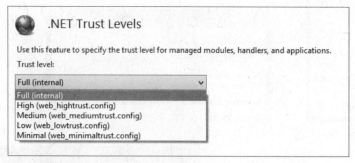

FIGURE D-29

By default, your application makes use of the `web.config` file, but specifying a different trust level causes the application to use a different `.config` file. You can find all of these `.config` files at `C:\Windows\ Microsoft.NET\Framework\v4.0.xxxxx\CONFIG`.

.NET Users

Probably one of the easiest ways to work with the ASP.NET membership system (covered in Chapter 19) is to create your users in the .NET Users section of the IIS Manager. Adding a user is easy to do through the dialog boxes provided, as illustrated in Figure D-30.

As shown in Figure D-30, you can provide the username, password, and security question and answer in a simple wizard. Figure D-31 shows the second screen of the wizard.

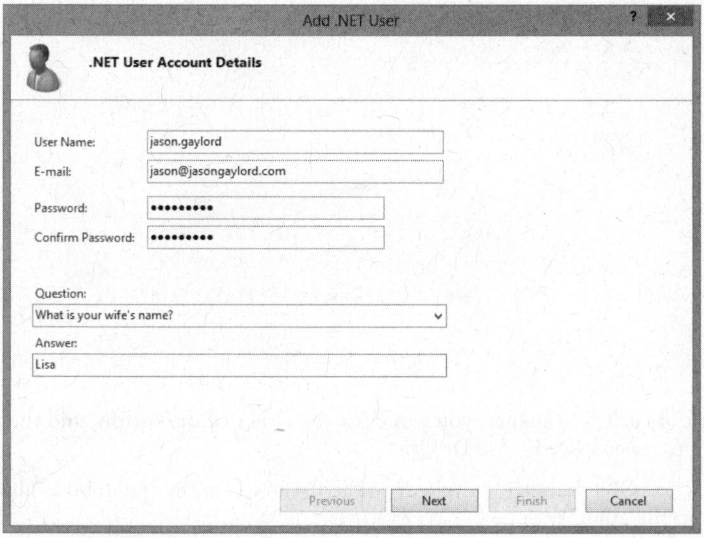

FIGURE D-30

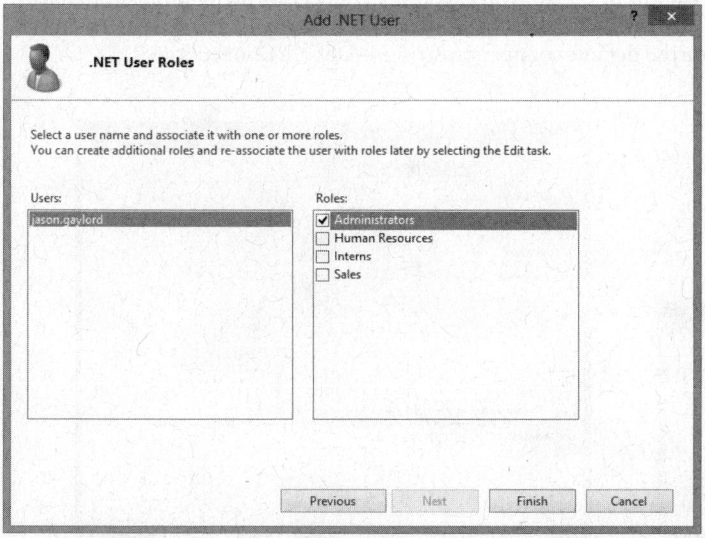

FIGURE D-31

In this second screen of the wizard, you can assign users to specific roles that are present in the role management system. Because the Administrators role was created earlier in this appendix, I am able to assign the user to this particular role because it exists in the system.

After a user is created, you can then see the entire list of users for this particular application from the main .NET Users screen, as illustrated in Figure D-32.

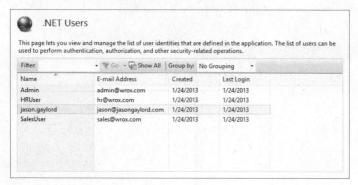

FIGURE D-32

Application Settings

In the IIS Application Settings section of the IIS Manager, you can click the Add or Edit button, and the Add/Edit Application Setting dialog box opens (see Figure D-33).

After you enter a key and value pair, click OK; the settings appear in the list in the main dialog box. Then you can edit or delete the settings from the application.

Connection Strings

In the Connection Strings section of the IIS Manager, you can add a connection string to your application by clicking its Add button. You also can edit or remove existing connection strings. Figure D-34 shows the Edit Connection String dialog box for the default connection string—DefaultConnection.

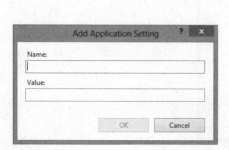

FIGURE D-33

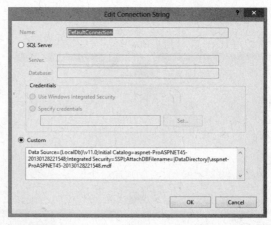

FIGURE D-34

Figure D-35 shows that adding a brand-new connection is also rather simple.

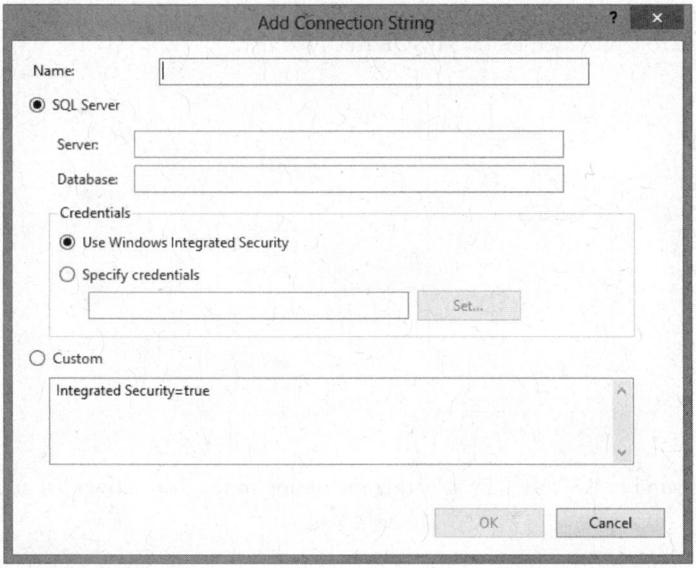

FIGURE D-35

Pages and Controls

The Pages and Controls section of the IIS Manager deals with a group of settings that control the overall ASP.NET pages (.aspx) and user controls in the application (.ascx). Figure D-36 shows the available settings for this section.

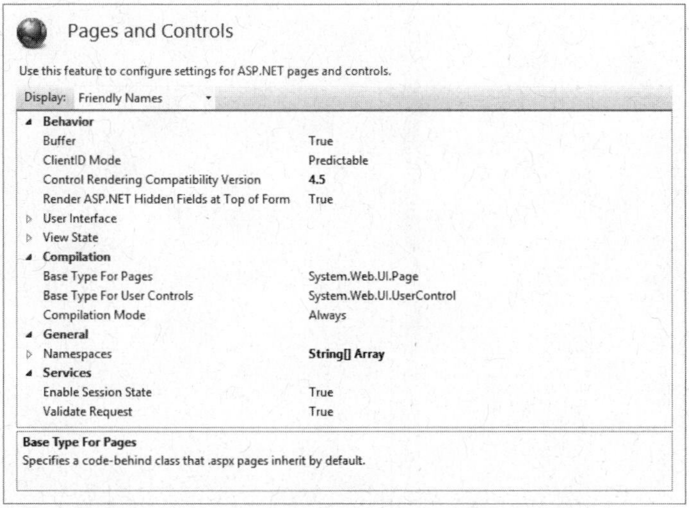

FIGURE D-36

Providers

The Providers section of IIS deals with all the providers that are defined within the application. From the example in Figure D-37, you can see that three providers are defined for the .NET Roles engine: a SQL Server role provider, a Windows Token role provider, and a MySQL role provider.

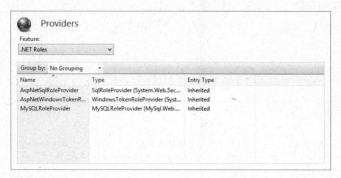

FIGURE D-37

You can look at all the other engines found in ASP.NET by selecting the option in the drop-down list at the top of the dialog box.

Session State

ASP.NET applications, being stateless in nature, are highly dependent on how state is stored. The Session State section of the IIS Manager (see Figure D-38) enables you to change a number of different settings that determine how state management is administered.

FIGURE D-38

You can apply state management to your applications in a number of ways, and this dialog box allows for a number of different settings— some of which are enabled or disabled based on what is selected. The following list describes the items available in the Session State Settings section:

➤ **Session state mode:** Determines how the sessions are stored by the ASP.NET application. The default option (shown in Figure D-38) is In process. Other options include Not enabled, Custom, State Server, and SQL Server. Running sessions in process means that the sessions are stored in the same process as the ASP.NET worker process. Therefore, if IIS is shut down and then brought up again, all the sessions are destroyed and unavailable to end users. Custom means you can specify a custom storage provider. For example, you may use a third-party session state provider. State Server means that sessions are stored out-of-process by a Windows service called ASPState. SQL Server is by far the most secure way to deal with your sessions; it stores them directly in SQL Server. State Server is also the least performance-efficient method.

➤ **Cookieless mode:** Changes how the identifiers for the end user are stored. The default setting uses cookies (UseCookies). Other possible settings include UseUri, AutoDetect, and UseDeviceProfile.

➤ **Session timeout:** Sessions are stored for only a short period of time before they expire. For years, the default has been 20 minutes. Modifying the value here changes how long the sessions created by your application are valid.

SMTP E-mail

If you need to work with an application that delivers e-mail, you must specify the settings to do this. You define the required settings for sending e-mail using SMTP through the SMTP E-mail section of the IIS Manager (see Figure D-39).

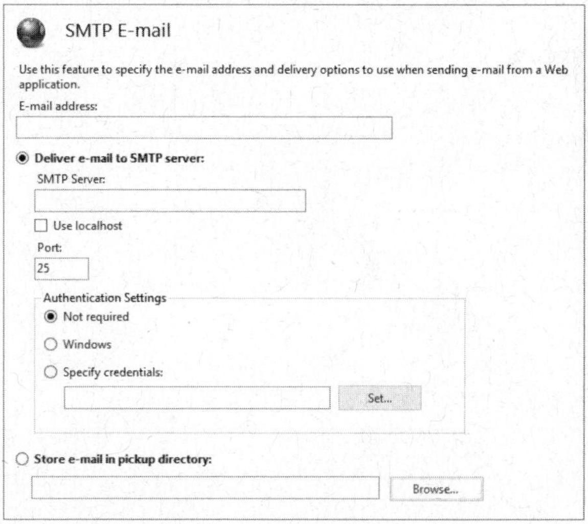

SUMMARY

This appendix showed you some of the management tools that are part of ASP.NET. These tools make the `web.config` file more manageable because they take care of setting the appropriate values in the application's configuration file.

The IIS Manager console in Windows 8 is a wonderful tool for managing applications that are configured to work with IIS. The ASP.NET Web Site Administration Tool provides even more value to administrators and developers by enabling them to easily manage settings.

FIGURE D-39

Dynamic Types and Languages

When Microsoft originally introduced .NET, many developers, especially those coming from Visual Basic 6 (or earlier), were brought into a new world of statically typed languages. No longer were developers allowed to create variant types, or easily create instances of objects at run time using late binding. The new .NET-based languages forced them to define all of their objects using a well-known type, and if the compiler did not recognize that type, it would throw errors back at them.

Purists out there will argue that .NET does indeed support late binding, and it is true that VB.NET can accommodate late binding through disabling the Option Strict command, though this is certainly discouraged in most situations. In C# if you want to simulate late binding you have to resort to reflection, which usually means a lot more lines of code and application complexity.

Although statically typed languages have many advantages, such as strict type safety and the ability to leverage the compiler to optimize based on well-known type information, you do lose a bit of flexibility that you get from a dynamically typed language. Additionally, the lack of dynamism does make interoperating between .NET and dynamic languages more difficult. You may have experienced this if you have ever had to create applications that require COM interop.

This appendix looks at some of the work Microsoft has done to embrace the concepts of dynamic languages and how it continues to make working directly with, as well as interoperating with, dynamic languages easier for developers.

IMPLICIT TYPES

Since implicit types were introduced in the .NET Framework, they have added flexibility to the way variables can be declared. Implicit types are expressed in C# using the var keyword or in VB.NET by declaring a variable without the As operator. They enable you to declare a variable whose type is implicitly inferred from the expression used to initialize the variable. In other words, implicit types enable you to declare variables in a fairly dynamic way in your code, while through a bit of compiler magic, retaining the benefits of a statically typed variable at run time. An example of using implicit types is shown here:

VB

```
Protected Sub Page_Load(ByVal sender As Object, ByVal e As System.EventArgs)
    Dim foo = 1
End Sub
```

C#

```
protected void Page_Load(object sender, EventArgs e)
{
    var foo = 1;
}
```

In this sample, a variable `foo` is declared as an implicit type, and immediately assigned a numeric value of 1. Because the variable is assigned a numeric, the compiler will automatically infer that the variable `foo` should actually be of type `Int32`. In fact if you decompile the code to its Intermediate Language (IL), you will see that the code actually output by the compiler emits the variable as the correct type. Trying to assign a different type to this variable as shown in the following results in a type mismatch exception:

VB

```
Protected Sub Page_Load(ByVal sender As Object, ByVal e As System.EventArgs)
    Dim foo = 1
    foo = "abc"
End Sub
```

C#

```
protected void Page_Load(object sender, EventArgs e)
{
    var foo = 1;
    foo = "abc";
}
```

Trying to compile this code results in a compiler error letting you know that a string cannot be assigned to the `foo` variable.

THE DYNAMIC LANGUAGE RUNTIME

To help developers gain back some of that flexibility, as well as bring the general goodness that the .NET Framework offers to a wider audience of developers, in 2007 Microsoft announced it had begun working on a new initiative called the *dynamic language runtime*, or DLR. With the release of .NET 4.0, the *Common Language Runtime* (CLR) was supplemented with the DLR. It brings to the CLR a dynamic type system, dynamic method dispatch, dynamic code generation, and a hosting API. The DLR enables dynamic languages to run with the .NET run time. Using the DLR, these dynamic languages get the best of both environments. They run in a dynamic environment in which types are discovered at run time and they have access to the richer .NET Base Class Libraries. IronPython and IronRuby, ports of two popular dynamic languages, currently take advantage of the DLR.

Both the IronRuby and IronPython languages were incubated from within Microsoft and released under open source licenses. The IronRuby and IronPython projects began as an effort for Microsoft to improve support for dynamic languages in the .NET Framework and to diversify its portfolio of programming languages. As of the last quarter of 2010, Microsoft turned the development of these Iron projects over to the community. Other dynamic languages are developed and maintained by third-party developers as well.

> **NOTE** *You can find more information on IronPython, the DLR implementation of Python, at* www.ironpython.net.
> *You can find more information on IronRuby, the DLR implementation of Ruby, at* www.ironruby.net.

Because the development of DLR-based languages was separate from the CLR-based languages, and support for the DLR-based languages has now been turned over to the community, support for these languages inside of Visual Studio is not very rich. Tools are available for both IronPython and IronRuby that integrate with Visual Studio, but the features vary to a large degree.

After you've loaded the languages on your system, you can develop standalone applications using them or leverage language libraries from other static languages like C# or VB.NET. Listing E-1 (IronPythonList .aspx in the IronPythonCS and IronPythonVB projects in the code download for this appendix) demonstrates using IronPython code from within an ASP.NET application using both C# and VB.NET. Note that to execute the example code, you will need to install version 2.7 of IronPython and reference both the `Microsoft.Scripting.dll` and `IronPython.dll` assemblies located in the default install location `\Program Files (x86)\IronPython 2.7\Platforms\Net40`.

LISTING E-1: Calling IronPython libraries from ASP.NET

VB

```
<%@ Page Language="VB" %>

<!DOCTYPE html>

<script runat="server">
    Dim items() As Integer = Enumerable.Range(1, 5).ToArray()
    Dim subitems() As Integer = Enumerable.Range(1, 7).ToArray()

    Dim random As Object

    Protected Sub Page_Load(ByVal sender As Object, ByVal e As System.EventArgs)
        System.IO.Directory.SetCurrentDirectory( _
            Environment.GetFolderPath( _
                Environment.SpecialFolder.ProgramFiles) & "\IronPython 2.7\Lib")

        Dim py As Microsoft.Scripting.Hosting.ScriptRuntime = _
            IronPython.Hosting.Python.CreateRuntime()

        random = py.UseFile("random.py")

        Me.Repeater1.DataSource = items
        Me.Repeater1.DataBind()

    End Sub

    Protected Sub Repeater1_ItemDataBound(ByVal sender As Object,
        ByVal e As System.Web.UI.WebControls.RepeaterItemEventArgs)

        Dim lbl As Label = CType(e.Item.FindControl("Label"), Label)
        lbl.Text = String.Format("List Number: {0}", e.Item.ItemIndex)

        Dim list As BulletedList = CType(e.Item.FindControl("BulletedList"), _
```

continues

```
            BulletedList)

        random.shuffle(subitems)

        list.DataSource = subitems
        list.DataBind()
    End Sub
</script>

<html xmlns="http://www.w3.org/1999/xhtml">
<head>
    <title></title>
</head>
<body>
    <form id="form1" runat="server">
        <div>
            <asp:Repeater ID="Repeater1" runat="server"
                OnItemDataBound="Repeater1_ItemDataBound">
                <ItemTemplate>
                    <p>
                        <asp:Label runat="server" ID="Label" />
                        <br />
                        <asp:BulletedList runat="server" ID="BulletedList" />
                    </p>
                </ItemTemplate>
            </asp:Repeater>
        </div>
    </form>
</body>
</html>
```

C#

```
<%@ Page Language="C#"%>

<!DOCTYPE html>

<script runat="server">
int[] items = Enumerable.Range(1, 5).ToArray();
int[] subitems = Enumerable.Range(1, 7).ToArray();
dynamic random;

protected void Page_Load(object sender, EventArgs e)
{
    System.IO.Directory.SetCurrentDirectory(
        Environment.GetFolderPath(
            Environment.SpecialFolder.ProgramFiles) + @"\IronPython 2.7\Lib");

    Microsoft.Scripting.Hosting.ScriptRuntime py =
        IronPython.Hosting.Python.CreateRuntime();
    random = py.UseFile("random.py");

    this.Repeater1.DataSource = items;
    this.Repeater1.DataBind();
}

protected void Repeater1_ItemDataBound(object sender, RepeaterItemEventArgs e)
{
    Label lbl = (Label)e.Item.FindControl("Label");
```

```
        lbl.Text = string.Format("List Number: {0}", e.Item.ItemIndex);

        BulletedList list = (BulletedList)e.Item.FindControl("BulletedList");
        random.shuffle(subitems);
        list.DataSource = subitems;
        list.DataBind();
    }
</script>

<html xmlns="http://www.w3.org/1999/xhtml">
<head>
    <title></title>
</head>
<body>
    <form id="form1" runat="server">
        <div>
            <asp:Repeater ID="Repeater1" runat="server"
                OnItemDataBound="Repeater1_ItemDataBound">
                <ItemTemplate>
                    <p>
                        <asp:Label runat="server" ID="Label" />
                        <br />
                        <asp:BulletedList runat="server" ID="BulletedList" />
                    </p>
                </ItemTemplate>
            </asp:Repeater>
        </div>
    </form>
</body>
</html>
```

You can see in this listing that when the page is loaded, the IronPython library `random.py` is loaded from the IronPython install directory using the DLR's hosting API. As each item in the `items` array is bound to the Repeater, its `subitems` are shuffled into a random order using the IronPython library.

DYNAMIC LOOKUP

In C# 4, a new feature was introduced called dynamic lookup. Although .NET developers have long been familiar with late binding using reflection, dynamic lookup brings a truly dynamic type declaration mechanism to C#. Dynamic lookup enables you to explicitly declare a variable as a dynamic type in your code and dynamically invoke methods against that type at run time. This differs from implicit typing in that dynamic types remain truly dynamic even at run time, whereas implicit types are converted to static types at compile-time. The following code shows a simple example of using the new `dynamic` keyword:

```
<script runat="server">
    protected void Page_Load(object sender, EventArgs e)
    {
        dynamic dynvalue =
            "Even though assigned a string, the type is still dynamic";
    }
</script>
```

In this sample, the property `dynvalue` is assigned a simple string as a value; however, unlike with implicit types, the variable remains typed as a dynamic type even at run time. You can see this dynamism if you are trying to access any member of the variable in Visual Studio. Normally, Visual Studio would show you a list of available properties and methods as well as the type of the variable. But because this type is dynamic, none of this information is known until run time. You can see this in Visual Studio by observing the tooltip on a dynamic variable as is shown in Figure E-1.

```
<script runat="server">

protected void Page_Load(object sender, EventArgs e)
{
    dynamic dynvalue = "Even though assigned a string, the type is still dynamic";
    dynvalue.
}                    (dynamic expression)
                     This operation will be resolved at runtime.

</script>
```

FIGURE E-1

At run time, the dynamic language runtime's dynamic dispatch system uses dynamic invocation to execute methods and properties of the type. This means that you can add and remove members from a type at run time. .NET provides two mechanisms to do this: the ExpandoObject class and the DynamicObject class.

You can use the ExpandoObject class in relatively simple scenarios where you need to add or remove members dynamically. The following code demonstrates using the ExpandoObject:

```
dynamic contact = new System.Dynamic.ExpandoObject();
contact.Name = "John Doe";
contact.Phone = "201-555-5555";
contact.Address = new System.Dynamic.ExpandoObject();
contact.Address.Street = "123 Main St";
contact.Address.City = "Anywhere";
contact.Address.State = "WA";
contact.Address.Postal = "12345";
```

In this sample code you can see that an ExpandoObject is created and several properties are added. These properties are added dynamically at run time and stored internally as an IDictionary<String,Object>, which the ExpandoObject implements internally to maintain the list of members.

An ExpandoObject is sealed and cannot be further inherited. If you need more control over what specific operations can be performed on a dynamic object, or what happens when an operation like getting and setting properties or calling a method occurs, you can create objects that derive from DynamicObject. An example of deriving from the DynamicObject class is shown using the JsonObject class (DynamicRest/JsonObject.cs in the DynamicRest project in the code download for this appendix). Part of this class is shown in the following code:

```
namespace DynamicRest {

    public sealed class JsonObject :
                                DynamicObject,
                                IDictionary<string, object>,
                                IDictionary
    {

        private Dictionary<string, object> _members;

        public JsonObject()
        {
            _members = new Dictionary<string, object>();
        }

        public JsonObject(params object[] nameValuePairs) : this() {
            if (nameValuePairs != null) {
                if (nameValuePairs.Length % 2 != 0) {
                    throw new ArgumentException(
                        "Mismatch in name/value pairs.");
```

```csharp
            }

            for (int i = 0; i < nameValuePairs.Length; i += 2) {
                if (!(nameValuePairs[i] is string)) {
                    throw new ArgumentException(
                        "Name parameters must be strings.");
                }

                _members[(string)nameValuePairs[i]] =
                    nameValuePairs[i + 1];
            }
        }
    }

    public override bool TryConvert(ConvertBinder binder,
                                    out object result)
    {
        Type targetType = binder.ReturnType;

        if ((targetType == typeof(IEnumerable)) ||
            (targetType ==
                typeof(IEnumerable<KeyValuePair<string, object>>)) ||
            (targetType == typeof(IDictionary<string, object>)) ||
            (targetType == typeof(IDictionary)))
        {
            result = this;
            return true;
        }

        return base.TryConvert(binder, out result);
    }

    public override bool TryDeleteMember(DeleteMemberBinder binder)
    {
        return _members.Remove(binder.Name);
    }

    public override bool TryGetMember(GetMemberBinder binder,
                                      out object result)
    {
        object value;
        if (_members.TryGetValue(binder.Name, out value))
        {
            result = value;
            return true;
        }

        return base.TryGetMember(binder, out result);
    }

    public override bool TrySetMember(SetMemberBinder binder,
                                      object value)
    {
        _members[binder.Name] = value;
        return true;
    }

    // ++++
    // Non-related interface implementations removed for clarity
    }
}
```

This JsonObject class is part of a larger library based on a sample written by Nikhil Kothari that simplifies retrieving and parsing JSON-formatted data. In .NET 4.5, the System.Json namespace was added, which provides the ability to more easily deal with JSON data. However, prior to that, to deal with JSON data in .NET, you would have to create proxy types that mirror the structure of the JSON and then perform complex parsing operations to parse the JSON data into collections of the custom types. Using the dynamic capabilities originally introduced in C# 4, you could simplify this by parsing the JSON data into generic types that expose the data via dynamic properties and methods, which are inferred at run time. Thus, the JsonObject class is a good example of the use of the DynamicObject. As you can see from the code example, you can override methods like TryGetMember and TrySetMember to control how to get and set properties on the type. In this case, members are stored in an internal Dictionary object in the JsonObject class.

The teams within Microsoft also leveraged the dynamic capabilities found in .NET 4.5 to make COM interop operations easier. The Office Primary Interop Assemblies (PIAs), which provide a managed layer over the Office COM Automation APIs, have been updated to leverage the dynamic capabilities of C#. The following code sample (ExcelInterop.vb and ExcelInterop.cs in the code download for this appendix) demonstrates how to interact with Excel from .NET using the PIAs:

VB

```vb
Dim excelApp As New Microsoft.Office.Interop.Excel.Application()
excelApp.Visible = True
excelApp.Workbooks.Add()

Dim workSheet As Microsoft.Office.Interop.Excel.Worksheet =
    excelApp.ActiveSheet
workSheet.Cells(1, "A") = "ID Number"
workSheet.Cells(1, "B") = "Current Balance"

Dim row = 1

For Each acct In accounts
    row = row + 1
    workSheet.Cells(row, "A") = acct.ID
    workSheet.Cells(row, "B") = acct.Balance
Next

workSheet.Columns(1).AutoFit()
workSheet.Columns(2).AutoFit()
```

C#

```csharp
var excelApp = new Microsoft.Office.Interop.Excel.Application();
excelApp.Visible = true;
excelApp.Workbooks.Add();

Microsoft.Office.Interop.Excel.Worksheet workSheet = excelApp.ActiveSheet;
workSheet.Cells[1, "A"] = "ID Number";
workSheet.Cells[1, "B"] = "Current Balance";

var row = 1;
foreach (var acct in accounts)
{
    row++;
    workSheet.Cells[row, "A"] = acct.ID;
    workSheet.Cells[row, "B"] = acct.Balance;
}

workSheet.Columns[1].AutoFit();
workSheet.Columns[2].AutoFit();
```

In prior versions of the PIAs, accessing certain APIs such as the `Columns` collection shown in the sample would have required you to cast the objects returned to the appropriate type to access that type's properties and methods. The newer versions, however, leverage the `dynamic` keyword to remove this requirement and allow for dynamic lookup of those properties and methods.

SUMMARY

Microsoft continues to expand the functionality of the .NET Framework and its languages by investing in features to bring more dynamism to the languages. These features give you additional programming tools in your tool belt, enabling you to leverage the features, or even the programming languages, that make the most sense for your specific application. From built-in features of C# and VB.NET such as implicit types and dynamic lookup, to entirely new languages such as IronPython and IronRuby, the choices available to you continue to expand.

ASP.NET Online Resources

AUTHOR BLOGS AND TWITTER IDS

Jason Gaylord: jasongaylord.com

    @jgaylord

Scott Hanselman: www.hanselman.com/blog/

    @shanselman

Todd Miranda: xperimentality.com

    @tmiranda

Pranav Rastogi: blogs.msdn.com/b/pranav_rastogi/

    @rustd

Christian Wenz: www.hauser-wenz.de/blog

    @chwenz

ASP.NET INFLUENTIAL BLOGS

Scott Guthrie: weblogs.asp.net/scottgu/

Rick Strahl: www.west-wind.com/weblog/

K. Scott Allen: odetocode.com/blogs/scott/

Phil Haack: www.haacked.com/

Steve Smith: www.stevesmithblog.com/

G. Andrew Duthie: http://devhammer.net/

Scott Mitchell: scottonwriting.net/sowBlog/

Nikhil Kothari: www.nikhilk.net/

WEBSITES

123ASPX Directory: www.123aspx.com

4 Guys from Rolla: www.4guysfromrolla.com

ASP Alliance: aspalliance.com

ASP Alliance Lists: aspadvice.com

The ASP.NET Developer Portal: msdn.microsoft.com/asp.net

ASP.NET Homepage: www.asp.net

ASP.NET Resources: www.aspnetresources.com

ASP.NET World: www.aspnetworld.com

International .NET Association: www.ineta.org

Microsoft's ASP.NET AJAX Site: www.asp.net/ajax/

Microsoft's ASP.NET MVC Site: www.asp.net/mvc/

Microsoft's ASP.NET Web API Site: http://www.asp.net/web-api

Microsoft Developer Centers: msdn.microsoft.com/developercenters

Microsoft Community Site: answers.microsoft.com

Microsoft's Open Source Project Community: www.codeplex.com

RegExLib: www.regexlib.com

XML for ASP.NET: www.xmlforasp.net

Stackoverflow: stackoverflow.com

Channel 9: channel9.msdn.com

TWITTER FOLKS WORTH FOLLOWING

@scottgu

@haacked

@brada

@ambroselittle

@sondreb

@chrislove

@wrox

@dseven

@randyholloway

@migueldeicaza

@donxml

@moon

@kvgros

@richcampbell

@christoc

@csells

@keyvan

@danwahlin

@devhammer

@jglozano

@shawnwildermuth

@julielermanvt

@codinghorror

@spolsky

@elijahmanor

@robconery

@jeremydmiller

@angrycoder

@rickstrahl

@csharpfritz

@DamianEdwards

@davidfowl

@coolcsh

Visual Studio Extensibility with NuGet

Over the years, the community of .NET developers has developed a large number of reusable libraries and utilities to help accomplish common tasks. Many of these third-party reusable libraries have found their way into the .NET developer's primary toolbox. In addition, .NET has become a thriving platform for open source development. Some of the most popular libraries have been published as open source projects.

In all aspects of .NET development, reusable libraries, whether open source or not, have become a valuable source of functionality. This fact is never more evident than in web development where the use of third-party .NET and JavaScript libraries is commonplace. In fact, many of the project templates in Visual Studio include third-party libraries.

Incorporating these libraries into your project can be as simple as including references to one or more assemblies. But more often, it is not as straight forward. If you don't already know the particular library that will give you the desired functionality, you need to find one. Once you have found a particular library, you need to download it. Often you have to choose the correct download from multiple versions or options. Don't forget to unblock the ZIP file after downloading the correct one. You should really verify the file using the hash provided by the download page. You then need to unzip the file into a folder within your solution. Often you create a `lib` folder to unzip the files into. You need to add a reference to the newly unzipped assembly or assemblies from within the Solution Explorer in Visual Studio. Now begins the process of setting the correct configuration settings in the `app.config` or `web.config` file and writing any initialization code required by the library. Determining the correct configuration settings often requires reading the documentation or researching forums and blogs.

As these libraries are developed, they incorporate and rely on other libraries, which in turn potentially need to be configured. The more dependencies, the more configuration headaches.

NuGet is a Visual Studio extension that makes it easy to add, remove, and update libraries and tools in Visual Studio projects that use the .NET Framework.

NuGet allows developers who build libraries to "package" their library and store it in a repository that makes it easy for others to find. The package, a .nupkg file, includes everything needed to install and configure the library in a solution. All the packages in a repository are bundled into feeds that can be accessed on the NuGet website or directly through Visual Studio. Developers who are looking for a library can search the feed and install the package through a command-line interface or a graphical interface.

USING NUGET IN VISUAL STUDIO

Prior to Visual Studio 2012, NuGet was installed using the Visual Studio Extension Manager. However, the NuGet client is already installed in Visual Studio 2012. In order to verify you have NuGet installed and to install NuGet if necessary, you can use the Visual Studio Extension Manager. Figure G-1 shows the Extension Manager in Visual Studio showing the extensions that are currently installed.

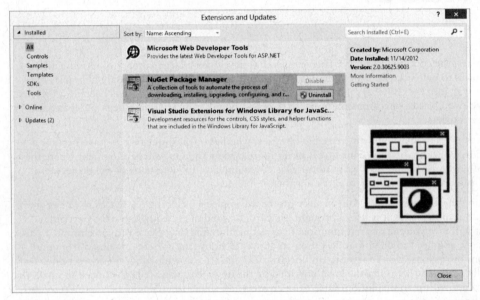

FIGURE G-1

The Extension Manager is also used to update NuGet when new versions are available. If an update is available for NuGet, you can see it in the Updates tab of the Extension Manager. Figure G-2 shows the Extension Manager displaying an update for NuGet. The update can be installed directly from this same interface.

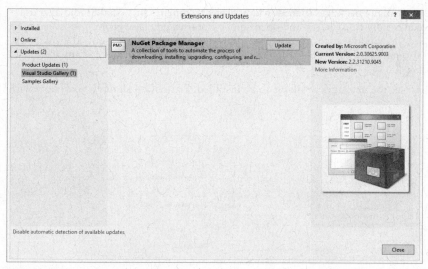

FIGURE G-2

Once NuGet is installed, you can find, install, and manage packages using either the Manage NuGet Packages window or using PowerShell commands in the Package Manager Console.

Managing NuGet Packages with the Window

The NuGet client for Visual Studio provides a graphical interface by way of the Manage NuGet Packages window. In order to use the interface, you need to have a solution loaded into Visual Studio. For the purpose of this example, create a new ASP.NET MVC 4 Web Application project and select Internet Application as the template type. In order to open the Manage NuGet Packages window, right-click on the project and select Manage NuGet Packages. Figure G-3 shows the Manage NuGet Packages window.

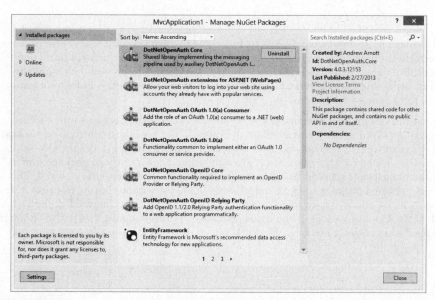

FIGURE G-3

Notice that there are already many packages loaded. Many project templates in Visual Studio also use NuGet packages to include certain third-party and open source libraries in a new project. As seen in Figure G-3, the left side of the window contains tabs that allow developers to see not only the currently installed packages, but also packages that are available to be installed. You can also see if any installed packages have updates.

Click on the Online tab to see the packages available to be installed. Figure G-4 shows the window with the Online tab selected.

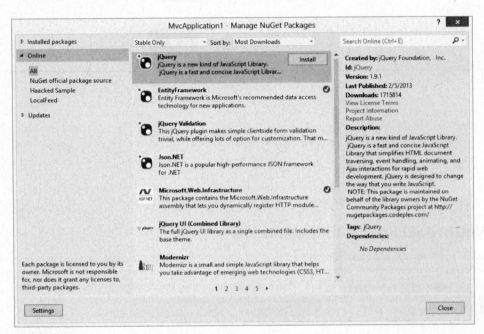

FIGURE G-4

There are a few things to make note of in Figure G-4. This first thing to mention is there are some packages in the list that have green checks in the upper-right corner of the package item. The checks indicate that the package is already installed in the current project. When a package is available to be installed, highlighting the package causes an Install button to appear. Highlighting a package also displays more information about the package in the right pane of the window.

NuGet packages are published to NuGet repositories. The repositories bundle the packages into a feed, which is what is ultimately displayed in the list of available packages. These repositories are called *package sources*. In Figure G-4, you can see that there is one default package source available under the Online tab. The default package source is hosted by Microsoft and is given the name "NuGet official package source." It is possible to add additional package sources. You can enable and disable package sources as well. This allows you to temporarily prevent a package source from showing in the list without having to delete it. In order to modify package sources, you will need to go into the Package Manager's settings. Click the Settings button in the lower left of the Manage Packages window to open the Options window. Figure G-5 shows the Options window with the Package Sources settings selected.

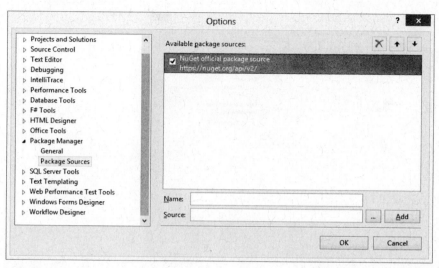

FIGURE G-5

In order to add a new package source, enter a name for the package source and its source URL. Note that you can also enter a folder path for the source. A folder containing NuGet packages is considered a valid package source. Different types of package sources are covered later in this appendix. Figure G-6 shows the Options window after adding a sample NuGet package source hosted by Phil Haack. The new package source is named Haacked Sample.

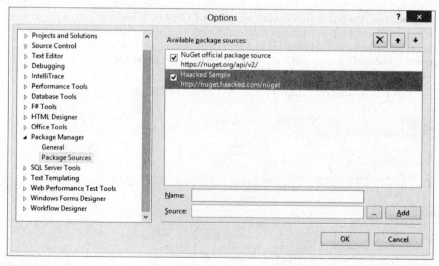

FIGURE G-6

After you close the Options window, the feed in the Manage NuGet Packages window is refreshed. Now it includes the packages from the Haacked Sample package source. By default, all of the packages from all of the enabled package sources are shown in the list and, if necessary, can be paged through. You can select a single package source to show only its packages. Figure G-7 shows the packages available only from the Haacked Sample package source.

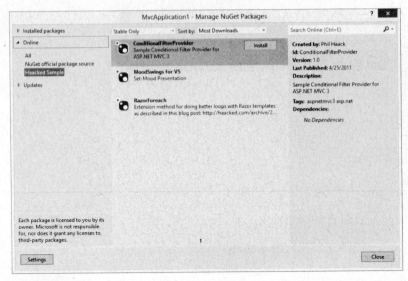

FIGURE G-7

Installing a NuGet Package

Installing a package is as simple as clicking the Install button on the package. But what really happens when you install a NuGet package? In order to see some of the changes a NuGet package makes when installed, find the package for the ELMAH.

ELMAH enables application-wide error logging for ASP.NET web applications. It is a good example because it has other dependencies and requires changes to the `web.config` file to configure it. From the Manage NuGet Packages window, use the search box to search for ELMAH. Note that you can also search for "logging" or "error logging" and find ELMAH in the search results. So you can search for content as well as the name of a package, which can be helpful if you don't know the name of a package but know what functionality you need. Figure G-8 shows the results of searching for ELMAH.

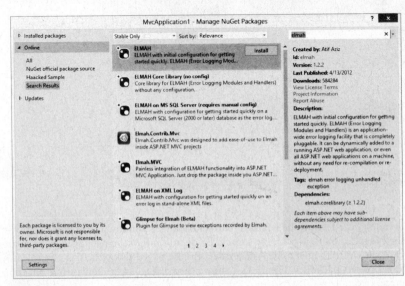

FIGURE G-8

Clicking the Install button will start the download and installation of the package. One of the additional things that happens when you install a package is that any packages it depends on are also downloaded and installed. As an example, Figure G-9 shows the installation window that is displayed during the download and installation process.

Notice the dependency on a version of `elmah.corelibrary` greater than 1.2.2. The package ELMAH depends on, called `elmah.corelibrary`, is also downloaded and installed. You didn't have to do anything special to get this to happen. NuGet packages contain this dependency information and handle the location and installation of any dependencies. Once the installation is done, a green check is shown next to the ELMAH package indicating that it has been installed. Sometimes after installing a package, a text file is displayed in Visual Studio with either additional directions or an indication of what was changed. Once the package is installed, you can use the library in your application immediately.

So what exactly happened when the package was installed? Figure G-10 shows that a reference to the ELMAH assembly was added to the project.

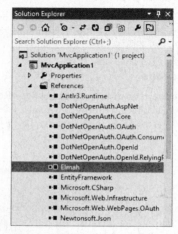

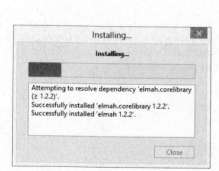

FIGURE G-9

FIGURE G-10

Not only was the assembly referenced, but changes were made to the `web.config` file to support and configure ELMAH and the handlers and modules it provides. Figure G-11 shows a portion of the `web.config` file with some changes made by the NuGet package.

```
Web.config    readme.txt
    <?xml version="1.0" encoding="utf-8"?>
<!--
    For more information on how to configure your ASP.NET application, please visit
    http://go.microsoft.com/fwlink/?LinkId=169433
    -->
<configuration>
    <configSections>
        <!-- For more information on Entity Framework configuration, visit http://go.microsoft.
        <section name="entityFramework" type="System.Data.Entity.Internal.ConfigFile.EntityFram
        <sectionGroup name="elmah">
            <section name="security" requirePermission="false" type="Elmah.SecuritySectionHandler
            <section name="errorLog" requirePermission="false" type="Elmah.ErrorLogSectionHandler
            <section name="errorMail" requirePermission="false" type="Elmah.ErrorMailSectionHandl
            <section name="errorFilter" requirePermission="false" type="Elmah.ErrorFilterSectionH
        </sectionGroup>
    </configSections>
    <connectionStrings>
        <add name="DefaultConnection" connectionString="Data Source=(LocalDb)\v11.0;Initial Cat
    </connectionStrings>
    <appSettings>
```

FIGURE G-11

The first package you install in a project creates a Packages folder. A subfolder is created in this folder for each package that is installed. In this particular example, the Visual Studio template for the project you created already installed some packages so the folder was already there. The folder will be located in the solution folder if there is one. If your project does not have a solution folder, the Packages folder will be created in the project folder. When you installed the ELMAH package, two subfolders were created. One was created for ELMAH and another was created for the package it depends

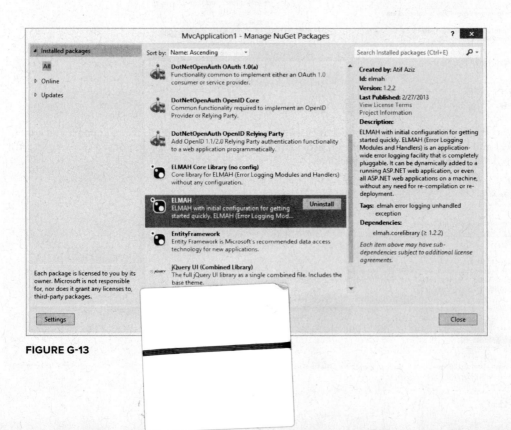

FIGURE G-12

on, the ELMAH core library. Figure G-12 shows the content of the packages folder showing the subfolders created by the ELMAH NuGet package.

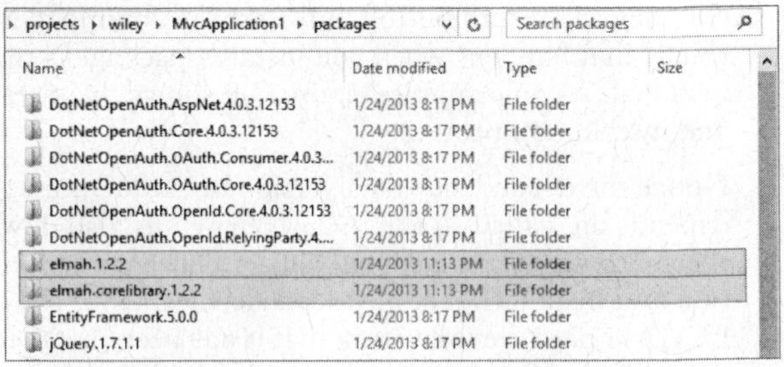

Each of these subfolders contains all of the files installed by the package, including the assemblies, the transform files defining the necessary configuration changes, the supporting documentation files, and the package file itself.

Uninstalling a NuGet Package

So what if you want to remove, or uninstall, a package? Removing a package is just as easy as installing it. Open the Manage NuGet Packages window again and select the Installed Packages tab. Figure G-13 shows the Manage NuGet Packages window with the installed ELMAH package selected.

FIGURE G-13

There is an Uninstall button on any package that has been installed. Note that the Uninstall button is shown only in the Installed Packages tab. If you have more than one project in your solution, you will have a Manage button instead of an Uninstall button. This scenario is covered in more detail later in this appendix. Click the Uninstall button. If the package depends on other packages, a window is displayed listing all of the packages that were installed along with the original package, asking if you want to uninstall them as well. Figure G-14 shows the window that is displayed when uninstalling the ELMAH package.

FIGURE G-14

Select Yes to uninstall the dependent packages. An uninstall progress window is displayed that's similar to the install progress window shown in Figure G-9. Once the package or packages have been uninstalled, the reference to the assembly is removed, any changes to the `web.config` file are removed, and the subfolders in the Packages folder are removed.

Managing Packages at the Solution Level

The previous example installed the ELMAH package for the ASP.NET MVC project in your solution. However, what if you have more than one project in a solution? You can manage packages at a solution level as well. If you have been following along with this appendix, add another project to the solution you have been using. In this case, a class library project is a good choice. After adding another project to the solution, right-click on the solution. In the context menu, instead of an option for Manage NuGet Packages, you will see an option for Manage NuGet Packages for Solution. Figure G-15 shows the context menu containing the new menu option.

FIGURE G-15

Clicking on this new menu option will open the Manage NuGet Packages window as before. The difference you see is that when viewing the list of currently installed packages, upon selecting a package, the Install button is now a Manage button.

Clicking on the Manage button for any installed package displays the Select Projects window. Figure G-16 shows the Select Projects window.

As you might have surmised, the Select Projects window allows you to choose which projects the package is installed for. This same window is used to remove a package from projects in the solution. If you wanted to install a new package, the process is the same as installing a package for a single project with the exception of this Select Projects window. When you install a package from the solution version of the Package Manager, you will be prompted to select which projects you want to install the package for.

FIGURE G-16

Installing a package into multiple projects is one of the reasons the Packages folder shown in Figure G-12 is placed in the Solution folder. If you are installing the package into multiple projects in a solution, you don't want to have multiple copies of the same files. Each project that will use the package simply references its files at the single solution-level location.

Managing NuGet Packages with the Console

If you prefer not to use the graphical interface, or if you are a developer who prefers to use the keyboard instead of the mouse, you can also work with NuGet packages using PowerShell commands. There is a console interface for working with NuGet. In order to open the console window, select Tools ⇨ Library Package Manager ⇨ Package Manager Console from the Visual Studio menu. This will open the Package Manager Console shown in Figure G-17.

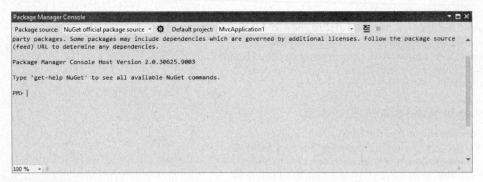

FIGURE G-17

There are two drop-downs in the Package Manager Console. The first allows you to select the default package source that will be used by the commands you type in the console. The second allows you to select the default project the commands will act against. These defaults can be overridden using parameters of the PowerShell commands. The first thing you may want to do is view the packages that are available to install. The following command lists all of the available packages from the source selected in the package source drop-down:

```
Get-Package -ListAvailable
```

Because this command lists all of the available packages, it will scroll until all packages have been displayed. You can click the red stop symbol to stop the list of packages being displayed in the console. As of the writing of this appendix, there are over 11,000 unique packages in the default package source feed. Displaying the entire list is probably not very helpful. You can filter the results by using the `Filter` parameter. You can specify the same terms used in the search box from the previous example as the arguments to the `Filter` parameter. The following command shows how to search for the ELMAH package:

```
Get-Package -Filter Elmah -ListAvailable
```

Running this command will list all packages that contain the term "elmah" in the description or in the title of the package. Figure G-18 shows the results of running this command.

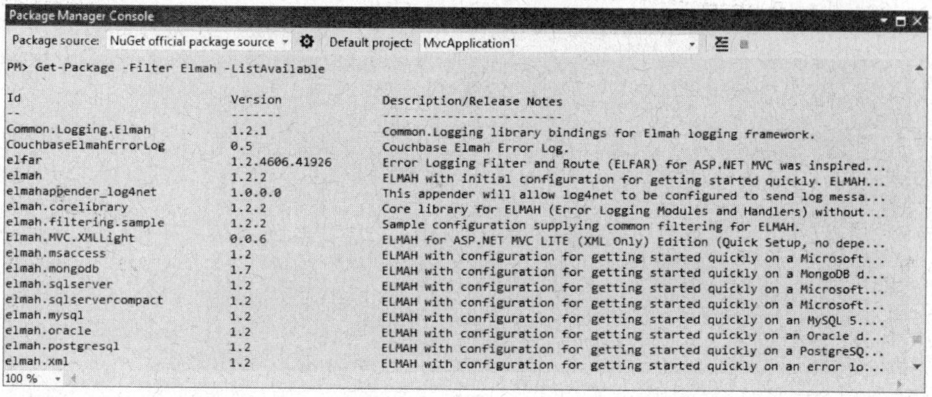

FIGURE G-18

If you want to know more about the `Get-Package` command, you can use the `Get-Help` command to list the parameters and get a description of the command. The following command displays help for the `Get-Package` command:

```
Get-Help Get-Package
```

Now that you can find the package that you want to install, you need to be able to install it. The command used to install a package is `Install-Package`. From the list of available packages shown in Figure G-18, you can see the package named `elmah`. To install the `elmah` package, you use this command:

```
Install-Package elmah
```

This will install the `elmah` package in the default project selected in the Default Project drop-down. As with installing a package using the Package Manager window, if the package you are installing has dependencies on other packages they will also be downloaded and installed. Figure G-19 shows the results of running the previous install command.

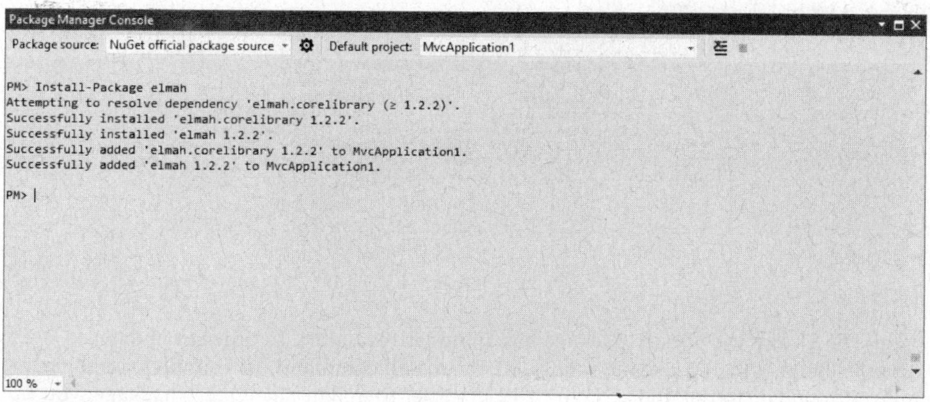

FIGURE G-19

Notice that the dependency on `elmah.corelibrary` was detected and that package was installed as well without you having to do anything special.

In order to view a list of packages that have already been installed, you can simply run the `Get-Package` command with no parameters. Figure G-20 shows the results of running this command.

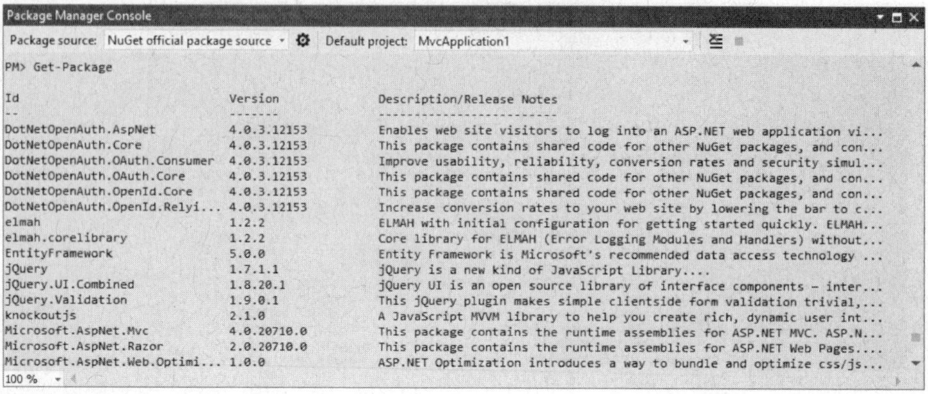

FIGURE G-20

Once you have installed a package, there may be a need to update it to the latest version. You can view a list of updates available using the `Updates` parameter to the `Get-Package` command. The following command can be used to determine if there are any updates to the installed packages:

```
Get-Package -Updates
```

Figure G-21 shows the results of running this command to view any available updates.

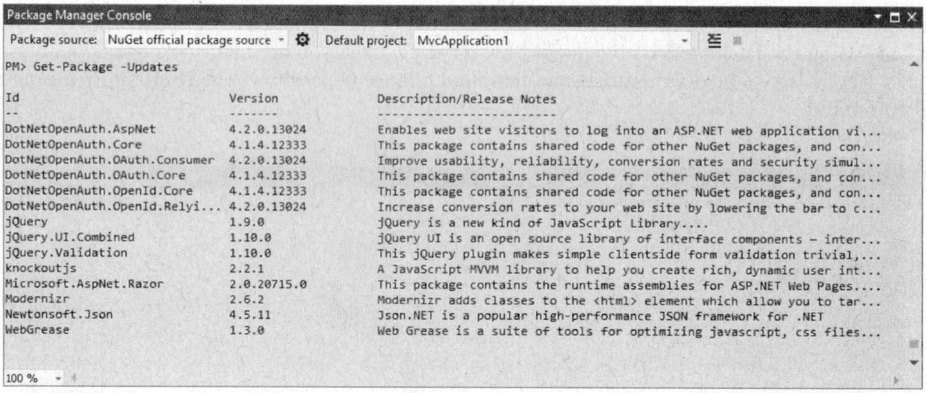

FIGURE G-21

You can see in Figure G-21 that the jQuery package has an update available. In order to update a package, you use the `Update-Package` command. Like the install command, you simply pass the name of the package you want to update to the update command. In order to update the jQuery package, you run the following command:

```
Update-Package jQuery
```

Figure G-22 shows the results of running this update command.

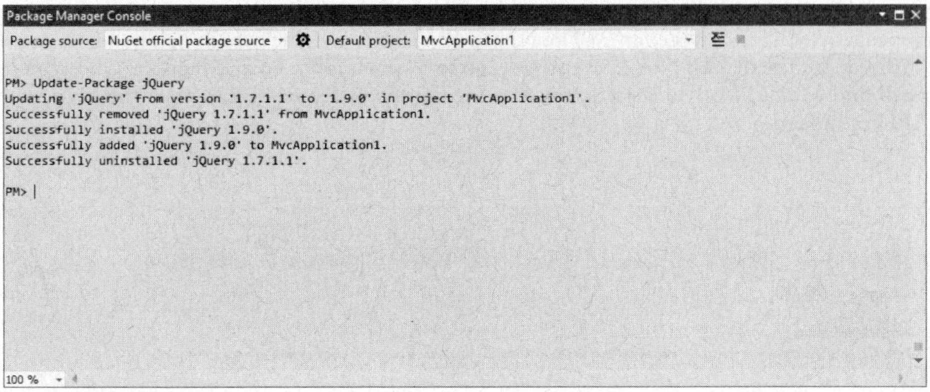

FIGURE G-22

You can also remove a package using the console. To remove a package, you use the `Uninstall-Package` command. Like both the install and the update commands, the uninstall command simply takes the name of the package you want to remove as a parameter. For example, in order to remove the `elmah` package you installed earlier, you run the following command:

```
Uninstall-Package elmah
```

CREATING A NUGET PACKAGE

The first step in creating a NuGet package is to create one or more assemblies that you want to publish as a NuGet package. As an example, you can create a simple class library project that contains a single class. For the purpose of this example, Listing G-1 shows some sample code that can be used to create a simple class.

LISTING G-1: Sample class in a class library

```
public class NugetMath
{
    public int AddNumbers(int number1, int number2)
    {
        return number1 + number2;
    }
}
```

Once you have one or more assemblies that you want to use to build a NuGet package, you need to download the NuGet.exe bootstrapper to create your packages. You can find the NuGet bootstrapper on the NuGet CodePlex site located at `nuget.codeplex.com`, from the Downloads page. Download NuGet.exe and put it somewhere accessible. To test that NuGet is accessible, open a command prompt and type `nuget help` to get help for the NuGet bootstrapper.

> **NOTE** *Note that you also need to tell NuGet that it can download any packages it needs to run. In order to do this, go into the Package Manager settings in the Visual Studio Options and check the option to Allow NuGet to Download Missing Packages During Build.*

If you are going to publish your NuGet package to a NuGet repository that requires an API key, like the default NuGet repository, you need to get an API key that will identify the package as belonging to you. In order to get an API key for the default NuGet repository, go to www.nuget.org and register. Once you have registered, you will find your API key located on the My Account page. Figure G-23 shows the My Account page with the API key hidden.

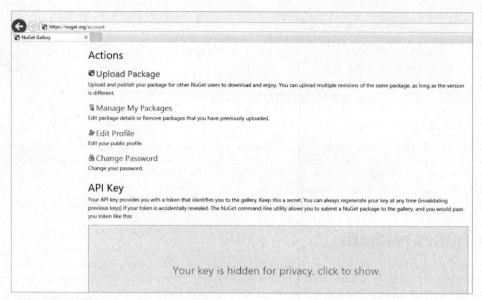

FIGURE G-23

Once you have your own API key, you can run NuGet with the setApiKey parameter in order to have it remember your API key. That way, you don't have to specify the key every time you create a NuGet package. The following command will cause NuGet to remember your API key, where *your-key* should be replaced with your actual API key:

```
nuget setApiKey your-key
```

There is more than one way to create a NuGet package. Which method you use depends on the complexity of your library. The first step to creating your NuGet package is to create the manifest file, which has a .nuspec file extension. A .nuspec file is an XML manifest that describes the NuGet package and any dependencies it has.

Creating a NuGet Package from an Assembly

You can create a .nuspec file from a single assembly. In order to create this file for a single assembly, you need to call the NuGet executable with the spec parameter and the path to the assembly. The command to generate a .nuspec file from your example assembly is as follows:

```
nuget spec NugetMath.dll
```

After running this command, a new file is created called NugetMath.dll.nuspec. Listing G-2 shows the content of the file that would be created by running this command.

LISTING G-2: Contents of the .nuspec file

```xml
<?xml version="1.0"?>
<package >
  <metadata>
    <id>NugetMath.dll</id>
    <version>1.0.0</version>
    <authors>Myname</authors>
    <owners>Myname</owners>
    <licenseUrl>http://LICENSE_URL_HERE_OR_DELETE_THIS_LINE</licenseUrl>
    <projectUrl>http://PROJECT_URL_HERE_OR_DELETE_THIS_LINE</projectUrl>
    <iconUrl>http://ICON_URL_HERE_OR_DELETE_THIS_LINE</iconUrl>
    <requireLicenseAcceptance>false</requireLicenseAcceptance>
    <description>Package description</description>
    <releaseNotes>
        Summary of changes made in this release of the package.
    </releaseNotes>
    <copyright>Copyright 2013</copyright>
    <tags>Tag1 Tag2</tags>
    <dependencies>
      <dependency id="SampleDependency" version="1.0" />
    </dependencies>
  </metadata>
</package>
```

Some of the content in the file is default content. However, some of the content was pulled from the assembly metadata. The reason you reference the assembly when creating the `.nuspec` file is simply to use the metadata to automatically fill in some of the `.nuspec` file content. You can edit the contents of this file as necessary. You can view the full specifications for the `.nuspec` files on the NuGet.org site at `http://docs.nuget.org/docs/reference/nuspec-reference`.

For now, just remove the dependencies section since you don't have any. Remove the lines that indicate they can be deleted, and edit any other fields as necessary. Listing G-3 shows the file contents after making the appropriate edits.

LISTING G-3: Contents of the .nuspec file after removing the dependencies section

```xml
<?xml version="1.0"?>
<package >
  <metadata>
    <id>NugetMath.dll</id>
    <version>1.0.0</version>
    <authors>Myname</authors>
    <owners>Myname</owners>
    <requireLicenseAcceptance>false</requireLicenseAcceptance>
    <description>A sample library to do addition</description>
    <releaseNotes>This is the initial release.</releaseNotes>
    <copyright>Copyright 2013</copyright>
    <tags>Sample Math Addition</tags>
  </metadata>
</package>
```

Now that you have your manifest, there is one additional step you must complete before creating the NuGet package. The NuGet bootstrapper uses a particular convention for subfolders and files when creating packages. In order to have your NuGet package automatically create a reference to your assembly when the package is installed in a project, you need to place the assembly in a folder named `lib`. In the folder containing the `.nuspec` file, create a subfolder named `lib` and move the `NuGetMath.dll` into it. In order to create the package for this `.nuspec` file, you simply run the NuGet command with the `pack` parameter followed by the name of the `.nuspec` file. You can see an example of the command here:

```
nuget pack NugetMath.dll.nuspec
```

This command generates a file named `NugetMath.dll.1.0.0.nupkg`. This is your NuGet package file. A `nupkg` file is just a renamed `.zip` file. If you change the extension from `.nupkg` to `.zip`, you will be able to unzip the file to see its contents. You should see the `.nuspec` file in the root of the ZIP file along with some other supporting files and folders. You will also see the `lib` subfolder containing your assembly. The `nupkg` file can now be published to a NuGet repository to be included in the feed of available packages from that repository.

Creating a NuGet Package from a Project

Generating a `.nuspec` file from an assembly is the simplest way to create the necessary manifest. However, you may have need for a slightly more complex scenario. For example, if you have installed one or more NuGet packages in your library project, those packages then become dependencies for your NuGet package. Generating the `.nuspec` file from the assembly won't pick up these dependencies. In this scenario, you can generate the `.nuspec` file from the .NET project. In order to demonstrate this, install a NuGet package into your class library project. Install Structuremap, which is an open source dependency injection/inversion of control library, into your project. If you have more than one project in your solution, make the project you want to install the package into the default project. You can search for Structuremap in the Package Manager window or issue the following command in the Package Manager Console:

```
Install-Package structuremap
```

Now that you have a NuGet package installed in your project, and thus have created a dependency on Structuremap, you can generate a `.nuspec` file from your project file. Doing so will take into account the dependency when you create the NuGet package. Open a console window and view the directory containing your `.csproj` or `.vbproj` file. From within that directory, issue the following command:

```
nuget spec
```

Issuing this command will generate a `.nuspec` file. If you look at the generated file, you will see some differences between it and the one generated directly from the assembly. Instead of reading metadata from the assembly to put into the .nuspec file, certain elements now contain tokens—such as $version$, $author$, and $description$—that will be replaced when you create the package. The value of these tokens is pulled for the project metadata, but it is not pulled until you create the package because their values may change over time. A good example of this is $version$. You also may notice that the `dependencies` section is missing. Listing G-4 shows the generated `.nuspec` file.

LISTING G-4: Contents of the .nuspec file generated from the project

```xml
<?xml version="1.0"?>
<package >
  <metadata>
    <id>$id$</id>
    <version>$version$</version>
    <title>$title$</title>
    <authors>$author$</authors>
    <owners>$author$</owners>
    <licenseUrl>http://LICENSE_URL_HERE_OR_DELETE_THIS_LINE</licenseUrl>
    <projectUrl>http://PROJECT_URL_HERE_OR_DELETE_THIS_LINE</projectUrl>
    <iconUrl>http://ICON_URL_HERE_OR_DELETE_THIS_LINE</iconUrl>
```

```xml
          <requireLicenseAcceptance>false</requireLicenseAcceptance>
          <description>$description$</description>
          <releaseNotes>
               Summary of changes made in this release of the package.
          </releaseNotes>
          <copyright>Copyright 2013</copyright>
          <tags>Tag1 Tag2</tags>
     </metadata>
</package>
```

As with the previous example, after generating the `.nuspec` file, you can edit it as necessary. In this case you will remove the lines that indicate they can be deleted, replace the author token with a hardcoded value, and change any other values that are related to your package. The tags that are changed are bolded in Listing G-4. Listing G-5 shows the file after the edits.

LISTING G-5: Contents of the .nuspec file after editing

```xml
<?xml version="1.0"?>
<package >
  <metadata>
     <id>$id$</id>
     <version>$version$</version>
     <title>$title$</title>
     <authors>Myname</authors>
     <owners>Myname</owners>
     <requireLicenseAcceptance>false</requireLicenseAcceptance>
     <description>$description$</description>
     <releaseNotes>Initial release.</releaseNotes>
     <copyright>Copyright 2013</copyright>
     <tags>Sample Math Addition</tags>
  </metadata>
</package>
```

Once the `.nuspec` file has been edited to your needs, you can create the NuGet package. To create the package from a project you will execute NuGet with the `pack` parameter and the name of the project file:

```
nuget pack NugetMath.csproj
```

Note that in the case of generating the NuGet package from a project, you specify the project file, not the `.nuspec` file when creating the package. The `.nuspec` file is still included in the package automatically. If you change the extension of the NuGet package to `.zip`, unzip the file, and view the `NugetMath.nuspec` file, you can see that all of the tokens have been replaced by values from the project metadata. Since there is a dependency on the Structuremap NuGet package, the `dependencies` section has also been added with an entry for the Structuremap dependency.

Publishing a NuGet Package

Now that you have created your NuGet package, you will want to publish it to a repository. You can publish your NuGet package directly on the `www.nuget.org` website. After logging on to the website and going to your account page, you can click on the Upload Package link and follow the directions online. Figure G-24 shows a portion of the Upload Your Package page.

FIGURE G-24

For those who would prefer to use the command line to publish their package, the process involves a single command. Once you have created your package as described, you will execute NuGet with the `push` parameter. The command to publish a NuGet package to the default Microsoft NuGet repository is shown:

```
nuget push NugetMath.1.0.0.0.nupkg
```

This command assumes you have previously stored your API key using the `setApiKey` parameter in a previous call to NuGet. You can override the API key and the package source location using command-line parameters.

HOSTING NUGET PACKAGES

NuGet packages would not be very helpful if you had no way to find them. A NuGet repository is often called a *NuGet Gallery*. The default NuGet Gallery is hosted by Microsoft. So far, this appendix has dealt with this default NuGet Gallery located at `www.nuget.org`. The packages located in the default NuGet Gallery are available to anyone searching the gallery. But what if you have a package that you want to be available only to you or to your organization or group? There are options for hosting your own NuGet Gallery.

File Share Hosting

The simplest option for hosting your own NuGet Gallery is to use a local folder or a file share. Although this option supports a read-only gallery that must be manually updated, it is a very quick way to set up a private gallery. To create a local gallery, create a folder on your local drive. Copy any NuGet packages (the `*.nupkg` files) you want to be available into the folder. That is it.

In the Visual Studio Package Manager options shown in Figure G-5, add a new package source. Specify the local gallery folder path as the source. Now when you view the available packages to install and specify the package source you just added, you will see all of the packages located in your gallery folder. This is a great option to allow you to test your own NuGet packages before publishing them to a public or private network gallery.

Creating a file share on a network drive works the same way. Access to a gallery on a network file share can be secured like any other file share. Whether you store your packages in a local folder or a network folder, you must update or add packages to the gallery manually. You have to copy any packages to the gallery folder manually. You also lose the ability to search packages using OData queries, which you can do when the gallery is hosted in IIS.

IIS Hosting

The next option for hosting a NuGet Gallery is to host it on IIS on an ASP.NET website. Luckily, and perhaps ironically, there is a NuGet package to help create your gallery. In order to create a NuGet Gallery hosted on IIS, begin by creating a new ASP.NET empty web application project in Visual Studio. Then you install the `nuget.server` NuGet package. If you are using the Package Manager window, search for the `nuget.server` package and install it. If you are using the Package Manager Console, use the following command to install the `nuget.server` package:

```
Install-Package nuget.server
```

The `nuget.server` package installs the files and creates the folders necessary to host your own NuGet Gallery. By default, packages are stored in the Packages folder. You can place any initial packages in that folder and mark them to be compiled as content so they are deployed with your website. You can change the folder used to store your packages by modifying the `packagesPath` key in the `appSettings` section of `web.config`. There are two additional `appSettings` that control whether the NuGet Gallery will allow packages to be published to it using the NuGet.exe bootstrapper. If the `requireApiKey` value is set to `false`, packages can be published to the gallery with no API key.

If the `requireApiKey` value is set to `true`, the determination of whether the gallery accepts packages to be published lies with the value of the `apiKey`. If the `apiKey` setting is deleted or its value is left blank, the gallery will be read-only and will not support publishing new packages using NuGet.exe. In order to support publishing packages, create a strong password and set the value of the `apiKey` to this value. This value is a shared public key that can be used by anyone publishing packages to the gallery.

> **NOTE** *Note that you should verify that there are not multiple* compilation *elements in the* system.web *section. Installing the* nuget.server *package on a website targeting .NET 4.5 can cause an additional* compilation *element specifying a target Framework of 4.0. If this is the case, simply remove the element instance targeting the 4.0 Framework.*

Without making any changes to the default settings (except for the note), the gallery is ready to run. If you have been following along with this appendix, copy the `NuGetMath` package created earlier into the Packages folder and run the website. Figure G-25 shows the default page of the gallery.

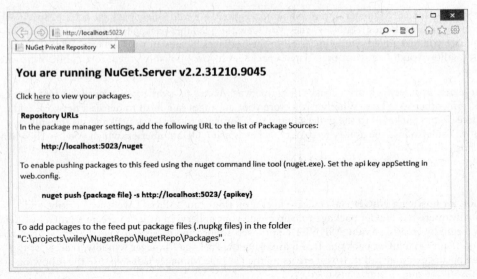

FIGURE G-25

Notice the line in Figure G-25 that says "Click here to view your packages." Clicking on the link displays the OData over ATOM feed of the packages in the gallery. Figure G-26 shows the page displayed when clicking on the link.

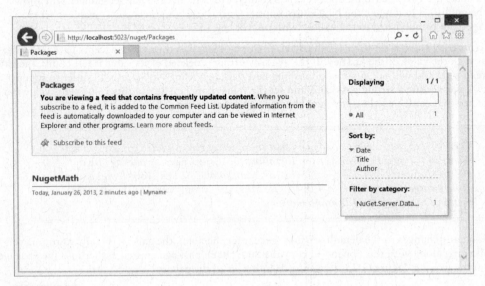

FIGURE G-26

If you want to test the gallery, you can add the address shown in Figure G-26 as a new package source in the Package Manager settings in Visual Studio. Publishing the website is no different than publishing any other website. After publishing, you have your own private NuGet Gallery.

EXTENDING VISUAL STUDIO WITH NUGET

The Package Manager Console is a PowerShell console within Visual Studio. So far, you have used the console to interact with NuGet. You can also use the console to interact with and automate Visual Studio. Using a NuGet package, you can add commands to the Package Manager Console that can perform standalone operations or interact with Visual Studio and your projects.

In the previous section on creating a NuGet package, you used the Nuget.exe bootstrapper to create your package. There is also a Windows GUI application for creating NuGet packages. The NuGet Package Explorer is a click-once application that makes creating packages very easy. It can also be used to view other NuGet packages to learn more about how they are structured. The NuGet Package Explorer is a CodePlex project and can be found at `npe.codeplex.com`. You can download and install the NuGet Package Explorer from there.

Creating the PowerShell Script Files

As an example of adding a command to the package manager, you will create a NuGet package that will add a command to generate a random password of variable length. Create a text file called `init.ps1`. The `init.ps1` file runs the first time a package is installed in a solution. It only runs one time per solution. If the same package is installed in multiple projects in the solution, the script is not run during those installations. The script also runs every time the solution is opened. Listing G-6 shows the content of the `init.ps1` file.

LISTING G-6: Contents of the init.ps1 file

```
param($installPath, $toolsPath, $package)
Import-Module (Join-Path $toolsPath GenRandomPassword.psm1)
```

The first line declares the set of parameters to the script. These parameters are passed into the script by NuGet. The second line of the script is used to import a PowerShell module. This listing specifies a script named `GenRandomPassword.psm1`.

Next you need to create this PowerShell module. Create a file called **GenRandomPassword.psm1**. Listing G-7 shows the contents of the `GenRandomPassword.psm1` file.

LISTING G-7: Contents of GenRandomPassword.psm1 file

```
$rand = New-Object System.Random

function Get-RndPassword($num1) {
    1..$num1 | ForEach {
        $NewPassword = $NewPassword + [char]$rand.next(33,127)
    }
    return $NewPassword
}

Export-ModuleMember Get-RndPassword
```

The first line creates a `System.Random` object that is used in the `Get-RndPassword` function defined in the next line. The `Get-RndPassword` function accepts a single input parameter that is used as the upper limit of the range of numbers piped into the `ForEach`. The `ForEach` picks a random character code between 33 and 127 for each number in the range and adds that character to a variable `$NewPassword`. After the `ForEach` finishes executing, the resulting `$NewPassword` is returned from the function. The last line calls `Export-Module` on the function, which makes it available in the Package Manager Console.

Adding Files to the NuGet Package

With the two files you have created, you will create your NuGet package using the NuGet Package Explorer. Open the NuGet Package Explorer. Select `Create a new package` from the Common tasks dialog. Figure G-27 shows the NuGet Package Explorer after selecting the option to Create a new package.

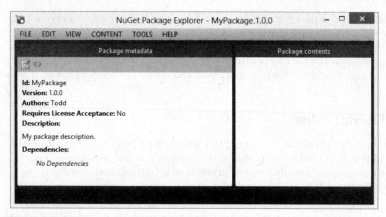

FIGURE G-27

Drag both the `init.ps1` and the `GenRandomPassword.psm1` files and drop them onto the pane in the NuGet Package Explorer titled Package contents. For both files, the NuGet Package Explorer will recognize the files as PowerShell scripts and ask if you would like the files placed in the tools folder. Answer Yes for both files to have the Package Explorer create the tools folder and place both files in the tools folder. Now you need to edit the metadata for the package.

Editing the NuGet Package Metadata

You need to edit the metadata for your package to customize it for your particular package. Select Edit ⇨ Edit Metadata from the menu. The main field that should be edited is the `Id` field. The `Id` field should be set to the name of your NuGet Package. In this example, change the `Id` field to **GenRandomPassword**. Figure G-28 shows the NuGet Package Explorer after editing the metadata.

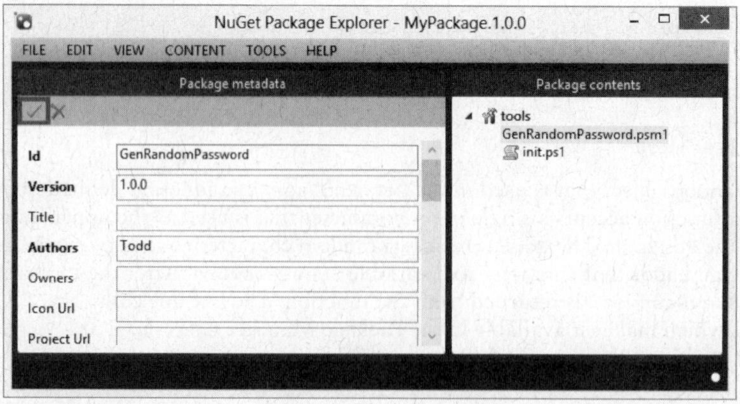

FIGURE G-28

Once you have finished editing the metadata, click the checkmark indicated in Figure G-28 in the upper left of the Package metadata pane.

Deploy the NuGet Package

Now you can publish the NuGet package. In order to publish your package to a hosted NuGet gallery, you can use the File ⇨ Publish menu item. But one of the best ways to test your package is to save it to a local or file share NuGet gallery. Choose File ⇨ Save from the NuGet Package Explorer menu and save the .nupkg file to the local folder or file share you used in the File Share Hosting section above.

Open the Package Manager Console and set the Package source to your local gallery. Type the following command to install the GenRandomPassword NuGet package:

```
Install-Package GenRandomPassword
```

Once you have installed the package, test the command you added to the console in your NuGet package. The following command will generate a random string of 12 characters.

```
Get-RndPassword 12
```

Figure G-29 shows the Package Manager Console after installing the NuGet package and executing the command added by the NuGet package.

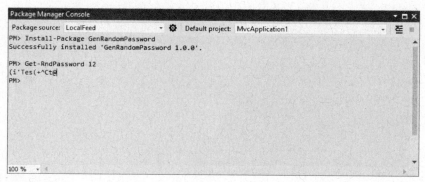

FIGURE G-29

SUMMARY

In the past, it could be difficult to find, install, and configure libraries in your .NET projects. With NuGet, the complexity of adding libraries to your projects has been greatly diminished, if not eliminated altogether. Finding various libraries that provide the functionality you need is also much easier thanks to the centralized feeds provided with the NuGet repositories.

For developers creating libraries for others to use, creating NuGet packages has become an easy way to publish your libraries so that they can be discovered and installed more easily. Using NuGet to find and install libraries has become the de-facto standard by developers. For those development groups that want or need more control over access to libraries and group standardization, there are various hosting options for NuGet repositories. These options include creating private repositories accessible only to those developers within certain groups or companies.

NuGet can also be used to provide Visual Studio extensibility through the use of PowerShell commands. NuGet continues to grow and provide an easy outlet for open source developers to distribute their projects. Its integration with Visual Studio also facilitates extending projects with reusable functionality that saves both time and resources.

INDEX

F

G

S